THE WORLD OF PSYCHOLOGY

THIRD CANADIAN EDITION

Samuel E. Wood
Lindenwood University

Ellen R. Green Wood
St. Louis Community College at Meramec

THIRD CANADIAN EDITION

Eileen Wood
Wilfrid Laurier University

Serge Desmarais
University of Guelph

Toronto

Canadian Cataloguing in Publication Data

Main entry under title:

The world of psychology

3rd Canadian ed.
Includes bibliographical references and index. Includes CD-ROM.
ISBN 0-205-36456-X

1. Psychology. I. Wood, Samuel E.

BF121.W67 2002 150 C00-933164-6

Original full-length edition published by Allyn and Bacon, Inc., a division of Pearson Education, Needham Heights, Massachusetts.

ISBN 0-205-36456-X

Vice-President, Editorial Director: Michael Young
Editor-in-Chief: David Stover
Acquisitions Editor: Jessica Mosher
Marketing Manager: Judith Allen
Senior Developmental Editor: Lise Dupont
Production Editor: Joe Zingrone
Copy Editor: Lisa Berland
Production Coordinator: Peggy Brown
Page Layout: Monica Kompter/Silver Birch Graphics
Permissions/Photo Research: Susan Wallace-Cox
Art Director: Mary Opper
Cover/Interior Design: Monica Kompter/Silver Birch Graphics
Cover Image: Juan Silva/Imagebank

2 3 4 5 06 05 04 03 02

Printed and bound in the United States of America.

To our families, our friends,
and Eileen's two smallest fans
— Alexander and Lochlain.

Brief Contents

Contents

Chapter 7 Intelligence, Cognition, and Language 212

Chapter 8 Development 250

Boxes

It Happened in Canada

On the Cutting Edge in Canada

World of Psychology

Remember It!

Try It!

Apply It!

An Invitation to the Student

We all learn best when we can apply new concepts to the world we know. The third edition of *The World of Psychology* allows you to do just that. Highly interactive and active, clearly written, and thoroughly up to date, this textbook will encourage you to think for yourself as you learn about, relate to, and apply the psychological principles that affect your life.

So that you can make the most of all the material in the following pages, this textbook package incorporates a number of helpful features and ancillary items.

A Clear, Engaging Writing Style

Few texts have received such positive responses from students as *The World of Psychology,* and first and foremost is praise for its writing style. In fact, class tests of the first edition got 100-percent positive feedback at a range of schools. The style is conversational and the text uses numerous everyday examples and real-life imagery to help you grasp even the most complex concepts.

Each chapter opens with a vignette—a dramatic real-life story or series of stories in the news—that draws you into the chapter topics and shows how psychology relates to the world around you. Each vignette is memorable and directly related to the chapter's content.

You'll be especially interested in the stories of

- The increase in work rage in Canada
- James Stone, Jr., a boy who could feel no pain
- Therapies and therapists offering services on the Web

It Happened in Canada boxes discuss interesting Canadian news events with the goal of drawing you into the section of the chapter that explains the psychology behind the event.

Interact with Your Textbook!

What better way to learn new material—to make it fresh, interesting, and memorable—than for you to demonstrate the principles for yourself? The unique *Try It!* feature will encourage you to learn by doing. This highly praised feature provides simple experiments that you can perform without elaborate equipment, usually as you read.

Research has shown that checking your progress at key points as you study will help you remember what you have read. One other way you can interact with your textbook is by taking the *Remember It!* quizzes at the end of many major sections.

Link It! icons appear at appropriate places throughout the text to alert you that related or updated information is available through related links.

Finally, you'll have a chance to relate psychological principles to your own life, in the *Apply It!* section at the end of each chapter. Each *Apply It!* helps you to apply psychology to your personal life and issues. Topics include

- Handedness: Does It Make a Difference?
- How to Win the Battle against Procrastination
- Improving Memory with Mnemonic Devices
- Stimulating Creativity

SQ3R: A Formula for Success

This textbook is organized to help you maximize your learning by following five steps: Survey, Question, Read, Recite, and Review. Together, these are known as the *SQ3R method*. You will learn and remember more if, instead of simply reading each chapter, you follow these steps. Here's how they work.

Survey

First, scan the chapter you plan to read. The *chapter outline* helps you preview the content and its organization.

Read all the section headings and the *learning objective questions*, which are designed to focus your attention on key information that you should learn and remember.

Glance at the illustrations and tables, including the *Review & Reflect tables*. Then read the chapter's Summary & Review. This survey process gives you an overview of the chapter.

Question

Before you actually read each section in the chapter, turn each topic heading into one or more questions. For some sections a learning objective study question is provided, but you can also jot in questions of your own. For example, one topic in Chapter 1 is "The Goals of Psychology." The question is "What are the four goals of psychology?" You might add this question of your own: "What is meant by 'control' as a goal of psychology?" Asking such questions helps to focus your reading.

Read

Read the section. As you read, try to answer the learning objective question and your own question(s). After reading the section, stop. If the section is very long or if the material seems especially difficult or complex, you should stop after reading only one or two paragraphs.

Recite

After reading part or all of a section, try to answer the learning objective question and your own question(s). To better grasp each topic, write a short summary of the material. If you have trouble summarizing a topic or answering the questions, scan or read the section once more before trying again.

When you have mastered one section, move on to the next. If the text does not include a learning objective question, formulate your own. Then read and recite, answering your question or writing a brief summary as before.

Review

Periodically you will find a *Remember It!* that consists of a few questions about the preceding topics. Answer the questions and check your answers. If you make errors, quickly review the preceding material until you know the answers. An average of six *Remember Its!* are interspersed throughout each chapter to cover the material emphasized in the learning objective questions.

When you have finished the chapter, revisit the *Remember Its!* and then review the *Key Terms*. If you don't know the meaning of a key term, turn to the page that features the term's definition in the corner of the page. These highlighted glossary terms and definitions provide a ready reference for important key terms that appear in boldface print in the text. All definitions also appear in the end-of-text Glossary. Phonetic pronunciations are provided for more than 100 potentially hard-to-pronounce terms.

Next, turn to the *Summary & Review* section. Review each study question in the summary and answer it in your own words. The answers provided are given only as condensed reminders, and you should be able to expand on them.

Finally, look at the three *Thinking Critically* questions: *Evaluation*, *Point/Counterpoint*, and *Psychology in Your Life*. Answering these questions requires more than simple memorization. The critical thinking questions give you the chance to show that you really understand the information presented in the chapter.

And for Some Extra Practice...

A variety of student ancillary items may be available from your bookstore. Check with your instructor.

Study Guide

By Dan Kelts and Tom Malcomson, this guide applies the tried-and-tested learning technique—SQ3R—to a variety of exercises for each chapter.

Website

Visit the Online Resources on the Pearson Education Canada website (www.pearsoned.ca/highered) to access this textbook's Companion Website for a wealth of information and assistance related to introductory psychology. Interact with an online study guide, chat with other students, or just browse.

Preface

In preparing the third edition of this book, our primary goals were to introduce critical issues in psychology accurately and clearly to students, using a format that is both interesting and memorable. We present the principles of psychology using a clear and engaging writing style and a pedagogically sound learning format that is accessible and appealing to students.

Having taught thousands of students their first course in psychology, we are sensitive to the complexities of the teaching/learning process, and are acutely aware of the tremendous changes that have occurred in the field of psychology over the years. With this in mind, we sought to create a textbook that is sensitive to the changing needs of modern students and their professors and that will provide a context in which readers may learn about psychology's past, present, and probable future.

New to This Edition

With such an overwhelming response to the first and second Canadian editions of *The World of Psychology*, we found it difficult to devise improvements to the book. In accordance with reviewer suggestions and the goals stated above, the third Canadian edition has been revised in the following ways:

- A new, more lively and colourful page layout has been designed to improve readability, emphasize content retention, highlight the text's learning aids, and appeal to today's students.
- Canadian and international research has been updated to reflect new trends in psychology and society.
- Sixty percent of the opening vignettes have been replaced to make the content relevant for the audience and the times.
- Emphasis on Canadian culture and psychology has been integrated throughout the text, illustrating how culture shapes and defines our experience and reflecting the multicultural and diverse reality of our society.
- The *It Happened in Canada* boxes and *Link Its!* have been thoroughly updated.

Features Retained from the Second Edition

We have retained many of the features from the second edition that generated such positive responses from instructors and students alike.

Canadian Context

Our Canadian colleagues and their students find that many introductory psychology texts target an American audience. The issues, research citations, and practical examples in these texts increasingly relate to U.S. events and experiences. We believe that students learn best when materials are relevant to their lives. The Canadian content in this text includes events in the media, current research, and historical references to Canadian facts and contributors. By including information that is more meaningful to Canadian students, we hope to enhance their understanding and retention of the material.

Part of the Canadian identity is our recognition of the diversity in society. To acknowledge this, we have made an effort to include the influential work of psychologists from around the world. Also, we have tried to include events and studies from different regions of Canada. We believe this added value makes *The World of Psychology,* Third Canadian Edition, a balanced, universal text.

A Clear, Understandable, Interesting Writing Style

First and foremost, a textbook is a teaching instrument. A good psychology text must communicate clearly to a wide audience of various ages and levels of academic ability. Our book is appealing to accomplished students, yet accessible to those whose academic skills are still developing.

We achieved this objective (we hope) by explaining concepts in much the same way as we do in our own psychology classes. Throughout the text we sought to ensure flow and continuity by using a conversational style and avoiding abrupt shifts in thought. In addition, the text is filled with everyday examples that are pertinent to students' lives.

A Series of High-Interest Features That Will Appeal to Today's Students

Every chapter opens with a vignette to capture student interest and build motivation. We have also included special features:

- *Apply It!* sections show the practical applications of the principles of psychology.
- *It Happened in Canada* boxes discuss Canadian news events that demonstrate concepts outlined in the text.
- *On the Cutting Edge in Canada* boxes highlight contemporary research being conducted in Canadian universities.
- *World of Psychology* boxes in selected chapters explore special diversity issues.

A Textbook That Encourages Students to Become Active Participants in the Learning Process

Reading about psychology is not enough. Students should be able to practise what they have learned, where appropriate. Many of the principles we teach can be demonstrated, often without elaborate equipment and sometimes as the student reads. What better way to teach new material and make it fresh, interesting, and memorable than to have students demonstrate principles for themselves using an important and innovative element of the book: *Try It!* sections. The response to *Try It!* demonstrations from professors and students has been so positive that this feature appears in every chapter. The *Try It!* sections personalize psychology and make it come alive.

Student involvement is also promoted through the use of rhetorical questions and by casting the student in the role of the participant in selected studies and descriptions of real-life events. Thus, students who use *The World of Psychology* become active participants in the learning process rather than simply passive recipients of information.

An Emphasis on Critical Thinking

Thinking critically does not call for being critical of all viewpoints other than one's own. Rather, critical thinking is a process of evaluating claims, propositions, or conclusions objectively, to determine whether they follow logically from the evidence presented. Critical thinkers are open-minded, objective, and unbiased, and they maintain a skeptical attitude that leads them to search for alternative explanations.

Critical thinking is too important to leave to chance. The first *Apply It!* section, "Being a Good Consumer of Psychological Research," provides students with an understanding of what critical thinking entails. In addition to promoting critical thinking throughout the text, we have also developed a systematic method of nurturing it. A *Critical Thinking* section at the end of each chapter features three types of questions:

1. Evaluation questions teach students to think critically as they take stock of psychological theories, techniques, approaches, perspectives, and research studies.
2. Point/counterpoint questions require students to comprehend, analyze, and formulate convincing arguments on both sides of important issues in psychology.
3. Real-life application questions allow students to apply psychological principles and concepts to their own lives and the everyday world.

Help for Students to Understand Human Diversity and More Fully Comprehend the Part Multicultural Issues Play in Modern Psychology

Human diversity issues are integrated throughout the book, both within the main text presentation and as highlighted special features. This form of presentation parallels the presence of diversity in Canada as a mainstream and special interest issue. Diversity issues include cultural, gender, and age concerns in selected topic areas in each chapter. For example, we focus on the problem of bias in a special section, "Avoiding Ageism, Sexism, and Cultural Bias in Research." Later, we discuss the impact of culture on memory, interpretation of emotion, and preferred forms of therapy. These, along with other segments, help to promote understanding of human diversity and how it is an integral part of our perception of the world.

Current Coverage That Preserves the Classic Contributions in Our Field

Advances in knowledge and research are occurring at an ever-increasing pace, and modern authors must keep abreast. This edition introduces students to the most up-to-date research on many topics that feature rapid change, including advanced technologies, neuropsychology, gender differences, sexual orientation, violence, aggression and stress, adolescent drug use, death and bereavement, and new therapies.

Yet we do not value newness for its own sake. We include, as well, studies that have stood the test of time, and we explore the classic contributions to psychology in depth.

An Appreciation of Psychology's History and an Understanding That Psychology is a Living, Growing, Evolving Science

A portion of Chapter 1 is devoted to psychology's history. But in our view, the history of psychology is best understood and appreciated in the context in which the contributions were made. Consequently, discussions of such topics as learning, memory, intelligence, emotion, and personality integrate the historical and recent research contributions to show how psychology has evolved up to the present day.

An Accurate and Thoroughly Researched Textbook That Features Original Sources

To accomplish our goal of introducing the world of psychology accurately and clearly, we have gone back to original sources and have read or reread the basic works of the major figures in psychology and the classic studies in the field. This has enabled us to write with greater clarity and assurance, without having to hedge or write tentatively when discussing what experts in the field have actually said. This book is one of the most carefully researched, up-to-date, and extensively referenced psychology textbooks available.

A Sound Pedagogical System in the Text and Learning Package

The pedagogical system in *The World of Psychology* consists of the following components:

- *Learning Objective Questions*. Learning objectives written in question form guide student reading by focusing attention on key information; providing a framework for the SQ3R approach; and assisting students in preparing for exams.
- *Remember It!* An average of six *Remember It!* memory checks have been included in each chapter. These checks are designed to encourage students to pause and test comprehension of material they have just read, and of content emphasized in the *Learning Objective Questions*.
- *Review & Reflect Tables*. We have expanded our use of the extremely popular summary tables, called *Review & Reflect*, which are useful for reviewing and comparing various perspectives, theories, and other concepts.
- *Text-Embedded Glossary*. A text-embedded glossary provides a ready reference for important key terms that appear in boldface in the text. At the end of each chapter, the key terms are listed along with the page numbers on which they appear. Definitions also appear in the back glossary. Phonetic pronunciations are provided for more than 100 potentially hard-to-pronounce terms.
- *Summary & Review*. These end-of-chapter sections provide answers to the *Learning Objective Questions*. The feature can be used both as a preview to the chapter and as a review in preparing for tests.

A Complete, Coordinated Teaching Package of the Highest Quality

The *Instructor's Resource Manual* (IRM) was developed to encourage student involvement and understanding with lecture examples, demonstrations, in-class activities, critical thinking topics, diversity issues, and guides to using other ancillary materials. *The World of Psychology* is also supported by a comprehensive *Test Bank* and *Computerized Test Item File* (for Macintosh and Windows). The test bank includes detailed explanations for answers to the more difficult questions.

Pearson Education Canada also allows you to seamlessly integrate an online component into your course. The content cartridge built to accompany *The World of Psychology*, Third Canadian Edition, is available for the WebCT, Blackboard, and CourseCompass platforms and provides course management functionality combined with our rich online content.

Also available is the *CBC/Prentice Hall Allyn and Bacon Canada Video Library for The World of Psychology*, featuring an exciting selection of CBC video clips from *The Health Show*.

Lastly, a superb set of acetate transparencies, CNN videos, CD-ROM-based learning materials, and much more, is available to instructors. Please speak to your Pearson Education Canada sales representative for more information about these and other ancillary materials.

Top-Quality, Innovative Supplements to Enhance Students' Learning

A comprehensive and innovative *Study Guide* accompanies the book. It features language enrichment, practice tests for each chapter, flash cards, graphics, and a variety of additional exercises to help students learn the material.

A new way to deliver educational content, the *Pearson Education Canada Companion Website* offers students and instructors a wide range of features, including an online study guide with instant feedback, and a syllabus builder. See the Companion Website spread for more detail.

Acknowledgments

We want to thank the following conscientious and knowledgeable reviewers, listed below in alphabetical order, whose suggestions have helped shape the third Canadian edition of this book.

Kathryn Bauer, Conestoga College

Jean Brown, Cambrian College

Tom Callaghan, St. Clair College

Dr. Dan Crocco, Mohawk College

Rick Grant, Loyalist College

Paul Hillock, Algonquin College

Louise Jarrold, Dawson College

Vivian Lucas, Sheridan College

Marilyn J. Quinn, Niagara College

Also, we are indebted to an incredible group of people at Pearson Education Canada for their contributions to *The World of Psychology*. First, we want to thank Clifford Newman and Rebecca Bersagel for getting the first and second editions of the book off the ground. Lise Dupont, developmental editor; Joe Zingrone, production editor; and Lisa Berland, copy editor, provided expert assistance throughout the writing process. Special thanks also to Silver Birch Graphics and Pearson's Creative Services department for creating this text's eye-catching new interior design.

About the Authors

Samuel E. Wood

Samuel E. Wood received his doctorate from the University of Florida. He has taught at West Virginia University and the University of Missouri–St. Louis and was a member of the doctoral faculty at both universities. From 1984 to 1996, he served as president of the Higher Education Center, a consortium of 14 colleges and universities in the St. Louis area. He was a co-founder of the Higher Education Cable TV channel (HEC-TV) in St. Louis and served as its president and CEO from its founding in 1987 until 1996. Dr. Wood is currently assistant to the president and adjunct professor of psychology at Lindenwood University.

Ellen R. Green Wood

Ellen Green Wood received her doctorate in educational psychology from St. Louis University and is currently an adjunct professor of psychology at St. Louis Community College at Meramec. Previously she taught in the clinical experiences program in education at Washington University and at the University of Missouri–St. Louis. In addition to her teaching, Dr. Wood has developed and taught seminars on critical thinking. She received the Telecourse Pioneer Award from 1982 through 1988 for her contributions to the field of distance learning.

Eileen Wood

Eileen Wood is an associate professor in the Department of Psychology at Wilfrid Laurier University. She conducts research in developmental and educational psychology. Her primary interest involves studying how people learn new information and how features of the learning environment affect the learner. She began teaching introductory psychology for nursing and broadcasting students in Ontario while she completed her Ph.D. She continued teaching introductory psychology when she moved to Wilfrid Laurier. Since then, she has taught a variety of courses, and her interaction with students has led to the development of this text.

Serge Desmarais

Dr. Serge Desmarais received his Ph.D. in social psychology from the University of Waterloo. He is an associate professor of psychology at the University of Guelph, where his responsibilities include teaching graduate and undergraduate courses and research supervision. His expertise involves social psychology, gender issues, close relationships, and social justice. Dr. Desmarais is an active researcher and the author of many articles and book chapters in the areas of interpersonal relations, social justice, work and pay expectations, and gender issues. He has been actively involved as a consultant to both public and private organizations, such as the Public Service Commission of Canada, the National Study on Gender and Work, the Correctional Service of Canada, and the Canadian Imperial Bank of Commerce.

The Pearson Education Canada companion Website...

Your Internet companion to the most exciting, state-of-the-art educational tools on the Web!

The Pearson Education Canada Companion Website is easy to navigate and is organized to correspond to the chapters in this textbook. The Companion Website comprises these distinct, functional features:

Customized Online Resources, including *Try Its!* and *Link Its!*

Online Interactive Study Guide

Study Break Sites

Table of Contents

Explore these areas in this Companion Website. Students and distance learners will discover resources for indepth study, research, and communication, empowering them in their quest for greater knowledge and maximizing their potential for success in the course.

A NEW WAY TO DELIVER EDUCATIONAL CONTENT

Course Management

Our Companion Websites provide instructors and students with the ability to access, exchange, and interact with material specially created for our individual textbooks.

- **Syllabus Manager** provides instructors with the option of creating online classes and constructing an online syllabus linked to specific modules in the Companion Website.
- **Grader** allows the student to take a test that is automatically marked by the program. The results of the test can be e-mailed to the instructor and then added to the student's record.
- **Help** includes an evaluation of the user's system and a tune-up area that makes updating browsers and plug-ins easier. This new feature will facilitate the use of our Companion Websites.

Instructor Resources

This section features modules with additional teaching material organized by chapter for instructors. Downloadable PowerPoint Presentations, Electronic Transparencies, and an Instructor's Manual are just some of the materials that may be available in this section. Where appropriate, this section will be password protected. To get a password, simply contact your Pearson Education Canada representative or call Faculty Sales and Services at 1-800-850-5813.

General Resources

This section contains information that is related to the entire book and that will be of interest to all users of the site. A Table of Contents and a Glossary are just two examples of the kind of information you may find in this section.

The General Resources section may also feature *Communication facilities* that provide a key element for distributed learning environments:

- **Message Board** – This module takes advantage of browser technology to provide the users of each Companion Website with a national newsgroup to post and reply to relevant course topics.
- **Chat Room** – This module enables instructors to lead group activities in real time. Using our chat client, instructors can display website content while students participate in the discussion.

1 Introduction to Psychology

Have you seen the T-shirt slogan "You are so off the island"?

Even if you haven't seen or heard the slogan, you know what it means. You and 5.6 million other Canadians and 50 million Americans were probably tuned into the last episode of Survivor. Even if you didn't watch the show yourself, you know about Rich and Kelly. You probably also know about Rudy. If you are like millions of other people, the summer of 2000 included watching 16 people begin a 49-day adventure on an island in Borneo. Each week one participant was voted off the island until finally it came down to Kelly and Rich. Rich walked away with a new car and one million dollars–Kelly with $100 000. Can you honestly say that you didn't support either Rich or Kelly in the final moments of their island experience? Apart from instantly capturing the fascination of millions of viewers, the show Survivor became a part of our culture. It was, and still is, part of our collective consciousness and knowledge. Even people who did not watch the show, or who tried actively to avoid watching it, could not escape the show's pres-

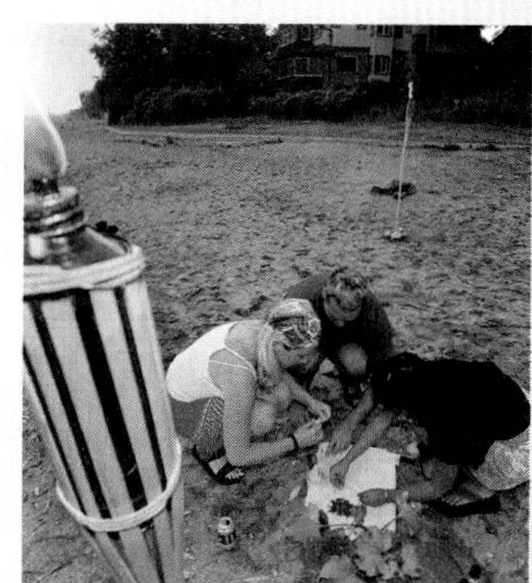

ence either in the media or in people's casual conversations. The evidence lies in the instant recognition of the slogan.

But why were *Survivor* and *Survivor: The Australian Outback* so popular? Why were so many people captivated by the weekly series? We suspect it is because people are simply curious about the behaviours of others; we are curious to see how people behave when facing unusual conditions. We ask ourselves how we may have handled the same conditions and we evaluate the appropriateness of others' responses. And our fascination with real people's lives is not new, but it appears that TV producers have finally realized that people's real lives matter to us.

When you hear the word *psychology*, what is the first thing that comes to mind? Would you say that it is how to handle yourself when on a deserted island hoping to win $1 000 000? Probably not. Most people's conception of the field of psychology consists of stories about Freud, some vague understanding of psychotherapy, and perhaps some exposure to recent self-help books—likely books about relationships and personal growth. However, the fact is that psychology covers more issues than you expect, including the often simple but sometimes complex situations encountered in our everyday lives (even those of the *Survivor* contestants!).

There are many branches of psychology (to which you will be introduced in this text) and psychologists specializing in different branches look at situations from different perspectives. For example, keeping in mind the show *Survivor,* a social psychologist might investigate whether we perceive ourselves as having better skills or better coping strategies than others when handling extreme situations. On the other hand, a personality psychologist may be interested in whether people who have certain types of personality might be better contestants or may be more successful in handling the types of situations to which the island contestants were exposed.

In contrast, a cognitive psychologist might be more concerned with the problem solving or thought processes that contestants expressed during the show. They may be interested to find out whether we can teach people the problem-solving skills that may help them deal better with the situations they encountered.

It is not possible in this brief introduction to portray the full range of research possibilities that might interest psychologists as well as the ways in which these various research avenues might be investigated. This book, *The World of Psychology*, is designed to expose you to psychological research and to help clarify some of the complexities of this academic discipline.

Introduction to Psychology

The word *psychology* makes people conjure up images of mental disorders, abnormal behaviour, and adjustment to difficult periods of life. As we pointed out above, however, though psychologists do sometimes study the strange and unusual, they are most often interested in day-to-day events—the normal and commonplace.

Just what is psychology? Psychology has changed over the years and so has its definition. In the late 1800s mental processes were considered to be the appropriate subject matter of psychology. Later there was a movement to restrict psychology to the study of observable behaviour alone. Today the importance of both areas is recognized, and **psychology** is now defined as the scientific study of behaviour and mental processes.

Answer the questions in *Try It!* to see how much you already know about some of the topics we will explore in *The World of Psychology*.

Try It!

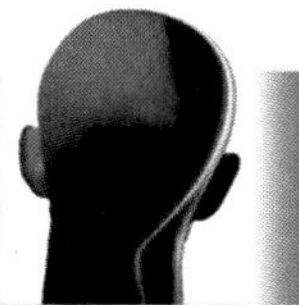

Test Your Knowledge of Psychology

Indicate whether each statement is true or false.

___ 1. Memory is more accurate under hypnosis.

___ 2. All people dream during a night of normal sleep.

___ 3. As the number of bystanders at an emergency increases, the time it takes for the victim to get help decreases.

___ 4. There is no maternal instinct in humans.

___ 5. Older adults tend to express less satisfaction with life in general than younger adults do.

___ 6. Eyewitness testimony is often unreliable.

___ 7. Children with high IQs tend to be less able physically than their peers.

___ 8. Creativity and high intelligence do not necessarily go together.

___ 9. When it comes to close personal relationships, opposites attract.

___ 10. The majority of teenagers have good relationships with their parents.

Psychology: Science or Common Sense?

Students begin their first course in psychology with various expectations about psychology. At first, many of them consider it more common sense than science. Will you be studying a collection of common-sense notions this semester? Or can we make a valid claim that psychology is a science?

While you were answering the *Try It!* questions, common sense may have led you astray. All the odd-numbered items are false, and all the even-numbered items are true. So common sense, on its own, will not take you very far in your study of psychology.

Many people believe that whether a field of study is a science depends on the nature of its body of knowledge. Physics, for example, is a science, and so is chemistry. But neither qualifies as a science solely because of its subject matter. A science is a science not because of the nature of its body of knowledge, but because of the approach—the standards, methods, values, and general principles—employed in acquiring that body of knowledge. Psychology is considered a science because it uses the scientific method, which minimizes biases, preconceptions, personal beliefs, and emotions (Christensen, 1997).

The Goals of Psychology

What are the four goals of psychology?

The goals of psychology are the description, explanation, prediction, and control of behaviour and mental processes. Psychological researchers always seek to accomplish one or more of these goals when they plan and conduct their studies.

The first goal, *description*, is usually the first step in understanding any behaviour or mental process. It is therefore more important in a very new area of research or in the early stages of research. Researchers describe the behaviour or mental process of interest as accurately and as completely as possible. A description tells "what" occurred.

The second goal, *explanation*, requires an understanding of the conditions under which a given behaviour or mental process occurs. An explanation enables researchers to state the causes of the behaviour or mental process. In other words, it tells "why" a given event or behaviour occurred. But researchers do not reach the goal of explanation until their results have been tested, retested, and confirmed. Researchers confirm an explanation by eliminating or ruling out other, competing explanations.

The goal of *prediction* is met when researchers can specify the conditions under which a behaviour or event is likely to occur. If researchers have identified all the prior conditions required for a behaviour or event to occur, they can predict the behaviour or event.

The goal of *control* is accomplished when researchers know how to apply a principle or change a condition to prevent unwanted occurrences or to bring about desired outcomes. A therapy could be designed to prevent anxiety attacks; a technique could be employed to improve one's memory.

psychology: The scientific study of behaviour and mental processes.

What Is a Theory?

Any science has a well-established body of theory to guide its research, and psychology is no exception. A **theory** is a general principle or set of principles that explains how a number of separate facts are related to one another. A theory enables researchers to fit many separate facts into a larger framework; thus, it imposes order on what otherwise would be a disconnected jumble of data. The value of a theory depends upon how well it accounts for the accumulated research findings in a given area and upon how accurately it can predict new findings.

A theory serves two important functions: (1) it organizes facts—a necessary step toward arriving at a systematic body of knowledge—and (2) it guides research.

Basic and Applied Research

What is the difference between basic and applied research?

The two main types of research psychologists pursue to accomplish their goals are (1) basic, or pure, research and (2) applied research. The purpose of **basic research** is to seek new knowledge and to explore and advance general scientific understanding. Basic research investigates such topics as the nature of memory, brain function, motivation, emotional expression, and the causes of mental disorders such as schizophrenia, depression, sleep and eating disorders, and so on. Psychologists doing basic research usually seek to accomplish the first three goals—description, explanation, and prediction. Basic research is not intended to solve specific problems, nor is it meant to investigate ways to apply what is learned to immediate real-world problems. Yet very often the findings of basic research are later applied in real-world settings.

Applied research is conducted specifically for the purpose of solving practical problems and improving the quality of life. Applied research focuses on such things as methods to improve memory or increase motivation, therapies to treat mental disorders, and ways to decrease stress. Applied psychologists are primarily concerned with the fourth goal—control—because it specifies ways and means of changing behaviour. You will learn more about some fields of applied psychology later in this text.

Descriptive Research Methods

The goals of psychological research—description, explanation, prediction, and control—are typically accomplished in stages. In the early stages of research, descriptive methods are usually the most appropriate. **Descriptive research methods** yield descriptions rather than identify causes of behaviour. Naturalistic observation, laboratory observation, the case study, and the survey are examples of descriptive research methods.

Naturalistic Observation: Caught in the Act of Being Themselves

What is naturalistic observation, and what are some of its advantages and limitations?

Naturalistic observation is a research method in which researchers observe and record behaviour in its natural setting without attempting to influence or control it. Ethnologists are researchers who study the behaviour patterns of animals in their natural environment. These researchers might observe their subjects through high-powered telescopes or from blinds that they build to conceal themselves.

Often human subjects are not aware that they are being observed. This can be accomplished by means

Although naturalistic observation allows researchers to study behaviour in everyday settings, observer bias may cause them to see what they expect to see.

of one-way mirrors—a technique researchers often use to observe children in nursery schools or special classrooms. You may have seen episodes of *W5, 20/20,* or *Candid Camera* in which hidden cameras or tape recorders were used to gather information from people "caught in the act of being themselves."

The major advantage of naturalistic observation is that it allows one to study behaviour in normal settings, where it occurs more naturally and spontaneously. Naturalistic observation may be the only feasible way to study certain phenomena when an experiment would be impossible or unethical—for example, to learn how people react during disasters like earthquakes or fires.

Naturalistic observation has its limitations, however. Researchers must wait for events to occur; they cannot speed the process up or slow it down. And because they have no control over the situation, the researchers cannot reach conclusions about cause-and-effect relationships. Another potential problem in naturalistic observation is observer bias, which is a distortion in researchers' observations. Observer bias can result when researchers' expectations about a situation cause them to see what they expect to see or to make incorrect inferences about the behaviour they observe.

Laboratory Observation: A More Scientific Look at the Subject

Another method of studying behaviour involves observation that takes place not in a natural setting but in the laboratory. There researchers can exert more control and use more precise equipment to measure responses. Much of our knowledge about sleep, for example, has been gained by laboratory observation of subjects who sleep for several nights in a sleep laboratory or sleep clinic.

The Case Study Method: Studying a Few Subjects in Depth

What is the case study method, and for what purposes is it particularly well-suited?

Another descriptive research method used by psychologists is the **case study**, or case history. In a case study, a single individual or a small number of people are studied in great depth, usually over an extended time. A case study involves observation, interviews, and sometimes psychological testing. A case study is exploratory in nature, and its purpose is to provide a detailed description of some behaviour or disorder. This method is particularly appropriate for studying people who have uncommon psychological or physiological disorders or brain injuries. Case studies often emerge in the course of treatment of these disorders. You may have read the book or seen the movie *Sybil,* the case study of a young woman who had multiple personalities. Much of what we know about unusual psychological disorders such as multiple personality comes from the in-depth analyses provided by case studies.

Although the case study has been useful in advancing knowledge in several areas of psychology, it has certain limitations. In a case study, researchers cannot establish the cause of observed behaviours. Moreover, because so few people are studied, researchers do not know how generalizable their findings are to larger groups or to different cultures.

Survey Research: The Art of Sampling and Questioning

What are the methods and purposes of survey research?

Psychologists are interested in many questions that cannot be investigated using naturalistic observation or case studies. With a **survey**, researchers

theory: A general principle or set of principles that explains how a number of separate facts are related to one another.

basic research: Research conducted for the purpose of advancing knowledge rather than for its practical application.

applied research: Research conducted for the purpose of solving practical problems.

descriptive research methods: Research methods that yield descriptions of behaviour rather than causal explanations.

naturalistic observation: A research method in which researchers observe and record behaviour without trying to influence or control it.

case study: An in-depth study of one or a few participants consisting of information gathered through observation, interviews, and perhaps psychological testing.

survey: A method whereby researchers use interviews and/or questionnaires to gather information about the attitudes, beliefs, experiences, or behaviours of a group of people.

use interviews and/or questionnaires to gather information about the attitudes, beliefs, experiences, or behaviours of a group of people. Well-designed and carefully conducted surveys have provided much of the information available to us about the incidence of drug use, about the sexual behaviour of particular segments of the population, and about the incidence of various mental disorders.

Selecting a Sample: There Are More Than Numbers to Consider

What is a representative sample, and why is it essential in a survey?

Researchers in psychology rarely conduct experiments or surveys using all members of the group they are studying. For example, researchers studying the sexual behaviour of Canadian women do not attempt to study every woman in Canada. Instead of studying the whole **population** (the entire group of interest), they study a sample. A **sample** is a part of the population that is selected and studied in order to reach conclusions about the entire larger population of interest.

However, researchers must ensure that the sample is representative. A **representative sample** is one that includes important subgroups in the same proportion as they are found in the larger population. That is, it should reflect the ethnic, cultural, and sexual diversity of the target population.

The Use of Questionnaires

Researchers using the survey method rely on information gathered through questionnaires or interviews, or through some combination of the two. Questionnaires can be completed more quickly and less expensively than interviews.

Many people believe that a survey becomes more accurate when more people answer it. In fact, the number of people who respond to a survey is not the critical element. A researcher can generalize findings from a sample only if it is representative of the entire population of interest. For example, the readers of *Flare* or *The Hockey News* do not represent a cross-section of Canadians. So questionnaires in magazines are not scientific; neither are TV phone-in surveys. Good surveys control wording, context, and format (Schwarz, 1999).

The Interview: A Better Way

"The best survey research uses the personal interview as the principal method of gathering information" (Kerlinger, 1986, p. 379). Skilled interviewers can gather accurate information by asking well-worded questions to a carefully selected sample of subjects.

When respondents feel comfortable with an interviewer, they feel freer to share personal information. Imagine that you are being interviewed about a sensitive subject such as your sexual behaviour. Will you be equally comfortable and truthful whether the interviewer is male or female? Young, middle-aged, or old? Chinese, black, francophone, or of another ethnic group? Christian or Jewish? Middle class or working class? The validity or truthfulness of responses can be affected by the interviewer's personal characteristics, which include gender, age, heritage, religion, social class, accent, and vocabulary.

Advantages and Disadvantages of Survey Research

Surveys, if conducted properly, can provide highly accurate information about large numbers of people and can show changes in attitudes and behaviour over time. Yet large-scale surveys can also be costly and time-consuming. Researchers must have expertise in many areas—in selecting a representative sample, constructing questionnaires, interviewing, and analyzing data.

The major limitation of the survey is that the respondents may provide inaccurate information. Respondents may give false information because of faulty memory or a desire to please the interviewer (saying what they think the interviewer wants to hear). Respondents may have a tendency to present themselves in a good light ("the social desirability response"). They may even deliberately mislead the researcher.

The Experimental Method: Searching for Causes

What is the main advantage of the experimental method?

Descriptive research methods (naturalistic observation, the case study, and the survey) are all well-suited for satisfying the first goal of psychology—namely,

Remember It!

Research Methods

1. Basic research is designed to solve practical problems. (true/false)
2. Researchers using naturalistic observation attempt to control the behaviour being observed. (true/false)
3. Much knowledge about sleep and the human sexual response has been gained through
   a. naturalistic observation.
   b. laboratory observation.
   c. the survey.
   d. the case study.
4. The case study is *not* useful for
   a. learning about rare physical and psychological disorders.
   b. learning the consequences of rare brain injuries.
   c. supplying detailed descriptions of behaviour that can provide the foundation for psychological theories.
   d. studying large numbers of people.
5. The survey is most useful when we wish to learn about
   a. rare psychological and physical disorders.
   b. behaviours, beliefs, or attitudes of a large group of people.
   c. how people react during natural disasters.
   d. how people respond under highly controlled conditions.
6. The most accurate surveys are those with the largest number of respondents. (true/false)
7. If the sample for a survey is relatively large, it should still be representative. (true/false)

Answers: 1. false 2. false 3. b 4. d 5. b 6. false 7. true

description. From descriptions, researchers may propose possible explanations for the behaviours they study. At some point researchers usually seek to determine the causes of behaviour and various other psychological phenomena.

What, for example, are the causes of depression, insomnia, stress, forgetting, and aggression? The **experimental method**, or the experiment, is the only research method that can be used to identify cause–effect relationships.

An experiment is designed to test a **hypothesis**—a prediction about a cause–effect relationship between two or more conditions or variables. A variable is any condition or factor that can be manipulated, controlled, or measured. One variable of interest to you is the grade you will receive in this psychology course. Another variable that probably interests you is how you should spend your time studying for this course. Do you suppose there is a cause–effect relationship between how you spend your time studying and the grades you will receive?

The answer to that question is yes. In 1990, Woloshyn and Willoughby of Brock University, Wood of Wilfrid Laurier University, and Pressley of the University of Notre Dame conducted an experiment to determine the impact of study strategies on learning factual material, such as that found in textbooks (Woloshyn, Willoughby, Wood, and Pressley, 1990). They wanted to see which of the three study strategies outlined below was most effective. Sixty students doing the introductory psychology course participated.

1. *Repetition.* Twenty students were asked to study by reading the information repeatedly, a study technique that many students prefer.
2. *Imagery.* Another 20 students were asked to generate a mental picture for each fact that they studied. This imagery method allowed them to create any mental picture as long as it contained the material to be learned.

population: The entire group of interest to researchers and to which they wish to generalize their findings; the group from which a sample is selected.

sample: The portion of any population that is selected for study and from which generalizations are made about the larger population.

representative sample: A sample of participants selected from the larger population in such a way that important subgroups within the population are included in the sample in the same proportions as they are found in the larger population.

experimental method: The research method whereby researchers randomly assign participants to groups and control all conditions other than one or more independent variables, which are then manipulated to determine their effect on some behaviour measured–the dependent variable in the experiment.

hypothesis: A prediction about the relationship between two or more variables.

3. *Why questions.* The last 20 students were taught how to answer "why" questions, such as "Why would that fact be true?" The questions encouraged them to draw on their own knowledge to make the facts more meaningful and hence more memorable.

In each case, all students were given the same amount of time and the same facts to study. After they had studied all the facts, students were given a memory test. The only thing that was different among the groups, then, was the type of study strategy that they used.

What were the results? As you might imagine, the participants who were asked to use the more sophisticated strategies, imagery and "why" questions, remembered more than the students who simply repeated the information. However, memory performance of students using imagery was the same as that of students answering "why" questions. The researchers concluded that although many students prefer to study by repeatedly reading the material they are trying to learn, they are much better off creating mental images or answering questions (see Figure 1.1 for results). We hope that these results will guide you in studying for this and other courses.

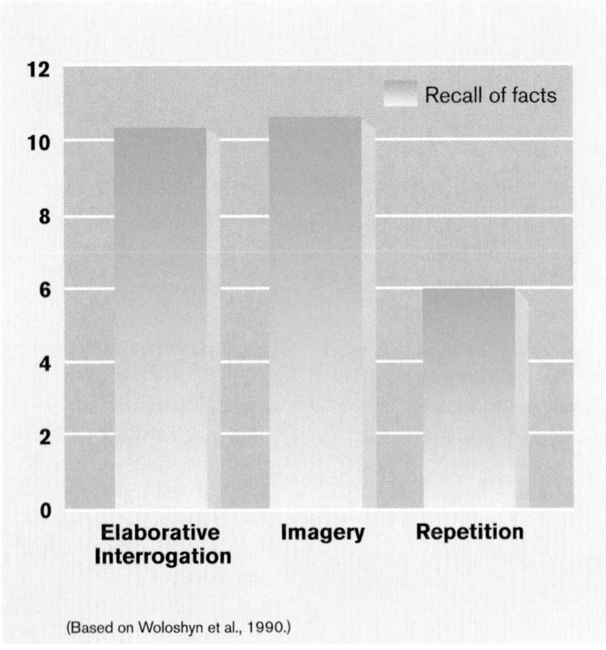

FIGURE 1.1
Study Strategies and Memory Performance

Independent and Dependent Variables

What is the difference between the independent variable and the dependent variable?

In all experiments there are two types of variables. First, there are one or more **independent variables**—variables that the researcher manipulates in order to determine whether they cause a change in another behaviour or condition. Sometimes the independent variable is referred to as the *treatment*. In the experiment by Woloshyn et al., there was one independent variable—the study strategy that was assigned.

The second type of variable found in all experiments is the **dependent variable.** It is measured at the end of the experiment and is presumed to vary (increase or decrease) as a result of the manipulations of the independent variable or variables. The dependent variable is presumed to depend on or to be affected by changes in the independent variable. In the study by Woloshyn et al., the dependent variable was memory of the factual information tested at the end of the study

Experimental and Control Groups: The Same Except for the Treatment

How do the experimental and control groups differ?

Most experiments are conducted using two or more groups of participants. There must always be at least one **experimental group**—a group of participants who are exposed to the independent variable or the treatment. In the experiment described above, Woloshyn and colleagues used two experimental groups:

Group 2: Imagery

Group 3: "Why" questions

In most experiments it is desirable to have a **control group**—a group that is similar to the experimental group and used for purposes of comparison. The control group is exposed to the same experimental environment as the experimental group but is not given the treatment. The first group in the Woloshyn experiment was not exposed to the independent variable—that is, this group was not taught to use a sophisticated study strategy. Because this group was similar to the experimental group and was exposed to the same experimental environment, it should be considered a control group. In an experiment, all groups, including the control group, are measured on the dependent variable at the end of the experiment.

Control in the Experiment: Attempting to Rule Out Chance

By conducting experiments in a laboratory, the experimenters can control the environmental setting to rule out other factors. For example, frustration, pain, and extreme noise or heat can change responses. Researchers carefully control the environment to ensure that these conditions are not present. They vary only the independent variables. That way, they can be reasonably certain that the manipulation of the independent variables is what causes any differences among the groups.

Generalizing the Experimental Findings: Do the Findings Apply to Other Groups?

What should we conclude from the Woloshyn experiment? Can we conclude that all students should use imagery or ask themselves "why" questions when studying? Before we reach such a conclusion, we should consider several factors:

- The only participants used in this experiment were introductory psychology students. Can we be sure that the same results would have occurred if individuals of other ages or groups had been used?
- The participants in this experiment were not classified according to their level of prior knowledge of the subject they were studying. Would the same results be true for both students who knew a lot in this area and those who did not?

To apply this experiment's findings to other groups, researchers would have to replicate, or repeat, the experiment using different populations of participants.

Potential Problems in Experimental Research

If an experiment is properly designed and conducted, the researcher should be able to attribute changes in the dependent variable to the manipulations of the independent variable. But several factors other than the independent variables can cause changes in the dependent variable, thereby destroying the validity of the experiment. Three of these potential problems are selection bias, the placebo effect, and experimenter bias. Researchers must design experiments to control for these and other problems, which could invalidate the results.

Selection Bias: Bias from the Start

What is selection bias, and what technique do researchers use to control for it?

Selection bias occurs when participants are assigned to groups in such a way that systematic differences among the groups are present at the beginning of the experiment. If selection bias occurs, differences at the end of the experiment may not reflect the manipulation of the independent variable; rather, they may be due to pre-existing differences in the groups.

To control for selection bias, researchers must use **random assignment.** This involves selecting participants through chance (such as drawing names out of a hat) to ensure that all have an equal probability of being assigned to any of the groups. Random assignment maximizes the likelihood that the groups will be similar at the beginning of the experiment. If there had been pre-existing differences in the level of prior knowledge in the Woloshyn experiment, random assignment would have spread those differences across the groups.

independent variable: In an experiment, the factor or condition that the researcher manipulates in order to determine its effect on another behaviour or condition known as the dependent variable.

dependent variable: The variable that is measured at the end of an experiment and that is presumed to vary as a result of manipulations of the independent variable.

control group: In an experiment, a group that is similar to the experimental group and that is exposed to the same experimental environment but is not exposed to the independent variable; used for purposes of comparison.

selection bias: The assignment of participants to experimental or control groups in such a way that systematic differences among the groups are present at the beginning of the experiment.

random assignment: In an experiment, the assignment of participants to experimental and control groups through a chance procedure, which guarantees that all participants have an equal probability of being placed in any of the groups; a control for selection bias.

The Placebo Effect: The Power of Suggestion (for the Participant)

What is the placebo effect, and how do researchers control for it?

Another factor that can influence the outcome of an experiment is the **placebo effect**. This occurs when the response to a treatment is due to the person's expectations rather than to the actual treatment itself. Suppose a drug is prescribed for a patient, and the patient reports improvement. The improvement could be a direct result of the drug, or it could be the result of the patient's expectation that the drug will work. Studies have shown that remarkable improvement in patients can sometimes be attributed solely to the power of suggestion—the placebo effect.

The researcher must use a control group to test whether results in an experiment are due to the treatment or to the placebo effect. So people in the control group are given a fake treatment. In drug experiments the control group is usually given a **placebo**—a harmless substance such as a sugar pill or an injection of saline solution. To control for the placebo effect, researchers do not let participants know whether they are in the *experimental* group (receiving the treatment) or in the *control* group (receiving the placebo). If getting the real drug or treatment results in a significantly greater improvement than receiving the placebo, the improvement can be attributed to the drug rather than to the power of suggestion.

But what about the expectations of those who conduct the experiments—the researchers or confederates (the experimenters or anyone else associated with the study) themselves?

Experimenter Bias: The Power of Suggestion (for the Experimenter)

What is experimenter bias, and how is it controlled?

The expectations of the experimenter are a third factor that can influence the outcome of an experiment. **Experimenter bias** occurs when researchers' preconceived notions or expectations cause them to find what they expect to find. A researcher's expectations can be communicated to the participants, perhaps unintentionally, through tone of voice, gestures, and facial expressions. These communications can influence the participants' behaviour. Expectations can also influence a researcher's interpretation of the experiment's results, even if no influence occurred during the experiment. When the interpretation supports the researcher's expectations in this way, it is called the *self-fulfilling prophecy*.

To control for experimenter bias, researchers must not know which participants are assigned to the experimental and control groups. The identities of both the experimental and control participants are coded, and their identities are not revealed to the researcher until after the research data are collected and recorded. (Obviously, someone assisting the researcher must know which participants are in which group.) When neither the participants nor the experimenters know which participants are getting the treatment and which are in the control group, the **double-blind technique** is being used. The double-blind technique is the most powerful procedure for studying cause–effect relationships.

Advantages and Limitations of the Experimental Method

The overwhelming advantage of the experiment is its ability to reveal cause–effect relationships. This is possible because researchers are able to exercise strict control over the experimental setting. This allows them to rule out factors other than the independent variable as possible reasons for differences in the dependent variable. But often, the more control the experimenter exercises, the more unnatural and contrived the research setting becomes, and the less generalizable the findings will be to the real world. When participants know that they are taking part in an experiment, they may behave differently than they would in a more natural setting. When a natural setting is considered to be an important factor in a study, researchers may run a field experiment (i.e., an experiment conducted in a real-life setting). The advantage of field studies is that participants behave more naturally. For example, in many studies, the researchers cannot control for background noise, amount of sunlight, temperature, and other environmental variables. These variables are, however, assumed to be less important.

A major limitation of the experimental method is that in many areas of interest to researchers, an experiment is either unethical or impossible. Some treatments cannot be given to humans because their physical or psychological health would be endangered, or their rights violated.

Remember It!

The Experimental Method

1. The experimental method is the *only* research method that can be used to identify cause–effect relationships between variables. (true/false)
2. Which of the following statements is *not* true about a control group?
   a. It should be similar to the experimental group.
   b It is exposed to the independent variable.
   c At the end of the experiment, it is measured on the dependent variable.
   d. It is used for purposes of comparison.
3. Match the description with the appropriate term.

____	1) A prediction about a relationship between two variables	a. independent variable
____	2) Any condition that can be manipulated, measured, or controlled	b. variable
____	3) The variable measured at the end of the experiment	c. hypothesis
____	4) The variable manipulated by the researcher	d. dependent variable

4. The placebo effect occurs when a participant responds according to
   a. the hypothesis.
   b. the actual treatment.
   c. how other subjects behave.
   d. his or her expectations.
5. The results of an experiment can be influenced by the expectations of either the participants or the researcher. (true/false)
6. Random assignment is used to control for
   a. experimenter bias.
   b. the placebo effect.
   c. selection bias.
   d. subject bias.

Answers: 1. true. 2. b 3. 1) c 2) b 3) d 4) a 4. d 5. true 6. c

Other Research Methods

The Correlational Method: Discovering Relationships, Not Causes

What is the correlational method, and when is it used?

We know that researchers are interested in finding the results and causes of various psychological phenomena. Does stress cause illness? Does arguing with friends cause a decline in the number of friendships? Does heavy marijuana use cause students to lose interest in school and get lower grades? Researchers would like to have answers to these questions, but none of them can be researched by the experimental method. It is often illegal and always unethical to assign

placebo (pluh-SEE-bo) effect: The phenomenon that occurs when a person's response to a treatment (or response to the dependent variable in an experiment) is due to expectations regarding the treatment rather than to the treatment itself.

placebo: Some inert substance, such as a sugar pill or an injection of saline solution, given to the control group in an experiment as a control for the placebo effect.

experimenter bias: A phenomenon that occurs when the researcher's preconceived notions in some way influence the participants' behaviour and/or the interpretation of experimental results.

double-blind technique: An experimental procedure in which neither the participants nor the experimenters know who is in the experimental and control groups until the results have been gathered; a control for experimenter bias.

humans randomly to experimental conditions that could be harmful. Also, individuals have features that the experimenter cannot manipulate, such as age and sex. Since people cannot be arbitrarily assigned an age, researchers instead look at the relationships between age and other factors.

To find out whether arguing with friends causes a decline in the number of friendships, no researcher would randomly assign students to an experimental study that would require those in the experimental groups to consistently argue with their friends. Can you imagine being asked to argue with all your friends for two years, for the good of scientific progress?

Much of our knowledge of the effects on human health of marijuana, cigarette smoking, stress, and even relationships has been gained through experiments on animals or through other research methods. When for ethical or practical reasons an experimental study cannot be performed to determine cause–effect relationships, the **correlational method** is usually used. This method determines the correlation, or relationship, between two characteristics, events, or behaviours—that is, the degree of association between the two variables under consideration. A group is selected for study, and the variables of interest are measured for each participant in the study. The variables might be the amount of marijuana used and grade-point average. Then the researcher applies a statistical formula to obtain a correlation coefficient.

The Correlation Coefficient: How Variables Relate

What is a correlation coefficient?

A **correlation coefficient** is a numerical value indicating the degree and direction of the relationship between two variables. A correlation coefficient ranges from + 1.00 (a perfect positive correlation) to .00 (no relationship) to –1.00 (a perfect negative correlation). The sign of a correlation coefficient (+ or –) indicates whether the two variables vary in the same or opposite directions. A positive correlation indicates that two variables vary in the same direction; in other words, an increase in the value of one variable is associated with an increase in the value of the other variable. Or, a decrease in the value of one variable is associated with a decrease in the value of the other. There is a positive though weak correlation between stress and illness, for example. When stress increases, illness is likely to increase; when stress decreases, illness tends to decrease.

A negative correlation means that an increase in the value of one variable is associated with a decrease in the value of the other variable. Think of a negative correlation as a seesaw—when one variable goes up, the other goes down. There is a negative correlation between the number of cigarettes people smoke and the number of years they can expect to live. The more people smoke, the shorter their life expectancy.

The number in a correlation coefficient indicates the relative *strength* of the relationship between two variables—the higher the number, the stronger the relationship. Examples of variables that are *not* correlated are grade-point average and height, and illness and shoe size.

Correlation and Prediction

Correlations are useful in making predictions. The stronger the relationship between the variables, the better the prediction. A perfect correlation (+ 1.00 or –1.00) would enable you to make completely accurate predictions.

The fact that there is a correlation between two variables does not necessarily mean that one variable causes the other. Only the experimental method allows us to reach conclusions about cause and effect. When two variables such as stress and illness are correlated, we cannot conclude that stress makes people sick. It might be that illness causes stress, or that a third factor such as poverty or poor general health increases susceptibility to both illness and stress, as shown in Figure 1.2.

Psychological Tests: Assessing the Participant

Psychologists have developed a wide range of tests for measuring intelligence, scholastic achievement, aptitudes, creativity, vocational interests, personality traits, and psychiatric problems. Depending on where you live in Canada, you may have taken some of these tests while in school—an IQ test, the Canadian Test of Cognitive Abilities, or the WISC-R, to name three. Psychological tests are used in a variety of situations—in schools, in the workplace, and in therapeutic settings. They are used to evaluate or compare individuals, to measure changes in behaviour, and to make predictions about behaviour. Test

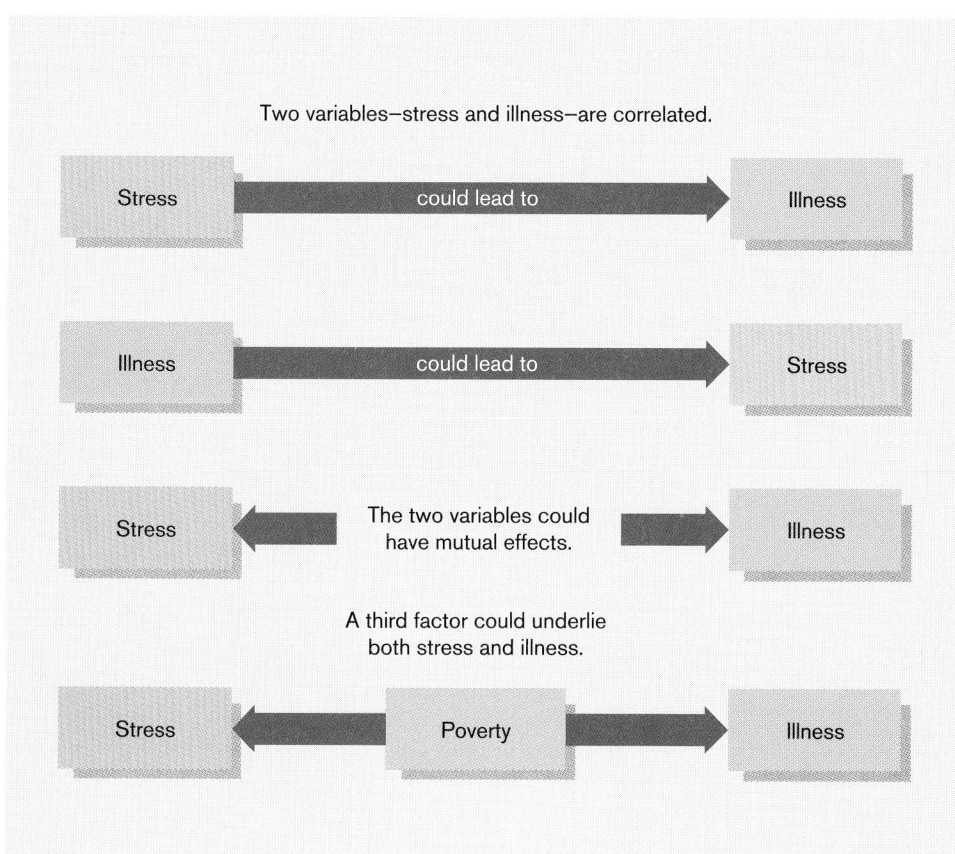
Two variables–stress and illness–are correlated.
Stress
could lead to
Illness
Illness
could lead to
Stress
Stress
The two variables could have mutual effects.
Illness
A third factor could underlie both stress and illness.
Stress
Poverty
Illness

FIGURE 1.2
Correlation Does Not Prove Causation A correction between two variables does not prove that a cause–effect relationship exists between them. There is a correlation between stress and illness, but that does not mean that stress necessarily causes illness. Both stress and illness may result from another factor, such as poverty or poor general health.

results also provide information that can be used in educational decision making, personnel selection, and vocational guidance. But these psychological tests, and all other tests, are useless unless they are both reliable and valid.

Reliability refers to the consistency of a test. A reliable test will yield nearly the same score time after time as the same person is tested and then retested. **Validity** is the test's ability to measure what it is intended to measure. Just as a clock is a valid instrument for measuring time but not speed, so a psychological test must be able to measure accurately and adequately the specific area it is designed to measure—achievement or vocational aptitude, for example.

Psychologists often use testing in conjunction with their research. Tests may be administered as part of a case study. And in an experiment, the dependent variable might be the score on a psychological test. For example, an educational psychologist who is experimenting with a new educational program might use an achievement test to compare the performances of experimental and control subjects.

Tests are also used in correlation studies. To determine the correlation between high school and university grades, researchers might statistically compare the actual high school grades of participants with their university grades. Review & Reflect 1.1 summarizes the different research methods discussed in this chapter.

correlational method: A research method used to establish the relationship (correlation) between two characteristics, events, or behaviours.

correlation coefficient: A numerical value that indicates the strength and direction of the relationship between two variables; ranges from +1.00 (a perfect positive correlation) to −1.00 (a perfect negative correlation).

reliability: The ability of a test to yield nearly the same scores when the same people are tested and then retested using the same test or an alternative form of the test.

validity: The ability of a test to measure what it is intended to measure.

Remember It!

The Correlational Method

1. A correlation coefficient shows a cause–effect relationship. (true/false)
2. Which of the following describes a negative correlation?
   a. When the value of one variable goes up, the value of the other variable goes down.
   b. When the value of one variable goes down, the value of the other goes down.
   c. When the value of one variable goes up, the value of the other goes up.
   d. When the value of one variable goes up or down, the value of the other variable remains unchanged.
3. Which of the following correlation coefficients indicates the strongest relationship?
   a. +.65
   b. −.78
   c. .00
   d. +.25
4. Psychological tests are sometimes used in experiments or correlation studies. (true/false)

Answers: 1. false 2. a 3. b 4. true

REVIEW & REFLECT 1.1
Research Methods in Psychology

Method	Description	Advantages	Limitations
Naturalistic observation	Researcher observes and records behaviour in its natural setting. Participants may or may not know they are being observed.	Good source of descriptive information. Can provide basis for hypotheses to be tested later. Behaviour studied in everyday setting is more natural.	Researchers' expectations can distort observations (observer bias). Presence of researcher may influence behaviour of participants. Little or no control over conditions.
Laboratory observation	Observation under more controlled conditions where sophisticated equipment can be used to measure responses.	More control than naturalistic observation.	Possible observer bias. Behaviour of participants may be less natural than in naturalistic observation.
Case study	In-depth study of one or a few participants using observation, interviews, psychological testing.	Source of information for rare or unusual conditions or events. Can provide basis for hypotheses to be tested later.	May not be representative of condition or event. Time-consuming. Subject to misinterpretation by researcher.
Survey	Interviews and/or questionnaires used to gather information about attitudes, beliefs, experiences, or behaviours of a group of people.	Can provide accurate information about large numbers of people.	Responses may be inaccurate. Sample may not be representative. Characteristics of interviewer may influence responses.
Experimental method	Random assignment of participants to groups. Manipulation of independent variables and measurement of their effects on the dependent variable.	Enables identification of cause–effect relationships.	Laboratory setting may inhibit natural behaviour of participants. Findings may not be generalizable to the real world. In some cases, experiment is unethical.
Correlational method	Method used to determine the relationship (correlation) between two events, characteristics, or behaviours.	Can assess strength of relationship between variables. Provides basis for prediction.	Does not demonstrate cause and effect.
Psychological tests	Tests used for measuring intelligence, scholastic achievement, aptitudes, vocational interests, personality traits, psychiatric problems.	Provide data for educational and vocational decision making, personnel selection, research, and psychological assessment.	Tests may not be reliable or valid.

Participants in Psychological Research

Human Participants in Psychological Research

For practical reasons, most studies with humans in the past 30 years have used college or university students. Students are a convenient group to study, and researchers/professors often encourage their participation by offering pay or points toward a course grade. Psychology studies have also used a disproportionate number of males (Gannon et al., 1992) and whites (Graham, 1992).

Heavy reliance on college and university students presents a problem. Students are a relatively select group in terms of age, socioeconomic status, educational level, and cultural diversity. How generalizable the findings of such studies are to the general population depends on the nature of the specific study. Studies that investigate basic psychological processes such as sensation, perception, and memory are likely to be relatively generalizable, because these processes probably function in similar ways in most adults. But in research on human social behaviour, there is great individual and cultural variation and thus a problem in generalizing the results of studies with college and university students to other segments of the population. (See the discussion of ageism, sexism, and cultural bias in psychological research in the *World of Psychology* box.)

LINK IT!

www.sshrc.ca/english/programinfo/policies/ethics.htm
SSHRC Policies: Ethical Conduct for Research Involving Humans

The Use of Animals in Research

Why are animals used in research?

Where would psychology be today without Pavlov's dogs, Skinner's pigeons, the ubiquitous white rat, and the many other species of animals used to advance scientific knowledge? Psychologists recognize that laboratory animals have been and still are immensely important in research; most psychologists favour their continued use. Animals are used in 7 to 8 percent of psychological experiments; 95 percent of the animals used are rodents (American Psychological Association, 1984).

LINK IT!

www.cpa.ca/guide7.html
Guidelines for Use of Animals in Research (Canadian Psychological Association)

Those conducting animal research in Canada are bound by the Canadian Code of Ethics for Psychologists (Canadian Psychological Association, 1988) as well as by the ethical code of the Canadian Council on Animal Care (1989). These documents support the humane treatment of animals. This means that researchers must do everything possible to minimize discomfort, pain, and illness in animal subjects. The Canadian Council on Animal Care is also responsible for checking active laboratories, usually on a three-year cycle. Furthermore, research with animals is supported only when there is a reasonable expectation that valuable knowledge will be obtained.

Many of the marvels of modern medicine would not have been available today without the use of animals in research. Why are animals used in research? There are at least five reasons: (1) They provide a simpler model for studying processes that operate

Most psychologists recognize that many scientific advances would not have been possible without animal research. Where do you stand on this issue?

similarly in humans. (2) Researchers can exercise far more control over animal subjects and thus be more certain of their conclusions. (3) A wider range of medical and other manipulations can be used with animals. (4) It is easier to study the entire life span and multiple generations in some animal species. (5) Animals are cheaper to use and are available at the researcher's convenience. (Of course, researchers also use animals when they want to learn more about the animals themselves.)

Nevertheless, controversy has long surrounded the use of animals in research. Animal rights advocates are becoming more militant in their efforts to stop animal research. They have broken into research laboratories, freed laboratory animals, destroyed research records, and wrecked laboratory equipment and other property. One animal rights group has demanded that all animal research studies be stopped immediately. Many activists are also against using animals for food, clothing, or any other purpose.

WORLD OF PSYCHOLOGY

Avoiding Ageism, Sexism, and Cultural Bias in Psychological Research

In planning and conducting psychological inquiries, researchers need to consider many factors besides scientific methodology. For example, they must be sensitive to human differences and show respect for the dignity of human participants. Several researchers have cited evidence of bias in psychological research. Our awareness of biases makes us more careful when designing and interpreting studies.

For example, ageism is a continuing source of bias. This is seen both in the language used in psychological research (Schaie, 1993) and in clinicians' preferences for younger clients (Zivian et al., 1992, 1994). Titles of research papers on aging often focus on loss, deterioration, decline, and dependency. According to Schaie, "Most research on adulthood shows that differences between those in their 60s and those in their 80s are far greater than those between 20- and 60-year-olds" (1993, p. 50). These observations demonstrate how important it is to guard against descriptions or conclusions that imply that all members of a group are defined by deterioration, forgetfulness, and deficits. The research with Canadian clinicians also makes it clear that clinicians should be sensitive to how they select clients. Overall, clinicians preferred younger clients over middle-aged clients, and middle-aged clients over senior clients (Zivian et al., 1992). These preferences may make it more difficult for older adults to get psychological assistance. The researchers suggest that "education about, exposure to, and experience with psychotherapy with older adults" would probably help moderate these preferences.

Research also suggests that familiarity with clients' cultural heritage and gender issues facilitates effective counselling (Malone, 2000) and research investigations (Darou, Kurtness, & Hum, 2000). Seven out of eight researchers were expelled from a Cree community because their research techniques were too rigid and insensitive to traditional Cree values (Darou et al., 2000). The lack of flexibility on the part of the researchers not only had a negative impact on the community, but it had the potential to restrict their ability to investigate a unique population and, hence, limit our understanding of this group. Fortunately, one researcher was able to employ a design that was sensitive to the cultural expectations of the community while maintaining scientific standards. In a similar way, greater awareness of cultural orientations, expectations, and traditional techniques (such as healing techniques within Native communities) makes clinicians more effective counsellors for their clients (Malone, 2000).

Inequities regarding gender issues have aroused concern among psychologists and researchers in psychology. In 1984, two Canadian researchers, Connie Stark-Adamec and Meredith Kimball, wrote a position paper that highlighted the possible harm that sexism could cause to psychological research. In their view, sexism is present when there exists "the premise that men, and the behaviour patterns characteristic of males, are superior to and more representative of the human experience than women or behaviour characteristics of females" (1984, p. 24). Fortunately, gender bias in the selection of research participants has decreased over the last decade (Ader & Johnson, 1994). In addition, there is a growing body of literature that advocates for a greater awareness of gender, culture, and age issues in order to promote more effective research and counselling.

Ethics in Research: First and Foremost

What are some ethical guidelines governing the use of human participants in research?

In 1991, the Canadian Psychological Association adopted a new set of ethical standards governing research with humans (with recent proposed changes; Hadjistavropoulos & Malloy, 2000). These standards safeguard the rights of experimental participants while supporting the goals of scientific inquiry. Participation must be voluntary, and there must be respect for confidentiality. Moreover, participants must be free to withdraw from the study at any time. At a more local level, colleges and universities usually have ethics committees that must approve any research studies proposed by professors or students.

Can studies that use deception be justified on scientific grounds? Many psychologists believe they can be. Others are against deception in any circumstances. Diane Baumrind (1985) opposes research using deception because of the potential harm to the participants. She also believes that such practices will damage the reputation of psychology and psychologists and cause people to lose confidence in the profession.

Even so, deception is used in many research studies, particularly in the field of social psychology. Today the Canadian Psychological Association's code of ethical standards allows deception

1. If it is justified by the value of the potential findings, in circumstances where equally effective procedures that do not involve deception cannot be used;
2. If participants are not deceived about "physical risks, discomfort, or unpleasant emotional experiences" that might affect their willingness to participate; *and*
3. If participants are debriefed as soon as possible after the experiment.

The debriefing sessions are designed to provide participants with information about the nature of the research and to clear up any misconceptions they may have had about what occurred during the study. Researchers want to erase any harmful effects of the deception and to ensure that participants understand that no other participants were actually harmed.

IT HAPPENED IN CANADA

Ethics of Government Data Collection

Psychologists are not the only ones who have to be sensitive to ethical issues when they conduct research or gather information. In May 2000, several newspapers reported that the Canadian Ministry of Human Resources had collected a computer database that held over 2000 pieces of information about every Canadian citizen (Ayed, 2000; Stone, 2000). Labelled the "Big Brother Database," the data include personal information, such as ethnicity, education, marital status, family disabilities, and tax, employment, and medical records, among other things. The Privacy Commissioner raised serious concerns that the government, or anyone else, who accessed the data could potentially misuse the information. Above all, from an ethical perspective, critics are concerned that the government is quietly tracking the lives of Canadians without their knowledge, without the right to do so. The government defended creating the database by pointing to the advantages of planning potential labour shortages and other trends, and also indicated that the personal information was masked to ensure that anyone using the database could not link it to a specific person. In your opinion, has the federal Ministry of Human Resources acted unethically?

LINK IT!

www.cpa.ca/ethics.html
Canadian Code of Ethics for Psychologists

The Historical Progression of Psychology: Exploring the Different Perspectives

If we were to trace the development of psychology from the beginning, we would need to stretch far back to the earliest pages of recorded history, even beyond the early Greek philosophers, such as Aristotle and Plato. People have always had questions about human nature and human behaviour. For centuries these questions were considered to be in the realm of philosophy.

LINK IT!

serendip.brynmawr.edu/Mind/Table.html
Mind and Body: René Descartes to William James

Remember It!

Research Participants and Ethics

1 Which of the following groups has *not* been overrepresented as participants in psychological research?
   a. whites
   b. males
   c. females
   d. university students
2. Psychologists are required to debrief participants thoroughly after a research study when the study
   a. violates participants' privacy.
   b. deceives participants about the true purpose of the research.
   c. exposes participants to unreasonable risk or harm.
   d. wastes taxpayers' money on trivial questions.
3. Investigators use animals in psychological research to learn more about humans. (true/false)
4. The Canadian Psychological Association has guidelines for ethical treatment for human participants but not for animal subjects. (true/false)
5. Which of the following has *not* been identified as a source of bias in psychological research, according to the text?
   a. age
   b. gender
   c. race
   d. religion

Answers: 1. c 2. b 3. true 4. false 5. d

IT HAPPENED IN CANADA

Our History Highlights

Psychology has been an active discipline in Canada since 1838, when the first course in psychology was offered at Dalhousie University. A significant milestone for the advancement of psychology in Canada was the founding of the Canadian Psychological Association in 1939. In conjunction with the American Psychological Association, the Canadian Psychological Association serves as the governing body, providing ethical guidelines and research initiatives. For more milestones in Canadian psychology, check the inside cover of your text!

Wilhelm Wundt: The Founding of Psychology

What was Wilhelm Wundt's contribution to psychology?

It was not until experimental methods were applied to the study of psychological processes that psychology became recognized as a formal academic discipline. Three German physiologists—Ernst Weber, Gustav Fechner, and Hermann von Helmholtz—were the first to apply experimental methods to the study of psychological processes. In so doing, they profoundly influenced the early development of psychology.

Although a number of early researchers contributed to the new field of psychology, Wilhelm Wundt is generally thought of as the founder of psychology. His psychological laboratory in Leipzig, Germany, founded in 1879, is considered the "birthplace" of psychology as a formal academic discipline. However, the studies and experiments that Wundt, his associates, and his students performed in that early laboratory were very different from psychology as we know it today.

For Wundt, the subject matter of psychology was experience—the actual, immediate, conscious experiences of individuals. Wundt believed that mental experiences could be reduced to basic elements, just as the early chemists were able to describe water as composed of the basic elements of hydrogen and oxygen (H_2O). In other words, Wundt was searching for the structure of conscious experience.

Wundt and his associates conducted experiments on reaction times and on attention span. They also studied the perception of a variety of visual (sight), tactile (touch), and auditory (hearing) stimuli, including rhythm patterns.

Titchener and Structuralism: Psychology's Blind Alley

What were the goals and methods of structuralism, the first school of psychology?

Wundt's most famous student, Edward Bradford Titchener, introduced psychology to North America. Although Titchener differed from Wundt on some points, he pursued similar goals. He gave the name **structuralism** to this first school of thought in psychology, which aimed at analyzing the basic elements, or the structure, of conscious mental experience.

Structuralism was most severely criticized for its primary method, introspection. Introspection was not objective, even though it involved observation, measurement, and experimentation. When different introspectionists were exposed to the same stimulus, such as the click of a metronome, they often reported different experiences. And when the same person was exposed to exactly the same stimulus at different times, he or she often reported somewhat different experiences. Structuralism was not considered a viable school of thought for long. Later schools of thought in psychology were established partly in reaction against structuralism, which collapsed as an approach when Titchener died.

Functionalism: The First North American School of Psychology

What was the goal of the early school of psychology known as functionalism?

As structuralism was losing its influence in the early 1900s, a new school of psychology called *functionalism* was taking shape. **Functionalism** was concerned not with the structure of consciousness but with how mental processes function—that is, with how humans and animals use mental processes in adapting to their environment.

An influential book by Charles Darwin, *On the Origin of Species by Means of Natural Selection* (1859), had a strong impact on the leading proponents of functionalism. Darwin's ideas about evolution and the continuity of species were largely responsible for the increasing use of animals in psychological experiments.

Another British thinker (and a cousin of Darwin) was Sir Francis Galton, who did pioneering work in the study of individual differences and the role of genetic inheritance in mental abilities. He also made a significant contribution in the areas of measurement and statistics.

Darwin's and Galton's ideas contributed much to the new school of functionalism. The American psychologist William James (1842–1910) was an advocate of functionalism, even though he did much of his writing before this school of psychology appeared. James's best-known work is his highly regarded *Principles of Psychology*, published more than 100 years ago (1890). James taught that mental processes are fluid and that they have continuity rather than a rigid or fixed structure (which is what the structuralists suggested). James spoke of the "stream of consciousness," which he said functioned to help humans adapt to their environment.

Functionalism broadened the scope of psychology to include the study of behaviour as well as mental processes. It also included the study of children, animals, and people who were mentally impaired. These groups had not been studied by the structuralists because they could not be trained to use introspection. Functionalists also established the subfield of applied psychology—for example, the psychology of education, the workplace, and individual differences.

LINK IT!

www.emory.edu/EDUCATION/mfp/james.html
An award-winning William James site.

Gestalt Psychology: The Whole Is More Than Just the Sum of Its Parts

What is the emphasis of Gestalt psychology?

Several schools of thought arose in part as a reaction against structuralism. Gestalt psychology was one of these. This school appeared in Germany in 1912, at around the same time that Watson was launching behaviourism. The

structuralism: The first formal school of psychology, aimed at analyzing the basic elements, or structure, of conscious mental experience through the use of introspection.

functionalism: An early school of psychology that was concerned with how mental processes help humans and animals adapt to their environments; developed as a reaction against structuralism.

Gestalt psychologists objected to the central idea of structuralism—that we can best understand conscious experience by reducing it to its basic elements. **Gestalt psychology** emphasized that individuals perceive objects and patterns as whole units, and that the whole thus perceived is more than just the sum of its parts. The German word *Gestalt* roughly means "whole, form, or pattern."

The leader of the Gestalt psychologists was Max Wertheimer (1880–1943), who introduced a famous experiment demonstrating the *phi* phenomenon. Perhaps you have seen flashing neon lights that you perceive as figures moving back and forth. Actually, the separate lights are being flashed on and off with precision timing: this is the phi phenomenon. We perceive wholes or patterns, not collections of separate and independent sensations. For the Gestaltists, the phi phenomenon proved that perceptions do not all arise from independent sensations, as the structuralists contended.

Other prominent Gestalt psychologists were Kurt Koffka and Wolfgang Köhler. Gestalt psychologists are still influential in the psychology of perception, which will be discussed in Chapter 3.

LINK IT!

www.enabling.org/ia/gestalt/gerhards/
Society for Gestalt Theory and its Applications (GTA)

Behaviourism: Never Mind the Mind

How did behaviourism differ from previous schools of psychology?

Psychologist John B. Watson (1878–1958) looked at the study of psychology as defined by the structuralists and functionalists and disliked virtually everything he saw. In Watson's view, the study of mental processes, the concepts of mind and consciousness, and the primary investigative technique of introspection were not scientific. Watson pointed out that each person's introspection is strictly individual. He further maintained that self-reflection and internal pondering cannot be observed, verified, understood, or communicated in objective, scientific terms. He argued that all the strictly subjective techniques and concepts in psychology must be thrown out. He did not deny the existence of conscious thought or experience. He simply did not view them as appropriate topics for psychology.

Watson proposed a radically new approach to psychology. This new school of psychology, called **behaviourism,** redefined psychology as the "science of behaviour." Behaviourism confined itself to the study of behaviour because it was observable and measurable and, therefore, objective and scientific. Behaviourism also emphasized that behaviour is determined primarily by factors in the environment.

B.F. Skinner: Continuing the Behaviourist Tradition

Behaviourism soon became the most influential school of thought in North American psychology. It is still a major force in modern psychology, in large part because of the profound influence of B.F. Skinner (1904–1990).

Skinner agreed with Watson that concepts such as mind, consciousness, and feelings were neither objective nor measurable and, therefore, were not the appropriate subject matter of psychology. Furthermore, Skinner argued that these concepts were not needed to explain behaviour. We can explain behaviour, he maintained, by analyzing conditions that were present before the behaviour occurred and by analyzing the consequences of the behaviour.

Skinner's research on operant conditioning emphasized the importance of reinforcement in learning and in the shaping and maintaining of behaviour. When a behaviour is reinforced (i.e., followed by pleasant or rewarding consequences), it is more likely to be performed again. Skinner's work has had a powerful influence on modern psychology.

Behaviourism has been criticized for ignoring inner mental processes such as thoughts and feelings. Many behaviourists today do not take as extreme a view as Skinner and his colleagues did. They still emphasize the study of behaviour, but they are also willing to consider how mental processes explain behaviour.

LINK IT!

www.bfskinner.org/
The B.F. Skinner Foundation

Psychoanalysis: It's What's Deep Down That Counts

What was the role of the unconscious in psychoanalysis, Freud's approach to psychology?

The behaviourists completely ignored unobservable mental forces in their explanations of behaviour. This is precisely where Sigmund Freud (1856–1939) looked in formulating his theory. Freud emphasized that unseen, unconscious mental forces were the key to understanding human nature and behaviour.

Freud developed a theory called **psychoanalysis.** He maintained that human mental life is like an iceberg. The smallest, visible part of the iceberg represents the conscious mental experience of the individual. But underwater, hidden from view, floats a vast store of unconscious impulses, thoughts, wishes, and desires. Although people are not aware of them directly or consciously, it is these unconscious forces that have the largest impact on behaviour.

Freud believed that the unconscious acts as a storehouse for material that threatens the conscious life of the individual—for disturbing sexual and aggressive impulses as well as traumatic experiences that have been repressed or "pushed down" to the unconscious. Once there, rather than resting quietly, the unconscious material festers and seethes.

Freud's psychological theory does not paint a very positive or hopeful picture of human nature. He believed that we do not consciously control our thoughts, feelings, and behaviours, but rather that these are determined by unconscious forces that we cannot see or control.

The overriding importance that Freud placed on sexual and aggressive impulses caused much controversy, both inside and outside the field of psychology. The most notable of Freud's famous students—Carl Jung, Alfred Adler, and Karen Horney—broke away from their mentor and developed their own theories of personality. These three are often referred to as the *neo-Freudians.*

Freud's influence on psychology is not nearly as strong as it once was (Robins et al., 1999). When people think of Freud, most imagine a psychiatrist psychoanalyzing a patient who is lying on a couch. The general public is familiar with such terms as the unconscious, repression, rationalization, and the Freudian slip. Such familiarity has made Freud a larger-than-life figure.

plaza.interport.net/nypsan/freudarc.html
Sigmund Freud and the Freud Archives

Humanistic Psychology: Looking at Human Potential

What is the focus of humanistic psychology?

Humanistic psychology emerged in part as a reaction against behaviourism and psychoanalysis. **Humanistic psychology** focuses on the uniqueness of human beings and their capacity for choice, growth, and psychological health. The humanists reject the behaviourist notion that people have no free will and are shaped and controlled strictly by the environment. Humanists also reject Freud's theory that people are determined and driven from within, acting and marching to the dark drums of the unconscious.

Abraham Maslow and other prominent humanistic psychologists, such as Carl Rogers, emphasized a much more positive view of human nature. They maintained that people are innately good and possess free will. Humanists believe that people are capable of making conscious, rational choices that can lead to growth and psychological health.

Maslow proposed a theory of motivation that consists of a hierarchy of needs. He considered the need for self-actualization (developing to one's fullest potential) to be the highest need in this hierarchy. Carl Rogers developed his person-centred therapy and,

Gestalt psychology (gehSHTALT): The school of psychology that emphasizes that individuals perceive objects and patterns as whole units and that the perceived whole is more than just the sum of its parts.

behaviourism: The school of psychology founded by John B. Watson that views observable, measurable behaviour as the appropriate subject matter for psychology and emphasizes the role of environment as a determinant of behaviour.

psychoanalysis (SY-ko-ah-NAL-ih-sis): The term Freud used for both his theory of personality and his therapy for the treatment of psychological disorders; the unconscious is the primary focus of psychoanalytic theory.

humanistic psychology: The school of psychology that focuses on the uniqueness of human beings and their capacity for choice, growth, and psychological health.

with other humanists, popularized encounter groups and other techniques that are part of the human potential movement.

Cognitive Psychology: Focusing on Mental Processes

What is the focus of cognitive psychology?

Cognitive psychology is a special branch of psychology that focuses on mental processes such as memory, problem solving, concept formation, reasoning and decision making, language, and perception. Just as behaviourism developed in part as a reaction against the focus on mental processes that was characteristic of structuralism and functionalism, so cognitive psychology grew and developed partly in response to strict behaviourism. Ironically, several psychologists who were behaviourists during the 1950s provided the greatest impetus to the development of cognitive psychology (Viney, 1993).

Cognitive psychologists see humans not as passive recipients who are pushed and pulled by environmental forces, but as active participants who seek out experiences, who alter and shape them, and who use mental processes to transform information in the course of their own cognitive development.

Pervasive in the research of cognitive psychology is the information-processing approach. According to this approach, our brain processes information in sequential stages, or levels, much as a computer does. "Increasingly, parallel processing models are developed in addition to stage models of processing" (Haberlandt, 1997, p. 2). Indeed, some cognitive psychologists have extended their study of problem solving, decision making, and other human mental processes to artificial intelligence. In this research, sophisticated computers are used to simulate the intellectual processes of the human brain.

Moreover, unlike the early behaviourists, psychologists today *can* observe some mental processes directly. Thanks to modern brain-imaging techniques, such as the PET scan, and sophisticated computer technology, researchers can observe the action (behaviour) of specific clusters of brain cells (neurons) as they carry out various mental processes (Raichle, 1994b). Such men-

Remember It!

Historical Perspectives in Psychology

1. Match the description with the appropriate school of psychology.

___	1) the scientific study of behaviour	a. Gestalt psychology
___	2) the perception of whole units or patterns	b. structuralism
___	3) the unconscious	c. functionalism
___	4) analysis of the basic elements of conscious mental experience	d. psychoanalysis
		e. humanistic psychology
___	5) the uniqueness of human beings and their capacity for conscious choice and growth	f. behaviourism
		g. cognitive psychology
___	6) the function of conscious mental experience	
___	7) the study of mental processes	

2. Match the major figures with the appropriate school of psychology.

___	1) James	a. behaviourism
___	2) Freud	b. structuralism
___	3) Watson and Skinner	c. functionalism
___	4) Wundt and Titchener	d. psychoanalysis
___	5) Maslow and Rogers	e. humanistic psychology

Answers: 1. 1) f 2) a 3) d 4) b 5) e 6) c 7) g. 2. 1) c 2) d 3) a 4) b 5) e.

REVIEW & REFLECT 1.2
Traditional and Modern Schools of Thought in Psychology

School	Description
Structuralism Wilhelm Wundt Edward Titchener	The first formal school of psychology. Focused on analyzing the basic elements or structures of conscious mental experience through the use of introspection.
Functionalism William James	The first North American school of psychology. Concerned with the study of mental processes and their role in facilitating adaptation to the environment. Broadened the scope of psychology to include the study of behaviour as well as mental processes, and the study of children, people who are mentally impaired, and animals.
Gestalt psychology Max Wertheimer Kurt Koffka Wolfgang Köhler	Emphasizes that individuals perceive objects and patterns as whole units. The perceived whole is more than just the sum of its parts and is not best understood by analysis of its elemental parts (as suggested by the structuralists).
Behaviourism John Watson B. F. Skinner	Views observable, measurable behaviour rather than internal mental processes as the appropriate subject matter of psychology. Stresses the roles of learning and the environment in determining behaviour.
Psychoanalysis Sigmund Freud	Emphasizes the role of unconscious mental forces and conflicts in determining behaviour.
Humanistic psychology Abraham Maslow Carl Rogers	Focuses on the uniqueness of human beings and their capacity for choice, growth, and psychological health. Called the "third force in psychology" (behaviourism and psychoanalysis being the other two forces).
Cognitive psychology	Focuses on mental processes such as memory, problem solving, reasoning, decision making, language, and perception. Uses information-processing approach.

tal activities as thinking, remembering, solving a problem, listening to a melody, speaking, viewing images and colours, and so on, have all been "observed," and this has provided a rich field of knowledge that cognitive psychologists use in their work.

LINK IT!

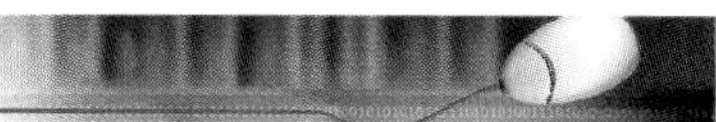

web.psych.ualberta.ca/%7emike/Pearl_Street/Dictionary/dictionary.html
University of Alberta Cognitive Science Dictionary

www.psych.purdue.edu/~coglab/
Cognitive Psychology Online Lab: "The purpose of this site is to help acquaint you with some of the influential research in cognitive psychology and give you the opportunity to experience these experiments yourself."

Review & Reflect 1.2 summarizes the various traditional and modern schools of thought in psychology.

Psychology Today

Perspectives in Psychology: Recent Views on Behaviour and Thinking

Modern psychologists are not easily categorized by specific schools of thought. There are no structuralists roaming the halls of psychology departments, and to our knowledge there are no professors who call themselves functionalists. Today, rather than discussing schools of psychology, it is more appropriate to refer to psychological perspectives—points of view used for explaining people's behaviour and thinking, whether normal or abnormal. Psychologists need not limit themselves to only one perspective or approach.

cognitive psychology: A speciality that studies mental processes such as memory, problem solving, reasoning, decision making, language, perception, and other forms of cognition; often uses the information-processing approach.

Some take an eclectic position, choosing a combination of approaches to explain a particular behaviour or psychological problem.

Biological Perspective: It's What's Inside That Counts

What is the focus of the biological perspective?

Psychologists who adopt the **biological perspective** emphasize biological processes and heredity as the keys to understanding behaviour and thinking. To explain thinking, emotion, and behaviour—both normal and abnormal—biologically oriented psychologists study the structures of the brain and central nervous system, the functioning of the neurons, the delicate balance of neurotransmitters and hormones, and the impact of genes. For example, we know that having too many or too few different neurotransmitters in the brain is related to various mental disorders such as schizophrenia and depression. Some drugs now being used to treat some of these disorders are designed to restore the brain's biochemical balance.

Researchers and theorists who adopt the biological perspective are often referred to as physiological psychologists, psychobiologists, or neuropsychologists. The continuing development of medical technology in recent decades has spurred the research efforts of physiological psychologists. Many important findings in psychology have resulted from their work.

Evolutionary Perspective: Adapting to the Environment

What is the focus of the evolutionary perspective?

The **evolutionary perspective** focuses on how humans have evolved and adapted behaviours required for survival in the face of various environmental pressures over the long course of evolution (Nesbitt, 1990). Evolutionary psychologists study how inherited tendencies and dispositions in humans influence a wide range of behaviours. For example, they tell us much about the way we select mates, the level of intellectual performance we demonstrate, and the reason why we help others of our species. However, most evolutionary psychologists recognize that our genes alone do not control our destiny: our inherited tendencies are *not* set in concrete.

Sociocultural Perspective: The Cultural Impact of Our World

What is the focus of the sociocultural perspective?

The **sociocultural perspective** emphasizes social and cultural influences on human behaviour. In the same way that someone who is quoted out of context is misunderstood, we may misinterpret the actions or gestures of those from other cultures if we do not understand the cultural context in which they occur. Writers such as Kenneth Gergen et al. (1996) assert that we are in "desperate need" of culturally sensitive research about people's behaviour in areas such as health, "birth control, child abuse, drug addiction, ethical and religious conflict, and the effects of technology on society" (p. 502).

Psychologists at Work

What are some specialties in psychology, and in what settings are they employed?

We know that psychologists have many different orientations toward the practice of psychology. Some teach at colleges and universities; others have private clinical practices and counsel patients. Psychologists work in hospitals and other medical facilities, in elementary and secondary schools, and in business and industry. Wherever you

Psychologists work in a wide range of settings

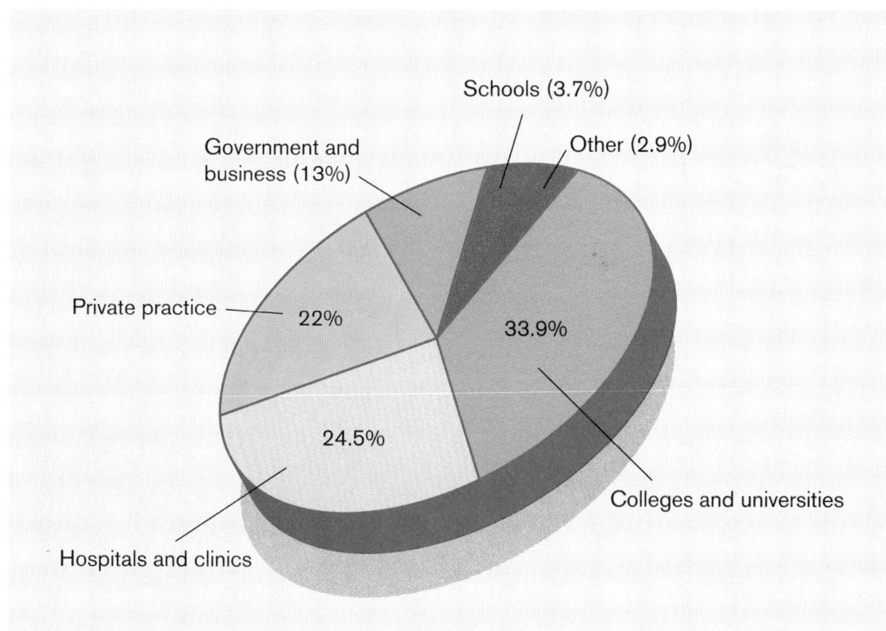

FIGURE 1.3
Where Psychologists Work
Psychologists work in a variety of settings. About 34 percent of psychologists work in colleges and universities, 24.5 percent work in hospitals and clinics, and 22 percent are in private practice. (Data from Howard et al., 1986.)

find human activity, you will likely find psychologists. Figure 1.3 shows the settings in which psychologists work. And Review & Reflect 1.3 outlines the modern perspectives in psychology.

With so much information available about psychology, it is important to become a good consumer of that information. The *Apply It!* box tells you how to go about doing this.

REVIEW & REFLECT 1.3
Modern Perspectives in Psychology

Perspective	Emphasis
Biological	The role of biological processes and structures, as well as heredity, in explaining behaviour.
Psychoanalytic	The role of unconscious motivation and early childhood experiences in determining behaviour and thought.
Behavioural	The role of environment in shaping and controlling behaviour.
Cognitive	The importance of mental processes–perception, thinking, and memory–that underlie behaviour.
Humanistic	The importance of the individual's subjective experience as a key to understanding behaviour.
Evolutionary	The role of inherited tendencies that have proven adaptive in humans.
Sociocultural	The effect of society and culture on behaviour.

biological perspective: A perspective that emphasizes biological processes and heredity as the keys to understanding behaviour.

evolutionary perspective: A perspective that focuses on how humans have evolved behaviours required for survival against various environmental pressures over the long course of evolution.

sociocultural perspective: A perspective that emphasizes social and cultural influences on human behaviour and stresses the importance of understanding those influences when we interpret the behaviour of others.

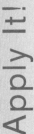

Remember It!

Recent Perspectives in Psychology

Match the psychological perspective with its major emphasis.

___ 1) the role of biological processes and heredity
___ 2) the role of learning and environmental factors
___ 3) the role of mental processes
___ 4) the role of the unconscious and early-childhood experiences
___ 5) the importance of the individual's own subjective experience
___ 6) the role of social and cultural influences
___ 7) the role of inherited tendencies that have proven adaptive in humans

a. psychoanalytic
b. biological
c. behavioural
d. cognitive
e. humanistic
f. evolutionary
g. sociocultural

Answers: 1) b 2) c 3) d 4) a 5) e 6) g 7) f

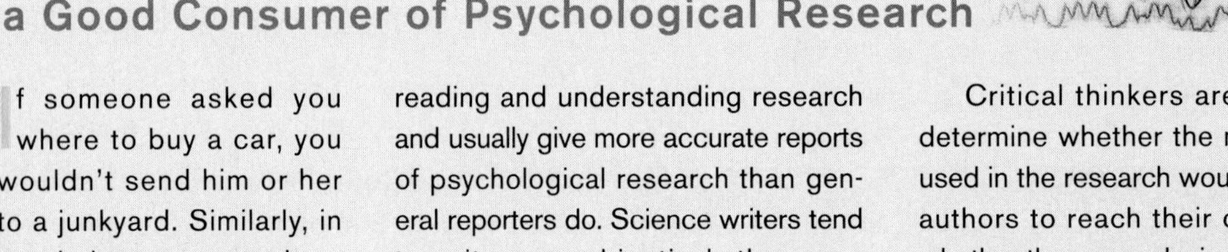

Being a Good Consumer of Psychological Research

Apply It!

If someone asked you where to buy a car, you wouldn't send him or her to a junkyard. Similarly, in psychology you must be a wise consumer in order to get accurate information—become a critical thinker.

Some publications are more scientifically respectable than others—*Science News* and *Psychology Today* are more credible than the *National Enquirer* and the *Toronto Sun.* Science writers have more experience reading and understanding research and usually give more accurate reports of psychological research than general reporters do. Science writers tend to write more objectively than non-science writers and are less likely to suggest that the researchers' findings are the last word on the subject. General reporters, on the other hand, are much more likely to make sweeping statements and extreme claims: "The most important study of our time," "Amazing new cure," "Dramatic new results show...."

To evaluate the information, James Bell suggests, you must be able to answer three key questions: "Who says so? What do they say? How do they know?" (1991, p. 36).

To critically evaluate research, you need to know who conducted the study and the methodology used. You need a description of the participants—their number, how they were selected, whether they were human or animal, and, if they were human, information such as their age, gender, and other characteristics that are relevant to evaluating the researcher's conclusions.

Critical thinkers are those who determine whether the methodology used in the research would enable the authors to reach their conclusions, whether those conclusions are logical, whether they are supported by the data, and whether there are alternative explanations for the findings.

Critical thinkers understand the difference between scientific and non-scientific research evidence. Testimonials and accounts of personal experience are non-scientific evidence. Testimonials most often appeal to emotions rather than to intellect.

Critical thinkers carefully consider the biases of the writers or researchers. Do they have "axes to grind"? Are they expressing information that can be confirmed as factual, or are they merely expressing their opinion?

Finally, critical thinkers do not accept the results of one study as definitive evidence. They want to know whether the research has been replicated and what other studies have been published on the subject. As a critical thinker, you would not modify your life on the basis of one study that you read.

KEY TERMS

applied research, p. 6
basic research, p. 6
behaviourism, p. 22
biological perspective, p. 26
case study, p. 7
cognitive psychology, p. 24
control group, p. 10
correlation coefficient, p. 14
correlational method, p. 14
dependent variable, p. 10
descriptive research methods, p. 6
double-blind technique, p. 12
evolutionary perspective, p. 26
experimental group, p. 10
experimental method, p. 9
experimenter bias, p. 12
functionalism, p. 21
Gestalt psychology, p. 22
humanistic psychology, p. 23
hypothesis, p. 9
independent variable, p. 10
naturalistic observation, p. 6
placebo, p. 12
placebo effect, p. 12
population, p. 8
psychoanalysis, p. 23
psychology, p. 4
random assignment, p. 11
reliability, p. 15
representative sample, p. 8
sample, p. 8
selection bias, p. 11
sociocultural perspective, p. 26
structuralism, p. 21
survey, p. 7
theory, p. 6
validity, p. 15

THINKING CRITICALLY

Evaluation

Consider the three major forces in psychology: behaviourism, psychoanalysis, and humanistic psychology. Which do you like most? Which do you like least? Explain.

Point/Counterpoint

This chapter discussed the issue of deception in research. Prepare convincing arguments to support each of these opinions:

a. Deception is justified in research studies.
b. Deception is *not* justified in research studies.

Psychology in Your Life

In this chapter you've learned something about experimental research and survey research. How will this new knowledge affect the way you evaluate research studies in articles you read or in reports you hear in the future?

SUMMARY & REVIEW

Introduction to Psychology

What are the four goals of psychology?

The four goals of psychology are the description, explanation, prediction, and control of behaviour and mental processes.

What is the difference between basic and applied research?

Basic research is conducted to advance knowledge rather than to discover any practical application. Applied research is conducted for the purpose of solving practical problems.

Descriptive Research Methods

What is naturalistic observation, and what are some of its advantages and limitations?

In naturalistic observation, researchers observe and record the behaviour of participants in a natural setting without attempting to influence or control it. The limitations include the researcher's lack of control over the observed situation and the potential for observer bias.

What is the case study method, and for what purposes is it particularly well suited?

The case study is an in-depth study of one or several participants through observation, interview, and sometimes psychological testing. It is particularly appropriate for studying people who have rare psychological or physiological disorders.

What are the methods and purposes of survey research?

The survey is a research method in which investigators use interviews and/or questionnaires to gather information about the attitudes, beliefs, experiences, or behaviours of a group of people.

What is a representative sample, and why is it essential in a survey?

A representative sample is a sample of participants selected from the population of interest in such a way that important subgroups within the whole population are included in the same proportions in the sample. A sample must be representative for the findings to be applied to the larger population.

The Experimental Method: Searching for Causes

What is the main advantage of the experimental method?

The experimental method is the only research method that can be used to identify cause–effect relationships.

What is the difference between the independent variable and the dependent variable?

In an experiment, an independent variable is a condition or factor manipulated by the researcher to determine its effect on the dependent variable. The dependent variable, measured at the end of the experiment, is presumed to vary as a result of the manipulations of the independent variable.

How do the experimental and control groups differ?

The experimental group is exposed to the independent variable. The control group is similar to the experimental group and is exposed to the same experimental environment but is *not* exposed to the independent variable.

What is selection bias, and what technique do researchers use to control for it?

Selection bias occurs when there are systematic differences among the groups before the experiment begins. Random assignment–assignment of participants to groups by means of a chance procedure–maximizes the probability that groups are similar at the beginning of the experiment.

What is the placebo effect, and how do researchers control for it?

The placebo effect occurs when a person's expectations influence the outcome of a treatment or experiment. To control for the placebo effect, the researcher must ensure that the participants do not know whether they are members of the experimental group (receiving the treatment) or the control group (receiving the placebo).

What is experimenter bias, and how is it controlled?

Experimenter bias occurs when the researcher's expectations affect the outcome of the experiment. Its control is the double-blind technique, in which neither the experimenters nor the participants know which participants are in an experimental group and which are in a control group.

Other Research Methods

What is the correlational method, and when is it used?

The correlational method is used to determine the correlation or relationship between two variables. It is often used when an experimental study cannot be conducted because it is either impossible or unethical.

What is a correlation coefficient?

A correlation coefficient is a numerical value that indicates the strength and direction of the relationship between two variables.

Participants in Psychological Research

Why are animals used in research?

Animals are used because they provide a simpler model for studying similar processes in humans; because researchers can exercise more control over animals and use a wider range of medical and other manipulations; because it is easier to study the entire lifespan (and even several generations in some species); and because animals are readily available and more economical to study.

What are some ethical guidelines governing the use of human participants in research?

Participation in research must be strictly voluntary; there must be respect for confidentiality; participants must be free to withdraw from the study at any time; and participants must be debriefed as soon as possible after they participate.

The Historical Progression of Psychology: Exploring the Different Perspectives

What was Wilhelm Wundt's contribution to psychology?

Wundt, considered the founder of psychology, established the first psychological laboratory in 1879 and launched the study of psychology as a formal academic discipline.

What were the goals and methods of structuralism, the first school of psychology?

Structuralism's main goal was to analyze the basic elements or structures of conscious mental experience through the use of introspection.

What was the goal of the early school of psychology known as *functionalism*?

Functionalism was concerned with how mental processes help humans and animals adapt to their environment.

What is the emphasis of Gestalt psychology?

Gestalt psychology emphasizes that individuals perceive objects and patterns as whole units and that the perceived whole is more than just the sum of its parts.

How did behaviourism differ from previous schools of psychology?

Behaviourism, the school of psychology founded by John B. Watson, views observable, measurable behaviour as the only appropriate subject matter for psychology. Behaviourism also emphasizes the environment.

What was the role of the unconscious in psychoanalysis, Freud's approach to psychology?

According to Freud's theory of psychoanalysis, our thoughts, feelings, and behaviour are determined primarily by the unconscious—the part of the mind that we cannot see and cannot control.

What is the focus of humanistic psychology?

Humanistic psychology focuses on the uniqueness of human beings and their capacity for choice, growth, and psychological health.

What is the focus of cognitive psychology?

Cognitive psychology focuses on mental processes such as memory, problem solving, concept formation, reasoning and decision making, language, and perception.

Psychology Today

What is the focus of the biological perspective?

The biological perspective emphasizes biological processes and heredity as the keys to understanding behaviour.

What is the focus of the evolutionary perspective?

The evolutionary perspective looks at inherited tendencies that have proved adaptive in humans.

What is the focus of the sociocultural perspective?

The sociocultural perspective emphasizes the role of cultural and social influences on behaviour.

What are some specialties in psychology, and in what settings are they employed?

There are clinical and counselling psychologists, physiological psychologists, experimental psychologists, developmental psychologists, educational and school psychologists, and social psychologists, as well as industrial and organizational psychologists. Psychologists are found in many different settings—in colleges and universities, elementary and secondary schools, medical settings, business and industry, and private practice.

2 Biology and Behaviour

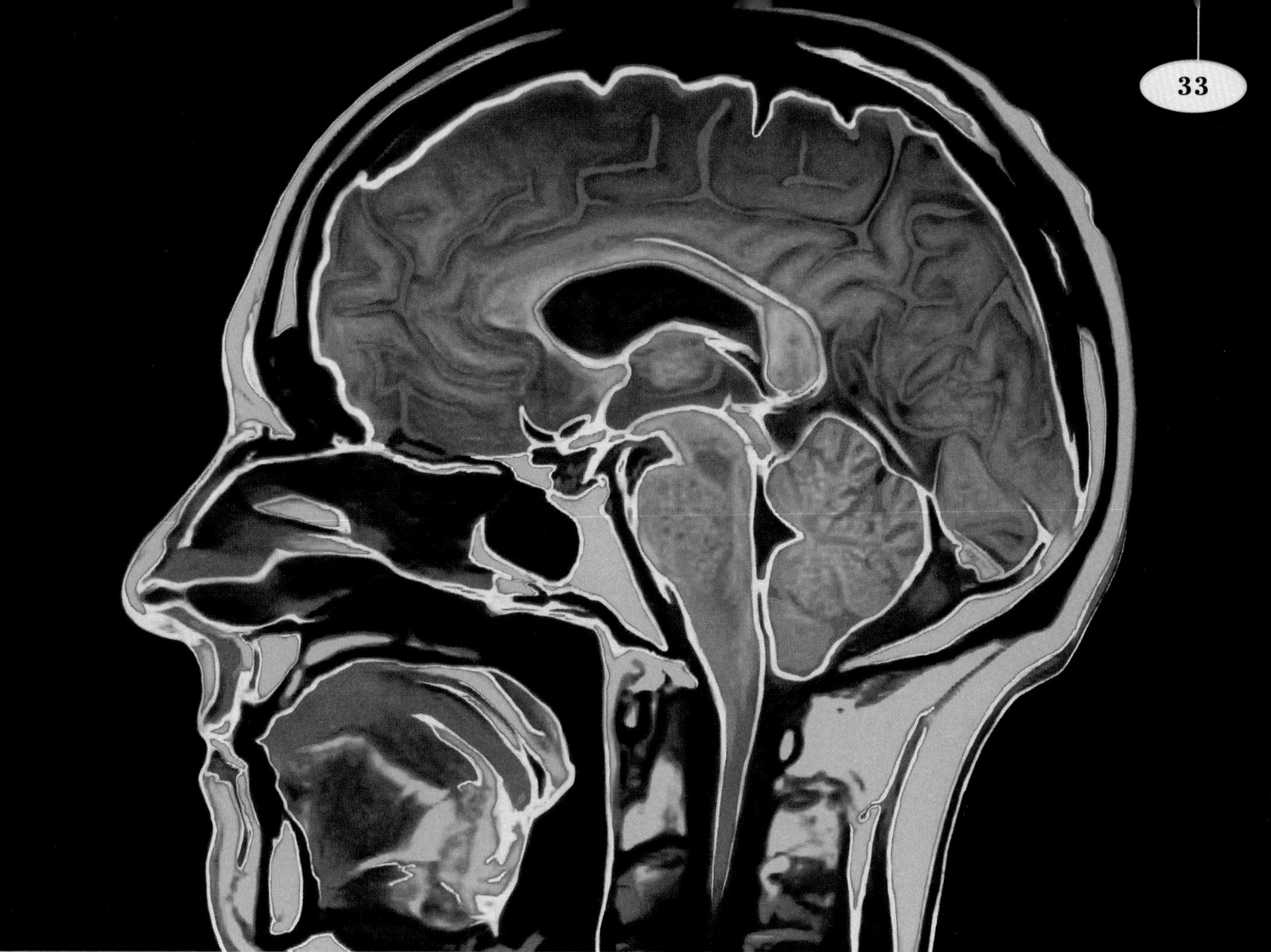

Lori and Reba Schappell are middle-aged sisters who are intimately aware of every aspect of each other's lives. They have never spent a day, or even a moment apart—they are conjoined twins (also known as Siamese twins). Not only are they conjoined, they happen to fall into the rare 2 percent of conjoined twins who are attached at the head. Lori and Reba are attached at the left temple just above the eye—each one facing the other. The true extent of their attachment became evident only recently when MRI technology indicated that the twins shared a significant portion of their frontal lobes—the part of the brain associated with personality, emotion, and higher intellectual functions. Given such a strong fusion of brain and nerve tissue, it might have been expected that these two sisters would share the same personality, likes and dislikes, and feelings about things ("Conjoined twins," 2000). Exactly how similar these twins are is not yet known; however, we do know that the sisters do not share thoughts—even emotional ones—or dreams, and they do not share all interests. For example, Reba is pursuing a country and western singing career but Lori prefers just to listen to her sister perform (Sunday Times, 2000). Information gathered from conjoined twins is challenging our beliefs and knowledge about how the brain works.

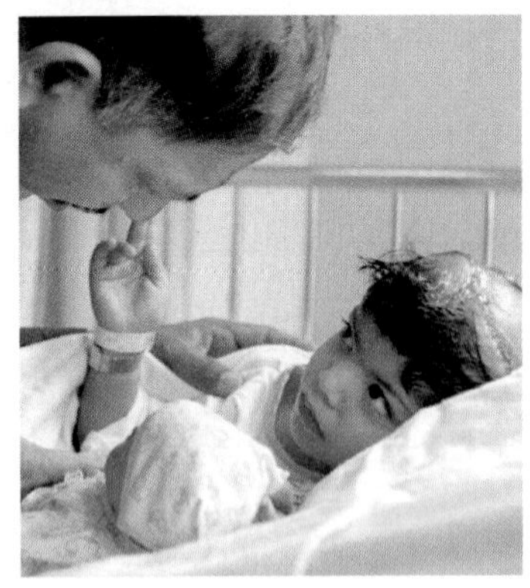

In a more recent case, the decision of how to handle shared brain tissue and the circulatory systems that support the brain and body became a more critical issue. Among the triplet sisters Faryal, Nida, and Hira, two–Hira and Nida–were joined at the head and shared some brain matter and cerebral circulation. Doctors recommended that the conjoined sisters be separated, but the medical expertise required for this type of surgery just wasn't available in their homeland, Pakistan ("Separate lives," 2000, p. 1). The future looked grim until Dr. Hoffman, at Toronto's Hospital for Sick Children, and his team of neurosurgeons, neuroradiologists, plastic surgeons, anesthetists, urologists, cardiologists, and surgical nurses agreed to try the surgery.

The twins were just two years old when they underwent surgery to separate them for the first time in their lives. The shared brain matter was in the parietal region and it was thought to be nonfunctional, so it was divided among the two sisters. A special clip was used to block part of the cerebral circulation shared by the twins. Excessive bleeding from this area during surgery would spell disaster. The 17-hour surgery ended in both success and failure. Within a month Nida died of a heart attack. Hira flourished. In 1997, she received the last treatment for her scalp, after which she would return home to continue her normal life as an independent, healthy five-year-old (Murray, 1999). (Story adapted from "Conjoined twins," 2000; Duce, 2000; Murray, 1999; "Separate lives," 2000.)

In Chapter 1 we defined psychology as the scientific study of behaviour and mental processes. Before we can understand and appreciate our behaviour and mental processes, we must first explore the all-important biological connection. Every thought we think, every emotion we feel, every sensation we experience, every decision we reach, every move we make—in short, all human behaviour—is rooted in a biological event. Therefore, we launch our exploration of psychology with the study of biology and behaviour. Our story begins where the action begins, in the smallest functional unit of the brain—the nerve cell, or neuron.

LINK IT!

Conjoined Twins
www.bbc.co.uk/science/horizon/conjoined_twins_transcript.shtml

www.med.harvard.edu/AANLIB/home.html
The Whole Brain Atlas

www.bic.mni.mcgill.ca/brainweb/
BrainWeb: Simulated Brain Database

The Neurons and the Neurotransmitters

The Neurons: Billions of Brain Cells

What is a neuron, and what are its three parts?

All our thoughts, feelings, and behaviour can ultimately be traced to the activity of specialized cells called **neurons.** Most experts estimate that there are as many as 100 billion neurons in the brain (Swanson, 1995). This means that you have about 17 times as many neurons as there are people living on this planet right now.

Neurons perform several important tasks: (1) Afferent (sensory) neurons relay messages from the sense organs and receptors—eyes, ears, nose, mouth, and skin—to the brain or spinal cord. (2) Efferent (motor) neurons convey signals from the brain and spinal cord to the glands and muscles, enabling us to move. (3) Interneurons, thousands of times more numerous than motor or sensory neurons, carry information between neurons in the brain and between neurons in the spinal cord.

Anatomy of a Neuron: Looking at Its Parts

Neurons transmit signals through the nervous system. Although no two neurons are exactly alike, nearly all are made up of three important parts: cell body (soma), dendrites, and axon. Figure 2.1 shows the structure of a neuron. The **cell body** contains the nucleus and carries out the metabolic, or life-sustaining, functions of the neuron. Branching out from the cell body are the **dendrites**, which look much like the leafless branches of a tree. The dendrites are the primary receivers of signals from other neurons, but the cell body can also receive the signals directly. Dendrites do not merely receive signals from other neurons and relay them to the cell body. Dendrites relay messages backward—from the cell body to their own branches (a process called back propagating). These backward messages may shape the dendrites responses to future signals they receive (Magee & Johnston, 1997; Sejnowski, 1997).

The **axon** is the slender, tail-like extension of the neuron that sprouts into many branches, each ending in a rounded axon terminal. The axon terminals transmit signals to the dendrites, to the cell bodies of other neurons, and to muscles, glands, and other parts of the body. In humans, some axons are short—only

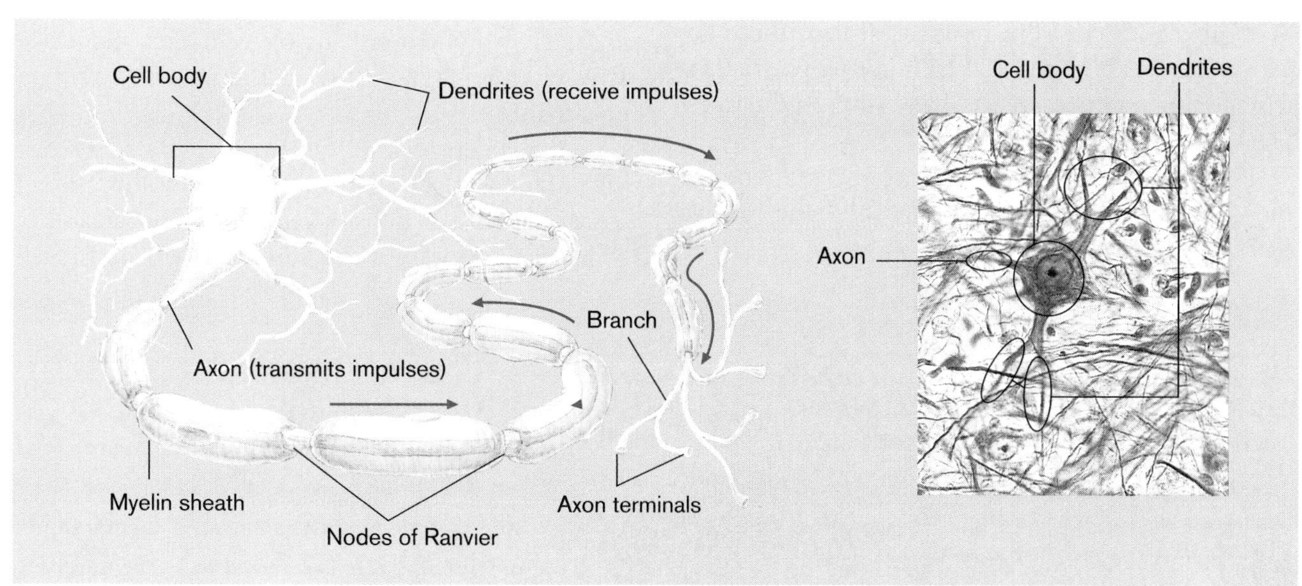

FIGURE 2.1

The Structure of a Neuron **Neurons have three important parts: (1) a cell body, which carries out the metabolic functions of the neuron; (2) branched fibres called dendrites, which are the primary receivers of the impulses from other neurons; and (3) a slender, tail-like extension called an axon, the transmitting end of the neuron, which sprouts into many branches, each ending in an axon terminal. The photograph shows human neurons greatly magnified.**

neuron (NEW-ron): A specialized cell that conducts impulses through the nervous system and contains three major parts–a cell body, dendrites, and an axon.

cell body: The part of the neuron, containing the nucleus, that carries out the metabolic functions of the neuron.

dendrites (DEN-drytes): The branch-like extensions of a neuron that receive signals from other neurons.

axon (AK-sahn): The slender, tail-like extension of the neuron that transmits signals to the dendrites or cell body of other neurons or to the muscles or glands.

thousandths of a centimetre. Others can be up to a metre long—long enough to reach from the brain to the tip of the spinal cord, or from the spinal cord to remote parts of the body.

The Synapse

What is a synapse?

Remarkably, the billions of neurons that send and relay signals are not physically connected. The axon terminals are separated from the receiving neurons by tiny, fluid-filled gaps called *synaptic clefts*. The **synapse** is the junction where the axon terminal of a sending neuron communicates with a receiving neuron across the synaptic cleft. There may be as many as 100 trillion synapses in the human nervous system (Swanson, 1995), with each neuron potentially connecting with thousands of other neurons (Kelner, 1997).

How big is one trillion? Numbers in the trillions are hard for us to comprehend. You know how short a time one second is. It takes almost 32 000 years for one trillion seconds to pass. Now try to imagine how incredibly complex your brain must be if there are between 10 trillion and 100 trillion synapses across which your neurons are passing and receiving messages.

If neurons are not physically connected, how do they communicate? How do they send and receive their messages?

The Neural Impulse: The Beginning of Thought and Action

What is the action potential?

Cells in the brain, the spinal cord, and the muscles generate electrical potentials. Every time we move a muscle, experience a sensation, or have a thought or a feeling, a small but measurable electrical impulse is present.

How does this biological electricity work? Even though the impulse that travels down the axon is electrical, the axon does not transmit it the way a wire conducts an electrical current. Rather, bodily fluids contain certain types of chemical molecules known as ions, some with a positive charge and others with a negative charge. What actually moves through the axon is a change in the permeability of the cell membrane. When this process occurs, ions move through the membrane, into and out of the neuron. Every neuron (like every other living cell) has a membrane. Inside this membrane there are normally more negative than positive ions. When at rest (not firing), a neuron carries a negative electrical potential relative to the environment outside the cell. This slight negative charge is referred to as the neuron's **resting potential**.

When a neuron is sufficiently stimulated, its resting potential becomes disturbed. As a result, the cell membrane of the neuron changes its permeability. This causes more positive ions to flow into the cell

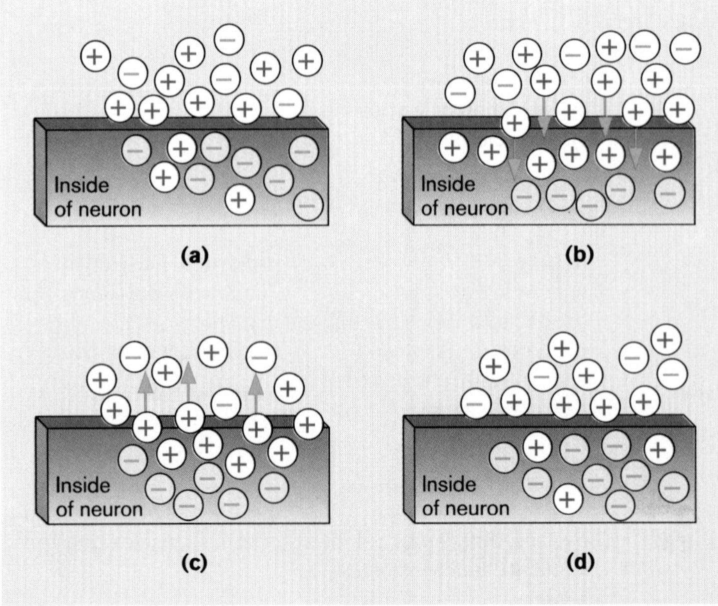

FIGURE 2.2

The Action Potential (a) When a neuron is at rest (not firing), the inside of the neuron has a slight negative electrical charge compared to the outside; this is referred to as the neuron's "resting potential." (b) When a neuron is stimulated, more positively charged particles flow into the cell, making the inside suddenly positive compared to the outside of the cell. This sudden reversal is the action potential. (c) Immediately after the neuron fires, some positive particles are actively pumped out of the cell. (d) The neuron returns to its resting potential and is ready to fire again if stimulated.

and other ions to flow out. If the disturbance reaches a minimum intensity known as the threshold, the neuron's resting membrane potential is suddenly reversed—it becomes positive. This sudden reversal of the resting potential is the **action potential**. The action potential operates according to the "all or none" law—the neuron either fires completely or does not fire at all. Immediately after the neuron reaches its action potential and fires, it returns to its resting potential until stimulated again. But its rest may be very short, because neurons can fire up to 1 000 times per second. Figure 2.2 illustrates the movement of positive ions across the cell membrane, which stimulates the neuron to its action potential.

Consider this important question: If a neuron only fires or does not fire, how can we tell the difference between a very strong and a very weak stimulus? a jarring blow and a soft touch? a blinding light and a dim one? a shout and a whisper? The answer lies in the number of neurons firing at the same time and their rate of firing (the number of times per second). A weak stimulus may cause relatively few neurons to fire; a strong stimulus may cause thousands of neurons to fire at the same time. Furthermore, a weak stimulus may cause neurons to fire very slowly; a strong stimulus may cause neurons to fire hundreds of times per second (normally the firing rate is much slower).

Nerve impulses travel at speeds between about 1 metre per second and about 100 metres per second (about 360 kilometres per hour). The speed of the impulse is related to the size of the axon. Neurons with larger, longer axons—those that reach from the brain through the spinal cord, and from the spinal cord to remote parts of the body—send impulses at a faster speed than those with smaller, shorter axons. How can they do this?

The most important factor in the speed of the impulse is the **myelin sheath**—a white, fatty coating wrapped around some axons that acts as insulation. If you look again at Figure 2.1, you will see that this coating has numerous gaps called *nodes of Ranvier*. These nodes cause the myelin sheath to look like links of sausage strung together. The electrical impulse is retriggered or regenerated at each node (or naked gap) along the axon. Thus impulses travel up to 100 times faster along axons with myelin sheaths.

Neurotransmitters: The Chemical Messengers of the Brain

What are neurotransmitters, and what role do they play in the transmission of signals from one neuron to another?

Once a neuron fires, how does it get its message to other neurons? Messages are transmitted between neurons by one or more of a large group of chemical substances known as **neurotransmitters** (Hokfelt et al., 1984).

Where are the neurotransmitters located? Inside the axon terminal are many small, sphere-shaped containers with thin membranes, called *synaptic vesicles*, which hold the neurotransmitters. When an action potential arrives at the axon terminal, synaptic vesicles move toward the cell membrane, fuse with it, and release their neurotransmitter molecules. This process is shown in Figure 2.3.

The Receptor Sites: Locks for Neurotransmitter Keys

Once released, neurotransmitters do not simply flow into the synaptic cleft and stimulate all the adjacent neurons. Each neurotransmitter has a distinctive molecular shape. Numerous **receptor sites** on the surfaces of dendrites and cell bodies also have distinctive shapes. Neurotransmitters can affect only those neurons that contain receptor sites designed to receive molecules matching their particular shape. In

synapse (SIN-aps): The junction where the axon of a sending neuron communicates with a receiving neuron across the synaptic cleft.

resting potential: The membrane potential of a neuron at rest, about −70 millivolts.

action potential: The firing of a neuron that results when the charge within the neuron becomes more positive than the charge outside the cell's membrane.

myelin sheath (MY-uh-lin): The white, fatty coating wrapped around some axons that acts as insulation and enables impulses to travel much faster.

neurotransmitter (NEW-ro-TRANS-miter): A chemical that is released into the synaptic cleft from the axon terminal of the sending neuron, crosses the synapse, and binds to appropriate receptor sites on the dendrites or cell body of the receiving neuron, influencing the cell either to fire or not to fire.

receptor site: A site on the dendrite or cell body of a neuron that will receive only specific neurotransmitters.

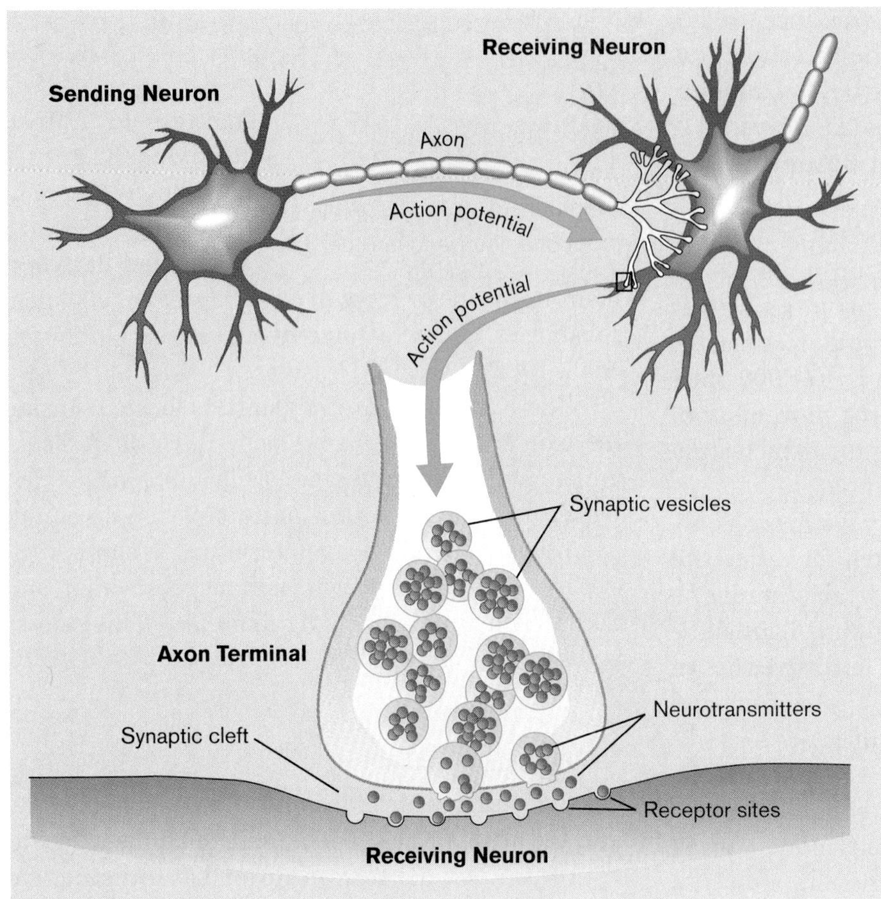

FIGURE 2.3
Synaptic Transmission **Sending neurons transmit their messages to receiving neurons by electrochemical action. When a neuron fires, the action potential arrives at the axon terminal and triggers the release of neurotransmitters from the synaptic vesicles. Neurotransmitters flow into the synaptic cleft and move toward the receiving neuron, which has numerous receptor sites. The receptor sites will receive only neurotransmitters with distinctive molecular shapes that match them. Neurotransmitters influence the receiving neuron only to fire or not to fire.**

other words, each receptor site is like a locked door that only certain neurotransmitter "keys" can unlock.

However, the process by which neurotransmitters bind with receptor sites is not as fixed and rigid as keys fitting locks or jigsaw puzzle pieces interlocking. Receptor sites in the brain are living matter; they can expand and contract their enclosed volumes. The interaction where the neurotransmitter and the receptor meet is controlled not by the direct influence of one on the other, but by their *mutual influence* on each other. Thus, a certain neurotransmitter may be competing for the same receptor with another neurotransmitter of a slightly different shape. The receptor will admit only one of the competing neurotransmitters—the one that fits it most perfectly. This means that a neurotransmitter may be received by a receptor at one time, but not at other times if another neurotransmitter molecule is present whose "affinity with the receptor is even stronger. As in dating and mating, what is finally settled for is always a function of what is available" (Restak, 1993, p. 28).

The Action of Neurotransmitters

When neurotransmitters enter receptor sites on the dendrites or cell bodies of receiving neurons, their action is either excitatory (influencing the neurons to fire) or inhibitory (influencing them not to fire). Because a single neuron may connect with thousands of other neurons at the same time, there will always be both excitatory and inhibitory influences on receiving neurons. For the neuron to fire, the excitatory influences must exceed the inhibitory influences of neurotransmitter substances by a sufficient amount (the threshold).

For many years researchers believed that each individual neuron responded to only one neurotransmitter. But it is now known that individual neurons may respond to several different neurotransmitters. This suggests a greater flexibility of response, even at the level of a single neuron.

You may wonder how the synaptic vesicles can continue to pour out their neurotransmitters, yet have a ready supply so that the neuron can respond to continuing stimulation. First, the cell body of the neuron is always working to manufacture more of the neurotransmitter substance. Second, after accomplishing its mission, the neurotransmitter may be broken down into its component molecules and reclaimed by the axon terminal to be recycled and used again. Third, by an important process called **reuptake**, the neurotransmitter substance may be taken intact back into the axon terminal, ready for immediate use. This ends the neurotransmitter's excitatory or inhibitory effect on the receiving neuron.

The important point to remember is that signals travel between neurons by way of the neurotransmitters, the chemical messengers of the brain.

LINK IT!

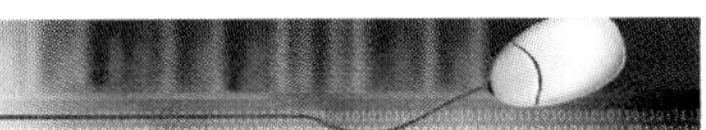

neuroscience.about.com/science/neuroscience/cs/neurotransmitters/
Neurotransmitters

www.pharmcentral.com/neurotransmitters.htm
Neurotransmitters

The Variety of Neurotransmitters: Some Excite and Some Inhibit

What are some of the ways in which neurotransmitters affect our behaviour, and what are some of the major neurotransmitters?

Neurotransmitters are manufactured in the brain, the spinal cord, the glands, and a few other parts of the body. Each kind of neurotransmitter affects the activity of the brain in a different way. Some neurotransmitters regulate the actions of glands and muscles; others affect learning and memory; still others promote sleep or stimulate mental and physical alertness. Some neurotransmitters orchestrate our feelings and emotions, from depression to euphoria. Others (endorphins) provide relief from pain.

To date, researchers have identified some 60 chemical substances manufactured by the body that may act as neurotransmitters (Greden, 1994). It was long believed that an individual neuron could secrete only one neurotransmitter. But more recently it has been demonstrated that some single neurons may secrete several different neurotransmitters (Changeux, 1993). We have already seen that neurotransmitters have two possible general effects on receiving neurons—excitatory and inhibitory. Some neurotransmitters are always excitatory, others are always inhibitory; still others can be either, depending on the receptor with which they bind.

Acetylcholine

The neurotransmitter **acetylcholine** may produce either excitatory or inhibitory effects. Acetylcholine has an excitatory effect on the skeletal muscle fibres, causing them to contract so that we can move. But it has an inhibitory effect on the muscle fibres in the heart.

The acetylcholine receptor, the first neurotransmitter receptor to be isolated, has been studied extensively (Changeux, 1993). Acetylcholine is involved in a variety of functions, including learning and memory, and in rapid eye movement (REM) sleep, the stage of sleep during which dreaming occurs.

The Monoamines

An important class of neurotransmitters known as monoamines includes four neurotransmitters—dopamine, norepinephrine (noradrenalin), epinephrine (adrenalin), and serotonin. Like acetylcholine, **dopamine** (DA) produces both excitatory and inhibitory effects and is involved in several functions, including learning, attention, movement, and reinforcement. A deficiency in dopamine is related to Parkinson's disease, a condition characterized by tremors and rigidity in the limbs. To treat Parkinson's disease, then, can doctors simply give dopamine to patients through injections or in pill form? No, because dopamine, like many other substances, cannot cross from the bloodstream directly into the brain. The symptoms of Parkinson's disease can, however, be controlled by a drug called *L-dopa* that can cross the blood–brain barrier and be converted into dopamine.

reuptake: The process by which neurotransmitter molecules are taken from the synaptic cleft back into the axon terminal for later use, thus terminating their excitatory or inhibitory effect on the receiving neuron.

acetylcholine: A neurotransmitter that plays a role in learning, memory, and rapid eye movement (REM) sleep and causes the skeletal muscle fibres to contract.

dopamine (DOE-pah-meen): A neurotransmitter that plays a role in learning, attention, and movement; a deficiency of dopamine is associated with Parkinson's disease, and an oversensitivity is associated with some cases of schizophrenia.

Norepinephrine affects eating habits (it stimulates the intake of carbohydrates) and it plays a major role in alertness and wakefulness. It is also one of two neurotransmitters that are believed to facilitate female sexual behaviour. *Epinephrine* also acts as a neurotransmitter in the brain, but its role is minor compared to that of norepinephrine. Epinephrine affects the metabolism of glucose and causes the nutrient energy stored in muscles to be released during strenuous exercise.

Serotonin produces inhibitory effects at most of the receptors with which it forms synapses. It plays an important role in regulating mood, sleep, impulsivity, aggression, and appetite (Greden, 1994). A deficiency in serotonin has also been associated with such behaviours as suicide and impulsive violence (Sandou et al., 1994). Both serotonin and norepinephrine are related to positive moods and a deficiency in them has been linked to depression. Some antidepressant drugs relieve the symptoms of depression by blocking the uptake of seratonin or norepinephrine, thus increasing the neurotransmitter's availability in the synapses.

Amino Acids

Researchers believe that eight or more amino acids also serve as neurotransmitters. Two of particular importance—they are found more commonly than any others in the central nervous system—are glutamate (glutamic acid) and GABA (gamma-aminobutyric acid). Glutamate is the primary excitatory neurotransmitter in the brain (Riedel, 1996). It may be released by some 40 percent of neurons and is active in higher brain centres that are involved in learning, thought, and emotions (Coyle & Draper, 1996).

GABA is the main inhibitory neurotransmitter in the brain (Miles, 1999) and is widely distributed throughout the brain and spinal cord. It is thought to facilitate the control of anxiety in humans. Researchers believe that an abnormality in the neurons that secrete GABA is one of the causes of epilepsy, a serious neurological disorder in which neural activity can become so heightened that seizures result.

Endorphins

Over 25 years ago, Candace Pert and her colleagues (1974) demonstrated that a localized region of the brain contains neurons with receptors that respond to the opiates—drugs such as opium, morphine, and heroin. It is now known that the brain produces its own opiate-like substances, known as **endorphins.** Endorphins provide relief from pain and produce feelings of pleasure and well-being.

Generally, one single neurotransmitter is not responsible for a given mental function. Memory, for example, is modified by a collection of neurotransmitters, including acetylcholine, epinephrine, norepinephrine, and (probably) serotonin. Review & Reflect 2.1 summarizes the major neurotransmitters and the behaviours with which they seem to be most strongly associated.

Glial Cells: The Neurons' Helper Cells

Glial cells are specialized cells in the brain that form the myelin coating and perform many other important functions. *Glia* means "glue," and these cells hold the neurons together. Glial cells remove waste products such as dead neurons from the brain by engulfing and digesting them; they also handle other manufacturing, nourishing, and clean-up tasks. Glial cells serve another function when the brain is being formed and as it grows and develops: they act as guides, taking the specialized neurons from where

REVIEW & REFLECT 2.1
Major Neurotransmitters and Their Functions

Neurotransmitter	Believed to Affect
Acetylcholine (ACh)	Movement, learning, memory, REM sleep
Dopamine (DA)	Learning, attention, movement
Norepinephrine (NE)	Eating habits, sleep, female sexual behaviour
Epinephrine	Metabolism of glucose, energy release during exercise
Serotonin	Neurobiological functions such as mood, sleep, and appetite
GABA	Neural inhibition in the central nervous system, possibly sleep
Endorphins	Relief from pain; feelings of pleasure and well-being

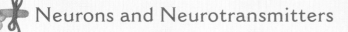

Remember It!

Neurons and Neurotransmitters

1. The branch-like extensions of neurons that act as the primary receivers of signals from other neurons are the
   a. dendrites.
   b. axons.
   c. glia.
   d. cell bodies.
2. The junction where the axon of a sending neuron communicates with a receiving neuron is called the
   a. reuptake site.
   b. receptor site.
   c. synapse.
   d. axon terminal.
3. When a neuron fires, neurotransmitters are released from the synaptic vesicles in the ______________ terminal into the synaptic cleft.
   a. dendrite
   b. cell body's
   c. receptor
   d. axon
4. The resting potential is the firing of a neuron that results when the charge within the neuron becomes more positive than the charge outside the cell membrane. (true/false)
5. Receptor sites on the receiving neuron
   a. receive any available neurotransmitter molecules.
   b. receive only neurotransmitter molecules of a specific shape.
   c. can be influenced only by neurotransmitters from a single neuron.
   d. are located only on the dendrites.
6. Which of the following substances cross the synaptic cleft and enter receptor sites on the dendrites and cell bodies of receiving neurons?
   a. Sodium ions
   b. Potassium ions
   c. Neurotransmitters
   d. Synapse modulators
7. Endorphins, norepinephrine, dopamine, and serotonin are all examples of
   a. hormones.
   b. neurotransmitters.
   c. neuropeptides.
   d. neuromodulators.

Answers: 1.a 2.c 3.d 4.false 5.b 6.c 7.b

they are formed to where they will finally function (Hoekfelt et al., 2000).

Glial cells are smaller than neurons but outnumber them about nine to one (Travis, 1994). Remarkably, glial cells make up more than half the volume of the human brain. It is now known that they interact with neurons in complex ways and that they play a part in creating a more efficient brain (Abbott & Raff, 1991).

The Central Nervous System

We have discussed how neurons function individually and in groups through electrochemical action. But human functioning involves much more than the actions of individual neurons. Collections of neurons, brain structures, and organ systems must also be explored. The nervous system is divided into two parts: (1) the **central nervous system (CNS)**, which is composed of the brain and the spinal cord, and (2) the peripheral nervous system, which connects the CNS to all other parts of the body (see Figure 2.4, or, for a complete depiction, Figure 2.12).

norepinephrine: A neurotransmitter affecting eating and sleep; a deficiency of norepinephrine is associated with depression.

serotonin: A neurotransmitter that plays an important role in regulating mood, sleep, aggression, and appetite; a serotonin deficiency is associated with anxiety, depression, and suicidal feelings.

endorphins (en-DOOR-fins): Chemicals produced naturally by the brain that reduce pain and affect mood positively.

glial cells (GLEE-ul): Cells that help to make the brain more efficient by holding the neurons together, removing waste products such as dead neurons, making the myelin coating for the axons, and performing other manufacturing, nourishing, and clean-up tasks.

central nervous system (CNS): The brain and the spinal cord.

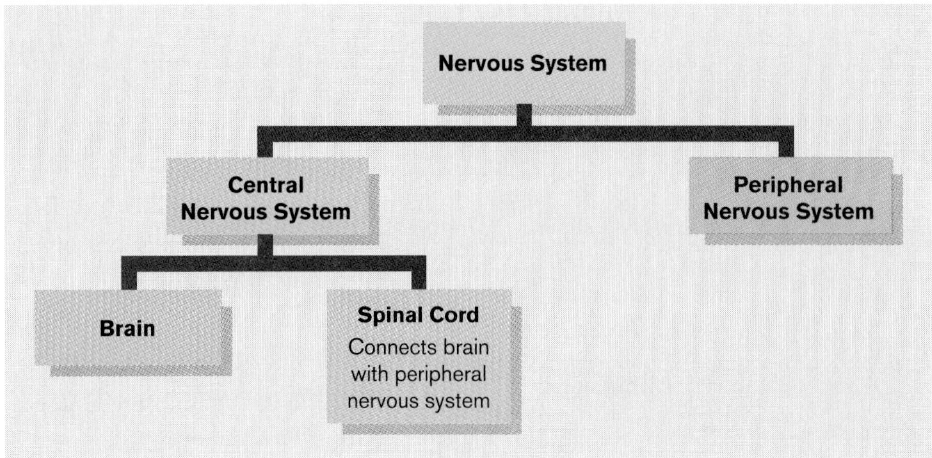

FIGURE 2.4
Divisions of the Human Nervous System The human nervous system is divided into two parts: (1) the central nervous system, consisting of the brain and the spinal cord; and (2) the peripheral nervous system.

The Spinal Cord: An Extension of the Brain

Why is an intact spinal cord important to normal functioning?

The **spinal cord** can best be thought of as an extension of the brain. Like the brain, it has grey matter as well as white matter and is loaded with glial cells. A cylinder of neural tissue about the diameter of your little finger, the spinal cord reaches from the base of the brain, through the neck, and down the hollow centre of the spinal column. The spinal cord is protected by bone and also by spinal fluid, which serves as a shock absorber. The spinal cord literally links the body with the brain. It transmits messages between the brain and the peripheral nervous system. Thus sensory information can reach the brain, and messages from the brain can be sent to the muscles, the glands, and other parts of the body.

Although the spinal cord and the brain usually function together, the spinal cord can act without help from the brain to protect us from injury. For example, the spinal reflex that causes you to withdraw your hand quickly from a hot stove is controlled by the spinal cord without the initial involvement of the brain. The brain, however, quickly becomes aware and involved when the pain signal reaches it. At that point you might plunge your hand into cold water to relieve the pain.

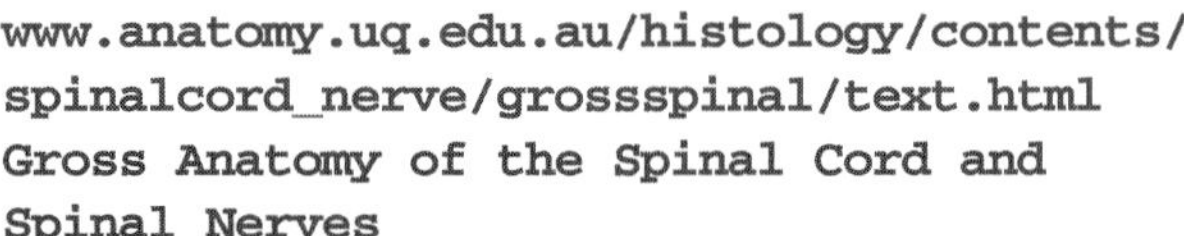

www.anatomy.uq.edu.au/histology/contents/spinalcord_nerve/grossspinal/text.html
Gross Anatomy of the Spinal Cord and Spinal Nerves

The Brainstem: The Most Primitive Part of the Brain

What are the crucial functions handled by the brainstem?

The **brainstem** begins at the site where the spinal cord enlarges as it enters the skull. The brainstem includes the medulla, the pons, and the reticular formation, as shown in Figure 2.5. The brainstem handles functions that are vital to our physical survival; damage to it is life-threatening. The **medulla** is the part of the brainstem that controls heartbeat, breathing, blood pressure, coughing, and swallowing. Fortunately, the medulla handles these functions automatically, so you do not have to decide consciously to breathe or remember to keep your heart beating.

Extending through the brainstem into the pons is another important structure, the **reticular formation**, sometimes called the *reticular activating system* (RAS). Find it in Figure 2.5. The reticular formation plays a crucial role in arousal and attention. Every day our sense organs are bombarded with stimuli, but we cannot possibly pay attention to everything we see or hear. The reticular formation screens messages entering the brain. It blocks some messages and sends others on to higher brain centres for processing.

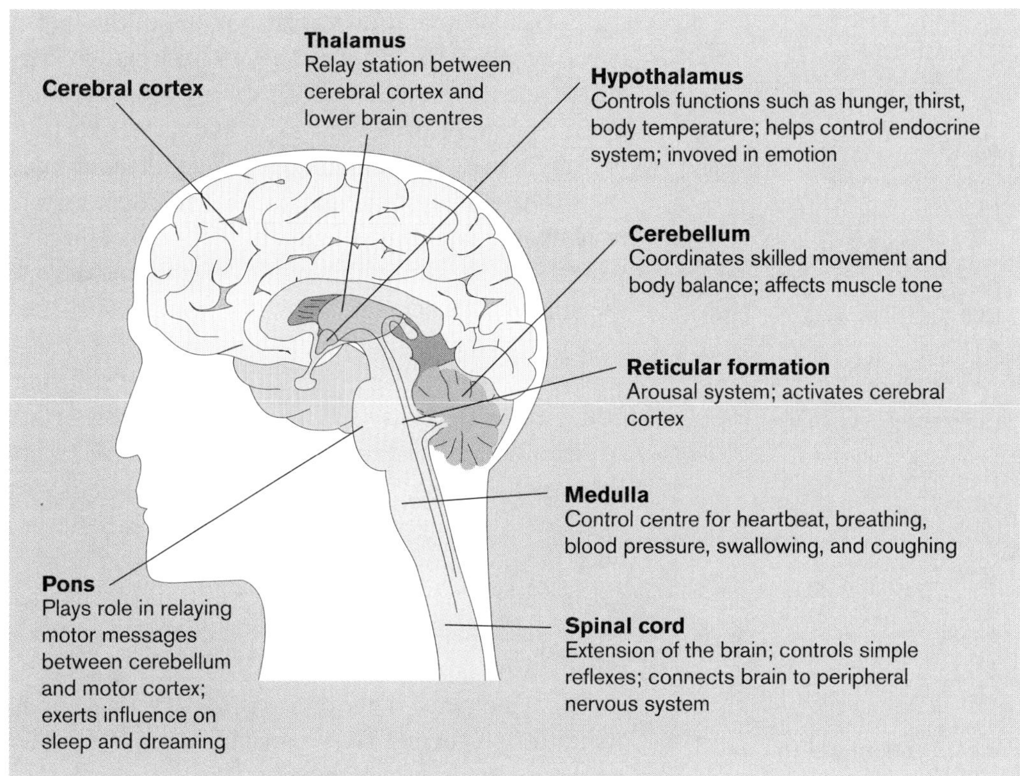
Thalamus
Relay station between cerebral cortex and lower brain centres
Cerebral cortex
Hypothalamus
Controls functions such as hunger, thirst, body temperature; helps control endocrine system; invoved in emotion
Cerebellum
Coordinates skilled movement and body balance; affects muscle tone
Reticular formation
Arousal system; activates cerebral cortex
Medulla
Control centre for heartbeat, breathing, blood pressure, swallowing, and coughing
Pons
Plays role in relaying motor messages between cerebellum and motor cortex; exerts influence on sleep and dreaming
Spinal cord
Extension of the brain; controls simple reflexes; connects brain to peripheral nervous system

FIGURE 2.5
Major Structures of the Human Brain Some of the major structures of the brain are shown in the drawing, and a brief description of the function of each is provided. The brain stem contains the medulla, the reticular formation, and the pons.

The reticular formation also determines how alert we are. When it slows down, we doze off or go to sleep. But like an alarm clock, it also can jolt us into consciousness. Thanks to the reticular formation, important messages get through even when we are asleep. That is why parents may be able to sleep through a thunderstorm but will awaken to the slightest cry of their baby. (The next time you sleep through your alarm and are late for class, blame it on your reticular formation.)

Above the medulla and at the top of the brainstem is a bridge-like structure called the *pons* (Latin for "bridge"). The pons extends across the top front of the brainstem and connects to the left and right halves of the cerebellum. The pons plays a role in body movement and exerts an influence on sleep and dreaming. Hobson and McCarley (1977) report that the neurons in the pons begin firing rapidly just as a sleeper begins to dream.

LINK IT!

www.uic.edu/~upaul1/brainstem/index-new.html
University of Illinois at Chicago, Brainstem Tutorial

The Cerebellum: A Must for Graceful Movement

What are the primary functions of the cerebellum?

Cerebellum means "little cerebrum." With its two hemispheres, it resembles the large cerebrum, which rests above it (see Figure 2.5). Its main functions are to execute smooth, skilled movements and to regulate muscle tone and posture (Lalonde & Botez, 1990). It

spinal cord: An extension of the brain, reaching from the base of the brain through the neck and spinal column, that transmits messages between the brain and the peripheral nervous system.

brainstem: The structure that begins at the point where the spinal cord enlarges as it enters the brain—and that includes the medulla, the pons, and the reticular formation.

medulla (muh-DUL-uh): The part of the brainstem that controls heartbeat, blood pressure, breathing, coughing, and swallowing.

reticular formation: A structure in the brainstem that plays a crucial role in arousal and attention that screens sensory messages entering the brain.

cerebellum (sehr-uh-BELL-um): The brain structure that executes smooth, skilled body movements and regulates muscle tone and posture.

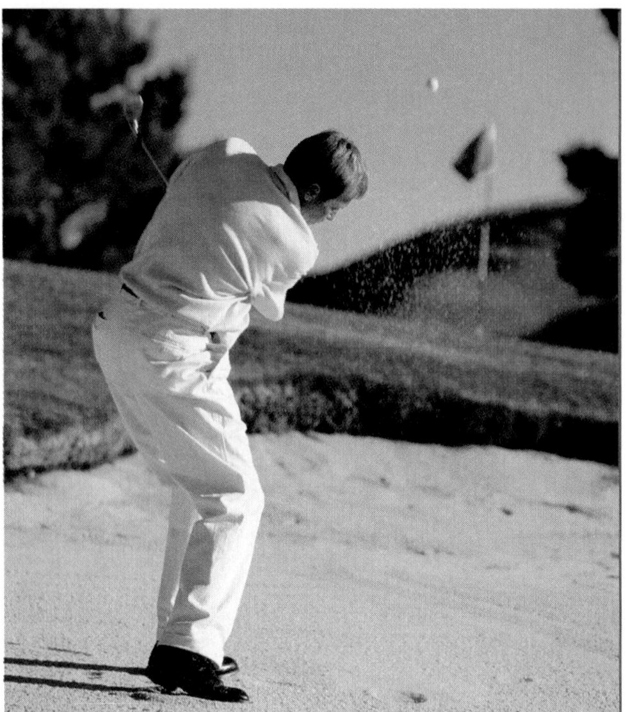

The major functions of the cerebellum are to execute smooth, skilled movements and to regulate muscle tone and posture.

has been found to play a role in motor learning and in retaining memories of motor activities. The cerebellum coordinates and orchestrates the movements necessary to perform many everyday activities without studied, conscious effort. It enables you to guide food from the plate to your mouth, walk in a straight line, or touch the tip of your nose. But with a damaged cerebellum, or one that is temporarily impaired by alcohol, such simple acts may be difficult or impossible to perform. Recent studies suggest that the cerebellum is involved in cognitive as well as motor functions (Allen et al., 1997; Fiez, 1996).

The Thalamus: The Relay Station between Lower and Higher Brain Centres

What is the primary role of the thalamus?

Above the brainstem lie two extremely important structures—the thalamus and the hypothalamus (refer to Figure 2.5). The **thalamus,** which looks like two egg-shaped structures, serves as the relay or switching station for virtually all the information that flows into and out of the higher brain centres. This includes sensory information from all the senses except smell. Incoming sensory information from the eyes, ears, skin, and taste buds travels first to parts of the thalamus or hypothalamus and then to the area of the cortex that handles vision, hearing, touch, or taste. Pain signals connect directly with the thalamus, which sends the pain message to the appropriate sensory areas of the cerebral cortex.

The thalamus—at least one small part of it—apparently affects our ability to learn new information, especially if it is verbal. This structure also plays a role in the production of language (Albert & Helm-Estabrooks 1988a; Metter 1991). The thalamus also regulates sleep cycles in cooperation (it is believed) with the pons and the reticular formation. The synchronized firing of networks of neurons in one part of the thalamus has been observed during slow-wave (deep) sleep (Krosigk, 1993).

What a diverse range of activities this single brain structure performs! Now consider a much smaller structure, the hypothalamus.

The Hypothalamus: A Master Regulator

What are some of the processes regulated by the hypothalamus?

Nestled directly below the thalamus and weighing only about 56 grams, the **hypothalamus** is, for its weight, the most influential structure in the brain. It regulates hunger, thirst, sexual behaviour, and a wide variety of emotional behaviours. The hypothalamus also regulates internal body temperature, starting the process that causes us to perspire when we are too hot and to shiver to conserve body heat when we are too cold. It also regulates the biological clock—our body rhythms and the timing of our sleep/wakefulness cycle (Ginty et al., 1993). As small as it is, the hypothalamus maintains nearly all our bodily functions except blood pressure, heart rhythm, and breathing.

The physiological changes in the body that accompany strong emotion are initiated by neurons concentrated mainly in the hypothalamus. You have felt these physical changes—sweaty palms, a pounding heart, a hollow feeling in the pit of your stomach, or a lump in your throat.

Electrical stimulation of parts of the hypothalamus has elicited some unusual reactions in animals. In 1969, José Delgado implanted an electrode in a

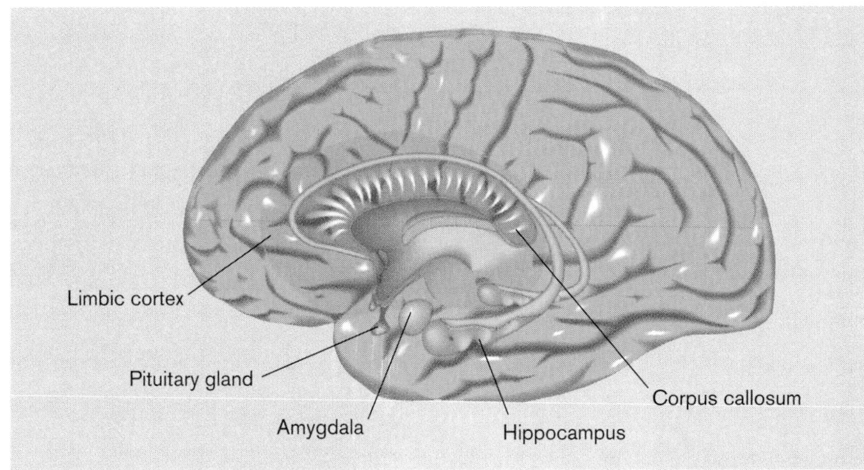

FIGURE 2.6
The Principal Structures in the Limbic System **The amygdala plays an important role in emotion; the hippocampus is essential in the formation of conscious memory.**

particular spot in the hypothalamus of a bull that had been bred specifically for bullfighting. Delgado stood calmly in the ring as the bull charged him. He then pressed a remote-control box that stimulated an area of the bull's hypothalamus. The bull stopped abruptly in its tracks. (Fortunately for Delgado, the batteries in the remote were working.) Apparently, aggression in animals can be turned on and off by stimulating specific areas of the hypothalamus. Pleasurable sensations can also be produced this way (Olds, 1956).

The Limbic System: Primitive Emotion and Memory

What is the role of the limbic system?

The **limbic system** is a group of brain structures involved in emotional expression, memory, and motivation. The **amygdala** plays an important role in our responses to aversive (i.e., unpleasant) stimuli (LeDoux, 1994). It is also prominently involved in various aspects of learning, such as learned fear responses that help humans and other animals avoid dangerous situations and aversive consequences (LeDoux, 1995). Specifically, the amygdala helps us form associations between external events (including social ones) and the emotions related to those events (Aggleton, 1993). Damage to the amygdala can also impair one's ability to recognize (1) facial expressions showing fear or anger, and (2) tone of voice expressing these emotions (Scott et al., 1997).

The **hippocampus** is another important part of the limbic system, located in the interior temporal lobes (see Figure 2.6). The hippocampus is absolutely essential in the formation of conscious memory (Squire, 1992). If your hippocampus were destroyed, you would not be able to store or recall any new information of a personal or cognitive nature (Eichenbaum, 1977; Gluck & Myers, 1997). Yet memories stored before the hippocampus was destroyed would remain intact. The hippocampus also plays a role in the brain's internal representation of space in the form of neural "maps" that help us learn our way around new environments and remember where we have been (Thompson & Best, 1990; Wilson & McNaughton, 1993).

Researchers at McGill University suggest that the components of the limbic system work together to help us remember emotion-based information (McDonald & White, 1993).

thalamus (THAL-uh-mus): The structure located above the brainstem that acts as a relay station for information flowing into or out of the higher brain centres.

hypothalamus (HY-po-THAL-uh-mus): A small but influential brain structure that controls the pituitary gland and regulates hunger, thirst, sexual behaviour, body temperature, and a wide variety of emotional behaviours.

limbic system: A group of structures in the brain, including the amygdala and hippocampus, that are collectively involved in emotion, memory, and motivation.

amygdala (ah-MIG-da-la): A structure in the limbic system that plays an important role in emotion, particularly in response to aversive stimuli.

hippocampus (hip-po-CAM-pus): A structure in the limbic system that plays a central role in the formation of long-term memories.

Remember It!

The Central Nervous System

1. The brain and the spinal cord make up the peripheral nervous system. (true/false)
2. The hypothalamus regulates all of the following except
   a. internal body temperature.
   b. hunger and thirst.
   c. coordinated movement.
   d. sexual behaviour.
3. Match each function with the appropriate structure.
   ___ 1) Connects the brain with the peripheral nervous system
   ___ 2) Controls heart rate, breathing, and blood pressure
   ___ 3) Consists of the medulla, the pons, and the reticular formation
   ___ 4) Influences attention and arousal
   ___ 5) Coordinates complex body movements
   ___ 6) Serves as a relay station for sensory information flowing into the brain

   a. medulla
   b. spinal cord
   c. reticular formation
   d. thalamus
   e. cerebellum
   f. brainstem

Answers: 1. false 2. c 3. true 4. 1) b 2) a 3) f 4) c 5) e 6) d

The Cerebral Hemispheres

What are the cerebral hemispheres, the cerebral cortex, and the corpus callosum?

The most extraordinary and the most essentially human part of the magnificent human brain is the cerebrum and its cortex. If you could peer into your skull and look into your own brain, you would see a structure that resembles the inside of a huge walnut (see Figure 2.7). Just as a walnut has two matched halves connected to each other, the **cerebrum** is composed of two **cerebral hemispheres**—a left and a right. These are physically connected at the bottom by a thick band of nerve fibres called the **corpus callosum**. This connection makes possible the transfer of information and the coordination of activity between the hemispheres. In general, the right cerebral hemisphere controls the left side of the body (i.e., movement and feeling); the left cerebral hemisphere controls the right side of the body. In over 95 percent of people, the left hemisphere also controls language functions (Hellige, 1990).

The cerebral hemispheres have a thin outer covering about half a centimetre thick called the **cerebral cortex,** which is primarily responsible for the higher mental processes of language, memory, and thinking. The presence of the cell bodies of billions of neurons in the cortex gives it a greyish appearance. Thus, the cortex is often referred to as grey matter. Beneath the cortex are the white myelinated axons (white matter) that connect cortex neurons with those in other brain regions. It is arranged in numerous folds or wrinkles called "convolutions." About two-thirds of the cortex is hidden from view in the folds. The cortex of less intelligent animals is much smaller in proportion to total brain size and, therefore, is much less convoluted.

The cerebral cortex contains three types of areas: (1) sensory input areas, where vision, hearing, touch, pressure, and temperature register; (2) motor areas, which control voluntary movement; and (3) **association areas**, which house our memories and are involved in thought, perception, and language.

The Lobes of the Brain

In each cerebral hemisphere there are four lobes—the frontal lobe, the parietal lobe, the occipital lobe, and the temporal lobe. Find them in Figure 2.8. Each of the lobe's functions are also reviewed in the *Apply It!* box near the end of the chapter.

The Frontal Lobes: For Moving, Speaking, and Thinking

What are some of the main areas within the frontal lobes, and what are their functions?

Of the lobes in the brain, the **frontal lobes** are by far the largest. They begin at the front of the brain and extend to the top centre of the skull. They contain the motor cortex, Broca's area, and the frontal association areas.

FIGURE 2.7

Two Views of the Cerebral Hemispheres The two hemispheres rest side by side like two matched halves, physically connected by the corpus callosum, shown in (a). An inside view of the right hemisphere of the cerebrum and cerebellum is shown in (b).

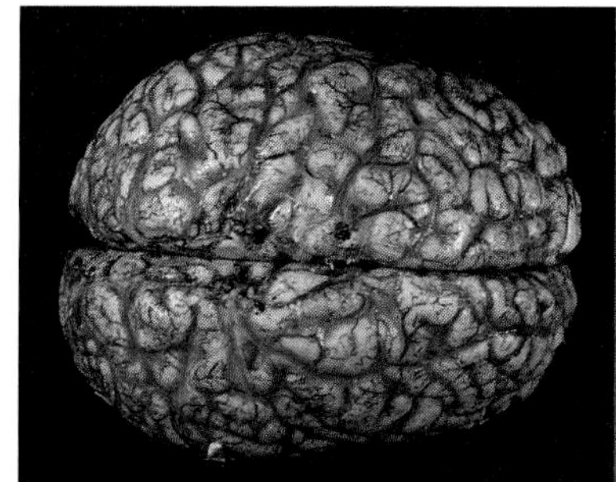

The two cerebral hemispheres show up clearly in this view looking down on an actual brain.

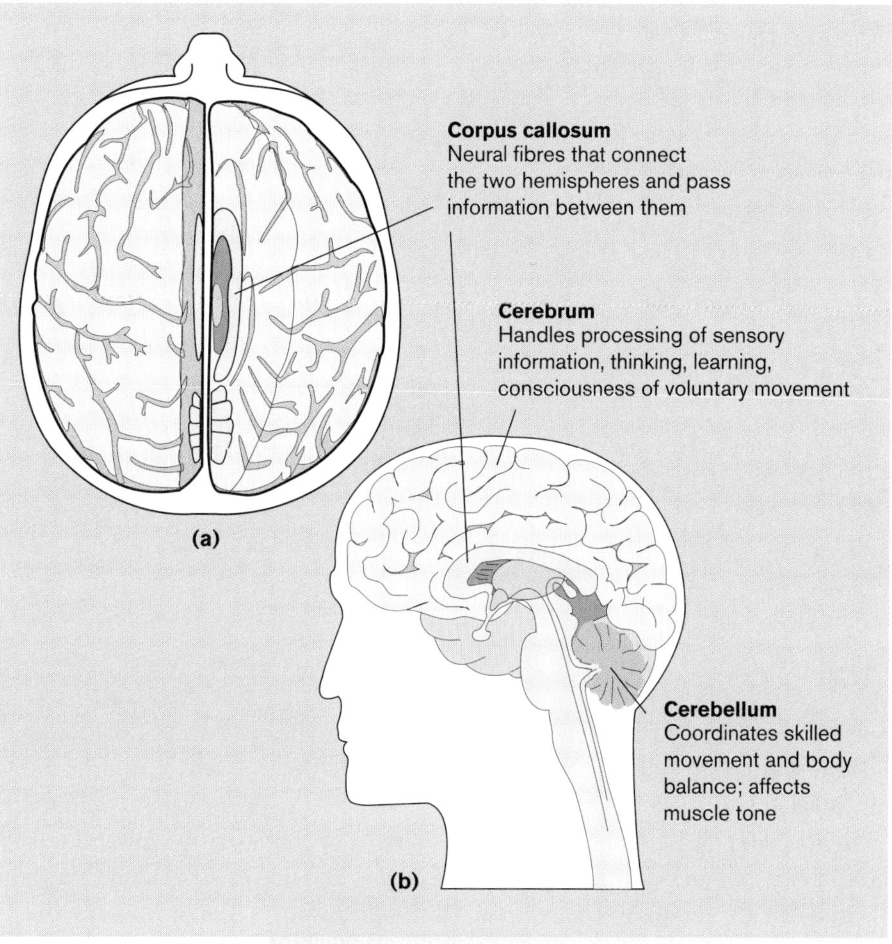
Corpus callosum
Neural fibres that connect the two hemispheres and pass information between them
Cerebrum
Handles processing of sensory information, thinking, learning, consciousness of voluntary movement
(a)
Cerebellum
Coordinates skilled movement and body balance; affects muscle tone
(b)

THE MOTOR CORTEX The **motor cortex** controls voluntary body movement (see Figure 2.8). The right motor cortex controls movement on the left side of the body, and the left motor cortex controls movement on the right side of the body. Research, however, has established that the left motor cortex is involved in the control of voluntary movement on the left side of the body as well (Kim et al., 1993).

Examine Figure 2.9. Notice the motor homunculus, or "little man," drawn next to the cross-section of the motor cortex. The body parts are drawn in proportion to the amount of motor cortex that controls each body part. The parts of the body that are capable of the most finely coordinated movements, such as the fingers, lips, and tongue, have a larger share of the motor cortex. Areas such as the legs and the trunk, which are capable only of gross movement, have a smaller amount of motor cortex. The lower parts of the body are controlled mainly by neurons at the top of the motor cortex; upper-body parts (face, lips, and tongue) are controlled mainly by neurons near the

cerebrum (seh-REE-brum): The largest structure of the human brain, consisting of the two cerebral hemispheres connected by the corpus callosum and covered by the cerebral cortex.

cerebral hemispheres (seh-REE-brul): The right and left halves of the cerebrum, covered by the cerebral cortex and connected by the corpus callosum.

corpus callosum (KOR-pus-kah-LO-sum): The thick band of nerve fibres that connects the two cerebral hemispheres and makes possible the transfer of information and the synchronization of activity between them.

cerebral cortex (seh-REE-brul-KOR-tex): The grey, convoluted covering of the cerebral hemispheres that is responsible for higher mental processes such as language, memory, and thinking.

association areas: Areas of the cerebral cortex that house memories and are involved in thought, perception, learning, and language.

frontal lobes: The lobes that control voluntary body movements, speech production, and such functions as thinking, motivation, planning for the future, impulse control, and emotional responses.

motor cortex: The strip of tissue at the rear of the frontal lobes that controls voluntary body movement.

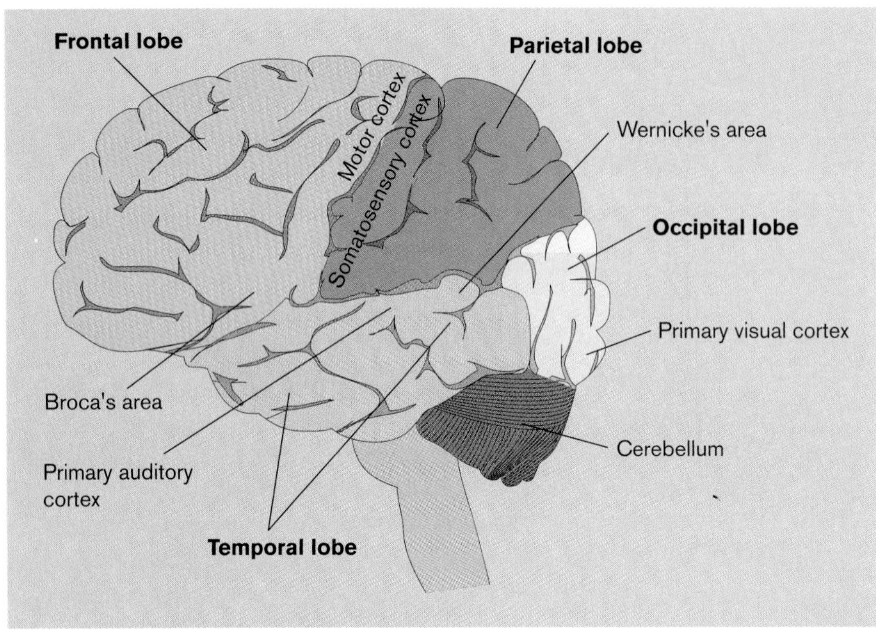

FIGURE 2.8

The Cerebral Cortex of the Left Hemisphere This illustration of the left cerebral hemisphere shows the four lobes: (1) the frontal lobe, including the motor cortex and Broca's area; (2) the parietal lobe, with the somatosensory cortex; (3) the occipital lobe, with the primary visual cortex; and (4) the temporal lobe, with the primary auditory cortex and Wernicke's area.

bottom of the motor cortex. For example, when you wiggle your right big toe a cluster of brain cells firing at the top of the left motor cortex is chiefly responsible for producing the movement. This "map" of the motor cortex is based upon the pioneering work of Canadian neurosurgeon Wilder Penfield, who recorded the responses of patients who received electrical stimulation of this area while under surgery.

Recent research indicates that the clusters of neurons responsible for moving a body part—a finger, for example—are active over a wider area of the cortex than was earlier assumed. This means that there is considerable overlap in the neurons that fire to move a finger (Scheiber & Hibbard, 1993).

What happens when part of the motor cortex is damaged? Depending on the severity of the damage, either paralysis or some impairment of coordination can result. Sometimes damage in the motor cortex causes the seizures of grand mal epilepsy. On the other hand, if an arm or leg is amputated, many of the neurons in the corresponding area of the motor cortex will eventually be dedicated to another function (Murray, 1995).

BROCA'S AREA In 1861, Paul Broca performed autopsies on two bodies—one of a person who had been totally without speech, the other of a person who had been able to say only four words (Jenkins et al., 1975). Broca found that both persons had had damage in the left hemisphere, slightly in front of the part of the motor cortex that controls movement of the jaw, lips, and tongue. Broca was among the first scientists to demonstrate the existence of localized functions in the cerebral cortex (Schiller, 1993). He concluded that the site of damage, now called **Broca's area,** was the part of the brain responsible for speech production (refer to Figure 2.8). Broca's area is involved in directing the muscle movements required to produce speech sounds.

If Broca's area is damaged, **Broca's aphasia** may result. **Aphasia** is a general term for a loss or impairment of the ability to use or understand language, resulting from damage to the brain (Goodglass, 1993). Characteristically, patients with Broca's aphasia know what they want to say but can speak very little or not at all. If they are able to speak, their words are produced very slowly, with great effort, and are poorly articulated.

LINK IT!

www.epub.org.br/cm/n02/historia/broca.htm
Sabbatini, R.M.E.: A Brief Biography of Pierre Paul Broca

FRONTAL ASSOCIATION AREAS Much of the frontal lobes consists of association areas that are involved in thinking, motivation, planning for the future, impulse control, and emotional responses (Stuss et al., 1992).

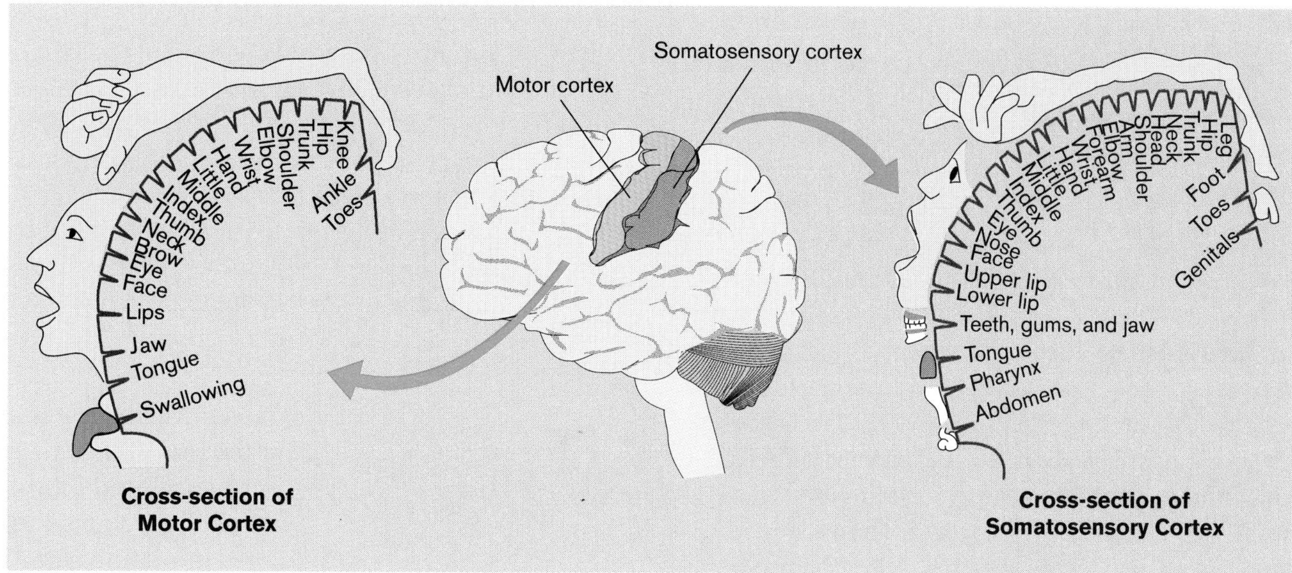

FIGURE 2.9

The Motor Cortex and the Somatosensory Cortex from the Left Hemisphere **The left motor cortex controls voluntary movement in the right side of the body. The left somatosensory cortex is the site where touch, pressure, temperature, and pain sensations from the right side of the body register. The more sensitive the body parts and the more capable they are of finely coordinated movements, the greater the areas of somatosensory cortex and motor cortex dedicated to those body parts. Note what large sections of cortex serve the head, face, hands, and fingers, and what small sections serve such large areas as the trunk, arms, and legs.**

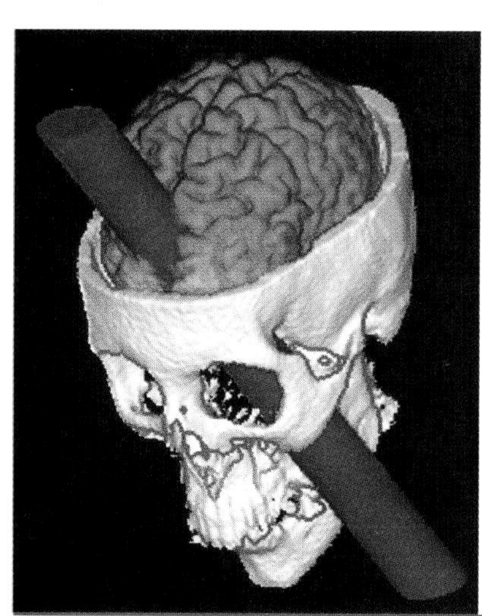

This computer-generated image shows the likely path of the bar that tore through Phineas Gage's skull.

Sometimes pronounced changes in emotional responses occur when the frontal lobes are damaged. One famous case involved Phineas Gage, a 25-year-old man who had a metal rod driven through the bottom of his left cheekbone and out through the top of his skull. The damage to the frontal lobes drastically altered impulse control and emotional responses. Using measurements from Gage's skull and modern brain-imaging techniques, researchers have been able to identify the probable location of the damage Gage's brain suffered (Damasio et al., 1994). The photo above shows the most likely trajectory of the metal rod that tore through his skull.

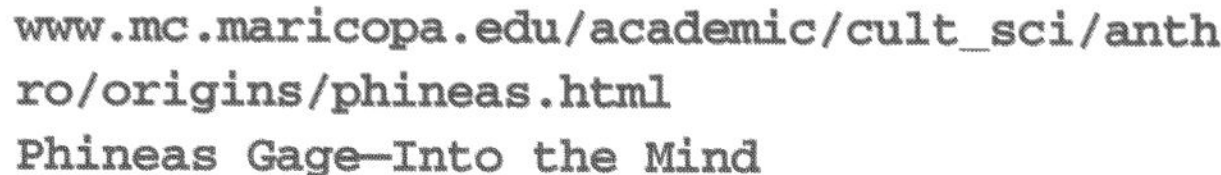

www.mc.maricopa.edu/academic/cult_sci/anthro/origins/phineas.html
Phineas Gage—Into the Mind

Broca's area (BRO-kuz): The area in the frontal lobe, usually in the left hemisphere, that controls production of the speech sounds.

Broca's aphasia (BRO-kuz uh-FAY-zyah): An impairment in the ability to physically produce speech sounds, or in extreme cases an inability to speak at all; caused by damage to Broca's area.

aphasia (uh-FAY-zyah): A loss or impairment of the ability to understand or communicate through the written or spoken word, which results from damage to the brain.

The Parietal Lobes: Vital to Our Sense of Touch

What are the primary functions of the parietal lobes in general and the somatosensory cortex in particular?

The **parietal lobes** lie directly behind the frontal lobes, in the top-middle portion of the brain. The parietal lobes are involved in the reception and processing of touch stimuli. The front strip of brain tissue in the parietal lobes, called the **somatosensory cortex**, is where touch, pressure, temperature, and pain register in the cortex (refer back to Figure 2.8). The somatosensory cortex also makes us aware of our body movements and the positions of our body parts at any given moment.

Dusser de Bareene discovered the function of the somatosensory cortex in 1916, when he applied a small amount of strychnine to a number of points along a monkey's somatosensory cortex. The strychnine stimulated the neurons to fire. As he touched each point, the monkey scratched a different location on its skin. Using this technique, de Bareene was able to map the monkey's somatosensory cortex.

If various points on your own somatosensory cortex were electrically stimulated, you would feel either a tingling sensation or a numbness in a corresponding part of your body. A person with damage to the somatosensory cortex of one hemisphere loses some sensitivity to touch on the opposite side of the body. If the damage is severe enough, the person may not be able to feel the difference between sandpaper and silk. Or the affected part of the body may feel numb.

The two halves of the somatosensory cortex (i.e., in the left and right parietal lobes) are wired to opposite sides of the body. Also, cells at the top of the somatosensory cortex govern feeling in the lower extremities of the body. When you drop a brick on your right foot, the topmost brain cells of the left somatosensory cortex fire and register the pain sensation. (Note: This is not a *Try It!* exercise.) Notice in Figure 2.9 the large somatosensory areas connected to sensitive body parts such as the tongue, lips, face, and hand, particularly the thumb and index finger. Observe the small amount of cortex connected to the trunk of the body, which is a large area.

Under unusual circumstances, the somatosensory cortex may reorganize itself to accommodate unusual demands made upon it (Diamond et al., 1994). For example, among blind people, experienced Braille readers have a larger area of the somatosensory cortex dedicated to the fingertips they use for reading than to their other fingertips (Pascual-Leone & Torres, 1993).

Other parts of the parietal lobes are responsible for spatial orientation and sense of direction. There are association areas in the parietal lobes that house our memory of how objects feel so that we can identify objects by touch. People with damage to these areas could hold a pencil, scissors, or a ball in their hand but not be able to identify it by touch alone.

The Occipital Lobes: The Better to See You With

What are the primary functions of the occipital lobes in general and the primary visual cortex in particular?

Behind the parietal lobes at the rear of the brain lie the **occipital lobes**, which are involved in the reception and interpretation of visual information (refer back to Figure 2.8). At the very back of the occipital lobes is the **primary visual cortex**, the site where vision registers in the cortex.

Each eye is connected to the primary visual cortex in both the right and left occipital lobes. Look straight ahead and draw an imaginary line down the middle of what you see. Everything to the left of the line is referred to as the left visual field and registers in the right visual cortex. Everything to the right of the line is the right visual field and registers in the left visual cortex. A person who sustains damage to one primary visual cortex will still have partial vision in both eyes. This is described by University of Lethbridge researcher Brian Kolb (1990), who reports on the long process of recovering from this type of damage.

The association areas in the occipital lobes are involved in the interpretation of visual stimuli. The association areas hold memories of past visual experiences and enable us to recognize what is familiar among the things we see. When these areas are damaged, people can lose their ability to identify objects visually, although they are still able to identify the same objects by touch or through some other sense.

The Temporal Lobes: Hearing's Here

What are the major areas within the temporal lobes, and what are their functions?

The **temporal lobes**, located slightly above the ears, are involved in the reception and interpretation of auditory stimuli. The site in the cortex where hearing registers is known as the **primary auditory cortex**. When this

Remember It!

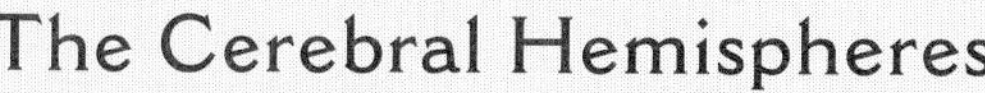

The Cerebral Hemispheres

1. What is the thick band of fibres connecting the two cerebral hemispheres?
   a. cortex
   b. cerebrum
   c. corpus callosum
   d. motor cortex
2. The thin outer covering of the cerebrum is the
   a. cerebral cortex.
   b. myelin sheath.
   c. cortex callosum.
   d. white matter.
3. Match the lobes with the brain areas they contain.
   ___ 1) primary auditory cortex, Wernicke's area
   ___ 2) primary visual cortex
   ___ 3) Broca's area, motor cortex
   ___ 4) somatosensory cortex

   a. frontal lobes
   b. parietal lobes
   c. occipital lobes
   d. temporal lobes
4. Match the specialized area with the appropriate description of function.
   ___ 1) site where hearing registers
   ___ 2) site where vision registers
   ___ 3) site where touch, pressure, and temperature register
   ___ 4) speech production
   ___ 5) voluntary movement
   ___ 6) formulation and understanding of the spoken and written word
   ___ 7) thinking, motivation, impulse control

   a. primary visual cortex
   b. motor cortex
   c. frontal association area
   d. primary auditory cortex
   e. somatosensory cortex
   f. Wernicke's area
   g. Broca's area

Answers: 1. c 2. a 3. 1) d 2) c 3) a 4) b 4. 1) d 2) a 3) e 4) g 5) b 6) f 7) c

area is stimulated with an electrical probe, the person hears bursts of sound. The primary auditory cortex in each temporal lobe receives sound inputs from both ears. Injury to one of these areas results in reduced hearing in both ears; the destruction of both areas causes total deafness.

WERNICKE'S AREA Adjacent to the primary auditory cortex in the left temporal lobe is **Wernicke's area,** which is the area involved in comprehending the spoken word and in formulating coherent written and spoken language (refer back to Figure 2.8). In about 95 percent of people, Wernicke's area is in the left hemisphere. When you listen to someone speak, the sound registers first in the primary auditory cortex. The sound is then sent to Wernicke's area, where the speech sounds are unscrambled into meaningful patterns of words. The same areas that are active when we listen to someone speak are also active in deaf individuals when they watch a person using sign language (Nishimura et al., 1999). Wernicke's area is also involved when we select the words to use in speech and written expression.

Wernicke's aphasia is a type of aphasia resulting from damage to Wernicke's area. Although speech

parietal lobes (puh-RY-uh-tul): The lobes that contain the somatosensory cortex (where touch, pressure, temperature, and pain register) and other areas that are responsible for body awareness and spatial orientation.

somatosensory cortex (so-MAT-o-SENS-or-ee): The strip of tissue at the front of the parietal lobes where touch, pressure, temperature, and pain register in the cortex.

occipital lobes (ahk-SIP-uh-tul): The lobes that contain the primary visual cortex, where vision registers, and association areas involved in the interpretation of visual information.

primary visual cortex: The area at the rear of the occipital lobes where vision registers in the cerebral cortex.

temporal lobes: The lobes that contain the primary auditory cortex, Wernicke's area, and association areas for interpreting auditory information.

primary auditory cortex: The part of the temporal lobes where hearing registers in the cerebral cortex.

Wernicke's area: The language area in the temporal lobe involved in comprehension of the spoken word and in formulation of coherent speech and written language.

Wernicke's aphasia: Aphasia resulting from damage to Wernicke's area, in which the patient's spoken language is fluent, but the content is either vague or incomprehensible to the listener.

is fluent and words are clearly articulated, the actual message does not make sense to others (Maratsos & Matheney, 1994). The content may be vague or bizarre; or it may contain inappropriate words and parts of words, or a gibberish of non-existent words. People with Wernicke's aphasia are not aware that anything is wrong with their speech.

Another kind of aphasia is auditory aphasia, or word deafness. It can occur if there is damage to the nerves connecting the primary auditory cortex with Wernicke's area. The person is able to hear normally but may not understand spoken language. As if hearing a foreign language spoken, the person hears the sounds but has no idea what the speaker is saying.

THE TEMPORAL ASSOCIATION AREAS The other parts of the temporal lobes consist of the association areas that house memories and are involved in the interpretation of auditory stimuli. For example, you have an association area where your memories of various sounds are stored, so that you instantly recognize the sounds of running water, fire engine sirens, dogs barking, and so on. There is also a special association area where familiar melodies are stored.

Specialization of the Cerebral Hemispheres

The two cerebral hemispheres make different but complementary contributions to our mental and emotional life. Research has shown that some **lateralization** of the hemispheres exists—that is, each hemisphere is specialized, to some extent, for certain functions. Yet functions are usually not handled exclusively by one hemisphere; the two hemispheres always work together (Bradshaw, 1989; Efron, 1990). Much of what we know about lateralization is derived from pioneering research conducted by Doreen Kimura at the University of Western Ontario (1961, 1973). She studied tasks in which different information could be presented to each of the hemispheres at the same time, thus demonstrating hemispheric specialization.

Functions of the Left Hemisphere: Language First and Foremost

What are the main functions of the left hemisphere?

In 95 percent of right-handers and in about 62 percent of left-handers, the **left hemisphere** handles most of the language functions, including speaking, writing, reading, and understanding the spoken word (Hellige, 1990). American Sign Language (ASL), which is used by deaf persons, is processed by both hemispheres (Neville et al., 1998). The left hemisphere is specialized for mathematical abilities, particularly calculation; it also processes information in an analytical and sequential, or step-by-step, manner (Corballis, 1989). Logic is primarily though not exclusively a left-brain specialty.

The left hemisphere coordinates complex movements by directly controlling the right side of the body and by indirectly controlling the movements of the left side of the body. It accomplishes this by sending orders across the corpus callosum to the right hemisphere so that the proper movements will be coordinated and executed smoothly. (Remember that the cerebellum also plays an important role in coordinating complex movements.)

Functions of the Right Hemisphere: The Leader in Visual-Spatial Tasks

What are the primary functions of the right hemisphere?

The **right hemisphere** is generally considered to be better at visual-spatial relations. Artists, sculptors, architects, and household do-it-yourselfers have strong visual-spatial skills. When you put together a jigsaw

Because the left hand of a professional string player must rapidly and accurately execute fine movements and slight pressure variations, it is not surprising that these musicians have an unusually large area of the somatosensory cortex dedicated to the fingers of that hand.

puzzle, draw a picture, or assemble a piece of furniture according to instructions, you are calling primarily on your right hemisphere.

The right hemisphere processes information holistically rather than part by part or piece by piece (Corballis, 1989). While auditory, visual, and touch stimuli register in both hemispheres, the right hemisphere appears to be more specialized for complex perceptual tasks. Consequently, the right hemisphere is better at recognizing patterns, whether of familiar voices (Van Lancker et al., 1988), melodies (Springer & Deutsch, 1985), or visual patterns.

Although the left hemisphere is generally considered the language hemisphere, the right hemisphere makes an important contribution to how we "hear" language. According to Howard Gardner, the right hemisphere is involved "in understanding the theme or moral of a story, in grasping metaphor ... and even in supplying the punch line for a joke" (1981, p. 74). It is the right hemisphere that is able to understand familiar idiomatic expressions such as "turning over a new leaf." If the right hemisphere is damaged, a person can understand only the literal meaning of such a statement.

To experience an effect of the specialization of the cerebral hemispheres, try your hand at the *Try It!*

Creativity and intuition are typically considered right hemisphere specialties, but the left hemisphere shares these functions. The right hemisphere controls singing and seems to be more specialized for musical ability in untrained musicians (Kinsella et al., 1988). But in trained musicians, both hemispheres play important roles in musical ability. In fact, parts of the left auditory cortex are significantly larger in musicians with perfect pitch (Schlaug et al., 1995)

Patients with right-hemisphere damage may have difficulty with spatial orientation, such as in finding their way around, even in familiar surroundings. They may have attentional deficits and be unaware of objects in the left visual field—a condition called "unilateral neglect" (Bellas et al., 1988; Halligan & Marshall, 1994). Unilateral neglect patients may eat only the food on the right side of their plate, read only the words on the right half of a page, and even groom only the right half of their body (Bisiach, 1996). And remarkably, some patients may even deny that their arm on the side opposite the brain damage belongs to them (Posner, 1996).

The Right Hemisphere's Role in Emotion: Recognizing and Expressing Emotion

According to Phil Bryden and his colleagues at the University of Waterloo, the right hemisphere is also more active in recognizing and expressing emotion (Bryden & MacRae, 1988). Reading and interpreting non-verbal behaviour, such as gestures and facial expressions, is primarily a right-hemisphere task (Hauser, 1993). Look at the two faces in the next *Try It!* (Jaynes, 1976).

Try It!

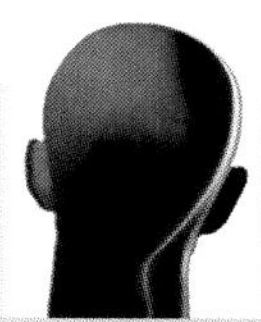

Testing the Hemispheres

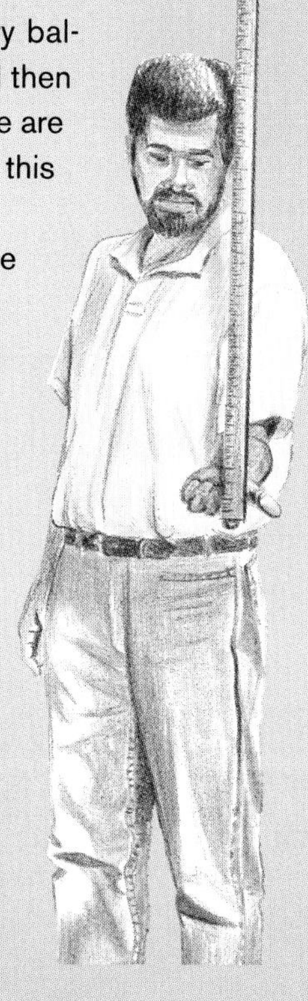

Get a metre stick or yardstick. Try balancing it across your left hand and then across your right hand. Most people are better with their dominant hand. Is this true for you?

Now try this: Begin reciting the alphabet out loud as fast as you can while balancing the stick with your *left* hand. Do you have less trouble this time? Why? The right hemisphere controls the act of balancing with the left hand. However, your left hemisphere, though poor at controlling the left hand, still tries to coordinate your balancing efforts. When you distract the left hemisphere with a steady stream of talk, the right hemisphere can orchestrate more efficient balancing with your left hand, without interference.

lateralization: The specialization of one of the cerebral hemispheres to handle a particular function.

left hemisphere: The hemisphere that controls the right side of the body, coordinates complex movements, and (in 95 percent of people), controls the production of speech and written language.

right hemisphere: The hemisphere that controls the left side of the body and that, in most people, is specialized for visual-spatial perception and for understanding of non-verbal behaviour.

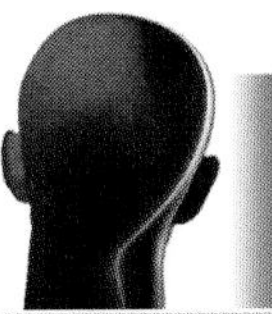

Try It!

Handedness and Perception

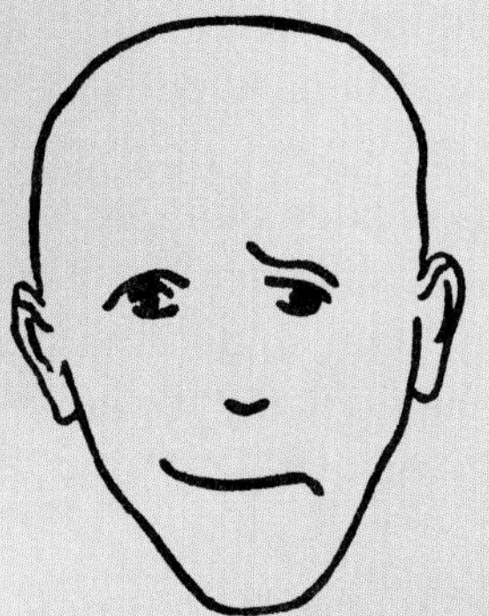

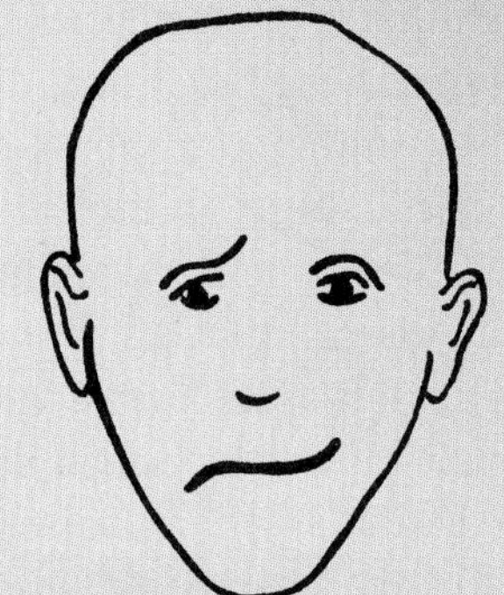

Pick out the happy face and the sad face.

Even though the faces in the drawings are mirror images, right-handed people tend to see the face on the left as the happier face. If you are right-handed, you are likely to perceive the emotional tone revealed by the part of the face to your left as you view it (McGee & Skinner, 1987). The right hemisphere processes information from the left visual field, so right-handed people tend to be more emotionally affected by the left side of the faces they view.

It is also the right hemisphere that responds to the emotional messages conveyed by another's tone of voice (Heilman et al., 1975). For example, say a professor sarcastically tells a student who enters the class late, "Well, I'm so glad you could come today." A student with right-hemisphere damage might respond only to the actual meaning of the words rather than to the sarcastic tone.

The right hemisphere is involved in our tone of voice and particularly in our facial expressions. The left side of the face, controlled by the right hemisphere, usually conveys stronger emotion than the right side of the face (Sackeim et al., 1978). Lawrence Miller (1988) describes the facial expressions and the voice inflections of people with right-hemisphere damage as "often strangely blank—almost robotic" (p. 39).

Evidence is accumulating that brain mechanisms responsible for negative emotions reside in the right hemisphere, while those responsible for positive emotions are found in the left hemisphere (Hellige, 1993). Recent research shows that patients suffering from major depression experience decreased activity in the left prefrontal cortex, where positive emotions are produced (Drevets et al., 1997).

The Split Brain: Separate Halves or Two Separate Brains?

What is the significance of the split-brain operation?

The fact that parts of the human brain are specialized for some functions does not mean that some people are left-brained while others are right-brained. Unless the hemispheres have been surgically separated, they do not operate in isolation and cannot be educated separately. Although each has important specialized functions, the cerebral hemispheres are always in intimate and immediate contact, thanks to the corpus callosum.

In very rare cases, people have been born with no corpus callosum or have had their corpus callosum severed in a drastic surgical procedure called the **split-brain operation**. Neurosurgeons Joseph Bogen and Philip Vogel (1963) found that patients with severe epilepsy, suffering frequent grand mal seizures, could be helped by surgery that severed the corpus callosum. In this way, the pulsing waves of neural activity that occur during a seizure could be confined to one brain hemisphere. For more information about epilepsy, read *On the Cutting Edge in Canada*.

The split-brain operation surgically separates the hemispheres, making the transfer of information between them impossible. The patient is left with two independently functioning hemispheres. In some cases the operation has been quite successful, completely eliminating seizures. And it causes no major changes in personality, intelligence, or behaviour.

Research with split-brain patients by Roger Sperry (1964, 1966) and colleagues Michael Gazzaniga (1967, 1970, 1989) and Jerre Levy (1985) has expanded our knowledge of the unique capabilities of the individual hemispheres. Sperry (1968) found that when surgically separated, each hemisphere continued to have individual and private experiences, sensations, thoughts, and perceptions. However, most sensory experiences were shared almost simultaneously, because each ear and eye has direct sensory connections to both hemispheres. For his work, Sperry won the Nobel Prize in Medicine in 1981.

on the cutting edge in canada

Epilepsy

Epilepsy is a disorder in which the normal electrical activity of the brain is disrupted. When a disruption occurs, the person may experience strange sensations, feelings, and behaviour, and sometimes the person has muscle spasms, convulsions, or loses consciousness (National Institute of Neurological Disorders and Stroke, 2000). There are several types of epileptic seizures, and they reflect the different parts of the brain that are involved in the disruption. *Generalized seizures* (also called grand mal) occur when the whole brain is involved. Grand mal seizures usually involve a loss of consciousness accompanied by convulsions. *Absence seizures* involve a sudden but fleeting loss of consciousness such that the person may not even be aware that a seizure has occurred (Encarta, 2000). Although the grand mal seizure is the one most often depicted in movies, it is the partial seizure that is most common.

Partial seizures involve only one area of the brain and are classified as simple, complex, and absence/petit mal seizures. *Simple partial seizures* may produce jerky body motions, some impairment in vision or hearing, nausea, and fear, but there is no loss of awareness. *Complex partial seizures,* also called temporal lobe epilepsy, interrupt normal behaviour and involve loss of awareness. Individuals may continue to be active but may appear to be in a trance. They have no control over body movements; therefore, their behaviour may appear random and inappropriate relative to the setting they are in or the activity in which they were engaged prior to the seizure. Often auras precede the seizure. Auras vary and can include unusual sensations or smells, dizziness, or fearfulness (Encarta, 2000).

People with epilepsy may develop behavioural and emotional problems as a result of the unpredictability, embarrassment, or frustration of having seizures or as a result of the ridicule or stigma associated with the disorder (National Institute of Neurological Disorders and Stroke, 2000). Epileptics often experience physical and social restrictions imposed by themselves or others.

Drugs and surgery are the most common treatments. Historically, evaluation of treatment effectiveness involved measuring seizure frequency (Wiebe & Derry, 2000). More recently, Dr. Paul Derry, a psychologist at the London Health Sciences Centre in London, Ontario, and his colleagues, have begun to assess the quality of life of individuals undergoing treatments for epilepsy. In a series of recent studies, Dr. Derry has examined psychological outcomes in patients who have undergone surgery for temporal lobe epilepsy (Derry et al., 1997; Derry & Wiebe, 2000; Wiebe & Derry, 2000). Brain surgery is performed to relieve seizures so as to optimize the patient's quality of life. The best results occur when brain surgery results in a 90 percent reduction of seizures or a seizure-free patient.

Surgical reduction of seizures by itself does not predict good outcomes. Pre-existing personality and social variables can also predict quality of life. Individuals who take an active role in their own health and believe they have some personal control, who have less overall anxiety and emotional distress, and who have had previous success in coping under stress and adequate social support report the best outcomes (Derry & Wiebe, 2000). Timing in assessment is also critical because adjustment occurs over time—sometimes one or two years are required for adjustment to occur (Wiebe & Derry, 2000). Derry and colleagues are continuing their study of psychological factors that predict adjustment both when surgical procedures are perceived to be successful or not.

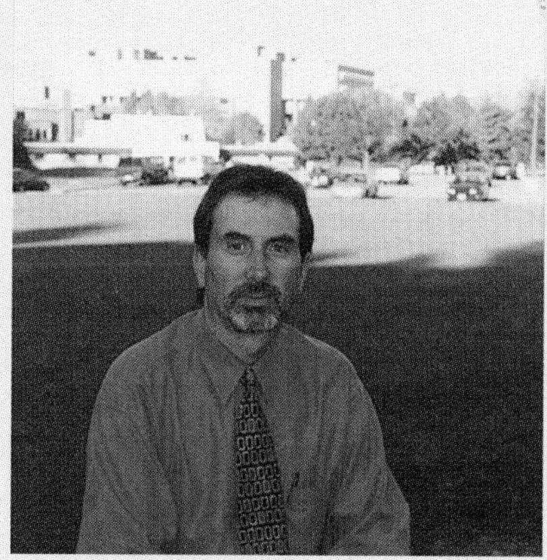

Paul Derry

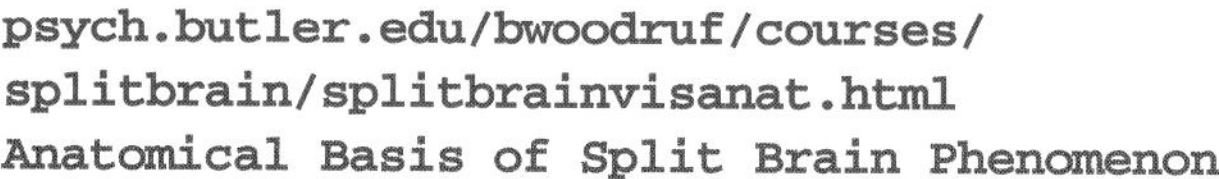

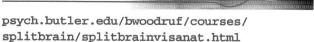

psych.butler.edu/bwoodruf/courses/splitbrain/splitbrainvisanat.html
Anatomical Basis of Split Brain Phenomenon

split-brain operation: An operation, performed in severe cases of epilepsy, in which the corpus callosum is cut, separating the cerebral hemispheres and usually lessening the severity and frequency of grand mal seizures.

www.macalester.edu/~psych/whathap/UBNRP/Split_Brain/Split_Brain_Consciousness.html
Split Brain Consciousness

www.tbidoc.com
Brain Injury and Neuropsychology

www.epub.org.br/cm/n02/historia/psicocirg_i.htm
R.M.E. Sabbatini. (1997, June/August), The history of psychosurgery, Brain & Mind Magazine, 1(2)

Testing the Split-Brain Person

Sperry's research revealed some fascinating findings. In Figure 2.10, a split-brain patient sits in front of a screen that separates the right and left fields of vision. If an orange is flashed to the right field of vision, it will register in the left (verbal) hemisphere. If asked what he saw, the patient will readily reply, "I saw an orange." But suppose that an apple is flashed to the left visual field and is relayed to the right (non-verbal) hemisphere. If asked what he saw, the patient will reply, "I saw nothing."

How could the patient report that he saw the orange but not the apple? Sperry maintains that in split-brain patients, only the verbal left hemisphere can report what it sees. In these experiments, the left hemisphere does not see what is flashed to the right hemisphere, and the right hemisphere is unable to report verbally what it has viewed. But did the right hemisphere actually see the apple that was flashed in the left visual field? Yes, because with his left hand (which is controlled by the right hemisphere), the patient can pick out from behind a screen the apple or any other object shown to the right hemisphere. The right hemisphere knows and remembers what it sees just as well as the left; but unlike the left hemisphere, the right cannot name what it has seen. (In these experiments, images must be flashed for no more than one or two tenths of a second so that the participants do not have time to refixate their eyes and send the information to the opposite hemisphere.)

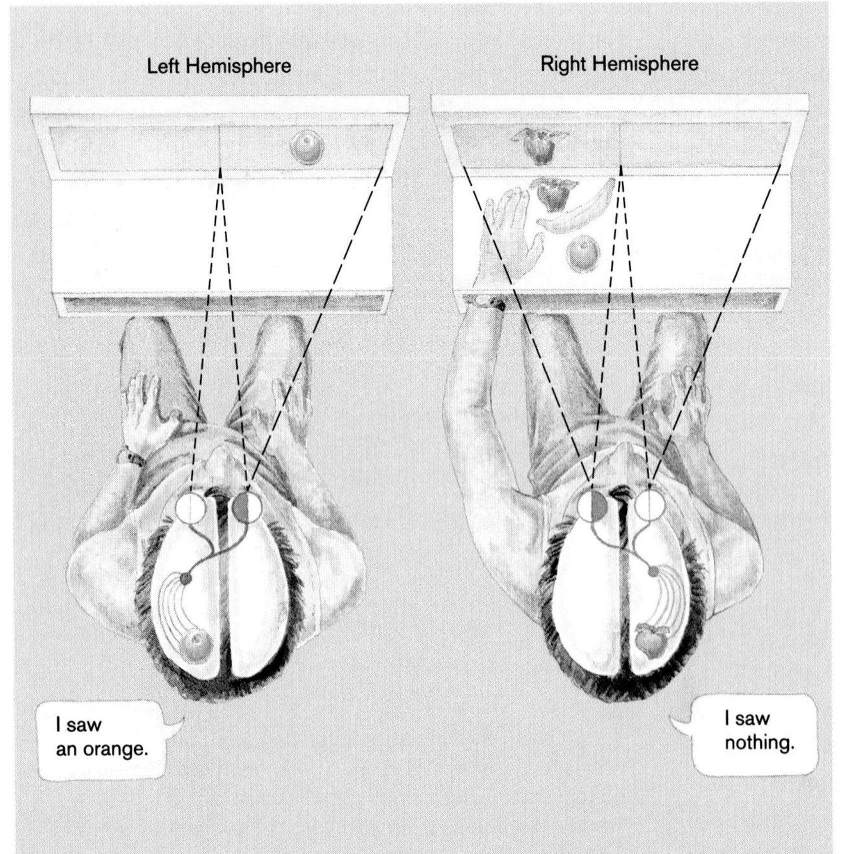

FIGURE 2.10

Testing a Split-Brain Person Using special equipment, researchers are able to study the independent functioning of the hemispheres in split-brain persons. In this experiment, when a visual image (an orange) is flashed on the right side of the screen, it is transmitted to the left (talking) hemisphere. When asked what he saw, the split-brain patient replies, "I saw an orange." When an image (an apple) is flashed on the left side of the screen, it is transmitted only to the right (non-verbal) hemisphere. Because the split-brain patient's left (language) hemisphere did not receive the image, he replies, "I saw nothing." But he can pick out the apple by touch if he used his left hand, proving that the right hemisphere "saw" the apple. (Based on Gazzaniga, 1983.)

Remember It!

Specialization in the Cerebral Hemispheres

1. Match the hemisphere with the specialized abilities usually associated with it.

   ___ 1) visual-spatial skills
   ___ 2) speech
   ___ 3) recognition and expression of emotion
   ___ 4) singing
   ___ 5) mathematics

   a. right hemisphere
   b. left hemisphere

2. Which of these statements is *not* true of the split-brain operation?
   a. It is used for people suffering from severe epilepsy.
   b. It provides a means of studying the functions of the individual hemispheres.
   c. It causes major changes in intelligence, personality, and behaviour.
   d. It makes transfer of information between the hemispheres impossible.

Answers: 1. 1) a 2) b 3) a 4) a 5) b 2. c

Discovering the Brain's Mysteries

What are some methods that researchers have used to learn about brain function?

Today, researchers are unlocking the mysteries of the human brain using electrical stimulation, the electroencephalograph (EEG), and the microelectrode, as well as modern scanning devices such as computerized axial tomography (CT scan), magnetic resonance imaging (MRI), positron-emission tomography (PET scan), functional MRI, and others.

The EEG and the Microelectrode

What is the electroencephalogram (EEG), and what are three of the brain-wave patterns it reveals?

In 1924, Austrian psychiatrist Hans Berger invented the electroencephalograph, a machine that amplifies a million times the electrical activity occurring in the brain. This electrical activity, detected by electrodes placed at various points on the scalp, produces a record of brain-wave activity called an **electroencephalogram (EEG)**. The EEG measures three types of waves. **Beta waves** are associated with mental or physical activity. **Alpha waves** are associated with deep relaxation, and **delta waves** with deep sleep. Figure 2.11 shows the various brain-wave patterns and their associated psychological states.

The most recent application of EEG studies employs a computerized imaging technique in which various colours are generated to represent the different levels of electrical activity occurring every millisecond on the surface of the brain.

While the EEG is able to detect electrical activity in different areas of the brain, it cannot reveal what is happening in individual neurons. Microelectrodes can. A **microelectrode** is a wire so small it can be inserted into a single neuron without damaging it. Microelectrodes can be used to monitor the electrical activity of a single neuron or to stimulate activity within it. Researchers have used microelectrodes to

electroencephalogram (EEG) (ee-lek-tro-en-SEFF-uh-lo-gram): The record of an individual's brainwave activity made by the electroencephalograph.

beta wave (BAY-tuh): The brain wave of 13 or more cycles per second that occurs when an individual is alert and mentally or physically active.

alpha wave: The brain wave of 8–12 cycles per second that occurs when an individual is awake but deeply relaxed, usually with the eyes closed.

delta wave: The slowest brain wave, having a frequency of 1–3 cycles per second and associated with slow-wave (deep) sleep.

microelectrode: An electrical wire so small that it can be used either to monitor the electrical activity of a single neuron or to stimulate activity within it.

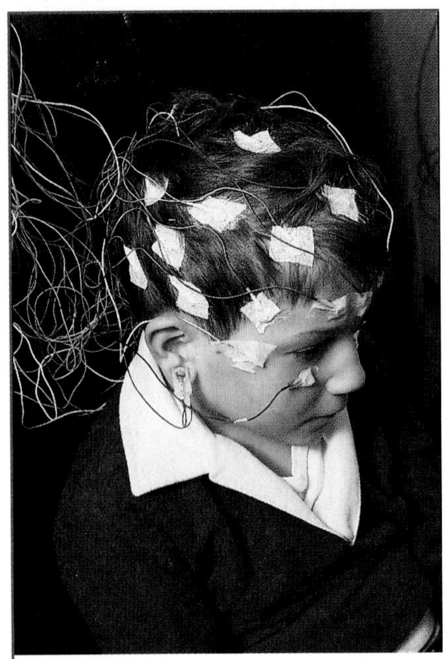

The electroencephalograph (EEG) uses electrodes placed on the scalp to amplify and record electrical activity in the brain.

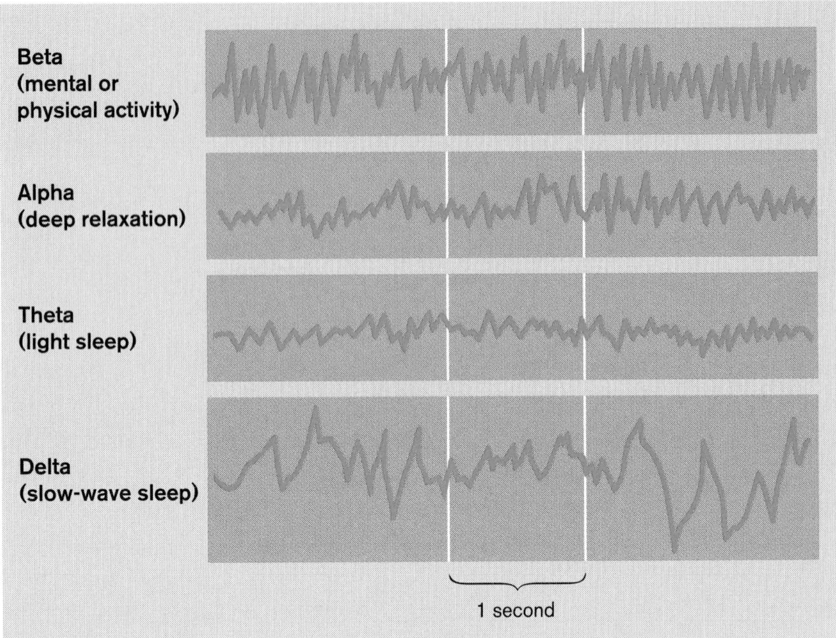

FIGURE 2.11

EEG Patterns Associated with Various Waking and Sleeping States

EEG patterns vary according to the level of brain activity monitored. Beta waves occur when a person is mentally or physically active.

discover the exact functions of single cells within the primary visual cortex and the primary auditory cortex.

The CT Scan and MRI

The patient undergoing a **CT scan (computerized axial tomography)** is placed inside a large, doughnut-shaped structure. An X-ray tube then circles the patient's entire head and shoots pencil-thin X-rays through the brain. A series of computerized cross-sectional images results; these images reveal the structures within the brain (or other parts of the body) as well as abnormalities and injuries, including tumours and old or recent strokes.

Another technique, **MRI (magnetic resonance imaging)**, produces clearer and more detailed images without exposing patients to the hazards of X-ray photography (Potts et al., 1993). MRI is a powerful diagnostic tool that can be used to find abnormalities in the central nervous system and in other systems of the body.

Although the CT scan and MRI do a remarkable job of showing what the brain looks like both inside and out, they cannot reveal what the brain is doing. But other technological marvels can.

The PET Scan, the Functional MRI, and Other Imaging Techniques

The **PET scan (positron-emission tomography)** is a powerful instrument for identifying malfunctions that cause physical and psychological disorders and also for studying normal brain activity (Volkow & Tancredi, 1991). The PET scan can map the patterns of blood flow, oxygen use, and consumption of glucose (the food of the brain). It can also show the action of drugs and other biochemical substances in the brain and other bodily organs (Farde, 1996).

The patient undergoing a PET scan either is injected with radioactive glucose or inhales oxygen laced with low-level radioactivity. The more active any part of the brain is, the more oxygen and glucose it consumes. The PET scan produces a computerized image in colours that vary with the amount of radioactive substance left behind as the brain uses different levels of oxygen or glucose.

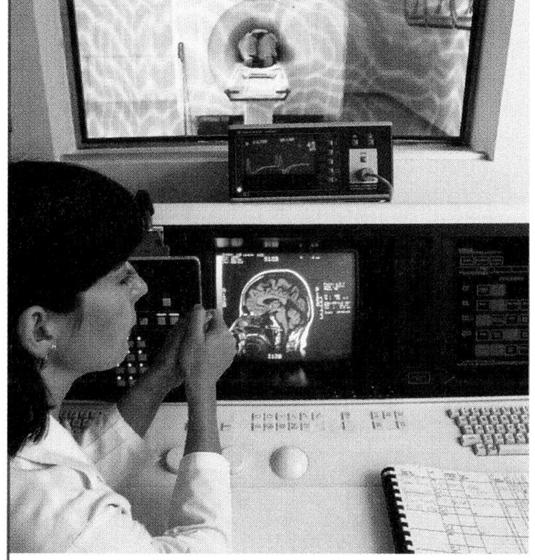

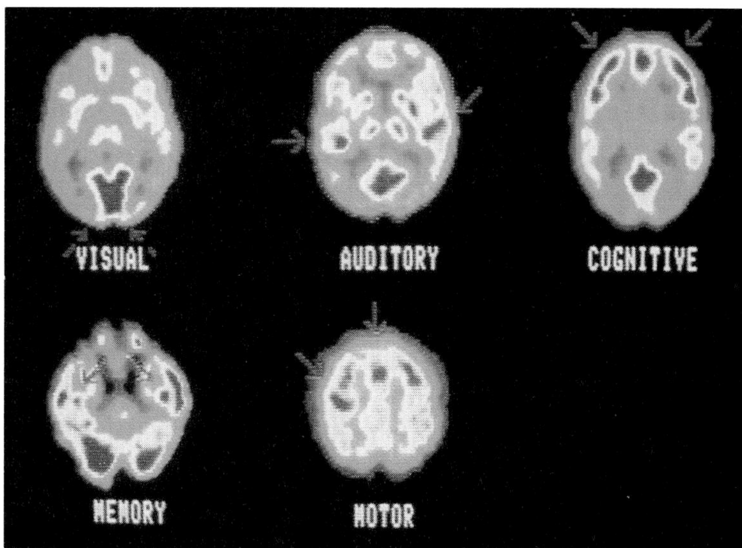

MRI (left) is a powerful tool for revealing what the brain looks like. Unlike PET scans, however, it cannot show us what the brain is doing. PET scans (right) show activity in specific areas of the brain.

The PET scan can detect only *changes* in blood flow and in oxygen and glucose consumption as they occur in the various brain areas. Many parts of the brain are always active, even when a person is doing nothing observable. How do researchers separate the activities of specific brain locations from those of other, unrelated brain locations? Thanks to sophisticated computers and creative mathematical techniques, researchers can "subtract" all other brain activities from the activities involved in the specific mental tasks the participants are performing at a given time (Raichle, 1994b).

One new application, functional MRI (fMRI), can image both brain structure and brain activity. It has several advantages over other imaging techniques: it requires nothing (radioactive or otherwise) to be injected into participants. Its ability to image precise locations of activity clearly is better than PET's and it can detect changes that take place in less than a second compared to around a minute for PET ("Brain Imaging," 1997). The major limitation of fMRI is that the participant's entire body must be confined within a long, narrow tube—a claustrophobic person's worst nightmare—during the entire imaging period.

For more information about these discoveries, read *On the Cutting Edge in Canada.*

Brain Damage: Causes and Consequences

What must occur in the brain for there to be some recovery from brain damage?

How can a person survive such massive brain damage as in the case of Phineas Gage, while a small bullet fired into the brain in particular places can result in instant death? The precise location of a brain injury is the most important factor determining whether a person lives or dies. Had the metal rod torn through Gage's brainstem, that would have been the end of him. Brain damage has many causes. Stroke, head injuries, diseases, tumours, and the abuse of drugs can leave people with a variety of disabilities.

CT scan (computerized axial tomography): A brain-scanning technique involving a rotating X-ray scanner and a high-speed computer analysis that produces slice-by-slice, cross-sectional images of the structure of the brain.

magnetic resonance imaging (MRI): A diagnostic scanning technique that produces high-resolution images of the structures of the brain.

PET scan (positron-emission tomography): A brain-imaging technique that reveals activity in various parts of the brain on the basis of the amount of oxygen and glucose consumed.

on the cutting edge in canada

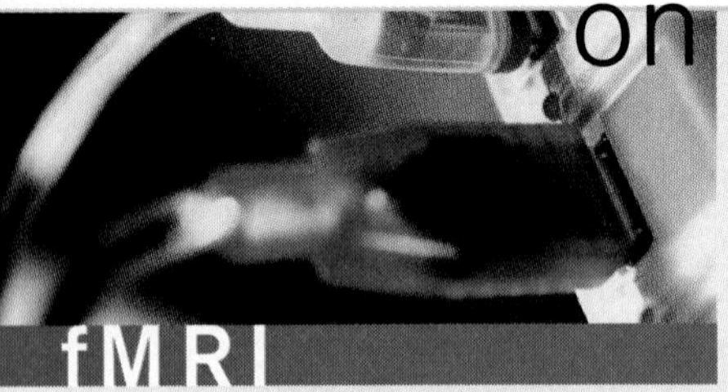

fMRI

One of the most exciting developments in the new field of cognitive neuroscience (an area of science that examines the neural bases of perception, cognition, and motor control) is *functional magnetic resonance imaging* (fMRI). How does it work? It has been known for some time that more active brain areas require more oxygen and, consequently, more blood is distributed to those regions. For example, suppose a given part of the brain is involved in reading. Whenever you read (this passage for example!), the neurons in that part of your brain will require more oxygen.

In Canada, at the Robarts Research Institute affiliated with the University of Western Ontario, research is being conducted with a "4 Tesla" MR system (one of six in the world). Dr. Ravi Menon, a Canadian physicist, and a research team composed of psychologists and physiologists, including Philip Servos from Wilfrid Laurier University, have been making important discoveries about the neural bases of visual and touch perception and visually guided action such as eye and arm movements.

Using the fMRI technology, Servos was able to map out the brain regions responsible for sensory information about the face. He demonstrated that there are errors in Penfield's original map. The face portion of the homunculus that Penfield mapped out was found to be upside down. Servos continues to map out the details of the sensory homunculus using fMRI. Such studies make possible the identification of brain regions that are as small as one cubic millimetre (the size of the head of a pin)! Although most fMRI work done in the world today can only monitor changes in the brain that occur over several seconds, recent groundbreaking work by Dr. Menon and his colleagues has made it possible to monitor changes in the brain that occur in the subsecond range.

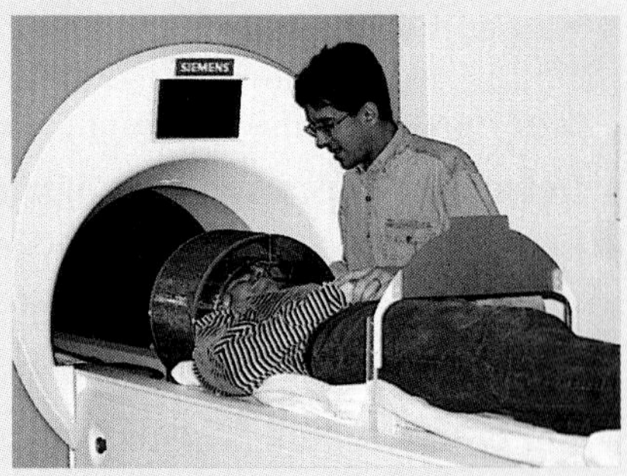

Dr. Ravi Menon

Recovering from Brain Damage

It was formerly thought that once neurons are destroyed, they were gone forever. However, research indicates that the hippocampus can regenerate neurons (Jones, 1999), damaged neurons can sprout new dendrites and re-establish connections with other neurons to assume some of the functions of the brain cells that were lost, and axons are able to regenerate and grow (Fawcett, 1992).

Some abilities lost through brain damage can be regained if areas near the damaged site take over the lost function. The brain's ability to reorganize and to compensate for brain damage is termed **plasticity**. Plasticity is greatest in young children, whose hemispheres haven't yet been completely lateralized (Bach-y-Rita & Bach-y-Rita, 1990). Some individuals who have had an entire hemisphere removed early in life because of uncontrollable epilepsy have been able to lead near-normal intellectual lives (Bower, 1988).

The Peripheral Nervous System

What is the peripheral nervous system?

The **peripheral nervous system (PNS)** is made up of all the nerves that connect the central nervous system to the rest of the body. Without the peripheral nervous system, the brain and spinal cord, encased in their bone coverings, would be isolated and unable to send information to or receive information from other parts of the body. The peripheral nervous system has two subdivisions—the somatic nervous system and the autonomic nervous system. Figure 2.12 shows the subdivisions within the peripheral nervous system.

The Somatic Nervous System

The somatic nervous system consists of all the *sensory* nerves, which transmit information from the sense receptors—eyes, ears, nose, tongue, and skin—to the central nervous system; and all the *motor* nerves, which relay messages from the central nerv-

Remember It!

Studying the Brain

1. The CT scan and MRI are used to
   a. show the amount of activity in various parts of the brain.
   b. produce images of the structures within the brain.
   c. measure electrical activity in the brain.
   d. observe neural communication at synapses.
2. Which of the following reveals the electrical activity of the brain by producing a record of brain waves?
   a. electroencephalograph
   b. CT scan
   c. PET scan
   d. MRI
3. Which of the following reveals brain activity and function, rather than the structure of the brain?
   a. CT scan   b. EEG
   c. PET scan   d. MRI
4. Match the brain-wave pattern with the state associated with it.
   ___ 1) Slow-wave (deep) sleep   a. beta wave
   ___ 2) Deep relaxation while awake   b. delta wave
   ___ 3) Physical or mental activity   c. alpha wave
5. Plasticity of the brain increases with age. (true/false)

Answers: 1. b 2. a 3. c 4. 1) b 2) c 3) a 5. false

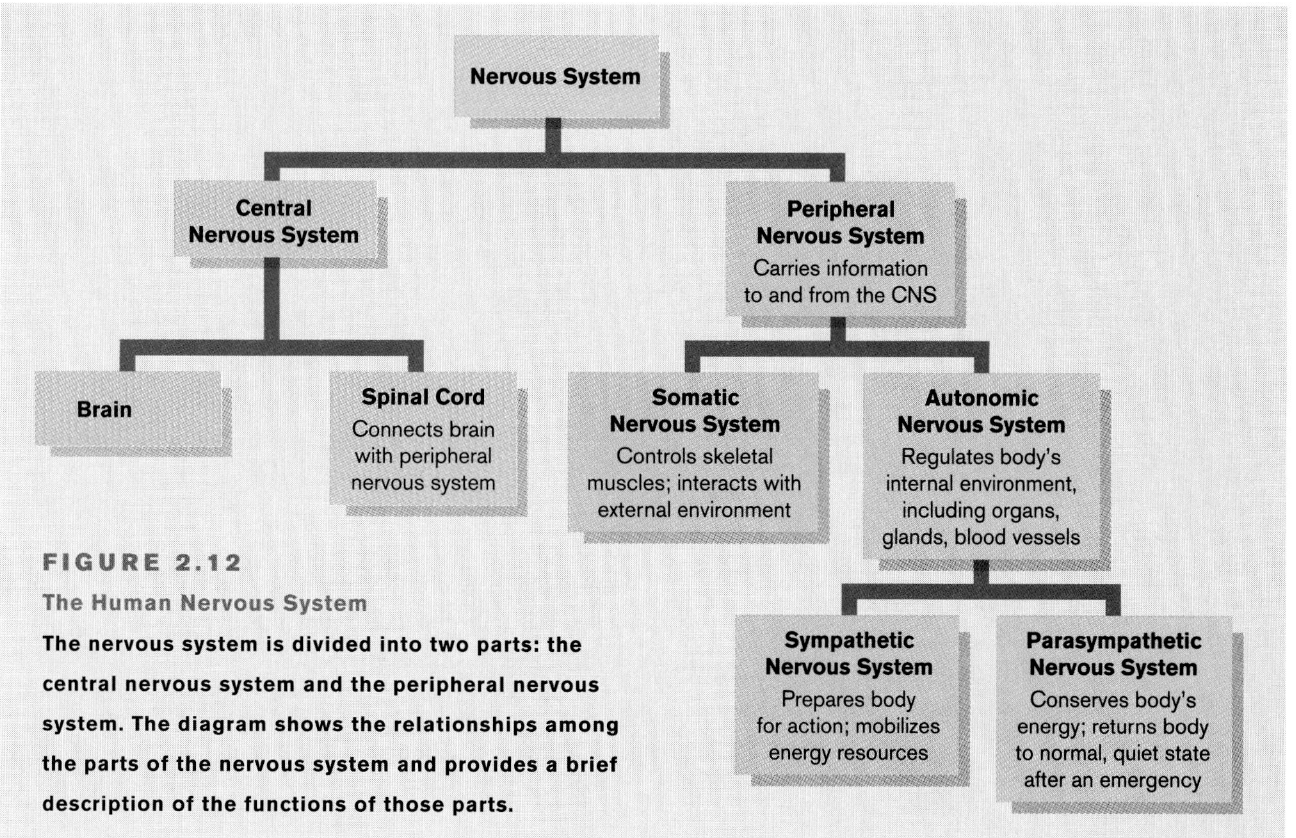

FIGURE 2.12
The Human Nervous System
The nervous system is divided into two parts: the central nervous system and the peripheral nervous system. The diagram shows the relationships among the parts of the nervous system and provides a brief description of the functions of those parts.

ous system to all the skeletal muscles of the body. In short, the nerves of the somatic nervous system make it possible for us to sense our environment and to move, and they are primarily under our conscious control.

plasticity: The ability of the brain to reorganize and compensate for brain damage.

peripheral nervous system (PNS) (peh-RIF-er-ul): The nerves connecting the central nervous system to the rest of the body; has two subdivisions–the autonomic and the somatic nervous systems.

The Autonomic Nervous System

What are the roles of the sympathetic and parasympathetic nervous systems?

The word *autonomic* is sometimes misread by students as *automatic.* That is not a bad synonym, because the autonomic nervous system operates quite well automatically, without our being conscious of it. It transmits messages between the central nervous system and the glands, the cardiac (heart) muscle, and the smooth muscles (such as those in the large arteries, the gastrointestinal system, and the small blood vessels), which are not normally under voluntary control.

The autonomic nervous system is further divided into two parts—the sympathetic and the parasympathetic nervous systems. Any time you are under stress or faced with an emergency, the **sympathetic nervous system** automatically mobilizes the body's resources, preparing you for action. This physiological arousal produced by the sympathetic nervous system is called the "fight or flight" response. If an ominous-looking stranger started following you and quickened his pace as you turned down a dark, deserted street, your sympathetic nervous system would automatically set to work. Your heart would begin to pound, your pulse rate would increase rapidly, your breathing would quicken, and your digestive system would nearly shut down. The blood flow to your skeletal muscles would be enhanced, and all of your bodily resources would be made ready to handle the emergency—RUN!

But once the emergency is over, something must happen to bring these heightened bodily functions back to normal. The **parasympathetic nervous system** is responsible for this. As a result of its action, your heart stops pounding and slows to normal, your pulse rate and breathing slow down, and the digestive system resumes its normal functioning. As you can see in Figure 2.13, the sympathetic and parasympathetic branches act as opposing but complementary forces in the autonomic nervous system. Their balanced functioning is essential for our health and survival.

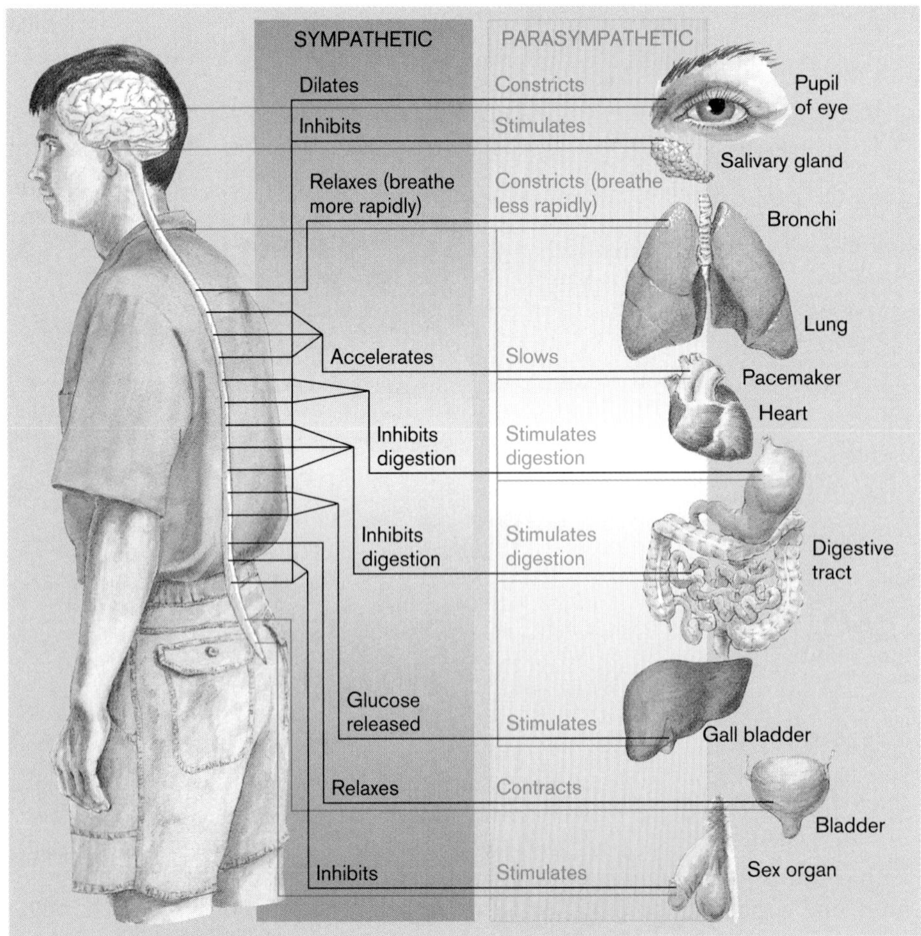

FIGURE 2.13

The Autonomic Nervous System **The autonomic nervous system consists of (1) the sympathetic nervous system, which mobilizes the body's resources during emergencies or during stress, and (2) the parasympathetic nervous system, which is associated with relaxation and which brings the heightened bodily responses back to normal after an emergency. This diagram shows the opposite effects of the sympathetic and parasympathetic nervous systems on various parts of the body.**

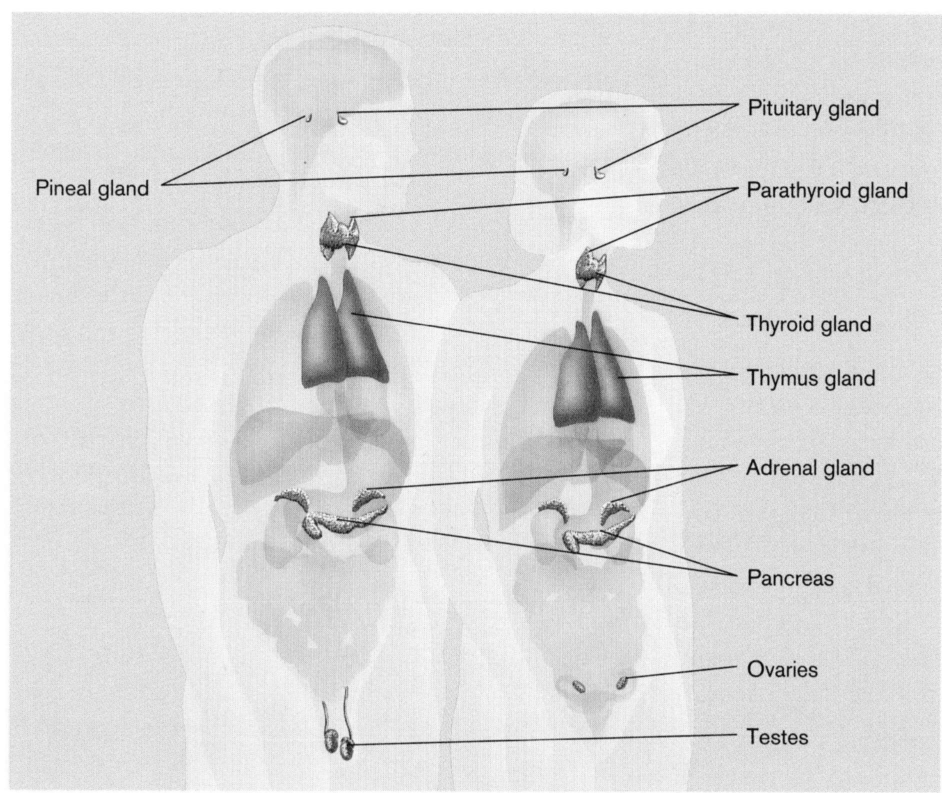

FIGURE 2.14

The Endocrine System The endocrine system is a series of glands that manufacture and secrete hormones. The hormones travel through the circulatory system and have important effects on many bodily functions.

The Endocrine System

What is the endocrine system, and what are some of the glands within it?

We have seen how chemical substances called neurotransmitters influence the 100 billion or so neurons in the nervous system. There is another system that stimulates and regulates important functions in the body by means of chemical substances. The **endocrine system** is a series of ductless glands, found in various parts of the body, that manufacture and secrete chemicals known as hormones (from the Greek word for "excite"). **Hormones** are manufactured and released in one part of the body but have an effect on other parts of the body. Hormones are released into the bloodstream and travel throughout the circulatory system, but each hormone performs its assigned job only when it connects with the body cells having receptors for it. Some neurotransmitters act as hormones as well—norepinephrine and vasopressin, to name two (Bergland, 1985). Figure 2.14 shows the glands in the endocrine system and their locations in the body.

The Pituitary Gland

The **pituitary gland** rests in the brain just below the hypothalamus and is controlled by it (refer to Figure 2.14). The pituitary is considered to be the master gland of the body because it releases the hor-

sympathetic nervous system: The division of the autonomic nervous system that mobilizes the body's resources during stress, emergencies, or heavy exertion, preparing the body for action.

parasympathetic nervous system: The division of the autonomic nervous system that is associated with relaxation and the conservation of energy and that brings the heightened bodily responses back to normal after an emergency.

endocrine system (EN-duh-krin): A system of ductless glands in various parts of the body that manufacture and secrete hormones into the bloodstream or lymph fluids, thus affecting cells in other parts of the body.

hormone: A substance manufactured and released in one part of the body that affects other parts of the body.

pituitary gland: The endocrine gland located in the brain and often called the "master gland," which releases hormones that control other endocrine glands and also releases a growth hormone.

mones that "turn on," or activate, the other glands in the endocrine system—a big job for a tiny structure about the size of a pea. The pituitary also produces the hormone that is responsible for body growth (Howard et al., 1996). Too little of this powerful substance will make one a dwarf, whereas too much will produce a giant.

The Thyroid Gland

The thyroid gland rests in the front lower part of the neck just below the voice box (larynx). The thyroid produces the important hormone thyroxin, which regulates the rate at which food is metabolized, or transformed into energy. Too much thyroxin can result in hyperthyroidism, a condition in which people are nervous and excitable, find it hard to be still and relax, and are usually thin. Hypothyroidism, an underproduction of thyroxin, has just the opposite effect. An adult with hypothyroidism may feel sluggish, lack energy, and be overweight.

The Pancreas

Curving around between the small intestine and the stomach is the pancreas (refer to Figure 2.14). The pancreas regulates the body's blood sugar levels by releasing the hormones insulin and glucagon into the bloodstream. The pancreas also produces digestive enzymes. In people with diabetes, too little insulin is produced. Without insulin to break down the sugars we ingest, the level of blood sugar can get dangerously high. In hypoglycemia, the opposite effect occurs—too much insulin is produced, resulting in low blood sugar. Both conditions may be partly controlled by diet, but in many cases the diabetic must also take daily insulin injections.

The Adrenal Glands

Lower in the body are the two **adrenal glands**, which rest just above the kidneys, as shown in Figure 2.14. The adrenal glands produce epinephrine and norep-

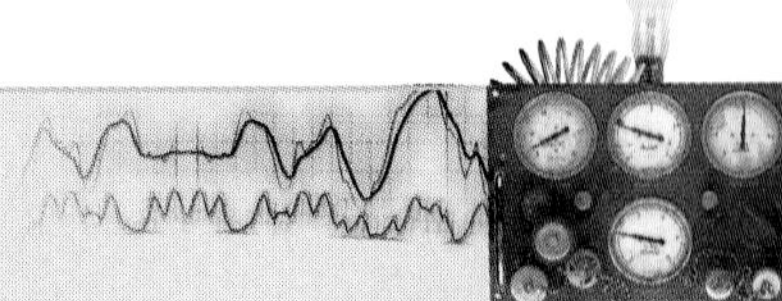

Handedness: Does It Make a Difference?

Apply It!

If you are left-handed, you are in good company. Among the better-known lefties of earlier centuries were Alexander the Great, Michelangelo, Leonardo da Vinci, and Joan of Arc. Other famous lefties include Albert Einstein and Marilyn Monroe; among left-handers of more recent times are Martina Navratilova, Howie Mandel, Dan Aykroyd, Marshall McLuhan, and Wayne Gretzky.

Stanley Coren and his colleagues at the University of British Columbia have studied the implications of being left-handed. They found that most people—about 90 percent of the world's population—are right-handed (Coren & Porac, 1977). Left-handedness occurs more often in males than in females. People who are left-handed are generally also left-footed, and to a lesser extent left-eyed and left-eared as well. There is a difference in the motor control provided by the two hemispheres of the brain. Thus, in a person whose left hand is dominant, the right hemisphere provides superior motor control for that hand.

Scholars and scientists have long wondered why such a small percentage of humans are left-handed. Some researchers propose a genetic cause (Annett, 1985; Levy & Nagylaki, 1972); others maintain that handedness is learned (Porac, 1993; Provins, 1997). No theory yet proposed is able to explain all the facts, although there is strong evidence that there is a genetic element in handedness.

Some research evidence is even more controversial. Investigators at McMaster University have proposed that handedness and sexual orientation are linked. For example, Witelson (1990) found that the percentage of right-handers drops sharply among homosexual men and women. The same investigator has identified a number of physiological differences between right-handed and left-handed

inephrine, two hormones that activate the sympathetic nervous system. The adrenal glands release the corticoids, which control the body's salt balance, and also release small amounts of the sex hormones.

The Sex Glands

The gonads are the sex glands—the ovaries in females and the testes in males (refer to Figure 2.14). Activated by the pituitary gland, the gonads release sex hormones that make reproduction possible and that are responsible for the secondary sex characteristics—pubic and underarm hair in both sexes, breasts in females, and facial hair and a deepened voice in males.

Androgens, the male sex hormones, influence sexual motivation. Estrogen and progesterone, the female sex hormones, help regulate the menstrual cycle. Although both males and females have androgens and estrogens, males have considerably more androgens, and females have considerably more estrogens.

Biology and behaviour are intimately related. However, there is much more to the scientific study of behaviour and mental processes than the biological connection can teach us. Later chapters in this text expand on other aspects of behaviour and mental processes.

LINK IT!

www.indiana.edu/~primate/brain.html
Handedness and Brain Lateralization

www.indiana.edu/~primate/forms/hand.html
Hand Preference Questionnaire: Participate in on-going research on human handedness

www.carleton.ca/49.663/web.htm
Neuropsychology and the Corpus Callosum

people. On average, the corpus callosum of left-handers is 11 percent larger and contains up to 2.5 million more nerve fibres (Witelson, 1985). In about 60 percent of left-handers, language functions are controlled by the left hemisphere; in 25 percent, by the right hemisphere; and in about 15 percent, by both hemispheres. In general, left-handers appear to be less lateralized than right-handers, meaning that the two sides of the brain are less specialized (Hellige et al., 1994). Because of this characteristic, left-handers tend to experience less language loss following an injury to either hemisphere (Geschwind, 1979); and they are more likely to recover, because the undamaged hemisphere can more easily take over the speech functions.

In many respects, left-handed people are at a disadvantage compared with right-handed people. Left-handers are five times more likely to suffer serious accidents, and they are sometimes said to be clumsier than right-handers. A more extreme suggestion is that left-handers, on average, have a shorter life span than right-handers (Coren & Halpern, 1991). This can probably be explained by the fact that they must function in a world designed for right-handers (Coren, 1989).

For example, the seats found in many college and university classrooms have a large writing surface at the end of the right arm, allowing right-handed people to rest that arm while writing. In cars with a standard shift, the gear shift is located on the right side of the driver's seat. The markings on measuring cups, thermometers, and other measuring devices cannot be read unless the object is held in the right hand. Table settings and doorknobs also assume right-handedness. The bias toward right-handedness even extends to feet: the arrangement of pedals in a car favours right-footed people.

Most left-handed people are able to adapt to these conditions. Some actually become ambidextrous as a result of using both hands for certain activities. (For example, Roberto Alomar hits from both sides in baseball.) Fortunately, some items–scissors and golf clubs, for example–are manufactured in left-hander versions.

Most children show a consistent preference for one hand over the other by the age of five; some begin to rely on the use of one hand at 18 months. Most experts in child development agree that it is harmful, if not futile, to interfere with the hand preference of a young child. It can cause emotional distress and lead to speech or reading problems.

adrenal glands (ah-DREE-nal): A pair of endocrine glands that release hormones that prepare the body for emergencies and stressful situations and also release small amounts of the sex hormones.

Remember It!

The Peripheral Nervous System

1. The ____________ nervous system connects the brain and spinal cord to the rest of the body.
   a. central b. peripheral
   c. somatic d. autonomic
2. The ____________ nervous system mobilizes the body's resources during times of stress; the ____________ nervous system brings the heightened bodily responses back to normal when the emergency is over.
   a. somatic; autonomic
   b. autonomic; somatic
   c. sympathetic; parasympathetic
   d. parasympathetic; sympathetic
3. The endocrine glands secrete ________ directly into the ________.
   a. hormones; bloodstream
   b. enzymes; digestive tract
   c. enzymes; bloodstream
   d. hormones; digestive tract
4. Match the endocrine gland with the appropriate description.

___ 1) Keeps body's metabolism in balance		
___ 2) Acts as a master gland that activates the other glands		a. pituitary gland
___ 3) Regulates blood sugar		b. adrenal glands
___ 4) Makes reproduction possible		c. gonads
___ 5) Releases hormones that prepare the body for emergencies		d. thyroid gland
		e. pancreas

Answers: 1. b 2. c 3. a 4. 1) d 2) a 3) e 4) c 5) b

KEY TERMS

acetylcholine, p. 39
action potential, p. 37
adrenal glands, p. 64
alpha wave, p. 57
amygdala, p. 45
aphasia, p. 48
association areas, p. 46
axon, p. 35
beta wave, p. 57
brainstem, p. 42
Broca's aphasia, p. 48
Broca's area, p. 48
cell body, p. 35
central nervous system, p. 41
cerebellum, p. 43
cerebral cortex, p. 46
cerebral hemispheres, p. 46
cerebrum, p. 46
corpus callosum, p. 46
CT scan, p. 58
delta wave, p. 57
dendrites, p. 35
dopamine, p. 39
electroencephalogram (EEG), p.57
endocrine system, p. 63
endorphins, p. 40
fMRI, p. 60
frontal lobes, p. 46
glial cells, p. 40
hippocampus, p. 45
hormone, p. 63
hypothalamus, p. 44
lateralization, p. 52
left hemisphere, p. 52
limbic system, p. 45
medulla, p. 42
microelectrode, p. 57
motor cortex, p. 47
MRI, p. 58
myelin sheath, p. 37
neuron, p. 34
neurotransmitter, p. 37
norepinephrine, p. 40
occipital lobes, p. 50
parasympathetic nervous system, p. 62
parietal lobes, p. 50
peripheral nervous system, p. 60
PET scan, p. 58
pituitary gland, p. 63
plasticity, p. 60
primary auditory cortex, p. 50
primary visual cortex, p. 50
receptor site, p. 37
resting potential, p. 36
reticular formation, p. 42
reuptake, p. 39
right hemisphere, p. 52
serotonin, p. 40
somatosensory cortex, p. 50
spinal cord, p. 42
split-brain operation, p. 54
sympathetic nervous system, p. 62
synapse, p. 36
temporal lobes, p. 50
thalamus, p. 44
Wernicke's aphasia, p. 51
Wernicke's area, p. 51

THINKING CRITICALLY

Evaluation

Using your knowledge about how the human brain has been studied in the past and today, point out the advantages and the disadvantages of the older investigative methods: the case study, the autopsy, and the study of people with brain injuries or who have had brain surgery (including the split-brain operation). Follow the same procedure to discuss the more modern techniques: EEG, CT scan, MRI, and PET scan.

Point/Counterpoint

A continuing controversial issue is whether animals should be used in biological research. Review the chapter and find each occasion in which animals were used to advance our knowledge of the brain. Using what you have read in this chapter and any other information you have acquired, prepare arguments to support each of the following positions:

a. The use of animals in research projects is ethical and justifiable because of the possible benefits to humankind.
b. The use of animals in research projects is not ethical or justifiable on the grounds of possible benefits to humankind.

Psychology in Your Life

How would your life change if you had a massive stroke in your left hemisphere? How would it change if the stroke were in your right hemisphere? Which stroke would be more tragic for you, and why?

SUMMARY & REVIEW

The Neurons and the Neurotransmitters

What is a neuron, and what are its three parts?

A neuron is a specialized cell that conducts messages through the nervous system. Its three main parts are the cell body, dendrites, and axon.

What is a synapse?

A synapse is the junction where the axon terminal of the sending neuron communicates with the receiving neuron across the synaptic cleft.

What is the action potential?

The action potential is the firing of a neuron that results when the charge within the neuron becomes more positive than the charge outside the cell's membrane.

What are neurotransmitters, and what role do they play in the transmission of signals from one neuron to another?

Neurotransmitters are chemicals released into the synaptic cleft from the axon terminal of the sending neuron. They cross the synapse and bind to receptor sites on the receiving neuron, influencing the cell to fire or not to fire.

What are some of the ways in which neurotransmitters affect our behaviour, and what are some of the major neurotransmitters?

Neurotransmitters regulate the actions of our glands and muscles, affect learning and memory, promote sleep, stimulate mental and physical alertness, and influence our moods and emotions, from depression to euphoria. Some of the major neurotransmitters are acetylcholine, dopamine, norepinephrine, serotonin, glutamate, GABA, and endorphins.

The Central Nervous System

Why is an intact spinal cord important to normal functioning?

The spinal cord is an extension of the brain, connecting it to the peripheral nervous system so that sensory information can reach the brain, and messages from the brain can reach the muscles and glands.

What are the crucial functions handled by the brainstem?

The brainstem contains (1) the medulla, which controls heartbeat, breathing, blood pressure, coughing, and swallowing; and (2) the reticular formation, which plays a crucial role in arousal and attention.

What are the primary functions of the cerebellum?

The main functions of the cerebellum are to execute smooth, skilled movements and to regulate muscle tone and posture.

What is the primary role of the thalamus?

The thalamus acts as a relay station for information flowing into or out of the higher brain centres.

What are some of the processes regulated by the hypothalamus?

The hypothalamus controls the pituitary gland and regulates hunger, thirst, sexual behaviour, body temperature, and a variety of emotional behaviours.

What is the role of the limbic system?

The limbic system is a group of structures in the brain, including the amygdala and the hippocampus, that are collectively involved in emotion, memory, and motivation.

The Cerebral Hemispheres

What are the cerebral hemispheres, the cerebral cortex, and the corpus callosum?

The cerebral hemispheres are the two halves of the cerebrum, connected by the corpus callosum and covered by the cerebral cortex, which is responsible for higher mental processes such as language, memory, and thinking.

What are some of the main areas within the frontal lobes, and what are their functions?

The frontal lobes contain (1) the motor cortex, which controls voluntary motor activity; (2) Broca's area, which functions in speech production; and (3) the frontal association areas, which are involved in thinking, motivation, planning for the future, impulse control, and emotional responses.

What are the primary functions of the parietal lobes in general and the somatosensory cortex in particular?

The parietal lobes are involved in the reception and processing of touch stimuli. They contain the somatosensory cortex, where touch, pressure, temperature, and pain register.

What are the primary functions of the occipital lobes in general and the primary visual cortex in particular?

The occipital lobes are involved in the reception and interpretation of visual information. They contain the primary visual cortex, where vision registers in the cerebral cortex.

What are the major areas within the temporal lobes, and what are their functions?

The temporal lobes contain (1) the primary auditory cortex, where hearing registers in the cortex; (2) Wernicke's area, which is involved in comprehending the spoken word and in formulating coherent speech and written language; and (3) association areas, where memories are stored and auditory stimuli are interpreted.

Specialization of the Cerebral Hemispheres

What are the main functions of the left hemisphere?

The left hemisphere controls the right side of the body, coordinates complex movements, and handles most of the language functions, including speaking, writing, reading, and understanding the spoken word.

What are the primary functions of the right hemisphere?

The right hemisphere controls the left side of the body; is specialized for visual-spatial perception, singing, reading, and non-verbal behaviour; and is more active in the recognition and expression of emotion.

What is the significance of the split-brain operation?

In the split-brain operation, a surgeon cuts the corpus callosum. This prevents the transfer of information between the hemispheres. Research on split-brain patients has extended our knowledge of the functions of the hemispheres.

Discovering the Brain's Mysteries

What are some methods that researchers have used to learn about brain function?

Researchers have learned about brain function from clinical studies of patients, through electrical stimulation of the brain, and from studies using the EEG, microelectrodes, the CT scan, MRI, and the PET scan.

What is the electroencephalogram (EEG), and what are three of the brain-wave patterns it reveals?

The electroencephalogram (EEG) is a record of brain-wave activity. Three normal brain-wave patterns are the beta wave, alpha wave, and delta wave.

Brain Damage: Causes and Consequences

What must occur in the brain for there to be some recovery from brain damage?

In recovery from brain damage, (1) damaged neurons may sprout new dendrites and reestablish connections with other neurons, (2) areas near the damaged site may take over the lost function, or (3) the undamaged hemisphere may assume the lost language function (as in aphasia).

The Peripheral Nervous System

What is the peripheral nervous system?

The peripheral nervous system connects the central nervous system to the rest of the body. It has two subdivisions: (1) the somatic nervous system, which consists of the nerves that make it possible for us to sense and move; and (2) the autonomic nervous system.

What are the roles of the sympathetic and parasympathetic nervous systems?

The autonomic nervous system has two parts: (1) the sympathetic nervous system, which mobilizes the body's resources during emergencies or during stress; and (2) the parasympathetic nervous system, which is associated with relaxation and brings the heightened bodily responses back to normal after an emergency.

The Endocrine System

What is the endocrine system, and what are some of the glands within it?

The endocrine system is a system of glands in various parts of the body that manufacture hormones and secrete them into the bloodstream. The hormones then affect cells in other parts of the body. The pituitary gland releases hormones that control other glands in the endocrine system and also releases a growth hormone. The thyroid gland produces thyroxin, which regulates metabolism. The adrenal glands release epinephrine and norepinephrine, which prepare the body for emergencies and stressful situations, and also release small amounts of the sex hormones. The pancreas produces insulin and regulates blood sugar. The gonads are the sex glands, which produce the sex hormones and make reproduction possible.

Sensation and Perception

James Stone, Jr., was born with a rare and unusual neurological condition–he could feel no pain. You might think of him as lucky. Imagine never feeling any physical pain! Imagine all the things you could do without ever feeling any sense of discomfort: exercise with no feeling of exhaustion, fall down when snowboarding without feeling any pain, and never be bothered by cuts or bruises. The reality of it is that James's condition made his life a living hell. Because he could feel no pain, James was unable to care for himself or to be concerned about his own safety. As a result, even when he was a very young boy, James bit off his own fingers, chewed his lips raw, and never noticed when he had burned or cut himself. By the time James reached the age of three, his body was covered with scars.

James's condition was a great burden to his parents, who lived in great poverty and were forced to protect him with the few resources they had. They padded all areas of his bed and bedroom with foam rubber; they took turn staying awake at night so someone was always with him in case he hurt himself without noticing; they constantly checked James's body for bruises. And because of his condition, James never got to feel the warm touch of his parents' hands, the softness of the wind, or sun on his skin.

Although no one knows what happened to James as he grew up and became an adult, odds are that his unfortunate condition would have forced him into a life of misery with the constant need to pay attention to his physical condition, without any of the pleasures associated with human physical contact. (Based on Marion, 1990.)

What is the difference between sensation and perception?

There may have been times in your life during which you wished you would not feel pain—in an extreme sport competition, during a race, when you broke a bone or hit your thumb with a hammer. However, as the story James Stone, Jr., reveals, feeling pain is one of the most important sensations associated with human survival.

Sensation and perception are intimately related in everyday experience, but they are not the same. **Sensation** is the process by which the senses detect visual, auditory, and other sensory stimuli and transmit them to the brain. **Perception** is the process by which sensory information is actively organized and interpreted by the brain. Sensation furnishes the raw material of sensory experience; perception provides the finished product.

To a large extent we must learn to perceive, and people who are unable to feel pain or who cannot see or hear may never be able to develop useful perception even if their sense is restored.

In this chapter we will explore the five primary senses—vision, hearing, touch, taste, and smell—and some of the secondary ones, such as balance and pain. You will learn how the senses detect sensory information and how this information is actively organized and interpreted by the brain. We begin with a closer look at sensation.

Sensation: The Sensory World

Our senses serve as ports of entry for all information about our world. Virtually everything we call experience is detected initially by our senses. Yet it is amazing how little of this sensory world we actually sense. For example, we see only a thin slice of the vast spectrum of electromagnetic energy. With the unaided eye we cannot see microwaves, X-rays, or ultraviolet light. We are unable to hear the ultrasonic sound of a dog whistle, and our ears can detect a scant 20 percent of the sounds that a dolphin or bat can hear; nor can we see the outline of a warm-blooded animal from its infrared heat pattern at night, though rattlesnakes and other pit vipers can. Yet all of these sensory stimuli exist in the real, physical world.

Whichever of our senses we select for comparison, humans are not at the top of the list for quality or sensitivity. Some animals have a superior sense of hearing (bats and dolphins); others have sharper vision (hawks); still others have a superior sense of smell (bloodhounds); and so on. Even so, we humans have remarkable sensory abilities and superior abilities of perception.

LINK IT!

www.sciencenet.org.uk/database/Social/Senses/s00096b.html
Sensory Reception

www.ucl.ac.uk/~smgxt01/
Neurotransmitters in Sensory Systems

The Absolute Threshold: To Sense or Not to Sense

What is the difference between the absolute threshold and the difference threshold?

What is the softest sound you can hear, the dimmest light you can see, the most diluted substance you can taste? What is the lightest touch you can feel, the faintest odour you can smell? Researchers in sensory psychology and psychophysics have performed many experiments over the years to answer these questions. Their research has established measures for the senses known as *absolute thresholds.* Just as the threshold of a doorway is the dividing point between being outside a room and being inside it, the **absolute threshold** of a sense marks the difference between not being able to hear a sound (or see a light) and being just barely able to hear it (or see it). Psychologists have arbitrarily defined this absolute threshold as the minimum amount of sensory stimulation that can be detected 50 percent of the time. For example, the absolute thresholds established for the five primary senses in humans are equivalent to the following: (1) for vision, a candle flame 48 kilometres away on a clear night; (2) for hearing, a watch ticking six metres away; (3) for taste, one teaspoon of sugar dissolved in nine litres of water; (4) for smell, a single drop of perfume in a three-room house; and (5) for touch, a bee's wing falling a distance of one centimetre onto your cheek.

Important as it is, the absolute threshold, once crossed, says nothing about the broad range of sensory experiences. Do we or don't we sense it? That is the only question the absolute threshold answers. But read on—there are other questions to be answered.

The Difference Threshold: Detecting Differences

If you are listening to music, the very fact that you can hear it means that the absolute threshold has been crossed. But how much must the volume be turned up or down for you to notice a difference? Or, if you are carrying a load of books, how much weight must be added or subtracted for you to be able to sense that your load is heavier or lighter? The **difference threshold** is a measure of the smallest increase or decrease in a physical stimulus that is required to produce the **just noticeable difference (JND)**. The JND is the smallest change in sensation that we are able to detect 50 percent of the time. If you were holding a 2-kilogram weight and 500 grams were added, you could easily tell the difference. But if you were holding 50 kilograms and one additional 500-gram weight were added, you could not sense the difference. Why not? After all, the weight added was the same.

More than 100 years ago, Ernst Weber observed that the JND for all our senses depends on a proportion or percentage of change rather than on a fixed amount of change. This observation became known as **Weber's law**. A weight we are holding must increase or decrease by 2 percent for us to notice the difference. According to Weber's law, the greater the original stimulus, the more it must be increased or decreased for us to tell the difference.

The difference threshold is not the same for all the senses. We need a very large (20 percent) difference to detect some changes in taste. In contrast, if you were listening to music, you would notice a difference if a tone changed in pitch by only 0.3 percent.

Aren't some people more sensitive to sensory changes than others? Yes they are. The difference thresholds for the various senses are not the same for all people. In fact, there are huge individual differences. Expert wine tasters would know if a particular vintage was a little too sweet, even if it varied by only a fraction of the 20 percent change. Professionally trained musicians would know if they were singing or playing slightly out of tune long before the 0.3 percent difference in pitch appeared. Actually, Weber's law best fits people with average sensitivities, and

sensation: The process through which the senses pick up visual, auditory, and other sensory stimuli and transmit them to the brain; sensory information that has registered in the brain but has not been interpreted.

perception: The process by which sensory information is actively organized and interpreted by the brain.

absolute threshold: The minimum amount of sensory stimulation that can be detected 50 percent of the time.

difference threshold: The smallest increase or decrease in a physical stimulus required to produce a difference in sensation that is noticeable 50 percent of the time.

just noticeable difference (JND): The smallest change in sensation that we are able to detect 50 percent of the time.

Weber's law: The law stating that the just noticeable difference (JND) for all our senses depends on a proportion or percentage of change in a stimulus rather than on a fixed amount of change.

sensory stimuli that are neither very strong (loud thunder) nor very weak (a faint whisper).

Signal Detection Theory

You may have realized that the classic methods for measuring sensory thresholds have a serious limitation. They focus exclusively on the physical stimulus—how strong or weak it is or how much the stimulus must change for the difference to be noticed. But there is significant variation among individuals in sensory sensitivities; and within the same individual, sensory capabilities vary both across time and according to the conditions. Factors that affect a person's ability to detect a sensory signal are (besides the strength of the stimulus) the motivation to detect it, previous experience, the expectation that it will occur, and the level of alertness (or fatigue).

Another approach takes into account these factors. **Signal detection theory** is the view that the detection of a sensory stimulus involves both noticing a stimulus from background "noise" and a decision as to whether the stimulus is actually present. Deciding whether a stimulus is present depends partly on the probability that the stimulus will occur and partly on the potential gain or loss associated with deciding that it is present or absent.

Suppose you were given the description of a cousin you had never seen before and were asked to pick her up at the gate when her plane arrived at the airport. Your task would be to scan a sea of faces for someone fitting the description and then to decide which of the several people who fit the description was actually your cousin. All the other faces and objects in your field of vision would be considered background noise. How certain you felt before you would be willing to approach someone would depend on several factors—for example, the embarrassment you might feel approaching the wrong person as opposed to the distress you would feel if you failed to find your cousin.

Signal detection theory has special relevance to people in many occupations—air traffic controllers, police officers, military personnel on guard duty, medical professionals, and poultry inspectors, to name a few. Whether these professionals detect certain stimuli can have important consequences for the health and welfare of us all (Swets, 1992, 1998).

Transduction: Transforming Sensory Stimuli into Neural Impulses

How are sensory stimuli in the environment experienced as sensations?

You may be surprised to learn that our eyes do not actually see; nor do our ears hear. Our sense organs provide only the beginning point of sensation, which must be completed by the brain. As you learned in Chapter 2, specific clusters of neurons in specialized parts of the brain must be stimulated for us to see, hear, taste, and so on. The brain itself cannot respond directly to light, sound waves, odours, and tastes. How, then, does it get the message? The answer involves the sensory receptors.

All our senses are equipped with specialized cells called **sensory receptors**, which detect and respond to various stimuli—light, sound waves, odours, and so on. Through a process known as **transduction**, the receptors change the sensory stimulation into neural impulses. The neural impulses are then transmitted to their own special locations in the brain, such as the visual cortex for vision and the primary auditory cortex for hearing. We experience a sensation only when the appropriate part of the brain is stimulated. Our sense receptors provide the essential links between the physical sensory world and the brain.

Sensory Adaptation

All of our senses are more receptive, more finely tuned, to changes in sensory stimuli than to sameness. After a time, the sensory receptors grow accustomed to constant, unchanging levels of stimuli—sights, sounds, smells—so that we notice them less and less, or not at all. This process of becoming less sensitive to an unchanging sensory stimulus over time is known as **sensory adaptation**.

Have you ever taken part in the polar bear swim that is held every year on New Year's Day in Vancouver? If you have, when you first entered the water the temperature receptors in your skin would vigorously signal "ice water." But gradually, sensory adaptation would occur and the water would feel comfortable. Well, maybe not—it's a little *too* cold. Similarly, you have undoubtedly noticed the distinctive odour of your home when you first walk through the door. But after a few minutes you are not aware of it. A continuous odour will stimulate the smell recep-

Remember It!

The Sensory World

1. The process through which the senses detect sensory information and transmit it to the brain is called (sensation/perception).
2. The point at which you can barely sense a stimulus 50 percent of the time is called the (absolute/difference) threshold.
3. The difference threshold is the same for all individuals. (true/false)
4. Which of the following is not true of sensory receptors?
   a. They are specialized to detect certain sensory stimuli.
   b. They transduce sensory stimuli into neural impulses.
   c. They are located in the brain.
   d. They provide the link between the physical sensory world and the brain.
5. The process by which a sensory stimulus is converted into a neural impulse is called ________________.
6. Each morning when Jackie goes to work at the dry cleaners she smells the strong odour of cleaning fluid. After she is there for a few minutes, she is no longer aware of it. What accounts for this?
   a. Signal detection theory
   b. Sensory adaptation
   c. Transduction
   d. The just noticeable difference

Answers: 1. sensation 2. absolute 3. false 4. c 5. transduction 6. b

People who swim in icy water experience a degree of sensory adaptation, which helps their bodies adjust to the frigid temperature. What other examples of sensory adaptation can you think of?

tors to respond only for a while. Then, if there is no change in the odours, the receptors will steadily diminish their firing rate, and smell adaptation will occur. However, sensory adaptation is not likely to occur in the presence of very strong stimuli—the smell of ammonia, an ear-splitting sound, or the taste of rancid food.

Vision

For most of us, vision is the most valued sensory experience, and it is the sense that has been most investigated. Before looking at how we see, consider *what* we see. We cannot see any object unless light is reflected from it or given off by it.

LINK IT!

www.yorku.ca/eye/
The Joy of Visual Perception: A Web Book

signal detection theory: The view that detection of a sensory stimulus involves both discriminating a stimulus from background "noise" and deciding whether the stimulus is actually present.

sensory receptors: Specialized cells in each sense organ that detect and respond to sensory stimuli—light, sound, odours, etc.—and transduce (convert) the stimuli into neural impulses.

transduction: The process by which sensory receptors convert sensory stimulation–light, sound, odours, etc.–into neural impulses.

sensory adaptation: The process of becoming less sensitive to an unchanging sensory stimulus over time.

Light: What We See

Light, one form of electromagnetic rays, is made up of tiny light particles called *photons,* which travel in waves. The vast majority of these waves are either too long or too short for humans and other animals to see. Our eyes can respond only to a very narrow band of electromagnetic waves, a band called the **visible spectrum** (see Figure 3.1).

The length of a light wave determines the colour we perceive. The shortest light waves we can see appear violet, and the longest ones we can see appear red. *What* we see is confined to the visible spectrum, but *how* we see depends on the many parts of the eye and brain that bring us the world of sight.

The Eye: Window to the Visual Sensory World

Our eyes are our most important sensory connections to the world. Vision provides most of the information on which our brain feeds. Look at the parts of the eye (shown in Figure 3.2), and read in the text the role each part plays in vision.

The Cornea, Iris, and Pupil: Up Front in the Eye

How do the cornea, the iris, and the pupil function in vision?

The round, globe-shaped human eyeball measures about 2.2 centimetres in diameter. Bulging from its front surface is the **cornea**—the tough, trans-

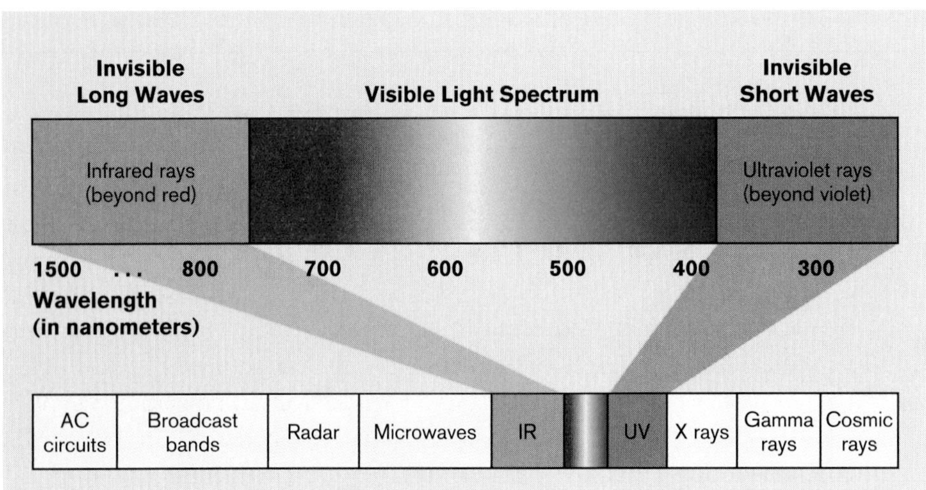

FIGURE 3.1
The Electromagnetic Spectrum The electromagnetic spectrum is composed of waves ranging in wavelength from many miles long (radio and other broadcast bands) to only 10 trillionths of an inch (cosmic rays). Our eyes can perceive only a very thin brand of electromagnetic waves, known as the visible spectrum.

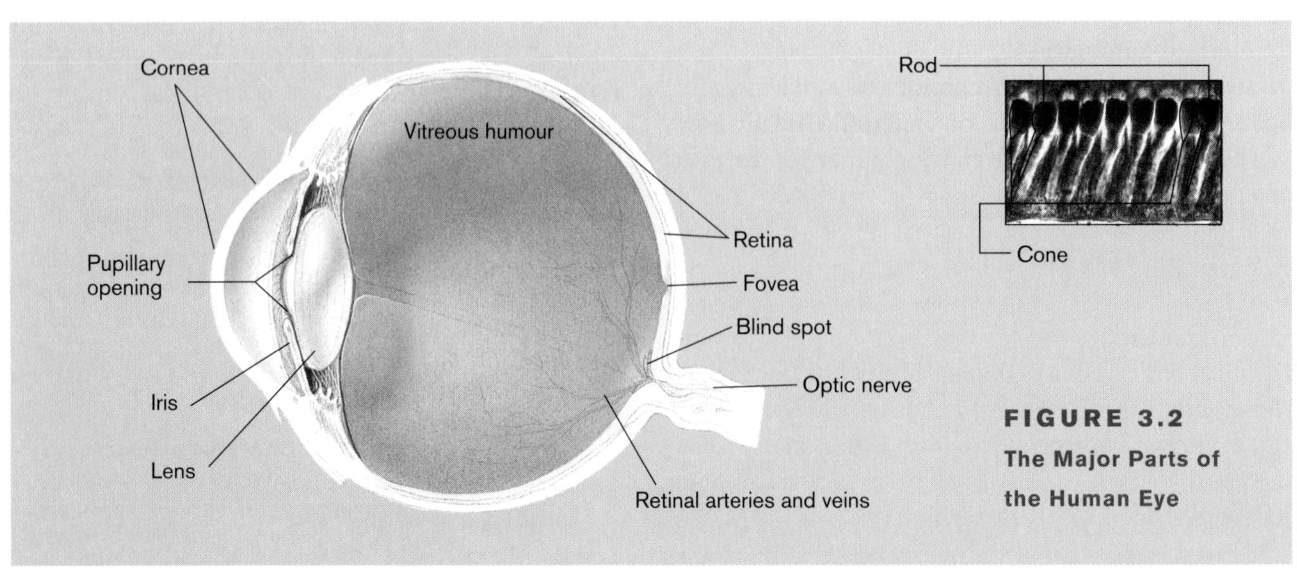

FIGURE 3.2
The Major Parts of the Human Eye

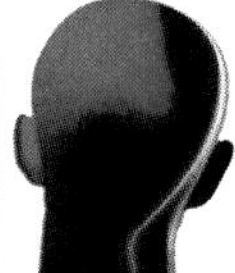

Try It!

How the Retina Works

Take an ordinary teaspoon–one in which you can see your reflection. Looking at the bottom (the convex surface) of the spoon, you will see a large image of your face that is right side up–the way the image enters the eye. Turn the spoon over and look in the inside (the concave surface) and you will see your face upside down and reversed left to right–the way the image appears on the retina. The brain, however, perceives images right side up.

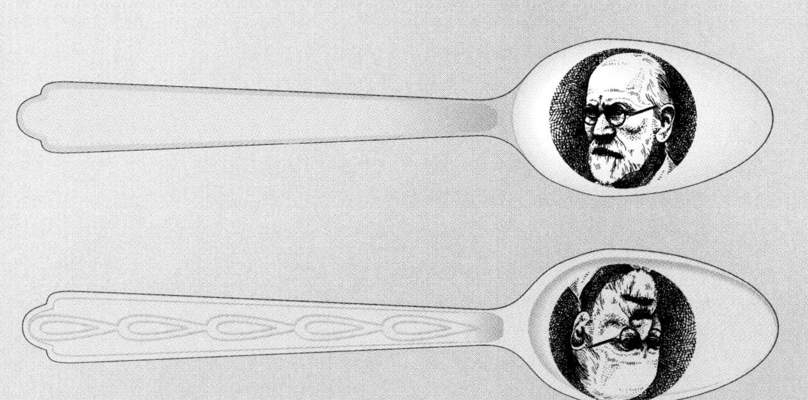

parent, protective layer covering the front of the eye. About the size of a dime, the cornea performs the first step in vision by bending the light rays inward. It herds the light rays through the pupil—the small, dark opening in the centre of the iris.

The iris is the circular, coloured part of the eye, which is even more unique to individuals than their fingerprints (Farah, 2000; Johnson, 1996). Two muscles in the iris dilate and contract the pupil, thus regulating the amount of light entering the eye. Although the pupil never closes completely, in very bright light it can contract to the size of the head of a pin; in very dim light it can dilate to the size of a pencil eraser (Freese, 1977). We have no control over the dilation and contraction of our pupils; the motion is a reflex, completely automatic.

The pupils respond to emotions as well as to light. When we look at someone or something highly desirable, our pupils dilate as if to take in more of the view (Hess, 1965). Pupils also dilate when we are frightened, telling a lie, or sexually aroused. Our pupil size is also related to mental effort—the more intense the mental activity, the larger our pupils become (Janisse & Peavler, 1974).

From Lens to Retina: Focusing Images

What are the lens and the retina?

Suspended just behind the iris and the pupil, the **lens** is composed of many thin layers and looks like a transparent disc. The lens performs the task of focusing on objects closer than 6.5 metres. It flattens as it focuses on objects viewed at a distance; it bulges in the centre as it focuses on close objects. This flattening and bulging action is referred to as **accommodation**. As we grow older, the lens loses some elasticity—that is, it loses the ability to change its shape to accommodate for near vision, a condition called *presbyopia* ("old eyes"). This is why many people over 40 must hold a book or newspaper at arm's length or use reading glasses to magnify the print.

The lens focuses the image we see onto the **retina**—a membrane about the size of a small postage stamp and as thin as onion skin. The retina contains the sensory receptors for vision. The image projected onto the retina is upside down and reversed left to right. You can demonstrate this for yourself in *Try It!*

visible spectrum: The narrow band of electromagnetic rays that are visible to the human eye.

cornea (KOR-nee-uh): The transparent covering of the coloured part of the eye that bends light rays inward through the pupil.

lens: The transparent structure behind the iris that changes in shape as it focuses images on the retina.

accommodation: The changing in shape of the lens as it focuses objects on the retina; it becomes more spherical for near objects and flatter for far objects.

retina: The tissue at the back of the eye that contains the rods and the cones and onto which the retinal image is projected.

In some people, the distance through the eyeball (from the lens to the retina) is either too short or too long for proper focusing. Nearsightedness (myopia) occurs when the lens focuses images of distant objects in front of, rather than on, the retina. A person with this condition will be able to see near objects clearly, but distant images will be blurred. Farsightedness (hyperopia) occurs when the focal image is longer than the eye can handle, as if the image should focus behind the retina (see Figure 3.3). The individual is able to see far objects clearly, but close objects are blurred. Both conditions are correctable with eyeglasses or contact lenses, and nearsightedness is now correctable with a surgical procedure known as radial keratotomy.

The Rods and Cones: Receptors for Light and Colour

What roles do the rods and cones play in vision?

At the back of the retina is a layer of light-sensitive receptor cells—the **rods** and the **cones**. The rods look like slender cylinders; the cones are shorter and more rounded. There are about 120 million rods and 6 million cones in each retina.

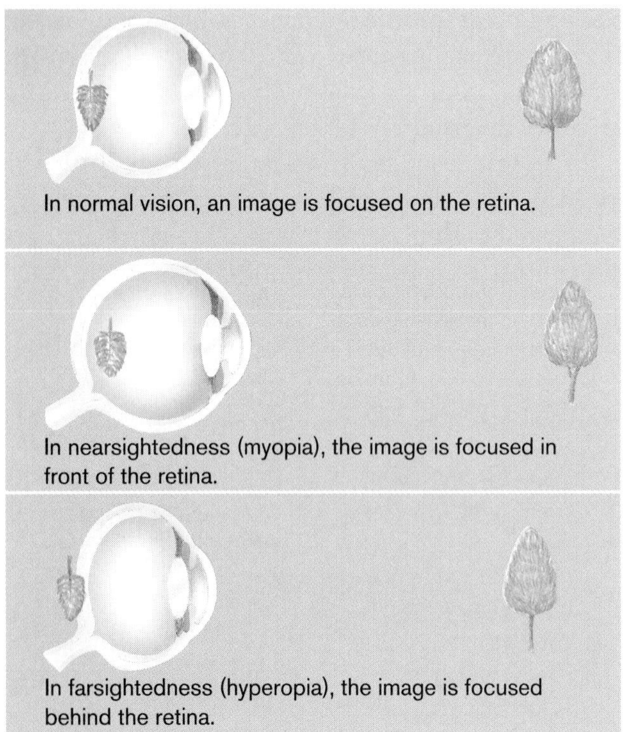

In normal vision, an image is focused on the retina.
In nearsightedness (myopia), the image is focused in front of the retina.
In farsightedness (hyperopia), the image is focused behind the retina.

FIGURE 3.3
Normal Vision, Nearsightedness, and Farsightedness

The cones enable us to see colour and fine detail in adequate light. They do not function in very dim light. There are three types of cones, each sensitive to red, green, or blue (Roorda & Williams, 1999).

If we were to plot an imaginary line through the middle of your pupil, the line would strike the centre of the retina at the **fovea**, a pit-like area about the size of the period at the end of this sentence (refer to Figure 3.2). When you look directly at an object, the image of the object is focused on the centre of your fovea. The clearest point of your vision, the fovea is the part of the retina that you use for fine detail work.

The fovea, which is only $\frac{1}{100}$ of a centimetre in diameter, contains no rods but has some 30 000 cones tightly packed together (Beatty, 1995). Cones are most densely packed at the centre of the fovea, and their density decreases sharply just a few degrees beyond the fovea's centre and levels off more gradually to the periphery of the retina (Abramov & Gordon, 1994; Farah 2000).

The rods respond to black and white; while they encode all other visible wavelengths, they do so in shades of grey instead of in colour. More sensitive to light than the cones, the rods enable us to see in very dim light and provide us with night vision. A single rod can respond to the smallest possible quantity of light (Stryer, 1987). Though the rods are more sensitive to light and enable us to see in dim light, they do not provide the sharp, clear images that the cones make possible.

Dark Adaptation

Step from bright sunlight into a darkened movie theatre and at first you can hardly tell which seats are occupied and which are empty. After a few moments in the dark, your eyes begin to adapt and you can see dimly. Yet it takes half an hour or more for your eyes to adapt completely. After complete **dark adaptation**, you can see light that is 100 000 times less bright than daylight. You may have thought that dark adaptation was a direct result of the dilation of your pupils, but this accounts for only a 16-fold difference in your sensitivity to light.

When you leave a movie theatre, your eyes are "dark-adapted," so the return to bright sunlight is a "blinding" experience. However, it takes only about 60 seconds, not half an hour, to become light-adapted again. In light adaptation, a reflexive action occurs; the pupils immediately become smaller, permitting less light to enter the eyes.

From the Retina to the Brain: From Visual Sensation to Visual Perception

What path does the neural impulse take from the retina to the visual cortex?

The rods and cones are the receptors in the eye. They change light waves into neural impulses that are eventually fed through a pencil-sized cable that extends through the wall of the retina and leaves the eye on its way to the brain.

Where the cable runs through the retinal wall, there can be no rods or cones, and so we are blind in that spot in each eye. After the cable leaves the retinal wall, it becomes known as the **optic nerve**. You can find your own blind spot if you perform *Try It!*

After leaving each eye, the optic nerves come together at a point where some of the nerve fibres cross to the opposite side of the brain. The visual fibres from the right half of each retina go to your left hemisphere, and the visual fibres from the left half of each retina go to the right hemisphere. This switching allows visual information from a single eye to be represented on the visual cortex of both hemispheres of the brain. It also plays an important part in depth perception.

The optic nerve then travels to the thalamus, where neural fibres transmit the impulses to the primary visual cortex. About one-quarter of the primary visual cortex is dedicated exclusively to analyzing input from the fovea, which, as we have seen, is a very small but extremely important part of the retina.

Colour Vision: A Multicoloured World

What are the three dimensions that combine to provide the colours we experience?

Some light waves striking an object are absorbed by it, and others are reflected from it. We see only the wavelengths that are reflected, not those that are absorbed. Our everyday visual experience goes far beyond the colours in the rainbow. We detect thousands of subtle colour shadings. What enables us to make these fine colour distinctions? Researchers have identified three dimensions that combine to provide the rich world of colour we experience: (1) The chief dimension is **hue**, which refers to the actual colour we view—red, green, and so forth. (2) **Saturation** refers to the purity of a colour. A colour becomes less saturated, or less pure, as other wavelengths of light are mixed with it. (3) **Brightness** refers to the intensity of the light

Try It!

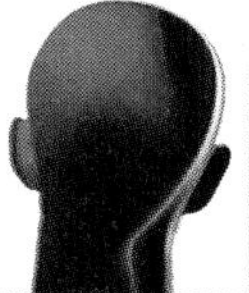

Find Your Blind Spot

To locate your blind spot, hold this book at arm's length. Close your right eye and look directly at the magician's eyes. Now slowly bring the book closer, keeping your eye fixed on the magician. When the rabbit disappears, you have found the blind spot in your left eye.

You might wonder why the blind spot in each eye is not perceived as a black hole in each visual field. The reason is that we usually have both eyes open, and each eye provides a slightly different view. The right eye can see the tiny area that is blind to the left eye, and vice versa.

rods: The light-sensitive receptors in the retina that provide vision in dim light in black, white, and shades of grey.

cones: The receptor cells in the retina that enable us to see colour and fine detail in adequate light, but that do not function in dim light.

fovea (FO-vee-uh): A small area of the retina that provides the clearest and sharpest vision because it has the largest concentration of cones.

dark adaptation: The eye's increasing ability to see in dim light; results partly from dilation of the pupils.

optic nerve: The nerve that carries visual information from the retina to the brain.

hue: The property of light commonly referred to as "colour" (red, blue, green, and so on), determined primarily by the wavelength of light reflected from a surface.

saturation: The degree to which light waves producing a colour are of the same wavelength; the purity of a colour.

brightness: The dimension of visual sensation that is dependent on the intensity of light reflected from a surface and that corresponds to the amplitude of the light wave.

energy we perceive. Figure 3.4 illustrates the dimensions of hue, saturation, and brightness.

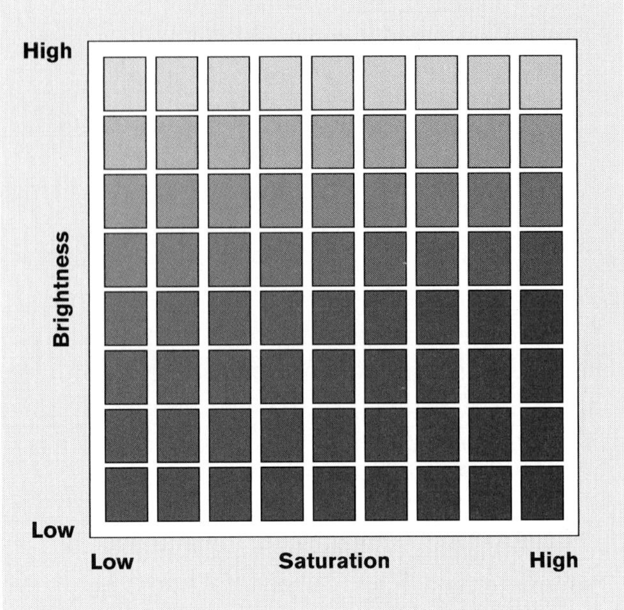

FIGURE 3.4

Hue, Saturation, and Brightness Three dimensions combine to produce the rich world of colour we experience. They are (1) hue, the actual colour we see (blue, green, and so on); (2) saturation, the purity of a colour; and (3) brightness, the intensity of the light energy reflected from a surface. The colours shown here are of the same hue but differ in saturation and brightness.

Theories of Colour Vision: How We Sense Colour

What two major theories attempt to explain colour vision?

Two major theories have been offered to explain colour vision. Both were formulated before the development of laboratory technology capable of testing them. The **trichromatic theory**, first proposed by Thomas Young in 1802, was modified by Hermann von Helmholtz about 50 years later. This theory states that there are three kinds of cones in the retina and that each kind makes its maximum chemical response to one of three colours—blue, green, or red, as shown in Figure 3.5. Research in the 1950s and 1960s by Nobel Prize winner George Wald (1964; Wald et al., 1954) supports the trichromatic theory. Wald discovered that even though all cones have basically the same structure, the retina does indeed contain three kinds of cones.

The trichromatic theory alone, however, cannot explain how we are able to perceive such a rich variety of colours.

The other major attempt to explain colour vision is the **opponent-process theory**, which was first proposed by physiologist Ewald Hering in 1878 and revised in 1957 by Leon Hurvich and Dorthea

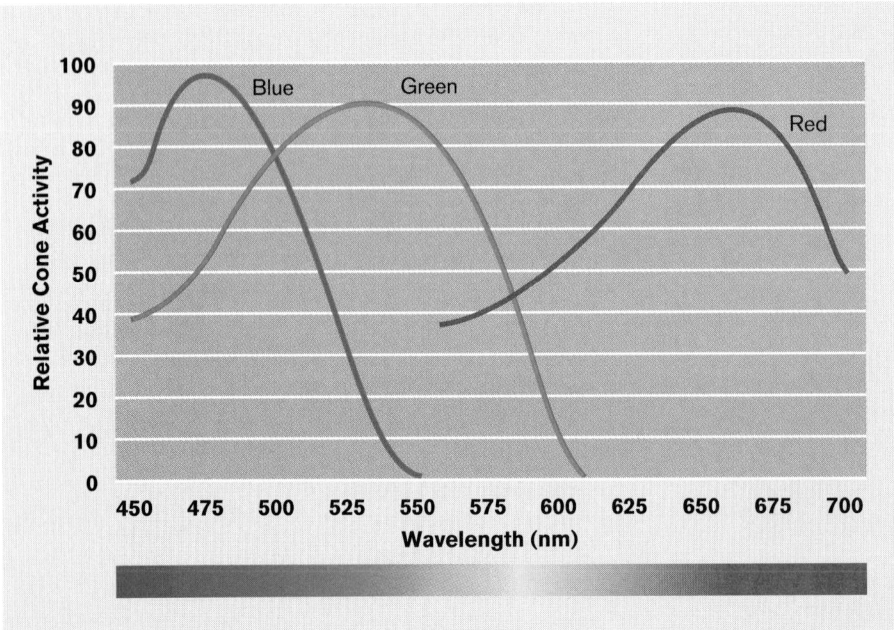

FIGURE 3.5

Relative Sensitivity of the Three Types of Cones Colour vision is largely dependent on three types of cones. Each type responds maximally to a restricted range of wavelengths. The maximal response for one cone type is to short wavelengths of 450–500 nm (blue), for another type it is to medium wavelengths of 500–570 nm (green), and for another type it is to long wavelengths of 620–700 nm (red).

Jamison. According to this theory, the cells increase or decrease their rate of firing when different colours are present. The red/green cells increase their firing rate when red is present and decrease it when green is present. The yellow/blue cells increase to yellow and decrease to blue. Another type of cell increases to white light and decreases to the absence of light. Think of the opponent-process theory as opposing pairs of cells on a seesaw. As one of this pair goes up, the other goes down. The relative firing rates of the three pairs of cells transmit colour information to the brain.

Does the opponent process operate in the cones, or elsewhere? Researchers now believe that the cones pass on information about wavelength colour to higher levels of visual processing. DeValois and DeValois (1975) proposed that the opponent processes might operate at the ganglion cells in the retina and in the higher brain centres rather than at the ı the receptors, the cones.

If you look long enough at one colour in the o nent-process pair and then look at a white surfac your brain will give you the sensation of the opposite colour—a negative **afterimage**. After you have stared at one colour in an opponent-process pair (red/green, yellow/blue, black/white), the cell responding to that colour tires and the opponent cell begins to fire, producing the afterimage. Demonstrate this for yourself in *Try It!*

Try It

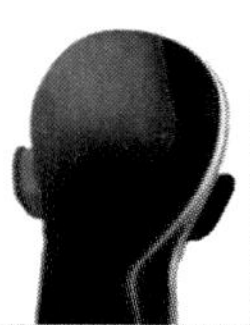

Testing the Opponent-Process Theory

Stare at the dot in the green and black flag for about one minute. Then shift your gaze to the dot in the white space. You will see the Canadian flag in its true colours–the opponent-process colours of red and white.

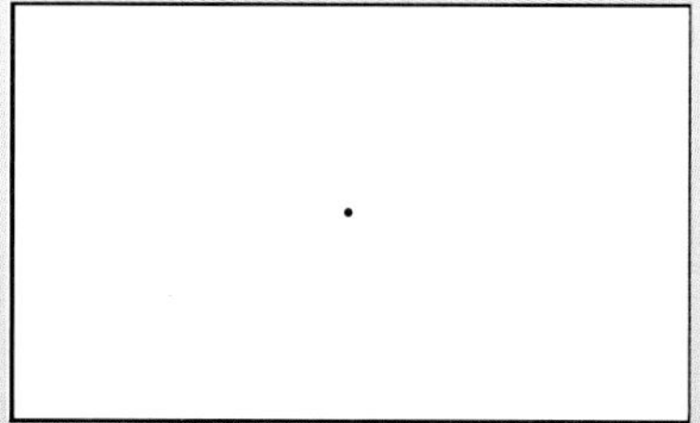

Colour Blindness: Weakness for Sensing Some Colours

Not all of us see the world in the same colours. If normal genes for the three colour pigments are not present, there will be some form of **colour blindness**—the inability to distinguish some colours or, in rare cases, the total absence of colour vision. Total colour blindness affects only about 1 in 100 000 people (Nathans et al., 1989). We know what the world looks like to a colour-blind person because of research with people who have normal vision in one eye but some form of colour blindness in the other. Most colour vision defects are actually weaknesses, or colour confusion, rather than colour blindness. Many people who have some type of colour defect are not even aware of it.

Until recently, scientists believed that in order to have normal colour vision, a person must inherit three genes for colour: one gene for blue on chromosome 7 and one gene each for red and green on the X chromosome. Recent DNA evidence has revealed that this is not the case and that the number of genes for red and green colour pigment range from two to nine

trichromatic theory: The theory of colour vision suggesting that there are three types of cones, which are maximally sensitive to red, green, or blue, and that varying levels of activity in these receptors can produce all of the colours.

opponent-process theory: The theory that certain cells in the visual system increase their firing rate to signal one colour and decrease their firing rate to signal the opposing colour (red/green, yellow/blue, white/black).

afterimage: The visual sensation that remains after a stimulus is withdrawn.

colour blindness: The inability to distinguish some or all colours in vision, resulting from a defect in the cones.

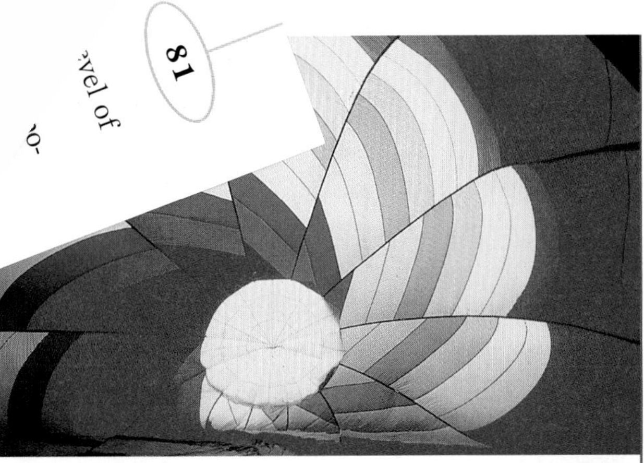

On the top a hot air balloon is shown as it would appear to a person with normal colour vision; on the bottom is the same balloon as it would appear to a person with red-green colour blindness.

(Neitz & Neitz, 1995). This finding suggests that colour vision exists on a continuum, from red-green colour blindness in those missing either one or both of the genes for red and green pigment, to exceptional red-green colour vision for those with multiple colour genes on the X chromosome. Some form of what is commonly referred to as "red-green colour blindness" is found in about 8 percent of males, compared with less than 1 percent of females (Neitz et al., 1996). The large difference is due to the fact that males have only one X chromosome. The photos on the next page show how a balloon would look to someone with red-green colour blindness.

Before leaving the topic of vision, let us dispel the myth that some mammals, especially dogs, lack colour vision. Research shows that some form of colour vision is present in every species of mammals (Jacobs, 1993).

Hearing

Many years ago the frightening science fiction movie *Alien* was advertised this way: "In space no one can hear you scream!" Although the movie was fiction, the statement is true. Light can travel through the vast nothingness of space, a vacuum, but sound cannot. In the following section, you will learn why.

Remember It!

Vision

1. Match the parts of the eye with their descriptions.

____ 1)	The coloured part of the eye	a. retina
____ 2)	The opening in the iris that dilates and constricts	b. cornea
____ 3)	The transparent covering of the iris	c. pupil
____ 4)	The transparent structure that focuses an inverted image on the retina	d. iris
____ 5)	The thin, photosensitive membrane at the back of the eye on which the lens focuses an inverted image	e. lens

2. The receptor cells in the retina that enable us to see in dim light are the (cones/rods); the cells that enable us to see colour and sharp images are (cones/rods).
3. Most people who are colour blind see no colour at all. (true/false)

Answers: 1. 1) d 2) c 3) b 4) e 5) a 2. rods; cones 3. false

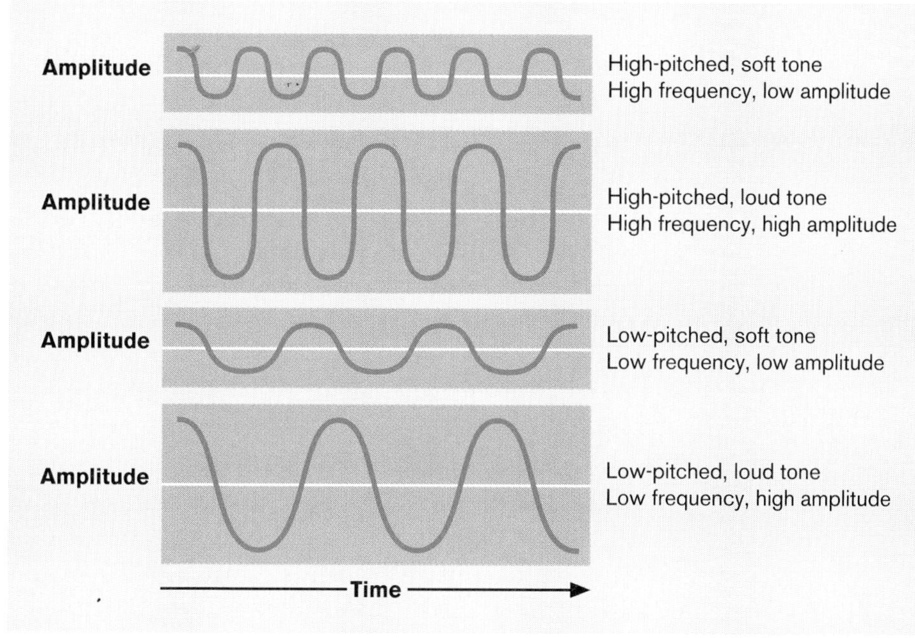

FIGURE 3.6
The Frequency and Amplitude of a Sound Wave
The frequency of a sound wave–the number of cycles completed per second–determines the pitch of the sound. Loudness is determined by amplitude–the energy or height of the sound wave.

Sound: What We Hear

What determines the pitch and the loudness of sound, and how is each quality measured?

Sound requires a medium through which to move, such as air, water, or a solid object. This was first demonstrated in 1660 by Robert Boyle, who suspended a ringing pocket watch by a thread inside a specially designed jar. When Boyle pumped all the air out of the jar, he could no longer hear the watch ringing. But when he pumped the air back into the jar, he could again hear the watch ringing.

If you have ever attended a very loud rock concert, you not only heard but actually felt the mechanical vibrations. The pulsating speakers may have caused the floor, your seat, the walls, and the air around you to shake or vibrate. You were feeling the moving air molecules being pushed toward you in waves as the speakers blasted their vibrations outward.

Frequency is an important characteristic of sound and is determined by the number of cycles completed by a sound wave in one second. The unit used to measure frequency, or cycles per second, is the hertz (Hz). The pitch—how high or low the sound—is chiefly determined by frequency: the higher the frequency (the more vibrations per second), the higher the sound.

The human ear can hear sound frequencies from low bass tones of around 20 Hz up to high-pitched sounds of about 200 Hz. Amazingly, dolphins can respond to sounds up to 100 000 Hz.

The loudness of a sound is determined largely by its **amplitude**. Amplitude depends on the energy of the sound wave. Loudness is determined mainly by the force or pressure with which the air molecules are moving. Figure 3.6 shows how sound waves vary in frequency and amplitude. We can measure the pressure level (loudness) of sounds using a unit called the *bel,* named for the Canadian inventor Alexander Graham Bell. Because the bel is a rather large unit, we usually express the measure in tenths of a bel, or **decibels** (dB). The threshold of human hearing is set at 0 dB, which does not mean the absence of sound but the softest sound that can be heard in a very quiet setting. Each increase of 10 dB makes a sound 10 times louder. A whisper is about 20 dB, but that is 100 times louder (10 dB × 10) than 0 dB. A normal conversation, around 60 dB, is 10 000 times louder

frequency: Measured in the unit hertz, the number of sound waves or cycles per second, determining the pitch of the sound.

amplitude: Measured in decibels, the magnitude or intensity of a sound wave, determining the loudness of the sound; in vision, the amplitude of a light wave affects the brightness of a stimulus.

decibel (DES-ih-bel): A unit of measurement of the intensity or loudness of sound based on the amplitude of the sound wave.

than a soft whisper at 20 dB. Figure 3.7 shows the comparative decibel levels for a variety of sounds.

If pitch and loudness were the only perceptual dimensions of sound, we could not tell the difference between two instruments if both were playing exactly the same note at the same decibel level. A third characteristic of sound, **timbre**, refers to the distinct quality of a sound that distinguishes it from other sounds of the same pitch and loudness. Unlike the pure sound of a tuning fork, which has only one frequency, most sounds we hear consist of several different frequencies.

The frequencies that form the sound pattern above any tone a musical instrument is playing are called *overtones,* or *harmonics.* Overtones are not actually heard as tones, but they give musical instruments their characteristic quality of sound, or timbre. The rich, full sound of a French horn is due to the large number of overtones present above the note being played. The almost pure sound of the flute is produced because relatively few overtones are generated above the notes sounded on that instrument.

LINK IT!

ear.berkeley.edu/auditory_lab/
University of California at Berkeley, Department of Psychology, Auditory Perception Lab

www.campanellaacoustics.com/faq.htm
Acoustics FAQ (Frequently Asked Questions)

The Ear: More to It Than Meets the Eye

How do the outer, middle, and inner ears function in hearing?

The part of the body that we call the ear plays only a minor role in **audition** in humans. In fact, if your visible outer ears were cut off, your hearing would suffer very little (Warren, 1999). Let us travel more deeply within the ear and learn how each part contributes to our ability to hear.

The Structure of the Ear: The Outer, Middle, and Inner Ears

The oddly shaped, curved flap of cartilage and skin called the *pinna* is the visible part of the **outer ear** (see Figure 3.8). Inside the ear, your auditory canal is about 2.5 centimetres long. Its entrance is lined with hairs. At the end of the auditory canal is the eardrum (the tympanic membrane), a thin, flexible membrane about a centimetre in diameter. The eardrum moves in response to the sound waves that strike it.

The **middle ear** is no larger than an aspirin tablet. Inside its chamber are the ossicles, the three smallest bones in your body, each "about the size of a grain of rice" (Strome & Vernick, 1989). Named for their shapes, the three connected ossicles—the hammer, the anvil, and the stirrup—link the eardrum to the oval window. The ossicles amplify the sound some 22 times (Békésy, 1957).

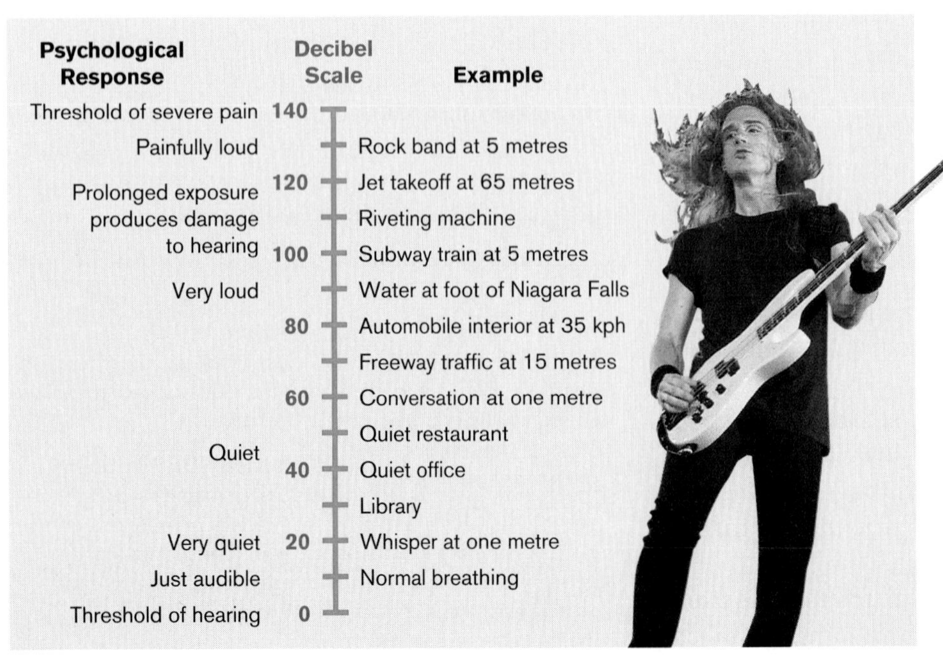

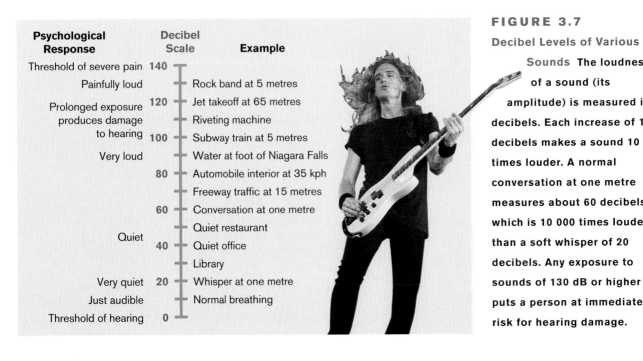

FIGURE 3.7

Decibel Levels of Various Sounds **The loudness of a sound (its amplitude) is measured in decibels. Each increase of 10 decibels makes a sound 10 times louder. A normal conversation at one metre measures about 60 decibels, which is 10 000 times louder than a soft whisper of 20 decibels. Any exposure to sounds of 130 dB or higher puts a person at immediate risk for hearing damage.**

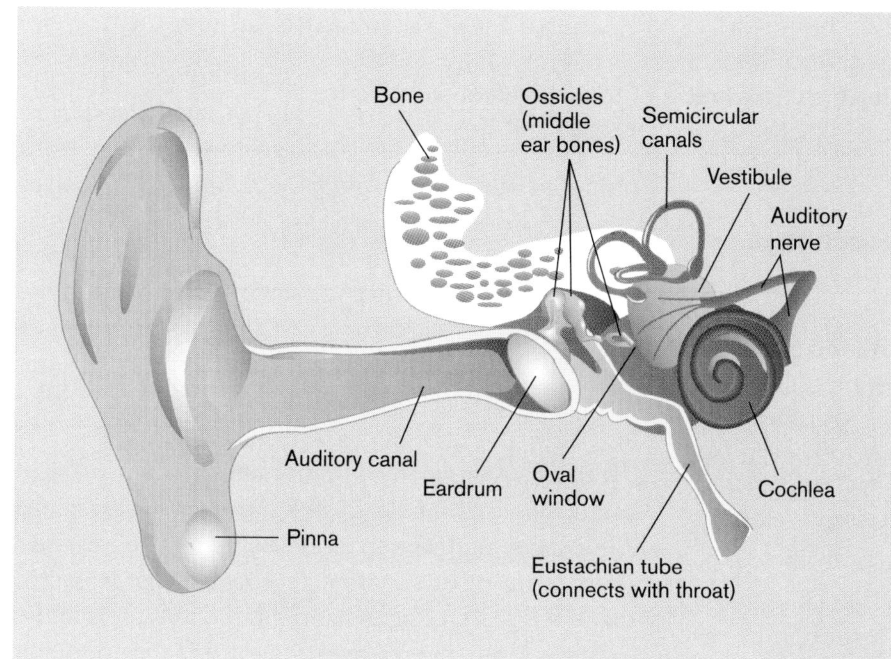

FIGURE 3.8

Anatomy of the Human Ear
Sound waves pass through the auditory canal to the eardrum, causing it to vibrate and set in motion the ossicles in the middle ear. When the stirrup pushes against the oval window, it sets up vibrations in the inner ear. This moves the fluid in the cochlea back and forth and sets the hair cells in motion, causing a message to be sent to the brain via the auditory nerve.

The **inner ear** begins at the inner side of the oval window in the base of the **cochlea**, a fluid-filled, snail-shaped, bony chamber. When the stirrup pushes against the oval window, it sets up vibrations that move the fluid in the cochlea back and forth in waves. The movement of the fluid sets in motion the thin basilar membrane that runs through the cochlea. Attached to the basilar membrane are about 15 000 sensory receptors called **hair cells**, each with a bundle of tiny hairs protruding from it. The tiny hair bundles are pushed and pulled by the motion of the fluid inside the cochlea. This produces an electrical impulse, which is transmitted to the brain by way of the auditory nerve (Hudspeth, 1983).

Having two ears, one on either side of the head, enables us to determine the direction from which sounds are coming (Konishi, 1993). Unless a sound is directly above, below, in front of, or behind us, it reaches one ear slightly before it reaches the other (Spitzer & Semple, 1991). The brain detects differences as small as $\frac{1}{10\,000}$ of a second and interprets them, telling us the direction of the sound (Rosenzweig, 1961). The source of a sound may also be determined by the difference in intensity of the sound reaching each ear (Middlebrooks & Green, 1991).

Theories of Hearing: How Hearing Works

What two major theories attempt to explain hearing?

In the 1860s, Hermann von Helmholtz helped develop **place theory**, one of the two major theories of hearing. This theory holds that each individual pitch we hear is determined by the particular spot or place along the basilar membrane that vibrates the most.

timbre (TIM-burr): The distinctive quality of a sound that distinguishes it from other sounds of the same pitch and loudness.

audition: The sensation of hearing; the process of hearing.

outer ear: The visible part of the ear, consisting of the pinna and the auditory canal.

middle ear: The portion of the ear containing the ossicles, which connect the eardrum to the oval window and amplify the vibrations as they travel to the inner ear.

inner ear: The innermost portion of the ear, containing the cochlea, the vestibular sacs, and the semicircular canals.

cochlea (KOK-lee-uh): The snail-shaped, fluid-filled organ in the inner ear that contains the hair cells (the sound receptors).

hair cells: Sensory receptors for hearing, found in the cochlea.

place theory: The theory that sounds of different frequencies or pitch cause maximum activation of hair cells at certain locations along the basilar membrane.

By observing the living basilar membrane, researchers have verified that different locations do indeed vibrate in response to differently pitched sounds (Ruggero, 1992). Even so, place theory cannot really explain how we perceive frequencies below 150 Hz.

Another attempt to explain hearing is **frequency theory**. According to this theory, the hair cell receptors vibrate the same number of times per second as the sounds that reach them. Thus, a tone of 500 Hz would stimulate the hair cells to vibrate 500 times per second as well. Frequency theory seems valid for low- and medium-pitched tones, but it has a major problem with high-frequency tones. Individual neurons cannot fire more than about 1 000 times per second. Therefore, they could not signal to the brain the higher-pitched tones of 1 000 to 20 000 Hz.

The *volley principle* suggests that groups, or volleys, of neurons, if properly synchronized, could together produce the firing rate required for tones somewhat higher than 1 000 Hz (Wever, 1949). Yet even with the help of the volley principle, frequency theory cannot explain how we hear tones with frequencies higher than about 4 000 Hz. Today, researchers believe that frequency theory best explains how we perceive low frequencies, and that place theory best explains how we perceive the remaining frequencies (Matlin & Foley, 1997; Warren, 1999).

Hearing Loss: Kinds and Causes

What are some major causes of hearing loss?

About two million people in Canada have hearing problems, and that number is growing rapidly. Hearing loss and deafness can be caused by disease, birth defects, injury, excessive noise, and old age. *Conductive* hearing loss, or conduction deafness, is usually caused by disease or injury to the eardrum or the bones of the middle ear, with the result that soundwaves cannot be conducted to the cochlea. People with conductive hearing loss can usually be helped with a hearing aid.

The vast majority of conductive hearing losses can be repaired medically or surgically by physicians specializing in disorders of the ear. And in rare cases, people can be fitted with a hearing aid that bypasses the middle ear and uses bone conduction to reach the cochlea. Many people over the age of 60 (more men than women) suffer from gradual hearing loss that involves damage either to the cochlea or to the auditory nerve. In cases where damage to the cochlea is not too severe, conventional hearing aids may be fitted to reduce the hearing loss (Bramblett, 1997). But hearing aids are useless if the damage is to the auditory nerve that connects the cochlea to the brain.

There are some indications that lifelong exposure to excessive noise may be more of a factor than aging

Remember It!

Hearing

1. Pitch is chiefly determined by ____________; loudness is chiefly determined by ____________.
   a. amplitude; frequency
   b. wavelength; frequency
   c. intensity; amplitude
   d. frequency; amplitude
2. Pitch is measured in (hertz/decibels); loudness is measured in (decibels/hertz).
3. Match the part of the ear with the structures it contains.
   ____ 1) ossicles — a. outer ear
   ____ 2) pinna, auditory canal — b. middle ear
   ____ 3) cochlea, hair cells — c. inner ear
4. The receptors for hearing are found in the
   a. ossicles.
   b. auditory canal.
   c. auditory membrane.
   d. cochlea.
5. The two major theories that attempt to explain hearing are
   a. conduction theory and place theory.
   b. hair cell theory and frequency theory.
   c. place theory and frequency theory.
   d. conduction theory and hair cell theory.
6. According to the text, lifelong exposure to excessive noise may be more of a factor in hearing loss than aging is. (true/false)

Answers: 1. d 2. hertz; decibels 3. 1) b 2) a 3) c 4. d 5. c 6. true

in explaining hearing loss (Kalb, 1997). Perhaps this is why the Mabaan people of the Sudan don't seem to suffer much hearing loss as they age. When hearing tests were conducted on that group, it was found that some 80-year-olds could hear as well as 20-year-olds in industrialized countries. The Mabaan pride themselves on their sensitive hearing and consider it important never to raise their voices. Even their festivals and celebrations are quiet affairs, featuring dancing and soft singing. The loudest sounds they usually hear in their everyday world are made by their own domestic animals, such as sheep or roosters (Bennett, 1990).

Smell and Taste

Smell: Sensing Scents

Consider what it would be like to live in a world without smell. "Not really so bad," you might say. "Although I could not smell flowers, perfume, or my favourite foods, I would never again have to endure the foul odours of life. It's a trade-off, so what's the difference?"

The difference is large indeed. Your ability to detect odours close at hand and at a distance is an aid to survival. You smell smoke and can escape before the flames of a fire envelop you. Your nose broadcasts an odour alarm to the brain when certain poisonous gases or noxious fumes are present. But the survival value of odour detection in humans does not stop there. Smell, aided by taste, is the last line of defence—your final chance to avoid putting spoiled food or drink into your body.

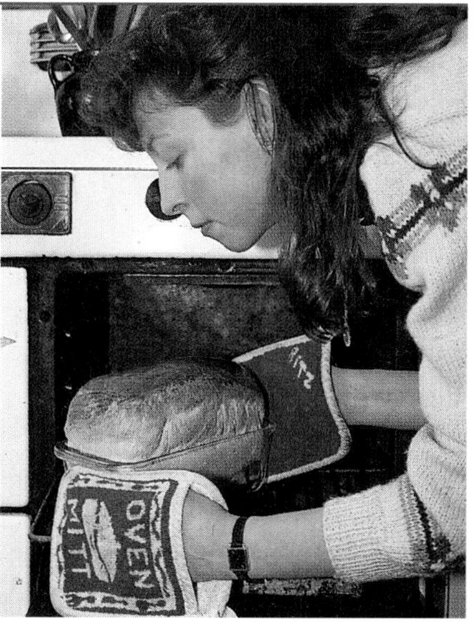

Odours have a powerful ability to evoke memories and stir up emotions.

It is well known that odours alone have a powerful ability to call forth old memories and rekindle strong emotional feelings, even decades after events in our lives. This is not surprising when we consider that the olfactory system sends information to the limbic system, an area in the brain that plays an important role in emotions and memories as well (Horvitz, 1997).

There are large individual differences in smell sensitivity. Perfumers and whiskey blenders can distinguish about 100 000 odour compounds; the average person with training can distinguish from 10 000 to about 40 000 (Dobb, 1989).

The Mechanics of Smell: How the Nose Knows

What path does a smell message take on its journey from the nose to the brain?

Olfaction—the sense of smell—is a chemical sense. We cannot smell a substance unless some of its molecules vaporize—pass from a solid or liquid into a gaseous state. Heat speeds up the evaporation of molecules, which is why food that is cooking has a stronger and more distinct odour than uncooked food. When odour molecules vaporize, they become airborne and make their way up our nostrils to the **olfactory epithelium**. The olfactory epithelium consists of two patches of tissue, one at the top of each nasal cavity, that together contain about 10 million olfactory neurons—the receptor cells for smell. Each of these neurons contains only 1 of the 1 000 different types of odour receptors (Bargmann, 1996). The intensity of the smell stimulus—how strong or weak it is—is apparently determined by the number of olfactory neurons firing at the same time (Freeman, 1991). Figure 3.9 shows a diagram of the human olfactory system.

frequency theory: The theory that hair cell receptors vibrate the same number of times as the sounds that reach them, thereby accounting for the way variations in pitch are transmitted to the brain.

olfaction (ol-FAK-shun): The sensation of smell; the process of smell.

olfactory epithelium: A patch of tissue at the top of the nasal cavity, that contains about 10 million receptors for smell.

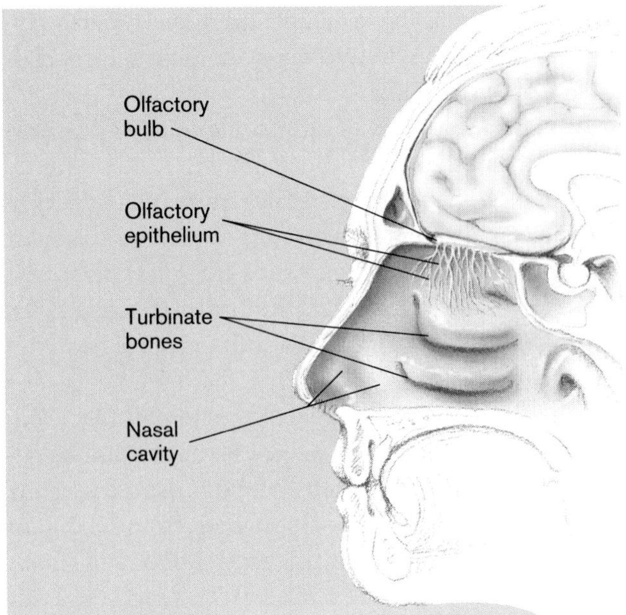

FIGURE 3.9

The Olfactory Sense **Odour molecules travel up the nostrils to the olfactory epithelium, which contains the receptor cells for smell. Olfactory receptors are special neurons with axons that form the olfactory nerve. The olfactory nerve relays smell messages to the olfactory bulbs and on to other parts of the brain.**

The olfactory neurons are different from all other sensory receptors. They are special types of neurons that come into direct contact with sensory stimuli and reach directly into the brain. Unlike all other neurons, olfactory neurons have a short life span—between 30 and 60 days—and are continuously being replaced (Buck, 1996). The axons of the olfactory receptor cells relay smell messages directly to the **olfactory bulbs**—two brain structures the size of matchsticks that rest above the nasal cavities (refer to Figure 3.9). From the olfactory bulbs, messages are relayed to different parts of the brain.

LINK IT!

www.cf.ac.uk/biosi/staff/jacob/teaching/sensory/olfact1.html
Olfaction

neuroscience.about.com/science/neuroscience/library/blxSystOlf.htm
Supplementary Olfactory Resources

Pheromones

Many animals excrete chemicals called **pheromones**, which can have a powerful effect on the behaviour of other members of the same species. Animals use pheromones to mark off territories and to signal sexual receptivity (Dobb, 1989).

Some studies suggest that humans, although not consciously aware of it, may also be receptive to pheromones when it comes to mating. Viennese researcher Karl Grammer (cited in Holden, 1996) analyzed the saliva of young men who had used an inhalant to sniff pheromones found in female vaginal secretion. Women's ovulatory secretions were the only ones to cause a rise in testosterone levels in the men's saliva. The men apparently recognized, though not consciously, which of the women were most likely to be fertile. A later study also indicates that humans can communicate by pheromones (Stern & McClintock, 1998).

Taste: What the Tongue Can Tell

What are the four primary taste sensations, and how are they detected?

A sizzling steak, hot buttered popcorn, chocolate cake—does your sense of taste alone tell you what these foods taste like? Surprisingly, no. **Gustation**, or the sense of taste, gives us only four distinct kinds of sensations—sweet, sour, salty, and bitter. When we say that a food tastes good or bad, we are actually referring to **flavour**—the combined sensory experience of taste, smell, and touch. As we taste, we feel the texture and temperature of foods we put in our mouths. But most of the pleasure we attribute to our sense of taste is actually due to smell, which comes from odour molecules forced up the nasal cavity by the action of the tongue, cheeks, and throat when we chew and swallow. Colour can also contribute to our sense of taste. In one study, many participants could not even recognize the taste of root beer when it was coloured red (Hyman, 1983). Can you identify some common foods by taste alone? *Try It!*

The Taste Receptors: Taste Detectors

If you look at your tongue in a mirror, you will see many small bumps called *papillae.* There are four different types of papillae, and three of them contain **taste buds**, which cluster around the cracks and

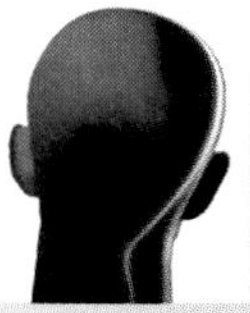

Try It!

Taste Test

Cover your eyes and hold your nose tightly. Ask a friend to feed you small pieces of food with a similar texture, such as raw potato, apple, and even onion. See if you can identify the food by taste alone. Most people cannot.

crevices between the papillae. Each taste bud is composed of 60 to 100 receptor cells, which resemble the petals of a flower (Kinnamon, 1988). Taste receptors are also found in the palate, in the mucous lining of the cheeks and lips, and in parts of the throat, including the tonsils (Bradley, 1971; G.H. Parker, 1922). The lifespan of the receptor cells for taste is very short, only about 10 days, and they are continually replaced (Beidler & Smallman, 1965).

Taste buds are most densely packed on the tip of the tongue, less densely packed on the rear edges, and absent from the centre of the tongue (Bartoshuk, 1989). But taste is poorly localized, and taste sensations appear to come from all over the mouth. Even people with damage over large areas of the mouth are usually unaware of the loss of taste buds, because very intense sensations can be produced by rather small areas of normal tissue (Bartoshuk et al., 1987).

For many years textbooks included a "tongue map" showing the four basic tastes spatially distributed over different areas of the tongue. But the tongue map is an error that resulted from a mistranslation of a 1901 article written in German. Researchers who have performed extensive spatial testing for the four taste sensations report that all four tastes can be detected by taste buds on all locations of the tongue (Bartoshuk & Beauchamp, 1994).

Although aging is typically accompanied by a decline in the other senses, people lose very little of their ability to detect the four primary taste sensations as they age (Bartoshuk et al., 1987). When older people complain that food doesn't taste as good as it once did, the reason is usually a loss of smell rather than a failing sense of taste (Bartoshuk, 1989).

Researchers, using videomicroscopy, have actually counted the number of taste buds on the tongues of different individuals (Miller & Reedy, 1990). Not surprisingly, people with a reduced ability to taste had the smallest number of taste buds per square centimetre—an average of 96. Medium tasters averaged nearly twice as many taste buds (184), and supertasters had more than four times as many taste buds (425). But the fact that supertasters do not taste all substances with greater intensity suggests that the number of taste buds alone does not explain general taste sensitivity.

Our Other Senses

Other senses are our sense of touch (the tactile sense), our sense of balance (the vestibular sense), and our kinesthetic sense.

The Skin Senses: Information from Our Natural Clothing

Our own natural clothing, the skin, is the largest organ of the body. It performs many important bio-

olfactory bulbs: Two matchstick-sized structures above the nasal cavities, where smell sensations first register in the brain.

pheromones: Chemicals excreted by humans and other animals that act as signals to and elicit certain patterns of behaviour from members of the same species.

gustation: The sensation of taste.

flavour: The combined sensory experience of taste, smell, and touch.

taste buds: The structures that are composed of 60 to 100 sensory receptors for taste.

Remember It!

Smell and Taste

1. The technical name for the process or sensation of smell is (gustation/olfaction).
2. The olfactory, or smell, receptors are located in the
   a. olfactory tract.
   b. olfactory nerve.
   c. olfactory epithelium.
   d. olfactory bulbs.
3. The four primary taste sensations are ________, ________, ________, and ________.
4. Our ability to identify foods with similar texture is most influenced by our sense of (taste/smell).
5. Each (papilla/taste bud) contains from 60 to 100 receptor cells.
6. Taste receptor cells have a very short life span and are continually replaced. (true/false)
7. Supertasters have the same number of taste buds as medium tasters and non-tasters. (true/false)

Answers: 1. olfaction 2. c 3. sweet, salty, sour, bitter 4. smell 5. taste bud 6. true 7. false

logical functions while also yielding much of what we know as sensual pleasure. Your skin can detect heat, cold, pressure, pain, and a vast range of touch sensations—caresses, pinches, punches, pats, rubs, scratches, and the feel of many different textures, from silk to sandpaper.

The Mechanism of Touch: How Touch Works

How does the skin provide sensory information?

Tactile information is conveyed to the brain when an object touches and depresses the skin, stimulating one or more of the several distinct types of nerve cell receptors. These sensitive nerve endings in the skin send the touch message through nerve connections to the spinal cord. The message travels up the spinal cord and through the brainstem and the lower brain centres, finally reaching the brain's somatosensory cortex. Only then do we become aware of where and how hard we have been touched. Remember from Chapter 2 that the somatosensory cortex is the strip of tissue at the front of the parietal lobes where touch, pressure, temperature, and pain register.

If we examine the skin from the outermost to the deepest layer, we find a variety of nerve endings that differ markedly in appearance. Most or all of these nerve endings appear to respond in some degree to all different types of tactile stimulation.

In the 1890s, one of the most prominent researchers of the tactile sense, Max von Frey, discovered the two-point threshold, which measures how far apart two points must be before we feel them as two separate touches. Demonstrate the two-point threshold yourself in the *Try It!* box below.

Try It!

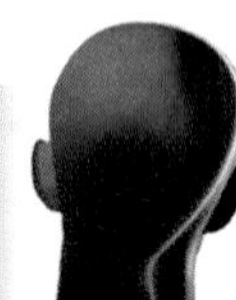

Testing the Two-Point Threshold

Have someone touch the middle of your back with two toothpicks held about four centimetres apart. Do you feel one point or two? How far apart do the toothpicks have to be before you perceive them as two separate touch sensations? How far apart do they have to be on your face? on your hands? on your fingers? on your toes? Which of these body parts are the most sensitive? Which are the least sensitive?

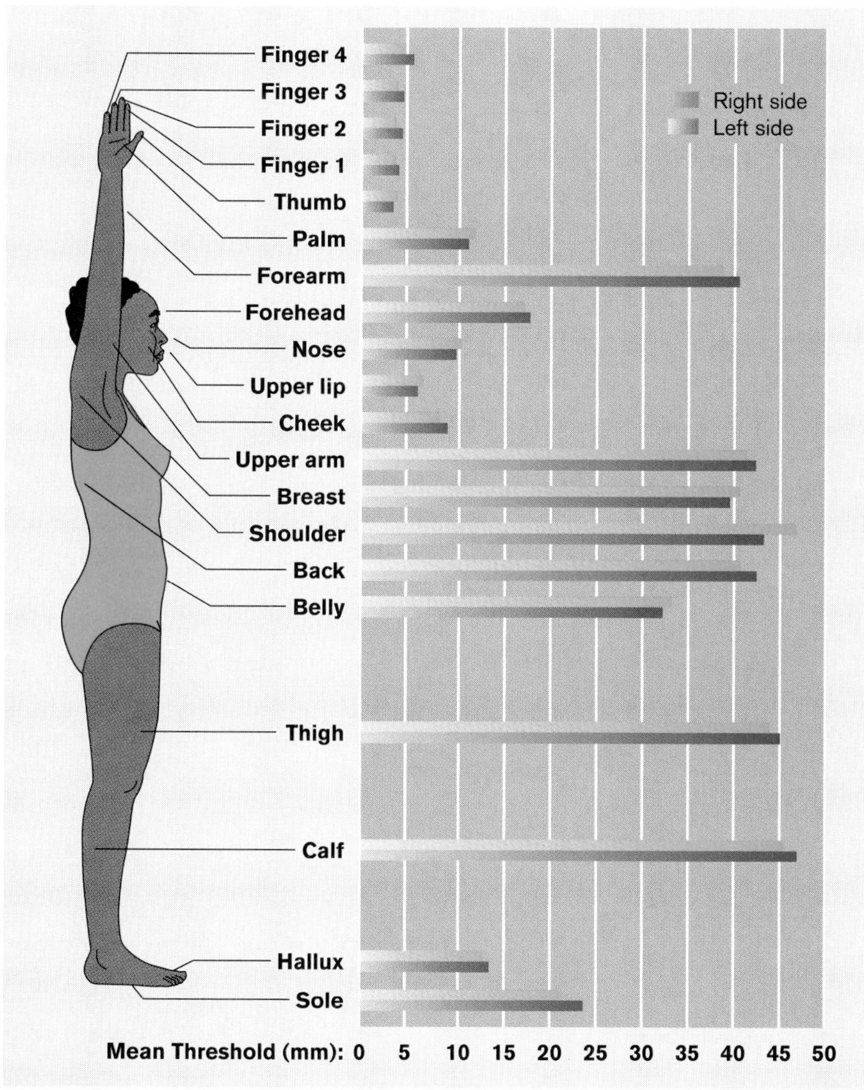

FIGURE 3.10

The Two-Point Threshold The two-point threshold measures how far apart two points must be to be felt as two separate touches. The drawing shows the average two-point thresholds for different parts of the body. The shortest bars on the graph indicate the greatest sensitivity; the longest bars, the least sensitivity. The thumb and fingers, being the most sensitive body parts, have the lowest two-point thresholds (less than 5 mm). The calves, being the least sensitive body parts, have two-point thresholds of about 45 mm. (After Weinstein, 1968).

Figure 3.10 illustrates two-point thresholds for different body parts, showing the actual distance apart at which two-point discriminations can be made by most people.

Recent Canadian research shows that even young infants (five and one-half months old) are sensitive to subtle changes in their mothers' touching, and that a mother's touch is perceived as a positive experience (Stack & Arnold, 1998; Stack & Lepage, 1996).

Pain: Physical Hurts

What beneficial purpose does pain serve?

Although our sense of touch brings us a great deal of pleasure, it delivers pain as well. Recall the opening story, in which we described the life of James Stone, Jr., the boy who could feel no pain. Although he had never had a headache or a toothache, and never felt the pain of a cut or a burn, he also was unable to feel the many adaptive cues revealed by pain. His arms and legs were twisted and bent. Some of his fingers were missing and bloody wounds would often cover his body, as he never noticed that he was repeatedly injuring himself.

This story shows that pain functions as a valuable warning and protective mechanism. It motivates us to tend to our injuries, restrict our activity, and seek medical help if we need it. Pain also teaches us to avoid pain-producing circumstances in the future.

tactile: Pertaining to the sense of touch.

Chronic pain, however, persists long after it serves any useful function and is a serious medical problem for many Canadians. The three major types of chronic pain are low-back pain, headache, and arthritis pain. For its victims, chronic pain is like a fire alarm that no one can turn off.

The Gate-Control Theory: Conducting Pains Great and Small

What is the gate-control theory of pain?

Pain is probably the least understood of all the sensations. We are not certain how pain works, but one major theory seeks to explain it—the **gate-control theory** of McGill researchers Melzack and Wall (1965, 1983). They contend that there is an area in the spinal cord that can act as a "gate" and either inhibit pain messages or transmit them to the brain. Only so many messages can go through the gate at any one time. We feel pain when pain messages carried by the small, slow-conducting nerve fibres reach the gate and cause it to open. Large, fast-conducting nerve fibres carry other sensory messages from the body; these can effectively tie up traffic at the gate so that it will close and keep many of the pain messages from getting through.

What is the first thing you do when you stub your toe or pound your finger with a hammer? If you rub or apply gentle pressure to the injury, you are stimulating the large, fast-conducting nerve fibres to send their message to the spinal gate first; this blocks some of the pain messages from the slower nerve fibres. Applying ice, heat, or electrical stimulation to the painful area also stimulates the large nerve fibres and closes the spinal gate.

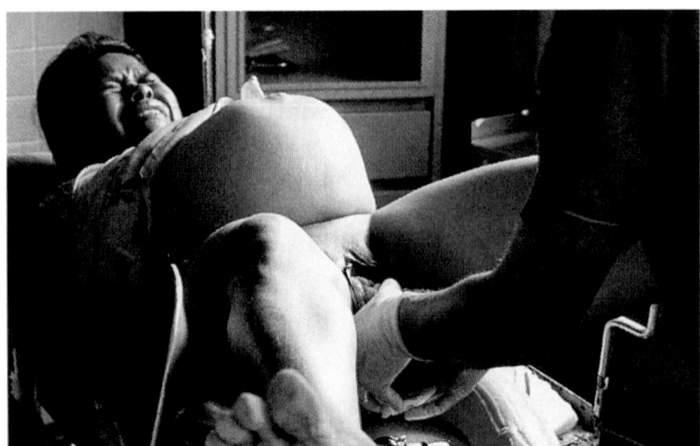

The experience of pain is affected by cultural background, and this influence extends even to childbirth, which is endured more stoically by women in some cultures.

In his newer formulation of the gate-control theory, Melzack (1999a; 1999b) argues that pain is a multidimensional experience produced by a widely distributed neural network. In other words, psychological, cognitive, and emotional factors can influence the perception of pain. Messages from the brain can thus inhibit the transmission of pain messages at the spinal gate and thereby affect the perception of pain. This may explain why some people can undergo surgery under hypnosis and feel little or no pain, and why athletes injured during games are so distracted that they often do not experience pain until some time after the injury.

Endorphins: Our Own Natural Pain Relievers

What are endorphins?

Throughout the world, people spend more effort and money trying to get rid of pain than for any other medical purpose. In fact, Canadians spend over $1 billion each year on treatments for chronic pain, ranging from over-the-counter medications to surgery and psychotherapy.

In Chapter 2 we read that our body produces its own natural painkillers, the **endorphins**, which block pain and produce a feeling of well-being (Hendler & Fenton, 1979). Endorphins are released when we are injured, when we experience stress or extreme pain, and when we laugh, cry, or exercise (Terman et al., 1984). "Runner's high" and an elevated mood after exercising are often attributed to an increase in endorphin levels (Goldberg, 1988).

Some people release endorphins even when they only *think* they are receiving pain medication. When hospital patients recovering from surgery ask for pain medication, they are sometimes given, instead, a placebo in the form of a sugar pill or an injection of saline solution. Nevertheless, 35 percent of the patients who receive placebos report relief from pain (Melzack & Wall, 1983). Why? When patients believe that they have received a drug for pain, apparently that belief stimulates the release of natural pain relievers, the endorphins.

Such may be the case when people use acupuncture, the ancient Chinese technique for relieving pain. Acupuncture seems to relieve pain by stimulating the

Try It!

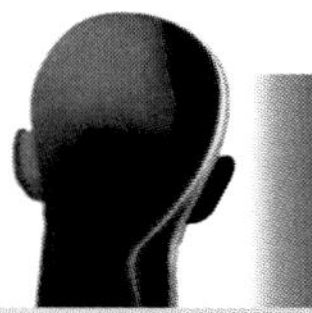

Controlling Pain

If you experience pain, you can try any of the following techniques for controlling it:

- Distraction can be particularly effective for controlling brief or mild pain. Generally, activities or thoughts that require a great deal of attention will provide more relief than passive distractions.
- Counterirritation–stimulating or irritating one area of the body to mask or diminish pain in another area–can be accomplished with ice packs, heat, massage, mustard packs, or electrical stimulation.
- Relaxation techniques are useful for reducing the stress and muscular tension that usually accompany pain.
- Positive thoughts can help you cope with pain, whereas negative thoughts tend to increase your anxiety.
- Attention and sympathy from family members and friends should be kept at a moderate level; too much attention may prove to be so reinforcing that it serves to prolong pain.

release of endorphins. The next time you experience pain, you may want to try some other pain-controlling techniques in *Try It!*

The Kinesthetic Sense: Keeping Track of Our Body Parts

What kind of information does the kinesthetic sense provide, and how is this sensory information detected?

The **kinesthetic sense** provides information about (1) the position of the body parts in relation to one another, and (2) the movement in various body parts. This information is detected by receptors in the joints, ligaments, and muscles. The other senses, especially vision, provide additional information about body position and movement, but our kinesthetic sense works well on its own. Thanks to our kinesthetic sense, we are able to perform smooth and skilled body movements without visual feedback or a studied, conscious effort. A companion sense, the vestibular sense, involves equilibrium, or the sense of balance.

The Vestibular Sense: Sensing Up and Down and Changes in Speed

What is the vestibular sense, and where are its sensory receptors located?

Our **vestibular sense** detects movement and provides information about where we are in space. The vestibular sense organs are located in the semicircular canals and the vestibular sacs in the inner ear. The **semicircular canals** sense the rotation of your head, such as when you are turning your head from side to side or when you are spinning around (see Figure 3.11). The tube-like canals are filled with fluid; rotating movements of the head in any direction send this fluid coursing through them. In the canals, the moving fluid bends the hair cells, which act as receptors and send neural impulses to the brain. Because there are three canals, each positioned on a different plane, the hair cells in one canal will bend more than the hair cells in the other canals, depending on the direction of rotation.

gate-control theory: The theory that the pain signals transmitted by slow-firing nerve fibres can be blocked at the spinal gate if fast-firing fibres get their message to the spinal cord first, or if the brain itself inhibits the transmission of the pain messages.

endorphins (en-DOR-fins): Chemicals, produced naturally by the pituitary gland, that reduce pain and affect mood positively.

kinesthetic sense: The sense that provides information about the position of body parts and about body movement, detected by sensory receptors in the joints, ligaments, and muscles.

vestibular sense (ves-TIB-yu-ler): The sense that provides information about movement and our orientation in space through sensory receptors in the semicircular canals and the vestibular sacs, which detect changes in the movement and orientation of the head.

semicircular canals: Three fluid-filled tubular canals in the inner ear that provide information about rotating head movements.

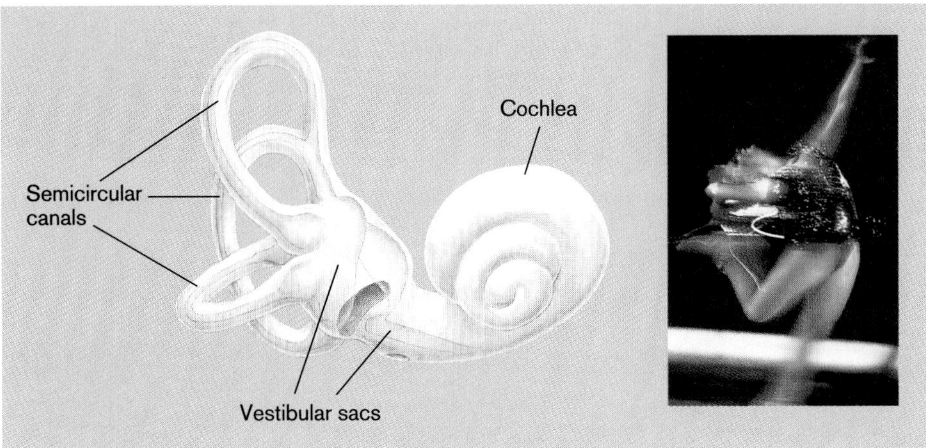

FIGURE 3.11
Sensing Balance and Movement **We sense the rotation of the head in any direction because the movement sends fluid coursing through the tubelike semicircular canals in the inner ear. The moving fluid bends the hair cell receptors, which in turn send the message to the brain.**

The semicircular canals and the vestibular sacs signal only *changes* in motion or orientation. If you were blindfolded and had no visual or other external cues, you would not be able to sense motion once your speed reached a constant rate. For example, in an airplane you feel the takeoff and landing or sudden changes in speed. But once the pilot levels off and maintains about the same speed, your vestibular organs do not signal to the brain that you are moving, even if you are travelling hundreds of kilometres per hour.

Remember It!

Other Senses

1. Each skin receptor responds only to touch, pressure, warmth, or cold. (true/false)
2. The two-point threshold varies for different body parts. (true/false)
3. People would be better off if they could not feel pain. (true/false)
4. The (kinesthetic/vestibular) sense provides information about the position of our body parts in relation to one another and about movement in those body parts.
5. The receptors for the (kinesthetic/vestibular) sense are located in the semicircular canals and vestibular sacs in the (middle ear/inner ear).

Answers: 1. false 2. true 3. false 4. kinesthetic 5. vestibular; inner ear

Perception: Ways of Perceiving

In the first part of this chapter, you learned how the senses detect visual, auditory, and other sensory information and transmit it to the brain. Now we will explore **perception**—the process by which this sensory information is actively organized and interpreted by the brain. We *sense* sounds in hertz and decibels, but we *perceive* melodies. We *sense* light of certain wavelengths and intensities, but we *perceive* a multicoloured world of objects and people. Sensations are the raw materials of human experiences; perceptions are the finished products.

We know that physical objects can be analyzed down to their smallest parts, even to the atoms that make up the object. Can perception be analyzed and understood in the same way—broken down into its smallest sensory elements? The answer is no, according to Gestalt psychology, a school of thought that began in Germany in the early 1900s.

The Gestalt Principles of Perceptual Organization

What are the Gestalt principles of perceptual organization?

The Gestalt psychologists maintained that we cannot understand our perceptual world by breaking down experiences into tiny parts and analyzing them separately. When sensory elements are brought together, something new is formed. They insisted that the whole is more than just the sum of its parts. The German word **Gestalt** has no exact English equivalent, but it roughly refers to the whole form, pattern, or configuration that we perceive.

How do we organize the world of sights, sounds, and other sensory stimuli in order to perceive the way we do? The Gestalt psychologists argued that we organize our sensory experience according to certain basic principles of perceptual organization. These principles include the figure–ground relationship and other principles of perceptual grouping.

Figure and Ground: One Stands Out

The **figure–ground** relationship is the most fundamental principle of perceptual organization and is, therefore, the best place to start analyzing how we perceive. As you view your world, some objects (the figure) seem to stand out from the background (the ground).

Many psychologists believe that figure–ground perceptual ability is **innate** (that is, an ability we do not have to learn). We know that figure–ground perception is present very early in life. It is also the first ability to appear in patients who were blind from birth and who became sighted as adults. We also know that figure–ground perception is not limited to vision. If you listen to a symphony orchestra or a rock band, the melody line tends to stand out as figure, while the chords and the rest of the accompaniment are heard as ground. An itch or a pain would immediately get your attention, while the remaining tactile stimuli you feel would fade to ground.

How can we be sure that knowing the difference between figure and ground is a result of our perceptual system, and that the difference isn't part of the sensory stimulus itself? The best proof is represented by reversible figures, where figure and ground seem to shift back and forth between two equal possibilities, as shown in Figure 3.12.

FIGURE 3.12 **Reversing Figure and Ground** **In this illustration, you can see a white vase as figure against a black background, or two black faces in profile on a white background. Exactly the same visual stimulus produces two opposite figure–ground perceptions.**

Sometimes a figure or an object blends so well with its background that we can hardly see it. When there are no sharp lines of contrast between a figure and its background, a figure is camouflaged. For many animals, camouflage provides protection from predators.

Gestalt Principles of Grouping: Perceptual Arrangements

The Gestalt psychologists believed that when we see figures or hear sounds, we organize them according to the simplest, most basic arrangement possible. They proposed the following principles of grouping: similarity, proximity, continuity, and closure (Wertheimer, 1958).

SIMILARITY We tend to group visual, auditory, and other stimuli according to the principle of similarity. Objects that have similar characteristics are perceived as a unit. In Figure 3.13(a), dots of a similar colour are perceived as belonging together to form horizontal rows (on the left) and vertical columns (on the right). When we listen to music, we group the instruments and perceive them as units—the violins, trumpets, and so on—on the basis of similarity in sound.

PROXIMITY Objects that are close together in space or time are usually perceived as belonging together, because of a principle of grouping called *proximity*. Because of their spacing, the lines in Figure 3.13(b) are perceived as four pairs of lines rather than as eight separate lines. Musical notes sounded close together in time are perceived as belonging together to produce musical phrases.

CONTINUITY The principle of continuity suggests that we perceive figures or objects as belonging together if they appear to form a continuous pattern, as in Figure 3.13(c). When two singers sing or two instruments are played in harmony, we perceive the notes in the melody line as belonging together, and

perception: The process by which sensory information is actively organized and interpreted by the brain.

Gestalt (geh-SHTALT): A German word roughly meaning *form* or *pattern*.

figure–ground: A principle of perceptual organization whereby the visual field is perceived in terms of an object (figure) standing out against a background (ground).

innate: Inborn, unlearned.

the notes in the harmony line as belonging together, even if they converge on the same note and then cross over.

CLOSURE The principle of closure attempts to explain our tendency to complete figures with gaps in them. Even though parts of the figure in Figure 3.13(d) are missing, we use closure and perceive them as a triangle. If you were listening to your favourite song on the radio and interference periodically interrupted it, you would fill in the gaps to perceive the whole song.

Perceptual Constancy

What is perceptual constancy, and what are its four types?

As we view people and objects from different angles and distances and under different lighting conditions, we tend to see them as maintaining the same size, shape, brightness, and colour. We call this phenomenon **perceptual constancy**.

Size Constancy: When Smaller Means Farther Away

When you say goodbye to friends and watch them walk away, the image they cast on your retina grows smaller and smaller until they finally disappear in the distance. But the shrinking-size information that the retina sends to your brain (the sensation) does not fool the perceptual system. As objects or people move farther away from us, we continue to perceive them as about the same size.

This perceptual phenomenon is known as **size constancy**. We do not make a literal interpretation about the size of objects from the **retinal image**—the image projected onto the retina of objects in the visual field. If we did, we would believe that objects we see become larger as they approach us and smaller as they move away from us. Some evidence suggests that size constancy is learned. People who are blind from birth and later become sighted usually have trouble perceiving visual sensations they have never experienced and grossly misjudge distances.

Shape Constancy: Seeing Round as Round from Any Angle

The shape or image of an object projected onto the retina changes according to the angle from which we view it. But our perceptual ability gives us **shape constancy**—the tendency to perceive objects as having a stable or unchanging shape regardless of changes in the retinal image resulting from differences in viewing angle. In other words, we perceive a door as rectangular and a plate as round from whatever angle we view them (see Figure 3.14).

Brightness Constancy: Perceiving Brightness in Sunlight and Shadow

We normally see objects as maintaining a constant level of brightness regardless of differences in lighting conditions—a phenomenon known as **brightness constancy**. Nearly all objects reflect some part of the light that falls upon them, and we know that white objects reflect more light than black objects. However, a black asphalt driveway actually reflects more light at noon in bright sunlight than a white shirt reflects indoors at night in dim lighting. Nevertheless, the driveway still looks black and the shirt still looks white. Why? We learn to infer the brightness of objects by comparing them with the brightness of all other objects viewed at the same time.

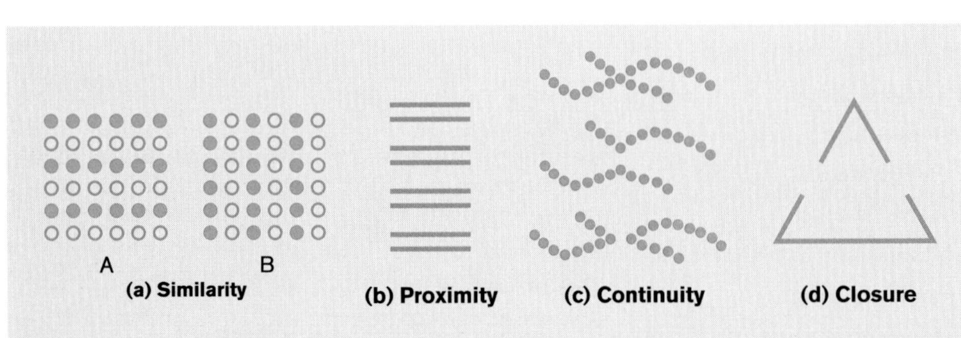

FIGURE 3.13 Gestalt Principles of Grouping Gestalt psychologists proposed four principles of perceptual grouping: similarity, proximity, continuity, and closure.

FIGURE 3.14
Shape Constancy The door projects very different images on the retina when viewed from different angles. But because of shape constancy, we continue to perceive the door as rectangular.

Colour Constancy: When Colours Stay the Same in Sunlight or Shadow

Colours can change considerably under different lighting conditions. But when objects are familiar to us, they appear to look about the same colour under different conditions of illumination. This is called **colour constancy**. Like brightness constancy, colour constancy depends on the comparisons we make between differently coloured objects we view at the same time (Brou et al., 1986).

Imagine what a strange world you would live in if it were not for the perceptual constancies. If your brain made a literal interpretation of all retinal images, the familiar sizes, shapes, and colours you view would appear to change back and forth before your eyes. Fortunately, the perceptual constancies, so natural and commonplace, provide a stable perceptual world.

Depth Perception: Perceiving What's Up Close and What's Far Away

Depth perception is the ability to perceive the visual world in three dimensions and to judge distances accurately. We judge how far away from us are the objects we grasp and the people we reach out to touch. We climb and descend stairs without stumbling, and perform other visual tasks too numerous to list, all requiring depth perception.

Depth perception has three dimensions, yet each eye is able to provide us with only two dimensions. The images cast upon the retina do not contain depth; they are flat, just like a photograph. How, then, do we perceive depth so vividly?

Binocular Depth Cues: The Cues Only Two Eyes Reveal

What are the binocular depth cues?

Some cues to depth perception depend on our two eyes working together. These are called **binocular depth cues**, and they

perceptual constancy: The tendency to perceive objects as maintaining stable properties, such as size, shape, and brightness, despite differences in distance, viewing angle, and lighting.

size constancy: The tendency to perceive objects as the same size regardless of changes in the retinal image.

retinal image: The image of objects in the visual field projected onto the retina.

shape constancy: The tendency to perceive objects as having a stable or unchanging shape regardless of differences in viewing angle.

brightness constancy: The tendency to see objects as maintaining the same brightness regardless of differences in lighting conditions.

colour constancy: The tendency to see objects as maintaining about the same colour regardless of differences in lighting conditions.

depth perception: The ability to see in three dimensions and to estimate distance.

binocular depth cues: Depth cues that depend on two eyes working together; convergence and binocular disparity.

Remember It!

Ways of Perceiving

1. Camouflage blurs the distinction between
   a. sensation and perception.
   b. figure and ground.
   c. continuation and closure.
   d. proximity and similarity.
2. The Gestalt principle of (continuity/closure) refers to our tendency to complete figures with gaps in them.
3. Which of the perceptual constancies cause us to perceive objects as being different from the retinal image they project?
   a. brightness constancy and colour constancy
   b. colour constancy and shape constancy
   c. shape constancy and size constancy
   d. colour constancy and size constancy
4. Which of the constancies depend on our comparing one object with other objects viewed under the same lighting conditions?
   a. brightness constancy and colour constancy
   b. colour constancy and shape constancy
   c. shape constancy and size constancy
   d. colour constancy and size constancy

Answers: 1. b 2. closure 3. c 4. a

include convergence and binocular disparity. **Convergence** occurs when our eyes turn inward as we focus on nearby objects—the closer the object, the greater the convergence. Hold the tip of your finger about 30 centimetres in front of your nose and focus on it. Now slowly begin moving your finger toward your nose. Your eyes will turn inward so much that they virtually cross when the tip of your finger meets the tip of your nose. Many psychologists believe that the tension of the eye muscles as they converge conveys information to the brain that serves as a cue for distance and depth perception.

Fortunately, our eyes are just far enough apart, about six centimetres or so, to give each eye a slightly different view of the objects we focus on and, consequently, a slightly different retinal image. The difference between the two retinal images, known as **binocular disparity** (or retinal disparity), provides an important cue for depth and distance. The farther away from us the objects we view (up to six metres or so), the less the disparity or difference between the two retinal images. The brain integrates these two slightly different retinal images and gives us the perception of three dimensions (Wallach, 1985b). Ohzawa and colleagues (1990) suggest that there are specific neurons in the visual cortex that are particularly suited to detecting disparity. Ordinarily we are not aware that each eye provides a slightly different view of the objects we see. You can prove this for yourself in *Try It!*

Try It!

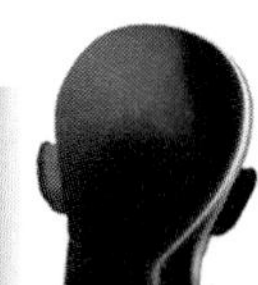

Testing Binocular Disparity

Hold your forefinger or a pencil at arm's length straight in front of you. Close your left eye and focus on the pencil. Now quickly close your right eye at the same time that you open your left eye. Repeat this procedure, closing one eye just as you open the other. The pencil will appear to move from side to side in front of your face.

Now slowly bring the pencil closer and closer until it almost reaches your nose. The closer you bring the pencil, the more it appears to move from side to side. This is because there is progressively more disparity between the two retinal images as we view objects closer and closer.

Convergence and binocular disparity provide depth or distance cues only for nearby objects. Fortunately, each eye by itself provides cues for objects at greater distances.

Monocular Depth Cues: The Cues One Eye Can Detect

What are seven monocular depth cues?

Close one eye and you will see that you can still perceive depth. The visual depth cues perceived by one eye alone are called **monocular depth cues**. The following is a description of seven monocular depth cues, many of which artists have used to give the illusion of depth to their paintings.

- *Interposition.* Some psychologists consider interposition, or overlapping, to be the most powerful depth cue of all (Haber, 1980). When one object partly blocks our view of another, we perceive the partially blocked object as farther away.
- *Linear perspective.* Linear perspective is a depth cue in which parallel lines that are known to be the same distance apart appear to grow closer together or converge as they recede into the distance. Linear perspective was used extensively by the Renaissance artists (in the 1400s).
- *Relative size.* Larger objects are perceived as being closer to us, and smaller objects as being farther away, as shown in Figure 3.15. We know that most adults are between 160 and 185 centimetres tall, so when images of the people we view are two, three, or many times smaller than their normal size, we perceive them as being two, three, or as many times farther away.
- *Texture gradient.* Texture gradient is a depth cue in which near objects appear to have a sharply defined texture, while similar objects appear progressively smoother and fuzzier as they recede into the distance.
- *Atmospheric perspective.* Atmospheric perspective, sometimes called "aerial perspective," is a depth cue in which objects in the distance have a bluish tint and appear more blurred than objects close at hand.
- *Shadow or shading.* When light falls on objects, shadows are cast. We can distinguish bulges from indentions by the shadows they cast. This ability appears to be learned (Hess, 1961).
- *Motion parallax.* When we ride in a moving vehicle and look out the side window, the objects we see outside appear to be moving in the opposite

Parallel lines appear to converge as they recede into the distance. This effect is known as linear perspective.

FIGURE 3.15

Relative Size: A Monocular Depth Cue **If we assume that these playing cards are all the same size, we perceive the largest card as closest and the smaller cards as progressively farther away.**

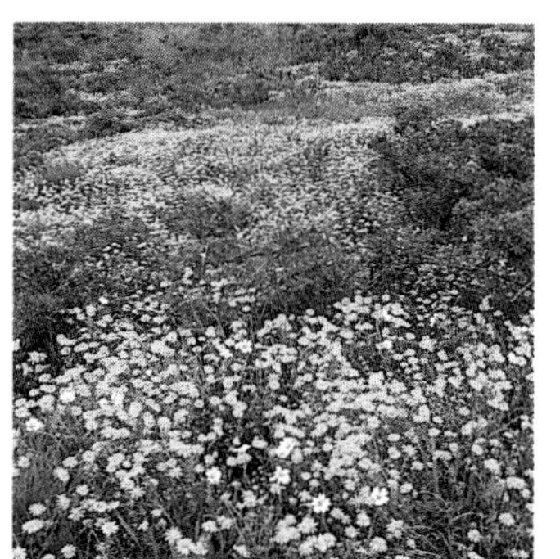

The texture of objects can provide depth cues. The flowers in the foreground appear sharp and well-defined, whereas those in the distance are blurred and fuzzy.

convergence: A binocular depth cue in which the eyes turn inward as they focus on nearby objects—the closer an object, the greater the convergence.

binocular disparity: A binocular depth cue resulting from differences between the two retinal images cast by objects at distances up to about six metres.

monocular depth cues (mah-NOK-yu-ler): Depth cues that can be perceived by only one eye.

direction. The objects also seem to be moving at different speeds—those closest to us appear to be moving faster than objects in the distance. This phenomenon, called "motion parallax," provides another monocular cue to depth perception. Objects very far away, such as the moon and the sun, appear to move in the *same* direction as we are moving.

Figure 3.16 summarizes the binocular and monocular depth cues.

Extraordinary Perceptions

We perceive ambiguous figures, impossible figures, and illusions as well.

Ambiguous Figures: More Than One Way to See Them

When we are faced for the first time with the ambiguous figure, we have no experience to call on. Our perceptual system is puzzled and tries to work its way out of the quandary by seeing the ambiguous figure first one way and then another, but not both at once. We never get closure with ambiguous figures, which seem to jump back and forth beyond our control.

In some ambiguous figures, two different objects or figures are seen alternately. The best known of these, "Old Woman/Young Woman," by E.G. Boring, is shown in Figure 3.17. If you direct your gaze to the left of the drawing, you are likely to see an attractive young woman, her face turned away. But the young woman disappears when you suddenly perceive the image of the old woman. Such examples of object ambiguity offer striking evidence that our perceptions are more than the mere sum of sensory parts. It is hard to believe that the same drawing (the same sum of sensory parts) can convey such dramatically different perceptions.

Impossible Figures: This Can't Be

At first glance, the pictures of impossible figures do not seem so unusual—not until we examine them more closely. Would you invest your money in a com-

FIGURE 3.17 **"Old Woman/Young Woman" by E.G. Boring** **The most famous ambiguous figure can be seen alternately as a young woman or an old woman depending on where your eyes fixate.**

FIGURE 3.16 **Binocular and Monocular Depth Cues** **Depth cues that require two eyes working together are binocular; those that require only one eye are monocular.**

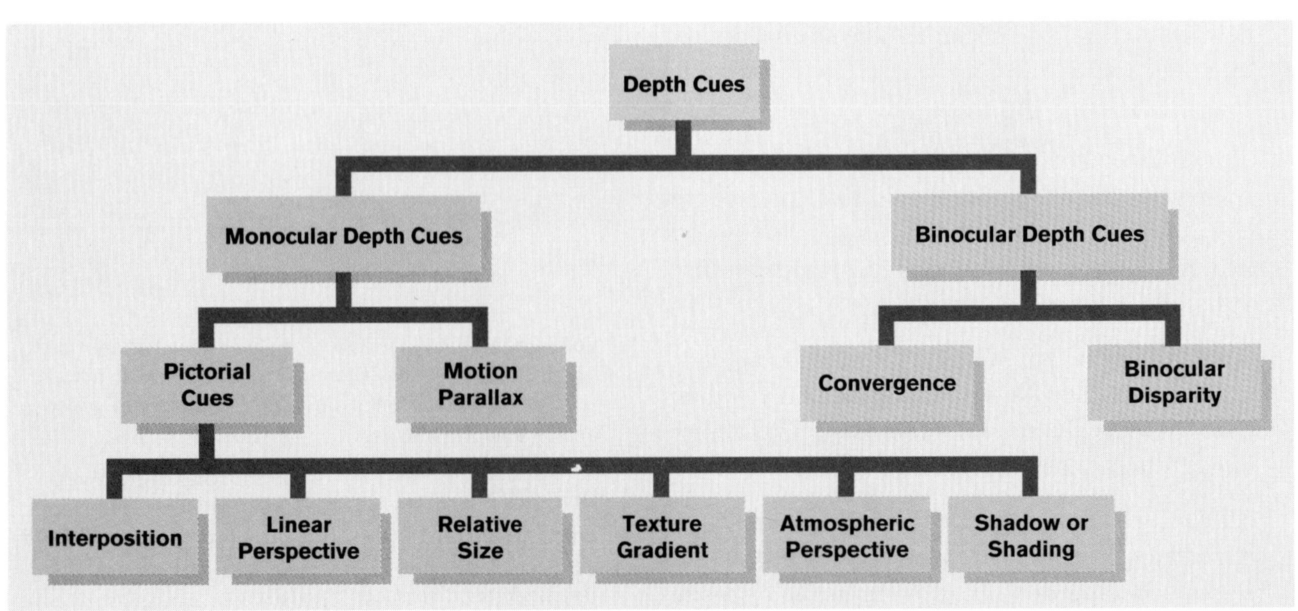

pany that manufactured three-pronged tridents as shown in Figure 3.18? Such an object could not be made as pictured because the middle prong appears to be in two different places at the same time. However, this type of impossible figure is more likely to fool the depth-perception sensibilities of people from Western cultures. People in some African cultures do not represent three-dimensional visual space in their art, and they do not perceive depth in drawings that contain pictorial depth cues. These people see no ambiguity in drawings similar to the three-pronged trident, and they can draw the figure accurately from memory much more easily than people from Western cultures (Bloomer, 1976).

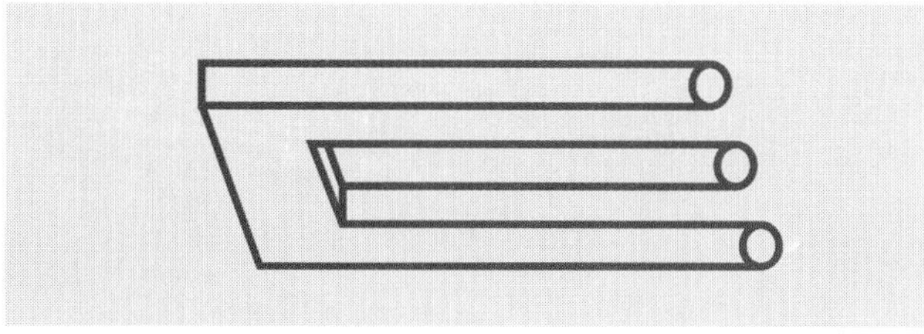

FIGURE 3.18

The Three-Pronged Trident This is an impossible figure because the middle prong appears to be in two places at the same time.

Illusions: False Perceptions

An **illusion** is a false perception or a misperception of an actual stimulus in the environment. We can misperceive size, shape, or the relationship of one element to another. We need not pay to see illusions performed by magicians: illusions occur naturally and we see them all the time. An oar in the water appears to be bent where it meets the water. The moon looks much larger at the horizon than it does overhead. Why? One explanation of the moon illusion involves relative size. The suggestion is that the moon looks very large on the horizon because it is viewed in comparison to trees, buildings, and other objects. When viewed overhead, the moon cannot be compared with other objects, and it appears smaller. People have been speculating about the moon illusion for 22 centuries and experimenting for 50 years to determine its cause, but there is still no agreement (Hershenson, 1989).

THE MÜLLER-LYER ILLUSION Look at Figure 3.19(a). Which line is longer? Actually, they are the same length. The same is true of 3.19(b). British psychologist R. L. Gregory (1978) has suggested that the Müller-Lyer illusion is actually a misapplication of size constancy. When two lines are the same length, the line we perceive to be farther away will look longer.

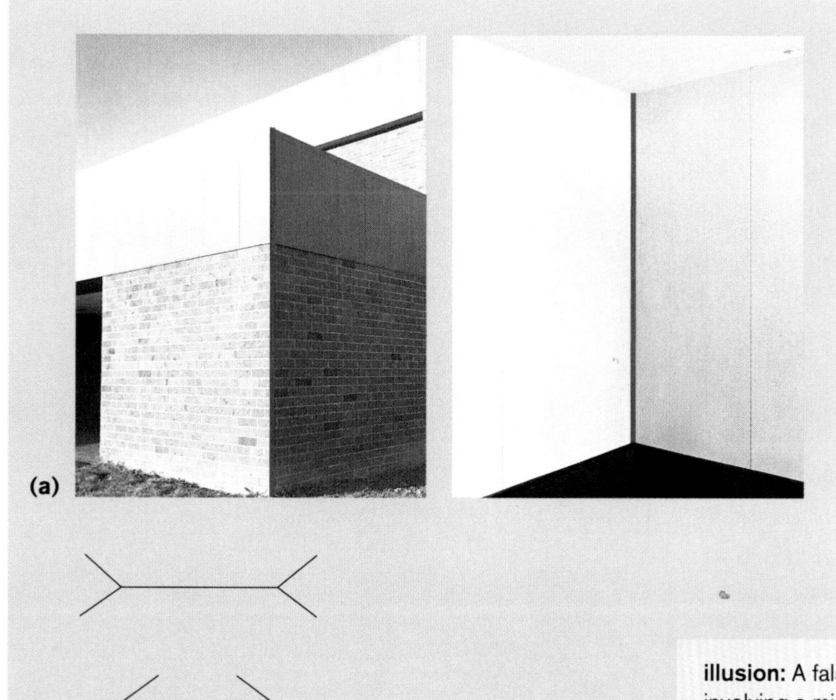

FIGURE 3.19

The Müller-Lyer Illusion Although the two vertical lines in (a) are the same length, the line on the left seems to project forward and appears closer than the line on the right, which seems to recede. The two horizontal lines in (b) are identical in length. When two lines are the same length, the one perceived as farther away will appear longer. (Based on Gregory, 1978.)

illusion: A false perception of actual stimuli involving a misperception of size, shape, or the relationship of one element to another.

THE PONZO ILLUSION The Ponzo illusion also plays an interesting trick. Look at Figure 3.20. Which obstruction on the railway tracks looks larger? You have undoubtedly guessed by now, contrary to your perceptions, that A and B are the same size. Again, our perceptions of size and distance, which we trust and which are normally accurate in informing us about the real world, can be wrong. If we saw two obstructions on real railway tracks identical to the ones in the illusion, the one that looked larger would indeed be larger. So the Ponzo illusion is not a natural illusion but rather a contrived one. In fact, all these illusions are really misapplications of principles that nearly always work properly in our normal everyday experience.

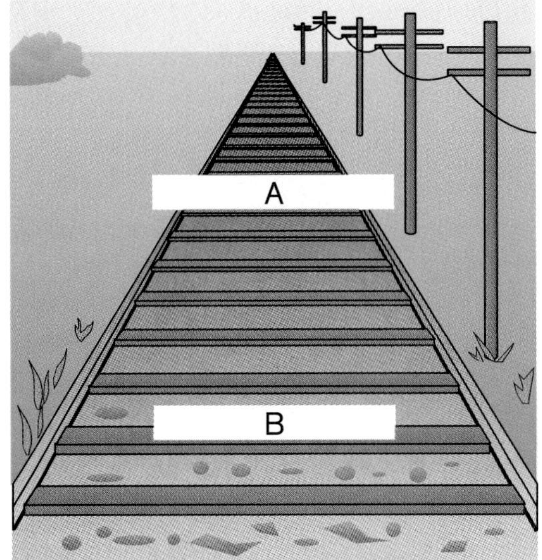

FIGURE 3.20
The Ponzo Illusion
The two white bars superimposed on the railway track are actually identical in length. Because A appears farther away than B, we perceive it as longer.

CULTURAL DIFFERENCES IN VISUAL ILLUSIONS Note that our susceptibility to visual illusions is not necessarily inborn. Several studies have examined the influence of culture or experience on people's perceptions of visual illusions. Segall and his colleagues (1966) tested over 1800 adults and children from 15 different countries and found "marked differences in illusion susceptibility across cultural groups" (p. 137). People from all cultures showed some tendency to see the illusions but experience different perceptions. Zulus from Africa who have round houses and see few corners of any kind were not as fooled by the Muller-Lyer illusion. In similar research, Pedersen and Wheeler (1983) studied Native American responses to the Muller-Lyer illusion among Navajos and found that those who had lived in round houses, like the Zulus, tended not to see the illusion.

Remember It!

Depth Perception and Illusion

1. Retinal disparity and convergence are two (monocular/binocular) depth cues.
2. Match the appropriate monocular depth cue with each example.
   ____ 1) One building partly blocking another
   ____ 2) Railway tracks converging in the distance
   ____ 3) Closer objects appearing to move faster than far objects
   ____ 4) Far objects looking smaller than near objects

   a. motion parallax
   b. linear perspective
   c. interposition
   d. relative size
4. An illusion is
   a. an imaginary sensation.
   b. an impossible figure.
   c. a misperception of a real stimulus.
   d. a figure–ground reversal.

Answers: 1. binocular 2. 1) c 2) b 3) a 4) d 3. stroboscopic motion 4. c

Additional Influences on Perception

Why don't all people perceive sights, sounds, odours, and events in the same way? The reason is that our perceptions involve more than just the sensory stimuli themselves.

Bottom-Up and Top-Down Processing

In what types of situations do we rely more on bottom-up or top-down processing?

Psychologists distinguish between two distinct information-processing techniques that we use in recognizing patterns—bottom-up processing and top-down processing.

Bottom-up processing begins with the individual components of a stimulus that are detected by the sensory receptors. The information is then transmitted to areas in the brain where it is combined and assembled into the whole patterns that we perceive.

In **top-down processing**, on the other hand, past experience and knowledge of the context plays a role in forming our perceptions. In other words, what we perceive is more than the sum of the individual elements taken in by our sensory receptors. If you have ever tried to decipher a prescription written by your doctor (bottom-up processing), you may have been amazed that your pharmacist could fill it. But prior knowledge and experience enabled the pharmacist to use top-down processing.

Of course, we use both bottom-up and top-down processing when we form perceptions. In situations unfamiliar to us, we are likely to use bottom-up processing. In familiar situations, where we have some prior knowledge and experience, we tend to use top-down processing.

So far we have considered perceptions that are formed above the threshold of our awareness and perceptions that arise from our known sensory abilities. Can we be influenced by persuasive messages below our level of awareness, through subliminal persuasion? And are we able to gain information by some means other than our known sensory channels, through extrasensory perception?

Subliminal Persuasion: Does It Work?

Over 30 years ago, it was reported that moviegoers in a New Jersey theatre were exposed to advertising messages flashed on the screen so briefly that they were not aware of them. An advertising executive, James Vicary, argued that the words "Eat Popcorn" and "Drink Coca-Cola" were projected on the screen for only 1/3000 of a second every five seconds during the movie. The purpose of the messages was to influence the audience to buy popcorn and Coca-Cola, not by getting their conscious attention, but by sending persuasive messages below their level of awareness—a technique called **subliminal persuasion**. During the six-week period the messages ran, popcorn sales supposedly rose by 57.5 percent and Coca-Cola sales rose by more than 18 percent (McConnell et al., 1958).

Technically, **subliminal perception** would be defined as the perception of sensory stimuli that are below the absolute threshold. But the subliminal persuasion experiment was limited to messages flashed so quickly that they could never be normally perceived at all. Can we actually perceive information that is completely below our level of awareness? Some people say we can (for example, see Channouf et al., 1999), and today subliminal persuasion is aimed at selling much more than popcorn and Coke. Subliminal self-help tapes, popularized by the New Age movement, are brisk sellers.

Is subliminal persuasion in audiotapes effective? This question was asked by Timothy Moore (1995) at Glendon College, York University. He found that audiotapes that claimed to influence behaviour with subliminal messages were not effective. Similarly, Merikle and Skanes (1992), at the University of Waterloo, investigated whether weight-loss tapes would influence eating behaviour. The researchers dismissed them as ineffective in therapy. So why do some users insist that tapes have helped them quit smoking or lose weight? The change is likely due to the power of suggestion or the placebo effect, and not the messages on the tapes (Pratkanis et al., 1994).

bottom-up processing: Information processing in which individual components or bits of data are combined until a complete perception is formed.

top-down processing: Application of previous experience and conceptual knowledge to first recognize the whole of a perception and thus easily identify the simpler elements of that whole.

subliminal persuasion: Sending persuasive messages below the recipient's level of awareness.

subliminal perception: Perceiving sensory stimulation that is below the absolute threshold.

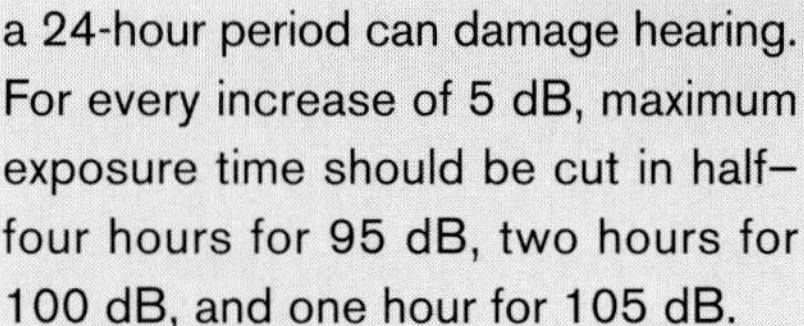

Apply It!

Noise and Hearing Loss: Bad Vibrations

Hearing loss is increasing rapidly in the industrialized world, and the main reason is NOISE. Jet engines, power mowers, radios, firecrackers, motorcycles, chain saws, and other power tools are well-known sources of noise that can injure the ear. For centuries we have known that noise can cause hearing loss.

We are in more danger of losing our hearing off the job than at the work site. Without proper protection, recreational hunting, rock concerts, and some sports events can cause more damage to hearing than industrial noise.

Exposure to hazardous noise can begin long before we are old enough to listen to a Sony Walkman, experience a rock concert, or attend a baseball game at a covered or domed stadium. Some babies and toddlers get an early start on hearing loss. Axelsson and Jerson (1985) tested seven squeaking toys that, at a distance of 10 centimetres, squeaked out pure sound levels loud enough to put toddlers at risk for hearing loss with "minutes of exposure each day."

If older children play with toy weapons, noise-induced hearing loss can occur within seconds. The same researchers tested several toy weapons and found that at a distance of 50 centimetres, the guns produced explosive sound levels ranging from 144 to 152 dB. All exceeded the 130 dB peak level that is considered the upper limit for exposure to short-lived explosive sounds.

Explosions, gun blasts, and other extremely loud noises may burst the eardrums, or fracture or dislocate the tiny ossicles in the middle ear. Often these injuries can be repaired surgically, but noise injuries to the inner ear cannot (Bennett, 1990). It doesn't take an explosion or years of exposure to noise to injure hair cells. Rock musician Kathy Peck lost 40 percent of her hearing in one evening after her band opened a stadium concert for Duran Duran.

In 1986 the rock group The Who entered the *Guiness Book of World Records* as the loudest rock band ever, blasting out deafening sound intensities that measured 120 dB at a distance of 164 feet from the speakers. Unless their ears were protected, every person within that 164-foot radius probably suffered some irreversible damage to the ears. And the band members? Pete Townshend of The Who has severely damaged hearing and, in addition, is plagued by tinnitus, an annoying condition in which there is a continuous ringing in the ears.

How can you tell when noise levels are high enough to jeopardize your hearing? You are putting yourself at risk if you have difficulty talking over the noise level, or if the noise exposure leaves you with a ringing in your ears or a temporary hearing loss (Dobie, 1987).

Experts maintain that exposure to noise of 90 dB (a lawn mower, for example) for more than eight hours in a 24-hour period can damage hearing. For every increase of 5 dB, maximum exposure time should be cut in half—four hours for 95 dB, two hours for 100 dB, and one hour for 105 dB.

What can you do to protect yourself from noise?

- If you must be exposed to loud noise, use earplugs (not the kind used for swimming) or earmuffs to reduce noise by as much as 15 to 30 dB (Dobie, 1987).
- If you must engage in an extremely noisy activity, such as cutting wood with a chain saw, limit periods of exposure so that stunned hair cells can recover.
- Keep the volume down on Walkman-type radios or tape players. If the volume control is numbered 1 to 10, a volume above 4 probably exceeds standards for noise. If you have a ringing in your ears, if sounds seem muffled, or if you have a tickling sensation after you remove your headset, you may have sustained some hearing loss.
- Begin humming before you are exposed to loud noise. Humming will set in motion the very tiny muscles in the middle ear; this will dampen the sound and provide some measure of protection (Borg & Counter, 1989).

Extrasensory Perception: Does It Exist?

Perception refers to the process by which we organize and interpret sensory input. Is it possible to perceive information that does *not* come through the senses? Is there such a thing as **extrasensory perception (ESP)**—gaining information about objects, events, or another's thoughts through some means other than the known sensory channels? Can some people read minds or foretell the future? How many of you have gone to see a fortune teller or called "Jojo's Psychic Hotline"? Extrasensory perception is part of a larger area of interest known as **parapsychology**—the study of psychic phenomena. Reported cases of ESP fall into three rough categories—telepathy, clairvoyance, and precognition.

Telepathy means gaining awareness of the thoughts, the feelings, or the activities of another without the use of the senses—in other words, reading a person's mind. *Clairvoyance* means gaining information about objects or events without use of the senses, such as knowing the contents of a letter without opening it. *Precognition* refers to an awareness of an event before it occurs. Most of the reported cases of precognition in everyday life have occurred while people were dreaming. One researcher revealed the poor record of well-known psychics who made New Year's predictions for the *National Enquirer* between 1978 and 1985. Only two of their 425 predictions proved to be accurate (Strentz, 1986). But probably the most telling blow against precognition is the failure of any of these psychics to predict some of the most astounding world events of the century.

Because psychic phenomena violate what we know about the real, measurable, physical world, scientists and skeptics naturally demand proof of their existence (Hansel, 1966, 1980; Randi, 1980). Time after time, investigators have discovered trickery when examining the claims of psychics that they can read minds or communicate with the dead.

What is the truth about psychic phenomena? Do they exist but have not yet been proved to exist, or do they exist but cannot be verified under laboratory conditions, or do they not exist at all? What do you believe?

Earlier we noted that sensation and perception are so closely linked in everyday experience that it is hard to be certain where one ends and the other begins. In this chapter you have seen many examples of what is sensed and what is perceived. Our perceptual system is continuously trying to complete what we merely sense.

extrasensory perception (ESP): Gaining awareness of or information about objects, events, or another's thoughts through some means other than the known sensory channels.

parapsychology: The study of psychic phenomena, which include extrasensory perception (ESP) and psychokinesis.

KEY TERMS

absolute threshold, p. 73
accommodation, p. 77
afterimage, p. 81
amplitude, p. 83
audition, p. 84
binocular depth cues, p. 97
binocular disparity, p. 98
bottom-up processing, p. 103
brightness, p. 79
brightness constancy, p. 96
cochlea, p. 85
colour blindness, p. 81
colour constancy, p. 97
cones, p. 78
convergence, p. 98
cornea, p. 76
dark adaptation, p. 78
decibel, p. 83
depth perception, p. 97
difference threshold, p. 73
endorphins, p. 92
extrasensory perception, p. 105
figure–ground, p. 95
flavour, p. 88
fovea, p. 78
frequency, p. 83
frequency theory, p. 86
gate-control theory, p. 92
Gestalt, p. 94
gustation, p. 88
hair cells, p. 85
hue, p. 79
illusion, p. 101
innate, p. 95
inner ear, p. 85
just noticeable difference, p. 73
kinesthetic sense, p. 93
lens, p. 77
middle ear, p. 84
monocular depth cues, p. 99
olfaction, p. 87
olfactory bulbs, p. 88
olfactory epithelium, p. 87
opponent-process theory, p. 80
optic nerve, p. 79
outer ear, p. 84
parapsychology, p. 105
perception, p. 72
perceptual constancy, p. 96
pheromones, p. 88
place theory, p. 85
retina, p. 77
retinal image, p. 96
rods, p. 78
saturation, p. 79
semicircular canals, p. 93
sensation, p. 72
sensory adaptation, p. 74
sensory receptors, p. 74
shape constancy, p. 96
signal detection theory, p. 74
size constancy, p. 96
subliminal perception, p. 103
subliminal persuasion, p. 103
tactile, p. 90
taste buds, p. 88
timbre, p. 84
top-down processing, p. 103
transduction, p. 74
trichromatic theory, p. 80
vestibular sense, p. 93
visible spectrum, p. 76
Weber's law, p. 73

THINKING CRITICALLY

Evaluation

Using what you have learned about the factors that contribute to hearing loss, prepare a statement indicating what the government should do to control noise pollution, even to the extent of banning certain noise hazards. Consider the workplace, the home, toys, machinery, rock concerts, and so on.

Point/Counterpoint

Recent polls indicate that nearly 49 percent of people believe in ESP. Prepare a sound, logical argument supporting one of the following positions:

a. There is evidence to suggest that ESP exists.
b. There is no evidence to suggest that ESP exists.

Psychology in Your Life

Vision and hearing are generally believed to be the two most highly prized senses. How would your life change if you lost your sight? How would your life change if you lost your hearing? Which sense would you find more traumatic to lose? Why?

SUMMARY & REVIEW

Sensation: The Sensory World

What is the difference between sensation and perception?

Sensation is the process through which the senses pick up sensory stimuli and transmit them to the brain. Perception is the process by which this sensory information is actively organized and interpreted by the brain.

What is the difference between the absolute threshold and the difference threshold?

The absolute threshold is the minimum amount of sensory stimulation that can be detected 50 percent of the time. The difference threshold is a measure of the smallest increase or decrease in a physical stimulus that can be detected 50 percent of the time.

How are sensory stimuli in the environment experienced as sensations?

For each of our senses, there are sensory receptors, which detect and respond to sensory stimuli. Through a process known as *transduction,* the receptors convert sensory stimuli into neural impulses, which are then transmitted to their own special locations in the brain.

Vision

How do the cornea, the iris, and the pupil function in vision?

The cornea bends light rays inward through the pupil—the small, dark opening in the eye. The iris dilates and contracts the pupil to regulate the amount of light entering the eye.

What are the lens and the retina?

The lens changes its shape as it focuses images of objects from varying distances on the retina, a thin membrane containing the sensory receptors for vision.

What roles do the rods and cones play in vision?

The cones detect colour, provide our sharpest vision, and function best in high illumination. The rods enable us to see in dim light. Rods respond to black and white, and they encode all other visible wavelengths in shades of grey.

What path does the neural impulse take from the retina to the visual cortex?

The rods and the cones transduce light waves into neural impulses that pass from the bipolar cells to the ganglion cells, whose axons form the optic nerve. At the optic chiasma, some of the fibres of the optic nerve cross to the opposite side of the brain, before reaching the thalamus. From the thalamus, the neural impulses travel to the visual cortex.

What are the three dimensions that combine to provide the colours we experience?

The three dimensions are hue, saturation, and brightness.

What two major theories attempt to explain colour vision?

Two major theories that attempt to explain colour vision are the trichromatic theory and the opponent-process theory.

Hearing

What determines the pitch and the loudness of sound, and how is each quality measured?

The pitch of a sound is determined by frequency, which is measured in hertz. The loudness of a sound is determined largely by the amplitude of the sound wave and is measured in decibels.

How do the outer, middle, and inner ears function in hearing?

Sound waves enter the pinna, the visible part of the outer ear, and travel to the end of the auditory canal, causing the eardrum to vibrate. This sets in motion the ossicles in the middle ear, which amplify the sound waves. The vibration of the oval window causes activity in the inner ear, setting in motion the fluid in the cochlea and moving the hair cell receptors, which transduce the vibrations into neural impulses. The auditory nerve carries the neural impulses to the brain.

What two major theories attempt to explain hearing?

Two major theories that attempt to explain hearing are place theory and frequency theory.

What are some major causes of hearing loss?

Some major causes of hearing loss are disease, birth defects, aging, injury, and noise.

Smell and Taste

What path does a smell message take on its journey from the nose to the brain?

The act of smelling begins when odour molecules reach the smell receptors in the olfactory epithelium at the top of the nasal cavity. The axons of these receptors form the olfactory nerve, which relays the smell message to the olfactory bulbs. From there the smell message travels to other parts of the brain.

What are the four primary taste sensations, and how are they detected?

The four primary taste sensations are sweet, salty, sour, and bitter. The receptor cells for taste are found in the taste buds on the tongue and in other parts of the mouth and throat.

Our Other Senses

How does the skin provide sensory information?

Nerve endings in the skin (the sensory receptors) respond to different kinds of stimulation, including heat and cold, pressure, pain, and a vast range of touch sensations. The neural impulses ultimately register in the somatosensory cortex.

What beneficial purpose does pain serve?

Pain can be a valuable warning and protective mechanism, motivating us to tend to an injury, to restrict our activity, and to seek medical help if needed.

What is the gate-control theory of pain?

Melzack and Wall's gate-control theory holds that pain signals transmitted by slow-conducting fibres can be blocked at the spinal gate (1) if fast-conducting fibres get their message to the gate first, or (2) if the brain itself inhibits their transmission.

What are endorphins?

Endorphins, released when we are stressed or injured, are the body's natural painkillers; they block pain and produce a feeling of well-being.

What kind of information does the kinesthetic sense provide, and how is this sensory information detected?

The kinesthetic sense provides information about the position of body parts and movement in those body parts. The position or motion is detected by sensory receptors in the joints, ligaments, and muscles.

What is the vestibular sense, and where are its sensory receptors located?

The vestibular sense provides information about movement and our orientation in space. Sensory receptors in the semicircular canals and in the vestibular sacs detect changes in the movement and orientation of the head.

Perception: Ways of Perceiving

What are the Gestalt principles of perceptual organization?

Gestalt principles of perceptual organization include the figure–ground relationship and four principles of perceptual grouping–similarity, proximity, continuity, and closure.

What is perceptual constancy, and what are its four types?

Perceptual constancy is the tendency to perceive objects as maintaining the same size, shape, brightness, and colour despite changes in lighting conditions or changes in the retinal image that result when objects are viewed from different angles and distances.

What are the binocular depth cues?

The binocular depth cues are convergence and binocular disparity; they depend on two eyes working together for depth perception.

What are seven monocular depth cues?

The monocular depth cues–those that can be perceived by one eye–include interposition, linear perspective, relative size, texture gradient, atmospheric perspective, shadow or shading, and motion parallax.

Additional Influences on Perception

In what types of situations do we rely more on bottom-up processing or top-down processing?

We use bottom-up processing more in unfamiliar situations, top-down processing more in situations in which we have some prior knowledge and experience.

4 States of Consciousness

"Car crash kills baby: Man, 44, faces drunk-driving charges causing death," *Toronto Sun*, July 31, 2000 (Bill, 2000).

"Police officer drank, drove, killed three," Canadian Press, July 25, 2000 (Canadian Press, 2000).

"Dad pleads guilty in crash that killed daughter," *Ottawa Sun,* June 22, 2000 (Roik, 2000).

We are all aware of the problems associated with alcohol and driving. Every day we are told of yet another unfortunate event that affects people's lives–the lives of our friends, our family, our community. All regions of our country have laws that specify how much alcohol can be consumed before driving skills are affected. The impact of drunk driving is serious both for the driver and, even more so, for the potential victims. This is why many advocacy groups are active in making the public aware that drinking is a personal choice and that drunk driving is not an uncontrollable event.

Obviously, all of us should be concerned about drunk driving. However, alcohol is not the only factor that affects our state of consciousness–and therefore our driving skills. For example, one Canadian researcher, Stanley Coren, at the University of British Columbia, says, "Canadians are so sleep deprived that even little things–like the switch to daylight savings time . . . generate a marked increase in traffic accidents" (Munro, 1996). Coren (1997) suggests that most of us need $9\frac{1}{2}$ to 10 hours of sleep per day. How many of you are getting enough sleep? If you are getting less than this, you may be sleep-deprived. According to Coren, sleep deprivation may "make us clumsy, stupid, unhappy, and dead" (Munro 1996). In fact, Coren's work on U.S. data suggests that many accidental causes of death, such as falling off a ladder, occur when people do not have enough sleep. So maybe there's something to that old adage, "Early to bed, early to rise, makes a person healthy, wealthy, and wise."

What Is Consciousness?

What are some different states of consciousness?

As the research outlined above suggests, much of our lives and many of our life experiences are determined by our state of **consciousness**. And our state of consciousness, in turn, is greatly influenced by things such as the amount of sleep we get and the drugs we may take (including caffeine, cough medicine, alcohol, and illicit drugs). Given the importance of our state of consciousness, it is surprising that our ability to define and explain consciousness is still imprecise. Some liken consciousness to a flowing stream; others argue that it is an underlying "mechanism" that combines attention and short-term memory.

When we are at the highest level of consciousness, we are fully absorbed, and our thoughts are fixed on the details of what we are concentrating on, whether it be our studies, a new skill, or a basketball game on TV. A lower level of awareness involves such states as daydreaming; still lower levels involve sleep. We will now explore the various states of consciousness and examine the many ways in which consciousness may be altered. Ordinary waking consciousness can be altered by substances—alcohol or drugs, for example—and by focused concentration such as in meditation and hypnosis. This chapter will explore these **altered states of consciousness**.

The most fundamental altered state is one in which we spend about one-third of our lives, the one we visit for several hours nearly every night—sleep.

Circadian Rhythms: Our 24-Hour Highs and Lows

What is a circadian rhythm, and which rhythms are most relevant to the study of sleep?

Do you notice changes in the way you feel throughout the day—fluctuations in your energy level, mood, or efficiency? More than 100 of our bodily functions and behaviours fluctuate in 24-hour cycles (Dement, 1974). These daily fluctuations, called **circadian rhythms**, are controlled largely by the brain (Ginty et al., 1993; Ralph, 1989). Blood pressure, heart rate, appetite, secretion of hormones and digestive enzymes, sensory acuity, elimination, and even our body's responses to medication all follow circadian rhythms (Hrushesky, 1994). Our learning efficiency ebbs and flows by daily rhythms, which also affect our mood (Boivin et al., 1997) and our ability to perform a wide variety of tasks (Johnson et al., 1992).

Two cycles of particular importance to the study of sleep relate to alertness and body temperature. Normal human body temperature can range from a low of about 36.1 degrees Celsius between 4:00 and 5:00 a.m., to a high of about 37 degrees Celsius between 5:00 and 8:00 p.m. People sleep best when their body temperature is lowest, and they are most alert when their body temperature is at its daily high point (Monk & Carrier, 1998). Alertness also follows a circadian rhythm, one that is quite separate from the sleep/wakefulness rhythm (Monk, 1989). For most of us, alertness decreases between 2:00 and 5:00 p.m. and between

2:00 and 7:00 a.m. (Mitler et al., 1988; Webb 1995). During the afternoon decrease in alertness, body temperature also dips (Barrett et al., 1993).

LINK IT!

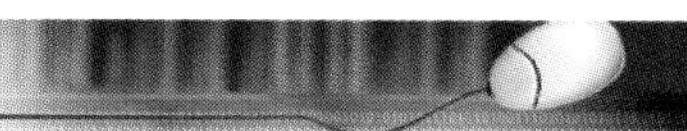

www.mrs.umn.edu/~goochv/Circadian/circadian.html
Circadian Rhythms

www.websciences.org/sltbr/
Society for Light Treatment and Biological Rhythms Home Page

The Suprachiasmatic Nucleus: The Body's Timekeeper

What is the suprachiasmatic nucleus?

So, what part of our brain acts as a biological clock? Studies suggest that it is a tiny piece of brain tissue smaller than the head of a pin located in the hypothalamus called the **suprachiasmatic nucleus** (SCN) (Ginty et al., 1993; Moore-Ede, 1993).

Are circadian rhythms strictly biological, or do environmental cues play a part? Canadian researchers Mistlberger and Rusak (1989) attempted to answer this question by placing people in an environment with no cues indicating the time of day. Most people naturally fell into a 25-hour schedule. But external stimuli—day and night, alarm clocks, job or school demands—cause us to modify our biological clock's preference for a 25-hour rhythm to conform to a 24-hour schedule. Circadian rhythms are slightly disrupted each year when daylight saving time begins and ends. An even greater disruption occurs when people fly across a number of time zones or when they work rotating shifts.

Jet Lag: Where Am I and What Time Is It?

Suppose you fly from Toronto to Paris, and the plane lands at 12:00 midnight Toronto time, about the time you usually go to sleep. When it is midnight in Toronto, it is 6:00 a.m. in Paris, almost time to get up. Everything in Paris, including the clocks and the sun, tells you it is early morning, but you still feel like it is 12:00 midnight. You are experiencing jet lag.

The problem is not simply the result of losing a night's sleep. You are fighting your own biological clock, which is synchronized with your usual time zone and not the time zone you are visiting (Graeber, 1989). It is difficult to sleep when your biological clock is telling you to wake up and feel alert. It is even harder to remain awake and alert when your internal clock is telling you to sleep. Some research suggests that jet lag is less troublesome for women, younger people, extroverts, and night owls (Kiester, 1997).

Shift workers experience a similar problem without the benefit of a trip to Europe or Asia.

Shift Work: Working Day and Night

What are some problems experienced by employees who work rotating shifts?

Many Canadians work the night shift or engage in various other patterns of shift work. The health care, data processing, and transportation industries are the largest employers of shift workers, along with police and fire departments. When people must work at night, they experience a disruption in the rhythms of many bodily functions that are normally synchronized for daytime. These rhythm disruptions can cause a variety of physical and psychological problems.

In a report by the Canadian Centre for Occupational Health and Safety (1988), health risks of shift workers were assessed. Not surprisingly, shift workers complain of sleepiness and sleeping difficulties. Shift workers average two to four hours less sleep than non-shift workers of the same age (Campbell, 1995). Forced to remain awake when their body temperature is low, they use more caffeine. Trying to sleep when their body temperature is high, they use more alcohol and sleeping pills (Gordon et al., 1986). Moreover, digestive problems such as appetite

consciousness: The continuous stream of perceptions, thoughts, feelings, or sensations of which we are aware from moment to moment.

altered state of consciousness: A mental state other than ordinary waking consciousness, such as sleep, meditation, hypnosis, or a drug-induced state.

circadian rhythm (sur-KAY-dee-un): Within each 24-hour period, the regular fluctuation from high to low points of certain bodily functions.

suprachiasmatic nucleus (SCN): A tiny structure in the brain's hypothalamus that controls the timing of circadian rhythms; the biological clock.

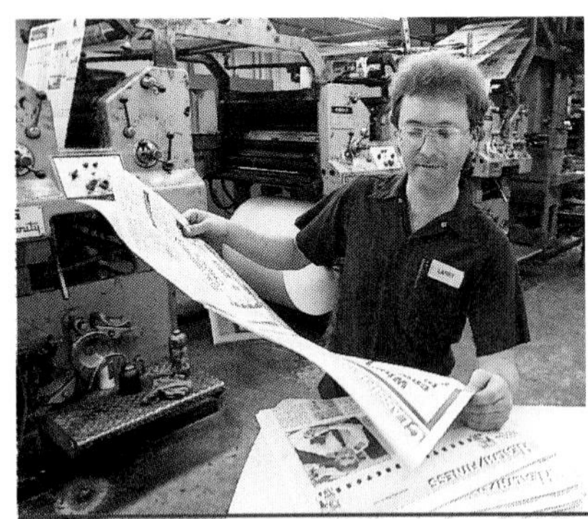

What are the physical and psychological effects of disturbing the normal sleep/wakefulness cycle when a person works the night shift, as this printing press operator does?

loss, diarrhea, and irregularity are common, because shift workers eat at times not in synchrony with the circadian rhythms (Regestein & Monk, 1991; Vener et al., 1989).

What about performance on the job? Alertness and performance deteriorate if people work during **subjective night,** when their biological clock is telling them to go to sleep (Åkerstedt, 1990; Folkard, 1990). During subjective night, energy and efficiency reach their lowest point, reaction time is slowest, and productivity is diminished.

Many air, rail, marine, and highway accidents have occurred when the shift workers in charge suffered sleep loss and fatigue because of the disruption of their circadian rhythms (Lauber & Kayten, 1988). More errors in judgment and most accidents occur during the night shift (Webb, 1975). The nuclear disasters at Three Mile Island and Chernobyl, and the Challenger disaster, are thought to have occurred in part because those responsible were dangerously fatigued (Moore-Ede, 1993).

Can anything be done to make shift rotation less disruptive? Rotating work schedules forward—from days to evenings to nights—and changing work shifts every three weeks rather than every week have resulted in increased job satisfaction, health, and productivity (Czeisler et al., 1982).

In several experiments of real significance to shift workers, researchers found that exposure to appropriately timed bright- or medium-intensity light reset workers' biological clocks and improved their performance (Martin & Eastman, 1998). Even a four-hour exposure to bright light between midnight and 4:00 a.m. on one night can improve performance and reduced sleepiness during the same period the following night (Thessing et al., 1994). Factories, police departments, and hospitals should seriously consider the research in this field to help workers adjust to shift changes.

Sleep: That Mysterious One-Third of Our Lives

Over a lifetime, a person spends about 25 years sleeping. For decades, sleep researchers argued about the function of sleep. Some believed sleep simply served a restorative function; others argued that sleep evolved

Remember It!

Consciousness and Circadian Rhythms

1. Which of the following best defines consciousness?
   a. awareness
   b. wakefulness
   c. receptiveness
   d. rationality
2. The two circadian rhythms most relevant to the study of sleep are the sleep/wakefulness cycle and
   a. blood pressure.
   b. secretion of hormones.
   c. body temperature.
   d. heart rate.
3. We sleep best when our body temperature is at the low point in our 24-hour cycle. (true/false)
4. Which is not characteristic of people who work rotating shifts?
   a. disturbed sleep
   b. digestive problems
   c. increased efficiency and alertness during subjective night
   d. greater use of caffeine, alcohol, and sleeping pills
5. For swing-shift workers, work schedules should be rotated from nights to evenings to days. (true/false)

Answers: 1. a 2. c 3. true 4. c 5. false

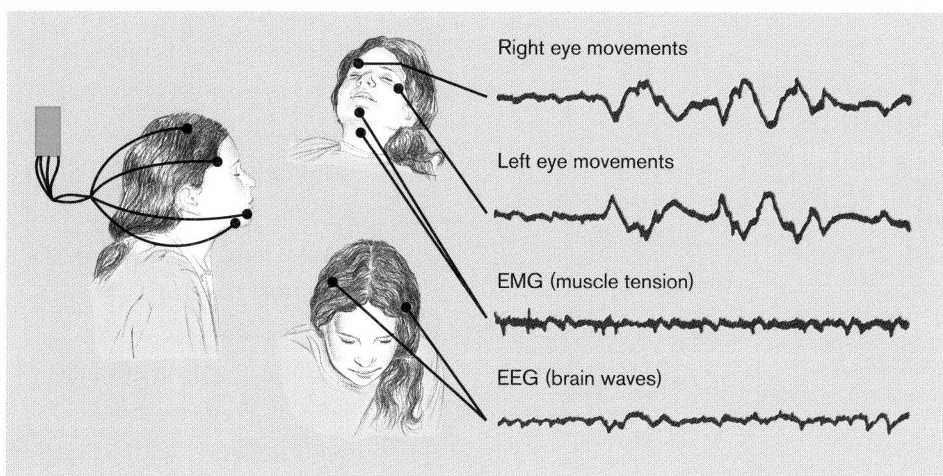

FIGURE 4.1
How Researchers Study Sleeping Participants
Researchers study participants in a sleep laboratory or sleep clinic by taping electrodes to the participant's head to monitor brain-wave activity, eye movements, and muscle tension. (After Dement, 1974.)

to keep animals out of harm's way. But neither of these theories alone accounts for many of the research findings about sleep. For example, if you miss a night's sleep, why are you very sleepy during the middle of the night, but less so the next day? Today most sleep researchers believe that sleep should be viewed as a circadian rhythm that, in part, serves a restorative function (Webb, 1994). This view accommodates the variety of findings about sleep that we will explore in the following pages.

www.sleepfoundation.org
National Sleep Foundation Home Page: Non-profit organization that promotes public understanding of sleep and sleep disorders

bisleep.medsch.ucla.edu/SRS/srs_main.htm
Sleep Research Society Home Page

NREM and REM Sleep: Watching the Eyes

Before the 1950s there was no understanding of what goes on during the state of consciousness we call sleep. Then, in the 1950s, several universities set up sleep laboratories where people's brain waves, eye movements, chin-muscle tension, heart rate, and respiration rate were monitored through a night of sleep. From the data they gathered, researchers discovered that there are two major categories of sleep: NREM (non–rapid eye movement) sleep and REM (rapid eye movement) sleep. Figure 4.1 shows a sleep research participant whose brain activity, eye movement, and chin-muscle activity are being recorded.

NREM Sleep: From Light to Deep Sleep in Stages

How does a sleeper act physically during NREM sleep?

NREM (pronounced NON-rem) **sleep** is the sleep in which there are no rapid eye movements. It is often called "quiet sleep," because heart rate and respiration are slow and regular, there is little body movement, and blood pressure and brain activity are at their lowest points of the 24-hour period.

There are four stages of NREM sleep, with Stage 1 being the lightest sleep and Stage 4 being the deepest. We pass gradually rather than abruptly from one stage to the next. Each stage can be identified by its brain-wave pattern, as shown in Figure 4.2. Growth hormone is secreted mainly during Stage 3 and Stage 4 sleep (Gronfier et al., 1996).

subjective night: The time during a 24-hour period when your body temperature is lowest and your biological clock is telling you to go to sleep.

NREM sleep: Non–rapid eye movement sleep, consisting of the four sleep stages and characterized by slow, regular respiration and heart rates, an absence of rapid eye movements, and blood pressure and brain activity that are at a 24-hour low point.

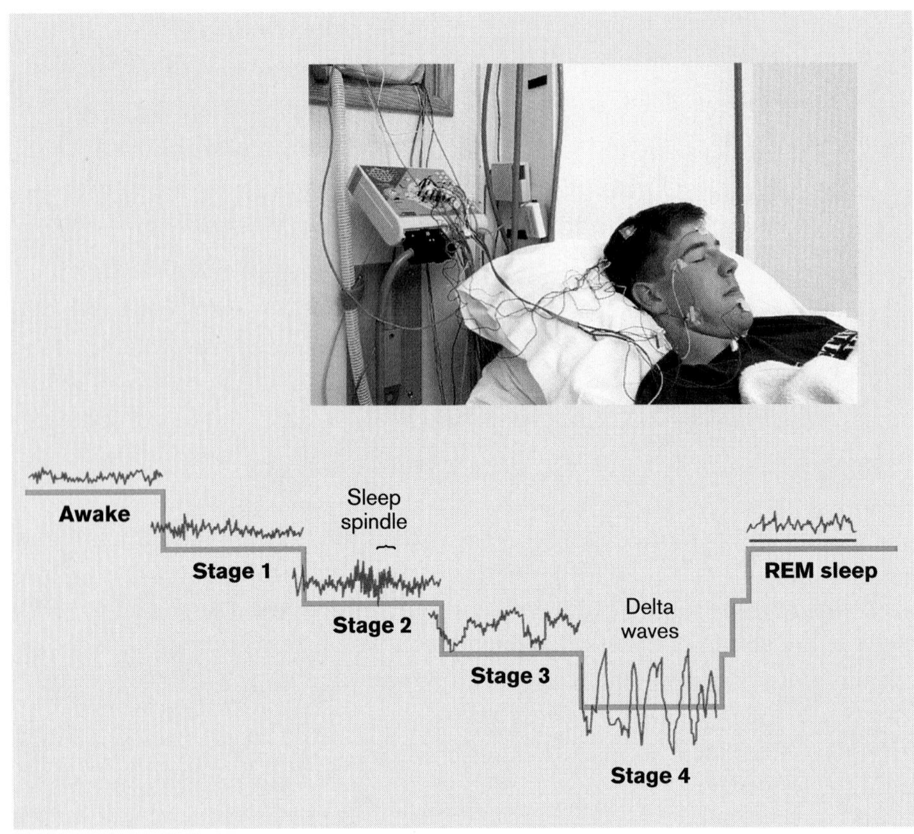

FIGURE 4.2
Brain-Wave Patterns Associated with Different Stages of Sleep By monitoring brain-wave activity with the EEG throughout a night's sleep, researchers have identified the brain-wave patterns associated with different stages of sleep. As sleepers progress through the four NREM stages, the brain-wave pattern changes from faster, low-voltage waves in Stages 1 and 2 to the slower, larger delta waves in Stages 3 and 4. Notice that the brain-wave activity during REM sleep is similar to that of the subject when awake. (After Hobson, 1989.)

REM Sleep: Rapid Eye Movements and Dreams

How does the body respond physically during REM sleep?

Most of us envision sleep as a time of deep relaxation and calm. But **REM sleep**, sometimes called "active sleep," is anything but calm, and it constitutes 20 to 25 percent of a normal night's sleep in adults. During the REM state, there is intense brain activity, and our body reacts as if to a daytime emergency. Epinephrine (adrenaline) shoots into the system, blood pressure rises, and heart rate and respiration become faster and irregular and brain temperature increases (Krueger & Takabashi, 1997). In contrast to this storm of internal activity, there is an external calm during REM sleep. The large muscles of the body—arms, legs, trunk—become paralyzed (Chase & Morales, 1990). Some researchers suggest that the reason for this paralysis is to prevent us from acting out our dreams.

If you observe a sleeper during the REM state, you can see the eyes darting around under the eyelids. Eugene Azerinsky discovered these bursts of rapid eye movements in 1952. Five years later, William Dement and Nathaniel Kleitman made the connection between rapid eye movements and dreaming. It is during REM periods that most of our vivid dreams occur. When awakened from REM sleep, 80 percent of people report dreaming (Carskadon & Dement, 1989).

Almost from birth, regardless of the content of their dreams, males have a full or partial erection during REM sleep, and women experience vaginal swelling and lubrication. Because sleepers are more likely to awaken naturally at the end of a REM period than during the NREM stages of sleep, men usually wake up with an erection (Campbell, 1985). In males suffering from impotence, the presence of an erection during REM sleep indicates that the impotence is psychological; its absence indicates that the impotence has physical causes.

If you are awakened during REM sleep and remain awake for several minutes, you will not go back into REM sleep for at least 30 minutes. This explains why most of us have experienced the disappointment of waking in the middle of a wonderful dream and not being able to get quickly back to sleep and into the dream.

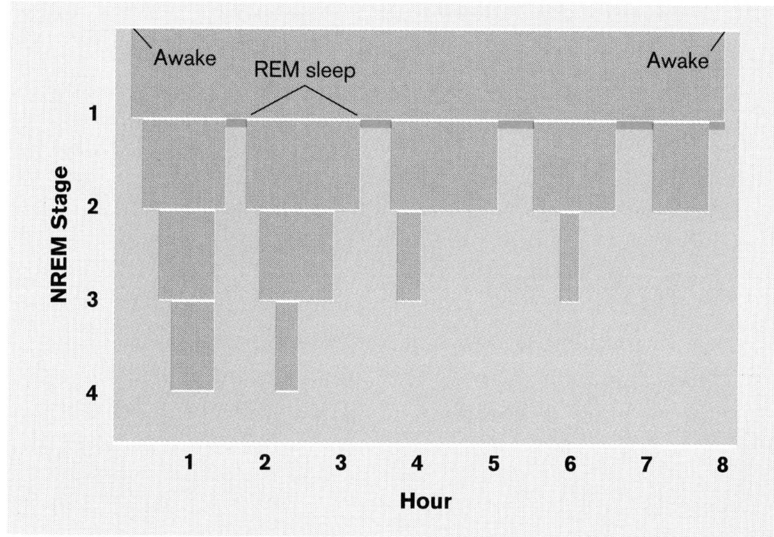

FIGURE 4.3

The Typical Composition of Sleep Cycles for Young Adults **A typical night's sleep for young adults consists of about five sleep cycles of about 90 minutes each. Stage 4 sleep occurs during the first two sleep cycles. People spend progressively more time in REM sleep with each succeeding 90-minute cycle. (After Hartmann, 1967.)**

Sleep Cycles: The Nightly Pattern of Sleep

What is the progression of NREM stages and REM sleep that a person goes through in a typical night of sleep?

Many people are surprised to learn that sleep follows a fairly predictable pattern each night. We sleep in cycles. During each **sleep cycle**, which lasts about 90 minutes, we have one or more stages of NREM sleep followed by a period of REM sleep. Let us go through a typical night of sleep for a young adult (see Figure 4.3).

The first sleep cycle begins with a few minutes in Stage 1 sleep, sometimes called "light sleep." Stage 1 is actually a transition stage between waking and sleeping. Then sleepers descend into Stage 2 sleep, in which they are somewhat more deeply asleep and harder to awaken. About 50 percent of the total night's sleep is spent in Stage 2 sleep. Next, sleepers enter Stage 3 sleep, the beginning of **slow-wave sleep** (or deep sleep). As sleep gradually becomes deeper, brain activity slows and more **delta waves** (slow waves) appear in the EEG. When there are more than 50 percent delta waves on the EEG, people are said to be in **Stage 4 sleep**, the deepest sleep, when people are hardest to awaken (Carskadon & Rechtschaffen, 1989; Cooper, 1994). Perhaps you have taken an afternoon nap and awakened confused, not knowing whether it was morning or night, a weekday or a weekend. If so, you probably awakened during Stage 4 sleep.

After about 40 minutes in Stage 4 sleep, brain activity increases and the delta waves begin to disappear from the EEG. Sleepers make an ascent back through Stage 3 and Stage 2 sleep, then enter the first REM period of the night, which lasts 10 or 15 minutes. At the end of this REM period, the first sleep cycle is complete, and the second sleep cycle begins. Unless people awaken after the first sleep cycle, they go directly from REM sleep into Stage 2 sleep. They then follow the same progression as in the first sleep cycle, through Stages 3 and 4 and back again into REM sleep.

After the first two sleep cycles of about 90 minutes each (three hours in total), the sleep pattern changes and sleepers usually get no more Stage 4 sleep. From this point on, during each 90-minute sleep cycle, people alternate mainly between Stage 2

REM sleep: Sleep characterized by rapid eye movements, paralysis of large muscles, fast and irregular heart rate and respiration rate, increased brain-wave activity, and vivid dreams.

sleep cycle: A cycle of sleep lasting about 90 minutes and including one or more stages of NREM sleep followed by a period of REM sleep.

slow-wave sleep: Stages 3 and 4 sleep; deep sleep.

delta wave: The slowest brain-wave pattern, associated with Stage 3 sleep and Stage 4 sleep.

Stage 4 sleep: The deepest NREM stage of sleep, characterized by an EEG pattern of more than 50 percent delta waves.

and REM sleep for the remainder of the night. With each sleep cycle, the REM periods (the "dreaming times") get progressively longer. By the end of the night, REM periods may be 30 to 40 minutes long. In a night, most people sleep about five sleep cycles (7.5 to 8 hours) and get about 1.5 hours of slow-wave sleep and 1.5 hours of REM sleep.

Variations in Sleep: How We Differ

There are great individual variations in sleep patterns. The major factor contributing to these variations is age.

The Older We Get, the Less We Sleep

How do sleep patterns change over the lifespan?

Infants and young children have the longest sleep times and the highest percentages of REM and deep sleep. However, people get even more REM sleep *before* birth. The fetus spends up to 80 percent of its time in REM sleep (Hobson, 1989).

Children between age six and puberty are the champion sleepers and wakers. They fall asleep easily, sleep soundly for 8.5 to 9 hours at night, and feel awake and alert during the day. Between puberty and the end of adolescence, teenagers average about 7.2 hours of sleep but would need about two hours more to be as alert as they should for school (Wolfson & Carskadon, 1998).

As people age, they usually experience a decrease in quality and quantity of sleep (Reyner & Horne, 1995). Older people have more difficulty falling asleep, and they typically have lighter sleep and more and longer awakenings than younger people (Foley et al., 1995). They spend more time awake in bed but less time asleep, averaging about 6.5 hours of sleep (Prinz et al., 1990). Slow-wave sleep decreases substantially from age 30 to 50 (Mourtazaev et al., 1995). The percentage of REM sleep stays about the same (Moran & Stoudemire, 1992).

Larks and Owls: Early to Rise and Late to Bed

Some people awaken early every morning and leap out of bed with enthusiasm, eager to start the day. Others of us fumble for the alarm clock and push in the snooze button to get a few more precious minutes of sleep. Sleep researchers have names for these two types—larks and owls—and there is a physical explanation for the differences in how they feel. About 25 percent of people are larks—people whose body temperature rises rapidly after they awaken and stays high until about 7:30 p.m. Larks turn in early and have the fewest sleep problems. Then there are the 25 percent who are owls and the 50 percent who are somewhere in between. The body temperature of an owl rises gradually throughout the day, peaking in the afternoon and not dropping until later in the evening. It is not surprising that larks have more difficulty than owls in adapting to night shifts. They are sleepier during their subjective night and are more likely to complain of difficulty sleeping (Hilliker et al., 1992). Differences in one of the genes that run the biological clock are responsible, in part, for the differences between larks and owls (Katzenberg et al., 1998).

"Larks see owls as lazy; owls see larks as party poopers" (Coleman, 1986, p. 15). Can an owl turn into a lark with a little self-discipline? The authors have been trying unsuccessfully to accomplish this for years. However, preliminary work with animals being conducted by Ralph Mistlberger (1991) at Simon Fraser University suggests that it may be possible to alter these roles. Researchers note that even when owls change their sleep schedule to match the early risers, they still *feel* like owls in the morning.

How Much Sleep Do We Need? More Than We Probably Get

What factors influence our sleep needs?

Perhaps you have wondered how much sleep you need in order to feel good, and perhaps you are hoping to find the answer in this chapter. When it comes to sleep, the expression "one size fits all" does *not* apply. Although adults average about 7.5 hours of sleep daily, with an extra hour on weekends, this is too much for some people and too little for others. Short sleepers are the 20 percent who require less than 6 hours; long sleepers are the 10 percent who require more than 9. There seems to be a limit below which most of us cannot go. In one study, not a single participant could get by with less than 4.5 hours of sleep. It seems that 6.5 hours is the minimum for most people.

What accounts for the large variation in the need for sleep? Genetics appears to play a part. Identical twins, for example, have strikingly similar sleep patterns compared with fraternal twins (Webb & Campbell, 1983). Laboratory animals have been bred to be short or long sleepers. But genetics aside, people

Remember It!

Types, Cycles, and Patterns of Sleep

1. State the type of sleep–NREM or REM–that corresponds to each characteristic.

   ___ 1) Paralysis of large muscles
   ___ 2) Slow, regular respiration and heart rate
   ___ 3) Rapid eye movements
   ___ 4) Penile erection and vaginal swelling
   ___ 5) Vivid dreams

   a. REM
   b. NREM

2. The average length of a sleep cycle in adults is
   a. 30 minutes.
   b. 60 minutes.
   c. 90 minutes.
   d. 120 minutes.

3. After the first two sleep cycles, most people get equal amounts of deep sleep and REM sleep. (true/false)

4. Match the age group with the appropriate description of sleep.

   ___ 1) Have most difficulty sleeping, most awakenings
   ___ 2) Sleep best at night; feel best during day
   ___ 3) Have highest percentage of REM and deep sleep
   ___ 4) Are usually sleepy during the day regardless of the amount of sleep at night

   a. infancy
   b. middle childhood
   c. adolescence
   d. old age

Answers: 1. 1) a 2) b 3) a 4) a 5) a 2. c 3. false 4. 1) d 2) a 3) c 4) b

need more sleep when they are depressed, under stress, or experiencing significant life changes such as changing jobs or schools. Increases in mental, physical, or emotional effort also increase our need for sleep (Hartmann, 1973). Contrary to popular opinion, the amount of activity required in an occupation does not affect the amount of sleep a person needs.

Do most people sleep enough? The answer is no, according to data from a number of North American studies. In fact, more than 36 percent of the population are chronically sleep-deprived (Bonnet & Arand, 1995).

How much sleep does the average person need? Probably more than he or she gets. And a temporary increase in mental activity can increase the need for sleep.

Sleep Deprivation: How Does It Affect Us?

What happens when people are deprived of REM sleep? What function does REM sleep appear to serve?

What is the longest you have ever stayed awake—one day, two days, three days, or four days? According to the *Guinness Book of World Records,* Californian Robert McDonald stayed awake 453 hours and 40 minutes (almost 19 days) in a 1986 rocking-chair marathon. Unlike McDonald, most of us have missed no more than a few consecutive nights of sleep, perhaps while studying for final exams. If you have ever missed two or three nights of sleep, you may remember having had difficulty concentrating, lapses in attention, and general irritability. After 60 hours without sleep, some people even have minor hallucinations. Most people who try to stay awake for long periods of time will have **microsleeps,** two- to three-second lapses from wakefulness into sleep. You may have experienced a microsleep if you have ever caught yourself nodding off for a few seconds in class or on a long automobile trip.

microsleep: A momentary lapse from wakefulness into sleep, usually occurring when one has been sleep-deprived.

Recent studies, with over 2000 participants, indicated that sleep deprivation seriously impairs functioning (Pilcher & Huffcutt, 1996). It has a negative impact on mood, alertness, and performance (Bonnet & Arand, 1995). Even partial sleep deprivation impairs one's ability to attend and process relevant stimuli from the environment (McCarthy & Waters, 1997). But do not despair if you are one of these people who tends to wake up often during the night, as this will not reduce your alertness the next day.

When people are deprived of REM sleep as a result of general sleep loss, illness, or too much alcohol (or other drugs), their bodies will make up for the loss by getting an increased amount of REM sleep after the deprivation (Vogel, 1975). This increase in the percentage of REM sleep to make up for REM deprivation is called a **REM rebound**. Because the intensity of REM sleep is increased during a REM rebound, nightmares often occur. But why do we need REM sleep?

The Function of REM Sleep: Necessary, but Why?

The fact that newborns have such a high percentage of REM sleep has led to the conclusion that REM sleep is necessary for maturation of the brain in infants.

Recent research has shown that REM sleep is involved in the consolidation of memories after learning. Karni and colleagues (1994) found that research participants learning a new perceptual skill showed an improvement in performance, with no additional practice, 8 to 10 hours later if they had a normal night's sleep or if their NREM sleep was disturbed. Performance did not improve, however, in those who were deprived of REM sleep (Marks et al., 1995).

An opposite view is proposed by Francis Crick and Graeme Mitchison (1983, 1995). They suggest that REM sleep is a type of "mental housecleaning" that erases trivial and unnecessary memories and clears overloaded neural circuits that might interfere with memory and rational thinking. In other words, they say, people dream in order to forget.

Dreaming: Mysterious Mental Activity While We Sleep

How do REM and NREM dreams differ?

People have always been fascinated by dreams. The vivid dreams we remember and talk about are **REM dreams**—the type that occur almost continuously during each REM period. But there are also **NREM dreams,** which occur during NREM sleep (Foulkes, 1996). REM dreams have a story-like or dream-like quality and are more visual, vivid, emotional, and bizarre than NREM dreams, which typically have a thought-like quality (Hobson, 1989; Webb & Cartwright, 1978). As the night wears on, our REM dreams become longer and more complex (Cipolli & Poli, 1992).

Have you ever heard that an entire dream takes place in an instant? Did you find that hard to believe? In fact, it is not true. Sleep researchers have discovered that it takes about as long to dream a dream as it would to experience the same thing in real life (Kleitman, 1960). Let's take a closer look at the dream state.

What do we dream about? REM dreams have a story-like quality and are more visual, vivid, and emotional than NREM dreams.

LINK IT!

www.ASDreams.org
The Association for the Study of Dreams

Dream Memories: We Remember Only a Few

Very few dreams are memorable enough to be retained very long. Sleep researchers have learned that sleepers have the best recall of a dream if they are awakened during the dream; the more time that passes after the dream ends, the poorer the recall (Kleitman, 1960). Perhaps the reason for the quick loss of memory is that human brain chemistry during sleep appears to differ from that in the waking state and does not facilitate the storing of memories (Hobson, 1996; Hobson & Stickgold, 1995).

The Content of Dreams: Bizarre or Commonplace?

In general, what have researchers found regarding the content of dreams?

What do we dream about? You may be surprised to learn that dreams are less bizarre and less filled with emotion than is generally believed (Cipolli et al., 1993; Hall & Van de Castle, 1966; Snyder, 1971). Because dreams are notoriously hard to remember, the features that stand out tend to be those that are bizarre or emotional.

Sleep researchers generally agree that dreams reflect our preoccupations in waking life—our fears, wishes, plans, hopes, and worries. Most dreams have rather commonplace settings with real people, half of whom are known to the dreamer. In general, dreams are more unpleasant than pleasant, and they contain more aggression than friendly interactions and more misfortune than good fortune. Fear and anxiety, often quite intense, are common in REM dreams (Hobson, 1996). Some dreams are in "living colour," whereas others are in black and white.

Table 4.1 (on the next page) lists the 20 most common dream themes among 250 university students. Although the study was conducted in 1958, a study today would probably yield similar results. Compare the results of your dream themes in *Try It!* with the results of the study shown in Table 4.1.

Try It!

What's in Your Dreams?

Read this list of 20 common dream themes. Check each one you have dreamed about.

____ Falling
____ Finding money
____ Being attacked or pursued
____ Swimming
____ Trying repeatedly to do something
____ Being dressed inappropriately
____ Snakes
____ School, teachers, studying
____ Being smothered
____ Sexual experiences
____ Being nude in public
____ Arriving too late
____ Fire
____ Eating
____ Failing an examination
____ Being frozen with fright
____ Flying
____ Death of a loved person
____ Seeing self as dead
____ Being locked up

REM rebound: The increased amount of REM sleep that occurs after REM deprivation; often associated with unpleasant dreams or nightmares.

REM dreams: Having a dream-like and story-like quality; the type of dream that occurs almost continuously during each REM period; more vivid, visual, emotional, and bizarre than NREM dreams.

NREM dreams: Mental activity occurring during NREM sleep that is more thought-like in quality than REM dreams are.

TABLE 4.1

Common Dream Themes

These are the 20 most common dream themes reported by 250 university students and the percentage of students having each type of dream.

Type of Dream	Percentage of Students
Falling	83
Being attacked or pursued	77
Trying repeatedly to do something	71
School, teachers, studying	71
Sexual experiences	66
Arriving too late	64
Eating	62
Being frozen with fright	58
Death of a loved person	57
Being locked up	56
Finding money	56
Swimming	52
Snakes	49
Being dressed inappropriately	46
Being smothered	44
Being nude in public	43
Fire	41
Failing an examination	39
Flying	34
Seeing self as dead	33

Source: Griffith, Miyago, & Tago, 1958.

Some people are troubled by unpleasant recurring dreams. The two most common themes involve being chased or falling (Stark, 1984). People who have recurring dreams seem to have more minor physical complaints, greater stress, and more anxiety and depression than other people (Brown & Donderi, 1986). Is there anything that can be done to stop recurring dreams? Some people have been taught to use *lucid dreaming* to bring about satisfactory resolutions to their unpleasant recurring dreams.

Have you ever experienced a **lucid dream**—one during which you were aware that you were dreaming? If so, you are among the 10 percent who possess this ability. Many lucid dreamers are able to change a dream while it is in progress, and a few virtuosos claim to be able to dream about any subject at will (Gackenbach & Bosveld, 1989; La Berge, 1981).

LINK IT!

www.cris.com/~Mbreck/lucid.shtml
The Lucid Dreamer's Reference Guide

www.lucidity.com
Lucidity Institute: Lucid Dreaming

Interpreting Dreams: Are There Hidden Meanings in Our Dreams?

Freud believed that dreams function to satisfy unconscious sexual and aggressive wishes. Because such wishes are unacceptable to the dreamer, they have to be disguised and therefore appear in dreams in symbolic form. Freud (1900/1953a) asserted that objects like sticks, umbrellas, tree trunks, and guns symbolize the male sex organ; objects like chests, cupboards, and boxes represent the female sex organ. Freud differentiated between the "manifest" content of the dream—the dream as recalled by the dreamer—and the underlying meaning of the dream, called the "latent" content, which he considered more significant.

In recent years there has been a major shift away from the Freudian interpretation of dreams. The greater focus now is on the manifest content—the actual dream itself—rather than on the search for symbols that can be decoded to reveal some inner conflict. The symbols in dreams, when analyzed, are now perceived as being specific to the individual rather than as having standard or universal meanings for all dreamers.

J. Allan Hobson (1988) rejects the notion that nature would equip us with a capability and a need to dream dreams that only a specialist could interpret. Hobson and McCarley (1977) advanced the activation-synthesis hypothesis of dreaming. This hypothesis suggests that dreams are simply the brain's attempt to make sense of the random firing of brain cells during REM sleep.

But Hobson (1989) now believes that our dreams do have psychological significance because they are woven from our personal experiences, remote memories, and "associations, drives, and fears" (p. 5).

Remember It!

Sleep and Dreams

1. Which factor *least* affects the amount of sleep people need?
   a. their heredity
   b. their emotional state
   c. the amount of stress in their lives
   d. the amount of physical activity required in their occupation
2. Following REM deprivation, there is usually
   a. an absence of REM sleep.
   b. an increase in REM sleep.
   c. a decrease in REM sleep.
   d. no change in the amount of REM sleep.
3. Which type of sleep seems to aid in learning and memory in humans and other animals?
   a. Stage 1
   b. Stage 2
   c. Stages 3 and 4
   d. REM sleep
4. Dream memories usually do not persist for more than 10 minutes after a dream has ended. (true/false)
5. Compared with REM dreams, NREM dreams are
   a. more emotional.
   b. more visual.
   c. more thought-like.
   d. more confusing.
6. According to researchers, each of the following statements about the content of dreams is correct *except*
   a. dreams are generally bizarre and filled with emotion.
   b. dreams generally reflect our waking preoccupations.
   c. dreams are generally more unpleasant than pleasant.
   d. dreams contain more aggression than friendly interactions.

Answers: 1.d 2.b 3.d 4.true 5.c 6.a

LINK IT! 

psychclassics.yorku.ca/Freud/Dreams/
Classics in the History of Psychology: Freud

Sleep Disorders

So far our discussion has centred on a typical night for a typical sleeper. But one-third of North American adults report sleep problems (Rosekind, 1992), and many children also experience sleep disturbances. Sleep problems range from mild to severe and from problems that affect only sleep to those that affect a person's entire life. Yet even today, most medical schools provide less than two hours' instruction on sleep and sleep disorders (Rosen et al., 1993).

LINK IT! 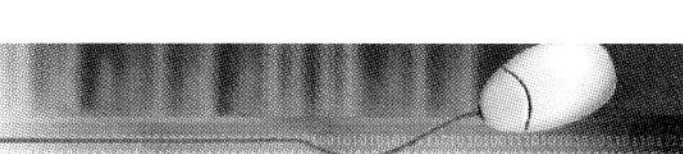

www.asda.org
American Sleep Disorders Association

Parasomnias: Unusual Behaviours During Sleep

Parasomnias are sleep disturbances in which behaviours and physiological states that normally occur only in the waking state take place during sleep or the transition from sleep to wakefulness. Sleepwalking and sleep terrors are two parasomnias that occur during Stage 4 sleep.

Sleepwalking and Sleep Terrors: Their Shared Characteristics

What are the characteristics common to sleepwalking and night terrors?

Sleepwalking (**somnambulism**) and **sleep terrors** are parasomnias that often run in families (Dement, 1974). They occur during a partial arousal from Stage 4 sleep in which the sleeper does not come to full consciousness.

lucid dream: A dream during which the dreamer is aware of dreaming; the dreamer is often able to influence the content of the dream while it is in progress.

parasomnias: Sleep disturbances in which behaviours and physiological states that normally occur only in the waking state take place during sleep or the transition from sleep to wakefulness (e.g., sleepwalking, sleep terrors).

somnambulism (som-NAM-bue-lism): Sleepwalking that occurs during a partial arousal from Stage 4 sleep.

sleep terror: A sleep disturbance in which a person partially awakens from Stage 4 sleep with a scream, in a dazed, groggy, and panicky state, and with a racing heart.

Typically, there is no memory of the episode the following day (Moldofsky et al., 1995). Most cases begin in childhood and are attributed primarily to a delayed development of the nervous system (Masand et al., 1995). The disturbances are usually outgrown by adolescence, and treatment is generally not advised. If the problems persist, however, or develop later in adulthood, the origin is thought to be psychological, and treatment is recommended.

Sleepwalking (Somnambulism): Walking Around but Sound Asleep

Cartoonists often depict sleepwalkers groping about with their eyes closed and their arms extended forward as if to feel their way about. Actually, sleepwalkers have their eyes open with a blank stare, and rather than walking normally, they shuffle about. Their coordination is poor, and if they talk, their speech is usually unintelligible.

If an EEG recording were made during a sleepwalking episode, it would show a combination of delta waves, indicating deep sleep, and alpha and beta waves, signalling the waking state. Sleepwalkers are awake enough to carry out activities that do not require their full attention, but asleep enough not to remember having done so the following day. Sleepwalkers may get up and roam through the house or simply stand for a short time and then go back to bed (Ferber, 1989; Karacan, 1988). Occasionally they get dressed, eat a snack, or go to the bathroom. The most important concern in sleepwalking is safety. Because of their reduced alertness and coordination, sleepwalkers are at risk of hurting themselves. They have been known to walk out of windows, fall down stairs, and more.

Finally, let us dispel a myth about sleepwalking. You may have heard that it is dangerous to awaken a sleepwalker. This piece of conventional wisdom is not true.

Sleep Terrors: Screams in the Night

What is a sleep terror?

Sleep terrors usually begin with a piercing scream. The sleeper springs up in a state of panic—eyes open, perspiring, breathing rapidly, with the heart pounding at two to four times the normal rate (Karacan, 1988). Episodes usually last from 5 to 15 minutes, and then the person falls back to sleep. If not awakened during a night terror, children usually have no memory of the episode the next morning. If awakened, however, they may recall a single frightening image (Hartmann, 1981).

Parents should not be unduly alarmed by sleep terrors in young children, since up to 5 percent of them have sleep terrors (Keefauver & Guilleminault, 1994). However, episodes that continue through adolescence into adulthood are more serious. Fewer than 1 percent of adults experience sleep terrors (Hublin et al., 1999), and they often indicate extreme anxiety or other psychological problems.

Nightmares: The Worst of Dreams

How do nightmares differ from sleep terrors?

Nightmares are very frightening dreams that occur during REM sleep and are likely to be remembered in vivid detail. The most common themes are being chased, threatened, or attacked. Nightmares can be a reaction to traumatic life experiences (Hefez et al., 1987), and are more frequent at times of high fever, anxiety, and emotional upheaval. REM rebound during drug withdrawal or after long periods without sleep can also produce nightmares. Sleep terrors occur early in the night during Stage 4 sleep, whereas anxiety nightmares occur toward morning, when the REM periods are longest.

Sleeptalking (Somniloquy): Might We Reveal Secrets?

Do you sometimes talk in your sleep? Are you afraid that you might confess to something embarrassing, or reveal some deep, dark secret? Relax. Sleeptalkers rarely reply to questions, and they usually mumble words or phrases that make no sense to the listener. Sleepers can talk during any sleep stage, but most often sleeptalking occurs in Stage 1 or Stage 2 sleep (Aldrich ,1989). There is no evidence at all that sleeptalking is related to a physical or psychological disturbance—not even to a guilty conscience (Arkin, 1981).

Major Sleep Disorders

Some sleep disorders can be so debilitating that they affect a person's entire life. These disorders are narcolepsy, sleep apnea, and insomnia.

Narcolepsy: Sudden Attacks of REM Sleep

What are the major symptoms of narcolepsy?

Narcolepsy is an incurable sleep disorder characterized by excessive daytime sleepiness and uncontrollable attacks of REM sleep, usually lasting 10 to 20 minutes (American Psychiatric Association, 1994). People with narcolepsy are often unfairly stigmatized as lazy, depressed, and uninterested in their work.

Anything that causes an ordinary person to be tired can trigger a sleep attack in a narcoleptic—a heavy meal, sunbathing at the beach, or a boring lecture. A sleep attack can also be brought on by any situation that is exciting (narcoleptic attacks often occur during lovemaking) or that causes a strong emotion, such as anger or laughter.

Narcolepsy is a physiological disorder caused by an abnormality in the part of the brain that regulates sleep, and it appears to have a strong genetic component (Billiard et al., 1994; Partinen et al., 1994). Although there is no cure for narcolepsy, stimulant medications improve daytime alertness in most patients (Guilleminault, 1993; Mitler et al., 1994). Many experts also recommend scheduled naps to relieve sleepiness (Hawkins et al., 1992; Mullington & Broughton, 1993).

LINK IT!

www.websciences.org/narnet/
Narcolepsy Network

Sleep Apnea: Can't Sleep and Breathe at the Same Time

What is sleep apnea?

Sleep apnea consists of periods during sleep when breathing stops and the individual must awaken briefly to breathe (White, 1989). The major symptoms of sleep apnea are excessive daytime sleepiness and extremely loud snoring (as loud as a jackhammer), often accompanied by snorts, gasps, and choking noises.

In very severe cases, apnea may last throughout the night, with as many as 800 partial awakenings to gasp for air. Alcohol and sedative drugs aggravate the condition (Langevin et al., 1992). Severe sleep apnea can lead to chronic high blood pressure, heart problems, and even death (Lavie et al., 1995).

Sleep researcher William Dement holds a dog that is experiencing a narcoleptic sleep attack. Much has been learned about narcolepsy through research with dogs.

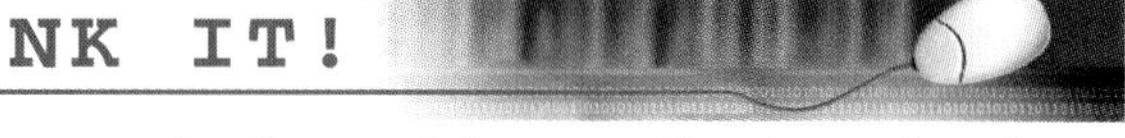

LINK IT!

www.newtechpub.com/phantom/faq/osa_faq.htm
Sleep Apnea FAQ

Insomnia: When You Can't Fall Asleep

What is insomnia?

People with **insomnia** suffer distress and impairment in daytime functioning owing to difficulty falling or staying asleep or to experiencing sleep that is light, restless, or of poor quality. Temporary insomnia, lasting three weeks or less, can result from jet lag, emotional highs or lows, or a brief illness or injury that interferes with sleep. Much more serious is chronic insomnia, which lasts for months or even years (Costa E Silva et al., 1996).

Chronic insomnia may begin as a reaction to a psychological or medical problem but persist long after the problem has been resolved.

In *Apply It!* at the end of this chapter, we examine some ways to overcome insomnia.

nightmare: A very frightening dream occurring during REM sleep.

narcolepsy (NAR-co-lep-see): A serious sleep disorder characterized by excessive daytime sleepiness and sudden, uncontrollable attacks of REM sleep.

sleep apnea: A sleep disorder characterized by periods when breathing stops during sleep and the person must awaken briefly to breathe; major symptoms are excessive daytime sleepiness and loud snoring.

insomnia: A sleep disorder characterized by difficulty falling or staying asleep or by light, restless, or poor sleep; causing distress and impaired daytime functioning.

Remember It! Sleep Disorders

1. Which is *not* a characteristic common to sleepwalking and sleep terrors in children?
   a. They occur during partial arousals from Stage 4 sleep.
   b. Episodes are usually forgotten the next morning.
   c. The disturbances occur most often in children.
   d. The disturbances indicate a psychological problem that should be treated by a mental health professional.

2. Match the disorder with the description or associated symptom.

___	1) sleep attacks during the day	a. narcolepsy
___	2) cessation of breathing during sleep; loud snoring	b. sleep apnea
___	3) difficulty falling or staying asleep	c. sleep terror
___	4) a very frightening REM dream	d. insomnia
___	5) partial awakening from Stage 4 sleep in a panic state related to a frightening dream image	e. nightmare

Answers: 1. d 2. 1) a 2) b 3) d 4) e 5) c

Altering Consciousness through Concentration and Suggestion

Sleep is an altered state of consciousness and a necessary one. We must sleep. But there are other, voluntary forms of altered consciousness. Meditation and hypnosis are two of these.

Meditation: Expanded Consciousness or Relaxation?

For what purposes is meditation used?

Meditation is a group of techniques that involve focusing attention on an object, a word, one's breathing, or body movement to block out all distractions and achieve an altered state of consciousness. Some forms of meditation—yoga, Zen, and transcendental meditation (TM)—have their roots in Eastern religions and are practised by followers of those religions to attain a higher state of spirituality. Others use these approaches to increase relaxation, reduce arousal, or expand consciousness.

Some meditators sit in a comfortable chair with eyes closed, both feet flat on the floor, and hands in the lap or simply resting on the arms of the chair. They might begin meditation by relaxing their muscles from the feet up, to achieve a deep state of relaxation. Other people concentrate on their breathing—slowly, rhythmically, in and out. In transcendental meditation, the meditator is given a mantra, a word (such as *om*) assigned by the teacher. The meditator repeats the mantra over and over during meditation to block out unwanted thoughts and facilitate the meditative state. Dr. Herbert Benson (1975) suggests that any word or sound will do. Moreover, he asserts that the benefits of meditation can be achieved through simple relaxation techniques. Do *Try It!* to experience Benson's relaxation response.

Try It!

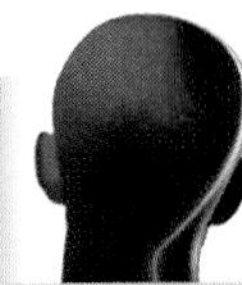

Relaxing through Meditation

Find a quiet place and sit in a comfortable position.

1. Close your eyes.
2. Relax all your muscles deeply. Begin with your feet and move slowly upward, relaxing the muscles in your legs, buttocks, abdomen, chest, shoulders, neck, and finally your face. Allow your whole body to remain in this deeply relaxed state.
3. Now concentrate on your breathing, and breathe in and out through your nose. Each time you breathe out, silently say the word *om* to yourself.
4. Repeat this process for 20 minutes. (You can open your eyes to look at your watch periodically, but don't use an alarm.) When you are finished, remain seated for a few minutes–first with your eyes closed, and then with them open.

Benson recommends that you maintain a passive attitude. Don't try to force yourself to relax. Just let it happen. If a distracting thought comes to mind, ignore it and just repeat *one* each time you exhale. It is best to practise this exercise once or twice each day, but not within two hours of your last meal. Digestion interferes with the relaxation response.

Hypnosis: Look into My Eyes

What is hypnosis, and when is it most useful?

Have you ever been hypnotized? Many people are fascinated by this unusual, somewhat mysterious phenomenon. Other people doubt that it even exists.

Hypnosis is a trance-like state of concentrated and focused attention, heightened suggestibility, and diminished response to external stimuli. In the hypnotic state, people suspend their usual rational and logical ways of thinking and perceiving, and allow themselves to experience distortions in perceptions, memories, and thinking. Under hypnosis, people may experience positive hallucinations, in which they see, hear, touch, smell, or taste things that are not present in the environment; or they may have negative hallucinations and fail to perceive those things that are present.

About 80 to 95 percent of people are hypnotizable to some degree, but only 5 percent can reach the deepest levels of trance (Nash & Baker, 1984). The ability to become completely absorbed in imaginative activities is characteristic of highly hypnotizable people (Nadon et al., 1991). Silva and Kirsch (1992) found that individuals' fantasy-proneness and their expectations of responding to hypnotic suggestions were predictors of hypnotizability.

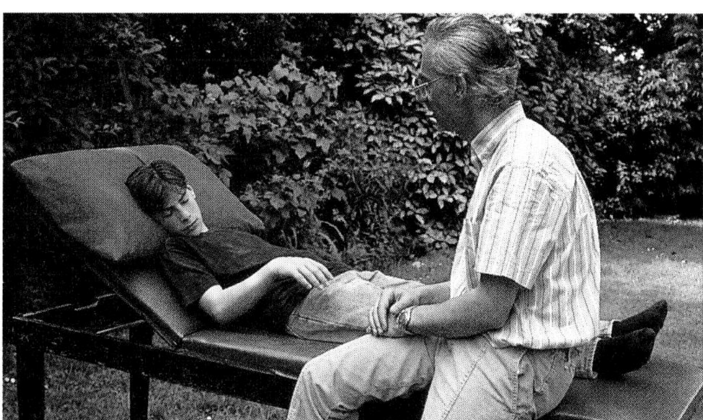

Hypnosis is a trance-like state of concentrated attention and heightened suggestibility. This hypnotherapist suggested to the youth that a balloon was tied to his right hand—and the youth began to raise his arm accordingly.

LINK IT!

www.hypnosis.com/faq
Hypnosis FAQ

serendip.brynmawr.edu/Mind/Trance.html
Trance and Trauma: Functional Nervous Disorders and the Subconscious Mind

Hypnosis: Separating Fact from Fiction

Hypnosis has been studied extensively in Canada—for example, by Nick Spanos and colleagues at Carleton University and by Kenneth Bowers and colleagues at the University of Waterloo. There are many misconceptions about hypnosis. Here are the facts.

- Hypnotized subjects *are* aware of what is going on during hypnosis.
- Individuals will *not* violate their moral values under hypnosis.
- Individuals *cannot* demonstrate superhuman strength or perform amazing feats because they are hypnotized.
- Memory is *not* more accurate under hypnosis.
- Hypnotized individuals will *not* reveal embarrassing secrets.
- Hypnotized individuals will *not* relive events as they believe the events should have occurred (i.e., rather than as they actually took place in childhood).
- Hypnotized individuals are *not* under the complete control of the hypnotist.
- The hypnotized person's responses are often automatic and involuntary (Bowers & Woody, 1996).

meditation: A group of techniques that involve focusing attention on an object, a word, one's breathing, or body movement in order to block out all distractions and achieve an altered state of consciousness.

hypnosis: A trance-like state of concentrated, focused attention, heightened suggestibility, and diminished response to external stimuli.

Medical Uses of Hypnosis: It's Not Just Entertainment

Hypnosis is now recognized as a viable technique for use in medicine, dentistry, and psychotherapy. It has been particularly helpful in the control of pain (Spanos et al., 1990). It has also been used successfully to treat a wide range of disorders, including high blood pressure, bleeding, psoriasis, severe morning sickness, side effects of chemotherapy, and burns (Kelly & Kelly, 1985). Other problems that have responded well to hypnosis are asthma, severe insomnia, some phobias (Orne, 1983), and multiple personality disorder (Kluft, 1992). Furthermore, recent studies suggest that hypnosis can be useful in treating warts (Ewin, 1992), repetitive nightmares (Kingsbury, 1993), and sexual dysfunctions such as inhibited sexual desire (Hammond, 1992) and impotence (Crasilneck, 1992).

Suppose you are overweight, or you smoke or drink heavily. Would a quick trip to a hypnotist rid you of overeating or other bad habits? Hypnosis has been only moderately effective in weight control and virtually useless in overcoming drug and alcohol abuse (Orne, 1983).

Critics' Explanations of Hypnosis: Is It Really What It Seems?

Because there is no reliable way to determine whether a person is truly hypnotized, some critics offer other explanations for behaviour occurring during this state. One explanation is that people are simply acting out the role suggested by the hypnotist (Spanos, 1991). Although some people who declare that they are hypnotized may be role-playing, this theory does not adequately explain how people can undergo surgery with hypnosis rather than a general anesthetic (Kroger & Fezler, 1976).

Another idea is that behaviour under hypnosis is no different from behaviour of other highly motivated individuals. Barber (1970) found that "both hypnotic and waking control subjects are responsive to suggestions for analgesia [pain relief], age regression, hallucinations and amnesia if they have positive attitudes toward the situation and are motivated to respond" (p. 27).

Next we will explore how psychoactive substances produce altered states of consciousness.

Altered States of Consciousness and Psychoactive Drugs

The altered states of consciousness we have examined thus far are natural ones. We will now explore effect of psychoactive drugs. A **psychoactive drug** is any substance that alters mood, perception, or thought. Some of these drugs are legal, but most are

Remember It!

Meditation and Hypnosis

1. Which is *not* a proposed use of meditation?
   a. to promote relaxation
   b. to substitute for anesthesia during surgery
   c. to bring a person to a higher level of spirituality
   d. to alter consciousness
2. A special mantra is used in transcendental meditation. (true/false)
3. According to Dr. Herbert Benson, the beneficial effects of meditation cannot be duplicated with simple relaxation techniques. (true/false)
4. Which of the following statements is true of people under hypnosis?
   a. They will often violate their moral code.
   b. They are much stronger than in the normal waking state.
   c. They can be made to experience distortions in their perceptions.
   d. Their memory is more accurate than during the normal waking state.
5. For a moderately hypnotizable person, which use of hypnosis would probably be most successful?
   a. for relief from pain
   b. for surgery instead of a general anesthetic
   c. for treating drug addiction
   d. for improving memory

Answers: 1. b 2. true 3. false 4. c 5. a

TABLE 4.2

Risk Factors and Protective Factors for Adolescent Drug Use and Abuse

	Risk Factors	Protective Factors
Peer Influences	Peers use and encourage use Peers provide substances	Peers are not users
Educational variables	Poor school performance Low educational aspirations	Good grades High educational aspirations
Social/family variables	Family conflict Family alcohol and/or drug abuse Lack of religious commitment	Positive family relationships Perceived sanctions against drug use Involvement in religious community
Environmental variables	Extreme poverty Neighbourhood disorganization Availability of drugs	
Psychological/ behavioural variables	Low self-esteem Antisocial behaviour Need for excitement Poor impulse control Stressful life events Depression Anxiety Apathy and pessimism Alienation and rebelliousness	Self-acceptance Law abidance Perceived future opportunities

Source: Adapted from Hawkins et al., 1992; Newcomb, 1997; Newcomb & Felix-Ortiz, 1992.

not. When these drugs are approved for medical use only, they are called *controlled substances*.

In Canada, there is considerable concern about the sale and use of illicit drugs. But in terms of "damage to users, harm to society, and numbers of addicts," alcohol and tobacco are "the most serious problem drugs by far" (Goldstein & Kalant, 1990, p. 151b).

Why do so many Canadians use psychoactive drugs? There are many reasons for taking drugs, and users often do not recognize their real motives. Some people take drugs to cope with or relieve anxiety, depression, or boredom (Baker, 1988). Others use drugs just to feel good, experience a thrill, or conform to social pressures. Others use psychoactive drugs for their medical benefits.

Peer influence is the factor most highly correlated with adolescents' use of illicit drugs, cigarettes, and alcohol. According to Dinges and Oetting (1993), there is a "90 percent correspondence between an adolescent's use of particular drugs and the use of those exact drugs by friends" (p. 264). Table 4.2 summarizes the risk factors and protective factors associated with adolescent drug use and abuse.

Drug Dependence: Slave to a Substance

What is the difference between physical and psychological drug dependence?

The effects of drugs are not always predictable. Some drugs create a physical or chemical dependence; others create a psychological dependence. **Physical drug dependence** comes about as a result of the body's natural ability to protect itself against harmful substances by developing a **drug tolerance**. This means that the user becomes progressively less affected by the drug

psychoactive drug: A drug that alters normal mental functioning–mood, perception, or thought; if used medically, called a controlled substance.

drug dependence (physical): A compulsive pattern of drug use in which the user develops a drug tolerance coupled with unpleasant withdrawal symptoms when the drug is discontinued.

drug tolerance: A condition in which the user becomes progressively less affected by the drug so that larger and larger doses are necessary to maintain the same effect.

and must take larger doses to get the same effect or high (Ramsey & Woods, 1997). Tolerance grows because the brain adapts to the presence of the drug by responding less intensely to it. The various bodily processes adjust in order to continue to function with the drug in the system.

Once drug tolerance is established, a person cannot function normally without the drug. If the drug is taken away, the user begins to suffer withdrawal symptoms. The **withdrawal symptoms**, both physical and psychological, are usually the exact opposite of the effects produced by the drug. For example, withdrawal from stimulants leaves a person exhausted and depressed; withdrawal from tranquilizers leaves a person nervous and agitated.

If physical dependence alone explained drug addiction, there would be no problem with drugs long thought to be physically non-addictive. Once the period of physical withdrawal was over, the desire for the drug would end along with the withdrawal symptoms. But this is not the case—there is more to drug addiction than physical dependence. **Psychological drug dependence** is a craving or irresistible urge for the drug's pleasurable effects, and it is more difficult to combat than physical dependence (O'Brien, 1996).

Four factors influence the addictive potential of a drug: (1) how quickly the effects of the drug are felt; (2) how pleasurable the drug's effects are; (3) how long the pleasurable effects last; and (4) how much discomfort is experienced when the drug is discontinued (Medzerian, 1991). With the most addictive drugs, the pleasurable effects are felt almost immediately but are short-lived. For example, the intensely pleasurable effects of crack cocaine are felt in seven seconds but last only about five minutes. Because the discomfort is intense after the pleasurable effects wear off, the user is highly motivated to continue taking the drug. With any drug, the abuse potential is higher if the drug is injected rather than taken orally, and higher still if it is smoked rather than injected.

Psychoactive drugs alter consciousness in a variety of ways. Let's consider the various alterations produced by the major categories of drugs: stimulants, hallucinogens (or psychedelics), and depressants.

LINK IT!

itsa.ucsf.edu/~ddrc
Drug Dependence Research Center Home Page

www.arf.org
Addiction Research Foundation

www.health.org/index.htm
U.S. National Clearinghouse for Alcohol and Drug Information

Stimulants: Speeding Up the Nervous System

How do stimulants affect the user?

Stimulants, often called **uppers,** speed up the central nervous system, suppress appetite, and can make a person feel more awake, alert, and energetic. Stimulants increase pulse, blood pressure, and respiration rate; they also reduce cerebral blood flow (Mathew & Wilson, 1991). In higher doses, they make people feel nervous, jittery, and restless, and they can cause shaking or trembling and can interfere with sleep.

No stimulant actually delivers energy to the body. Instead, a stimulant forces the body to use some of its stored-up energy sooner and in greater amounts than it would naturally. When the stimulant's effect wears off, the body's natural energy is depleted. This leaves the person feeling exhausted and depressed.

There are *legal* stimulants such as caffeine and nicotine, *controlled* stimulants such as amphetamines, and *illegal* stimulants such as cocaine.

Caffeine: The Most Widely Used Drug

Caffeine is the world's most widely used drug. If you cannot start your day without a cup of coffee (or two, or more), you may be addicted to it. Coffee, tea, cola drinks, chocolate, and more than 100 prescription and over-the-counter drugs contain caffeine. They provide a mild jolt to the nervous system, at least temporarily. Caffeine makes us more mentally alert and can help us stay awake. Many people use caffeine to lift their mood, but laboratory studies reveal that one hour after consuming medium or high doses of caffeine, subjects show significantly higher levels of anxiety, depression, and hostility (Veleber & Templer, 1984).

Nicotine: A Deadly Poison

Nicotine is a poison so strong that the body must develop a tolerance for it almost immediately—in only hours, in contrast to days or weeks for heroin, and usually months for alcohol. It is estimated that 20 to 30 percent of Canadians smoke, and that 40 000 Canadians die each year from cigarette smoking. "Cigarette smoking results in the premature death of approximately 50 percent of smokers" (Henningfield et al., 1996, p. 1857). The many health problems associated with smoking are discussed in Chapter 11.

Amphetamines: Energy to Burn—at a Price

What effects do amphetamines have on the user?

Amphetamines form a class of stimulants that increase arousal, relieve fatigue, suppress the appetite, and give a rush of energy. In low to moderate doses, these stimulants may temporarily improve athletic and intellectual performance. A person who takes amphetamines becomes more alert and energetic, experiences mild euphoria, and usually becomes more talkative, animated, and restless.

In high doses—100 milligrams or more—amphetamines can cause confused and disorganized behaviour, extreme fear and suspiciousness, delusions and hallucinations, aggressiveness and antisocial behaviour, and even manic behaviour and paranoia. One powerful amphetamine, known as *methamphetamine* ("crank" or "speed"), now comes in a smokable form—"ice," which is highly addictive and can be fatal.

Withdrawal from amphetamines leaves a person physically exhausted, sleeping for 10 to 15 hours or more. The user awakens in a stupor, extremely depressed and intensely hungry. Victims of fatal overdoses of stimulants usually have multiple hemorrhages in the brain.

Cocaine: Snorting White Powder, Smoking Crack

How does cocaine affect the user?

Cocaine, a stimulant derived from coca leaves, can be sniffed as a white powder, injected intravenously, or smoked in the form of crack. The rush of well-being is dramatically intense and powerful, but it is just as dramatically short-lived. In the case of cocaine, the euphoria lasts no more than 30 to 45 minutes; with crack, however, the effect lasts no more than 5 to 10 minutes (Julien, 1995). In both cases, the euphoria is followed by an equally intense **crash** that is marked by depression, anxiety, agitation, and a powerful craving for more of the drug (Gawin, 1991).

Cocaine stimulates the reward or "pleasure" pathways in the brain, which use the neurotransmitter dopamine (Landry, 1997). With continued use, the reward systems fail to function normally and the user becomes incapable of feeling any pleasure except from the drug (Gawin, 1991). The main withdrawal symptoms are psychological—the inability to feel pleasure and the craving for more cocaine (Gawin & Ellinwood, 1988).

Cocaine constricts the blood vessels, raises blood pressure, speeds up the heart, quickens respiration, and can even cause epileptic seizures in people who have no history of epilepsy (Pascual-Leone et al., 1990). Over time, or even quickly in high doses, cocaine can cause heart palpitations, an irregular heartbeat, and heart attacks (Lange et al., 1989). Smart and Adlaf (1992), at the Addiction Research Foundation in Toronto, note that cocaine use is relatively rare in Canada. For instance, in Ontario fewer than 2 percent of adolescents have used cocaine.

The cheapest and perhaps the most dangerous form of cocaine, **crack** can produce a powerful dependency in several weeks. Crack may be "the most addicting form of the most addicting drug" (Lundgren, 1986, p. 7).

withdrawal symptoms: The physical and psychological symptoms (usually the opposite of those produced by the drug) that occur when a regularly used drug is discontinued and that terminate when the drug is taken again.

drug dependence (psychological): A craving or irresistible urge for a drug's pleasurable effects.

stimulants: A category of drugs that speed up activity in the central nervous system, suppress appetite, and cause a person to feel more awake, alert, and energetic.

uppers: A slang term for stimulants.

amphetamines: A class of central nervous system stimulants that increase arousal, relieve fatigue, and suppress the appetite.

cocaine: A stimulant that produces a feeling of euphoria.

crash: The feelings of depression, exhaustion, irritability, and anxiety that occur following an amphetamine, a cocaine, or a crack high.

crack: The most potent, inexpensive, and addictive form of cocaine, and the form that is smoked.

Remember It!

Drug Tolerance, Drug Dependence, and Stimulants

1. Which of the following does not necessarily occur with drug tolerance?
   a. The body adjusts to functioning with the drug in the system.
   b. The person needs larger and larger doses of the drug to get the desired effect.
   c. The user becomes progressively less affected by the drug.
   d. The user develops a craving for the pleasurable effects of the drug.
2. During withdrawal from a drug, the user experiences symptoms that are the opposite of the effects produced by the drug. (true/false)
3. Psychological dependence on a drug is more difficult to combat than physical dependence. (true/false)
4. Match the stimulant with the appropriate description.

___ 1) responsible for the most deaths	a. caffeine
___ 2) used to increase arousal, relieve fatigue, and suppress appetite	b. cigarettes
___ 3) found in coffee, tea, chocolate, and colas	c. amphetamines
___ 4) snorted or injected	d. crack
___ 5) most dangerous, potent, and addictive form of cocaine	e. cocaine

Answers: 1. d 2. true 3. true 4. 1) b 2) c 3) a 4) e 5) d

Hallucinogens: Seeing, Hearing, and Feeling What Is Not There

What are the main effects of hallucinogens, and what are three psychoactive drugs classified as hallucinogens?

The **hallucinogens**, or psychedelics, are drugs that can alter and distort perceptions of time and space, alter mood, and produce feelings of unreality. Hallucinogens have been used for recreation and in religious rituals and ceremonies in diverse cultures since ancient times (Millman & Beeder, 1994). As the name implies, hallucinogens also cause **hallucinations**, sensations that have no basis in external reality (Andreasen & Black, 1991; Miller & Gold, 1994).

Rather than producing a relatively predictable effect as do most other drugs, hallucinogens usually magnify the mood or the frame of mind of the user at the time the drug is taken. The hallucinogens we will discuss are LSD, Ecstasy, and marijuana.

LSD: Mind Altering, Not Mind Expanding

LSD, sometimes referred to simply as "acid," is the acronym for lysergic acid diethylamide. The average LSD "trip" lasts 10 to 12 hours and usually produces extreme perceptual changes—visual hallucinations and distortions. Emotions can become very intense and unstable, ranging from euphoria to anxiety, panic, and depression (Miller & Gold, 1994). LSD sometimes causes bad trips, which can leave the user in a state of terror. Some bad LSD trips have ended in accidents, death, or suicide. Sometimes a person who has taken LSD experiences a **flashback**—a brief, sudden recurrence of a trip. Flashbacks can occur as many as five years after LSD use (APA, 1994). Marijuana and some other drugs may trigger LSD flashbacks (Gold, 1994).

The Newest Trend in Designer Drug: Ecstasy (MDMA)

Ecstasy is a designed drug—a laboratory creation—that is a cross between a hallucinogen and an amphetamine. As many young people already know, it is a popular drug of abuse with teenagers, especially those who attend raves (Schwartz & Miller, 1997). The drug's main appeal is its psychological effect—a feeling of relatedness and connectedness with others (Taylor, 1996). But animal experiments with MDMA have revealed some disturbing findings—irreversible destruction of serotonin-releasing neurons (Green & Goodwin, 1996). MDMA is also more toxic than most other hallucinogens and should be considered a dangerous drug.

Marijuana: More Harmful Than We Once Believed

In Canada, marijuana is probably the most widely used illicit drug. **Marijuana** tends to produce a feeling of well-being, promotes relaxation, and lowers inhibitions and anxiety. The user may experience an increased sensitivity to sights, sounds, and touch, as well as perceptual distortions and a "slowing" of time.

THC (tetrahydrocannabinol), the ingredient in marijuana that produces the high, remains in the body for days or even weeks (Julien, 1995). A person who smokes only one marijuana cigarette, or joint, every few weeks is never completely free of THC. Marijuana impairs attention and coordination and slows reaction time; these effects make operating complex machinery such as an automobile dangerous, even after the feeling of intoxication has passed.

Marijuana can interfere with concentration, logical thinking, and the ability to form new memories. It can produce fragmentation in thought as well as confusion in remembering recent occurrences (Fletcher et al., 1996; Herkenham, 1992). Many of the receptor sites for marijuana are in the hippocampus, which explains why memory is affected (Matsuda et al., 1990). Chronic use of marijuana has been associated with loss of motivation, general apathy, and decline in school performance—referred to as the amotivational syndrome (Andreasen & Black, 1991).

Marijuana can cause respiratory damage even faster than cigarette smoking (Tzu-Chin et al., 1988). Marijuana abuse affects the reproductive system in males, causing a 20 percent impotence rate, a 44 percent reduction in testosterone levels (Kolodny et al., 1979), a 30 to 70 percent reduction in sperm count, and an abnormal appearance of sperm cells (Hembree et al., 1979). In women, failure to ovulate, other menstrual irregularities, and lower-birth-weight babies have been associated with heavy marijuana smoking (Hingson et al., 1982; Kolodny et al. 1979).

Marijuana has been prescribed by doctors to treat the eye disease glaucoma (Restak, 1993) and in controlling nausea and stimulating appetite in patients receiving chemotherapy for cancer or AIDS (Fackelmann, 1997). But, as discussed in the *It Happened in Canada* box on the next page, there is a continuing controversy about whether marijuana should be legalized for medical purposes.

Depressants: Slowing Down the Nervous System

What are some of the effects of depressants, and what drugs make up this category?

Depressants (sometimes called **downers**) decrease activity in the central nervous system, slow down body functions,

Marijuana, the most widely used illicit drug in North America, has been associated with loss of motivation, general apathy, and decline in school performance.

hallucinogens (hal-lu-SIN-o-jenz): A category of drugs, sometimes called psychedelics, that alter perception and mood and can cause hallucinations.

hallucination: An imaginary sensation.

LSD (lysergic acid diethylamide): A powerful hallucinogen with unpredictable effects ranging from perceptual changes and vivid hallucinations to states of panic and terror.

flashback: The brief recurrence of effects a person has experienced while taking LSD or other hallucinogens, occurring suddenly and without warning at a later time.

Ecstasy (MDMA): A designer drug that is a hallucinogen-amphetamine and can produce permanent damage of the serotonin-releasing neurons.

marijuana: A hallucinogen with effects ranging from relaxation and giddiness to perceptual distortions and hallucinations.

THC tetrahydrocannabinol: The principal psychoactive ingredient in marijuana and hashish.

and reduce sensitivity to outside stimulation. Within this category of drugs are the sedative-hypnotics (alcohol, barbiturates, and minor tranquilizers) and the narcotics, or opiates.

IT HAPPENED IN CANADA

Medicinal Use of Marijuana

Should marijuana be available to people who need it for medicinal purposes? This is a difficult question that has been at the forefront of many court debates and decisions all across Canada. The debate is complicated by the fact that while marijuana possession and use is illegal in Canada, recent research suggests that it may just be a very effective treatment for a variety of side effects associated with many medical conditions. For instance, marijuana appears to be an effective treatment for AIDS-related syndrome, intro-ocular pressure caused by glaucoma, chemotherapy-related nausea, as well as muscle spasticity arising from spinal cord injuries, epilepsy, and multiple sclerosis. It is also estimated that over 200 000 Canadians might benefit from marijuana's medical effects. And perhaps these findings are changing the way the public thinks about the use of marijuana for both medical and non-medical purposes. According to a recent poll conducted by the *National Post,* 65 percent of Canadians would like to see possession of small amounts of marijuana decriminalized, and 92 percent of them believe that marijuana should be legal for medical purposes.

Recent efforts on the part of Federal Government have tended to be consistent with the change in public opinion. Section 56 of the Controlled Drugs and Substances Act now allows Canadians to obtain exemptions to the nation's marijuana laws. The amendment has already had an effect in the courts. For instance, in August 2000, the Ontario Court of Appeal decided that Terrance Parker could be both a legal marijuana grower and user as long as the substance was required for medical purposes. Similar judgments have been made in courts across the country. But the application of this new amendment to the Drug Act has not been without complications. Police authorities in many localities have been inconsistent in recognizing the new law and have either seized or even arrested some people who have been given permission to possess marijuana as a therapeutic drug. (Based on Handelman, 2000; "Marijuana as medicine," 2000; "Just say yes," 2000.)

Alcohol: The Nation's Number One Drug Problem

Even though **alcohol** is a depressant, the first few drinks seem to relax and enliven at the same time. But the more alcohol is put into the bloodstream, the more the central nervous system is depressed. As drinking increases, the symptoms of drunkenness mount—slurred speech, poor coordination, staggering. Men tend to become more aggressive (Pihl et al., 1997) and more sexually aroused (Roehrich & Kinder, 1991) but less able to perform sexually (Crowe & George, 1989). Too much alcohol can cause a person to lose consciousness, and extremely large amounts can kill. The dangers from overdrinking were made obvious when one student at the University of Guelph died in 1988 after a night of partying. Similar incidents have been reported both in Canada and the United States (Cohen, 1997). Table 4.3 shows the effects of various blood alcohol levels.

Barbiturates: Sedatives That Can Kill in Overdose

Barbiturates depress the central nervous system and, depending on the dose, can act as a sedative or a sleeping pill. People who abuse barbiturates become drowsy and confused. Their thinking and judgment suffer, and their coordination and reflexes are affected (Henningfield & Ator, 1986). Barbiturates can kill if taken in overdose, and a lethal dose can be as little as only three times the prescribed dose. The popular **minor tranquilizers**, the benzodiazepines, came on the scene in the early 1960s and are sold under the brand names Valium, Librium, Dalmane, and, more recently, Xanax (also used as an antidepressant). About 90 million prescriptions for minor tranquilizers are filled each year. Benzodiazepines are prescribed for several medical and psychological disorders and are considered to be generally effective and safe (Cole & Chiarello, 1990). They are rarely used recreationally (Woods et al., 1987). Alcohol and benzodiazepines, when taken together, are a potentially fatal combination.

Narcotics: Drugs from the Opium Poppy

What are the general effects of narcotics, and what are several drugs in this category?

The word *narcotic* comes from a Greek word meaning "stupor." **Narcotics** produce both a pain-relieving and a calming effect. All

TABLE 4.3

Behavioural Effects Associated with Different Blood Alcohol Levels

Blood Alcohol Level (in milligrams of alcohol per millilitre of blood)	Behavioural Effects
0.05	Alertness is lowered, judgment is impaired, inhibitions are lowered, and the user relaxes and feels good.
0.10	Reaction is slowed, motor functions are impaired, and the user is less cautious.
0.15	Reaction time is slowed markedly; the user may stagger, slur speech, and act impulsively.
0.20	Perceptual and motor capabilities are markedly depressed; the user shows obvious intoxication.
0.25	Motor functions and sensory perceptions are severely distorted. The user may see double and fall asleep.
0.30	The user is conscious but in a stupor and not able to comprehend events in the environment.
0.35	The user is completely anesthetized.
0.40–0.80	The user is unconscious. Respiration and heartbeat stop. User dies (blood level of 0.40 causes death for 50% of people; death comes by 0.80 for the rest.)

Source: Adapted from Hawkins et al., 1992; Newcomb, 1997; Newcomb & Felix-Ortiz, 1992.

narcotics originate from opium, a dark, gummy substance derived from the opium poppy. Opium affects mainly the brain and the bowel. It paralyzes the intestinal muscles, which is why it is used medically to treat diarrhea. If you have ever taken paregoric, you have had a little tincture of opium. Because opium suppresses the cough centre, it is used in some cough medicines. Both morphine and codeine, two drugs prescribed for pain, are natural constituents of opium.

A highly addictive narcotic derived from morphine is **heroin**. Heroin addicts describe a sudden "rush," or euphoria, followed by drowsiness, inactivity, and impaired concentration. Withdrawal symptoms begin about 6 to 24 hours after use, and the addict becomes physically sick (APA, 1994). Nausea, diarrhea, depression, stomach cramps, insomnia, and pain grow worse and worse until they become intolerable—unless the person gets another fix. Heroin use has doubled since the mid-1980s (Leland, 1996).

Review & Reflect 4.1 provides a summary of the effects and withdrawal symptoms of the major psychoactive drugs.

How Drugs Affect the Brain

Eating, drinking, and sexual activity—in fact, all the natural reinforcers—have one thing in common with all addictive drugs. They increase the availability of the neurotransmitter dopamine in a part of the brain's limbic system known as the *nucleus accumbens*. The stimulation of the nucleus accumbens by dopamine

depressants: Drugs that decrease activity in the central nervous system, slow down bodily functions, and reduce sensitivity to outside stimulation.

downers: A slang term for depressants.

alcohol: A central nervous system depressant.

barbiturates: A class of central nervous system depressants used as sedatives, sleeping pills, and anesthetics; addictive, and in overdose can cause coma or death.

tranquilizer (minor): A central nervous system depressant that calms the user (examples: Valium, Librium, Dalmane, Xanax).

narcotics: Derived from the opium poppy, a class of depressant drugs that have pain-relieving and calming effects.

heroin: A highly addictive, partly synthetic narcotic derived from morphine.

plays an important role in reinforcement and reward (Di Chiara, 1997).

There is now ample evidence that dopamine is involved in the rewarding and motivational effects produced by a long list of drugs, including alcohol, amphetamines, cocaine (Landry, 1997), marijuana, heroin (Tanda et al., 1997), and nicotine (Pich et al., 1997). Amphetamines, alcohol, and nicotine stimulate the release of dopamine, whereas both cocaine and amphetamines slow the reuptake of dopamine at the synapses, and thus increase and prolong its reinforcing effects (Volkow et al., 1997a; 1997b).

Opiates such as morphine and heroin mimic the effects of the brain's own endorphins, which make us feel good, and have analgesic, or pain-relieving, properties.

Alcohol, barbiturates, and benzodiazepines (which include Valium and Librium) act upon GABA receptors (Harris et al., 1992). GABA is primarily an inhibitory neurotransmitter that slows down the central nervous system. Thus, stimulating the release of GABA by ingesting alcohol or tranquilizers has a calming and sedating effect. If enough GABA is released, it can shut down the brain. This is why the combination of alcohol and tranquilizers is potentially so deadly.

Unfortunately, most addicts experience a virtually irresistible compulsion to use drugs and are apparently unable to consider the likely consequences of their acts—the loss of the love and respect of family and friends, of money, of jobs, of health, and even their lives (Leshner, 1999).

REVIEW & REFLECT 4.1
The Effects and Withdrawal Symptoms of Some Psychoactive Drugs

Psychoactive Drug	Effects	Withdrawal Symptoms
Stimulants		
Tobacco (nicotine)	Effects range from alertness to calmness; lowers appetite for carbohydrates; increases pulse rate and other metabolic processes.	Irritability, anxiety, increased appetite.
Caffeine	Produces wakefulness and alertness; increases metabolism but slows reaction time.	Headache, depression.
Amphetamines	Increase metabolism and alertness; elevate mood, cause wakefulness, suppress appetite.	Fatigue, increased appetite, depression, long periods of sleep, irritability.
Cocaine	Brings on euphoric mood, energy boost, feeling of excitement; suppresses appetite.	Depression, fatigue, increased appetite, long periods of sleep, irritability.
Hallucinogens		
Marijuana	Generally produces euphoria, relaxation; affects ability to store new memories.	Anxiety, difficulty sleeping, decreased appetite, hyperactivity.
LSD	Produces excited exhilaration, hallucinations, experiences perceived as insightful and profound.	
Depressants		
Alcohol	First few drinks stimulate and enliven while lowering anxiety and inhibitions; higher doses have a sedative effect, slowing reaction time, impairing motor control and perceptual ability.	Tremors, nausea, sweating, depression, weakness, irritability, and in some cases hallucinations.
Tranquilizers (e.g., Valium, Xanax)	Lower anxiety, have calming and sedative effect, decrease muscular tension.	Restlessness, anxiety, irritability, muscle tension, difficulty sleeping.
Barbiturates (e.g., phenobarbital)	Promote sleep, have calming and sedative effect, decrease muscular tension, impair coordination and reflexes.	Sleeplessness, anxiety; sudden withdrawal can cause seizures, cardiovascular collapse, and death.
Narcotics		
Opium, morphine, heroin	Produces euphoria, relaxes muscles, suppresses pain, causes constipation.	Anxiety, restlessness, diarrhea, nausea, muscle spasms, chills and sweating, runny nose.

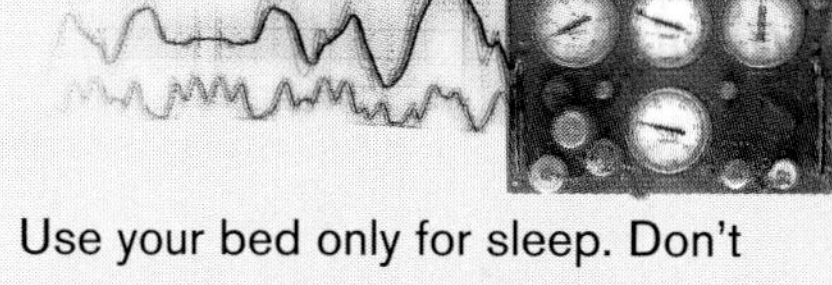

Apply It!

Battling Insomnia

As we saw in this chapter, insomnia is a sleep disorder whereby a person has trouble falling or staying asleep or whereby sleep is light, restless, or of poor quality.

What causes insomnia? Sleep researchers believe that most causes are psychological in origin. Some of the major causes include the following (Bootzin & Perlis, 1992; Costa E Silva et al., 1996; Mendelson, 1995; Morin & Ware, 1996):

- Psychological disorders, such as depression, anxiety disorders, or alcohol or other drug abuse.
- Medical problems such as chronic pain, breathing problems, or gastrointestinal disorders.
- Circadian rhythm disturbances caused by shift work, jet lag, or a chronic mismatch between a person's body time and clock time.
- Use of various drugs, such as caffeine, prescription drugs, nicotine, alcohol, tranquilizers, sleeping pills, and so on.
- Poor sleep environment with conditions that may be too noisy, hot, cold, or bright.
- Poor sleep habits, such as spending too much non-sleep time in bed, taking unnecessary naps, or having irregular sleep times; or association of bedtime with the frustration of not being able to get to sleep.

Sleeping Pills: Do They Help?

A person whose sleep is disturbed by insomnia may resort to a variety of sleep "aids," including tranquilizers, over-the-counter sleep products, and the most widely used drug of all—alcohol. A few drinks at bedtime may get you to sleep faster, but there is a price to be paid: lighter sleep, more awakenings, and less sleep overall (Johnson et al., 1998). Over-the-counter sleep aids are useless in serious cases of insomnia because instead of actually inducing sleep, they simply cause grogginess (Morin & Wooten, 1996). These products can be dangerous if taken in higher-than-recommended doses (Meltzer, 1990). Research also indicates, however, that some medications prescribed by physicians can reduce the effects of temporary insomnia. These drugs are called benzodiazepines (Dement, 1992; Vogel, 1992).

Hints for a Better Night's Sleep

So what can you do to battle insomnia and improve the quality of your sleep? Here are some good, research-based suggestions (Murtagh & Greenwood, 1995).

- Use your bed only for sleep. Don't read, study, write letters, watch television, eat, or talk on the phone on your bed.
- Leave the bedroom whenever you cannot fall asleep after 10 minutes. Go to another room and read, watch television, or listen to music. Don't return to bed for another try until you feel more tired. Repeat the process as many times as necessary until you fall asleep within 10 minutes.
- Establish a consistent, relaxing ritual to follow each night just before bedtime. For example, take a warm bath, eat a small snack, brush your teeth, pick out your clothes for the next day, and so on.
- Set your alarm and wake up at the same time every day, including weekends, regardless of how much you have slept. No naps are allowed during the day.
- Exercise regularly—but not within several hours of bedtime. (Exercise raises body temperature and makes it more difficult to fall asleep.)
- Establish regular mealtimes. Don't eat heavy or spicy meals close to bedtime. If you must eat then, try milk and a few crackers.
- Beware of caffeine and nicotine—they are sleep disturbers. Avoid caffeine within six hours and smoking within one or two hours of bedtime.
- Avoid wrestling with your problems when you go to bed. Try counting backward from 1000 by twos; or try a progressive relaxation exercise.

Remember It!

Hallucinogens and Depressants

1. Which category of drugs alters perception and mood and can cause hallucinations?
   a. stimulants
   b. depressants
   c. hallucinogens
   d. narcotics
2. Which of the following is *not* associated with long-term use of marijuana?
   a. respiratory damage
   b. loss of motivation
   c. reproductive problems
   d. increased risk of heart attack and stroke
3. Decreased activity in the central nervous system is the chief effect of
   a. stimulants.
   b. depressants.
   c. hallucinogens.
   d. narcotics.
4. Which of the following is a narcotic?
   a. cocaine
   b. heroin
   c. LSD
   d. Valium
5. Narcotics have
   a. pain-relieving effects.
   b. stimulating effects.
   c. energizing effects.
   d. perception-altering effects.
6. Cocaine and amphetamines increase the effect of the neurotransmitter
   a. acetylcholine.
   b. GABA.
   c. dopamine.
   d. serotonin.

Answers: 1. c 2. d 3. b 4. b 5. a 6. c

KEY TERMS

alcohol, p. 134
altered state of consciousness, p. 112
amphetamines, p. 131
barbiturates, p. 134
circadian rhythm, p. 112
cocaine, p. 131
consciousness, p. 112
crack, p. 131
crash, p. 131
delta wave, p. 117
depressants, p. 134
downers, p. 134
drug dependence (physical), p. 129
drug dependence (psychological), p. 130
drug tolerance, p. 129
Ecstasy (MDMA), p. 132
flashback, p. 132
hallucinations, p. 132
hallucinogens, p. 132
heroin, p. 135
hypnosis, p. 127
insomnia, p. 125
LSD (lysergic acid diethylamide), p. 132
lucid dream, p. 122
marijuana, p. 133
meditation, p. 126
microsleep, p. 119
narcolepsy, p. 125
narcotics, p. 134
nightmare, p. 124
NREM dreams, p. 120
NREM sleep, p. 115
parasomnias, p. 123
psychoactive drug, p. 128
REM dreams, p. 120
REM rebound, p. 120
REM sleep, p. 116
sleep apnea, p. 125
sleep cycle, p. 117
sleep terror, p. 123
slow-wave sleep, p. 117
somnambulism, p. 123
Stage 4 sleep, p. 117
stimulants, p. 130
subjective night, p. 114
suprachiasmatic nucleus, p. 113
THC (tetrahydrocannabinol), p. 133
tranquilizer, p. 134
uppers, p. 130
withdrawal symptoms, p. 130

THINKING CRITICALLY

Evaluation

The famous sleep researcher Wilse Webb wrote a book called *Sleep, the Gentle Tyrant.* From what you have learned about sleep, explain why this is or is not a fitting title.

Point/Counterpoint

You hear much debate about the pros and cons of legalizing drugs. Present the most convincing argument possible to support each of these positions:

a. Illicit drugs should be legalized.
b. Illicit drugs should not be legalized.

Psychology in Your life

You have been asked to make a presentation to Grades 7 and 8 students about the dangers of drugs. What are the most persuasive general arguments you can give to convince them not to get involved with drugs? What are some convincing, specific arguments against using each of these drugs: alcohol, marijuana, cigarettes, and cocaine?

SUMMARY & REVIEW

What Is Consciousness?

What are some different states of consciousness?

Various states of consciousness include ordinary waking consciousness, daydreaming, sleep, and altered states brought about through meditation, hypnosis, or the use of psychoactive drugs.

Circadian Rhythms: Our 24-Hour Highs and Lows

What is a circadian rhythm, and which rhythms are most relevant to the study of sleep?

A circadian rhythm is the regular fluctuation in certain body functions from a high point to a low point within a 24-hour period. Two rhythms that are highly relevant to sleep are the sleep/wakefulness cycle and body temperature.

What is the suprachiasmatic nucleus?

The suprachiasmatic nucleus is the body's biological clock, which regulates circadian rhythms and signals the pineal gland to secrete or suppress secretion of melatonin.

What are some problems experienced by employees who work rotating shifts?

People working rotating shifts experience a disruption in their circadian rhythms that causes sleep difficulties, digestive problems, and lowered alertness, efficiency, productivity, and safety during subjective night.

Sleep: That Mysterious One-Third of Our Lives

How does a sleeper act physically during NREM sleep?

During NREM sleep, heart rate and respiration are slow and regular, blood pressure and brain activity are at a 24-hour low point, and there is little body movement and no rapid eye movements.

How does the body respond physically during REM sleep?

During REM sleep, the large muscles of the body are paralyzed, respiration and heart rates are fast and irregular, brain activity increases, and the sleeper has rapid eye movements and vivid dreams.

What is the progression of NREM stages and REM sleep that a person goes through in a typical night of sleep?

During a typical night, a person sleeps in sleep cycles, each lasting about 90 minutes. The first sleep cycle contains Stages 1, 2, 3, and 4, and REM sleep; the second contains Stages 2, 3, and 4, and REM sleep. In the remaining sleep cycles, the sleeper alternates mainly between Stage 2 and REM sleep, with each sleep cycle having progressively longer REM periods.

How do sleep patterns change over the lifespan?

Infants and young children have the longest sleep time and largest percentage of REM and deep sleep. Children from age six to puberty sleep best. The elderly typically have shorter total sleep time, more awakenings, and a virtual lack of deep sleep.

What factors influence our sleep needs?

Factors that influence our sleep needs are heredity, the amount of stress in our lives, and our emotional state.

What happens when people are deprived of REM sleep? What function does REM sleep appear to serve?

Following REM deprivation, people experience REM rebound, an increase in the percentage of REM sleep. REM sleep appears to aid in learning and memory.

How do REM and NREM dreams differ?

Dreams usually reflect the dreamer's preoccupations in waking life. Dreams tend to have commonplace settings, to be more unpleasant than pleasant, and to be less emotional and bizarre than people remember them.

In general, what have researchers found regarding the content of dreams?

REM dreams have a dream-like, story-like quality and are more vivid, visual, emotional, and bizarre than the more thought-like NREM dreams.

Sleep Disorders

What are the characteristics common to sleepwalking and night terrors?

Sleepwalking and sleep terrors occur during a partial arousal from slow-wave sleep, and the person does not come to full consciousness. Episodes are rarely recalled. These disorders are typically found in children and outgrown by adolescence, and they tend to run in families.

What is a sleep terror?

A sleep terror is a parasomnia in which the sleeper awakens from Stage 4 sleep with a scream, in a dazed, groggy, and panicky state, and with a racing heart.

How do nightmares differ from sleep terrors?

Nightmares are frightening dreams occurring during REM sleep and remembered in vivid detail. Sleep terrors occur during Stage 4 sleep, are rarely remembered, and often involve a single, frightening dream image.

What are the major symptoms of narcolepsy?

The symptoms of narcolepsy include excessive daytime sleepiness and sudden attacks of REM sleep.

What is sleep apnea?

Sleep apnea is a serious sleep disorder in which breathing stops during sleep and the person must awaken briefly to breathe. Its major symptoms are excessive daytime sleepiness and loud snoring.

What is insomnia?

Insomnia is a sleep disorder that involves difficulty falling or staying asleep, or sleep that is light, restless, or of poor quality. It can be transient or chronic, and it affects from 10 to 15 percent of the adult population.

Altering Consciousness through Concentration and Suggestion

For what purposes is meditation used?

Meditation is used by some to promote relaxation and reduce arousal, and by others to expand consciousness or attain a higher level of spirituality.

What is hypnosis, and when is it most useful?

Hypnosis, which has been used most successfully for the control of pain, is a trance-like state of consciousness characterized by focused attention, heightened suggestibility, and diminished response to external stimuli.

Altered States of Consciousness and Psychoactive Drugs

What is the difference between physical and psychological drug dependence?

With physical drug dependence, the user develops a drug tolerance so that larger and larger doses are needed to get the same effect. Withdrawal symptoms appear when the drug is discontinued and disappear when the drug is taken again. Psychological drug dependence involves an intense craving for the drug.

How do stimulants affect the user?

Stimulants speed up activity in the central nervous system, suppress appetite, and make a person feel more awake, alert, and energetic.

What effects do amphetamines have on the user?

Amphetamines increase arousal, relieve fatigue, and suppress the appetite; with continued use they result in exhaustion, depression, and agitation.

How does cocaine affect the user?

Cocaine, a stimulant, causes a feeling of euphoria and is highly addictive. Heavy use can cause heart damage, seizures, and even heart attacks.

What are the main effects of hallucinogens, and what are three psychoactive drugs classified as hallucinogens?

Hallucinogens–LSD, Ecstasy, and marijuana–can alter perception and mood, and cause hallucinations.

What are some harmful effects associated with heavy marijuana use?

There is some evidence that heavy marijuana use can cause memory problems, respiratory damage, loss of motivation, impotence, lowered testosterone levels and sperm count, irregular menstrual cycles, and lower-birth-weight babies.

What are some of the effects of depressants, and what drugs make up this category?

Depressants decrease activity in the central nervous system, slow down body functions, and reduce sensitivity to outside stimulation. Depressants include sedative-hypnotics (alcohol, barbiturates, and minor tranquilizers) and narcotics (opiates).

What are the general effects of narcotics, and what are several drugs in this category?

Narcotics, which include opium, codeine, morphine, and heroin, have both pain-relieving and calming effects.

5 Learning

Is Canada becoming a more violent society? The answer depends on whom you ask and what information you use to form your opinion. Crime statistics suggest that per capita rates of criminal offences are dropping throughout Canada and are at their lowest rate in 25 years. Yet most people would argue that this is a more violent and less friendly society than it once was. Certainly, the media play a role in our perception of crimes and have reported on some disturbing new crime trends in Canada. Since the beginning of 1997, several gangs of young girls, aged 14 to 17, have been in the news for committing crimes that have shocked us all. In Toronto, a gang called "the Spadina girls" has been linked to a series of vicious extortions and other crimes against fellow students at a local high school; police have described their actions as a "reign of terror" (Lamberti, 1998). In Victoria, seven girls were charged and some of them found guilty of murdering another teenage girl. In Saskatchewan, two teenage girls were charged with murdering a woman at a youth offender facility. Other similar events have been reported across Canada.

Teenage violence and gang behaviour have traditionally been seen as the exclusive domain of males. Like everyone in the community, psychologists and other social scientists are wondering what aspects of our society have changed to cause these new violent trends. Psychologists interested in learning theory, which is described in this chapter, would likely suggest that the young women involved in the crimes described above suffer from having poor role models at home. This negative role modelling is reinforced by movies and TV shows that portray high levels of teen violence as an acceptable way of solving conflict. But role models have also been shown to define acceptable behaviour and to reinforce proper societal values.

Our opening story provides one interpretation that accounts for societal behaviours that are very hard to understand—that is, observational learning through modelling. In observational learning, we learn by observing the behaviour of others, usually those in positions of authority or those we admire and respect, and then we may imitate that behaviour.

Psychologists study two other types of learning: operant conditioning and classical conditioning. In *operant conditioning,* an association is formed between a behaviour and its consequences—for example, between acting out violently and being rewarded by your peers for that behaviour. A third form of learning, *classical conditioning,* may also account for some of the behaviours reported above. In classical conditioning, an association is learned between one **stimulus** and another. A stimulus is any event or object in the environment to which an organism responds. Certain environmental cues (the presence of your gang, the gang's colours, the gang leader) become associated with violence.

These three kinds of learning are all-powerful forces that influence human thought and behaviour for good or for ill. They are perhaps involved in establishing and maintaining inappropriate and violent behaviour in youth gangs. But not all consequences of learning principles are negative. The same principles also help people break addictions, lose weight, study harder, and improve their lives, as you will learn.

Learning may be defined as a relatively permanent change in behaviour, capability, or attitude that is acquired through experience and cannot be attributed to illness, injury, or maturation. Several parts of this definition warrant further explanation. First, defining learning as a "relatively permanent change" excludes temporary changes in our behaviour or attitudes that could result from illness, fatigue, or fluctuations in mood. Second, by referring to changes that are "acquired through experience," we exclude some relatively permanent, readily observable changes in behaviour that occur as a result of brain injury or certain diseases. Moreover, there are observable changes as we grow and mature that have nothing to do with learning. For example, a young male at puberty does not *learn* to speak in a deeper voice; rather, his voice changes to a lower pitch as a result of maturation.

We cannot observe learning directly; instead, we must infer whether it has occurred. We draw our inferences from changes in observable behaviour or from changes in measurable capabilities and attitudes. Certainly, much learning occurs that we are not able to observe or measure. As a student, you surely remember times when you learned much more than your test scores reflected. Finally, learning does not always result in a change in behaviour or performance: sometimes we learn or acquire a capability that we may not demonstrate until we are motivated to do so.

Learning is one of the most important topics in the field of psychology, and available evidence suggests that we learn through many different avenues. This chapter explores the three basic forms of learning: classical conditioning, operant conditioning, and observational learning.

Classical Conditioning

Classical conditioning is one of the simplest forms of learning, yet it has a powerful effect on our attitudes, likes and dislikes, and emotional responses. We have all learned to respond in specific ways to a variety of words and symbols. Santa Claus, Canada Revenue, the Montreal Canadiens, and the GST are just sounds and symbols, but they tend to evoke strong emotional responses because of their associations.

The explanation for these feelings is simple—learning by association. We associate one thing with another—a positive or a negative attitude with a name, a particular gesture, a style of dress, or a manner of speaking. Our lives are profoundly influenced by the associations we learn through classical conditioning. We will now explore the work of Ivan Pavlov, whose research on the conditioned reflex in dogs revealed much of what we know about the principles of classical conditioning (sometimes referred to as "respondent" or "Pavlovian conditioning").

www.as.wvu.edu/~sbb/comm221/chapters/pavlov.htm
Classical Conditioning

Pavlov and Classical Conditioning

Ivan Pavlov (1849–1936) organized and directed research in physiology at the Institute of Experimental Medicine in St. Petersburg, Russia, from 1891 until his death 45 years later. For his classic experiments on the physiology of digestion, he won a Nobel Prize in 1904—the first Russian to be so honoured. Pavlov's study of the conditioned reflex in dogs brought him fame, and he pursued this research from about 1898 until the end of his career. His book *Conditioned Reflexes* is one of the classic works in the field of psychology.

Pavlov's contribution to psychology came about quite by accident. To conduct his study of the salivary response, Pavlov made a small incision in the side of each experimental dog's mouth. Then he attached a tube so that the flow of saliva could be diverted from the animal's mouth, through the tube, and into a container, where the saliva was collected and measured.

The purpose of this was to collect the saliva that the dogs secreted naturally in response to food placed in the mouth. But Pavlov noticed that in many cases, the dogs began to salivate even before the food was presented. Pavlov observed drops of saliva collecting in the container when the dogs heard the footsteps of the laboratory assistants coming to feed them. And he observed saliva collecting when the dogs only heard their feeding dishes rattling, when they saw the attendant who fed them, and at the mere sight of their food. How could an involuntary response such as salivation come to be associated with the sights and sounds accompanying the act of feeding? Pavlov spent the rest of his life studying this question. The type of learning that he studied is known today as "classical conditioning."

Pavlov was a meticulous researcher; he wanted an experimental environment in which he could carefully control all the factors that could affect the dogs

Ivan Pavlov (1849–1936) earned fame by studying the conditioned reflex in dogs.

stimulus (STIM-yu-lus): Any event or object in the environment to which an organism responds; plural is *stimuli.*

learning: A relatively permanent change in behaviour, capability, or attitude that is acquired through experience and cannot be attributed to illness, injury, or maturation.

classical conditioning: A process through which a response previously made only to a specific stimulus is made to another stimulus that has been paired repeatedly with the original stimulus.

during the experiments. To accomplish this, he planned and built at the institute a laboratory specifically for his purposes.

The dogs were isolated inside soundproof cubicles and placed in harnesses that restrained their movements. From an adjoining cubicle, the experimenter observed the dogs through a one-way mirror. Food and other stimuli could be presented and the flow of saliva measured by remote control (see Figure 5.1). What did Pavlov and his colleagues learn?

The Elements and Processes in Classical Conditioning

The Reflex: We Can't Help It

A **reflex** is an involuntary response to a particular stimulus. Two examples are the eye-blink response to a puff of air and salivation when food is placed in the mouth. There are two kinds of reflexes—conditioned and unconditioned. Think of the term *conditioned* as meaning "learned" and the term *unconditioned* as meaning "unlearned." Salivation in response to food is called an "unconditioned reflex" because this behaviour is an inborn, automatic, unlearned response to a particular stimulus. Unconditioned reflexes are built into the nervous system.

When Pavlov observed that his dogs salivated at the sight of food or the sound of rattling dishes, he realized that this salivation reflex was the result of learning. He called these learned involuntary responses **conditioned reflexes**.

The Conditioned and Unconditioned Stimulus and Response

How is classical conditioning accomplished?

Pavlov continued to investigate the circumstances under which a conditioned reflex is formed. He used tones, bells, buzzers, lights, geometric shapes, electric shocks, and metronomes in his conditioning experiments. In a typical experiment, food powder was placed in the dog's mouth, causing salivation. Dogs do not need to be conditioned to salivate in response to food, so salivation in response to food is an unlearned or **unconditioned response (UR)**. Any stimulus, such as food, that without learning will automatically elicit, or bring forth, an unconditioned response is called an **unconditioned stimulus (US)**.

Remember that a reflex is made up of both a stimulus and a response. Following is a list of some common unconditioned reflexes, showing their two components—the unconditioned stimulus and the unconditioned response.

Unconditioned Reflexes

Unconditioned Stimulus (US)		**Unconditioned Response (UR)**
food	→	salivation
onion juice	→	tears
heat	→	sweating
loud noise	→	startle
light in eye	→	contraction of pupil
puff of air in eye	→	blink
touching hot stove	→	hand withdrawal

FIGURE 5.1

The Experimental Apparatus Used in Pavlov's Classical Conditioning Studies In Pavlov's classical conditioning studies, the dog was restrained in a harness in the cubicle and isolated from all distractions. An experimenter observed the dog through a one-way mirror and, by remote control, presented the dog with food and other conditioning stimuli. A tube carried the saliva from the dog's mouth to a container where it was measured.

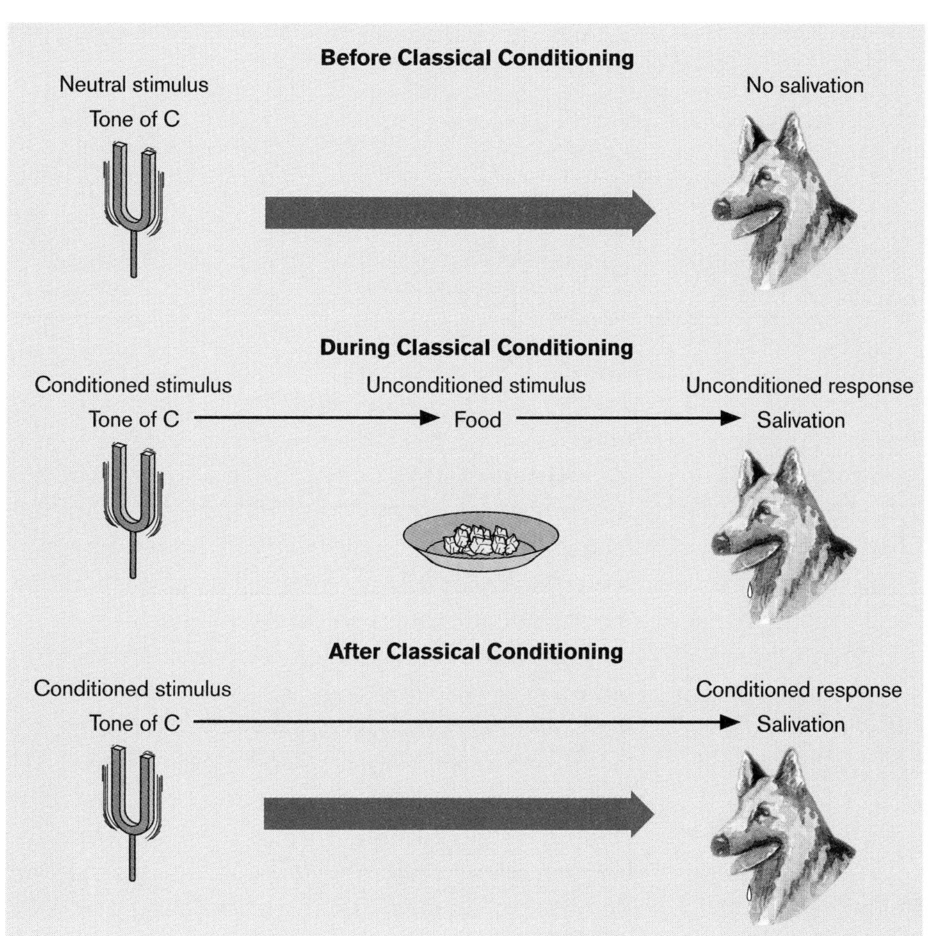

FIGURE 5.2
Classically Conditioning a Salivation Response **A neutral stimulus (a tone) elicits no salivation until it is repeatedly paired with the unconditioned stimulus (food). After many pairings, the neutral stimulus (now called conditioned stimulus) alone produces salivation. Classical conditioning has occurred.**

Pavlov demonstrated that dogs could be conditioned to salivate in response to a variety of stimuli that had never before been associated with food. During the conditioning or acquisition process, the researcher would present a neutral stimulus such as a musical tone shortly before placing food powder in the dog's mouth. The food powder would cause the dog to salivate. After pairing the tone and food many times—usually 20 or more—Pavlov (1960) found that the tone alone would elicit salivation (p. 385). Because dogs do not naturally salivate in response to musical tones, he concluded that this salivation was a learned response. Pavlov called the tone the *learned* or **conditioned stimulus (CS)**, and salivation to the tone the *learned* or **conditioned response (CR)** (see Figure 5.2).

In a modern view of classical conditioning, the conditioned stimulus can be thought of as a signal that the unconditioned stimulus will follow (Schreurs, 1989). In Pavlov's experiment, the tone became a signal that food would follow shortly. So the signal (conditioned stimulus) gives advance warning, and a person or animal is prepared with the proper response (conditioned response) even before the unconditioned stimulus arrives.

reflex: An involuntary response to a particular stimulus, like the eye-blink response to a puff of air or salivation in response to food placed in the mouth.

conditioned reflex: A learned reflex rather than a naturally occurring one.

unconditioned response (UR): A response that is invariably elicited by the unconditioned stimulus without prior learning.

unconditioned stimulus (US): A stimulus that elicits a specific response without prior learning.

conditioned stimulus (CS): A neutral stimulus that, after repeated pairing with an unconditioned stimulus, becomes associated with it and elicits a conditioned response.

conditioned response (CR): A response that comes to be elicited by a conditioned stimulus as a result of its repeated pairing with an unconditioned stimulus.

Extinction and Spontaneous Recovery: Gone but Not Forgotten

How does extinction occur in classical conditioning?

After conditioning an animal to salivate to a tone, what happens when you continue to sound the tone but no longer pair it with food? Pavlov found that salivation to the tone without the food became weaker and weaker and then finally disappeared altogether—a process known as **extinction**.

By extinction, we do not mean that the conditioned response has been completely erased or forgotten. Rather, the animal learns that the tone is no longer a signal that food will follow shortly, and the old conditioned response is gradually inhibited or suppressed. Animals are better able to adapt to a changing environment if they have the ability to discard conditioned responses that are no longer useful or needed.

How did Pavlov determine whether the conditioned response, once extinguished, had been inhibited rather than permanently erased or forgotten? If, after the response had been extinguished, the dog was allowed to rest and was then brought back to the laboratory, Pavlov found that the dog would again salivate to the tone. He called this recurrence **spontaneous recovery**. The spontaneously recovered response, however, was weaker and shorter in duration than the original conditioned response. Figure 5.3 illustrates the processes of extinction and spontaneous recovery.

Generalization: Responding to Similarities

What is generalization?

Assume that you have conditioned a dog to salivate when it hears the tone middle C on the piano. If in your experiment, you accidentally played the tone D or E, would that note produce salivation? Or would the dog not salivate to this slightly different tone? Pavlov found that a tone similar to the original conditioned stimulus produced the conditioned response, a phenomenon called **generalization**. If you are as careful a researcher as Pavlov, you will observe that as you move further away from the original tone, salivation decreases. Eventually the tone will be so different that the dog will not salivate at all (see Figure 5.4).

It is easy to see the impact of generalization in our everyday experience. Suppose that as a child you had been bitten by a large, grey dog. To experience fear in the future, you would not need to see exactly the same dog or another of the same breed or colour coming toward you: your original fear would probably generalize to all large dogs of any description. Because of generalization, we do not need to learn a conditioned response to every stimulus. Rather, we learn to approach or avoid a range of stimuli similar to the one that produced the original conditioned response.

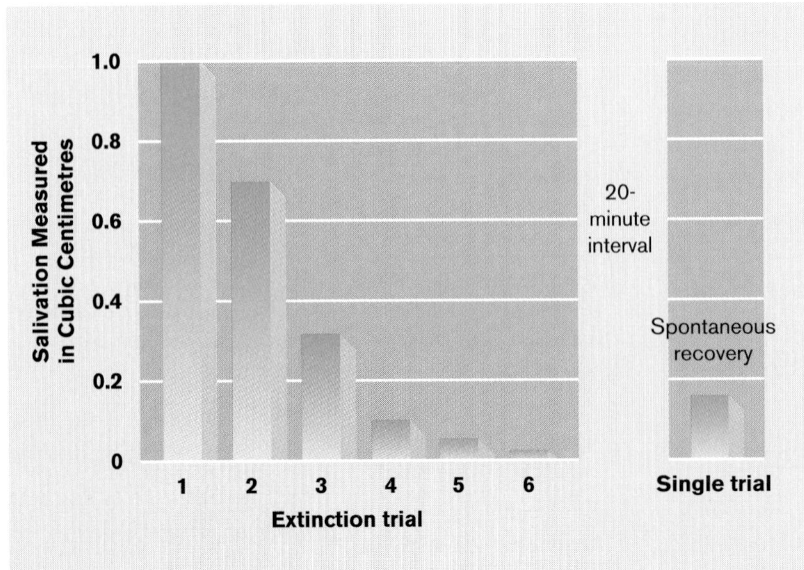

FIGURE 5.3

Extinction of a Classically Conditioned Response **When a classically conditioned stimulus (the tone) was presented in a series of trials without the unconditioned stimulus (the food), Pavlov's dogs salivated less and less until there was virtually no salivation. But after a 20-minute rest, with one sound of the tone, the conditioned response would reappear in a weakened form (producing only a small amount of salivation), a phenomenon Pavlov called "spontaneous recovery." (Data from Pavlov, 1927, p. 58.)**

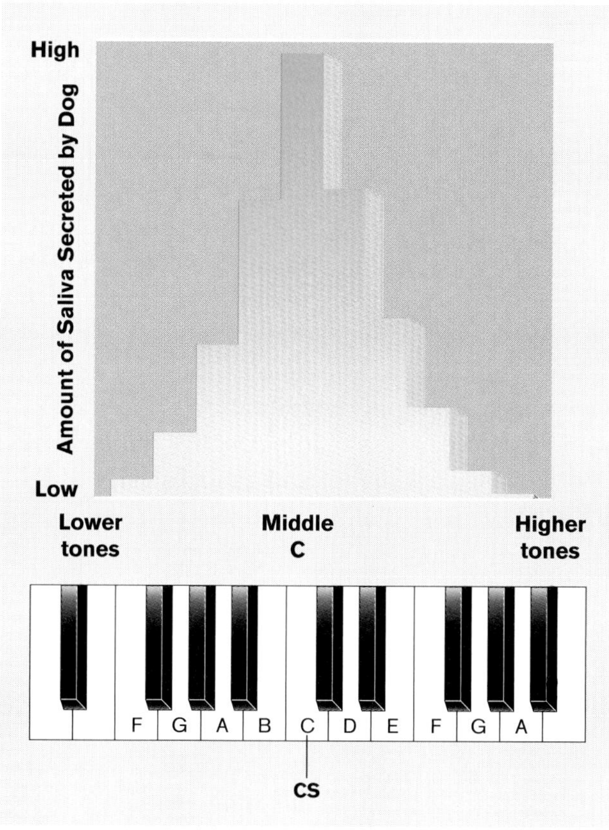

FIGURE 5.4

Generalization in Classical Conditioning **Because of the phenomenon of generalization, a dog conditioned to salivate to middle C (the CS) on the piano also salivates to similar tones—but less and less so as the tone moves away from middle C.**

A child attacked by a dog can easily develop a long-lasting fear of all dogs, through the process of generalization.

Discrimination: Learning That They're Not All Alike

What is discrimination in classical conditioning?

We must learn not only to generalize, but also to distinguish between similar stimuli. Using the previous example of a dog being conditioned to a musical tone, we can trace the process of **discrimination:**

Step 1: The dog is conditioned to the tone C.

Step 2: Generalization occurs, and the dog salivates to a range of musical tones above and below tone C. The dog salivates less and less as the note moves away from C.

Step 3: The original tone C is repeatedly paired with food, but when neighbouring tones are sounded, they are not followed with food. The dog is being conditioned to discriminate. Gradually, the salivation response to the neighbouring tones is extinguished, while salivation to the original tone C is strengthened (as demonstrated below).

Conditioned Stimulus	Conditioned Response
Tone C →	More salivation
Tones A, B, D, E →	Progressively less salivation

Step 4: Eventually, discrimination is achieved (as demonstrated below).

Conditioned Stimulus	Conditioned Response
Tone C →	Stronger salivation response
Tones A, B, D, E →	No salivation

extinction: The weakening and often eventual disappearance of a learned response (in classical conditioning, the conditioned response is weakened by repeated presentation of the conditioned stimulus without the unconditioned stimulus).

spontaneous recovery: The reappearance of an extinguished response (in a weaker form) when an organism is exposed to the original conditioned stimulus following a rest period.

generalization: In classical conditioning, the tendency to make a conditioned response to a stimulus that is similar to the original conditioned stimulus; in operant conditioning, the tendency to make the learned response to a stimulus that is similar to the one for which it was originally reinforced.

discrimination: The learned ability to distinguish between similar stimuli so that the conditioned response occurs only to the original conditioned stimulus but not to similar stimuli.

Like generalization, discrimination has survival value. Discriminating between the odours of fresh and spoiled milk will spare you an upset stomach. Knowing the difference between a rattlesnake and a garter snake could save your life.

Higher-Order Conditioning

Classical conditioning would be somewhat limited in its effect on behaviour if a conditioned response could be produced in only two ways, (1) by the pairing of a conditioned stimulus with an unconditioned stimulus, or (2) through generalization. Fortunately, classical conditioning can occur in another way—through higher-order conditioning. **Higher-order conditioning** takes place when a neutral stimulus is paired with an existing conditioned stimulus, becomes associated with it, and gains the power to elicit the same conditioned response. Suppose that after Pavlov conditioned the dogs to salivate to a tone, he presented a light (a neutral stimulus) immediately before the tone a number of times. The light would become associated with the tone, and the dogs would learn to give the salivation response to the light alone.

John Watson, Little Albert, and Peter

Little Albert and the Conditioned Fear Response: Learning to Fear

How did John B. Watson demonstrate that fear could be classically conditioned?

John Watson believed that in humans all fears except those of loud noises and loss of support are classically conditioned. In 1919, Watson and his laboratory assistant, Rosalie Rayner, conducted a now-famous study to prove that fear could be classically conditioned. The participant in the study, known as "Little Albert," was a healthy and emotionally stable infant. When tested, he showed no fear except of the loud noise Watson made by striking a hammer against a steel bar. In this classic experiment, Watson tested whether he could condition 11-month-old Albert to fear a white rat by causing Albert to associate the rat with a loud noise.

John B. Watson

Remember It!

Classical Conditioning: Knowing the Basics

1. Classical conditioning was originally researched most extensively by ________.
2. The dog's salivation in response to a musical tone was a/an (conditioned/unconditioned) response.
3. The gradual weakening and disappearance of a conditioned response–when the conditioned stimulus is presented repeatedly without the unconditioned stimulus–is termed
   a. generalization.
   b. discrimination.
   c. extinction.
   d. spontaneous recovery.
4. Juanita had an automobile accident on a bridge, and now she becomes very nervous whenever she has to cross any bridge. Which process accounts for this feeling?
   a. generalization
   b. discrimination
   c. extinction
   d. spontaneous recovery
5. Five-year-old Jesse was bitten by his neighbour's collie. He won't go near that dog but seems to have no fear of other dogs, even other collies. Which process accounts for his behaviour?
   a. generalization
   b. discrimination
   c. extinction
   d. spontaneous recovery
6. For higher-order conditioning to occur, a neutral stimulus must be paired repeatedly with
   a. another neutral stimulus.
   b. an existing conditioned stimulus.
   c. an unconditioned stimulus.
   d. a conditioned reflex.

Answers: 1. Ivan Pavlov 2. conditioned 3. c 4. a 5. b 6. b

In the laboratory, Rosalie presented Little Albert with a white rat. As Albert reached for the rat, Watson struck a steel bar with a hammer just behind Albert's head. This procedure was repeated, and Albert "jumped violently, fell forward and began to whimper" (Watson & Rayner, 1920, p. 4). A week later, the rat was paired with the loud noise five more times. Then at the sight of the white rat alone, Albert began to cry.

Conditioned Stimulus		**Unconditioned Stimulus**		**Unconditioned Response**
white rat	→	loud noise	→	fear reaction
Conditioned Stimulus				**Conditioned Response**
white rat	→			fear reaction

When Albert returned to the laboratory five days later, his fear had generalized to a rabbit and (to a lesser degree) to a dog, a seal coat, Watson's hair, and a Santa Claus mask. When he made his final visit to the laboratory 30 days later, his fears remained, although they were somewhat less intense. The researchers concluded that conditioned fears "persist and modify personality throughout life" (Watson & Rayner, 1920, p. 12).

Watson had already formulated techniques for removing conditioned fears, but Albert left the city before they could be tried on him. (Watson apparently knew he would.) Some of Watson's ideas for removing fears were excellent and laid the groundwork for therapies that are used today. One method involved conditioning a new association between the feared object and a positive stimulus. In Albert's case, candy or other food could have been given just as the white rat was presented. Another procedure involved "modelling"—that is, Albert could have observed other children playing happily with the white rat.

It is difficult not to conclude that Watson, in his study of the conditioned fear response, showed a disregard for the welfare of Little Albert. Fortunately, the American Psychological Association (APA) and the Canadian Psychological Association (CPA) now have strict ethical standards for the use of both humans and animals in research. Neither the APA nor the CPA would sanction an experiment such as Watson's today.

Little Albert demonstrates that his fear of the white rat has generalized to a rabbit.

Removing Peter's Fears: The Triumph of Candy and Patience

Three years after the experiment with Little Albert, Watson and a colleague, Mary Cover Jones (1924), found three-year-old Peter, who, like Albert, was afraid of white rats. He was also afraid of rabbits, a fur coat, feathers, cotton, and a fur rug. Peter's fear of the rabbit was his strongest fear, and this became the target of these two researchers' fear-removal techniques.

Peter was brought into the laboratory, seated comfortably in a high chair, and given candy to eat. A white rabbit in a wire cage was brought into the room but kept far enough away from Peter that it would not upset him. Over the course of 38 therapy sessions, the rabbit was brought closer and closer to Peter, who continued to enjoy his candy. Occasionally some of Peter's friends were brought into the laboratory to play with the rabbit (at a safe distance) so that Peter could see first-hand that the rabbit did no harm. Toward the end of the therapy, the rabbit was taken out of the cage and eventually put in Peter's lap. By the final session, Peter had grown fond of the rabbit. Moreover, he had lost all fear of the fur coat, cotton, and feathers, and he could tolerate the white rats and the fur rug.

higher-order conditioning: Occurs when a neutral stimulus is paired with an existing conditioned stimulus, becomes associated with it, and gains the power to elicit the same conditioned response.

So far we have considered classical conditioning primarily in relation to Pavlov's dogs and Watson's human subjects. How does classical conditioning work in everyday life? First let us outline the factors that influence how classical conditioning affects our lives.

Factors Influencing Classical Conditioning

What are four factors that influence classical conditioning?

There are four major factors that affect the strength of a classically conditioned response and the length of time required for conditioning.

1. *The number of pairings of the conditioned stimulus and the unconditioned stimulus.* The number of pairings required varies considerably, depending on the individual characteristics of the person or animal being conditioned. Generally, the greater the number of pairings, the stronger the conditioned response.
2. *The intensity of the unconditioned stimulus.* If a conditioned stimulus is paired with a very strong unconditioned stimulus, the conditioned response will be stronger and will be acquired more rapidly than if it is paired with a weaker unconditioned stimulus (Gormezano, 1984). Striking the steel bar with the hammer produced stronger and faster conditioning in Little Albert than would have occurred if Watson had merely clapped his hands behind Albert's head.
3. *How reliably the conditioned stimulus predicts the unconditioned stimulus.* Robert Rescorla (1967, 1968) has shown that classical conditioning does not occur automatically just because a neutral stimulus is repeatedly paired with an unconditioned stimulus. The neutral stimulus must also reliably predict the occurrence of the unconditioned stimulus. A smoke alarm that never goes off except in response to a fire will elicit more fear than one that occasionally gives false alarms. A tone that is *always* followed by food will elicit more salivation than one that is followed by food only some of the time.
4. *The temporal relationship between the conditioned stimulus and the unconditioned stimulus.* Conditioning takes place fastest if the conditioned stimulus occurs shortly before the unconditioned stimulus. It takes place more slowly or not at all when the two stimuli occur at the same time. Conditioning rarely takes place when the conditioned stimulus follows the unconditioned stimulus (Spetch et al., 1981; Spooner & Kellogg, 1947).

The ideal time between the presentation of the conditioned and the unconditioned stimulus is about half a second, but this varies according to the type of response being conditioned and the nature and intensity of the conditioned and unconditioned stimulus (Wasserman & Miller, 1997). Some studies indicate that the age of the subject may also affect the optimal time interval (Solomon et al., 1991). In general, if the conditioned stimulus occurs too long before the unconditioned stimulus, an association between the two will not form. One notable exception to this general principle relates to the conditioning of taste aversions.

Classical Conditioning in Everyday Life

What types of responses can be learned through classical conditioning?

Do certain songs have special meaning because they remind you of a current or past love? Do you find the scent of a certain perfume or aftershave pleasant or unpleasant because it reminds you of a particular person? Many of our emotional responses, whether positive or negative, result from classical conditioning (often higher-order conditioning). Classical conditioning occurs in everyday life when neutral cues become associated with particular people, objects, locations, situations, or even words, and develop the power to elicit the same feelings as the original stimulus.

Fears and phobias largely result from classical conditioning. For example, many people who have had painful dental work develop a dental phobia. Not only do they come to fear the dentist's drill, but they develop anxiety in response to a wide range of environmental stimuli associated with it—the dental chair, the waiting room, or even the building where the dentist's office is located.

When businesspeople wine and dine customers, they are hoping that they and their product or service will elicit the same positive response as the pleasant setting and fine food. Advertisers are trying to classically condition us when they show us their prod-

Classical conditioning is very effective in advertising. Here a neutral product (clothing) has been paired with images of very attractive people.

ucts along with great-looking models or celebrities, or in situations where people are enjoying themselves. The advertisers are relying on the probability that if the "neutral" product is associated with people, objects, or situations we particularly like, then in time the product will elicit a similarly positive response. Pavlov found that presenting the tone slightly before the food was the most efficient way to condition salivation. Television advertisements, too, are most effective when the products are presented *before* the beautiful people or situations are shown (van den Hout & Merckelbach, 1991).

You might want to see just how much the principles of classical conditioning are applied in advertising by doing *Try It!*

Try It!

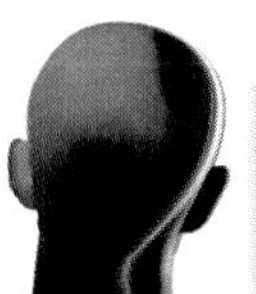

Classical Conditioning in Commercials

Some commercials simply give information about a product or place of business. Others are designed to classically condition the viewer to form a positive association. One night while you are watching TV, keep a record of the commercials you see. What proportion rely on classical conditioning? What are the kinds of cues (people, objects, or situations) with which the products are to be associated? Are the products introduced slightly before, during, or after these cues?

Drug Use and Classical Conditioning

Researchers are discovering that drug abuse in combination with classical conditioning can be deadly. Why do many drug addicts treated for overdoses in hospital emergency rooms report that they had taken only their usual dose but were *not* in their usual drug-taking environment when they overdosed?

All drugs produce characteristic physiological effects. As a person continues to use a drug, the body makes adjustments to decrease the drug's effects. These adjustments enable the body to *tolerate* the drug. For example, opiates elevate skin temperature and decrease respiratory function; the body compensates by lowering skin temperature and increasing the respiratory response. Over time a **drug tolerance** develops—that is, the user becomes progressively less affected by the drug and must take higher and higher doses to maintain the same effects.

If drug tolerance were solely a physiological phenomenon, it wouldn't make any difference where or in what circumstances the addict took the drug. But it does make a difference. In many cases, addicts suffer overdoses (some of them fatal) in unfamiliar surroundings—a hotel room, for example—not in a place where they habitually took the drug. Why should the same amount of a drug produce stronger physiological effects in an unfamiliar environment than in a familiar one? The answer involves classical conditioning. Here is how the process works.

Environmental cues associated with the setting where drugs are usually taken—the familiar surroundings, sights, sounds, odours, and drug paraphernalia, and the familiar drug-use ritual—can act as conditioned stimuli that become associated with the unconditioned stimulus, which is the drug itself (Dworkin, 1993; O'Brien et al., 1992; Siegel et al., 1982). These environmental cues come to signal to the user that the drug is on the way and initiate the compensatory mechanisms. In other words, these cues stimulate physiological effects that are primarily the opposite of the physiological effects of the drug. When the user takes the usual dose of the drug in unfamiliar surroundings, the environmental cues that initiate these protective mechanisms are not pres-

drug tolerance: A condition in which the user becomes progressively less affected by a drug so that larger and larger doses are necessary to maintain the same effect.

Classical conditioning helps explain why certain environmental cues or social situations can lead to continued drug use.

ent. Consequently, the effects of the drugs are more powerful—sometimes even fatal. This explains why drug counsellors strongly urge recovering addicts to avoid any environmental cues associated with their past drug use—the people, the places, the drug paraphernalia, and so on. Relapse is far more common in people who do not avoid the associated environmental cues.

Classically Conditioned Taste Aversions

Taste Aversions

The experience of nausea and vomiting after eating a certain food is often enough to condition a long-lasting taste aversion. A **taste aversion** is an intense dislike and/or avoidance of a particular food associated with nausea or discomfort. Taste aversions can be classically conditioned when the delay between the conditioned stimulus (food) and the unconditioned stimulus (nausea) is as long as 12 hours. Researchers believe that many taste aversions begin when we are between two and three years old, so we may not remember how our taste aversions originated (Rozin & Zellner, 1985). Taste aversions are more likely to develop to "less preferred, less familiar foods," and they can be acquired even when people are convinced that the food did not cause the nausea (Logue, 1985, p. 27). Once developed, taste aversions frequently generalize to similar foods (Logue et al., 1981). For example, an aversion to chili is likely to include sloppy joes as well.

Using Conditioned Taste Aversions to Help Cancer Patients

One unfortunate result of chemotherapy is that patients often associate nausea with the foods they ate several hours before treatment (Bovbjerg et al., 1992). As a result, they often develop taste aversions to the foods they normally eat—even favourite foods. This can lead to a loss of appetite and weight at a time when good nutrition is particularly important.

Bernstein and colleagues (1982, 1985) devised a technique to help patients avoid developing aversions to desirable foods. A group of cancer patients were fed a novel-tasting, maple-flavoured ice cream before chemotherapy. The nausea caused by the treatment resulted in a taste aversion to the ice cream. It was found that when an unusual or unfamiliar food became the "scapegoat" or target for taste aversion, other foods in the patient's diet were often protected, and the patient continued to eat them regularly. Perhaps cancer patients should refrain from eating preferred or nutritious foods before a chemotherapy session. Instead, they should be given unusual-tasting foods at that time.

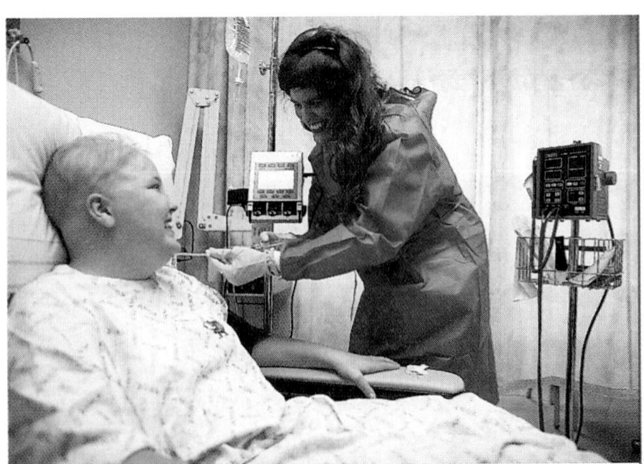

Chemotherapy treatments can result in conditioned taste aversions, but providing patients with a "scapegoat" target for the taste aversion can help them maintain a proper diet.

Remember It!

Classical Conditioning: Albert and Everyday Life

1. In Watson's experiment on Little Albert, the white rat was the (conditioned/unconditioned) stimulus, and Albert's crying when the hammer struck the steel bar was the (conditioned/unconditioned) response.
2. Albert's fear of the white rat transferred to the rabbit, dog, fur coat, and mask. What process did this demonstrate?
   a. generalization
   b. discrimination
   c. extinction
   d. spontaneous recovery
3. In everyday life, which of the following are *not* acquired through classical conditioning?
   a. positive feelings
   b. negative feelings
   c. skills
   d. fears and phobias
4. Which of the following does *not* increase the strength of the conditioned response in classical conditioning?
   a. more pairings of the conditioned with the unconditioned stimulus
   b. presenting the conditioned stimulus a considerable time before the unconditioned stimulus
   c. increasing the intensity of the unconditioned stimulus
   d. always following the conditioned stimulus with the unconditioned stimulus
5. Which element in classical conditioning is the signal?
   a. unconditioned response
   b. unconditioned stimulus
   c. conditioned response
   d. conditioned stimulus
6. In order for classical conditioning to occur, the unconditioned stimulus should occur immediately after the conditioned stimulus and the two must be paired repeatedly. Which of the following is an exception to this statement?
   a. conditioned salivation response
   b. conditioned immune response
   c. conditioned taste aversion
   d. conditioned drug tolerance

Answers: 1. conditioned; unconditioned 2. a 3. c 4. b 5. d 6. c

Operant Conditioning

Skinner and Operant Conditioning

How are responses acquired through operant conditioning?

Recall that in classical conditioning, the organism does not learn a new response. Rather, it learns to make an old or existing response to a new stimulus. Classically conditioned responses are involuntary or reflexive, and in most cases the person or animal cannot help but respond in expected ways.

Let's now examine a method for conditioning *voluntary* responses, known as **operant conditioning**. Operant conditioning does not begin, as does classical conditioning, with the presentation of a stimulus to elicit a response. Rather, the response comes first, and the consequence tends to modify this response in the future. In operant conditioning, the consequences of behaviour are manipulated to increase or decrease the frequency of a response or to shape an entirely new response. Behaviour that is reinforced—followed by rewarding consequences—tends to be repeated. A **reinforcer** is anything that strengthens a response or increases the probability that the response will occur. Behaviour that is ignored or punished is less likely to be repeated.

Operant conditioning permits the learning of a wide range of new responses. A simple response can be operantly conditioned if we merely wait for it to appear and then reinforce it. But this can be time-consuming. The process can be speeded up with a technique called "shaping." Shaping can also be used to condition responses that would never occur naturally.

taste aversion: The dislike and/or avoidance of a particular food that has been associated with nausea or discomfort.

operant conditioning: A type of learning in which the consequences of behaviour tend to modify that behaviour in the future (behaviour that is reinforced tends to be repeated; behaviour that is ignored or punished is less likely to be repeated).

reinforcer: Anything that strengthens a response or increases the probability that it will occur.

LINK IT!

www.biozentrum.uni-wuerzburg.de/genetics/behavior/learning/operant.html
Tutorial in Operant Conditioning

Shaping Behaviour: Just a Little Bit at a Time

How is shaping used to condition a response?

Shaping is a technique that was employed by B.F. Skinner at Harvard University. Skinner is seen by many as the great authority on operant conditioning, which is particularly useful in conditioning complex behaviours. In shaping, rather than waiting for the desired response to occur and then reinforcing it, we reinforce any movement in the direction of the desired response, gradually guiding the responses closer and closer to the ultimate goal.

B.F. Skinner

Influenced by the early work of Thorndike on animal influence (Thorndike, 1920, 1970), Skinner designed a soundproof operant-conditioning apparatus, commonly called a **Skinner box**, with which he conducted his experiment. One type of box is equipped with a lever or bar that a rat presses to gain a reward of food pellets or water from a dispenser. A complete record of the animal's bar-pressing responses is registered on a device called a "cumulative recorder," also invented by Skinner.

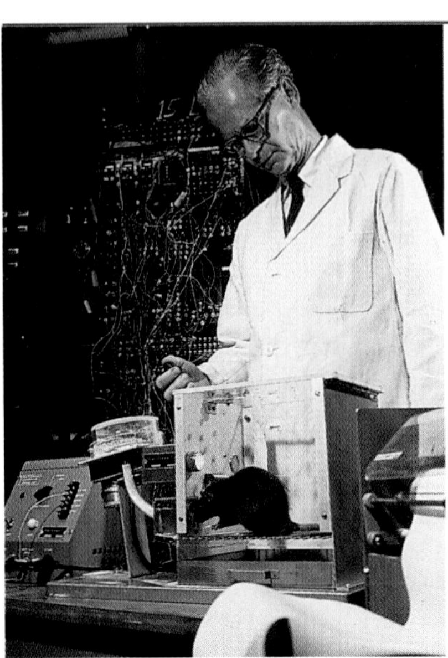

B.F. Skinner shapes a rat's bar-pressing behaviour in a Skinner box.

Rats in a Skinner box are conditioned through the use of shaping to press a bar for rewards. A rat may be rewarded first for simply turning toward the bar. Once this behaviour is established, the next reward comes only when the rat moves closer to the bar. Each step closer to the bar is rewarded. Next the rat may touch the bar and receive a reward; finally, the rat is rewarded only when it presses the bar.

Shaping—rewarding gradual **successive approximations** toward the terminal or desired response—has been used effectively to condition complex behaviours in people as well as in non-human animals. Parents may use shaping to help their children develop good table manners, praising them each time they show gradual improvements. Teachers often use shaping with disruptive children, rewarding them at first for very short periods of good behaviour and then gradually expecting them to work productively for longer and longer periods. Through shaping, circus animals have learned to perform a wide range of amazing feats, and pigeons have learned to bowl and play table tennis. You might even want to try shaping your own behaviour using the next *Try It!*

LINK IT!

www.bfskinner.org
The B.F. Skinner Foundation

Superstitious Behaviour: Mistaking a Coincidence for a Cause

Sometimes a rewarding event follows a response but is not caused by or connected with it. Superstitious behaviour occurs when an individual believes that a connection exists between an act and its consequences although, in fact, there is no relationship between the two.

A gambler in Windsor, Ontario, blows on the dice just before he rolls them and wins $1000. On the next roll, he follows the same ritual and wins again. Although this rewarding event follows the ritual of blowing on the dice, the connection between the two is accidental. Nevertheless, the gambler will probably persist in this superstitious behaviour at least as long as his winning streak continues. Some professional athletes have been known to carry superstitious behaviour to remarkable extremes. Baseball star Keith Hernandez reportedly wears his lucky socks (the same pair) for the entire season.

Extinction: Withholding Reinforcers

How does extinction occur in operant conditioning?

We have seen that responses followed by reinforcers tend to be repeated and that responses no longer followed by reinforcers will occur less and less often and eventually die out. A rat in a Skinner box will eventually stop pressing a bar when it is no longer rewarded with food pellets. In operant conditioning, **extinction** occurs when reinforcers are withheld.

In humans and other animals, extinction can lead to frustration or even rage. Consider a child having a temper tantrum. If whining and loud demands do not bring the reinforcer, the child may progress to kicking and screaming. If a vending machine takes your coins but fails to deliver candy or pop, your button-pushing or lever-pulling behaviour may become erratic and more forceful. You might even shake the machine or kick it before giving up. Not getting what we expect makes us angry.

The process of spontaneous recovery, which we discussed in relation to classical conditioning, also occurs in operant conditioning. A rat whose bar pressing has been extinguished may again press the bar a few times when returned to the Skinner box after a period of rest.

Generalization and Discrimination

Skinner conducted many of his experiments with pigeons placed in a Skinner box specially designed for them. The box contained small, illuminated disks that the pigeons could peck to receive bits of grain from a food tray. Skinner found that generalization occurs in operant conditioning. A pigeon rewarded for pecking at a yellow disk is likely to peck at another disk similar in colour. The less similar a disk is to the original colour, the lower the rate of pecking will be.

Try It!

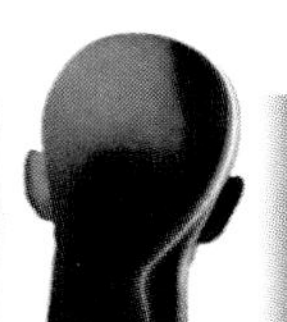

Can You Modify Your Own Behaviour?

Use conditioning to modify your own behaviour.

1. *Identify the target behaviour.* It must be both observable and measurable. You might choose, for example, to increase the amount of time you spend studying.
2. *Gather and record baseline data.* Keep a daily record of how much time you spend on the target behaviour for about a week. Also note where the behaviour takes place and what cues (or temptations) in the environment precede any slacking off from the target behaviour.
3. *Plan your behaviour modification program.* Formulate a plan and set goals to either decrease or increase the target behaviour.
4. *Choose your reinforcers.* Any activity you enjoy more can be used to reinforce any activity you enjoy less. For example, you could reward yourself with a game of basketball after a specified period of studying.
5. *Set the reinforcement conditions and begin recording and reinforcing your progress.* Be careful not to set your reinforcement goals so high that it becomes nearly impossible to earn a reward; remember Skinner's concept of shaping–rewarding small steps to reach a desired outcome. Be perfectly honest with yourself and claim a reward only when the goals are met. Chart your progress as you work toward gaining more and more control over the target behaviour.

shaping: Gradually moulding a desired behaviour by reinforcing responses that become progressively closer to it; reinforcing successive approximations of the desired response.

Skinner box: Invented by B.F. Skinner for conducting experiments in operant conditioning; a soundproof chamber with a device for delivering food and either a bar for rats to press or a disk for pigeons to peck.

successive approximations: A series of gradual training steps, with each step becoming more like the final desired response.

extinction: The weakening and often eventual disappearance of a learned response (in operant conditioning, the conditioned response is weakened by the withholding of reinforcement).

Discrimination in operant conditioning involves learning to distinguish between a stimulus that has been reinforced and other stimuli that may be very similar. We learn discrimination when our response to the original stimulus is reinforced but responses to similar stimuli are not reinforced. For example, to encourage discrimination, a researcher would reward the pigeon for pecking at the yellow disk but not for pecking at the orange or red disk.

There are certain cues that have come to be associated with reinforcement or punishment. For example, children are more likely to ask their parents for a treat when the parents are smiling than when they are frowning. The stimulus that signals whether a certain response or behaviour is likely to be rewarded, ignored, or punished is called a **discriminative stimulus**. If a pigeon's peck at a lighted disk results in a reward but a peck at an unlighted disk does not, the pigeon will soon be pecking at the lighted disk but not at the unlighted one. The presence or absence of the discriminative stimulus, in this case the lighted disk, will control whether or not the pecking takes place.

We may wonder why children sometimes misbehave with a grandparent but not with a parent, or why they make one teacher's life miserable but are model students for another. The children may have learned that in the presence of some people (the discriminative stimuli), misbehaviour will almost certainly lead to punishment, whereas in the presence of certain other people, it may even be rewarded.

Reinforcement: What's the Payoff?

Positive and Negative Reinforcement: Adding the Good, Taking Away the Bad

What are the goals of both positive and negative reinforcement, and how are the goals accomplished for each?

Reinforcement is a key concept in operant conditioning and may be defined as any event that increases the probability of the response that it follows. There are two types of reinforcement, positive and negative. **Positive reinforcement**, roughly the same thing as a reward, refers to any *positive* consequence that, if applied after a response, increases the probability of that response. We know that many people will work hard for a raise or a promotion, that salespeople will increase their efforts to get awards and bonuses, that students will study to get good grades, and that children will throw temper tantrums to get candy or ice cream. In these examples, raises, promotions, awards, bonuses, good grades, candy, and ice cream are positive reinforcers.

Just as people engage in behaviours to get positive reinforcers, they also engage in behaviours to avoid or escape unpleasant conditions. Terminating an unpleasant stimulus to increase the probability of a response is called **negative reinforcement**. When people find that a response successfully ends an aversive condition, they are likely to repeat it. People will turn on their air conditioner to terminate the heat, and they will get out of bed to turn off a faucet to

Remember It!

Operant Conditioning

1. Operant conditioning was researched most extensively by
   a. Watson.
   b. Wundt.
   c. Skinner.
   d. Pavlov.
2. Operant conditioning can be used effectively for all of the following *except*
   a. learning new responses.
   b. learning to make an existing response to a new stimulus.
   c. increasing the frequency of an existing response.
   d. decreasing the frequency of an existing response.
3. Even though the B that Billy wrote looked more like a D, his teacher, Mrs. Chen, praised him because it was better than his previous attempts. Mrs. Chen is using a procedure called ______________.
4. Which of the following processes occurs in operant conditioning when reinforcers are withheld?
   a. generalization
   b. discrimination
   c. spontaneous recovery
   d. extinction

Answers 1. c 2. b 3. shaping 4. d

avoid listening to the annoying "drip, drip, drip." Heroin addicts will do almost anything to obtain heroin to terminate their painful withdrawal symptoms. In these instances, negative reinforcement involves putting an end to the heat, the dripping faucet, and the withdrawal symptoms.

Responses that end discomfort and responses that are followed by rewards are likely to be strengthened or repeated because *both* lead to a more positive outcome. Some behaviours are influenced by a combination of positive and negative reinforcement. If you eat a plateful of rather disgusting leftovers to relieve intense hunger, then eating probably has been negatively reinforced. You are eating solely to remove hunger, a negative reinforcer. But if your hunger is relieved by a gourmet dinner at a fine restaurant, both positive and negative reinforcement will have played a role. Your hunger has been removed, and the delicious dinner has been a reward in itself.

Do the *Try It!* to see how your behaviour is influenced by positive and negative reinforcers in everyday life.

LINK IT!

server.bmod.athabascau.ca/html/prtut/reinpair.htm
Positive Reinforcement: A Self-Instructional Exercise

Primary and Secondary Reinforcers: The Unlearned and the Learned

A **primary reinforcer** is one that fulfills a basic physical need for survival and does not depend on learning. Food, water, sleep, and termination of pain are examples of primary reinforcers. And sex too is a powerful reinforcer. Fortunately, learning does not depend solely on primary reinforcers. If that were the case, we would need to be hungry, thirsty, or sex-starved before we would respond at all. Much observed behaviour in humans is in response to secondary rather than primary reinforcers. A **secondary reinforcer** is acquired or learned by association with other reinforcers. Some secondary reinforcers (money, for example) can be exchanged at a later time for other reinforcers. Praise, good grades, awards, bonuses, applause, and signals of approval such as a smile or a kind word are all examples of secondary reinforcers.

Attention is a secondary reinforcer of great general worth. To obtain the reinforcers we seek from other people, we must first get their attention. Children vie for the attention of parents because they represent the main source of a child's reinforcers. But often parents reward children with attention for misbehaviour and ignore their good behaviour. When this happens, misbehaviour is strengthened, and good behaviour may be extinguished for lack of reinforcement.

Try It!

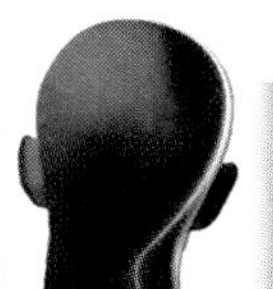

Reinforcement in Everyday Life

List all of your behaviours during the course of a day that have been influenced by either positive or negative reinforcement. Also list the behaviours that have been influenced by a combination of the two. During that day, were more behaviours positively or negatively reinforced?

Behaviour	Positive Reinforcement	Negative Reinforcement	Combination
Ate breakfast			
Attended class			
Totals:			

discriminative stimulus: A stimulus that signals whether a certain response or behaviour is likely to be followed by reward or punishment.

reinforcement: An event that follows a response and increases the strength of the response and/or the likelihood that it will be repeated.

positive reinforcement: A reward or pleasant consequence that follows a response and increases the probability that the response will be repeated.

negative reinforcement: The termination of an unpleasant stimulus after a response in order to increase the probability that the response will be repeated.

primary reinforcer: A reinforcer that fulfills a basic physical need for survival and does not depend on learning (examples: food, water, sleep, termination of pain).

secondary reinforcer: A neutral stimulus that becomes reinforcing after repeated pairing with other reinforcers.

Schedules of Reinforcement: When Will I Get My Reinforcers?

What are the four major schedules of reinforcement, and which schedule yields the highest response rate and the greatest resistance to extinction?

In conditioning the bar-pressing response in rats, every time the rat pressed the bar, the experimenter reinforced the response with a food pellet. Reinforcing every correct response, known as **continuous reinforcement**, is the most efficient way to condition a new response. However, after a response has been conditioned, partial or intermittent reinforcement is more effective if we want to maintain or increase the rate of response (Nation & Woods, 1980). **Partial reinforcement** is operating when some but not all of an organism's responses are reinforced. In real life, reinforcement is almost never continuous. Partial reinforcement is the rule.

Partial reinforcement may be administered according to different **schedules of reinforcement**. Different schedules produce distinct rates and patterns of responses, as well as varying degrees of resistance to extinction when reinforcement is discontinued. Although several varieties of reinforcement schedules are possible, the two basic types are the ratio and interval schedules. Ratio schedules require that a certain *number of responses* be made before one of the responses is reinforced. With interval schedules, a given *amount of time* must pass before a reinforcer is administered. These schedules are further subdivided into fixed and variable categories.

Following are descriptions of the four most basic schedules of reinforcement: the fixed-ratio schedule, the variable-ratio schedule, the fixed-interval schedule, and the variable-interval schedule.

THE FIXED-RATIO SCHEDULE On a **fixed-ratio schedule**, a reinforcer is administered after a fixed number of non-reinforced correct responses. If the fixed ratio is set at 30 responses (FR-30), a reinforcer is given after 30 correct responses. Examples of this schedule are factory workers whose payment depends on the number of units produced, and farm workers who are paid by the basket for the fruit they pick.

The fixed-ratio schedule is a very effective way to maintain a high response rate, because the number of reinforcers received depends directly on the response rate. The faster people respond, the more reinforcers they earn. When large ratios are used, people and animals tend to pause after each reinforcement but then return to the characteristic high rate of responding.

THE VARIABLE-RATIO SCHEDULE Pauses after reinforcement do not occur when the variable-ratio schedule is used. On a **variable-ratio schedule**, a reinforcer is administered on the basis of an average ratio after a varying number of non-reinforced correct responses. With a variable ratio of 30 responses (VR-30), you might be reinforced one time after 10 responses, another after 50, another after 30, and so on. You cannot predict exactly which responses will be reinforced, but in this example, reinforcement would average 1 in 30.

Variable-ratio schedules result in higher, more stable rates of responding than fixed-ratio schedules. Skinner (1953) reports that on this schedule "a pigeon may respond as rapidly as five times per second and maintain this rate for many hours" (p. 104). According to Skinner (1988), the variable-ratio schedule is useful because "it maintains behavior against extinction when reinforcers occur only infrequently. The behavior of the dedicated artist, writer, businessman, or scientist is sustained by an occasional, unpredictable reinforcement" (p. 174).

An insurance salesperson working on a variable-ratio schedule may sell policies to two clients in a row but then may have to contact 20 more prospects before making another sale. The best example of the seemingly addictive power of the variable-ratio schedule is

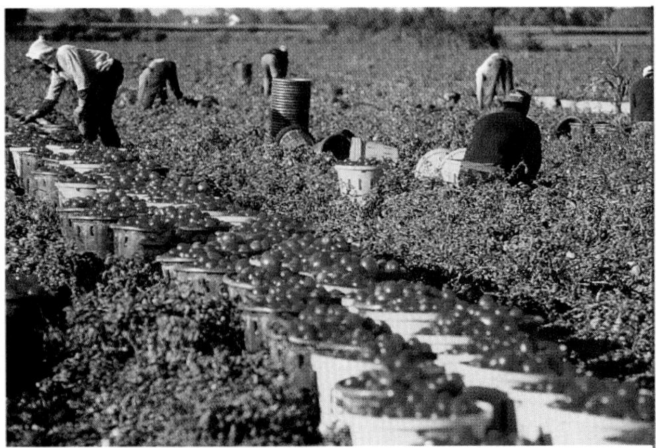

Migrant farm workers are paid according to a fixed-ratio schedule. Since their earnings depend on the number of bushels of tomatoes they pick, they are motivated to work quickly.

the gambling casino. Slot machines, roulette wheels, and most other games of chance pay on this schedule (see *It Happened in Canada*). The variable-ratio schedule, in general, produces the highest response rate and the most resistance to extinction.

THE FIXED-INTERVAL SCHEDULE On a **fixed-interval schedule**, a specific time interval must pass before a response is reinforced. For example, on a 60-second fixed-interval schedule (FI-60), a reinforcer is given for the first correct response that occurs 60 seconds after the last reinforced response. People working on salary are reinforced on the fixed-interval schedule.

IT HAPPENED IN CANADA

Reinforcement: Video Lottery Terminals

A new addiction has been in the news lately: the addiction to video lottery terminals (VLTs). Perhaps you have seen or even used these electronic slot machines, or "one-armed bandits." On the surface, VLTs appear to be no worse than regular video games, but critics of video gambling have a very different opinion. Researchers who study gambling behaviour now refer to VLTs as "the crack cocaine of gambling." VLTs are widely available, even in many corner stores across Canada. They require no skill or knowledge to operate, cost very little, and tempt the user by the potential for high returns. Not surprisingly, VLTs are highly addictive: Canadians spend more on VLTs than they spend on movies, CDs, and books combined.

With VLTs within easy reach, it should not be surprising that gambling in Canada is on the rise. For instance, casino gambling and VLTs are now generating almost $2.8 billion in net revenue in Canada, which is 100 times more than was the case just eight years earlier. And according to a study conducted by the National Council on Welfare, up to 1.2 million Canadians are problem gamblers. Gambling especially affects the poor, who tend to spend over four times more on lottery tickets and VLTs than wealthier Canadians.

Why are VLTs so addictive? According to the learning principles described in this chapter, the appeal of these machines may be related to the fact that they use a "variable-ratio schedule" of reinforcement. As Skinner (1988) himself pointed out, this form of reinforcement schedule has the highest response rate and is the most resistant to extinction. (Based on Duffy & Everson, 1996; Gombu, 2000; Schwartz, 1997.)

Unlike ratio schedules, reinforcement on interval schedules does not depend on the number of responses made, only on the one correct response made after the time interval has passed. Characteristic of the fixed-interval schedule is a pause or a sharp decline in responding immediately after each reinforcement and a rapid acceleration in responding just before the next reinforcer is due.

As an example of this schedule, think of a psychology test as a reinforcer (that's a joke, isn't it?) and studying for the test as the desired response. Suppose you have four tests scheduled during the semester. Your study responses will probably drop to zero immediately after the first test, gradually accelerate, and perhaps reach a frenzied peak just before the next scheduled exam; then your study responses will immediately drop to zero again, and so on. As you may have guessed, the fixed-interval schedule produces the lowest response rate.

THE VARIABLE-INTERVAL SCHEDULE Variable-interval schedules eliminate the pause after reinforcement that is typical of the fixed-interval schedule. On a **variable-interval schedule**, a reinforcer is administered on the basis of an average time after the first correct response following a varying time of non-reinforced responses. Rather than reinforcing a response every 60 seconds, for example, a reinforcer might be

continuous reinforcement: Reinforcement that is administered after every desired or correct response; the most effective method of conditioning a new response.

partial reinforcement: A pattern of reinforcement in which some portion, rather than 100 percent, of the correct responses are reinforced.

schedule of reinforcement: A systematic program for administering reinforcements that has a predictable effect on behaviour.

fixed-ratio schedule: A schedule in which a reinforcer is administered after a fixed number of non-reinforced correct responses.

variable-ratio schedule: A schedule in which a reinforcer is administered on the basis of an average ratio after a varying number of non-reinforced correct responses.

fixed-interval schedule: A schedule in which a reinforcer is administered following the first correct response after a fixed period of time has elapsed.

variable-interval schedule: A schedule in which a reinforcer is administered on the basis of an average time after the first correct response following a varying time of non-reinforcement.

given after a 30-second interval, with others following after 90-, 45-, and 75-second intervals. But the average time elapsing between reinforcers would be 60 seconds (VI-60). Although this schedule maintains remarkably stable and uniform rates of responding, the response rate is typically lower than that of the ratio schedules, because reinforcement is not tied directly to the *number* of responses made.

Again, with another flight into fantasy, we could think of the psychology exam as the reinforcer and studying for the exam as the response. Rather than a regularly scheduled exam, however, we need pop quizzes to illustrate the variable-interval schedule. Because you cannot predict when a pop quiz will be given, your study responses will be more uniform and stable. Also, the response rate tends to be higher with shorter intervals and lower with longer ones. If your professor gives a pop quiz once a week on the average, your study response will be higher than if you average only one quiz per month.

Review & Reflect 5.1 summarizes the characteristics of the four schedules of reinforcement.

The Effect of Continuous and Partial Reinforcement on Extinction

What is the partial-reinforcement effect?

One way to understand extinction in operant conditioning is to consider how consistently a response is followed by reinforcement. On a continuous schedule, a reinforcer is expected without fail after each correct response. When a reinforcer is withheld, it is noticed immediately. But on a partial-reinforcement schedule, a reinforcer is not expected after every response. Thus, no immediate difference is apparent between the partial-reinforcement schedule and the onset of extinction.

When you put money in a vending machine and pull the lever but no candy or pop appears, you know immediately that something is wrong with the machine. But if you are playing a broken slot machine, you could have many non-reinforced responses before suspecting that the machine is malfunctioning.

Partial reinforcement results in a greater resistance to extinction than does continuous reinforcement (Lerman et al., 1996). This result is known as the **partial-reinforcement effect**. There is an inverse relationship between the percentage of responses that have been reinforced and resistance to extinction—that is, the lower the percentage of responses that are reinforced, the longer extinction will take when reinforcement is withheld (Weinstock, 1954). The strongest resistance to extinction that we can find on record occurred in one experiment in which pigeons were conditioned to peck at a disk. According to Holland and Skinner (1961), "After the response had been maintained on a fixed ratio of 900 and reinforcement was then discontinued, the pigeon emitted 73,000 responses during the first $4\frac{1}{2}$ hours of extinction" (p. 124).

Parents often wonder why their children continue to nag to get what they want, even though the par-

REVIEW & REFLECT 5.1

Reinforcement Schedules Compared According to Response Rate, Pattern of Responses, and Resistance to Extinction

Schedule of Reinforcement	Response Rate	Pattern of Responses	Resistance to Extinction
Fixed ratio	Very high	Steady response with low ratio. Brief pause after each reinforcement with very high ratio.	The higher the ratio, the more resistant to extinction.
Variable ratio	Highest response rate	Constant response pattern, no pauses.	Most resistant to extinction.
Fixed interval	Lowest response rate	Long pause after reinforcement, followed by gradual acceleration.	The longer the interval, the more resistant to extinction.
Variable interval	Moderate	Stable, uniform response.	More resistant to extinction than fixed-interval schedule with same average interval.

Remember It!

Reinforcement

1. Negative reinforcement (increases/decreases) the likelihood of a response.
2. Many people take aspirin to terminate a painful headache. Taking aspirin is a behaviour that is likely to continue because of the effect of (positive/negative) reinforcement.
3. (Partial/Continuous) reinforcement is most effective in conditioning a new response; afterward, (partial/continuous) reinforcement is best for maintaining the response.
4. Jennifer and Ashley are both employed raking leaves. Jennifer is paid $1 for each bag of leaves she rakes; Ashley is paid $4 per hour. Jennifer is paid according to the ____________ schedule; Ashley is paid according to the ____________ schedule.
   a. fixed-interval/fixed-ratio
   b. variable-ratio/fixed-interval
   c. variable-ratio/variable-interval
   d. fixed-ratio/fixed-interval
5. Which schedule of reinforcement yields the highest response rate and the greatest resistance to extinction?
   a. variable-ratio
   b. fixed-ratio
   c. variable-interval
   d. fixed-interval
6. Danielle's parents have noticed that she has been making her bed every day, and they would like this to continue. They understand the partial-reinforcement effect, so they will want to reward her *every* time she makes the bed. (true/false)

Answers: 1. increases 2. negative 3. Continuous, partial 4. d 5. a 6. false

ents *usually* do not give in to the nagging. Unwittingly, the parents are reinforcing their children's nagging on a variable-ratio schedule, which results in the most persistent behaviour. For this reason experts always caution parents to be consistent. If parents *never* reward nagging, the behaviour will extinguish; if they give in occasionally, it will persist and be extremely hard to extinguish.

Factors Influencing Operant Conditioning

What three factors, in addition to the schedule of reinforcement, influence operant conditioning?

We know that responses are acquired more quickly with continuous rather than partial reinforcement, and that the schedule of reinforcement influences both response rates and resistance to extinction. Several other factors affect how quickly a response is acquired, response rate, and resistance to extinction.

The first factor is the *magnitude of reinforcement.* In general, as the magnitude of reinforcement increases, acquisition of a response is faster, the rate of responding is higher, and resistance to extinction is greater (Clayton, 1964). People would be motivated to work harder and faster if they were paid $30 for each yard mowed rather than only $10. Other research indicates that level of performance is also influenced by the relationship between the amount of reinforcement expected and what is actually received (Crespi, 1942). For example, your performance on the job would undoubtedly be affected if your salary were suddenly cut in half. Also, it might improve dramatically if your employer doubled your pay.

The second factor affecting operant conditioning is the *immediacy of reinforcement.* In general, responses are conditioned more effectively when reinforcement is immediate. One reason people become addicted to crack cocaine so quickly is that its euphoric effects are felt almost instantly (Medzerian, 1991). As a rule, the longer the delay in reinforcement, the more slowly the response will be acquired (R. A. Church, 1989; Mazur, 1993; and see Figure 5.5 on the next page.) Overweight people have difficulty changing their eating habits because of the long delay between their behaviour change and the rewarding consequences of weight loss and better health.

The third factor influencing conditioning is the *level of motivation* of the learner. If you are highly

partial-reinforcement effect: The greater resistance to extinction that occurs when a portion, rather than 100 percent, of the correct responses have been reinforced.

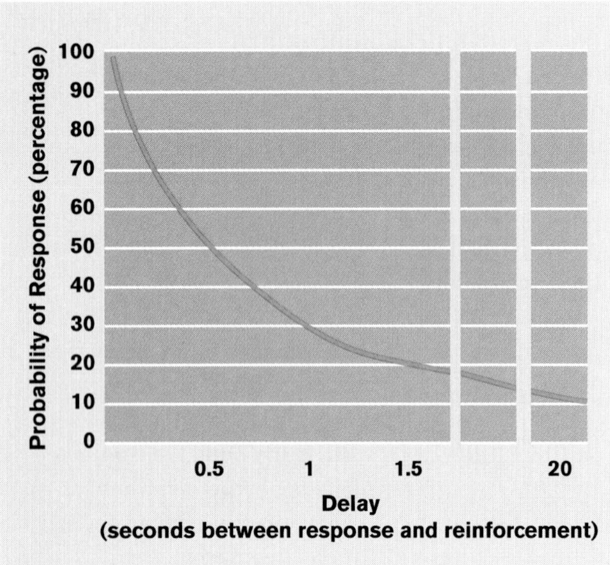

FIGURE 5.5

The Effect of Delay in Reinforcement on Conditioning of a Response **In general, responses are conditioned more effectively when reinforcement is immediate. The longer the delay in reinforcement, the lower the probability that a response will be acquired.**

motivated to learn to play tennis, you will learn faster and practise more than if you have no interest in the game. Skinner found that when food is the reinforcer, a hungry animal will learn faster than a full animal. To maximize motivation, he used rats that had been deprived of food for 24 hours and pigeons that were maintained at 75 to 80 percent of their normal body weight.

Punishment: That Hurts!

How does punishment differ from negative reinforcement?

Punishment is in many ways the opposite of reinforcement. Punishment tends to lower the probability of a response. It can be accomplished by the addition of an unpleasant stimulus or by the removal of a pleasant stimulus. The added unpleasant stimulus might be a scolding, criticism, a disapproving look, a fine, or a prison sentence. The removal of a pleasant stimulus might involve withholding affection and attention, suspending a driver's licence, or taking away a privilege such as watching television.

Students often confuse negative reinforcement and punishment. Unlike punishment, negative reinforcement increases the probability of a desired response by removing an unpleasant stimulus when the correct response is made (see Review & Reflect 5.2). "Grounding" can be used in either punishment or negative reinforcement. When a teenager fails to clean her room after many requests to do so, her parents could ground her for the weekend—a punishment. An alternative approach would be to use negative reinforcement—tell her she is grounded *until* her room is clean. Which approach is likely to be more effective?

The Disadvantages of Punishment: Its Downside

What are some disadvantages of punishment?

Skinner always argued that punishment does not extinguish an undesirable behaviour; rather, it suppresses that behaviour when the punishing agent is present. But the behaviour is likely to continue when the threat of punishment is removed and in settings where punishment is unlikely. There is ample empirical support for Skinner's argument. If punishment (imprisonment, fines, and so on) did extinguish criminal behaviour, there would be fewer repeat offenders in our criminal justice system.

Another problem with punishment is that it indicates which behaviours are unacceptable but does not help people develop more appropriate behaviours. If punishment is used, it should be administered in conjunction with reinforcement or rewards for appropriate behaviour.

Controlling behaviour by punishment has a number of other potential disadvantages. The person who is severely punished often becomes fearful and feels angry and hostile toward the punisher. These reactions may be accompanied by a desire to avoid or escape from the punisher and the punishing situation, or to find a way to retaliate. Many runaway teenagers leave home to escape physical abuse.

Punishment frequently leads to aggression. Those who administer physical punishment may become models of aggressive behaviour—people who demonstrate aggression as a way of solving problems and discharging anger. Children of abusive, punishing parents are at greater risk than other children of becoming aggressive and abusive themselves (Widom, 1989b).

Alternatives to Punishment: There's More Than One Way to Change Behaviour

Because of the many disadvantages of punishment, parents and teachers should explore alternative ways of handling misbehaviour. Often the use of extinction and positive and negative reinforcement leads to the desired outcomes without the negative side effects of punishment.

Many psychologists believe that *removing the rewarding consequences of undesirable behaviour* is the best way to extinguish a problem behaviour. According to this view, parents should extinguish a child's temper tantrums not by punishment but by *never* giving in to the child's demands during a tantrum. A parent might best extinguish problem behaviour that is performed merely to get attention by ignoring it and giving attention to more appropriate behaviour. Sometimes, simply explaining why certain behaviours are not appropriate is all that is required to extinguish the behaviour.

Using positive reinforcement such as praise will make good behaviour more rewarding for children. This approach brings with it the attention that children want and need—attention that too often is given only when they misbehave. And as we saw in our earlier example of grounding, negative reinforcement can often be more effective than punishment in bringing about desired outcomes.

It is probably unrealistic to believe that punishment can be dispensed with entirely. If a young child runs into the street, puts a finger near an electrical outlet, or reaches for a hot pan on the stove, a swift punishment may save the child from a potentially disastrous situation. It is important to be aware of some ways to make punishment more effective.

Review & Reflect 5.2 summarizes the differences between reinforcement and punishment.

REVIEW & REFLECT 5.2
The Effects of Reinforcement and Punishment

Reinforcement (increases or strengthens a particular behaviour)	**Punishment (decreases or suppresses a particular behaviour)**
Adding a Positive Positive Reinforcement Presenting food, money, praise, attention, or other rewards.	*Adding a Negative* Delivering a pain-producing or otherwise aversive stimulus such as a spanking or an electric shock.
Subtracting a Negative Negative Reinforcement Removing or terminating some pain-producing or otherwise aversive stimulus, such as electric shock.	*Subtracting a Positive* Removing some pleasant stimulus or taking away privileges such as TV watching, use of automobile.

Making Punishment More Effective: Some Suggestions

What three factors increase the effectiveness of punishment?

Research has revealed several factors that influence the effectiveness of punishment: its *timing*, its *intensity*, and the *consistency* of its application (Parke, 1977). Punishment is most effective when it is applied during the misbehaviour or as soon afterward as possible. Interrupting the problem behaviour is most effective because it abruptly halts the rewarding aspects of the misbehaviour. The longer the delay between the response and the punishment, the less effective the punishment will be in suppressing the response (Azrin & Holz, 1966; Camp et al., 1967). If the punishment is delayed, the punisher should remind the perpetrator of the incident and explain why the behaviour was inappropriate.

Animal studies have revealed that the more intense the punishment, the greater the suppression of the undesirable behaviour (Church, 1963). But that does not mean that the severity of punishment should be the same for major and minor misbehaviours alike. The intensity of the punishment should match the seriousness of the misdeed. Ideally, punishment should be the minimum necessary to suppress the problem behaviour. Unnecessarily severe punishment is likely to be accompanied by the negative side effects mentioned earlier. But if the initial punishment is too mild, it will have no effect.

What if the intensity of the punishment is gradually increased? The perpetrator will gradually adapt to it, and the unwanted behaviour will persist (Azrin & Holz, 1966; Solomon, 1964). At a minimum, if a behaviour is to be suppressed, the punishment must be more punishing than the misbehaviour is rewarding. In human terms, a $2 speeding ticket would not

punishment: The removal of a pleasant stimulus or the application of an unpleasant stimulus, which tends to suppress a response.

be much of a deterrent; a $200 ticket is more likely to suppress the urge to speed.

If it is to be effective, punishment also must be applied consistently. For example, a parent cannot ignore an act of misbehaviour one day and punish the same act the next. There should also be consistency between different people administering the punishment. Both parents ought to react to the same misbehaviour in a consistent manner. And an undesired response will be suppressed more effectively when the probability of punishment is high. Few people would speed while observing a police car in the rear-view mirror.

Finally, punishment should not be administered in anger. The purpose of punishment must always be clearly understood: it is not to vent anger but rather to modify behaviour. Also, punishment meted out in anger is likely to be more intense than necessary to bring about the desired result.

Escape and Avoidance Learning

Learning to perform a behaviour because it terminates an aversive event is called "escape learning," and it reflects the power of negative reinforcement. Running away from a punishing situation and taking aspirin to relieve a pounding headache are examples of escape behaviour. In these situations the aversive event has begun and an attempt is being made to escape it.

Avoidance learning depends on two types of conditioning. First, through classical conditioning, an event or condition comes to signal an aversive state. Drinking and driving may be associated with automobile accidents and death. Then, because of such associations, people may engage in behaviours to avoid the anticipated aversive consequences. Making it a practice to avoid driving with people who have had too much to drink is sensible avoidance behaviour.

Many avoidance behaviours are maladaptive, however, and occur in response to phobias. Students who have had a bad experience speaking in front of a class may begin to fear any situation that involves speaking before a group. Such students may avoid taking classes that require class presentations, or avoid taking leadership roles that require public speaking. Avoiding such situations prevents them from suffering the perceived dreaded consequences. But the avoidance behaviour is negatively reinforced and thus strengthened through operant conditioning. Maladaptive avoidance behaviours are very difficult to extinguish, because people never give themselves a chance to learn that the dreaded consequences probably will not occur or are greatly exaggerated.

Learned Helplessness

It is fortunate that we (like other animals) can easily learn to escape and avoid punishing or aversive situations. Research on learned helplessness, however, suggests that if we are exposed to repeated aversive events that we can neither escape nor avoid, we may learn to do nothing—simply to sit or stand helplessly and suffer the punishment. **Learned helplessness** is a passive resignation to aversive conditions learned by repeated exposure to aversive events that are inescapable and unavoidable.

The initial experiment on learned helplessness was conducted by Overmeier and Seligman (1967), who used dogs as their subjects. The experimental group of dogs were strapped, one at a time, into a harness from which they could not escape and were exposed to electric shocks. Later, these same dogs were placed in a shuttle box with two experimental compartments separated by a low barrier. The dogs then experienced a series of trials in which a warning signal was followed by an electric shock. The floor on one side was electrified, and the dogs should have learned quickly to escape the electric shocks simply by jumping the barrier. Surprisingly, the dogs did not do so; they simply suffered as many shocks as the experimenter chose to deliver, *as if* they could not escape.

Another group of dogs, the control group, had not previously experienced the inescapable shock, and they behaved in an entirely different manner. They quickly learned to escape the shock by jumping the barrier when the warning signal sounded. Seligman reported that the dogs experiencing the inescapable shock were less active, had less appetite, and showed other depression-like symptoms.

Seligman (1975, 1991) later reasoned that humans who have suffered painful and negative experiences they could not avoid and from which they could not escape may experience learned helplessness. Having experienced helplessness, they may simply give up and react to disappointment in life by becoming inactive, withdrawn, and depressed. Learned helplessness has been suggested as one cause of depression.

REVIEW & REFLECT 5.3
Classical and Operant Conditioning Compared

Characteristics	Classical Conditioning	Operant Conditioning
Type of association	Between two stimuli	Between a response and its consequence
State of subject	Passive	Active
Focus of attention	On what precedes response	On what follows response
Type of response typically involved	Involuntary or reflexive response	Voluntary response
Bodily response typically involved	Internal responses: emotional and glandular reactions	External responses: muscular and skeletal movement and verbal responses
Range of responses	Relatively simple	Simple to highly complex
Responses learned	Emotional reactions: fears, likes, dislikes	Goal-oriented responses

LINK IT! 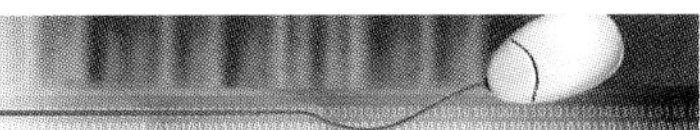

www.psych.upenn.edu/~fresco/helplessness.html
The Learned Helplessness Forum

Comparing Classical and Operant Conditioning: What's the Difference?

In summary, the processes of generalization, discrimination, extinction, and spontaneous recovery occur in both classical and operant conditioning. Both types of conditioning depend on associative learning. In classical conditioning, an association is formed between two stimuli—for example, a tone and food, a white rat and a loud noise, or a product and a celebrity. In operant conditioning, the association is established between a response and its consequences—studying hard and a high test grade, good table manners and praise from a parent, or (in the world of rats and pigeons) bar pressing and food, or disk pecking and food.

In classical conditioning, the focus is on what precedes the response. Pavlov focused on what led up to the salivation in his dogs, not on what happened after they salivated. In operant conditioning, the focus is on what follows the response. If a rat's bar pressing or your studying is followed by a reinforcer, that response is more likely to occur in the future.

Generally, in classical conditioning, the subject is passive and responds to the environment rather than acting upon it. In operant conditioning, the subject is active and *operates* on the environment. Children *do* something to get their parents' attention or their praise. Review & Reflect 5.3 highlights the major differences between classical and operant conditioning.

Exceptions can be found to most general principles. Research in biofeedback indicates that internal responses, once believed to be completely involuntary, can be brought under a person's voluntary control.

Behaviour Modification: Changing Our Act

What is behaviour modification?

Behaviour modification is a method of changing behaviour through a systematic program based on the principles of learning—classical conditioning, operant conditioning, or observational learning (which we will discuss soon). Most behaviour modification programs use the principles of operant conditioning.

avoidance learning: Learning to avoid events or conditions associated with dreaded or aversive outcomes.

learned helplessness: The learned response of resigning oneself passively to aversive conditions, rather than taking action to change, escape, or avoid them; learned through repeated exposure to inescapable or unavoidable aversive events.

behaviour modification: The systematic application of the learning principles of operant conditioning, classical conditioning, or observational learning to individuals or groups in order to eliminate undesirable behaviour and/or encourage desirable behaviour.

Many institutions—schools, mental hospitals, homes for young offenders, prisons—have used behaviour modification programs with varying degrees of success. Institutions lend themselves well to such techniques because they provide a restricted environment where the consequences of behaviour can be more strictly controlled. Some institutions such as prisons or mental hospitals use a **token economy**—a program that motivates socially desirable behaviour by reinforcing it with tokens. The tokens (poker chips or coupons) may later be exchanged for desired goods like candy or cigarettes and privileges such as weekend passes, free time, or participation in desired activities. People in the program know in advance exactly what behaviours will be reinforced and how they will be reinforced. Token economies have been used effectively in mental hospitals to encourage patients to attend to grooming, to interact with other patients, and to carry out housekeeping tasks (Ayllon & Azrin, 1965, 1968). Although the positive behaviours generally stop when the tokens are discontinued, this does not mean that the programs are not worthwhile. After all, most people who are employed would probably quit their jobs if they were no longer paid.

Classroom teachers have used behaviour modification to modify undesirable behaviour and to encourage learning. "Time out" is a useful technique in which a child who is misbehaving is removed for a short time from sources of positive reinforcement. (Remember that according to operant conditioning, a behaviour that is no longer reinforced will be extinguished.)

Some research indicates, however, that it may be unwise to reward students for participating in learning activities they already enjoy. Reinforcement in such cases may lessen students' natural interest in the tasks, so that when reinforcers are withdrawn, it may disappear (Deci, 1975; Lepper et al., 1973).

Behaviour modification has been used successfully in business and industry to increase profits and to modify employee behaviour in health, safety, and learning. To reduce costs associated with automobile accidents and auto theft, automobile insurance companies attempt to modify the behaviour of their policyholders. They offer incentives in the form of reduced insurance premiums for installing airbags and burglar alarm systems. To encourage their employees to take company-approved college and university courses, many companies offer tuition reimbursement contingent on course grades. Many companies promote sales by giving salespeople special bonuses, awards, trips, and other prizes for increasing sales.

Remember It!

Learning Paradigms and Punishment

1. Punishment is roughly the same as negative reinforcement (true/false)
2. Which of the following is *not* presented in the text as one of the major factors influencing the effectiveness of punishment?
   a. timing
   b. consistency
   c. intensity
   d. frequency
3. Punishment usually does *not* extinguish undesirable behaviour. (true/false)
4. People often engage in behaviour that is reinforcing in the short term but not in their long-term interest. This reflects the influence of
   a. the magnitude of reinforcement.
   b. level of motivation.
   c. the immediacy of reinforcement.
   d. the schedule of reinforcement.
5. Recall what you have learned about classical and operant conditioning. Which of the following is descriptive of operant conditioning?
   a. An association is formed between a response and its consequence.
   b. The responses acquired are usually emotional reactions.
   c. The subject is usually passive.
   d. The response acquired is usually an involuntary or reflexive response.
6. Applying the principles of learning to eliminate undesirable behaviour and/or encourage desirable behaviour is called (operant conditioning/behaviour modification).

Answers: 1. false 2. d 3. true 4. c 5. a 6. behaviour modification

One of the most successful applications of behaviour modification has been in the treatment of psychological problems ranging from phobias to addictive behaviours. In this context, behaviour modification is called "behaviour therapy." This kind of therapy is discussed in Chapter 13.

You can learn how to use behaviour modification in shaping your own behaviour in the *Apply It!* box at the end of this chapter.

Cognitive Learning

So far, we have explored relatively simple types of learning. In classical and operant conditioning, learning is defined in terms of observable or measurable changes in behaviour. Early behaviourists believed that learning through operant and classical conditioning could be explained without reference to internal mental processes. Today, however, a growing number of psychologists stress the role of mental processes. They choose to broaden the study of learning to include such **cognitive processes** as thinking, knowing, problem solving, remembering, and forming mental representations. According to cognitive theorists, these processes are critically important to a more complete understanding of learning.

Here we will focus on observational learning and the work of Albert Bandura.

Observational Learning: Watching and Learning

What is observational learning?

In our exploration of operant conditioning, you read how people and other animals learn by directly experiencing the consequences, positive or negative, of their behaviour. But must we experience rewards and punishments directly in order to learn? Not according to Albert Bandura (1986), who contends that many of our behaviours or responses are acquired through observational learning. **Observational learning**, sometimes called **modelling**, is learning that results when we observe the behaviour of others and the consequences of that behaviour.

The person who demonstrates a behaviour or whose behaviour is imitated is called the **model**. Parents, movie stars, and sports personalities are often powerful models. The effectiveness of a model is related to his or her status, competence, and power. Other important factors are the age, sex, attractiveness, and ethnic status of the model. Whether or not learned behaviour is actually performed depends largely on whether the observed models are rewarded or punished for their behaviour and whether the individual expects to be rewarded for the behaviour (Bandura, 1969a, 1977a).

We use observational learning to acquire new responses or to strengthen or weaken existing responses. Consider your native language or accent, your attitudes, gestures, personality traits, good habits (or bad habits, for that matter), moral values, food preferences, and so on. Do you share any of these with your parents? While you were growing up, their example probably influenced your behaviour for better or worse. Look around the classroom and observe the clothes, hairstyles, and verbal patterns of the other students. Most people have been greatly influenced by observing others.

Children can learn effectively by observing and imitating others.

token economy: A program that motivates and reinforces socially acceptable behaviours with tokens that can be exchanged for desired items or privileges.

cognitive processes (COG-nuh-tiv): Mental processes such as thinking, knowing, problem solving, and remembering.

observational learning: Learning by observing the behaviour of others and the consequences of that behaviour; learning by imitation.

modelling: Another name for observational learning.

model: The individual who demonstrates a behaviour or serves as an example in observational learning.

Observational learning is particularly useful when we find ourselves in unusual situations. Picture yourself as a guest at an elaborate dinner with the prime minister. More pieces of silverware extend from the plate than you have ever seen before. Which fork should be used for what? How should you proceed? You might decide to take your cue from the other guests—observational learning.

Inhibitions can be weakened or lost as a result of our observation of the behaviour of others. Adolescents can lose whatever resistance they may have to drinking, drug use, or sexual activity by seeing or hearing about peers engaging in these behaviours. With peer pressure, there is often an overwhelming tendency to conform to the behaviour and accept the values of the peer group. But inhibitions can also be strengthened through observational learning. A person does not need to experience the unfortunate consequences of dangerous behaviour to avoid it.

Fears, too, can be acquired through observational learning. A parent with an extreme fear of the dentist or of thunderstorms might serve as a model for these fears in a child. For instance, Muris and his colleagues (1996) found that children whose mothers expressed fears of animals, injuries, or medical problems had significantly higher levels of fear than children whose mothers did not express such fears. Note too that observational learning is not restricted to humans, as it has been shown by research on monkeys (Cook et al., 1985), octopuses (Fiorito & Scotto, 1992), and pigeons.

Try It!

Learning in Everyday Life

Think about everything you did yesterday from the time you woke up until the time you went to sleep. List 10 behaviours and indicate whether observational learning (OL), operant conditioning (OC), and/or classical conditioning (CC) played some role in the acquisition of each one. Remember, a behaviour may originally have been learned by some combination of the three types of learning and then been maintained by one or more of the types.

You probably learned to brush your teeth through a combination of observational learning (watching a parent demonstrate) and operant conditioning (being praised as your technique improved–shaping). Now the behaviour is maintained through operant conditioning, specifically negative reinforcement (getting rid of the terrible taste in your mouth). Avoiding cavities and the scorn of everyone around you is an extra bonus.

Which kind of learning had the most checks on your chart?

	Acquired through:			Maintained through:		
Behaviour	**OL**	**OC**	**CC**	**OL**	**OC**	**CC**
Brushing teeth	X	X			X	

Learning Aggression: Copying What We See

Albert Bandura suspected that aggressive behaviour is particularly subject to observational learning and that aggression and violence on television and in cartoons tend to increase aggression in children. His pioneering work has greatly influenced current thinking on these issues. In several classic experiments, Bandura demonstrated how children are influenced by exposure to aggressive models.

One study (Bandura et al., 1961) involved three groups of preschool children. Children in one group individually observed an adult model punching, kicking, and hitting an inflated plastic "Bobo Doll" (a large, plastic doll that is weighted at the bottom so that it doesn't fall over) with a mallet, while uttering aggressive words such as "Sock him in the nose ..." "Throw him in the air ..." "Kick him ..." "Pow ..." (p. 576). Children in the second group observed a non-aggressive model who ignored the Bobo Doll and sat quietly assembling Tinker Toys. Children in the control group were placed in the same setting as those in the two other groups, but with no adult present. Later, each child was observed through a one-way mirror. Participants exposed to the aggressive model imitated much of the aggression and also engaged in significantly more non-imitative aggression than either of the other groups. Participants in the second group, who had observed the non-aggressive model, showed less aggressive behaviour than the control group.

A further study (Bandura et al., 1963) compared the degree of aggression in children following exposure to (1) a live aggressive model, (2) a filmed version of the episode, and (3) a film depicting an aggressive cartoon character using the same aggressive behaviours in a fantasy-like setting. A control group was not exposed to any of the three situations of aggression. The groups exposed to aggressive models used significantly more aggression than the control group. The researchers concluded that "of the three experimental conditions, exposure to humans on film portraying aggression was the most influential in eliciting and shaping aggressive behaviour" (p. 7).

Bandura's research provided the impetus for studying the effects of television violence and aggression in both cartoons and regular programming. Although there has been some consciousness-raising about the negative impact of media violence, the amount of television violence is still excessive. The problem is compounded by the fact that the average family watches more than seven hours of television each day. Watching excessive violence gives people an exaggerated view of the pervasiveness of violence in our society, while making them less sensitive to the victims of violence. Media violence also encourages aggressive behaviour in children by portraying aggression as an acceptable and effective way to solve problems and by teaching new forms of aggression (Wood et al., 1991). But just as children imitate the aggressive behaviour they observe on television, they also imitate the prosocial, or helping, behaviour they observe. Programs like *Sesame Street* have been found to have a positive influence on children (Coates et al., 1976).

Of course, learning principles can also have many positive outcomes, such as those described in the *Apply It!* box below.

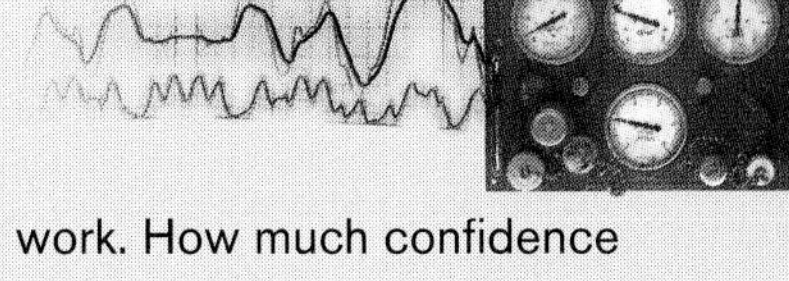

Apply It!

Steps to Take in Overcoming Procrastination

Procrastinators of all types can profit from the following 10 steps for overcoming procrastination. We'll use studying as our example in each step:

- Identify the environmental cues that habitually interfere with your studying. What competing interests are most likely to cause you to put off studying or to interrupt your studying—television, bed, refrigerator, telephone, friends, family members?
- Select a place to study that you associate only with studying, preferably away from the distracting environmental cues you have identified.
- Schedule your study time in advance so your decisions about when to start work will not be ruled by the whim of the moment.
- The most difficult part is getting started. Give yourself an extra reward for starting on time and, perhaps, a penalty for not starting on time.
- Much procrastination results from a failure to consider its negative consequences. Visualizing the consequences of not studying can be an effective tool. Suppose you are considering going out of town with friends for the weekend instead of studying for a midterm test on Monday. Picture this! You walk into the classroom Monday morning unprepared; you know the answers to very few questions; you flunk the test. Now visualize the outcome if you stay home for the weekend and study.
- Estimate how long it will take to complete an assignment, and then keep track of how long it actually takes.
- Avoid jumping to another task when you reach a difficult part of an assignment.
- Avoid preparation overkill. Busy procrastinators may spend hours preparing for the task rather than on the task itself. This enables them to postpone the task.
- Keep a record of the reasons you give yourself for postponing studying or completing important assignments.
- Procrastinators are notorious for breaking their own promises to get to work. How much confidence would you have in a friend who made promises to you but never followed through?

  "I'll do this tomorrow." Why is tomorrow going to be a better day? You told yourself this yesterday, and now you are not following through.
  "I'll go out with my friends, but only for a few hours." As a rule, does your time with friends turn out to be a few hours or the whole day or night?
  "I'll get some sleep and set my alarm for 3:00 a.m. and then study." Are you usually able to get up at 3:00 a.m.?
  "I'll watch TV for a few minutes and then get back to studying." Does a few minutes often turn into several hours?
  "I'll rest for a few minutes and clear my mind so I can think better." Does your ability to think *really* improve?

Apply the steps outlined here to gain more control over your behaviour. A good source for finding other suggestions on this topic is *Overcoming Procrastination* by Albert Ellis and William J. Knaus (1977).

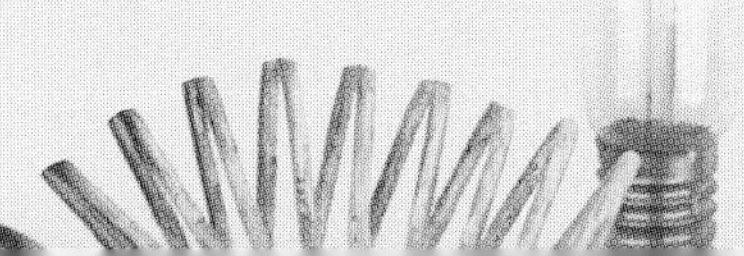

KEY TERMS

avoidance learning, p. 166
behaviour modification, p. 167
classical conditioning, p. 145
cognitive processes, p. 169
conditioned reflex, p. 146
conditioned response (CR), p. 147
conditioned stimulus (CS), p. 147
continuous reinforcement, p. 160
discrimination, p. 149
discriminative stimulus, p. 158
drug tolerance, p. 153
extinction, pp. 148 and 157
fixed-interval schedule, p. 161
fixed-ratio schedule, p. 160
generalization, p. 148
higher-order conditioning, p. 150
learned helplessness, p. 166
learning, p. 144
model, p. 169
modelling, p. 169
negative reinforcement, p. 158
observational learning, p. 169
operant conditioning, p. 155
partial reinforcement, p. 160
partial-reinforcement effect, p. 162
positive reinforcement, p. 158
primary reinforcer, p. 159
punishment, p. 164
reflex, p. 146
reinforcement, p. 158
reinforcer, p. 155
schedule of reinforcement, p. 160
secondary reinforcer, p. 159
shaping, p. 156
Skinner box, p. 156
spontaneous recovery, p. 148
stimulus, p. 144
successive approximations, p. 156
taste aversion, p. 154
token economy, p. 168
unconditioned response (UR), p. 146
unconditioned stimulus (US), p. 146
variable-interval schedule, p. 161
variable-ratio schedule, p. 160

THINKING CRITICALLY

Evaluation

Prepare statements outlining the strengths and limitations of classical conditioning, operant conditioning, and observational learning in explaining how behaviours are acquired and maintained.

Point/Counterpoint

The use of behaviour modification has been a source of controversy among psychologists and others. Prepare arguments supporting each of the following positions:

a. Behaviour modification should be used in society to shape the behaviour of others.
b. Behaviour modification should not be used in society to shape the behaviour of others.

Psychology in Your Life

Think of a behaviour of a friend, a family member, or a professor that you would like to change. Using what you know about classical conditioning, operant conditioning, and observational learning, formulate a detailed plan for changing the behaviour of the target person.

SUMMARY & REVIEW

Classical Conditioning

What was Pavlov's major contribution to psychology?

Ivan Pavlov's study of the conditioned reflex provided psychology with a model of learning called *classical conditioning.*

How is classical conditioning accomplished?

During classical conditioning, a neutral stimulus (tone) is presented shortly before an unconditioned stimulus (food), which naturally elicits, or brings forth, an unconditioned response (salivation). After repeated pairings, the conditioned stimulus (tone) by itself will elicit the conditioned response (salivation).

How does extinction occur in classical conditioning?

If the conditioned stimulus (tone) is presented repeatedly without the unconditioned stimulus (food), the conditioned response (salivation) will become progressively weaker and eventually disappear—a process called *extinction*.

What is generalization?

Generalization occurs when an organism makes a conditioned response to a stimulus that is similar to the original conditioned stimulus.

What is discrimination in classical conditioning?

Discrimination is the ability to distinguish between similar stimuli, so that the conditioned response is made only to the original conditioned stimulus.

How did John B. Watson demonstrate that fear could be classically conditioned?

John Watson demonstrated that fear could be classically conditioned when, by presenting a white rat along with a loud, frightening noise, he conditioned Little Albert to fear the white rat.

What are four factors that influence classical conditioning?

Four factors influencing classical conditioning are (1) the number of pairings of conditioned stimulus and unconditioned stimulus, (2) the intensity of the unconditioned stimulus, (3) how reliably the conditioned stimulus predicts the unconditioned stimulus, and (4) the temporal relationship between the conditioned stimulus and the unconditioned stimulus.

What types of responses can be learned through classical conditioning?

Positive and negative emotional responses (including likes, dislikes, fears, and phobias), conditioned immune responses, and conditioned drug tolerance in drug users are some types of responses acquired through classical conditioning.

Operant Conditioning

How are responses acquired through operant conditioning?

Operant conditioning is a method for conditioning voluntary responses. The consequences of behaviour are manipulated to shape a new response or to increase or decrease the frequency of an existing response.

How is shaping used to condition a response?

In shaping, rather than waiting for the desired response to be produced, we selectively reinforce successive approximations toward the goal response until the desired response is achieved.

How does extinction occur in operant conditioning?

In operant conditioning, extinction occurs when reinforcement is withheld.

What are the goals of both positive and negative reinforcement, and how are the goals accomplished for each?

Both positive reinforcement and negative reinforcement are used to strengthen or increase the probability of a response. With positive reinforcement the desired response is followed with a reward; with negative reinforcement it is followed with the termination of an aversive stimulus.

What are the four major schedules of reinforcement, and which schedule yields the highest response rate and the greatest resistance to extinction?

The four major schedules of reinforcement are the fixed-ratio, variable-ratio, fixed-interval, and variable-interval schedules. The variable-ratio schedule provides the highest response rate and the greatest resistance to extinction.

What is the partial-reinforcement effect?

The partial-reinforcement effect is the greater resistance to extinction that occurs when responses are maintained under partial reinforcement rather than under continuous reinforcement.

What three factors, in addition to the schedule of reinforcement, influence operant conditioning?

In operant conditioning, the acquisition of a response, the response rate, and the resistance to extinction are influenced by the magnitude of reinforcement, the immediacy of reinforcement, and the motivation of the organism.

How does punishment differ from negative reinforcement?

Punishment is used to decrease the frequency of a response; negative reinforcement is used to increase the frequency of a response.

What are some disadvantages of punishment?

Punishment generally suppresses rather than extinguishes behaviour; it does not help people develop more appropriate behaviours; and it can cause fear, anger, hostility, and aggression in the punished person.

What three factors increase the effectiveness of punishment?

Punishment is most effective when it is administered immediately after undesirable behaviour, when it is consistently applied, and when it is fairly intense.

What is behaviour modification?

Behaviour modification involves the systematic application of learning principles to individuals or groups in order to eliminate undesirable behaviour and/or encourage desirable behaviour.

Cognitive Learning

What is observational learning?

Observational learning is learning by observing the behaviour of others, called models, and the consequences of that behaviour.

Memory

"No, no, not me. Not me!" cried Hen Van Nguyen in halting English. This unfortunate Vietnamese immigrant, on trial for murder, protested his innocence for two full days at the trial before it was discovered that he was not the real defendant. Before the trial, Nguyen had been charged with theft and was being held in a Georgia county jail. In the same jail was another Vietnamese man, who had been accused of stabbing to death the woman he lived with.

The jailer had mistakenly delivered the wrong man to the courtroom. Yet unbelievably, during the trial, two eyewitnesses identified Nguyen and swore that he had committed the murder. Even more astonishing, the defence attorney, who had met several times with his client to prepare his defence, sat with the wrong man in the courtroom and defended him for two days. The county sheriff remarked, "How the defence attorney did not know his client, I don't know" ("Wrong man," 1985).

In this case, the defence attorney, the sheriff, and the eyewitnesses were all members of a racial group different from Mr. Nguyen's.

In another case, however, even though the eyewitness was of the same race as the suspect, she picked the wrong man. Can someone be in two

Donald Thomson, psychologist

places at once? No! And this saved psychologist Donald Thomson.

One night, Thomson was a guest on an Australian talk show about eyewitness testimony. He was with other experts, including the chief of police. He argued that a good eyewitness must notice specific features of the face. He pointed to his important features (eyes, smile, and so on). A woman who was watching him on the show was, at that time, assaulted and raped. Later, when she regained consciousness, she identified Thomson as her assailant. Fortunately for Thomson, it was a live taping and he had witnesses to support his alibi.

This case is ironic in that Thomson studies the very phenomenon that led to his arrest.

Do these cases simply reflect the rare and unusual in human memory, or are memory errors common occurrences? This and many other questions you may have about memory will be answered in this chapter. We will describe three memory systems: sensory, short-term, and long-term. You will learn how much information each system holds, for how long, and in what form. You will discover why virtually everyone finds it harder to remember names than faces. Is memory like a video recorder, in which the sights and sounds we experience are captured intact and simply played back in exact detail? Or do we "reconstruct" the past when we remember, leaving out certain bits and pieces of events that actually happened and adding others that did not?

Would you like to improve your memory? You will learn some techniques that can help you study more effectively, and some mnemonic devices (memory strategies) that can be used in practical ways every day as memory aids. Now read on … and remember.

Remembering

Our memory is the storehouse for everything we know. It enables us to know who and where we are when we awaken each morning. Memory provides the continuity of life—the long thread to which are tied our joys and sorrows, our knowledge and skills, our triumphs and failures, and the people and places that form our lives.

Most current efforts to understand human memory have been conducted within a framework known as the *information-processing approach* (Klatzky, 1984). This approach makes use of modern computer science and related fields to provide models that help us understand the processes involved in memory.

The Three Processes in Memory: Encoding, Storage, and Retrieval

What three processes are involved in the act of remembering?

What must occur to enable us to remember a friend's name, a fact from history, or an incident from our past? The act of remembering requires the successful completion of three processes: encoding, storage, and retrieval. The first process, **encoding**, involves transforming information into a form that can be stored in memory. Sometimes we encode information automatically, without any effort; but often we must do something with the information to remember it. For example, if you met someone named Brian at a party, you might associate his name with

Bryan Adams or Brian Mulroney. Such simple associations can markedly improve your ability to recall names and other information. Carefully encoding information greatly increases the chances that you will remember it.

This sounds easier than it actually is. To ensure that we encode information appropriately we must focus our *attention*. At any given time, we are bombarded with all kinds of sensory information. Imagine yourself in your classroom, and recall how hard it is to focus on your instructor's voice when you can also hear overhead fans and papers rustling; or you are distracted by how hot you feel, how uncomfortable your chair is, or how hungry or thirsty you are. All of these events compete for our attention. Because we cannot absorb every piece of information in our environment, we have to *selectively attend* to some information and let the other information fade into the background. **Selective attention** is the tool that allows us to eliminate interference from the relevant information.

The second memory process, **storage**, involves keeping or maintaining information in memory. For encoded information to be stored, some physiological change in the brain must take place—a process called **consolidation**. Consolidation occurs automatically in normal circumstances. If a person loses consciousness for any reason, the process can be disrupted and a permanent memory will not form (Deutsch & Deutsch, 1966). That is why someone who has been in a serious car accident may awaken in a hospital and not remember what has happened.

The final process, **retrieval**, occurs when information stored in memory is brought to mind. Calling Brian by name the next time you meet him shows that you have retrieved his name from memory. To remember, we must perform all three of these processes—encode the information, store it, and then retrieve it. Memory failure can result from the failure of any one of the three processes (see Figure 6.1).

Similar steps are required in the information processing of computers. Information is encoded (entered in some form the computer is able to use), then stored on the hard drive or floppy disks, and later retrieved on the screen or through the printer. You would not be able to retrieve the material if you had failed to enter it, if a power failure occurred before you could save what you had entered, or if you forgot which disk or file contained the needed information. Of course, human memory is far more complex than even the most advanced computer systems, but computer processing provides a useful analogy to memory, provided we don't take it too literally.

The Three Memory Systems: The Long and the Short of It

How are memories stored? According to one widely accepted view, the Atkinson–Shiffrin model, there are three different, interacting memory systems: sensory, short-term, and long-term (Atkinson & Shiffrin, 1968; Broadbent, 1958; Shiffrin & Atkinson, 1969). Considerable research in the biology of memory lends support to the model (Squire et al., 1993). We will

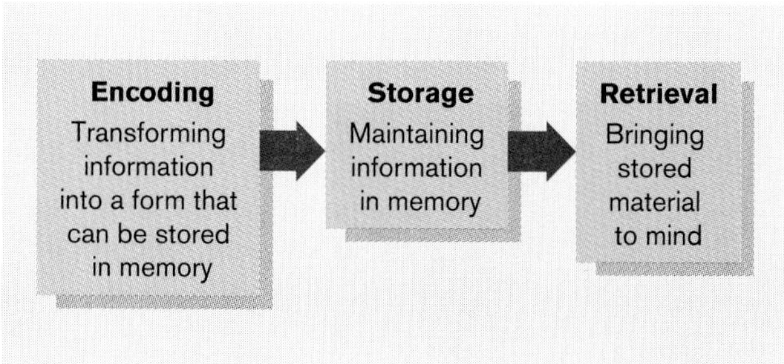

FIGURE 6.1

The Processes Required in Remembering **The act of remembering requires the successful completion of three processes: encoding, storage, and retrieval. Memory failure can result from the failure of any one of the three processes.**

encoding: Transforming information into a form that can be stored in short-term or long-term memory.

selective attention: Focusing on one piece of information while placing other information in the background.

storage: The act of maintaining information in memory.

consolidation: The presumed process, believed to involve the hippocampus, by which a permanent memory is formed.

retrieval: The act of bringing to mind material that has been stored in memory.

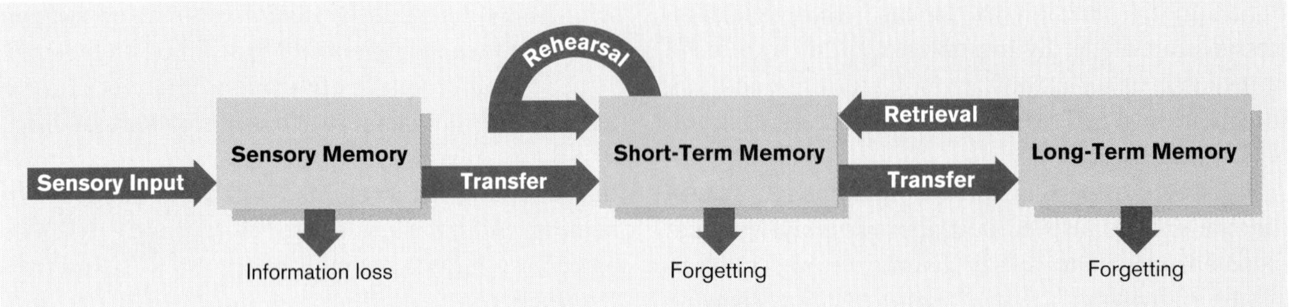

FIGURE 6.2

The Three Memory Systems **According to the Atkinson–Schiffrin model, there are three separate memory systems: sensory memory, short-term memory, and long-term memory.**

examine each of these three memory systems, which are shown in Figure 6.2.

Sensory Memory: Images and Echoes

What is sensory memory?

As information comes in through the senses, virtually everything we see, hear, feel, or otherwise sense is held in **sensory memory**, but only for the briefest period of time. Sensory memory normally holds visual images for a fraction of a second and holds sounds for about two seconds (Crowder, 1992).

Visual sensory memory lasts just long enough to keep whatever you are viewing from disappearing when you blink your eyes. You can demonstrate visual sensory memory for yourself by doing the *Try It!*

For a fraction of a second, glance at the three rows of letters and numbers shown below and then close your eyes. How many of the items can you recall?

X B D F
M P Z G
L C N H

Most people can correctly recall only four or five of the items when they are briefly presented. Does this indicate that visual sensory memory can hold only four or five items at a time? No. Researcher George Sperling (1960) knew that our visual sensory capacity should enable us to take in most or all of the 12 items at a single glance. Could it be that sensory memory is so short-lived that while we are reporting some items, others have already faded from sensory memory? Sperling thought of an ingenious method to test this notion. He briefly flashed 12 items like those above to his participants. Immediately upon turning the display off, he sounded a high, medium, or low tone that signalled the participants to report

Try It!

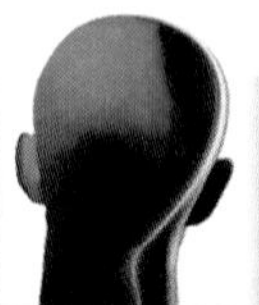

Testing Sensory Memory

To prove the existence of the visual sensory memory, move your forefinger back and forth rapidly in front of your face. You will see what appears to be the blurred images of many fingers. This occurs because your sensory memory briefly holds a trace of the various positions that your finger occupies as it moves.

Sensory memory holds a visual image, such as a lightning bolt, for a fraction of a second—just long enough for us to perceive a flow of movement.

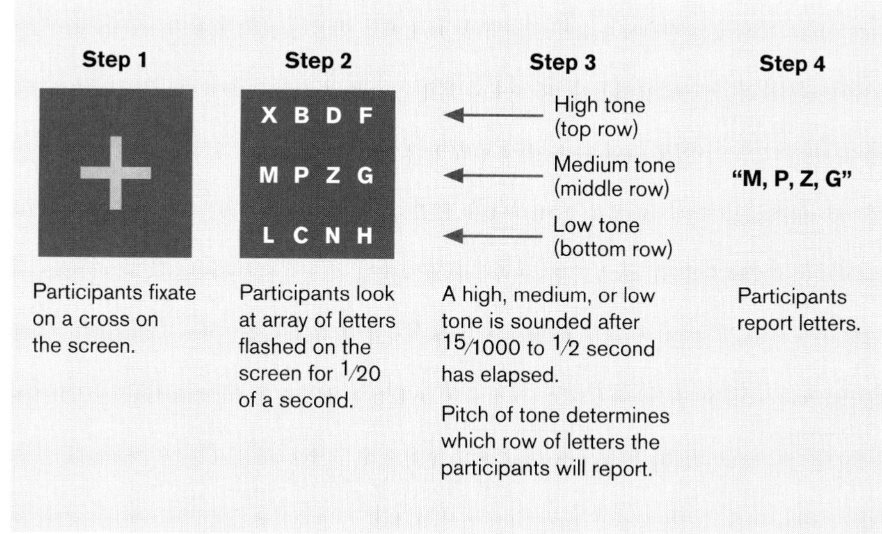
Step 1
Step 2
Step 3
Step 4
X B D F
M P Z G
L C N H
High tone (top row)
Medium tone (middle row)
Low tone (bottom row)
"M, P, Z, G"
Participants fixate on a cross on the screen.
Participants look at array of letters flashed on the screen for 1/20 of a second.
A high, medium, or low tone is sounded after 15/1000 to 1/2 second has elapsed.
Pitch of tone determines which row of letters the participants will report.
Participants report letters.

FIGURE 6.3
Sperling's Study of the Capacity of Sensory Memory Sperling demonstrated that sensory memory holds more information than participants are able to report completely because the visual afterimage fades so quickly. Sperling proved that people could retain 12 items in sensory memory, but only long enough to report 4 items in the designated row. (Based on Sperling, 1960.)

only the top, middle, or bottom row of items. Before they heard the tone, the participants had no way of knowing which row they would have to report. Sperling found that when the participants could view the letters for 0.0015 to 0.5 seconds, they could report correctly all the items in any row nearly 100 percent of the time. But the items fade from sensory memory so quickly that during the time it takes to report three or four of the items, the other eight or nine have already disappeared. Figure 6.3 shows the steps that were involved in Sperling's research study.

Sensory memory for sound is similar to that for vision. You have experienced auditory sensory memory when the last few words someone has spoken seem to echo briefly in your mind. Auditory sensory memory usually lasts about two seconds, compared with the fractions of a second for visual sensory memory (Klatzky, 1980).

We have seen that an abundance of information in raw, natural form can be stored briefly in sensory memory. This brief period is just long enough for us to begin to process the sensory stimuli and to select the most important information for further processing in the second memory system—short-term memory.

Short-Term Memory: Short Life, Small Capacity

What are the characteristics of short-term memory?

Whatever you are thinking about right now is in your **short-term memory** (STM). We use short-term memory when we carry on a conversation, solve a problem, or look up a telephone number and remember it just long enough to dial it.

Short-term memory does not hold sensory stimulus the way sensory memory does. Short-term memory usually codes information according to sound—that is, in acoustic form (Conrad, 1964). The letter *T* is coded as the sound "tee," not as the shape T. Short-term memory can also hold visual images, and store information in semantic form (i.e., according to meaning) (Shulman, 1972).

LINK IT!

www.ucs.mun.ca/~mathed/Stats/memory14.htm
Investigating short-term memory

www.alzheimer.ca
Alzheimer Society of Canada

THE CAPACITY OF SHORT-TERM MEMORY Unlike sensory memory, which can hold a vast amount of information briefly, short-term memory has a very limited

sensory memory: The memory system that holds information coming in through the senses for a period ranging from a fraction of a second to several seconds.

short-term memory: The second stage of memory, which holds about seven (a range of five to nine) items for less than 30 seconds without rehearsal; working memory; the mental workspace we use to keep in mind tasks we are thinking about at any given moment.

capacity—about seven (plus or minus two) different items or bits of information at one time (Miller, 1956). Test the capacity of your short-term memory in the *Try It!*

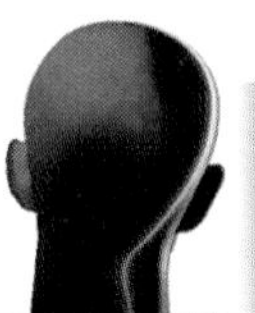

Try It!

Testing Short-Term Memory

Read aloud the digits in the first row (row "a" below) at a steady rate of about two per second. Then, from memory, write them down on a sheet of paper.

Repeat the process, row by row.

a. 3 8 7 1

b. 9 6 4 7 3

c. 1 8 3 0 5 2

d. 8 0 6 5 9 1 7

e. 5 2 9 7 3 1 2 5

f. 2 7 4 0 1 9 6 8 3

g. 3 9 1 6 5 8 4 5 1 7

How well did you do in *Try It*? You just learned that most people recall about seven items. This is just enough for phone numbers and postal codes. When short-term memory is filled to capacity, **displacement** can occur (Waugh & Norman, 1965). In displacement, each incoming item pushes out an existing item, which is then forgotten.

One way to overcome the limitation of seven or so bits of information is to use a technique that George A. Miller (1956) calls "chunking." Chunking means organizing or grouping separate bits of information into larger units, or chunks. A chunk is an easily identifiable unit such as a syllable, a word, an acronym, or a number (Cowan, 1988). For example, the numbers 5 2 9 7 3 1 2 5 could be chunked 52 97 31 25, leaving the short-term memory with the easier task of dealing with four chunks of information instead of eight separate bits. Complete the next *Try It*! and see if chunking works for you.

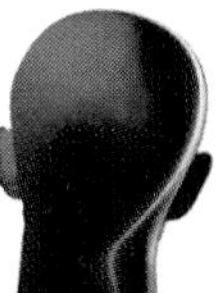

Try It!

Chunking

Read the following letters individually at the rate of about one per second and then see if you can repeat them.

N - H - L - C - B - C - P - E - I - V - C - R - R - C - M - P

Did you have difficulty? Probably, because there are 16 different letters. But now try this:

NHL CBC PEI VCR RCMP

Did you find that five chunks are easier to remember than 16 separate items?

Chunking is a very useful technique for increasing the capacity of short-term memory, but there are limits. Simon (1974) suggests that the larger the chunks, the fewer chunks we can remember.

THE DURATION OF SHORT-TERM MEMORY Items in short-term memory are lost very quickly, in less than 30 seconds, unless we repeat them over and over to ourselves, silently or out loud, to retain them. This process is known as **rehearsal**. We rehearse telephone numbers that we have looked up to keep them in short-term memory long enough to dial the number. But short-term memory is easily disrupted. It is so fragile, in fact, that an interruption or a distraction can cause information to be lost in just a few seconds.

Researchers have tried to determine how long short-term memory lasts if rehearsal is prevented. In a series of early studies, participants were briefly shown three consonants, such as H, G, and L, and were then asked to count backward by threes from a given number (738, 735, 732, and so on). After intervals lasting from 3 to 18 seconds, participants were instructed to stop their backward counting and recall the three letters (Brown, 1958; Peterson & Peterson, 1959). Following a delay of nine seconds, the participants could recall an average of only one of the three letters. After 18 seconds, there was practically no recall whatsoever. An 18-second distraction had completely erased the three letters from short-term memory.

SHORT-TERM MEMORY AS WORKING MEMORY Short-term memory is more than just a system that holds information received from sensory memory until we are able to store it in long-term memory. Allan Baddeley (1990, 1992, 1995) suggests that *working memory* is a more fitting term than *short-term memory*. More than just a temporary way station between sensory memory and long-term memory, working memory is a kind of mental workspace that temporarily holds incoming information from sensory memory or information retrieved from long-term memory in order to perform some conscious cognitive activity. "Without it you couldn't understand this sentence, add up a restaurant tab in your head, or find your way home. Working memory is an erasable mental blackboard that allows you to hold briefly in your mind and manipulate the information, whether it be words, menu prices, or a map of your surroundings" (Wickelgren, 1997, p. 1580).

Research shows that the prefrontal cortex is the primary area responsible for working memory (Courtney et al., 1997; Rao et al., 1997).

Long-Term Memory: As Long as a Lifetime

What is long-term memory, and what are its subsystems?

Some information from short-term memory makes its way into long-term memory. **Long-term memory** (LTM) is our vast storehouse of permanent or relatively permanent memories. There are no known limits to the storage capacity of long-term memory. Long-term memories last a long time, some of them for a lifetime.

When we talk about memory in everyday conversation, we are usually referring to long-term memory. Long-term memory holds all the knowledge we have accumulated, the skills we have acquired, and the memories of our past experiences. Although visual images, sounds, and odours can be stored in long-term memory, information in long-term memory is usually stored in semantic form.

But how does this vast store of information make its way from short-term memory into long-term memory? We seem to remember some information with ease, almost automatically, but other kinds of material require great effort. Sometimes, through mere repetition or rehearsal, we are able to transfer information into long-term memory. Your teachers may have used a drill to try to cement the multiplication tables in your long-term memory. This rote rehearsal, however, is not necessarily the best way to transfer information to long-term memory (Craik & Watkins, 1973). When you relate new information to the information already safely tucked away in long-term memory, you increase the chances that you will be able to retrieve the new information (Symons & Johnson, 1997; Willoughby et al., 2000). These skills would surely be useful in games such as that described in the *It Happened in Canada* box. Figure 6.4 summarizes the three memory systems.

IT HAPPENED IN CANADA

Trivial Pursuit

Where was the game Trivial Pursuit invented? If you guessed Canada, you were right. And if you were playing Trivial Pursuit, you might have earned a piece of the pie! If you like to play, try these questions:

1. Into how many languages has Trivial Pursuit been translated?
2. In how many countries can you buy the game?

As you can see, the game involves recalling facts from memory. Have you ever noticed that some categories are easier for you to answer than others? This has to do with the way that you store information and how valuable the information is to you when you learn it. Now try to answer the following question: What type of memory are you using when you play Trivial Pursuit?

The answers are 19 and 33.

displacement: The event that occurs when short-term memory is holding its maximum and each new item entering short-term memory pushes out an existing item.

rehearsal: The act of purposely repeating information to maintain it in short-term memory or to transfer it to long-term memory.

long-term memory: The relatively permanent memory system with a virtually unlimited capacity.

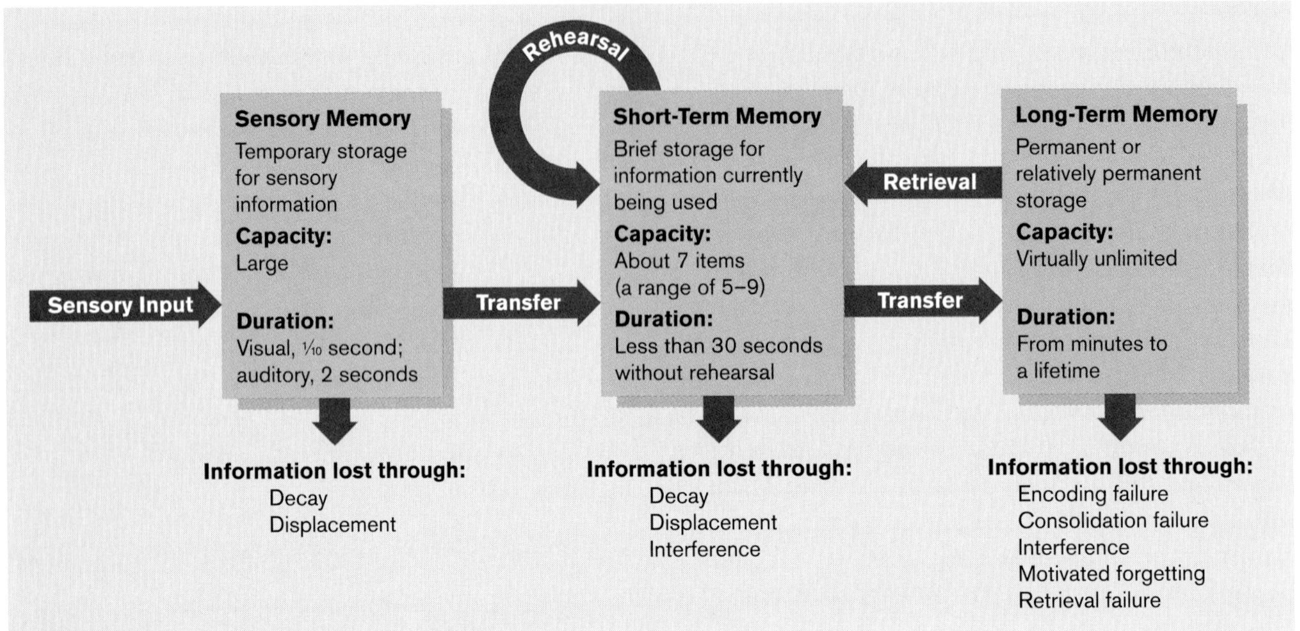

FIGURE 6.4
Characteristics of and Processes Involved in the Three Memory Systems

Declarative Memory and Non-Declarative Memory

A number of experts believe that there are two main subsystems within long-term memory—declarative memory and non-declarative memory.

Declarative memory (also called "explicit memory") stores facts and information. There are two types of declarative memory—episodic memory and semantic memory.

EPISODIC MEMORY **Episodic memory** is the subpart of declarative memory that contains the memory of events we have experienced personally (Wheeler et al., 1997). Endel Tulving (1985) at the University of Toronto describes it as something like a mental diary that records the episodes of our lives—the people we have known, the places we have seen, and the personal experiences we have had. According to Tulving,

> The episodic system stores and makes possible subsequent recovery of information about personal experiences from the past. It enables people to travel back in time, as it were, into their personal past, and to become consciously aware of having witnessed or participated in events and happenings at earlier times. (1989, p. 362)

SEMANTIC MEMORY **Semantic memory**, the second subpart of declarative memory, is our memory for general knowledge and is made up of objective facts and information. In other words, semantic memory is our mental dictionary or encyclopedia of stored knowledge such as the following:

> The three memory systems are sensory, short-term, and long-term memory.
>
> Dictionary is spelled d-i-c-t-i-o-n-a-r-y.
>
> 10 times 10 equals 100.

When you play Trivial Pursuit, you are calling on semantic memory almost exclusively to answer the questions. As a rule, the semantic facts you have stored are not personally referenced to time and place, as episodic memories are. You probably do not remember exactly where and when you learned to spell *dictionary* or to multiply 10 times 10.

Non-declarative memory (also called "implicit memory") consists of motor skills, habits, and simple classically conditioned responses (Squire et al., 1993). Motor skills are acquired through repetitive practice and include such things as eating with a fork, riding a bicycle, and driving a car. Although acquired

Declarative memory stores facts, information, and personal life events, such as a trip to a foreign country. Non-declarative memory encompasses motor skills, such as dance movements, which–once learned–can be carried out with little or no conscious effort.

slowly, once learned, these skills become habit, are quite reliable, and can be remembered and carried out with little or no conscious effort. For example, you probably use the keyboard on a computer without consciously being able to name the keys in each row from left to right.

Figure 6.5 shows the subsystems of long-term memory.

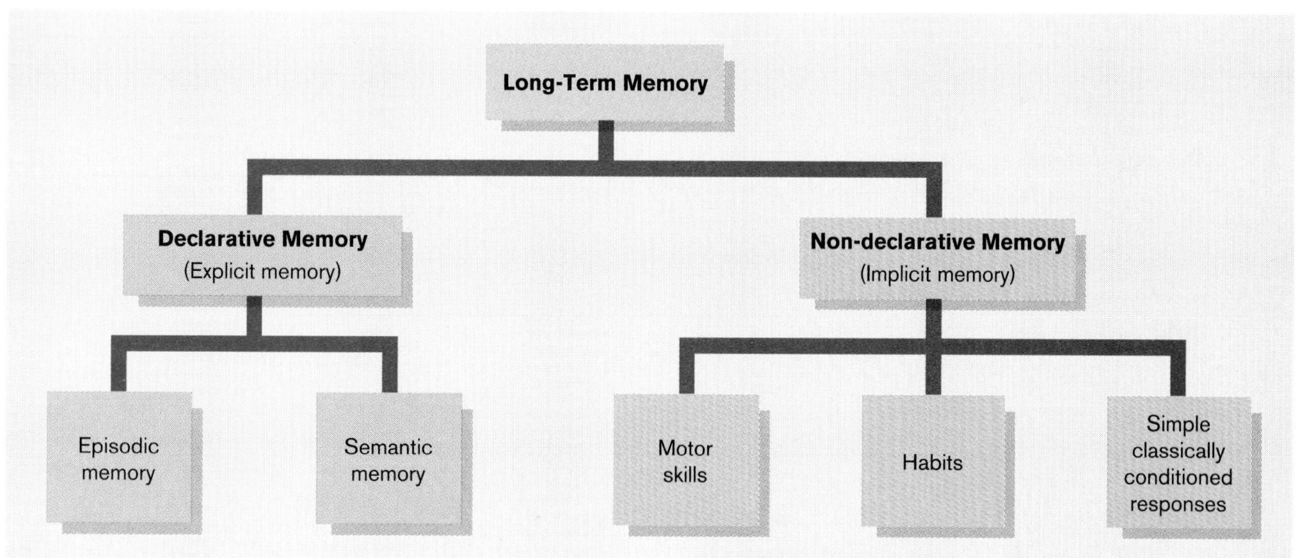

FIGURE 6.5

Subsystems of Long-Term Memory **Non-declarative memory consists of motor skills acquired through repetitive practice, habits, and simple classically conditioned responses. Declarative memory can be divided into two subparts–episodic memory, which stores memories of personally experienced events, and semantic memory, which stores facts and information.**

declarative memory: The subsystem within long-term memory that stores facts, information, and personal life experiences; also called explicit memory.

episodic memory (ep-ih-SOD-ik): The subpart of declarative memory that contains memories of personally experienced events.

semantic memory: The subpart of declarative memory that stores general knowledge; our mental encyclopedia or dictionary.

non-declarative memory: The subsystem within long-term memory that consists of skills acquired through repetitive practice, habits, and simple classically conditioned responses; also called implicit memory.

The Levels-of-Processing Model: Another View of Memory

Not all psychologists support the notion of three memory systems. University of Toronto researchers Craik and Lockhart (1972) proposed instead a **levels-of-processing model** (see also Lockhart & Craik, 1990). They suggest that whether we remember an item for a few seconds or a lifetime depends on how deeply we process the information. With the shallowest levels of processing, we are merely aware of the incoming sensory information. Deeper processing takes place only when we do something more with the information—when we form a relationship, make an association, or attach meaning to a sensory impression.

Craik and Tulving (1975) tested the levels-of-processing model. They had students answer *yes* or *no* to questions asked about words just before the words were flashed to them for 0.2 seconds. The students had to process the words *visually* (was the word in capital letters?), *acoustically* (does the word rhyme with another particular word?), and *semantically* (does the word make sense when used in a particular sentence?). Read the material in the next *Try It!*

The test required shallow processing for the first question, deeper processing for the second question, and the deepest processing for the third question. Later the students were unexpectedly given a retention test to see whether deeper levels of processing would facilitate memory. The deeper the level of processing, the higher the accuracy rate of memory. However, this conclusion would be equally valid for the three-system model. Now, test their conclusions yourself. Without looking back, name the three words you read in *Try It!* Were any easier to remember?

Brain-imaging studies with fMRI have revealed that semantic (deeper) encoding causes greater activity in the prefrontal cortex (Gabrieli et al., 1996).

Remember It!

Basic Memory Processes

1. Transforming information into a form that can be stored in memory is called ______; bringing the material that has been stored to mind is called ______.
   a. encoding; decoding
   b. consolidation; retrieval
   c. consolidation; decoding
   d. encoding; retrieval

2. Match the memory system with the best description of its capacity and the duration of time it holds information.
   ____ 1) sensory memory
   ____ 2) short-term memory
   ____ 3) long-term memory

   a. virtually unlimited capacity; long duration
   b. large capacity; short duration
   c. very limited capacity; short duration

3. Match the example with the appropriate memory system.
   ____ 1) semantic memory
   ____ 2) episodic memory
   ____ 3) non-declarative memory
   ____ 4) working memory

   a. playing tennis
   b. remembering your high school graduation
   c. deciding what you will do tomorrow
   d. naming the premiers of the provinces.

4. Which subsystem of long-term memory does not require conscious awareness?
   a. episodic memory
   b. semantic memory
   c. non-declarative memory
   d. declarative memory

Answers: 1.d 2.1) b 2) c 3) a 3.1) d 2) b 3) a 4) d 4.c

Try It!

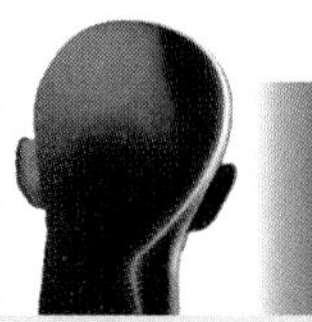

Testing the Levels-of-Processing Model

Answer *yes* or *no* to each of the following questions:

1. Is the word *LARK* in capital letters?
2. Does the word *speech* rhyme with *sleet*?
3. Would the word *park* make sense in this sentence?

   The woman passed a ______ on her way to work.

Now continue reading.

Measuring Memory

Three Methods of Measuring Memory

What are three methods of measuring retention?

Psychologists have used three main methods of measuring memory: recall, recognition, and the relearning method.

Recall

Recall tasks are usually the most difficult. In **recall** we must produce the required information by searching our memory without the help of **retrieval cues**. Remembering someone's name, recalling items on a shopping list, memorizing a speech or a poem word for word, and remembering appointments are all recall tasks. Essays and fill-in-the-blank questions require recall. Try to answer the following question:

> The three processes involved in memory are ________, ________, and ________.

In recalling, we must remember information "cold." Recall tasks are a little easier if cues are provided to jog our memory. Such cues might consist of the first letters of the required words for fill-in-the-blank questions. If you did not recall the three terms in the first question, try again with cued recall:

> The three processes involved in memory are e________, s________, and r________.

Sometimes serial recall is required—that is, information must be recalled in a specific order. This is the way you learned the alphabet, memorized poems, and learned any tasks that had to be carried out in a certain sequence.

Recognition

Recognition is exactly what the name implies: we simply recognize something as familiar—a face, a name, a taste, a melody. Some multiple-choice, matching, and true/false questions are examples of recognition test items. Consider a version of the question that was posed before:

> Which of the following is *not* one of the processes involved in memory?
>
> a. encoding b. assimilation
> c. storage d. retrieval

Was this recognition question easier than the recall version? The main difference between recall and recognition is that a recognition task does not require you to supply the information but only to recognize it when you see it. The correct answer is included along with the other items in a recognition question.

The Relearning Method

There is yet another way to measure memory that is even more sensitive than recognition. With the **relearning method** (the savings method), retention is expressed as the percentage of time saved when material is relearned compared with the time required

levels-of-processing model: A single-memory-system model in which retention depends on how deeply information is processed.

recall: A measure of retention that requires one to remember material with few or no retrieval cues, as in an essay test.

retrieval cue: Any stimulus or bit of information that aids in the retrieval of particular information from long-term memory.

recognition: A measure of retention that requires one to identify material as familiar, or as having been encountered before.

relearning method: Measuring retention in terms of the percentage of time or learning trials saved in relearning material compared with the time required to learn it originally; also called the *savings method*.

to learn the material originally. Suppose it took you 40 minutes to memorize a list of words, and one month later you were tested, using recall or recognition, to see how many of the words you remembered. If you could not recall or recognize a single word, would this mean that you had absolutely no memory of anything on the test? Or could it mean that the recall and the recognition methods of testing were not sensitive enough to pick up what little information you may have stored? How could we measure what is left of this former learning? Using the relearning method, we could time how long it would take you to relearn the list of words. If it took 20 minutes to relearn the list, this would represent a 50 percent savings over the original learning time of 40 minutes. The percentage of time saved—the **savings score**—reflects how much material remains in long-term memory.

Often parents wonder if the time they spend reading to their young children or exposing them to good music has any lasting influence. Do some traces of such early exposure remain? Many years ago, H.E. Burtt (1932) carried out a unique relearning experiment on his son Benjamin to study this question.

Every day Burtt read to his son three passages from Sophocles's *Oedipus Tyrannus* in the original Greek. He would repeat the same three passages for three months and then read three new passages for the next three months. This procedure continued from the time Benjamin was 15 months until he was three years old. Nothing more was done for five years until the boy reached the age of eight. Then Burtt tested Benjamin by having him memorize some of the passages read to him originally and some similar passages that he had never heard before. It took Benjamin 27 percent fewer trials to memorize the original passages. This 27 percent savings score suggests that a considerable amount of information remained in his memory for an extended period of time—information that could not have been detected through recall or recognition tests. The study also suggests that even information we do not understand can be stored in memory. Between 15 months and three years of age, young Benjamin did not speak or understand Greek, yet much of the information remained in his memory for years.

Students demonstrate this each semester when they study for comprehensive final exams. Relearning material for the final exams takes less time than it took to learn the material originally.

Hermann Ebbinghaus and the First Experimental Studies on Learning and Memory

What was Ebbinghaus's major contribution to psychology?

Hermann Ebbinghaus (1850–1909) conducted the first experimental studies on learning and memory. Ebbinghaus realized that some materials are easier than others to understand and remember. To study memory objectively, he was faced with the task of selecting materials that would all be equally difficult to memorize. To accomplish this, he originated the use of **nonsense syllables**, which are consonant-vowel-consonant combinations that are not actual words. Examples are LEJ, XIZ, LUK, and ZOH. The use of nonsense syllables largely accomplished Ebbinghaus's goal. But did you notice that some of the syllables sound more like actual words than others and would, therefore, be easier to remember?

Ebbinghaus conducted his famous studies on memory using 2300 nonsense syllables as his material and using himself as his only subject. He carried out all his experiments in the same surroundings at about the same time of day, and he kept away all possible distractions. Ebbinghaus's method was to learn lists of nonsense syllables, repeating them over and over at a constant rate of 2.5 syllables per second, marking time with a metronome or the ticking of a watch. He repeated a list until he could recall it twice without error, a point that he called *mastery*.

Ebbinghaus recorded the amount of time or the number of learning trials it took to memorize his lists to mastery. Then, after different periods of time had passed and forgetting had occurred, he recorded the amount of time or the number of trials he needed to relearn the same list to mastery. Ebbinghaus compared the time or the trials required for relearning with those of the original learning and then computed the percentage of time saved, or *savings score*. For him, the percentage of savings represented the percentage of the original learning that remained in memory.

Ebbinghaus's famous curve of forgetting, shown in Figure 6.6, consists of savings scores at various time intervals after the original learning. What does the curve of forgetting show about how rapidly this type of material is forgotten? Forgetting begins very quickly and then gradually tapers off. Ebbinghaus found that

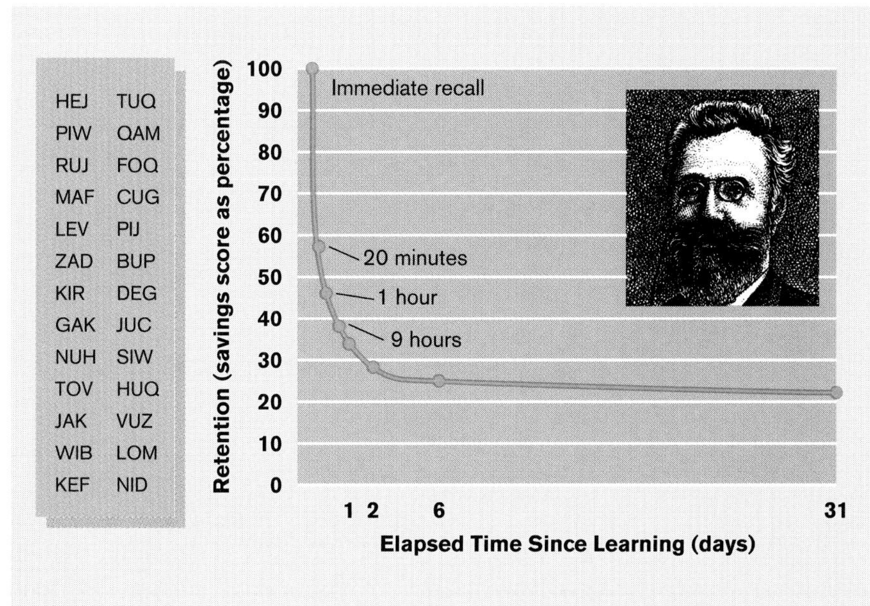

FIGURE 6.6

Ebbinghaus's Curve of Forgetting

After memorizing lists of nonsense syllables similar to those on the left of the figure, Ebbinghaus measured his retention after varying intervals of time using the relearning method. Forgetting was most rapid at first, as shown by his retention of only 58 percent after 20 minutes and 44 percent after 1 hour. Then the rate of forgetting tapered off, with a retention of 34 percent after 1 day, 25 percent after 6 days, and 21 percent after 31 days. (Data from Ebbinghaus, 1913.)

if he retained information as long as a day or two, very little more would be forgotten even a month later. But remember, this curve of forgetting applies to nonsense syllables. The forgetting of meaningful, carefully encoded, deeply processed, or frequently rehearsed material usually occurs more slowly.

What Ebbinghaus learned about the rate of forgetting is relevant for all of us. Do you, like most students, cram before a big exam? If so, don't assume that everything you memorize on Monday can be held intact until Tuesday. Because a significant amount of forgetting can occur within the first 24 hours, it is wise to spend at least some time reviewing the material on the day of the test. The less meaningful the material is to you, the more forgetting you can expect and the more necessary a review will be.

Forgetting

Patient: Doctor, you've got to help me. I'm sure I'm losing my memory. I hear something one minute and forget it the next. I don't know what to do!

Doctor: When did you first notice this?

Patient: Notice what?

Most of us think of forgetting as a problem to be overcome, but forgetting is not all bad. Wouldn't it be depressing if you were condemned to remember in stark detail all the bad things that ever happened to you? Forgetting clearly has its advantages.

The Causes of Forgetting

What are six causes of forgetting?

There are many reasons why we fail to remember. Among them are encoding failure, consolidation failure, decay, interference, motivated forgetting, and retrieval failure.

Encoding Failure

There is a distinction between forgetting and not being able to remember. Forgetting is "the inability to recall something now that could be recalled on an earlier occasion" (Tulving, 1974, p. 74). But often when we say we cannot remember, we have not actually forgotten. Our inability to remember may be a result of **encoding failure**—the information never entered our long-term memory in the first place. Of

savings score: The percentage of time or learning trials saved in relearning material over the amount of time or number of learning trials taken in the original learning.

nonsense syllable: A consonant-vowel-consonant combination that does not spell a word; used to control for the meaningfulness of the material.

encoding failure: Forgetting resulting from material never having been put into long-term memory.

Remember It!

Measures of Retention

1. Which of the following methods is the most sensitive way of measuring retention and can detect learning where other methods cannot?
   a. recall
   b. recognition
   c. relearning
   d. retrieval
2. Who invented the nonsense syllable, conceived the relearning method for testing retention, and plotted the curve of forgetting?
   a. George Sperling
   b. H. E. Burtt
   c. Frederick Bartlett
   d. Hermann Ebbinghaus
3. The curve of forgetting shows that memory loss
   a. occurs most rapidly at first and then levels off to a slow decline.
   b. begins to occur about 3 to 4 hours after learning.
   c. occurs at a fairly steady rate over a month's time.
   d. occurs slowly at first and increases steadily over a month's time.
4. Match all examples with the corresponding method of measuring retention.

   ____ 1) recognition
   ____ 2) relearning
   ____ 3) recall

   a. identifying a suspect in a lineup
   b. answering a fill-in-the-blank question on a test
   c. having to study less for a comprehensive final exam than for the sum of the previous exams
   d. answering questions on this Remember It!

Answers: 1. c 2. d 3. a 4. 1) a, d 2) c 3) b

the many things we encounter every day, it is sometimes surprising how little we actually encode. Can you recall accurately, or even recognize, something you have seen thousands of times before? Do the *Try It!* to find out.

Try It!

Check Your Recall

On a separate sheet of paper, draw a sketch of a one-cent coin from memory using recall. In your drawing, show the direction the Queen's image is facing and the location of the date, and include all the words on the "heads" side of the cent.

Once your drawing is complete, check the accuracy of your recall by comparing your drawing to a real coin. How accurate were you?

In your lifetime you have seen thousands of pennies, but unless you are a coin collector, you probably have not encoded the details of a penny. If you did poorly on the *Try It!*, you have plenty of company. Nickerson and Adams (1979) reported that few people can reproduce a penny from recall. In fact, only a handful of subjects could even recognize a drawing of a real penny when it was presented along with incorrect drawings.

In preparing for tests, do you usually assume a passive role? Do you merely read and reread your textbook and notes and assume that this process will eventually result in learning? If you don't test yourself, you may find that you have been the unwitting victim of encoding failure.

Consolidation Failure

Consolidation is the process by which encoded information is stored in memory. When a disruption in the consolidation process occurs, a permanent memory usually does not form. **Consolidation failure** can result from anything that causes a person to lose consciousness—a car accident, a blow to the head, a grand mal seizure, or an electroconvulsive shock treatment given for severe depression. Memory loss of the experiences that occurred shortly before the loss of consciousness is called **retrograde amnesia** (Lynch & Yarnell, 1973; Stern, 1981).

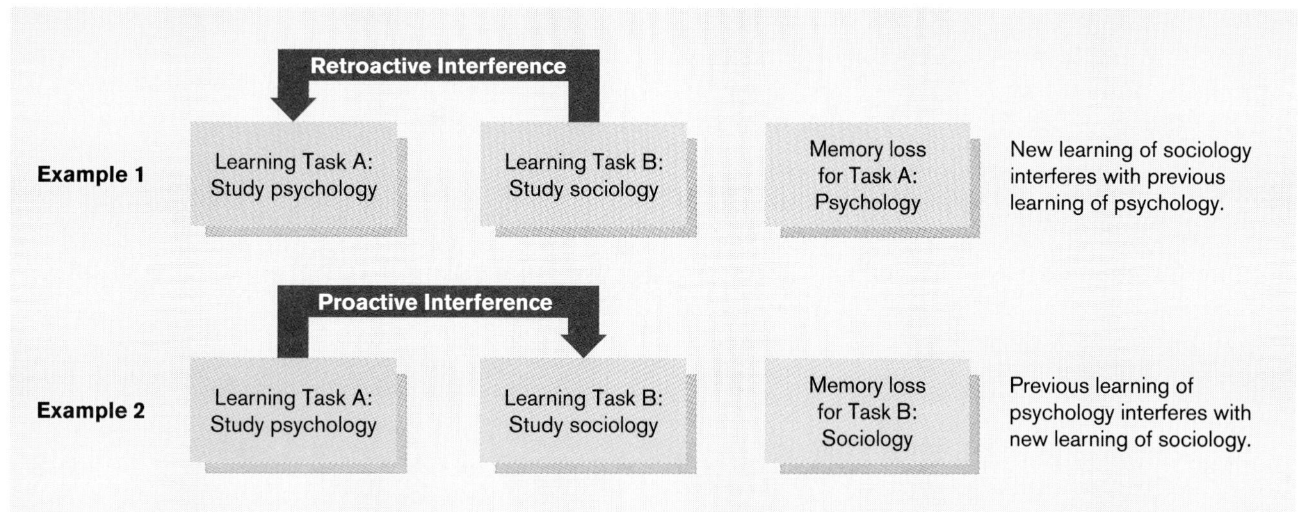

FIGURE 6.7

Retroactive and Proactive Interference **In Example 1, retroactive interference occurs when new learning hinders the ability to recall information learned previously. In Example 2, proactive interference occurs when prior learning hinders new learning.**

Decay

Decay theory, probably the oldest theory of forgetting, assumes that memories, if not used, fade with time and ultimately disappear entirely. The term *decay* implies a physiological change in the neural trace that recorded the experience. According to this theory, the neural trace may decay or fade within seconds or days, or over a much longer period of time.

Today most psychologists accept the notion of decay, or fading of the memory trace, as a cause of forgetting in sensory and short-term memory but not in long-term memory. If there were a gradual, inevitable decay of the memory trace in long-term memory, Harry Bahrick and colleagues (1975) would not have found that after 35 years, people recognized 90 percent of their high school classmates' names and photographs—the same percentage as for recent graduates.

Interference

What is interference, and how can it be minimized?

A major cause of forgetting, and one that affects us every day, is **interference**. Interference refers to those times when new information or information you have already learned interferes with what you are now learning or trying to recall (see Figure 6.7). There are two forms of interference: proactive and retroactive (Underwood, 1964).

PROACTIVE INTERFERENCE Laura's romance with her new boyfriend, Todd, got off to a bad start when she accidentally called him Dave, her former boyfriend's name. How many cheques written early in January do you suppose have the wrong year? Such mistakes happen frequently, and the reason for that is proactive interference. Proactive interference occurs when information or experiences already stored in long-term memory hinder our ability to remember newer information (Underwood, 1957). When you buy a new car, it may take a while to feel comfortable with the new arrangement of the dashboard. Your memory of the old car's dashboard may at first interfere with your driving. This type of proactive interference is called *negative transfer.* One explanation for interference is that old and new responses are competing with each other (Bower et al., 1994).

consolidation failure: Any disruption in the consolidation process that prevents a permanent memory from forming.

retrograde amnesia (RET-ro-grade): A loss of memory for events occurring during a period of time preceding a brain trauma that caused a loss of consciousness.

decay theory: A theory of forgetting that holds that the memory trace, if not used, disappears with the passage of time.

interference: The cause of memory loss that occurs when information or associations stored either before or after a given memory hinder our ability to remember it.

RETROACTIVE INTERFERENCE New learning or experience that interferes with our ability to remember information previously stored is called "retroactive interference." The more similar the new learning or experience is to the previous learning, the more interference there is. You may be surprised to learn that of all the activities we engage in, sleep interferes with previous learning the least.

What can you do to lessen the effects of retroactive interference on memory?

- When possible, study before going to sleep.
- If you can't study before going to sleep, at least review at that time the material you need to remember.
- Try not to study similar subjects back-to-back. Better yet, after studying one subject, take a short break before beginning the next subject.
- Schedule your classes so that courses with similar subject matter do not follow each other.

We have discussed ways to avoid forgetting. But there are times when we may need to avoid remembering—when we *want* to forget.

Motivated Forgetting: Don't Remind Me

Victims of assault and survivors of disasters (natural or human) may be haunted by their experiences for years. They are motivated to forget. However, even people who have not suffered any trauma use **motivated forgetting** to protect themselves from experiences that are painful, frightening, or otherwise unpleasant.

With one form of motivated forgetting, *suppression,* a person makes a conscious, active attempt to put a painful or disturbing memory out of mind, but the person is still aware that the painful event occurred. With another type of motivated forgetting, **repression**, unpleasant memories are literally removed from consciousness, and the person is no longer aware that the unpleasant event ever occurred (Freud, 1922). People who have **amnesia** (memory loss) that is not due to loss of consciousness or brain damage have actually repressed the events they no longer remember. To deal with unpleasant memories, more people probably use motivated forgetting than any other method. Humans, it seems, have a natural tendency to forget the unpleasant circumstances of life and to remember the pleasant ones (Linton, 1979; Matlin, 1989; Meltzer, 1930).

Retrieval Failure: Misplaced Memories

How many times have these experiences happened to you? You are with a friend when you meet an acquaintance, but you can't introduce the two because you cannot recall the name of your acquaintance. Or while taking a test, you can't remember the answer to a question that you are sure you know. Often we are certain that we know something, but we are not able to retrieve the information when we need it. This type of forgetting is called "retrieval failure" (Shiffrin, 1970).

Tulving (1974) asserts that much of what we call "forgetting" is really our inability to locate the information we seek. The information is in our long-term memory, but we cannot retrieve it. Tulving found that participants could recall a large number of items they seemed to have forgotten if he provided retrieval cues to jog their memory. For example, odours often provide potent reminders of experiences from the past, and they can serve as retrieval cues for information learned when certain odours were present (Schab, 1990).

A common retrieval failure experience is known as the "tip-of-the-tongue" (TOT) phenomenon (Brown & McNeil, 1966). Surely you sometimes try to recall a name, a word, or some other bit of information, fully aware that you know the item almost as well as your own name. You can almost recall the word or name, and perhaps even know the number of syllables and the beginning or ending letter of the word. It is on the tip of your tongue, but it just won't quite come out.

Prospective Forgetting: Forgetting to Remember

Do you have trouble remembering appointments? Do you forget to mail birthday cards on time, pick up your clothes at the cleaners, pay your bills, or water your plants? If you do, you are not alone. In a study of everyday forgetting, Terry (1988) had 50 people keep a diary of the instances of forgetting that occurred each day. Of the 751 recorded instances of forgetting, most did not involve forgetting names, facts, or other information already known. Rather, they involved prospective memory—remembering to carry out an action in the future.

Remember It!

Forgetting

1. Match the example with the appropriate cause of forgetting.
   ____ 1) encoding failure
   ____ 2) consolidation failure
   ____ 3) retrieval failure
   ____ 4) repression
   ____ 5) interference

   a. failing to remember the answer on a test until after you turn the test in
   b. forgetting a humiliating experience from childhood
   c. not being able to describe the back of a five-dollar bill
   d. calling a friend by another's name
   e. waking up in the hospital and not remembering you had an automobile accident

2. To minimize interference, it is best to follow learning with
   a. rest.
   b. recreation.
   c. sleep.
   d. unrelated study.

3. According to the text, the major cause of forgetting is interference. (true/false)

Answers: 1. 1) c 2) e 3) a 4) b 5) d 2. c 3. true

The Nature of Remembering and Forgetting

Memory as a Permanent Record: The Video Recorder Analogy

For hundreds of years, people have speculated about the nature of memory. Aristotle suggested that the senses imprint memories in the brain like signet rings stamping impressions in wax. Freud believed that all memories are permanently preserved, with some lying deep in the unconscious. Wilder Penfield (1969), a Canadian neurosurgeon, asserted that experiences leave a "permanent imprint on the brain ... as though a tape recorder had been receiving it all" (p. 165). What would lead him to such a conclusion?

Penfield (1975) performed more than 1100 operations on patients with epilepsy. He found that when parts of the temporal lobes were stimulated with an electrical probe, a small number of patients (3.5 percent) reported flashback experiences, as though they were actually reliving parts of their past. After reviewing Penfield's findings, other researchers offered different explanations for his patients' responses. Neisser (1967) suggested that the experiences patients reported were "comparable to the content of dreams," rather than the recall of actual experiences (p. 169).

Memory as a Reconstruction: Partly Fact and Partly Fiction

What is meant by the statement "Memory is reconstructive in nature"?

Other than Penfield's work, there is no research to suggest that memory works like a video recorder, capturing every part of an experience exactly as it happens. Normally, what we recall is not an exact replica of an event (Schachter et al., 1998). Rather, it is a **reconstruction**—a piecing together of a few highlights, using information that may or may not be accurate (Loftus & Loftus, 1980). Even for

motivated forgetting: Forgetting through suppression or repression in order to protect oneself from material that is too painful, anxiety- or guilt-producing, or otherwise unpleasant.

repression: Removing from one's consciousness disturbing, guilt-provoking, or otherwise unpleasant memories so that one is no longer aware that a painful event occurred.

amnesia: A partial or complete loss of memory resulting from brain trauma or psychological trauma.

When people recall an event, such as a car accident, they are actually reconstructing it from memory by piecing together bits of information that may or may not be totally accurate.

those of us with the most accurate memories, recall is partly truth and partly fiction (Conway et al., 1996). We supply what we *think* are facts to flesh out or complete those fragments of our experiences that we do recall accurately. This was the finding of another pioneer in memory research, Sir Frederick Bartlett.

Sir Frederick Bartlett

What is Bartlett's contribution to our understanding of memory?

Sir Frederick Bartlett (1886–1969) studied memory using rich and meaningful material learned and remembered under more life-like conditions. Bartlett (1932) gave participants stories to read and drawings to study. Then at varying time intervals he had them reproduce the original material. Accurate reports were rare. His participants seemed to reconstruct rather than actually remember the material they had learned. They recreated the stories, making them shorter and more consistent with their own individual points of view. They rationalized puzzling features of the stories to fit their own expectations; and they often changed details and substituted more familiar objects or events. Bartlett also found that errors in memory increased with time and that his participants were not aware that they had partly remembered and partly invented. Ironically, the parts his participants had created were often the very parts that they most adamantly claimed to have remembered.

Bartlett concluded that we systematically distort the facts and the circumstances of our experiences and that we do not simply remember new experiences as isolated events. Rather, information already stored in long-term memory exerts a strong influence on how we remember new information and experiences.

Schemas and Memory

What are schemas, and how do they affect memory?

Bartlett suggested that the inaccuracies in the participants' memories reflected **schemas**—integrated frameworks of knowledge and assumptions about people, objects, and events. Schemas help us process large amounts of material by providing us with means to incorporate new information and experience. They also provide association cues that can help us with retrieval. For example, you probably have a schema for fast-food restaurants. You typically order at a counter, pay immediately, wait for your food, carry your food to a table, and put your tray away when you're finished. We are often made aware of our schemas when they are violated. For example, if you went into a restaurant that you expected to serve fast food, you would be surprised if someone gave you a menu and tried to seat you.

Once formed, our schemas influence what we notice and how we encode and recall information. When we encounter new information or have a new experience related to an existing schema, we try to make it "fit" that schema. To this end, we may have to distort some aspects of the information and ignore or forget other aspects. Some of the distorting and ignoring occurs as the material is being encoded; more can occur when we try to remember or reconstruct the original experience (Brewer & Nakamura, 1984).

Distortion in Memory

When we reconstruct our memories, we do not purposely try to distort the actual experience—unless, of course, we are lying. But all of us tend to omit some facts that actually occurred and to supply other details from our own imaginations. Distortion occurs when we alter the memory of an event or of our experience so that it fits our beliefs, expectations, logic, or prejudices.

The tendency toward systematic distortion of actual events has been demonstrated many times. Try your own demonstration of distortion in memory in *Try It!*

Try It!

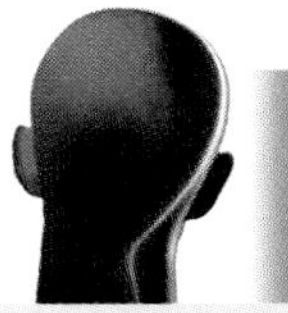

Testing Memory Distortion

Read this list of words aloud at a rate of about one word per second. Then close your book and write all the words you can remember.

bed	rest	awake	tired
dream	wake	snooze	doze
nap	yawn	snore	slumber

Now check your list. Did you "remember" the word *sleep*? Many people do, even though it is not one of the words on the list (Deese, 1959).

Try It! shows that we are very likely to alter or distort what we see or hear to make it fit with what we believe *should* be true. Since all the words on the list are related to sleep, it seems logical that *sleep* should be one of the words. In a a recent study that used word lists similar to the one in the *Try It!* box, Roediger and McDermott (1995) found that 40 to 55 percent of the participants "remembered" the very word that was not on the list.

Our tendency to distort makes the world more understandable and lets us organize our experiences into our existing systems of beliefs and expectations. This tendency is, however, also frequently responsible for gross inaccuracies in what we remember. We tend to distort memories in a positive way. Bahrick and others (1996) found that 89 percent of college students accurately remembered the A's they earned in high school, but only 29 percent accurately recalled the D's. Some of the most dramatic examples of systematic distortion are found in eyewitness testimony.

Eyewitness Testimony: Is It Accurate?

When people say, "I ought to know—I saw it with my own eyes," we are likely to accept their statement almost without question. After all, seeing is believing. Or is it?

Studies on the accuracy of human memory suggest that eyewitness testimony is highly subject to error and should always be viewed with caution (Brigham et al., 1982; Loftus, 1993a). Nevertheless, eyewitness testimony does play a vital role in our justice system. Says Loftus (1984), "We can't afford to exclude it. Sometimes, as in cases of rape, it is the only evidence available, and it is often correct" (p. 24). In fact, researchers at the University of British Columbia argue that eyewitness testimony may not be as problematic as others suggest. Yuille and Tollestrup (1992) believe that in most crime incidents, the victim is involved and "invested" (unlike participants in laboratory research). Hence, their memories tend to be more accurate.

Fortunately, there are ways in which eyewitness mistakes can be minimized. Eyewitnesses to crimes typically identify suspects from a lineup. The composition of the lineup is important. Other subjects in a lineup must resemble the suspect in age, body build, and certainly in race. Even then, if the lineup does not contain the guilty party, eyewitnesses may identify the person who most resembles the perpetrator (Gonzalez et al., 1993). Eyewitnesses are less likely to identify the culprit incorrectly and just as likely to make a correct identification if a sequential lineup is used—that is, if the members of the lineup are viewed one after the other, rather than simultaneously (Loftus, 1993a). Some police officers and researchers prefer a "showup" to a lineup. In a showup, one suspect is presented and the witness indicates whether that person is or is not the perpetrator. There are fewer misidentifications with a showup, but also more failures in making positive identifications (Gonzalez et al., 1993; Wells, 1993). However, Yarmey and his colleagues (1996) at the University of Guelph caution that lineups may provide greater accuracy than showups when the time interval between the occurrence and identification is lengthened.

In the case of children, fast "elimination lineups" seem to be most effective. In a Canadian study (Pozzulo & Lindsay, 1999), children were most accurate when asked to eliminate lineup members until only one suspect was left. Then, the children were told about the consequences of incorrectly identifying

reconstruction: A memory that is not an exact replica of an event but has been pieced together from a few highlights, with the use of information that may or may not be accurate.

schemas: The integrated frameworks of knowledge and assumptions we have about people, objects, and events, which affect how we encode and recall information.

an innocent person as a criminal. This procedure enhanced children's performance to the level of adults.

Regardless of age, the race of the individual is also a critical concern because eyewitnesses are more likely to identify the wrong person if the person's race is different from their own. According to Egeth (1993), misidentifications are about 15 percent higher in cross-race than in same-race identifications.

Questioning witnesses after a crime also can influence what they later remember. Because leading questions can substantially change a witness's memory of an event, it is critical that interviewers ask neutral questions (Leichtman & Ceci, 1995). Misleading information supplied after the event can result in erroneous recollections of the actual event, a phenomenon known as the *misinformation effect* (Loftus, 1997). Furthermore, after eyewitnesses have repeatedly recalled information, whether accurate or inaccurate, they become even more confident when they testify in court because the information is so easily retrieved (Shaw, 1996).

Witnessing a crime is highly stressful. How does stress affect eyewitness accuracy? Research suggests that eyewitnesses do tend to remember the central, critical details of the event even though their arousal is high. It is the memory of *peripheral* details that suffers as a result of high arousal (Burke et al., 1992; Christianson, 1992).

Hypnosis for Eyewitnesses

Does hypnosis improve the memory of eyewitnesses?

Research suggests that under controlled laboratory conditions, people do not show improved memory under hypnosis (Buckhout et al., 1981). Hypnotized subjects supply more information and are more confident of their recollections, but they supply more *inaccurate* information as well (Dywan & Bowers, 1983; Nogrady et al., 1985). Because subjects are much more confident of their memories after hypnosis, they become very convincing witnesses. Some critics of hypnosis are against using it as an aid for eyewitness testimony, but they believe that it can be a valuable investigative tool for police.

Recovering Repressed Memories: A Controversy

Since the late 1980s, thousands of people, most of them adult women under the age of 50, have come forward claiming to have been sexually abused as children. Given the fact that childhood sexual abuse is widespread and underreported, the growing number of claims of sexual abuse, including incest, should not be surprising. But many of these new claims are controversial in that the accusers maintain that they had repressed all memory of the abuse until they underwent therapy or read a self-help book for survivors of childhood sexual abuse. Is it likely that people could endure repeated episodes of childhood sexual abuse for years, selectively repress all memories of their abuse, and then recover the repressed memories as adults? On this issue, psychologists are divided.

Critics of repressed memory therapy are especially skeptical of recovered memories of events that occurred in the first few years of life. According to Loftus (1994), "Not a single piece of empirical work in human memory provides support for the idea that adults have concrete episodic memories of events from the first years of their lives" (p. 443). In fact, most people have few if any memories from the second and third year of life, in part because the hippocampus, which is vital in the formation of declarative memories, is not fully developed; nor, according to Squire and colleagues (1993), are the areas of the cortex where memories are stored. Furthermore, children are still limited in their language ability during these years and therefore do not store memories in the categories that would be accessible to them later in life. This relative inability of older children and adults to recall events from the first few years of life is referred to as **infantile amnesia**.

In contrast, Connie Kristiansen (1994), at Carleton University, argues that the question is not whether repressed memory occurs but how often it occurs. Even those who contest the existence of repressed memories (e.g., Loftus, 1993b) report finding them in some people. In her recent research, Kristiansen reports that false memory syndrome is not occurring in "epidemic proportions" (Hovdestad & Kristiansen, 1996). In fact, only 3.9 to 13.6 percent of individuals with recovered memories satisfy the criteria for diagnosis. Kristiansen also suggests that "repressed" memory might be better called "dissociated" memory to reflect the trauma that would lead a person to dissociate himself or herself from an event.

We have seen that conscious memory, even at its best, is a mixture of accurate recall and fragments of our own imagination. And at best, factual recall is not a faithful, point-by-point, detail-by-detail rendering of what actually occurred. There is strong evidence that the memory of an event is not like a photograph or recording that sits awaiting retrieval and is capable of being recalled intact. Rather, memory, like other brain functions, is fluid, plastic, and malleable. Like a living thing, it grows and changes over the years.

LINK IT!

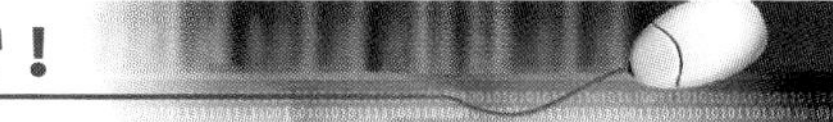

www.brown.edu/Departments/Taubman_Center/Recovmem/Archive.html
Recovered Memory Project

www.jimhopper.com/memory
Recovered memories of sexual abuse: scientific research & scholarly resources

www.csicop.org/si/9503/memory.html
Committee for the Scientific Investigation of Claims of the Paranormal (CSICOP), Skeptical Inquirer, "Remembering Dangerously"

www.fmsfonline.org
Website of the False Memory Syndrome Foundation

www.kspope.com/memory.shtml
Memory, Abuse, and Science

www.vix.com/pub/men/falsereport/child.html#recover
False allegations of child molestation and abuse

Unusual Memory Phenomena

Flashbulb Memories: Extremely Vivid Memories

Most of you remember New Year's Eve for the coming of the year 2000, and many of you may have unusually vivid memories of exactly when and where you were when the final countdown occurred. This type of extremely vivid memory is called a **flashbulb memory** (Bohannon, 1988; Brown & Kulik, 1977). Brown and Kulik suggest that a flashbulb memory is formed when an individual learns of an event that is highly shocking and emotional. You may have a flashbulb memory of the time you received the news of the death or serious injury of a close family member or a friend.

Reisberg and colleagues (1988) suggest that the vividness of a memory is related to the strength of the emotion we feel rather than to the element of surprise or whether the emotion is positive or negative. Other researchers remind us that a memory remains vivid because the person has probably talked about the circumstance with others or thought about it on many occasions.

A flashbulb memory is formed when a person learns of an event that is shocking and highly emotional, such as the death of Princess Diana in 1997. Where were you when you first heard the news of the car accident?

Pillemer (1990) argues that flashbulb memories do not constitute a different type of memory altogether. Rather, he suggests that all memories vary on the dimensions of emotion, importance, and rehearsal (how often people think or talk about the event after-

infantile amnesia: The relative inability of older children and adults to recall events from the first few years of life.

flashbulb memory: An extremely vivid memory of the conditions surrounding one's first hearing of the news of a surprising, shocking, or highly emotional event.

ward). Since flashbulb memories rank high in all three dimensions, they should be the most accurate of any memories. But are they infallible? Hardly.

Several studies suggest that flashbulb memories may not be as accurate as people believe them to be. Neisser and Harsch (1992) questioned first-year university students about the Challenger disaster the following morning. When the same students were questioned again three years later, one-third gave accounts that differed markedly from those they gave initially, even though they were extremely confident of their recollections.

Eidetic Imagery: Almost Like "Photographic Memory"

Have you ever wished you had a photographic memory? Perhaps you have heard of someone who is able to read a page in a book and recall it word for word. More than likely, this person has developed such an enviable memory by learning and applying principles of memory improvement. Psychologists doubt that there are more than a few rare cases of truly photographic memory, which captures all the details of any experience and retains them perfectly. But some studies do show that about 5 percent of children apparently have something akin to photographic memory, which psychologists call "eidetic imagery" (Haber, 1980). **Eidetic imagery** is the ability to retain the image of a visual stimulus, such as a picture, for several minutes after it has been removed from view and to use this retained image to answer questions about the visual stimulus (see Figure 6.8).

Children with eidetic imagery generally have no better long-term memory than children without it, and virtually all children who have eidetic imagery lose it before adulthood. One exception, however, is Elizabeth, a highly intelligent teacher and a skilled artist. Elizabeth can project on her canvas an exact duplicate of a remembered scene with all its rich detail. Even more remarkable is her ability to retain visual images other than scenes and pictures. "Years after having read a poem in a foreign language, she can fetch back an image of the printed page and copy the poem from the bottom line to the top line as fast as she can write" (Stromeyer, 1970, p. 77).

Some impressive memory abilities develop through cultural needs, as the *World of Psychology* box illustrates.

FIGURE 6.8

Test for Eidetic Imagery Researchers test children for eidetic imagery by having them stare for 30 seconds at a picture like the one in (a). A few minutes later, the drawing in (b) is shown to the children, who are asked to report what they see. Those with eidetic imagery usually maintain that they see a face and describe the composite sketch in (c). The face can be perceived only if the participant retains the image of the first picture and fuses it with the middle drawing. (From Haber, 1980.)

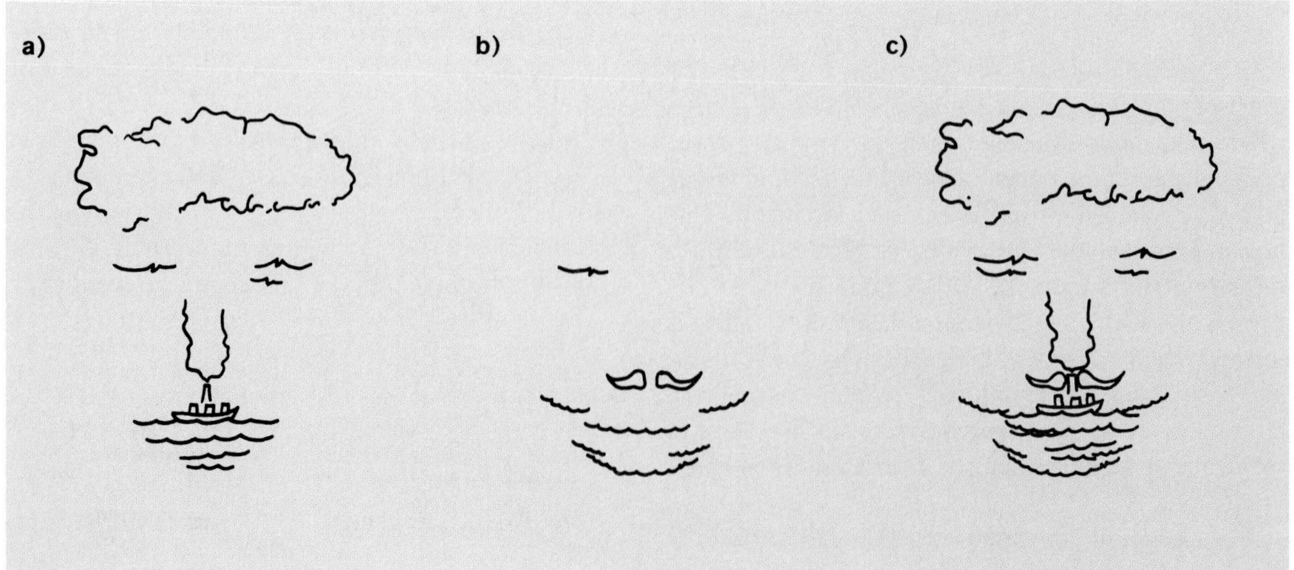

WORLD OF PSYCHOLOGY

Memory and Culture

Sir Frederick Bartlett believed that memory operates within a social or cultural context and cannot be understood as a pure process. He stated that "both the manner and matter of recall are often predominantly determined by social influences" (1932, p. 244).

In studying memory in a cultural context, Bartlett described the amazing ability of the Swazi people of Africa to remember the slight differences in individual characteristics of their cattle. One Swazi herdsman, Bartlett said, could remember details of every head of cattle bought the year before by the owner of the herd. Such a feat is less surprising when we consider that the key component of traditional Swazi culture consists of the herds of cattle the people depend upon for their living. Do the Swazi people have super powers of memory? Bartlett performed experiments comparing young Swazi men with young European men of comparable ages. Asked to recall a message consisting of 25 words, the young Swazis had no better recall ability than the young Europeans.

Among many peoples of Africa, tribal history is preserved orally. For this reason, an oracle, or specialist, must be able to encode, store, and retrieve huge volumes of historical data (D'Azevedo, 1982). In New Guinea, elders of the Iatmul people are said to have committed to memory the lines of descent for the various clans of their people stretching back generation upon generation (Bateson, 1982). The unerring memory of the elders for the kinship patterns of generations of their people are used to resolve disputed property claims (Mistry & Rogoff, 1994).

Barbara Rogoff, an expert in cultural psychology, maintains that such phenomenal, prodigious memory feats are best explained and understood in the cultural context in which they occur (Rogoff & Mistry, 1985). The tribal elders perform their impressive memory feats because doing so is an integral and critically important part of the culture in which they live. Most likely, their ability to remember lists of nonsense syllables would be no better than your own.

In summary, memory is not a pure process that exists apart from cultural context, social influences, or our individual interests. We remember what we are interested in, what we think about, and the daily transactions that occur in our cultural and social world.

Remember It!

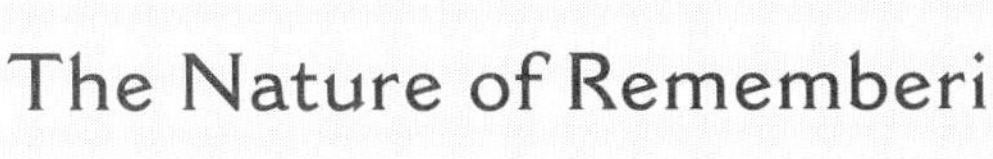

The Nature of Remembering and Forgetting

1. What early memory researcher found that, rather than accurately recalling information detail by detail, people often reconstruct and systematically distort facts to make them more consistent with past experiences?
   a. Hermann Ebbinghaus
   b. Frederick Bartlett
   c. Wilder Penfield
   d. William James
2. Which of the following is *not* true of schemas?
   a. Schemas are the integrated frameworks of knowledge assumptions we have about people, objects, and events.
   b. Schemas affect the way we encode information.
   c. Schemas affect the way we retrieve information.
   d. When we use schemas, our memories are accurate.
3. As a rule, people's memories are more accurate under hypnosis. (true/false)
4. The ability to retain a visual image several minutes after it has been removed is called
   a. photographic memory.
   b. flashbulb memory.
   c. eidetic imagery.
   d. sensory memory.

Answers: 1. b 2. d 3. false 4. c

eidetic imagery (eye-DET-ik): The ability to retain the image of a visual stimulus several minutes after it has been removed from view.

Factors Influencing Retrieval

Researchers in psychology have identified several factors that influence memory. We can control some of these factors, but not all of them.

The Serial Position Effect: To Be Remembered, Be First or Last but Not in the Middle

What is the serial position effect?

If you were introduced to a dozen people at a party, you would most likely recall the names of the first few people you met and the last one or two, but forget most of the names in the middle. A number of studies have revealed the **serial position effect**—the finding that for information learned in sequence, recall is better for items at the beginning and the end than for items in the middle of the sequence.

Information at the beginning of a sequence has a fairly high probability of being recalled because there has been time to rehearse it and encode it into long-term memory. This is called the **primacy effect**. Information at the end of a sequence has an even higher probability of being recalled because it is still in short-term memory and being rehearsed and encoded at the time you need to remember it. This is known as the **recency effect**. The poorer recall of information in the middle of a sequence occurs because that information is no longer in short-term memory and has not yet been placed in long-term memory. The serial position effect lends strong support to the notion of separate systems for short-term and long-term memory (Glanzer & Cunitz, 1966; Postman & Phillips, 1965).

Primacy and recency effects can also have an impact on information stored for longer periods of time (Roediger, 1991). For example, children learning the alphabet are likely to remember the first and last several letters of the alphabet better than many of the letters in the middle.

Environmental Context and Memory

How does environmental context affect memory?

Have you ever stood in your living room and thought of something you needed from your bedroom, only to forget what it was when you went there? Did the item come to mind when you returned to the living room? Some research has revealed that we tend to recall information better when we are in the same location—the same environmental context—as when the information was originally encoded.

Tulving and Thompson (1973) suggest that many elements of the physical setting in which we learn information are encoded along with the information and become part of the memory trace. If part or all of the original context is reinstated, it may serve as a retrieval cue. Then the information previously learned in that context may come to mind. This is known as the *encoding specificity hypothesis.*

Godden and Baddeley (1975) conducted one of the early studies of context and memory with members of a university scuba diving club. Students memorized a list of words when they were either 10 feet under water or on land. They were later tested for recall of the words in the same or in a different environment. The results of the study suggest that recall of information is strongly influenced by environmental context (see Figure 6.9). Words learned under water were best recalled under water, and words learned on land were best recalled on land. In fact, when the scuba divers learned and recalled the words in the same context, their scores were 47 percent higher than when the two contexts were different.

Godden and Baddeley (1980) found that changes in context did not affect the outcome when they measured memory using recognition rather than recall. Why? The original context seems to provide retrieval cues that make recall easier. In a recognition task, people have only to recognize the information as being familiar, so there is less need for the extra retrieval cues that the original context provides (Eich, 1980).

Going from 10 feet under water to dry land is a rather drastic change in context. Some researchers find the same effects in more subtle context changes, such as going from one room to another.

Odours can also supply powerful and enduring retrieval cues for memory. Experimental participants who experienced a pleasant odour during learning and again when tested five days later had greater recall than those who did not experience the odour during both learning and recall (Morgan, 1996).

Not all studies have found that memory is enhanced when students learn and are tested in the same environment (Fernandez & Glenberg, 1985;

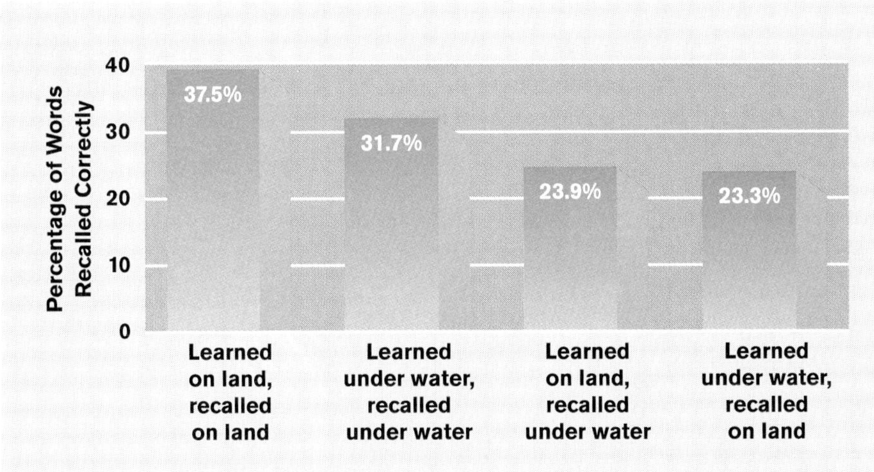

FIGURE 6.9
Context-Dependent Memory
Godden and Baddeley showed the strong influence of environmental context on recall. Scuba divers who memorized a list of words, either on land or under water, had significantly better recall in the same physical context in which the learning had taken place. (Data from Godden & Baddeley, 1975.)

Saufley et al., 1985). How can the discrepancy be explained? McDaniel and colleagues (1989) reasoned that the more completely and carefully people encode material to be remembered, the less dependent they are on reinstating the original context or environment. But we have already learned that people do not always carefully encode information and events to be remembered. Consequently, authorities investigating crimes often bring eyewitnesses back to the crime scene or ask them to visualize it to help them recall more details of the crime.

The State-Dependent Memory Effect

What is the state-dependent memory effect?

Does our internal state (e.g., happy or sad mood, intoxicated or sober) influence our memory? Yes it does. We tend to recall information better if we are in the same internal state as when the information was encoded. Psychologists call this the **state-dependent memory effect**.

Alcohol, Other Drugs, and Memory

Some studies have shown a state-dependent memory effect for alcohol and drugs such as marijuana, amphetamines, and barbiturates (Eich, 1980). People learned (encoded) material while sober or intoxicated, and later were tested in either the sober or the intoxicated state. Recall was found to be best when the subjects were in the same state for both learning and testing (Weingartner et al., 1976). As in other studies, the state-dependent memory effect was evident for recall but not for recognition. Research by Bruce and colleagues (1999) suggests that alcohol affects memory by intensifying the processes of interference.

Mood and Memory

Researchers have not been able to reliably demonstrate that recall is best if participants are in the same mood (happy or sad) when they encode or learn material as when they try to recall it. However, some evidence does suggest that pleasant experiences are more likely to be recalled when people are in a happy mood, and negative experiences when people are in a negative mood (Bower, 1992; Eich et al., 1994; Teasdale & Fogarty, 1979). Adults who are clinically depressed tend to recall more negative life experiences (Clark & Teasdale, 1982) and are likely to recall their parents as unloving and rejecting (Lewinsohn & Rosenbaum, 1987). But as depression lifts, the tendency toward negative recall reverses itself (Lloyd & Lishman, 1975).

serial position effect: The tendency to recall the beginning and ending items on a list better than the middle items.

primacy effect: The tendency to recall the first items on a list more readily than the middle items.

recency effect: The tendency to recall the last items on a list more readily than those in the middle of the list.

state-dependent memory effect: The tendency to recall information better if one is in the same pharmacological or psychological (mood) state as when the information was encoded.

Stress, Anxiety, and Memory: Relax and Remember

Have you ever watched a quiz show on television, convinced that you could have easily won the prize? Would your memory work as well under the stress of TV cameras, lights, and millions of people watching as it does in the privacy and comfort of your own home? Psychologists who study stress and memory say that either too much or too little stress and emotional arousal can hinder memory performance (Loftus, 1980).

Biology and Memory

We have learned a great deal about how we remember and why we forget. And we know that our vast store of information must exist physically somewhere in the brain. But where?

Brain Damage: A Clue to Memory Formation

Modern researchers are finding some specific locations in the brain that house and mediate functions and processes in memory. One important source of information comes from people who have suffered memory loss as a result of damage to specific brain areas. One such person is H.M., who has had a major influence on present-day knowledge of human memory. Much of what we know about H.M. was recorded by Canadian researcher Brenda Milner.

The Case of H.M.

What has the study of H.M. revealed about the role of the hippocampus in memory?

H.M. suffered from such severe epilepsy that, out of desperation, he agreed to a radical surgical procedure. The surgeon removed the site responsible for his seizures, the medial portions of both temporal lobes—the amygdala and the *hippocampal region,* which includes the hippocampus itself and the underlying cortical areas. It was 1953, and H.M. was 27 years old.

> After his surgery, H.M. remained intelligent and psychologically stable, and his seizures were drastically reduced. But unfortunately, the tissue cut from H.M.'s brain housed more than the site of his seizures. It also contained his ability to form new, conscious, long-term memories. Though his short-term memory is still as good as ever and he easily remembers the events of his life stored well before the operation, H.M. suffers from **anterograde amnesia.** He has not been able to remember a single event that has

Remember It!

Factors That Influence Memory

1. When children learn the alphabet, they often are better at learning and recalling the first few (a, b, c, d) and last few (x, y, z) letters of the alphabet, before learning the letters in between. This is called the
   a. primacy effect.
   b. recency effect.
   c. serial position effect.
   d. state-dependent memory effect.
2. Recall is about as good when people visualize the context in which learning occurred as it is when recall and learning occur in the same context. (true/false)
3. Scores on recognition tests (either multiple-choice or true/false) will be higher if testing and learning take place in the same physical environment. (true/false)
4. The fact that drugs such as alcohol and marijuana can interfere with recall if the participant is under the influence of drugs during learning but not during retrieval can best be explained on the basis of
   a. the consistency effect.
   b. state-dependent memory.
   c. context-dependent memory.
   d. consolidation failure.
5. Compared with non-depressed people, depressed people tend to have
   a. more sad memories.
   b. fewer memories.
   c. more pleasant memories.
   d. memories about the same in emotional content.

Answers: 1. c 2. true 3. false 4. b 5. a

occurred since the surgery over 40 years ago. Though H.M. turned 74 in the year 2000, as far as his conscious long-term memory is concerned, it is still 1953 and he is still 27 years old.

Surgery affected only H.M.'s declarative, long-term memory—his ability to store facts, personal experiences, and names, faces, telephone numbers, and the like. Researchers were surprised to discover that he could still form non-declarative memories—that is, he could still acquire skills through repetitive practice, although he could not remember having done so. For example, since the surgery, H.M. has learned to play tennis and improve his game, but he has no memory of having played. (Adapted from Milner, 1966, 1970; Milner et al., 1968.)

H.M.'s case was one of the first indications that the hippocampal region is involved in the formation of long-term memories. Other patients who, like H.M., have suffered similar brain damage exhibit the same types of memory loss (Squire, 1992). The most recent research indicates that the hippocampus is critically important in forming episodic memories (Eichenbaum, 1997; Gluck & Myers, 1997). Semantic memory, however, depends not on the hippocampus itself, but on the other parts of the hippocampal region underlying it (Vargha-Khadem et al., 1997).

Other research suggests that the hippocampus is needed for only a limited time after learning (Kim & Fanselow, 1992). The hippocampus plays a continuing role during the process of reorganization and consolidation through which memories are finally stored in other areas of the cortex. At that point, the memory can be recalled without the involvement of the hippocampus (Frackowiak, 1994; Squire & Zola-Morgan, 1991).

The Case of K.C.

To support the distinction between semantic and episodic memory, Tulving cites the case of K.C., a Toronto resident who sustained a severe head injury from a motorcycle accident (1989; Tulving et al., 1988). K.C. suffered massive damage to his left frontal lobe and other parts of the brain as well.

> K.C.'s case is remarkable in that he cannot remember, in the sense of bringing back to conscious awareness, a single thing that he has ever done or experienced. He cannot remember himself experiencing situations and participating in life's events. This total absence of personal recollections makes K.C.'s case unique; no other reports exist of amnesiac patients who have been incapable of recollecting *any* personal happenings. (Tulving, 1989, p. 362)

Although his episodic memory was erased, K.C.'s semantic memory was largely spared. His storehouse of knowledge from fields such as geography, history, politics, and music is still large, enabling him to answer questions about many topics. Tulving concludes that episodic memory depends upon the functioning of parts of the frontal lobe. Studies using PET scans have confirmed that, in addition to the hippocampus, the left prefrontal lobe plays a role in encoding episodic memories, while the right prefrontal lobe is involved in their retrieval (Nyberg et al., 1996, 1996b).

We have described how researchers have been able to identify some of the brain structures that play a part in memory. But what processes within these structures make new memories?

Neuronal Changes in Memory: Brain Work

Some researchers are exploring memory more minutely, by studying the actions of single neurons. Others are studying collections of neurons and their synapses, and the neurotransmitters whose chemical action begins the process of recording and storing a memory. The first close look at the nature of memory in single neurons was provided by Eric Kandel and his colleagues, who traced the effects of learning and memory in the sea snail *Aplysia* (Dale & Kandel, 1990; Dash et al., 1990). Using tiny electrodes implanted in several single neurons in the sea snail, Kandel and his fellow researchers have been able to map neural circuits that are formed and maintained as the animal learns and remembers. Furthermore, they have discovered the different types of protein synthesis that facilitate short-term and long-term memory (Kandel et al., 1987; Sweatt & Kandel, 1989)

anterograde amnesia: The inability to form long-term memories of events occurring after brain surgery or a brain injury, although memories formed before the trauma are usually intact.

But the studies of learning and memory in *Aplysia* reflect only simple classical conditioning, which is a type of non-declarative memory. Other researchers are studying mammals and report that physical changes occur in the neurons and synapses in brain regions involved in declarative memory.

Long-Term Potentiation: Prolonged Action at the Synapses

What is long-term potentiation, and why is it important?

As far back as 1949, Canadian psychologist Donald O. Hebb argued that the necessary neural ingredients for learning and memory must involve the enhancement of transmission at the synapses. Hebb (1949) proposed that some process must operate at the synapse to initiate and maintain the continuous and simultaneous interaction of the presynaptic (sending) neurons and the postsynaptic (receiving) neurons. Such a process, he asserted, would strengthen the synaptic connection.

Today the most widely studied model for learning and memory at the level of the neurons is **long-term potentiation**, or LTP (Cotman & Lynch, 1989; Stein et al., 1993). LTP meets the requirements of the mechanism Hebb described (Fischbach, 1992). To *potentiate* means to make potent or to strengthen. LTP is a long-lasting increase in the efficiency of neural transmission at the synapses (Schuman & Madison, 1994). LTP has become the leading model for the facilitation of some types of long-term memory in mammals because it can last for days and even weeks (Bliss & Lomo, 1973; Nguyen et al., 1994). LTP is important because it may be the basis for learning and memory at the level of the neurons.

LTP does not take place unless *both* the presynaptic and postsynaptic neurons are activated at the same time by intense high-frequency stimulation. Also, the postsynaptic neuron must be depolarized (ready to fire) when stimulation arrives, or LTP will not occur. Increased neural activity at very fast frequencies (20–70 cycles per second) occurs at the synapses when learning and memory tasks are performed (Miltner et al., 1999) LTP is a common occurrence in the hippocampus, which, as you have learned, is essential in the formation of declarative memories. Much of the research on LTP has been conducted in various areas of the hippocampus (Eichenbaum & Otto, 1993).

If the types of changes in synapses produced by LTP are the same neural changes that take place in learning, then blocking or interfering with LTP should likewise interfere with learning. And it does. It appears that LTP is also involved in structural change in the neurons, as Hebb envisioned (Pinel, 1993).

Research in the biology of memory is exceedingly complex, and scientists are only beginning to provide compelling answers about the neurochemical nature of learning and memory.

Hormones and Memory

How do memories of threatening situations compare with ordinary memories?

The strongest and most lasting memories are usually those fuelled by emotion. Research by Cahill and colleagues (1995) suggests that there may be two pathways for forming memories—one for ordinary information and another for memories that are fired by emotion. When a person is emotionally aroused, the adrenal glands release the hormones adrenalin (epinephrine) and noradrenalin (norepinephrine) into the bloodstream. Long known to be involved in the "fight or flight response," these hormones enable humans to survive, and they also imprint powerful and enduring memories of the circumstances surrounding threatening situations.

Such emotionally laden memories activate the amygdala (known to play a central role in emotion) and other parts of the memory system (Gabrieli, 1998). Emotional memories are lasting memories, and this may be the most important factor in explaining the intensity and durability of flashbulb memories.

Other hormones may have important effects on memory. Estrogen, the female sex hormone, appears to improve learning and memory, not only in healthy women but in patients with Alzheimer's disease as well. Estrogen appears to exert this effect by helping to build and maintain synapses between neurons in brain areas known to be involved in memory, such as the hippocampal region (Woolley et al., 1997).

Improving Memory

Study Habits That Aid Memory

What are four study habits that can aid memory?

There are no magic formulas for improving your memory. Remembering is a skill and, like any other skill, requires knowledge and practice. In this section we will show you several study habits and techniques that can improve your memory.

Organization: Everything in Its Place

A telephone directory would be of little use to you if the names and phone numbers were listed in random order. In a similar way, you are giving your memory a task it probably will not accept if you try to remember large amounts of information in a haphazard fashion. Organizing material to be learned is a tremendous aid to memory. You can prove this for yourself by completing *Try It!*

We tend to retrieve information from long-term memory according to the way we have organized it for storage. Almost anyone can name the months of the year in about 12 seconds, but how long would it take to recall them in alphabetical order? The same 12 items, all well known, are much harder to retrieve in alphabetical order because they are not organized that way in memory. When you study, it is helpful to organize items in some meaningful way (in alphabetical order, or according to categories, historical sequence, size, or shape) to make retrieval easier.

Overlearning: Reviewing Again, and Again, and Again

What is overlearning, and why is it important?

Do you still remember the words to songs that were popular when you were in high school? Can you recite many of the nursery rhymes you learned as a child even though you haven't heard them in years? You probably can because of **overlearning**.

Let us say that you wanted to memorize a list of words, and you studied until you could recite the words once without error. Would this amount of study or practice be sufficient? Many studies suggest that we remember material better and longer if we overlearn it—that is, if we practise or study beyond the minimum needed to barely learn it (Ebbinghaus, 1885/1964). A pioneering study in overlearning by Krueger (1929) showed very substantial long-term gains for participants engaged in 50 and 100 percent overlearning. Furthermore, overlearning makes material more resistant to interference. It is perhaps your best insurance against stress-related forgetting.

The next time you study for a test, don't stop studying as soon as you think you know the material. Spend another hour or so going over it, and you will be surprised at how much more you will remember.

Spaced Versus Massed Practice: A Little at a Time Beats All at Once

We have all tried cramming for examinations, but spacing study over several different sessions generally is more effective than **massed practice**—learn-

Try It!

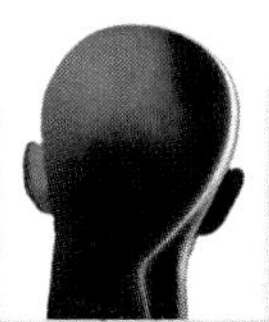

Organizing Information to Aid Memory

Have a pencil and a sheet of paper handy. Read the following list of items out loud and then write down as many as you can remember.

peas	ice cream	fish	perfume	bananas
toilet paper	onions	apples	cookies	ham
carrots	shaving cream	pie	grapes	chicken

If you organize this list, the items are much easier to remember. Now read each category heading and the items listed beneath it. Write down as many items as you can remember.

Desserts	Fruits	Vegetables	Meat	Toilet Articles
pie	bananas	carrots	chicken	perfume
ice cream	apples	onions	fish	shaving cream
cookies	grapes	peas	ham	toilet paper

long-term potentiation: A long-lasting increase in the efficiency of neural transmission at the synapses.

overlearning: Practising or studying material beyond the point where it can be repeated once without error.

massed practice: One long learning practice session as opposed to spacing the learning in shorter practice sessions over an extended period.

ing in one long practice session without rest periods (Bahrick & Phelps, 1987; Glover & Corkill, 1987). The spacing effect applies to learning motor skills as well as to learning facts and information. All music students can tell you that it is better to practise for half an hour each day, every day, than to practise for many hours in a row once a week.

You will remember more with less total study time if you space your study over several sessions. Long periods of memorizing make material particularly subject to interference and often result in fatigue and lowered concentration. Moreover, when you space your practice, you probably create a new memory that may be stored in a different place, and this increases your chances of recalling it.

Active Learning Versus Rereading: Active Learning Wins

Many students simply read and reread their textbook and notes when they study for an exam. Research over many years shows that you will recall more if you increase the amount of active learning in your study. For example, it is better to read a page or a few paragraphs and then practise recalling what you have just read. Even better, you should ask yourself questions as you read (Wood et al., 1990; Willoughby et al. 2000).

The *Apply It!* box offers a useful technique to help you remember certain material.

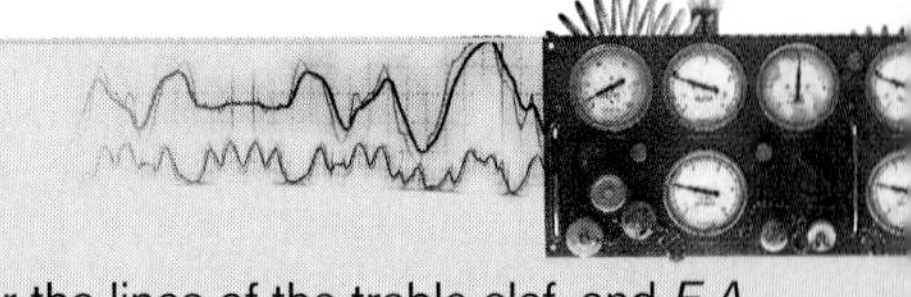

Improving Memory with Mnemonic Devices

Apply It!

We all use external aids to remember things. Writing notes, making lists, writing on a calendar, or keeping an appointment book is often more reliable and accurate than trusting our own memory. What if you need information at unpredictable times, when you do not have external aids handy?

Several *mnemonics*, or memory devices, have been developed over the years to aid memory. The mnemonic techniques we explore here are rhyme, the first-letter technique, and the keyword method (see Pressley et al., 1998; Wood et al., 1995).

Rhyme

Many of us use rhymes to help us remember material. Perhaps as a child you learned the alphabet by using a rhyming song:

A - B - C - D
E - F - G
H - I - J - K
L - M - N - O - P

You may repeat the verse "Thirty days hath September" when you try to recall the number of days in each month, or the saying "*i* before *e* except after *c*" when you are trying to spell a word. Rhymes are useful because they ensure that information is recalled in the proper sequence. Otherwise there is no rhyme.

The First-Letter Technique

Another useful technique is to take the first letter of each item to be remembered and form a word, a phrase, or a sentence with those letters (Matlin, 1989). For example, if you had to memorize the seven colours of the visible spectrum in their proper order, you could use the first letter of each colour to form the name Roy G. Biv. Three chunks are easier to remember than seven different ones.

Red Orange Yellow Green
Blue Indigo Violet

As a child taking music lessons, you may have learned the saying "*E*very *g*ood *b*aby *d*oes *f*ine" to remember the lines of the treble clef, and *F A C E* to remember the spaces.

The Method of Loci: "In the First Place"

The *method of loci* is a mnemonic device that you can use to remember things in a specific order. The word *loci* is the plural of *locus*, which is Latin for "location" or "place."

To use the method of loci, select any familiar location—your home, for example—and simply associate the items to be remembered with places there. You begin by picturing the first locus, for example, your driveway; the second locus, your garage; the third locus, the walk leading to your front door; and the fourth locus, perhaps the front hall closet. You progress through your house from room to room in an orderly fashion. Then you visualize the first item or idea you want to remember in its place on the driveway, the second item in your garage, the third at your front door, and so on until you have associated each word, idea, or item you want to remember with a

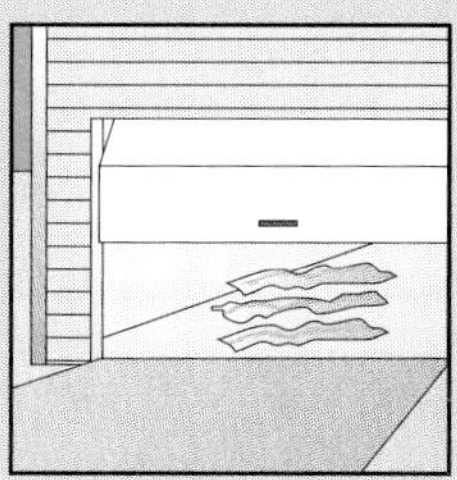

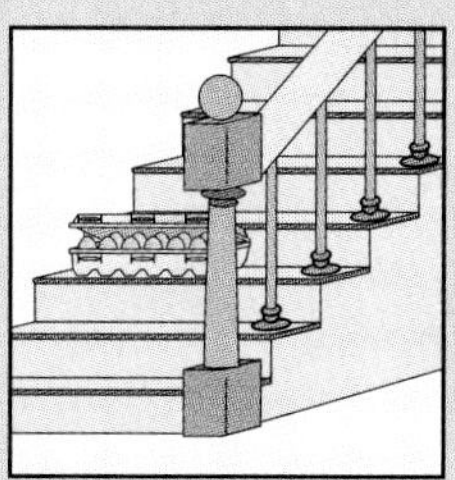

FIGURE 6.10

The Method of Loci **Begin by thinking of locations, perhaps in your home, that are in a sequence. Then visualize one of the items to be remembered in each location.**

specific place. You will probably find it helpful to conjure up exaggerated images of the items that you place at each location, as the examples in Figure 6.10 illustrate.

When you want to recall the items, take an imaginary walk starting at the first place, and the first idea will pop into your mind. When you think of the second place, the second idea will come to mind, and so on through all the places you visualize. The use of loci as a memory aid may be the origin of the phrase "in the first place."

The Keyword Method

The keyword method is used primarily to assist in vocabulary and second-language learning. It has three steps, as illustrated in Figure 6.11. In Step 1, you take the new or foreign word that you have to remember and look for a familiar homonym (a word that sounds alike). For example, as an English speaker, I want to learn the French word for *duck* (*canard*). One homonym might be *canner*. This is a good homonym because it is easy to make a mental picture of someone making a can. In Step 2, you construct an image of the homonym and the meaning of the word (canard = duck). The image would be of a duck sitting in a can. Vivid images work better, so my duck is flapping his wings in the can. In Step 3, you try to remember. When you see the word "canard," you think of the homonym (canner) and ask yourself, "Who in my picture was in the can?" The answer is "duck." If, on the other hand, you are asked for a translation for the word "duck," you try to imagine what the duck was doing. This gives you "canner," which acts as a cue for the word "canard."

Extensive work was done on the keyword method and foreign language learning by Michael Pressley at the University of Western Ontario.

FIGURE 6.11

The Keyword Method **Here are the two steps for the keyword strategy. In Step 1, you picture something that sounds like the word you have to learn, such as "canner" for "canard." In Step 2, you make an interactive image with the sound-alike picture and a picture of the real word you have to learn ("duck in a can" for "canard").**

Remember It!

The Biology of Memory and Ways to Improve Memory

1. The hippocampus is the brain structure involved in the formation of permanent memories of
   a. motor skills.
   b. facts and personal experiences.
   c. motor skills, facts, and personal experiences.
   d. motor skills and personal experiences.
2. What is the term for the long-lasting increase in the efficiency of neural transmission at the synapses that may be the basis for learning and memory at the level of the neurons?
   a. long-term potentiation
   b. synaptic facilitation
   c. synaptic potentiation
   d. presynaptic potentiation
3. When studying for an exam, it is best to spend
   a. more time reciting than rereading.
   b. more time rereading than reciting.
   c. equal time rereading and reciting.
   d. all of the time reciting rather than rereading.
4. Being able to recite a number of nursery rhymes from childhood is probably due mainly to
   a. spaced practice.
   b. organization.
   c. mnemonics.
   d. overlearning.

Answers: 1. b 2. a 3. d 4. d

KEY TERMS

THINKING CRITICALLY

Evaluation

Some studies cited in this chapter involved only one or a few participants.

a. Select two of these studies and discuss the possible problems in drawing conclusions on the basis of studies using so few participants.
b. Suggest several possible explanations for the researchers' findings other than those proposed by the researchers.
c. In your view, should such studies even be mentioned in a textbook? Why or why not?

Point/Counterpoint

Using what you have learned in this chapter on memory, prepare an argument citing cases and specific examples to support each of these positions:

a. Long-term memory is a permanent record of our experiences.
b. Long-term memory is not necessarily a permanent record of our experiences.

Psychology in Your Life

Drawing upon your knowledge, formulate a plan that you can put into operation to help improve your memory and avoid the pitfalls that cause forgetting.

SUMMARY & REVIEW

Remembering

What three processes are involved in the act of remembering?

Three processes involved in remembering are (1) encoding–transforming information into a form that can be stored in memory; (2) storage–maintaining information in memory; and (3) retrieval–bringing stored material to mind.

What is sensory memory?

Sensory memory holds information coming in through the senses for up to several seconds, just long enough for us to begin to process the information and send some on to short-term memory.

What are the characteristics of short-term memory?

Short-term (working) memory holds about seven unrelated items of information for less than 30 seconds without rehearsal. Short-term memory also acts as our mental workspace while we carry out any mental activity.

What is long-term memory, and what are its subsystems?

Long-term memory is the permanent or relatively permanent memory system with a virtually unlimited capacity. Its subsystems are (1) declarative memory, which holds facts and information (semantic memory) and personal life experiences (episodic memory); and (2) non-declarative memory, which consists of motor skills acquired through repetitive practice, habits, and simple classically conditioned responses.

Measuring Memory

What are three methods of measuring retention?

Three methods of measuring retention are (1) recall, whereby information must be supplied with few or no retrieval cues; (2) recognition, whereby information must simply be recognized as having been encountered before; and (3) the relearning method, which measures retention in terms of time saved in relearning material compared with the time required to learn it originally.

What was Ebbinghaus's major contribution to psychology?

Hermann Ebbinghaus conducted the first experimental studies of learning and memory. He invented the nonsense syllable, conceived the relearning method as a test of memory, and plotted the curve of forgetting.

Forgetting

What are six causes of forgetting?

Six causes of forgetting are encoding failure, consolidation failure, decay, interference, motivated forgetting, and retrieval failure.

What is interference, and how can it be minimized?

Interference occurs when information or associations stored either before or after a given memory hinder our ability to remember it. To minimize interference, follow a learning activity with sleep, and arrange learning so that similar subjects are not studied back to back.

The Nature of Remembering and Forgetting

What is meant by the statement "Memory is reconstructive in nature"?

Our memory does not work like a video recorder. We reconstruct memories, piecing them together from a few highlights and using information that may or may not be accurate.

What is Bartlett's contribution to our understanding of memory?

Sir Frederick Bartlett found that people do not recall facts and experiences detail by detail. Rather, they systematically reconstruct and distort them to fit information already stored in memory.

What are schemas, and how do they affect memory?

Schemas are the integrated frameworks of knowledge and assumptions we have about people, objects, and events; schemas affect how we encode and recall information.

What conditions reduce the reliability of eyewitness testimony?

The reliability of eyewitness testimony is reduced when witnesses view a photograph of the suspect before viewing the lineup, when members of a lineup are viewed at the same time rather than one by one, when the perpetrator is of a different race from that of the eyewitness, when a weapon has been used in the crime, and when leading questions are asked to elicit information.

Does hypnosis improve the memory of eyewitnesses?

Hypnotized subjects supply more information and are more confident of their recollections, but they supply more inaccurate information as well.

Factors Influencing Retrieval

What is the serial position effect?

The serial position effect is the tendency, when a person is recalling a list of items, to remember the items at the beginning of the list (primacy effect) and the items at the end of the list (recency effect) better than items in the middle.

How does environmental context affect memory?

People tend to recall material more easily if they are in the same physical location during recall as during the original learning.

What is the state-dependent memory effect?

The state-dependent memory effect is our tendency to recall information better if we are in the same pharmacological or psychological state as when the information was learned.

Biology and Memory

What has the study of H.M. revealed about the role of the hippocampus in memory?

The case of H.M. reveals that the hippocampus is essential in forming declarative memories but not in forming non-declarative memories.

What is long-term potentiation, and why is it important?

Long-term potentiation (LTP) is a long-lasting increase in the efficiency of neural transmission at the synapses. LTP is important because it may be the basis for learning and memory at the level of the neurons.

How do memories of threatening situations compare with ordinary memories?

Memories of threatening situations tend to be more powerful and enduring than ordinary memories.

Improving Memory

What are four study habits that can aid memory?

Four study habits that can aid memory are organization, overlearning, the use of spaced rather than massed practice, and the use of a higher percentage of time reciting than rereading material.

What is overlearning, and why is it important?

Overlearning means practising or studying material beyond the point where it can be repeated once without error. Material that is overlearned is remembered better and longer, and it is more resistant to interference and stress-related forgetting.

7 Intelligence, Cognition, and Language

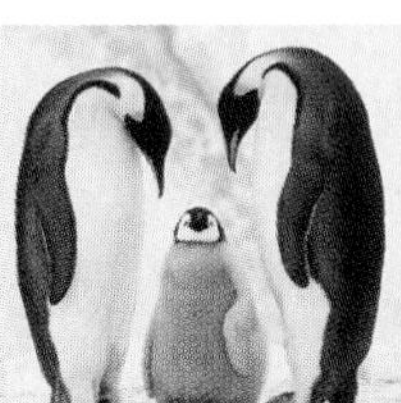
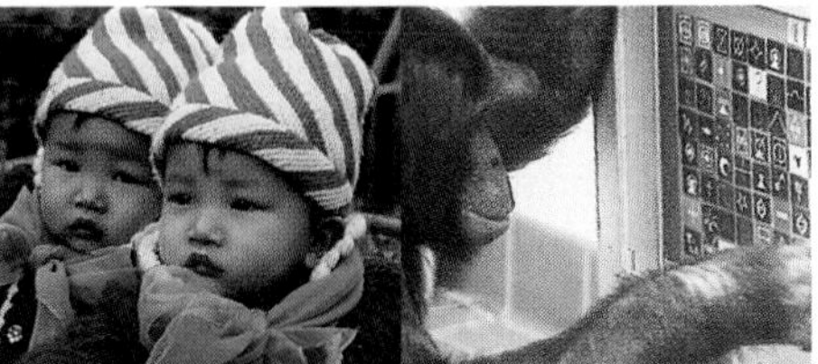

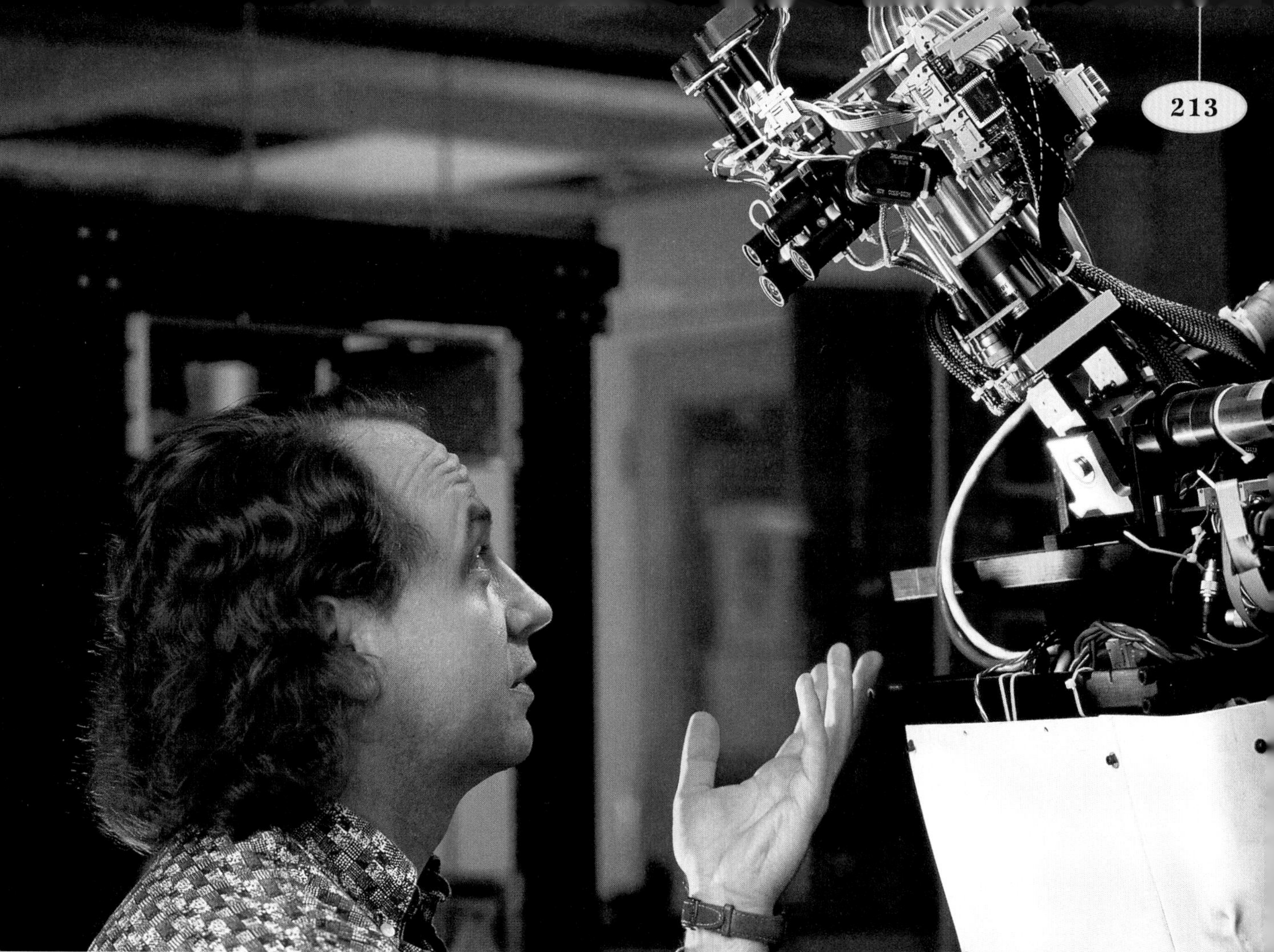

Imagine being able to explore Einstein's genius today. Well, that dream is a reality for Canadian researchers at McMaster University. Although Einstein died in 1955 at the age of 76, his legacy in physics and math continues today—and so does his brain. It is Einstein's brain that is the focus of interest for neuroscientist Dr. Sandra Witelson. Einstein's brain was removed and carefully cut into sections during an autopsy shortly after his death. The pathologist who did the autopsy, Dr. Thomas Harvey, still retains most of the pieces of the brain in his lab in Wichita, Kansas ("Have brain," 1999). Some of the brain, however, has travelled extensively and has been examined by medical and psychological researchers.

Most recently, Dr. Witelson examined Einstein's brain to see if the physical brain would reveal anything about his genius. In her preliminary work she noted some unique characteristics. For example, the portion of the brain associated with mathematics was wider in Einstein's brain than it is for most brains (Chang, 2000). The brain also has a different shape. One area in the middle of the brain, the inferior parietal lobes, has a shortened groove where most people have

a long groove running from the back to the front. Interestingly, it is this area of the brain that is often associated with higher-level thinking–such as that involved in mathematics. Researchers believe that this shortened groove might have allowed the neurons in that area to work together more easily and to make more interconnections (Chang, 2000). Although no one is saying that it is just the anatomy that accounts for the intelligence of Einstein, it is interesting that there seems to be some physical evidence that matches his extraordinary abilities.

There is more to intelligence than simple anatomy. As yet, our knowledge of the anatomical differences between geniuses and ordinary people is quite primitive. In many ways we are limited in our ability to pick out those few people who will, through their innovation, creativity, or brilliance, change all of our lives. For example, many highly prominent people tested poorly in school. Among them are Thomas Edison, Winston Churchill, whose teachers thought he was mentally limited, and Albert Einstein, who was labelled a dunce in math. These examples show us how important it is to understand the breadth of intelligence and intelligent thinking.

In this chapter we will explore intelligence, thinking skills, creativity, and language. You will learn about the nature of intelligence and how it is measured. Where does our intelligence come from—our genes, or experiences provided by our environment, or both? We will look at people who are mentally gifted and those who are mentally disabled. Then we will consider how we think and examine the approaches we use to solve problems. Finally, we will explore language.

First, let us ask the most obvious question: What is intelligence? A recent task force of experts from the American Psychological Association defined intelligence as an individual's "ability to understand complex ideas, to adapt effectively to the environment, to learn from experience, to engage in various forms of reasoning, and to overcome obstacles by taking thought" (Neisser et al., 1996, p. 77)

The Nature of Intelligence

Is intelligence a single trait or capability? Is it many capabilities unrelated to each other? Or is it something in between? As you might expect, there are many different points of view about the nature of intelligence.

LINK IT!

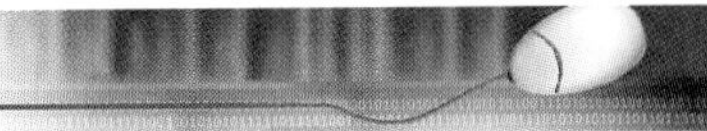

www.educ.drake.edu/romig/cogito/intelligence.html
Brain and mind

www2.psy.mq.edu.au/~tbates/104/104-theories.html
Major Descriptive Theories of Intelligence

The Search for Factors Underlying Intelligence

What factors underlie intelligence, according to Spearman, Thurstone, and Guilford?

Are there certain common factors that underlie intelligence? If so, what might they be?

Spearman and General Intelligence: The g Factor

English psychologist Charles Spearman (1863–1945) observed that people who are bright in one area are usually bright in other areas as well. In other words, they tend to be generally intelligent. Spearman (1927) came to believe that intelligence involves a general ability, or ***g* factor**, that underlies all intellectual functions.

Spearman arrived at his "g theory" when he found that there were positive relationships between scores on the subtests of intelligence tests. People who score high on one subtest tend to score high on the other subtests. Spearman theorized that this positive relationship between the scores on the subtests meant that the tests were measuring something in common—that general ability was being expressed to some degree in all of them. This, according to Spearman, was evidence of the g factor—general intelligence. The influence of Spearman's thinking can be seen in the intelligence tests, such as the Stanford-Binet, that yield one IQ score to indicate the level of general intelligence.

But some of the correlations between subtests are higher than others. If the g factor alone defined the whole of what intelligence tests measure, then all of the correlations would be nearly perfect. Because they are not, some other abilities in addition to the g factor must be present. These other abilities Spearman named "*s* factors" for specific abilities. Spearman concluded that intelligence tests tap an individual's g factor, or general intelligence, and a number of *s* factors, or specific intellectual abilities.

Thurstone's Primary Mental Abilities: Primarily Seven

Louis L. Thurstone (1938), another early researcher in testing, rejected Spearman's notion of general ability, or g factor. After analyzing the scores of a large number of people on some 50 separate ability tests, Thurstone identified seven **primary mental abilities**: verbal comprehension, numerical ability, spatial relations, perceptual speed, word fluency, memory, and reasoning. He maintained that all intellectual activities involve one or more of these primary mental abilities. Thurstone and his wife, Thelma G. Thurstone, developed their Primary Mental Abilities Tests to measure these seven abilities.

The Thurstones believed that a single IQ score obscured more than it revealed. They suggested that a profile showing relative strengths and weaknesses on the seven primary abilities would provide a more accurate picture of a person's mental ability.

Guilford's Structure of Intellect: A Mental House with 180 Rooms

Still another effort to shed light on the nature of intelligence was J.P. Guilford's **structure of intellect**. In 1967, Guilford proposed that the structure of intelligence has three dimensions: mental operations, contents, and products.

When we think, we perform a mental operation or activity. According to Guilford's theory, the mental operation can be cognition, memory, evaluation, divergent production, or convergent production. But we can't think in a vacuum; we must think *about* something. The something we think about, Guilford called "contents," which can be visual, auditory, figural, symbolic, semantic, or behavioural. The result of bringing some mental activity to bear on some contents is a "product."

Guilford (1967) hypothesized that there are 120 different intellectual abilities, depending on how the different operations, contents, and products are combined in a task. Shortly before his death, Guilford (1988) expanded his theory so that there were 180 abilities, and he divided the operation of memory into two categories: memory recording and memory retention.

Intelligence: More Than One Type?

What types of intelligence did Gardner and Sternberg identify?

Some theorists, instead of searching for the factors that underlie intelligence, propose that there are different types of intelligence. For example, some researchers distinguish between two types of intelligence (Horn, 1982). *Crystallized intelligence* refers to verbal ability and accumulated knowledge, whereas *fluid intelligence* refers to abstract reasoning and mental flexibility. Some theorists have made very refined distinctions in the types of intelligence we have. Two such modern theorists are Howard Gardner and Robert Sternberg.

g factor: Spearman's term for a general intellectual ability that underlies all mental operations to some degree.

primary mental abilities: According to Thurstone, seven relatively distinct abilities that singularly or in combination are involved in all intellectual activities.

structure of intellect: The model proposed by Guilford consisting of 180 different intellectual abilities, which involve all of the possible combinations of the three dimensions of intellect—mental operations, contents, and products.

Gardner's Theory of Multiple Intelligences: Seven Frames of Mind

Howard Gardner (1983) denies the existence of a *g* factor—a general intellectual ability. Instead he proposes seven forms of intelligence, which he declares are independent and of equal importance. Gardner's multiple intelligences are as follows:

1. *Linguistic*—language skills
2. *Logical/mathematical*—math and quantitative skills
3. *Musical*
4. *Spatial*—skills used by painters, sculptors, and architects to manipulate and create forms
5. *Bodily kinesthetic*—body control necessary in athletics, and skill and dexterity in handling objects
6. *Interpersonal*—understanding the behaviour and reading the moods, desires, and intentions of others
7. *Intrapersonal*—understanding one's own feelings and behaviour

Gardner (1983) developed his theory of multiple intelligences after studying patients with different types of brain damage that affected some forms of intelligence but left others intact. He also studied reports of "idiot savants"—individuals who possess a strange combination of mental disability and unusual talent or ability. Finally, he considered how various abilities and skills have been valued differently in other cultures and periods of history.

Gardner's theory "has enjoyed wide popularity, especially among educators, but Gardner's ideas are based more on reasoning and intuition than on the results of empirical studies" (Aiken, 1997, p. 196). Recently his theory has been expanded to include other intelligences, such as "naturalistic" intelligence. His theory is criticized by those who do not believe that all seven frames of mind are of equal value in education and in life. For example, Robert Sternberg (1985b) contends that "the multiple intelligences might better be referred to as multiple talents" (p. 1114). He asks whether an adult who is tone-deaf and has no sense of rhythm can be considered mentally limited in the same way as another person who has never developed any verbal skills. But Sternberg is not merely a critic; he has developed his own theory of intelligence.

Sternberg's Triarchic Theory of Intelligence: The Big Three

Sternberg uses the information-processing approach to understanding intelligence. This approach involves a step-by-step analysis of the cognitive processes people employ as they acquire knowledge and use it to solve problems.

Though now a respected theorist and researcher in the area of intelligence, Sternberg admits that when he was young he never did well on traditional intelligence tests. "I really stunk on IQ tests. I was just ter-

FIGURE 7.1

Sternberg's Triarchic Theory of Intelligence

According to Sternberg, there are three types of intelligence: componential, experiential, and contextual.

Componential Intelligence
Mental abilities most closely related to success on traditional IQ and achievement tests

Experiential Intelligence
Creative thinking and problem solving

Contextual Intelligence
Practical intelligence or "street smarts"

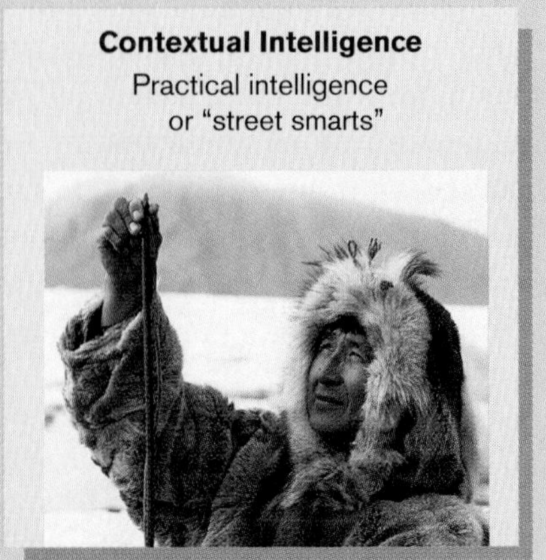

rible," he says (Trotter, 1986, p. 56). Believing that he possessed more intellectual power than conventional intelligence tests revealed, he made up an intelligence test of his own—the Sternberg Test of Mental Abilities—when he was in junior high school.

Sternberg (1985a, 1986b) has formulated a **triarchic theory of intelligence**, which, as the term *triarchic* implies, proposes that intelligence consists of three main parts: the componential, the experiential, and the contextual (see Figure 7.1). The first part, the *componential,* refers to the mental abilities that are most closely related to success on conventional IQ and achievement tests. He maintains that traditional intelligence tests tap only the componential, or analytical, aspect of intelligence.

The second part, the *experiential,* encompasses creativity and insight, although creativity has not yielded easily to conventional measurement efforts. The third leg of the triarchic model is *contextual* or practical intelligence, which some might equate with common sense or "street smarts." People with high contextual intelligence are survivors who capitalize on their strengths and compensate for their weaknesses. They adapt well to their environment, or change the environment to improve their success, or find a new environment. People who have succeeded in spite of hardships and adverse circumstances probably have a great deal of contextual intelligence. Sternberg and his colleagues (1995) maintain that testing both academic and practical intelligence yields more accurate predictions about real-world performance than relying on either kind alone.

Remember It!

Theories of Intelligence

Match the theorist with the theory of intelligence.

1) triarchic theory of intelligence
2) seven primary mental abilities
3) structure of intellect
4) the *g* factor

a. Spearman
b. Thurstone
c. Guilford
d. Sternberg
e. Gardner

Answers: 1) d 2) b 3) c 4) a

You have now read several competing explanations of how intelligence is structured and how intellectual processes work. But even before a workable definition of intelligence was formulated, attempts were made to measure intelligence.

Measuring Intelligence

Alfred Binet and the First Successful Intelligence Test

What was Binet's major contribution to psychology?

The first successful effort to measure intelligence resulted not from a theoretical approach but as a practical means of solving a problem. The Ministry of Public Instruction in Paris was trying to find some objective means of identifying children's intelligence. The ministry wanted to ensure that average or brighter children would not be wrongly assigned to special classes and that children of limited ability would not be subjected to the regular program of instruction. In 1903 a commission was formed to study the problem. One of its members was French psychologist Alfred Binet (1857–1911).

Alfred Binet

triarchic theory of intelligence: Sternberg's theory that intelligence consists of three parts–the componential, the contextual, and the experiential.

With the help of his colleague, psychiatrist Theodore Simon, he began testing the schoolchildren of Paris. They used a wide variety of tests, some of which Binet had tried with his own daughters. They kept only those test items that discriminated well between older and younger children. Binet and Simon published their intelligence scale in 1905 and revised it in 1908 and again in 1911. The Binet-Simon Intelligence Scale was an immediate success in most Western countries.

Test items on the scale were structured according to increasing difficulty, with the easiest item first and each succeeding item more difficult than the last. Children went as far as they could, and then their progress was compared with that of others of the same age. A child with the mental ability of a normal five-year-old was said to have a mental level of five. (Binet and Simon used the term *mental level*, but since then the term *mental age* has been used instead.) Binet established the concept that mental disability and mental superiority are based on the difference between chronological age (one's actual age) and mental age. An eight-year-old with a mental age of eight is normal or average. An eight-year-old with a mental age of five is mentally deficient, whereas an eight-year-old with a mental age of eleven is mentally superior.

LINK IT!

www.yorku.ca/dept/psych/classics/Binet/binet1.htm
Text of Binet's New Methods for the Diagnosis of the Intellectual Achievements of Subnormals (1905)

The Intelligence Quotient, or IQ

What does IQ mean, and how was it originally calculated?

Binet believed that children with a mental age two years below chronological age were disabled and should be placed in special education classes. But there was a flaw in his thinking: a four-year-old with a mental age of two is far more retarded than a 12-year-old with a mental age of 10. How could a similar degree of retardation at different ages be expressed?

German psychologist William Stern (1914) came up with the answer. In 1912 he devised a simple formula for calculating intelligence—the **intelligence quotient**, or **IQ**. He divided a child's mental age by his or her chronological age. This formula was revised later by Lewis Terman who eliminated the decimal and multiplied by 100:

Here's how IQ is calculated:

$$\frac{\text{Mental age}}{\text{Chronological age}} \times 100 = \text{IQ}$$

Here is how some IQs for 10-year-olds would be calculated:

$$\frac{14}{10} \times 100 = 1.40 \times 100 = \text{IQ } 140 \text{ (superior IQ)}$$

$$\frac{10}{10} \times 100 = 1.00 \times 100 = \text{IQ } 100 \text{ (normal IQ)}$$

$$\frac{6}{10} \times 100 = 0.60 \times 100 = \text{IQ } 60 \text{ (below normal IQ)}$$

It is interesting to note that Binet and his partner Simon were totally against the use of IQ scores. They believed that trying to represent human intelligence with a single number was impossible and that doing so was not only misleading but dangerous (Hothersall, 1984).

Intelligence Testing in North America

The Stanford-Binet Intelligence Scale

What is the Stanford-Binet Intelligence Scale?

Henry H. Goddard translated the Binet-Simon scales of 1908 and 1911 into English. Lewis M. Terman of Stanford University in California published a thorough revision of the Binet-Simon scale in 1916. Terman established new **norms**—standards based on the scores of a large number of people and used as bases for comparison. Terman's revision, known as the **Stanford-Binet Intelligence Scale**, was the first test to make use of Stern's IQ score (von Mayrhauser, 1992). Within two-and-a-half years, four million children had taken the test.

The Stanford-Binet is an individually administered IQ test developed for persons aged 2 to 23. Last revised in 1986, it now contains four subscales: verbal reasoning, quantitative reasoning, abstract visual reasoning, and short-term memory. An overall IQ score is derived from scores on the four subscales. The Stanford-Binet is highly regarded and correlates well with achievement test scores (Laurent et al., 1992).

LINK IT!

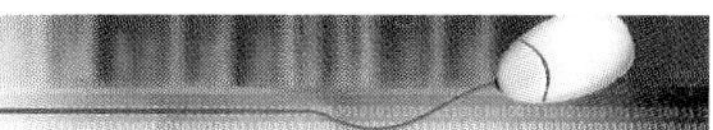

www.abacon.com/slavin/t26.html
The Modern Stanford-Binet Intelligence Scale

Intelligence Testing for Adults

It quickly became obvious that the Stanford-Binet Intelligence Scale was not useful for testing adults. The original IQ formula could not be applied to adults because at a certain age, maturity in intelligence is reached, as it is for height and for other physical characteristics. According to the original IQ formula, a 40-year-old who scored the same on an IQ test as the average 20-year-old would be mentally disabled, with an IQ of only 50. Obviously, something went wrong when the formula was applied to adults. Today we still use the term IQ; however, for adults, IQ is a **deviation score** calculated by comparing an individual's score with scores of others of the *same age* on whom the test's norms were formed. The deviation score is one of the contributions of David Wechsler, another pioneer in mental testing.

The Wechsler Intelligence Tests

What did Wechsler's tests provide that the Stanford-Binet did not?

In 1939 David Wechsler developed the first successful individual intelligence test for people aged 16 and older. The original test has been revised, restandardized, and renamed the **Wechsler Adult Intelligence Scale (WAIS-R)** and is now one of the most common psychological tests. The test contains both verbal and performance (non-verbal) subtests, which yield separate verbal and performance IQ scores as well as an overall IQ score. This test is a departure from the Stanford-Binet, which yields just one IQ score.

Wechsler also published the Wechsler Intelligence Scale for Children (WISC), as well as the Wechsler Preschool and Primary Scale of Intelligence (WPPSI), which has established norms for children aged four to six and a half.

The latest revision, the WISC III, was tested for Canadian populations. Researchers tested shorter alternative scoring frameworks in order to reduce testing times for subjects. The General Ability Index (GAI) is a good alternative system that is appropriate for Canadian children (Weiss et al., 1999). The WPPSI was also tested for Canadian children. Researchers found it appropriate when the whole scale was used to make assessments. Canadian children showed much greater variability, which would make them less accurate in assessing performance (French et al., 2000).

Group Intelligence Tests

Administering individual intelligence tests such as the Stanford-Binet and the Wechsler is expensive and time-consuming. The tests must be administered to one individual at a time by a psychologist or other qualified testing professional. When large numbers of people must be tested in a short period of time on a limited budget, individual IQ testing is out of the question. A number of widely used group intelligence tests now exist, such as the California Test of Mental Maturity, the Canadian Cognitive Abilities Test, and the Otis-Lennon Mental Ability Test. You may have taken one or more of these tests, all of which are good. But not all tests are created equal, as we will see in the following discussion.

Requirements of Good Tests: Reliability, Validity, and Standardization

What is meant by the terms *reliability, validity,* and *standardization*?

If your watch gains six minutes one day and loses three or four minutes the next day, it is not reliable. You want a watch that you can rely on to give the correct time day after day. Like a watch, an

intelligence quotient (IQ): An index of intelligence originally derived by dividing mental age by chronological age and then multiplying by 100.

norms: Standards based on the range of test scores of a large group of people who are selected to provide the bases of comparison for those who will take the test later.

Stanford-Binet Intelligence Scale: An individually administered IQ test for those aged 2 to 23; Lewis Terman's adaptation of the Binet-Simon Scale.

deviation score: A test score calculated by comparing an individual's score with the scores of others of the same age on whom the test's norms were formed.

Wechsler Adult Intelligence Scale (WAIS-R): An individual intelligence test for adults that yields separate verbal and performance (non-verbal) IQ scores as well as an overall IQ score.

intelligence test must have **reliability**; the test must consistently yield nearly the same scores when the same people are retested on the same test or an alternative form of the test. The higher the correlation between the two scores, the more reliable the test. A correlation coefficient of 1.0 would indicate perfect reliability. Most widely used tests, such as the Stanford-Binet and Wechsler tests, boast high reliabilities of about .90.

Even highly reliable tests are worthless if they are not valid. A test has **validity** if it measures what it is intended to measure. For example, a thermometer is a valid instrument for measuring temperature; a bathroom scale is valid for measuring weight. But no matter how reliable your bathroom scale is, it will not take your temperature. It is valid only for weighing.

Once a test is proven to be valid and reliable, the next requirement is for **standardization**. There must be standard procedures for administering and scoring the test. Exactly the same directions must be given, whether written or oral, and the same amount of time must be allowed for every test taker. But even more important, standardization involves establishing norms by which all scores are interpreted. The creators of a test standardize it by administering it to a large sample of people representative of those who will be taking the test in the future. The group's scores are analyzed, and then the average score, standard deviation, percentile rankings, and other measures are computed. These comparative scores become the norms, which are used as the standard against which all other test takers will be measured.

The Range of Intelligence

What are the ranges of IQ scores that are considered average, superior, and in the range of mental disability?

When large populations are measured on mental characteristics such as intelligence or on physical characteristics such as height or weight, the test scores or results usually conform to the bell-shaped distribution known as the *normal curve.* Most of the scores cluster around the mean (average). The farther the scores deviate, or move away, from the mean, above *or* below, the fewer people there are (see Figure 7.2).

The average IQ test score for all people in the same age group is arbitrarily assigned a value of 100. On the Wechsler intelligence tests, about 50 percent of all scores fall in the average range, between 90 and 110. About 68 percent fall between 85 and 115, and about 95 percent fall between 70 and 130. About 2 percent of the scores are above 130, which is considered superior, and about 2 percent fall below 70, in the range of mental disability.

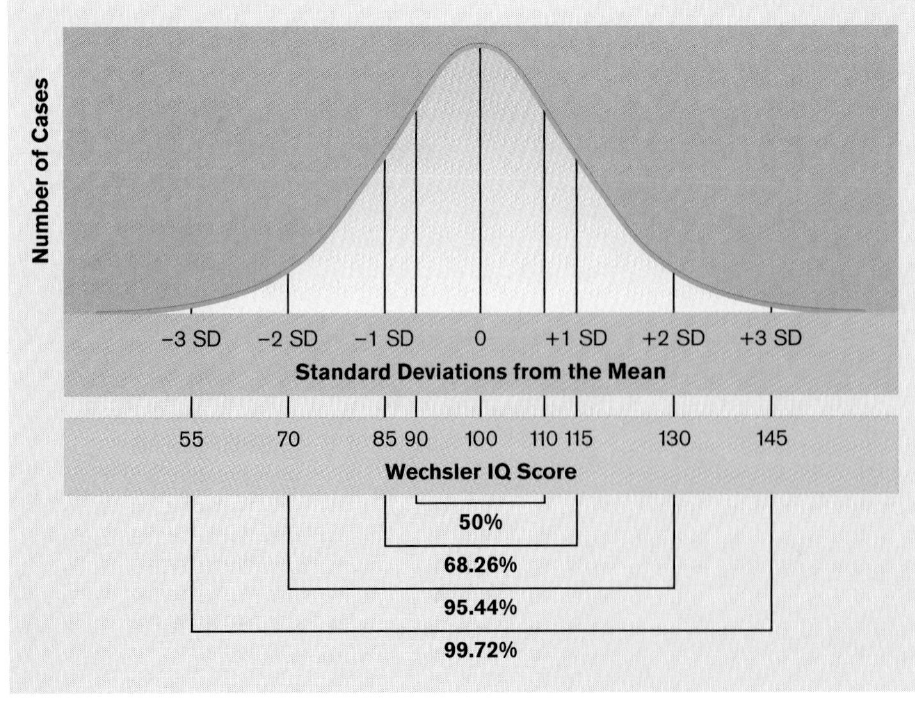

FIGURE 7.2

The Normal Curve When a large number of test scores are compiled, they are typically distributed in a normal (bell-shaped) curve. On the Wechsler scales, the average or mean IQ score is set at 100. As the figure shows, about 68 percent of the scores fall between 15 IQ points (1 standard deviation) above and below 100 (from 85 to 115), and about 95.5 percent of the scores fall between 30 points (2 standard deviations) above and below 100 (from 70 to 130).

Terman's Study of Gifted People: 1528 Geniuses and How They Grew

According to the Terman study, how do gifted people differ from the general population?

In 1921 Lewis M. Terman began a **longitudinal study**, now a classic, in which 1528 gifted students were measured at different ages throughout their lives. The 857 males and 671 females were students who had unusually high IQs on the Stanford-Binet, ranging from 135 to 200, with a mean (or average) of 151. Terman assumed the Stanford-Binet was "a measure of innate intelligence" and that IQ was fixed at birth (Cravens, 1992).

Terman's early findings ended the myth that mentally superior people are more likely to be physically inferior. Terman's gifted participants excelled in almost all of the abilities he studied—intellectual, physical, emotional, moral, and social. Terman also exploded many other myths about mentally gifted people (Terman & Oden, 1947). For example, you may have heard the saying that there is a thin line between genius and madness. Actually, Terman's gifted group enjoyed better mental health than the general population. Also, they were more likely to be successful in the real, practical world than their less mentally gifted peers.

The Terman study continues today, with most of the participants in their 80s. Shneidman (1989) states its basic findings of the study—that "an unusual mind, a vigorous body, and a relatively well-adjusted personality are not at all incompatible" (p. 687).

Who Is Gifted?

In the early 1920s, the term *giftedness* was used to describe those with IQs in the upper 2 or 3 percent of the population. Since that time, the term has been expanded to include both the exceptionally creative and those excelling in the visual or performing arts.

Traditionally, special programs for gifted people have involved either acceleration or enrichment. Acceleration programs enable students to progress at a rate that is consistent with their abilities; students may skip grades, progress through subject matter more quickly, or enter university early. Enrichment programs broaden or extend students' knowledge in foreign languages, music appreciation, and the like, or develop more advanced thinking skills.

People with Mental Disabilities

What two criteria must a person meet to be classified as mentally disabled?

At the opposite end of the continuum from the intellectually gifted are the 2 percent of Canadians whose IQ scores place them in the range of **mental disability.** People are not classified as mentally disabled unless their IQ is below 70 and they find it very hard to care for themselves and relate to others (Grossman, 1983). Individuals with IQs ranging from 55 to 70 are considered mildly disabled; from 40 to 55, moderately disabled; from 25 to 40, severely disabled; and below 25, profoundly disabled. Table 7.1 shows the level of functioning expected for various categories of mental disability.

Before the late 1960s, mentally disabled children were educated almost exclusively in special schools. Since then there has been a movement toward **mainstreaming**, which involves educating mentally disabled students in regular schools, often in classes with "abled" students.

Some mentally disabled individuals may have exceptional abilities in a narrow area of accomplishment. This is known as *savant syndrome* (also referred to as "splinter skills"), and it allows individuals to excel in one area such as arithmetic, memory tasks, music, art, or sculpture (Miller, 1999).

reliability: The ability of a test to yield nearly the same score each time a person takes the test or an alternative form of the test.

validity: The ability of a test to measure what it is intended to measure.

standardization: The establishment of norms for comparing the scores of people who will take the test in the future; administering tests using a prescribed procedure.

longitudinal study: A type of developmental study in which the same group of participants is followed and measured at different ages.

mental disability: Subnormal intelligence reflected by an IQ below 70 and by adaptive functioning severely deficient for one's age.

mainstreaming: Educating mentally disabled students in regular rather than special schools by placing them in regular classes for part of the day or having special classrooms in regular schools.

TABLE 7.2

Mental Disability as Measured on the Wechsler Scales

Classification	IQ Range	Percentage of Mentally Disabled People	Characteristics of Disabled Persons at Each Level
Mild	55–70	90%	Are able to grasp learning skills up to Grade 6 level; may become self-supporting and can be profitably employed in various occupations.
Moderate	40–55	6%	Probably are not able to grasp more than Grade 2 academic skills but can learn self-help skills and some social and occupational skills; may work in sheltered workshops.
Severe	25–40	3%	Can be trained in basic health habits; can learn to communicate verbally; learn through repetitive habit training.
Profound	Below 25	1%	Rudimentary motor development; may learn very limited self-help skills.

Remember It!

Measuring Intelligence

1. The first valid intelligence test was the
   a. Stanford-Binet.
   b. Binet-Simon.
   c. Wechsler.
   d. Terman.
2. According to Stern's formula, what is the IQ of a child with a mental age of 12 and a chronological age of 8?
   a. 75
   b. 150
   c. 125
   d. 100
3. The Stanford-Binet and Wechsler intelligence tests must be administered individually rather than in groups. (true/false)
4. Wechsler developed intelligence tests for adults and children. (true/false)
5. The largest percentage of people taking an IQ test will score in the range from
   a. 80 to 100.
   b. 90 to 109.
   c. 100 to 130.
   d. 65 to 90.
6. In his study of gifted people, Terman found that mentally superior individuals tend to be physically smaller and weaker. (true/false)
7. People are considered mentally disabled if they are clearly deficient in adaptive functioning and their IQ is below
   a. 100.
   b. 90.
   c. 80.
   d. 70.
8. A test that measures what it claims to measure has ________; a test that gives consistent results has __________.
   a. reliability; validity
   b. equivalence; reliability
   c. validity; reliability
   d. objectivity; validity

Answers: 1. a 2. b 3. true 4. true 5. b 6. false 7. d 8. c

The IQ Controversy: Brainy Dispute

The Uses and Abuses of Intelligence Tests

Since Binet's time, intelligence testing has become a major growth industry. Virtually every college and university student in Canada has taken one or more intelligence or aptitude tests. And many people have come to believe that an IQ score gives a precise indication of a person's intellectual capacity, ability, or potential.

Intelligence Test Scores: Can They Predict Success and Failure?

What do intelligence tests predict well?

What can intelligence tests really tell us? IQ scores are fairly good predictors of academic achievement and success in school. Both the Stanford-Binet Intelligence Scale and the Canadian Cognitive Abilities Test correlate highly with school grades. This is not surprising, since these scales test the same things as schoolwork—verbal and test-taking ability. But IQ tests and aptitude tests are far from infallible.

Another important question is whether there is a high correlation between IQ and success in real life. While it is true that people in the professions (doctors, dentists, lawyers) tend to have higher IQs than people in lower-status occupations, the exact relationship between IQ score and occupational status is not clearly understood. Nevertheless, intelligence scores are related to a wide range of social outcomes including job performance, income, social status, and years of education completed (Neisser et al., 1996).

The Abuses of Intelligence Tests: Making Too Much of a Single Number

What are some of the abuses of intelligence tests?

Abuses occur when people are judged solely on their scores on intelligence tests. Intelligence tests do not measure attitude and motivation, which are critical ingredients of success. Many people who probably should not be are admitted to schools; but more important, many people are denied admission to schools who could profit from them and possibly make significant contributions to society.

Many poor and minority children (particularly those for whom English is a second language) and visually impaired or hearing-impaired children have been placed into special education programs. IQ tests predicted that they were not mentally able to profit from regular classroom instruction. There would be no problem with this if tests were unfailingly accurate. But in fact they are not.

Many people maintain that IQ tests are designed for the white middle class and that other groups are at a disadvantage when they are assessed with these tests. For example, Native populations often score lower on IQ tests (Darou, 1992). Attempts have been made to develop **culture-fair intelligence tests**. Such tests are designed to minimize cultural bias; the questions do not penalize individuals whose cultural experience or language differs from that of the urban middle or upper classes. See Figure 7.3 for an example of the type of test item found on a culture-fair test.

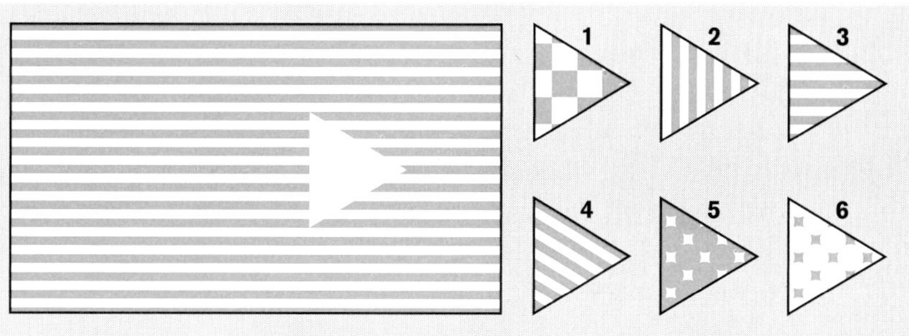

FIGURE 7.3

An Example of a Test Item on a Culture-Fair Test This culture-fair test item does not penalize test takers whose language or cultural experiences differ from those of the urban middle or upper classes. Participants are to select, from the six samples on the right, the patch that would complete the pattern. Patch number 3 is the correct answer. (Adapted from the Raven Standard Progressive Matrices Test.)

culture-fair intelligence test: An intelligence test designed to minimize cultural bias by using questions that will not penalize individuals whose culture or language differs from that of the urban middle or upper class.

The Nature–Nurture Controversy: Battle of the Centuries

How does the nature–nurture controversy apply to intelligence?

The most vocal area of disagreement concerning intelligence has been the **nature–nurture controversy**, the debate over whether intelligence is primarily the result of heredity or environment. Most psychologists today agree that both nature and nurture contribute to intelligence, but they continue to debate the proportions.

Behavioural Genetics: Investigating Nature and Nurture

What is behavioural genetics, and what are the primary methods used in the field today?

Behavioural genetics is a field of research that investigates the relative effects of heredity and environment on behaviour and ability (Plomin et al., 1997). Two of the primary methods used by behavioural geneticists are the twin study method—first used by Galton (1875) in his studies of heredity—and the adoption method.

In the **twin study method**, researchers study **identical twins** (monozygotic twins) and **fraternal twins** (dizygotic twins) to determine how much they resemble each other on a variety of characteristics. *Identical* twins have exactly the same genes: a single sperm cell of the father fertilizes a single egg of the mother, forming a cell that then splits to form two human beings—"carbon copies." *Fraternal* twins are no more alike genetically than other siblings born to the same parents: two separate sperm cells fertilize two separate eggs that happen to be released at the same time during ovulation.

Twins who are raised together, whether identical or fraternal, have similar environments. If identical twins raised together are found to be more alike than fraternal twins on a certain trait, that trait is assumed to be more influenced by heredity. If identical and fraternal twins from similar environments do not differ on a trait, that trait is assumed to be influenced more by environment. The term **heritability** refers to the index of the degree to which a characteristic is estimated to be influenced by heredity. Figure 7.4 shows estimates of the contribution of genetic and environmental factors to intelligence.

Behavioural geneticists also use the **adoption method** and conduct longitudinal studies of children adopted shortly after birth. By comparing their abilities and personality traits with those of the adoptive family members with whom they live and with those of their biological parents (whom they may never

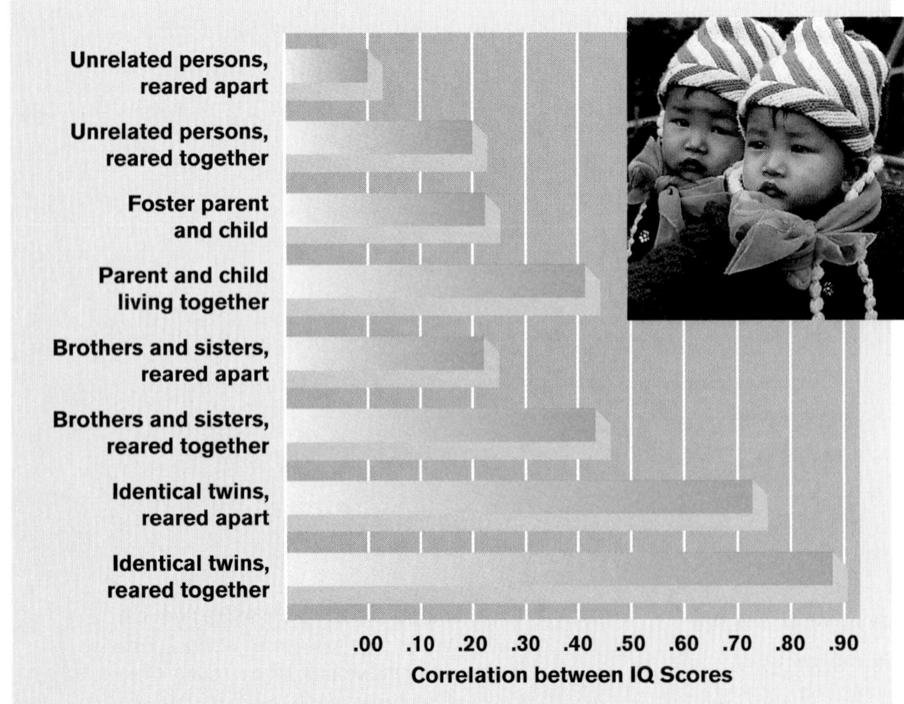

FIGURE 7.4
Correlations between the IQ Scores of Persons with Various Relationships The more closely related two individuals are, the more similar their IQ scores tend to be. Thus, there is a strong genetic contribution to intelligence. (Based on data from Bouchard & McGue, 1981; Erlenmeyer-Kimling & Jarvik, 1963.)

have met), researchers can disentangle the effects of heredity and environment (Plomin et al., 1988).

A Natural Experiment: Identical Twins Reared Apart

How do twin studies support the view that intelligence is inherited?

Probably the best way to assess the relative contributions of heredity and environment is to study identical twins who have been separated at birth and raised apart. When separated twins are found to have strikingly similar traits, it is assumed that heredity has been a major contributor. When separated twins differ on a given trait, the influence of the environment is thought to be greater.

Since 1979 researchers headed by Thomas Bouchard have studied some 60 pairs of fraternal twins and 80 pairs of identical twins who were reared apart. They conclude that *"general intelligence or IQ is strongly affected by genetic factors"* (1990, p. 227). Bouchard (1997) reports that various types of twin studies have consistently revealed heritability estimates to be .60 to .70 for intelligence, indicating that 60 to 70 percent of the variation in IQ can be attributed to genetic factors. Not all researchers agree with Bouchard's estimate. Having combined data from a number of twin studies, Plomin and colleagues (1994) estimate heritability for general intelligence to be .52 and other larger studies seem to concur with Plomin's estimates (McClearn et al., 1997).

Psychologists who consider environmental factors to be the chief contributors to differences in intelligence take issue with Bouchard's findings. They maintain that most separated identical twins are raised by adoptive parents who have been matched as closely as possible to the biological parents. This fact, the critics say, could account for the similarities in IQ. In response to their critics, Bouchard (1997) points out that studies comparing non-biologically related siblings reared in the same home reveal that IQ correlations are close to zero by the time the participants reach adolescence.

Adoption studies reveal that children adopted shortly after birth have IQs closer to their biological than to their adoptive parents' IQs. The family environment influences IQ early in life, but that influence seems to diminish; as participants reach adulthood, it is the genes that are most closely correlated with IQ (Loehlin et al., 1988, 1989; McCartney et al., 1990; Plomin & Rende, 1991). Bouchard and others (1990) assert that "although parents may be able to affect their children's rate of cognitive skill acquisition, they may have relatively little influence on the ultimate level attained" (p. 225). But does this mean that the degree to which intelligence is inherited is the degree to which it is absolutely fixed and immune to environmental intervention?

Intelligence: Is It Fixed or Changeable?

What kinds of evidence suggest that IQ is changeable rather than fixed?

Probably the most important issue in intelligence is whether IQ is fixed or changeable. There is little doubt that the great similarity in intelligence scores between identical twins reared apart makes a strong case that genetics is a powerful influence. But even Bouchard and his colleagues (1990, 1997) admit that only a few of the identical twins studied were raised in impoverished environments or by illiterate parents. Consequently, they caution against trying to generalize their findings to people raised in disadvantaged environments. Moreover, they point out that their findings do not argue that IQ cannot be enhanced in a more optimal environment.

Several studies indicate that IQ test scores are not fixed but can be modified with an enriched environ-

nature–nurture controversy: The debate over whether intelligence and other traits are primarily the result of heredity or environment.

behavioural genetics: A field of research that investigates the relative effects of heredity and environment on behaviour and ability.

twin study method: Studying identical and fraternal twins to determine the relative effects of heredity and environment on a variety of characteristics.

identical twins: Twins with identical genes; monozygotic twins.

fraternal twins: Twins who are no more alike genetically than ordinary brothers and sisters; dizygotic twins.

heritability: An index of the degree to which a characteristic is estimated to be influenced by heredity.

adoption method: A method researchers use to study the relative effects of heredity and environment on behaviour and ability in children who are adopted shortly after birth, by comparing them with their biological and adoptive parents.

ment. More than two decades ago, Sandra Scarr and Richard Weinberg (1976) studied 130 black and interracial children who had been adopted by highly educated, upper-middle-class white families; 99 of the children had been adopted in the first year of life. The adoptees were fully exposed to middle-class cultural experiences and vocabulary, the "culture of the tests and the school" (p. 737).

How did the children perform on IQ and achievement tests? For these children, the average 15-point black–white IQ gap was bridged by an enriched environment. Instead of an average IQ score of 90 (which would have been expected had they been reared by their biological parents), these adoptees had an average IQ of 106.3. And their achievement test scores were slightly *above* the national average. Studies in France also show that IQ scores and achievement are substantially higher when children from lower-class environments are adopted by middle- and upper-middle-class families (Duyme, 1988; Schiff & Lewontin, 1986). Zajonc and Mullaly (1997) suggest that the gains might be due to the fact that family size has decreased over the decades. First- and second-born children tend to do better on intelligence and achievement tests than those born later in larger families. With the decrease in family size, there has been a naturally corresponding increase in the proportion of first- and second-born children.

Other evidence also suggests that environmental factors have a strong influence on IQ scores. In industrialized countries all over the world there have been huge IQ gains over the past 50 years. These IQ gains are known as the *Flynn effect,* after James Flynn, who analyzed 73 studies involving some 7 500 participants ranging in age from 12 to 48. He found that "every Binet and Wechsler sample from 1932 to 1978 has performed better than its predecessor" (1987b, p. 225). The gain, about one-third of an IQ point per year (three points per decade), has been continuing for 50 years. That is, average IQ in industrial nations is currently about 15 IQ points, or one standard deviation, higher than 50 years ago.

In regard to the black–white IQ gap among American adults, Flynn (1987b) asserts that "the environmental advantage whites enjoy over blacks is similar to what whites (adults) of today enjoy over their own parents or grandparents of 50 years ago" (p. 226).

Drastic changes in the environment can have major effects on intelligence. For example, malnutrition, especially early in life, can harm intellectual development (Brown & Pollitt, 1996).

Race and IQ: The Controversial Views

What are Jensen's and Herrnstein and Murray's controversial views on race and IQ?

Some studies over the past several decades have reported that, on average, blacks score about 15 points lower than whites on standardized IQ tests (Herrnstein & Murray, 1994; Jensen, 1985; Loehlin et al., 1975). In 1969 Arthur Jensen published an article in the *Harvard Educational Review* in which he attributed the IQ gap to genetic factors. He also maintained that because heredity is such a strong influence on intelligence, environment cannot make a significant difference. Jensen's views on race and intelligence sent a shock wave through the scientific community.

In a similar vein, a Canadian researcher, J. Philippe Rushton, argued that races could be ranked in order of intelligence, with Asians being the highest, followed by whites, and then blacks. His conclusions are based on differences in head circumference, brain size, and estimated cranial space (Rushton, 1991, 1992). This argument has been challenged by other researchers who question the methodology of the research, the accuracy of the measurements, and whether the studies actually test intelligence. Active among Rushton's critics are Guelph University researchers Michael Peters (1995a, 1995b) and Andrew Winston (1996).

A book called *The Bell Curve* (1994) is the most recent fuel for this same controversy. The authors, Herrnstein and Murray, argue that more than any other factor, IQ explains how those at the top rungs of society got there and why those on the lower rungs remain there. For the authors, IQ is primarily genetic and cannot be changed by environmental interventions.

Jensen's views and those of Rushton and Herrnstein and Murray run counter to the beliefs of those who argue that an enriched, stimulating environment can overcome the deficits of poverty and cultural disadvantage and thus reduce or wipe out the IQ deficit.

IS THE GAP DUE TO RACE ALONE? If average IQ differences were genetically determined by race, then the mean IQ scores of mixed-race individuals should fall somewhere between the mean scores for blacks and whites. But studies over the decades have not

Remember It! IQ Controversies

1. IQ tests are good predictors of success in school. (true/false)
2. What field of research investigates the relative effects of heredity and environment on behaviour and ability?
   a. genetics
   b. behavioural genetics
   c. biology
   d. physiology
3. Twin studies suggest that environment is a stronger factor than heredity in shaping IQ differences. (true/false)
4. Jensen and Herrnstein and Murray maintain that the black–white IQ gap is due primarily to
   a. genetics.
   b. environment.
   c. discrimination.
   d. racism.
5. Several adoption studies have revealed that when infants from disadvantaged environments are adopted by middle- and upper-middle-class parents, their IQ scores are raised about 15 points. (true/false)

Answers: 1. true 2. b 3. false 4. a 5. true

found such a relationship between IQ and mixed ancestry. Among the earliest such research was a study by Witty and Jenkins (1936), who reported no relationship between test scores and white ancestry as reported by blacks. Other studies showed that blacks whose blood types were identical to those most commonly found in whites did not score higher than blacks with other blood types (Loehlin et al., 1973; Scarr et al., 1977).

At the end of World War II, American soldiers stationed in Germany, both black and white, fathered thousands of children with German women. Fifteen years later, Eyeferth (1961) randomly selected samples of these children (183 with black fathers and 83 with white fathers). The mean IQs of the two groups were virtually identical. Having a white father conferred no measurable IQ advantage at all.

LINK IT!

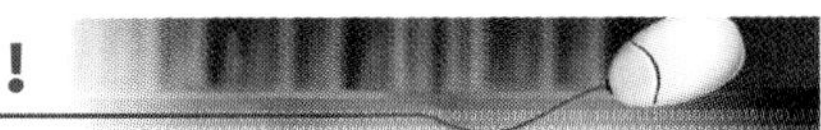

www.mugu.com/cgi-bin/Upstream/Issues/bell-curve/index.html
Materials Relating to the Book The Bell Curve

webusers.anet-stl.com/~civil/bellcurveillustration2.html
Compilation of Web sites and scholarly articles on The Bell Curve

Emotional Intelligence

Daniel Goleman (1995) claims that success in life is more markedly influenced by emotional intelligence than by IQ. **Emotional intelligence** refers to a set of capabilities that are separate from IQ but necessary for success in life—in the workplace, in intimate personal relations, and in social interactions. Goleman (1995) has extended the work of Peter Salovey and John Mayer (1990; Mayer & Salovey, 1993, 1995, 1997), who first introduced the concept of emotional intelligence.

Personal Components of Emotional Intelligence

What are the personal components of emotional intelligence?

The foundation of emotional intelligence is self-knowledge. It involves an awareness of emotions, an ability to manage those emotions, and self-motivation.

Awareness of our own emotions—recognizing and acknowledging feelings as they happen—is at the very heart of emotional intelligence. It means being aware

emotional intelligence: A type of intelligence that includes an awareness of and an ability to manage one's own emotions, the ability to motivate oneself, empathy, and the ability to handle relationships successfully.

not only of our moods, but of thoughts about those moods, as well. Those who are able to monitor their feelings as they arise are more likely to be able to manage them rather than being ruled by them.

Managing emotions does not mean suppressing them, any more than it means giving free rein to every feeling and impulse. To manage emotions is to express them in an appropriate manner and not let them run out of control. For example, if not tempered with reason, uncontrolled anger can lead to rage and violence. People high in emotional intelligence have learned how to regulate their moods and not let anger, boredom, or depression ruin their day (or their lives). You manage your emotions when you do something to cheer yourself up, soothe your own hurts, reassure yourself, or otherwise temper an inappropriate or out-of-control emotion.

Self-motivation refers to a strength of emotional self-control that enables a person to get moving and pursue worthy goals, persist at tasks even when frustrated, and resist the temptation to act on impulse.

The ability to postpone immediate gratification and to persist in working toward some greater future gain is most closely related to success—whether one is trying to build a business, get a college degree, or even stay on a diet.

Interpersonal Components of Emotional Intelligence

What are the interpersonal components of emotional intelligence?

The interpersonal aspects of emotional intelligence are empathy and the ability to handle relationships.

The ability to empathize—to recognize and understand the motives and emotions of others—is the cornerstone of successful interpersonal relations. Empathy appears to be a higher level of development that springs from self-awareness. If we have no insight into our own emotions, it is unlikely that we will develop sensitivity and understanding of the emotions of others.

One key indicator, or hallmark, of the empathy component of emotional intelligence is the ability to read and interpret non-verbal behaviour—the gestures, vocal inflections, tones of voice, and facial expressions of others. Non-verbal behaviour is, in a sense, the language of the emotions, because our feelings are most genuinely expressed this way. People may fail to communicate their feelings verbally or even lie about them, but their non-verbal behaviour often reveals their true feelings.

A person with high emotional intelligence shows empathy–recognizing non-verbal signals from others and making appropriate responses.

For most people, hardly anything in life is more important than their relationships—intimate love relationships; family, professional, and work relationships; and relationships with friends. Without rewarding relationships, life would be lonely indeed. What does emotional intelligence have to do with forming and maintaining successful relationships? Virtually everything. Some people are inept at forming and handling mutually satisfying relationships; others seem to be masters of the art.

Two components of emotional intelligence that are prerequisites for handling relationships are (1) the ability to manage one's own emotions, and (2) empathy. These two components combine to produce the ability to respond appropriately to emotions in others. And this, Goleman (1995) maintains, is the very centre of the art of handling relationships. But he does not mean "handling" in an autocratic, dominating sense. People who handle relationships well, says Goleman, are able to shape encounters, "to mobilize and inspire others to thrive in intimate relationships, to persuade and influence, to put others at ease" (p. 113).

Optimism also appears to be a component of emotional intelligence. People who are optimistic have a "strong expectation in general [that] things will turn out all right in life" (p. 88). The most significant aspect of optimism in the context of emotional intelligence is the way in which optimists explain their successes and failures. When optimists fail, they attribute their failure to something in the situation that can be changed. Thus, they believe that by trying harder, they can succeed the next time. But when pessimists fail, they blame themselves and attribute their failure to some personal characteristic or flaw that cannot be changed.

Imagery and Concepts: Tools of Thinking

In our discussion of intelligence, we reviewed the basic components of IQ tests. Some of these components assess verbal skills, spatial abilities, problem solving, and logic. These underlying competencies are also important when we consider the tools of thinking.

What *are* the tools of thinking? All of us have an intuitive notion of what thinking is. We say, "I think it's going to rain" (a prediction); "I think this is the right answer" (a choice); "I think I will resign" (a decision). But our everyday use of the word *think* does not suggest the processes we use to perform the act itself. Sometimes our thinking is free-flowing rather than goal-oriented. At other times, it is directed at a goal such as solving a problem or making a decision. Just how is the act of thinking accomplished? There is general agreement that at least two tools are commonly used when we think—images and concepts.

Imagery: Picture This—Elephants with Purple Polka Dots

What is imagery?

Can you imagine hearing a recording of your favourite song or someone calling your name? Can you picture yourself jogging or walking, pouring ice water over your hands, or kissing someone you love? The vast majority of us are able to produce mental **imagery**—that is, we can represent or picture a sensory experience in our mind.

In a survey of 500 adults conducted by McKellar (1972), 97 percent said they had visual images; 93 percent reported auditory images (imagine your psychology instructor's voice); 74 percent said they had motor imagery (imagine raising your hand); 70 percent, tactile or touch images (imagine rubbing sandpaper); 6 percent, gustatory images (imagine the taste of a dill pickle); and 66 percent, olfactory images (imagine smelling a rose). Visual imagery is certainly the most common, although auditory imagery is not far behind.

Our images may be dimmer and less vivid than when we are experiencing the real thing, but images are not limited to time, space, size, or other physical realities. We can imagine ourselves flying through the air like an eagle, singing to the thundering applause of adoring fans, or performing all sorts of amazing feats. But normally our imaging is quite similar to the real world we are thinking about.

When we construct visual mental images, we may believe that we form the entire image all at once. But according to Stephen Kosslyn (1988), we do not. Rather, we mentally construct the objects we image, one part at a time. Studies with split-brain patients and normal people suggest that two types of processes are used in the formation of visual images. First, we retrieve stored memories of how parts of an object look; then we use mental processes to arrange or assemble those parts into the proper whole. Both hemispheres participate in the processes of forming visual images. Try forming visual images as you do *Try It!*

Try It!

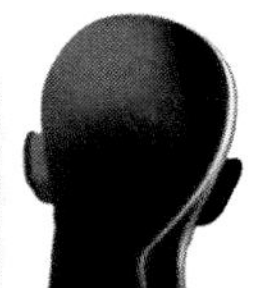

Forming Visual Images

A. Picture an ant crawling on a newspaper about one metre away. How many legs does the ant have?

B. Picture an ant perched on the end of a toothpick right in front of your eyes. Does the ant have eyelashes?

In which mental picture is the ant larger, A or B? Which mental picture provided more detail of the ant? (After Finke, 1985.)

imagery: The representation in the mind of a sensory experience–visual, auditory, gustatory, motor, olfactory, or tactile.

Kosslyn (1975, 1983) asked research participants many questions like those in *Try It!* and found that they answered questions about larger images about 0.2 seconds faster than questions about small images. It takes us slightly longer to zoom in on smaller images than on larger ones, just as it does when we actually look at real objects (Kosslyn & Ochsner, 1994).

But what if we are forming new images rather than answering questions about large and small images already formed? Picture an elephant standing about a metre away. Now picture a rabbit standing at the same distance. Which image took longer to form? Kosslyn (1975) discovered that it takes people longer to form large mental images—an elephant as opposed to a rabbit. It takes longer to view the elephant because there is more of it to view, and likewise more of it to image.

Not only do we form a mental image of an object, but we manipulate and move it around in our mind much as we would if we were actually holding and looking at the object (Cooper & Shepard, 1984). Shepard and Metzler (1971) asked eight participants to judge some 1600 pairs of drawings like the ones in Figure 7.5. They had to rotate the objects in their imagination to see if they matched. In Figure 7.5 the objects in (a) and (b) are a match; those in (c) are not. But the important finding is that the more the objects had to be rotated in imagery, the longer it took participants to decide whether they matched. This is precisely what happens if the participants rotate real objects; the more they need to be rotated, the longer it takes to make the decision. As this study demonstrates, we manipulate objects in mental imagery in the same way as we manipulate real physical objects.

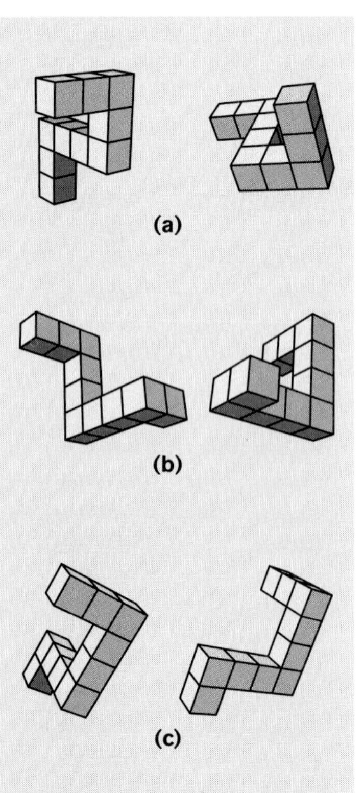

FIGURE 7.5 Samples of Geometric Patterns in Shepard and Metzler's Mental Rotation Study Mentally rotate one of the patterns in each pair–(a), (b), and (c)–and decide whether the two patterns match. Do you find that the more you have to rotate the objects mentally, the longer it takes to decide if they match? (From Shepard & Metzler, 1971.)

Similarities in the Processes of Imaging and Perceiving

If we form mental images (visual, auditory, etc.) in the brain much as we actually perceive them, then is imaging subject to interference, just like our perceptions? Close your eyes and form a mental image of your psychology instructor. Now keep the visual image and open your eyes. Doesn't the mental image fade or disappear as soon as you see a real object? But if viewing an actual object interferes with a visual image, is the reverse also true? Will a vivid visual image interfere with a real object?

Yes, according to Craver-Lemley and Reeves (1992). In an earlier study, Segal and Fusella (1970) asked students to form either a visual image of a tree or an auditory image of the sound of a typewriter. The researchers then made a faint sound on a harmonica, or flashed a small, dimly lighted blue arrow, or did nothing at all. Students holding the visual image of a tree were less likely to see the blue arrow but more likely to hear the harmonica. Students imaging the sound of a typewriter had the opposite experience: they saw the arrow but missed the sound of the harmonica. To the researchers, this meant that both perceiving and imaging probably use some of the same mental processes and that using the same processes *simultaneously* on two different tasks causes interference.

But not all researchers who study imagery and perception agree (Roland & Gulyás, 1994). There is agreement that certain higher-order visual areas in the temporal and parietal lobes are involved in both imagery and perception (Moscovitch et al., 1994). But some researchers say that the primary visual cortex is not necessarily active during imaging unless the person is actually scrutinizing the features of some object stored in memory—as you did in *Try It!* (Sakai & Miyashita, 1994). Kosslyn and Ochsner (1994; also Kosslyn, 1994), on the other hand, maintain that the primary visual cortex is also involved in most imaging. They believe that the same brain pathways are used both in perceiving and in imaging objects, although the pathways for imaging are activated in reverse order from the pathways for perceiving. Patients who have experienced damage in a particular region of the right hemisphere may have a loss of perception in the left half of their visual field. (Remember that information from the left and right visual fields is fed into the opposite brain hemispheres.) Some males with such damage will shave the right side of their face but completely ignore the left side. When these same patients are asked to produce a mental image of an object or a location they know well, they identify only the details on the right half of the object or location (Bisiach & Luzzati, 1978).

Concepts: Our Mental Classification System (Is a Penguin a Bird?)

What are concepts, and how are they formed?

Thinking is not limited to conjuring up a series of pictures, sounds, touches, tastes, and smells. We humans are capable of conceptualizing as well. A **concept** is a label that represents a class or group of objects, people, or events that share common characteristics or attributes. Concepts are useful tools that help us order our world and think and communicate with speed and efficiency.

Imagine that you are walking down the street with a friend, and you see approaching in the distance a hairy, brown-and-white, four-legged animal with two eyes and two ears, its mouth open, its tongue hanging out, and a long, wagging tail. You simply say to your friend, "Here comes a dog." Thanks to our ability to use concepts, we are not forced to consider and describe everything in great detail before we make an identification. We do not need a different name to identify and describe every single rock, tree, animal, or situation we meet. *Dog* is a concept that stands for a family of animals that share similar characteristics or attributes, even though they may differ in significant ways (in this case, according to breed).

We have concepts for abstractions as well as for tangible objects and organisms. Love, beauty, and justice are abstract concepts, yet we can identify and consider aspects of beauty and justice because we have formed concepts of them. We also use relational concepts in our thinking—larger than, smaller than, older than, younger than, and so on—to compare individuals, objects, and ideas.

Concept Formation: Learning What Fits a Concept

How do we acquire concepts, and how do we know what fits or does not fit a given concept? We can form concepts (1) from a formal definition of the concept, (2) by systematically memorizing a concept's common features, (3) through our experiences with positive and negative instances of the concept, (4) through the use of prototypes, or (5) through the use of exemplars.

SYSTEMATIC OR FORMAL APPROACHES Studies have been conducted and theories proposed to explain how we form concepts. Some theorists maintain that we approach concept formation in an active, orderly, and systematic way, rather than in a random, informal, and haphazard way (Bruner et al., 1956). Sometimes we learn a concept from a formal definition or from a formal classification system. You surely have memorized several such systems while studying biology, chemistry, English, or similar subjects.

POSITIVE AND NEGATIVE INSTANCES We acquire many simple concepts through experiences with examples or positive instances of the concept. When children are young, parents may point out examples of a car—the family car, the neighbour's car, cars on the street, and pictures of cars in a book. But if a child points to some other type of moving vehicle and says "car," the parent will say, "No, that is a truck," or "This is a bus." "Truck" and "bus" are negative instances, or "non-examples," of the concept "car." After experience with positive and negative instances of the concept, a child begins to grasp some of the properties of a car that distinguish it from other wheeled vehicles.

PROTOTYPES Eleanor Rosch (1973, 1978) argues that formal theories of concept formation, and the experiments on which they are based, tend to be rather artificial, contrived, and unrelated to our actual experience. She and her colleagues have studied concept formation in its natural setting and have concluded

concept: A label that represents a class or group of objects, people, or events sharing common characteristics or attributes.

that in real life, our thinking and concept formation are somewhat fuzzy, not clear-cut and systematic. Sometimes we identify objects based on a memorized list of features or attributes that are common to instances of a concept. But in addition, we are likely to picture a **prototype** of the concept—an example that embodies the most common and typical features of the concept.

What is your prototype for the concept *bird?* Chances are it is not a penguin, an ostrich, or a kiwi. All three are birds that cannot fly. A more likely bird prototype is a robin or perhaps a sparrow. Most birds can fly, but not all; most mammals cannot fly, but bats are mammals, have wings, and can fly. So not all examples within a concept fit equally well. Nevertheless, the prototype most closely fits a given concept, and items and organisms belonging to the concept share more attributes with their prototype than with the prototype of any other concept.

EXEMPLARS A recent theory of concept formation suggests that concepts are represented by their **exemplars**—individual instances, or examples, of a concept that we have stored in memory from our own experience (Estes, 1994). To decide whether an unfamiliar item belongs to a concept, we compare it with exemplars (other examples) of that concept.

The concepts we form do not exist in isolation. We form them in hierarchies. For example, the canary and the cardinal are subsets of the concept *bird*; at a higher level, birds are subsets of the concept *animal*; and at a still higher level, animals are a subset of the concept *living things*.

A prototype is an example that embodies the most typical features of a concept. Which of the animals shown here best fits your prototype for the concept *bird*?

Remember It! Imagery and Concepts

1. The two most common forms of imagery are
   a. visual and motor imagery.
   b. auditory and tactile imagery.
   c. visual and auditory imagery.
   d. visual and gustatory imagery.
2. Our images are generally as vivid as the real thing. (true/false)
3. A label that represents a class or group of objects, people, or events that share common characteristics or attributes is called a(n)
   a. image.
   b. concept.
   c. positive instance.
   d. prototype
4. A prototype is the most ____________ example of a concept.
   a. abstract
   b. unusual
   c. recent
   d. typical
5. A stork is an exemplar of the concept *bird.* (true/false)

Answers: 1. c 2. false 3. b 4. d 5. true

Problem Solving and Creativity

Approaches to Problem Solving: How Do We Begin?

What are three problem-solving techniques, and how are they used?

All of us are faced every day with a variety of problems needing to be solved. Most of our problems are simple and mundane, like what to have for dinner or what clothes to put on in the morning. But some of our problems are more far-reaching, such as what career to pursue, how to sustain or improve a relationship, or how to stretch our income from one paycheque to the next. Then there are the problems we meet in our schoolwork, which we must think through using problem-solving techniques. Among these techniques are trial and error, algorithms, and heuristics. How would you solve the problem in the *Try It!* box?

Trial and Error

How did you choose to solve the *Try It!* problem? Many people simply start placing the numbers in the boxes and then change them around when a combination doesn't work. This is called **trial and error**. It occurs when we try one solution after another, in no particular order, until by chance we hit upon the answer.

However, other techniques are far more effective and less time-consuming.

Algorithms

Another major problem-solving method is the algorithm (Newell & Simon, 1972). An **algorithm** is a systematic, step-by-step procedure that guarantees a solution to a problem of a certain type if the algorithm is appropriate and executed properly. Formulas used in mathematics and other sciences are algorithms. Another type of algorithm is a systematic strategy for exploring every possible solution to a problem until the correct one is reached. In some cases there may be millions or even billions or more possibilities that one would have to try before reaching a solution. Often computers are programmed to solve such problems, because with a computer an accurate solution is guaranteed and millions of possible solutions can be tried in a few seconds.

Many problems do not lend themselves to solution by algorithms, however. Suppose you were a contestant on *Wheel of Fortune,* trying to solve this missing-letter puzzle: P_Y_ _OL_ _ _. An exhaustive search algorithm would be out of the question—even Vanna White's smile would fade long before the nearly nine billion possibilities could be considered. An easier way to solve such problems is by heuristics.

Heuristic Strategies in Problem Solving

A **heuristic** is a problem-solving method that does not guarantee success but offers a promising way to

Try It!

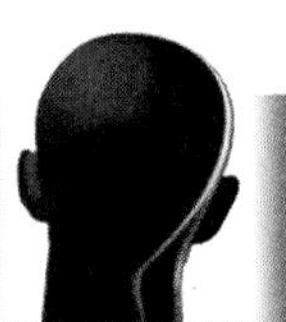

Testing Problem Solving

Insert the numbers 1 through 7 in the seven boxes, one digit to a box, in such a way that no consecutive numbers are next to each other horizontally, vertically, or diagonally. Several solutions are possible.

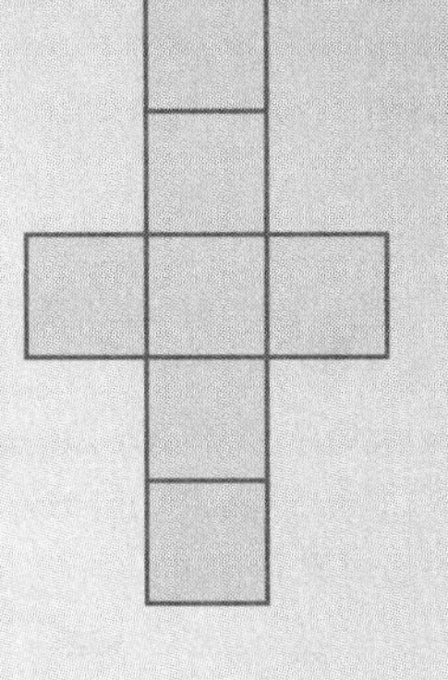

(Printed upside down:)
5 / 7 / 1 4 2 / 6 / 3
3 / 1 / 4 7 5 / 2 / 6
6 / 4 / 1 7 2 / 5 / 3
3 / 1 / 7 4 6 / 2 / 5

prototype: An example that embodies the most common and typical features of a particular concept.

exemplars: The individual instances of a concept that we have stored in memory from our own experience.

trial and error: An approach to problem solving in which one solution after another is tried in no particular order until a workable solution is found.

algorithm: A systematic, step-by-step procedure, such as a mathematical formula, that guarantees a solution to a problem of a certain type if the algorithm is appropriate and executed properly.

heuristic (hyu-RIS-tik): A problem-solving method that offers a promising way to attack a problem and arrive at a solution, although it does not guarantee success.

attack a problem and arrive at a solution. Chess players must use heuristics because there is not enough time in a lifetime to consider all of the moves and countermoves that are possible in a single game of chess (Bransford et al., 1986).

We use heuristics to eliminate useless steps and take the shortest probable path toward a solution. The missing-letter puzzle presented earlier is easily solved through a simple heuristic approach that makes use of our existing knowledge of words (prefixes, roots, suffixes). For example, we would probably try the most common letters (E, R, S, A, T, O, L, N) rather than every possible letter to fill the blank spaces. Next we would identify likely letter combinations first (PSY rather than PNY). Then we would supply the missing letters and spell out PSYCHOLOGY.

MEANS–END ANALYSIS One popular heuristic strategy is **means–end analysis**, in which the current position is compared with a desired goal, and a series of steps are formulated and then taken to close the gap between the two (Sweller & Levine, 1982). Many problems are large and complex and must be broken down into smaller steps or sub-problems. If your professor assigns a term paper, for example, you probably do not simply sit down and write it. You must first determine how you will deal with your topic, research the topic, make an outline, and then probably write the subtopics over a period of time. At last you are ready to assemble the complete term paper, write several drafts, and put the finished product in final form before handing it in.

WORKING BACKWARD Another heuristic that is effective for solving some problems is **working backward**, sometimes called the "backward search." In this approach we start with the solution—a known condition—and work our way backward through the problem. Once our backward search has revealed the steps to be taken and their order, we can solve the problem. Try working backward to solve the water lily problem in *Try It!*

Impediments to Problem Solving: Mental Stumbling Blocks

What are the two major impediments to problem solving?

Sometimes the difficulty in problem solving lies not with the problem but with ourselves. The two major impediments to problem solving are functional fixedness and mental set.

Try It!

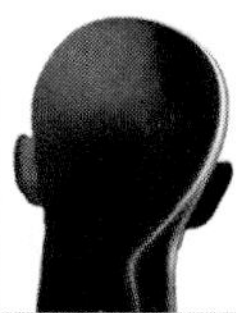

Working Backward to Solve a Problem

Water lilies double the area they cover every 24 hours. At the beginning of the summer there is one water lily on a lake. It takes 60 days for the lake to become covered with water lilies. On what day is the lake half covered?

Answer: The most important fact is that the lilies double in number every 24 hours. If the lake is to be completely covered on the 60th day, it has to be half covered on the 59th day.

Functional Fixedness

Many of us are hampered in our efforts to solve problems in daily living because of **functional fixedness**—the failure to use familiar objects in novel ways to solve problems. We tend to see objects only in terms of their customary functions. Just think of all the items we use daily—tools, utensils, and other equipment—that help us perform certain functions. Often the normal functions of objects become fixed in our thinking so that we do not consider using them in new and creative ways.

What if you wanted a cup of coffee, but the decanter to your coffeemaker was broken? If you suffered from functional fixedness, you might come to the conclusion that there was nothing you could do to solve your problem at that moment. The solution? Rather than thinking about the object or utensil that you don't have, think about the function you need served in order to solve your problem. What you need is something to catch the coffee, rather than the specific glass decanter that came with the coffeemaker. Could you catch the coffee in some other type of bowl or cooking utensil, or even in a coffee mug?

Mental Set

Another impediment to problem solving, similar to functional fixedness but much broader, is mental set. **Mental set** means that we get into a mental rut in our approach to solving problems, continuing to use the same old methods even though other approaches might be better. Perhaps we hit on a way to solve a problem once in the past and continue to use the same technique in similar situations, even though it is not highly effective or efficient. We are much more susceptible to mental set when we fail to consider the special requirements of a problem. Not surprisingly, the same people who are subject to mental set are also more likely to have trouble with functional fixedness when they attempt to solve problems (McKelvie, 1984).

Creativity: Unique and Useful Productions

What is creativity, and what tests have been designed to measure it?

Creativity can be thought of as the ability to produce original, appropriate, and valuable ideas and/or solutions to problems. But can creativity be measured, and does it differ from conventional thought? According to psychologist J.P. Guilford, who studied creativity for several decades, creative thinkers are proficient in **divergent thinking**. Divergent thinking is the ability to produce multiple ideas, answers, or solutions to a problem rather than a single, correct response. Divergent thinkers can conceive of novel or original ideas that involve the combination and synthesis of unusual associations that lead to an abundant quantity of ideas (Csikszentmihalyi, 1996).

Obviously, creative thinking is divergent. But is divergent thinking necessarily creative thinking? No! All creative thought is divergent, but not all divergent thought is creative. Novelty is not synonymous with creativity. We are not surprised, then, to find that high scores on tests of divergent thinking do not have a very high correlation with creative thinking in real life. Guilford himself admitted (1967) that in studies of students from elementary through high school, the correlations of his divergent-thinking tests with actual creative thinking were not spectacular.

Other researchers have also tried to design tests to measure creative ability. Mednick and Mednick (1967) reasoned that the essence of creativity is the thinker's ability to fit ideas together that might appear remote or unrelated to the less creative thinker. They created the Remote Associates Test (RAT) as a means of measuring creative ability. Try your creative skills in the next *Try It!*

Mednick and Mednick point out that some studies show a relationship between high scores on the RAT and creative thinking in the workplace; other studies, however, have not found this relationship (Matlin, 1983). For more information about creativity, see *Apply It!* at the end of this chapter.

Creativity and Intelligence: How Do They Relate?

Is creativity related to intelligence? There is a modest correlation between the two: highly creative people tend to be well above average in intelligence. However, in the upper IQ ranges (120 +) there seems to be little correlation (Barron & Harrington, 1981).

means-end analysis: A heuristic problem-solving strategy in which the current position is compared with the desired goal, and a series of steps are formulated and taken to close the gap between them.

working backward: A heuristic strategy in which a person discovers the steps needed to solve a problem by defining the desired goal and working backward to the current condition.

functional fixedness: The failure to use familiar objects in novel ways to solve problems because of a tendency to view objects only in terms of their customary functions.

mental set: The tendency to apply a familiar strategy to the solution of a problem without carefully considering the special requirements of the problem.

creativity: The ability to produce original, appropriate, and valuable ideas and/or solutions to problems.

divergent thinking: Producing one or more possible ideas, answers, or solutions to a problem rather than a single, correct response.

Try It!

Testing Creative Ability

One indication of creativity may be the ability to make associations among several elements that seem only remotely related or unrelated. Test your ability to find associations for these 10 sets of words, which are similar to those on the Remote Associates Test. Think of a fourth word that is related in some way to all three of the words in each row. For example, the words *keeper, text,* and *worm* are related to the word *book* and become *bookkeeper, textbook,* and *bookworm.*

1. sales, collector, income
2. flower, room, water
3. red, shot, dog
4. ball, hot, stool
5. rock, man, classical
6. story, true, sick
7. news, plate, waste
8. stuffed, sleeve, sweat
9. class, temperature, bath
10. wrist, man, stop

Answers: 1. tax 2. bed 3. hot 4. foot 5. music 6. love 7. paper 8. shirt 9. room 10. watch

Remember the young geniuses studied by Lewis Terman? Not a single one of them produced a highly creative work in later years (Terman & Oden, 1959). They were geniuses, yes, but not creative geniuses.

Language

Without language, there would be no books to read, no papers to write, no lectures to endure. Not bad so far, you may be thinking. But consider: Without language we would each live in a largely solitary and isolated world, unable to communicate or receive any information, from simple requests to our most intimate thoughts and feelings. Our knowledge would be restricted to the direct and immediate, our own experience locked within us.

Thanks to language, we can profit from the experience, the knowledge, and the wisdom of others and can benefit others with our own. Language is not confined to time and space. The wisdom of the ages from every corner of the world and spanning the centuries of recorded history is available to us through language. Truly, language is one of the most important capabilities of the human species. Civilization could not exist without it. Whether spoken, written, or signed, language is vital to us. What are the components and the structure of this most amazing tool of human communication?

Remember It!

Problem Solving and Creativity

1. Which of the following is guaranteed, if properly applied, to result in the correct answer to a problem?
   a. an algorithm
   b. a heuristic
   c. trial and error
   d. applying prior knowledge
2. Working backward and means–end analysis are examples of
   a. algorithms.
   b. heuristics.
   c. mental sets.
   d. functional fixedness.
3. John uses a wastebasket to keep a door from closing. In solving his problem, he was not hindered by
   a. a heuristic.
   b. an algorithm.
   c. functional fixedness.
   d. mental set.
4. One characteristic of good problem solvers is mental set. (true/false)
5. Divergent thinking tests and the Remote Associates Test are used to measure
   a. imaging ability.
   b. concept formation.
   c. problem-solving ability.
   d. creativity.

Answers: 1. a 2. b 3. c 4. false 5. d

The Structure of Language

What are the four important components of language?

Psycholinguistics is the study of how language is acquired, produced, and used and how the sounds and symbols of language are translated into meaning. Psycholinguists devote much of their time to the study of the structure of language and the rules governing its use. The structure and rules governing language involve four different components—phonemes, morphemes, syntax, and semantics.

LINK IT!

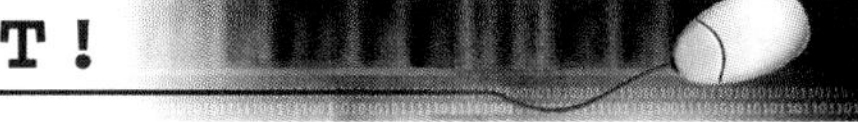

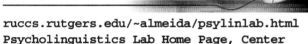

ruccs.rutgers.edu/~almeida/psylinlab.html
Psycholinguistics Lab Home Page, Center for Cognitive Science, Rutgers University

www.ugcs.caltech.edu/~egnor/psycho/
Participate in a psycholinguistic survey

Phonemes

The smallest units of sound in a spoken language are known as **phonemes**. Phonemes form the basic building blocks of a spoken language. Three phonemes together form the sound of the word *cat*—the *c* (which sounds like *k*), *a*, and *t*. Phonemes do not sound like the single letters of the alphabet as we recite them, *a-b-c-d-e-f-g*, but like the sounds of the letters as they are used in words, like the *b* in *boy*, the *p* in *pan*, and so on. The sound of the phoneme *c* in the word *cat* is different from the sound of the phoneme *c* in the word *city*.

Letters combined to form sounds are also phonemes, such as the *th* in *the* and the *ch* in *child*. The same sound (phoneme) may be represented by different letters in different words, as in the *a* in *stay* and the *ei* in *sleigh*. And, as we saw with *c*, the same letter can serve as different phonemes. The letter *a*, for example, can be sounded as three different phonemes, as in *day*, *cap*, and *law*.

How many phonemes are there? There are perhaps 100 or so different sounds that could serve as phonemes, but most languages have far fewer. English uses about 45 phonemes; some languages may have as few as 15 or so and other languages as many as 85 (Solso, 1991). Though phonemes are the basic building blocks of language, they alone, with a few exceptions, do not provide language with meaning. For meaning, we must move to the next component of language, the morphemes.

Morphemes

Morphemes are the smallest units of meaning in a language. In almost all cases in the English language, a morpheme is made of two or more phonemes. But a few phonemes also serve as morphemes, such as the article *a* and the personal pronoun *I*. Many words in English are single morphemes—*book*, *word*, *learn*, *reason*, and so on. In addition to root words, morphemes may also be prefixes (such as *re* in *relearn*) or suffixes (such as *ed* to show past tense—*learned*). The single morpheme *reason* becomes the two-morpheme *reasonable*. The letter *s* gives a plural meaning to a word and is thus a morpheme. The morpheme *book* (singular) becomes the two-morpheme *books* (plural).

So morphemes, singly and in combination, form the words in a language and provide meaning. But sounds and single words alone are not enough. A language also requires rules for structuring or putting together words in an orderly and meaningful fashion. This is where syntax enters the picture.

Syntax

Syntax is the aspect of grammar that specifies the rules for arranging and combining words to form phrases and sentences. An important rule of syntax in English is that adjectives usually come before nouns. So we refer to the caution lights at intersections as yellow lights or amber lights. But in French the noun usually comes before the adjective, and speakers would say *le feu jaune,* or "the light yellow." So the rules of word order, or syntax, differ from one language to another. In English we ask, "Do you speak German?" But speakers of German would ask *Sprechen Sie Deutsch?* or, "Speak you German?"

psycholinguistics: The study of how language is acquired, produced, and used, and how the sounds and symbols of language are translated into meaning.

phonemes: The smallest units of sound in a spoken language.

morphemes: The smallest units of meaning in a language.

syntax: The aspect of grammar that specifies the rules for arranging and combining words to form phrases and sentences.

Semantics

Semantics refers to the meaning we derive from morphemes, words, and sentences. The same word can have different meanings depending upon how it is used in sentences: "I don't mind." "Mind your manners." "He has lost his mind." Or consider another example, "Loving to read, the young girl read three books last week." Here, the word *read* is pronounced two different ways and in one case is in the past tense.

Language is a universal human phenomenon, yet there is great diversity in the way language is used around the world—there are some 6000 spoken languages (Berreby, 1994). But however it is spoken, written, signed, or otherwise used, language is one of the most complex human capabilities.

Language Development

At birth, the infant's only means of communication is crying, but at age 17, the average high school graduate has a vocabulary of 80 000 words (Miller & Gildea, 1987).

Children do much more than simply add new words to their vocabulary. They acquire an understanding of the way words are put together to form sentences (syntax) and the way language is used in social situations. Children acquire most of their language without any formal teaching and discover the rules of language on their own. During their first few months, infants communicate distress or displeasure through crying (Shatz, 1983). The cry is their innate reaction to an unpleasant internal state, such as hunger, thirst, discomfort, or pain.

Cooing and Babbling

During the second or third month, infants begin cooing—repeatedly uttering vowel sounds such as "ah" and "oo."

At about six months, infants begin **babbling**. They utter phonemes. Consonant-vowel combinations are repeated in a string, like "ma-ma-ma" or "ba-ba-ba." During the first part of the babbling stage, infants babble all the basic speech sounds that occur in all the languages of the world. Language up to this point seems to be biologically determined, because all babies throughout the world, even deaf children, vocalize this same range of speech sounds.

At about eight months, babies begin to focus attention on those phonemes common to their native tongue and on the rhythm and intonation of the language. Gradually they cease making the sounds not found in their native language. At about one year, a French-speaking child's babbling sounds like French, and an English-speaking child's babbling sounds like English (Levitt & Wang, 1991). Deaf children who are exposed to sign language from birth babble manually. That is, they make the hand movements that represent the phonemes in sign language (Petitto & Marentette, 1991).

The One-Word Stage

At about one year, the babbling stage gives way to the one-word stage, and infants utter their first real words. The first words usually represent objects that move or those that infants can act upon or interact with. Early words usually include food, animals, and toys—"cookie," "mama," "dada," "doggie," and "ball," to name a few (Nelson, 1973).

Sometimes infants use one-word sentences, called "holophrases," in which the same word is used to convey different meanings depending on the context. "Cookie" can mean "This is a cookie," "I want a cookie," or, if the child is looking down from a high chair, "The cookie is on the floor."

Initially their understanding of words differs from that of an adult. On the basis of some shared feature and because they lack the correct word, children may apply a word to a broader range of objects than is appropriate. This is known as **overextension**. For example, any man may be called "dada," any four-legged animal, "doggie." **Underextension** occurs, too, when children fail to apply a word to other members of the class. Their poodle is a "doggie," but the German shepherd next door is not.

The Two-Word Stage and Telegraphic Speech

Between 18 and 20 months, when the vocabulary is about 50 words, children begin to put nouns, verbs, and adjectives together in two-word phrases and sentences. At this stage children depend to a great extent on gesture, tone, and context to convey their meaning (Slobin, 1972). Depending on intonation, their sentences may indicate questions, statements, or possession. Children adhere to a rigid word order. You might hear "mama drink," "drink milk," or "mama milk," but not "drink mama," "milk drink," or "milk mama."

By two years, their vocabulary has increased to about 272 words (Brown, 1973). At about two and a half years, short sentences are used, which may contain three or more words. Labelled **telegraphic speech** by Roger Brown (1973), these short sentences follow a rigid word order and contain only essential content words, leaving out plurals, possessives, conjunctions, articles, and prepositions. Telegraphic speech reflects the child's understanding of syntax—the rules governing how words are ordered in a sentence. When a third word is added to a sentence, it usually fills in the word missing from the two-word sentence (for example, "Mama drink milk").

Suffixes, Function Words, and Grammatical Rules

After using telegraphic speech for a time, children gradually begin to add modifiers to make words more precise. Suffixes and function words—pronouns, articles, conjunctions, and prepositions—are acquired in a fixed sequence, although the rate of acquisition varies (Brown, 1973; Maratsos 1983).

Overregularization is the kind of error that results when a grammatical rule is misapplied to a word that has an irregular plural or past tense (Kuczaj, 1978). Thus children who have learned and correctly used words such as "went," "came," and "did" incorrectly apply the rule for past tenses and begin to say "goed," "comed," and "doed." What the parent sees as a regression in speech actually means that the child has acquired a grammatical rule (Marcus et al., 1992).

Theories of Language Development: How Do We Acquire It?

How do learning theory and the nativist position explain the acquisition of language?

The ability to acquire language has fascinated researchers and philosophers alike. Two explanations that explain how language is acquired are the learning theory and the nativist approach.

Learning Theory

Learning theorists have long maintained that language is acquired in the same way that other behaviours are acquired—as a result of learning through reinforcement and imitation. B.F. Skinner (1957) asserted that language is shaped through reinforcement. He said that parents selectively criticize incorrect speech and reinforce correct speech through praise, approval, and attention. Thus the child's utterances are progressively shaped in the direction of grammatically correct speech. Others believe that children acquire vocabulary and sentence construction mainly through imitation (Bandura, 1977a).

On the surface, what the learning theorists propose appears logical, but there are some problems with learning theory as the sole explanation for language acquisition. Imitation cannot account for patterns of speech such as telegraphic speech or for systematic errors such as overregularization. Children do not hear telegraphic speech in everyday life, and "I comed" and "He goed" are not forms commonly used by parents.

There are also problems with reinforcement as an explanation for language acquisition. First, parents seem to reward children more for the content of the utterance than for the correctness of the grammar (Brown et al., 1968). And parents are much more likely to correct children for saying something untrue than for making a grammatical error. Regardless, correction does not seem to have much impact on a child's grammar.

Nevertheless, reinforcement plays an important part in language learning. Responsiveness to infants' vocalizations increases the amount of vocalization, and reinforcement can help children with language deficits improve (Lovaas, 1967; Whitehurst et al., 1989).

semantics: The meaning or the study of meaning derived from morphemes, words, and sentences.

babbling: Vocalization of the basic speech sounds (phonemes), which begins between the ages of four and six months.

overextension: The act of using a word, on the basis of some shared feature, to apply to a broader range of objects than is appropriate.

underextension: Restricting the use of a word to only a few, rather than to all, members of a class of objects.

telegraphic speech: Short sentences that follow a strict word order and contain only essential content words.

overregularization: The act of inappropriately applying the grammatical rules for forming plurals and past tenses to irregular nouns and verbs.

The Nativist Position

A very different theory was proposed by Noam Chomsky (1957), who believes that language ability is largely innate. Chomsky (1968) maintains that the brain contains a language acquisition device (LAD), which enables children to acquire language and discover the rules of grammar. This mechanism predisposes children to acquire language easily and naturally. Language develops in stages that occur in a fixed order and appear at about the same time in most normal children—babbling at about six months, the one-word stage at about one year, and the two-word stage at 18 to 20 months. Deaf children exposed to sign language from birth proceed along the same schedule (Meier, 1991; Petitto & Marentette, 1991). Lenneberg (1967) believes that biological maturation underlies language development in much the same way that it underlies physical and motor development.

Very young infants do seem to have an innate mechanism that allows them to perceive and differentiate phonemes present in any language (Eimas, 1985). But by the end of the first year, their power to distinguish between speech sounds that do not differentiate words in their own language is greatly reduced (Kuhl et al., 1992). This is why adults whose native tongue is Japanese have so much difficulty discriminating between the *r* and *l* sounds in English.

The nativist position accounts more convincingly than does the learning theory for the fact that children throughout the world go through the same basic stages in language development. It can account, too, for the similarity in errors that they make when they are first learning to form plurals, past tenses, and negatives—errors not acquired through imitation or reinforcement. There remain, however, aspects of language development that the nativist position cannot explain.

Remember It!

Language Acquisition

1. Which aspect of language acquisition is learning theory *not* able to explain?
   a. how reinforcement is used to encourage language
   b. why children are able to generate sentences they have not heard or used before
   c. why children imitate adults and other children in their speech
   d. why children overgeneralize the concepts expressed in words
2. Which explanation best accounts for the early stages of babbling and telegraphic speech?
   a. reinforcement
   b. imitation
   c. cognitive mapping
   d. the nativist position

Answers: 1. b 2. d

Having More Than One Language

Many countries in the world, including Canada, have more than one official language (Snow, 1993). Even within countries that formally acknowledge only one official language, considerable variation exists in the languages that are spoken by the inhabitants. The diversity in language can be attributed to many variables, such as immigration, restoration of traditional or native languages, and the introduction of technological advances that have made communication outside one's own land commonplace. In some cases, these changes have made the acquisition of a second language necessary, and in other cases, they have made it desirable or at least noteworthy. Read about Canada's experience with bilingualism in *It Happened in Canada*.

Psychological interests in second language acquisition range from psycholinguistic concerns (that is, structures of language) to social issues. One important concern that affects the study of language acquisition is the age of onset. Learners can acquire a second language at any time in their lifetime and for the most part it can be achieved by almost all learners (e.g., Humes-Bartlo, 1989). A second language can be learned either simultaneously with the first language or at a later time. A learner who is fluent in two languages is considered *bilingual*; a learner who is fluent in many languages is called *multilingual.* Many learners, however, are often more skilled in one language than in others. Children raised in multilingual homes, who have consistent and equivalent access to each language, tend to follow the same steps in language development as monolingual children. It is important to note that the data do not support the myth that fluency in a second language is possible only if learners are introduced to that second language at a very early age (e.g., Genessee, 1978). Learning a second language later in life requires motivation, a positive attitude, and effort and opportunity to practise the language (e.g., Gardner & Lysynchuk, 1990; Hakuta, 1987; Shulz, 1991).

Acquiring a second language can result in a number of benefits, such as higher scores on aptitude and math tests (Lambert et al., 1993) and reducing ethnocentricity. Canadian research by Lambert, Tucker, and d'Anglejan (1973) suggests that people who have learned a second language tend to hold more positive opinions about the second language group, and are less likely to favour their own language group than are their monolingual counterparts. By comparison, people who can speak only one language are more likely to be intolerant of other linguistic groups (Guimond & Palmer, 1993). Therefore, second-language learning may be an important mediator for enhancing both social perceptions and intellectual ability.

To maximize second language learning we have to be sensitive to the prevalence of the languages that are to be learned. In some cases when a minority language is presented in tandem with a majority language, the minority language is poorly acquired. This phenomenon is called *subtractive bilingualism* because one language detracts from the acquisition of the other and, overall, there is less learned. Researchers suggest that one way to circumvent this problem is to provide early instruction in the minority language (Wright et al., 2000). For example, when Inuit children were provided early instruction in their heritage language (Inuktitut) and maintained that instruction over three years, their heritage language and second language skills were stronger than other Inuit children trained in the second language (English or French). Early instruction in the minority heritage language alleviated the problem of subtractive bilingualism.

IT HAPPENED IN CANADA

Bilingualism

In 1985 the Official Languages Act was introduced. It was later repealed and then by 1993 it was amended and accepted. The official Languages Act recognizes and promotes the use of Canada's two official languages. Although the inhabitants of Canada reflect many first languages, the two official languages are English and French. The proportion of people in each province with French or English as a first language varies. English tends to be the predominant language for most provinces. Across Canada, approximately 73.4 percent of the population identify themselves as English speakers and 26.4 percent identify themselves as French speakers (Statistics Canada, 1996).

Since the introduction of the act, government agencies and educators have been trying to enhance bilingualism and understanding of both official languages. At present, most schools offer instruction in the minority language. Two primary forms of instruction are immersion programs and core language programs. Immersion programs typically start in kindergarten or grade six and involve 100 percent exposure early on with some reduction over the years. Core language programs involve taking a language as a subject in school. In the 1997–1998 school year, approximately 317 000 students were enrolled in French immersion programs and two million were enrolled in core French instruction (Canadian Parents for French, 2000).

Animal Language

How does language in trained chimpanzees differ from human language?

Humans value their ability to communicate with one another. Non-human species also have complex ways of communicating. Our earliest attempt to share communication with non-humans dates back more than 70 years. As early as 1933 researchers attempted to teach chimpanzees to speak by raising the chimps in their homes. These experiments failed because the vocal tract in chimpanzees and the other apes is not adapted to human speech.

Researchers next turned to the American Sign Language system used by deaf people in North America. Allen and Beatrix Gardner (1969) took in a one-year-old chimp they named Washoe and taught her sign language. Washoe learned signs for objects, as well as certain commands and concepts such as "flower," "give me," "come," "open," and "more." Though it took Washoe an entire year to learn only 12 signs, by the end of her fifth year she had mastered about 160 (Fleming, 1974).

Another chimp, Sarah, was taught to use signs by David Premack (1971). Premack developed an artificial language consisting of magnetized, metal-backed plastic chips of various shapes, sizes, and colours, as shown in Figure 7.6. Premack used operant conditioning techniques. Sarah learned to select the plastic chip representing a fruit (apple, banana, etc.) and place it on a magnetized language board. The trainer would then reward Sarah with the fruit she had requested. Later, to receive the reward, Sarah had to add the name of her trainer, Mary, and select chips that symbolized "Mary apple." Still later, rewards would come only when Sarah identified herself as well, and signalled, "Mary give apple Sarah."

Sarah mastered the concepts of similarities and differences, and eventually her performance in signalling whether two objects were the same or different was close to perfect (Premack & Premack, 1983). She even performed well on part–whole relationships and could match such things as half an apple and a glass half-filled with water. Even more remarkable was that Sarah could view a whole apple and a cut apple and, even though she had not seen the apple being cut, match the apple with the utensil needed to cut it—a knife.

Another chimp, Lana, participated in a computer-controlled language training program. She learned to press keys imprinted with geometric symbols that represented words in an artificial language. Sue Savage-Rumbaugh (1977, 1986) varied the location, colour, and brightness of the keys so that Lana had to learn which symbols to use no matter where they were located. One day her trainer, Tim, had an orange that she wanted. Lana had available symbols for many fruits—apple, banana, and so on—but none for an orange. But there was a coloured symbol for the colour orange, so Lana improvised and signalled, "Tim give apple which is orange." Impressive!

But the most impressive performance to date is that of a rare species of ape known as the pygmy chimpanzee. One pygmy chimp, Kanzi, developed an amazing ability to communicate with his trainers without having formally been taught by them. Researchers worked with Kanzi's mother, Matata, during the mid-1980s, teaching her to press symbols representing words. Her progress was not remarkable, but her infant son, Kanzi, who stood by and observed her during training, learned rapidly (thanks to observational learning). When researchers gave Kanzi a chance at the symbol board, his performance quickly surpassed that of his mother and of every other chimp the researchers had tested.

Kanzi demonstrated an advanced understanding (for chimps) of spoken English and could respond correctly even to new commands, such as "Throw your ball to the river," or "Go to the refrigerator and get out a tomato" (Savage-Rumbaugh, 1990; Savage-

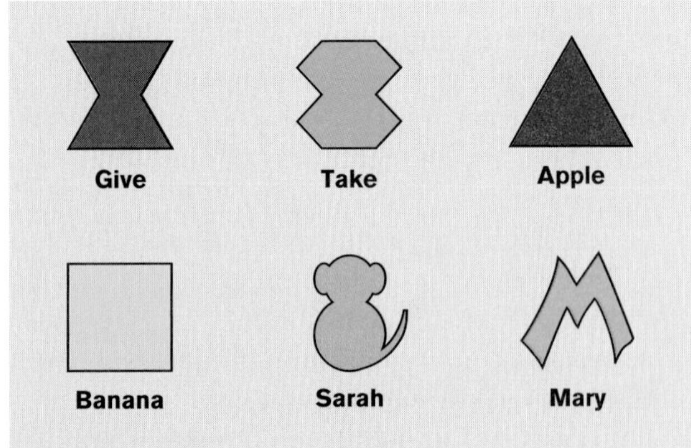

FIGURE 7.6
Sarah's Symbols **A chimpanzee named Sarah learned to communicate using plastic chips of various shapes, sizes, and colours to represent words in an artificial language developed by her trainer, David Premack.**

From their studies of communication among chimps and other animals, researchers have gained useful insights into the nature of language. The pygmy chimp Kanzi is skilled in using a special symbol board to communicate.

Rumbaugh et al., 1992). By the time Kanzi was six years old, a team of researchers who worked with him had recorded more than 13 000 "utterances" and were reporting that he could communicate using some 200 different geometric symbols (Gibbons, 1991). Kanzi could press symbols to ask someone to play chase with him and even to ask two others to play chase while he watched. Furthermore, if Kanzi signalled someone to "chase and hide," it mattered greatly to him that his first command, "chase," be done first (Gibbons, 1991).

On the basis of research with chimps and other animals (especially dolphins), many investigators now believe that language is not necessarily unique to humans (Herman et al., 1993).

Language and Thinking

Does the fact that you speak English or French mean that you reason, think, and perceive your world differently from someone who speaks Spanish, Chinese, or Swahili? According to one hypothesis presented some 45 years ago, it does.

The Linguistic Relativity Hypothesis

What is the linguistic relativity hypothesis, and is it supported by research?

Benjamin Whorf (1956) in his **linguistic relativity hypothesis** suggested that the language a person speaks largely determines the nature of that person's thoughts. According to this hypothesis, our world view is constructed primarily by the words in our language. As proof, Whorf offered his classic example. The languages used by the Inuit have a number of different words for snow: "*apikak*, first snow falling; *aniv*, snow spread out; *pukak*, snow for drinking water," whereas the English-speaking world has but one word, *snow* (Restak, 1988, p. 222). Whorf contended that this rich and varied selection of words for snow provided the Inuit with a different thinking process about snow relative to people whose languages lack specific words for various snow conditions. But do the Inuit perceive snow differently because they have so many words for it? Or do they have so many words for it because they think about and experience snow differently? Whatever language you speak, you can perceive and think about snow according to whether it is falling or on the ground, powdery or slushy, fluffy or packed, without specific words for those conditions.

Eleanor Rosch (1973) tested the linguistic relativity hypothesis. If language determines thinking, she reasoned, then people whose language contains many names for colours will be better at thinking about and discriminating among colours than people whose language has only a few colour names. Her participants for the comparative study were English-speaking Americans and the Dani, a remote New Guinea people whose language has only two names for colours—*mili* for dark, cool colours and *mola* for bright, warm colours. How well would these two groups perform in perceiving, discriminating, and remembering coloured chips of many different hues?

Rosch showed both groups single-colour chips of 11 colours—black, white, red, yellow, green, blue, brown, purple, pink, orange, and grey—for 5 seconds each. After 30 seconds, she had the participants select the 11 colours they had viewed from a larger group of 40 colour chips. If Whorf's hypothesis was accurate, she reasoned, the English speakers would perform with far greater accuracy than the Dani, for whom brown, black, purple, and blue are all *mili*, or dark. But this was not the case. Between the two groups, Rosch found no significant differences in discriminating, remembering, or thinking about the 11 basic colours used in the experiment.

Whorf appeared to go too far in suggesting that language determines how we think. But let us not go too far in the opposite direction and assume that language has little influence on how people think. Language and thought have a mutually supportive relationship.

Sexism in Language

The words we use matter a great deal. Consider the generic use of the pronoun *he* to refer to people in general. If your professor says, "I expect each student in this class to do the best he can," does this announcement mean the same to males and females? Not according to research conducted by Gastil (1990), in which participants read sentences worded in three

linguistic relativity hypothesis: The notion that the language a person speaks largely determines the nature of that person's thoughts.

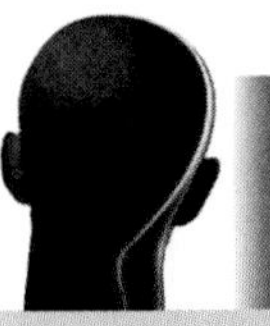

Try It!

Generic Pronouns and Sexist Language

After reading each of these three sentences, pause and jot down any image that comes to mind.

1. The average Canadian believes he watches too much television.
2. The average Canadian believes he/she watches too much television.
3. Average Canadians believe they watch too much television.

different forms. Use the *Try It!* exercise to see how Gastil's study worked.

The odds are that after reading the first sentence you, like most of Gastil's participants, imagined that the sentence was about a male. Many other studies have confirmed that the generic *he* is interpreted heavily in favour of males (Hamilton, 1988; Henley, 1989; Ng, 1990).

It is important to be aware of the full message in everything we say.

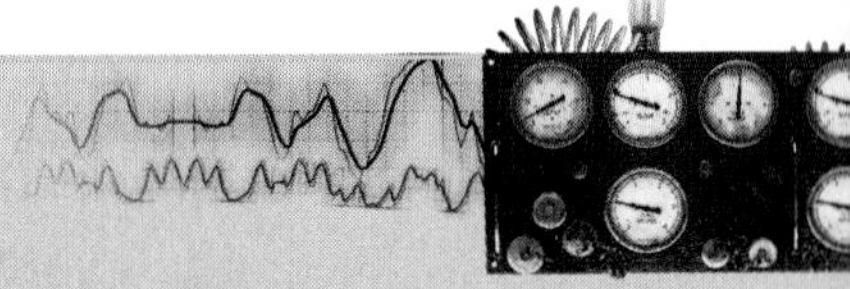

Apply It!

Stimulating Creativity

Creativity is certainly not limited only to "special" people, who are naturally gifted with flair and imagination. Everyone has some potential for creativity. What can you do to become more creative? Psychologists have suggested a variety of techniques for stimulating creativity.

- *"Tune in" to your own creativity and have confidence in it.* The more you develop the habit of thinking of yourself as a creative person and the higher you value creativity as a personal goal, the more likely it is that you will come up with creative ideas and solutions to problems (Hennessey & Amabile, 1988).
- *Challenge yourself to develop your special interests.* Maybe you enjoy cooking or photography? Whatever your creative interest, set small challenges for yourself. Go beyond simply cooking a tasty meal or taking pictures of friends and family. Start inventing new recipes or taking photographs of subjects in original ways. The more you stretch yourself beyond the ordinary, the more creative you will become.
- *Broaden yourself.* The more knowledge and expertise you acquire, the greater potential for creative output you will develop (Epstein, 1996).
- *Change your normal routine.* Have lunch at a different time. Take a new route to school or work. Don't ask yourself why you're making these changes; just do them for the sake of change.
- *Spend more time with creative people.* This will stimulate whatever creativity abilities you might have (Amabile, 1983).
- *Be flexible and open to new possibilities.* Free your thoughts from arbitrary restraints. Learn to avoid mental set, or the failure to consider alternative solutions to common problems.
- *Avoid self-censorship.* Ignore the inner voice that tells you something can't possibly work. Don't be critical of your thoughts or efforts during

Remember It!

Language

1. Match the component (language) with its description.
   ____ 1) the smallest units of meaning
   ____ 2) the meaning derived from phonemes, morphemes
   ____ 3) grammatical rules for arranging and combining words to form phrases and sentences
   ____ 4) the smallest units of sound in a spoken language

   a. syntax
   b. morphemes
   c. semantics
   d. phonemes

2. The linguistic relativity hypothesis is not supported by research. (true/false)

Answers: 1. 1) b 2) c 3) a 4) d 2. true

the early stages of the creative process. Fretting over the correctness of the output inhibits the very process itself (Amabile, 1983).

- *Don't be afraid to make mistakes.* For the creative person, mistakes are valuable learning experiences, not something to be feared and avoided at all costs. In fact, creative people tend to make more mistakes than less imaginative people. Why? Because they make more attempts, try more experiments, and come up with more ideas to be tested (Goleman et al., 1992).
- *Capture your creative thoughts.* Become more attentive to your creative thoughts, and be prepared to preserve them no matter where you might be (Epstein, 1996). Use a notepad, tape recorder, or any other device to capture your good ideas when you get them. It is highly unlikely that they will reappear in the same form at a more convenient time.
- *Relax.* One way to stimulate creative thinking is to relax. Go for a walk, take a long shower, sit in a comfortable chair and daydream, lie on the beach. Relaxing gives the you a chance to play with ideas and combine them in new ways.

In group settings, creativity appears to be fostered by humour. Groups whose members joke, kid around, and laugh easily often have been found to be more creative than groups whose members interact more formally.

Organizations that seek to encourage creativity and innovation should allow employees more leeway in solving problems and more control over performance of their assigned tasks. Moreover, employees should be given sufficient time to allow them to do quality work, should be allowed to work independently where appropriate, and should be free of continuous monitoring.

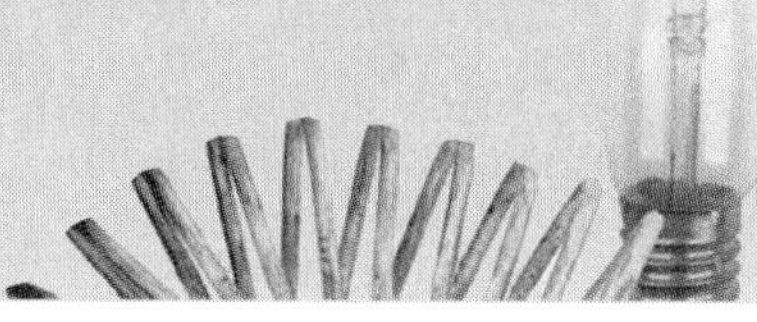

KEY TERMS

THINKING CRITICALLY

Evaluation

Which of the theories of intelligence best fits your notion of intelligence? Why?

Point/Counterpoint

Prepare an argument supporting each of the following positions:

a. Intelligence tests should be used in the schools.
b. Intelligence tests should not be used in the schools.

Psychology in Your Life

Give several examples of how tools of thinking (imagery and concepts) and problem-solving strategies (algorithms and heuristics) can be applied in your educational and personal life.

SUMMARY & REVIEW

The Nature of Intelligence

What factors underlie intelligence, according to Spearman, Thurstone, and Guilford?

Spearman believed that intelligence is composed of a general ability (*g* factor), which underlies all intellectual functions, and a number of specific abilities (*s* factors). Thurstone points to seven primary mental abilities, which singly or in combination are involved in all intellectual activities. Guilford's model consists of 180 different intellectual abilities that involve all of the possible combinations of the three dimensions of intellect–mental operations, contents, and products.

What types of intelligence did Gardner and Sternberg identify?

Gardner believes that there are seven independent and equally important types of intelligence. Sternberg's triarchic theory of intelligence identifies three: the componential (conventional intelligence), the experiential (creative intelligence), and the contextual (practical intelligence).

Measuring Intelligence

What was Binet's major contribution to psychology?

Binet's major contribution to psychology was the concept of mental age and a method for measuring it–the intelligence test.

What does IQ mean, and how was it originally calculated?

IQ stands for intelligence quotient, an index of intelligence originally derived by dividing a person's mental age by his or her chronological age and then multiplying by 100.

What is the Stanford-Binet Intelligence Scale?

The Stanford-Binet Intelligence Scale is a highly regarded individual intelligence test for those aged 2 to 23. It has been revised several times since Lewis Terman's original, extensive adaptation of the Binet-Simon Intelligence Scale.

What did Wechsler's tests provide that the Stanford-Binet did not?

David Wechsler developed the first successful individual intelligence test for adults, the Wechsler Adult Intelligence Scale (WAIS-R). His tests for adults, children, and preschoolers yield separate verbal and performance (non-verbal) IQ scores as well as an overall IQ score.

What is meant by the terms *reliability, validity,* and *standardization*?

Reliability is the ability of a test to yield nearly the same score each time a person takes the test or an alternative form of the test. Validity is the power of a test to measure what it is intended to measure. Standardization refers to prescribed procedures for administering a test and to established norms that provide a means of evaluating test scores.

What are the ranges of IQ scores that are considered average, superior, and in the range of mental disability?

Fifty percent of North Americans have IQ scores ranging from 90 to 109; 2 percent have scores above 130, considered superior; and 2 percent have scores below 70, in the range of mental disability.

According to the Terman study, how do gifted people differ from the general population?

Terman's longitudinal study revealed that, in general, gifted people enjoy better physical and mental health and are more successful than their less gifted counterparts.

What two criteria must a person meet to be classified as mentally disabled?

To be classified as mentally disabled, one must have an IQ score below 70 and show severe deficiencies in everyday adaptive functioning.

The IQ Controversy: Brainy Dispute

What do intelligence tests predict well?

IQ tests are good predictors of success in school but not good predictors of occupational success among people of the same social class and level of education.

What are some of the abuses of intelligence tests?

Abuses occur when IQ tests are the only criterion for admitting people to educational programs, for tracking children, or for placing people in classes for those with mental disabilities. Many people maintain that IQ tests are biased in favour of the urban middle or upper class.

How does the nature–nurture controversy apply to intelligence?

The nature–nurture controversy is the debate over whether intelligence is primarily the result of heredity or environment.

What is behavioural genetics, and what are the primary methods used in the field today?

Behavioural genetics is the field that investigates the relative effects of heredity and environment on behaviour and ability. The twin study method and the adoption method are the primary methods used.

How do twin studies support the view that intelligence is inherited?

Twin studies provide evidence that intelligence is primarily inherited because identical twins are more alike in intelligence than fraternal twins, even if they have been reared apart.

What kinds of evidence suggest that IQ is changeable rather than fixed?

Several adoption studies have revealed that when infants from disadvantaged environments are adopted by middle- and upper-middle-class parents, their IQ scores are about 15 points higher on average than they would otherwise be expected to be. Furthermore, IQ scores have been rising steadily over the past 50 years in many countries, including the United States and Canada, presumably because of increases in the standard of living and educational opportunities.

What are Jensen's and Herrnstein and Murray's controversial views on race and IQ?

These researchers assert that the black–white IQ gap is due to genetic differences between the races that are too strong to be changed significantly through environmental intervention.

What are the personal components of emotional intelligence?

The personal components are an awareness of and ability to control one's own emotions and the ability to motivate oneself.

What are the interpersonal components of emotional intelligence?

The interpersonal components are empathy and the ability to handle relationships.

Imagery and Concepts: Tools of Thinking

What is imagery?

Imagery is the representation in the mind of a sensory experience–visual, auditory, gustatory, motor, olfactory, or tactile.

What are concepts, and how are they formed?

Concepts are labels that represent classes or groups of objects, people, or events sharing common characteristics or attributes. We can form a concept (1) from a formal definition of the concept, (2) by systematically memorizing features or attributes common to members of a concept (as in formal classification systems), (3) through our experiences with positive and negative instances of the concept, (4) through the use of prototypes, or (5) through the use of exemplars.

Problem Solving and Creativity

What are three problem-solving techniques, and how are they used?

Trial and error is an unsystematic problem-solving technique whereby we try one solution after another until we hit on one that works. An algorithm is a step-by-step procedure that guarantees a solution, such as a mathematical formula or a systematic exploration of every possible solution. A heuristic method does not guarantee success but offers a promising way to solve a problem and arrive at a solution, such as working backward or means–end analysis.

What are the two major impediments to problem solving?

Two major impediments to problem solving are functional fixedness, which is the failure to use familiar objects in novel ways to solve problems, and mental set, which is the tendency to apply familiar problem-solving strategies before carefully considering the special requirements of the problem.

What is creativity, and what tests have been designed to measure it?

Creativity is the ability to produce original, appropriate, and valuable ideas and/or solutions to problems. Two tests used to measure creativity are divergent-thinking tests and the Remote Associates Test.

Language

What are the four important components of language?

The four important components of language are (1) phonemes, the smallest units of sound in a spoken language; (2) morphemes, the smallest units of meaning; (3) syntax, grammatical rules for arranging and combining words to form phrases and sentences; and (4) semantics, the meanings derived from phonemes, morphemes, and sentences.

How do learning theory and the nativist position explain the acquisition of language?

Learning theory focuses on external information that is provided by parents, friends, media, and so on, as sources of information from which we develop our knowledge of language. Nativists believe that the mechanisms for acquiring language are innate.

How does language in trained chimpanzees differ from human language?

Chimpanzees do not have a vocal tract adapted to speech, and their communication using sign language or symbols consists of constructions strung together rather than sentences.

What is the linguistic relativity hypothesis, and is it supported by research?

The linguistic relativity hypothesis suggests that the language a person speaks largely determines the nature of the person's thoughts, but this theory has not been supported by research.

8 Development

North of Kampala, Uganda, in Africa, the jungle is dark, dense, and lush with a rich variety of exotic plant life and an abundance of animal species. But civil war disturbed the peace and beauty of Uganda for many years, and brutal massacres claimed the lives of many men, women, and children.

In 1984 Ugandan soldiers retreating through the jungle came upon one of the strangest sights they had ever seen. In one tribe of monkeys, they saw a larger creature unlike the others, who was playfully hopping around with them. Intrigued, they came closer and were amazed to discover that this strange creature was a human child.

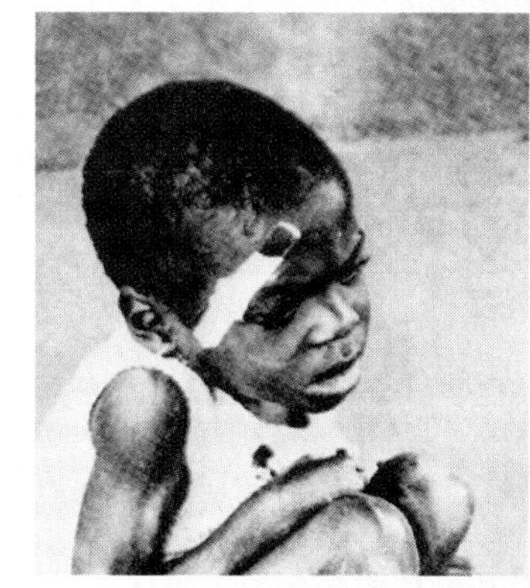
Robert

The soldiers captured the young boy and took him to an orphanage in Kampala, Uganda. Here staff members named him Robert. They estimated that he was between five and seven years old, and they were amazed by his behaviour. He squealed and grunted but could not speak. He didn't walk normally but jumped from one place to another the way a monkey would. He scratched people when they approached him;

he ate grass or any other edible thing he could find; and he did not sit but squatted when he was not moving around. Small for his age, Robert was less than a metre tall when he was found and weighed only 10 kilograms. One staff member at the orphanage said that Robert always looked miserable: no one ever saw him smile. Those who studied Robert's case believed that his parents had been slaughtered when he was about a year old and that somehow he had managed to escape the massacre and make his way deep into the jungle.

Genetically, Robert is fully as human as any other human. But for most of his young life he was "adopted" by a monkey tribe whose members protected and nurtured him as though he were one of their own. Developmental psychologists are intrigued by cases like Robert's because they show the profound effect that extreme environmental conditions can have on the course of human development.

Developmental Psychology: Basic Issues and Methodology

Developmental psychology is the study of how we grow, develop, and change throughout the lifespan. Some developmental psychologists specialize in a particular age group, almost anywhere along the continuum from infancy through childhood and adolescence, and into early, middle and late adulthood. Others concentrate on a specific area of interest such as physical development, language or cognitive development, or moral development.

LINK IT!

www.investinkids.ca
Invest in Kids Foundation

lpcwww.grc.nia.nih.gov
Laboratory of Personality & Cognition, National Institute on Aging

www.aoa.dhhs.gov
Administration on Aging

Controversial Issues in Developmental Psychology

Developmental psychologists must consider several controversial issues as they pursue their work.

1. *To what degree do heredity and environment influence development?* This is the **nature–nurture controversy** that was discussed in the previous chapter. Some take the view that our abilities are determined almost exclusively by our heredity and are transmitted to us through our genes. Others maintain that our environment—the circumstances in which we are raised—determines what we become. Today the question is not whether nature or nurture affects development, but how much each affects various aspects of development.
2. *Is development continuous or does it occur in stages?* Physical growth during middle childhood is usually gradual, continuous, and cumulative. Children change quantitatively as they grow taller, heavier, and stronger. Are other aspects of development—cognitive and moral development, for example—best understood in terms of gradual, continuous, cumulative change? Or does change in some aspects of development occur in spurts in the form of stages, with one stage *qualitatively* different from the next?
3. *To what extent are personal characteristics stable over time?* In this chapter we will discuss whether certain personal traits, such as intelligence, aggression, and aspects of temperament, tend to be stable or changeable over time. How do developmental psychologists study changes over the lifespan?

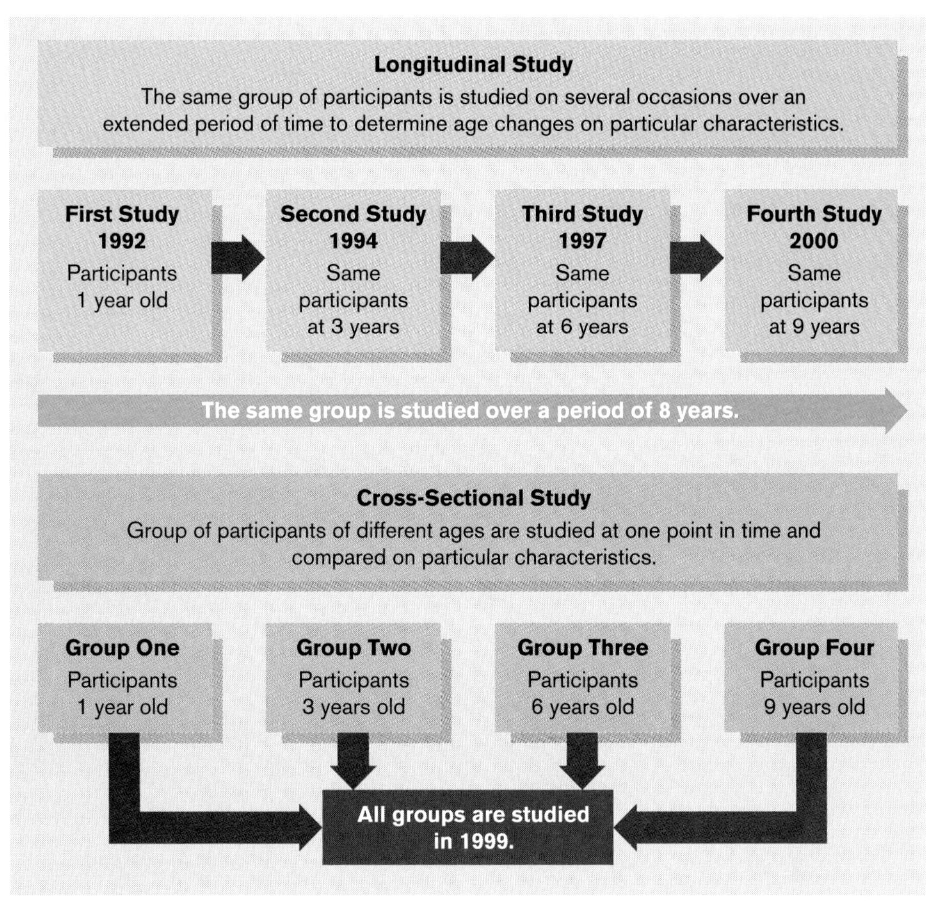

FIGURE 8.1
A Comparison of Longitudinal and Cross-Sectional Studies To study age-related changes using a longitudinal study, researchers examine the same group of individuals over an extended period of time. When using a cross-sectional study, researchers examine and compare groups of different ages at one point in time.

Approaches to Studying Developmental Change

What are two types of studies that developmental psychologists use to investigate age-related changes?

Developmental psychologists use longitudinal and cross-sectional studies to investigate age-related changes. A **longitudinal study** is one in which the same group is followed and measured at different ages, and it may take years to complete. There are some drawbacks to the longitudinal study. It is time-consuming and expensive, and people may drop out of the study, possibly leaving the researcher with a biased sample.

A **cross-sectional study** is a less expensive and less time-consuming method in which researchers compare groups of different ages with respect to various characteristics to determine age-related differences. But in a cross-sectional study, differences found in age groups are based on group averages, and so this approach cannot provide answers to some questions. For example, it cannot be used to determine whether the temperament of individuals is stable over time. Moreover, there may be certain relevant differences among groups that have less to do with ages than with the eras in which the participants grew up. Figure 8.1 compares the longitudinal and cross-sectional studies.

Development begins before birth. We will trace its course from the beginning.

developmental psychology: The study of how humans grow, develop, and change throughout the lifespan.

nature-nurture controversy: The debate concerning the relative influences of heredity and environment on development.

longitudinal study: A type of developmental study in which the same group of individuals is followed and measured at different ages.

cross-sectional study: A type of developmental study in which researchers compare groups of individuals of different ages with respect to certain characteristics to determine age-related differences.

Heredity and Prenatal Development

The Mechanism of Heredity: Genes and Chromosomes

How are hereditary traits transmitted?

Genes are the biological blueprints that determine and direct the transmission of all of our hereditary traits. Genes are segments of DNA located on each of the rod-shaped structures called **chromosomes**, which are found in the nuclei of the body cells. Normal body cells, with two exceptions, have 23 pairs of chromosomes (so that there are 46 chromosomes in all). The two exceptions are the sperm cells and the mature egg cells, each of which has 23 single chromosomes. At conception the sperm adds its 23 single chromosomes to the 23 of the egg. This union forms a single cell called a *zygote,* which has the full 46 chromosomes (23 pairs), which in turn contain about 100 000 genes—the genetic information needed to make a human being.

Twenty-two of the 23 pairs of chromosomes are matching pairs, called *autosomes.* Each member of these pairs carries genes for particular physical and mental traits. The chromosomes in the 23rd pair are called **sex chromosomes** because they carry the genes that determine a person's sex, primary and secondary sex characteristics, and other sex-linked traits such as red-green colour blindness, male pattern baldness, and hemophilia.

The sex chromosomes of females consist of two X chromosomes (XX); males have an X chromosome and a Y chromosome (XY). Because the egg cell always contains an X chromosome, the sex of a child depends on whether the egg is fertilized by a sperm carrying an X chromosome, which produces a female, or a sperm carrying a Y chromosome, which produces a male. Half of a man's sperm cells carry an X chromosome, and half carry a Y. Consequently, the chances of conceiving a boy or a girl are about equal.

Each pair of chromosomes contains genes responsible for particular traits and body functions. Genes also determine the sequence of growth and the biological timetable responsible for many of the changes occurring over the lifespan. The majority of genes on each chromosome carry the same information in all humans; this ensures the transmission of the characteristics that we all have in common. For example, we breathe through lungs rather than gills; we have four fingers and an opposable thumb, rather than claws; and so on.

In some cases a single gene from each pair of chromosomes provides the genetic influence for a particular trait. In many other cases, such as intelligence, height, and weight, a number of genes collectively produce the genetic influence for a particular trait or ability. The Human Genome Project is aimed at identifying the functions of all of the genes and locating them on the chromosomes. Its ultimate goal is to decipher the complete instructions for making a human being. As illustrated in the *It Happened in Canada* box, research on genetics raises some thorny ethical issues.

IT HAPPENED IN CANADA

A Market for Genes

How much are your genes worth? If you lived in Newfoundland, they could potentially be worth billions ("Who owns life," 2000). On February 14, 2000, the people of Newfoundland embarked on a unique business venture that could have a significant impact on their health and economy. The company responsible for all this excitement is called Newfound Genomics. The name *genomics* refers to the study of the relationship between human genes and human health and/or disease. Dr. Wayne Gulliver, a Newfoundlander, helped to initiate this venture to collect the DNA from Newfoundlanders, along with other clinical measures, and sell it to genetics, pharmaceutical, and other biotechnology companies.

Newfoundlanders are particularly interesting because most of the inhabitants descend from a limited "founding" population of English, Irish, and Scottish immigrants who settled the islands between the 17th and 19th centuries (Gemini Genomics, 2000). This means that the gene pool in Newfoundland is more homogeneous than in other parts of Canada where the gene pool is more diverse. When researchers want to find mutations that may be responsible for diseases, they look for a homogeneous sample because differences are more likely to stick out when the genes are similar. In Newfoundland there is a higher level of diseases such as psoriasis, rheumatoid arthritis, and diabetes, and Dr Gulliver hopes that some of the researchers will devote their energy toward discovering the genetic causes and treatments for these diseases. Now, Canadians must quickly grapple with the ethics involved in selling the rights to an entire population's genetic code.

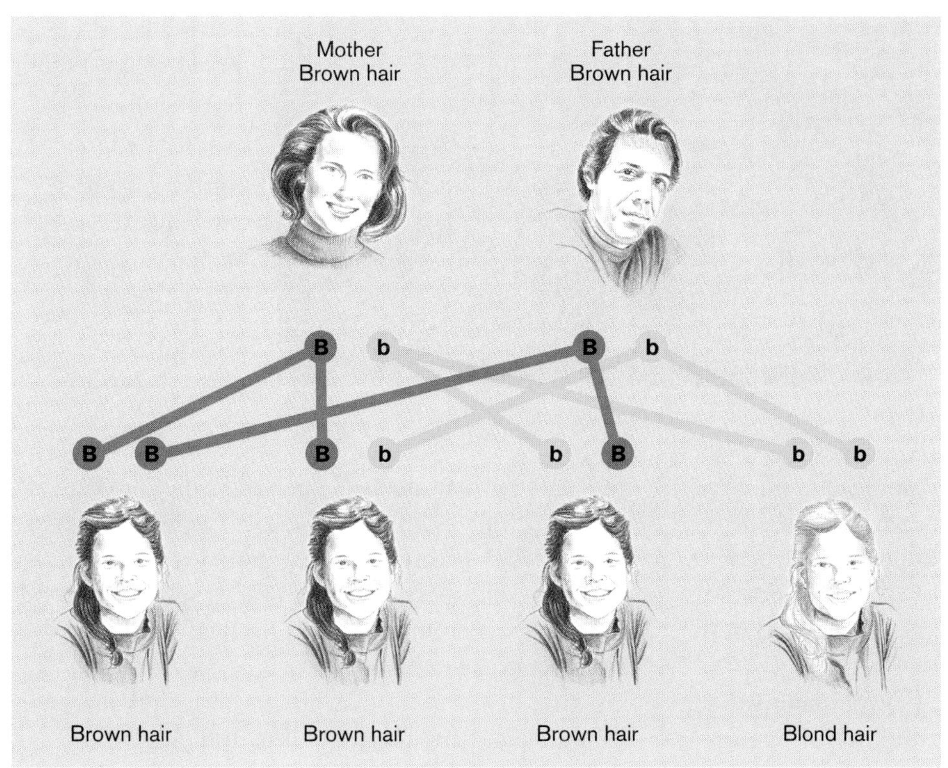

FIGURE 8.2
Gene Transmission for Hair Colour **This figure shows all the possible combinations in children when both parents carry a gene for brown hair (B) and a gene for blond hair (b). The chance of their having a blond-haired child (bb) or a brown-haired child (BB) is 25 percent in each case. There is a 50 percent chance of having a brown-haired child who carries both the dominant gene (B) and the recessive gene (b).**

LINK IT!

ibgwww.colorado.edu/index.html
Institute for Behavioral Genetics

Dominant and Recessive Genes: Dominants Call the Shots

When are dominant or recessive genes expressed in a person?

When two different genes are transmitted for the same trait, one of the genes is usually a **dominant gene**—that is, one that causes the dominant trait to be expressed in the individual. The gene for brown hair, for instance, is dominant over the gene for blond hair. An individual having one gene for brown hair and one gene for blond hair will have brown hair. And of course, two dominant genes will produce brown hair (see Figure 8.2).

The gene for blond hair is recessive. A **recessive gene** will be expressed if it is paired with another recessive gene. Therefore, blond-haired people have two recessive genes for blond hair. A recessive gene will not be expressed if it is paired with a dominant gene. Yet a person with such a pair can pass either the recessive gene or the dominant gene along to his or her offspring.

The Stages of Prenatal Development: Unfolding According to Plan

What are the three stages of prenatal development?

Conception occurs the moment a sperm cell fertilizes the ovum (egg cell), forming the single-celled zygote. Conception usually takes place in one of the fallopian tubes. Within the next two weeks the zygote travels to the uterus and attaches itself to the uterine wall. During the first five or six days the zygote engages in cell division and produces two parts. The

genes: Within the chromosomes, the segments of DNA that are the basic units for the transmission of hereditary traits.

chromosomes: Rod-shaped structures, found in the nuclei of body cells, that contain all the genes and carry all the hereditary information.

sex chromosomes: The 23rd pair of chromosomes, which carry the genes that determine one's sex and primary and secondary sex characteristics.

dominant gene: The gene that is expressed in the individual.

recessive gene: A gene that will not be expressed if paired with a dominant gene, but will be expressed if paired with another recessive gene.

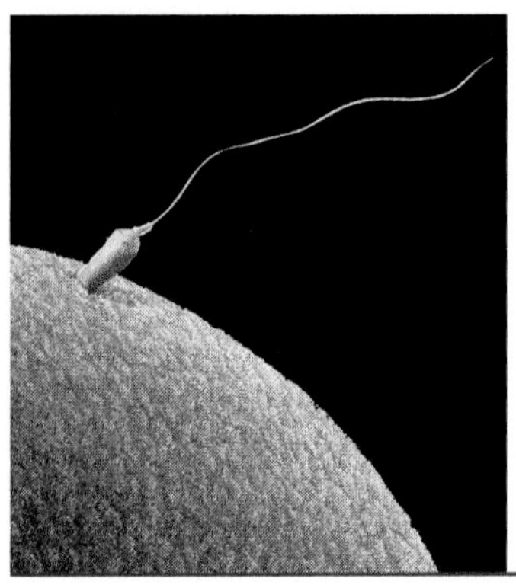
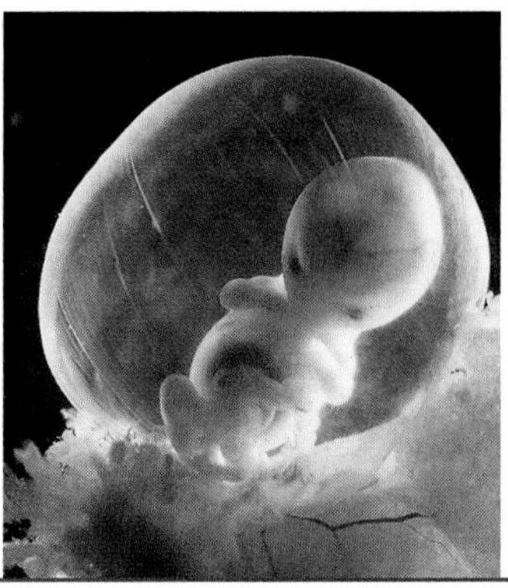
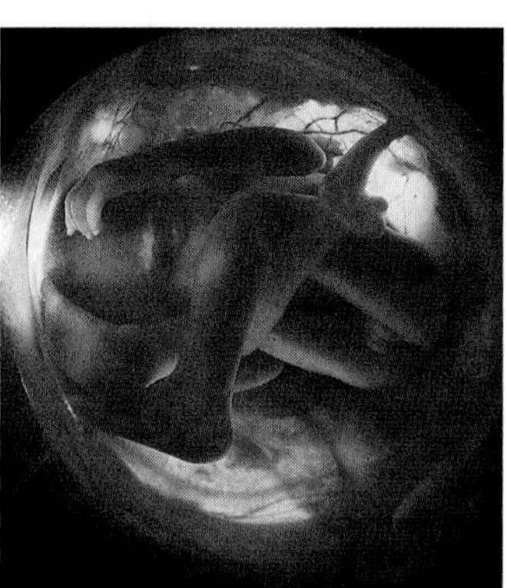

This sequence of photos shows the fertilization of an egg by a sperm (left), an embryo at seven weeks (middle), and a fetus at 22 weeks (right).

cluster of cells in the centre will later lead to the development of the fetus, while the complex outside cell mass becomes the placenta and supporting structures. At the end of this first stage of **prenatal** development, the zygote is only the size of the period at the end of this sentence.

The second stage of prenatal development is the period of the **embryo**, when the major systems, organs, and structures of the body develop. Lasting from week three through week eight, this period ends when the first bone cells form. Though about 2.5 centimetres long and weighing about 4 grams, the embryo already has enough rudimentary features that it can be recognized as a human embryo.

The final stage, called the period of the **fetus**, lasts from the end of the second month until birth. It is a time of rapid growth and further development of the structures, organs, and systems of the body. Table 8.1 describes the characteristics of each stage of prenatal development.

Multiple Births: More Than One at a Time

The types of multiple births described in the *It Happened in Canada* box are two example of the rarest and most unusual cases ever recorded. Of course, most multiple births are those of twins. In the case of **identical (monozygotic) twins**, one egg is fertilized by one sperm, but the zygote splits and develops into two embryos with identical genetic codes. Thus, identical twins are always of the same sex. This splitting of the zygote seems to be a chance occurrence, accounting for about 4 in 1000 births.

Fraternal (dizygotic) twins develop when two eggs are released during ovulation and are fertilized by two different sperm. The two zygotes develop into two siblings who are no more alike genetically than ordinary brothers and sisters. The likelihood of fraternal twins is greater if there is a family history of multiple births, if the woman is between 35 and 40, and if she has recently stopped taking birth control pills. Fertility drugs also often cause the release of more than one egg, and some fertility procedures involve the implantation of multiple fertilized eggs. When multiple eggs are released during ovulation, when one or more eggs split before or after fertilization, when multiple eggs are implanted, or when these events occur in combination, multiple births ranging from twins even to sextuplets can result. In July 2000

TABLE 8.1

Stages of Prenatal Development

Stage	Time after Conception	Major Activities of the Stage
Period of the zygote	1 to 2 weeks	Zygote attaches to the uterine lining. At 2 weeks, zygote is the size of the period at the end of this sentence.
Period of the embryo	3 to 8 weeks	Major systems, organs, and structures of the body develop. Period ends when first bone cells appear. At 8 weeks, embryo is about 2.5 cm long and weighs about 4 g.
Period of the fetus	9 weeks to birth (38 weeks)	Rapid growth and further development of the body structures, organs, and systems.

the body representing Canadian obstetricians and gynecologists appealed to the government for more support for families with multiple births because the rate of multiple births has increased dramatically with greater access and use of fertility procedures.

Negative Influences on Prenatal Development: Sabotaging Nature's Plan

What are some negative influences on prenatal development, and when is their impact greatest?

Teratogens are agents in the prenatal environment that can cause birth defects and other problems. The damage done by a teratogen depends on its intensity and on when it is present during prenatal development. Most teratogens (e.g., drugs, diseases, environmental hazards such as X-rays or toxic waste) do the most harm during the first three months of development (the first trimester). During this time there are **critical periods** when certain body structures develop. If drugs or infections interfere with development during a critical period, the structure or body part will not form properly and development will not occur at a later time (Kopp & Kaler, 1989).

Researchers have known for many years that viruses and other infectious agents can have devastating effects on the fetus. Many of the most devastating viruses do their damage during the first trimester, although some viruses impact throughout the pregnancy and delivery stages. Probably the best-known viral example is rubella (German measles), which can cause deafness, blindness, mental disability, heart defects, and damage to the central nervous system if the mother contracts it during the first trimester.

Although physical abnormalities are always possible, exposure to risks during the second trimester of pregnancy—the fourth, fifth, and sixth months—is more likely to result in intellectual and social impairment.

Prenatal malnutrition can negatively affect development of the embryo and the fetus; it can have particularly harmful effects on brain development during the final trimester. To maximize the chances

IT HAPPENED IN CANADA

Multiple Births

In the middle of the Great Depression, Annette, Cecile, Emilie, Marie, and Yvonne Dionne attained celebrity status. Why? They were the first quintuplets on record to survive. They were born on May 28, 1934, in a small town called Corbeil, a few kilometres outside North Bay, Ontario. Although multiple births are now more common (a recent dramatic example is the McCaughey sextuplets, born in Iowa in November 1998), the Dionne quints were unique even by modern standards. Their parents hadn't used fertility drugs, and the five sisters were identical, having developed from a single fertilized egg. Furthermore, they were two months premature and were delivered in a small farmhouse with none of the technology often used to assist premature infants.

The Dionne quints' story is, however, not a completely happy one. They were separated from their parents and raised in a special nursery operated by the Ontario government. Thousands of tourists paid to peer at them through one-way mirrors. In 1997, the three surviving Dionnes, in ill health and living together in financial hardship on Montreal's south shore, sued the Ontario government for compensation for their past exploitation. On March 8, 1998, the government of Ontario announced that it had made a settlement of $4 million. It also apologized to the Dionne quintuplets and their family for the pain and suffering they endured while growing up.

prenatal: Occurring between conception and birth.

embryo: The developing organism during the period (week three through week eight) when the major systems, organs, and structures of the body develop.

fetus: The developing organism during the period (week nine until birth) when rapid growth and further development of the structures, organs, and systems of the body take place.

identical (monozygotic) twins: Twins with exactly the same genes, who develop after one egg is fertilized by one sperm, and the zygote splits into two parts.

fraternal (dizygotic) twins: Twins, no more alike genetically than ordinary siblings, who develop after two eggs are released during ovulation and are fertilized by two different sperm.

teratogens: Harmful agents in the prenatal environment that can have a negative impact on prenatal development and even cause birth defects.

critical period: A period that is so important to development that a harmful environmental influence can keep a bodily structure or behaviour from developing normally.

of having a healthy baby, a woman needs proper nutrition and possibly multivitamin supplements (especially folic acid, to minimize the chances of neural tube defects) before as well as during pregnancy (Bendich & Keen, 1993; Menard, 1997).

The Hazard of Drugs

Many drugs cross the placental barrier and directly affect the embryo or fetus. Consequently, both prescription and non-prescription drugs (for example, aspirin, nose sprays, laxatives, douches, weight-reducing aids, baking soda, and vitamin supplements) should be taken only with the approval of a physician (Apgar & Beck, 1982). Some prescription drugs, such as certain antibiotics, tranquilizers, and anticonvulsants, are known to cause specific damage.

HEROIN, COCAINE, AND CRACK The use of heroin, cocaine, and crack during pregnancy has been linked to miscarriage, prematurity, low birth weight, physical defects, and fetal death. Infants prenatally exposed to cocaine often suffer lasting physical development complications (Christmas, 1992; Held et al., 1999). Cocaine use by the father at the time of conception also can be harmful, in that tiny specks of cocaine can bind to sperm and "piggyback" their way into the zygote (Yazigi et al., 1991). Pregnant women who take heroin, cocaine, or crack risk having babies born addicted to those drugs.

ALCOHOL Few people would think of giving a newborn baby a bottle full of beer, wine, or hard liquor, but many people do not realize that even a small amount of alcohol consumed during pregnancy crosses the placental barrier. In fact, alcohol levels in the fetus almost match the alcohol levels in the mother's blood (Little et al., 1989). And researchers believe that alcohol can alter brain development throughout pregnancy (Streissguth et al., 1989).

Women who drink heavily during pregnancy risk having babies with **fetal alcohol syndrome**. Babies with this syndrome are mentally disabled and have abnormally small heads with wide-set eyes, a short nose, and other anatomical abnormalities. In addition, they exhibit behavioural abnormalities such as hyperactivity (Julien, 1995). Some children prenatally exposed to alcohol may have *fetal alcohol effects*—some of the characteristics of fetal alcohol syndrome but in less severe form (Mattson & Riley, 2000). And it does not take a lot of alcohol—the fetal brain can be adversely affected if women drink only moderately (Braun, 1996).

Because drinking even small moderate amounts is related to IQ deficits, fine and gross motor deficits, and other problems, it is recommended that women abstain from alcohol altogether during pregnancy (Barr et al., 1990; Guerri et al., 1999). In addition, there is now some evidence that when men ingest large amounts of alcohol, changes in sperm cells occur that can inhibit conception or cause complications in development (Cicero, cited in Dryden, 1994).

SMOKING Smoking decreases the amount of oxygen and increases the amount of carbon monoxide crossing the placental barrier. The embryo or fetus is exposed to nicotine and to several thousand other chemicals as well. Smoking increases the probability that a baby will be premature or of low birth weight (Fourn, 1999; McDonald et al., 1992; Nordentoft et al., 1996). Women smoking one pack per day are at three times the risk for premature birth. Smoking has also been associated with higher rates of spontaneous abortion (Ness et al., 1999), stillbirth, infant mortality, and sudden infant death syndrome (Lincoln, 1986).

CAFFEINE Infante-Rivard and colleagues (1993) reported that miscarriage was linked to caffeine intake during pregnancy and during the month before conception. Animal studies also reveal a link between the intake of caffeine and miscarriage, stillbirth, increased heart rate, fearfulness, and other problems (Reznick, 1999; Schuetze & Zeskind, 1999). Even though some researchers have found no adverse effects (Barr & Streissguth, 1991; Hinds et al., 1996), the wisest course of action is to limit caffeine consumption during pregnancy.

Newborns at High Risk

Low-birth-weight babies—babies weighing less than 2.5 kilograms—and **preterm infants** (born at or before the 37th week) are at risk for survival. The smaller and more premature the baby, the greater the risk (Hoy et al., 1988; Lukeman & Melvin, 1993). According to Apgar and Beck (1982), the handicaps of prematurity range from subtle learning and behaviour problems (in babies closer to normal birth weight) to "severe retardation, blindness, hearing loss, and even death" in the smallest newborns (p. 69).

Poor nutrition, poor prenatal care, smoking, drug use, maternal infection, and too short an interval

Remember It!

Developmental Issues, Heredity, and Prenatal Development

1. The cross-sectional study takes longer to complete than the longitudinal study. (true/false)
2. In humans, genes are located on how many pairs of chromosomes?
   a. 22 b. 23
   c. 44 d. 46
3. Females have an X and a Y chromosome. (true/false)
4. A dominant gene will not be expressed if the individual carries
   a. two dominant genes for the trait.
   b. one dominant gene and one recessive gene for the trait.
   c. two recessive genes for the trait.
   d. either one or two dominant genes for the trait.
5. Fraternal twins are no more alike than ordinary brothers and sisters. (true/false)
6. Match the stage of prenatal development with its description:
   ____ 1) first 2 weeks of life
   ____ 2) rapid growth and further development of body structures and systems
   ____ 3) major systems, organs, and structures

   a. period of the fetus
   b. period of the embryo
   c. period of the zygote
7. Negative influences such as drugs, illness, and environmental hazards cause the most devastating consequences during the
   a. first trimester.
   b. second trimester.
   c. third trimester.
   d. any trimester.

Answers: 1. false 2. b 3. false 4. c 5. true 6. 1) c 2) a 3) b 7. a

between pregnancies all increase the likelihood of the birth of a low-birth-weight baby with complications.

Physical Development and Learning

The Neonate

Although **neonates** (newborn babies) may be beautiful to their parents, they do not yet resemble the babies who pose for the baby ads. They arrive with dry and wrinkled skin, a rather flat nose, and an elongated forehead—the temporary result of the journey through the birth canal. Nevertheless, newborns come equipped with an impressive range of **reflexes**, built-in responses to certain stimuli needed to ensure survival in their new world.

Reflexes: Built-In Responses

Sucking, swallowing, coughing, and blinking are some important behaviours that newborns can perform right away. They will move an arm, leg, or other body part away from a painful stimulus, and they will try to remove a blanket or a cloth placed over their face, which might hamper breathing. Stroke a baby on the cheek and you will trigger the rooting reflex—the baby's mouth opens and actively searches for a nipple. Neonates also have some reflexes that serve no apparent function; these reflexes are believed to be remnants of our evolutionary past. As the brain develops, behaviours that were initially reflexive—controlled by the lower brain centres—gradually come under the voluntary control of the higher brain centres. The presence of these reflexes at birth (as well as their

fetal alcohol syndrome: A condition, caused by maternal alcohol intake during pregnancy, in which the baby is born mentally disabled, abnormally small, and with facial, organ, and limb abnormalities.

low-birth-weight baby: A baby weighing less than 2.5 kilograms.

preterm infant: An infant born before the 37th week and weighing less than 2.5 kilograms; a premature infant.

neonate: Newborn infant up to one month old.

reflexes: Inborn, unlearned, automatic responses to certain environmental stimuli (examples: coughing, blinking, sucking, grasping).

disappearance between the second and fourth months) provides a means of assessing development of the nervous system.

Perceptual Development in Infancy

What are the perceptual abilities of the newborn?

The five senses, although not fully developed, are functional at birth. The newborn already has preferences for certain odours, tastes, sounds, and visual configurations. Hearing is much better developed than vision in the neonate and is functional even before birth (Busnel et al., 1992; Kisilevsky et al., 1992). Newborns are able to turn their head in the direction of a sound and show a general preference for female voices—especially their mother's voice (DeCasper & Fifer, 1980). A preference for the father's voice over a strange male voice does not develop until later. Newborns are able to discriminate among and show preferences for certain odours and tastes (Bartoshuk & Beauchamp, 1994). They favour sweet tastes and are able to differentiate between salty, bitter, and sour solutions. Newborns are also sensitive to pain (Porter et al., 1988) and are particularly responsive to touch, reacting positively to stroking and fondling.

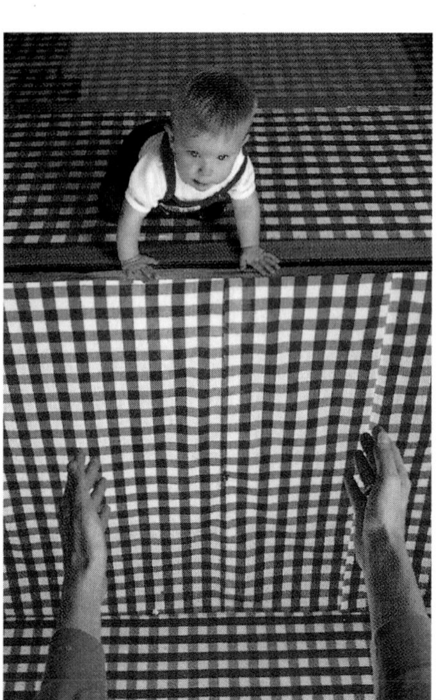

When placed on the visual cliff, most infants older than six months will not crawl out over the deep side, indicating that they can perceive depth.

Vision: What Newborns Can See

The infant's vision at birth is about 20/600 and does not reach an adult level until about age two (Held, 1993). Newborns focus best on objects about 20 centimetres away, and they can follow a moving object (MacFarlane, 1978). Infants 22 to 93 hours old already indicate a preference for their own mother's face over that of an unfamiliar female (Field et al., 1984). At two months, infants can see all or almost all of the colours adults see (Brown, 1990) However, they prefer red, blue, green, and yellow (Bornstein & Marks, 1982).

Gibson and Walk (1960) measured depth perception by having infants crawl across a glass table top that had a checkered pattern below it to simulate depth. This made it appear that there was a large drop-off, a "visual cliff," on one side. Babies from 6 to 14 months could be coaxed by their mothers to crawl to the shallow side, but few would crawl onto the deep side. Gibson and Walk concluded that "most human infants can discriminate depth as soon as they can crawl" (p. 64).

Later, Campos and colleagues (1970) found that six-week-old infants had distinct changes in heart rate when they faced the deep side of the cliff, but no change when they faced the shallow side. Researchers suggested that the change in heart rate indicated fear and showed that the infants could perceive depth.

Learning in Infancy

What types of learning occur in the first few days of life?

When are babies first capable of learning? We know that learning begins even before birth, because infants' experiences in the womb can affect their preferences shortly after birth. DeCasper and Spence (1986) had pregnant women read *The Cat in the Hat* to their developing fetuses twice a day during the final six and a half weeks of pregnancy. A few days after birth the infants could adjust their sucking on specially designed, pressure-sensitive nipples wired to electronic equipment to hear their mothers reading either *The Cat in the Hat* or *The King, the Mice, and the Cheese,* a story they had never heard before. Which story did the infants prefer? You guessed it—their sucking behaviour signalled a clear preference for the familiar sound of *The Cat in the Hat*.

Researchers have demonstrated both classical conditioning and operant conditioning in infants in the first few days of life (Lipsitt, 1990; Rovee-Collier & Lipsitt, 1982). The simplest evidence of learning in infants is the phenomenon of **habituation**. When presented with a new or interesting stimulus, infants respond by generally becoming quieter. Their heart rate slows, and they fixate on the stimulus. But when they become accustomed to the stimulus, they stop responding—that is, they habituate to it. Later, if the familiar stimulus is presented along with a new stimulus, infants will usually pay more attention to the new stimulus, indicating that they remember the original stimulus but prefer the new one. Memory can be measured by (1) the speed with which habituation occurs and (2) the relative amounts of time infants spend looking at or listening to a new and an old stimulus. Amazing as it may seem, babies only 42 minutes old can imitate gestures such as sticking out the tongue (Anisfeld, 1996; Meltzoff & Moore, 1977).

Physical and Motor Development: Growing, Growing, Grown

Although physical and motor development persists throughout childhood, the most obvious periods of change are during infancy and adolescence. Some of the changes are due to learning and others are due to maturation. Maturation occurs naturally according to the individual's own genetically determined biological timetable. In some cases some maturational processes may be slowed down or speeded up, but in appropriate environments, these will only be temporary differences.

Infancy

In infancy, many motor milestones, such as sitting, standing, and walking (shown in Figure 8.3), are primarily a result of maturation and ultimately depend on the growth and development of the central nervous system. The rate at which these milestones are achieved is slowed when the infant is subjected to extremely unfavourable environmental conditions, such as severe malnutrition or maternal and sensory deprivation. In some cultures the milestones are achieved earlier because infants are exposed to special motor-training techniques (Kilbride & Kilbride, 1975). However, the faster learning of motor skills has no lasting impact on development.

Although infants follow their own individual timetables, there is a sequence in which the basic motor skills usually appear. Physical and motor development proceeds from the head downward to the trunk and legs, so babies lift their heads before they sit, and sit before they walk. Development also proceeds from the centre of the body outward—trunk to shoulders to arms to fingers. Thus, control of the arms develops before control of fingers.

Puberty

What physical changes occur during puberty?

Adolescence begins with the onset of **puberty**—a period of rapid physical growth and change that culminates in sexual maturity (Rice, 1992). The average age for onset of puberty is 10 for girls and 12 for boys; the normal *range* is 7 to 14 for girls and 9 to 16 for boys (Chumlea, 1982). Every individual's timetable for adolescence is influenced mainly by heredity, although environmental factors also exert some influence.

Puberty begins with a surge in hormone production, which in turn causes a number of physical changes. The most startling change during puberty is the marked acceleration in growth known as the **adolescent growth spurt**. The growth spurt occurs from age $10\frac{1}{2}$ to 13 in girls and about two years later in boys (Tanner, 1961). Because various parts of the body grow at different rates, the adolescent often has a lanky, awkward appearance. Girls attain their full height at 16 or 17, boys between 18 and 20 (Roche & Davila, 1972).

In both sexes, during puberty the reproductive organs develop and **secondary sex characteristics** appear—those physical characteristics not directly involved in reproduction that distinguish mature males from mature females. In girls the breasts develop and the hips round; in boys the voice deepens and

habituation: A decrease in response or attention to a stimulus as an infant becomes accustomed to it.

puberty: A period of rapid physical growth and change that culminates in sexual maturity.

adolescent growth spurt: A period of rapid physical growth that peaks in girls at about age 12 and in boys at about age 14.

secondary sex characteristics: Those physical characteristics not directly involved in reproduction but distinguishing the mature male from the mature female.

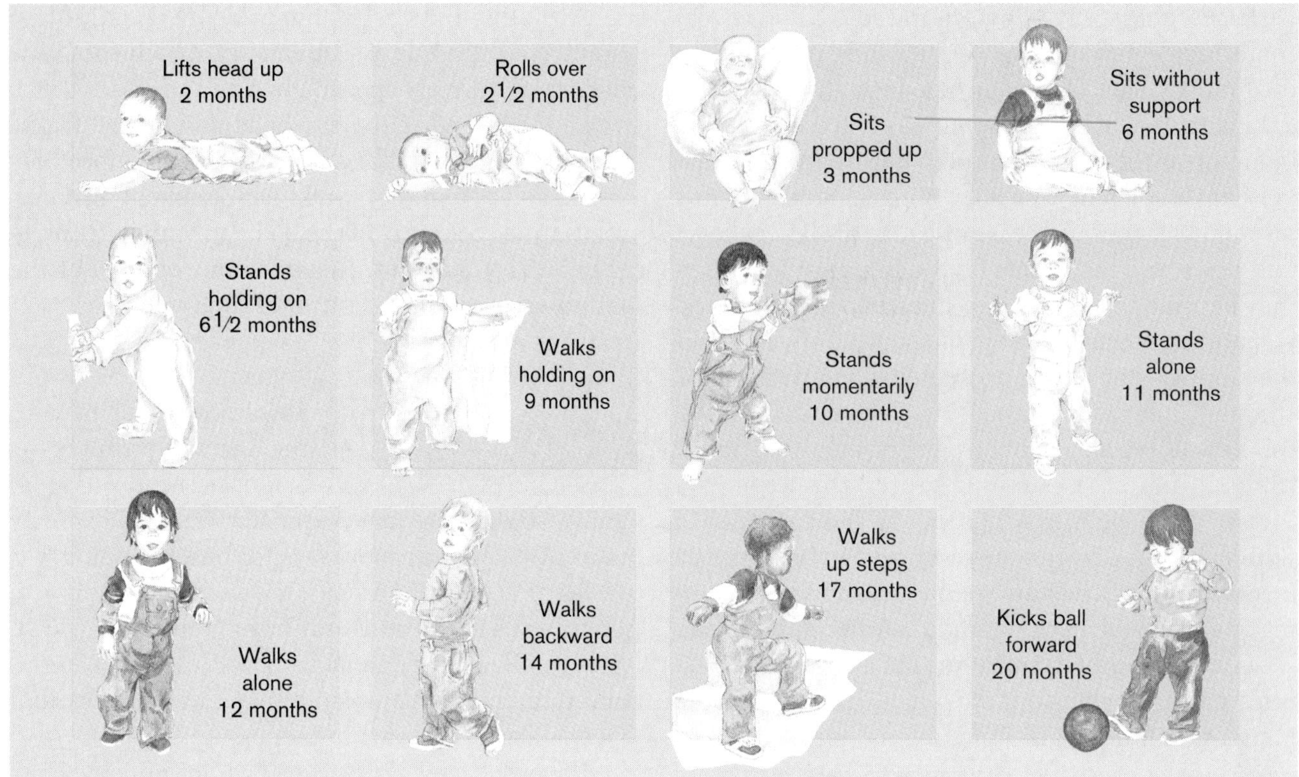

FIGURE 8.3

The Progression of Motor Development Most infants develop motor skills in the sequence shown in the figure. The ages indicated are only averages, so normal, healthy infants may develop any of these milestones a few months earlier or later than the average.

facial and chest hair appears. In both sexes there is growth in pubic and underarm (axillary) hair.

For males, the first major sign of puberty is the first ejaculation, which occurs on average at age 13 (Jorgensen & Keiding, 1991). For females, the major landmark is **menarche**—the onset of menstruation—which typically occurs at age 12, with 10 to 15 being the normal age range (Tanner, 1990). Some research suggests that environmental stress, such as parental divorce or conflict, is related to an earlier onset of menarche (Belsky et al., 1991; Wierson et al., 1993).

See the *Apply It!* box at the end of this chapter for a discussion of teenage pregnancy.

Middle Age

What are the physical changes associated with middle age?

The major biological event for women during middle age is **menopause**—the cessation of menstruation—which occurs between ages 45 and 55 and signifies the end of reproductive capacity. Probably the most common symptom associated with menopause and the sharp decrease in the level of estrogen is hot flashes—sudden feelings of being uncomfortably hot. Some women also experience anxiety, irritability, mood swings, or depression, but most do not experience psychological problems (Busch et al., 1994). Most women find that menopause is less upsetting than they had anticipated (Jackson et al., 1991; Matthews et al., 1990).

Men experience a gradual decline in their testosterone levels from about age 20 (their peak) until age 60. During late middle age, men may also experience a reduction in the functioning of the prostate gland that affects the production of semen. Usually, the reduction in testosterone and semen production leads to a reduction in the sex drive.

With advancing age, the elderly typically become more farsighted, have increasingly impaired night vision, and suffer hearing loss in the higher frequencies (Slawinski et al., 1993).

Remember It!

Physical Development and Learning

1. Compared with a neonate, the number of reflexes you possess is
   a. much larger.
   b. slightly larger.
   c. the same.
   d. smaller.
2. Which of the following statements about infant sensory development is not true?
   a. Vision, hearing, taste, and smell are all fully developed at birth.
   b. Vision, hearing, taste, and smell are all functional at birth.
   c. Infants can show preferences in what they want to look at, hear, taste, and smell shortly after birth.
   d. Hearing is better developed at birth than vision.
3. What type(s) of learning occur(s) in the first few days of life?
   a. classical conditioning
   b. operant conditioning
   c. observational learning
   d. classical and operant conditioning and observational learning
4. Two-month-old Michael likes to look at the soft, multicoloured ball in his crib, but the new black-and-white ball has recently gained his attention. Habituation has occurred, meaning that
   a. Michael has gotten used to a stimulus (the multicoloured ball).
   b. Michael no longer remembers the stimulus he has seen previously.
   c. Michael has a short attention span.
   d. a complex form of learning has taken place.
5. The main factor influencing the attainment of the major motor milestones is
   a. experience.
   b. maturation.
   c. learning.
   d. habituation.
6. The secondary sex characteristics
   a. are directly involved in reproduction.
   b. appear at the same time in all adolescents.
   c. distinguish mature males from mature females.
   d. include the testes and ovaries.

Answers: 1. d 2. a 3. d 4. a 5. b 6. c

The Cognitive Stages of Development: Climbing the Steps to Cognitive Maturity

Piaget's Stages of Cognitive Development

What were Piaget's beliefs regarding stages of cognitive development?

Jean Piaget formulated a comprehensive theory that systematically describes and explains how intellect develops (Piaget, 1963b, 1964; Piaget & Inhelder, 1969). He believed that cognitive development occurs in four stages, which differ not according to the amount of knowledge accumulated, but in the way individuals at different ages reason. Each stage reflects a qualitatively different way of reasoning and understanding the world. The stages occur in a fixed sequence; the accomplishments of one stage provide the foundation for the next. Although everyone is thought to progress through the stages in the same order, there are individual differences in the rates at which they pass through them. And these rates are influenced by maturation and experience.

According to Piaget, cognitive development begins with a few basic **schemas**—cognitive structures or concepts that are used to

Jean Piaget

menarche (men-AR-kee): The onset of menstruation.

menopause: The cessation of menstruation, occurring between ages 45 and 55 and signifying the end of reproductive capacity.

schema: Piaget's term for a cognitive structure or concept used to identify and interpret information.

identify and interpret objects, events, and other information in the environment. When confronted with new objects, events, experiences, and information, learners attempt to fit these into their existing schemas, a process known as **assimilation**. But not everything can be assimilated into the existing schemas. If children call a stranger "daddy" or the neighbour's cat "doggie," assimilation is not appropriate. When parents and others correct them, or when they discover for themselves that something cannot be assimilated into an existing schema, children will use a process known as accommodation. In **accommodation**, existing schemas are modified or new schemas are created to process new information. It is through the processes of assimilation and accommodation, then, that schemas are formed, differentiated, and broadened.

LINK IT!

www.cogsci.indiana.edu
Center for Research on Concepts and Cognition

The Sensorimotor Stage (Birth to Age Two)

What is Piaget's sensorimotor stage?

In the first stage, the **sensorimotor stage**, infants gain an understanding of the world through their senses and their motor activities (actions or body movements)—hence the term *sensorimotor*. An infant's behaviour, which is mostly reflexive at birth, becomes increasingly complex and gradually evolves into intelligent behaviour. At this stage, the intelligence is one of action rather than of thought, and it is confined to objects that are present and events that are directly perceived. The child learns to respond to and manipulate objects, and to use them in goal-directed activity.

At birth, infants are incapable of thought, and they are unable to differentiate themselves from others or from the environment. Living in a world of the here and now, infants are aware that objects exist only when they can actually see them. Take a stuffed animal away from a five-month-old and it ceases to exist as far as the child is concerned. At this age, out of sight is always out of mind.

The major achievement of the sensorimotor period is the development of **object permanence**, which is the realization that objects (including people) continue to exist even when they are out of sight. This concept develops gradually and is complete when the child is able to represent objects mentally in their absence. This marks the end of the sensorimotor period.

The Preoperational Stage (Ages Two to Seven)

What cognitive limitations characterize a child's thinking during the preoperational stage?

The **preoperational stage** is a period of rapid development in language. Children become increasingly able to represent objects and events mentally with words and images. Now their thinking is no longer restricted to objects and events that are directly perceived and present in the environment. Evidence of representational thought is the child's ability to imitate the behaviour of a person who is no longer present (deferred imitation). Other evidence is the child's ability to engage in imaginary play using one object to stand for another, such as using a broom to represent a horse.

Although children's thinking at the preoperational stage is more advanced than at the previous stage, it is still quite restricted. Thinking is dominated by perception, and the children at this stage exhibit egocentrism in thought. They believe that everyone sees what they see, thinks as they think, and feels as they feel.

At this stage children also show animistic thinking, believing that inanimate objects such as a tree, the sun, and a doll are alive and have feelings and intentions as well (Piaget, 1960, 1963a). That explains why two-year-old Meghan says "hello" to her food before she eats it, and why three-year-old Beth shows distress when her brother throws her doll into her toy box. Children also believe that all things, even the sun, the moon, and the clouds, are made for people and usually even by people.

The preoperational stage is so named because children are not yet able to perform mental operations (manipulations) that follow logical rules. Children at this stage are not aware that a given quantity of matter (a given number, mass, area, weight, or volume of matter) remains the same if it is rearranged or changed in its appearance, as long as nothing has been added or taken away. This concept is known as **conservation** and is illustrated in *Try It!*

Centration and irreversibility are two restrictions on thinking that lead children to wrong conclusions.

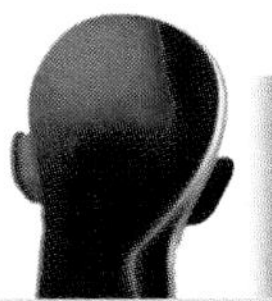

Try It!

Understanding the Conservation Concept

If you know a child of preschool age, try this conservation experiment. Show the child two glasses of the same size, and then fill them with the same amount of juice. After the child agrees they are the same, pour the juice from one glass into a tall, narrow glass. Now ask the child if the two glasses have the same amount of juice, or if one glass has more than the other. Children at this stage will insist that the taller, narrower glass has more juice, although they will quickly agree that you neither added juice nor took it away.

Centration is the tendency to focus on only one dimension of a stimulus and ignore the other dimensions. For example, in *Try It!*, children focused on the tallness of the glass and failed to notice that it was also narrower. At this stage, taller means more.

Preoperational children have not developed **reversibility** in thinking—the realization that after any change in shape, position, or order, matter can be returned mentally to its original state. The preoperational child in *Try It!* cannot mentally return the juice to the original glass and realize that once again the two glasses of juice are equal.

The Concrete Operations Stage (Ages Seven to Eleven or Twelve)

What cognitive abilities do children acquire during the concrete operations stage?

In the third stage, the **concrete operations stage** (ages 7 to 11 or 12), children gradually overcome the obstacles to logical thought associated with the preoperational period. Their thinking is less egocentric, and they come to realize that other people have thoughts and feelings that may be different from their own. Children acquire the ability to mentally carry out the operations essential for logical thought. They can now decentre their thinking—that is, attend to two or more dimensions of a stimulus at the same time. They can also understand the concept of reversibility, which is crucial in problem solving. Finally, during this stage children acquire the concept of conservation. But children are able to apply logical operations only to

assimilation: The process by which new objects, events, experiences, or pieces of information are incorporated into existing schemas.

accommodation: The process by which existing schemas are modified and new schemas are created to incorporate new objects, events, experiences, or information.

sensorimotor stage: Piaget's first stage of cognitive development (birth to age two), culminating in the development of object permanence and the beginning of representational thought.

object permanence: The realization that objects continue to exist even when they are no longer perceived.

preoperational stage: Piaget's second stage of cognitive development (ages two to seven), characterized by rapid development of language, and thinking that is governed by perception rather than logic.

conservation: The concept that a given quantity of matter remains the same despite rearrangement or change in its appearance, as long as nothing has been added or taken away.

centration: The child's tendency during the preoperational stage to focus on only one dimension of a stimulus and ignore the other dimensions.

reversibility: The realization, during the concrete operations stage, that any change occurring in shape, position, or order of matter can be returned mentally to its original state.

concrete operations stage: Piaget's third stage of cognitive development (ages 7 to 11 or 12), during which a child acquires the concepts of reversibility and conservation and is able to apply logical thinking to concrete objects.

concrete problems that they can perceive directly. They cannot apply these mental operations to verbal, abstract, or hypothetical problems. Surprisingly, the concepts of conservation of number, substance (liquid, mass), length, area, weight, and volume are not all acquired at once. They come in a certain sequence and usually at the ages shown in Figure 8.4.

The Formal Operations Stage (Age Eleven or Twelve and Beyond)

What new capability characterizes the formal operations stage?

In the **formal operations stage**, adolescents and adults can apply reversibility and conservation to abstract, verbal, or hypothetical situations and to problems in the past, present, or future.

Not all people attain full formal-operational thinking (Kuhn, 1984; Neimark, 1981; Papalia & Bielby, 1974) and those who do attain it usually apply it only in those areas where they are most proficient (Ault, 1983; Martorano, 1977). Some suggest that it is because this level of thinking requires training (Siegler, 1991) that some adults do not attain it.

Piaget's four stages of development are summarized in Review & Reflect 8.1.

LINK IT! 

www.piaget.org
The Jean Piaget Society

An Evaluation of Piaget's Contribution

Although Piaget's genius and his monumental contribution to our knowledge of mental development are rarely disputed, his methods and some of his findings and conclusions have been criticized (Halford, 1989).

Piaget was limited in the information he could gather about infants because he relied on observation and on the interview technique, which depended on verbal responses. Newer techniques requiring nonverbal responses—sucking, looking, heart-rate changes, reaching, and head turning—have shown that infants and young children are more competent than Piaget proposed (Flavell, 1992).

Few developmental psychologists believe that cognitive development takes place in the general stage-like fashion proposed by Piaget. If it did, children's cognitive functioning would be similar across all cognitive tasks and content areas (Flavell, 1992). Neo-Piagetians believe that while there are impor-

FIGURE 8.4
Piaget's Conservation Tasks Pictured here are two of Piaget's conservation tasks. The ability to answer correctly develops over time according to the ages indicated for each task. (From Berk, 1997.)

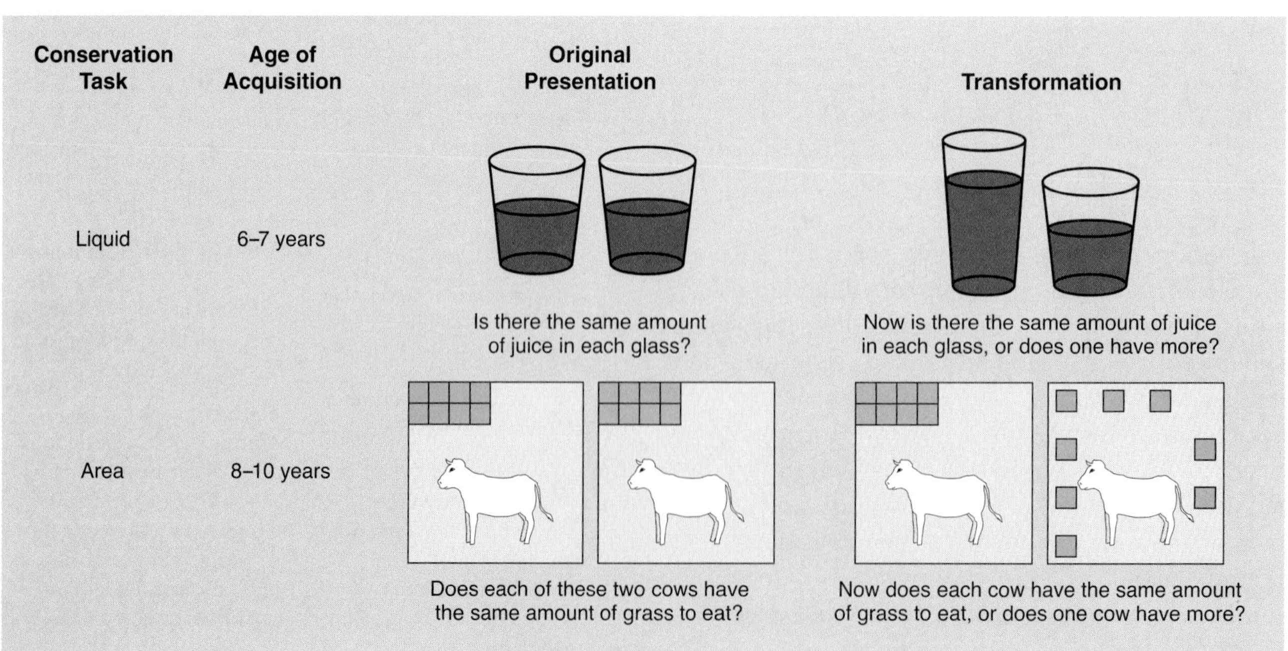

REVIEW & REFLECT 8.1
Piaget's Stages of Cognitive Development

Stage		Description
Sensorimotor (birth to age 2)	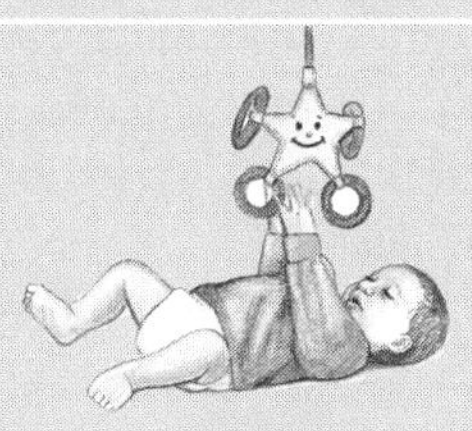	Infants experience the world through their senses, actions, and body movements. At the end of this stage, toddlers develop the concept of object permanence and can mentally represent objects in their absence.
Preoperational (ages 2 to 7)		Children are able to represent objects and events mentally with words and images. They can engage in imaginary play (pretend), using one object to represent another. Their thinking is dominated by their perceptions, and they are unable to consider more than one characteristic of an object at the same time (centration). Their thinking is egocentric–that is, they fail to consider the perspective of others.
Concrete operational (ages 7 to 11 or 12)		Children at this stage become able to think logically in concrete situations. They acquire the concepts of conservation and reversibility, and can order objects in a series and classify them according to multiple dimensions.
Formal operational (age 11 or 12 and beyond)		At this stage, adolescents learn to think logically in abstract situations, learn to test hypotheses systematically, and become interested in the world of ideas. Not all people attain full formal operational thinking.

tant general properties in cognitive development, there is also more variability in how children perform on certain tasks than Piaget described (Case, 1987, 1992). This variability results from the expertise children acquire in different content areas through extensive practice and experience (Flavell 1992). This also applies to adults: the expertise they have in a particular content area will influence whether they use formal operational reasoning or fall back on concrete operational reasoning when they approach a given task.

It is fair to say that Piaget has stimulated more research in developmental psychology than any other theorist in recent times (Beilin, 1992). Piaget's work has had a profound impact on the fields of psychology and education. His influence has led teachers to arrange richer learning environments in which children gain knowledge and improve cognitive skills through exploration and discovery.

Intellectual Capacity during Early, Middle, and Late Adulthood

In general, can adults look forward to an increase or decrease in intellectual performance from their 20s to their 60s?

Conventional wisdom has held that intellectual ability reaches its peak in the late teens or early 20s, and that it's all downhill after that. Fortunately, conventional wisdom is wrong. Although younger people tend to do better on tests requiring speed or rote memory, intellectual performance in adults continues to increase in other areas. In tests measuring general information, vocabulary, reasoning

formal operations stage: Piaget's fourth and final stage, characterized by the ability to apply logical thinking to abstract problems and hypothetical situations.

ability, and social judgment, older individuals usually do better than younger ones because of their greater experience and education (Horn, 1982; Horn & Donaldson, 1980). Adults actually continue to gain knowledge and skills over the years, particularly when they lead intellectually challenging lives. Neil Charness (1989), while at the University of Waterloo, found no differences in recall performance for young and older populations when participants were tested in their area of expertise.

Canadian data from the Victoria Longitudinal study were used to determine whether actively participating in the activities of everyday life could buffer individuals against cognitive decline as they aged. Findings from this research, and others, suggest that living an "engaged" life protects against cognitive decline (Hultsch et al., 1999; Pushkar et al. 1999; Shimamura et al., 1995). Several factors that are positively correlated with good cognitive functioning in the elderly are education level (Lykestsos et al., 1999), a complex work environment, a long marriage to an intelligent spouse, and a higher income (Schaie, 1990). Women also have the advantage as they generally live longer and do not experience the same level of cognitive decline.

It was long assumed that the number of neurons declined sharply in later adulthood, but this assumption appears to be false (Gallagher & Rapp, 1997). Recent research suggests that the shrinking volume of the aging cortex is due more to breakdown of the myelin that covers the axons in the white matter than to loss of the neurons that make up the grey matter (Wickelgren, 1996). As you learned in Chapter 2, the myelin sheath facilitates the rapid conduction of neural impulses. The breakdown of myelin thus explains one of the most predictable characteristics of aging—the slowing of behaviour. When the myelin breaks down, the brain takes longer to process information, and reaction time is slower.

Socialization and Social Relationships

Every one of us is born into a society. To function effectively and comfortably within that society, we must come to know the patterns of behaviour that it considers desirable and appropriate. The process of learning socially acceptable behaviours, attitudes, and values is called **socialization**. Many people play a role in our socialization, including parents and peers. School, the media, and religion are also important influences.

Remember It!

Piaget's Stages of Cognitive Development

1. Which statement reflects Piaget's thinking about the cognitive stages?
   a. All people pass through the same stages but not necessarily in the same order.
   b. All people progress through the stages in the same order but not at the same rate.
   c. All people progress through the stages in the same order and at the same rate.
   d. Very bright children sometimes skip stages.
2. Three-year-old Danielle says "Airplane!" when she sees a helicopter for the first time. She is using the process Piaget called
   a. assimilation. b. accommodation.
   c. centration. d. conservation.
3. Four-year-old Kendra rolls her ball of clay into the shape of a wiener to make "more" clay. Her actions demonstrate that she has *not* acquired the concept of
   a. reversibility. b. animism.
   c. centration. d. conservation.
4. Not all individuals reach the stage of formal operations. (true/false)
5. Match the stage with the relevant concept.
   ____ 1) abstract thought
   ____ 2) conservation, reversibility
   ____ 3) object permanence
   ____ 4) egocentrism, centration

   a. concrete operations
   b. sensorimotor stage
   c. formal operations
   d. preoperational stage

Answers: 1. b 2. a 3. d 4. true 5. 1) c 2) a 3) b 4) d

Erikson's Theory of Psychosocial Development

What is Erikson's theory of psychosocial development?

Erik Erikson proposed a theory that emphasizes the role of social forces on human development throughout the lifespan. He was the first to stress that society plays an important role in personality development, and that so do the individuals themselves; that is, he did not focus exclusively on the influence of parents. Erikson's is the only major theory of development to include the entire lifespan.

According to Erikson, individuals progress through eight **psychosocial stages** during the lifespan. Each stage is defined by a conflict involving the individual's relationship with the social environment that must be resolved satisfactorily in order for healthy development to occur. Although failure to resolve a conflict impedes later development, resolution may occur at a later stage and reverse any damage done earlier.

LINK IT!

snycorva.cortland.edu/%7EANDERSMD/ERIK/welcome.HTML
Erikson Tutorial Home Page

Stage 1: Basic Trust versus Basic Mistrust (Birth to 12 Months)

During the first stage, **basic trust versus basic mistrust**, infants develop a sense of trust or mistrust depending on the degree and regularity of care, love, and affection they receive from the mother or primary caregiver. Erikson (1980) considered "basic trust as the cornerstone of a healthy personality" (p. 58).

Stage 2: Autonomy versus Shame and Doubt (Ages One to Three)

The second stage, **autonomy versus shame and doubt** (ages one to three), is one in which infants are developing their physical and mental abilities and want to do things for themselves. They begin to express their will or independence and develop a "sudden violent wish to have a choice" (Erikson, 1963, p. 252). "No!" becomes one of their favourite words. Erikson believed that parents must set appropriate limits but at the same time facilitate children's desires for autonomy by encouraging their appropriate attempts at independence. If parents are impatient or overprotective, they may make children feel shame and doubt about their efforts to express their will and explore their environment.

Stage 3: Initiative versus Guilt (Ages Three to Six)

In the third stage, **initiative versus guilt** , children go beyond merely expressing their autonomy and begin to develop initiative. Enjoying their new locomotor and mental powers, they begin to plan and undertake tasks. They initiate play and motor activities and ask questions.

If children's appropriate attempts at initiative are encouraged and their inappropriate attempts are handled firmly but sensitively, they will leave this stage with a sense of initiative that will form "a basis for a high and yet realistic sense of ambition and independence" (Erikson, 1980, p. 78).

Stage 4: Industry versus Inferiority (Age Six to Puberty)

During the fourth stage, **industry versus inferiority**, children develop enjoyment and pride in making things and doing things. The encouragement of teachers as well as parents is important for a positive resolution of this stage. "But parents who see

socialization: The process of learning socially acceptable behaviours, attitudes, and values.

psychosocial stages: Erikson's eight developmental stages, which are each defined by a conflict that must be resolved in order for healthy personality development to occur.

basic trust versus basic mistrust: Erikson's first psychosocial stage (birth to 12 months), when infants develop trust or mistrust depending on the quality of care, love, and affection provided.

autonomy versus shame and doubt: Erikson's second psychosocial stage (ages one to three), when infants develop autonomy or shame depending on how parents react to their expression of will and their wish to do things for themselves.

initiative versus guilt: Erikson's third psychosocial stage (ages three to six), when children develop a sense of initiative or guilt depending on how parents react to their initiation of play, their motor activities, and their questions.

industry versus inferiority: Erikson's fourth psychosocial stage (age six to puberty), when children develop a sense of industry or inferiority depending on how parents and teachers react to their efforts to undertake projects.

their children's efforts at making and doing as 'mischief' and as simply 'making a mess,' help to encourage in children a sense of inferiority" (Elkind, 1970, pp. 89–90).

Stage 5: Identity versus Role Confusion (Adolescence)

Erikson's fifth stage of psychosocial development, **identity versus role confusion**, is the developmental struggle of adolescence. "Who am I?" becomes the critical question at this stage, as adolescents seek to establish their identity and find values to guide their lives (Erikson, 1963). They must develop a sense of who they are, where they have been, and where they are going. Adolescents are seriously looking to the future for the first time and considering an occupational identity—what they will choose as their life's work. Erikson (1968) believed that "in general it is the inability to settle on an occupational identity that most disturbs young people" (p. 132). The danger at this stage, he said, is that of role confusion—not knowing who one is or where one belongs.

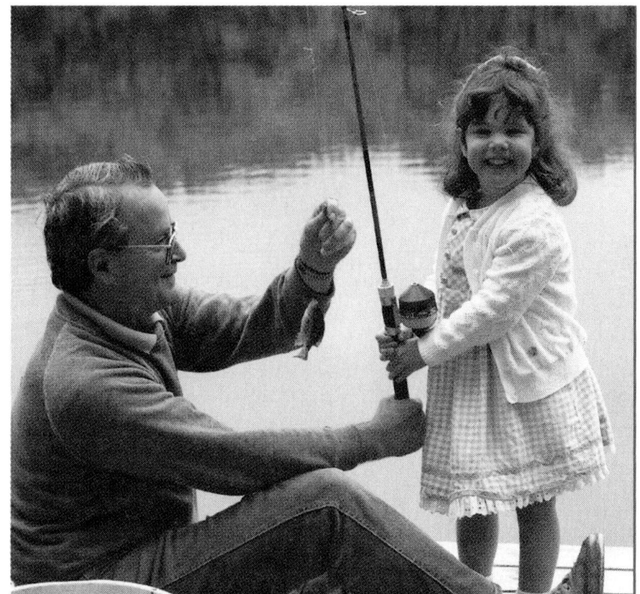

According to Erikson, in middle adulthood people develop generativity—an interest in guiding the next generation.

Stage 6: Intimacy versus Isolation (Young Adulthood)

Erikson contended that if healthy development is to continue, young adults must establish intimacy in a relationship. This sixth stage of psychosocial development he called **intimacy versus isolation**.

What kind of intimacy was Erikson referring to? He meant more than sexual intimacy alone. Intimacy means the ability to share with, care for, make sacrifices for, and commit to another person. Erikson believed that avoiding intimacy results in a sense of isolation and loneliness. Erikson and others argue that young adults must first establish their own identity before true intimacy is possible.

Stage 7: Generativity versus Stagnation (Middle Adulthood)

Erikson's seventh psychosocial stage is called **generativity versus stagnation**. Erikson (1980) maintained that in order for mental health to continue into middle adulthood, individuals must develop generativity—an "interest in establishing and guiding the next generation" (p. 103). This interest should extend beyond the immediate family to include making the world a better place for all young people.

People who do not develop generativity become self-absorbed and "begin to indulge themselves as if they were their own one and only child" (p. 103). Personal impoverishment and a sense of stagnation often accompany such self-absorption. We enlarge ourselves when we have concern for others.

Stage 8: Ego Integrity versus Despair (Late Adulthood)

In Erikson's eighth stage, **ego integrity versus despair**, the outcome depends primarily on whether a person has resolved the conflicts at the previous stages (Erikson et al., 1986). Those who have a sense of ego integrity believe their life has had meaning. They can look back on their life with satisfaction and a sense of accomplishment, and they are not burdened with major regrets:

> At the other extreme is the individual who looks back upon [his or her] life as a series of missed opportunities and missed directions; now in the twilight years [she or he] realizes that it is too late to start again. For such a person the inevitable result is a sense of despair at what might have been. (Elkind, 1970, p. 112)

Remember It!

Erikson's Psychosocial Stages of Development

1. According to Erikson, if the basic conflict of a given stage is not resolved satisfactorily, the individual
   a. will not enter the next stage.
   b. will acquire the unhealthy basic attitude associated with the stage, which will adversely affect development at the next stage.
   c. will be permanently damaged regardless of future experiences.
   d. will be fixed at that stage.
2. Match the psychosocial stage with the appropriate phrase.

____ 1) needs regular care and love	a. basic trust versus mistrust
____ 2) initiates play and motor activities, asks questions	b. industry versus inferiority
____ 3) strives for sense of independence	c. initiative versus guilt
____ 4) undertakes projects, makes things	d. autonomy versus shame and doubt

3. Which of the following was *not* identified by Erikson as a developmental task in his psychosocial stage for adolescence?
   a. forming an intimate relationship
   b. planning for an occupation
   c. forming an identity
   d. finding values to live by
4. Erikson believed that an active interest in guiding the next generation is necessary for good mental health in
   a. adolescence.
   b. young adulthood.
   c. middle age.
   d. old age.
5. Erikson believed that the main task in young adulthood is to
   a. develop generativity.
   b. forge an identity.
   c. start a family.
   d. form an intimate relationship.
6. According to Erikson, older people who feel they did not reach many of their goals or contribute positively to others will experience
   a. stagnation.
   b. despair.
   c. isolation.
   d. inferiority.

Answers: 1. b 2. 1) a 2) c 3) d 4) b 3. a 4. c 5. d 6. b

Review & Reflect 8.2 on the next page describes Erikson's stages.

The Parents' Role in the Socialization Process

For children, the parents' role in the socialization process consists of the examples they set, their teachings, and their approach to discipline. Parents are usually more successful if they are loving, warm, nurturant, and supportive (Maccoby & Martin, 1983). In fact, a longitudinal study (Franz et al., 1991) that followed individuals from ages 5 to 41 revealed that "children of warm, affectionate parents were more likely to be socially accomplished adults who, at age

identity versus role confusion: Erikson's fifth psychosocial stage, when adolescents need to establish their own identity and to form values to live by; failure can lead to an identity crisis.

intimacy versus isolation: Erikson's sixth psychosocial stage, when the young adult must establish intimacy in a relationship in order to avoid feeling isolated and lonely.

generativity versus stagnation: Erikson's seventh psychosocial stage, occurring during middle age, when the individual becomes increasingly concerned with guiding and assisting the next generation rather than becoming self-absorbed and stagnating.

ego integrity versus despair: Erikson's eighth and final psychosocial stage, occurring during old age, when individuals look back on their lives with satisfaction and a sense of accomplishment or have major regrets about missed opportunities and mistakes.

REVIEW & REFLECT 8.2
Erikson's Psychosocial Stages of Development

Stage	Ages	Description
Trust vs. mistrust	Birth to 12 months	Infant learns to trust or mistrust depending on the degree and regularity of care, love, and affection from mother or primary caregiver.
Autonomy vs. shame and doubt	Ages 1 to 3	Children learn to express their will and independence, to exercise some control, and to make choices. If not, they experience shame and doubt.
Initiative vs. guilt	Ages 3 to 6	Children begin to initiate activities, to plan and undertake tasks, and to enjoy developing motor and other abilities. If not allowed to initiate or if made to feel stupid and are considered a nuisance, they may develop a sense of guilt.
Industry vs. inferiority	Age 6 to puberty	Children develop industriousness and feel pride in accomplishing tasks, making things, and doing things. If not encouraged, or if rebuffed by parents and teachers, they may develop a sense of inferiority.
Identity vs. role confusion	Adolescence	Adolescents must make the transition from childhood to adulthood, establish an identity, develop a sense of self, and consider a future occupational identity. Otherwise, role confusion can result.
Intimacy vs. isolation	Young adulthood	Young adults must develop intimacy–the ability to share with, care for, and commit themselves to another person. Avoiding intimacy brings a sense of isolation.
Generativity vs. stagnation	Middle adulthood	Middle-aged people must find some way of contributing to the development of the next generation. Failing this, they may become self-absorbed, personally impoverished, and reach a point of stagnation.
Ego integrity vs. despair	Late adulthood	Individuals review their lives. If they are satisfied and feel a sense of accomplishment, ego integrity will result. If dissatisfied, they may sink into despair.

41, were mentally healthy, coping adequately, and psychosocially mature in work, relationships, and generativity" (p. 593).

The first social relationship in our lives is the one we forge with our caretakers. Human newborns are among the most helpless and dependent of all animal species and cannot survive alone. Fortunately, infants form a strong attachment to their primary caregivers. Because their attachment is a two-way affair, the term *bonding* has been used to describe this mutual attachment (Brazelton et al., 1975).

What precisely is the glue that binds caregiver and infant? For decades people believed that an infant's attachment to its caregiver was formed primarily because the caregiver provided the nourishment that sustains life. However, a series of classic studies by Harry Harlow on attachment in rhesus monkeys suggests that life-sustaining physical nourishment is not enough to bind infants to their primary caregivers.

Attachment in Infant Monkeys: Like Humans in So Many Ways

What did Harlow's studies reveal about maternal deprivation and attachment in infant monkeys?

Harlow found that the behaviour of monkeys deprived of mothering was not unlike that of children raised in orphanages. Typically, motherless monkeys would "sit in their cages and stare fixedly into space, circle their cages in a repetitive stereotyped manner and clasp their heads in their hands or arms and rock for long periods of time" (Harlow & Harlow, 1962, p. 138).

To investigate systematically the nature of attachment and the effects of maternal deprivation on infant monkeys, Harlow constructed two artificial monkey "mothers." One was a plain wire-mesh cylinder with a wooden head; the other was a wire-mesh cylinder that was padded, covered with soft terry cloth, and

Harlow found that infant monkeys developed a strong attachment to a cloth-covered surrogate mother and little or no attachment to a wire surrogate mother–even when the wire mother provided nourishment.

fitted with a somewhat more monkey-like head (see the photograph above). A baby bottle could be attached to one or the other "mother" for feeding.

Newborn monkeys were placed in individual cages with equal access to a cloth surrogate and a wire surrogate. The source of their nourishment (cloth or wire surrogate) was unimportant. "The infants developed a strong attachment to the cloth mothers and little or none to the wire mothers" (Harlow & Harlow, 1962, p. 141). Harlow found that it was contact comfort—the comfort supplied by bodily contact—rather than nourishment that formed the basis of the infant monkey's attachment to its mother.

The Necessity for Love

Harlow's research reveals the disastrous effects that maternal deprivation can have on infant monkeys. Human infants, too, need love in order to grow physically and psychologically. Between 1900 and 1920 many infants under a year old who were placed in orphanages did not survive, even though they were given adequate food and medical care (Montagu, 1962). Usually kept in cribs, the sides draped with sheets, these unfortunate infants were left to stare at the ceiling. Lacking a warm, close, personal caregiver and the all-important ingredient of love, the infants who survived their first year failed to gain weight and grow normally—a condition known as "deprivation dwarfism" (Gardner, 1972). And they were far behind other children in their mental and motor development (Spitz, 1946). To survive, infants need to become attached to someone. That someone can be nearly anyone.

The Development of Attachment in Humans

When does the infant have a strong attachment to the mother?

No strong emotional attachment between mother and infant is present at birth; nor does it develop suddenly. Rather, as a result of the mother and the infant responding to each other with behaviours that provide mutual satisfaction, the attachment develops gradually. The mother holds, strokes, talks to, and responds to the baby; and the baby gazes at and listens to the mother and even moves in synchrony with her voice (Condon & Sander, 1974; Lester et al., 1985). The baby's responses reinforce the mother's attention and care. Even crying can promote attachment, because the mother is motivated to relieve the baby's distress and feels rewarded when she is successful.

John Bowlby (1951), one of the foremost theorists on attachment, maintains that to grow up mentally healthy, infants and young children "should experience a warm, intimate, and continuous relationship" with their attachment figure that is mutually satisfying and enjoyable (p. 13).

Once the attachment has formed, infants show **separation anxiety**—fear and distress when the parent leaves them with another caretaker.

Ainsworth's Study of Attachment: The Importance of Being Securely Attached

What are the four attachment patterns identified in infants?

Virtually all infants will develop an attachment to a caregiver by age two, but vast differences exist in the quality of that attachment. In a classic study of mother–child attachment, Mary Ainsworth (1973, 1979) observed mother–child interactions in a laboratory procedure called the "Strange Situation." On the basis of infants' reactions to their mothers after two brief separations, Ainsworth and others identified four patterns of attachment: secure, avoidant, resistant, and disorganized/disoriented (Ainsworth et al., 1978; Main & Solomon, 1990).

separation anxiety: The fear and distress an infant feels when left with another caretaker.

SECURE ATTACHMENT Securely attached infants (about 65 percent of North American infants) are usually distressed when separated from their mothers. They eagerly seek to re-establish contact after separation and then show an interest in play. Moreover, securely attached infants use their mothers as a "safe base" from which to explore, much as Harlow's monkeys had done when unfamiliar objects were placed in their cages. Securely attached infants are the most responsive, obedient, and content. They also cry less than babies who are less strongly attached (Ainsworth et al., 1978). The mothers of securely attached infants tend to be the most sensitive, accepting, and affectionate, as well as the most responsive to their infants' cries and needs (Isabella et al., 1989; Pederson et al., 1990). This finding contradicts the notion that mothers who respond promptly to an infant's cries end up with spoiled babies who cry more.

Securely attached infants are likely to grow up to be more sociable, more effective with peers, more interested in exploring the environment, and generally more competent than less securely attached infants (Masters, 1981). Furthermore, their interactions with friends tend to be more harmonious and less controlling (Park & Walters, 1989).

Secure attachment is the most common type across cultures. However, cross-cultural research has revealed a higher incidence of insecure attachment patterns in Israel, Japan, and Germany than in the United States (Collins & Gunnar, 1990). But Ainsworth's procedure, the Strange Situation, may not be valid for assessing mother–child attachment in all cultures. Some also argue that the laboratory setting of the strange situation is not necessarily what would be observed in naturalistic settings.

AVOIDANT ATTACHMENT About 20 percent of North American infants are considered to have an avoidant attachment to their mothers. Infants with this attachment pattern are usually unresponsive to the mother when she is present and are not troubled when she leaves. When the mother returns, the infant may actively avoid contact with her or, at least, not readily greet her. The mother of an avoidant infant tends to show little affection and to be generally unresponsive to her infant's needs and cries.

RESISTANT ATTACHMENT Between 10 and 15 percent of North American infants show a resistant attachment pattern toward their mothers. Prior to a period of separation, resistant infants seek and prefer close contact with their mothers. Yet they do not tend to branch out and explore like securely attached infants. And when the infant's mother returns to the room after a period of separation, the resistant infant displays anger, and many push the mother away or hit her. When picked up, the infant is hard to comfort and may continue crying.

DISORGANIZED/DISORIENTED ATTACHMENT Between 5 and 10 percent of North American infants show a disorganized/disoriented attachment pattern, which is the most puzzling and apparently least secure pattern. When reunited with their mothers, these infants exhibit contradictory and disoriented responses. Rather than looking at the parent while being held, the infant may purposely look

Remember It!

Attachment

1. Which of the following was *not* true of infant monkeys raised with surrogate mothers?
   a. They showed inappropriate aggression.
   b. They would not interact with other monkeys.
   c. Their learning ability was impaired.
   d. They became abusive mothers.
2. A strong attachment between infant and mother usually occurs shortly after birth. (true/false)
3. Ainsworth found that most infants had a secure attachment. (true/false)
4. The most common type of interaction most fathers have with their infant is in the context of caregiving–feeding, changing, and bathing. (true/false)
5. Infants raised with adequate physical care but without the attention of a close, personal caregiver often become mentally and/or physically disabled. (true/false)

Answers: 1. c 2. false 3. true 4. false 5. true

away or approach the parent with an expressionless or depressed demeanour.

Parenting Styles: What Works and What Doesn't

What are the three parenting styles discussed by Baumrind, and which did she find most effective?

Diane Baumrind (1971, 1980, 1991) has identified three parenting styles—the authoritarian, the authoritative, and the permissive. She related these styles first to different patterns of behaviour in preschool children and later to those in older children and adolescents. The outcomes found for each parenting style are based on research with predominantly white, middle-class children.

AUTHORITARIAN PARENTS **Authoritarian parents** make the rules, expect unquestioned obedience from their children, punish misbehaviour (often physically), and value obedience to authority. Rather than giving a rationale for a rule, authoritarian parents consider "because I said so" a sufficient reason for obedience. Parents using this parenting style tend to be uncommunicative, unresponsive, and somewhat distant. Baumrind (1967) found preschool children disciplined in this manner to be withdrawn, anxious, and unhappy.

If the goal of discipline is eventually to have children internalize parental standards, the authoritarian approach leaves much to be desired. When parents fail to provide a rationale for rules, children find it hard to see any reason for following them. When a parent says, "Do it because I said so" or "Do it or you'll be punished," the child may do what is expected when the parent is present, but not when the parent is not around.

AUTHORITATIVE PARENTS **Authoritative parents** set high but realistic and reasonable standards, enforce limits, and at the same time encourage open communication and independence. They are willing to discuss rules and supply rationales for them. When children know why the rules are necessary and important, they find it easier to internalize and follow them, whether or not their parents are present. Authoritative parents are generally warm, nurturant, supportive, and responsive; they also show respect for their children and their opinions. Children raised in this way are the most mature, happy, self-reliant, self-controlled, assertive, socially competent, and responsible. Furthermore, this parenting style is associated with higher academic performance, independence, higher self-esteem, and internalized moral standards in middle childhood and adolescence (Dornbusch et al., 1987; Lamborn et al., 1991; Steinberg et al., 1989).

Authoritative parents are warm, nurturant, supportive, and responsive.

Michael Pratt and Mary Lou Arnold (1995) at Wilfrid Laurier University interviewed mothers and fathers and their teenagers about moral values and family discussions. They found that children of authoritative parents reported a more positive "family climate." These teens enjoyed moral discussions with their parents and tended to adopt some of their parents' ways of thinking about and discussing moral issues.

PERMISSIVE PARENTS **Permissive parents,** although rather warm and supportive, make few rules or demands and usually do not enforce those that are made. They allow children to make their own decisions and control their own behaviour. Children raised in this manner are the most immature, impulsive, and dependent; they also seem to be the least self-controlled and the least self-reliant.

authoritarian parents: Parents who make arbitrary rules, expect unquestioned obedience from their children, punish transgressions, and value obedience to authority.

authoritative parents: Parents who set high but realistic standards, reason with the child, enforce limits, and encourage open communication and independence.

permissive parents: Parents who make few rules or demands and allow children to make their own decisions and control their own behaviour.

Permissive parents also come in the indifferent, unconcerned, and uninvolved variety (Maccoby & Martin, 1983). In adolescents, this parenting style is associated with drinking problems, promiscuous sex, delinquent behaviour, and poor academic performance.

Peer Relationships

How do peers contribute to the socialization process?

Infants begin to show an interest in each other at a very young age. At only six months they already demonstrate an interest in other infants by looking, reaching, touching, smiling, and vocalizing (Vandell & Mueller, 1980). Friendships begin to develop by age three or four. Relationships with peers become increasingly important, and by middle childhood, membership in a peer group is central to a child's happiness. At a time when adolescents feel the need to become more independent from their family, friends become a vital source of emotional support and approval. Adolescents usually choose friends who have similar values, interests, and backgrounds (Duck, 1983; Epstein, 1983).

The peer group serves a socializing function by providing models of appropriate behaviour, dress, and language. It is a continuing source of both reinforcement for appropriate behaviour and punishment for deviant behaviour. The peer group also provides an objective measure against which individuals can evaluate their own traits and abilities (e.g., how smart or how good at sports they are).

Adolescent Egocentrism: On Centre Stage, Unique, and Indestructible

David Elkind (1967, 1974) believes that the early teenage years are marked by adolescent egocentrism, which takes two forms—the imaginary audience and the personal fable.

Do you remember, as a teenager, picturing how your friends would react to the way you looked when you made your grand entrance at a big party? At this stage of life, it never occurred to us that most of the other people at the party were preoccupied not with us, but with the way *they* looked and the impression *they* were making. This **imaginary audience** of admirers (or critics) that an adolescent conjures up exists only in the imagination; "but in the young person's mind, he/she is always on stage" (Buis & Thompson, 1989, p. 774).

Teenagers also have an exaggerated sense of personal uniqueness and indestructibility that Elkind calls the **personal fable**. They cannot fathom that anyone has ever felt as deeply as they feel or loved as they love. Elkind suggests that this compelling sense of personal uniqueness may be why many adolescents believe they are somehow protected from the misfortunes that befall others, such as unwanted pregnancies, car accidents, or drug overdoses. Belief in the personal fable may account for many of the risks teens take during adolescence.

Quadrel and colleagues (1993) dispute Elkind's explanation for adolescent risk taking. They found that both high-risk adolescents (from group homes or juvenile centres) and middle-class, low-risk adolescents were more likely than adults (the parents of the group of middle-class adolescents) to anticipate experiencing certain negative events—injury in an auto accident, alcohol dependency, mugging, and so forth. Apparently adolescents are willing to engage in high-risk behaviours *in spite of* the risks involved, perhaps because of peer pressure, or because the pleasure outweighs the risk.

And according to Bjorklund and Green (1992), risk taking may have some positive consequences. It may enable adolescents to "experiment with new ideas and new tasks and generally behave more independently. Many of these experiences will be adaptive for adult life and for making the transition to adulthood" (p. 49).

Remember It!

Parenting Style and Peer Relationships

1. Match the parenting style with the approach to discipline.

____ 1) expect unquestioned obedience

____ 2) set high standards, give rationale for rules

____ 3) set few rules or limits

a. permissive parents

b. authoritative parents

c. authoritarian parents

2. The peer group is usually a negative influence on social development. (true/false)

Answers: 1. 1) c 2) b 3) a 2. false

Kohlberg's Theory of Moral Development

What are Kohlberg's three levels of moral reasoning?

How do we develop our ideas of right and wrong? Lawrence Kohlberg (1981, 1984, 1985) believed that moral reasoning is closely related to cognitive development and that it, too, evolves in stages. Kohlberg (1969) studied moral development by presenting a series of moral dilemmas to male participants from a number of countries.

Read one of his best-known dilemmas in the *Try It!*

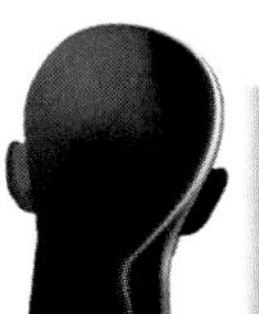

Try It!

Test Your Moral Judgment

In Europe a woman was near death from a special kind of cancer. There was one drug that the doctors thought might save her. It was a form of radium that a druggist in the same town had recently discovered. The drug was expensive to make, and the druggist was charging 10 times what the drug cost him to make. He paid $200 for the radium and charged $2000 for a small dose of the drug. The sick woman's husband, Heinz, went to everyone he knew to borrow the money, but he could only get together $1000, which was half of what it cost. He told the druggist that his wife was dying and asked him to sell it cheaper or let him pay later. But the druggist said, "No, I discovered the drug, and I am going to make money from it." So Heinz got desperate and broke into the man's store to steal the drug for his wife (Colby et al., 1983, p. 77).

What moral judgment would you make about the dilemma? Should Heinz have stolen the drug? Explain.

Levels of Moral Reasoning

Kohlberg was less interested in how people judged Heinz's behaviour than in the *reasons* for their responses. He found that moral reasoning had three levels, with each level having two stages.

THE PRECONVENTIONAL LEVEL At the **preconventional level**, moral reasoning is governed by the standards of others rather than an individual's own internalized standards of right and wrong. An act is judged good or bad on the basis of its physical consequences. In Stage 1, "right" is whatever avoids punishment; in Stage 2, "right" is whatever is rewarded, benefits the individual, or results in a favour being returned. "You scratch my back and I'll scratch yours" is the thinking common at this stage. Children through age 10 usually function at the preconventional level.

THE CONVENTIONAL LEVEL At the **conventional level,** the individual has internalized the standards of others and judges right and wrong in terms of those standards. Stage 3 is sometimes called the "good boy–nice girl orientation." "Good behaviour is that which pleases or helps others and is approved by them" (Kohlberg, 1968, p. 26). At Stage 4, the orientation is toward "authority, fixed rules, and the maintenance of the social order. Right behaviour consists of doing one's duty, showing respect for authority, and maintaining the given social order for its own sake" (p. 26). Kohlberg believed that a person must have reached Piaget's concrete operations stage in order to reason morally at the conventional level.

THE POSTCONVENTIONAL LEVEL Kohlberg's highest level of moral reasoning is the **postconventional level**, which requires the ability to think at Piaget's level of formal operations. According to Kohlberg, most often this level is found among middle-class, well-educated people. At this level, people do not simply internalize the standards of others. Instead, they weigh moral alternatives, realizing that at times the law may conflict with basic human rights. At Stage 5,

imaginary audience: A belief of adolescents that they are or will be the focus of attention in social situations and that others will be as critical or approving as they are of themselves.

personal fable: An exaggerated sense of personal uniqueness and indestructibility, which may be the basis of the risk taking that is common during adolescence.

preconventional level of moral reasoning: Kohlberg's lowest level, based on the physical consequences of an act; "right" is whatever avoids punishment or gains a reward.

conventional level of moral reasoning: Kohlberg's second level, in which right and wrong are based on the internalized standards of others; "right" is whatever helps or is approved of by others, or whatever is consistent with the laws of society.

postconventional level of moral reasoning: Kohlberg's highest level, in which moral reasoning involves weighing moral alternatives; "right" is whatever furthers basic human rights.

the person believes that laws are formulated to protect both society and the individual and should be changed if they fail to do so. At Stage 6, ethical decisions are based on universal ethical principles, which emphasize respect for human life, justice, equality, and dignity for all people. People who reason morally at Stage 6 believe that they must follow their conscience even if it results in a violation of the law.

Couldn't this kind of moral reasoning provide a convenient justification for any act at any time? Not according to Kohlberg, who insisted that an action must be judged in terms of whether it is right and fair from the perspective of *all* the people involved. In other words, the person must be convinced that the action would be proper even if he or she had to change positions with any individual, from the most favoured to the least favoured, in the society.

We should point out that Kohlberg had second thoughts about this sixth stage and was unsure whether it exists except as a matter of theoretical and philosophical speculation (Levine et al., 1985).

Review & Reflect 8.3 describes Kohlberg's stages of moral development.

The Development of Moral Reasoning

According to Kohlberg, we progress through moral stages one stage at a time in a fixed order. We do not skip stages, and if movement occurs, it is to the next higher stage. Postconventional reasoning is not possible, Kohlberg said, until people fully attain Piaget's level of formal operations. They must be able to think in terms of abstract principles and be able to think through and apply ethical principles in hypothetical situations (Kohlberg & Gilligan, 1971; Kuhn et al., 1977). Attaining a high level of cognitive development, however, does not guarantee advanced moral reasoning. Current research by Joan Grusec, at the University of Toronto, and by Jacqueline Goodnow (1994), suggests that in order for children to acquire moral values from their parents they must listen to and understand the information given *and* they must also accept it.

REVIEW & REFLECT 8.3
Kohlberg's Stages of Moral Development

Method	Limitations
Level I: Preconventional Level (ages 4 to 10) Moral reasoning is governed by the standards of others; an act is good or bad depending on its physical consequences–whether it is punished or rewarded.	Stage 1 The stage where whatever avoids punishment is right. Children obey out of fear of punishment. Stage 2 The stage of self-interest. Whatever benefits the individual or gains a favour in return is right. "You scratch my back and I'll scratch yours."
Level II: Conventional Level (ages 10 to 13) The person internalizes the standards of others and judges right and wrong according to those standards.	Stage 3 The morality of mutual relationships. The "good boy–nice girl" orientation. Child acts to please and help others. Stage 4 The morality of the social system and conscience. Orientation toward authority. Morality is doing one's duty, respecting authority, and maintaining the social order.
Level III: Postconventional Level (after age 13, at young adulthood, or never) Moral conduct is under internal control; this is the highest level and the mark of true morality.	Stage 5 The morality of contract; respect for individual rights and laws that are democratically agreed on. Rational valuing of the wishes of the majority and welfare of the people. Belief that society is best served if citizens obey the law. Stage 6 The highest stage of the highest social level. The morality of universal ethical principles. The person acts according to internal standards independent of legal restrictions or opinions of others.

Research on Kohlberg's Theory

What do cross-cultural studies reveal about the universality of Kohlberg's theory?

In a review of 45 studies of Kohlberg's theory conducted in 27 countries, Snarey (1985) found support for the virtual universality of Stages 1 through 4, and for the invariant sequence of these stages in all groups studied. Stage 5 was evident in almost all samples from urban or middle-class populations and absent in all of the tribal or village societies studied. And a more recent study by Snarey (1995) supports the conclusions reached a decade earlier.

Kohlberg indicated that most women remain at Stage 3, while most men attain Stage 4. Do men typically attain a higher level of moral reasoning than women? Carol Gilligan (1982) asserts that Kohlberg's theory is sex-biased. Not only did Kohlberg fail to include any females in his original research, Gilligan points out, but he limited morality to abstract reasoning about moral dilemmas. Furthermore, at his highest level, Stage 6, Kohlberg emphasized justice and equality but not mercy, compassion, love, or concern for others. Gilligan and others (Wark & Krebs, 1996) suggest that females tend more than males to view moral behaviour in terms of compassion, caring, and concern for others. Thus Gilligan agrees that the content of moral reasoning differs between the sexes, but she contends that males and females do not differ in the complexity of their moral reasoning. Kohlberg's theory does emphasize rights and justice over concern for others; even so, researchers have found that females score as high as males in their moral reasoning (Walker, 1989; Walker et al., 1987).

Adult Social Relationships

Marriage

A review of 93 studies of life satisfaction revealed that married people report much higher levels of well-being than unmarried people, and that married women report slightly higher levels of well-being than married men (Mookherjee, 1997). Inglehart (1990) reported that studies in Europe and North America show that married couples were happier than people who were unmarried, separated, or divorced. Lesbian couples, too, report being happier than lesbians living alone (Wayment & Peplau, 1995). Levenson and others (1993) found that older couples tended to be happier in their marriages than middle-aged couples, experiencing less conflict and more sources of pleasure than their younger counterparts.

Divorce and Staying Single

The marriages most likely to fail are teenage marriages, those in which the bride was pregnant, and those between people whose parents were divorced.

Remember It!

More on Socialization and Social Relationships

1. Match Kohlberg's level of moral reasoning with the rationale for engaging in a behaviour.
   ____ 1) to avoid punishment or gain a reward
   ____ 2) to ensure that human rights are protected
   ____ 3) to gain approval or to follow the law

   a. conventional
   b. preconventional
   c. postconventional

2. For adolescents, the most effective parenting style is the _________; the least effective is the _________.
   a. authoritative; authoritarian
   b. authoritarian; permissive
   c. authoritative; permissive
   d. permissive; authoritarian

3. For most adolescents, the peer group serves some useful functions. (true/false)

Answers: 1. 1) b 2) c 3) a 2. c 3. true

Note that marriages that do survive are not necessarily happy. Many couples stay together for reasons other than love—because of religious beliefs, for the sake of the children, for financial reasons, or out of fear of facing the future alone.

Recently, greater interest has been directed toward adults who remain single throughout their lives. Some report lower life satisfaction for this group (Frazier et al., 1996) but this finding appears to be moderated by available social support. When social support is higher, life satisfaction is also higher (Barrett, 1999; Newtson & Keith, 1997).

Parenthood

What effect does parenthood have on marital satisfaction?

Even though most couples want children, satisfaction with marriage does tend to decline after the birth of the first child (Belsky et al., 1989; Cowan & Cowan, 1992). Women in general find the period of child rearing the least satisfying time of marriage. The problems centre mainly on the division of work—who does what. Even though men are helping with children more than in the past, child care still generally ends up being primarily the responsibility of the woman. Unless a woman holds very traditional views of sex roles, her dissatisfaction after the birth of the first child often depends on how much help with child care and housework she receives relative to what she expected (Hackel & Ruble, 1992).

The *On the Cutting Edge in Canada* box discusses studies that have been done on adoption.

Remaining Childless

Some couples are choosing not to have children. Recent studies suggest that the advantages for this decision include "fewer worries or problems, financial benefits, greater freedom, and career flexibility" (Connidis & McMullin, 2000). A few studies indicate that such couples are happier and find their marriages more satisfying than couples with children (Campbell, 1975; Somers, 1993). However, this same sense of satisfaction may not continue into middle and old age, when couples may wonder if their decision to remain childless was a good one (Connidis & McMullin, 2000).

on the cutting edge in canada

Adoption Research

Perhaps the most central debate in psychology is whether who we are–our sense of self, identity, or personality–develops as a result of our genetic coding passed on from our parents and family of origin, or whether our upbringing and early parental socialization determines who we become. The resolution of the "nature–nurture debate" has been hotly disputed for decades, but most psychologists would now agree that both factors influence our development.

Adoption research has contributed immensely to our understanding of human development, especially in the consideration of the similarities and differences that arise in the sense of identity of children raised in either a biological or adoptive family. Early Canadian research documented the various differences between adoptive and birth families. While both types of families may provide an excellent environment for the positive development of children, adoptive and birth families are not necessarily similar.

Michael Sobol

For well over twenty years, Michael Sobol, a psychologist at the University of Guelph, has been active both as a researcher and lobbyist on issues of adoption. His work focuses on the centrality of a personal history–a connection with one's past that may only be understood once a person is aware of his or her family of origin.

In his research, Dr. Sobol has argued for the need to create more

Life at Work

Today, nearly one out of three young adults will not only change jobs but will even change occupational field (Phillips & Blustein, 1994). Probably no other part of life is so central to identity and self-esteem as a person's occupation or profession, with the possible exception of motherhood for some women. A career often becomes a basic part of a person's definition of self and a major factor in the way others define him or her. A career can define your lifestyle—the friends you choose, the neighbourhood you live in, your habits, and even your ideas and opinions. And job satisfaction affects general life satisfaction. Yet, most retirees are happy to leave the world of work. Generally, those most reluctant to retire are better-educated, hold high-status jobs with a good income, and find fulfillment in their work. Life satisfaction also appears to be related to participation community service and social activities (Harlow & Cantor, 1996).

Personality and Social Development in Middle Age

Many people consider middle age the prime of life. Reaching middle age, men and women begin to express personality characteristics that they had earlier suppressed. Men generally become more nurturant and women more assertive (Neugarten, 1968). Many women "feel that the most conspicuous characteristic of middle age is the sense of increased freedom" (Neugarten, 1968, p. 96).

Wink and Helson (1993) found that after children leave home, most women work at least part-time and tend to experience an increase in self-confidence and a heightened sense of competence and independence. Contrary to the conventional wisdom—that parents feel empty and depressed when their children grow up and leave—most parents seem to be happier when their children are on their own (Campbell, 1975; Miller, 1976; Rollins & Feldman, 1970). Parents have more time and money to pursue their own goals and interests, and they are happy about it. "For the majority of women in middle age, the departure of teenage children is not a crisis, but a pleasure. It is when the children do *not* leave home that a crisis occurs (for both parent and child)" (Neugarten, 1982 , p. 163). For most people, an empty nest is a happy nest.

openness in adoption policies. Adoption laws, he argues, must recognize the right of an individual to understand where he or she comes from, to know his or her background or family history. His research has shown, for instance, that learning about the adoptee's family of origin need not become a threat to the adopted family. Instead, he suggests that adoptive parents and the adopted child should work together on "a journey of discovery in which the adoptee begins to write chapter 1 of his or her life. Without that information, the adoptee's own self-understanding is destined to start at chapter 2" (Sobol, personal communication, 2000). The biological mother, too, should have the option of reconnecting with her child at some point in the future. Her decision to part with a child is often related to difficult personal circumstances beyond her control. The choice to reconnect at some point in the future should not be discouraged by a rigid adoption system.

Dr. Sobol's research has examined some of the psychological ramifications of the adoption process (Sobol & Cardiff, 1983; Sobol & Daly, 1992). He has shown that the adopted family's negative discussions about the birth family is often associated with a greater desire on the part of the adoptee to search for the family of origin. Similarly, openness in adoption, the early positive discussion of the fact that one is adopted, and more information provided about the birth family tend to be associated with better outcomes. It is also interesting to note that greater similarity between adopted parents and the adoptee in terms of aptitudes and interests also tends to be connected with more positive psychological outcomes for the adoptee (Sobol et al., 2000).

But Dr. Sobol's interests in adoption issues have not been strictly limited to research. He has also been very active in lobbying efforts to change Canadian laws to open adoption records. In a contribution to the Royal Commission on New Reproductive Technology (Sobol & Daly, 1992), he argued for the need of offspring made possible through reproductive technology to have access to identifying genetic material. For his efforts, he received the David Kirk Award for research in Adoption given by the Adoption Council of Canada and, more recently, the 2000 Adoption Activist Award by the North American Council on Adoptable Children.

Special Concerns in Later Adulthood

Age 65 or 70 is generally considered the beginning of old age. What are your perceptions of life after 65? Complete *Try It!* by answering *true* or *false* to the statements about older adults.

Try It!

Testing Perceptions of Older Adults

Are the following statements true or false?

____ 1. Older adults tend to express less satisfaction with life in general than younger adults do.

____ 2. A lack of money is a serious problem for most people over 65.

____ 3. Marital satisfaction declines in old age.

____ 4. Mandatory retirement forces most workers out of jobs before they are ready to leave.

____ 5. The majority of retirees do not adjust well to retirement.

____ 6. A large percentage of individuals over 85 end up in nursing homes or institutions.

Answers: All of the statements are false!

Most people give the wrong answers to questions such as these about older adults. The statements are all false. But one thing we do know is that when we reach our 70s or 80s, strenuous physical activity is definitely out for us—right? Wrong! Many older adults are physically (and mentally) running circles around younger people.

Fitness and Aging

Men and women in their 60s and 70s who exercise properly and regularly can have the energy and fitness of people 20 to 30 years younger (deVries, 1986).

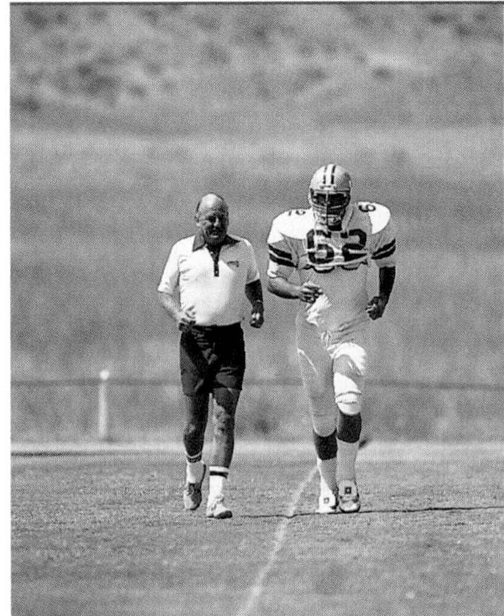

Older adults who stay fit and active have a better chance of remaining healthy.

Recent research suggests that physical exercise enhances the performance of older adults on tests of reaction time, working memory, and reasoning (Clarkson-Smith & Hartley, 1990). "People rust out faster from disuse than they wear out from overuse" (Horn & Meer, 1987, p. 83). In a recent study, 100 frail nursing-home residents, whose average age was 87, exercised their thigh and hip muscles vigorously on exercise machines for 45 minutes three times a week. At the end of 10 weeks, they had increased their stair-climbing power by 28.4 percent and their walking speed by 12 percent, and four were able to exchange a walker for a cane (Fiatarone et al., 1994). Most of us have the potential to remain fit and vigorous as we age. As pointed out in recent research by Benjamin Schlesinger (1996), even the pleasures of sex are still enjoyed by many who are well advanced in years.

Terminal Illness and Death

One of the developmental tasks for the elderly is to accept the inevitability of death and to prepare themselves for it. At no time does this become more critical than when people face a terminal illness.

Kübler-Ross on Death and Dying

According to Kübler-Ross, what stages do terminally ill patients experience as they come to terms with death?

Psychiatrist Elisabeth Kübler-Ross (1969) interviewed some 200 terminally ill people and found commonalities in their reactions to dying. In her book *On Death and Dying,* she identifies five stages that most of those she interviewed went through in coming to terms with death.

In the first stage, *denial and isolation,* most patients feel shock and disbelief. When denial can no longer be maintained, it gives way to the second stage, *anger,* which is marked by envy of those who are young and healthy, and resentment. "Why me?" is the question that rages inside. In the third stage, *bargaining,* the person attempts to postpone death for a specific period of time in return for "good behaviour."

Eventually the bargaining gives way to the fourth stage, *depression.* This stage brings a great sense of loss—physical loss, loss of ability to work, loss of the role of mother, father, husband, or wife. This depression takes two forms—depression over past losses and over impending losses.

If enough time remains, patients usually reach the final stage, *acceptance,* in which they are neither depressed nor angry. They stop struggling against death and are able to contemplate its coming without fear or despair. Kübler-Ross found that the family also goes through stages similar to those experienced by the patient.

Kübler-Ross has made the public aware of the needs and feelings of the dying. Although other researchers acknowledge that her proposed stages often do occur, they deny their universality and their invariant sequence (Butler & Lewis, 1982; Kastenbaum, 1992). We must keep in mind that each person is unique. We should not expect the reactions of all the terminally ill to conform to some rigid sequence of stages; nor should we dismiss their anguish as merely a stage they are going through.

Bereavement

Many of us have experienced the grieving process—the period of bereavement that follows the death of a loved one and sometimes lingers long after. Contrary to what many believe, those who suffer the most intense grief initially, who weep inconsolably and feel the deepest pain, do not get through their bereavement more quickly than others (Bonanno et al., 1995). For most people the loss of a spouse is the most stressful event of a lifetime. Both widows and widowers are at a greater risk for health problems and have a higher mortality rate, particularly within the first six months, than their age mates who are not bereaved (Martikainen & Valkonen, 1996). Folkman and her colleagues (1996) found that the grieving process for male caregivers whose partners were dying of AIDS was similar to that experienced by spouses.

Death and dying are not pleasant subjects, but remember that life itself is a terminal condition, and each day of life should certainly be treasured like a precious gift.

Remember It!

Adults

1. The highest levels of life satisfaction are reported by ______; the lowest levels by ______.
   a. singles; married people
   b. married people; widowed people
   c. married people; singles
   d. married people; divorced people
2. Compared with older adults who are mentally and physically active, younger adults do better on
   a. tests requiring speed.
   b. comprehension tests.
   c. general information tests.
   d. practical problem solving.
3. According to Kübler-Ross, the first stage experienced by terminally ill patients in coming to terms with death is ________; the last stage is ________.
   a. anger; depression
   b. denial; depression
   c. bargaining; acceptance
   d. denial; acceptance

Answers: 1. c 2. a 3. d

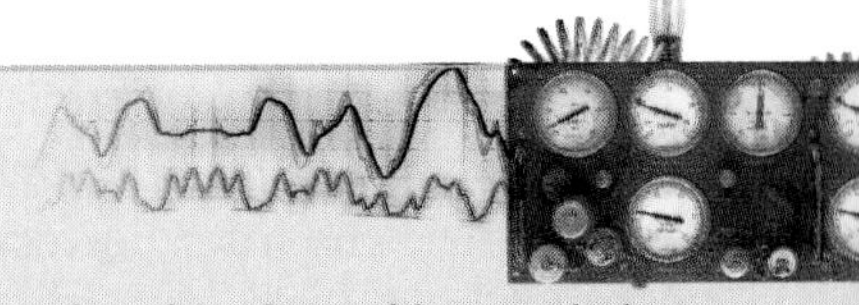

Teenage Pregnancy

Apply It!

The Consequences for Mother and Child

Among teens who give birth before 18 and choose to keep their babies, half will never complete high school. As a group, their earning power will be about half that of those who did not have babies at this early age (National Research Council, 1993), and many will eventually go on welfare (Brooks-Gunn & Furstenberg, 1986). About one-third of pregnant teenagers marry the baby's father, but the divorce rate for these marriages is two to three times the national average.

Early pregnancy can have serious physical consequences. Teen mothers are 60 percent more likely than women in their 20s to suffer complications or death during pregnancy or delivery. And pregnant teens who do not have abortions are more likely to come from poor backgrounds, which means that they are less likely to receive early prenatal medical care and may suffer from inadequate nutrition. As a result, they are twice as likely to give birth to premature or low-birth-weight infants than mothers who are over 18, and their babies are at greater risk for poor health and emotional and educational problems (Brooks-Gunn & Furstenberg, 1986; Furstenberg et al., 1989). Moreover, their babies have two to three times the normal risk of dying in infancy. And since teen mothers are more likely than older mothers to be single parents living in poverty, their children often grow up in an environment where economic security, discipline, and attention are all lacking.

Teen mothers often are unable to attend school because there is no one to care for the baby. They also face economic barriers. Although most teen mothers have some work experience, they find it difficult to earn enough to support themselves and pay for child care.

Little research has been done on teen fathers. The few studies that have been conducted have found that many young fathers want to play a part in the lives of the mother and child, but they also want to complete their education and find a good job. They therefore experience stresses similar to those affecting the mother. A teen father is more likely to marry the mother of his child if he can find a job that provides enough income to support a family. However, few such jobs are available to young people who have not completed high school.

Preventing Pregnancy and Cultural Contradictions

Many sexually active teens between 15 and 19 do not use contraception at all; many others use it only occasionally.

Why are teenagers unwilling to use contraceptives? Some feel guilty about their sexual activity; to them, planning to have sex seems more wrong than simply letting it happen spontaneously. Some find it too embarrassing to buy contraceptives. Others believe contraceptives interfere with sexual pleasure. In addition, many sexually active teens greatly underestimate the risk of getting pregnant. As a result, 62 percent of those who are sexually active and fail to use contraceptives do become pregnant (Zelnik et al., 1979).

Parents are divided on the question of sex education in schools. Some favour it; others fear that teaching children about sex will encourage them to engage in sexual activities. Scores of magazines and TV programs focus on sex and casual sexual activity, yet frank discussion of sexual behaviour in homes and schools is not common. Thus, teenagers are led to desire sex but not taught much about how to control their desires or avoid the ill consequences of sexual behaviour if they engage in it.

For whatever reasons, (including fear of AIDS), a growing number of teens have decided to postpone sex until the time is right for them.

There are two competing schools of thought on how best to deal with teen sex and its consequences (White & DeBlassie, 1992). One view accepts teen sex as inevitable and natural and focuses on preventing its negative consequences through condom distribution and other birth control measures. The other view holds that teens can be taught to avoid sexual intercourse, or to delay it until they are older, and recommends helping them understand their sexual desires and how to deal with them.

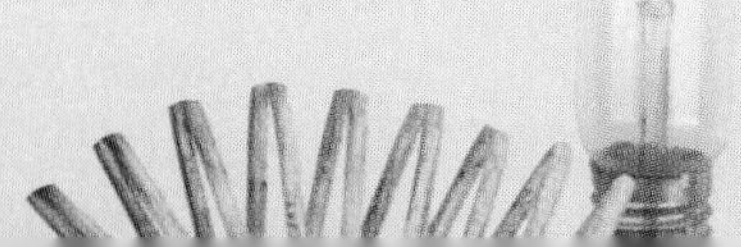

KEY TERMS

accommodation, p. 264
adolescent growth spurt, p. 262
assimilation, p. 264
authoritarian parents, p. 275
authoritative parents, p. 275
autonomy versus shame and doubt, p. 269
basic trust versus basic mistrust, p. 269
centration, p. 265
chromosomes, p. 254
concrete operations stage, p. 265
conservation, p. 265
conventional level of moral reasoning, p. 277
critical period, p. 257
cross-sectional study, p. 253
developmental psychology, p. 252
dominant gene, p. 255
ego integrity versus despair, p. 270
embryo, p. 256
fetal alcohol syndrome, p. 258
fetus, p. 256
formal operations stage, p. 266
fraternal (dizygotic) twins, p. 256
generativity versus stagnation, p. 270
genes, p. 254
habituation, p. 261
identical (monozygotic) twins, p. 256
identity versus role confusion, p. 270
imaginary audience, p. 276
industry versus inferiority, p. 269
initiative versus guilt, p. 269
intimacy versus isolation, p. 270
longitudinal study, p. 253
low-birth-weight baby, p. 258
menarche, p. 262
menopause, p. 262
nature–nurture controversy, p. 252
neonate, p. 259
object permanence, p. 264
permissive parents, p. 275
personal fable, p. 276
postconventional level of moral reasoning, p. 277
preconventional level of moral reasoning, p. 277
prenatal, p. 256
preoperational stage, p. 264
preterm infant, p. 258
psychosocial stages, p. 269
puberty, p. 262
recessive gene, p. 255
reflexes, p. 259
reversibility, p. 265
schema, p. 263
secondary sex characteristics, p. 262
sensorimotor stage, p. 264
separation anxiety, p. 273
sex chromosomes, p. 254
socialization, p. 268
teratogens, p. 257

THINKING CRITICALLY

Evaluation

In your opinion, do Erikson's psychosocial stages for adolescence and early adulthood accurately represent the major conflicts of these periods of life? Explain.

Point/Counterpoint

Prepare an argument supporting each of these positions:

a. Physical development peaks in the early adult years and declines thereafter.
b. Physical development can be maintained throughout life.

Psychology in Your Life

Using Erikson's theory, try to relate the first four stages of psychosocial development to your life.

Using Baumrind's scheme, classify the parenting style your mother and/or father used in rearing you.

a. Cite examples of techniques they used that support your classification.
b. Do you agree with Baumrind's conclusions about the effects of that parenting style on children? Explain.

SUMMARY & REVIEW

Developmental Psychology: Basic Issues and Methodology

What are two types of studies that developmental psychologists use to investigate age-related changes?

To investigate age-related changes, developmental psychologists use (1) the longitudinal study, in which the same group of participants is followed and measured at different ages; and (2) the cross-sectional study, in which researchers compare groups of participants of different ages with respect to various characteristics to determine age-related differences.

Heredity and Prenatal Development

How are hereditary traits transmitted?

Hereditary traits are transmitted by genes, which are located on each of our 23 pairs of chromosomes.

When are dominant or recessive genes expressed in a person?

When there are alternative forms of a gene for a specific trait, the dominant gene will be expressed. A recessive gene is expressed when it is paired with another recessive gene.

What are the three stages of prenatal development?

The three stages of prenatal development are the period of the zygote, the period of the embryo, and the period of the fetus.

What are some negative influences on prenatal development, and when is their impact greatest?

Some common hazards in the prenatal environment include certain prescription and non-prescription drugs, psychoactive drugs, poor maternal nutrition, and maternal infections and illnesses. Their impact is greatest during the first trimester.

Physical Development and Learning

What are the perceptual abilities of the newborn?

All of the newborn's senses are functional at birth, and the neonate already has preferences for certain odours, tastes, sounds, and visual configurations.

What types of learning occur in the first few days of life?

Newborns are capable of habituation and can acquire new responses through classical and operant conditioning and observational learning.

What physical changes occur during puberty?

Puberty is a period marked by rapid physical growth (the adolescent growth spurt), further development of the reproductive organs, and the appearance of the secondary sex characteristics. The major event for girls is menarche (first menstruation); for boys it is the first ejaculation.

What are the physical changes associated with middle age?

Physical changes associated with middle age are a need for reading glasses, a greater susceptibility to life-threatening disease, menopause (for women), and a declining reproductive capacity (for men).

The Cognitive Stages of Development: Climbing the Steps to Cognitive Maturity

What were Piaget's beliefs regarding stages of cognitive development?

Piaget believed that intellect develops in four stages, each representing a qualitatively different form of reasoning and understanding. He also believed the stages to be universal and to occur in an invariant sequence, although the rate at which children progress through them might differ.

What is Piaget's sensorimotor stage?

During the sensorimotor stage (birth to age two), infants gain knowledge and understanding of the world through their senses and motor activities. The major accomplishment of this stage is object permanence.

What cognitive limitations characterize a child's thinking during the preoperational stage?

Children at the preoperational stage (ages two to seven) are increasingly able to represent objects and events mentally, but they exhibit egocentrism and centration, and they have not developed the concepts of reversibility and conservation.

What cognitive abilities do children acquire during the concrete operations stage?

When working on concrete problems, children at the concrete operations stage (ages 7 to 11 or 12 years) become able to decentre their thinking and to understand the concepts of reversibility and conservation.

What new capability characterizes the formal operations stage?

At the formal operations stage (ages 11 or 12 years and beyond) adolescents are able to apply logical thinking to abstract problems and hypothetical situations.

In general, can adults look forward to an increase or decrease in intellectual performance from their 20s to their 60s?

Although younger people tend to do better on tests requiring speed or rote memory, intellectual performance shows modest gains until the mid-40s. A modest decline occurs from the 60s to the 80s. Scholars, scientists, and those in the arts are usually most productive in their 40s.

Socialization and Social Relationships

What is Erikson's theory of psychosocial development?

Erikson believed that individuals progress through eight psychosocial stages during the lifespan, each defined by a conflict with the social environment that must be resolved. The four stages in childhood are basic trust versus basic mistrust (birth to age two), autonomy versus shame and doubt (ages one to three), initiative versus guilt (ages three to six), and industry versus inferiority (age six to puberty). Adolescents experience the fifth stage, identity versus role confusion. The three stages of adulthood are intimacy versus isolation (young adulthood), generativity versus stagnation (middle adulthood), and ego integrity versus despair (late adulthood).

What did Harlow's studies reveal about maternal deprivation and attachment in infant monkeys?

Harlow found that the basis of attachment in infant monkeys is contact comfort, and that monkeys raised with surrogates showed normal learning ability but abnormal social, sexual, and emotional behaviour.

When does the infant have a strong attachment to the mother?

The infant has usually developed a strong attachment to the mother at six to eight months.

What are the four attachment patterns identified in infants?

Ainsworth identified four attachment patterns: secure, avoidant, resistant, and disorganized/disoriented attachments.

What are the three parenting styles discussed by Baumrind, and which did she find most effective?

The three parenting styles discussed by Baumrind are the authoritarian, the permissive, and the authoritative; she found authoritative to be best.

How do peers contribute to the socialization process?

The peer group serves a socializing function by modelling and reinforcing behaviours it considers appropriate, by punishing inappropriate behaviour, and by providing an objective measurement against which children can evaluate their own traits and abilities.

What are Kohlberg's three levels of moral reasoning?

At Kohlberg's preconventional level, moral reasoning is based on the physical consequences of an act—"right" is whatever averts punishment or brings a reward. At the conventional level, right and wrong are based on the internalized standards of others—"right" is whatever helps or is approved of by others, or whatever is consistent with the laws of society. Postconventional moral reasoning involves weighing moral alternatives—"right" is whatever furthers basic human rights.

What do cross-cultural studies reveal about the universality of Kohlberg's theory?

Cross-cultural studies support the universality of Kohlberg's Stages 1 through 4 and their invariant sequence. Stage 5 was found in almost all urban or middle-class samples but was absent in the tribal and village folk societies.

What effect does parenthood have on marital satisfaction?

Even though most couples want children, satisfaction with marriage, particularly in women, tends to decline after children arrive. This decline can be explained in part by the unequal workload carried by mothers employed outside the home.

Special Concerns in Later Adulthood

According to Kübler-Ross, what stages do terminally ill patients experience as they come to terms with death?

Kübler-Ross maintains that terminally ill patients go through five stages in coming to terms with death: denial, anger, bargaining, depression, and acceptance.

Motivation and Emotion

They were on their way to "Gold Mountain"–their name for Canada. There were almost 500 of them in four rusted cargo ships. Each of them had their own story, their own thoughts, their own hopes, and their own limitations. The one thing they had in common was a desire to live in Canada–no matter what the cost and no matter what the means.

Starting in May 1998 until September 1999, these "boat people" as they came to be known, ventured across the Pacific to start a new life. In all cases, the boats were detected by the Canadian Coast Guards and guided into the port of Manama in British Columbia. The refugees, primarily young men with a few women and children, were detained awaiting the decision of the Canadian government regarding their future. Canadians responded quickly and vocally. Some reacted with anger because migrants were trying to enter their country by illegal means, others with compassion for the difficult and life-threatening ordeal the migrants had suffered in order to enter a promised land. Some people

responded by writing letters, protesting and demanding action; others offered their services, aid, and support; and others merely watched as the events unfolded. Canadians' concept of fairness, the openness of our country, and the diversity of our people were tested. The fates of the "boat people" were mixed. Some were detained for long periods with no resolution. Others were released and allowed to place refugee claims. A final group was returned to their homeland ("Canada praised," 2000; Harper, 2000).

This story touched every Canadian. It challenged us emotionally, cognitively, and, for some on the front lines, physically. Psychologists have always had a strong interest in determining why people do the things they do. It may be difficult for us to imagine the circumstances that prompted each of the Chinese refugees to make such a drastic decision. The risks of embarking on such a dangerous voyage and the ramifications of being caught make their decisions all the more remarkable. Nonetheless, given what we have learned about these people, and given what we know about ourselves, the question arises, "Would we have done the same?" Are the things that motivated them different from what motivates us? The story of the refugees and other similar feats expose us to the extraordinary drive, spectacular efforts, and acts of courage or heroism that individuals demonstrate everyday. Are such individuals born with special talents or exceptional genes? What motivates them? Perhaps more importantly, what motivates us?

Introduction to Motivation

What is the difference between intrinsic and extrinsic motivation?

In this chapter on **motivation**, we look at the underlying processes that initiate, direct, and sustain behaviour in order to satisfy physiological and psychological needs. At any given time our behaviour may be explained by one or a combination of **motives**—needs or desires that energize and direct behaviour toward a goal. Motives can arise from an internal need, such as when we are hungry and look for something to eat. In such cases we are pushed into action from within. Other motives come from outside: some external stimulus, or **incentive**, pulls or entices us to act. After finishing a huge meal, some people yield to the temptation of a delicious dessert. At times like this, it is the external tempter, not the internal need for food, that moves us.

The intensity of our motivation, which depends on the number and strength of the motives involved, has a bearing on the effort and the persistence with which we pursue our goals. Sometimes we pursue an activity as an end in itself simply because it is enjoyable, not because any external reward is attached to it. This type of motivation is known as **intrinsic motivation**. On the other hand, when we engage in activities not because they are enjoyable but to gain some external reward or to avoid some undesirable consequence, we are pulled by **extrinsic motivation**. If you are working hard in this course solely because you find the subject interesting, your motivation is intrinsic. But if you are studying only to meet a requirement or to satisfy some other external need, your motivation is extrinsic. In real life, the motives for many activities are both intrinsic and extrinsic. You may love your job, but you would probably be motivated to leave if your salary—an important extrinsic motivator—were taken away. Table 9.1 gives examples of intrinsic and extrinsic motivation.

What do the experts say about the motives behind our behaviour? Consider some theories of motivation and find out.

Theories of Motivation

Do we act the way we do because of our inherent nature—the inborn, biological urges that push us from within? Or do we act because of the incentives that pull us from without? Obviously, both forces

TABLE 9.1

Intrinsic and Extrinsic Motivation

	Description	Examples
Intrinsic motivation	An activity is pursued as an end in itself because it is enjoyable and rewarding.	A person anonymously donates a large sum of money to a university to fund scholarships for hundreds of deserving students. A child reads several books each week because reading is fun.
Extrinsic motivation	An activity is pursued to gain an external reward or to avoid an undesirable consequence.	A person agrees to donate a large sum of money to a university for the construction of a building, provided it will bear the family name. A child reads two books each week to avoid losing television privileges.

influence us; theories of motivation differ in the relative power they attribute to each. The most thoroughly biological theories of motivation are the instinct theories.

Instinct Theories of Motivation

How do instinct theories explain motivation?

Scientists have learned much about instincts by observing animal behaviour. Spiders instinctively spin their intricate webs without having *learned* the technique from other spiders. It is neither a choice they make nor a task they learn, but an instinct. An **instinct** is an inborn, unlearned, fixed pattern of behaviour that is characteristic of an entire species. An instinct does not improve with practice, and an animal will perform it the same way even if it has never seen another member of its species. Even when their web-spinning glands are removed, spiders still perform the complex spinning movements and then lay their eggs in the imaginary web they have spun. So instincts tell us a great deal about animal behaviour.

But can human motivation be explained by **instinct theory**—the notion that we are motivated by certain innate, unlearned tendencies that are part of the genetic makeup of all individuals? Instinct theory was widely accepted by psychologists and others for the first 20 or 30 years of the 20th century. Over the course of those decades, the list of instincts expanded until thousands of instincts were being proposed to explain human behaviour. Common experience alone suggests that human behaviour is too richly diverse, and often too unpredictable, to be considered fixed and invariant across our species (Hood, 1995). Today, most psychologists reject the instinct theory as an explanation of human motivation.

Drive-Reduction Theory: Striving to Keep a Balanced Internal State

What is the drive-reduction theory of motivation?

Another major attempt to explain motivation, human and otherwise, is the **drive-reduction theory**, or the drive theory, popularized by Clark Hull (1943). According to Hull, all living organisms have certain

motivation: The process that initiates, directs, and sustains behaviour to satisfy physiological or psychological needs.

motives: Needs or desires that energize and direct behaviour toward a goal.

incentive: An external stimulus that motivates behaviour (examples: money, fame).

intrinsic motivation: The desire to perform an act because it is satisfying or pleasurable in and of itself.

extrinsic motivation: The desire to perform an act in order to gain a reward or to avoid an undesirable consequence.

instinct: An inborn, unlearned, fixed pattern of behaviour that is characteristic of an entire species.

instinct theory: The notion that human behaviour is motivated by certain innate tendencies, or instincts, shared by all individuals.

drive-reduction theory: A theory of motivation suggesting that a need creates an unpleasant state of arousal or tension called a drive, which impels the organism to engage in behaviour that will satisfy the need and reduce tension.

biological needs that must be met if they are to survive. A need gives rise to an internal state of tension or arousal called a **drive,** and we are motivated to reduce it. For example, when we are deprived of food or go too long without water, our biological need causes a state of tension, in this case the hunger or thirst drive. We become motivated to seek food or water to reduce the drive and satisfy our biological need.

Drive-reduction theory is derived largely from the biological concept of **homeostasis**—the tendency of the body to maintain a balanced, internal state to ensure physical survival. Body temperature, blood sugar, water balance, oxygen—in short, everything required for physical existence—must be maintained in a state of equilibrium, or balance. When this state is disturbed, a drive is created to restore the balance, as shown in Figure 9.1. But drive theory cannot fully account for the broad range of human motivation.

It is true that we are sometimes motivated to reduce tension, as the drive-reduction theory states, but often we are just as motivated to increase it. Why do people seek activities that actually create a state of tension—hang-gliding, horror movies, bungee-jumping, and so on? Why do animals and humans alike engage in exploratory behaviour when it does not serve to reduce any primary drive?

Arousal Theory: Striving for an Optimal Level of Arousal

How does arousal theory explain motivation?

Arousal theory can answer some of the puzzling questions that drive-reduction theory cannot answer. **Arousal** refers to a person's state of alertness and mental and physical activation. It ranges from no arousal (as in comatose), to moderate arousal (when we are pursuing normal day-to-day activities), to high arousal (when we are excited and highly stimulated).

Unlike drive-reduction theory, **arousal theory** does not suggest that we are always motivated to reduce arousal or tension. Arousal theory states that we are motivated to maintain an optimal level of arousal. If arousal is less than the optimal level, we do something to stimulate it; if arousal exceeds the optimal level, we seek to reduce it.

Biological needs, such as the needs for food and water, increase our arousal. But we also become aroused when we encounter new stimuli or when the intensity of stimuli is increased, as with loud noises, bright lights, or foul odours. And of course, certain kinds of drugs—stimulants such as caffeine, nicotine, amphetamines, and cocaine—also increase arousal.

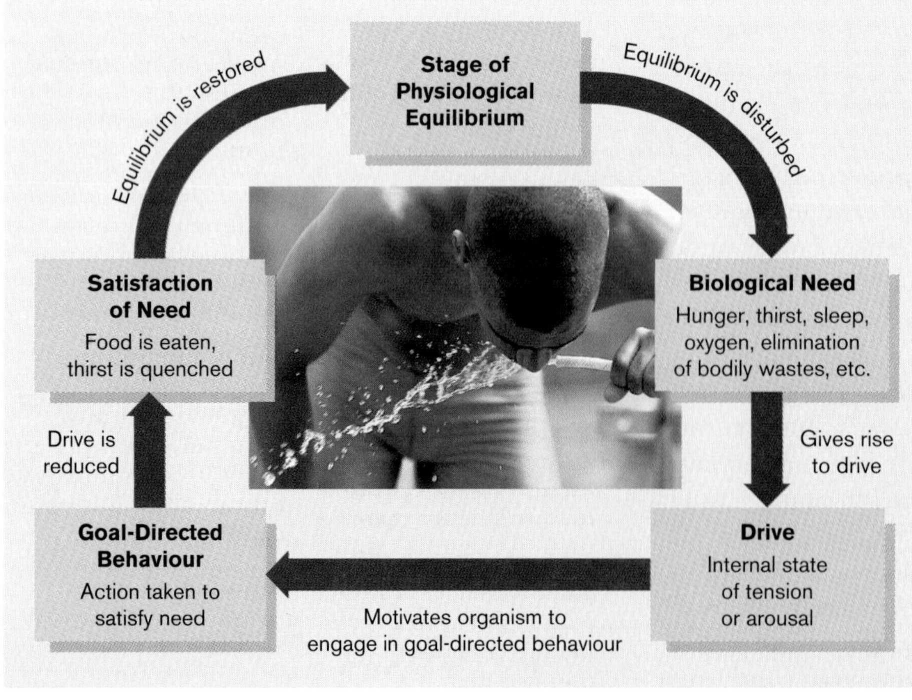

FIGURE 9.1

Drive-Reduction Theory

Drive-reduction theory is based on the biological concept of homeostasis–the body's natural tendency to maintain a state of internal balance, or equilibrium. When the equilibrium becomes disturbed (e.g., when we are thirsty and need water), a drive (internal state of arousal) emerges. Then the organism is motivated to take action to satisfy the need, thus reducing the drive and restoring equilibrium.

REVIEW & REFLECT 9.1
Theories of Motivation

Theory	View	Example
Instinct Theory	Behaviour is the result of innate, unlearned tendencies. (This view has been rejected by most modern psychologists.)	Two people fight because of their aggressive instinct.
Drive-Reduction Theory	Behaviour results from the need to reduce an internal state of tension or arousal.	Eating to reduce hunger.
Arousal Theory	Behaviour results from the need to maintain an optimal level of arousal.	Climbing a mountain for excitement; listening to classical music for relaxation.

Psychologists once believed that people generally felt better when their arousal level was moderate (Berlyne, 1971). But current theories suggest that people differ in the level of arousal they prefer. Some people are sensation seekers who love the thrills of new experiences, while others prefer the routine of a predictable life (McCourt et al., 1993).

Review & Reflect 9.1 summarizes the three major motivation theories that we have discussed: instinct, drive reduction, and arousal.

Stimulus Motives: Increasing Stimulation

When arousal is too low, **stimulus motives,** such as curiosity and the motives to explore, to manipulate objects, and to play, cause us to increase stimulation. Young monkeys will play with mechanical puzzles for long periods just for the stimulation of doing so (Harlow, 1950, 1953). Rats will explore intricate mazes when they are neither thirsty nor hungry and when no reinforcement is provided (Dashiell, 1925). Animals, including humans, will spend more time exploring novel objects than familiar ones.

Arousal and Performance

There is often a close link between arousal and performance. According to the **Yerkes-Dodson law**, performance on tasks is best when arousal level is appropriate to the difficulty of the task. Although optimal levels of arousal vary from person to person (Ebbeck & Weiss, 1988), we tend to perform better on simple tasks when arousal is relatively high. Tasks of moderate difficulty are best accomplished when our arousal is moderate; we do better on complex or difficult tasks when arousal is lower. Performance suffers when arousal level is either too high or too low for the task. You may have experienced too much or too little arousal when taking an exam. Perhaps your arousal was so low that your mind was sluggish and you didn't even finish the test; or you may have been so keyed up that you couldn't remember much of what you had studied.

The Effects of Sensory Deprivation: Sensory Nothingness

How would you like to be paid to do absolutely nothing? In an early experiment, Bexton and colleagues (1954) at McGill University gave student volunteers this opportunity when they studied the effects of **sensory deprivation**—a condition in which sensory stimulation is reduced to a minimum or eliminated.

drive: A state of tension or arousal brought about by an underlying need, which motivates one to engage in behaviour that will satisfy the need and reduce the tension.

homeostasis: The tendency of the body to maintain a balanced internal state with regard to oxygen level, body temperature, blood sugar, water balance, and so forth.

arousal: A state of alertness and mental and physical activation.

arousal theory: A theory suggesting that the aim of motivation is to maintain an optimal level of arousal.

stimulus motives: Motives that cause us to increase stimulation and that appear to be unlearned (examples: curiosity and the need to explore, manipulate objects, and play).

Yerkes-Dodson law: The principle that performance on tasks is best when arousal level is appropriate to the difficulty of the task–higher arousal for simple tasks, moderate arousal for tasks of moderate difficulty, and lower arousal for complex tasks.

sensory deprivation: A condition in which sensory stimulation is reduced to a minimum or eliminated.

Students had to lie motionless in a specially designed sensory-deprivation chamber in which sensory stimulation was severely restricted, as in the photograph. The participants could eat, drink, and go to the bathroom when they wanted to. Occasionally they were tested for motor and mental function. Otherwise they were confined to their sensationless prison.

Did they enjoy the experience? Hardly! Half the participants quit the experiment after the first two days. Those who remained eventually became irritable, confused, and unable to concentrate. They began to have visual hallucinations. Some began to hear imaginary voices and music and felt as if they were receiving electric shocks or being hit by pellets. Their performance on motor and cognitive tasks deteriorated. None said they liked the experiment.

But are the effects associated with sensory deprivation always negative? Not at all, according to University of British Columbia researcher Peter Suedfeld (Suedfeld & Borrie, 1999; Suedfeld & Coren, 1989). He and his colleagues developed a milder form of sensory deprivation known as "restrictive environmental stimulation (REST)," which has produced beneficial effects ranging from better control over cigarette smoking (Suedfeld, 1990) and other addiction (Borrie, 1991) to relief from tension headaches (Wallabaum et al., 1991). One study has even reported beneficial effects for autistic children (Harrison & Barabasz, 1991).

LINK IT!

www.nacd.org/articles/sensdep.html
Sensory deprivation

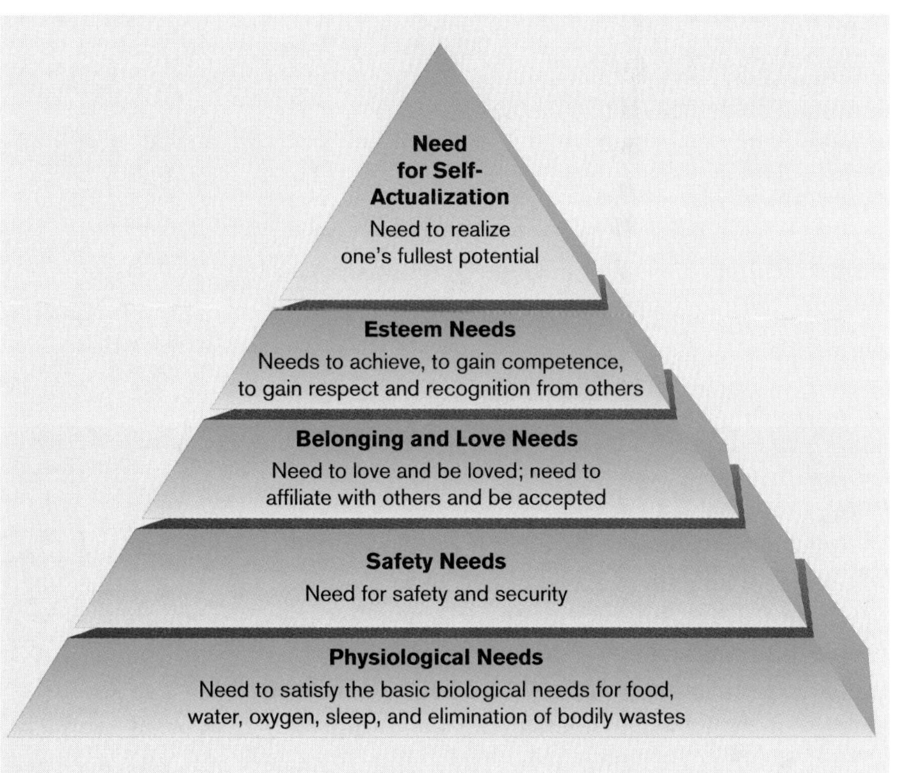

FIGURE 9.2
Maslow's Hierarchy of Needs

Maslow's Hierarchy of Needs: Putting Our Needs in Order

How does Maslow's hierarchy of needs account for human motivation?

Humans have a variety of needs or motives. Clearly some needs are more critical to sustaining life than others. We could live without self-esteem, but obviously we could not live long without air to breathe, water to drink, or food to eat.

Abraham Maslow (1970) proposed a **hierarchy of needs** (see Figure 9.2) to account for the range of human motivation. He placed physiological needs such as food and water at the base of the hierarchy, stating that these needs must be adequately satisfied before higher ones can be considered.

Once our physiological needs (for water, food, sleep, sex, and shelter) are met, the motives at the next higher level—the safety and the security needs—come into play. Once these needs are satisfied, we climb to the next level to satisfy our needs to belong,

Remember It!

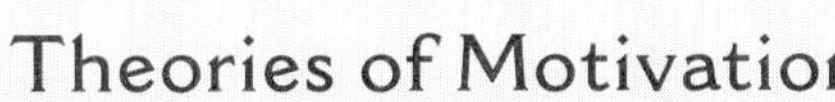

Theories of Motivation

1. When you engage in an activity to gain a reward or to avoid an unpleasant consequence, your motivation is (intrinsic/extrinsic).
2. In its original form, drive-reduction theory focused primarily on which of the following needs and the drives they produce?
   a. cognitive
   b. psychological
   c. biological
   d. emotional
3. Which theory suggests that human behaviour is motivated by certain innate, unlearned tendencies that are shared by all individuals?
   a. arousal theory
   b. instinct theory
   c. Maslow's theory
   d. drive-reduction theory
4. According to arousal theory, people seek ________ arousal.
   a. minimized
   b. increased
   c. decreased
   d. optimal
5. According to Maslow's hierarchy of needs, which needs must be satisfied before a person will try to satisfy the belonging and love needs?
   a. safety and self-actualization needs
   b. self-actualization and esteem needs
   c. physiological and safety needs
   d. physiological and esteem needs

Answers: 1. extrinsic 2. c 3. b 4. d 5. c

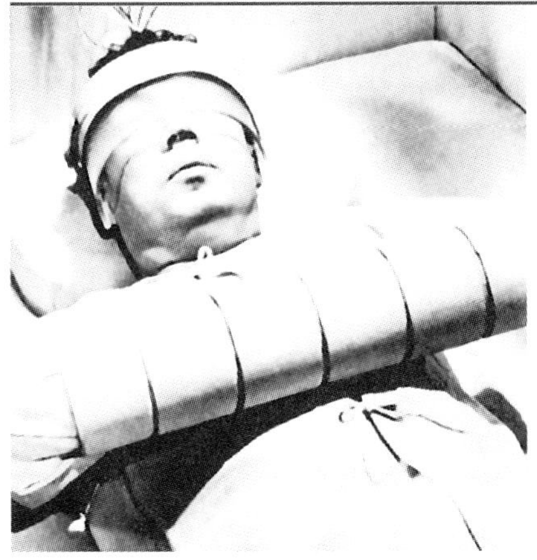

Sensory stimulation is reduced to a minimum for participants in sensory-deprivation experiments.

and to love and be loved. Maslow believed that failure to meet the belonging and love needs deprives individuals of acceptance, affection, and intimacy and is the most prominent factor in human adjustment problems. Still higher in the hierarchy are the needs for self-esteem and the esteem of others. These needs involve our sense of worth and competence, our need to achieve and be recognized for it, and our need to be respected. At the top of Maslow's hierarchy is the need for **self-actualization**, the need to realize our full potential. People may reach self-actualization through achievement in virtually any area of life's work.

Maslow's hierarchy of needs has been a popular notion, appealing to many, but much of it has not been verified by empirical research. The steps on the hierarchy may not be the same for all people (Goebel & Brown, 1981; Wahba & Bridwell, 1976). It is well known that in some people the desire for success and recognition is so strong that they are prepared to sacrifice safety, security, and personal relationships to achieve it. A few people are willing to sacrifice their very lives for others or for a cause to which they are committed. Perhaps they, too, have a hierarchy, but one in which the order of needs is somewhat different.

LINK IT!

www.maslow.com/index.html
Abraham Maslow publications site

hierarchy of needs: Maslow's theory of motivation, in which needs are arranged in order of urgency ranging from physical needs to security needs, belonging needs, esteem needs, and finally the need for self-actualization.

self-actualization: The development of one's full potential; the highest need on Maslow's hierarchy.

The Primary Drives: Hunger and Thirst

Drive-reduction theory, as we have seen, suggests that motivation is based largely on the **primary drives**, those that are unlearned and that seek to satisfy biological needs. Two of the most important primary drives are thirst and hunger.

Thirst: We All Have Two Kinds

Under what kinds of conditions do the two types of thirst occur?

Thirst is a basic biological drive. Adequate fluid is critical because the body itself is about 75 percent water. Without any intake of fluids, we can survive only about four or five days.

But how do we know when we are thirsty? When we have a dry mouth and throat, or a powerful urge to drink? Yes, of course. But thirst is more complex than that. There are two types of thirst signalling us to drink. One type, extracellular thirst, occurs when fluid is lost from the body tissues. When you are exercising heavily or doing almost anything in hot weather, you perspire and lose bodily fluid. Bleeding, vomiting, and diarrhea also rob your body of fluid. Perhaps you have heard that it is not a good idea to drink a cold beer or any other type of alcohol to quench your thirst on a very hot day. Alcohol increases extracellular fluid loss. This is why most people awaken with a powerful thirst after drinking heavily the night before.

Another type of thirst, intracellular thirst, involves the loss of water from inside the body cells. When we eat a lot of salty food, the water-sodium balance in the blood and in the tissues outside the cells is disturbed. The salt cannot readily enter the cells, so the cells release some of their own water to restore the balance. As the body cells become dehydrated, thirst is stimulated so that we drink to increase the water volume (Robertson, 1983). Might this explain why salted peanuts and pretzels are provided at many bars free of charge?

The Biological Basis of Hunger: Internal Hunger Cues

Hunger is a biological drive operating in all animals. But what happens in our bodies to make us feel hungry, and what causes satiety—the feeling of being full or satisfied?

The Role of the Hypothalamus: Our Feeding and Satiety Centre

What are the roles of the lateral hypothalamus and the ventromedial hypothalamus in the regulation of eating behaviour?

Researchers have found two areas of the hypothalamus that are of central importance in regulating eating behaviour and thus affect the hunger drive (Steffens et al., 1988). The **lateral hypothalamus (LH)** acts in part as a feeding centre to excite eating. Stimulating the feeding centre causes animals to eat even when they are full (Delgado & Anand, 1953). When the feeding centre is destroyed, animals initially refuse to eat (Anand & Brobeck, 1951).

The **ventromedial hypothalamus (VMH)** presumably acts as a satiety centre. When active, it inhibits eating (Hernandez & Hoebel, 1989). Electrically stimulating the satiety centre causes animals to stop eating (Duggan & Booth, 1986). If the VMH is surgically removed, experimental animals soon eat their way to gross obesity (Hetherington & Ranson, 1940; Parkinson & Weingarten, 1990). One rat whose satiety centre was destroyed weighed nearly six times as much as a normal rat. In human terms this would be like a person who weighs 67 kilograms ballooning up to 405 kilograms.

Some researchers believe that destruction of the VMH causes animals to lose the ability to adjust their metabolism and thereby stabilize their body weight (Vilberg & Keesey, 1990).

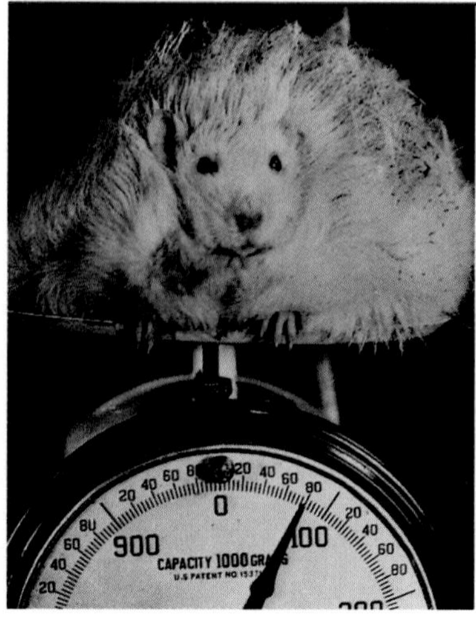

A rat whose satiety centre has been destroyed can weigh up to six times as much as a normal rat.

Hunger regulation, however, is not as simple as an off/on switch regulated by the LH and VMH. These two areas of the hypothalamus are just components of the brain's complex system for regulating hunger (Stricker & Verbalis, 1987). Other organs and substances in the body also play a role in our feelings of hunger and satiety.

The Role of the Stomach: Hunger Pangs

What are some of the body's hunger and satiety signals?

The fullness of the stomach affects our feeling of hunger. The stomach has a capacity of about 0.5 litres when empty and stretches to hold 1.2 litres when full (Avraham, 1989). Generally, the fuller or more distended the stomach, the less hunger we feel (Pappas et al., 1989).

How do you know when you are hungry? Does your stomach growl? Do you have stomach contractions, or "hunger pangs"? In a classic experiment, Cannon and Washburn (1912) demonstrated a close correlation between stomach contractions and the perception of hunger. But their discovery does not necessarily mean that the sensation of hunger is caused by stomach contractions. Additional research has confirmed that humans and other animals continue to experience hunger even when it is impossible for them to feel stomach contractions. Human cancer and ulcer patients who have had their entire stomachs removed still report that they feel hunger pangs (Janowitz & Grossman, 1950).

Other Hunger and Satiety Signals

Templeton and Quigley (1930) found that the blood of an animal that has eaten its fill is different from the blood of an excessively hungry animal. The difference was related to the blood levels of glucose—a simple sugar resulting from the digestion of carbohydrates. Glucose is highly associated with our perceptions of hunger. For instance, nutrient detectors in the liver constantly monitor blood levels of glucose and send this information to the brain (Friedman et al., 1986). Hunger is stimulated when the brain receives the message that blood glucose levels are low. Insulin, a hormone produced by the pancreas, chemically converts glucose into energy that is usable by the cells. Elevations in insulin cause an increase in hunger, in food intake, and in a desire for sweets (Rodin et al., 1985). Chronic oversecretion of insulin often leads to obesity.

Hunger is also influenced by some of the substances secreted by the gastrointestinal tract during digestion, which are released into the blood and act as satiety signals (Flood et al., 1990). The hormone cholecystokinin (CCK) is one satiety signal that causes people to limit the amount of food they eat during a meal (Bray, 1991).

We are pushed to eat not only by our hunger drive within. There are also external factors that stimulate hunger.

Other Factors Influencing Hunger: External Eating Cues

What are some non-biological factors that influence what and how much we eat?

Smell that coffee brewing. Look at that mouth-watering chocolate cake. Listen to the bacon sizzling in the morning. Apart from our internal hunger, there are external factors influencing what, where, and how much we eat. Sensory cues such as the taste, smell, and appearance of food stimulate the appetite. For many, the hands

Just the sight of mouth-watering foods can make us want to eat, even when we aren't actually hungry.

primary drive: A state of tension or arousal arising from a biological need; one not based on learning.

lateral hypothalamus (LH): The part of the hypothalamus that supposedly acts as a feeding centre and, when activated, signals an animal to eat; when the LH is destroyed, the animal refuses to eat.

ventromedial hypothalamus (VMH): The part of the hypothalamus that presumably acts as a satiety centre and, when activated, signals an animal to stop eating; when the area is destroyed, the animal overeats, becoming obese.

of the clock alone, signalling mealtime, are enough to prompt a quest for food. And when we eat with other people, we tend to eat more than when we are eating alone (de Castro & de Castro, 1989).

Susceptibility to External Eating Cues: Can You Resist Them?

Are we all equally susceptible to such external eating cues? Psychologist Judith Rodin (1981) has shown that our responsiveness to internal or external cues does not strongly correlate with the degree of overweight. But external cues *can* trigger internal processes that motivate a person to eat. The sight and smell of appetizing food can trigger the release of insulin, particularly in those who are externally responsive (Rodin et al., 1977). Even in rats, environmental cues previously associated with food cause an increase in insulin levels (Detke et al., 1989). For some individuals, "simply seeing and thinking about food" can cause an elevated level of insulin. Such people have a greater tendency to gain weight (Rodin, 1985).

The Palatability of Food: Tempting Tastes

How good a particular food tastes—that is, how palatable the food is—seems to work somewhat independently of hunger and satiety in determining how much we eat (Rogers, 1990); otherwise, most of us would refuse the pie after eating a big dinner.

Foods that are sweet and high in fat tend to stimulate the human appetite (Ball & Grinker, 1981), even when the sweetness is provided by artificial sweeteners (Blundell et al., 1988; Tordoff ,1988). Figure 9.3 summarizes the factors that stimulate and inhibit eating.

Understanding Body Weight: Why We Weigh What We Weigh

What are some factors that account for variations in body weight?

Pencil-thin models seen in television commercials and fashion magazines have come to represent the ideal body for many women. But most of these models have only 10 to 15 percent body fat, far below the 22 to 26 percent considered normal for women (Brownell, 1991). Fat has become a negative term, even though some body fat is necessary. Men need 3 percent and women 12 percent just for survival. And in order for a woman's reproductive system to function properly, she must maintain 20 percent body fat. Of course, there is a range of weight that is considered healthy and this range varies according to height, as illustrated in Figure 9.4.

Extremes in either fatness or thinness can pose health risks. An abnormal desire for thinness can result in eating disorders such as anorexia nervosa (self-starvation) and bulimia nervosa (a pattern of bingeing and purging). Read the *Apply It!* box later in this chapter for more details on eating disorders. At the other extreme are those Canadians—perhaps as many as one-third (Flegal, 1996)—who suffer from obesity, which increases the risk of high blood pressure, coronary heart disease, stroke, and cancer (Whelan & Stare, 1990). The term **obesity** means excessive fat-

FIGURE 9.3

Factors That Inhibit and Stimulate Eating **Both biological and environmental factors combine to inhibit or to stimulate eating.**

Factors That Inhibit Eating

Biological	Environmental
▪ Activity in ventromedial hypothalamus ▪ Raised blood glucose levels ▪ Distended (full) stomach ▪ CCK (hormone that acts as satiety signal) ▪ Sensory-specific satiety	▪ Smell, taste, and appearance of unappetizing food ▪ Acquired taste aversions ▪ Learned eating habits ▪ Desire for thinness ▪ Reaction to stress, unpleasant emotional state

Factors That Stimulate Eating

Biological	Environmental
▪ Activity in lateral hypothalamus ▪ Low blood levels of glucose ▪ Increase in insulin ▪ Stomach contractions ▪ Empty stomach	▪ Aroma of food ▪ Sight of appetizing food ▪ Taste of appetizing food ▪ Acquired food preferences ▪ Being around others who are eating ▪ Foods high in fat and sugar ▪ Learned eating habits ▪ Reaction to boredom, stress, unpleasant emotional states

ness and is applied to men whose body fat exceeds 20 percent of their weight and to women whose body fat exceeds 30 percent (Williams, 1986).

The Role of Genetic Factors in Body Weight

Studies of adopted children and twins reveal the strong influence of heredity on body size (Bouchard, 1997; de Castro, 1998). Genes are particularly likely to be involved when obesity begins before age 10 (Price et al., 1990). Across all weight classes, from very thin to very obese, children adopted at birth tend to resemble their biological parents more than their adoptive parents in body size (Price et al., 1987; Stunkard et al., 1990). Still, environmental characteristics and lifestyle make an even stronger contribution than the genes to overall body mass (Bouchard, 1997).

Researchers have discovered a gene in rats that leads to gross obesity when mutated—a gain of up to three times normal weight (Friedman & Ramirez, 1994). The normal gene may produce a protein that keeps weight under control. Could there be a similar gene in humans? Yes, say the researchers, who have also found a gene in humans that produces a protein very similar to the one produced by the rat gene. A mutation of this receptor gene can cause obesity as well as pituitary abnormalities (Clément et al., 1998).

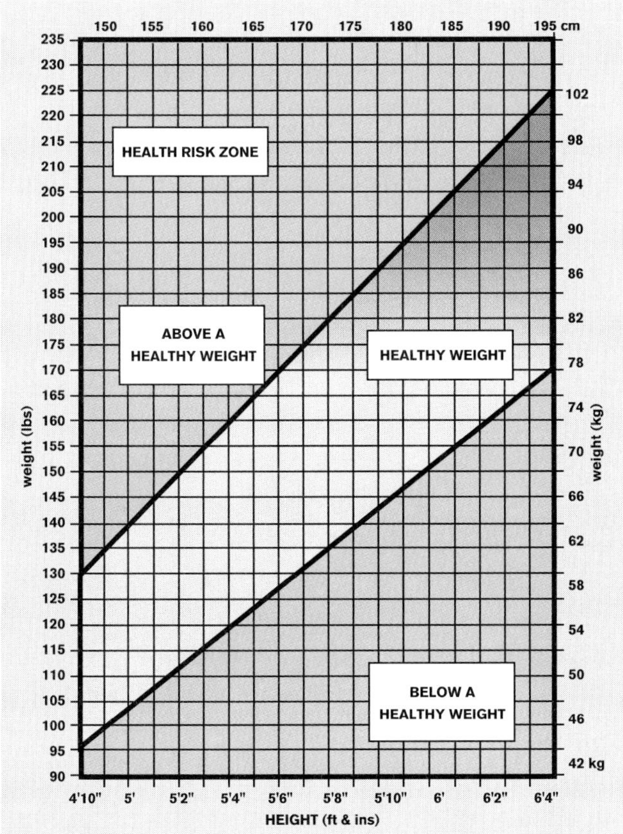

FIGURE 9.4

Healthy Weight by Height This comparison chart shows healthy and potentially unhealthy weight.

Metabolic Rate: Burning Energy—Slow or Fast

The term *metabolism* refers to all the physical and chemical processes that are carried out in the body to sustain life. Food provides the energy required to carry out these processes. The rate at which the body burns calories to produce energy is called the **metabolic rate**. Physical activity uses up only about one-third of our energy; the other two-thirds is consumed by the maintenance processes that keep us alive (Shah & Jeffery, 1991). When there is an imbalance between energy intake (how much we eat) and output (how much energy we use), our weight changes. If our calorie intake exceeds our daily energy requirement, we gain weight. If our daily energy requirement exceeds our caloric intake, we lose weight.

Fat-Cell Theory: Tiny Storage Tanks for Fat

Fat-cell theory proposes that fatness is related to the number of **fat cells** in the body. It is estimated that each of us has between 30 and 40 billion fat cells (adipose cells) and that the number is determined by both our genes and our eating habits (Bennett & Gurin, 1982; Grinker, 1982). Fat cells serve as storehouses for liquefied fat. When we lose weight, we do not lose the fat cells themselves. We lose the fat that is stored in them—the cells simply shrink (Dietz, 1989). Also, researchers now believe that when people overeat beyond the point at which the fat cells reach their capacity, the number of fat cells increases (Rodin & Wing, 1988).

obesity (o-BEE-sih-tee): Excessive fatness; a term applied to men whose body fat exceeds 20 percent of their weight and to women whose body fat exceeds 30 percent of their weight.

metabolic rate (meh-tuh-BALL-ik): The rate at which the body burns calories to produce energy.

fat cells: Numbering 30 to 40 billion, cells that serve as storehouses for liquefied fat in the body; with weight loss, they decrease in size but not in number.

Set-Point Theory: Thin/Fat Thermostat

How does set point affect body weight?

Set-point theory suggests that humans and other mammals are genetically programmed to carry a certain amount of body weight (Keesey, 1988). **Set point** is affected by the number of fat cells in the body and by metabolic rate, both of which are influenced by the genes (de Castro, 1993; Gurin, 1989).

According to set-point theory, an internal homeostatic system functions to maintain set-point weight, much as a thermostat works to keep temperature near the point at which it is set. Whether we are lean, overweight, or average, when our weight falls below our set point, our appetite increases. When our weight climbs above our set point, our appetite decreases so as to restore the original weight.

The theory also holds that our rate of energy expenditure adjusts to maintain the body's set-point weight (Keesey & Powley, 1986). When people gain weight, their metabolic rate increases (Dietz, 1989). When people restrict calories to lose weight, their metabolic rate *decreases*; this causes the body to burn fewer calories, which in turn makes further weight loss more difficult. Increasing the amount of physical activity is the one method recommended for lowering the set point so that the body will store less fat (Foreyt et al., 1996).

Social Motives

What is Murray's contribution to the study of motivation?

Do you have a strong need to be with other people (affiliation), or a need for power, or a need for achievement? These needs are three examples of **social motives**, which we learn or acquire through social and cultural experiences. Each of us differs in the strength of various social motives and in the priorities we assign to them. Our highest aspirations, the professions we choose, the partners we are drawn to, and the methods we use to achieve our sense of importance result primarily from our social motives.

In 1938 Henry Murray drew up a list of social motives or needs, which included the needs for achievement, recognition, affiliation, dominance, and order. Murray believed that people have social motives in varying degrees. To investigate the strength of those various needs, Murray (1938) developed the **Thematic Apperception Test (TAT)**, which consists of a series of pictures of ambiguous situations. People are asked to write a story about each picture—to describe what is going on in the picture, what the person or persons pictured are thinking about, what they may be feeling, and what is likely to be the outcome of the situation. The stories are presumed to reveal the individual's needs and the strength of those

Remember It!

The Primary Drives: Hunger and Thirst

1. Body cells lose water and become dehydrated when an individual
   a. perspires heavily.
   b. consumes too much salt.
   c. has diarrhea or vomiting.
   d. drinks too much alcohol.
2. The lateral hypothalamus (LH) acts as a (feeding/satiety) centre; the ventromedial hypothalamus (VMH) acts as a (feeding/satiety) centre.
3. All of the following are hunger signals *except*
   a. activity in the lateral hypothalamus.
   b. low levels of glucose in the blood.
   c. the hormone CCK.
   d. high insulin level.
4. Foods that are sweet and high in fat tend to stimulate the appetite. (true/false)
5. Which factor is most responsible for how fast your body burns calories to produce energy?
   a. set point
   b. fat cells
   c. eating habits
   d. metabolic rate
6. According to set-point theory, the body works to (increase/decrease/maintain) body weight.
7. Fat cells never decrease in number. (true/false)
8. Increased exercise during dieting is important to counteract the body's tendency to
   a. increase the fat in the fat cells.
   b. increase the number of fat cells.
   c. lower its metabolic rate.
   d. raise its metabolic rate.

Answers: 1. b 2. feeding, satiety 3. c 4. true 5. d 6. maintain 7. true 8. c

needs. The TAT has also been used as a more general personality test.

Complete *Try It!*, which describes a game that is said to reveal high or low achievement motivation.

The Need for Achievement: The Drive to Excel

What is the need for achievement?

Both men and women are driven by social motives. Among these is the **need for achievement**, defined by Murray (1938) as the need "to accomplish something difficult.... To overcome obstacles and attain a high standard. To excel one's self" (p. 164). This need has been researched vigorously. Unfortunately, the participants in these studies have been almost exclusively male (McClelland, 1958, 1961, 1985).

Atkinson's Theory of Achievement Motivation: When Do We Try?

Atkinson (1964) suggests that when we approach any situation, two conflicting factors are operating—our hope for success and our fear of failure. Motivation to avoid failure can cause us to work harder at a task to try to ensure success, or it can cause us to avoid the task altogether.

Whether you strive for a goal depends on three factors: (1) the strength of your need to achieve, (2) your expectation of success, and (3) the incentive value of success or failure at a particular activity—that is, how much you value success in the activity and how distressed you would be if you failed at it (Wigfield & Eccles, 2000). For example, whether you try to achieve an A in psychology will depend on how important an A is to you, on whether you believe an A is possible, and on how much pride you will feel in getting an A as opposed to how upset you will be if you do not.

People with a high need for achievement can overcome even serious disabilities in their efforts to succeed.

Try It!

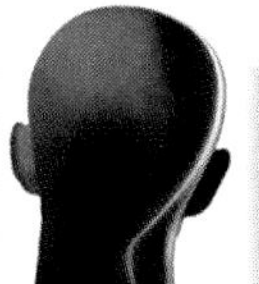

Test Your Need for Achievement

Imagine yourself involved in a ring-toss game. You have three rings to toss at any of the six pegs pictured here. You will be paid a few pennies each time you are able to ring a peg.

Which peg would you try to ring with your three tosses—peg 1 or 2 nearest you, peg 3 or 4 at a moderate distance, or peg 5 or 6 at the far end of the room?

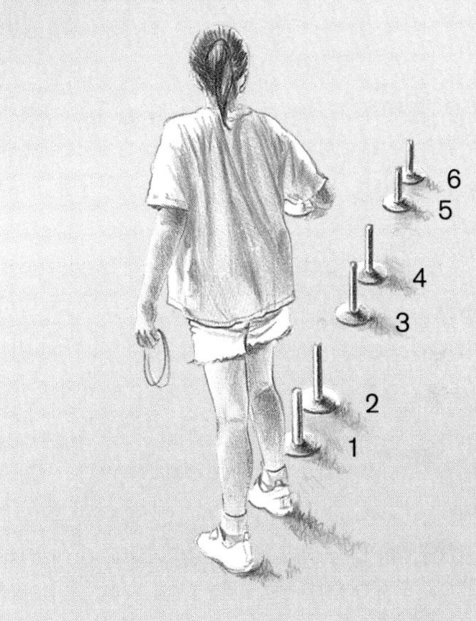

set point: The weight the body normally maintains when one is trying neither to gain nor to lose weight (if weight falls below the normal level, appetite increases and metabolic rate decreases; if weight is gained, appetite decreases and metabolic rate increases so that the original rate is restored).

social motives: Motives acquired through experience and interaction with others (examples: need for achievement, need for affiliation).

Thematic Apperception Test (TAT): A projective test consisting of drawings of ambiguous human situations, which the subject describes; thought to reveal inner feelings, conflicts, and motives.

need for achievement: The need to accomplish something difficult and to perform at a high standard of excellence.

Characteristics of Achievers: Successful People Have Them

What are some characteristics shared by people who are high in achievement motivation?

McClelland and colleagues (1953) found that high achievers differ from low achievers in several ways. People with a high achievement motivation tend to set goals of moderate difficulty. They pursue goals that are challenging yet attainable with hard work, ability, determination, and persistence. Goals that are too easy—that anyone can reach—offer no challenge and hold no interest, because success would not be rewarding (McClelland, 1985). Impossibly high goals and high risks are also not pursued, because they offer little chance of success and are considered a waste of time.

People with a low need for achievement are not willing to take chances when it comes to testing their own skills and abilities. They are motivated more by their fear of failure than by their hope and expectation of success. This is why they set either ridiculously low goals, which anyone can attain, or else impossibly high goals (Geen, 1984). After all, who can fault a person for failing to reach a goal that is impossible for almost anyone?

In view of this description, which peg in the ring toss game in *Try It!* would people low in achievement motivation try for? If you guessed peg 1 or 2, or peg 5 or 6, you are right. People low in achievement motivation are likely to stand right over peg 1 so they can't possibly fail. Or they may toss the rings at peg 6, hoping they might get lucky. People with a high need for achievement tend to toss their rings at peg 3 or 4, an intermediate distance that offers some challenge. Which peg did you aim for?

People with high achievement motivation see their success as a result of their own talents, abilities, persistence, and hard work (Kukla, 1972). They typically do not credit luck or the influence of other people for their successes; nor do they blame luck or other people for their failures. When individuals with low achievement motivation fail, they usually give up quickly and attribute their failure to lack of ability. They also believe that luck or fate, rather than effort, is responsible for accomplishment (Weiner, 1972, 1974).

Developing Achievement Motivation: Can We Learn It?

If achievement motivation, like the other social motives, is primarily learned, *how* is it learned? Some experts believe that child-rearing practices and values in the home are important factors in developing achievement motivation (McClelland, 1985; McClelland & Pilon, 1983). Parents may be more likely to have children with high achievement motivation if they give their children responsibilities, stress independence when the children are young, and praise them sincerely for genuine accomplishments (Ginsburg & Bornstein, 1993; Gottfried et al., 1994). Birth order appears to be related to achievement motivation; first-born and only children show a higher

Remember It!

Social Motivation

1. Social motives are, for the most part, unlearned. (true/false)
2. According to Atkinson's theory of achievement motivation, which of the following is *not* a major factor in determining whether an individual approaches a goal?
   a. the strength of the individual's need to achieve
   b. the person's expectation of success
   c. how much pride the person has in achieving the goal as opposed to how upsetting failure would be
   d. the financial reward attached to the goal
3. Which of these statements is *not* true of people high in achievement motivation?
   a. They set very high goals for which success will be extremely difficult to obtain.
   b. They set goals of moderate difficulty.
   c. They attribute their success to their talents, abilities, and hard work.
   d. They are likely to choose careers as entrepreneurs.

Answers: 1. false 2. d 3. a

need for achievement than younger siblings (Falbo & Polit, 1986). Younger siblings, however, tend to be more sociable and likable than first-born or only children, and this has its rewards too.

The What and Why of Emotions

Motivation and Emotion: What Is the Connection?

Motivation does not occur in a vacuum. Much of our motivation to act is fuelled by our emotional state. In fact, the root of the word **emotion** means "to move," indicating the close relationship between motivation and emotion. When we observe the emotion of sadness in another, we often feel empathy, and this may motivate us to acts of altruism (helping behaviour). Fear motivates us either to flee (to escape danger) or to perform protective behaviours that provide security and safety (Izard, 1992). Emotions prepare and motivate us to respond adaptively to a variety of situations in life. They enable us to communicate our feelings and intentions more effectively than we could with words alone; thus, they make it more likely that others will respond to us. But what, precisely, are emotions?

The Components of Emotions: The Physical, the Cognitive, and the Behavioural

What are the three components of emotions?

What are emotions—nothing more than feelings? Is that what emotions are? We say that we feel lonely or sad, happy or content, or angry, embarrassed, or afraid. Most people describe emotions in terms of feeling states; psychologists, however, study emotions according to their three components—physical, cognitive, and behavioural.

The *physical* component is the physiological arousal (the internal body state) that accompanies the emotion. Without the physiological arousal, we would not feel the emotion in all its intensity. The surge of powerful feeling we know as emotion is due largely to the physiological arousal we experience.

The *cognitive* component, the way we perceive or interpret a stimulus or situation, determines the

IT HAPPENED IN CANADA

Canadians' Outpouring of Emotions

Canadians often perceive themselves to be well in control of their emotions. It is part of the traditional norms of many Canadians to act calmly and rationally when faced with sad or potentially upsetting events. Our reserved nature is especially pronounced when we are in the presence of others. But some events are out of the ordinary and, since the beginning of the year 2000, a few such events have definitely touched many of us.

In the spring of 2000, Maurice "le Rocket" Richard passed away. Richard was a well-loved and admired hockey legend who broke many records during his playing days with the Montreal Canadiens in the 1940s and 1950s. Following the announcement of his death, over 110 000 people came forward to mourn. Crowds overflowed the Notre-Dame Basilica in Montreal, with more than 2000 people lining the street in front of the church. Several times during the funeral service, many of the 2700 mourners dissolved into tears. For days after his death, the media reviewed the life and achievements of one of Canada's most respected hockey greats (Bird, 2000).

Near the end of the summer, Canadians were informed of another sad event of national proportion. Pierre Elliot Trudeau, who many believed to be Canada's most influential prime minister, died after a prolonged illness. Tens of thousands of Canadians visited Parliament Hill and waited as long as four hours to pay their respects. Thousands sent flowers; many wrote highly personal comments to thank Mr. Trudeau for his vision and the impact he had on their lives (McKinnon, 2000). Trudeau's death clearly struck a chord with many Canadians. Conversations in restaurants, at work, and on the radio and television were filled with anecdotes and stories about how Mr. Trudeau's spirit affected Canadians personally and changed the country as a whole (Winsor, 2000).

In both these stories, the outpouring of emotions was likely beneficial to all those who were touched by the lives of Mr. Richard and Mr. Trudeau. It is perhaps time to reconsider our perceptions of Canadians as reserved and generally unemotional, as touching events will clearly affect us all.

emotion: A feeling state involving physiological arousal, a cognitive appraisal of the situation arousing the state, and an outward expression of the state.

TABLE 9.2
The Components of Emotions

Physical Component	Cognitive Component	Behavioural Component
Physiological arousal (internal bodily state accompanying the emotion).	The way we interpret a stimulus or situation.	Outward expression of the emotion (facial expressions, gestures, body posture, tone of voice).

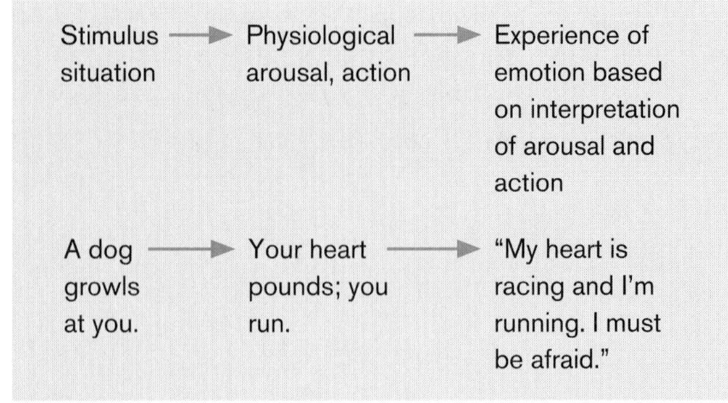

FIGURE 9.5
The James-Lange Theory of Emotion The James-Lange theory of emotion is the exact opposite of what our subjective experience tells us. If an angry dog growls at you, the James-Lange interpretation is this: The dog growls, your heart begins to pound, and only by observing that your heart is pounding do you conclude that you must be afraid.

specific emotion we feel. If you are home alone and the wind is banging a tree limb on your roof, you may become fearful if you perceive the knocking and the banging as a burglar trying to break into your house. An emotional response to an imaginary threat is every bit as powerful as a response to a real threat. Perceptions make it so. Have you ever worked yourself into a frenzy before a first date, a job interview, or an oral presentation for one of your classes? Then your thinking was contributing to your emotional state.

The *behavioural* component of emotions is the outward expression of the emotions. Our facial expressions, gestures, body posture, and tone of voice stem from and convey the emotions we are feeling within. Some of the facial expressions that accompany emotion are innate and are the same across cultures. But some of our emotional expressions are more influenced by our culture and its rules for displaying emotion. Table 9.2 summarizes the components of emotions.

Theories of Emotion: Which Comes First, the Thought or the Feeling?

There is no doubt that we react to certain experiences with emotion. For example, if you think you are making a fool of yourself in front of your friends, the emotion you feel is embarrassment, which triggers a physiological response that may cause you to blush. This type of reaction seems logical—it seems to fit our everyday experience. But is this sequence of events the course that an emotional experience really follows?

LINK IT!

emotion.salk.edu/emotion.html
Emotion Home Page

The James-Lange Theory

According to the James-Lange theory, what sequence of events occurs when we experience an emotion?

William James (1884) argued that the sequence of events in an emotional experience is exactly the reverse of what our subjective experience tells us. James believed that first an event causes physiological arousal and a physical response. Only then do we perceive or interpret the physical response as an emotion. In other words, saying something stupid causes us to blush, and we interpret our physical response, the blush, as an emotion, embarrassment. James (1890) went on to suggest that "we feel sorry *because* we cry, angry *because* we strike, afraid *because* we tremble" (p. 1066).

At about the same time that James proposed his theory, a Danish physiologist and psychologist, Carl Lange, independently formulated nearly the same theory. Hence, we have the **James-Lange theory** of emotion (Lange & James, 1922). The theory suggests that different patterns of arousal in the autonomic nervous system produce the different emotions we feel, and that the physiological arousal appears before the emotion is perceived. See Figure 9.5.

If the physical arousal itself were the sole cause of what we know as emotion, however, there would have to be a distinctly different set of physical changes associated with each emotion. Otherwise we wouldn't know whether we were sad, embarrassed, frightened, or happy.

The Cannon-Bard Theory

What is the Cannon-Bard theory of emotion?

An early theory of emotion that challenged the James-Lange theory was proposed by Walter Cannon (1927), who claimed that the bodily changes caused by the various emotions are not sufficiently distinct to allow people to distinguish one emotion from another.

Physiologist Philip Bard (1934) later expanded Cannon's original theory. The **Cannon-Bard theory** suggests that the following chain of events occurs when we feel an emotion: Emotion-provoking stimuli are received by the senses and are then relayed simultaneously to the cerebral cortex, which provides the conscious mental experience of the emotion, and the sympathetic nervous system, which produced the physiological state of arousal. In other words, your feeling of emotion (e.g., fear) occurs at about the same time that you experience physiological arousal (e.g., pounding heart). One does not cause the other.

The Schachter-Singer Theory

According to the Schachter- Singer theory, what two things must occur in order for us to experience an emotion?

Stanley Schachter looked at these early theories of emotion and concluded that they left out a critical component—our own cognitive interpretation of why we become aroused. Schachter and Singer (1962) proposed a two-factor theory. According to the **Schachter-Singer theory**, two things must happen for a person to feel an emotion: (1) The person must first experience physiological arousal. (2) Then there must be a cognitive interpretation or explanation of the physiological arousal so that the person can label it as a specific emotion. Thus, according to this theory, a true emotion can occur only if we are physically aroused and can find some reason for it. However, attempts to replicate the findings of Schachter and Singer have been largely disappointing (Marshall & Zimbardo, 1979).

The Lazarus Cognitive-Appraisal Theory

According to Lazarus, what sequence of events occurs when an individual feels an emotion?

Richard Lazarus (1991a, 1991b, 1995) has proposed a theory of emotion that most heavily emphasizes cognition. According to the **Lazarus theory** of emotion, a cognitive appraisal is the first step in an emotional response, and all other aspects of an emotion, including physiological arousal, depend on the cognitive appraisal. Contrary to what Schachter and Singer proposed, Lazarus believes that when faced with a stimulus or event, a person first appraises it. This cognitive appraisal determines whether the person will have an emotional response and, if so, what type of response it should be. The physiological arousal and all other aspects of the emotion flow from the appraisal. In short, Lazarus contends that emotions are provoked when cognitive appraisals of events are positive or negative—but not neutral.

Critics of the Lazarus theory point out that some emotional reactions are instantaneous—occurring too rapidly to pass through cognitive appraisal (Zajonc, 1980, 1984, 1998). Lazarus (1991b) responds that some mental processing occurs without conscious awareness, and that there must be some form of cognitive realization, however brief, or else a person would not know what he or she is supposed to feel. This issue is still hotly debated among experts. What do you think? Do emotions or cognitions come first?

Review & Reflect 9.2 summarizes the four major theories of emotion: James-Lange, Cannon-Bard, Schachter-Singer, and Lazarus.

James-Lange theory: The theory that emotional feelings result when we become aware of our physiological response to an emotion-provoking stimulus (in other words, we are afraid because we tremble).

Cannon-Bard theory: The theory that physiological arousal and the feeling of emotion occur simultaneously after an emotion-provoking stimulus is relayed to the thalamus.

Schachter-Singer theory: A two-stage theory stating that for an emotion to occur, there must be (1) physiological arousal and (2) an explanation for the arousal.

Lazarus theory: The theory that an emotion-provoking stimulus triggers a cognitive appraisal, which is followed by the emotion and the physiological arousal.

The Expression of Emotion

Expressing emotions comes as naturally to humans as breathing. No one has to be taught how to smile or frown, or how to express fear, sadness, surprise, or disgust. Only actors practise making the facial expressions to convey various emotions. And the facial expressions of the basic emotions are much the same across human cultures all over the world.

The Range of Emotion: How Wide Is It?

What are basic emotions?

How many emotions are there? The number of emotions people list depends on their culture, the language they speak, and other factors. Two leading researchers in the field, Paul Ekman (1993) and Carroll Izard (1992), insist that there are a limited number of basic emotions. **Basic emotions** are unlearned and universal—that is, they are found in all cultures, are reflected in the same

REVIEW & REFLECT 9.2
Theories of Emotion

Theory	View	Example
James-Lange Theory	An event causes physiological arousal. We experience an emotion only after we interpret the physical response.	You are walking home late at night and hear footsteps behind you. Your heart pounds and you begin to tremble. You interpret these physical responses as fear.
Cannon-Bard Theory	An event causes a physiological *and* an emotional response simultaneously. One does not cause the other.	You are walking home late at night and hear footsteps behind you. Your heart pounds, you begin to tremble, *and* you feel afraid.
Schachter-Singer Theory	An event causes physiological arousal. We must then be able to identify a reason for the arousal in order to label the emotion.	You are walking home late at night and hear footsteps behind you. Your heart pounds and you begin to tremble. You know that walking alone at night can be dangerous, and so you feel afraid.
Lazarus Theory	An event occurs, a cognitive appraisal is made, and then the emotion and physiological arousal follow.	You are walking home late at night and hear footsteps behind you. You think it could be a mugger. So you feel afraid, and your heart starts to pound and you begin to tremble.

Remember It!

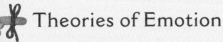

Theories of Emotion

1. According to the text, emotions have all of the following *except* a ________ component.
   a. physical
   b. cognitive
   c. sensory
   d. behavioural
2. Which theory of emotion holds that we feel a true emotion only when we become physically aroused and can identify some cause for the arousal?
   a. Schachter-Singer theory
   b. James-Lange theory
   c. Cannon-Bard theory
   d. Lazarus theory
3. Which theory of emotion suggests that we feel fearful *because* we were shaking?
   a. Schachter-Singer theory
   b. James-Lange theory
   c. Cannon-Bard theory
   d. Lazarus theory
4. Which theory suggests that our feeling of an emotion and our physiological response to an emotional situation occur at about the same time?
   a. Schachter-Singer theory
   b. James-Lange theory
   c. Cannon-Bard theory
   d. Lazarus theory

Answers: 1. c 2. a 3. b 4. c

facial expressions, and emerge in children according to their own biological timetable of development. Fear, anger, disgust, surprise, joy or happiness, and sadness or distress are usually considered basic emotions. Izard (1992, 1993) suggests that there are distinct neural circuits that underlie each of the basic emotions; and Levenson and colleagues (1990) point to specific autonomic nervous system activity associated with the basic emotions. Panksepp (1992; Panksepp et al. 1998) believes there is strong evidence that emotional systems in the brain underlie at least these: rage, fear, expectancy, and panic. Not all researchers, however, subscribe to the notion of basic emotions (Turner & Ortony, 1992).

Ekman (1993, 1999) suggests that we consider studying emotions as families. Clearly there are gradients, or degrees, of intensity within a single emotion. For example, people experience fear in various degrees, from mild uneasiness to outright terror. Anger as a "family" could range from annoyance to irritation to rage. It could also include resentment, outrage, and vengefulness.

Obviously, the facial expression for annoyance is quite different from the facial expression for rage. But can you imagine 60 different facial expressions for the different types and intensities of anger? Ekman and Friesen identified 60 anger expressions; each was different from the others but all shared the basic properties of the face of anger (Ekman, 1993). Just as there are many words in our vocabulary to describe the variations in any emotion, there are subtle distinctions in the facial expression of a single emotion that convey its intensity.

How do we learn to express our emotions? Or *do* we learn? There is considerable evidence that the basic emotions (fear, anger, sadness, happiness, disgust, and surprise), or the facial expressions we make when we feel them, are biologically rather than culturally determined.

The Development of Facial Expressions in Infants: Smiles and Frowns Come Naturally

How does the development of facial expressions of different emotions in infants suggest a biological basis for emotional expression?

According to the biological timetable of maturation (Greenberg, 1977), facial expressions of emotions develop naturally, just as do the motor skills of crawling and walking. By three months, babies can express happiness and sadness (Lewis, 1995), and laughter appears somewhere around three and a half to four months (Provine, 1996). Between the ages of four and six months, the emotions of anger and surprise appear, and by about seven months, infants show fear. The self-conscious emotions do not emerge until later. Between 18 months and three years, children begin to show first empathy, envy, and embarrassment, followed by shame, guilt, and pride (Lewis, 1995).

Another strong indication that the facial expressions of emotion are biologically determined, rather than learned, comes from studies done on children who were blind and deaf from birth. Their smiles and frowns, their laughter and crying, and their facial expressions of anger, surprise, and pouting were the same as those of children who could hear and see (Eibl-Eibesfeldt, 1973).

Although recent studies have contributed much to our understanding of facial expressions, the biological connection between emotions and facial expressions was proposed many years ago, as described in the next *World of Psychology* box.

Cultural Rules for Displaying Emotion

While the facial expressions of the basic emotions are much the same in cultures around the world, cultures can have very different **display rules**—cultural rules that dictate how emotions should generally be expressed and where and when their expression is appropriate (Ekman, 1993; Ekman & Friesen, 1975; Scherer & Wallbott, 1994). Society often expects us to give evidence of certain emotions that we may not actually feel. We are expected to be sad at funerals, to hide our disappointment when we lose, and to refrain from showing disgust if the food we are served tastes bad to us. In one study, Cole (1986) found that three-year-old girls, when given an unattractive gift, smile nevertheless. They have learned the display

basic emotions: Emotions that are found in all cultures, that are reflected in the same facial expressions across cultures, and that emerge in children according to their biological timetable (e.g., anger, disgust, happiness, sadness, distress).

display rules: Cultural rules that dictate how emotions should be expressed, and when and where their expression is appropriate.

WORLD OF PSYCHOLOGY

Facial Expressions for the Basic Emotions: A Universal Language

The relationship between emotions and facial expressions was first studied by Charles Darwin (1872, 1965). He believed that the facial expression of emotion was an aid to survival in that it enabled people, before they developed language, to communicate their internal states and react to emergencies. Darwin maintained that most of the emotions we feel and the facial expressions that convey them are genetically inherited and characteristic of the entire human species. To test his belief, he asked missionaries and people of different cultures around the world to record the facial expressions that accompany the basic emotions. On the basis of those data, he concluded that facial expressions were similar across cultures.

In some cases, modern research supports Darwin's view that facial expressions are universal (Ekman & Friesen, 1971). More recent research, however, suggests that cultural differences do exist.

Ekman and Friesen showed photographs portraying facial expressions of the primary emotions—sadness, surprise, happiness, anger, fear, and disgust—to members of the Fore tribe in a remote area in New Guinea. The Fore people were able to identify the emotional expressions of happiness, sadness, anger, and disgust; however, they had difficulty distinguishing fear and surprise.

Ekman then had the tribespeople make faces to reflect the same emotional expressions, and he videotaped them. The tapes were shown to students in the United States, who could readily identify the emotions portrayed except for the same two expressions that had posed a problem for the Fore—surprise and fear.

Recent studies by James Russell (1993, 1994) at the University of British Columbia suggest that for some facial expressions, recognition varies between cultures. For example, the facial expressions that Canadian participants recognized as fear were perceived as surprise by Japanese participants, although most participants agreed on which faces were happy. Russell argues that the differences in some of the "primary" emotions show that culture may affect how we interpret facial expressions; this conflicts with Darwin's idea that facial expressions are a genetic trait shared by all humans.

Do Ekman's test in *Try It!* and see if you can identify the faces of emotion.

rules and signal an emotion that they very likely do not feel. Davis (1995) found that among first to third graders, girls were better able to hide disappointment than were boys. Gender differences in display rules have been reported with some consistency in a variety of contexts (Brody, 2000).

Different cultures, neighbourhoods, and even families may have very different display rules. Display rules in Japanese culture dictate that negative emotions must be disguised when others are present (Ekman, 1972; Triandis, 1994). In many Western societies, women are expected to smile often, whether they feel happy or not. And in East Africa, young males from traditional Masai society are expected to appear stern and stony-faced and to "produce long, unbroken stares" (Keating, 1994). It appears that much of our communication of emotion is not authentic, not truly felt.

Most of us learn display rules very early and abide by them most of the time. Yet we may not be fully aware that the rules we have learned dictate where, when, how, and even how long certain emotions should be expressed.

Emotion as a Form of Communication

Why is emotion considered a form of communication?

Emotions enable us to communicate our feelings, intentions, and needs more effectively than just words alone; thus they make it more likely that others will respond to us. And researchers maintain that not only are we biologically wired to convey certain emotion signals, but we are biologically predisposed to read and interpret them as well (Dimberg, 1990; Oatley & Jenkins, 1992).

By communicating emotions, we motivate others to act. When we communicate sadness or distress, people close to us are likely to be sympathetic and to try to help us. By expressing emotions, infants com-

Try It!

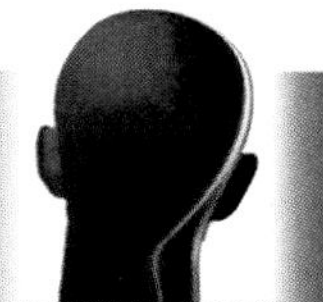

Identifying Facial Expression of Emotion

Look carefully at the six photographs. Which basic emotion is portrayed in each?

Match the number of the photograph with the basic emotion it portrays:

a. happiness c. fear e. surprise

b. sadness d. anger f. disgust

1. ________

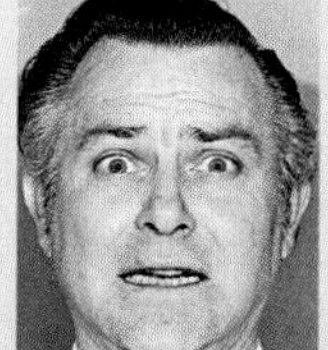

2. ________

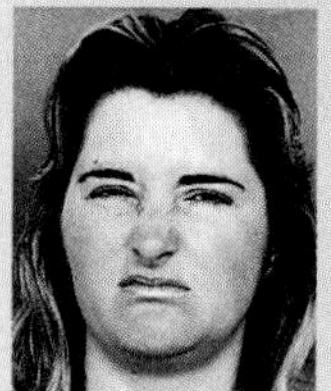

3. ________

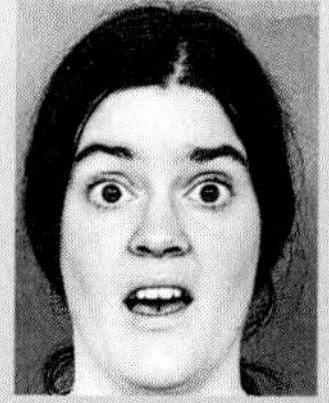

4. ________

5. ________

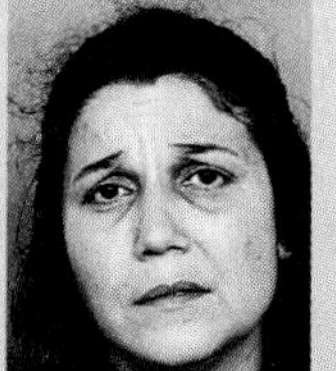

6. ________

Answers: 1.d 2.c 3.f 4.e 5.a 6.b

municate their feelings and needs before they can speak. In an early study, Katherine Bridges (1932) observed emotional expression in Canadian infants over a period of months. She reported that the first emotional expression to appear is that of distress, which occurs at three weeks. In terms of survival, the expression of distress enables helpless newborns to get the attention of their caretakers so that their needs can be met.

Do you feel happier when you are around others who are happy? You may already know that emotions are contagious. Infants will usually begin to cry when they hear another infant cry. Your own emotional expressions can infect others with the same emotion.

The stern faces of these two young Masai warriors from Kenya reflect their culture's display rules banning the public expression of emotion.

Parents seem to know this intuitively when they display happy expressions to infect their babies with happy moods (Keating, 1994). Researchers have found that mothers in many cultures—Trobriand Island, Yanomamo, Greek, German, and Japanese—attempt to regulate the moods of their babies through facial communication of emotions (Kanaya et al., 1989; Keller et al., 1988; Termine & Izard, 1988).

From as early as our first year of life, we perceive the emotions of others and use this information to guide our own behaviour (Sternberg & Hagekull, 1997). Infants pay close attention to the facial expressions of others, especially their mother. And when they are confronted with an ambiguous situation, they use the mother's emotion as a guide to whether they should approach or avoid the situation. This phenomenon is known as *social referencing* (Klinnert et al., 1983).

In fact, by adulthood, we become very sensitive to even subtle cues. For example, Gosselin and colleagues (1995, 1997), at the University of Ottawa, demonstrated that adults can often tell the difference between actors just acting an emotion and actors truly experiencing an emotion.

LINK IT!

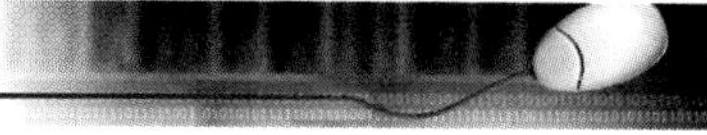

www.hc.t.u-tokyo.ac.jp/~jikken/index-e.html
Home Page of the Facial Image Processing World

mambo.ucsc.edu/psl/fanl.html
Facial Analysis Resources

Remember It!

Expressing Emotion

1. All of the following are true of the basic emotions *except* that
   a. they are reflected in distinctive facial expressions.
   b. they are found in all cultures.
   c. there are several hundred known to date.
   d. they are unlearned.
2. Which of the following is *not* one of the emotions represented by a distinctive facial expression?
   a. happiness
   b. hostility
   c. surprise
   d. sadness
3. Facial expressions associated with the basic emotions develop naturally according to a child's own biological timetable of maturation. (true/false)
4. All of the following are true of display rules *except* that they
   a. are the same in all cultures.
   b. dictate when and where emotions should be expressed.
   c. dictate what emotions should not be expressed.
   d. often cause people to display emotions they do not feel.
5. Which of the following statements is *not* true about emotion as a form of communication?
   a. Emotions communicate our feelings better than just words alone.
   b. Emotions communicate our intentions.
   c. Emotions are often contagious.
   d. Infants under one year of age are unable to use the emotions of others to guide their behaviour.

Answers: 1. c 2. b 3. true 4. a 5. d

Experiencing Emotion

How are expressions of emotion related to our experience of emotion? Some researchers go so far as to suggest that the facial expression alone can actually produce the experience.

The Facial-Feedback Hypothesis: Does the Face Cause the Feeling?

What is the facial-feedback hypothesis?

Sylvan Tomkins (1962, 1963) suggested that facial expressions of the basic emotions are genetically programmed. But he went a step further: he asserted that the facial expression itself—that is, the movement of the facial muscles producing the expression—triggers both the physiological arousal and the conscious feeling associated with the emotion. The notion that the muscular movements involved in certain facial expressions produce the corresponding emotion is called the **facial-feedback hypothesis** (Izard, 1971, 1977, 1990; Strack et al., 1988).

In an extensive review of research on the facial-feedback hypothesis, Adelmann and Zajonc (1989) found impressive evidence to support an association between facial expression and the subjective experience of the emotion. In addition, they found considerable support for the notion that simply the act of making the facial expression can initiate the subjective feeling of the emotion.

The Simulation of Facial Expressions: Put On a Happy Face

Over 125 years ago, Darwin (1872, 1965) wrote, "Even the simulation of an emotion tends to arouse it in our minds" (p. 365). Ekman and colleagues (1983) put this notion to the test using 16 participants (12 professional actors and 4 scientists). They were guided to contract specific muscles in the face so that they could assume the facial expressions of six basic emotions—surprise, disgust, sadness, anger, fear, and happiness. However, they were never actually told to smile, frown, or put on an angry face.

They were hooked up to electronic instruments, which monitored changes in heart rate, skin response (to measure perspiring), muscle tension, and hand temperature. Measurements were taken as they made each facial expression. While hooked up to the devices, the participants were also asked to imagine or relive six actual experiences in which they had felt each of the six emotions.

Ekman reported that a distinctive physiological response pattern emerged for the emotions of fear, sadness, anger, and disgust, whether the participants relived one of their emotional experiences or simply made only the corresponding facial expression. In fact, in some cases the physiological measures of emotion were greater when the actors and scientists made the facial expression than when they imagined an actual emotional experience (Ekman et al., 1983). The researchers found that both anger and fear accelerate heart rate, and fear produces colder fingers than does anger.

Do you think that making particular facial expressions will affect your emotions? A simple experiment you can try alone or with friends or classmates is described in the next *Try It!* When you hold a pencil between your teeth, you activate the facial muscles used to express happiness. When you hold it between your lips, you activate the muscles involved in the expression of anger.

Try It!

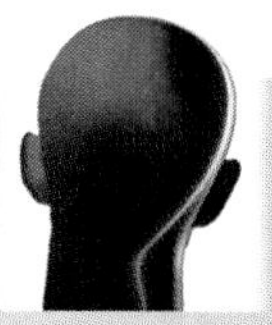

Do Facial Expressions Affect Emotions?

Hold a pencil between your lips with your mouth closed, as shown in the left-hand drawing, for about 15 seconds. Pay attention to your feelings. Now hold the pencil between your teeth, letting your teeth show, as shown in the right-hand drawing, for about 15 seconds.

Did you have more pleasant feelings with the pencil between your lips or your teeth? Why? (Adapted from Strack et al.. 1988.)

Controlling Our Facial Expressions to Regulate Our Feelings

If facial expressions can activate emotions, is it possible that intensifying or weakening a facial expression can intensify or weaken the corresponding state of feeling?

Izard (1990) believes that by learning to regulate our own emotional expressions, we may be able to gain control over our emotions. We may learn to change the intensity of an emotion by inhibiting or amplifying its expression, or change the emotion by simulating another emotion. Izard proposes that this might be a useful adjunct to psychotherapy.

Regulating or modifying an emotion by simulating an expression of its opposite may be effective if the emotion is not unusually intense. What is it about intense emotional states that makes them so difficult to control or regulate?

Emotion and Rational Thinking

Have you ever been so "swept away" by emotion that your ability to reason deserted you and you did something you later regretted? Could there be a negative correlation between emotional intensity and objective, rational thinking? The proposition has been posed this way: as emotion intensifies, rational thinking decreases (Brandt-Williams, personal communication, 1994).

Intense emotional states are frequently described in phrases that suggest these states are devoid of rational thinking—"insanely jealous," "blinded by love," "frozen with fright," "consumed by passion," "burning with envy." Can you think of examples that would suggest that rational thinking lessens as emotional states intensify?

Some dramatic examples of how extreme emotional states can diminish rational thinking and result in tragedy are major depression resulting in suicide, and rage resulting in spousal abuse, child abuse, or murder. Do the next *Try It!* to find other emotion-causing events that could affect rational thinking.

Emotional experience is a central part of human existence. But do we all, male and female alike, expe-

facial-feedback hypothesis: The idea that the muscular movements involved in certain facial expressions trigger the corresponding emotions (for example, smiling makes us happy).

Try It!

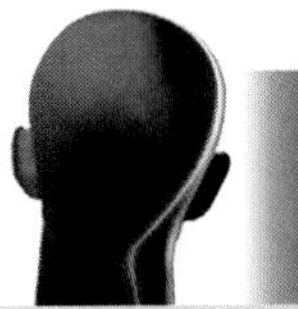

Events That Cause Extreme Emotion

List as many news events as you can that seem to support the notion that when people are consumed by emotion, rational thinking can decrease or disappear, with disastrous consequences.

Event	Extreme Emotion
________________	________________
________________	________________
________________	________________
________________	________________

rience our emotions in identical ways? The *World of Psychology* box addresses this question.

Love: The Strongest Emotional Bond

The emotion of love comes in many varieties. And although we often use the term rather loosely or casually—"I love ice cream," "I love to dance"—it is usually experienced as a deep and abiding affection. We feel love for our parents, for our sisters and brothers, for our children, and ideally for our friends and neighbours and other humans. There is also love of country and love of learning. There seems to be a virtually endless list of people, things, and situations that may produce in humans the emotion of love.

The variety of love most written about by poets, most set to music by composers, and most longed for by virtually all of us is—romantic love.

But the first question to ask is, How many components are there to this thing we call love?

WORLD OF PSYCHOLOGY

Gender Differences in the Experience of Emotion

Do females and males differ significantly in how they experience their emotions? Do women tend to be more intensely emotional than men? Some research suggests that the answer to both questions may be yes (Brody, 2000).

What emotion would you feel first if you were betrayed or criticized harshly by another person? When asked to respond to this hypothetical situation, males were more likely to report they would feel angry, and females were more likely to say they would feel hurt, sad, or disappointed (Brody, 1985).

But the most puzzling gender difference found in emotional experience is the following: In surveys of happiness, women report greater happiness and life satisfaction (Wood et al., 1989); but they also report more sadness, are twice as likely to report being depressed, and admit to greater fear (Scherer et al., 1986). How can women be both happier and sadder than men? Another gender difference may explain it: researchers have found sex differences in the intensity of emotional response. Grossman and Wood (1993) tested males and females for intensity of emotional response on five basic emotions–joy, love, fear, sadness, and anger. They found that "women reported more intense and more frequent emotions than men did, with the exception of anger" (p. 1013).

More joy, more sadness, more fear, more love! But these were self-reports. How do we know that the women actually *felt* four of the five emotions more intensely than the males? The researchers also measured physiological arousal. The participants viewed slides depicting the various emotions while they were hooked up to an electromyogram to measure tension in the facial muscles. It was found that "women not only reported more intense emotional experience than men, but they also generated more extreme physiological reactions" (Grossman & Wood, 1993, p. 1020). Other researchers agree that, in general, women respond with greater emotional intensity than men and thus can experience both greater joy and greater sorrow (Fujita et al., 1991).

Remember It!

Experiencing Emotion

1. The idea that making a happy, sad, or angry face can actually trigger the physiological response and feeling associated with the emotion is called the
   a. emotion production theory.
   b. emotion control theory.
   c. facial-feedback hypothesis.
   d. facial expression theory.
2. Heightened emotion tends to facilitate rational thinking. (true/false)
3. Some research supports the notion that women tend to experience emotions more intensely than men. (true/false)
4. Which of the following is *not* one of the central components of love, according to Sternberg's triangular theory?
   a. compatibility
   b. passion
   c. commitment
   d. intimacy
5. What is the complete form of love, according to Sternberg?
   a. romantic love
   b. fatuous love
   c. companionate love
   d. consummate love

Answers: 1. c 2. false 3. true 4. a 5. d

Romantic Love: Lost in Each Other

When we say we have "fallen" in love, it is probably romantic love we have fallen into. Romantic love (sometimes called "passionate love") is an intense emotional response characterized by a turmoil of emotion, coupled with sexual arousal and a tremendous longing for that person (Hatfield, 1988). Does it mean that love is over when passion fades? Probably not. Love often changes into what has been termed *companionate love* (Hatfield, 1988). This is characterized by a less sexualized sense of affection. As love grows, couples often focus on the stability of the relationship, on the commitment and sense of liking for the other person.

The Six Styles of Love

Canadian psychologist John Allan Lee (1973, 1988) proposed that love is characterized by six different "styles of loving," all of which may be present in differing degrees for each individual. These dimensions of love are (a) romantic and passionate, (b) friendly, (c) game-playing, (d) possessive, (e) pragmatic, and (f) unselfish.

Sternberg's Theory of Love: Three Components, Seven Types

How does Sternberg's triangular theory of love account for the different kinds of love?

Robert Sternberg (1986b, 1987, 1997), whose triarchic theory of intelligence was discussed earlier, proposes a three-component **triangular theory of love**. The three components are intimacy, passion, and commitment. Sternberg (1987) explains intimacy as "those feelings in a relationship that promote closeness, bondedness, and connectedness" (p. 339). Passion refers to those drives in a loving relationship "that lead to romance, physical attraction, [and] sexual consummation" (1986b, p. 119). The decision/commitment component consists of a short-term aspect (i.e., the decision that one person loves another) and a long-term aspect (i.e., the commitment the person makes to maintaining that love over time).

Sternberg proposes that these three components combine in various ways to form different kinds of love. Each component can vary in intensity, from very strong to very weak, and the kind of love that is experienced depends on the strengths of each of the three components relative to one another. *Liking,* for example, has only one of the love components—intimacy. *Infatuated love* consists of strong passion combined with little intimacy and weak decision/commitment, while *romantic love* is a combination of strong passion and great intimacy with weak decision/commitment. **Consummate love** is the only type that

triangular theory of love: Sternberg's theory that three components–intimacy, passion, and decision/commitment–singly or in various combinations produce seven different kinds of love.

consummate love: According to Sternberg's theory, the most complete form of love, consisting of three components–intimacy, passion, and decision/commitment.

Eating Disorders: The Tyranny of the Scale

Apply It!

Imagine this: The thought of even the slightest layer of fat on your body repels you. You have been dieting and exercising strenuously for months, but you still feel fat, even though your friends comment that you're nothing but skin and bones. And you're unbelievably hungry: your dreams and daydreams are all about food–delicious food, lots of it, elegantly served. You leaf through cookbooks, go grocery shopping, and prepare meals whenever you get a chance, but when you sit down to eat you merely play with your food, because if you ate it you might get fat.

Now imagine this: Driven by an uncontrollable urge, you buy a dozen packages of cookies, some pop, perhaps a box of doughnuts. You take them home, lock the door, and start eating them. Once you've started, you can't stop–you gorge yourself on cookies and doughnuts until you feel as if you're about to explode. At that point you are overcome with disgust and anger at yourself; you take a double dose of laxative in an effort to get rid of the excess volume of food you have consumed.

These two scenarios are not as unusual as you might think. They represent two surprisingly common eating disorders: anorexia nervosa and bulimia nervosa. What causes these disorders, and how can they be treated?

Although there are some similarities between them, anorexia and bulimia are very different disorders. *Anorexia nervosa* is characterized by an overwhelming, irrational fear of gaining weight or becoming fat, compulsive dieting to the point of self-starvation, and excessive weight loss. Some anorexics lose as much as 20 to 25 percent of their original body weight. Anorexia typically begins in adolescence, and 90 percent of those afflicted are females (American Psychiatric Association, 1994). About 1 percent of females between 12 and 40 suffer from this disorder (Johnson et al., 1996).

Anorexia often begins with dieting, perhaps in reaction to a gain in weight after the onset of menstruation. Gradually the dieting develops into an obsession. Anorexic individuals continue to feel hunger and are strangely preoccupied with food. They spend inordinate amounts of time thinking about food, reading recipes, shopping for food, preparing it, and watching other people eat.

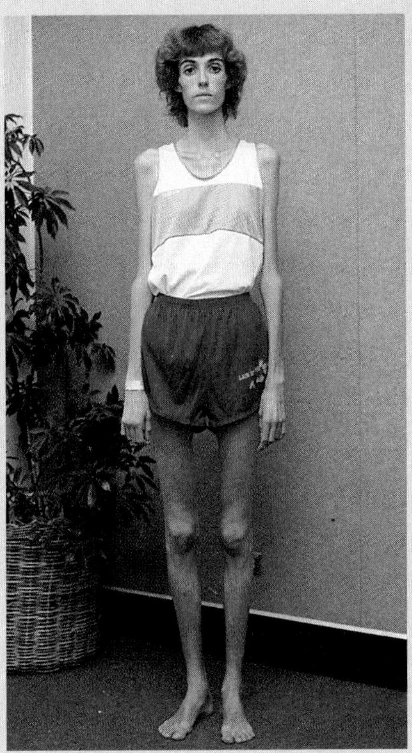

has all three components in great intensity and is certainly perceived to be the ideal type of love relationship for which many people strive. However, Sternberg cautions that maintaining consummate love may be even harder than achieving it!

Sternberg stresses the importance of translating the components of love into action. "Without expression," he warns, "even the greatest of loves can die" (1987, p. 341).

Love in all its fullness, its richness, and its power is such an intense and consuming human experience that researchers find it hard to capture. It is almost too personal to be viewed and studied with passionless objectivity. Love, the strongest emotional bond, is the most satisfying human experience imaginable for those fortunate enough to find it.

LINK IT!

www.ams.queensu.ca/anab
Anorexia Nervosa and Bulimia Association

www.nedic.on.ca
National Eating Disorder Information Centre

Anorexic individuals also have a gross distortion in the perception of their body size. No matter how thin they become, they continue to perceive themselves as fat. They are so obsessed with their weight that frequently they not only starve themselves but also exercise relentlessly and excessively in an effort to accelerate their weight loss.

It is difficult to pinpoint the cause of this disorder. Some investigators believe that young women who refuse to eat are attempting to control a portion of their lives, which they may feel unable to control in other respects.

Most anorexics are steadfast in their refusal to eat; about 20 percent of them starve themselves to death while insisting that nothing is wrong with them (Brotman, 1994).

Up to 50 percent of anorexics also develop symptoms of bulimia nervosa, a chronic disorder characterized by repeated and uncontrolled episodes of binge eating, often in secret (American Psychiatric Association 1993). An episode of binge eating has two main features: (1) much larger amounts of food than most people would eat during the same period of time, and (2) a feeling of inability to stop the eating or control the amount eaten. Binges are frequently followed by purging: self-induced vomiting and/or the use of large quantities of laxatives and diuretics. Bulimics may also engage in excessive dieting and exercise. Athletes are especially susceptible to this disorder. Many bulimics are average in size, and they purge after an eating binge simply to maintain their weight.

Bulimia nervosa can cause a number of health problems. The stomach acid in vomit eats away at the teeth and may cause them to rot, and the delicate balance of body chemistry is destroyed by excessive use of laxatives and diuretics. The disorder also has a strong emotional component; the bulimic individual is aware that the eating pattern is abnormal and feels unable to control it. Depression, guilt, and shame often accompany the binges and subsequent purging.

Bulimia nervosa tends to appear in the late teenage years and affects about one in 25 women during their lifetime (Kendler et al., 1991). An even larger number of young women regularly binge and purge, but not frequently enough to warrant the diagnosis of bulimia nervosa (Drewnowski et al., 1994). About 10 to 15 percent of all bulimics are males (Carlat et al., 1997).

Bulimia, like anorexia, is difficult to treat. Cognitive-behavioural therapy has been used successfully to help modify eating habits and abnormal attitudes about body shape and weight (Agras et al., 2000; Halmi, 1996; Johnson et al., 1996). Certain antidepressant drugs result in significant attitudinal change (Agras et al., 1994; "Eating disorders," 1997), but it appears that cognitive-behavioural therapy is more effective (Whittal et al., 1999).

If you or someone you know is showing signs of suffering from either of these disorders, you can get help by contacting the National Eating Disorder Information Centre, College Wing, Rm. 1–211, 200 Elizabeth St., Toronto ON, M5G 2C4, (416) 340-4156. Or contact a local agency through the public health department or your local hospital.

KEY TERMS

arousal, p. 292
arousal theory, p. 292
basic emotions, p. 306
Cannon-Bard theory, p. 305
consummate love, p. 313
display rules, p. 307
drive, p. 292
drive-reduction theory, p. 291
emotion, p. 303
extrinsic motivation, p. 290
facial-feedback hypothesis, p. 310
fat cells, p. 299
hierarchy of needs, p. 294
homeostasis, p. 292
incentive, p. 290
instinct, p. 291
instinct theory, p. 291
intrinsic motivation, p. 290
James-Lange theory, p. 304
lateral hypothalamus (LH), p. 296
Lazarus theory, p. 305
metabolic rate, p. 299
motivation, p. 290
motives, p. 290
need for achievement, p. 300
obesity, p. 299
primary drive, p. 296
Schachter-Singer theory, p. 305
self-actualization, p. 294
sensory deprivation, p. 293
set point, p. 300
social motives, p. 300
stimulus motives, p. 293
Thematic Apperception Test (TAT), p. 300
triangular theory of love, p. 313
ventromedial hypothalamus (VMH), p. 296
Yerkes-Dodson law, p. 293

THINKING CRITICALLY

Evaluation

In your view, which theory or combination of theories best explains motivation: drive-reduction theory, arousal theory, or Maslow's hierarchy of needs? Which theory do you find least convincing? Support your answers.

Using what you have learned about body weight and dieting, select any well-known weight-loss plan (for example, Weight Watchers, Jenny Craig, Slim-Fast) and evaluate it, explaining why it is or is not an effective way to lose weight and keep it off.

Point/Counterpoint

Present a convincing argument for each of these positions:

a. Polygraph testing should not be allowed in the legal system or in business and industry.
b. Polygraph testing should be allowed in the legal system and in business and industry.

Psychology in Your Life

Which level of Maslow's hierarchy (shown in Figure 9.2) provides the strongest motivation for your behaviour in general? Give specific examples to support your answer.

SUMMARY & REVIEW

Introduction to Motivation

What is the difference between intrinsic and extrinsic motivation?

With intrinsic motivation, an act is performed because it is satisfying or pleasurable in and of itself; with extrinsic motivation, an act is performed to bring a reward or to avert an undesirable consequence.

Theories of Motivation

How do instinct theories explain motivation?

Instinct theories suggest that human behaviour is motivated by certain innate, unlearned tendencies, or instincts, that are shared by all individuals.

What is the drive-reduction theory of motivation?

Drive-reduction theory suggests that a biological need creates an unpleasant state of arousal or tension called a *drive,* which impels the organism to engage in behaviour that will satisfy the need and reduce tension.

How does arousal theory explain motivation?

Arousal theory suggests that the aim of motivation is to maintain an optimal level of arousal. If arousal is less than optimal, we engage in activities that stimulate arousal; if arousal exceeds the optimal level, we seek to reduce stimulation.

How does Maslow's hierarchy of needs account for human motivation?

Maslow's hierarchy of needs arranges needs in order of urgency—from physical needs (food, water, air, shelter) to security needs, belonging needs, esteem needs, and finally the need for self-actualization (developing to one's full potential) at the top of the hierarchy. Theoretically, the needs at the lower levels must be satisfied adequately before a person will be motivated to fulfill the higher needs.

The Primary Drives: Hunger and Thirst

Under what kinds of conditions do the two types of thirst occur?

One type of thirst results from a loss of bodily fluid that can be caused by perspiration, vomiting, bleeding, diarrhea, or excessive intake of alcohol. Another type of thirst results from excessive intake of salt, which disturbs the water-sodium balance.

What are the roles of the lateral hypothalamus and the ventromedial hypothalamus in the regulation of eating behaviour?

The lateral hypothalamus (LH) apparently acts as a feeding centre: when activated, it signals the animal to start eating; when it is destroyed, the animal refuses to eat. The ventromedial hypothalamus (VMH) evidently acts as a satiety centre: when activated, it signals the animal to stop eating; when it is destroyed, the animal overeats, becoming obese.

What are some of the body's hunger and satiety signals?

Some biological hunger signals are stomach contractions, low blood glucose levels, and high insulin levels. Some satiety signals are a full or distended stomach, high blood glucose levels, and the presence in the blood of other satiety substances (such as CCK) that are secreted by the gastrointestinal tract during digestion.

What are some non-biological factors that influence what and how much we eat?

External eating cues, such as the taste, smell, and appearance of food, the variety of food offered, and the time of day, can cause people to eat more food than they actually need.

What are some factors that account for variations in body weight?

Variations in body weight are influenced by heredity, metabolic rate, activity level, number of fat cells, and eating habits.

How does set point affect body weight?

Set-point theory suggests that an internal homeostatic system functions to maintain body weight by adjusting appetite and metabolic rate.

Social Motives

What is Murray's contribution to the study of motivation?

Murray defined a list of social motives, or needs, and developed the Thematic Apperception Test (TAT) to assess a person's level of these needs.

What is the need for achievement?

The need for achievement is the need to accomplish something difficult and to perform at a high standard of excellence.

What are some characteristics shared by people who are high in achievement motivation?

People high in achievement motivation enjoy challenges and like to compete. They tend to set goals of moderate difficulty, are more motivated by hope of success than by fear of failure, attribute their success to their ability and hard work, and are most often drawn to business, frequently becoming entrepreneurs.

The What and Why of Emotions

What are the three components of emotions?

An emotion is a feeling state that involves physiological arousal, a cognitive appraisal of the situation arousing the emotion, and outward expression of the emotion.

According to the James-Lange theory, what sequence of events occurs when we experience an emotion?

According to the James-Lange theory of emotion, environmental stimuli produce a physiological response, and then our awareness of this response causes the emotion.

What is the Cannon-Bard theory of emotion?

The Cannon-Bard theory suggests that emotion-provoking stimuli received by the senses are relayed to the thalamus, which simultaneously passes the information to the cortex, giving us the mental experience of the emotion, and to the internal organs, producing physiological arousal.

According to the Schachter-Singer theory, what two things must occur in order for us to experience an emotion?

The Schachter-Singer theory states that for an emotion to occur, (1) there must be physiological arousal, and (2) the person must perceive some reason for the arousal in order to label the emotion.

According to Lazarus, what sequence of events occurs when an individual feels an emotion?

An emotion-provoking stimulus triggers a cognitive appraisal, which is followed by the emotion and the physiological arousal.

The Expression of Emotion

What are basic emotions?

The basic emotions (happiness, sadness, disgust, etc.) are those that are unlearned and that are reflected in the same facial expressions in all cultures.

How does the development of facial expressions of different emotions in infants suggest a biological basis for emotional expression?

The facial expressions of different emotions develop in a particular sequence in infants and seem to be the result of maturation rather than learning. The same sequence occurs even in children who have been blind and deaf since birth.

Why is emotion considered a form of communication?

Emotions enable us to communicate our feelings, intentions, and needs more effectively than just words alone and thus make it more likely that others will respond to us.

Experiencing Emotion

What is the facial-feedback hypothesis?

The facial-feedback hypothesis suggests that the muscular movements involved in certain facial expressions trigger the corresponding emotion (for example, smiling makes us happy).

How does Sternberg's triangular theory of love account for the different kinds of love?

In his triangular theory of love, Sternberg proposes that three components–intimacy, passion, and decision/commitment–singly or in various combinations produce seven different kinds of love–infatuated, empty, romantic, fatuous, companionate, and consummate love, as well as liking.

Personality Theory and Assessment

What makes us the way we are? Are the personality characteristics we exhibit influenced more markedly by genes or by the environment in which we live, grow, and develop? Environments can be strikingly different. Consider the environments described in the next two paragraphs.

Oskar Stohr was raised as a Catholic by his grandmother in Nazi Germany. As part of Hitler's youth movement, Oskar was expected to be an obedient Nazi. Book burnings, military parades, hatred of Jews, and the right hand raised with the salute "Heil Hitler" were all part of Oskar's early environment. How did this environment affect his personality?

Jack Yufe, the same age as Oskar, was raised by his Jewish father on the island of Trinidad. Far removed from the goose-stepping storm troopers in Nazi Germany, Jack enjoyed all of the educational advantages and social supports of a middle-class Jewish upbringing. How did Jack's environment affect his personality?

Though raised in starkly different environments, Oskar and Jack are amazingly alike. They have quick tempers, are domineering toward women, enjoy surprising people by faking sneezes in elevators, and flush the toilet before using it. They both read magazines from back to front, store rubber bands on their wrists, like spicy foods and sweet liqueurs, and dip buttered toast in their coffee.

The list of similarities between Oskar and Jack is much longer, but there is a good reason for them. The men are identical twins. They were separated shortly after birth when their father took Jack with him to the island of Trinidad, and their maternal grandmother raised Oskar in Germany.

Researchers at the Minnesota Center for Twin and Adoption Research are studying the effects of genetics and environment on identical twins reared apart. When Oskar and Jack first arrived at the centre to take part in the study, they looked almost exactly alike physically, and both of them were wearing double-breasted blue shirts with epaulets, identical neatly trimmed mustaches, and wire-rimmed glasses. How powerfully the genes influence personality!

Joan Gardiner and Jean Nelson are another pair of identical twins in the Minnesota study. They were also raised apart, but their environments did not differ so markedly. Joan's adoptive mother and Jean's adoptive father were sister and brother, so the twins were together quite often.

Like Oskar and Jack, Joan and Jean have many similarities and a few differences. But one difference between the twins is so unusual that researchers are especially intrigued by it. Joan is musical; Jean is not. Although her adoptive mother was a piano teacher, Jean does not play. But Joan, whose adoptive mother was not a musician, plays piano very well—so well, in fact, that she has performed with the Minnesota Symphony Orchestra. Joan's mother made her practise piano several hours every day, while Jean's mother allowed her to pursue whatever interests she chose.

Duplicate genes but differences in musical ability—how do the researchers explain this? David Lykken of the Minnesota Center suggests that both twins have the same genetic musical capability, but the reason one plays and the other does not shows the effects produced by the environment. How powerfully the environment influences personality!

It is often said that no two people are exactly alike, that each of us is unique. When people talk about someone's uniqueness, they are usually referring to personality. **Personality** is defined as an individual's unique and stable pattern of characteristics and behaviours. And personalities are indeed different—consider, for example, Shania Twain and k.d. lang, Jean Chrétien and Stockwell Day, Elvis Stojko and Toller Cranston. What makes these people so different?

A number of theories attempt to account for our personality differences and explain how we come to be the way we are. This chapter explores some of the major personality theories and the variety of tests and inventories used to assess personality.

Sigmund Freud and Psychoanalysis

To what two aspects of Freud's work does the term *psychoanalysis* apply?

Most textbooks begin their exploration of personality theory with Sigmund Freud, and for good reason. Freud created one of the first and most controversial personality theories. Using information gained from the treatment of his patients and from his own life experiences, Freud developed the theory of **psychoanalysis**. When you hear the term "psychoanalysis," you may picture a psychiatrist treating a troubled patient on a couch. But psychoanalysis is much more than that. The term refers not only to a therapy for treating psychological disorders but also to a personality theory.

Freud's theory of psychoanalysis is largely original, and it was revolutionary and shocking to the 19th- and early 20th-century European audience to which it was introduced. The major components of Freud's theory, and perhaps the most controversial, are (1) the central role of the sexual instinct, (2) the concept of infantile sexuality, and (3) the dominant part played by the unconscious in moving and shaping our thoughts and behaviour. Freud's theory assumes a psychic determinism, the view that there is a cause for our every thought, idea, feeling, action, or behaviour. Nothing happens by chance or accident; everything we do and even everything we forget to do has an underlying cause.

LINK IT!

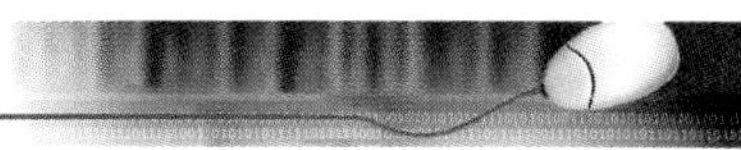

plaza.interport.net/nypsan/freudarc.html
Sigmund Freud and the Freud Archives

home.ican.net/~analyst
Canadian Psychoanalytic Society

The Conscious, the Preconscious, and the Unconscious: Levels of Awareness

What are the three levels of awareness in consciousness?

Freud believed that there are three levels of awareness in consciousness: the conscious, the preconscious, and the unconscious. The **conscious** consists of whatever we are aware of at any given moment—a thought, a feeling, a sensation, or a memory. When we shift our attention or our thoughts, a change occurs in the content of the conscious.

Freud's **preconscious** is very much like the present-day concept of long-term memory. It contains all the memories, feelings, experiences, and perceptions that we are not consciously thinking about at the moment, but that may be brought to consciousness—which high school you went to or the year in which you were born, for example. This information resides in your preconscious but can easily be brought to consciousness.

The most important of the three levels is the **unconscious**, which Freud believed to be the primary motivating force of our behaviour. The unconscious holds memories that once were conscious but were so unpleasant or anxiety-provoking that they were repressed (involuntarily removed from consciousness). The unconscious also contains all of the

personality: A person's unique and stable pattern of characteristics and behaviours.

psychoanalysis (SY-co-ah-NAL-ih-sis): Freud's term for his theory of personality and for his therapy for the treatment of psychological disorders.

conscious (KON-shus): Those thoughts, feelings, sensations, and memories of which we are aware at any given moment.

preconscious: The thoughts, feelings, and memories that we are not consciously aware of at the moment but that may be brought to consciousness.

unconscious (un-KON-shus): Considered by Freud to be the primary motivating force of behaviour, containing repressed memories as well as instincts and wishes that have never been conscious.

instincts (sexual and aggressive), wishes, and desires that have never been allowed into consciousness. Freud traced the roots of psychological disorders to these impulses and repressed memories.

The Id, the Ego, and the Superego: Warring Components of the Personality

What are the roles of the id, the ego, and the superego?

Freud (1961) proposed a new conception of personality that contained three systems: the id, the ego, and the superego. These systems do not exist physically; they are only concepts, or ways of looking at personality.

The **id** is the only part of the personality that is present at birth. It is inherited, primitive, inaccessible, and completely unconscious. The id contains (1) the life instincts, which are the sexual instincts and the biological urges such as hunger and thirst; and (2) the death instinct, which accounts for our aggressive and destructive impulses (Freud, 1965). The id operates according to the **pleasure principle**—that is, to seek pleasure, avoid pain, and gain immediate gratification of its wishes. The id is the source of the **libido**, the psychic energy that fuels the entire personality; yet the id cannot act on its own. It can only wish, image, fantasize, demand.

The **ego** is the logical, rational, realistic part of the personality. The ego evolves from the id and draws its energy from the id. One of the ego's functions is to satisfy the id's urges. But the ego, which is mostly conscious, acts according to the reality principle; it must consider the constraints of the real world in determining appropriate times, places, and objects to gratify the id's wishes. It allows compromises to be made—for example, it is due to the ego that on a given day you might choose a cookie instead of cheesecake.

When a child is five or six years old, the **superego**—the moral component of the personality—is formed. The superego has two parts: (1) the *conscience,* which consists of all the behaviours for which we have been punished and about which we feel guilty; and (2) the *ego ideal,* which contains the behaviours for which we have been praised and rewarded and about which we feel pride and satisfaction. At first the superego reflects only the parents' expectations of what is good and right, but it expands over time to incorporate teachings from the broader social world. In its quest for moral perfection, the superego sets moral guidelines that define and limit the flexibility of the ego.

Figure 10.1 describes the three systems of the personality.

Defence Mechanisms: Protecting the Ego

What is a defence mechanism?

All would be well if the id, the ego, and the superego had compatible aims. But the id's demands for sensual pleasure are

FIGURE 10.1

Freud's Conception of the Personality According to Freud, personality is composed of three structures, or systems: the id, the ego, and the superego. Their characteristics are diagrammed and described here.

Structure	Level of Consciousness	Characteristics
Id	Unconscious	Primitive component containing the sexual instincts, biological urges, and aggressive and destructive impulses. Source of the libido. Operates according to the pleasure principle, seeking immediate gratification. Impulsive, amoral, and selfish.
Ego	Largely conscious, partly unconscious	Logical, rational component, which functions to satisfy the id's urges and carry out transactions in the real world. Acts according to the reality principle.
Superego	Both conscious and unconscious	The moral component, consisting of the conscience and the ego ideal. Sets moral guidelines, which limit the flexibility of the ego.

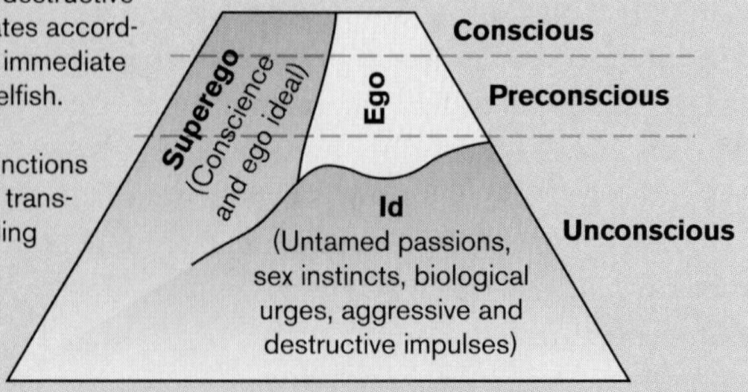

often in direct conflict with the superego's desire for moral perfection. At times the ego needs some way to defend itself against the anxiety created by the excessive demands of the id, by the harsh judgments of the superego, or by the sometimes threatening conditions in the environment. Often the ego can relieve anxiety by solving its problems rationally and directly. When it cannot do so, it must resort to irrational defences against anxiety called *defence mechanisms.* Freud's daughter Anna (1966), also a psychoanalyst, contributed much to our understanding of defence mechanisms.

A **defence mechanism** is a technique used to defend against anxiety and to maintain self-esteem, but it involves self-deception and the distortion of internal and external reality (Vaillant, 1994, 1998). We use defence mechanisms to protect ourselves from failure and from guilt-arousing desires or actions (Vaillant, 2000).

Repression: Out of Mind, Out of Sight

What are two ways in which repression operates?

Repression is the most important and the most frequently used defence mechanism, and it is present to some degree in all other defence mechanisms. Repression operates in two ways: (1) it can remove painful or threatening memories, thoughts, ideas, or perceptions from consciousness and keep them in the unconscious; or (2) it can prevent unconscious but disturbing sexual and aggressive impulses from breaking into consciousness.

Even though repressed, the memories lurk in the unconscious and exert an active influence on personality and behaviour. This is why repressed traumatic events of childhood can cause psychological disorders (neuroses) in adults. Freud believed that the way to cure such disorders is to bring the repressed material back to consciousness. This was what he tried to accomplish through his therapy, psychoanalysis.

Other Defence Mechanisms: Excuses, Substitutions, and Denials

What are some other defence mechanisms?

There are several other defence mechanisms that we may use from time to time. We use **projection** when we attribute our own undesirable impulses, thoughts, personality traits, or behaviour to others, or when we minimize the undesirable in ourselves and exaggerate it in others.

Denial is a refusal to consciously acknowledge or to believe that a danger or a threatening condition exists. For instance, smokers use denial when they refuse to admit that cigarettes are a danger to their health.

Rationalization occurs when we unconsciously supply a logical, rational, or socially acceptable reason rather than the real reason for an action or event. When we rationalize, we make excuses for, or justify, our failures and mistakes. A teacher may blame students for their low grades, arguing that they are unmotivated and lazy, rather than evaluating the impact of his or her teaching techniques.

Sometimes, when frustrated or anxious, we may use **regression**—that is, revert to behaviour that might have reduced anxiety at an earlier stage of development. A five-year-old child with a new baby sibling may regress and suck her thumb.

id (IHD): The unconscious system of the personality, which contains the life and death instincts and operates on the pleasure principle.

pleasure principle: The principle by which the id operates to seek pleasure, avoid pain, and obtain immediate gratification.

libido (lih-BEE-doe): Freud's name for the psychic or sexual energy that comes from the id and provides the energy for the entire personality.

ego (EE-go): In Freudian theory, the rational and largely conscious system of one's personality; operates according to the reality principle and tries to satisfy the demands of the id without violating moral values.

superego (sue-per-EE-go): The moral system of the personality, which consists of the conscience and the ego ideal.

defence mechanism: An unconscious, irrational means used by the ego to defend against anxiety; involves self-deception and the distortion of reality.

repression: The act of removing unpleasant memories from one's consciousness so that one is no longer aware of the painful event.

projection: The act of attributing our own undesirable thoughts, impulses, or behaviours to others.

denial: The act of refusing to consciously acknowledge the existence of a danger or a threatening condition.

rationalization: The act of supplying a logical, rational, socially acceptable reason rather than the real reason for an unacceptable thought or action.

regression: The act of reverting to a behaviour that might have reduced anxiety at an earlier stage of development.

Reaction formation is at work when people express exaggerated ideas and emotions that are the opposite of their disturbing, unconscious impulses and desires. In reaction formation, the conscious thought or feeling masks the unconscious one. Unconscious hatred may be expressed as love and devotion, cruelty as kindness. For example, a former chain smoker becomes irate and complains loudly at the faintest whiff of cigarette smoke.

Displacement occurs when we substitute a less threatening object or person for the original object of a sexual or aggressive impulse. If your boss makes you angry, you may take out your hostility on your boyfriend or girlfriend.

With **sublimation**, we rechannel sexual or aggressive energy into pursuits or accomplishments that society considers acceptable or even praiseworthy. An aggressive person may rechannel that aggression and become a football or hockey player, a boxer, a surgeon, or a butcher. Freud viewed sublimation as the only completely healthy ego defence mechanism. In fact, Freud (1930/1962) considered all advances in civilization to be the result of sublimation. Review & Reflect 10.1 describes and provides additional examples of the defence mechanisms.

The Psychosexual Stages of Development: Centred on the Erogenous Zones

The sex instinct, Freud said, is the most important factor influencing personality; but it does not just suddenly appear full-blown at puberty. It is present at birth and then develops through a series of **psychosexual stages**. Each stage centres on a particular erogenous zone, a part of the body that provides pleasurable sensations and around which a conflict arises (Freud, 1953b; 1963b). If the conflict is not resolved without undue difficulty, the child may develop a **fixation**. This means that a portion of the libido (psychic energy) remains invested at that stage, leaving less energy to meet the challenges of future stages. Overindulgence at a stage may leave a person unwilling psychologically to move on to the next stage. But too little gratification may leave the person trying to make up for previously unmet needs. Freud believed that certain personality characteristics develop as a

REVIEW&REFLECT 10.1
Traditional and Modern Schools of Thought in Psychology

Defence Mechanism	Description	Example
Repression	Involuntarily removing an unpleasant memory from consciousness or barring disturbing sexual and aggressive impulses from consciousness.	Jill forgets a traumatic incident from childhood.
Projection	Attributing one's own undesirable traits or impulses to another.	A very lonely divorced woman accuses all men of having only one thing on their minds.
Denial	Refusing to consciously acknowledge the existence of danger or a threatening situation.	Amy is severely injured when she fails to take a storm warning seriously.
Rationalization	Supplying a logical, rational reason rather than the real reason for an action or event.	Fred tells his friend that he didn't get the job because he didn't have connections.
Regression	Reverting to a behaviour characteristic of an earlier stage of development.	Susan bursts into tears whenever she is criticized.
Reaction formation	Expressing exaggerated ideas and emotions that are the opposite of disturbing, unconscious impulses and desires.	A former purchaser of pornography, Bob is now a tireless crusader against it.
Displacement	Substituting a less threatening object for the original object of an impulse.	After being spanked by his father, Bill hits his baby brother.
Sublimation	Rechannelling sexual and aggressive energy into pursuits that society considers acceptable or even admirable.	Tim goes to a gym to work out when he feels hostile and frustrated.

Remember It!

Psychoanalysis and Defence Mechanisms

1. Psychoanalysis is both a theory of personality and a therapy for the treatment of mental disorders. (true/false)
2. Freud considered the (conscious/unconscious) to be the primary motivating force of our behaviour.
3. The part of the personality that would make you want to eat, drink, and be merry is your
   a. id. b. ego.
   c. superego. d. unconscious.
4. You just found a gold watch in a darkened movie theatre. Which part of your personality would urge you to turn it in to the lost-and-found?
   a. id b. ego
   c. superego d. unconscious
5. The part of the personality that must determine the most appropriate ways and means of satisfying your biological urges is the
   a. id b. ego
   c. superego d. unconscious
6. Defence mechanisms are used only by psychologically unhealthy individuals. (true/false)
7. Match the example with the corresponding defence mechanism.
   ____ 1) sublimation
   ____ 2) repression
   ____ 3) displacement
   ____ 4) rationalization
   a. forgetting a traumatic childhood experience
   b. supplying a logical reason for arriving late
   c. creating a work of art
   d. venting anger on a friend or spouse after getting a speeding ticket from a police officer

Answers: 1. true 2. unconscious 3. a 4. c 5. b 6. false 7. 1) c 2) a 3) d 4) b

result of difficulty at one or another of the psychosexual stages.

The Oral Stage (Birth to 12 or 18 Months)

During the **oral stage**, the mouth is the primary source of sensual pleasure (Freud, 1920/1963b). The conflict at this stage centres on weaning. Too much or too little gratification may result in an oral fixation—an excessive preoccupation with oral activities such as eating, drinking, smoking, gum chewing, nail biting, and even kissing. Freud believed that difficulties at the oral stage can result in personality traits such as excessive dependence, optimism, and gullibility or extreme pessimism, sarcasm, hostility, and aggression.

The Anal Stage (12 or 18 months to Age Three)

During the **anal stage**, children derive sensual pleasure from expelling and withholding feces. A conflict arises when toilet training begins, because this is one of the parents' first attempts to have children withhold or postpone gratification. When parents are harsh in their approach, children may rebel openly, defecating whenever and wherever they please. This may lead to an anal expulsive personality—someone who

reaction formation: The process of denying an unacceptable impulse, usually sexual or aggressive, by giving strong conscious expression to its opposite.

displacement: Substitution of a less threatening object for the original object of an impulse; taking out frustrations on objects or people who are less threatening than those who provoked us.

sublimation: The rechannelling of sexual or aggressive energy to pursuits or accomplishments that society considers acceptable or even praiseworthy.

psychosexual stages: A series of stages through which the sexual instinct develops; each stage is defined by an erogenous zone that becomes the centre of new pleasures and conflicts.

fixation: Arrested development at a psychosexual stage occurring because of excessive gratification or frustration at that stage.

oral stage: The first of Freud's psychosexual stages (birth to 12 or 18 months), in which sensual pleasure is derived mainly through stimulation of the mouth (examples: sucking, biting, chewing).

anal stage: Freud's second psychosexual stage (ages 12 or 18 months to three years), in which the child derives sensual pleasure mainly from expelling and withholding feces.

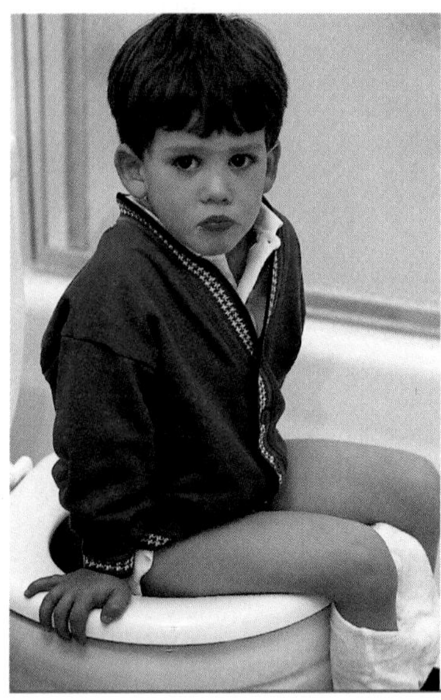

Freud believed that a fixation at the anal stage, resulting from harsh parental pressure, could lead to an anal retentive personality–characterized by excessive stubbornness, rigidity, and neatness.

is sloppy, irresponsible, rebellious, hostile, and destructive. Other children may defy their parents and gain attention by withholding feces. They may develop anal retentive personalities, gaining security through what they possess and becoming stingy, stubborn, rigid, and excessively neat and clean, orderly, and precise (Freud, 1965).

The Phallic Stage (Ages Three to Five or Six)

What is the Oedipus complex?

During the **phallic stage**, children learn that they can get pleasure by touching their genitals, and masturbation is common. They become aware of the anatomical differences in males and females and may begin to play "Doctor."

The conflict that develops at this stage is a sexual desire for the parent of the opposite sex and a hostility toward the same-sex parent. Freud (1963a) called this the **Oedipus complex** (after the central character in the Greek tragedy *Oedipus Rex,* by Sophocles). "Boys concentrate their sexual wishes upon their mother and develop hostile impulses against their father as being a rival" (p. 61). But the young boy eventually develops castration anxiety—an intense fear that his father might retaliate and harm him by cutting off his penis (Freud, 1965). This fear becomes so intense, Freud believed, that the boy usually resolves the Oedipus complex by identifying with his father and repressing his sexual feelings for his mother. With identification, the child takes on his father's behaviours, mannerisms, and superego standards. In this way the superego develops (Freud, 1962).

TABLE 10.1

Freud's Psychosexual Stages of Development

In Freud's view, the most important factor influencing personality is the sex instinct, which develops through a series of psychosexual stages. Each stage is centred on a particular erogenous zone. Certain adult personality traits can result from a failure to resolve problems or conflicts at one of the psychosexual stages.

	Oral	Anal	Phallic	Latency	Genital
Stage	Birth to 12–18 months	12–18 months to 3 years	3 to 5–6 years	5–6 years to puberty	Puberty onward
Erogenous zone	Mouth	Anus	Genitals	None	Genitals
Conflicts/ experiences	Weaning; oral gratification from sucking, eating, biting	Toilet training; gratification from expelling and withholding feces	Oedipal conflict; sexual curiosity; masturbation	Period of sexual calm; interest in school, hobbies, same-sex friends	Revival of sexual interests; establishment of mature sexual relationships
Adult traits associated with problems at this stage	Optimism, gullibility, dependency, pessimism, passivity, hostility, sarcasm, aggression	Excessive cleanliness, orderliness, stinginess, messiness, rebelliousness, destructiveness	Flirtatiousness, vanity, promiscuity, pride, chastity		

Remember It!

Freud's Psychosexual Stages

1. According to Freud, the sex instinct
   a. is present before birth.
   b. is present at birth.
   c. first appears during the phallic stage.
   d. first appears at puberty.
2. Which of the following presents Freud's psychosexual stages in the order in which they occur?
   a. anal; oral; genital; phallic
   b. genital; anal; oral; phallic
   c. oral; phallic; anal; genital
   d. oral; anal; phallic; genital
3. Excessive concern with cleanliness and order could indicate a fixation at the ________ stage.
   a. oral b. anal
   c. phallic d. genital
4. When a boy develops sexual feelings toward his mother and hostility toward his father, he is experiencing the stage of internal struggle called the ____________________.
5. According to Freud, which of the following represents a primary source of influence on our personality?
   a. our heredity
   b. life experiences after we begin school
   c. the relative strengths of our id, ego, and superego
   d. the problems we experience during adolescence

Answers: 1. b 2. d 3. b 4. Oedipus complex 5. c

Girls experience a similar conflict, often referred to as the Electra complex, although Freud did not use that term. Freud (1965) contended that when young girls discover that they have no penis, they develop "penis envy" and turn to their father because he has the desired organ. They feel sexual desires for him and develop a jealous rivalry with their mother. But eventually girls, too, experience anxiety as a result of their hostile feelings. They repress their sexual feelings toward the father and identify with the mother, and this leads to the formation of their superego (Freud, 1930/1962).

According to Freud, failure to resolve these conflicts can have serious consequences for both boys and girls. Freud thought that tremendous guilt and anxiety could be carried over into adulthood and cause sexual problems, great difficulty relating to members of the opposite sex, and even homosexuality.

The Latency Period (Age Five or Six to Puberty)

The **latency period** is one of relative calm. The sex instinct is repressed and temporarily sublimated in school and play activities, hobbies, and sports.

The Genital Stage (from Puberty On)

In the **genital stage**, for the vast majority of people the focus of sexual energy gradually shifts to the opposite sex. This culminates in heterosexual love and the attainment of full adult sexuality. Freud believed that the few who reach the genital stage without having fixations at earlier stages can achieve the state of psychological health that he equated with the ability to love and work.

Table 10.1 provides a summary of the psychosexual stages of development.

Freud's Explanation of Personality

According to Freud, what are the two primary sources of influence on the personality?

According to Freud, personality is almost completely formed by age five or six, when the Oedipal conflict is resolved and the superego is formed. He believed that there are two primary influences on personality: (1) the traits

phallic stage: The third of Freud's psychosexual stages (ages three to five or six), during which sensual pleasure is derived mainly through touching the genitals; the stage when the Oedipus complex arises.

Oedipus complex (ED-uh-pus): Occurring in the phallic stage, a conflict in which the child is sexually attracted to the opposite-sex parent and feels hostility toward the same-sex parent.

latency period: The period following Freud's phallic stage (age five or six to puberty), in which the sex instinct is largely repressed and temporarily sublimated in school and play activities.

genital stage: The last of Freud's psychosexual stages (from puberty on), in which for most people the focus of sexual energy gradually shifts to the opposite sex, culminating in the attainment of full adult sexuality.

that develop because of fixations at any of the psychosexual stages, and (2) the relative strengths of the id, the ego, and the superego. In psychologically healthy people, there is a balance among the three components. If the id is too strong and the superego too weak, people will take pleasure and gratify desires, and feel no guilt, no matter who is hurt or what the cost. But a tyrannical superego will leave people with perpetual guilt feelings, unable to enjoy sensual pleasure.

Evaluating Freud's Contribution

Freud's theory is so comprehensive (he wrote more than 24 volumes) that its elements must be evaluated separately. His belief that women are inferior to men sexually, morally, and intellectually and that they suffer penis envy seems ridiculous today. Moreover, research contradicts Freud's notion that personality is almost completely formed by age five or six. However, we are indebted to him for emphasizing the influence of early childhood experiences on later development.

Critics of Freud's theory argue that it interprets behaviour after the fact (Stanovich, 1989), though some even go as far as to say that the entire theory can neither be supported scientifically nor justified therapeutically (Crews, 1996; Erwin, 1996).

Even so, Freud's contribution has influenced an enormous body of research across many areas of psychology (Westen, 1998). For instance, research in neuroscience and social psychology supports the existence of unconscious mental processing (Loftus & Klinger, 1992) but this unconscious is not what Freud had envisioned. Rather, unconscious mental activity is now viewed as information processing that takes place below the level of awareness (Bargh & Chartrand, 1999; Wegner & Bargh, 1998).

The Neo-Freudians

Several personality theorists, referred to as neo-Freudians, started their careers as followers of Freud but began to disagree on some of the basic principles of psychoanalytic theory. They modified some aspects of the theory and presented their own original ideas about personality. We will discuss Carl Jung (analytical psychology), Alfred Adler (individual psychology), and Karen Horney.

Carl Gustav Jung

Carl Jung (1875–1961) differed with Freud on many major points. He did not consider the sexual instinct to be the main factor in personality, nor did he believe that the personality is almost completely formed in early childhood. He maintained that middle age is an important period for personality development (Jung, 1933). He even disagreed with Freud on the basic structure of personality.

LINK IT!

www.cgjungpage.org
The C. G. Jung Page

Jung's View of the Personality: A Different View of the Unconscious

According to Jung, what are the three components of personality?

Jung conceived of the personality as consisting of three parts: the ego, the personal unconscious, and the collective unconscious. He saw the ego as the conscious component of personality, which carries out our normal daily activities. Like Freud, he believed the ego to be secondary in importance to the unconscious.

The **personal unconscious** develops as a result of our own individual experience and is therefore unique to each individual. It contains all the experiences, thoughts, and perceptions accessible to the conscious, as well as repressed memories, wishes, and impulses. The personal unconscious resembles a combination of Freud's preconscious and unconscious.

Carl Jung

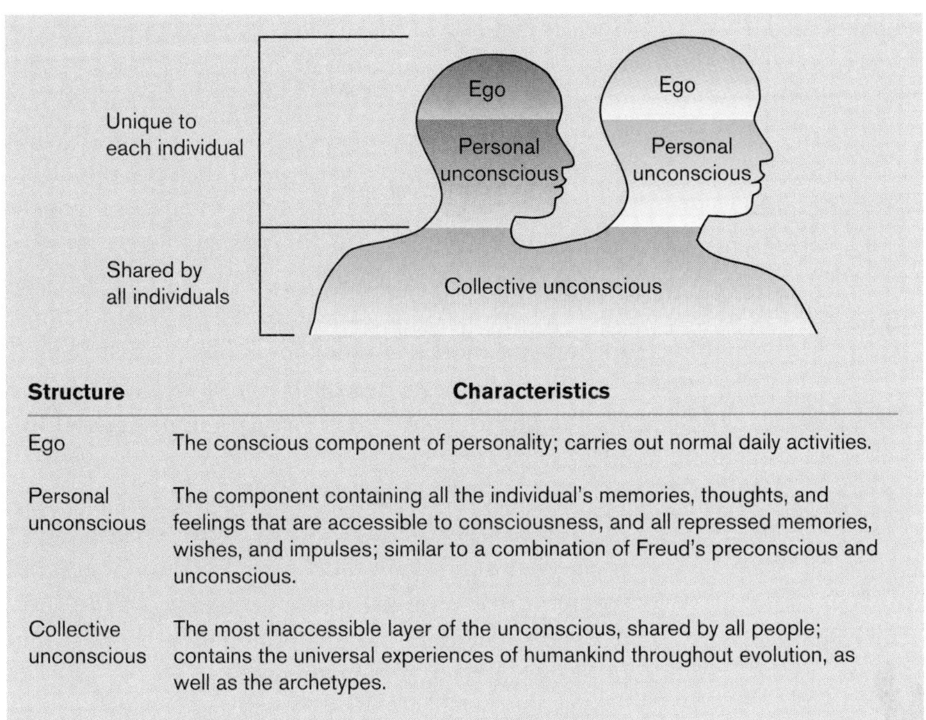

Structure	Characteristics
Ego	The conscious component of personality; carries out normal daily activities.
Personal unconscious	The component containing all the individual's memories, thoughts, and feelings that are accessible to consciousness, and all repressed memories, wishes, and impulses; similar to a combination of Freud's preconscious and unconscious.
Collective unconscious	The most inaccessible layer of the unconscious, shared by all people; contains the universal experiences of humankind throughout evolution, as well as the archetypes.

FIGURE 10.2
Jung's Conception of Personality **Like Freud, Carl Jung saw three components in personality. The ego and the personal unconscious are unique to each individual. The collective unconscious is shared by all people and accounts for the similarity of myths and beliefs in diverse cultures.**

The **collective unconscious** is the deepest and most inaccessible layer of the unconscious. Jung thought that the universal experiences of humankind throughout evolution are transmitted to each individual through the collective unconscious. This is how he accounted for the similarity of certain myths, dreams, symbols, and religious beliefs in cultures widely separated by distance and time.

The collective unconscious contains what Jung called *archetypes*. An **archetype** is an inherited tendency to respond to universal human situations in particular ways. Jung would say that the tendencies of people to believe in a god, a devil, evil spirits, and heroes, and to have a fear of the dark, all result from inherited archetypes that reflect the shared experience of humankind.

Figure 10.2 provides a summary of Jung's conception of the personality.

Alfred Adler: Overcoming Inferiority

What did Adler consider to be the driving force of the personality?

Alfred Adler (1870–1937) disagreed with most of Freud's basic beliefs; on many points his views were the exact opposite. Adler emphasized the unity of the personality rather than the separate warring components of id, ego, and superego. He believed that our behaviour is motivated more by the conscious than by the unconscious and that we are influenced more by future goals than by early childhood experiences.

Unlike Freud, who believed that sex and pleasure-seeking are our primary motives, Adler (1927, 1956) maintained that we are driven by the need to compensate for inferiority and to strive for superiority or significance. He believed that feelings of weakness and inferiority are an inevitable experience in every child's early life. Adler himself had felt a particularly keen sense of inferiority as a child because he was small, sickly, and unable to walk until he was four.

personal unconscious: In Jung's theory, the layer of the unconscious containing all of the thoughts and experiences that are accessible to the conscious, as well as repressed memories and impulses.

collective unconscious: In Jung's theory, the most inaccessible layer of the unconscious, which contains the universal experiences of humankind transmitted to each individual.

archetype (AR-keh-type): Existing in the collective unconscious, an inherited tendency to respond in particular ways to universal human situations.

According to Adler (1956), people at an early age develop a "style of life"—a unique way in which the child and later the adult will go about the struggle to achieve superiority. Sometimes inferiority feelings are so strong that they prevent personal development. Adler originated a term to describe this condition—the "inferiority complex" (Dreikurs, 1953). Adler (1964) also maintained that birth order influences personality, making first-born children more likely than their siblings to be high achievers.

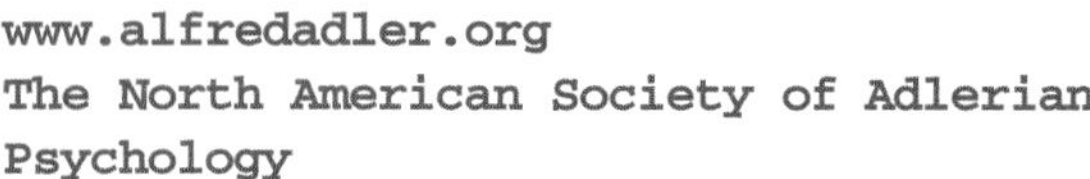

www.alfredadler.org
The North American Society of Adlerian Psychology

Karen Horney: Champion of Feminine Psychology

Why is Horney considered a pioneer in psychology?

Karen Horney's work centred on two main themes—the neurotic personality (1937, 1945, 1950) and feminine psychology (1967). She considered herself a disciple of Freud, accepting his emphasis on unconscious motivation and the basic tools of psychoanalysis. However, she disagreed with many of his basic beliefs. She did not accept his division of personality into id, ego, and superego, and she flatly rejected his psychosexual stages and the concepts of the Oedipus complex and penis envy. Furthermore, she thought Freud overemphasized the role of the sexual instinct and neglected cultural and environmental influences on personality. While she did stress the importance of early childhood experiences (1939), she believed that personality could continue to develop and change throughout life. She argued forcefully against Freud's notion that a woman's desire to have a child and a man is nothing more than a conversion of the unfulfilled wish for a penis.

Horney insisted that what women really want are the same opportunities, rights, and privileges that society grants to men. She argued convincingly that women must be given the opportunity to find their own personal identities, to develop their abilities, and to pursue careers if they choose.

Horney believed that to be psychologically healthy, we all need safety and satisfaction. But these needs can be frustrated in early childhood by parents who are indifferent, unaffectionate, rejecting, or hostile. Such early experiences may cause a child to develop basic anxiety—"the feeling a child has of being isolated and helpless in a potentially hostile world" (Horney, 1945, p. 41). To minimize this basic anxiety and to satisfy the need for safety, children develop coping strategies that form their basic attitude toward life—either moving *toward* people, moving *against* people, or moving *away from* people. If we are normal, we move in all three ways as different situations demand. But if we are neurotic, we are restricted to only one way to reduce anxiety, and we use it excessively and inappropriately.

Horney (1950) believed that the idealized self brings with it the "tyranny of the should"—unrealistic demands for personal perfection that "no human being could fulfill" (p. 66). The irrational, neurotic thinking that may spring from the "tyranny of the should" is an important part of Horney's theory. Her influence may be seen in modern cognitive-behavioural therapies, especially the rational-emotive therapy of Albert Ellis, which we explore in a later chapter.

LINK IT!

www.1w.net/karen/index.html
Karen Horney

Karen Horney insisted that, rather than envying the penis, as Freud believed, women really want the same opportunities and privileges as men—to play sports at the Olympic and professional levels, for example.

Remember It!

The Neo-Freudians

1. In Jung's theory, the inherited part of the personality that stores the experiences of humankind is the
   a. ego.
   b. collective conscious.
   c. personal unconscious.
   d. collective unconscious.
2. Which personality theorist believed that our basic drive is to overcome and compensate for inferiority feelings and strive for superiority and significance?
   a. Sigmund Freud
   b. Carl Jung
   c. Alfred Adler
   d. Karen Horney
3. Horney traced the origin of psychological maladjustment to
   a. the inferiority feelings of childhood.
   b. basic anxiety resulting from the parents' failure to satisfy the child's needs for safety and satisfaction.
   c. excessive frustration or overindulgence of the child at early stages of development.
   d. the failure to balance opposing forces in the personality.

Answers: 1. d 2. c 3. b

Trait Theories

What are trait theories of personality?

How would you describe yourself—cheerful, moody, talkative, quiet, shy, friendly, outgoing? When you describe your own personality or that of someone else, you probably list several relatively stable and consistent personal characteristics called **traits. Trait theories** are attempts to explain personality and differences between people in terms of personal characteristics.

Gordon Allport: Personality Traits in the Brain

How did Allport differentiate between cardinal and central traits?

Gordon Allport (1897–1967) asserted that personality traits are real entities, physically located somewhere in the brain (Allport & Odbert, 1936). Each of us inherits a unique set of raw materials for given traits, which are then shaped by our experiences. Traits describe how we respond to the environment and the consistency of that response. If we are shy, we respond to strangers differently than if we are friendly; if we are self-confident, we approach tasks differently than if we feel inferior.

Allport (1961) identified two main categories of traits: common and individual. Common traits are those traits we share or hold in common with most others in our own culture. For example, quiet, polite behaviour is a common trait of some Asian cultures. Far more important to Allport were three types of individual traits: cardinal, central, and secondary traits.

A **cardinal trait** is "so pervasive and so outstanding in a life that ... almost every act seems traceable to its influence" (Allport, 1961, p. 365). It is so strong a part of a person's personality that he or she may become identified with or known for that trait. **Central traits** are those we would "mention in writing a careful letter of recommendation" (Allport, 1961). Do the next *Try It!* to learn more about central traits.

We also possess numerous secondary traits, but these are less obvious, less consistent, and not as critical as the cardinal and central traits in defining our personality. Secondary traits are such things as food preferences, favourite music, and specific attitudes. We have many more secondary traits than cardinal or central traits.

trait: A personal characteristic that is used to describe or explain personality.

trait theories: Theories that attempt to explain personality and differences between people in terms of personal characteristics.

cardinal trait: Allport's name for a personal quality that is so strong a part of a person's personality that he or she may become identified with that trait.

central trait: Allport's name for the type of trait you would use in writing a letter of recommendation.

Try It!

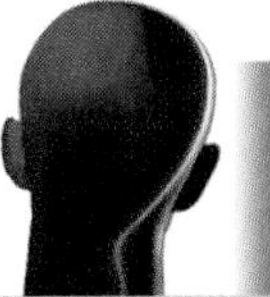

Identifying Central Traits

Which adjectives in this list best describe you? Which characterize your mother or your father? In Allport's terms you are describing her or his central traits.

decisive	funny	intelligent
disorganized	shy	fearful
jealous	controlled	responsible
rigid	outgoing	inhibited
religious	arrogant	loyal
competitive	liberal	friendly
compulsive	quiet	generous
sloppy	laid-back	rebellious
calm	good-natured	nervous
serious	humble	lazy
industrious	deceptive	cooperative
reckless	sad	honest
happy	selfish	organized

Raymond Cattell's 16 Personality Factors

How did Cattell differentiate between surface and source traits?

Raymond Cattell (1950) considered personality to be a pattern of traits providing the key to understanding and predicting a person's behaviour. He identified two types: surface traits and source traits.

If you were asked to describe your best friend, you might list such traits as kind, honest, helpful, generous, and so on. These observable qualities of personality Cattell called **surface traits**. (Allport called these qualities "central traits.") Using observations and questionnaires, Cattell studied thousands of people; he found certain clusters of surface traits that appeared together time after time. He thought these were evidence of deeper, more general personality factors. Using a statistical technique called "factor analysis," Cattell tried to identify these factors, which he called "source traits."

Source traits make up the most basic personality structure and, according to Cattell, cause behaviour. We all possess the same source traits; however, we do not all possess them in the same degree. Intelligence is a source trait, and every person has a certain amount of it, but obviously not exactly the same amount or the same kind. The level of people's intelligence can influence whether they pursue a university degree, the profession or job they choose, the type of leisure activities they pursue, and the kinds of friends they have.

Cattell found 23 source traits in normal individuals, 16 of which he studied in great detail. Cattell's Sixteen Personality Factor Questionnaire, commonly called the "16 P. F.," yields a personality profile (Cattell et al., 1950, 1977).

You can chart your own source traits in *Try It!*

The Cattell Personality Profile can be used to provide a better understanding of a single individual or to compare individuals. When later researchers tried to confirm Cattell's 16 factors, no one could find more than seven factors, and most found five (Digman, 1990).

Try It!

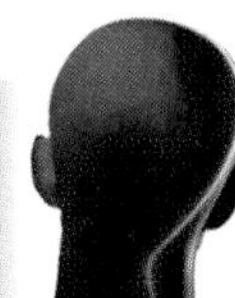

Charting a Personality Profile

This hypothetical personality profile is based on Cattell's Sixteen Personality Factor Questionnaire. Using it as a model, circle the point along each of the 16 dimensions of bipolar traits that best describes your personality.

Reserved	■ ■ ■ ■ ■ ■ ■ ■ ■ ■	Warm
Concrete	■ ■ ■ ■ ■ ■ ■ ■ ■ ■	Abstract
Reactive	■ ■ ■ ■ ■ ■ ■ ■ ■ ■	Emotionally stable
Avoids conflict	■ ■ ■ ■ ■ ■ ■ ■ ■ ■	Dominant
Serious	■ ■ ■ ■ ■ ■ ■ ■ ■ ■	Lively
Expedient	■ ■ ■ ■ ■ ■ ■ ■ ■ ■	Rule-conscious
Shy	■ ■ ■ ■ ■ ■ ■ ■ ■ ■	Socially bold
Utilitarian	■ ■ ■ ■ ■ ■ ■ ■ ■ ■	Sensitive
Trusting	■ ■ ■ ■ ■ ■ ■ ■ ■ ■	Suspicious
Practical	■ ■ ■ ■ ■ ■ ■ ■ ■ ■	Imaginative
Forthright	■ ■ ■ ■ ■ ■ ■ ■ ■ ■	Private
Self-assured	■ ■ ■ ■ ■ ■ ■ ■ ■ ■	Apprehensive
Traditional	■ ■ ■ ■ ■ ■ ■ ■ ■ ■	Open to change
Group-oriented	■ ■ ■ ■ ■ ■ ■ ■ ■ ■	Self-reliant
Tolerates disorder	■ ■ ■ ■ ■ ■ ■ ■ ■ ■	Perfectionistic
Relaxed	■ ■ ■ ■ ■ ■ ■ ■ ■ ■	Tense

Hans Eysenck: Stressing Two Factors

What does Eysenck consider to be the two most important dimensions of personality?

British psychologist Hans Eysenck (1990) has always believed that personality is largely determined by the genes, and that environmental influences are slight at best. Although Eysenck maintains that three higher-order factors or dimensions are needed to capture the essence of personality, he places particular emphasis on two dimensions: **extraversion** (versus **introversion**) and neuroticism (versus emotional stability). Extraverts are sociable, outgoing, and active, whereas introverts are withdrawn, quiet, and introspective. Emotionally stable people are calm, even-tempered, and often easygoing, whereas emotionally unstable people are anxious, excitable, and easily distressed.

Eysenck (1981) believes that individual variability on the two dimensions may be partly due to differences in nervous system functioning. He suggests that extraverts have a lower level of cortical arousal than introverts and as a result seek out more stimulation to increase arousal, while introverts are more easily aroused and thus more likely to show emotional instability.

The Five-Factor Theory of Personality: The Big Five

What are the Big Five personality dimensions in the five-factor theory as described by McCrae and Costa?

Today, the most talked-about theory of personality is the **five-factor theory**, also known as the "Big Five" (Wiggins, 1996). Each of the five factors is composed of a constellation of traits, all of which are specific components of a larger, broader personality factor.

Some of the researchers who accept these five broad dimensions of personality still disagree as to what they should be named. We will describe the Big Five dimensions using the names assigned by Robert McCrae and Paul Costa (1987; McCrae, 1996), the most influential proponents of the five-factor theory:

- *Extraversion.* This dimension contrasts such traits as sociable, outgoing, talkative, assertive, persuasive, decisive, and active with more introverted traits such as withdrawn, quiet, passive, retiring, reserved.
- *Neuroticism.* People high on neuroticism are prone to emotional instability. They tend to experience negative emotions and to be moody, irritable, nervous, and prone to worry. Neuroticism differentiates people who are anxious, excitable, and easily distressed from those who are emotionally stable and thus calm, even-tempered, easygoing, and relaxed.
- *Conscientiousness.* This factor differentiates individuals who are dependable, organized, reliable, responsible, thorough, hard-working, and persevering from those who are undependable, disorganized, impulsive, unreliable, irresponsible, careless, negligent, and lazy.
- *Agreeableness.* This factor is composed of a collection of traits that range from compassion to antagonism toward others. A person high on agreeableness would be a pleasant person, good-natured, warm, sympathetic, and cooperative; whereas one low on agreeableness would tend to be unfriendly, unpleasant, aggressive, argumentative, cold, and even hostile and vindictive.
- *Openness to Experience.* The naming of this factor has been the subject of lively debate, but there is general agreement that openness to experience contrasts individuals who are imaginative, curious, broad-minded, and cultured with those who are concrete-minded and practical, and whose interests are narrow (King et al., 1996).

Researchers from many different traditions have found five factors when they have subjected self-ratings, observer ratings, and peer ratings to analysis. Five factors have emerged, as well, from studies in many

surface traits: Cattell's name for observable qualities of personality, such as those used to describe a friend.

source traits: Cattell's name for the traits that underlie the surface traits, make up the most basic personality structure, and cause behaviour.

extraversion: The tendency to be outgoing, adaptable, and sociable.

introversion: The tendency to focus inward.

five-factor theory: A trait theory that attempts to explain personality using five broad dimensions, each of which is composed of a constellation of personality traits.

different languages; across different age groups; with females and males; and in various cultures, including German, Chinese, Korean, Israeli, Portuguese, Turkish, British, and Spanish (McCrea & Costa, 1997; McCrea et al., 2000). Still more support for the five-factor theory comes from two cross-cultural studies by Paunonen and colleagues (1996, 2000) involving participants from Canada and several other countries. In addition, a large-scale study by Williams and colleagues (1998) found consistent personality patterns along the Big Five dimensions in 20 countries.

Most studies that examine the Big-Five personality factors have used a personality measure called the NEO Personality Inventory (NEO-PI) which was originally developed by Costa and McCrae (1985, 1992, 1997) and has been recently revised (NEO-PI-R).

There certainly has been a lot of recent research support for the Big-Five theory of personality and acceptance is growing, but this model also has its critics. Block (1995) maintains that there is inconsistency in the model and a lack of clarity about how the factors ought to be understood. McAdams (1992) argues that the model fails to address "core constructs of personality functioning beyond the level of traits" and to provide "compelling causal explanations for human behaviour and experience" (p. 329). Because the five-factor theory describes personality on a very general level, knowing how high or low a person scored on the five dimensions would not enable one to predict that person's behaviour in a specific situation. But the Big Five may be helpful in predicting general trends of behaviour in a wide variety of situations.

Evaluating the Trait Perspective

Do we possess stable and enduring traits that predictably guide the way we will act across time and changing situations? Critics of trait theories say no and maintain that the consistency of our behaviour across situations is very low and not predictable on the basis of personality traits. After several decades of study, the weight of evidence supports the view that there are internal traits that strongly influence behaviour across situations (Carson, 1989; McAdams, 1992). According to Funder and Colvin (1991), "Even though situations profoundly affect what people do, people can still manage to preserve their distinctive behavioural styles across situations" (p. 791). Additional support for the trait theorists has come from longitudinal studies. McCrae and Costa (1987) studied personality traits of subjects over time and found them to be stable for periods of 3 to 30 years. They concluded that "aging itself has little effect on personality" (p. 862). According to McCrae (1993), "Stable individual differences in basic dimensions are a universal feature of adult personality" (p. 577).

Even the most talkative and boisterous among us tend to be quiet during a religious service or a funeral.

Remember It!

Trait Theories

1. According to Allport, the kind of trait that is used in a letter of recommendation is a __________; the kind of trait that is a defining characteristic of one's personality is a __________.
   a. common trait; secondary trait
   b. cardinal trait; common trait
   c. cardinal trait; central trait
   d. central trait; cardinal trait
2. Which of the following statements is *not* true of source traits, according to Cattell?
   a. Differences in personality can be explained primarily in terms of the degree to which people possess the same source traits.
   b. Source traits can be viewed as the cause of behaviour.
   c. The differences between people are explained by the number of source traits they possess.
   d. Source traits can be used to compare one person with another.
3. We can best understand personality by assessing people on two major dimensions: extraversion and neuroticism. This view is championed by:
   a. Hans Eysenck.
   b. Gordon Allport.
   c. Raymond Cattell.
   d. Carl Jung.
4. According to a growing number of trait theorists, there are ______ major dimensions of personality.
   a. 3
   b. 5
   c. 7
   d. 16

Answers: 1. d 2. c 3. a 4. b

According to the trait theorists, characteristic traits determine how we behave *most* of the time, not *all* of the time. And we would agree that even the most optimistic, happy, and outgoing people have "down" days, fall ill, and frown occasionally.

Learning Theories and Personality

According to the learning perspective, personality consists of the learned tendencies that have been acquired over a lifetime.

The Behaviourist View of B.F. Skinner

How did Skinner account for what most people refer to as personality?

B.F. Skinner and other behaviourists have an interesting view of personality: they deny that there is any such thing. What we call personality, they believe, is nothing more or less than a collection of learned behaviours or habits that have been reinforced in the past. Skinner denied that a personality or self initiates and directs behaviour. The causes of behaviour, he stated, lie outside the person, and they are based on past and present rewards and punishments. Thus, Skinner did not use the term "personality." He simply described the variables in the environment that shape an individual's observable behaviour. Healthy experiences in a healthy environment make a healthy person.

But what about the psychologically unhealthy individual? Where does abnormal behaviour originate? Skinner (1953) believed that psychologically unhealthy people have been reinforced by the environment for behaving abnormally. For example, an overly dependent person may have been punished by his parents for asserting his independence and reinforced for dependency. To change an individual's behaviour, then, we must restructure the environment so that it will reinforce normal rather than abnormal behaviour. What a contrast this is to psychoanalytic theory and trait theory, which see internal forces as the major shapers and determinants of behaviour.

LINK IT!

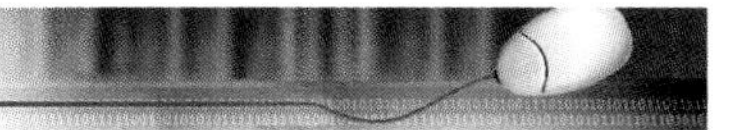

www.bfskinner.org
The B.F. Skinner Foundation

The Social-Cognitive Theorists: Expanding the Behaviourist View

There is no doubt that some of our behaviours can be traced to classical and operant conditioning; but can all of personality, or even all of learning, be explained in this way? Not according to social-cognitive theorists, who consider both the environment *and* personal/cognitive factors in their attempts to understand human personality and behaviour. Personal/cognitive factors include personal dispositions, feelings, expectancies, perceptions, and cognitions, such as thoughts, beliefs, and attitudes.

Albert Bandura's Views on Personality

What are the components that make up Bandura's concept of reciprocal determinism, and how do they interact?

The chief advocate of the social-cognitive theory is Albert Bandura, who maintains that personal/cognitive factors, our behaviour, and the external environment all influence each other and are influenced by each other (Bandura, 1989). This mutual relationship he calls **reciprocal determinism.** Figure 10.3 provides a diagram of Bandura's model of reciprocal determinism.

Consider how Bandura's concept of reciprocal determinism might work in the following situation: A waiter who normally works in a section of a restaurant where good tippers habitually sit is reassigned to tables in an area where tips are normally poor. This new environment influences the waiter's beliefs and expectancies (personal/cognitive factors). Now, because he believes that good service will not be appropriately rewarded, his behaviour changes. He is inattentive, is not very pleasant, and provides poor service. Consequently, the waiter's attitude and behaviour work reciprocally on the customers, affecting their thinking, feelings, and attitudes. And these, in turn, influence their behaviour. Not surprisingly, these customers *do* tip poorly.

One of the personal/cognitive factors Bandura (1997a, 1997b) considers especially important is self-

reciprocal determinism: Bandura's concept that behaviour, personal/cognitive factors, and environment all influence and are influenced by each other.

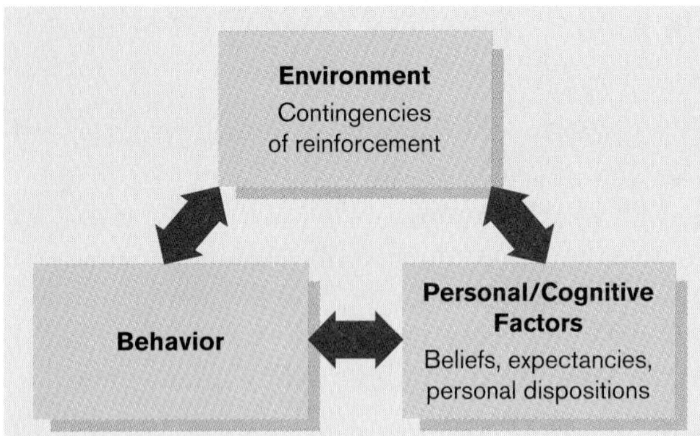

FIGURE 10.3

Albert Bandura's Reciprocal Determinism **Albert Bandura takes a social-cognitive view of personality. He suggests that three components–our environment, our behaviour, and personal/cognitive factors such as our beliefs, expectancies, and personal dispositions–play reciprocal roles in determining personality and behaviour.**

efficacy. **Self-efficacy** is the perception people hold of their ability to perform competently and successfully in whatever they attempt. People high in self-efficacy will approach new situations confidently and will persist in their efforts because they believe success is likely. People low in self-efficacy, on the other hand, will expect failure and avoid challenges, will "give up in the face of difficulty, recover slowly from setbacks and easily fall victims to stress and depression" (Bandura 1997a, p. 5).

Locus of Control

What is meant by the terms *internal* and *external locus of control*?

Julian Rotter (1966, 1971, 1990) proposes another concept, **locus of control**, which provides additional insight into why people behave as they do. Some people see themselves as primarily in control of their behaviour and its consequences. That is, they exhibit an *internal* locus of control. Others perceive that whatever happens to them is in the hands of fate, luck, or chance; they exhibit an *external* locus of control and may contend that it does not matter what they do because "whatever will be, will be." Herbert Lefcourt at the University of Waterloo supports the locus-of-control concept. His 1966 article in *Psychological Bulletin*, one of the most highly recognized psychology journals, is one of the 10 most cited articles in this journal. Both Rotter and Lefcourt contend that people with an external locus of control are less likely to change their behaviour as a result of reinforcement, because they do not see reinforcers as being tied to their own actions.

Evaluating the Social-Cognitive Perspective

The social-cognitive perspective cannot be criticized for lacking a strong research base. Yet some argue that it emphasizes the *situation* too strongly. They

Remember It!

Learning Theories and Personality

1. Which of the following concepts does Skinner find useful in explaining behaviour?
   a. Behaviour is initiated by inner forces called personality.
   b. Behaviour is caused by forces outside the person and based upon past rewards and punishments.
   c. Behaviour is an interaction of inner forces and situational forces.
   d. Behaviour and personality are for the most part determined by our heredity.
2. Bandura's concept of reciprocal determinism refers to the mutual effects of
   a. our behaviour, personality, and thinking.
   b. our feelings, attitudes, and thoughts.
   c. our behaviour, personal/cognitive factors, and the environment.
   d. classical and operant conditioning and observational learning.
3. Which statement is *not* true of people low in self-efficacy?
   a. They persist in their efforts.
   b. They lack confidence.
   c. They expect failure.
   d. They avoid challenge.
4. Who proposed the concept of *locus of control*?
   a. B.F. Skinner
   b. Albert Bandura
   c. Hans Eysenck
   d. Julian Rotter

Answers: 1.b 2.c 3.a 4.d

ask: What about *unconscious* motives or *internal* dispositions (traits) that we exhibit fairly consistently across many different situations? Other critics point to the accumulating evidence that heredity may explain 40 to 50 percent or more of the variation in personality characteristics (Bouchard, 1994).

Humanistic Personality Theories

Who were the two pioneers in humanistic psychology, and how did they view human nature?

Humanistic psychology seeks to give a more complete and positive picture of the human personality than the two other major forces in psychology—behaviourism and psychoanalysis. Humanistic psychologists developed their own unique view of human nature, a view that is considerably more flattering. They see human nature as innately good and contend that people have a natural tendency toward growth and the realization of their fullest potential. The humanists largely deny that there is a dark or evil side of human nature. They do not believe that people are shaped strictly by the environment or ruled by mysterious, unconscious forces. Rather, they see people as creative beings with an active, conscious free will who can chart their own course in life.

The pioneering humanistic psychologists were Abraham Maslow and Carl Rogers.

Abraham Maslow: The Self-Actualizing Person

What is self-actualization, and how did Maslow study it?

For Abraham Maslow (1970), motivational factors were at the root of personality. As we saw in Chapter 9, Maslow constructed a hierarchy of needs, with physiological needs at the bottom and the need for self-actualization at the top. **Self-actualization** means developing to one's fullest potential. A healthy person is one who is always growing and becoming all that he or she can be.

Maslow maintained that if you want to know what makes a healthy personality, you must study people who are healthy. So he studied individuals he believed were using their talents and abilities to their fullest—in other words, individuals who exemplified self-actualization. Maslow studied historical figures, and figures who made significant contributions during their lifetime, to identify characteristics that self-actualizing people seem to share.

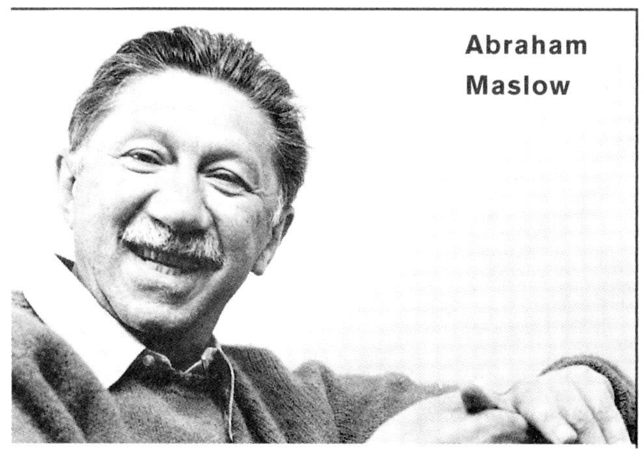
Abraham Maslow

Maslow found self-actualizers to be accurate in perceiving reality—able to judge honestly and to spot quickly the fake and the dishonest. Self-actualizers are comfortable with life; they accept themselves and others, and nature as well, with good humour and tolerance. Most of them believe they have a mission to accomplish or the need to devote their life to some larger good. Self-actualizers tend not to depend on external authority or on other people; rather, they seem to be inner-driven, autonomous, and independent. They feel a strong fellowship with humanity, and their relationships with others are characterized by deep and loving bonds. They can laugh at themselves, and their sense of humour, though well-developed, never involves hostility or criticism of others. Finally, self-actualizers often have

self-efficacy: A person's belief in his or her ability to perform competently in whatever is attempted.

locus of control: A concept used to explain how people account for what happens in their lives–people with an *internal locus of control* see themselves as primarily in control of their behaviour and its consequences; those with an *external locus of control* perceive what happens to be in the hands of fate, luck, or chance.

humanistic psychology: An approach to psychology that stresses the uniquely human attributes and a positive view of human nature.

self-actualization: Developing to one's fullest potential.

peak experiences—experiences of harmony within and with the universe.

Maslow concluded that each of us has the capacity for self-actualization. If we apply our talent and energy to doing our best in whatever endeavour we choose, then we, too, can lead creative lives and be considered self-actualizing.

LINK IT!

www.maslow.com/index.html
Abraham Maslow publications site

Carl Rogers: The Fully Functioning Person

According to Rogers, why don't all people become fully functioning persons?

Carl Rogers (1951, 1961) developed his theory of personality through insights gained from his patients in therapy sessions. Rogers viewed human nature as basically good. If left to develop naturally, he thought, people would be happy and psychologically healthy.

According to Rogers, each of us lives in a private subjective reality, the *phenomenological field*. It is in this personal, subjective field, rather than in the objective, real, physical environment, that we act, think and feel. In other words, the way we see it is the way it is—for us. Gradually a part of the phenomenological field becomes differentiated as the self. The self-concept emerges as a result of repeated experiences involving such terms as "I," "me," and "mine." With the emerging self comes the need for positive regard. We need such things as warmth, love, acceptance, sympathy, and respect from the people who are significant in our lives. While positive regard from others is crucial to the self, it alone is not enough. We also need positive self-regard. But the road to positive self-regard can be long and rocky indeed, because we need the positive regard of others all along the way. And there are usually strings attached to positive regard from others.

Usually our parents do not view us positively regardless of our behaviour. They set up **conditions of worth**—conditions on which their positive regard hinges. Conditions of worth force us to live and act according to someone else's values rather than our own. In our efforts to gain positive regard, we deny our true self by inhibiting some of our behaviour, denying and distorting some of our perceptions, and closing ourselves to parts of our experience. In so doing, we experience stress and anxiety, and our whole self-structure may be threatened.

For Rogers, a major goal of psychotherapy is to enable individuals to open themselves up to experiences and begin to live according to their own values rather than the values of others. He calls his therapy "person-centred therapy," preferring not to use the term *patient*. Rogers believes that the therapist must give the client **unconditional positive regard**—that is, the therapist must give positive regard no matter what the client says, does, has done, or is thinking of doing. Unconditional positive regard is designed to reduce threats, eliminate conditions of worth, and bring the person back in tune with his or her true self.

Evaluating the Humanistic Perspective

Humanism has become much more than a personality theory and an approach to therapy. Its influence has spread significantly as a social movement in the schools and in society in general. Some of its severest critics charge that an all-consuming personal quest for self-fulfilment can lead to a self-centred, self-serving, self-indulgent personality that lacks moral restraint or genuine concern for others (Campbell & Sprecht, 1985; Wallach & Wallach, 1983).

Humanistic psychologists do not accept such criticisms as valid. By and large, they trust in the inherent goodness of human nature, and their perspective on personality is consistent with that trust. But how do humanists explain the evil we see around us—assaults, murder, rape? Where does this originate? Rogers replied, "I do not find that this evil is inherent in human nature … I have never known an individual to choose the cruel or destructive path … So my experience leads me to believe that it is cultural influences which are the major factor in our evil behaviors" (1981, p. 16).

Though the humanists have been criticized for being unscientific and for seeing, hearing, and finding no evil within the human psyche, they have inspired the study of the positive qualities—altruism, cooperation, love, and acceptance of self and others.

Humanistic and Behavioural Theories of Personality

Remember It!

1. Humanistic psychologists would *not* say that
   a. human nature is innately good.
   b. human beings have a natural tendency toward self-actualization.
   c. human beings have free will.
   d. researchers' focus should be primarily on observable behaviour.
2. Which psychologist studied individuals he believed exemplified self-actualization in order to identify characteristics that self-actualizing persons share?
   a. Carl Rogers
   b. Gordon Allport
   c. Abraham Maslow
   d. Hans Eysenck
3. Which psychologist believed that individuals often do not become fully functioning persons because, in childhood, they failed to receive unconditional positive regard from their parents?
   a. Carl Rogers
   b. Gordon Allport
   c. Abraham Maslow
   d. Hans Eysenck
4. Many behavioural geneticists believe that personality may be as much as __________ inherited.
   a. 10 to 20 percent
   b. 25 to 35 percent
   c. 40 to 50 percent
   d. 65 to 75 percent

Answers: 1. d 2. c 3. a 4. c

Personality: Is It in the Genes?

What has research in behavioural genetics revealed about the influence of the genes and the environment on personality?

Behavioural genetics is a field of research that investigates the relative effects of heredity and environment on behaviour and ability (Plomin & Rende, 1991).

The Twin Study Method: Studying Identical and Fraternal Twins

One approach used in behavioural genetics is the twin study method, in which identical (monozygotic, or MZ) twins and fraternal (dizygotic, or DZ) twins are studied to determine how much they resemble each other with respect to a variety of characteristics. An ideal way to assess the relative contribution of heredity and environment is to study identical twins who were separated at birth and reared apart. When identical twins who were reared apart have strikingly similar traits, it is assumed that heredity has been a major contributor. When twins differ on a given trait, the influence of the environment is thought to be greater.

Tellegen and colleagues (1988) found that identical twins were quite similar on several personality factors whether they were raised together or apart. The term **heritability** refers to the degree to which a characteristic is estimated to be influenced by heredity. Altruism and aggressiveness—traits one would expect to be strongly influenced by parental upbringing—also appear to be more strongly influenced by heredity (Miles & Carey, 1997). After studying heritability of traits in 573 adult twin pairs, Rushton and colleagues (1986) at the University of Western Ontario found that aggressiveness, nurturance, empathy, assertiveness, and altruism are substantially influenced by heredity.

Twin studies have also revealed a genetic influence on social attitudes such as traditionalism, that is, whether we endorse traditional moral values and follow rules and authority (Finkel & McGue, 1997). There even seems to be a genetic influence on how people view their environment (Chipuer et al., 1993; Plomin & Bergeman, 1991), on how they perceive

conditions of worth: Conditions upon which the positive regard of others rests.

unconditional positive regard: Unqualified caring and non-judgmental acceptance of another.

behavioural genetics: The field of research that investigates the relative effects of heredity and environment on behaviour and ability.

heritability: An index of the degree to which a characteristic is estimated to be influenced by heredity.

life events (particularly controllable ones), on people's sense of well-being (Plomin & Rende, 1991), and on alcoholism in men (Prescott & Kendler, 1999).

The genetic influences we have been discussing are not the result of one or even a few genes. Rather, they involve many genes, each with small effects (Plomin et al., 1994). While these findings indicate that most personality traits are influenced by genes, "behavioural genetic research clearly demonstrates that both nature and nurture are important in human development" (Plomin, 1989, p. 110). To learn that most psychological traits are significantly heritable does not lessen the value or reduce the importance of environmental factors such as social influences, parenting, and education.

IT HAPPENED IN CANADA

I Am Canadian!

Can a country have a personality? From the success of the recent advertising campaign that focuses on Joe Canadian, the answer appears to be a resounding "yes." No one really expected the level of success achieved by the ad that attacked often held stereotypes of Canadians. "We definitely didn't expect the ad to have the impact it had, beyond its value as a beer ad," commented Molson Vice-President Brett Marchand. "The ad is what more Canadians wish people would do—scream that they're proud to be Canadian" ("Beer ad," 2000).

Psychological research has not really examined whether a country can have a personality, but some studies do suggest that culture has a significant influence on people's personality. Work by Hofstede in the 1980s revealed several dimensions that link culture and personality—the most important factor being the individualism/collectivism dimension. In individualist cultures, more emphasis is placed on individual rather than group achievement, and high-achieving individuals are accorded honour and prestige. People in collectivist cultures, on the other hand, tend to be more interdependent and define themselves and their personal interests in terms of their group membership. Perhaps you will not be surprised to hear that the United States ranked as the most individualist culture, although Canada was not far behind. But it is also true that the Canada of today differs greatly from what it once was, even as recently as in the 1980s.

The many cultures that are now represented in Canada's cultural mosaic vary greatly in their values, with many of them, especially those from Asia, being far more collectivist than others. Native Canadians, too, share many collectivist values such as the importance of family, community, cooperation, helpfulness and generosity. For Native Canadians, such behaviours bring more honour and prestige than accumulating property and wealth. This is certainly food for thought when we consider what type of "personality" is characteristic of our country, and of its members.

LINK IT!

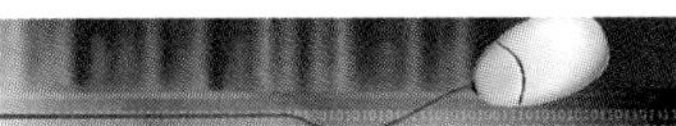

web.mit.edu/afs/athena/user/j/g/jganger/Public/ourhome.html
The MIT Twins Study Home page

Personality Assessment

What are the three major methods used in personality assessment?

Just as there are many different personality theories, there are many different methods for measuring personality. Various personality tests are used by clinical and counselling psychologists, psychiatrists, and counsellors to diagnose patients and assess progress in therapy. Personality assessment is also used by businesses and industries to aid in hiring decisions, and by counsellors for vocational and educational counselling. Personality assessment methods can be grouped in a few broad categories: (1) observation, interviews, and rating scales; (2) inventories; and (3) projective tests.

Observation, Interviews, and Rating Scales

Observation

All of us use observation, though informally, to form opinions about other people. Psychologists use observation in personality assessment and evaluation in a variety of settings, including hospitals, clinics, schools, and workplaces.

Using an observational technique known as *behavioural assessment*, psychologists can count and record the frequency of particular behaviours they are studying. This method is often used in behaviour modification programs in settings such as mental hospitals, where psychologists may chart the progress of patients in reducing aggressive acts or other undesirable or abnormal behaviours.

Although much can be learned from observation, it has its shortcomings; it is time-consuming and expensive (observers must be trained and paid); what is observed may be misinterpreted; and two observers may interpret the same event differently. Probably the most serious limitation is that the very presence of the observer can alter the behaviour that is observed. And assessing personality through observation can sometimes be misleading.

Interviews

Clinical psychologists and psychiatrists use interviews to help diagnose and treat patients. Counsellors use interviews to screen applicants for admission to colleges, universities, and special programs. Employers use them to evaluate job applicants and candidates for job promotions.

Interviewers consider not only a person's answers but also tone of voice, speech, mannerisms, gestures, and general appearance. Psychologists and other professionals use both structured and unstructured interviews in making their assessments. In unstructured situations, the direction the interview will take and the questions to be asked are not all planned beforehand; thus, the interview can be highly personalized. In structured situations, the content of the questions and the manner in which they are asked are carefully planned ahead of time. The interviewer tries not to deviate in any way from the structured format so that more reliable comparisons can be made between different participants.

Rating Scales

Sometimes examiners use rating scales to record data from interviews or observations. Rating scales are useful because they provide a standardized format, including a list of traits or behaviours on which the subject is to be evaluated. The rating scale helps to focus the rater's attention on all relevant traits so that some are not overlooked or weighed too heavily.

But there are problems with rating scales. Often there is low agreement among raters in their evaluation of the same individual. One way to overcome this is to train the judges or raters to a point where they can achieve high agreement when the same person or event is rated. Another problem is the **halo effect**—the tendency of raters to be excessively influenced in their overall evaluation of a person by one or a few favourable or unfavourable traits. Often traits or attributes that are not even on the rating scale, such as physical attractiveness or similarity to the rater, heavily influence a rater's perception of a participant.

Personality Inventories: Taking Stock

What is an inventory, and what are the MMPI-2 and the JPI designed to reveal?

There is an objective method for measuring personality, a method in which the personal opinions and ratings of observers or interviewers do not unduly influence the results. This method is the **inventory**, a paper-and-pencil test with questions about an individual's thoughts, feelings, and behaviours, which measures several dimensions of personality and can be scored according to a standard procedure. Psychologists favouring the trait approach to personality prefer the inventory because it can assess where people fall on various dimensions of personality, and the results are plotted on a personality profile. Many personality inventories have been developed; none has been more widely used than the Minnesota Multiphasic Personality Inventory.

The MMPI and MMPI-2

The **Minnesota Multiphasic Personality Inventory-2 (MMPI-2)** is a revision of the most popular, the most heavily researched, and the most widely used personality test for screening and diagnosing psychiatric problems and disorders, and for use in psychological research (Butcher & Rouse, 1996).

There have been more than 115 recognized translations of the MMPI, which is used in more than 65 countries (Butcher & Graham, 1989). Published in 1943 by McKinley and Hathaway, the MMPI was originally intended to identify tendencies toward various psychiatric disorders.

Because it was published back in 1943, some aspects of the MMPI had become outdated by the 1980s. It was revised, and the MMPI-2 was published in 1989 (Butcher et al., 1989). Most of the original

halo effect: The tendency of raters to be excessively influenced in their overall evaluation of a person by one or a few favourable or unfavourable traits.

inventory: A paper-and-pencil test with questions about a person's thoughts, feelings, and behaviours, which can be scored according to a standard procedure.

Minnesota Multiphasic Personality Inventory-2 (MMPI-2): A revision of the most extensively researched and widely used personality test; used to screen and diagnose psychiatric problems and disorders.

test items were retained, but some were deleted because they were obsolete or because they contained sexual or religious references that offended some people (Kingsbury, 1991). New items were added to provide more adequate coverage of areas such as alcoholism, drug abuse, and suicidal tendencies. Although the MMPI-2 now has 567 items, updating has made it more user-friendly and easier for the person being tested (Butcher & Hostetler, 1990).

The MMPI-2 provides scores on four validity scales and ten clinical scales. Here are examples of questions on the test:

> I wish I were not bothered by thoughts about sex.
>
> When I get bored I like to stir up some excitement.
>
> In walking I am very careful to step over sidewalk cracks.
>
> If people had not had it in for me, I would have been much more successful.

Evaluating the MMPI-2

The MMPI-2 is reliable, easy to administer and score, and inexpensive to use. It is useful in the screening, diagnosis, and clinical description of abnormal behaviour; however, it is not very good at revealing differences among normal personalities.

Both the MMPI and the MMPI-2 can claim only modest success in predicting a clinical diagnosis. Morrison and colleagues (1994) found that both instruments agreed with the diagnosis made by clinicians only 39 percent of the time. Other researchers have cautioned against making diagnoses based exclusively on the MMPI and MMPI-2 (Brems, 1991; Libb et al., 1992). Rather, clinicians should integrate MMPI results with other sources of clinical information before making a diagnosis.

The Jackson Personality Inventory and the Personality Research Form

Are there instruments to assess the personality of a normal person? Yes. D. N. Jackson at the University of Western Ontario developed the **Jackson Personality Inventory** (JPI) (Jackson, 1976) and the Personality Research Form (PRF) (Jackson, 1984). Both are highly regarded personality tests that have been developed especially for normal populations.

The JPI and PRF are valuable for predicting behaviour. The JPI measures 16 personality traits, the PRF measures 20. Each test assesses different characteristics. For example, the JPI measures risk taking. The PRF is the fourth most highly cited personality inventory in the psychology literature (Mitchell, 1983).

on the cutting edge in canada

Personality Scales for French-speaking Canadians

So far in this chapter, we have discussed how personality inventories are used to assess people's personalities on particular dimensions, such as self-esteem, motivation, or self-control. But do these personality constructs hold across cultures? Research suggests that this is the case, but careful test development must take place to ensure the reliability and validity of these instruments when they are used in different cultures. How then do psychologists make sure that they are measuring the same dimensions when people are from different linguistic groups? This is a question that has been at the forefront of much research by Quebec psychologists.

In the past 10 years, psychologists at the Université du Quebec à Montréal and Trois-Rivieres, Université Laval, and the Université de Montréal have worked to develop new French personality inventories and have translated existing English inventories to be used in Quebec and other francophone communities throughout Canada.

Creating a new inventory is not a simple task. Scale development requires that data be collected on hundreds and often thousands of participants. Recent work by Quebec researchers has led to the development of scales that assess educational motivation (Vallerand et al., 1993), adolescent autonomy (Deslandes et al., 1999), motivation toward family activities (Senecal & Vallerand, 1999), self-control (Levesque et al., 1995), conflict resolution (Laferriee & Bouchard, 1996), and reasons for living (Labelle et al., 1996), to name a few. Such research efforts have provided French-speaking researchers and practitioners with more valid methods of assessments that take into consideration cultural and linguistic differences.

Could such differences help predict the success of relationships?

The *On the Cutting Edge in Canada* box describes Canadian researchers' work in translating popular personality tests into French.

Projective Tests: Projections from the Unconscious

How do projective tests provide insight into personality, and what are several of the most commonly used ?

Responses on interviews and questionnaires are conscious responses; for this reason, they are less useful to therapists who wish to probe the unconscious. Such therapists may choose a completely different technique called a projective test. A **projective test** is a personality test consisting of inkblots, drawings of ambiguous human situations, or incomplete sentences for which there are no obvious correct or incorrect responses. People respond by projecting their own inner thoughts, feelings, fears, or conflicts onto the test materials, just as a movie projector projects film images onto a screen.

The Rorschach Inkblot Test: What Do You See?

One of the oldest and most popular projective tests is the **Rorschach Inkblot Test**, developed by Swiss psychiatrist Hermann Rorschach in 1921. It consists of 10 inkblots, which people are asked to describe (see Figure 10.4).

To develop his test, Rorschach put ink on paper and then folded the paper so that symmetrical patterns resulted. Earlier, psychologists had used standardized series of inkblots to study imagination and other personal attributes; Rorschach was the first to use inkblots to investigate personality (Anastasi & Urbina, 1997). He experimented with thousands of inkblots on different groups of people and found that 10 of the inkblots could be used to discriminate between different diagnostic groups: manic depressives, paranoid schizophrenics, and so on. These 10 inkblots—five black and white, and five in colour—were standardized and are still widely used.

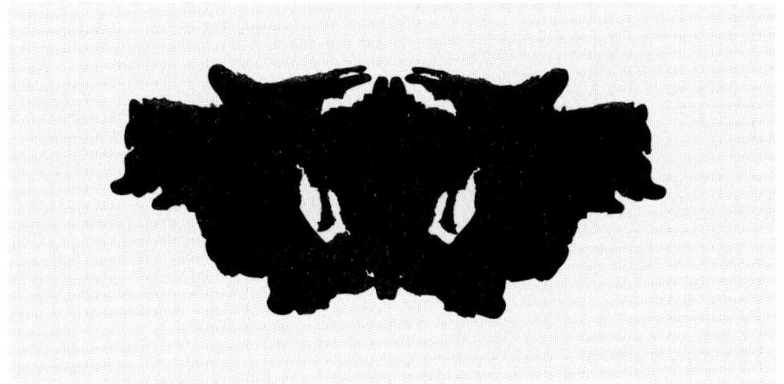

FIGURE 10.4

An Inkblot Similar to One on the Rorschach Inkblot Test

ADMINISTRATION AND SCORING OF THE RORSCHACH

The 10 inkblots are shown to the person, who is asked to tell everything that each inkblot looks like or resembles. The examiner writes down the person's responses and then goes through the cards again, asking questions to clarify what the person has reported.

Reliable interpretation remains a problem. For the most part, researchers have found low reliability and validity (Walsh & Betz, 1990; Wood et al., 2000). Weiner (1994) suggests that the Rorschach might best be thought of as a method that "generates useful information about personality functioning" (pp. 499–500). But despite these criticisms, the Rorschach has been second in popularity over the past 20 years (MMPI is first) for use in research and clinical assessment (Butcher & Rouse, 1996).

The Thematic Apperception Test: Seeing Ourselves in Scenes of Others

Another projective test is the **Thematic Apperception Test (TAT)** developed by Henry Murray and his colleagues in 1935 (Morgan & Murray, 1935; Murray, 1938). The TAT consists of one blank card and 19 other cards showing vague or ambiguous black-and-white drawings of human fig-

Jackson Personality Inventory (JPI): A highly regarded personality test used to assess the normal personality.

projective test: A personality test in which people respond to inkblots, drawings of ambiguous human situations, incomplete sentences, and the like, by projecting their own inner thoughts, feelings, fears, or conflicts into the test materials.

Rorschach Inkblot Test (ROR-shok): A projective test composed of 10 inkblots to which a participant responds; used to reveal unconscious functioning and the presence of psychiatric disorders.

Thematic Apperception Test (TAT): A projective test consisting of drawings of ambiguous human situations, which the subject describes; thought to reveal inner feelings, conflicts, and motives, which are projected onto the test materials.

ures in various situations. The test taker is asked to make up a story about each scene in the test.

"The test is based upon the well-recognized fact that when a person interprets an ambiguous social situation he is apt to expose his own personality as much as the phenomenon to which he is attending" (Morgan & Murray, 1962, p. 531). If many of a person's story themes are about illness (or sex, or fear of failure, or aggression, or power, or interpersonal conflicts, etc.), it is thought to reveal a problem in the person's life. Murray (1965) also maintains that the strength of the TAT is "its capacity to reveal things that the patient is unwilling to tell or is unable to tell because he is unconscious of them" (p. 427).

The TAT is time-consuming and difficult to administer and score. Although it has been used extensively in personality research, it suffers from the same weaknesses as other projective techniques: (1) It relies heavily on the interpretation skills of the examiner; and (2) it may reflect too strongly a person's temporary motivational and emotional state and not get at the more permanent aspects of personality.

The Sentence-Completion Method: Filling in the Blanks

Another projective technique, the sentence-completion method, may be one of the most valid projective techniques of all. It consists of a number of incomplete sentences to be completed by the individual, such as these:

I worry a great deal about ________.

I sometimes feel ________.

I would be happier if ________.

My mother ________.

In a comprehensive review, Goldberg (1965) summarized 50 validity studies and concluded that sentence completion is a valuable technique appropriate for widespread clinical and research use.

The Value of Projective Tests

How effective are projective tests? Research evidence concerning the validity of projective techniques as a whole is very disappointing: projective tests continue to suffer from a lack of objectivity in scoring and an absence of adequate norms (Halperin & McKay, 1998). Nevertheless, in clinical practice projective tests continue to be a popular and valued diagnostic tool (Archer et al., 1991; Butcher & Rouse, 1996; Lubin et al., 1986; Weiner, 1997).

Review & Reflect 10.2 summarizes the different types of personality tests. We also summarize the major theories of personality, their assumptions, and assessment techniques in Review & Reflect 10.3.

Remember It!

Personality Assessment

1. Match the personality test with its description.

____ 1) MMPI-2	a. inventory used to diagnose psychopathology
____ 2) Rorschach	b. inventory used to assess normal personality
____ 3) TAT	c. projective test using inkblots
____ 4) JPI	d. projective test using drawings of ambiguous human situations

2. Dr. X and Dr. Y are both experts in personality assessment. They would be most likely to agree on their interpretation of results from the

a. Rorschach. b. MMPI-2.
c. TAT. d. sentence-completion method.

3. George has an unconscious resentment toward his father. Which test might best detect this?

a. MMPI-2 b. JPI
c. Rorschach d. TAT

Answers: 1. 1) a 2) c 3) d 4) b 2. b 3. d

REVIEW & REFLECT 10.2
Three Approaches to Personality Assessment

Method	Examples	Description
Observation and rating	Observation Interviews Rating scales	Performance (behaviour) is observed in a specific situation, and personality is assessed on the basis of observation. In interviews, the responses to questions are taken to reveal personality characteristics. Rating scales are used to score or rate subjects on the basis of traits, behaviours, or results of interviews. Assessment is subjective, and accuracy depends largely on the ability and experience of the evaluator.
Inventories	Minnesota Multiphasic Personality Inventory-2 (MMPI-2) Jackson Personality Inventory (JPI)	Subjects reveal their beliefs, feelings, behaviour, and/or opinions on paper-and-pencil tests. Scoring procedures are standardized and responses are compared to group norms.
Projective tests	Rorschach Inkblot Test Thematic Apperception Test (TAT) Sentence-completion method	Subjects respond to ambiguous test materials and presumably reveal elements of their own personality. This is done through an analysis of the themes each person describes, either orally or in writing. Scoring is subjective, and accuracy depends largely on the ability and experience of the evaluator.

REVIEW & REFLECT 10.3
Summary of Five Approaches to Personality

Approach	Associated Theorists	Assumptions about Behaviour	Assessment Techniques	Research Methods
Psychoanalytic	Freud	Behaviour arises mostly from unconscious conflicts between pleasure-seeking id and moral-perfectionist superego, with reality-oriented ego as mediator.	Projective tests to tap unconscious motives; interviews for purposes of analysis.	Case studies.
Trait	Allport Cattell Eysenck McCrae and Costa	Behaviour springs from personality traits that may be influenced by both heredity and environment.	Self-report inventories; adjective checklists; inventories.	Analysis of test results for identifying strength of various traits.
Learning behaviourist	Skinner	Behaviour is determined strictly by environmental influences.	Direct observation of behaviour; objective tests; interviews; rating scales; self-report.	Analysis of observations of behaviour; quantifying behaviours; analysis of person-situation interactions.
Social-cognitive	Bandura Rotter	Behaviour results from an interaction between internal cognitive factors and environmental influences.	Direct observation of behaviour; objective tests; interviews; self-reports	Analysis off interactions between internal cognitive factors and environmental influences.
Humanistic	Maslow Rogers	Behaviour springs from the person's own unique perception of reality and conscious choices. Humans are innately good.	Interviews and tests designed to assess the person's self-concept and perceptions of control.	Analysis of the relationship between the person's feelings or perceptions and behaviour.

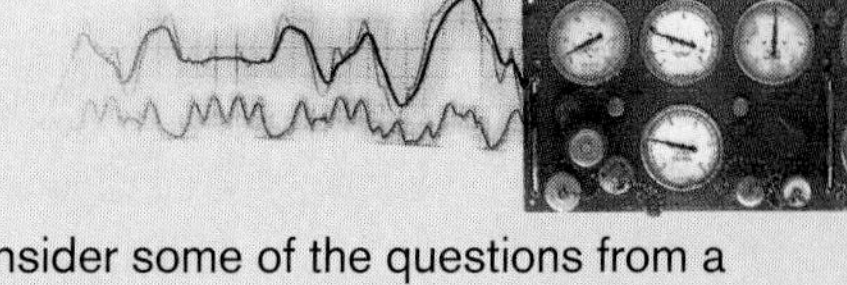

Is There Really a Sucker Born Every Minute?

Apply It!

Scorpio (Oct. 23–Nov. 22): You will start to feel more in control of your life than in recent weeks. You are beginning to understand why several things went wrong. Though you may not be in a position to fix them immediately, you can begin to plan how to do it in the near future. Put your best foot forward, and be gentle in trying to win a point.

Aquarius (Jan. 21–Feb. 19): Your reputation has been up and down several times in the last few months. This week you are poised to make a remarkable comeback. Young Aquarians may receive their first real job offers, or start to develop an interest that will eventually lead to a long and satisfying career. (Accurso, 1994, p. 44)

These two horoscopes are products of the "science" of astrology, which is based on the notion that the relative positions of the stars and planets at the time of a person's birth will influence that individual's personality traits and behaviour throughout life. Each day a horoscope is published for the 12 "signs"–Gemini, Leo, Capricorn, Pisces, and so on.

If you're a Scorpio or an Aquarius, one of these horoscopes applies to you, right? Look again. When you read them carefully, you see that all horoscopes contain advice and predictions that could apply to almost anyone.

In fact, horoscopes apply to no one. Researchers have found no correlation between the signs of the zodiac and individual personality traits (Gauguelin, 1982). The same can be said for graphology. Graphologists claim to be able to measure personality and predict job success by analyzing an individual's handwriting. But scientific studies have found little connection between the characteristics of a person's handwriting and his or her personality traits or success at a particular job (Beyerstein & Beyerstein, 1992; Dean et al., 1992).

We can see the same problem in the "personality tests" often published in popular magazines. For instance, consider some of the questions from a test apparently designed to examine whether you are "too hard on yourself":

A few of your co-workers decide to get together one night to watch a TV show, but the invitation never makes it your way. You

- Figure it was an oversight and show up anyway.
- Stay up the whole night baking batches of cookies for the office–you'll win them over if it's the last thing you do.
- Shrug it off, but make sure the TV buddies know for next time that you're always game for a get-together.

During your year-end review, your boss reveals you could improve in a few minor areas. You:

- Stare blankly, imagining the minor area in which she can stick her report.
- Ask her to explain further so you can work on your weaknesses.

KEY TERMS

anal stage, p. 327
archetype, p. 331
behavioural genetics, p. 340
cardinal trait, p. 333
central trait, p. 333
collective unconscious, p. 331
conditions of worth, p. 340
conscious, p. 323
defence mechanism, p. 325
denial, p. 325
displacement, p. 326
ego, p. 324
extraversion, p. 335
five-factor theory, p. 335
fixation, p. 326
genital stage, p. 329
halo effect, p. 343
heritability, p. 341
humanistic psychology, p. 339
id, p. 324
introversion, p. 335
inventory, p. 343
Jackson Personality Inventory (JPI), p. 344
latency period, p. 329
libido, p. 324
locus of control, p. 338
Minnesota Multiphasic Personality Inventory-2 (MMPI-2), p. 343
Oedipus complex, p. 328
oral stage, p. 327
personal unconscious, p. 330
personality, p. 323
phallic stage, p. 328
pleasure principle, p. 324
preconscious, p. 323
projection, p. 325
projective test, p. 345
psychoanalysis, p. 323
psychosexual stages, p. 326
rationalization, p. 325
reaction formation, p. 326
reciprocal determinism, p. 337
regression, p. 325
repression, p. 325

- Get so freaked out about being fired that you work your butt off all weekend. (Moore, 2000)

The odds are that for each of these questions you will select the answer that reflects most favourably on your personality. Even if you select a "negative" answer, the chances are that you are doing so because of a temporary problem, not because you behave that way all the time. The results of such a quiz have little chance of being scientifically accurate. "Pop psych" articles in magazines have "a little something for everybody," but the reader who takes them seriously is in danger of illustrating a famous saying attributed to P.T. Barnum: "There's a sucker born every minute."

The descriptions of personality that are often published in astrological charts share some of the characteristics of the personality analyses in popular magazines. At first glance, you might consider the description under "your" sign wonderfully accurate. But if you look more closely, you'll see that most of the traits contained in the description are desirable ones. Even when the description includes both positive and negative traits you may find it remarkably accurate. Two effects are operating here. The first is referred to as the *self-serving bias*: we are more likely to accept a positive description of ourselves than a negative one. The second is known as the *fallacy of positive instances*: a person is likely to notice or remember something that matches his or her expectations and not to notice other information that might contradict those expectations. Personality profiles and horoscope charts capitalize on these tendencies by presenting "descriptions" that are so general that they apply to almost anyone and are so flattering that almost anyone will accept them as accurate (French et al., 1991).

By now it should be obvious that the same principles apply to fortune-telling and palmistry. Both contain such general statements that they seem to fit almost anyone. An observation such as, "At times you are extraverted, affable, sociable, while at other times you are introverted, wary, and reserved" could describe most of the people on this planet.

You can avoid being a "sucker" if you critically evaluate personality profiles, horoscopes, fortunes, and the like. Be alert to vague, all-purpose descriptions. Notice the negative statements as well as the positive ones. And watch out for flattery disguised as science. This is not to say that you should never read your horoscope or have your fortune told—these activities can be entertaining.

Rorschach Inkblot Test, p. 345
self-actualization, p. 339
self-efficacy, p. 338
source traits, p. 334
sublimation, p. 326
superego, p. 324
surface traits, p. 334
Thematic Apperception Test (TAT), p. 345
trait, p. 333
trait theories, p. 333
unconditional positive regard, p. 340
unconscious, p. 323

THINKING CRITICALLY

Evaluation

In your opinion, which personality theory is the most accurate, reasonable, and realistic? Which is the least accurate, reasonable, and realistic? Support your answers.

Point/Counterpoint

Are personality characteristics mostly learned? Or are they mostly transmitted through the genes? Using what you have learned in this chapter and other evidence you can gather, make a case for each position. Support your answers with research and expert opinion.

Psychology in Your Life

Consider your own behaviour and personality attributes from the standpoint of each of the theories: psychoanalysis, trait theory, and the learning, humanistic, and genetic perspectives. Which theory or theories best explain your personality? Why?

SUMMARY & REVIEW

Sigmund Freud and Psychoanalysis

To what two aspects of Freud's work does the term *psychoanalysis* apply?

Psychoanalysis is the term Freud used for both his theory of personality and his therapy for the treatment of psychological disorders.

What are the three levels of awareness in consciousness?

The three levels of awareness in consciousness are the conscious, the preconscious, and the unconscious.

What are the roles of the id, the ego, and the superego?

The id is the primitive, unconscious part of the personality, which contains the instincts and operates on the pleasure principle. The ego is the rational, largely conscious system, which operates according to the reality principle. The superego is the moral system of the personality, consisting of the conscience and the ego ideal.

What is a defence mechanism?

A defence mechanism is an unconscious, irrational means that the ego uses to defend against anxiety and to maintain self-esteem; it involves self-deception and the distortion of reality.

What are two ways in which repression operates?

Through repression, (1) painful memories, thoughts, ideas, or perceptions are involuntarily removed from consciousness, and (2) disturbing sexual or aggressive impulses are prevented from breaking into consciousness.

What are some other defence mechanisms?

Other defence mechanisms are projection, denial, rationalization, regression, reaction formation, displacement, and sublimation.

What are the psychosexual stages, and why did Freud consider them so important in personality development?

Freud believed that the sexual instinct is present at birth, develops through a series of psychosexual stages, and provides the driving force for thought and activity. The psychosexual stages are the oral stage, anal stage, phallic stage (followed by the latency period), and genital stage.

What is the Oedipus complex?

The Oedipus complex, occurring in the phallic stage, is a conflict in which the child is sexually attracted to the opposite-sex parent and feels hostility toward the same-sex parent.

According to Freud, what are the two primary sources of influence on the personality?

Freud believed that differences in personality result from the relative strengths of the id, the ego, and the superego and from the personality traits that develop as a result of problems during the psychosexual stages.

The Neo-Freudians

According to Jung, what are the three components of personality?

Jung conceived of the personality as having three parts: the ego, the personal unconscious, and the collective unconscious.

What did Adler consider to be the driving force of the personality?

Adler maintained that the predominant force of the personality is the drive to overcome and compensate for feelings of weakness and inferiority and to strive for superiority or significance.

Why is Horney considered a pioneer in psychology?

Horney took issue with Freud's sexist view of women and added the feminine dimension to the world of psychology.

Trait Theories

What are trait theories of personality?

Trait theories of personality are attempts to explain personality and differences between people in terms of their personal characteristics.

How did Allport differentiate between cardinal and central traits?

Allport defined a cardinal trait as a personal quality that is so strong a part of a person's personality that he or she may become identified with that trait or known for it. A central trait is the type you would mention in writing a letter of recommendation.

How did Cattell differentiate between surface and source traits?

Cattell used the term *surface traits* to refer to observable qualities of personality, which you might use in describing a friend. *Source traits* underlie the surface traits, exist in all of us in varying degrees, make up the most basic personality structure, and cause behaviour.

What does Eysenck consider to be the two most important dimensions of personality?

Eysenck considers extraversion (versus introversion) and neuroticism (versus emotional stability) to be the most important dimensions of personality.

What are the Big Five personality dimensions in the five-factor theory as described by McCrae and Costa?

According to McCrae and Costa, the Big Five factors are neuroticism, extraversion, conscientiousness, agreeableness, and openness to experience.

Learning Theories and Personality

How did Skinner account for what most people refer to as personality?

B.F. Skinner viewed personality as simply a collection of behaviours and habits that have been reinforced in the past.

What are the components that make up Bandura's concept of reciprocal determinism, and how do they interact?

The external environment, behaviour, and personal/cognitive factors are the three components of reciprocal determinism, each influencing and being influenced by the others.

What is meant by the terms *internal* and *external locus of control*?

According to Rotter, people with an internal locus of control see themselves as primarily in control of their behaviour and its consequences; those with an external locus of control believe their destiny is in the hands of fate, luck, or chance.

Humanistic Personality Theories

Who were the two pioneers in humanistic psychology, and how did they view human nature?

Abraham Maslow and Carl Rogers, the two pioneers in humanistic psychology, believed that human nature is innately good and that people have free will and a tendency toward growth and realization of their potential.

What is self-actualization, and how did Maslow study it?

Self-actualization means developing to one's fullest potential. Maslow studied people who had made significant contributions in their lifetime and who exemplified self-actualization, to determine what characteristics they share.

According to Rogers, why don't all people become fully functioning persons?

Individuals often do not become fully functioning persons because in childhood they fail to receive unconditional positive regard from their parents. In order to gain positive regard, they must meet their parents' conditions of worth.

Personality: Is It in the Genes?

What has research in behavioural genetics revealed about the influence of the genes and the environment on personality?

Research in behavioural genetics has revealed that about 40 to 50 percent of personality can be attributed to the genes, and that the environmental influences on personality are mainly from the non-shared environment.

Personality Assessment

What are the three major methods used in personality assessment?

The major methods used in personality assessment are (1) observation, interviews, and rating scales, (2) inventories, and (3) projective tests.

What is an inventory, and what are the MMPI-2 and the JPI designed to reveal?

An inventory is a paper-and-pencil test with questions about a person's thoughts, feelings, and behaviours, which can be scored according to a standard procedure. The MMPI-2 is designed to screen and diagnose psychiatric problems, and the JPI is designed to assess the normal personality.

How do projective tests provide insight into personality, and what are several of the most commonly used?

In a projective test, people respond to inkblots, drawings of ambiguous human situations, incomplete sentences, and the like by projecting their own inner thoughts, feelings, fears, or conflicts onto the test materials. Examples are the Rorschach Inkblot Test, the Thematic Apperception Test (TAT), and the sentence-completion method.

11 Health and Stress

How angry do you get at work or school? Imagine you have to get your course's textbook and you have one hour for lunch and you've waited in line for 45 minutes and someone butts in front of you. Would you be angry? Then you rush to the cafeteria and they're going to close but you know that they haven't turned off the cash machines yet and they still won't let you buy the sandwich you want to purchase. Now are you angry? You get to your class and you find out that the instructor has changed the day of the final exam to coincide with a trip out of town that you've planned for over six months. Angry yet?

Like most people, we like to think of ourselves as rational, sensible, and calm. But the mounting tensions of our work environments sometimes take us right to the edge. And some people cross the line and engage in something called work rage. Take the case of Pierre LeBrun, who in April 1999 walked into his workplace at an Ottawa transit station and shot four co-workers before shooting himself. For LeBrun, there was a history of persistent taunting by co-workers about his stuttering. In response, he physically assaulted one co-worker. His employer handled the situation by moving him from one job to

another without ever disciplining his co-workers. Eventually, LeBrun just couldn't take it anymore. (Adapted from Flavelle, 2000).

A similar event happened in June 1999 when Andrew Alan was stabbed when delivering a courier package. Although you would rarely consider delivering packages to be a life-threatening job, it is dangerous when you have to deal with others who might be engaging in road rage. Edmonton police suggest that Alan was the unfortunate victim of another driver 's road rage while en route to his drop-off site. The charges against his alleged attacker were subsequently dropped ("Charge stayed," 2000).

All of the above share a common theme—*work rage*. Work rage involves all levels of violence from name-calling, to pushing and shoving, to murder. The violence can be against co-workers, customers, or management. Although Canadian statistics on workplace violence are not presently available, Ottawa is now collecting data. Early findings suggest that workplace conflict is on the rise. People who deal with the public, such as teachers and retail clerks, are at greatest risk. Intimidating managers pose the second greatest threat, followed by co-workers. Experts suggest that downsizing and other social stresses outside the job are contributing to the higher level of perceived stress on the job, and hence higher levels of work rage. Advocates are calling for companies to be more attentive to work rage issues and to adopt zero-tolerance standards to protect their employees.

Work rage is only one expression of stress in our society. Stress can be the cause for lashing out and it can cause a number of internally directed psychological concerns. Our personal well-being and psychological and physical health is integrally tied to social and psychological influences. In this chapter we examine health and stress.

Two Approaches to Health and Illness

How do the biomedical and biopsychosocial models differ in their approaches to health and illness?

There are two main approaches to health and illness. The **biomedical model**, the predominant view in medicine, focuses on illness rather than health. It explains illness in terms of biological factors without considering psychological and social factors that might contribute to the condition.

Another approach that is gaining serious attention is the **biopsychosocial model** of health and wellness (see Figure 11.1). This approach focuses on health as well as illness, and holds that both are determined by a combination of biological, psychological, and social factors (Engel, 1977, 1980; Schwartz 1982). This model, which most health psychologists endorse, goes beyond disease prevention to include health promotion (Breslow, 1999).

But first, what is **health psychology**? Health psychology is "the field within psychology devoted to understanding psychological influences on how people stay healthy, why they become ill, and how they respond when they do get ill" (Taylor, 1991, p. 6). Health psychologists study psychological factors asso-

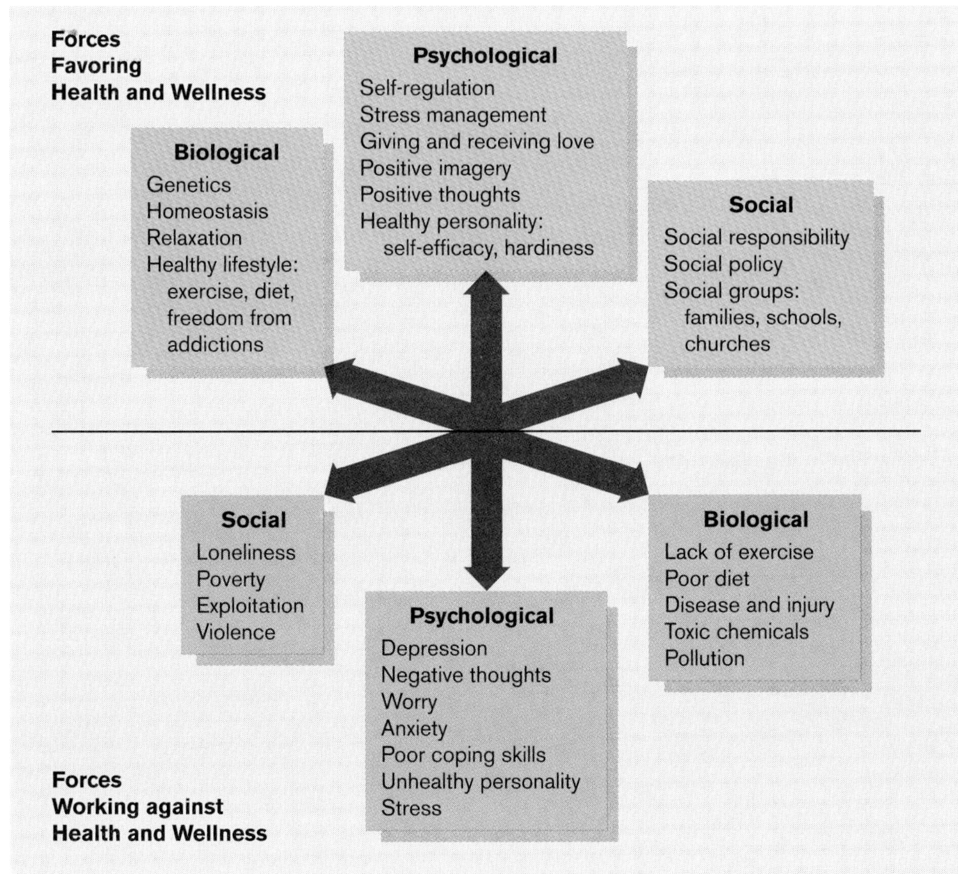

FIGURE 11.1
The Biopsychosocial Model of Health and Wellness **The biopsychosocial model focuses on health as well as illness, and holds that both are determined by a combination of biological, psychological, and social factors. Most health psychologists endorse the biopsychosocial model. (From Green & Shellenberger, 1990.)**

ciated with health and illness, and they promote interventions that foster good health and aid recovery from illness.

Why do people become ill in the modern age? At the beginning of the 20th century, the primary causes of death in Canada were pneumonia and infectious diseases such as diphtheria and tuberculosis. The health menaces of modern times are diseases related to unhealthy lifestyle and stress—heart attack, stroke, hardening of the arteries, cancer, and cirrhosis of the liver. In this chapter we will discuss stress, disease, and behaviours that promote and compromise health.

Theories of Stress

How would you define stress? Is stress something in the environment? Is it a physiological or psychological reaction that occurs within a person? Is it something we should avoid at all costs? As with most issues in psychology, there are different ways to view stress. Some researchers emphasize the physiological effects of stress, whereas others focus on the role that our thinking plays in stress (Carpi, 1996). Most psychologists define **stress** as the physiological and psychological response to a condition that threatens or challenges the individual and requires some form of adaptation or adjustment.

LINK IT!

www.stresscanada.org
The Canadian Institute of Stress

biomedical model: A perspective that focuses on illness rather than health, explaining illness in terms of biological factors without regard to psychological and social factors.

biopsychosocial model: A perspective that focuses on health as well as illness, and holds that both are determined by a combination of biological, psychological, and social factors.

health psychology: The field concerned with the psychological factors that contribute to health, illness, and recovery.

stress: The physiological and psychological response to a condition that threatens or challenges a person and requires some form of adaptation or adjustment.

Hans Selye and the General Adaptation Syndrome

An early, classic contribution to stress research was made by Walter Cannon (1932), who described the fight-or-flight response. Cannon discovered that when any threat is perceived by an organism (animal or human), the sympathetic nervous system and the endocrine glands prepare the body to fight the threat or flee from it. Cannon considered the fight-or-flight response wonderfully adaptive, because it helps the organism respond rapidly to threats. He also considered it potentially harmful in the long run if an organism is not able to fight or flee and experiences prolonged stress and continuing physical arousal (Sapolsky, 1994).

Canadian scientist Hans Selye (1907–1982) is the researcher most prominently associated with the study of stress and health. Selye spent most of his pioneering career at McGill University (1932 to 1945) and the Université de Montréal (1945 to 1977). At McGill, he conducted research on the effects of sex hormones. In one experiment he injected rats with hormone-rich extracts of cow ovaries. What happened to the rats? To Selye's amazement, (1) their adrenal glands became swollen, (2) their immune systems were weakened, and (3) they developed bleeding ulcers in the stomach and intestines. Never before had a hormone been shown to cause such clear physical symptoms. Selye thought he might be on the verge of discovering a new hormone. But after further experiments he found that he could produce the same symptoms by trying almost anything on the rats—for example, exposing them to toxic chemicals or freezing temperatures. Even extreme muscle fatigue caused the same symptoms. It seemed that Selye had not discovered anything at all. He was crushed. Then brooding gave way to reflection.

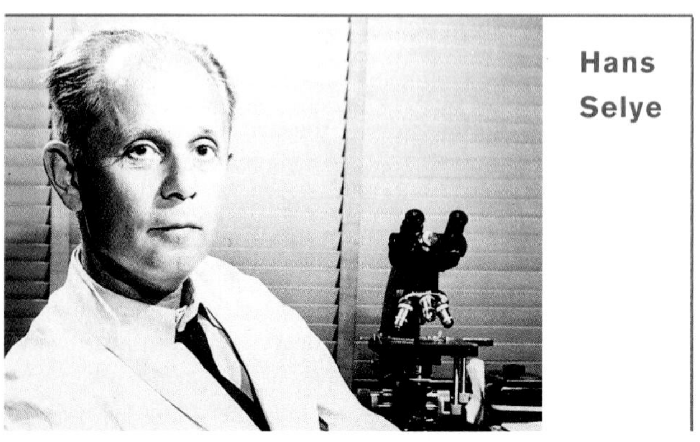

Hans Selye

He realized that the body responds in much the same way to all harmful agents (toxic substances, injuries, electric shock) and a host of other stressors. The physical response was so predictable, so general, that Selye named it the "general adaptation syndrome." As a medical student in the 1920s, Selye had been struck by the fact that patients admitted to the hospital with an amazingly wide variety of illnesses all had many of the same physical symptoms. Now he was seeing general symptoms in rats exposed to a variety of stressors.

Selye was elated by his discovery, but the medical world was skeptical. The notion that organisms react in the same way to a wide range of dangers was completely contrary to the orthodox medical thinking of the day. Within five years, however, Selye had proved that the general stress reaction was indeed the body's way of responding to stress.

The General Adaptation Syndrome: A General Physical Response to Many Stressors

What is the general adaptation syndrome?

Selye knew that all living organisms are constantly confronted with **stressors**—stimuli or events that place a demand on the organism for adaptation or readjustment. Each stressor causes both specific and non-specific responses. Extreme cold, for example, causes the *specific* response of shivering. Apart from this, the body makes a *non-specific* response to a wide variety of stressors. The heart of Selye's concept of stress is the **general adaptation syndrome (GAS)**, his term for the non-specific response to stress (see Figure 11.2). The GAS consists of three stages: alarm, resistance, and exhaustion (Selye, 1956).

The body's first response to a stressor is the **alarm stage**, when emotional arousal occurs and the body prepares its defensive forces to meet the threat. In the alarm stage the sympathetic nervous system, through the release of hormones, mobilizes the body to fight or flee. If the stressor cannot be quickly conquered or avoided, the organism enters the **resistance stage**, which is characterized by intense physiological efforts to either resist or adapt to the stressor. During the resistance stage the adrenal glands pour out powerful hormones (glucocorticoids) to help the body resist stressors. Resistance may last a long time. According to Selye, the length of the resistance stage depends both on the strength or intensity of the stressor and on the body's power to adapt.

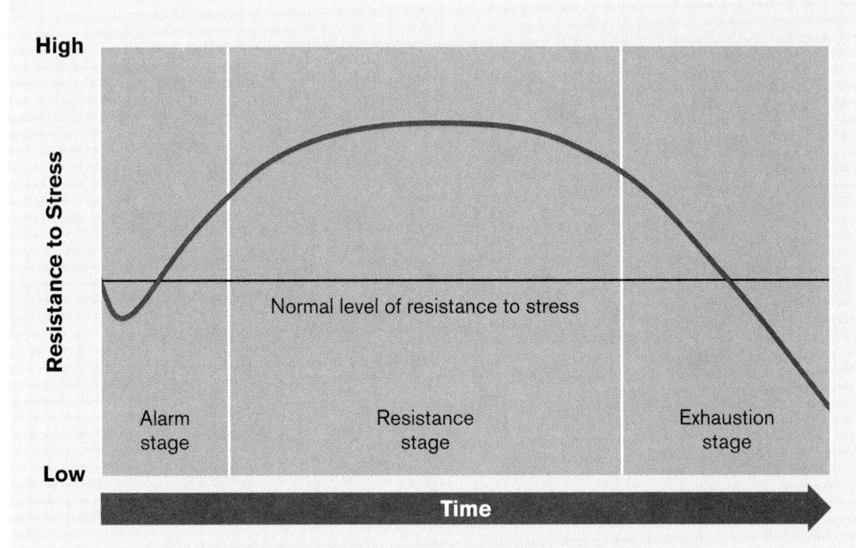

FIGURE 11.2

The General Adaptation Syndrome

The three stages in Hans Selye's general adaptation syndrome are (1) the alarm stage, during which tere is emotional arousal and the defensive forces of the body are mobilized for fight or flight; (2) the resistance stage, in which intense physiological efforts are exerted to resist or adapt to the stressor; and (3) the exhaustion stage, when the organism fails in its efforts to resist the stressor. (Based on Selye, 1956.)

If the organism fails in its efforts to resist, it reaches the **exhaustion stage**. "The stage of exhaustion after a temporary demand upon the body, is reversible, but the complete exhaustion of all stores of deep adaptation energy is not" (Selye, 1974, p. 29). If exposure to the stressor continues, all the stores of deep energy are depleted, and disintegration, disease, or death may follow.

Selye claimed that any event requiring a readjustment, positive or negative, will produce stress in an organism. He did, however, differentiate between the positive and negative aspects of stress. "Eustress" is positive or good stress, including exhilaration, excitement, and the thrill of accomplishment. "Distress" is damaging or unpleasant stress, such as frustration, inadequacy, loss, disappointment, insecurity, helplessness, or desperation.

Criticisms of Selye's Theory: A Missing Cognitive Factor

The connection between extreme, prolonged stress and certain diseases is now widely accepted by medical experts, but some criticism of Selye's work seems justified. The major criticism is directed at Selye's contention that the intensity of the stressor determines one's physical reaction to it. His theory does not provide for a psychological component—that is, it does not consider how a person perceives and evaluates the stressor. This criticism led to the development of the cognitive theory of stress.

Richard Lazarus's Cognitive Theory of Stress

Richard Lazarus contends that it is not the stressor itself that causes stress, but a person's perception of the stressor (Lazarus, 1966; Lazarus & Folkman, 1984). Because Lazarus emphasizes the importance of perceptions and the appraisal of stressors, his is a cognitive theory of stress and coping. To Lazarus, the stress process can be understood in terms of four phases. First, there is a causal agent, either external or internal, commonly referred to as stress or the stressor. Second, the mind or the body evaluates the stressor as either threatening or benign. Third, the mind or the body uses coping processes to deal with the stressor. Finally, there is the stress reaction—the

stressor: Any event capable of producing physical or emotional stress.

general adaptation syndrome (GAS): The predictable sequence of reactions (the alarm, resistance, and exhaustion stages) that organisms show in response to stressors.

alarm stage: The first stage of the general adaptation syndrome, when there is emotional arousal and the defensive forces of the body are prepared for fight or flight.

resistance stage: The second stage of the general adaptation syndrome, during which there are intense physiological efforts to resist or adapt to the stressor.

exhaustion stage: The final stage of the general adaptation syndrome, occurring if the organism fails in its efforts to resist the stressor.

"complex pattern of effects on mind and body" (Lazarus, 1993, p. 4). Lazarus believes that physiological and psychological stress must be analyzed differently. He argues that while Selye's general adaptation syndrome describes how the body copes with physiological stress, his model focuses on how we cope with psychological stressors.

The Cognitive Appraisal of Stressors: Evaluating the Stressor and Considering Your Options

What are the roles of primary and secondary appraisal when people are confronted with a potentially stressful event?

According to Lazarus, when people are confronted with a potentially stressful event, they engage in a cognitive process that involves a primary and a secondary appraisal. A **primary appraisal** is an evaluation of the meaning and significance of a situation—whether its effect on our well-being is positive, irrelevant, or negative. An event appraised as negative or stressful could involve (1) harm or loss—damage that has already occurred; (2) threat—the potential for harm or loss; or (3) challenge—the opportunity to grow or gain. An appraisal of threat, harm, or loss can be made in relation to anything important to us—a friendship, a part of our body, our property, our finances, or our self-esteem.

The same event can be appraised differently by different people. Some students may welcome the opportunity to give an oral presentation in class, seeing it as a challenge and a chance to impress their professor and raise their grade. Other students may feel threatened, fearing that they may embarrass themselves in front of their classmates and lower their grade in the process. Still others may view the assignment as both a challenge and a threat. When we appraise a situation as one involving harm, loss, or threat, we have negative emotions such as anxiety, fear, anger, and resentment (Folkman, 1984). A challenge appraisal, on the other hand, is usually accompanied by positive emotions such as excitement, hopefulness, and eagerness. Stress for younger people is more likely to take the form of challenges; for older people, stress involving losses and threats is more common (El-Shiekh et al., 1989).

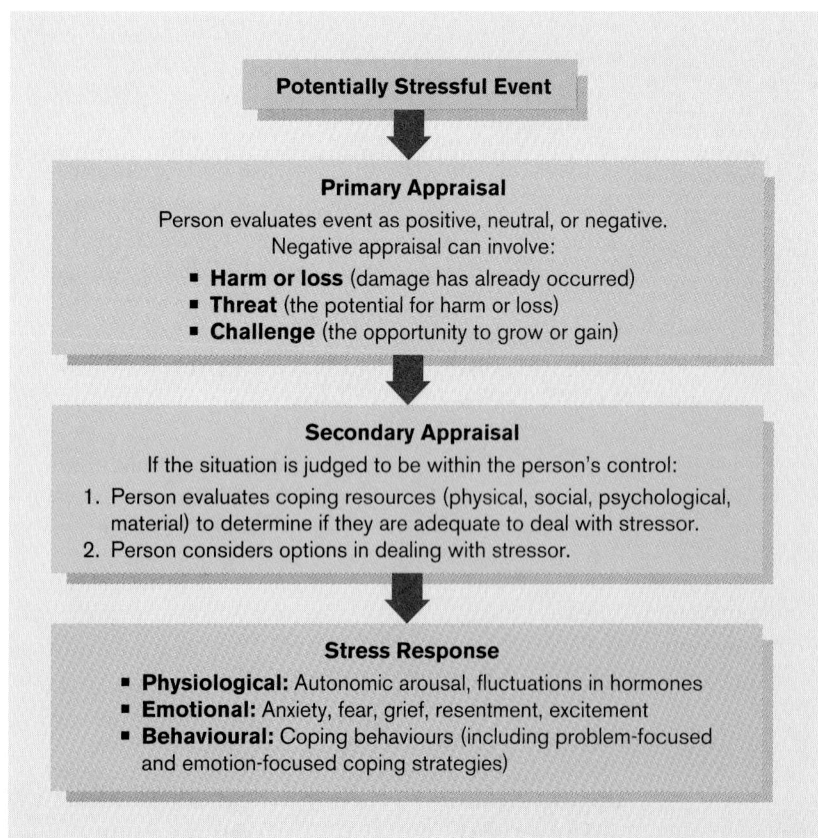

Potentially Stressful Event
Primary Appraisal
Person evaluates event as positive, neutral, or negative.
Negative appraisal can involve:
▪ Harm or loss (damage has already occurred)
▪ Threat (the potential for harm or loss)
▪ Challenge (the opportunity to grow or gain)
Secondary Appraisal
If the situation is judged to be within the person's control:
1. Person evaluates coping resources (physical, social, psychological, material) to determine if they are adequate to deal with stressor.
2. Person considers options in dealing with stressor.
Stress Response
▪ Physiological: Autonomic arousal, fluctuations in hormones
▪ Emotional: Anxiety, fear, grief, resentment, excitement
▪ Behavioural: Coping behaviours (including problem-focused and emotion-focused coping strategies)

FIGURE 11.3
Lazarus and Folkman's Psychological Model of Stress
Lazarus and Folkman emphasize the importance of a person's perceptions and appraisal of stressors. The stress response depends on the outcome of the primary and secondary appraisals, whether the person's coping resources are adequate to cope with the threat, and how severely the resources are taxed in the process. (Based on Folkman, 1984.)

Remember It!

Approaches to Health and Theories of Stress

1. The biomedical model focuses on _______; the biopsychosocial model focuses on _______.
   a. illness; illness
   b. health and illness; illness
   c. illness; health and illness
   d. health and illness; health and illness
2. Which stage of the general adaptation syndrome is marked by intense physiological efforts to adapt to the stressor?
   a. readjustment stage
   b. resistance stage
   c. alarm stage
   d. exhaustion stage
3. Susceptibility to illness increases during what stage of the general adaptation syndrome?
   a. readjustment stage
   b. resistance stage
   c. alarm stage
   d. exhaustion stage
4. During secondary appraisal, we
   a. evaluate our coping resources and consider options in dealing with the stressor.
   b. determine whether an event is positive, neutral, or negative.
   c. determine whether an event involves loss, threat, or challenge.
   d. determine whether an event causes physiological or psychological stress.
5. Selye focused on the _______ aspects of stress; Lazarus focused on the _______ aspects of stress.
   a. physiological; physiological
   b. physiological; psychological
   c. psychological; physiological
   d. psychological; psychological

Answers: 1. c 2. b 3. d 4. a 5. b

When we assess an event as stressful, we engage in a **secondary appraisal**. During secondary appraisal, if we judge the situation to be within our control, we make an evaluation of our available coping resources: physical (health, energy, stamina), social (support network), psychological (skills, morale, self-esteem), material (money, tools, equipment), and time. Then we consider our options and decide how we will deal with the stressor. The level of stress we feel depends largely on whether our resources are adequate to cope with the threat, and how severely our resources will be taxed in the process. Figure 11.3 summarizes Lazarus and Folkman's psychological model of stress.

Research support exists for Lazarus and Folkman's contention that the physiological, emotional, and behavioural reactions to stressors depend partly on whether the stressors are appraised as challenging or threatening. Tomaka and colleagues (1993) found that active coping with stressors that are appraised as challenging was associated with increased heart rate, better performance, and positive emotions. Active coping with stressors appraised as threatening was related to increased blood pressure, poorer performance, and negative emotional tone.

Sources of Stress: The Common and the Extreme

Some stressors produce temporary stress, whereas others produce chronic stress—a state of stress that continues unrelieved over time. Chronic health problems, physical handicaps, poverty, and unemployment are sources of chronic stress. The burden of chronic stress is disproportionately heavy for the poor, for minorities, and for the elderly.

Everyday Sources of Stress

How do approach–approach, avoidance–avoidance, and approach–avoidance conflicts differ?

Sometimes conflicting motives can be sources of stress. When we must make a choice between two desirable

primary appraisal: Evaluating the significance of a potentially stressful event according to how it will affect one's well-being—whether it is perceived as irrelevant or as involving harm or loss, threat, or challenge.

secondary appraisal: Evaluating one's coping resources and deciding how to deal with a stressful event.

alternatives, we are facing an **approach–approach conflict**, and stress may be the result. Some approach–approach conflicts are minor, such as deciding which movie to see. Others can have major consequences, such as whether to continue building a promising career or to interrupt the career to raise a child. In approach–approach conflicts, both choices are desirable.

In **avoidance–avoidance conflicts** we must choose between two undesirable alternatives. You may want to avoid studying for an exam, but at the same time want to avoid failing the test. In an **approach–avoidance conflict** we are simultaneously drawn to and repelled by a choice; for example, we may want to take a wonderful vacation but we would have to empty our savings account to do so.

Unpredictability and Lack of Control: Factors That Increase Stress

How do the unpredictability of and lack of control over a stressor affect its impact?

Our physical and psychological well-being is profoundly influenced by the degree to which we feel a sense of control over our lives (Rodin & Salovey, 1989). Langer and Rodin (1976) studied the effects of control on nursing-home residents. One group of residents was given some measure of control over their lives, such as choices in arranging their rooms and in the times they could see movies. They showed improved health and well-being and had a lower death rate than another group that was not given control. Within 18 months, 30 percent of the residents given no choices had died, compared to only 15 percent of those who had been given some control over their lives. Control is important for cancer patients as well. Some researchers suggest that for cancer patients a sense of control over their daily physical symptoms and emotional reactions may be even more important than control over the course of the disease itself (Thompson et al., 1993).

Several studies suggest that we are less subject to stress when we have the power to do something about it, whether we exercise that power or not. Glass and Singer (1972) subjected two groups of subjects to the same loud noise, but the subjects in one group were told that they could, if necessary, terminate the noise by pressing a switch. Subjects in the group that had the control suffered less stress even though they never did exercise the control they were given. Friedland and colleagues (1992) suggest that when people experience a loss of control because of a stressor, they are motivated to try to re-establish control in the stressful situation, as is illustrated in the next *It Happened in Canada* story. If they fail in this, they often attempt to increase their sense of control in other areas of life.

Racial Stress

A significant source of everyday stress is being a member of a minority group in a majority culture. A study of white and black participants' responses to a survey about ways of coping suggests that a person may experience racial stress from simply being one of the few or only members of a particular race in any of a variety of settings (classroom, workplace, or a social setting). The feeling of stress can be intense, even in the absence of racist attitudes, discrimination, or any other overt evidence of racism (Plummer & Slane, 1996).

Catastrophic Events and Chronic Intense Stress

How do people typically react to catastrophic events?

Environmental, social, bodily, and emotional stressors are a fact of life for most people. Some people have the misfortune to experience a catastrophic event such as a plane crash, a fire, or an earthquake. Panic reactions are rare except in situations such as fires, which people feel they must escape immediately. Many victims of catastrophic events initially appear dazed, stunned, and emotionally numb. They seem disoriented and may wander about aimlessly, often unaware of their own injuries and without attempting to help themselves or others. Following this stage, the victims show a concern for others; although unable to act efficiently on their own, they are willing to follow the directions of rescue workers. You may have observed these reactions in TV coverage of the earthquake in Los Angeles, or the floods in Manitoba and Quebec, or the ice storm that devastated southern Quebec and eastern Ontario.

As victims begin to recover, this shock is replaced by generalized anxiety. Recovering victims typically have recurring nightmares and feel a compulsive need to retell the event over and over. Perhaps re-experiencing the event through dreaming and retelling helps desensitize them to the horror of the experience. Crisis intervention therapy can provide victims with both

IT HAPPENED IN CANADA

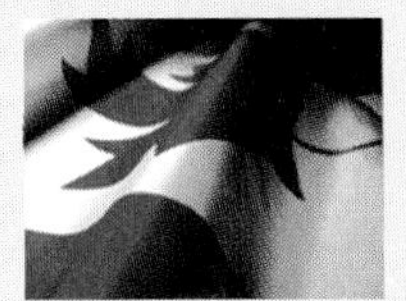

Disaster

How do people respond in the face of uncontrollable events? Clinical and social psychologists alike have extensively researched this issue. Studies try to imitate, often in a laboratory, the pressures that people would experience under traumatic conditions. But nothing can fully capture the experience of losing control over your life in the way that happens when a chaotic event hits you unexpectedly. The holiday makers at Green Acres Campground in Alberta and the residents of Walkerton, Ontario, know the full extent of what is involved in either a natural or man-made disaster.

It was around suppertime and many campers at the Green Acres Campground in Alberta were in the process of starting or clearing up after their evening meal when the sky began to blacken and winds and hail the size of golf balls swept through the trailer campground. Anticipating a storm, campers began to reel in their trailer awnings, but no one was prepared for the funnel cloud that engulfed the site. With winds exceeding 300 kilometres an hour, trees were snapped like twigs, boats were overturned, vehicles and trailers were picked up and scattered like toys. The result was devastation. In only minutes the campground was transformed to rubble. Ten people died and at least 130 were injured; for the others the trauma will be with them for the rest of their lives (Benedict & Cameron, 2000; Mahoney, 2000).

For the people of Walkerton, Ontario, the trauma was much slower and involved mounting fear as the residents of their community started to become fatally ill and no one could tell them why. At first it was children who showed the characteristic bloody diarrhea indicating contamination of food or water. But the public utilities company assured residents and medical health authorities that the water was safe and secure, so health officials began to search the town for possible food contaminants (Bruce-Grey-Owen Sound Health Unit, 2000). Meanwhile, more people were falling ill; so many that they had to be flown to neighboring communities for medical help. Finally, the community was informed that their water supply was contaminated with a deadly strain of E. coli bacteria. But the news and replacement water didn't come until after five people had already died and 400 were being treated in hospital emergency departments (Wickens & Hawkes, 2000).

For some people, these events led to stress, frayed tempers, extraordinary fear, frustration, and crying spells. Other people reacted by trying to help those around them. And now many are trying to make some sense of these events as they pull their lives together.

coping strategies and realistic expectations about the problems they may face in connection with the trauma.

Posttraumatic Stress Disorder: The Trauma Is Over, but the Stress Remains

What is posttraumatic stress disorder?

Posttraumatic stress disorder (PTSD) is a prolonged and severe stress reaction to a catastrophic event (such as a plane crash, an earthquake, or rape) or to chronic intense stress (such as occurs in combat or during imprisonment as a hostage). The disorder may show up immediately, or it may not appear until six months or more after the traumatic experience, in which case it is called *delayed* posttraumatic stress disorder. The most

When writer Pico Iyer's home was destroyed by arson, he saved only his cat and his manuscript. A fairly common reaction to such catastrophic events is posttraumatic stress disorder.

approach–approach conflict: A conflict arising from having to choose between desirable alternatives.

avoidance–avoidance conflict: A conflict arising from having to choose between equally undesirable alternatives.

approach–avoidance conflict: A conflict arising when a choice has both desirable and undesirable features, so that you are both drawn to and repelled by the same choice.

posttraumatic stress disorder (PTSD): A prolonged and severe stress reaction to a catastrophic or otherwise traumatic event, characterized by anxiety, psychic numbing, withdrawal from others, and the feeling that one is reliving the traumatic experience.

serious cases of PTSD are found among those who have witnessed brutal atrocities: Cambodian refugees (Carlson & Rosser-Hogan, 1991), Holocaust survivors (Kuch & Cox, 1992), or victims of state-sanctioned terror and torture (Bloche & Eisenberg, 1993). High rates of PTSD were found among Canadian Vietnam veterans. Of 164 veterans, 90 had symptoms of PTSD (Stretch, 1990).

People with posttraumatic stress disorder often have flashbacks, nightmares, or intrusive memories in which they feel as if they are actually re-experiencing the traumatic event. They suffer from heightened anxiety and startle easily, particularly in response to anything that reminds them of the trauma (Green et al., 1985). Many survivors experience survivor guilt because they lived while others died. Some feel that perhaps they could have done more to save others.

Is there anything that can be done to lessen the stress that follows major trauma? According to Bloche and Eisenberg (1993), "Belief systems that give life a sense of purpose and meaning can prevent emotional damage" (p. 5).

LINK IT!

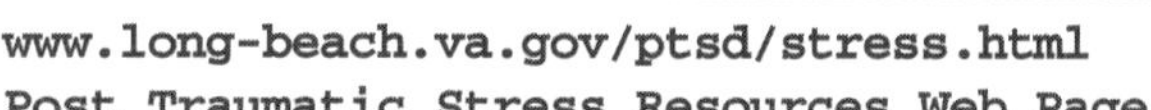

www.long-beach.va.gov/ptsd/stress.html
Post Traumatic Stress Resources Web Page

www.sover.net/~schwcof/ptsd.html
Post-Traumatic Stress Disorder Bibliography

play.psych.mun.ca/~dhart/trauma_net
Canadian Traumatic Stress Network

Coping with Stress

When we encounter stressful situations, we try either to alter them or to reinterpret them to make them seem more favourable. **Coping** refers to our efforts to deal with demands that we perceive as taxing or overwhelming (Lazarus, 1993).

Problem-Focused and Emotion-Focused Coping

What is the difference between problem-focused and emotion-focused coping?

Coping strategies fall into two categories: problem-focused and emotion-focused (Lazarus & Folkman, 1984). **Problem-focused coping** is direct; it involves reducing, modifying, or eliminating the source of stress. If you are getting a poor grade in history and appraise this as a

on the cutting edge in canada

Humour

Is laughter the best medicine? Rod Martin (1996), at the University of Western Ontario, recently investigated the positive impact of humour on general psychological well-being and coping with stress. He is now comparing the circumstances under which humour is healthy or not healthy.

Unhealthy uses of humour include putting people down, avoiding dealing with problems, or minimizing important issues (Kuiper & Martin, 1998).

Martin has demonstrated that people who report high levels of negative life events also have lower humour scores. Moreover, those with high humour scores may find stressful events somewhat invigorating rather than disturbing. In addition, people with higher levels of coping humour perceive themselves as having more control over their lives: they feel less overwhelmed, less anxious, and less stressed than people who have low levels of coping humour. Most impressive are the studies that demonstrate that a sense of humour may moderate physiological responses to stress. Using measures of secretions of immunoglobin-A—a physiological marker of stress—Martin and his colleagues were able to show that humour reduces physiological effects of stress on the immune system. This research may serve as the foundation for therapeutic interventions.

Rod Martin

REVIEW & REFLECT 11.1
Problem-Focused and Emotion-Focused Coping Strategies

Coping Strategy	Definition	Examples
Problem-focused	A response aimed at reducing, modifying, or eliminating the source of stress.	Acting to remove or lessen the threat. Removing oneself from the stressful situation. Enlisting the help of others in dealing with the threat. Seeking professional help or advice. Acting to prevent recurrence of similar stressful situations.
Emotion-focused	A response aimed at reducing the emotional distress caused by the stressor.	Viewing the stressor as a challenge rather than a threat. Using one of these responses: prayer, denial, wishful thinking, fantasizing, humour, relaxation, biofeedback, alcohol, drugs, overeating, promiscuous sex.

threat, you may study harder, talk over your problem with your professor, form a study group with other class members, get a tutor, or drop the course.

But what can we do when we face stress that we cannot fight, escape from, avoid, or modify in any way? We can use **emotion-focused coping** to change the way we respond emotionally. Emotion-focused coping may involve reappraising a stressor. If you lose your job, you may decide that it isn't a major tragedy and instead view it as a challenge—an opportunity to find a better job with a higher salary. To cope emotionally, people may use anything from religious faith, wishful thinking, or denial, to alcohol, drugs, or promiscuous sex (Lazarus & DeLongis, 1983). But misguided emotion-focused coping efforts can become additional sources of stress themselves.

Well-functioning people use a combination of problem-focused and emotion-focused coping in almost every stressful situation. Folkman and Lazarus (1980) studied the coping patterns of 100 individuals over a 12-month period and found that 98 percent of them used both types of coping in the 1300 stressful life events they had confronted. Not surprisingly, problem-focused coping strategies increased in situations that subjects appraised as changeable, and emotion-focused coping techniques increased in situations appraised as not changeable.

The two types of coping are summed up in the well-known saying: "Grant me the strength to change those things that I can change [problem-focused coping], the grace to accept those things that I cannot change [emotion-focused coping], and the wisdom to know the difference." Review & Reflect 11.1 summarizes the problem-focused and emotion-focused coping strategies.

Coping with Traumatic Events

A task force of experts on stress developed strategies for treating stress reactions in people who had experienced traumatic events (Hobfoll et al., 1991). These stress experts suggest a number of positive coping strategies:

- When you attempt to cope with complex stressful events, break the problems down into small goals and tasks that can be accomplished. Develop a system of rewards for small accomplishments.
- Begin to act now. Dealing with your problems will begin to restore a feeling of control over your life and increase your feeling of self-efficacy.

coping: Efforts through action and thought to deal with demands that are perceived as taxing or overwhelming.

problem-focused coping: A response aimed at reducing, modifying, or eliminating a source of stress.

emotion-focused coping: A response aimed at reducing the emotional impact of the stressor.

- Don't isolate yourself from other people.
- Seek the support you need. Help may be available from close family members or friends, a support group or religious group, clergy, school counsellors, psychologists, and other sources.
- Find ways to help others. You will feel less like a victim and more like a contributor.
- Use problem-focused coping to change aspects of your situation that are changeable; use emotion-focused coping to accept your situation and reduce your anxiety and arousal.
- Try to develop an optimistic attitude—a belief that your coping efforts will improve your situation.
- Avoid the temptation to use illicit drugs, alcohol, or large amounts of prescription drugs as a means of coping.

Evaluating Life Stress: Major Life Changes, Hassles, and Uplifts

There are two major approaches to evaluating life stress and its relation to illness. One approach focuses on major life events, which cause life changes that require adaptation. A second approach focuses on life's daily hassles.

Holmes and Rahe's Social Readjustment Rating Scale: Adding Up the Stress Score

What is the Social Readjustment Rating Scale designed to reveal?

Interested in the relationship between life changes and illness, Thomas Holmes and Richard Rahe (1967) developed the **Social Readjustment Rating Scale (SRRS)**. The SRRS is designed to measure stress by ranking different life events from most to least stressful. Each life event is assigned a point value. Life events that produce the greatest life changes and require the greatest adaptation are considered the most stressful, regardless of whether the events are positive or negative. The 43 life events range from death of a spouse (100 stress points) to such items as divorce (73 points), death of a close family member (63 points), marriage (50 points), pregnancy (40 points), and trouble with the boss (23 points) to minor law violations such as getting a traffic ticket (11 points). Would you like to learn the number of stress points in your life? Complete *Try It!*

Remember It!

Sources of and Coping with Stress

1. Rick cannot decide whether to go out or stay home and study for his test. What kind of conflict does he have?
   a. approach–approach conflict
   b. avoidance–avoidance conflict
   c. approach–avoidance conflict
   d. ambivalence–ambivalence conflict
2. Panic is the most common *initial* reaction to a catastrophic event. (true/false)
3. Victims of catastrophic events typically want to talk about their experience. (true/false)
4. What has research shown to increase stress?
   a. predictability of the stressor
   b. unpredictability of the stressor
   c. predictability of and control over the stressor
   d. unpredictability of and lack of control over the stressor
5. Posttraumatic stress disorder is a prolonged and severe stress reaction that results when a number of common sources of stress occur simultaneously. (true/false)
6. Coping aimed at reducing, modifying, or eliminating a source of stress is called ________ coping; coping aimed at reducing an emotional reaction to stress is called ________ coping.
   a. emotion-focused; problem-focused
   b. problem-focused; emotion-focused
   c. primary; secondary
   d. secondary; primary
7. People typically use a combination of problem-focused and emotion-focused coping when dealing with a stressful situation. (true/false)

Answers: 1. c 2. false 3. true 4. d 5. false 6. b 7. true

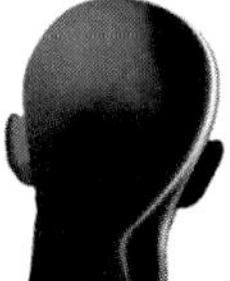

Try It!

Finding Your Stress Score

To assess your life in terms of life changes, check all the events listed that have happened to you in the past year. Add up the points to derive your stress score.

Rank	Life Event	Life Change Unit Value	Your Scores
1	Death of spouse	100	____
2	Divorce	73	____
3	Marital separation	65	____
4	Jail term	63	____
5	Death of close family member	53	____
6	Personal injury or illness	53	____
7	Marriage	50	____
8	Getting fired at work	47	____
9	Marital reconciliation	45	____
10	Retirement	45	____
11	Change in health of family member	44	____
12	Pregnancy	40	____
13	Sex difficulties	39	____
14	Gain of new family member	39	____
15	Business readjustment	39	____
16	Change in financial state	38	____
17	Death of close friend	37	____
18	Change to different line of work	36	____
19	Change in number of arguments with spouse	35	____
20	Taking out loan for major purchase (e.g., home)	31	____
21	Foreclosure of mortgage or loan	30	____
22	Change in responsibilities at work	29	____
23	Son or daughter leaving home	29	____
24	Trouble with in-laws	29	____
25	Outstanding personal achievement	28	____
26	Spouse beginning or stopping work	26	____
27	Beginning or ending school	26	____
28	Change in living conditions	25	____
29	Revision of personal habits	24	____
30	Trouble with boss	23	____
31	Change in work hours or conditions	20	____
32	Change in residence	20	____
33	Change in schools	20	____
34	Change in recreation	19	____
35	Change in church activities	19	____
36	Change in social activities	18	____
37	Taking out loan for lesser purchase (e.g., car or TV)	17	____
38	Change in sleeping habits	16	____
39	Change in number of family get-togethers	15	____
40	Change in eating habits	15	____
41	Vacation	13	____
42	Christmas	12	____
43	Minor violation of the law	11	____
	Total score:		____

Even positive life events, such as getting married, can cause stress.

Social Readjustment Rating Scale (SRRS): A stress scale, developed by Holmes and Rahe, which ranks 43 different life events from most to least stressful and assigns a point value to each.

Holmes and Rahe maintain that there is a connection between the degree of life stress and major health problems. After analyzing more than 5000 medical case histories, they concluded that major life changes often precede serious illness (Rahe et al., 1964).

However, one of the main shortcomings of the SRRS is that it assigns a point value to each life change without taking into account whether the change is for the better or the worse. For example, life changes such as divorce, separation, pregnancy, retirement from work, and changing jobs or residences may be either welcome or unwelcome.

The Hassles of Life: Little Things Stress a Lot

What roles do hassles and uplifts play in the stress of life, according to Lazarus?

Richard Lazarus disagrees with the rationale behind Holmes and Rahe's scale. He contends that one cannot weight life events for stressfulness without considering their meaning to the individual. He also believes that the little stressors, which he calls **hassles**, add up to more stress than major life events.

Daily hassles are the "irritating, frustrating, distressing demands and troubled relationships that plague us day in and day out" (Lazarus & DeLongis, 1983, p. 247). Kanner and colleagues (1981) developed the Hassles Scale to assess various categories of hassles. Unlike the Holmes and Rahe scale, the Hassles Scale takes into account that items may or may not represent stressors and that the amount of stress produced by an item varies from person to person. People completing the scale indicate which items have been a hassle for them and rate them for severity on a three-point scale. Research indicates that minor hassles that accompany stressful major life events are better predictors of the level of psychological distress than the major life events themselves (Pillow et al., 1996).

According to Lazarus, "A person's morale, social functioning, and health don't hinge on hassles alone, but on a balance between the good things that happen to people—that make them feel good—and the bad" (quoted in Goleman, 1979, p. 52). Table 11.1 shows the 10 most frequent hassles reported by students.

Fortunately, life's **uplifts**—that is, the positive experiences—may neutralize or cancel out many of the hassles. Lazarus and his colleagues also constructed an Uplifts Scale. As with the Hassles Scale, people make a cognitive appraisal in determining what they consider an uplift. Items viewed as uplifts by some people may actually be stressors for other people. Kanner and colleagues (1981) found that for middle-aged people, uplifts were often health- or family-related; for students, uplifts often came in the form of having a good time.

TABLE 11.1

The 10 Most Common Hassles for College and University Students*

Hassle	Percentage of Times Checked
1. Troubling thoughts about future	76.6
2. Not getting enough sleep	72.5
3. Wasting time	71.1
4. Inconsiderate smokers	70.7
5. Physical appearance	69.9
6. Too many things to do	69.2
7. Misplacing or losing things	67.0
8. Not enough time to do the things you need to do	66.3
9. Concerns about meeting high standards	64.0
10. Being lonely	60.8

**n* (number of participants in sample) = 34

Source: A.D. Kanner, J.C. Coyne, C. Schaefer, and R.S. Lazarus, 1981, "Comparison of Two Modes of Stress Measurement: Daily Hassles and Uplifts Versus Major Life Events," *Journal of Behavioral Medicine, 4,* pp. 1–39.

Health and Disease

Health psychologists study the myriad ways in which we respond to illness risk factors, and the factors that affect whether we seek treatment. Let's look at two examples: cancer and AIDS.

LINK IT!

www.canadian-health-network.ca
The Canadian Health Network

Remember It!

Evaluating Stress

1. On the Social Readjustment Rating Scale, only negative life changes are considered stressful. (true/false)
2. The Social Readjustment Rating Scale takes account of the individual's perceptions of the stressfulness of the life change in assigning stress points. (true/false)
3. According to Lazarus, hassles typically account for more life stress than major life changes. (true/false)
4. Lazarus's approach in measuring hassles and uplifts considers individual perceptions of stressful events. (true/false)

Answers: 1. false 2. false 3. true 4. true

Cancer: A Dreaded Disease

Cancer. The word alone is frightening. It is second only to heart disease as the leading cause of death. It was estimated that in 2000, 132 100 Canadians would be diagnosed with cancer and 65 000 would die of it (Cunningham, 2000). Young people are not spared the scourge of cancer, which takes the lives of more children between the ages of three and fourteen than any other disease.

We speak of cancer as a single disease, but actually it is a complicated collection of diseases. Cancer can invade the cells in any part of a living organism—humans, other animals, and even plants. Cancer always starts small, because it is a disease of the body's cells. Normal cells in all parts of the body reproduce (divide), and they have built-in instructions about when to stop doing so. If they did not, every part of the body would continue to grow as long as it lived. Unlike normal cells, cancerous cells do not stop dividing. Unless they can be caught in time and destroyed, they continue to grow and spread, eventually killing the organism.

Risk Factors for Cancer

Health psychologists warn that an unhealthy diet, smoking, excessive alcohol consumption, promiscuous sexual behaviour, and becoming sexually active in the early teens (especially for females) are all behaviours that increase the risk of cancer. Compared with those who do not get cancer, many cancer patients report that they faced more high-stress situations in their lives before their cancer was diagnosed.

Coping with Cancer

What can cancer patients do to help them cope with having cancer?

People who are diagnosed with cancer must adjust to the chronic stressors associated with it. They must cope with difficult therapies, "continued emotional distress, disrupted life tasks, social and interpersonal turmoil and fatigue and low energy" (Anderson et al., 1994, p. 390). The chronic stress associated with cancer can damage the autonomic, endocrine, and immune systems. Anderson and colleagues suggest that patients need more than medical treatment: their therapy should also involve helping them maintain their quality of life. Patients should be able to discuss their fears and anxieties, be given information about their disease and treatment, and be taught how to lower their arousal. In addition, researchers at the University of Manitoba (Degner et al., 1997) have found that a majority of women prefer to exercise some control over their treatment, with input from their physician, rather than selecting their own treatment or relinquishing the treatment plan to their physician.

What have health psychologists found that can help cancer patients? Carver and colleagues (1993) found that breast-cancer patients who maintained an optimistic outlook, accepted the reality of their situation, and maintained a sense of humour experienced less distress three months and six months after surgery. Patients who refused to accept the reality of the situation and who had thoughts of giving up experienced much higher levels of distress. Dunkel-Schetter and colleagues (1992) found that the most effective elements of a strategy for coping with cancer were social support (such as through self-help groups), a focus on the positive, and distraction. Avoidant coping strategies such as fantasizing, denial, and social withdrawal were associated with more emotional distress.

hassles: Little stressors that include the irritating demands and troubled relationships that are encountered daily and that, according to Lazarus, cause more stress than do major life changes.

uplifts: The positive experiences in life, which can neutralize the effects of many of the hassles.

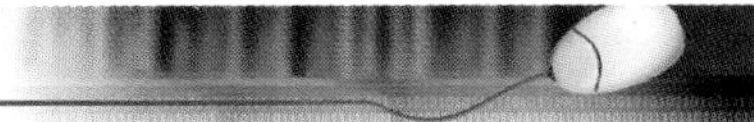

LINK IT!

www.cancer.ca/stats2000/highle.htm
Canadian Cancer Statistics 2000

The Immune System: An Army of Cells to Fight Off Disease

Most researchers today do not question that stress and health are closely related (Kiecolt-Glaser & Glaser, 1992). People who experience stress may indeed be more susceptible to coronary heart disease, stroke, and poorer pregnancy outcomes (Adler & Matthews, 1994; Davidson et al., 2000). But even more ominous is the growing evidence that stress can impair the functioning of the immune system itself.

The immune system, now known to be one of the most complex systems of the body, protects us from infection and disease. An army of highly specialized cells and organs, the immune system identifies and destroys any bacteria, viruses, fungi, parasites, and other foreign materials that enter the body. The immune system can identify a pathogen it has encountered before, sometimes over the entire lifespan (Ahmed & Gray, 1996). Cells of the immune system can distinguish instantly between self and non-self. Virtually every cell in your body carries distinctive molecules that mark it as self (Schindler, 1988). Non-self cells carry their own distinctive molecules, which mark them as foreign invaders to be attacked and destroyed. This is why transplanted organs are rejected by the immune system unless powerful immune-suppressant drugs are administered—they are foreign or non-self tissue to the recipient.

AIDS

What happens to a person from the time of infection with HIV to the development of full-blown AIDS?

The most feared disease related to the immune system is AIDS (acquired immune deficiency syndrome), which is caused by the human immunodeficiency virus (HIV). The virus attacks the helper cells, gradually but relentlessly weakening the immune system. The first case of AIDS was diagnosed in Canada in the early 1980s; there is still no cure for it and no vaccine to protect against it.

When a person is first infected, HIV enters the bloodstream. This initial infection usually causes no symptoms, and the immune system begins to produce HIV antibodies. It is these antibodies that are detected in the AIDS test. Individuals then progress to the asymptomatic carrier state, during which they experience no symptoms at all and thus can unknowingly infect others.

HIV attacks the immune system until it becomes essentially non-functional. The diagnosis of AIDS is made when the immune system is so damaged that victims develop rare forms of cancer or pneumonia or other "opportunistic" infections. Such infections would not usually affect people with a normal immune response; in people who have a very impaired immune system, these infections can be life-threatening. At this point patients typically experience progressive weight loss, weakness, fever, swollen lymph nodes, and diarrhea; a further 25 percent have a rare cancer that produces red-purple spots on the skin. Other infections develop as the immune system weakens further.

The average time from infection with HIV to advanced AIDS is about 10 years; but the time may range from 2 to 15 years (Nowak & McMichael, 1995). The disease progresses faster in smokers, in the very young, in people over 50, and (apparently) in women. AIDS also progresses faster in those who have been repeatedly exposed to the virus and in those who were infected by someone in an advanced stage of the disease.

The Transmission of AIDS

HIV is transmitted primarily through the exchange of blood, semen, or vaginal secretions during sexual contact or when IV (intravenous) drug users share contaminated needles or syringes (Des Jarlais & Friedman, 1994). Infected mothers can also infect the fetus prenatally, during childbirth, and when breastfeeding. Fortunately, recent research has identified a number of interventions that have reduced the transmission to rates as low as 4 to 10 percent, from previous levels of about 32 percent (Duong et al., 1999; Sullivan, 1997; Van de Perre, 1999).

The Psychological Impact of HIV Infection and AIDS

Most people are psychologically devastated when they are diagnosed with the AIDS virus. Not only are they being sentenced to an early death, but there is a social stigma associated with AIDS that few other diseases have.

To cope psychologically, AIDS patients and those infected with HIV need education and information about the disease. They can be helped by psychotherapy, self-help groups, and medications such as antidepressants and antianxiety drugs. Self-help groups and group therapy may serve as substitute family for some patients. An ever-present concern voiced by patients in psychotherapy is whether to tell others and, if so, what to tell them and how. Patients may feel a compelling need to confide in others and, at the same time, to conceal their condition.

The stigma associated with AIDS can compound the daily lives of AIDS patients. For example, Stewart Page (1999) conducted a study in which he compared the availability of rooms for rent when the interested renter was identified as having AIDS or not. Overall, in two Canadian cities, London and Windsor, and Detroit, Michigan, the probability of the rooms no longer being available was greatest when the potential renter was identified as having AIDS.

Protection against Sexually Transmitted Diseases: Minimizing Risk

Although everyone has seen or heard the messages about "safer" behaviours, many people still ignore the message. Researchers in Ontario surveyed adults at dating bars and found that even though people were concerned about contracting AIDS, many of them had not used any form of protection during their last sexual encounter (Herold & Mewhinney, 1993). People who choose to practise risky sex cannot be safe, but can reduce the risks by using a latex condom. Sexual abstinence or monogamous relationships with partners free of infection also reduce risk.

Stress and the Immune System

What are the effects of stress and depression on the immune system?

In a field of study known as **psychoneuroimmunology**, psychologists, biologists, and medical researchers combine their expertise to learn how psychological factors (emotions, thinking, and behaviour) affect the immune system.

Several studies show that psychological factors, emotions, and stress are related to immune system functioning (O'Leary, 1990). Moreover, the immune system exchanges information with the brain, and what goes on in the brain can apparently influence the immune system for good or ill.

Periods of high stress have been correlated with increased symptoms of many infectious diseases, including oral and genital herpes, mononucleosis, colds, and flu (Jemmott & Locke, 1984). People exposed to cold viruses are more likely to develop colds if they have experienced a greater number of life changes in the previous year (Cohen et al., 1993; Stone et al., 1992). Cohen and Williamson (1991) conclude from a review of studies that stress is associated with an increase in illness behaviours, such as reporting physical symptoms and seeking medical care.

Poor marital relationships, sleep deprivation, and exams and academic pressures have been linked to lowered immune response (Kiecolt-Glaser et al., 1987; Maier & Laudenslager, 1985). Severe, incapacitating depression is related to lowered immune activity (Irwin et al., 1987; Schleifer et al., 1983, 1985). For several months after the death of a spouse, the widow or widower suffers weakened immune system function (Bartrop et al., 1977) and is at a higher risk of mortality (Rogers & Reich, 1988).

McNaughton and colleagues (1990) report that immune suppression in the elderly is associated with depressed mood, severe stress, and dissatisfaction with social supports, whereas improved immune functioning is related to the use of problem-focused coping. Rodin (1986) found that nursing-home residents who were given training in coping skills developed fewer illnesses, suffered less deterioration from chronic conditions, and reported less stress than a similar group not given the training. Moreover, physicians have long observed that stress and anxiety can worsen autoimmune diseases. And, "if fear can produce relapses [in autoimmune diseases], then even the fear of a relapse may become a self-fulfilling prophecy" (Steinman, 1993, p. 112).

Personal Factors Reducing the Impact of Stress and Illness

What three personal factors are associated with health and resistance to stress?

Researchers have identified three personal factors that may contribute to better health: optimism, psychological hardiness, and social support.

psychoneuroimmunology (sye-ko-NEW-ro-IM-you-NOLL-oh-gee): A field in which psychologists, biologists, and medical researchers study the effects of psychological factors on the immune system.

Optimism and Pessimism

People who are generally optimistic tend to cope more effectively with stress, and this in turn may reduce their risk of illness (Seligman, 1990). Optimists generally expect good outcomes, and this helps make them more stress-resistant than pessimists, who tend to expect bad outcomes. Optimists are more likely to use problem-focused coping, to seek social support, and to find the positive aspects of a stressful situation and to better adjust to stress (Carver et al., 1993; Chang, 1998; Scheier & Carver, 1992). Pessimists are more likely to use denial or to focus on their stressful feelings (Scheier et al., 1986). Scheier and Carver (1985) found that optimistic college students reported fewer physical symptoms than those who were pessimistic. Another study, of patients who had undergone coronary bypass surgery, revealed that optimists recovered faster during their hospitalization and were able to resume their normal activities sooner after discharge than pessimists (Scheier et al., 1989). Apparently, happy thoughts are healthy thoughts.

Psychological Hardiness: Commitment, Challenge, and Control

Suzanne Kobasa (1979; Kobasa et al., 1982) wondered why some people under great stress succumb to illness while others do not. She studied 670 male executives, who identified stressful life events and symptoms of illness that they had experienced in the preceding three years. She then administered personality questionnaires to 200 executives who ranked high for both stress and illness and to 126 who had faced equally stressful life events but had few symptoms of illness. She found three qualities that distinguished those who remained healthy from those who had a high incidence of illness: commitment, control, and challenge. Kobasa collectively called these psychological **hardiness**.

Hardy individuals feel a strong sense of commitment to their work and personal life. They see themselves as having control over consequences and outcomes, and they welcome challenges. Florian and others (1995) found that commitment and control are sufficient to produce hardiness. Control provides the confidence that a person is in charge of the situation and capable of finding the right solution to a problem, and commitment provides the "staying power" to see it through.

Roth and colleagues (1989) suggest that "hardy individuals may possess a cognitive style such that troubling life events are interpreted less negatively and thereby rendered less harmful" (p. 141).

Social Support: Help in Time of Need

Another factor that seems to contribute to better health is **social support** (Kaplan et al., 1994). This includes support provided by a spouse or other family members, and by friends, neighbours, colleagues, support groups, and members of the larger community. Social support can direct help, information, and advice to the individual, as well as emotional support (Cohen, 1988). Social support provides the feeling that we are loved, valued, esteemed, and cared for by those for whom we feel a mutual obligation (Cobb, 1976).

Social support appears to have positive effects on the body's immune system as well as the cardiovascular and endocrine systems (Uchino et al., 1996). Social support may encourage health-promoting behaviours and reduce the impact of stress so that people are less likely to resort to unhealthy methods of coping, such as smoking and drinking (Adler & Matthews, 1994). Social support has been shown to reduce the impact of stress from unemployment, organizational restructuring, illness, retirement, and bereavement (Burke & Greenglass, 1999; Krantz et al., 1985). A study of 4775 people over a nine-year period found that people with low social support were twice as likely to die as those with high social support (Berkman & Syme, 1979).

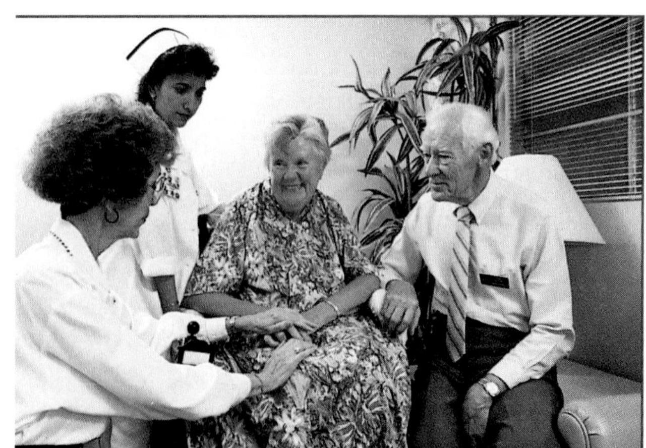

A strong social support network can help a person recover faster from an illness.

Remember It!

Health and Disease

1. Lowered immune response has been associated with
   a. stress.
   b. depression.
   c. stress and depression.
   d. neither stress nor depression.
2. Some research suggests that optimists are more stress-resistant than pessimists. (true/false)
3. Social support tends to reduce stress but is unrelated to health outcomes. (true/false)
4. Which of the following is *not* a dimension of psychological hardiness?
   a. a feeling that adverse circumstances can be controlled and changed
   b. a sense of commitment and deep involvement in personal goals
   c. a tendency to look upon change as a challenge rather than a threat
   d. close, supportive relationships with family and friends

Answers: 1. c 2. true 3. false 4. d

IT HAPPENED IN CANADA

Butt Out!

Grabbed a doughnut lately? If you pop into Tim Hortons you will most likely notice the absence of cigarette smoke. In fact, they were forerunners in a trend that is happening across our country. It's a subtle change but it is making a difference for the health of workers and customers everywhere—it is smoke-free legislation. Tim Hortons introduced their first totally smoke-free store in Hamilton in 1984. They introduced separately ventilated smoking rooms in 1994, and by 1999 the entire chain (except in Quebec) went smoke free or had a smoking room (5 percent). Now smoke-free rooms and smoke-free stores are being introduced in Quebec (Slopek, 2000).

Whole communities are now copying the move at Tim Hortons. At present, there are approximately 60 municipalities across Canada that have bylaws requiring smoke-free restaurants, and 44 requiring smoke-free bars. One of the most aggressive provinces is British Columbia, where the Workers' Compensation Board is fining businesses that fail to protect the safety of its workers by banning smoking in the workplace (Cunningham, 2000; Moore, 2000). The idea of smoke-free communities, where smoking is prohibited in all public areas, is the next step, and it is already starting to appear with the voluntary move toward smoke-free bowling alleys, shopping malls, casinos, play parks, and so on.

Recent research on natural disasters reveals that initial social support is common but that the support tends to deteriorate, because the needs of victims overwhelm the tangible and emotional resources of friends and family (Kaniasty & Norris, 1993). Similarly, chronic physical or mental illness may deplete the resources of those supplying care and social support, and lead to burnout (Schulz & Tompkins, 1990).

Your Lifestyle and Your Health

What constitutes an unhealthy lifestyle, and how serious a factor is lifestyle in illness and disease?

If you are not healthy or physically hardy, who or what is to blame? There are a number of enemies of good health: environmental pollutants; job, family, and personal stressors; genetic and congenital defects; accidents and injury; and others. But the number one concern with most people is lifestyle habits. The specific culprits are all well known: an unhealthy diet, overeating, lack of exercise, alcohol and drug abuse, too little sleep, and so on. But the most dangerous unhealthy behaviour of all is smoking.

hardiness: A combination of three psychological qualities shared by people who can undergo high levels of stress yet remain healthy: a sense of control over one's life, commitment to one's personal goals, and a tendency to view change as a challenge rather than as a threat.

social support: Tangible support, information, advice, and/or emotional support provided in time of need by family, friends, and others; the feeling that we are loved, valued, and cared for.

Smoking: Hazardous to Your Health

Why is smoking considered the single most preventable cause of death?

Today some 20 to 30 percent of Canadians smoke. Smoking is directly related to 35 000 deaths annually in Canada, according to Health and Welfare Canada. And those Canadians who don't smoke but who must breathe smoke-filled air suffer the ill effects of passive smoking (Kawachi et al., 1997). Add to this statistic the suffering from chronic bronchitis, emphysema, and other respiratory diseases; death and injury from fires caused by smoking; and low birth-weight and impaired fetal development in babies born to mothers who smoke.

Why do adult smokers continue the habit even though most admit they would prefer to be non-smokers? There seems little doubt that smoking is an addiction. Nicotine is a powerful substance that increases the release of acetylcholine, norepinephrine, dopamine, and other neurotransmitters, which improve mental alertness, sharpen memory, and reduce tension and anxiety (Pomerleau & Pomerleau, 1989). According to Parrott (1993), some people smoke primarily to increase arousal, whereas others smoke primarily to reduce stress and anxiety. Thus, smoking for most people is a coping mechanism for regulating moods.

Because smoking is so addictive, smokers have great difficulty breaking the habit. Even so, 90 percent of ex-smokers quit smoking on their own (Novello, 1990). The average smoker makes five or six attempts to quit before finally succeeding (Sherman 1994). Some aids, such as nicotine gum and the nicotine patch, help many people kick the habit. A meta-analysis involving 17 studies and more than 5000 people revealed that 22 percent of people who used the nicotine patch were smoke-free, compared with only 9 percent of those who received a placebo. And 27 percent of those receiving the nicotine patch *and* antismoking counselling or support remained smoke-free (Fiore, cited in Sherman, 1994). But even with the patch, quitting is difficult, because the patch only lessens withdrawal symptoms. Withdrawal symptoms typically last two to four weeks (Hughes, 1992). Half of all relapses occur within the first two weeks after people quit. Relapses are most likely when people are experiencing negative emotions or when they are using alcohol. It takes just one cigarette, sometimes only one puff, to cause a relapse.

Alcohol: A Problem for Millions

What are some health risks of alcohol consumption?

Although smoking is directly related to a greater number of deaths, alcohol undoubtedly causes more misery. The health and social costs of alcohol—in fatalities, lost work, family problems, and so on—are staggering. Alcohol abuse and dependence is three times more prevalent in males than in females (Grant et al., 1991). People who begin drinking before age 15 are more likely than those who begin later to become dependent on alcohol (Grant & Dawson, 1998; Prescott & Kendler, 1999). Although a higher percentage of white-collar workers use alcohol, the percentage of problem drinkers is higher among blue-collar workers (Harford et al., 1992). For many, alcohol provides a means of coping with life strains that they feel powerless to control (Seeman & Seeman, 1992).

Alcohol can damage virtually every organ in the body, but it is especially harmful to the liver and is the major cause of cirrhosis. Pregnant women should avoid all alcohol because of its potentially disastrous effects on the developing fetus. Alcohol also affects the brain. The only good news in recent studies is that some of alcohol's effects on the brain seem to be partially reversible with prolonged abstinence.

Alcoholism's toll goes beyond physical damage to the alcoholic. Drunk drivers kill and injure. Alcohol has also been implicated in drownings, suicides, rapes, burglaries, and assaults.

LINK IT!

www.arf.org
Addiction Research Foundation

www.aa-intergroup.org/faq.html
The On-line Intergroup of A.A.: Frequently Asked Questions

Alcoholism: Causes and Treatment

The Canadian Medical Association maintains that alcoholism is a disease, and "once an alcoholic, always an alcoholic." According to this view, even a small amount of alcohol causes an irresistible craving for more, leading alcoholics to lose control of their drinking (Jellinek, 1960). Total abstinence is seen as the only acceptable recourse. The medical establishment and Alcoholics Anonymous endorse both the disease concept and the total abstinence approach to treatment.

Some studies suggest that there is a genetic factor in alcoholism and lend support to the disease model. According to Goodwin (1985), about one-half of hospitalized alcoholics have a family history of alcohol abuse. Adoption studies have revealed that "sons of alcoholics were three or four times more likely to be alcoholic than were sons of non-alcoholics, whether raised by their alcoholic biologic parents or by non-alcoholic adoptive parents" (Goodwin, 1985, p. 172). Pihl, Peterson, and Finn (1990) at McGill University agree with Goodwin's findings that sons of male alcoholics have a heightened genetic risk for alcohol abuse. The data for daughters did not show this pattern.

The hypothesis that there is a greater genetic risk of alcoholism for men is also supported by research that involved 356 pairs of identical and fraternal twins (McGue et al., 1992). The study revealed a substantial genetic influence for male twins, especially if their first symptom of alcoholism appeared before they turned 20. A study of 1000 pairs of female identical and fraternal twins found that alcoholism in women is 50 to 60 percent heritable, which is a rate similar to that for male alcoholics (Kendler et al., 1994).

Is alcoholism a disease? Some experts reject the disease concept and contend that alcoholism can take various forms and have various causes (Pattison, 1982). Researchers caution against overlooking the environmental contribution to alcoholism, even in people who are genetically predisposed (Searles, 1988). Family and cultural influences are apparently the dominant factors in men whose drinking problems appear after adolescence. A recent Canadian study (McCreary et al., 1999) demonstrated that men who endorsed traditional male gender roles engaged in a higher level of alcohol consumption than others.

Some experts stress the role of behavioural, social, and cultural factors in alcoholism and advocate various approaches to treatment. One approach—*cue exposure*—systematically exposes the problem drinker to cues that have triggered drinking in the past (Neimark et al., 1994). The individual is prevented from drinking in the presence of those cues and gradually becomes less responsive to them.

With behaviour therapy, some (not all) problem drinkers can learn the skills necessary to drink socially without losing control (Cunningham et al., 1999; Peele, 1992; Sobell & Sobell, 1978). Advocates of this treatment—**controlled drinking**—generally suggest that it is most successful with younger drinkers who have less serious drinking problems and who are not yet physically dependent on alcohol (Marlatt, 1983; Polich et al., 1981).

Whatever treatment approach is used, social support is essential; this can be provided by friends, family members, therapists, or members of self-help groups. Alcoholics who have such support are often able to quit on their own, without any formal treatment. The key seems to involve developing the motivation to quit drinking and then doing so with the encouragement and support of others.

Exercise: Keeping Fit Is Healthy

What are some benefits of regular aerobic exercise?

For years medical experts, especially health psychologists, have promoted regular exercise. Yet "only 15 percent of the general population is highly active, and as much as 70 percent of the entire population can be characterized as inactive" (Rodin & Salovey, 1989, p. 554). Many studies show that regular **aerobic exercise** pays rich dividends in the form of physical and mental fitness.

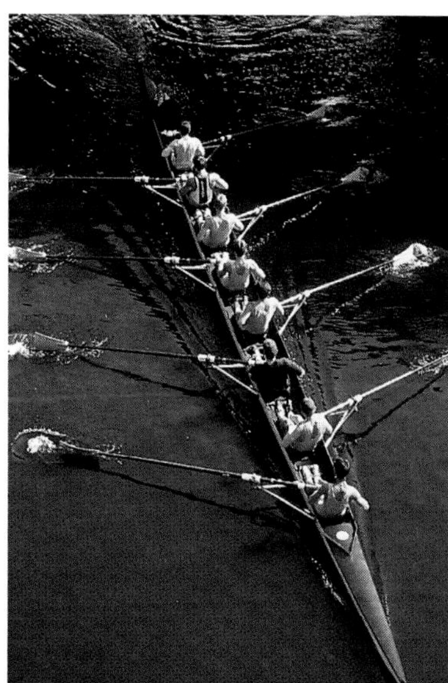

Regular aerobic exercise improves cardiovascular fitness in people of all ages and helps moderate the effects of stress.

controlled drinking: A behavioural approach in the treatment of alcoholism, designed to teach alcoholics the skills necessary to drink socially without losing control.

aerobic exercise (ah-RO-bik): Exercise involving the use of large muscle groups in continuous, repetitive action and requiring increased oxygen intake and increased breathing and heart rates.

Aerobic exercise (such as running, swimming, brisk walking, bicycling, rowing, and jumping rope) is exercise that uses the large muscle groups in continuous, repetitive action and requires increased oxygen intake and increased breathing and heart rates. Aerobic exercise should be performed regularly—three or four times a week for 20 to 30 minutes, with additional five- to ten-minute warm-up and cool-down periods (Alpert et al., 1990; Shepard, 1986). Less than 20 minutes of aerobic exercise three times a week has "no measurable effect on the heart," and more than three hours per week "is not known to reduce cardiovascular risk any further" (Simon, 1988, p. 3).

The importance of regular, systematic aerobic exercise in keeping the cardiovascular system healthy cannot be overemphasized. This is true for people of all ages. Even preschoolers receive cardiovascular benefits from planned exercise (Alpert et al., 1990). At the other end of the age spectrum, regular, planned exercise yields dramatic increases in muscle and bone strength in older people. Exercisers between the ages of 87 and 96 who were on a weight-lifting program for only two months showed the same absolute gains in rate of muscular strength as younger people (Allison, 1991). Strenuous workouts would not transform a Bob Hope into an Arnold Schwarzenegger, but significant increases in muscle strength have been recorded even in people pushing 100.

We do not need to become marathon runners or spend several hours a day sweating and grunting in a fitness centre to enjoy the maximum benefits of exercise. Low-intensity physical training improves physical fitness in older adults (DeVito et al., 1997). Even a daily brisk walk of 30 minutes or more helps to reduce stress and yields the fitness standard associated with a much lower death rate.

In case you are not yet convinced, consider the following benefits of exercise.

- It increases the efficiency of the heart, enabling it to pump more blood with each beat; it reduces the resting pulse rate and improves circulation.
- It raises HDL (good blood cholesterol) levels; this helps rid the body of LDL (bad blood cholesterol) and also removes plaque buildup on artery walls.
- It burns up extra calories, enabling you to lose weight or maintain your weight.
- It makes bones denser and stronger; this helps prevent osteoporosis in women.
- It moderates the effects of stress.
- It gives you more energy and increases your resistance to fatigue.
- It benefits the immune system by increasing natural killer cell activity (Fiatarone et al., 1988).

If you are a couch potato, you watch a lot of TV, and TV is a valued part of your social life, you might be in trouble! Donald McCreary, working in the health

Remember It!

Lifestyle and Health

1. Which is the most important factor leading to disease and death?
   a. unhealthy lifestyle
   b. a poor health care system
   c. environmental hazards
   d. genetic disorders
2. Which health-compromising behaviour is responsible for the most deaths?
   a. overeating
   b. smoking
   c. lack of exercise
   d. excessive alcohol use
3. (Alcohol/Smoking) damages virtually every organ in the body.
4. To improve cardiovascular fitness, aerobic exercise should be done
   a. 15 minutes daily.
   b. 1 hour daily.
   c. 20 to 30 minutes daily.
   d. 20 to 30 minutes 3 or 4 times a week

Answers: 1. a 2. b 3. Alcohol 4. d

area in Regina, and Stanly Sadava, at Brock University (2000), looked at the relation between TV viewing and health, weight, and physical fitness. Women who spent a lot of time watching TV believed they were in poorer health. Overall, both men and women who watched a lot of TV thought they were overweight more so than people who watched less TV. To feel better about yourself, you might want to get out and take a walk.

Managing Stress

Apply It!

Anyone who is alive is subject to stress, but some of us are more negatively affected by it than others.

If stress leaves you fretting and fuming, with your muscles in knots, try a few relaxation techniques.

Progressive Relaxation

The fight-or-flight response is our body's way of preparing us to deal with a threat. If we can neither fight nor flee, we are left with intense physiological arousal, or stress. There are several relaxation techniques that you can use to calm yourself and relieve muscle tension. Probably the most widely used relaxation technique is progressive relaxation (Rice, 1987). It consists of flexing and relaxing the different muscle groups throughout the body from the head to the toes. Here's how to do it:

1. Loosen or remove any tight-fitting clothing, take off your shoes, and situate yourself comfortably in an armchair with your arms resting on the chair's arms. Sit straight in the chair, but let your head fall forward so that your chin rests comfortably on your chest. Place your feet flat on the floor with your legs slightly apart in a comfortable position.
2. Take a deep breath. Hold the breath for a few seconds and then exhale slowly and completely. Repeat several times. Notice the tension in your chest as you hold the breath, and the relaxation as you let the breath out.
3. Flex the muscles in your right upper arm (in your left arm if you are left-handed). Hold the muscles as tight as you can for about 10 seconds. Feel the tension. Now relax the muscles completely and observe the feeling of relaxation. Repeat the flexing and the relaxing several times. Then do the same with the other arm.
4. After completing the opening routine with your arms, continue the procedure, tensing and then relaxing a group of muscles, starting with the muscles in the forehead. Progressively work your way down through all the muscle groups in the body, ending with your feet.

Managing Mental Stress

When we become angry, hostile, fearful, worried, and upset by things we think are going to happen, we cause our hearts to pound and our stomachs to churn. How often have you done this to yourself only to find that what you had imagined never actually materialized? The next time you begin to react to something you think will happen, stop yourself. Learn to use your own thinking to reduce stress, not create it.

Stress-Inoculation Training

Stress-inoculation training is a program designed by psychologist Donald Meichenbaum (1977) at the University of Waterloo. Test anxiety, stress over personal and social relationships, and various types of performance anxiety have been successfully treated with stress inoculation. Individuals are taught to recognize their own negative thoughts ("I'll never be able to do this" or "I'll probably make a fool of myself"), and to replace negative thoughts with positive ones. They learn how to talk to themselves using posi-

tive coping statements to dispel worry and provide self-encouragement. Here are some examples of these coping statements (adapted from Meichenbaum, 1977):

Preparing for the stressor
"I can come up with a plan to handle the problem."

Facing or confronting the stressor
"If I take one step at a time, I know that I can handle this situation."

Coping with the stressor
"I will keep my mind focused on the present, on what is happening now, and just concentrate on what I have to do."

When the coping attempt is finished
"I am really making progress."

Taking a Breather

To counteract the shallow, rapid breathing that occurs when you are stressed, you need to take deep abdominal breaths. To learn how, place one hand on your chest and the other on your abdomen. Practise inhaling in such a way that your abdomen, not your chest, rises. Once you are able to do this, you are ready to learn how to "take a breather" to counteract stress.

1. Slowly exhale through your mouth to remove the stale air from your lungs. Repeat until your lungs feel empty.
2. Inhale through your nose until your abdomen (not your lungs) begins to rise. Hold for five seconds, and then exhale.
3. Repeat four or five times whenever you feel tense and irritable.

Working Off Stress

Blow off steam physically by exercising or engaging in physical work (raking leaves, gardening, cleaning). Physical activity will provide a "fight" outlet for your mental stress.

Other Stress-Reducing Measures

Here are some additional suggestions for reducing the negative effects of stress.

- Make time for relaxation and activities you enjoy.
- Rely on social support to moderate the effects of stress.
- Don't expect perfection from yourself or from other people.
- If you suffer from "hurry sickness," slow down.
- Learn to be patient.
- Avoid overeating, drinking, or using drugs.
- Eat a balanced diet and get enough sleep.
- Use caffeine in moderation.

KEY TERMS

aerobic exercise, p. 373
alarm stage, p. 356
approach–approach conflict, p. 360
approach–avoidance conflict, p. 360
avoidance–avoidance conflict, p. 360
biomedical model, p. 354
biopsychosocial model, p. 354
controlled drinking, p. 373
coping, p. 362
emotion-focused coping, p. 363
exhaustion stage, p. 357
general adaptation syndrome (GAS), p. 356
hardiness, p. 370
hassles, p. 366
health psychology, p. 354
posttraumatic stress disorder (PTSD), p. 361
primary appraisal, p. 358
problem-focused coping, p. 362
psychoneuroimmunology, p. 369
resistance stage, p. 356
secondary appraisal, p. 359
Social Readjustment Rating Scale (SRRS), p. 364
social support, p. 370
stress, p. 355
stressor, p. 356
uplifts, p. 366

THINKING CRITICALLY

Evaluation

Can people always cure themselves of illnesses? What are the limits to what people can do to help themselves?

Point/Counterpoint

Prepare two arguments, one supporting the position that alcoholism is a genetically inherited disease, and the other supporting the position that alcoholism is not a medical disease but results from learning.

Psychology in Your Life

Choose several stress-producing incidents from your own life and explain what problem-focused and emotion-focused coping strategies you used. From the knowledge you have gained in this chapter, list other coping strategies that might have been more effective.

SUMMARY & REVIEW

Two Approaches to Health and Illness

How do the biomedical and biopsychosocial models differ in their approaches to health and illness?

The biomedical model focuses on illness rather than on health and explains illness in terms of biological factors. The biopsychosocial model focuses on health as well as on illness and holds that both are determined by a combination of biological, psychological, and social factors.

Theories of Stress

What is the general adaptation syndrome?

The general adaptation syndrome is the predictable sequence of reactions that organisms show in response to stressors. It consists of the alarm stage, the resistance stage, and the exhaustion stage.

What are the roles of primary and secondary appraisal when people are confronted with a potentially stressful event?

Lazarus maintains that when we are confronted with a potentially stressful event, we engage in a cognitive appraisal process consisting of (1) a primary appraisal, to evaluate the relevance of the event to our well-being (whether it will be positive, will be irrelevant, or will involve harm or loss, threat, or challenge); and (2) a secondary appraisal to determine how we will cope with the stressor.

Sources of Stress: The Common and the Extreme

How do approach–approach, avoidance–avoidance, and approach–avoidance conflicts differ?

In an approach–approach conflict, we must decide between equally desirable alternatives; in an avoidance–avoidance conflict, between two undesirable alternatives. In an approach–avoidance conflict, we are both drawn to and repelled by a choice.

How do the unpredictability of and lack of control over a stressor affect its impact?

Stressors that are unpredictable and uncontrollable are more stressful than those that are predictable and controllable.

How do people typically react to catastrophic events?

Victims of catastrophic events are initially dazed and stunned. When they begin to recover from the shock, they typically experience anxiety, nightmares, and a compulsive need to retell the event over and over.

What is posttraumatic stress disorder?

Posttraumatic stress disorder (PTSD) is a prolonged, severe stress reaction to a catastrophic event; the victim relives the trauma in flashbacks, nightmares, or intrusive memories.

Coping with Stress

What is the difference between problem-focused and emotion-focused coping?

Problem-focused coping is a response aimed at reducing, modifying, or eliminating the source of stress; emotion-focused coping is aimed at reducing the emotional impact of the stressor.

Evaluating Life Stress: Major Life Changes, Hassles, and Uplifts

What is the Social Readjustment Rating Scale designed to reveal?

The SRRS assesses stress in terms of life events that necessitate life change. Holmes and Rahe found a relationship between degree of life stress (as measured on the scale) and major health problems.

What roles do hassles and uplifts play in the stress of life, according to Lazarus?

According to Lazarus, daily hassles typically cause more stress than major life changes. The positive experiences in life—the uplifts—can neutralize the effects of many of the hassles.

Health and Disease

What can cancer patients do to help them cope with having cancer?

Cancer patients need medical treatment and social support that will help them maintain their quality of life. They need to have opportunities to discuss their treatment and emotions openly. In addition, if the patient maintains an optimistic outlook and is able to accept their condition, they may experience less distress.

What happens to a person from the time of infection with HIV to the development of full-blown AIDS?

When a person is initially infected with HIV, the body begins to produce HIV antibodies, eventually detectable in a blood test. For a period of time, the victim has no symptoms, but HIV gradually renders the immune system non-functional. The diagnosis of AIDS is made when the person succumbs to various opportunisitic infections.

What are the effects of stress and depression on the immune system?

Both stress and depression have been associated with lowered immune response, and stress has been linked to increased symptoms of various infectious diseases.

What three personal factors are associated with health and resistance to stress?

Personal factors related to health and resistance to stress are optimism, psychological hardiness, and social support.

Your Lifestyle and Your Health

What constitutes an unhealthy lifestyle, and how serious a factor is lifestyle in illness and disease?

Slightly over 50 percent of all deaths in this country can be attributed to unhealthy lifestyle factors, which include smoking, overeating, an unhealthy diet, too much coffee or alcohol, drug abuse, and/or too little exercise and rest.

Why is smoking considered the single most preventable cause of death?

Because each year in Canada, smoking results in tens of thousands of deaths from heart disease, cancer, lung disease, and stroke.

What are some health risks of alcohol consumption?

Alcohol damages virtually every organ in the body, including the liver, stomach, skeletal muscles, heart, and brain.

What are some benefits of regular aerobic exercise?

Regular aerobic exercise reduces risk of cardiovascular disease, increases muscle strength, moderates the effects of stress, makes bones denser and stronger, and helps maintain a desirable weight.

12 Psychological Disorders

It was early in January, and Sybil Dorsett was working with other students in the chemistry lab at Columbia University in New York. Suddenly the loud crash of breaking glass made her heart pound and her head throb. The room seemed to be whirling around, and the acrid smell of chemicals filled the air, stinging her nostrils.

That smell—so much like the old drugstore back in her native Wisconsin—and the broken glass, like a half-forgotten, far-off memory at home in her dining room when she was a little girl. Again Sybil heard the accusing voice, "You broke it." Frantically she seized her chemistry notes, stuffed them into her brown zipper folder, and ran for the door with all eyes—those of the professor and the other students—following her in astonishment.

Sybil ran down the long, dark hall on the third floor of the chemistry building, pushed the elevator button, and waited. Seconds seemed like hours.

The next thought that entered Sybil's awareness was that of clutching for her brown folder, but it was gone. Gone, too, were the elevator she was waiting for and the long, dark hallway. She found herself walking down a dark, deserted

street in a strange city. An icy wind whipped her face, and thick snowflakes filled the air. This wasn't New York. Where could she be? And how could she have gotten here in the few seconds between waiting for the elevator and now? Sybil walked on, bewildered, and finally came to a newsstand, where she bought a local paper. She was in Philadelphia. The date on the newspaper told her that five days had passed since she stood waiting for the elevator. Where had she been? What had she done?

A victim of sadistic physical abuse since early childhood, Sybil had experienced blackouts–missing days, weeks, and even longer periods, which seemed to have been taken from her life. Unknown to Sybil, other, very different personalities emerged during those periods to take control of her mind and body. Sixteen separate selves, 14 female and 2 male, lived within Sybil, each with different talents and abilities, emotions, ways of speaking and acting, moral values, and ambitions.

For many years Sybil (later identified as Shirley Mason) worked with her psychiatrist and eventually integrated her 16 personalities. After that, she lived a quiet, reclusive life, painting and running an arts business. She remained close to her therapist and eventually died of cancer at the age of 75 on February 26, 1998 (Miller & Kantrowitz, 1999). (Based on Schreiber, 1973.)

What you have just read is not fiction. These and even stranger experiences are part of the real-life story of "Sybil," who suffered from an unusual phenomenon, dissociative identity disorder, better known as multiple personality. Her life story, told in the book *Sybil*, and the life story of Chris Sizemore, told in the film *The Three Faces of Eve*, are two of the best-known cases of this disorder.

How can we know whether *our* behaviour is normal or abnormal? At what point do our fears, thoughts, mood changes, and actions move from normal to mentally disturbed? This chapter explores many psychological disorders, their symptoms, and their possible causes. But first let us ask the obvious question: What is abnormal?

What Is Abnormal?

What criteria might be used to differentiate normal from abnormal behaviour?

Because Sybil's case is such an extreme example, virtually everyone would agree that her behaviour was abnormal. But most abnormal behaviour is not so extreme and clear-cut. There are not two clearly separate and distinct kinds of human beings: one kind always mentally healthy and well-adjusted, and another kind always abnormal and mentally disturbed. Behaviour lies along a continuum, with most of us fairly well-adjusted and experiencing only occasional maladaptive thoughts or behaviour. At one extreme of the continuum are the unusually mentally healthy; at the other extreme are the seriously disturbed, like Sybil.

Abnormal behaviour is defined by each culture. For example, homelessness is considered abnormal in some cultures and completely normal in others.

But where along the continuum does behaviour become abnormal? Several questions can help determine what behaviour is abnormal:

- *Is the behaviour considered strange within the person's own culture?* What is considered normal and abnormal in one culture will not necessarily always be considered so in another. Even within the same culture, conceptions about what is normal can change from time to time.
- *Does the behaviour cause personal distress?* When people experience considerable emotional distress without any life experience that warrants it, they may be diagnosed as having a psychological or mental disorder. But not all people with psychological disorders feel distress. Some feel perfectly comfortable, even happy with the way they are and the way they feel.
- *Is the behaviour maladaptive?* Some experts believe that the best way to differentiate between normal and abnormal behaviour is to consider whether the behaviour is adaptive or maladaptive—that is, whether it leads to healthy or impaired functioning. Maladaptive behaviour interferes with the quality of people's lives and can cause a great deal of distress to family members, friends, and coworkers.
- *Is the person a danger to self or others?* Another consideration is whether people are a threat or danger to themselves or others. In order to be committed to a mental institution, a person has to be judged both mentally ill and a danger to himself or herself or to others.
- *Is the person legally responsible for his or her acts?* Traditionally, the term *insanity* was used to label those who behaved abnormally. "Not guilty due to mental disorder" is a legal phrase used by the Canadian courts to declare people not legally responsible for their acts; the term, however, is not used by mental health professionals.

Perspectives on the Causes and Treatment of Psychological Disorders

What are five current perspectives that attempt to explain the causes of psychological disorders?

The earliest explanation of psychological disorders was that disturbed people were possessed by evil spirits or demons. At present, there are five main perspectives that attempt to explain the causes of psychological disorders and to recommend the best methods of treatment: biological, psychodynamic, learning, cognitive, and humanistic. They are summarized in Review & Reflect 12.1.

Mental health professionals often disagree about the causes of abnormal behaviour and the best treatments; there is less disagreement about diagnosis. Standard criteria have been established and are used by most mental health professionals to diagnose psychological disorders.

REVIEW & REFLECT 12.1
Perspectives on Psychological Disorders: Summary

Perspective	Cause of Psychological Disorders	Treatment
Biological perspective	A psychological disorder is a symptom of an underlying physical disorder caused by a structural or biochemical abnormality in the brain, by genetic inheritance, or by infection.	Diagnose and treat like any other physical disorder Drugs, electroconvulsive therapy, or psychosurgery
Psychodynamic perspective	Early childhood experiences; unconscious sexual or aggressive conflicts; imbalance among id, ego, and superego.	Bring disturbing repressed material to consciousness and help patient work through unconscious conflicts Psychoanalysis
Learning perspective	Abnormal thoughts, feelings, and behaviours are learned and sustained like any other behaviours; or there is a failure to learn appropriate behaviour.	Use classical and operant conditioning and modelling to extinguish abnormal behaviours and to increase adaptive behaviour Behaviour therapy, behaviour modification
Cognitive perspective	Faulty and negative thinking can cause psychological disorders.	Change faulty, irrational, and/or negative thinking Beck's cognitive therapy, rational-emotive therapy
Humanistic perspective	Psychological disorders result from blocking of normal tendency toward self-actualization.	Increase self-acceptance and self-understanding; help patient become more inner-directed Client-centred therapy, Gestalt therapy

Defining and Classifying Psychological Disorders

What is the DSM-IV?

In 1952 the American Psychiatric Association (APA) published a diagnostic system for describing and classifying psychological disorders. Over the years this system has been revised several times. In 1994 the APA published its most recent edition—the *Diagnostic and Statistical Manual of Mental Disorders* (fourth edition), commonly referred to as the **DSM-IV**. It describes about 290 specific psychological disorders and lists the criteria for diagnosing them. The DSM-IV is the most widely accepted diagnostic system in Canada and the United States and is used by researchers, therapists, and mental health workers. It enables a diverse group of professionals to speak the same language when diagnosing, treating, researching, and conversing about a variety of psychological disorders. Review & Reflect 12.2 summarizes the major categories of disorders in the DSM-IV.

You may have heard the terms *neurotic* and *psychotic* used in relation to mental disturbances. The term **neurosis** (now obsolete) used to be applied to disorders that cause people considerable personal distress and some impairment in functioning but do not cause them to lose contact with reality or to violate important social norms. A **psychosis** is a more serious disturbance that greatly impairs everyday functioning. It can cause people to lose touch with reality and to suffer from delusions or hallucinations, or both; it sometimes requires hospitalization. The term *psychosis* is still used by mental health professionals.

REVIEW & REFLECT 12.1
Perspectives on Psychological Disorders: Summary

Disorder	Symptoms	Examples
Anxiety disorders	Disorders characterized by anxiety and avoidance behaviour.	Panic disorder Social phobia Obsessive-compulsive disorder Posttraumatic stress disorder
Somatoform disorders	Disorders in which physical symptoms are present that are psychological in origin rather than due to a medical condition.	Hypochondriasis Pain disorder Conversion disorder
Dissociative disorders	Disorders in which one handles stress or conflict by forgetting important personal information or one's whole identity, or by compartmentalizing the trauma or conflict into a split-off alter personality.	Dissociative amnesia Dissociative fugue Dissociative identity disorder
Schizophrenia and other psychotic disorders	Disorders characterized by the presence of psychotic symptoms including hallucinations, delusions, disorganized speech, bizarre behaviour, or loss of contact with reality.	Schizophrenia, disorganized type Schizophrenia, paranoid type Schizophrenia, catatonic type Delusional disorder, jealous type
Mood disorders	Disorders characterized by periods of extreme or prolonged depression or mania, or both.	Major depressive disorder Bipolar disorder
Personality disorders	Disorders characterized by long-standing, inflexible, maladaptive patterns of behaviour beginning early in life and causing personal distress or problems in social and occupational functioning.	Antisocial personality disorder Histrionic personality disorder Narcissistic personality disorder Borderline personality disorder
Substance-related disorders	Disorders in which undesirable behavioural changes result from substance abuse, dependence, or intoxication.	Alcohol abuse Cocaine abuse Cannabis dependence
Disorders usually first diagnosed in infancy, childhood, or adolescence	Disorders that include mental disability, learning disorders, communication disorders, pervasive developmental disorders, attention-deficit and disruptive behaviour disorders, tic disorders, and elimination disorders.	Conduct disorder Autism Tourette's syndrome Stuttering
Sleep disorders	Disorders including dyssomnias (disturbance in the amount, quality, or timing of sleep) and parasomnias (abnormal occurrences during sleep).	Primary insomnia Narcolepsy Sleep terror disorder Sleepwalking disorder
Eating disorders	Disorders characterized by severe disturbances in eating behaviour.	Anorexia nervosa Bulimia nervosa

Source: Based on DSM-IV (APA, 1994).

DSM-IV: *The Diagnostic and Statistical Manual of Mental Disorders* (fourth edition); it describes about 290 mental disorders and the symptoms that must be present for diagnosing each disorder.

neurosis (new-RO-sis): An obsolete term for a disorder causing personal distress and some impairment in functioning, but not causing one to lose contact with reality or to violate important social norms.

psychosis (sy-CO-sis): A severe psychological disorder, sometimes requiring hospitalization, in which one typically loses contact with reality, suffers delusions and/or hallucinations, and has a seriously impaired ability to function in everyday life.

Remember It!

What Is Abnormal?

1. It is relatively easy to differentiate normal behaviour from abnormal behaviour. (true/false)
2. Match the perspective with its suggested cause of abnormal behaviour.
   ____ 1) faulty learning
   ____ 2) unconscious, unresolved conflicts
   ____ 3) blocking of the natural tendency toward self-actualization
   ____ 4) genetic inheritance or biochemical or structural abnormalities in the brain
   ____ 5) faulty thinking

   a. psychodynamic
   b. biological
   c. learning
   d. humanistic
   e. cognitive
3. The DSM-IV is a manual published by the American Psychiatric Association that is used to
   a. diagnose psychological disorders.
   b. explain the causes of psychological disorders.
   c. outline treatments for various psychological disorders.
   d. assess the effectiveness of treatment programs.

Answers: 1. false 2. 1) c 2) a 3) d 4) b 5) e 3. a

Anxiety Disorders: When Anxiety Is Extreme

When is anxiety healthy, and when is it unhealthy?

Anxiety is a vague, general uneasiness or feeling that something bad is about to happen. Anxiety may be associated with a particular situation or object, or it may be free-floating—not associated with anything specific. None of us is a stranger to anxiety. We have all felt it.

Some anxiety is normal and appropriate. Imagine that you are driving on a highway late at night when you notice that your gas tank indicator is on empty. A wave of anxiety sweeps over you, and you immediately begin to look for a service station. You are feeling normal anxiety—a response to a real danger or threat. Normal anxiety prompts us to take useful action and is therefore healthy. Anxiety is abnormal if it is out of proportion to the seriousness of the situation, if it does not fade soon after the danger is past, or if it occurs in the absence of real danger (Goodwin, 1986).

Some of the psychological disorders characterized by severe anxiety are generalized anxiety disorder, panic disorder, phobias, and obsessive-compulsive disorder.

Generalized Anxiety Disorder

Generalized anxiety disorder is the diagnosis given to people who experience *excessive* anxiety and worry that they find difficult to control. They may be unduly worried about their finances or their own health or the health of family members. They may worry unnecessarily about their performance at work or their ability to function socially. Their excessive anxiety may cause them to feel tense, on edge, tired, and irritable, and to have difficulty concentrating and sleeping. Their symptoms may include trembling, palpitations, sweating, dizziness, nausea, diarrhea, and frequent urination. It is estimated that about 5 percent of North Americans will suffer from generalized anxiety disorder sooner or later. Kendler and colleagues (1992b) estimate the heritability of generalized anxiety disorder to be about 30 percent. Previously thought of as a mild disorder, generalized anxiety disorder is now considered to substantially reduce the quality of life for those who suffer from it (Brawman-Mintzer & Lydiard, 1997; Kranzler, 1996).

Panic Disorder

What are the symptoms of a panic disorder?

Mindy Markowitz is an attractive, stylishly dressed, 25-year-old art director for a trade magazine. She is seeking treatment for her "panic attacks," which have been escalating over the past year. These attacks—she now has two or three a day—begin with a sudden and intense wave of "horrible fear" that seems to come out of nowhere. Some of these strike her during the day, some wake her from sleep. She begins to tremble, sweats profusely, and feels nauseated. She also feels as though she is gagging and fears that she will lose control and do something crazy, like run screaming into the street. (Adapted from Spitzer et al., 1989, p. 154)

During **panic attacks**—attacks of overwhelming anxiety, fear, or terror—people commonly report a pounding heart, uncontrollable trembling or shaking, and a feeling of being choked or smothered. They may report being afraid that they are going to die or that they are "going crazy."

Markowitz was diagnosed with **panic disorder**, which is characterized by recurrent, unpredictable panic attacks that cause apprehension about the occurrence and consequences of further attacks. This apprehension can cause people to avoid situations that have been associated with previous panic attacks.

The biological perspective sheds some light on panic disorder. PET scans reveal that even in a nonpanic state, many panic-disorder patients show a greatly increased blood flow to parts of the right hemisphere of the limbic system—the part of the brain involved in emotion (Reiman et al., 1989). Family and twin studies, too, suggest that genetic factors play a role in panic disorder (Goldstein et al., 1994).

Faravelli and Pallanti (1989) found that high stress, particularly in the form of significant losses or threatening events, may be the precipitating factor in the first panic attack. Once people have had an attack, they may develop extreme anxiety that it will happen again (Gorman et al., 1989). Clark and colleagues (1997) offer a cognitive theory suggesting that panic attacks are associated with a catastrophic misinterpretation of bodily sensations. Roth and colleagues (1992) suggest that when panic disorder patients know that a stressor is coming, their anticipatory anxiety may set the stage for a panic attack.

Panic disorder can have significant social and health consequences (Sherbourne et al., 1996). Panic disorder patients tend to overuse the health-care system (Katon, 1996) and are at increased risk for abuse of alcohol and other drugs (Marshall, 1997).

LINK IT!

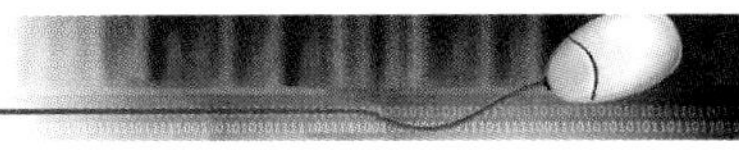

www.adaa.org
Anxiety Disorders Association of America

Phobias: Persistent, Irrational Fears

What are the characteristics of the three categories of phobias?

People suffering from a **phobia** experience a persistent, irrational fear of some specific object, situation, or activity that poses no real danger (or whose danger they blow out of proportion). Phobics realize their fear is irrational; they nevertheless feel compelled to avoid the feared object or situation. There are three classes of phobias—agoraphobia, social phobia, and specific phobia.

Agoraphobia

A person with **agoraphobia** has an intense fear of being in a situation where immediate escape is not possible or help would not be readily available. In some cases an individual's entire life must be planned around avoiding feared situations such as busy streets, crowded stores, restaurants, or public transportation. An agoraphobic often will not leave home unless accompanied by a friend or family member—and in severe cases, not even then.

anxiety: A generalized feeling of apprehension, fear, or tension that may be associated with a particular object or situation or may be free-floating, not associated with anything specific.

generalized anxiety disorder: An anxiety disorder in which people experience excessive anxiety or worry that they find difficult to control.

panic attack: An attack of overwhelming anxiety, fear, or terror.

panic disorder: An anxiety disorder in which a person experiences recurrent unpredictable attacks of overwhelming anxiety, fear, or terror.

phobia (FO-bee-ah): A persistent, irrational fear of an object, situation, or activity that the person feels compelled to avoid.

agoraphobia (AG-or-uh-FO-bee-uh): An intense fear of being in a situation where immediate escape is not possible or help is not immediately available in case of incapacitating anxiety.

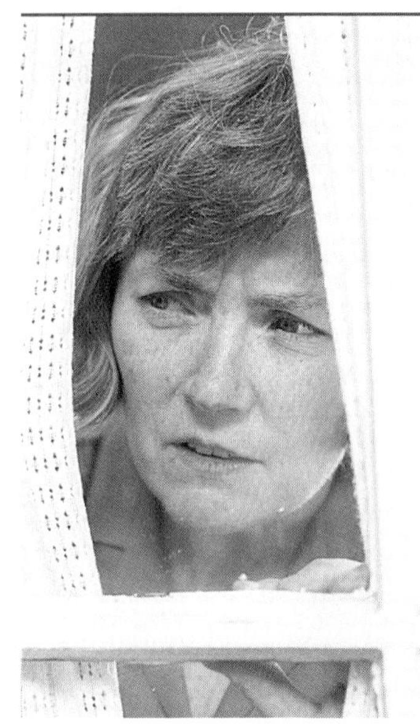

People with agoraphobia have an intense fear of public places and are often reluctant to leave home.

Although agoraphobia can occur without panic attacks, it typically begins during the early adult years with repeated panic attacks (Horwath et al., 1993). The intense fear of having another attack causes the person to avoid any place or situation where previous attacks have occurred. Some researchers believe that agoraphobia is actually an extreme form of panic disorder (Sheehan, 1983; Thyer et al., 1985).

A person is at greater risk of having agoraphobia if other family members have it. The closer the relative, the higher the risk (Rosenbaum et al., 1994). Some agoraphobics have been treated successfully with psychotherapy (Shear & Weiner, 1997); others have responded well to antidepressants (Marshall, 1997).

Social Phobia

Those with **social phobia** have an irrational fear of social or performance situations in which they might embarrass or humiliate themselves in front of others—where they might shake, blush, sweat, or in some other way appear clumsy, foolish, or incompetent. They may fear eating, talking, or writing in front of others, or doing anything else that would cause people to think poorly of them. Can you imagine being unable to cash a cheque, use a credit card, or even make notes or take a written exam in class because you feared writing in front of other people?

Although less debilitating than agoraphobia, social phobia in its extreme form can seriously harm people's prospects at work and at school, and severely restrict their social life (Greist, 1995). Those with social phobia often turn to alcohol and tranquilizers to lessen their anxiety in social situations (Kushner et al., 1990).

Specific Phobia

Specific phobia is a catchall category for any phobias other than agoraphobia and social phobia. The categories of specific phobias, in order of frequency of occurrence, are as follows: (1) situational phobias (fear of elevators, airplanes, enclosed places, public transportation, tunnels, bridges); (2) fear of the natural environment (storms, water, heights); (3) blood/injection/injury phobia (fear of seeing blood or injury, receiving an injection); and (4) animal phobias (fear of dogs, snakes, insects, mice). Two types of situational phobia—claustrophobia (fear of closed spaces) and acrophobia (fear of heights)—are the specific phobias treated most often by therapists. *Try It!* will introduce you to some others.

People with specific phobias generally fear the same things others fear, but their fears are grossly exaggerated. A fear is not considered a phobia unless it causes a great deal of distress or interferes with a person's life in a major way. Phobics experience intense anxiety when they are faced with the object or situation they fear, even to the point of shaking or screaming.

Try It!

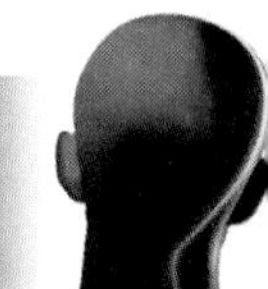

Identifying Some Specific Phobias

Can you match the following specific phobias with their descriptions?

____ 1. Acrophobia	a. Fear of high places
____ 2. Anthropophobia	b. Fear of fire
____ 3. Arachnophobia	c. Fear of animals
____ 4. Monophobia	d. Fear of human beings
____ 5. Pyrophobia	e. Fear of spiders
____ 6. Zoophobia	f. Fear of being alone

Answers: 1. a 2. d 3. e 4. f 5. b 6. c

Phobics will go to great lengths to avoid the feared object or situation. Some people with blood-injury phobia will not seek medical care even if it is a matter of life and death (Marks, 1988). Few of us are thrilled at the prospect of visiting the dentist, but some people with a dental phobia will actually let their teeth rot rather than visit the dentist.

Causes of Phobias

What do psychologists believe are some probable causes of phobias?

It is likely that most specific and social phobias result from learning; that is, direct conditioning, modelling, or the transmission of information (Eysenck, 1987; Thyer et al., 1985). Frightening experiences, most experts agree, set the stage for phobias, although not all phobics recall the experience that produced the phobia. A person with a dog phobia may be able to trace its beginning to a painful dog bite (King et al., 1997); a fear of heights may date from a frightening fall down a flight of stairs (Beck & Emory, 1985). A person may be humiliated by performing poorly in front of others and develop a social phobia (Rosenbaum et al., 1994).

Phobias may be acquired through observational learning. For example, children who hear their parents talk about frightening experiences with the dentist or with bugs or snakes or thunderstorms may develop similar fears themselves. In many cases phobias are acquired through a combination of conditioning and observational learning (Merckelbach et al., 1996).

Genes appear to play a role in specific phobias (particularly animal phobias), social phobia, and agoraphobia. People are at three times the risk if a close relative suffers from a phobia (Fyer et al., 1993).

Obsessive-Compulsive Disorder

What is obsessive-compulsive disorder?

What is wrong with a person who is endlessly counting, checking, or performing other time-consuming rituals over and over? Why would a person wash his or her hands 100 times a day until they are raw and bleeding? People with another form of anxiety disorder, **obsessive-compulsive disorder (OCD)**, suffer from recurrent obsessions, or compulsions, or both.

Obsessions

Have you ever had a tune or the words of a song run through your mind over and over without being able to stop it? If so, you have experienced obsessive thinking in a mild form. Imagine how miserable you would be if every time you touched something you thought you were being contaminated, or if the thought of stabbing your mother kept popping into your mind. **Obsessions** are persistent, recurring, involuntary thoughts, images, or impulses that invade consciousness and cause great distress.

Common themes of obsessions include worry about contamination and doubt as to whether a certain act was performed (Insel, 1990). People with obsessional doubt may have a persistent fear that they failed to turn off the stove or put out a cigarette. Other types of obsessions centre on aggression, religion, or sex. One minister reported obsessive thoughts of running naked down the church aisle and shouting obscenities at his congregation.

Do people ever act on their obsessive thoughts? It is not unheard of, but it is extremely rare. Yet many people are so horrified by their obsessions that they think they are going crazy.

Compulsions

A person who has a **compulsion** feels literally compelled to repeat certain acts over and over or to perform specific rituals repeatedly. The individual knows such acts are irrational and senseless, but resistance to performing them would result in an intolerable buildup of anxiety—anxiety that can be relieved only by yielding to the compulsion. Many of us have engaged in compulsive behaviour from time to time (e.g., stepping over cracks on the sidewalk, counting

social phobia: An irrational fear and avoidance of social situations in which people believe they might embarrass or humiliate themselves by appearing clumsy, foolish, or incompetent.

specific phobia: A catchall category for any phobia other than agoraphobia and social phobia.

obsessive-compulsive disorder (OCD): An anxiety disorder in which a person suffers from obsessions and/or compulsions.

obsession: A persistent, recurring, involuntary thought, image, or impulse that invades consciousness and causes great distress.

compulsion: A persistent, irresistible, irrational urge to perform an act or ritual repeatedly.

stairs). The behaviour becomes a psychological problem only when the person cannot resist performing it, when it is very time-consuming, and when it interferes with the person's normal activities and relationships.

Compulsions usually involve cleanliness, counting, checking, touching objects, hoarding, or excessive ordering (Leckman et al., 1997; Summerfeldt et al., 1999). Sometimes compulsive acts or rituals resemble "magical" thinking and must be performed faithfully in order to ward off some danger. People with OCD do not enjoy the time-consuming rituals—the endless counting, checking, hand washing, or cleaning. They realize that their behaviour is not normal but they simply cannot help themselves, as shown in the following example:

> Mike, a 32-year-old patient, performed checking rituals that were preceded by a fear of harming other people. When driving, he had to stop the car often and return to check whether he had run over people, particularly babies. Before flushing the toilet, he had to check to be sure that a live insect had not fallen into the toilet, because he did not want to be responsible for killing a living thing. At home he repeatedly checked to see that the doors, stoves, lights, and windows were shut or turned off. ... Mike performed these and many other checking rituals for an average of four hours a day. (Kozak et al., 1988, p. 88)

Are there many Mikes out there, or is his case unusual? Mike's checking compulsion is quite extreme. That being said, between 1.1 and 1.8 percent of Canadians, Americans, Puerto Ricans, Germans, Koreans, and New Zealanders (Weissman et al., 1994) suffer from obsessive-compulsive disorder.

About 70 percent of people in treatment for OCD have both obsessions and compulsions. This was long assumed to be the most common pattern. It has since been found, however, that in the general population, 50 percent of OCD cases involve obsessions only, 34 percent compulsions only, and 16 percent both obsessions and compulsions (Weissman et al., 1994). When both occur together, the compulsion most often serves to relieve the anxiety caused by the obsession. All age groups with this disorder—children, adolescents, and adults—show strikingly similar thoughts and rituals (Swedo et al., 1989).

Causes of Obsessive-Compulsive Disorder

For many years obsessive-compulsives were seen as extremely insecure individuals who viewed the world as threatening and unpredictable. Their ritualistic behaviour was thought to be a means for imposing some order, structure, and predictability on the world. From the psychodynamic perspective, obsessive-compulsive behaviour protects individuals from recognizing the real reasons for their anxiety—repressed hostility or unacceptable sexual urges. Thus a person, without knowing quite why, might wash hands compulsively to atone for "dirty thoughts."

Some evidence points to a biological basis for obsessive-compulsive disorder in some patients. Several twin and family studies suggest that a genetic factor may be involved (Rasmussen & Eisen, 1990). PET scans of OCD patients have revealed abnormally high rates of glucose consumption in two regions of the brain involved in emotional reactions (Rauch et al., 1994).

The most significant finding seems to be that many OCD patients have an imbalance in levels of the neurotransmitter serotonin (Pigott, 1996). Such patients are often helped by an antidepressant that restores the balance of serotonin (Murphy & Pigott, 1990). But because the drug treatment does not work for all OCD patients, some researchers suggest that OCD may have several different causes (Goodman et al., 1989).

Most people with OCD never get treatment; they know their symptoms are bizarre and are afraid to seek help for fear other people will think they are "crazy" (Rasmussen & Eisen, 1992).

Somatoform and Dissociative Disorders

Somatoform Disorders: Physical Symptoms with Psychological Causes

What are two somatoform disorders, and what symptoms do they share?

The word *soma* means "body." The **somatoform disorders** involve bodily symptoms that cannot be explained by known medical conditions. Although they are psychological in origin, patients are sincerely convinced

Remember It!

Anxiety Disorders

1. Anxiety serves no useful function. (true/false)
2. Match the psychological disorder with the example.

____ 1) Renée refuses to eat in front of others for fear her hand will shake.

____ 2) John is excessively anxious about his health and his job, even though there is no concrete reason for it.

____ 3) Betty has been housebound for four years.

____ 4) Jackson gets hysterical when a dog approaches him.

____ 5) Laura has incapacitating attacks of anxiety that come over her suddenly.

____ 6) Max repeatedly checks his doors, windows, and appliances before he goes to bed.

a. panic disorder
b. agoraphobia
c. specific phobia
d. generalized anxiety disorder
e. social phobia
f. obsessive-compulsive disorder

3. Most phobias result from frightening experiences and observational learning. (true/false)
4. Obsessive-compulsive disorder appears to be caused primarily by psychological rather than biological factors. (true/false)

Answers: 1. false 2. 1) e 2) d 3) b 4) c 5) a 6) f 3. true 4. false

that their symptoms spring from real physical disorders. People with somatoform disorders are not consciously faking illness to avoid work or other activities. Hypochondriasis and conversion disorder are two types of somatoform disorders.

Hypochondriasis

People with **hypochondriasis** are overly concerned about their health. They are preoccupied with the fear that their bodily symptoms are a sign of some serious disease, but their symptoms are not usually consistent with known physical disorders. Even when a medical examination reveals no physical problem, hypochondriacs are not convinced. They may "doctor shop," going from one physician to another, seeking confirmation of their worst fears. Unfortunately, hypochondriasis is not easily treated, and there is usually a poor chance of recovery.

Conversion Disorder: When Thoughts and Fears Can Paralyze

A man is suddenly struck blind, or an arm, a leg, or some other part of his body becomes paralyzed. Extensive medical tests find nothing wrong—no possible physical reason for the blindness or the paralysis. How can this be?

A diagnosis of **conversion disorder** is made when there is a loss of motor or sensory functioning in some part of the body that (a) is not due to a physical cause and (b) solves a psychological problem. Psychologists think that conversion disorder can act as an unconscious defence against any intolerable anxiety situation that the individual cannot otherwise escape. For example, a soldier who desperately fears going into battle may escape the anxiety by developing a paralysis or some other physically disabling symptom.

You would expect normal people to show great distress if they suddenly lost their sight or hearing or became paralyzed. Yet many patients with con-

somatoform disorders (so-MAT-uh-form): Disorders in which physical symptoms are present that are due to psychological rather than physical causes.

hypochondriasis (HI-poh-kahn-DRY-uh-sis): A somatoform disorder in which persons are preoccupied with their health and convinced they have some serious disorder despite reassurance from doctors to the contrary.

conversion disorder: A somatoform disorder in which a loss of motor or sensory functioning in some part of the body has no physical cause but solves some psychological problem.

version disorder exhibit a calm and cool indifference to their symptoms, called "la belle indifference." Furthermore, many seem to enjoy the attention, sympathy, and concern their disability brings them.

Dissociative Disorders: Mental Escapes

We are consciously aware of who we are. Our memories, our identity, our consciousness, and our perception of the environment are integrated. But some people, in response to unbearable stress, develop a **dissociative disorder** and lose this integration. Their consciousness becomes dissociated either from their identity or from their memories of important personal events. Dissociative disorders provide a mental escape from intolerable circumstances. Three types of dissociative disorders are dissociative amnesia, dissociative fugue, and dissociative identity disorder (commonly known as "multiple personality").

Dissociative Amnesia: "Who Am I?"

What is dissociative amnesia?

Amnesia is a complete or partial loss of the ability to recall personal information or identify past experiences that cannot be attributed to ordinary forgetfulness or substance use. Popular books, movies, and TV shows have used amnesia as a central theme in which, usually after a blow to the head, characters cannot remember who they are or anything about their past. In **dissociative amnesia**, however, no physical cause such as a blow to the head is present. Rather, a traumatic experience—a *psychological* blow, so to speak—or an unbearable anxiety situation causes the person to escape by "forgetting." Patients with dissociative amnesia can have a loss of memory about specific periods of their life or a complete loss of memory for their entire identity. For example, if a man experienced the very traumatic event of watching his child be struck and killed by a car, he might avoid facing the trauma by developing some form of dissociative amnesia. Yet such people do not forget everything. They forget only items of personal reference such as their name, their age, and where they live. They may also fail to recognize their parents, other relatives, and friends. But they do not forget how to read and write or solve problems, and their basic personality structure remains intact.

Dissociative Fugue: "Where Did I Go and What Did I Do?"

What is dissociative fugue?

Even more puzzling than dissociative amnesia is **dissociative fugue**. In a fugue state, people not only forget their identity, they also physically leave the scene and travel away from home. Some take on a new identity that is usually more outgoing and uninhibited than their former identity (APA, 1994). The fugue state may last for hours, days, or even months. The fugue is usually a reaction to some severe psychological stress, such as a natural disaster, a serious family quarrel, a deep personal rejection, or military service in wartime.

For most people, recovery from dissociative fugue is usually rapid, although there may be some amnesia for the initial stressor that brought on the fugue state. When people recover from the fugue, they often have no memory of events that occurred during the episode.

Dissociative Identity Disorder: Multiple Personality

What are some of the identifying symptoms of dissociative identity disorder?

In **dissociative identity disorder**, two or more distinct, unique personalities exist in the same individual, as in the case of Sybil, described at the beginning of this chapter. In 50 percent of cases of dissociative identity disorder, there are more than 10 different personalities (Sybil had 16). The change from one personality to another often occurs suddenly—usually during stress. The *host personality* is "the one who has executive control of the body the greatest percentage of time" (Kluft, 1984, p. 23). The alternate or *alter personalities* may differ radically in intelligence, speech, accent, vocabulary, posture, body language, hairstyle, taste in clothes, manners, and even handwriting. And incredibly, within the same individual, the alter personalities may differ in gender, age, and even sexual orientation. Almost all people with this disorder have "a number of child and infant personalities" (Putnam, 1992, p. 34). Some alters may be right-handed, others left-handed. Some alters may need different prescription glasses, have specific food allergies, or show different responses to alcohol or medications (Putnam et al., 1986). There are usually promiscuous alters who act on forbidden impulses (Putnam, 1992).

Remember It!

Somatoform and Dissociative Disorders

1. Match the psychological disorder with the example.

   ____ 1) Mark is convinced he has some serious disease although his doctors can find nothing physically wrong.

   ____ 2) David was found far away from his hometown, calling himself by another name and having no memory of his past.

   ____ 3) Theresa suddenly loses her sight, but doctors can find no physical reason for the problem.

   ____ 4) Larry has no memory of being in the boat with other family members on the day his older brother drowned.

   ____ 5) Nadine has no memory for blocks of time in her life and often finds clothing in her closet that she cannot remember buying.

   a. dissociative identity disorder
   b. dissociative fugue
   c. dissociative amnesia
   d. hypochondriasis
   e. conversion disorder

2. Somatoform disorders have physiological rather than psychological causes. (true/false)
3. Dissociative disorders are psychological in origin. (true/false)

Answers: 1. 1) d 2) b 3) e 4) c 5) a 2. false 3. true

Many multiple-personality patients report hearing voices and sometimes the sounds of crying or screaming or laughter. For this reason, such patients have often been misdiagnosed as schizophrenic.

In 80 percent of the cases of dissociative identity disorder, the host personality does not know of the alters, but "the alter personalities will possess varying levels of awareness for one another" (Putnam 1989, p. 114). The host and alter personalities commonly show amnesia for certain periods of time or for important life episodes (e.g., their wedding, the birth of a child). There is the common complaint of "lost time"—periods for which a given personality has no memory because he or she was not in control of the body.

CAUSES OF DISSOCIATIVE IDENTITY DISORDER Dissociative identity disorder usually begins in early childhood, but the condition is rarely diagnosed before adolescence (Vincent & Pickering, 1988). Colin Ross and his colleagues (1989) at the University of Manitoba studied many cases of people diagnosed with dissociative identity disorder. They found that about 90 percent of the treated cases were women. More than 95 percent had an early history of severe physical and/or sexual abuse (Gleaves, 1996; Ross et al., 1990). The splitting off of separate personalities is apparently a way of coping with such intolerable abuse. How can we account for the 5 percent of multiple-personality patients who were not abused? The psychodynamic perspective suggests that alternate personalities may come forth to express sexual or aggressive impulses that would be unacceptable to the original personality. However, this suggestion has not been experimentally verified. Regardless of cause, this disorder can be treated, often by psychotherapy, and empirical evidence suggests patients respond well to treatment (Ellason & Ross, 1997).

dissociative disorders: Disorders in which, under stress, one loses the integration of consciousness, identity, and memories of important personal events.

dissociative amnesia: A dissociative disorder in which there is a loss of memory for limited periods in one's life or for one's entire personal identity.

dissociative fugue (FEWG): A dissociative disorder in which one has a complete loss of memory for one's entire identity, travels away from home, and may assume a new identity.

dissociative identity disorder: A dissociative disorder in which two or more distinct personalities occur in the same individual, each taking over at different times; also called multiple personality.

Schizophrenia

To a mild degree we can identify with most people who suffer from most psychological disorders. We can imagine being anxious, fearful, depressed; we can picture ourselves having an obsession or a compulsion. But schizophrenia is so far removed from our common, everyday experience that it is all but impossible for us to imagine what it is like to be schizophrenic.

Schizophrenia is the most serious of the psychological disorders. It affects about one person in a hundred. Schizophrenia usually begins in adolescence or early adulthood, although it can appear later in life. It is probably the most devastating of all the psychological disorders because of the social disruption and misery it brings to those who suffer from it and to their families.

LINK IT!

www.schizophrenia.ca
Schizophrenia Society of Canada

www.schizophrenia.com
The Schizophrenia Home Page

The Symptoms of Schizophrenia: Many and Varied

There are many symptoms associated with schizophrenia. Any given individual with the disorder may have one or more of the major symptoms, but there is no one single symptom or brain abnormality that is shared by all schizophrenics (see Andreasen, 1999). The symptoms of schizophrenia fall into two categories: positive and negative.

Positive Symptoms

What are some of the major positive symptoms of schizophrenia?

Positive symptoms are so named not because they are desirable, but rather because they are present (as opposed to absent). Positive symptoms include hallucinations, delusions, disorganized thinking and speech, and grossly disorganized or bizarre behaviour (McGlashan & Fenton, 1992).

HALLUCINATIONS One of the clearest symptoms that suggests schizophrenia is the presence of **hallucinations**—imaginary sensations. Schizophrenic patients may see, hear, feel, taste, or smell strange things in the absence of any stimulus in the environment. Hearing voices is the most common type of hallucination. Schizophrenic patients may believe they hear the voice of God or Satan, the voices of family members or friends, and even their own voice broadcasting aloud what they are thinking. Most often the voices are unpleasant, accusing or cursing the patient or engaging in a running commentary on his or her behaviour. Sometimes the voices are menacing and order the patient to kill someone or commit suicide.

Visual hallucinations are less common than auditory ones. They are usually in black and white and commonly take the form of friends, relatives, God, Jesus, or the devil. Schizophrenics may also experience bodily sensations that are exceedingly frightening and painful. They may feel they are being beaten, burned, or sexually violated. One schizophrenic complained that "spiders were crawling all through his heart and vessels, eating his brain, and although he could not see them, he thought he could feel them crawling on his skin" (Salama & England, 1990, p. 86).

DELUSIONS Imagine how upset you would be if you believed that your every thought was being broadcast aloud for everyone to hear. What if you were convinced that some strange agent or force was stealing your thoughts or inserting in your head thoughts that were not your own? These are examples of **delusions**—false beliefs that are not generally shared by others in the culture. Usually patients cannot be persuaded that their beliefs are false, even in the face of strong evidence.

Delusions may be of several different types. Schizophrenics with **delusions of grandeur** may believe they are a famous person (the Queen or Jesus Christ, for example) or a powerful or important person who possesses some great knowledge, ability, or authority. Those with **delusions of persecution** have the false notion that some person or agency is trying to harass, cheat, spy on, conspire against, injure, kill, or in some other way harm them.

DISTURBANCES IN THE FORM OF THOUGHT OR SPEECH Schizophrenia is often marked by thought disturbance. The most common type involves a loosening of associations—the individual does not follow one line of thought to completion, but on the basis of vague connections shifts from one subject to another. The speech of schizophrenics is often very difficult, if not impossible, to understand. The content of the message may be extremely vague, or the person may invent words or use them inappropriately (Chaika, 1985):

> I am writing on paper. The pen I am using is from a factory called "Perry & Co." This factory is in England.... The city of London is in England. I know this from my school-days. Then, I always liked geography. My last teacher in that subject was ... a man with black eyes. I also like black eyes. There are also blue and gray eyes and other sorts, too. I have heard it said that snakes have green eyes. All people have eyes. There are some, too, who are blind. (Bleuler, 1950, p. 17)

GROSSLY DISORGANIZED BEHAVIOUR Grossly disorganized behaviour can include such things as child-like silliness, inappropriate sexual behaviour (masturbating in public), dishevelled appearance, and peculiar dress. There may also be unpredictable agitation, including shouting and swearing, and unusual or inappropriate motor behaviour, including strange gestures, facial expressions, or postures.

INAPPROPRIATE AFFECT Schizophrenics may have grossly **inappropriate affect** —that is, their facial expressions, tone of voice, and gestures may not reflect the emotion that would be expected under the circumstances. A person might cry when watching a TV comedy and laugh when watching a news story showing bloody bodies being removed from a fatal automobile accident.

Negative Symptoms

What are some of the major negative symptoms of schizophrenia?

Negative symptoms of schizophrenia involve a loss of or deficiency in thoughts and behaviours that are characteristic in normal functioning. Negative symptoms may include social withdrawal, apathy, loss of motivation, lack of goal-directed activity, very limited speech, slow movements, and poor hygiene and grooming (McGlashan & Fenton, 1992). Some schizophrenic patients show *flat affect*—practically no emotional response at all. They may speak in a monotone, and their facial expressions may be blank and emotionless. Such patients may act and move more like robots than humans.

Some researchers who have followed schizophrenics over a number of years have found that those with negative symptoms seem to have the poorest outcomes (Belitsky & McGlashan, 1993; Fenton & McGlashan, 1994). They tend to withdraw from others and retreat into their own world. Often their functioning is too impaired for them to hold a job or even care for themselves.

Brain Abnormalities in Some Schizophrenics

Several abnormalities in brain structure and function have been found in schizophrenic patients. Among these are defects in the neural circuitry of the cerebral cortex (Andreasen, 1999) and abnormally low neural activity in the frontal lobes (Buchsbaum et al., 1996). Some studies have revealed a decreased volume of the hippocampus, the amygdala (Nelson et al., 1998), and the thalamus (Buchsbaum et al., 1996). In many schizophrenics, there is a deficit in cortical grey matter (Lim et al., 1996), and the ventricles are larger than in the normal brain (Lieberman et al., 1992).

Types of Schizophrenia

What are the four subtypes of schizophrenia?

Various behavioural characteristics are shared by most schizophrenics; there are also certain features that distinguish one subtype of schizophrenia from

schizophrenia (SKIT-soh-FREE-nee-ah): A severe psychological disorder characterized by loss of contact with reality, hallucinations, delusions, inappropriate or flat affect, some disturbance in thinking, social withdrawal, and/or other bizarre behaviour.

hallucination: A sensory perception in the absence of any external sensory stimulus; an imaginary sensation.

delusion: A false belief, not generally shared by others in the culture, that cannot be changed despite strong evidence to the contrary.

delusion of grandeur: A false belief that one is a famous person or that one has some great knowledge, ability, or authority.

delusion of persecution: An individual's false belief that a person or group is trying in some way to harm him or her.

inappropriate affect: A symptom common in schizophrenia in which an individual's behaviour (including facial expression, tone of voice, and gestures) does not reflect the emotion that would be expected under the circumstances–for example, a person laughs at a tragedy, cries at a joke.

A person with catatonic schizophrenia may become frozen in an unusual position, like a statue, for hours at a time.

another. Four main types of schizophrenia exist: catatonic, disorganized, paranoid, and undifferentiated.

People with **catatonic schizophrenia** may display complete stillness and stupor, or great excitement and agitation. Frequently they alternate rapidly between the two. They may become frozen in a strange posture or position, as shown in the photograph, and remain there for hours without moving.

Disorganized schizophrenia is the most serious type, marked by extreme social withdrawal, hallucinations, delusions, silliness, inappropriate laughter, grimaces, grotesque mannerisms, and other bizarre behaviour. These people show flat or inappropriate affect and are frequently incoherent. They often exhibit obscene behaviour, masturbate openly, and swallow almost any kind of object or material. Disorganized schizophrenia tends to occur at an earlier age than the other types, and it results in the most severe disintegration of the personality (Beratis et al., 1994). Patients with this type of schizophrenia have the poorest chance of recovery (Fenton & McGlashan, 1991; Kane, 1993).

People with **paranoid schizophrenia** usually suffer from delusions of grandeur or persecution. They may be convinced that they have an identity other than their own. Their delusions may include the belief that they possess great ability or talent, or that they have some special mission. They may believe that they are in charge of the hospital or on a secret assignment for the government. Paranoid schizophrenics often show exaggerated anger and suspiciousness. If they have delusions of persecution and feel that they are being harassed or threatened, they may become violent in an attempt to defend themselves against their imagined persecutors. Usually the behaviour of the paranoid schizophrenic is not so obviously disturbed as that of the catatonic or disorganized type, and the chance for recovery is better (Fenton & McGlashan, 1991; Kendler et al., 1984).

Undifferentiated schizophrenia is a general catchall category for individuals who clearly have symptoms of schizophrenia but whose symptoms either do not conform to the criteria of any other type of schizophrenia or conform to more than one type.

The Causes of Schizophrenia

What are some suggested causes of schizophrenia?

During the 1950s and 1960s, many psychiatrists and some researchers pointed to unhealthy patterns of communication and interaction in the entire family as the breeding ground for schizophrenia (Bateson et al., 1956; Lidz et al., 1965). However, unhealthy family interaction patterns could be the *result* rather than the *cause* of schizophrenia. There is no convincing evidence to justify pointing the finger of blame at mothers, fathers, or other family members (Johnson, 1989; Torrey, 1983).

Research evidence continues to mount that biology is a factor in many cases of schizophrenia.

Genetic Inheritance

Research suggests that schizophrenia tends to run in families and that genetic factors play a major role (Gottesman, 1991; Kendler et al., 1993; Mortensen et al., 1999). Figure 12.1 shows how the likelihood of developing schizophrenia varies with the degree of relationship to a schizophrenic patient.

According to genetic theorists, what is inherited is not schizophrenia itself, but a predisposition to it (Zubin & Spring, 1977). People with a genetic predisposition may develop the disorder if exposed to sufficient environmental stressors, either in the womb or during childhood, adolescence, or adulthood. According to the **diathesis–stress model**, schizophrenia develops when there is *both* a genetic pre-

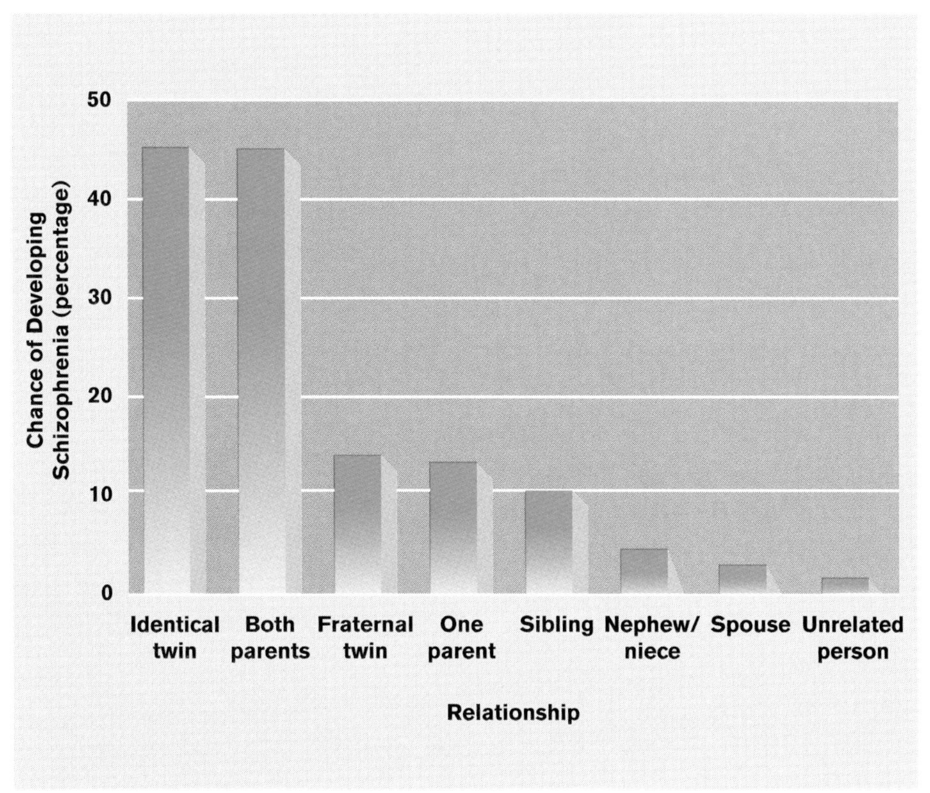

FIGURE 12.1

Genetic Similarity and Probability of Developing Schizophrenia Research strongly indicates a genetic factor operating in many cases of schizophrenia. Identical twins have identical genes, and if one twin develops schizophrenia, the other twin has a 46 percent chance of developing it also. In fraternal twins the chance is only 14 percent. A person with one schizophrenic parent has a 13 percent chance of developing schizophrenia, but a 46 percent chance if both parents are schizophrenic. (Data from Nicol & Gottesman, 1983.)

disposition toward the disorder (diathesis) and more stress than the person can handle (Fowles, 1992).

Whether predisposed people develop the disorder may depend on their life circumstances (Fowles, 1992; Johnson, 1989). Schizophrenia is more common in highly urbanized areas than in rural areas because of the greater stress of city life coupled with higher exposure to pollutants, toxins, and infectious diseases (Torrey & Bowler, 1990).

Excessive Dopamine Activity

Abnormal activity in the brain's dopamine systems is common in many schizophrenics (Winn, 1994). Much of the dopamine activity occurs in the limbic system, which is involved in human emotions (Davis et al., 1991). Drugs found to be effective in reducing the symptoms of schizophrenia block dopamine action (Iverson, 1979; Torrey, 1983), although about one-third of patients do not show improvement with such drugs (Wolkin et al., 1989).

The recent discovery of three more dopamine receptors, bringing the total to five in all, may increase our understanding of schizophrenia. As we reviewed in Chapter 2, drugs are being developed whose action is aimed at particular dopamine receptors (Seeman, 1995). Many questions remain about the causes of schizophrenia. Most likely, various factors play a role, including genetic predispositions, biochemical processes, environmental conditions, and life experiences.

catatonic schizophrenia (KAT-uh-TAHN-ik): A type of schizophrenia characterized by extreme stillness or stupor and/or periods of great agitation and excitement; patients may assume an unusual posture and remain in it for long periods.

disorganized schizophrenia: The most serious type of schizophrenia, marked by inappropriate affect, silliness, laughter, grotesque mannerisms, and bizarre behaviour.

paranoid schizophrenia (PAIR-uh-noid): A type of schizophrenia characterized by delusions of grandeur or persecution.

undifferentiated schizophrenia: A catchall category; marked by symptoms that do not conform to the other types or that conform to more than one type.

diathesis–stress model: The idea that people with a constitutional predisposition (diathesis) toward a disorder, such as schizophrenia, may develop the disorder if they are subjected to sufficient environmental stress.

Remember It! Schizophrenia

1. Match the symptom of schizophrenia with the example.

____ 1) Joe believes he is Moses.		a. delusions of grandeur
____ 2) Elena thinks her family is spreading rumours about her.		b. hallucinations
____ 3) Peter hears voices cursing him.		c. inappropriate affect
____ 4) Marco laughs at tragedies and cries when he hears a joke.		d. delusions of persecution

2. Match the subtype of schizophrenia with the example:

____ 1) Louise stands for hours in the same strange position.		a. paranoid schizophrenia
____ 2) Ron believes that CSIS is plotting to kill him.		b. disorganized schizophrenia
____ 3) Harry makes silly faces, laughs a lot, and masturbates openly.		c. catatonic schizophrenia
____ 4) Sue has the symptoms of schizophrenia but does not fit any one type.		d. undifferentiated schizophrenia

3. There is substantial research evidence that all of the following help to cause schizophrenia *except*
   a. genetic factors.
   b. stress in people predisposed to the disorder.
   c. excessive dopamine activity.
   d. unhealthy family interaction patterns.

Answers: 1. 1) a 2) d 3) b 4) c
2. 1) c 2) a 3) b 4) d 3. d

Mood Disorders

Mood disorders involve moods or emotions that are extreme and unwarranted. In the most serious disorders, mood ranges from the depths of severe depression to the heights of extreme elation. Mood disorders fall into two broad categories: depressive and bipolar.

LINK IT!

www.ndmda.org
National Depressive and Manic-Depressive Association

ww2.med.jhu.edu/drada
Depression and Related Affective Disorders Association (DRADA)

Depressive Disorders and Bipolar Disorder: Emotional Highs and Lows

Major Depressive Disorder

What are the symptoms of major depressive disorder?

It is normal to feel blue, down, sad, or depressed in response to many of life's common experiences—death of a loved one, loss of a job, or an unhappy ending to a long-term relationship. Major depression, however, is not normal. People with **major depressive disorder** feel an overwhelming sadness, despair, and hopelessness, and they usually lose their ability to experience pleasure. They may have appetite and weight changes, sleep disturbance, loss of energy, and difficulty thinking or concentrating. Key symptoms of major depressive disorder are psychomotor disturbances (Sobin & Sackheim, 1997). For example, body movements and speech are so slow that they seem to be doing everything in slow motion. Some depressed patients experience the other extreme: they are constantly moving and fidgeting, wringing their hands, and pacing. Depression can be so severe that its victims actually experience delusions or hallucinations, which are symptoms of psychotic depression (Coryell, 1996). The most common of all serious mental disorders, depression strikes people of all social classes, cultures, and nations around the world.

Women are reported to be twice as likely as men to suffer from depression (Culbertson, 1997), with one notable exception. Among Jews, males are equally as likely as females to have major depression (Levav et al., 1997). In recent years there has been an increase in depression in adolescents, particularly in adolescent girls and perhaps among Native people and homosexual young people (Petersen et al., 1993).

Why are women so much more likely to suffer from depression than men? Are they somehow biologically predisposed? Are they subject to more life stress than men? At least one major study has suggested that the higher rate of depression in women is largely due to social and cultural factors. The risk for depression in women is greater because they must play so many roles—mother, wife, lover, friend, daughter, neighbour (Scattolon & Stoppard, 1999). In fulfilling those roles, women are likely to put the needs of others ahead of their own. Having young children poses a particular risk. Women also suffer other stresses disproportionately, such as poverty and physical and sexual abuse. Canadian researchers also identified women's perceptions of "being demoralized" as a common theme among depressed women (Hurst, 1999). Typically, women became demoralized following betrayal, abuse, and being left out. Pribor and Dinwiddie (1992) found an alarming incidence of depression—88.5 percent—among female incest victims.

While some patients suffer only one major episode of depression, most (50 to 60 percent) will have a recurrence (APA, 1994). Risk of recurrence is greatest for females (Winokur et al., 1993), for those who experienced depression before age 20 (Brown, 1996), and for those with a family history of mood disorders (Akiskal, 1989). Recurrences may be frequent or infrequent. For 20 to 35 percent of patients, the depressive episodes are chronic, lasting two years or longer. Recurring episodes tend to be increasingly more severe and long-lasting (Greden, 1994; Maj et al., 1992). Unfortunately, about 80 percent of those suffering from depression never even receive treatment (Holden, 1986). About 15 percent of people with a major depressive disorder commit suicide (Coppen, 1994). To learn more about suicide, read the following *World of Psychology* box.

People experiencing major depression feel overwhelming sadness, despair, and hopelessness.

Many people suffer from a milder form of depression called *dysthymia,* which is nonetheless chronic (lasting two years or longer). Individuals with dysthymia suffer from depressed mood but have fewer of the symptoms associated with major depressive disorder.

Seasonal Depression

Many people find that their moods seem to change with the seasons (Kasper et al., 1989). People suffering from **seasonal affective disorder (SAD)** experience a significant depression that tends to come and go with the seasons (Wehr & Rosenthal, 1989). There is a spring/summer depression that remits in winter; but the most common type, winter depression, seems to be triggered by light deficiency (Molin et al., 1996). During the winter months, when the days are shorter, some people become very depressed and tend to sleep and eat more, gain weight, and crave carbohydrates

mood disorders: Disorders characterized by extreme and unwarranted disturbances in feeling or mood, which can include depressive or manic episodes, or both.

major depressive disorder: A mood disorder characterized by feelings of great sadness, despair, guilt, worthlessness, and hopelessness, and, in extreme cases, suicidal intentions.

seasonal affective disorder (SAD): A mood disorder in which depression comes and goes with the seasons.

WORLD OF PSYCHOLOGY

Teen Suicide in Canada

The rate of suicide among 15- to 19-year-olds has quadrupled over the past three decades, from 3.2 per 100 000 in 1962 to 13.5 per 100 000 now. Among industrialized nations, Canada now ranks third in rate of teen suicides (Nemeth, 1994). Teenage males are much more likely to commit suicide than teenage females (IASP, 1999; Leenaars & Lester, 1990), and especially males living in the Yukon and Northwest Territories (see Figure 12.2). Factors that may push a teenager "over the edge" include an underlying psychiatric condition, a precipitating circumstance such as the breakup of a relationship, family conflict, a disciplinary crisis, and school problems (Heikkinen et al., 1993). There is an elevated risk of suicide among adolescents who have been in trouble with the police or who have been incarcerated (Brent et al., 1993).

Researchers at the Université du Québec à Montréal suggest that poor care from fathers is related to suicide attempts (Tousignant et al., 1993). The suicide rate is highest among those who have made a previous suicide attempt (Beck et al., 1990). What is especially disconcerting is that young males who attempt suicide use more lethal methods than young females (Sigurdson et al., 1994).

Preventing Suicide

Although there are cultural differences in suicide rates, the methods used, the reasons, and the warning signs for suicide are very similar across ethnic, gender, and age groups. Most suicidal individuals communicate their intent; in fact, about 90 percent of them leave clues (Shneidman, 1994). They may communicate verbally: "You won't be seeing me again," "You won't have to worry about me any more," "Life isn't worth living." They may leave behavioural clues—for example, they may give away their most valued possessions; withdraw from friends, family, and associates; take unnecessary risks; show personality changes; act and look depressed; and lose interest in favourite activities. These warning signs should always be taken seriously. Suicidal individuals need compassion, emotional support, and the opportunity to express the feelings and problems that are the source of their psychological pain.

Hopelessness is a common characteristic of suicidal individuals (Beck et al., 1993; Wetzel & Reich, 1989). Proposing solutions or alternatives that could lessen hopelessness may lower the likelihood of suicide. Most people contemplating suicide are not totally committed to self-destruction. This may explain why many potential victims leave warnings or use less lethal means in attempted suicide.

But we should not be amateur psychologists if we are dealing with a suicidal person. Probably the best service you can render is to encourage the person to get professional help. There are 24-hour-a-day suicide hotlines all over the country. A call might save a life. One number to call is Kids Help Phone (1-800-668-6868).

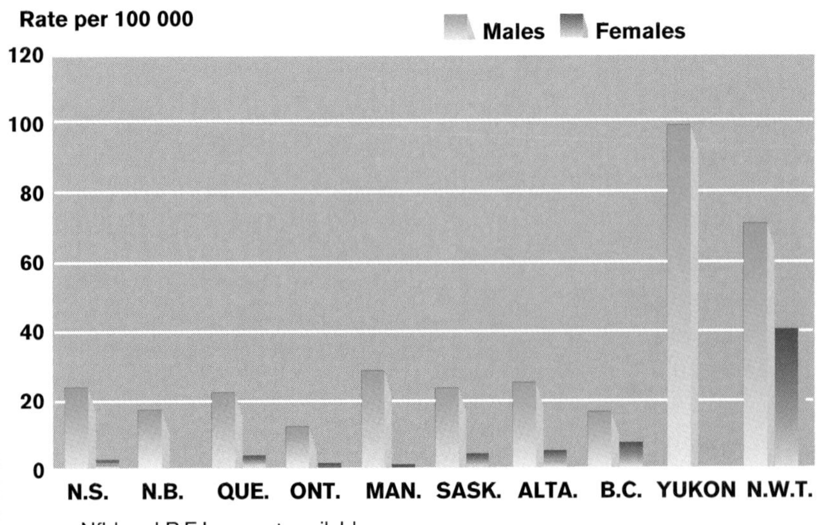

FIGURE 12.2
Teen Suicide Rates in Canada
Adapted from Fine, 1990.

The depressed moods of seasonal affective disorder (SAD) usually occur during the winter, when days are short, and can be improved using light therapy.

(Rosenthal et al., 1986; Wurtman & Wurtman, 1989). During the spring and summer months, they are in higher spirits and are more energetic, and say they function better (Wehr et al., 1986).

Reasoning that the obvious difference between the seasons was the amount and intensity of light, Rosenthal and colleagues (1985) exposed patients with winter depression to bright light, which simulated the longer daylight hours of summer. After several days of the light treatment, most of the participants improved.

In a recent Canadian study, admissions for manic depression and mixed states were examined over a 75-year period for one large psychiatric hospital. The researchers recorded when admissions occurred to see if there were seasonal variations. Contrary to expectations, the researchers found no seasonal pattern for manic depression but there was the expected seasonal peak for mixed state admissions (Whitney et al., 1999).

Bipolar Disorder

What are the extremes of mood suffered in bipolar disorder?

Another type of mood disorder is **bipolar disorder**, in which patients experience two radically different moods: extreme highs (called "manic episodes," or "mania") and extreme lows (major depression), usually with relatively normal periods in between. A **manic episode** is marked by excessive euphoria, inflated self-esteem, wild optimism, and hyperactivity. During a manic episode, people are wound up and full of energy. They rarely sleep, are frantically engaged in a flurry of activity, and talk loud and fast, skipping from one topic to another.

You may wonder what is wrong with being euphoric, energetic, and optimistic. Obviously nothing, as long as it is warranted. But people in a manic state have temporarily lost touch with reality. Their high-spirited optimism is not merely irrational, it is delusional. They may go on wild spending sprees or waste large sums of money on grand get-rich-quick schemes. If family members try to stop them or talk them out of their irrational plans, they are likely to become irritable, hostile, enraged, or even dangerous. Quite often, patients must be hospitalized during manic episodes to protect them and others from the disastrous consequences of their poor judgment.

Bipolar disorder is much less common than major depressive disorder. Its lifetime prevalence rate is about the same for males (1.6 percent) as for females (1.7 percent) (Kessler et al., 1994). Unfortunately, some 89 percent of those with bipolar disorder have recurrences (Winokur et al., 1994). In 60 to 70 percent of the cases, the manic episodes directly precede or follow the depressive episodes (APA, 1994). The good news is that 70 to 80 percent of patients return to normal after an episode (APA, 1994). However, some people with bipolar disorder are "rapid cyclers," who experience four or more episodes per year. Like depression, bipolar disorder may also follow a seasonal pattern (Faedda et al., 1993).

Causes of Major Depressive Disorder and Bipolar Disorder

What are some suggested causes of major depressive disorder and bipolar disorder?

The biological and cognitive perspectives offer some insight into the causes of mood disorders and suggest treatments that have been helpful to many people.

bipolar disorder: A mood disorder in which manic episodes alternate with periods of depression, usually with relatively normal periods in between.

manic episode (MAN-ik): A period of extreme elation, euphoria, and hyperactivity, often accompanied by delusions of grandeur and by hostility if activity is blocked.

The Biological Perspective

Biological factors such as genetic inheritance and abnormal brain chemistry play a major role in bipolar disorder and major depressive disorder. PET scans have revealed abnormal patterns of brain activity in both of these disorders (Drevets et al., 1992; George et al., 1993).

THE ROLE OF GENETIC INHERITANCE Does depression tend to run in families? Apparently so: people who have relatives with a mood disorder are at higher risk of developing mood disturbances, and this risk is due to shared genetic factors rather than shared environmental factors (Kendler et al., 1992d). On the basis of a study of 1721 identical and fraternal female twins, Kendler and colleagues (1993) estimated the heritability of major depression to be 70 percent. A person is three times more likely to develop depression if a close relative has had an early onset of depression and if the depression was recurring rather than single-episode (Bland et al., 1986; Weissman et al., 1984). Several recent twin studies have found genetic influences on depression to be similar in male twins and female twins (Kendler & Prescott, 1999; Lyons et al., 1998).

The genetic link is much stronger in bipolar disorder than in depression. The odds of developing bipolar disorder are 24 times greater among persons who have first-degree relatives (parents, children, or siblings) with the disorder (Weissman et al., 1984).

THE ROLE OF SEROTONIN AND NOREPINEPHRINE We all know that mood can be altered by the substances people put into their bodies. Alcohol, caffeine, various other uppers and downers, and a host of additional psychoactive substances are known to alter mood. Researchers now know that our moods are also altered and regulated by our own body's biochemicals, which of course include the neurotransmitters. Norepinephrine and serotonin are two neurotransmitters thought to play an important role in mood disorders. Both are localized in the limbic system and the hypothalamus, parts of the brain that help regulate emotional behaviour. Too little norepinephrine is associated with depression, and too much is related to mania (Schildkraut, 1970). It is interesting to note that amphetamines, which cause an emotional "high," are reported to stimulate the release of both serotonin and norepinephrine.

An important question remains: Do these biochemical differences in the brain cause psychological changes or result from them? Theorists who emphasize psychological causes see biochemical changes as the result, not the cause, of mood disorders.

Remember It!

Mood Disorders

1. Sanju has periods during which he is so depressed that he becomes suicidal. At other times he is energetic and euphoric. He would probably receive the diagnosis of
   a. dysthymia.
   b. seasonal mood disorder.
   c. bipolar disorder.
   d. major depressive disorder.
2. Match the theory of depression with the proposed cause.
   ____ 1) negative thoughts about oneself, the world, and one's future
   ____ 2) a deficiency of serotonin and norepinephrine
   ____ 3) turning resentment and hostility inward
   ____ 4) a family history of depression

   a. psychodynamic theory
   b. cognitive theory
   c. genetic theory
   d. biochemical theory

Answers: 1. d 2. 1) b 2) d 3) a 4) c

The Cognitive Perspective

Cognitive explanations, such as that of Aaron Beck (1967, 1991), maintain that depression is characterized by distortions in thinking. According to Beck, depressed individuals view themselves, their world, and their future negatively. They see their interactions with the world as defeating—a series of burdens and obstacles that end mostly in failure. Depressed persons believe they are deficient, unworthy, and inadequate, and they attribute their perceived failures to their own physical, mental, or moral inadequacies. Finally, according to the cognitive perspective, depressed patients believe that their future holds no hope. They may reason: "Everything always turns out wrong." "I never win." "Things will never get better." "It's no use."

In a review of a number of studies, Haaga and colleagues (1991) found that depression is related to distorted thinking. The cognitive perspective has much to offer for us to apply in our daily lives. Read the *Apply It!* box at the end of this chapter to learn more.

Other Psychological Disorders

Personality Disorders: Troublesome Behaviour Patterns

What are the main attributes of personality disorders?

A **personality disorder** is a long-standing, inflexible, maladaptive pattern of behaving and relating to others. It usually begins in childhood or adolescence (Widiger et al., 1988). People with this type of disorder tend to have problems in their social relationships and in their work; they may experience personal distress as well. Some realize that their behaviour is a problem, yet they seem unable to change. More commonly, they are self-centred and do not see themselves as responsible for their difficulties. Rather, they tend to blame other people or situations for their problems.

The DSM-IV lists ten categories of personality disorders; five are explained briefly in Table 12.1. Of particular interest is antisocial personality disorder.

LINK IT!

www.soulselfhelp.on.ca
Borderline Personality Disorder

Antisocial Personality Disorder

All too often we read or hear about people who commit horrible crimes and show no remorse whatsoever. Baffled, we ask ourselves how a person could do such things. Many of these people have antisocial personality disorder. Clifford Olson, the infamous serial killer, is thought to be one.

People with **antisocial personality disorder** have a "pervasive pattern of disregard for, and viola-

TABLE 12.1

Examples of DSM-IV Categories of Personality Disorders

Type of Disorder	Symptoms
Paranoid	Person is highly suspicious, untrusting, guarded, hypersensitive, easily slighted, lacking in emotion; holds grudges.
Antisocial personality	Person shows callous disregard for the rights and feelings of others; is manipulative, impulsive, selfish, aggressive, irresponsible, reckless; is willing to break the law, lie, cheat, or exploit others for personal gain, without remorse; fails to hold job.
Histrionic	Individual seeks attention and approval; is overly dramatic, self-centred, shallow; is demanding, manipulative, easily bored, suggestible; craves excitement; often is attractive and sexually seductive.
Narcissistic	Person has exaggerated sense of self-importance and entitlement, and is self-centred, arrogant, demanding, exploitive, envious; craves admiration and attention; lacks empathy.
Borderline	Individual is unstable in mood, behaviour, self-image, and social relationships; has intense fear of abandonment; exhibits impulsive and reckless behaviour, inappropriate anger; makes suicidal gestures and performs self-mutilating acts.

Source: Based on DSM-IV (APA, 1994).

personality disorder: A continuing, inflexible, maladaptive pattern of inner experience and behaviour that causes great distress or impaired functioning and differs significantly from the patterns expected in the person's culture.

antisocial personality disorder: A disorder marked by lack of feeling for others; selfish, aggressive, irresponsible behaviour; and willingness to break the law, lie, cheat, or exploit others for personal gain.

tion of, the rights of others that begins in childhood or early adolescence and continues into adulthood" (APA, 1994, p. 645). As children, they lie, steal, vandalize, initiate fights, skip school, and run away from home; they may be physically cruel to others. By early adolescence they usually drink excessively, use drugs, and engage in promiscuous sex. In adulthood, the antisocial personality typically fails to keep a job, to act as a responsible parent, to honour financial commitments, and to obey the law. Research suggests that 2 to 3 percent of Canadians suffer from this disorder (Weissman, 1993).

Many antisocial types are intelligent, and they may seem charming and very likable at first. Men make up a greater percentage of antisocial types than do women: as many as 5.8 percent of American men have this disorder, compared with less than 1.3 percent of American women (Kessler et al., 1994). One of the original studies of antisocial personality disorder revealed that persons who have it seem to lack the ability to love or to feel loyalty or compassion (Checkley, 1941). They seem to have no conscience; they feel little or no guilt or remorse for their actions, no matter how cruel or despicable those actions may be (Hare, 1995).

Years ago, people with antisocial personality disorder were referred to as "psychopaths" or "sociopaths." Con men, quack doctors, impostors, and today many drug pushers, pimps, delinquents, and criminals could be diagnosed as having this disorder. Some come to the attention of the authorities; others do not.

IT HAPPENED IN CANADA

Sex Change and Gender Identity

In 1965 twin boys, Bruce and Brian Reimer, were born in Winnipeg. There was nothing exceptional about the Reimer boys until at eight months of age doctors recommended that they be circumcised to correct their constricted foreskins. That's when things went wrong. The exact nature of the error that was to follow is not known–either the doctor used the wrong setting for an electronic cauterizing machine or used it incorrectly. In any case, Bruce's penis was severely burned, eventually falling off a few days later. This outcome started a chain of events that ended with Bruce becoming Brenda. The 19-month-old Bruce was introduced to Dr. John Money, the leading expert in sexual identity. It was Money who suggested the sex-change surgery, believing that gender identity developed as the child matured and that Bruce would stand a better chance as a girl than as an incomplete male. Bruce was castrated. Brenda was raised as a female and started estrogen therapy at 12.

The experimental data from Money indicated that everything was going well–Brenda was a well-adjusted girl. In reality, however, Brenda was not well adjusted–she didn't feel like a girl. At 14 she was finally told of her real sexual identity, and from that point on she was determined to live her life as a man. She became David, had a mastectomy, took testosterone, and had surgery to partially build a penis. David did not have a gender identity disorder–all the struggles he had experienced with his gender identity started to make sense–he was on the road to recovery. Eventually he married and is raising a family. David's willingness to share his story has cast doubt on the practice of sex-reassignment surgery for infants who have suffered accidental disfigurement or small abnormalities of their genitalia. (Based on Colapinto, 2000.)

Sexual and Gender Identity Disorders

What are the sexual and gender identity disorders?

The DSM-IV has two categories of sexual disorders: sexual dysfunctions and paraphilias. **Sexual dysfunctions** are persistent problems that cause marked distress and interpersonal difficulty; they may involve sexual desire, sexual arousal, or the pleasure associated with sex or orgasm. A person with a **paraphilia** has recurrent sexual urges, fantasies, or behaviours involving children, other non-consenting partners, non-human objects, or suffering or humiliation. To be diagnosed as having a paraphilia, the person must experience considerable psychological distress or an impairment in functioning in an important area of his or her life. **Gender identity disorders** involve difficulties accepting one's identity as male or female.

Table 12.2 describes a number of the sexual disorders listed in the DSM-IV. Note that homosexuality is *not* considered a sexual disorder.

Current Canadian research on pedophilia is described in *On the Cutting Edge in Canada*.

TABLE 12.2

DSM-IV Categories of Sexual Disorders

Type of Disorder	Symptoms
Paraphilias	Disorders in which recurrent sexual urges, fantasies, and behaviours involve non-human objects, children, other non-consenting persons, or the suffering or humiliation of the individual or his/her partner.
Fetishism	A disorder in which sexual urges, fantasies, and behaviour involve an inanimate object, such as women's undergarments or shoes.
Transvestic fetishism	A disorder in which sexual urges, fantasies, and behaviour involve cross-dressing.
Pedophilia	A disorder in which sexual urges, fantasies, and behaviour involve sexual activity with a prepubescent child or children.
Exhibitionism	A disorder in which sexual urges, fantasies, and behaviour involve exposing one's genitals to an unsuspecting stranger.
Voyeurism	A disorder in which sexual urges, fantasies, and behaviour involve watching unsuspecting people naked, undressing, or engaging in sexual activity.
Sexual masochism	A disorder in which sexual urges, fantasies, and behaviour involve being beaten, humiliated, bound, or otherwise made to suffer.
Sexual sadism	A disorder in which sexual urges, fantasies, and behaviour involve inflicting physical or psychological pain and suffering on another.
Frotteurism	A disorder in which sexual urges, fantasies, and behaviour involve touching or rubbing against a non-consenting person, usually in a crowded place.
Other paraphilias	Disorders in which sexual urges, fantasies, and behaviour involve, among other things, animals, feces, urine, corpses, filth, or enemas.
Sexual dysfunctions	Disorders involving low sexual desire; the inability to attain or maintain sexual arousal; a delay or absence of orgasm; premature ejaculation; and genital pain associated with sexual activity.

Source: Based on DSM-IV (APA, 1994).

Try It!

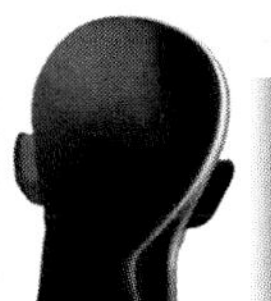

Portrayals of Psychological Disorders

Make a list of movies, TV shows, or plays you have seen or heard about in which a character with a psychological disorder plays a prominent role. One example is given to get you started.

As Good As It Gets	Jack Nicholson	Obsessive compulsive disorder
______	______	______
______	______	______
______	______	______

By now, you should know a great deal about psychological disorders. Apply your knowledge in the *Try It!*

sexual dysfunction: A persistent or recurrent problem that causes marked distress and interpersonal difficulty and that may involve any or some combination of the following: sexual desire, sexual arousal, or the pleasure associated with sex, or orgasm.

paraphilia: A sexual disorder in which sexual urges, fantasies, and behaviour generally involve children, other non-consenting partners, non-human objects, or the suffering and humiliation of oneself or one's partner.

gender identity disorders: Disorders characterized by a problem accepting one's identity as male or female.

on the cutting edge in canada

Pedophilia

A pedophile is an adult who is sexually attracted to prepubescent children. Pedophilia is both uncommon and very difficult to treat. One problem is that it comes in many forms. For instance, although most pedophiles are males, some prefer their victims to be a specific gender or age, whereas others do not.

Canadian researchers are renowned for their work on pedophilia. Some particularly prominent people include the late Dr. Kurt Freund and Michael Kuban (1993) at the Clarke Institute for Psychiatry, who examined the relation between childhood experiences and pedophilia. They found that many pedophiles reported that they had been sexually abused by adults during their childhood. Dr. William Marshall and colleagues (2000) at Queen's University also found high levels of sexual abuse in this population. Seto and colleagues (1999) at the Centre for Addiction and Mental Health in Toronto recently tested a theory that suggests that parental incest would occur only when parents are uninvolved in parenting and/or their pedophilic interest was at such a high level that it would override taboos against inbreeding. It was expected that pedophile biological fathers who were involved in their child's upbringing would have much higher pedophilic interest than others. The theory was not supported. They did not find differences in pedophilic interest. They did, however, note the importance of measuring pedophilic interest, and they are pursuing other explanations for sexual molestation within families.

Remember It!

Other Psychological Disorders

1. Which statement is true of personality disorders?
   a. Personality disorders usually begin in adulthood.
   b. Persons with these disorders usually realize their problem.
   c. Personality disorders typically cause problems in social relationships and at work.
   d. Persons with these disorders typically seek professional help.
2. Tim lies, cheats, and exploits others without feeling guilty. He most likely has __________ personality disorder.
   a. avoidant b. histrionic
   c. antisocial d. narcissistic
3. What is the name for disorders in which sexual urges, fantasies, and behaviours involve children, other non-consenting partners, or non-human objects?
   a. paraphilias
   b. gender identity disorders
   c. dysfunctional object disorder
   d. sexual dysfunctions
4. What is the general term used to describe disturbances in sexual desire, sexual arousal, or the ability to attain orgasm?
   a. paraphilias
   b. gender identity disorders
   c. dysfunctional object disorder
   d. sexual dysfunctions

Answers: 1. c 2. c 3. a 4. d

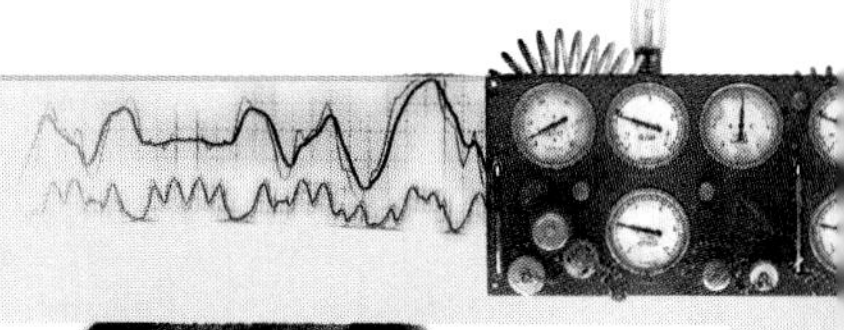

Depression: Bad Thoughts, Bad Feelings

Apply It!

Do you know that you can actually cause your own moods? Consider these thoughts: "I'll never pass this course." "He/she would never go out with me." "I can't do anything right." "I'm a failure." How do these thoughts make you feel? How about these thoughts? "My future looks bright and happy." "I have good friends and I am well liked." "I feel so happy I could laugh."

When it comes to physical health and well-being, you have probably heard it said, "You are what you eat." To a large extent, in the area of mental health, "You are what you think." Depression and other forms of mental misery can be fuelled by our own negative or irrational thoughts.

One step toward healthy thinking is to recognize and avoid the following five cognitive traps.

Cognitive Trap 1: The "Tyranny of the Should"

One certain path to unhappiness is to set unrealistic, unachievable standards for yourself. Unrealistic and unachievable standards are characterized by such words as *always, never, all, everybody,* and *everything*. Have you ever been tyrannized by any of the following *shoulds?*

I should always be the perfect friend, lover, spouse, parent, student, teacher, [or] employee.
I should never feel hurt and should always be calm.
I should be able to solve all of my problems and the problems of others in no time.
I should never be tired or fall ill.
(Adapted from Horney, 1950, pp. 64–66.)

Cognitive Trap 2: Negative, "What If" Thinking

Much unhappiness stems from a preoccupation with what might be. These are examples of "what if" thinking: "What if she/he turns me down?" "What if I lose my job?" "What if I flunk this test?" And if a "what if" comes to pass, the third cognitive trap may be sprung.

Cognitive Trap 3: Making Mountains Out of Molehills

A molehill becomes a mountain when a single negative event is perceived as catastrophic or allowed to become a definition of our total worth. "I failed this test" might become "I'll never pass this course," "I'll never graduate from school," "I'm too dumb to be in college," or "I'm a failure."

Cognitive Trap 4: The Perfection–Failure Dichotomy

Only on the rarest occasions can anyone's performance be considered absolutely perfect or a total failure. But people who fall into this cognitive trap judge anything short of perfection as total failure.

Cognitive Trap 5: Setting Impossible Conditions for Happiness

Don't let your happiness hinge on perfection in yourself and others.

Not everyone will love you or even like you, approve of you, or agree with you. If any of these are conditions upon which your happiness depends, you are setting the stage for disappointment or even depression.

Developing Healthier Thinking Habits

If negative or irrational thoughts are part of your habitual repertoire, you

need to develop healthier thinking habits. The next time you notice yourself entertaining negative thoughts or self-doubts, write them down and analyze them objectively and unemotionally. But don't go to the opposite extreme and substitute equally distorted positive thinking or mindless "happy talk." Self-delusion in either direction is not healthy. Your goal should be to monitor your thinking and systematically make it less distorted, more rational, more accurate, and more logical. For example:

- Instead of thinking, "It would be the end of everything if I lost my job!" think, "I would not want to lose my job, but I could find another."
- Instead of thinking, "I am a failure because this turned out so badly," substitute, "I am embarrassed about how this turned out, but I'll do better the next time."

Depression is a complex psychological disorder with both physiological and psychological causes. Not all depression can be controlled simply by a change in thinking. If symptoms such as those listed at the beginning of this box persist, seek professional treatment.

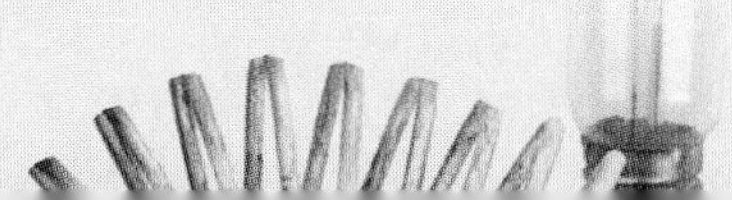

KEY TERMS

agoraphobia, p. 387
antisocial personality disorder, p. 404
anxiety, p. 386
bipolar disorder, p. 401
catatonic schizophrenia, p. 396
compulsion, p. 389
conversion disorder, p. 391
delusion, p. 394
delusion of grandeur, p. 394
delusion of persecution, p. 394
diathesis–stress model, p. 396
disorganized schizophrenia, p. 396
dissociative amnesia, p. 392
dissociative disorders, p. 392
dissociative fugue, p. 392
dissociative identity disorder, p. 392
DSM-IV, p. 384
gender identity disorders, p. 404
generalized anxiety disorder, p. 386
hallucination, p. 394
hypochondriasis, p. 391
inappropriate affect, p. 395
major depressive disorder, p. 398
manic episode, p. 401
mood disorders, p. 398
neurosis, p. 384
obsession, p. 389
obsessive compulsive disorder (OCD), p. 389
panic attack, p. 387
panic disorder, p. 387
paranoid schizophrenia, p. 396
paraphilia, p. 404
personality disorder, p. 403
phobia, p. 387
psychosis, p. 384
schizophrenia, p. 394
seasonal affective disorder (SAD), p. 399
sexual dysfunction, p. 404
social phobia, p. 388
somatoform disorders, p. 390
specific phobia, p. 388
undifferentiated schizophrenia, p. 396

THINKING CRITICALLY

Evaluation

Some psychological disorders are more common in women (depression, agoraphobia, and specific phobia), and some are more common in men (antisocial personality disorder, and substance abuse and dependence). Give some possible reasons why such gender differences exist in these disorders. Support your answer.

Point/Counterpoint

There is continuing controversy over whether specific psychological disorders are chiefly biological in origin (nature) or result primarily from learning and experience (nurture). Select any two disorders from this chapter and prepare arguments for both nature and nurture for both disorders.

Psychology in Your Life

Formulate a specific plan for your own life that will help you recognize and avoid the five cognitive traps that contribute to unhealthy thinking. You might enlist the help of a friend to monitor your negative statements.

SUMMARY & REVIEW

What Is Abnormal?

What criteria might be used to differentiate normal from abnormal behaviour?

Behaviour might be considered abnormal if it deviates radically from what is considered normal in one's own culture, if it leads to personal distress or impaired functioning, or if it results in one's being a danger to self and/or others.

What are five current perspectives that attempt to explain the causes of psychological disorders?

Five current perspectives on the causes of abnormal behaviour are (1) the biological perspective, which views it as a symptom of an underlying physical disorder; (2) the psychodynamic perspective, which maintains that it is caused by unconscious, unresolved conflicts; (3) the learning perspective, which argues that it is learned and sustained in the same way as other behaviour; (4) the cognitive perspective, which suggests that it results from faulty thinking; and (5) the humanistic perspective, which views it as a result of the blocking of one's natural tendency toward self-actualization.

What is the DSM-IV?

The DSM-IV, published by the American Psychiatric Association, is the system most widely used in North America to diagnose psychological disorders.

Anxiety Disorders: When Anxiety Is Extreme

When is anxiety healthy, and when is it unhealthy?

Anxiety–a generalized feeling of apprehension, fear, or tension–is healthy if it is a response to a real danger or threat; it is unhealthy if it is inappropriate or excessive.

What are the symptoms of a panic disorder?

Panic disorder is marked by recurrent, unpredictable panic attacks: attacks of overwhelming anxiety, fear, or terror, during which people experience palpitations, trembling or shaking, choking or smothering sensations, and the feeling that they are going to die or go crazy.

What are the characteristics of the three categories of phobias?

The three categories of phobic disorders are (1) agoraphobia, fear of being in situations in which escape is impossible or help is not available in case of incapacitating anxiety; (2) social phobia, fear of social situations in which one might be embarrassed or humiliated by appearing clumsy or incompetent; and (3) specific phobia, a marked fear of a specific object or situation and a catchall category for all phobias other than agoraphobia or social phobia.

What do psychologists believe are some probable causes of phobias?

Phobias result primarily from frightening experiences or through observational learning. Genes may also play a role.

What is obsessive-compulsive disorder?

Obsessive-compulsive disorder is characterized by obsessions (persistent, recurring, involuntary thoughts, images, or impulses that cause great distress) and/or compulsions (persistent, irresistible, irrational urges to perform an act or ritual repeatedly).

Somatoform and Dissociative Disorders

What are two somatoform disorders, and what symptoms do they share?

Somatoform disorders involve bodily symptoms that cannot be explained by known medical conditions. Hypochondriasis involves a preoccupation with the fear that bodily symptoms are the sign of some serious disease. Conversion disorder involves a loss of motor or sensory functioning in some part of the body, such as paralysis or blindness.

What is dissociative amnesia?

People with dissociative amnesia have a loss of memory for limited periods of their life or for their entire personal identity.

What is dissociative fugue?

In dissociative fugue, people forget their entire identity, travel away from home, and may assume a new identity somewhere else.

What are some of the identifying symptoms of dissociative identity disorder?

In dissociative identity disorder (often called multiple personality), two or more distinct, unique personalities occur in the same person, each taking over at different times. Most patients are female and victims of early, severe physical and/or sexual abuse. They typically complain of periods of "lost time."

Schizophrenia

What are some of the major positive symptoms of schizophrenia?

The "positive" symptoms of schizophrenia are abnormal behaviours and characteristics, including hallucinations, delusions, disorganized thinking and speech, bizarre behaviour, and inappropriate affect.

What are some of the major negative symptoms of schizophrenia?

The "negative" symptoms of schizophrenia represent deficiencies in thoughts and behaviour and include social withdrawal, apathy, loss of motivation, very limited speech, slow movements, flat affect, and poor hygiene and grooming.

What are the four subtypes of schizophrenia?

The four subtypes of schizophrenia are catatonic, disorganized, paranoid, and undifferentiated.

What are some suggested causes of schizophrenia?

Some suggested causes of schizophrenia are a genetic predisposition, sufficient stress in people who are predisposed to the disorder, and excessive dopamine activity in the brain.

Mood Disorders

What are the symptoms of major depressive disorder?

Major depressive disorder is characterized by feelings of great sadness, despair, guilt, worthlessness, hopelessness, and, in extreme cases, suicidal intentions.

What are the extremes of mood suffered in bipolar disorder?

Bipolar disorder is a mood disorder in which a person suffers from manic episodes (periods of extreme elation, euphoria, and hyperactivity) alternating with major depression, usually with relatively normal periods in between.

What are some suggested causes of major depressive disorder and bipolar disorder?

Some of the proposed causes are (1) a genetic predisposition; (2) an imbalance in the neurotransmitters norepinephrine and serotonin; (3) a tendency to turn hostility and resentment inward rather than expressing it; (4) distorted and negative views of oneself, the world, and the future; and (5) stress.

Other Psychological Disorders

What are the main attributes of personality disorders?

Personality disorders are continuing, inflexible, maladaptive patterns of behaviour and inner experience that cause personal distress and/or impairment in social and occupational functioning.

What are the sexual and gender identity disorders?

Three categories of sexual disorders are sexual dysfunctions (problems with sexual desire, sexual arousal, or orgasm); paraphilias (needing unusual or bizarre objects, conditions, or acts for sexual gratification); and gender identity disorders (having a problem accepting one's identity as male or female).

13 Therapies

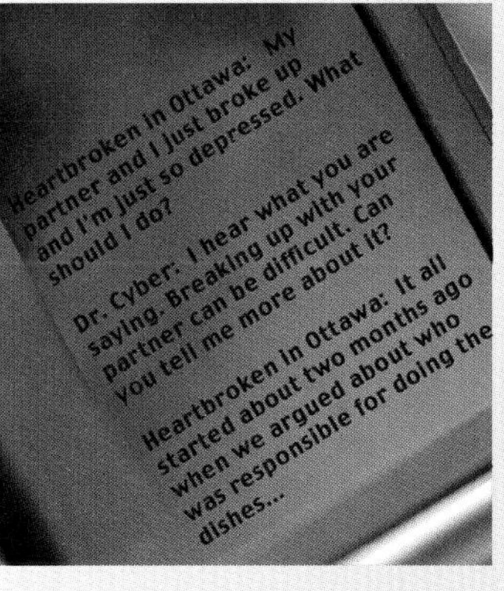

Heartbroken in Ottawa: My partner and I just broke up and I'm just so depressed. What should I do?
Dr. Cyber: I hear what you are saying. Breaking up with your partner can be difficult. Can you tell me more about it?
Heartbroken in Ottawa: It all started about two months ago when we argued about who was responsible for doing the dishes...

If you read what is on the screen on the computer above, you, like many of us, have just been a voyeur on a chat line. Chat rooms are a 24-hour-a-day meeting place where you can talk to anyone about anything. It's no wonder then that many counsellors have started to offer their services online. But what about you? Are you a computer user? Do you use chat lines? Would you use an online counsellor?

Some experts say that Web-based therapy is the wave of the future, but how does it stack up now? In a recent article, Rebecca Segall (2000) tried using several counsellors who offer their services on the Web. On the plus side was the potential for greater portability, greater accessibility, and more anonymity. Segall is a businesswoman who travels, but her computer goes wherever she goes. Having an online counsellor meant that she didn't have to be located in the same place, as traditional therapy would require, nor did she have to follow traditional office hours. She could contact a counsellor from any location at any time of day or night. She also found that there was a large variety of services offered and that using her computer allowed her to store all her correspondence, which gave her a permanent written record that she could review at her convenience.

If this is sounding good, think again! Although there are lots of services advertised, the challenge of finding a qualified therapist is much greater online. You don't have physical access to these individuals, their diplomas, their office, or colleagues, which means that you do not have any tangible evidence of their qualifications. Because online services cross provincial and international boundaries, the standards that operate in your community do not necessarily affect the person you are contacting. That makes the search for a qualified practitioner quite a bit more challenging. Anyone can post a website. Anonymity works two ways on the Web–you can be whoever you want to be, and so can other people!

It's also good to remember that a therapist's understanding of what's happening to you is based on more than just what you say. He or she observes nonverbal communications as well. On the Web, it's only you and your words. And how comfortable are you spilling your heart out when you're not sure who else is reading your mail? Although some websites are secure, you always run the risk of undesired external parties looking in on your most personal exchanges. Finally, limitations of servers, system crashes, and other unforeseen technical problems also exist on the Web and can interfere with access to the counsellor.

Although online services may seem attractive on the surface, they have yet to be proven an effective method of therapy. In this chapter we will discuss a variety of recognized and well-researched therapies designed to treat psychological disorders.

Insight Therapies

What comes into your mind when you hear the word ***psychotherapy***? Many people picture a patient on a couch talking to a grey-haired, bearded therapist with a heavy accent. But that picture is hopelessly out of date, as you will see. **Psychotherapy** uses psychological rather than biological means to treat emotional and behavioural disorders; it usually involves a conversation between the client and the therapist. There are therapies for every trouble, techniques for every taste—over 450 different psychotherapies (Karasu, 1986). Today, the couch has generally been replaced by a comfortable chair. And psychotherapy is now relatively brief, averaging about 18 sessions, with private therapists, instead of years (Goode, 1987). Furthermore, modern psychotherapy is not completely dominated by men—more women are becoming therapists.

Some forms of psychotherapy are collectively referred to as **insight therapies** because their assumption is that our psychological well-being depends on self-understanding—understanding of our thoughts, emotions, motives, behaviour, and coping mechanisms. The major insight therapies are psychoanalysis, person-centred therapy, existential therapy, and Gestalt therapy.

Psychodynamic Therapies: Freud Revisited

Freud proposed that the cause of psychological disorders lies in early childhood experiences and in unresolved, unconscious conflicts, usually of a sexual or aggressive nature. **Psychoanalysis** was the first formal psychotherapy, and it was the dominant influence on psychotherapy in the 1940s and 1950s (Garfield, 1981). The goals of psychoanalysis are to uncover repressed memories and to bring to consciousness the buried, unresolved conflicts believed to lie at the root of the person's problem.

Psychoanalysis: From the Couch of Freud

What are the four basic techniques of psychoanalysis, and how are they used to help disturbed patients?

Freudian psychoanalysis uses four basic techniques: free association, analysis of resistance, dream analysis, and analysis of transference.

FREE ASSOCIATION The central technique of psychoanalytic therapy is **free association**, in which the patient is instructed to reveal whatever thoughts, feelings, or images come to mind, no matter how embarrassing, terrible, or trivial they might seem. Freud believed that free assoc iation allows important unconscious material to surface—for example, repressed memories, threatening impulses, and traumatic episodes of childhood. The analyst pieces together the free-flowing associations, explains their meaning, and helps patients gain insight into the thoughts and behaviours that are troubling them.

ANALYSIS OF RESISTANCE How do you think you would react if an analyst told you to express *everything* that came into your mind? Would you try to avoid revealing certain painful or embarrassing thoughts? Freud's patients did, and he called this **resistance**.

If the patient hesitates, balks, or becomes visibly upset about any topic touched on, the analyst assumes that the topic is emotionally important to the patient. Freud also pointed out other forms of resistance, such as "forgetting" appointments with the analyst or arriving late.

DREAM ANALYSIS Freud believed that areas of emotional concern repressed in waking life are sometimes expressed in symbolic form in dreams. He believed that dreams convey hidden meanings and identify important repressed thoughts, memories, and emotions.

ANALYSIS OF TRANSFERENCE Freud said that at some point during psychoanalysis, the patient inevitably begins to react to the analyst with the same feelings and attitudes that were present in another significant

Freud's famous couch was used by his patients during psychoanalysis.

psychotherapy: The treatment for psychological disorders that uses psychological rather than biological means and primarily involves conversations between patient and therapist.

insight therapy: Any type of psychotherapy based on the notion that psychological well-being depends on self-understanding.

psychoanalysis (SY-ko-uh-NAL-ul-sis): The psychotherapy that uses free association, dream analysis, and analysis of resistance and transference to uncover repressed memories, impulses, and conflicts thought to cause psychological disorder.

free association: A psychoanalytic technique used to explore the unconscious; patients reveal whatever thoughts or images come to mind.

resistance: In psychoanalytic therapy, the patient's attempts to avoid expressing or revealing painful or embarrassing thoughts or feelings.

relationship—usually with the mother or father. This reaction he called **transference**. Transference allows the patient to relive or re-enact troubling experiences from the past with the analyst as parent substitute. The unresolved childhood conflicts can then be replayed in the present, this time with a parent figure who does not reject, provoke guilt, or punish as the actual parent did.

Psychodynamic Therapy Today: The New View

Traditional psychoanalysis can be a long and costly undertaking. Patients attend four or five therapy sessions per week for two to four years. In the mid-1980s, only about 2 percent of people undergoing psychotherapy chose classical psychoanalysis (Goode, 1987) and the numbers declined in the 1990s (Grünbaum, 1994). Psychoanalysis is most suitable for those with average or higher intelligence who are not severely disturbed, but who are interested in extensive self-exploration.

Many psychoanalysts practise brief psychodynamic therapy, which is also aimed at gaining insight into unconscious conflicts. The therapist and patient decide on the issues to explore at the outset rather than waiting for them to emerge in the course of treatment. The therapist assumes a more active role and places more emphasis on the present than is the case in traditional psychoanalysis (Davanloo, 1980). Brief psychodynamic therapy may require only one or two visits per week for as few as 12 to 20 weeks (Altshuler, 1989). In an analysis of 11 well-controlled studies, Crits-Christoph (1992) found brief psychodynamic therapy to be as effective as other kinds of psychotherapy.

Criticisms of Psychoanalytic Therapy

Traditional psychoanalysis has been criticized for its emphasis on the unconscious and the past and its virtual neglect of the conscious and the present. Moreover, the focus on unconscious motives as the major determinants of behaviour minimizes patients' responsibility for their behaviour and their choices. And from a practical standpoint, research does not suggest that the tremendous cost of psychoanalysis yields results that are superior to briefer, less costly therapy.

The Humanistic and Existential Therapies

Humanistic and existential therapies stand in stark contrast to psychoanalysis in that they are based on a more optimistic and hopeful picture of human nature and human potential. Individuals are viewed as unique and basically self-determining, with the ability and freedom to lead rational lives and make rational choices. Humanistic and existential therapists encourage personal growth; they seek to teach clients how to fulfill their potential and take responsibility for their behaviour and for what they become in life. The focus is primarily on current relationships and experiences.

LINK IT!

ahpweb.org/index.html
Association for Humanistic Psychology Home Page

Person-Centred Therapy: The Patient Becomes the Person

What is the role of the therapist in person-centred therapy?

Person-centred therapy, developed by Carl Rogers (1951), is based on the humanistic view of human nature. According to this view, people are innately good and, if allowed to develop naturally, will grow toward **self-actualization** (the realization of their inner potential).

If people grow naturally toward self-actualization, then why is everyone not self-actualized? The humanistic perspective suggests that psychological disorders result when a person's natural tendency toward self-actualization is blocked. Rogers (1959) insisted that individuals block their natural tendency toward growth and self-actualization when they act in ways

Carl Rogers (at upper right) facilitates discussion in a therapy group.

that are inconsistent with their true self in order to gain the positive regard of others.

In person-centred therapy, the focus is on conscious thoughts and feelings. The therapist attempts to create a warm, accepting climate in which clients are free to be themselves so that their natural tendency toward growth can be released. Person-centred therapy is a **non-directive therapy**. The direction of the therapy sessions is controlled by the client. The therapist acts as a facilitator of growth, giving understanding, support, and encouragement rather than proposing solutions, answering questions, or actively directing the course of therapy. Rogers rejected all forms of therapy that casts the therapist in the role of expert and clients in the role of patients who expect the therapist to tell them something or prescribe something that "cures" their problem.

According to Rogers, only three things are required of therapists. First, the therapist must have **unconditional positive regard** for, or total acceptance of, the client, regardless of the client's feelings, thoughts, or behaviour. In such an atmosphere, clients feel free to reveal their weakest points, relax their defences, and begin to accept and value themselves. Second, the therapist's feelings toward the client must be genuine—no façade, no putting up a professional front. Third, therapists must have empathy with the client—that is, they must be able to put themselves in the client's place. Therapists must show that they comprehend the client's feelings, emotions, and experiences, and that they understand and see the client's world as the client sees it. When clients speak, the therapist follows by restating or reflecting back their ideas and feelings. In this way clients begin to see themselves more clearly; eventually, they resolve their own conflicts and make positive decisions about their lives.

In the 1940s and 1950s, person-centred therapy was the only psychotherapy, other than psychoanalysis, with any following among psychologists. In the early 1980s a survey of 400 psychologists and counsellors revealed that Rogers was the most influential figure in counselling and psychotherapy (Smith, 1982).

Existential Therapy: Finding Meaning in Life

Existential therapy helps people to deal with the issues that are part of the human condition—to find meaning in life, to find values that are worth living and even dying for. The existential point of view tries to deal with alienation: the feeling that we are disconnected from the rest of the world, that we don't fit in, that we are lonely and stand apart.

The existential therapist stresses that we have both the freedom and the responsibility to choose the kind of person we want to become. Because each of us is unique, we must find our own personal meaning in our existence.

Gestalt Therapy: Getting in Touch with Your Feelings

What is the major emphasis in Gestalt therapy?

Gestalt therapy, developed by Fritz Perls (1969), emphasizes the importance of clients' fully experiencing, in the present moment, their feelings, thoughts, and actions, and then taking responsibility for both their feelings and their behaviour. Perls maintains that many of us block out aspects of our experience and are often not aware of how we really feel.

Gestalt therapy is a **directive therapy**, one in which the therapist takes an active role in determin-

transference: An intense emotional situation occurring in psychoanalysis when one comes to behave toward the analyst as one had behaved toward a significant figure from the past.

person-centred therapy: A non-directive, humanistic therapy in which the therapist creates a warm, accepting atmosphere, thus freeing clients to be themselves and releasing their natural tendency toward positive growth; developed by Carl Rogers.

self-actualization: Developing to one's fullest potential.

non-directive therapy: An approach in which the therapist acts to facilitate growth, giving understanding and support rather than proposing solutions, answering questions, or actively directing the course of therapy.

unconditional positive regard: A condition required of person-centred therapists, involving a caring for and acceptance of clients regardless of their feelings, thoughts, or behaviour.

existential therapy: A therapy that places an emphasis on finding meaning in life.

Gestalt therapy: A therapy originated by Fritz Perls that emphasizes the importance of clients' fully experiencing, in the present moment, their feelings, thoughts, and actions and taking personal responsibility for their behaviour.

directive therapy: An approach to therapy in which the therapist takes an active role in determining the course of therapy sessions and provides answers and suggestions to the patient.

ing the course of therapy sessions. "Getting in touch with one's feelings" is an ever-present objective for those in Gestalt therapy. The therapist helps, prods, or badgers clients to experience their feelings as deeply and genuinely as possible and then admit responsibility for them.

Perls suggests that those of us who need therapy carry around a heavy load of unfinished business, which may be in the form of resentments or conflicts with parents, siblings, lovers, employers, or others. If not resolved, these conflicts are carried forward into our present relationships. One method of dealing with unfinished business is the "empty chair" technique, which is used to help clients express their true feelings about significant people in their lives. The client imagines, for example, that a wife, husband, father, mother, or friend sits in the empty chair. The client then proceeds to tell the "chair" what he or she truly feels about that person. Then the client trades places and sits in the empty chair and role-plays the imagined person's response to what the client has said.

The ultimate goal of Gestalt therapy is not merely to relieve symptoms. Rather, it is to help clients achieve a more integrated self and become more authentic and self-accepting. In addition, clients must learn to assume personal responsibility for their behaviour rather than blame society, past experiences, parents, or others.

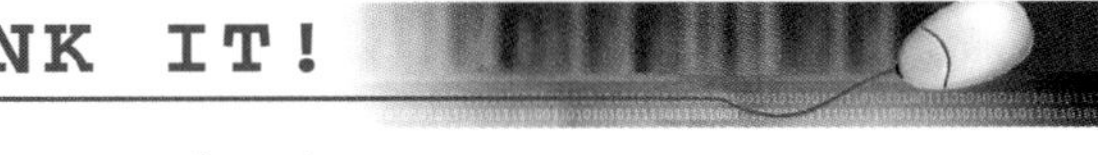

www.g-g.org/aagt
Association for the Advancement of Gestalt Therapy (AAGT) Home Page

Therapies Emphasizing Interaction with Others

Some therapies look not only at the individual's internal struggles but also at interpersonal relationships.

Interpersonal Therapy: Short Road to Recovery

What four problems commonly associated with major depression is interpersonal therapy designed to treat?

Interpersonal therapy (IPT) is a brief psychotherapy that has proven very effective in the treatment of depression (Elkin et al., 1989; Klerman et al., 1984). Interpersonal therapy is designed specifically to help patients cope with four types of problems commonly associated with major depression:

1. *Unusual or severe responses to the death of a loved one.* The therapist seeks to help the patient release strong negative feelings (e.g., guilt) and develop an active interest in the present.

Remember It!

Psychodynamic, Humanistic, and Existential Therapies

1. In psychoanalysis the technique whereby a patient reveals every thought, idea, or image that comes to mind is called __________; the patient's attempt to avoid revealing certain thoughts is called __________.
   a. transference; resistance
   b. free association; transference
   c. revelation; transference
   d. free association; resistance
2. What is the directive therapy that emphasizes the importance of the client's fully experiencing, in the present moment, his or her thoughts, feelings, and actions?
   a. person-centred therapy
   b. Gestalt therapy
   c. existential therapy
   d. psychoanalytic therapy
3. What is the non-directive therapy developed by Carl Rogers in which the therapist creates a warm, accepting atmosphere so that the client's natural tendency toward positive change can be released?
   a. person-centred therapy
   b. Gestalt therapy
   c. existential therapy
   d. psychoanalytic therapy
4. Which therapy presumes that the causes of the patient's problems are repressed memories, impulses, and conflicts?
   a. person-centred therapy
   b. Gestalt therapy
   c. existential therapy
   d. psychoanalytic therapy

Answers: 1.d 2.b 3.a 4.d

2. *Interpersonal role disputes.* Depression is often associated with mutually incompatible expectations about roles or responsibilities between patients and their partners, children, parents, co-workers or employers. These may be a source of conflict, resentment, and even hostility. The therapist helps the patient to comprehend what is at stake for those involved and to explore options for bringing about change. If the problem involves a family member, it is often helpful for that person also to attend a therapy session.
3. *Difficulty in adjusting to role transitions such as divorce, career change, and retirement.* Role transitions may involve a loss, such as a life change resulting from an illness or injury or the loss of a job. Other role transitions involve positive events, such as marriage, a new baby, or a promotion. Patients are helped to see the change not as a threat but as a challenge and an opportunity for growth.
4. *Deficits in interpersonal skills.* Some people lack the skills to make friends and are unable to sustain intimate relationships. Through role-playing and analysis of the patient's communication style, the therapist tries to help the patient develop the interpersonal skills necessary to initiate and sustain relationships.

Interpersonal therapy is brief, consisting of 12 to 16 weekly sessions. A large study conducted in the United States by the National Institute of Mental Health found IPT to be effective even for severe depression and to have a low dropout rate (Elkin et al., 1989, 1995). Research also indicates that patients who recover from major depression can enjoy a longer period without relapse when they continue with monthly sessions of IPT (Frank et al., 1991).

Family and Marital Therapy: Healing Our Relationships

For most of us, the most significant group to which we will ever belong is the family. But even the strongest families sometimes have problems, and there are therapists of all types who specialize in treating troubled families. Families who come to therapists include those in which abuse is occurring and those with troubled or troublesome teenagers or alcoholic parents. In **family therapy**, parents and children enter therapy as a group with one therapist, or perhaps more (in conjoint therapy). As you can imagine, there are some things a family member may want to discuss privately with the therapist. Family therapists realize this and do not conduct every session with the entire family together. Sometimes they work with only one or a few family members at a time.

The therapist's goal is to help the family reach agreement on certain changes that will help heal the wounds of the family unit, improve communication patterns, and create more understanding and harmony.

Therapists who work with married couples help them resolve their difficulties and stay together; or ease the emotional turmoil if a breakup is the best answer for the couple. Dr. Donald Meichenbaum at the University of Waterloo has contributed greatly to our understanding of family therapy and, in addition, has developed a stress inoculation technique for handling anxiety (see Chapter 11).

Family and marital therapists pay attention to the dynamics of the family unit–how members communicate, act toward each other, and view each other.

interpersonal therapy (IPT): A brief psychotherapy designed to help depressed people understand their problems in interpersonal relationships and develop more effective ways to solve them.

family therapy: Therapy based on the assumption that an individual's problem is caused and/or maintained in part by problems within the family unit; the entire family is involved in therapy.

Group Therapy: Helping One at a Time, Together

What are some advantages of group therapy?

Besides being less expensive than individual therapy, **group therapy** has other advantages. It gives the individual a sense of belonging and an opportunity to express feelings, get feedback from other members, and give and receive help and emotional support. Discovering that others share their problems leaves individuals feeling less alone and ashamed. Most of the therapies we have discussed can be used in a group setting; others are designed primarily for a group.

Psychodrama, originated by J.L. Moreno (1959) in the mid-1950s, is a technique whereby one client acts out a problem situation or relationship with the assistance and participation of the other group members. Sometimes the client plays the part of the person who is a problem—a technique called "role reversal." In doing so he or she may gain some understanding of the other person's feelings. When group members act out their own frustrations and role-play the frustrations of others, they often gain insight into the nature of their problems and troublesome relationships.

Group Help of a Different Sort

Some people seek help for their problems from sources other than mental health professionals, through encounter groups and self-help groups.

ENCOUNTER GROUPS: WHERE ANYTHING GOES **Encounter groups** claim to promote personal growth and self-knowledge and to improve personal relationships through intense emotional encounters with other group members. Groups are composed of 10 to 20 people who meet with a leader or leaders over a period of several weeks or months. Encounter group participants are urged to express their true feelings about themselves and others. Not all exchanges are oral. Relating to others physically (i.e., touching, hugging) is also encouraged.

Some studies indicate that about one-third of encounter group participants benefit from the experience, one-third are unaffected, and one-third are harmed (Lieberman et al., 1973).

SELF-HELP GROUPS: LET'S DO IT OURSELVES Self-help groups are not usually led by professional therapists. They are simply groups of people who share a common problem and meet to support one another.

One of the oldest and best-known self-help groups is Alcoholics Anonymous, which is believed to have 1.5 million members worldwide (Hurley, 1988). Other self-help groups, patterned after AA, have been formed to help individuals overcome many other addictive behaviours—for example, Overeaters Anonymous, Gamblers Anonymous, and Cocaine Anonymous. There are self-help groups for people with a variety of physical and mental illnesses, and groups to help people deal with crises, from divorce and bereavement to victimization.

Self-help groups offer comfort because people can talk about their problems with others who have "been there." They can exchange useful information, discuss their coping strategies, and gain hope by seeing

Remember It!

Interpersonal Therapies

1. Which depressed person would be *least* likely to be helped by interpersonal therapy (IPT)?
   a. Kirk, who is unable to accept the death of his wife
   b. Martha, who has been depressed since she was forced to retire
   c. Sharon, who was sexually abused by her father
   d. Tony, who feels isolated and alone because he has difficulty making friends
2. All of the following are true of group therapy *except* that it
   a. allows individuals to get feedback from other members.
   b. allows individuals to receive help and support from other members.
   c. is not conducted by trained therapists.
   d. is less expensive than individual therapy.
3. Self-help groups are generally ineffective, because they are not led by professionals. (true/false)

Answers: 1. c 2. c 3. false

people who are coping with the same problems successfully (Galanter, 1988). Lieberman (1986), after reviewing a number of studies of self-help groups, concluded that the results tend to be positive. For problems such as alcoholism and obesity, self-help groups are often as effective as psychotherapy (Zilbergeld, 1986).

Behaviour Therapy: Unlearning the Old, Learning the New

What is behaviour therapy?

Behaviour therapy is a treatment approach associated with the learning perspective on psychological disorders—the perspective that holds that abnormal behaviour is learned. According to the behaviourists, unless people are suffering from some physiological disorder, such as brain pathology, those who seek therapy need it for one of two reasons: (1) they have learned inappropriate or maladaptive responses, or (2) they have never had the opportunity to learn appropriate behaviour in the first place. Instead of viewing the maladaptive behaviour as a symptom of some underlying disorder, the behaviour therapist sees the behaviour itself as the disorder. Thus, if a person comes to a therapist with a fear of flying, that fear of flying is seen as the problem.

Behaviour therapy applies the principles of operant conditioning, classical conditioning, and/or observational learning to eliminate inappropriate or maladaptive behaviours and replace them with more adaptive responses. Sometimes this approach is referred to as **behaviour modification.** The goal is to change the troublesome behaviour, not to change the individual's personality structure or to search for the origin of the problem behaviour. "Behaviour therapy is educational rather than 'healing' " (Thorpe & Olson, 1990, p. 15). The therapist's role is active and directive.

LINK IT! 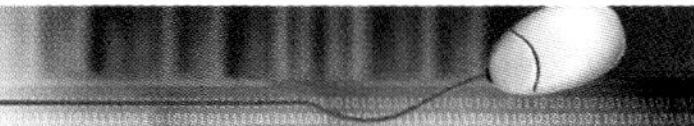

www.aabt.org
Association for Advancement of Behavior Therapy (AABT)

Behaviour Modification Techniques Based on Operant Conditioning

How do behaviour therapists modify behaviour using operant conditioning techniques?

Behaviour modification techniques based on operant conditioning seek to control the consequences of behaviour. Undesirable behaviour is eliminated by withholding or removing reinforcement for the behaviour. If children are showing off to get attention, behaviour therapists may recommend ignoring the behaviour. If children are whining or having temper tantrums to get their way, therapists will try to make sure that the whining and temper tantrums do not pay off. As you have learned, behaviour that is not reinforced will eventually stop.

Behaviour therapists also seek to reinforce desirable behaviour in order to increase its frequency; and they use reinforcement to shape entirely new behaviours. The process works best when it is applied consistently. Institutional settings such as hospitals, prisons, and school classrooms lend themselves well to these techniques, because they provide a restricted environment in which the consequences (or contingencies) of behaviour can be more tightly controlled.

group therapy: A form of therapy in which several clients (usually between seven and ten) meet regularly with one or two therapists to resolve personal problems.

psychodrama: A group therapy in which one group member acts out a personal problem situation or relationship, assisted by other members, to gain insight into the problem.

encounter group: An intense emotional group experience designed to promote personal growth and self-knowledge; participants are encouraged to let down their defences and relate honestly and openly with one another.

behaviour therapy: A treatment approach that employs the principles of operant conditioning, classical conditioning, and/or observational learning theory to eliminate inappropriate or maladaptive behaviours and replace them with more adaptive responses.

behaviour modification: The systematic application of learning principles to help a person eliminate undesirable behaviours and/or acquire more adaptive behaviours; sometimes the term is used interchangeably with "behaviour therapy."

Token Economies: What Would You Do for a Token?

Some institutions use behaviour modification programs called **token economies** that reward appropriate behaviour with poker chips, play money, gold stars, and the like. These can later be exchanged for desired goods (candy, gum, cigarettes) and/or privileges (weekend passes, free time, participation in desirable activities). For decades, mental hospitals have used token economies with chronic schizophrenics to improve self-care skills and social interaction, with good results (Ayllon & Azrin, 1965, 1968). Patients tend to perform chores when reinforced, and not to perform them when not reinforced. Symptoms of schizophrenia such as delusions and hallucinations, of course, are not affected.

Time Out: All Alone with No Reinforcers

Another effective method used to eliminate undesirable behaviour, especially in children and adolescents, is **time out** (Brantner & Doherty, 1983). The principle is simple. Children are told in advance that if they engage in certain undesirable behaviours, they will be removed calmly from the situation and will have to pass a period of time (usually no more than 15 minutes) in a place containing no reinforcers (no television, books, toys, friends, and so on). Theoretically, the undesirable behaviour will stop if it is no longer followed by attention or any other positive reinforcers.

Stimulus Satiation: Too Much of a Good Thing

Another behaviour modification technique, **stimulus satiation**, attempts to change problem behaviours by giving people too much of whatever they find reinforcing. The idea is that the reinforcer will lose its attraction and become something to be avoided.

The Effectiveness of Operant Approaches: Do They Work?

Behaviour therapies based on operant conditioning have been particularly effective in modifying some behaviours of seriously disturbed individuals (Ayllon & Azrin, 1968; Paul & Lentz, 1977). Although these techniques do not presume to cure severe psychological disorders, they can increase the frequency of desirable behaviours and decrease the frequency of undesirable ones.

Behaviour modification techniques can also be used to break bad habits such as smoking and overeating, or to develop good habits such as a regular exercise regime. If you want to modify any of your behaviours, devise a reward system for desirable behaviours, and remember the principles of shaping. Reward gradual changes in the direction of your ultimate goal. If you are trying to develop better eating habits, don't try to change a lifetime of bad habits all at once. Begin with a small step such as substituting frozen yogurt for ice cream. Set realistic and achievable weekly goals.

Therapies Based on Classical Conditioning

What behaviour therapies are based on classical conditioning?

Some behaviour therapies are based mainly on the principles of classical conditioning, which can account for how we acquire many of our emotional reactions. In classical conditioning, a neutral stimulus—some object, person, or situation that initially does not elicit any strong positive or negative emotional reaction—is paired with either a very positive or a very negative stimulus. After conditioning, our strong feeling toward the positive or negative stimulus transfers to the original, neutral stimulus.

Therapies based on classical conditioning can be used to rid people of fears and other undesirable behaviours. We will discuss four types of therapy based primarily on classical conditioning: systematic desensitization, flooding, exposure and response prevention, and aversion therapy.

Systematic Desensitization: Overcoming Fears One Step at a Time

How do therapists use systematic desensitization to rid people of fears?

Have you ever been both afraid and relaxed at the same time? Psychiatrist Joseph Wolpe (1958, 1973) came to the conclusion that these two responses are incompatible—that is, one inhibits the other. On the basis of this, he developed a therapy to treat fears and phobias, reasoning that if he could get you to relax and *stay* relaxed while you thought about a feared object, person, place, or situation, you could conquer your fear or phobia.

In Wolpe's therapy, **systematic desensitization**, clients are trained in deep muscle relaxation. Then they confront a hierarchy of anxiety-producing situations—either in real life or in their imagination—until they can remain relaxed even in the presence of the most feared situation. The therapy can be used for everything from fear of animals to acrophobia (fear of high places), claustrophobia (fear of enclosed places), test anxiety, and social and other situational fears.

What do you fear most? Many students would say that they fear speaking in front of a group. If that were your fear and you went to a behaviour therapist who used systematic desensitization, here is what she or he would have you do. First the therapist would ask you to identify the fear causing your anxiety and everything connected with it. Then all the aspects of the fear would be arranged in a hierarchy from least to most anxiety-producing.

After the hierarchy was prepared, you would be taught deep muscle relaxation—how to progressively relax parts of your body until you achieve a completely relaxed state. During the actual desensitization procedure, you would be asked to picture, as vividly as possible, the least fear-producing item on your hierarchy—for example, reading in the syllabus that the presentation will be assigned. Once you were able to remain relaxed while visualizing this item, the therapist would have you picture the next item—your professor assigning the oral presentation. This procedure would be followed until you were able to remain calm and relaxed while you vividly imagined the most fear-producing stimulus—actually making your presentation in class. If, during the desensitization process, anxiety crept in as you imagined items on the hierarchy, you would signal the therapist, who would instruct you to stop thinking about that item. You would then clear your mind, come back to a state of complete relaxation, and begin again. Try creating your own hierarchy in the next *Try It!*

How effective is systematic desensitization? Many experiments, demonstrations, and case reports confirm that it is highly successful in eliminating fears and phobias in a relatively short time (Kalish, 1981; Rachman & Wilson, 1980). It has proved effective for specific problems like test anxiety, stage fright, and anxiety related to sexual disorders such as impotence and frigidity.

Several other therapies used to treat phobias and obsessive-compulsive disorder use *exposure* as the key therapeutic element.

Try It!

Using Systematic Desensitization to Overcome Fear

Use what you have learned about systematic desensitization to create a step-by-step approach to help someone overcome a fear of making a class presentation. The person's hierarchy of fears begins with reading in the syllabus that an oral presentation will be assigned, and it culminates in actually making the oral presentation. Fill in the sequence of steps, according to a possible hierarchy of fears, that will lead to the final step. One possible solution appears here:

1. Being assigned the oral presentation and given a due date.
2. Preparing the oral presentation.
3. Practising the oral presentation one week before it is due.
4. Practising the oral presentation the night before it is due.
5. Waiting to give the presentation.
6. Walking to the front of the room to give the presentation.

token economy: A behavioural technique used to encourage desirable behaviours by reinforcing them with tokens that can be exchanged later for desired objects, activities, and/or privileges.

time out: A behavioural technique, used to decrease the frequency of undesirable behaviour, that involves withdrawing an individual from all reinforcement for a period of time.

stimulus satiation (say-she-A-shun): A behavioural technique in which a patient is given so much of a stimulus that it becomes something to avoid.

systematic desensitization: A behaviour therapy, used to treat phobias, that involves training clients in deep muscle relaxation and then having them confront a graduated series of anxiety-producing situations (real or imagined) until they can remain relaxed while confronting even the most feared situation.

Flooding: Confronting Our Fears All at Once

What is flooding?

Flooding is a behaviour therapy used in the treatment of phobias. Clients are exposed to the feared object or event (or asked to vividly imagine it) for an extended period until their anxiety decreases. Flooding is almost the opposite of systematic desensitization. The person is exposed to the fear all at once, not gradually and certainly not in a state of relaxation. A person with a fear of heights, for example, might have to go onto the roof of a tall building and remain there until the fear subsided.

The key to success is keeping the person in the feared situation long enough for it to become clear that none of the dreaded consequences actually come to pass (Marks, 1978). Flooding sessions typically last from 30 minutes to two hours and should not be terminated until patients are markedly less afraid than they were at the beginning of the session. It is rare for a patient to need more than six treatment sessions (Marshall & Segal, 1988).

Confronting the real object works faster and is more effective than simply imagining it, so this form of flooding should be used whenever possible (Chambless & Goldstein, 1979; Marks, 1972). Flooding may be quite painful for the patient. But flooding often works when other therapies have failed; and it works faster than other therapies, as you can see.

An acrophobic client wears a virtual-reality headset, which exposes him to the view from a high balcony (bottom) but allows him to experience moving toward or away from the railing. Such a realistic but safe exposure to the feared stimulus allows many people to overcome their phobias.

Exposure and Response Prevention: Cutting the Tie That Binds Fears and Rituals

How is exposure and response prevention used to treat people with obsessive-compulsive disorder?

Exposure and response prevention is a successful therapy for treating obsessive-compulsive disorder (Baer, 1996; Foa, 1995). The therapy consists of two components. The first involves *exposure*—patients are exposed to objects or situations they have been avoiding because they trigger obsessions and compulsive rituals. The second component is *response prevention*—patients agree to resist performing their compulsive rituals for progressively longer periods of time.

The therapist begins by identifying the thoughts, objects, or situations that trigger the compulsive ritual. For example, touching a doorknob, a piece of unwashed fruit, or garbage might ordinarily send people with a fear of contamination to the nearest bathroom to wash their hands. Patients are gradually exposed to stimuli that they find more and more distasteful and anxiety-provoking. They must agree not to perform the normal ritual (handwashing, bathing, or the like) for a specified period of time after exposure. Gradually, patients learn to tolerate the anxiety evoked by the various "contaminants." A typical treatment course—about 10 sessions over a period of three to seven weeks—can bring about considerable improvement in 60 to 70 percent of patients (Jenike, 1990).

Systematic desensitization, flooding, and exposure help people *stop* avoiding feared objects and situations. Even treatments using virtual reality as the means of exposure have been successful (Carlin et al., 1997). But what type of therapy exists to help people *start* avoiding situations? The answer: aversion therapy.

Aversion Therapy: Making Us Sick to Make Us Better

How does aversion therapy rid people of a harmful or undesirable behaviour?

Aversion therapy rids clients of a harmful or socially undesirable behaviour by pairing that behaviour with a painful, sickening, or otherwise aversive stimulus. Electric shock, emetics (which cause nausea and vomiting), and other unpleasant stimuli are paired with the undesirable behaviour time after time until a strong negative association is formed and the person comes to avoid that behaviour, habit, or substance. Treatment continues until the bad habit loses its appeal because it has become associated with pain or discomfort.

Alcoholics given a nausea-producing substance such as Antabuse (which reacts violently with alcohol) retch and vomit until their stomach is empty. Obviously the aversion therapist cannot show up at the alcoholic's house every morning with a bottle of Antabuse; however, nausea-based aversion therapy has produced abstinence rates of about 60 percent one year after treatment (Elkins, 1991; Parloff et al., 1986).

Therapies Based on Observational Learning: Just Watch This!

How does participant modelling help people overcome fears?

A great deal of what we learn in life, we learn from watching and then copying or imitating others. Much positive behaviour is learned this way; but so are bad habits, aggressive behaviours, and fears and phobias. Therapies derived from Albert Bandura's work on observational learning are based on the belief that people can overcome fears and acquire social skills through modelling.

For example, therapists have effectively treated fears and phobias by having clients watch a model (on film or in real life) responding to a feared situation in appropriate ways with no dreaded consequences. Usually the model approaches the feared object in gradual steps. Bandura (1967) describes how nursery school children lost their fear of dogs after watching a film showing a child who was not afraid of dogs first approaching a dog, then playing with it, petting it, and so on. Modelling films have been used to reduce the fears of children preparing for surgery (Melamed & Siegel, 1975) and to reduce children's fear of the dentist (Shaw & Thoresen, 1974).

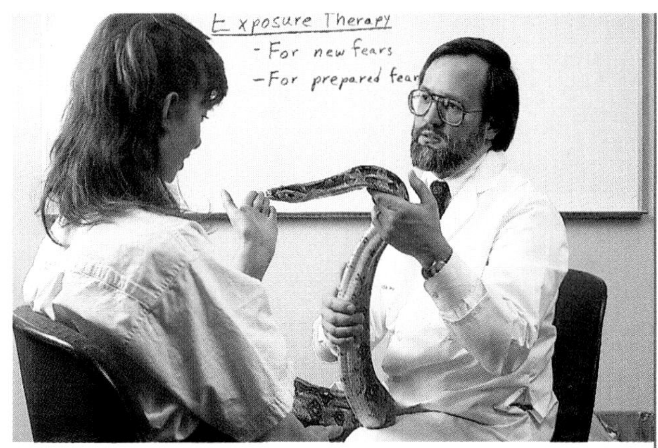

Most simple phobias, such as a fear of snakes, can be extinguished after only a few hours of modelling therapy with client participation.

The most effective type of therapy based upon observational learning is **participant modelling** (Bandura, 1977a; Bandura et al., 1975, 1977). Here the model demonstrates the appropriate response in graduated steps; the client attempts to imitate the model step by step while the therapist gives encouragement and support. The client benefits by being exposed to the feared stimulus.

flooding: A behavioural therapy used to treat phobias; clients are exposed to the feared object or event (or asked to imagine it vividly) for an extended period until their anxiety decreases.

exposure and response prevention: A behaviour therapy that exposes obsessive-compulsive disorder patients to stimuli generating increasing anxiety; patients must agree not to carry out their normal rituals for a specified period of time after exposure.

aversion therapy: A behaviour therapy used to rid clients of a harmful or socially undesirable behaviour by pairing it with a painful, sickening, or otherwise aversive stimulus until the behaviour becomes associated with pain and discomfort.

participant modelling: A behaviour therapy in which an appropriate response is modelled in graduated steps and the client attempts each step, encouraged and supported by the therapist.

Remember It!

Behaviour Therapy

1. Behaviour therapy techniques that try to change behaviour by reinforcing desirable behaviour and removing reinforcers for undesirable behaviour are based on
   a. operant conditioning.
   b. observational learning.
   c. classical conditioning.
   d. modelling.
2. Behaviour therapies based on classical conditioning are used mainly to
   a. shape new, more appropriate behaviours.
   b. rid people of fears and undesirable behaviours or habits.
   c. promote development of social skills.
   d. demonstrate appropriate behaviours.
3. Exposure and response prevention is a treatment for people with
   a. panic disorder.
   b. phobias.
   c. generalized anxiety disorder.
   d. obsessive-compulsive disorder.
4. Match the description with the therapy.

____ 1) flooding	a. practising deep muscle relaxation during gradual exposure to feared object
____ 2) aversion therapy	b. associating painful or sickening stimuli with undesirable behaviour
____ 3) systematic desensitization	c. being exposed directly to the feared object without relaxation
____ 4) participant modelling	d. imitating a model responding appropriately in the feared situation

Answers: 1. a 2. b 3. d 4. 1) c 2) b 3) a 4) d

Most specific phobias can be extinguished in only three or four hours of modelling therapy. Participant modelling is more effective than simple observation for some specific phobias (Bandura et al., 1969).

Cognitive Therapies: It's the Thought That Counts

We have seen that behaviour therapies based on classical and operant conditioning and modelling are effective in eliminating many types of troublesome behaviour. What if the problem is not an observable, undesirable behaviour but is rather in our thinking, attitudes, beliefs, or self-concept? There are therapies for these problems as well. **Cognitive therapies** assume that maladaptive behaviour can result from irrational thoughts, beliefs, and ideas, which the therapist tries to change. When cognitive therapy is combined with behavioural techniques such as relaxation training or exposure, it is called cognitive-behavioural therapy.

The emphasis in cognitive therapies is on conscious rather than unconscious processes, and on the present rather than the past. We will explore two types of cognitive therapy—rational-emotive therapy and Beck's cognitive therapy.

LINK IT!

iacp.asu.edu
International Association for Cognitive Psychotherapy Home Page

Rational-Emotive Therapy: Human Misery—The Legacy of False Beliefs

What is the aim of rational-emotive therapy?

Picture this scenario: Harry received two free tickets to a Saturday night concert featuring his favourite group. Excited and looking forward to a great time on Saturday, Harry called Sally, whom he had dated a couple of times, to ask her to share the evening with him. But she turned him down with some lame excuse like "I have to do my laundry." He was stunned and humiliated. "How could she do this to me?" he wondered. As the week dragged on, he became more and more depressed.

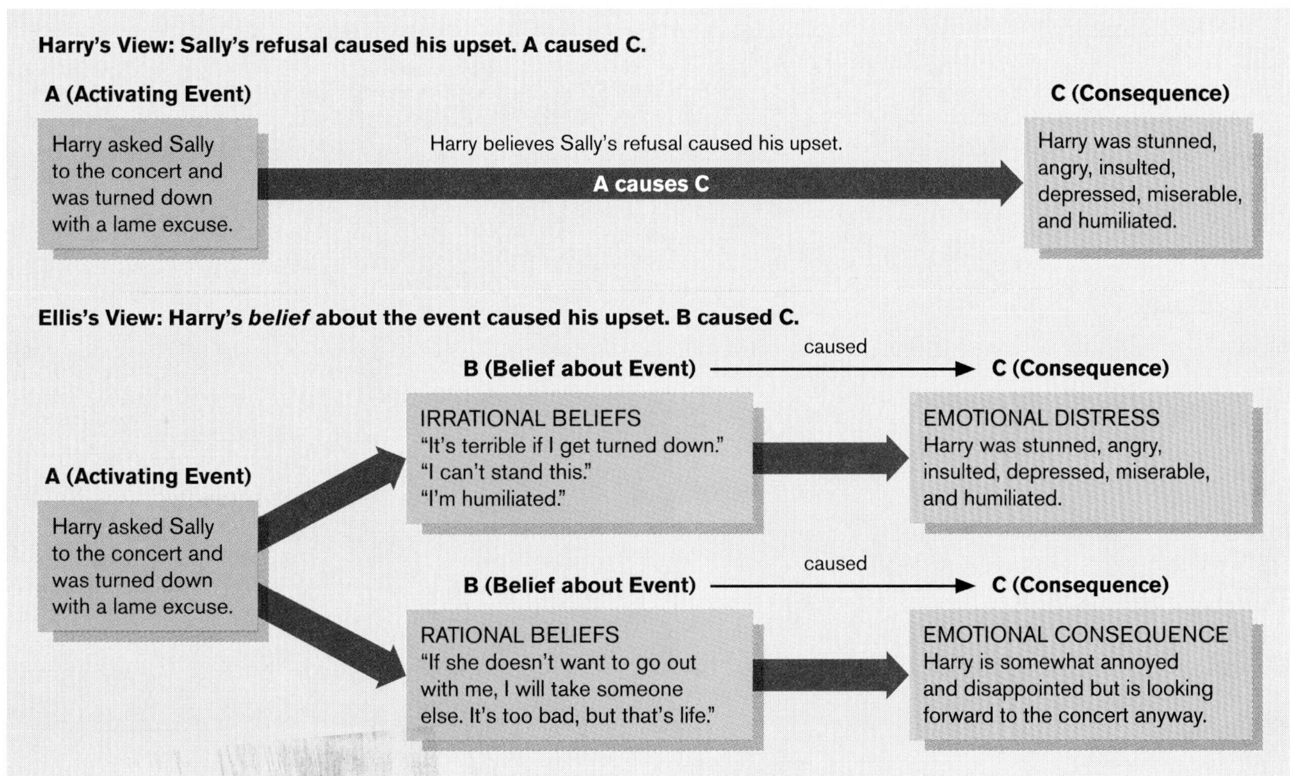
Harry's View: Sally's refusal caused his upset. A caused C.
A (Activating Event)
Harry asked Sally to the concert and was turned down with a lame excuse.
Harry believes Sally's refusal caused his upset.
A causes C
C (Consequence)
Harry was stunned, angry, insulted, depressed, miserable, and humiliated.
Ellis's View: Harry's *belief* about the event caused his upset. B caused C.
A (Activating Event)
Harry asked Sally to the concert and was turned down with a lame excuse.
B (Belief about Event)
caused
C (Consequence)
IRRATIONAL BELIEFS
"It's terrible if I get turned down."
"I can't stand this."
"I'm humiliated."
EMOTIONAL DISTRESS
Harry was stunned, angry, insulted, depressed, miserable, and humiliated.
B (Belief about Event)
caused
C (Consequence)
RATIONAL BELIEFS
"If she doesn't want to go out with me, I will take someone else. It's too bad, but that's life."
EMOTIONAL CONSEQUENCE
Harry is somewhat annoyed and disappointed but is looking forward to the concert anyway.

FIGURE 13.1

The ABCs of Albert Ellis's Rational-Emotive Therapy

Rational-emotive therapy teaches clients that it is not the activating event (A) that causes the upsetting consequences (C). Rather, it is the client's beliefs (B) about the activating event. Irrational beliefs cause emotional distress, according to Albert Ellis. Rational-emotive therapists help clients identify their irrational beliefs and replace them with rational ones.

What caused Harry's depression? Sally turning him down, right? Not according to Albert Ellis (1961, 1977, 1993), a clinical psychologist who developed **rational-emotive therapy** in the 1950s. Rational-emotive therapy is based on Ellis's ABC theory. A refers to the *activating* event, B to the person's *belief* about the event, and C to the emotional *consequence*. Ellis argues that it is not the event that causes the emotional consequence, but rather the person's belief about the event. In other words, A does not cause C; B causes C. If the belief is irrational, the emotional consequence can be extreme distress, as illustrated in Figure 13.1.

"Everyone should love me!" "I must be perfect!" Because reality does not conform to these and other irrational beliefs, people who hold them are doomed to frustration and unhappiness. Irrational beliefs cause people to view an undesirable event as a catastrophe rather than a disappointment or inconvenience; this leads them to say "I can't stand this," rather than "I don't like this." Irrational beliefs cause people to feel depressed, worthless, or enraged instead of simply disappointed or annoyed. To make matters worse, they go on to feel "anxious about their anxiety" and "depressed about their depression" (Ellis, 1987, p. 369).

Rational-emotive therapy is a directive, confrontational form of psychotherapy designed to challenge clients' irrational beliefs about themselves and

cognitive therapy: Any therapy designed to change maladaptive thoughts and behaviour, based on the assumption that maladaptive behaviour can result from one's irrational thoughts, beliefs, and ideas.

rational-emotive therapy: A directive, confrontational psychotherapy designed to challenge and modify the client's irrational beliefs, which are thought to cause their personal distress; developed by Albert Ellis.

others. As clients begin to replace irrational beliefs with rational ones, their emotional reactions become more appropriate, less distressing, and more likely to lead to constructive behaviour.

Try challenging an irrational belief of your own in the *Try It!*

Most clients in rational-emotive therapy are seen individually, once a week, for 5 to 50 sessions. In stark contrast to person-centred therapists (and most other therapists, for that matter), "rational-emotive therapists do not believe a warm relationship between counsellee and counsellor is a necessary or a sufficient condition for effective personality change" (Ellis, 1979, p. 186). In Ellis's view, "giving a client RET [rational-emotive therapy] with a good deal of warmth, approval and reassurance will tend to help this client 'feel better' rather than 'get better'" (p. 194).

One meta-analysis of 28 studies showed that patients receiving rational-emotive therapy did better than those receiving no treatment or a placebo, and about the same as those receiving systematic desensitization (Engles et al., 1993).

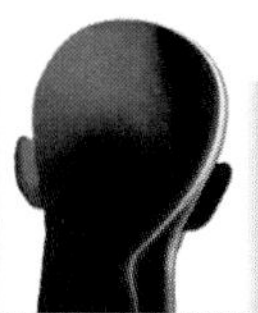

Try It!

Using Rational-Emotive Therapy

Use what you have learned about Albert Ellis's rational-emotive therapy to identify—and perhaps even eliminate—an irrational belief that *you* hold about yourself.

First, identify an irrational belief, preferably one that causes some stress in your life. For example, perhaps you feel that you must earn all A's in order to think of yourself as a good person.

Ask yourself the following questions, and write down your answers in as much detail as possible.

- Where does this belief come from? Can you identify the time in your life when it began?
- Why do you think this belief is true? What evidence can you provide that "proves" your belief?
- Can you think of any evidence to suggest that this belief is false? What evidence contradicts your belief? What people do you know who do not cling to this belief?
- How does holding this belief affect your life, both negatively and positively?
- How would your life be different if you stopped holding this belief? What would you do differently?

LINK IT!

rebt.org/index.html
Albert Ellis Institute

Beck's Cognitive Therapy: Overcoming "the Power of Negative Thinking"

How does Beck's cognitive therapy help people overcome depression and anxiety disorders?

"To be happy, I have to be successful in whatever I undertake."

"To be happy, I must be accepted (liked, admired) by all people at all times."

"If people disagree with me, it means they don't like me."

If you agree with all of these statements, you probably spend a good part of your time upset and unhappy. Psychiatrist Aaron T. Beck (1976) maintains that much of the misery of depressed and anxious people can be traced to **automatic thoughts**—unreasonable but unquestioned ideas that rule the person's life. Beck believes that depressed individuals hold "a negative view of the present, past, and future experiences" (1991, p. 369). They tend to view themselves as "deficient, defective, and/or undeserving"; their environment as "unduly demanding, depriving, and/or rejecting"; and their future as "without promise, value, or meaning" (Karasu, 1990a, p. 138). These people notice only negative, unpleasant things and

Aaron T. Beck

Remember It! Cognitive Therapies

1. Cognitive therapists believe that, for the most part, emotional disorders
   a. have physical causes.
   b. result from unconscious conflicts and motives.
   c. result from faulty and irrational thinking.
   d. result from environmental stimuli.
2. Rational-emotive therapy is a non-directive therapy that requires a warm, accepting therapist. (true/false)
3. The goal of Beck's cognitive therapy is best described as helping people
   a. develop effective coping strategies.
   b. replace automatic thoughts with more objective thoughts.
   c. develop an external locus of control.
   d. develop realistic goals and aspirations.
4. Beck's cognitive therapy has proved very successful in the treatment of
   a. depression and mania.
   b. schizophrenia.
   c. fears and phobias.
   d. anxiety disorders and depression.

Answers: 1. c 2. false 3. b 4. d

jump to upsetting conclusions. Anxious people expect the worst; they "catastrophize" and at the same time underestimate their ability to cope with situations.

The goal of **Beck's cognitive therapy** is to help patients stop their negative thoughts as they occur and replace them with more objective thoughts. The focus is on the present, not the past. No attempt is made to uncover hidden meanings in the patients' thoughts and responses. After challenging patients' irrational thoughts, the therapist sets up a plan and guides patients so that their own experience in the real world provides evidence to refute their false beliefs. Patients are given homework assignments, such as keeping track of automatic thoughts and the feelings evoked by them, and substituting more rational thoughts.

Beck's cognitive therapy is brief—usually only 10 to 20 sessions—and is therefore less expensive than many other types of therapy (Beck 1976). This therapy has been researched extensively and is reported to be highly successful in the treatment of mildly to moderately depressed patients (Antonuccio et al., 1995). There is some evidence that depressed people who have received Beck's cognitive therapy are less likely to relapse than those who have been treated with antidepressants (Scott, 1996).

Beck's cognitive therapy is also effective for generalized anxiety disorder (Beck, 1993), bulimia, and panic disorder (Barlow, 1997). An alternative to Beck's cognitive therapy was developed by University of Waterloo psychologist Donald Meichenbaum (1985). He proposed that individuals can be "inoculated" against negative events by being taught in advance to make positive and optimistic self-evaluations. In this way, the positive evaluations act as a buffer against negative experiences.

The Biological Therapies

What are the three main biological therapies?

Professionals who favour the biological perspective—the view that psychological disorders are symptoms of underlying physical disorders—usually favour a **biological therapy**. The three treatment categories in biological therapy are drug therapy, electroconvulsive therapy (ECT), and psychosurgery.

automatic thoughts: Unreasonable and unquestioned ideas that rule a person's life and lead to depression and anxiety.

Beck's cognitive therapy: A brief cognitive therapy for depression and anxiety, designed to help people recognize their automatic thoughts and replace them with more objective thoughts.

biological therapy: A therapy that is based on the assumption that most mental disorders have physical causes and that attempts to change or influence the biological mechanism involved (e.g., through drug therapy, ECT, or psychosurgery).

IT HAPPENED IN CANADA

Deinstitutionalization

In the 1960s, most psychiatric patients were placed in a hospital–usually a large psychiatric institution where they often resided for many years. Nowadays, however, many people who suffer from psychiatric problems are placed, as outpatients, in a group home, which is a semi-independent living arrangement; sometimes they may even be allowed to live completely on their own. This change is largely the result of *deinstitutionalization,* the effort by governments and health authorities to find alternatives to placing people in psychiatric institutions for long periods.

Thirty years ago there were almost 48 000 beds in Canadian psychiatric hospitals, whereas today there are fewer than 15 000. The move toward deinstitutionalization of psychiatric patients has, to a large extent, been made possible by our increased understanding of psychobiology, which has fundamentally changed the treatment of people diagnosed with psychiatric disorders. As we describe in this chapter, some psychiatric disorders can be regulated reasonably well with antipsychotic medications.

Many unresolved issues still remain regarding deinstitutionalization and the use of antipsychotic medications. For instance, antipsychotic drugs can have many side effects. In addition, psychiatric patients often feel they are "cured" and stop taking their medication. And too often, psychiatric patients find themselves without resources, out of work, and wandering the streets.

Clearly then, other forms of treatment, such as the many types of therapeutic interventions described in this chapter, can help psychiatric patients deal with the day-to-day pressures of their lives.

Drug Therapy: Pills for Psychological Ills

The favourite and by far the most frequently used biological treatment is drug therapy. A major breakthrough in drug therapy came in the mid-1950s, when antipsychotic drugs—sometimes called the major tranquilizers—began to be used to treat schizophrenia. In the late 1950s, antidepressants were discovered. Finally, in 1970, lithium, the miracle drug for bipolar disorder, was introduced into psychiatry (Snyder, 1984). Modern drug therapy is now capable of relieving the debilitating symptoms of schizophrenia, depression, bipolar disorder, and some anxiety disorders. This has had a tremendous impact on the treatment of psychological disorders.

Antipsychotic Drugs

How do antipsychotic drugs help schizophrenic patients?

Antipsychotic drugs, or *neuroleptics,* are prescribed mainly for schizophrenia to control severe psychotic symptoms, such as hallucinations, delusions, and other disorders in thinking. They are also effective in reducing restlessness, agitation, and excitement. You may have heard of these drugs under some of their brand names—Thorazine, Stelazine, Compazine, and Mellaril. These drugs apparently work by inhibiting the activity of the neurotransmitter dopamine. About 50 percent of patients have a good response to these drugs (Kane, 1996). However, even those patients who are helped by antipsychotics often stop taking them because of their very unpleasant side effects: causing restless pacing and fidgeting, muscle spasms and cramps, and a shuffling gait. Long-term use of antipsychotic drugs carries a high risk of the most severe side effect, *tardive dyskinesia.* Tardive dyskinesia involves almost continual twitching and jerking movements of the face and tongue, and squirming movements of the hands and trunk (Glazer et al., 1993).

Several newer "atypical" neuroleptics, such as asclozapine, help patients who have not benefitted from standard neuroleptics (Rosenheck et al., 1997). These drugs affect certain dopamine receptors differently than the standard neuroleptics, and they block serotonin receptors. Although it has fewer side effects it can cause a fatal blood defect for 1 to 2 percent of patients.

New drugs risperidone and olanzapine produce no fatalities and have fewer side effects than the standard antipsychotics (Casey, 1996). Risperidone is much more effective than the other antipsychotics in treating the negative symptoms of schizophrenia—apathy, emotional unresponsiveness, and social withdrawal (Marder, 1996).

While antipsychotic drugs help two-thirds of patients, they do not cure schizophrenia (Wolkin et al., 1989). Rather, they reduce and control many of the major symptoms so that patients can function. Most patients must continue to take them to keep the symptoms under control (Schooler et al., 1997).

Antidepressant Drugs

For what conditions are antidepressants prescribed?

Antidepressants work well as mood elevators for people who are severely depressed. They have also been helpful in the treatment of certain anxiety disorders.

Imbalances in the neurotransmitters serotonin and norepinephrine often accompany symptoms of depression. The *tricyclic antidepressants* (e.g., amitriptyline and imiprine, known as Elavil and Tofranil) are the drug treatment of first choice for major depression (Perry, 1996); they are effective for more than 60 percent of depressed patients (Karasu, 1990b). Tricyclics, however, can have some unpleasant side effects—sedation, dizziness, nervousness, fatigue, dry mouth, forgetfulness, and weight gain (Frazer, 1997). According to Noyes and colleagues, progressive weight gain—an average of more than 8.5 kilograms—is the main reason people stop taking tricyclics, in spite of the relief from distressing psychological symptoms (Noyes et al., 1989).

SEROTONIN-SELECTIVE REUPTAKE INHIBITORS (SSRIS)

Some more recently developed antidepressants, including Prozac, Zoloft, Paxil, and Anafranil, block the reuptake of serotonin, increasing its effect at the synapses (Goodwin, 1996). Prozac is one of the most widely used and is effective for less severe depression, (Avenoso, 1997; Nelson, 1991). It is also effective in the treatment of obsessive-compulsive disorder, which has been associated with a serotonin imbalance (Rapoport, 1989). Similar outcomes have been obtained with Zoloft and Paxil. In general, SSRIs have fewer side effects (Nelson, 1997) and are safer in overdose than tricyclics (Thase & Kupfer, 1996).

MONOAMINE OXIDASE INHIBITORS (MAO INHIBITORS)

Another line of treatment for depression is the monoamine oxidase inhibitors. By blocking the action of an enzyme that breaks down norepinephrine and serotonin in the synapses, MAO inhibitors increase the availability of norepinephrine and serotonin.

These drugs (e.g., Nardil and Marplan) are usually prescribed for depressed patients who do not respond to other antidepressants (Thase et al., 1992). They are also effective in treating panic disorder (Sheehan & Raj, 1988) and social phobia (Marshall et al., 1994). But MAO inhibitors have many of the same unpleasant side effects as tricyclic antidepressants, and patients taking MAO inhibitors must avoid certain foods or run the risk of stroke.

Lithium: A Natural Salt That Evens Moods

How does lithium help patients with bipolar disorder?

Lithium, a naturally occurring salt, is considered a wonder drug for 40 to 50 percent of patients with bipolar disorder (Thase & Kupfer, 1996). It is said to begin to calm the manic state within five to ten days. This is a noteworthy accomplishment, in that the average episode, if untreated, lasts between three and four months. The proper maintenance dose of lithium will usually even out the moods of the patient and reduce the number and severity of episodes of both mania and depression (Prien et al., 1984; Teuting et al., 1981). Patients who discontinue lithium are 6.3 times more likely to have a recurrence (Suppes et al., 1991). Careful and continuous monitoring of lithium levels in the patient's system is absolutely necessary to guard against lithium poisoning and permanent damage to the nervous system (Schou, 1989).

The Minor Tranquilizers

The minor tranquilizers known as *benzodiazepines* include Valium, Librium, and Xanax. Used primarily to treat anxiety, "benzodiazepines are the most widely prescribed class of psychoactive drugs in current therapeutic use" (Medina et al., 1993, p. 1; see also Famighetti, 1997).

Xanax is effective in treating panic disorder and works faster and has fewer side effects than antidepressants (Noyes et al., 1996). But there is a downside to Xanax: many patients, after they are panic-free, experience moderate to severe withdrawal symptoms, including severe anxiety, if they stop taking the drug (Otto et al., 1993).

Some Problems with Drug Therapy

What are some of the problems with drug therapy?

So far, one might conclude that drug therapy is the simplest and possibly the most effective way of treating schizophrenia, depression, panic disorder, and obsessive-compulsive disorder. There are, how-

antipsychotic drugs: Drugs used to control severe psychotic symptoms, such as the delusions and hallucinations of schizophrenics; also known as neuroleptics or major tranquilizers.

antidepressants: Drugs that are prescribed to treat depression and some anxiety disorders.

ever, a number of potential problems with the use of drugs. Antipsychotics and antidepressants have side effects that can be so unpleasant that many patients stop treatment before they have a reduction in symptoms.

Antipsychotics, antidepressants, and lithium do not cure psychological disorders, so patients usually experience a relapse if they stop taking the drugs when their symptoms lift. Maintenance doses of antidepressants following a major depression reduce the probability of recurrences (Prien & Kocsis, 1995). Maintenance doses are usually required with anxiety disorders as well, otherwise symptoms are likely to return (Ramussen et al., 1993).

The main problem with antidepressants is that they are relatively slow-acting. In addition, more often than not, depressed patients have to try several different antidepressants before finding one that is effective. A severely depressed patient needs at least two to six weeks to obtain relief, and 30 percent don't respond at all. This poses a risk for suicidal patients. If suicide is a danger, antidepressant drugs are not the treatment of choice.

Electroconvulsive Therapy: The Controversy Continues

For what purpose is electroconvulsive therapy (ECT) used, and what is its major side effect?

Electroconvulsive therapy (ECT), or electric shock, was widely used as a treatment for several mental disorders until the introduction of the antipsychotic and antidepressant drugs in the 1950s. ECT developed a bad reputation, partly because it was misused and overused in this country in the 1940s and 1950s. Often it was misused simply to make troublesome patients easier to handle. Some patients received hundreds of shock treatments. Today, electroconvulsive therapy is used mainly as a treatment for severe depression (Coryell, 1998). ECT has been found to result in marked improvement or remission in 80 percent of manic patients who have not been helped by lithium (Fink, 1997).

If you were to have electroconvulsive therapy, what could you expect? One or two electrodes would be placed on your head, and a mild electric current would be passed through your brain for one or two seconds. Immediately after the shock was administered, you would lose consciousness and experience a seizure lasting between 30 and 60 seconds. Apparently the seizure is necessary if ECT is to have any effect. The complete ECT procedure takes about five minutes. Medical complications following the procedure are said to be rare (Abrams, 1988). Usually there is no pain associated with the treatment, and patients have no memory of the experience when they wake up.

Although ECT can cut depression short, it is not a cure. Experts think that the seizure temporarily changes the biochemical balance in the brain, which in turn results in a lifting of depression.

The Side Effects of ECT

Some psychiatrists and neurologists have spoken out and written books and articles against the use of ECT, arguing that the procedure causes pervasive brain damage and memory loss (Breggin, 1979; Friedberg, 1976, 1977; Grimm, 1976). But advocates of ECT say that claims of brain damage are based on animal studies in which dosages of ECT were much higher than those now used in human patients (Devanand et al., 1994). No structural brain damage as a result of ECT has been revealed in studies in which MRI or CT scans were compared before and after a series of treatments (Devanand et al. 1994).

Even advocates of ECT acknowledge that there are side effects, the most disturbing of which is memory loss. The memory loss appears to result from a temporary disruption of memory consolidation that, in most cases, lasts for only a few weeks. Some patients have a spotty memory loss of events that happened before ECT (Sackeim et al., 1993; Squire, 1986). In a few patients the memory loss may last longer than six months (Sackeim, 1992).

A survey by the U.S. National Institute of Mental Health (1985) found that most psychiatrists believe that a legitimate place exists for ECT in the treatment of severely depressed patients who are suicidal or who have not been helped by any other therapy. In Canada, several position papers have been presented to the Canadian Psychiatric Association supporting the selective use of ECT. Psychologists Murray Enns and Jeffrey Reiss (1992) at the University of Manitoba reviewed the pros and cons of the procedure and also concluded that when used properly, ECT is a safe and effective treatment.

Remember It!

Biological Therapies

1. For the most part, advocates of biological therapies assume that psychological disorders have a physical cause. (true/false)
2. Match the disorder with the drug most often used for its treatment.

____ 1)	panic disorder and agoraphobia	a.	lithium
____ 2)	schizophrenia	b.	antipsychotic
____ 3)	bipolar disorder	c.	antidepressant
____ 4)	depression		
____ 5)	obsessive-compulsive disorder		

3. Medication that relieves the symptoms of schizophrenia is thought to work by blocking the action of
   a. serotonin.
   b. dopamine.
   c. norepinephrine.
   d. epinephrine.
4. Which of the following statements concerning drug therapy for psychological disorders is false?
   a. It is often difficult to determine the proper dose.
   b. Drugs often have unpleasant side effects.
   c. Patients often relapse if they stop taking the drugs.
   d. Drugs are usually not very effective.
5. For which disorder is ECT typically used?
   a. severe depression
   b. schizophrenia
   c. anxiety disorders
   d. panic disorder
6. The major side effect of ECT is tardive dyskinesia. (true/false)
7. Psychosurgery techniques are now so precise that the exact effects of the surgery can be predicted in advance. (true/false)

Answers: 1. true 2. 1) c 2) b 3) a 4) c 5) c 3. b 4. d 5. a 6. false 7. false

Psychosurgery: Cutting to Cure

What is psychosurgery, and for what problems is it used?

An even more drastic procedure than ECT is **psychosurgery**—brain surgery performed strictly to alleviate serious psychological disorders, such as severe depression, severe anxiety, or obsessions, or to provide relief in some cases of unbearable chronic pain. Psychosurgery is not the same as brain surgery performed to correct a physical problem, such as a tumour or blood clot.

The first such surgical procedure for human patients was developed by Portuguese neurologist Egas Moniz in 1935 to treat severe phobias, anxiety, and obsessions. In his technique, the **lobotomy**, surgeons severed the frontal lobes and the deeper brain centres involved in emotion. No brain tissue was removed. At first the procedure was considered a tremendous contribution, and it won for Moniz the Nobel Prize in Medicine in 1949. Not everyone considered it a contribution, however: one of Moniz's lobotomized patients curtailed the surgeon's activities by shooting him in the spine, leaving him paralyzed on one side.

Neurosurgeons performed tens of thousands of frontal lobotomies throughout the world from 1935 until 1955. Although the surgery was effective in calming many patients, it often left them in a severely deteriorated condition. Apathy, impaired intellect, loss of motivation, and a change in personality kept many from resuming a normal life.

In the mid-1950s, when antipsychotic drugs came into use, psychosurgery virtually stopped. Since that time there has been a "second wave" of psychosurgical procedures; these are far less drastic than the lobotomies of decades past. In some of the most modern procedures, electric currents are delivered through

electroconvulsive therapy (ECT): A treatment in which an electric current is passed though the brain, causing a seizure; usually reserved for the severely depressed who are either suicidal or unresponsive to other treatment.

psychosurgery: Brain surgery to treat some severe, persistent, and debilitating psychological disorder or severe chronic pain.

lobotomy: A psychosurgery technique in which the nerve fibres connecting the frontal lobes to the deeper brain centres are severed.

electrodes to destroy a much smaller, more localized area of brain tissue. This results in less intellectual impairment than in conventional surgery. In one procedure, called a *cingulotomy,* electrodes are used to destroy the cingulum, a small bundle of nerves connecting the cortex to the emotion centres of the brain. The cingulotomy has been helpful in some extreme cases of obsessive-compulsive disorder (Greist, 1992; Jenike et al., 1991). For recent Canadian work in this area, read about Paul Derry in *On the Cutting Edge in Canada* in Chapter 2.

Even today, the results of psychosurgery are still not predictable and, for better or for worse, the consequences are irreversible. For this reason, psychosurgery is considered a treatment of absolutely last resort.

Therapies and Therapists: Many Choices

Evaluating the Therapies: Do They Work?

How effective is psychotherapy? Several researchers have attempted to determine whether therapy helps and which therapies are most effective. Most studies suggest that the average person who receives therapy is better off than those who do not (Lipsey & Wilson, 1993; Smith et al., 1980).

It also appears that the different types of therapy—behavioural, psychodynamic, and cognitive—are more or less equally effective. Moreover, neither the length of treatment nor the therapist's years of

REVIEW & REFLECT 13.1
Summary and Comparison of Major Approaches to Therapy

Type of Therapy	Perceived Cause of Disorder	Goals of Therapy	Methods Used	Primary Disorders Treated
Psychoanalysis	Unconscious sexual and aggressive urges or conflicts; fixations; weak ego.	Help patient bring disturbing, repressed material to consciousness and work through unconscious conflicts; strengthen ego functions.	Psychoanalyst analyzes and interprets dreams, free associations, resistances, and transference.	General feelings of unhappiness; unresolved problems from childhood.
Person-centred	Blocking of normal tendency toward self-actualization; incongruence between real and desired self; overdependence on positive regard of others.	Increase self-acceptance and self-understanding; help patient become more inner-directed; increase congruence between real and desired self; enhance personal growth.	Therapist shows empathy, unconditional positive regard, and reflects client's expressed feelings back to client.	General feelings of unhappiness; interpersonal genuineness, and problems.
Behaviour	Learning of maladaptive behaviours or failure to learn appropriate behaviours.	Extinguish maladaptive behaviours and replace with more adaptive ones; help patient acquire needed social skills.	Therapist uses methods based on classical and operant conditioning and modelling, which include systematic desensitization, flooding, exposure and response prevention, aversion therapy, and reinforcement.	Fears, phobias, panic disorder, obsessive-compulsive disorder, bad habits.
Cognitive	Irrational and negative assumptions and ideas about self and others.	Change faulty, irrational, and/or negative thinking.	Therapist helps client identify irrational and negative thinking and substitute rational thinking.	Depression, anxiety, panic disorder; general feelings of unhappiness.
Biological	Underlying physical disorder caused by structural or biochemical abnormality in the brain; genetic inheritance.	Eliminate or control biological cause of abnormal behaviour; restore balance of neurotransmitters.	Physician prescribes drugs such as antipsychotics, antidepressants, lithium, or tranquilizers; ECT, psychosurgery.	Schizophrenia, depression, bipolar disorder, anxiety disorders.

experience appeared to be related to the effectiveness of treatment (Smith et al., 1980).

These findings have led some researchers to suggest that it may be the strength of the relationship between the therapist and the patient that accounts for the effectiveness of treatment, rather than the specific techniques of the various therapies (Blatt et al., 1996; Krupnick et al., 1996). Perhaps the elements that are *common* to virtually all therapies (the patient–therapist relationship, "acceptance and support of the patient," "the opportunity to express emotions," and so on), rather than the ones that are different, account for success (Altshuler 1989, p. 311).

Read Review & Reflect 13.1, which summarizes the five major approaches to therapy.

Mental Health Professionals: How Do They Differ?

What different types of mental health professionals conduct psychotherapy?

Who are mental health professionals, and for what problems are their services most appropriate?

For serious psychological disorders, a clinical psychologist or psychiatrist is the best source of help. A **clinical psychologist**, who usually has a Ph.D. in clinical psychology, specializes in assessing, treating, and/or researching psychological problems and behavioural disturbances. Clinical psychologists use various types of psychotherapy to treat a variety of psychological disorders and adjustment problems.

A **psychiatrist** is a medical doctor with a specialty in the diagnosis and treatment of mental disorders. Psychiatrists can prescribe drugs and other biological treatments; many also provide psychotherapy. A **psychoanalyst** is usually (not always) a psychiatrist with specialized training in psychoanalysis from a psychoanalytic institute.

For clients with other psychological problems (such as substance abuse, marital or family problems, and adjustment disorders), the choice of mental health professionals widens. A *counselling psychologist* usually has a doctorate in clinical or counselling psychology, or a doctor of education degree with a major in counselling. A *counsellor* typically has a master's degree in psychology or counsellor education. Often employed by colleges and universities, counselling psychologists and counsellors help students with personal problems and/or test or counsel them in academic or vocational areas. A *psychiatric social worker* usually has a master's degree in social work with specialized training in psychiatric problems, and may practise psychotherapy. Read *Apply It!* to learn how to go about selecting a therapist.

Therapy and Race, Ethnicity, and Gender

Why is it important to consider multicultural variables in the therapeutic setting?

There is a growing awareness that psychotherapists need to consider multicultural variables such as race, ethnicity, and gender in diagnosing and treating psychological disorders (Bernal & Castro, 1994; Heilbron & Guttman, 2000; Hogan & Barlow, 2000). According to Kleinman and Cohen (1997), people experience and suffer from biological and psychological disorders within a cultural context in which the meaning of symptoms, outcomes, and responses to therapy may differ dramatically. When the cultures of the therapist and patient differ markedly, behaviour that is normal for the patient can be misinterpreted as abnormal by the therapist (Lewis-Fernandez & Kleinman, 1994). Cultural values, social class, and non-verbal communication (gestures, facial expressions) that differ across cultures can all hinder effective counselling (Sue, 1994). Race has also been associated with differential treatment, as has gender (Strakowski et al., 1995; Yonkers & Hamilton, 1995). Canadian awareness of these issues can be seen through the integration of culturally familiar forms of therapy. For an example, see the work on healing circles in *On The Cutting Edge in Canada*.

clinical psychologist: A psychologist, usually with a Ph.D., whose training is in the diagnosis, treatment, or research of psychological and behavioural disorders.

psychiatrist: A medical doctor with a specialty in the diagnosis and treatment of mental disorders.

psychoanalyst (SY-ko-AN-ul-ist): A professional, usually a psychiatrist, with special training in psychoanalysis.

on the cutting edge in canada

"Culture is Healing"

In most cases, alcohol and substance abuse can be "cured" with the right kind of support. For aboriginal people, the success rate with typical approaches has been very low. Rod McCormick, at the University of British Columbia, has conducted ongoing research with aboriginal populations that suggests that aboriginal people feel reluctant to acknowledge the need for therapy and, if they become involved in therapy, they often drop out early because typical Euro-Western treatments are not sensitive to their cultural values.

Although there are considerable differences among aboriginal groups, they share some similar beliefs about health and illness. These beliefs integrate the individual within the broader, family, community, and spiritual network. Within the aboriginal worldview, healing and spirituality are integrated, not separated. Mainstream approaches focus primarily on the individual, without addressing the broader context. McCormick, among others, has recently advocated for the re-introduction of traditional healing practices to facilitate reconnection to cultural values and traditions and to treat aboriginal clients within familiar contexts (McCormick, 2000). Review of outcomes where traditional healing practices have been introduced suggests that traditional healing circles and healing practices are desired (Wyrostock & Paulston, 2000) and successful (McCormick, 1997, 2000). As McCormick points out, for aboriginal people, connection to "culture is treatment" (2000, p. 30).

Remember It!

Selecting Therapies and Therapists

1. What is true regarding the effectiveness of therapies?
   a. All are equally effective for any disorder.
   b. Specific therapies have proved effective in treating particular disorders.
   c. Insight therapies are consistently best.
   d. Therapy is no more effective than no treatment for emotional and behavioural disorders.
2. One must have a medical degree to become a
   a. clinical psychologist.
   b. psychoanalyst.
   c. psychiatrist.
   d. clinical psychologist, psychiatrist, or psychoanalyst.
3. Match the problem with the most appropriate therapy.

____ 1) eliminating fears, bad habits
____ 2) schizophrenia
____ 3) general unhappiness, interpersonal problems
____ 4) severe depression

a. behaviour therapy
b. insight therapy
c. drug therapy

Answers: 1. b 2. c 3. 1) a 2) c 3) b 4) c

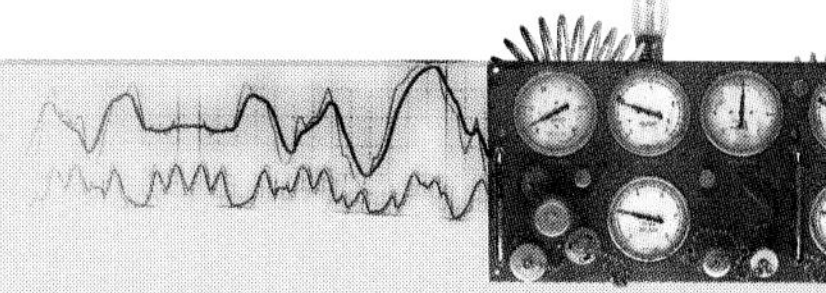

Finding a Therapist

Apply It!

People are often embarrassed to seek professional help or are afraid that friends and relatives will think less of them if they do. Sometimes they are afraid of the therapy itself, or afraid that seeking help means there is something fundamentally wrong with them. There is no reason for such feelings. Going to a psychotherapist when you are feeling anxious or depressed is no different from going to a doctor when you are feeling sick. If you have a problem that has made you unhappy for a significant length of time, you should seek help—especially if you feel overwhelmed by your problem and your friends or relatives have suggested that you seek help.

There are times when you need the help of a trained professional. That person may be a psychiatrist, psychologist, social worker, or mental health counsellor.

Just as you wouldn't select a doctor or lawyer at random, you shouldn't just go to any therapist who happens to be nearby. Professional training and academic credentials are important, but they do not guarantee that you will receive high-quality treatment. A good place to start your search for a therapist is to ask family members, friends, your doctor, or your psychology professor for recommendations. Another place to look is the psychology department or counselling centre at your school or the psychiatry department of a local hospital or medical school. Also, many cities have community mental health centres and human service agencies that can provide recommendations. In addition, some companies have employee-assistance programs that offer counselling to employees or will refer them to an appropriate therapist.

In considering a particular therapist, you should ask about his or her educational background, supervised experience, types of therapy practised, length of treatment, and fees. The therapist must be professionally trained to listen in a supportive fashion and help you understand and interpret your thoughts and feelings. Bear in mind that in Canada there are no restrictions on the use of the title "therapist." People who call themselves therapists may not actually be qualified to provide the kind of therapy you need. You can usually find out about a therapist's credentials simply by asking. If you want to check further, you can contact the local branch of the Mental Health Association, which will be listed in the white pages of the phone book.

Take your time when choosing a therapist. A "good" therapist is one who is able to create an atmosphere of acceptance and empathy. Because the relationship between client and therapist is an extremely important ingredient of successful therapy, it is essential to have a therapist whom you trust. The first step is to arrange for a brief consultation. If, during that initial interview, you find that you do not feel comfortable with the therapist, you should say so. Usually the therapist will be willing to recommend someone else.

Private therapists receive fees for their services that are comparable to those received by doctors, dentists, and other professionals. Some health insurance plans cover those fees; others do not. If you have insurance that covers psychotherapy, check to make sure your policy covers the type of therapy you will be receiving. Also note any restrictions contained in the policy, such as limits on the number of sessions allowed.

Group therapy tends to be less expensive than individual therapy because the cost is shared among several people. You can also receive free or less expensive therapy at public facilities such as community mental health centres. These are usually supported by tax revenues. The services of a student counselling centre are usually provided free or at a low cost.

You may be concerned about confidentiality, but you need not be. Confidentiality is fundamental to the client–therapist relationship. However, there are some limits that should be explained to you in your first interview with the therapist.

Of course, what we said earlier about taking your time when choosing a therapist doesn't apply in a crisis. In such situations it is essential to get help immediately. In most communities you can call a hotline and receive counselling at any time, day or night. If the crisis is non-violent in nature, you can call a mental health centre or go to a hospital emergency room. If the crisis is more urgent—for example, if a friend is threatening to commit suicide—call the police.

KEY TERMS

antidepressants, p. 431
antipsychotic drugs, p. 430
automatic thoughts, p. 428
aversion therapy, p. 425
Beck's cognitive therapy, p. 429
behaviour modification, p. 421
behaviour therapy, p. 421
biological therapy, p. 429
clinical psychologist, p. 435
cognitive therapy, p. 426
directive therapy, p. 417
electroconvulsive therapy (ECT), p. 432
encounter group, p. 420
existential therapy, p. 417
exposure and response prevention, p. 424
family therapy, p. 419
flooding, p. 424
free association, p. 415
Gestalt therapy, p. 417
group therapy, p. 420
insight therapy, p. 414
interpersonal therapy (IPT), p. 418
lobotomy, p. 433
non-directive therapy, p. 417
participant modelling, p. 425
person-centred therapy, p. 416
psychiatrist, p. 435
psychoanalysis, p. 415
psychoanalyst, p. 435
psychodrama, p. 420
psychosurgery, p. 433
psychotherapy, p. 414
rational-emotive therapy, p. 427
resistance, p. 415
self-actualization, p. 416
stimulus satiation, p. 422
systematic desensitization, p. 423
time out, p. 422
token economy, p. 422
transference, p. 416
unconditional positive regard, p. 417

THINKING CRITICALLY

Evaluation

In your opinion, what are the major strengths and weaknesses of the following approaches to therapy: psychoanalysis, person-centred therapy, behaviour therapy, cognitive therapy, and drug therapy?

Point/Counterpoint

From what you have learned in this chapter, prepare a strong argument to support each of these positions:

a. Psychotherapy is generally superior to drug therapy in the treatment of psychological disorders.
b. Drug therapy is generally superior to psychotherapy in the treatment of psychological disorders.

Psychology in Your Life

What questions would you ask a therapist before beginning treatment?

SUMMARY & REVIEW

Insight Therapies

What are the four basic techniques of psychoanalysis, and how are they used to help disturbed patients?

The four basic techniques of psychoanalysis–free association, analysis of resistance, dream analysis, and analysis of transference–are used to uncover the repressed memories, impulses, and conflicts presumed to cause the patient's problems.

What is the role of the therapist in person-centred therapy?

Person-centred therapy is a non-directive therapy in which the therapist provides an atmosphere of unconditional positive regard. Clients are free to be themselves so that their natural tendency toward positive growth will be released.

What is the major emphasis in Gestalt therapy?

Gestalt therapy emphasizes the importance of clients' fully experiencing, in the present moment, their feelings, thoughts, and actions, and taking personal responsibility for their behaviour.

What four problems commonly associated with major depression is interpersonal therapy designed to treat?

Interpersonal therapy (IPT) is designed to help depressed patients cope with severe responses to the death of a loved one, interpersonal role disputes, difficulties in adjusting to role transitions, and deficits in interpersonal skills.

What are some advantages of group therapy?

Group therapy is less expensive than individual therapy and gives people an opportunity to express feelings and get feedback from other members, and to give and receive help and emotional support.

Behaviour Therapy: Unlearning the Old, Learning the New

What is behaviour therapy?

Behaviour therapy is a treatment approach that employs the principles of operant conditioning, classical conditioning, and/or observational learning theory to replace inappropriate or maladaptive behaviours with more adaptive responses.

How do behaviour therapists modify behaviour using operant conditioning techniques?

Operant conditioning techniques involve the withholding of reinforcement to eliminate undesirable behaviours, as in time out, or the use of reinforcement to shape or increase the frequency of desirable behaviours, as in token economies.

What behaviour therapies are based on classical conditioning?

Behaviour therapies based on classical conditioning are systematic desensitization, flooding, exposure and response prevention, and aversion therapy.

How do therapists use systematic desensitization to rid people of fears?

Therapists using systematic desensitization train clients in deep muscle relaxation and then have them confront a series of graduated anxiety-producing situations, either real or imagined, until they can remain relaxed in the presence of even the most feared situation.

What is flooding?

With flooding, clients are exposed to the feared object or event or asked to imagine it vividly for an extended period until their anxiety decreases and they realize that none of the dreaded consequences come to pass.

How is exposure and response prevention used to treat people with obsessive-compulsive disorder?

In exposure and response prevention, people with obsessive-compulsive disorder are exposed to the anxiety-generating stimuli but gradually increase the time before they begin their compulsive rituals. Thus, they learn to tolerate their anxiety.

How does aversion therapy rid people of a harmful or undesirable behaviour?

Aversion therapy pairs the unwanted behaviour with an aversive stimulus until the bad habit becomes associated with pain or discomfort.

How does participant modelling help people overcome fears?

In participant modelling, an appropriate response is modelled in graduated steps and the client is asked to imitate each step with the encouragement and support of the therapist.

Cognitive Therapies: It's the Thought That Counts

What is the aim of rational-emotive therapy?

Rational-emotive therapy is a directive form of therapy designed to challenge and modify the client's irrational beliefs, which are believed to cause personal distress.

How does Beck's cognitive therapy help people overcome depression and anxiety disorders?

Beck's cognitive therapy helps people overcome depression and anxiety disorders by pointing out irrational thoughts that are causing them misery and by helping them learn other, more realistic ways of looking at themselves and their experience.

The Biological Therapies

What are the three main biological therapies?

The three main biological therapies are drug therapy, ECT, and psychosurgery.

How do antipsychotic drugs help schizophrenic patients?

Antipsychotic drugs control the major symptoms of schizophrenia by inhibiting the activity of dopamine.

For what conditions are antidepressants prescribed?

Antidepressants are prescribed for depression, generalized anxiety disorder, panic disorder, agoraphobia, and obsessive-compulsive disorder.

How does lithium help patients with bipolar disorder?

Lithium is used to control the symptoms in a manic episode and to even out the mood swings in bipolar disorder.

What are some of the problems with drug therapy?

Some problems are the sometimes unpleasant or dangerous side effects, the difficulty in establishing the proper dosages, and the fact that a relapse is likely if the drug therapy is discontinued.

For what purpose is electroconvulsive therapy (ECT) used, and what is its major side effect?

ECT is a treatment of last resort for people with severe depression; it is most often reserved for those who are in imminent danger of committing suicide. Its major side effect is some memory loss.

What is psychosurgery, and for what problems is it used?

Psychosurgery is brain surgery performed strictly to relieve some severe, persistent, and debilitating psychological disorder; it is considered experimental and highly controversial.

Therapies and Therapists: Many Choices

What different types of mental health professionals conduct psychotherapy?

Professionals trained to conduct psychotherapy fall into the following categories: clinical psychologists, counselling psychologists, counsellors, psychiatrists, psychoanalysts, and psychiatric social workers.

Why is it important to consider multicultural variables in the therapeutic setting?

Multicultural variables such as race, ethnicity, and gender have a profound influence on patients' responses to the therapy and the therapist and on therapists' responses to patients.

14 Social Psychology

Do you remember your first day in high school? How worried were you about the way you dressed, how cool you looked, and whether you fitted in? You may have experienced the same concerns when you started college or university or when you dated someone for the first time. The concerns that we all experience when faced with new events are often associated with our fears of violating a norm—doing something that seems inappropriate under the circumstances. Let's think about some other norms that you might have violated either by accident or on purpose. For instance, have you ever showed up in a costume at a Halloween party only to find out that it was not a costumed event? Have you ever dyed your hair blue or orange just to see your parents' reaction? Do you have any tattoos or piercings? Why? Because you like them? Because they make you look (or feel) different and cool? There is no easy explanation for why we choose to abide by norms or decide to violate them. But when we do violate a norm, we can experience a range of emotions, from satisfaction to humiliation. The "receiver," or person witnessing such a violation, can

also respond in a number of ways—with approval, anger, ostracism, or indifference.

One person who has experienced all of these responses is Gwen Jacob. In 1991, in Guelph, Ontario, Gwen Jacob was charged with indecency after walking topless in a public area on a hot day. This single event became the focus of attention of an entire province. It led to a court ruling that the requirement that women be covered is a gender-based inequality. As a result, women in Ontario, like their male counterparts, can choose to be topless or covered in public places. On the basis of a single act or norm violation based on a perception that rules were not fair, the norms of a province were rewritten.

The circumstances surrounding Gwen Jacob's decision to go topless and the subsequent court ruling should not be minimized. Whether or not we agree with Jacob's decision and that of the court, these events reflect some of our society's norms and stereotypes, roles and expectations. All of us are clearly affected by the norms of our community, but do they affect us all to the same extent? Do they influence our perceptions of ourselves and of others? We will explore this and other questions in our study of social psychology.

Social psychology is the area of study that attempts to explain how the actual, imagined, or implied presence of others influences the thoughts, feelings, and behaviour of individuals. No human being lives in a vacuum. How we think about, respond to, and interact with other people provides the scientific territory that social psychology explores. Research in social psychology yields some surprising and provocative explanations about human behaviour, from the atrocious to the altruistic.

In this chapter, we will first explore social perception—how we form impressions of other people, and how we try to understand why they behave as they do. Then we will consider the factors involved in attraction. What draws us to other people, and how do friendships and romantic relationships develop? We will look at factors influencing conformity and obedience, and we will examine groups and their influence on performance and decision making. We will also discuss attitudes and learn how they can be changed, and we will explore prejudice and discrimination. Finally, we will look at the conditions under which people are likely to help each other (prosocial behaviour) and hurt each other (aggression).

LINK IT!

www.wesleyan.edu/spn
Social Psychology Network

Social Perception

We spend a significant portion of our lives in contact with other people. Not only do we form impressions of others, but we also attempt to understand why they behave as they do.

Impression Formation: Sizing Up the Other Person

Why are first impressions so important and enduring?

When we meet people for the first time, we start forming impressions of them right away. And, of course, they are busy forming impressions of us. Naturally we notice the obvious attributes first—gender, ethnicity, age, dress, and physical attractiveness. The latter, as shallow as it may seem, has a definite impact on our first impressions. Beyond noticing physical appearance, we may wonder: What is her occupation? Is he married? Answers to our questions, combined with a conscious or unconscious assessment of the person's verbal and non-verbal behaviour, all play a part in forming a first impression. Our own moods also play a part—when we are happy, our impressions of others are usually more positive than when we are unhappy (Forgas & Bower, 1987). First impressions are powerful and can colour many of the later impressions we form about people.

A number of studies reveal that our overall impression or judgment of another person is influenced more by the first information we receive than by later information (Asch, 1946; Luchins, 1957; Park, 1986). This phenomenon is called the **primacy effect**. It seems that we attend to initial information more carefully, and once an impression is formed, it provides the framework through which we interpret later information. Any information that is consistent with the first impression is likely to be accepted, thus strengthening the impression. Information that does not fit with the earlier information is more likely to be disregarded. As you will read later in this chapter, people's tendency to minimize cognitive efforts, to use thinking strategies that are easy and fast, plays an important role in the way we evaluate others and in all social interactions (Fiske & Taylor, 1991).

Remember that any time you list your personal traits or qualities, always list your most positive ones first. It pays to put your best foot forward—first.

What first impression have you formed of the person shown here?

Expectations: Seeing What We Expect to See

Sometimes our expectations become a self-fulfilling prophecy and actually influence the way other people act. Expectations may be based on a person's gender, age, racial or ethnic group, social class, role or occupation, personality traits, past behaviour, relationship with us, and so on. Once formed, our expectations affect how we perceive the behaviour of others—what we pay attention to and what we ignore. Rarely do we consider that our own expectations may colour our attitude and manner toward other people—that we ourselves partly bring about the very behaviour we expect (Jones, 1986; Miller & Turnbull, 1986).

Attribution: Our Explanation of Behaviour

What is the difference between a situational attribution and a dispositional attribution for a specific behaviour?

How often do you ask yourself why people (ourselves included) do the things they do? When trying to explain behaviour, we make **attributions**—that is, we assign or attribute causes to explain the behaviour of others and to explain our own behaviour as well. We are particularly interested in the causes when behaviours are unexpected, when goals are not attained (Weiner, 1985), and when actions are not socially desirable (Jones & Davis, 1965).

Although we can actually observe behaviour, we usually can only infer its cause or causes. Whenever we try to determine why we or someone else behaved in a certain way, we can make two types of attributions. In some instances we make a **situational attri-**

social psychology: The study of the way in which the actual, imagined, or implied presence of others influences the thoughts, feelings, and behaviour of individuals.

primacy effect: The likelihood that an overall impression or judgment of another will be influenced more by the first information received about that person than by information that comes later.

attribution: An inference about the cause of our own or another's behaviour.

situational attribution: Attribution of a behaviour to some external cause or factor operating in the situation; an external attribution.

bution (an external attribution) and attribute the behaviour to some external cause or factor operating within the situation. After failing an exam, we might say, "The test was unfair" or "The professor didn't teach the material well." Or we might make a **dispositional attribution** (an internal attribution) and attribute the behaviour to some internal cause such as a personal trait, motive, or attitude. Thus, we might attribute a poor grade to our own lack of ability or to a poor memory.

Attributional Biases: Different Attributions for Ourselves and Others

How do the kinds of attributions we tend to make about ourselves differ from those we make about other people?

A basic difference exists in how we make attributions for our own behaviour and that of others—a phenomenon called the **actor–observer bias** (Jones, 1976, 1990; Jones & Nisbett, 1971). We tend to use situational attributions to explain our own behaviour, because we are aware of factors in the situation that influenced us to act the way we did. In addition, being aware of our past behaviour, we know whether our present actions are typical or atypical.

In explaining the behaviour of others, we focus more on the personal factors than on the factors within the situation (Gilbert & Malone, 1995; Leyens et al., 1996). Not knowing how a person has behaved in different situations in the past, we assume a consistency in his or her behaviour. Thus, we are likely to attribute the behaviour of the individual to some personal quality. The tendency to overemphasize internal factors and underemphasize situational factors when we explain other people's behaviour is so fundamental, so commonplace, that it has been named the **fundamental attribution error** (Ross, 1977).

There is one striking inconsistency in the way we view our own behaviour—the self-serving bias. We use the **self-serving bias** when we attribute our successes to internal or dispositional causes and blame our failures on external or situational causes (Baumgardner et al., 1986; Brown & Rogers, 1991; Miller & Ross, 1975). If we interview for a job and get it, it is probably because we have the right qualifications. If someone else gets the job, it is probably because he or she knew the right people. The self-serving bias allows us to take credit for our successes and to shift the blame for our failures to the situation. In some ways the self-serving bias can be adap-

Remember It!

Social Perception

1. Which of the following statements about first impressions is false?
   a. We usually pay closer attention to early information than to later information we receive about a person.
   b. Early information forms a framework through which other information is interpreted.
   c. First impressions often serve as self-fulfilling prophecies.
   d. The importance of first impressions is greatly overrated.
2. We tend to make __________ attributions to explain our own behaviour and __________ attributions to explain the behaviour of others.
   a. situational; situational
   b. situational; dispositional
   c. dispositional; situational
   d. dispositional; dispositional
3. The tendency of people to overemphasize dispositional causes and underemphasize situational causes when they explain the behaviour of others is called the
   a. fundamental attribution error.
   b. false consensus error.
   c. self-serving bias.
   d. actor-observer bias.
4. The tendency of people to emphasize situational explanations for their own behaviours but dispositional attributions for the behaviours of others is called the
   a. fundamental attribution error.
   b. false consensus error.
   c. self-serving bias.
   d. actor–observer bias.
5. Attributing Mike's poor grade to his lack of ability is a dispositional attribution. (true/false)

Answers: 1. d 2. b 3. a 4. d 5. true

tive: it helps protect our self-esteem and positive self-identity (Schlenker et al., 1990; Tesser, 1988) both of which are associated with well-being (Taylor & Brown, 1988).

Attraction

Think for a moment about the people you consider to be your closest friends. What causes you to like or even love one person yet ignore or react negatively to someone else? What factors influence interpersonal attraction—the degree to which we are drawn to or like one another?

Factors Influencing Attraction

Proximity: Close to You

Why is proximity an important factor in attraction?

One major factor influencing our choice of friends is physical **proximity**, or geographic closeness. If you live in an apartment complex, you are probably more friendly with people who live next door or only a few doors away (Festinger et al., 1950). The same is true in a dormitory (Priest & Sawyer, 1967). What about the people you like best in your classes? Do they sit next to you or not more than a seat or two away?

It is much easier to make friends or even fall in love with people who are close at hand. One possible explanation for this is that mere exposure to people, objects, and circumstances probably increases our liking for them (Zajonc, 1968). The **mere-exposure effect** refers to our tendency to feel more positive toward stimuli with repeated exposure. People, food, songs, and styles become more acceptable the more we are exposed to them. Advertisers rely on the positive effects of repeated exposure to increase our liking for products, trends, and even political candidates.

There are exceptions to the mere-exposure effect, however. If our initial reaction to a person is highly negative, frequent exposure can make us feel even more negative toward the person (Swap, 1977).

Reciprocal Liking: Liking Those Who Like Us

We tend to like people who like us—or who we believe like us. Curtis and Miller (1968) falsely led research participants to believe that another person either liked or disliked them after an initial encounter. This false information became a self-fulfilling prophecy. When the participants met the person again, those who believed they were liked "self-disclosed more, disagreed less, expressed dissimilarity less, and had a more positive tone of voice and general attitude than subjects who believed they were disliked" (p. 284). These positive behaviours, in turn, actually caused the other person to view them positively.

Attractiveness: Good Looks Attract

How important is physical attractiveness in attraction?

Although people are quick to deny that mere physical appearance is the main factor that attracts them to someone initially, a substantial body of evidence indicates that it is. People of all ages have a strong tendency to prefer physically attractive people (Dion, 1973, 1979; Feingold, 1992).

What constitutes physical beauty? Researchers Langlois and Roggman (1990) found that physical beauty consists not of rare physical qualities but of facial features that are more or less the average of the features in a given general population. Studies show, for instance, that symmetrical faces and bodies are seen as more attractive and sexually appealing (Singh, 1995; Thornhill & Gangestad, 1994). Judgments of physical attractiveness seem to have some definite consistency across cultures, especially for men. A study by Cunningham and others (1995) found that

dispositional attribution: Attribution of one's own or another's behaviour to some internal cause such as a personal trait, motive, or attitude; an internal attribution.

actor–observer bias: The tendency of observers to make dispositional attributions for the behaviours of others but situational attributions for their own behaviours.

fundamental attribution error: The tendency to overemphasize internal factors and underemphasize situational ones when explaining other people's behaviour.

self-serving bias: Our tendency to attribute our successes to dispositional causes, and our failures to situational causes.

proximity: Geographic closeness; a major factor in attraction.

mere-exposure effect: The tendency of people to develop a more positive evaluation of some person, object, or other stimulus with repeated exposure to it.

Native Asians, Hispanics, and black and white North American men reported a high level of agreement in rating the attractiveness of women's faces of different cultures. Whether this level of agreement is associated with similar views of beauty across cultures or the influence of the media on our perceptions of beauty is still debated.

Why is physical attractiveness so important? When people have one trait or quality that we either admire or dislike very much, we often assume that they also have other admirable or negative traits—a phenomenon known as the **halo effect** (Nisbett & Wilson, 1977; Thorndike, 1920). Dion and colleagues (1972) at the University of Toronto found that people generally attribute other favourable qualities to those who are attractive. Attractive people are seen as more exciting, personable, interesting, and socially desirable than unattractive people.

Feingold (1992) conducted several large studies that shed more light on the relationship between physical attractiveness and certain personality characteristics and social behaviours. One such study confirmed that positive characteristics are indeed attributed to physically attractive people.

Feingold also discovered a positive correlation between a person's *self-rated* physical attractiveness and many other attributes—self-esteem, popularity with the opposite sex, social comfort, extraversion, mental health, and sexual experience. In other words, if we believe we are physically attractive, others will be more likely to perceive us as attractive.

The halo effect–the attribution of other favourable qualities to those who are attractive–helps explain why physical attractiveness is so important.

Other than believing we are physically attractive, what else can we do to increase our attractiveness to others? Try smiling more. A study by Reis and colleagues (1990) revealed that smiling increases our perceived attractiveness among others and makes us appear more sincere, sociable, and competent.

Eagly and colleagues (1991) analyzed 76 studies of the physical attractiveness stereotype. They found that physical attractiveness has its greatest impact on judgments of popularity and sociability and less impact on judgments of adjustment and intellectual competence. They did find one negative, however: attractive people are perceived as more vain and less modest.

Other research suggests that job interviewers are more likely to recommend highly attractive people (Dipboye et al., 1975), and that attractive people have their written work evaluated more favourably (Landy & Sigall, 1974). Even the evaluation of the attractiveness of a person's voice is affected by the person's physical appearance (Zuckerman et al., 1991).

Being attractive is an advantage to children and adults, and to males and females. According to some studies, women's looks contribute more to how they are judged on other personal qualities than is the case with men (Bar-Tal & Saxe, 1976; Feingold, 1990). Not surprisingly, physical attractiveness seems to have its greatest impact in the context of romantic attraction, particularly in initial encounters (Hatfield & Sprecher, 1986; Feingold, 1988).

Does this mean that unattractive people don't have a chance? Fortunately not. Eagly and her colleagues (1991) suggest that the impact of physical attractiveness is strongest in the perception of strangers. But once we get to know people, other qualities assume more importance. In fact, as we come to like people, they begin to look more attractive to us, while people with undesirable personal qualities begin to look less attractive.

Similarity: A Strong Basis of Attraction

Are people, as a rule, more attracted to those who are opposite or to those who are similar to them?

To sum up research on attraction, the saying that "birds of a feather flock together" is more accurate than "opposites attract." Beginning in elementary school, people are more likely to pick friends of the same age, gender, ethnic background, and socioeconomic class. These sociological variables continue to influence the choice of friends through college or university and later in life. Of course, choosing friends who are similar to us could be related to proximity—that is, to the fact that we tend to come into contact with people who are more similar to us in a variety of ways.

For both sexes, liking people who have similar attitudes begins early in childhood and continues throughout life (Griffitt et al., 1972). We are likely to choose friends and lovers who have similar views on most things that are important to us. Similar interests and attitudes toward leisure activities make it more likely that time spent together is rewarding. Not only is similarity in attitudes an important ingredient in attraction (Newcomb, 1956), but people often have negative feelings toward others whose attitudes differ from their own (Byrne et al., 1986; Rosenbaum, 1986; Smeaton et al., 1989). People who share our attitudes validate our judgments; those who disagree with us suggest that we may be wrong and arouse negative feelings in us. It is similarities, then, not differences, that usually stimulate liking and loving (Alicke & Largo, 1995). But recent studies suggest that attitude similarity plays a more important role in attraction than attitude dissimilarity does in preventing it (Drigotas, 1993; Tan & Singh, 1995).

Romantic Attraction

The Matching Hypothesis

> Moderately attractive, unskilled, unemployed, 50-year-old divorced man with 7 children seeks beautiful, wealthy, exciting woman between ages 20 and 30 for companionship, romance, and possible marriage. No smokers or drinkers.

Can you imagine reading this ad in the personals column of your newspaper? Somehow, we all recognize that this "match" is not reasonable. Even though most of us may be attracted to beautiful people, the **matching hypothesis** suggests that we are more likely to end up with someone similar to ourselves in attractiveness and other assets (Berscheid et al., 1971; Feingold, 1988; Walster & Walster, 1969). Furthermore, couples mismatched in attractiveness are more likely to end the relationship (Cash & Janda, 1984).

It has been suggested that most people estimate their social assets and realistically expect to attract someone with more or less equal assets. In terms of physical attractiveness, some people might consider a current movie idol or supermodel to be the ideal man or woman, but they do not seriously consider the ideal to be a realistic, attainable possibility. Fear of rejection keeps many people from pursuing those who are much more attractive than they are.

Does the same process apply to same-sex friendships? In general, yes (Cash & Derlega, 1978), although this is more true of males (Feingold, 1988). A person's perceived attractiveness seems to be affected by the attractiveness of his or her friends (Geiselman et al., 1984).

Mate Selection: The Mating Game

In 1958 Robert Winch proposed that men and women tend to choose mates whose needs and personalities complement their own. Winch saw complementary needs not necessarily as opposite, but as needs that supply what the partner lacks. A talkative person might seek a quiet mate who prefers to listen. Although there is some research to support this view (Dryer & Horowitz, 1997), the weight of research suggests that *similarity* in needs leads to attraction (Buss, 1984; Phillips et al., 1988). Similarities in personality, as well as in "physical characteristics, cognitive abilities, age, education, religion, ethnic background, attitudes and opinions, and socioeconomic status," play a role in marital choice (O'Leary & Smith 1991, p. 196) and seem to be related to marital success. Similarities wear well.

If you were to select a marital partner, what qualities would attract you? Do the next *Try It!* to evaluate your own preferences.

halo effect: The tendency to infer generally positive or negative traits in a person as a result of observing one major positive or negative trait.

matching hypothesis: The notion that people tend to have spouses, lovers, or friends who are about equal in social assets such as physical attractiveness.

Try It!

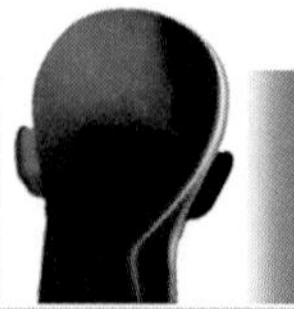

What Qualities Are You Looking for in a Mate?

In your choice of a mate, which qualities are most and least important to you? Rank these 18 qualities of a potential mate from most important (1) to least important (18) to you.

___ Ambition and industriousness
___ Chastity (no previous sexual intercourse)
___ Desire for home and children
___ Education and intelligence
___ Emotional stability and maturity
___ Favourable social status or rating
___ Good cooking and housekeeping skills
___ Similar political background
___ Similar religious background
___ Good health
___ Good looks
___ Similar education
___ Pleasing disposition
___ Refinement/neatness
___ Sociability
___ Good financial prospects
___ Dependable character
___ Mutual attraction/love

How do your selections compare with those of men and women from 33 countries and five major islands around the world? Generally, men and women across cultures agree on the first four values in mate selection: (1) mutual attraction/love, (2) dependable character, (3) emotional stability and maturity, and (4) pleasing disposition (Buss et al., 1990). Beyond these first four, however, they differ somewhat in the attributes they prefer. According to Buss (1994), "Men prefer to mate with beautiful young women, whereas women prefer to mate with men who have resources and social status" (p. 239). These preferences, he believes, have been adaptive in human evolutionary history (Buss & Kenrick, 1998). Others, however, see this as a simple reflection of men's greater economic power in our society (Carporael, 1989; Howard et al., 1987).

Conformity, Obedience, and Compliance

Conformity: Going Along with the Group

Whether we like it or not, we all conform to some norms. The real question is: To what do we conform? **Conformity** involves changing or adopting a behaviour or an attitude in order to be consistent with the norms of a group or the expectations of other people. **Norms** are the standards of behaviour and the attitudes that are expected of members of the group. Some conformity is necessary if we are to have a society at all. We cannot drive on either side of the street as we please, or park anywhere we want, or drive as fast as we choose. Norms are in place to create a predictable and stable environment.

We need other people, so we must conform to their expectations to some extent. It is easy to see why people conform to norms and standards of groups that are important to them, such as the family, the peer group, the social group, and the sports team. But to an amazing degree, people also conform to the majority opinion, even when they are among strangers.

Asch's Experiment: The Classic on Conformity

What did Asch find in his famous experiment on conformity?

The best-known experiment on conformity was conducted by Solomon Asch (1951, 1955), who designed the simple test shown in Figure 14.1. Look at the standard line at the top. Then pick the line—1, 2, or 3—that is the same length. Did you pick line 2? Can you imagine any circumstances in which you might tell the experimenter that either line 1 or line 3 matched the standard line? You could be surprised by your own behaviour if people around you insisted that the wrong line—say, line 3—was of the same length as the standard line. And many participants were, in Asch's classic experiment, even when the tests were so simple that they otherwise picked the correct line more than 99 percent of the time.

Remember It!

Attraction

1. Physical attractiveness is a very important factor in initial attraction. (true/false)
2. People are usually drawn to those who are more opposite than similar to themselves. (true/false)
3. Match the term at the right with the description at the left.
   ____ 1) Brian sees Susan at the library often and begins to like her.
   ____ 2) Liane assumes that because Boyd is handsome, he must be popular and sociable.
   ____ 3) Alan and Carol are going together and are both very attractive.

   a. matching hypothesis
   b. halo effect
   c. mere-exposure effect

Answers: 1. true 2. false 3. 1) c 2) b 3) a

Eight males were seated around a large table and were asked, one by one, to tell the experimenter which of the three lines matched the standard line as in Figure 14.1. Only one of the eight was an actual participant; the others were confederates assisting the experimenter. There were 18 trials—18 different lines to be matched. During 12 of these trials, the confederates all gave the same wrong answer, which of course puzzled the naive participant. Would the participant continue to believe his eyes and select the correct line, or would he feel pressure to conform to the group's selection and give the wrong answer himself?

Asch found that 5 percent of the participants conformed to the incorrect, unanimous majority *all* of the time; 70 percent conformed *some* of the time; and 25 percent remained completely independent and were *never* swayed by the group.

In this scene from Asch's experiment on conformity, all but one of the "participants" were really confederates of the experimenter. They deliberately chose the wrong line to try to influence the naive subject (second from right) to go along with the majority.

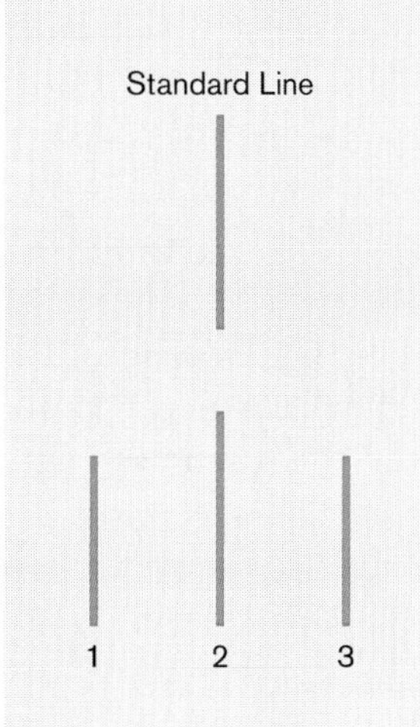

FIGURE 14.1
Asch's Classic Study of Conformity **If you were one of eight participants in the Asch experiment who were asked to pick the line (1, 2, or 3) that matched the standard line, which line would you choose? If the other participants all chose line 3, would you conform and answer line 3? (Based on Asch, 1955.)**

conformity: Changing or adopting an attitude or behaviour to be consistent with the norms of a group or the expectations of others.

norms: The attitudes and standards of behaviour expected of members of a particular group.

Asch wondered how group size would influence conformity. Varying the experiment with groups of two, three, four, eight, and ten to fifteen, he found that the tendency to "go along" with the majority opinion was in full force even when the unanimous majority consisted of only three confederates. Surprisingly, unanimous majorities of 15 produced no higher conformity rates than did those of three. Asch also found that if just one other person voiced a dissenting opinion, the tendency to conform was not as strong. When just one confederate in the group disagreed with the incorrect majority, the naive participants' errors dropped drastically, from 32 percent to 10.4 percent.

Other research on conformity reveals that people of low status are more likely to conform than those of high status (Eagly, 1987); but, contrary to the conventional wisdom, women are no more likely to conform than men (Eagly & Carli, 1981). And conformity is even greater if the sources of influence are perceived as belonging to one's own group (Abrams et al., 1990).

According to Wood and others (1994), those who hold minority opinions on an issue have more influence in changing a majority view if they present a well-organized, clearly stated argument. And minorities who are especially consistent in advocating their views are more influential.

Obedience: Following Orders

Some obedience is necessary if society is to function; however, unquestioned obedience can bring people to commit unbelievably horrible acts. In one of the darkest chapters in human history, officials in Nazi Germany obeyed Hitler's orders to exterminate six million Jews and other "undesirables." The civilized world was stunned and sickened by their actions, and nearly everyone wondered how human beings could be capable of committing such atrocities. Stanley Milgram, a young researcher at Yale University in the 1960s, designed a study to investigate how far ordinary citizens would go to obey orders.

The Milgram Study: The Classic on Obedience

What did Milgram find in his classic study of obedience?

In the 1960s this advertisement appeared in newspapers in New Haven, Connecticut, and in other communities near Yale:

> **Wanted:** Volunteers to serve as subjects in a study of memory and learning at Yale University.

Many people responded to the ad, and 40 males between the ages of 20 and 50 were selected, among them "postal clerks, high school teachers, salesmen, engineers, and laborers" (Milgram, 1963, p. 372). But no experiment on memory and learning was to take place. Instead, Milgram planned a staged drama. Imagine that you are one of the naive participants selected for the experiment.

The researcher actually wants to know how far you will go in obeying orders to administer what you believe are increasingly painful electric shocks to a "learner" who misses questions on a test. The cast of characters is as follows:

> **The experimenter:** A 31-year-old high school biology teacher dressed in a grey laboratory coat who assumes a stern and serious manner.
>
> **The learner:** A pleasant, heavyset accountant about 50 years of age (an accomplice of the experimenter).
>
> **The teacher:** You—the only naive member of the cast.

The experimenter leads you and the learner into one room. The learner is then strapped into an electric-chair apparatus. You, the teacher, are given a sample shock of 45 volts, which stings you and is supposedly for the purpose of testing the equipment and showing you what the learner will feel. The learner complains of a heart condition and says that he hopes the electric shocks will not be too painful. The experimenter admits that the stronger shocks will hurt but hastens to add, "Although the shocks can be extremely painful, they cause no permanent tissue damage" (p. 373).

Then the experimenter takes you to an adjoining room, out of sight of the learner. The experimenter seats you in front of an instrument panel (shown in the photograph on the left), on which 30 lever switches are set horizontally. The first switch on the left, you are told, delivers only 15 volts, but each successive switch is 15 volts stronger than the last—30 volts, 45 volts, and so on up to the last switch, which carries 450 volts. The instrument panel has verbal designations ranging from "Slight Shock" to "Danger: Severe Shock."

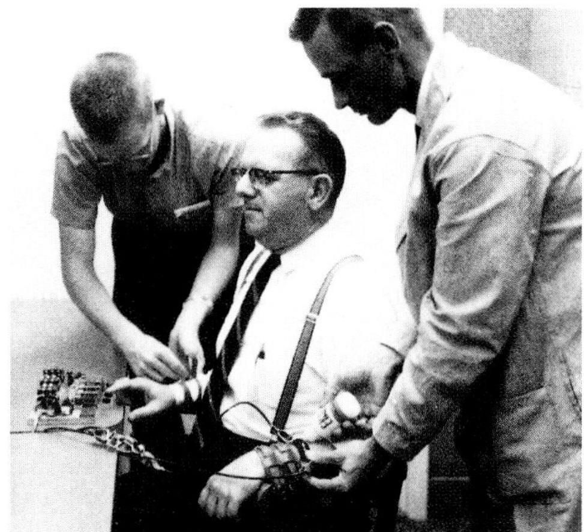

On the left is the shock generator used by Milgram in his famous experiment. On the right is the learner (actually an accomplice) being strapped into his chair by the experimenter and the unsuspecting participant.

The experimenter explains that you are to read a list of word pairs to the learner and then test his memory. When the learner makes the right choice, you go on to the next pair. If he misses a question, you are to flip a switch and shock him, moving one switch to the right—delivering 15 additional volts—for each miss. The learner does well at first but then begins missing about three out of every four questions. You begin pulling the switches, which you believe are delivering stronger and stronger shocks for each incorrect answer. When you hesitate, the experimenter urges you, "Please continue" or "Please go on." If you still hesitate, the experimenter orders you, "The experiment requires that you continue," or more strongly, "You have no other choice, you *must* go on" (p. 374).

At the 20th switch, 300 volts, the learner begins to pound on the wall and screams, "Let me out of here, let me out, my heart's bothering me, let me out!" (Meyer, 1972, p. 461). From this point on, the learner answers no more questions. Alarmed, you protest to the experimenter that the learner, who is pounding the wall frantically, does not want to continue. The experimenter answers, "Whether the learner likes it or not, you must go on" (Milgram, 1963, p. 374). When the learner fails to respond, you are told to count that as an incorrect response and shock him again.

Do you continue? If you do, you flip the next switch—315 volts—and only groans are heard from the learner. You look at the experimenter, obviously distressed, your palms sweating, your heart pounding. The experimenter states firmly: "You have no other choice, you *must* go on." If you refuse at this point, the experiment is ended. Would you refuse, or would you continue to shock a silent learner nine more times until you delivered the maximum of 450 volts?

How many of the 40 participants do you think obeyed the experimenter to the end—to 450 volts? The answer is quite disturbing: almost everyone in the study (87.5 percent) continued to administer the shock to the 20th switch, supposedly 300 volts, when the learner began pounding the wall. Amazingly, 26 people—65 percent of the sample—obeyed the experimenter to the bitter end, as shown in Figure 14.2. But this experiment took a terrible toll on the participants. "Subjects were observed to sweat, tremble, stutter, bite their lips, groan, and dig their fingernails into their flesh. These were characteristic rather than exceptional responses to the experiment" (p. 375).

Variations of the Milgram Study

Would the same results have occurred if the experiment had not been conducted at a famous university like Yale? The same experiment was carried out in a three-room office suite in a run-down building identified by a sign, "Research Associates of Bridgeport." Even there, 48 percent of participants administered the maximum shock, compared with the 65 percent in the Yale setting (Meyer, 1972).

Milgram (1965) conducted a variation of the original experiment in which each trial included three teachers; two were confederates and the third a naive participant. One confederate was instructed to refuse to continue after 150 volts, the other after

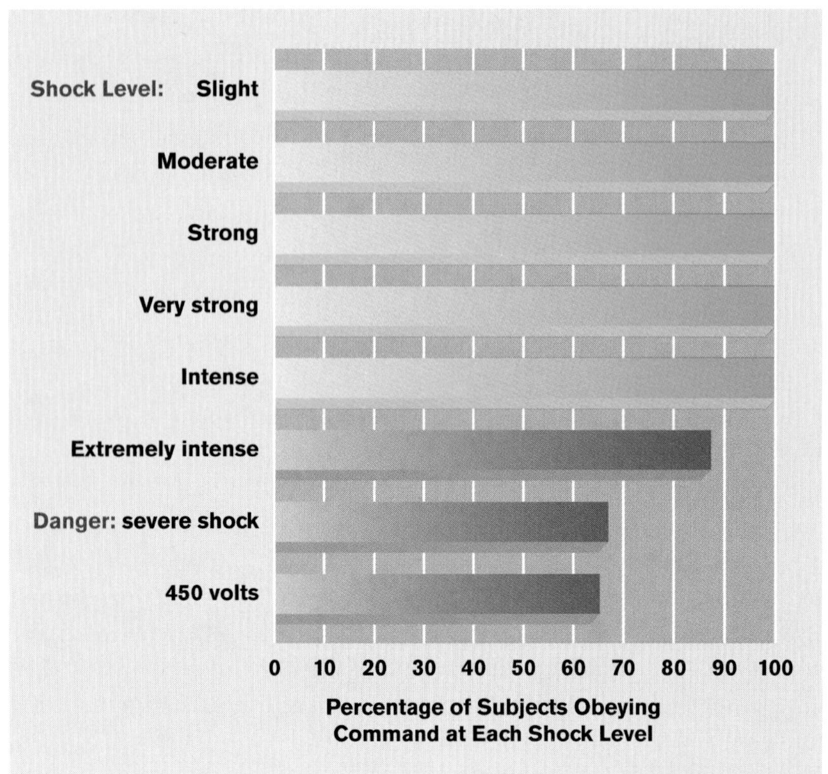

FIGURE 14.2
The Results of Milgram's Classic Experiment on Obedience In his classic study, Stanley Milgram showed that a large majority of his participants would obey authority even if obedience caused great pain or was life-threatening to another person. Milgram reported that 87.5 percent of the participants continued to administer what they thought were painful electric shocks of 300 volts to a victim who complained of a heart condition. Amazingly, 65 percent of the participants obeyed authority to the bitter end and continued to deliver what they thought were dangerous, severe shocks to the maximum of 450 volts. (Data from Milgram, 1963.)

210 volts. In this situation 36 out of 40 naive participants (90 percent) defied the experimenter before the maximum shock could be given, compared to only 14 in the original experiment (Milgram, 1965). In Milgram's experiment, as in Asch's conformity study, the presence of another person who *refused to go along* gave many of the participants the courage to defy authority.

Compliance: Giving In to Requests

What are three techniques used to gain compliance?

Often, people act not out of conformity or obedience but in accordance with the wishes, suggestions, or direct requests of another person. This type of action is called **compliance**. Almost daily we are confronted by people who make requests of one sort or another. Do we comply with these requests? Quite often we do. People use several techniques to gain the compliance of others.

The Foot-in-the-Door Technique: Upping the Ante

One strategy, the **foot-in-the-door technique**, is designed to secure a favourable response to a small request first. The intent is to make a person more likely to agree later to a larger request (the request that was desired from the beginning). In one study a researcher pretending to represent a consumers' group called a number of homes and asked whether the people answering the phone would mind answering a few questions about the soap products they used. Then a few days later, the same person called those who had agreed to the first request and asked if he could send five or six of his assistants to conduct an inventory of the products in their home. The researcher told the respondents that the inventory would take about two hours, and that the inventory team would have to search all drawers, cabinets, and closets in the house. Would you agree to such an imposition?

In fact, nearly 53 percent of the foot-in-the-door group agreed to this large request, compared with 22 percent of a control group who were contacted only once, with the large request (Freedman & Fraser, 1966). A review of many studies on the foot-in-the-door approach suggests that it is highly effective (Beaman et al., 1983; DeJong, 1979). But strangely enough, exactly the opposite approach will work just as well.

Remember It!

Conformity, Obedience, and Compliance

1. What percentage of the participants in the original Asch study never conformed to the majority's unanimous incorrect response?
   a. 70 percent b. 33 percent
   c. 25 percent d. 5 percent
2. What percentage of the participants in Milgram's original obedience experiment administered what they thought was the maximum 450 volt shock?
   a. 85 percen b. 65 percent
   c. 45 percent d. 25 percent
3. Match the compliance technique with the appropriate example.
   ____ 1) Julie agrees to sign a letter supporting an increase in taxes for road construction. Later she agrees to make 100 phone calls urging people to vote for the measure.
   ____ 2) Rick refuses a phone request for a $24 donation to send four needy children to the circus but does agree to give $6.
   ____ 3) Linda agrees to babysit for her next-door neighbours and then is informed that their three nephews will be there, too.

   a. door-in-the-face technique
   b. low-ball technique
   c. foot-in-the-door technique

Answers: 1. c 2. b 3. 1) c 2) a 3) c

The Door-in-the-Face Technique: An Unreasonable Request First

With the **door-in-the-face technique**, a large, unreasonable request is made first. The expectation is that the person will refuse but will then be more likely to respond favourably to a smaller request later (the request that was desired from the beginning). In one of the best-known studies of the door-in-the-face technique, university students were approached on campus. They were asked to agree to serve without pay as counsellors to young offenders for two hours each week for a minimum of two years. As you would imagine, not a single person agreed (Cialdini et al., 1975). Then the experimenters countered with a much smaller request, asking the students if they would agree to take a group of young offenders on a two-hour trip to the zoo. Half the students agreed—a fairly high compliance rate. The researchers used another group of university students as controls, asking them to respond only to the smaller request, the zoo trip. Only 17 percent agreed when the smaller request was presented alone. We should note that, of the foot-in-the-door and the door-in-the-face techniques, the former is more effective (Fern et al., 1986).

The Low-Ball Technique: Not Telling the Whole Truth Up Front

Another method used to gain compliance is the **low-ball technique**. A very attractive initial offer is made to get people to commit themselves to an action, and then the terms are made less favourable. In one study, university students were asked to enrol in an experimental course for which they would receive credit. But they were low-balled: only after the students had agreed to participate were they informed that the class would meet at 7:00 a.m. But 55 percent of the low-balled group agreed to participate anyway. When another group of students were told up-front that the class would meet at 7:00 a.m., only about 25 percent agreed to take the class (Cialdini et al., 1978).

compliance: Acting in accordance with the wishes, the suggestions, or the direct requests of another person.

foot-in-the-door technique: A strategy designed to secure a favourable response to a small request at first, with the aim of making the subject more likely to agree later to a larger request.

door-in-the-face technique: A strategy in which someone makes a large, unreasonable request with the expectation that the person will refuse but will then be more likely to respond favourably to a smaller request at a later time.

low-ball technique: A strategy to gain compliance by making a very attractive initial offer to get a person to agree to an action and then making the terms less favourable.

Group Influence

The Effects of the Group on Individual Performance

Our performance of tasks can be enhanced or impaired by the mere presence of others, and the decisions we reach as part of a group can be quite different from those we would make when acting alone.

Social Facilitation: Performing in the Presence of Others

Under what conditions does social facilitation have either a positive or a negative effect on performance?

The term **social facilitation** refers to any effect on performance, positive or negative, that can be attributed to the presence of others. Research on this phenomenon has focused on two types of effects: (1) **audience effects**—the impact of passive spectators on performance; and (2) **coaction effects**—the impact on performance of the presence of other people engaged in the same task.

One of the first studies in social psychology was conducted by Norman Triplett (1898), who looked at coaction effects. Triplett had observed in official bicycle records that bicycle racers pedalled faster when they were pedalling against other racers than when they were racing against the clock. Was this pattern of performance peculiar to competitive bicycling? Or was it part of a more general phenomenon in which individuals worked faster and harder in the presence of others than when performing alone? Triplett set up a study in which he told 40 children to wind fishing reels as quickly as possible under two conditions: (1) alone, and (2) in the presence of other children performing the same task. He found that the children worked faster when other reel turners were present.

Later studies on social facilitation found just the opposite effect—the presence of others, whether coacting or just watching, could impede individual performance. Robert Zajonc (1965; Zajonc & Sales, 1966) reasoned that we become aroused by the presence of others and that arousal facilitates the dominant response—that is, the one most natural to us. On simple tasks and on tasks at which we are skilled, the dominant response is the correct one (performing effectively). However, on tasks that are difficult or tasks we are first learning, the incorrect response

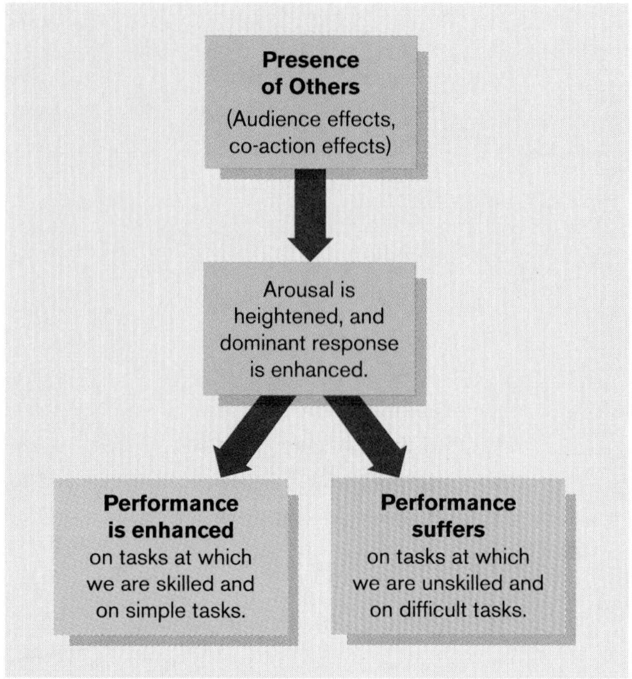

FIGURE 14.3
Social Facilitation: Performing in the Presence of Others **The presence of others (either as an audience or as coactors engaged in the same task) may have opposite effects, either helping or hindering our performance. Why? Robert Zajonc explained that (1) the presence of others heightens our arousal, and (2) heightened arousal leads to better performance on tasks we are good at and worse performance on tasks that are difficult for us. (Based on Zajonc & Sales, 1966.)**

(making a mistake) is dominant. This would account for the repeated findings that in the presence of others, performance improves on tasks that people do easily, but suffers on difficult tasks (Michaels et al., 1982) See Figure 14.3.

Other researchers have suggested that it is concern over the observers' evaluations of us that affects performance, particularly if we expect a negative evaluation (Sanna & Shotland, 1990; Seta et al., 1989).

Social Loafing: Not Pulling Our Weight in a Group Effort

What is social loafing, and what factors can lessen or eliminate it?

What happens in cooperative tasks in which two or more individuals are working together? Do they

Social loafing is people's tendency to exert less effort when working with others on a common task, such as pedalling a multiperson cycle.

increase their effort or slack off? Researcher Bibb Latané used the term **social loafing** for the tendency of people to exert less effort when they are working with others on a common task than when they are working alone on the same task. Social loafing takes place in situations in which no one person's contribution to the group can be identified, and in which individuals are neither praised for a good performance nor blamed for a poor one (Williams et al., 1981).

Several studies have found that social loafing disappears when participants in a group are led to believe that each person's output can be monitored and his or her performance evaluated (Harkins & Jackson, 1985; Weldon & Gargano, 1988). Even the *possibility* that the group's performance may be evaluated against some standard can be sufficient to eliminate the loafing effect (Harkins & Szymanski, 1989). When group size is relatively small and group evaluation is important, some members will even expend extra effort if they know that some of their co-workers are unwilling, unreliable, or incompetent (Karau & Williams, 1995; Williams & Karau, 1991). Social loafing is not likely to take place when participants can evaluate their own individual contributions (Szymanski & Harkins, 1987), when they are personally involved in the outcome or feel that the task is challenging (Brickner et al., 1986), and when they are working with close friends or teammates (Karau & Williams, 1993).

Social loafing is apparently not peculiar to any single culture but is typical of the human species. Some 50 studies conducted in places as diverse as Taiwan, Japan, Thailand, and India confirm that social loafing shows up when people are involved in performing cooperative tasks (Gabrenya et al., 1983).

The Effects of the Group on Decision Making

The group can have profound and predictable effects on decision making, depending on the group's attitudes before discussion begins.

Group Polarization: When Group Decisions Become More Extreme

How are the initial attitudes of group members likely to affect group decision making?

It is commonly believed that groups tend to make more moderate, conservative decisions than individuals make, but some research in social psychology tells us otherwise.

Group discussion often causes members of the group to shift to a more extreme position in whatever direction they were leaning initially—a phenomenon known as **group polarization** (Isenberg, 1986; Lamm, 1988). The group members, it seems, will decide to take a greater risk if they were leaning in a risky direction to begin with, but they will shift toward a more cautious position if they were somewhat cautious at the beginning of the discussion (Moscovici & Zavalloni, 1969; Myers & Lamm, 1975).

Why, then, aren't all group decisions either very risky or very cautious? The reason is that the members of a group do not always all lean in the same direction at the beginning of a discussion. When subgroups within a larger group hold opposing views, compromise rather than polarization is the likely outcome (Vinokur & Burnstein, 1978).

social facilitation: Any positive or negative effect on performance due to the presence of others, either as an audience or as coactors.

audience effects: The impact of passive spectators on performance.

coaction effects: The impact on performance caused by the presence of others engaged in the same task.

social loafing: The tendency to put forth less effort when working with others on a common task than when working alone.

group polarization: The tendency of members of a group, after group discussion, to shift toward a more extreme position in whatever direction they were leaning initially.

Groupthink: When Group Cohesiveness Leads to Bad Decisions

Group cohesiveness refers to the degree to which group members are attracted to the group and experience a feeling of oneness. **Groupthink** is the term that social psychologist Irving Janis (1982) applies to the decisions that are often reached by overly cohesive groups. When a tightly knit group is more concerned with preserving group solidarity and uniformity than with objectively evaluating all possible alternatives in decision making, individual members may hesitate to voice any dissent. The group may also discredit opposing views from outsiders and begin to believe it is invulnerable and incapable of making mistakes. Even plans bordering on madness can be hatched and adopted when groupthink prevails.

To guard against groupthink, Janis suggests that the group encourage an open discussion of alternative views and encourage the expression of any objections and doubts. He further recommends that outside experts sit in and challenge the views of the group. Finally, at least one group member should take the role of devil's advocate whenever a policy alternative is evaluated.

Groups exert an even more powerful influence on individuals by prescribing social roles.

Social Roles

The group is indispensable to human life. We are born into a family group, a culture, a racial and ethnic group, and usually a religious group. And as we grow and mature, we may choose to join many other groups, such as social groups and professional groups.

The groups to which we belong define certain roles. **Roles** are the behaviours considered to be appropriate for individuals occupying certain positions within a group.

Roles are useful because they tell us beforehand how people—even people we have never met before—are likely to act toward us in many situations. If you have ever been stopped for speeding by a police officer, you were at that moment unwillingly cast in the role of speeder, and you had few doubts about the role the officer would play. But both you and the police officer assume many different roles in life—family roles, social roles, work roles, and so on—and your behaviour can differ dramatically as you shift from role to role.

Roles can shape human behaviour to an alarming degree. This is best illustrated in a classic study by Philip Zimbardo.

Zimbardo's Prison Study: Our Roles Dictate Our Actions

Picture the following scene: On a quiet Sunday morning in a peaceful university town, the scream of sirens split the air as the local police conducted a surprise mass arrest, rounding up nine male university students. The students were searched, handcuffed, read their rights, and hauled off to jail. Here they were booked and fingerprinted, then transported to "Stanford County Prison." At the prison, each student was stripped naked, searched, deloused, given a uniform and a number, and placed in a cell with two other prisoners. All of this was more than sufficiently traumatic, but then there were the guards in their khaki uniforms, wearing reflector sunglasses that made eye-to-eye contact impossible and carrying clubs that resembled small baseball bats.

The prisoners had to get permission from the guards for the most simple, routine matters, such as writing a letter, smoking a cigarette, or even using the toilet. And the guards were severe in the punishments they imposed. Prisoners were made to do pushups while the guards sometimes stepped on them or forced another prisoner to sit on them. Some prisoners were placed in solitary confinement. (This anecdote is adapted from Zimbardo, 1972.)

But wait a minute! People are not arrested, charged, and thrown into prison without a trial. What happened? In truth the guards were not guards and the prisoners were not prisoners. All were university students who had been selected to participate in a two-week experiment on prison life (Zimbardo et al., 1973). Guards and prisoners were selected randomly from a pool of volunteers who had been judged to be mature, healthy, psychologically stable, law-abiding citizens. Those who were to be prisoners were not aware of their selection until they were "arrested" on that quiet Sunday morning.

This was only an experiment, but it became all too real—for the guards and especially for the prisoners. How could some of the guards, though mild-mannered pacifists, so quickly become sadistic, heartless tormentors in their new role? One guard remembered making prisoners clean the toilets with their bare hands—he virtually viewed them as cattle. The prisoners fell into their roles quickly as well.

Remember It!

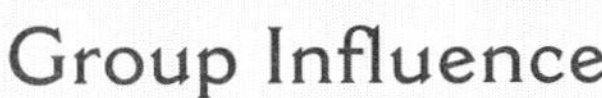

Group Influence

1. Which of the following statements regarding the effects of social facilitation is true?
   a. Performance improves on all tasks.
   b. Performance worsens on all tasks.
   c. Performance improves on easy tasks and worsens on difficult tasks.
   d. Performance improves on difficult tasks and worsens on easy tasks.
2. Social loafing is most likely to occur when
   a. individual output is monitored.
   b. individual output is evaluated.
   c. a task is challenging.
   d. individual output cannot be identified.
3. When group polarization occurs following group discussion, the group will decide to take a greater risk
   a. if members were leaning in a cautious direction to begin with.
   b. if members were leaning in a risky direction to begin with.
   c. if members were leaning in different directions to begin with.
   d. regardless of the initial position of the members.
4. What occurs when members of a very cohesive group are more concerned with preserving group solidarity than with evaluating all possible alternatives in making a decision?
   a. groupthink
   b. group polarization
   c. social facilitation
   d. social loafing

Answers: 1.c 2.d 3.b 4.a

How could autonomous, self-respecting students allow themselves to become debased and subservient in their captivity, to suffer physical and mental abuse, and to behave as if they were real prisoners? The experiment was to be run for two weeks but had to be called off after only six days.

Now, years later, social psychologists are still trying to answer the questions posed by the behaviour of the "prisoners" and the "guards."

Attitudes and Attitude Change

Attitudes: Cognitive, Emotional, and Behavioural Positions

What are the three components of an attitude?

What is your attitude toward abortion? or gun control? or premarital sex? An **attitude** is a relatively stable evaluation of a person, object, situation, or issue that varies along a continuum from negative to positive (Petty et al., 1997). Most of our attitudes have three components: (1) a cognitive component—our thoughts and beliefs about the attitudinal object; (2) an emotional component—our feelings toward the attitudinal object; and (3) a behavioural component—how we are predisposed to act toward the object (Breckler, 1984; Chaiken & Stanger, 1987; Petty & Wegener, 1998; Zanna & Rempel, 1988). Figure 14.4 on the next page shows the three components of an attitude.

Attitudes enable us to appraise people, objects, and situations; in this way they provide structure and consistency to our social environment (Fazio, 1989). Attitudes help us process social information (Pratkanis, 1989); they also guide our behaviour (Sanbonmatsu & Fazio, 1990) and influence our social judgments and decisions (Devine, 1989a; Jamieson & Zanna, 1989).

How do we form our attitudes? Some of our attitudes are acquired through firsthand experience with people, objects, situations, and issues. Others are acquired vicariously. When we hear parents, family, friends, and teachers express positive or negative attitudes toward certain issues or people, we may take

groupthink: The tendency for members of a very cohesive group to feel such pressure to maintain group solidarity and to reach agreement on an issue that they fail to adequately weigh available evidence or to consider objections and alternatives.

roles: The behaviours considered to be appropriate for individuals occupying certain positions within the group.

attitude: A relatively stable evaluation of a person, object, situation, or issue.

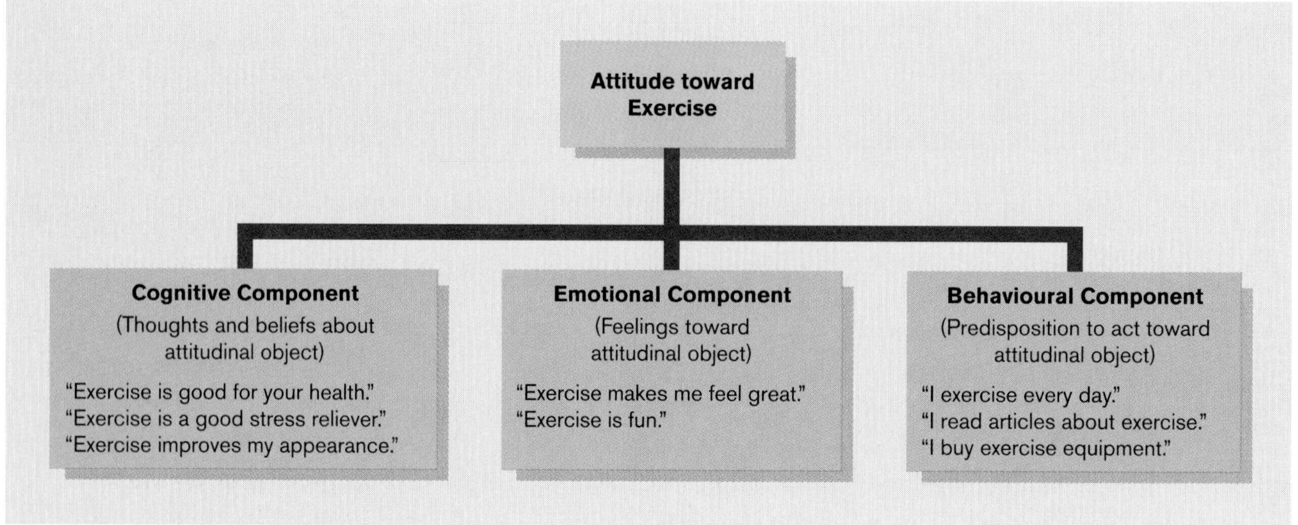

FIGURE 14.4

The Three Components of an Attitude **An attitude is a relatively stable evaluation of a person, object, situation, or issue. Most of our attitudes have (1) a cognitive component, (2) an emotional component, and (3) a behavioural component.**

the same attitudes as our own. The media, including advertisers, greatly influence our attitudes and reap billions of dollars annually for their efforts. As you might expect, however, the attitudes we form through direct experience are stronger than those we acquire vicariously and are more resistant to change (Wu & Shaffer, 1987).

Some research indicates that attitudes may have a partly genetic basis (Lykken et al., 1993). Tesser (1993) found that the greater the degree to which particular attitudes could be attributed to genetic influences, the more resistant those attitudes were to conformity pressures. But the controversial claim for a genetic influence on attitudes contradicts more conventional findings that emphasize the roles of learning and experience in attitude formation (Petty et al., 1997).

The Relationship between Attitudes and Behaviour

The general consensus among social scientists initially was that attitudes govern behaviour (Allport, 1935). But toward the end of the 1960s, one study after another failed to reveal a strong relationship between what people reported they believed on attitude measurement scales and their actual behaviour. Attitudes seemed to predict observed behaviour only about 10 percent of the time (Wicker, 1969).

Why aren't attitude measurements better predictors of behaviour? Attitude measurements may often be too general for this. People may express strong attitudes toward protecting the environment and conserving resources, but this doesn't mean they use their recycling boxes or join carpools. When attitudes correspond very closely to the behaviour of interest, they actually become good predictors of behaviour (Ajzen & Fishbein, 1977). Attitudes are also better predictors of behaviour if the attitudes are strongly held, are readily accessible in memory (Bassili, 1995; Fazio & Williams, 1986; Fazio et al., 1986; Kraus, 1995), and vitally affect our interests (Sivacek & Crano, 1982).

Cognitive Dissonance: The Mental Pain of Inconsistency

What is cognitive dissonance, and how can it be resolved?

If we discover that some of our attitudes are in conflict with others or are not consistent with our behaviour, we are likely to experience an unpleasant state. Leon Festinger (1957) called this **cognitive dissonance**. We usually try to reduce the dissonance by changing our behaviour or our attitude, or by somehow explaining away the inconsistency or reducing its importance (Aronson, 1973, 1976; Cooper & Fazio, 1984; Festinger 1957). A change in attitudes does seem to reduce the discomfort caused by dissonance (Elliot & Devine, 1994).

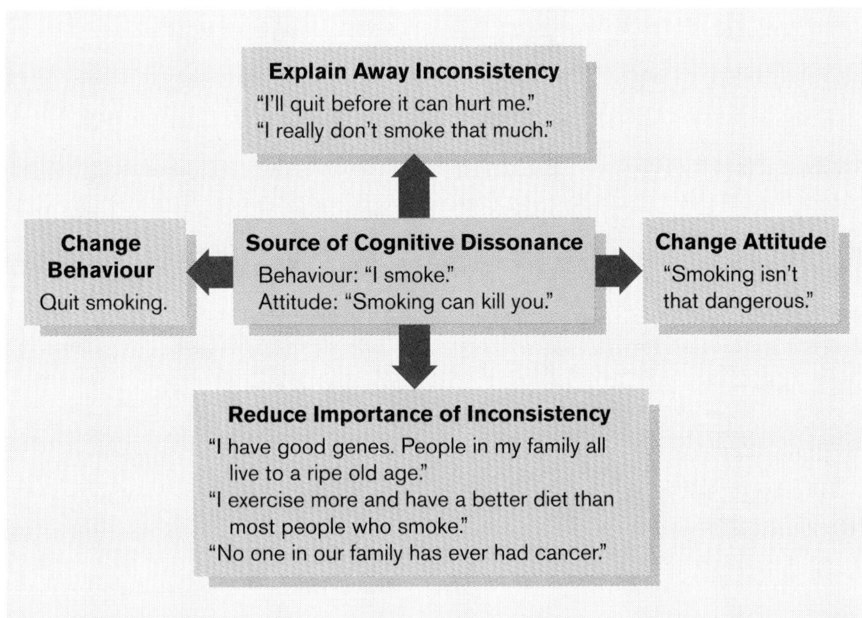

FIGURE 14.5
Methods of Reducing Cognitive Dissonance **Cognitive dissonance can occur when people become aware of inconsistencies in their attitudes or between their attitudes and their behaviour. People try to reduce dissonance by (1) changing their behaviour, (2) changing their attitude, (3) explaining away the inconsistency, or (4) reducing its importance. Here are examples of how a smoker might use these methods to reduce the cognitive dissonance created by his or her habit.**

Smoking provides a perfect example of cognitive dissonance. What are smokers to do? The healthiest, but perhaps not the easiest, way for them to reduce cognitive dissonance is to change their behaviour—quit smoking. Another way is to change their attitude—to convince themselves that smoking is not as dangerous as research suggests. Smokers can also tell themselves that they will stop smoking long before any permanent damage is done, or that medical science is advancing so rapidly that a cure for cancer is just around the corner. Figure 14.5 illustrates the methods that smokers can use to reduce cognitive dissonance.

If people voluntarily make a statement or take a position that is counter to what they believe, they will experience cognitive dissonance because of the inconsistency. To resolve this dissonance, they are likely to change their beliefs to make them more consistent with their behaviour (Festinger & Carlsmith, 1959). Cognitive dissonance can also be reduced by trivializing or minimizing the dissonant cognitions instead of changing one's attitudes (Simon et al., 1995).

Persuasion: Trying to Change Attitudes

What are the four elements in persuasion?

Persuasion is a deliberate attempt to influence the attitudes and/or the behaviour of another person. Persuasion is a pervasive part of our work experience, social experience, and family life.

Researchers have identified four elements in persuasion: (1) the source of the communication (who is doing the persuading), (2) the audience (who is being persuaded), (3) the message (what is being said), and (4) the medium (the means by which the message is transmitted).

The Source: Look Who's Talking

What qualities make a source most persuasive?

Some factors that make the source (communicator) more persuasive are credibility, attractiveness, and likability. Credibility refers to how believable a source is. A credible communicator is one who has expertise (knowledge of the topic at hand) and trustworthiness (truthfulness and integrity). The influence of a credible source is even greater if the audience knows the communicator's credentials beforehand. Moreover, we attach greater credibility to sources who have nothing to gain from persuading us or, better yet,

cognitive dissonance: The unpleasant state that can occur when people become aware of inconsistencies between their attitudes or between their attitudes and their behaviour.

persuasion: A deliberate attempt to influence the attitudes and/or behaviour of another.

who seem to be arguing against their own best interests. For example, arguments against pornography are more persuasive if they are made by a source known to be generally opposed to censorship.

In matters that involve our own personal tastes and preferences rather than issues, attractive people and celebrities can be very persuasive (Chaiken, 1979). Movie and TV stars, athletes, and even unknown but attractive fashion models have long been used by advertisers to persuade us to buy certain products. Likable, down-to-earth, ordinary people who are perceived to be similar to the audience are sometimes even more effective persuaders. Political candidates try to appear more likable, and more like voters, by donning hard hats and visiting construction sites and coal mines, by kissing babies, and by posing with farmers.

Persuasion is a deliberate attempt to influence the attitudes and/or behaviour of another person. What tactics do you use when trying to persuade others?

The Audience and the Message

Persuaders must consider the nature of their audience. In general, people with low intelligence are easier to persuade (Rhodes & Wood, 1992). Research suggests that a one-sided message (in which only one side of an issue is given) is usually most persuasive if the audience is not well-informed on the issue, is not overly intelligent, or is already in agreement with the point of view. A two-sided approach (in which both sides of an issue are mentioned) works best when the audience is well-informed, fairly intelligent, or initially opposed to the point of view. The two-sided approach usually sways more people than a one-sided appeal (Hovland et al., 1949; McGuire, 1969, 1985).

People tend to scrutinize arguments that are contrary to their existing beliefs more carefully and exert more effort refuting them; they are also more likely to judge such arguments as weaker than those that support their beliefs (Edwards & Smith, 1996).

A message can be well-reasoned, logical, and unemotional ("just the facts"); or it can be strictly

Remember It!

Attitudes and Attitude Change

1. Which of the following is *not* one of the three components of an attitude?
   a. cognitive component
   b. emotional component
   c. physiological component
   d. behavioural component
2. All of the following are ways to reduce cognitive dissonance *except*
   a. changing an attitude.
   b. changing a behaviour.
   c. explaining away the inconsistency.
   d. strengthening the attitude and behaviour.
3. People who have made a great sacrifice to join a group usually decrease their liking for the group. (true/false)
4. Credibility relates most directly to the communicator's
   a. attractiveness.
   b. expertise and trustworthiness.
   c. likability.
   d. personality.
5. With a well-informed audience, two-sided messages are more persuasive than one-sided messages. (true/false)
6. High-fear appeals are more effective than low-fear appeals if they provide definite actions that people can take to avoid dreaded outcomes. (true/false)

Answers: 1. c 2. d 3. false 4. b 5. true 6. true

emotional ("scare the hell out of them"); or it can be a combination of the two. Which type of message works best? Arousing fear seems to be effective for persuading people to adopt healthier attitudes and behaviours (Robberson & Rogers, 1988). Appeals based on fear are most effective when the presentation outlines definite actions the audience can take to avoid the feared outcome (Leventhal et al., 1965).

IT HAPPENED IN CANADA

Burnt Church

Despite the changing nature of Canada's cultural environment and the growing acceptance of our country as one that includes many traditions, norms, and beliefs, Canadians continue to be challenged and somewhat divided over how to deal with the way these different views affect perceptions and expectations. In the past few years, Canadians have witnessed an increasing tension over issues associated with the inherent rights of Native people.

In the summer of 2000, conflict between Natives and government officials took a serious turn when the Supreme Court ruled that Native Canadians had the treaty right to fish and hunt for a moderate livelihood, while also upholding Ottawa's right to regulate the fishery. Burnt Church, New Brunswick, a community of 1300 people, mainly Mi'kmaq, became the focal point of the conflict. There, Native and non-Native fishers fought over their apparent rights to fish for lobster. The clash of views and the differing interpretations of the Supreme Court ruling resulted in acts of vandalism and threats from members of both Native and non-Native groups, along with strong intervention from both RCMP and Fisheries officials. The daily occurrences of Burnt Church wrought constant headlines in our newscasts during the summer of 2000, and attempts to reconcile the two groups were not successful.

Conflicts such as these are infused with social psychological processes. They are based on each group's prejudicial attitudes regarding the other group. Those views involved a focus on differences between members of "our" versus the "other" group. Such perspectives serve to polarize each person's attitudes toward any member of the other group by casting everyone in the other group as being indistinguishable in attitudes and beliefs from any other member of that group. Such views lead to discrimination and make it virtually impossible for negotiators to find a solution. Can social psychologists help find a solution to such conflicts? (Based on Morris, 2000a, 2000b.)

Another important factor in persuasion is repetition. The more often a product or a point of view is presented, the more people will be persuaded to buy it or embrace it. Advertisers apparently believe in the mere-exposure effect, as they repeat their message over and over (Bornstein, 1989).

Prejudice and Discrimination

As we have seen, increasing cultural diversity is a fact of life in the modern world. And Canada is among the most culturally diverse nations in the world. Can we all learn to live and work peacefully no matter what racial, ethnic, cultural, or other differences exist among us? The answer is a conditional yes—we can do it *if* we can learn how to combat prejudice and discrimination.

The Roots of Prejudice and Discrimination

What is the difference between prejudice and discrimination?

Prejudice consists of attitudes (usually negative) toward others based on their gender, religion, race, or membership in a particular group. Prejudice involves beliefs and emotions (not actions) that can escalate into hatred. **Discrimination** consists of behaviour—that is, actions (usually negative) toward members of a group. Many people have experienced prejudice and discrimination—minority racial groups (racism), women (sexism), the elderly (ageism), disabled people, gays and lesbians, religious groups, and others. What, then, are the roots of prejudice and discrimination?

The Realistic Conflict Theory: When Competition Leads to Prejudice

One of the oldest explanations offered for prejudice is competition among various social groups for scarce economic resources—good jobs, land, political power,

prejudice: Negative attitudes toward others based on their gender, religion, race, or membership in a particular group.

discrimination: Behaviour, usually negative, directed toward others based on their gender, religion, race, or membership in a particular group.

and so on. Commonly called the **realistic conflict theory**, this view suggests that as competition increases, so does prejudice, discrimination, and hatred among the competing groups. Some historical evidence supports this theory. Prejudice and hatred were high between the Europeans and the Native Canadians who struggled over land during Canada's westward expansion. Many of the millions of immigrants to Canada have felt the sting of prejudice and hatred from native-born Canadians. This has been especially true in times of economic scarcity. As nations around the world experience hard economic times in the late new century, will we see an increase in prejudice and discrimination? The realistic conflict theory predicts that we will. But prejudice and discrimination are too complex to be explained simply by economic conflict. What are some other causes?

Us Versus Them: Dividing the World into In-Groups and Out-Groups

What is meant by the terms *in-group* and *out-group*?

Prejudice can also spring from the distinct social categories into which we divide our world—*us versus them* (Turner et al., 1987). An **in-group** is a social group with a strong feeling of togetherness and from which others are excluded. Fraternities and sororities often exhibit strong in-group feelings. An **out-group** consists of individuals or groups specifically identified by the in-group as not belonging. Us-versus-them thinking can lead to excessive competition, hostility, prejudice, discrimination, and even war.

Prejudiced individuals who most strongly identify with their racial in-group are most reluctant to admit others to the group if there is the slightest doubt about their racial purity (Blascovich et al., 1997). Note, however, that groups need not be composed of different races, religions, nations, or any other particular category for in-group/out-group hostility to develop (Tajfel, 1982). Sometimes, even the slightest form of affiliation can lead to in-group/out-group differences.

THE ROBBERS' CAVE EXPERIMENT A famous study by Sherif and Sherif (1967) shows how in-group/out-group conflict can escalate into prejudice and hostility rather quickly, even between groups that are very much alike. The researchers set up their experiment at the Robbers' Cave summer camp. Their subjects were 22 bright, well-adjusted, 11- and 12-year-old white, middle-class boys from Oklahoma City. Divided into two groups and housed in separate cabins, the boys were kept apart for all their daily activities and games. During the first week, in-group solidarity, friendship, and cooperation developed within each of the groups. One group called itself the Rattlers; the other group took the name Eagles.

During the second week of the study, competitive events were purposely scheduled so that the goals of one group could be achieved "only at the expense of the other group" (Sherif, 1958, p. 353). The groups were happy to battle each other, and intergroup conflict quickly emerged. Name-calling began, fights broke out, and accusations were hurled back and forth. During the third week of the experiment, the researchers tried to put an end to the hostility and to turn rivalry into cooperation. They simply brought the groups together for pleasant activities such as eating meals and watching movies. "But far from reducing conflict, these situations only served as opportunities for the rival groups to berate and attack each other.... They threw paper, food, and vile names at each other at the tables" (Sherif, 1956, pp. 57–58).

Finally, the last stage of the experiment was set in motion. The experimenters manufactured a series of crises that could be solved only if all the boys combined their efforts and resources, and cooperated. The water supply, sabotaged by the experimenters, could be restored only if all the boys worked together. After a week of several activities requiring cooperation, cutthroat competition gave way to cooperative exchanges. Friendships developed between groups, and before the end of the experiment, peace was declared. Working together toward shared goals had turned hostility into friendship.

The Social Learning Theory: Acquiring Prejudice through Modelling and Reinforcement

How does prejudice develop, according to the social learning theory?

According to the social learning theory, people learn attitudes of prejudice and hatred the same way they learn other attitudes. If children hear their parents, teachers, peers, and others openly express prejudices toward different racial, ethnic, or cultural groups, they may be quick to learn such attitudes. And if parents, peers, and others reward children with smiles and approval for mimicking their own prejudices (operant conditioning), children may learn these prejudices even more quickly.

Philips and Ziller (1997) suggest that people can also learn to be nonprejudiced. These researchers conceptualize *nonprejudice* as a set of attitudes about interpersonal relations that lead people to selectively pay attention to and emphasize the similarities between themselves and others, rather than the differences.

Social Cognition: Natural Thinking Processes Can Lead to Prejudice

What are stereotypes?

Social cognition also plays a role in giving birth to prejudice. **Social cognition** refers to the ways in which we typically process social information, or to the natural thinking processes whereby we notice, interpret, and remember information about our social world. The processes we use to simplify, categorize, and order our world are the very same processes we use to distort it. Thus, prejudice may arise not only from heated negative emotions and hatred toward other social groups, but also from cooler cognitive processes that govern how we think and process social information (Kunda & Oleson, 1995; Linville et al., 1989; Quattrone, 1986).

One way people simplify, categorize, and order their world is through stereotypes. **Stereotypes** are widely shared beliefs about the characteristics of members of various social groups (racial, ethnic, religious); among these beliefs is the assumption that *they* are usually all alike. Macrae and colleagues (1994) suggest that we resort to stereotypes because doing so requires less mental energy than trying to understand people as individuals. Research by Anderson and colleagues (1990) showed that people can process information more efficiently and answer questions more quickly when they are using stereotypes. But even though they help us process information more quickly, stereotypes may also carry *symbolic beliefs* about a specific group—that is, stereotypes may imply that a specific group threatens our values and norms (Esses et al., 1993).

Do you use stereotypes in your thinking? To find out, complete the *Try It!*

Are women nurturant and non-competitive, and men strong, dominant, and the best leaders? Are beautiful people more vain? All these beliefs are stereotypes. Once developed, stereotypes strongly influence our evaluations of incoming information about specific groups. The stereotypes we hold can powerfully affect our reactions to and judgments of people in various groups.

When you did the *Try It!* how many group characteristics could you list? We know that not *all* members of a group possess the same traits or characteristics, but we tend to use stereotypic thinking nonetheless.

Try It!

Do You Use Stereotypes?

Can you list characteristics for each of the following groups?

Jamaican Canadians
White, male top-level executives
Native Canadians
Gays
Feminists
Members of fundamentalist religious groups
Jews
Arabs
Italians
Germans

realistic conflict theory: The notion that prejudices arise when social groups must compete for scarce opportunities and resources.

in-group: A social group with a strong sense of togetherness and from which others are excluded.

out-group: A social group specifically identified by the in-group as not belonging.

social cognition: Mental processes that people use to notice, interpret, understand, remember, and apply information about the social world and that enable them to simplify, categorize, and order their world.

stereotypes: Widely shared beliefs about the characteristic traits, attitudes, and behaviours of members of various social groups (racial, ethnic, religious); these include the assumption that they are usually all alike.

Social stereotypes can involve more than overgeneralization about the traits or characteristics of members of certain groups (Judd et al., 1991; Park & Judd, 1990). People tend to perceive more variability within the groups to which they belong (in-groups) and less variability among members of other groups (out-groups) (Ostrom et al., 1993). Thus, whites see more diversity among themselves but more sameness within groups of Blacks and Asians. This tendency in thinking can extend from race to gender to age to any other category of people (Linville et al., 1989). Age stereotypes can often be more pronounced and negative than gender stereotypes (Kite et al., 1991).

Stereotypes can be positive or negative, but all are distortions of reality. One of the most insidious things about stereotypes is that we often are not even aware that we are using them. The *World of Psychology* box illustrates the way gender stereotyping affects women's income.

LINK IT!

www.psych.purdue.edu/~esmith/arcor.html
Social Cognition Archive: General Orientation

WORLD OF PSYCHOLOGY

Gender Stereotyping: Who Wins? Who Loses?

Most of the people on our planet are women, yet around the world women are vastly underrepresented in positions of power. Gender stereotypes define men as decisive, aggressive, unemotional, logical, and ambitious. These qualities are perceived by many men and women alike as precisely the "right stuff" for leaders, decision makers, and powerful people at all levels of society. But women, too, can be strong, bold, and decisive leaders–like former prime ministers Margaret Thatcher of Britain, Golda Meir of Israel, and Indira Gandhi of India.

Today, 99 percent of men and 98 percent of women *say* that women should receive equal pay for equal work (Newport, 1993). Yet the average female worker in Canada is paid about 72 cents for every dollar paid to a male worker (Statistics Canada, 1995). And women are more likely to hold low-paying, low-status jobs. Table 14.1 shows the male–female earnings gap in 10 different countries.

As you can see, wage discrimination against women is not confined to Canada. Of the 10 industrialized nations shown in Table 14.1, Australia has the smallest wage gap between men and women (88 cents to female workers for every dollar paid to male workers). Switzerland has the widest wage gap, with women paid, on the average, only about half as much as men (International Labour Organization, 1990).

TABLE 14.1

Average Earnings of Full-time Female Workers as a Percentage of Men's in 10 Industrialized Countries (Non-agricultural Activities), 1980 and 1988.

Country	Earnings Ratio (1980)	Earnings Ratio (1988)
Australia	85.9	87.9
Denmark	84.5	82.1
France	79.2	81.8*
Netherlands	78.2	76.8
Belgium	69.4	75.0
West Germany	72.4	73.5
United Kingdom	69.7	69.5
United States	66.7‡	70.2
Switzerland	53.8	50.7

*1987 data 1984 data ‡1983 data
Source: Renzetti & Curran, 1992, p. 192.

Reverse Discrimination: Bending Over Backward to Be Fair

What is reverse discrimination?

Another subtle form of discrimination is **reverse discrimination**. It occurs when people bend over backward to give favourable treatment to members of groups that have been discriminated against in the past. Those who practise reverse discrimination may be trying to show that they are not prejudiced. But reverse discrimination is not genuine, and it insults the dignity of the group to which it is directed. It assumes that the other group is indeed inferior and capable only of achieving a lower standard.

A study by Fajardo (1985) clearly illustrates reverse discrimination. A group of teachers (all of whom were white) were asked to grade essays that were identified as having been written by either black or white students. The researchers had purposely written the essays to be poor, low average, high average, or excellent in quality. If white teachers were practising reverse discrimination, they would rate the essays they believed were written by black students higher than those supposedly written by white students. This is exactly what happened, especially when the quality of the essays was in the average range.

A series of studies by Don Dutton and his colleagues (1971, 1973) at the University of British Columbia also demonstrated the presence of reverse discrimination. For instance, in one study, couples asked to be seated in a restaurant. The couples were either black or white, and in each case the man's attire violated the restaurant's dress code. About 30 percent of the white couples were seated, whereas 75 percent of the black couples were seated. Dutton (1971) argued that employees went out of their way to appear non-discriminatory.

Reverse discrimination may benefit people in the short run, but it deceives them and creates false hopes, setting them up for greater disappointment and failure in the long run. Students and workers alike need and deserve objective evaluations of their work and their progress.

Combating Prejudice and Discrimination

What are several strategies for reducing prejudice and discrimination?

Prejudice and discrimination have been pervasive in human societies throughout recorded history. We have seen that both may take many forms, ranging from bigotry and hatred to the kindness and compassion (though misplaced) of reverse discrimination. Given that prejudice and discrimination may grow from many roots, are there effective ways to reduce them? Many experts believe so. One way is through education: To the extent that prejudice is learned, it can also be unlearned. Sustained educational programs designed to increase teachers' and parents' awareness of the damage caused by prejudice and discrimination can be very effective (Aronson, 1990).

LINK IT!

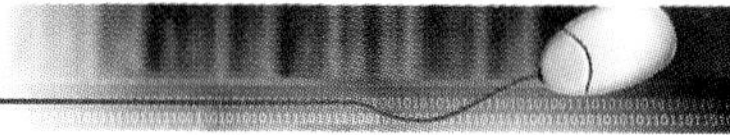

www.uwindsor.ca:7000/classical/king/me10.htm
Multiculturalism in Canada

www.auaa.org
Americans United for Affirmative Action (AUAA)

Direct Contact: Bringing Diverse Groups Together

Prejudice separates us, keeping us apart from other racial, ethnic, religious, and social groups. Can we reduce our prejudices and stereotypic thinking by increasing our contact and interaction with people in other social groups? Yes, according to the **contact hypothesis**.

Increased contacts with members of groups about which we hold stereotypes can teach us that *they* are not all alike. But the contact hypothesis works to reduce prejudice only under certain conditions. In fact, if people from diverse groups are simply thrown together, prejudice and even hostility are likely to increase rather than decrease, as we learned from Sherif and Sherif's Robbers' Cave experiment. We also learned from that experiment the conditions under which intergroup contact reduces prejudice. These findings have been confirmed and extended by others (Aronson, 1990; Finchilescu, 1988).

reverse discrimination: Giving special treatment or higher evaluations to individuals from groups that have been the target of discrimination.

contact hypothesis: The notion that prejudice can be reduced through increased contact among members of different social groups.

The contact hypothesis will work to reduce prejudice most effectively under the following conditions:

- Interacting groups should be about equal in social and economic status and in their ability to perform the tasks.
- The intergroup contact must be cooperative (not competitive) in nature, and work should be confined to shared goals.
- The contact should be informal, so that friendly interactions can develop more easily and group members can get to know each other individually.
- The conditions of the contact situation should favour group equality.
- The individuals involved should perceive each other as typical members of the groups to which they belong.

Us Versus Them: Extending the Boundaries of Narrowly Defined Social Groups

Our tendency to separate ourselves into social categories (in-groups and out-groups) creates an us-versus-them mentality. This mentality heightens prejudice, stereotypic thinking, and discrimination—for example, "Our group (or school, or country, or race, or religion) is better than theirs." But the boundary lines between us and them are not eternally fixed. If such boundaries can be extended, prejudice and in-group/out-group conflict can be reduced. We saw in the Sherif study that the Rattlers and the Eagles became a larger us group when they were brought together to work cooperatively on shared goals.

If your college or university wins the regional championship in a competitive event, then local rival colleges and universities will often join your group because you represent the region in national competition. Many researchers have shown that this recategorization reduces us-versus-them bias and prejudice (Gaertner et al., 1990; Wright et al., 1990).

Prejudice: Is It Increasing or Decreasing?

Few people would readily admit to being prejudiced. Gordon Allport (1954), a pioneer in research on prejudice, noted that while "defeated intellectually, prejudice lingers emotionally" (p. 328). Even those who are sincerely intellectually opposed to prejudice may still harbour some prejudicial feelings (Devine, 1989b).

Is there any evidence that prejudice is decreasing in our society? According to some researchers, we are not making much progress toward reducing either prejudice *or* discrimination (Crosby et al., 1980; Gaertner & Dovidio, 1986). But Devine and her colleagues (1991) are more optimistic. Their research

Remember It!

Prejudice and Discrimination

1. Match the example with the appropriate term.

____ 1) Joseph was promoted because the firm needed one French-Canadian manager.	a. stereotypic thinking
____ 2) Darlene thinks all whites are racists.	b. discrimination
____ 3) Betty's salary is $5000 less than that of her male counterpart.	c. reverse discrimination
____ 4) Bill can't stand Jews.	d. prejudice
____ 5) To make his Native employees feel good, Mr. Jones, who is white, gave them higher bonuses than he gave his white employees.	e. tokenism

2. From the in-group perspective, out-group members are often liked as individuals. (true/false)
3. Researchers have found that bringing diverse social groups together almost always decreases hostility and prejudice. (true/false)

Answers: 1. 1) e 2) a 3) b 4) d 5) c 2. false 3. false

suggests that "many people appear to be in the process of prejudice reduction" (p. 829).

Gallup polls reveal that whites are becoming more racially tolerant than they were in decades past (Gallup & Hugick, 1990). When whites were asked in 1990 whether they would move if blacks were to move in next door to them, 93 percent said no, compared with 65 percent 25 years earlier.

We can make things better for all by examining our own attitudes and actions, and then by using what we have learned here and elsewhere to combat prejudice and discrimination in ourselves. Prejudice has no virtues. It immediately harms those who feel its sting and ultimately harms those who practise it.

Prosocial Behaviour: Behaviour That Benefits Others

> Kitty Genovese was returning home alone late one night. But this was no ordinary night. Nearly 40 of her neighbours who lived in the apartment complex nearby watched as she was attacked and stabbed, but they did nothing. The attacker left. Kitty was still screaming, begging for help, and then … he returned. He dragged her around, stabbing her again while her neighbours watched. Some of them turned off their bedroom lights to see more clearly, pulled up chairs to the window, and watched. Someone yelled, "Leave the girl alone," and the attacker fled again. But even then, no one came to her aid. A third time the attacker returned. Again there was more stabbing and screaming, and still they only watched. Finally, Kitty Genovese stopped screaming. When he had killed her, the attacker fled for the last time. (Adapted from Rosenthal, 1964.)

This actual event might not seem so unusual today, but it was a rare occurrence in the early 1960s—so rare, in fact, that people wondered how Genovese's neighbours could have been so callous and cold-hearted to do nothing but watch as she begged for help that never came. Social psychologists Bibb Latané and John Darley looked deeper for an explanation. Perhaps there were factors in the situation itself that would help explain why so many people only watched and listened.

The Bystander Effect: The Greater the Number of Bystanders, the Less Likely They Are to Help

What is the bystander effect, and what factors have been suggested to explain why it occurs?

If you were injured or ill and needed help, would you feel safer if one or two other people were near, or if a large crowd of onlookers were present? You may be surprised to learn of the **bystander effect:** as the number of bystanders at an emergency increases, the probability that the victim will be helped by them decreases, and the help, if given, is likely to be delayed.

Why should this be? Darley and Latané (1968a) set up a number of experiments to study helping behaviour. In one study, participants were placed one at a time in a small room and told they would be participating in a discussion group by means of an intercom system. It was explained that because personal problems were being discussed, a face-to-face group discussion might be inhibiting. Some participants were told they would be communicating with only one other person, some believed that two other participants would be involved, and some were told that five other people would be participating. In fact, there were no other participants in the study—only the prerecorded voices of confederates assisting the experimenter.

Shortly after the discussion began, the voice of one confederate was heard over the intercom calling for help, indicating that he was having an epileptic seizure. Of the participants who believed that they alone were hearing the victim, 85 percent went for help before the end of the seizure. When they believed that one other person was hearing the seizure, 62 percent sought help. When they believed there were four other people, only 31 percent sought help. Figure 14.6 shows how the number of bystanders affects both the number of people who try to help and the speed of response.

bystander effect: As the number of bystanders at an emergency increases, the probability that the victim will receive help decreases, and help, if given, is likely to be delayed.

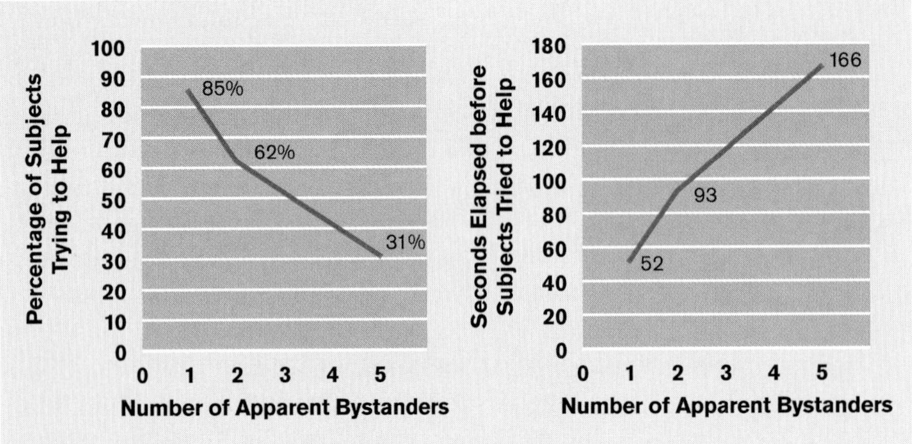

FIGURE 14.6

The Bystander Effect In their intercom experiment, Darley and Latané showed that the more people a participant believed were present during an emergency, the longer it took that participant to respond and help a person in distress. (Data from Darley & Latané, 1968a.)

Latané and Darley suggest two possible explanations for the bystander effect: diffusion of responsibility and the influence of apparently calm bystanders.

Diffusion of Responsibility: An Explanation for the Bystander Effect

When bystanders are present in an emergency, they generally feel that the responsibility for helping is shared by the group, a phenomenon known as **diffusion of responsibility**. Consequently, each person feels less compelled to act than if she or he were alone and thus totally responsible. Kitty Genovese's neighbours were aware that other people were watching because they saw lights go off in the other apartments. They did not feel that the total responsibility for action rested only on their shoulders. Or they may have thought, "Somebody else must be doing something" (Darley & Latané, 1968a, p. 378).

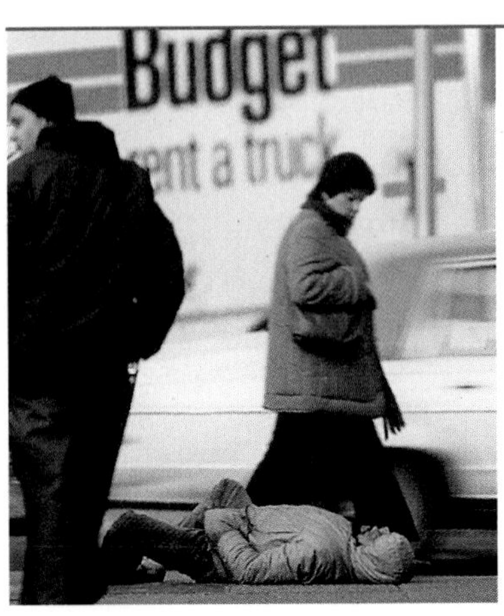

Why do people often ignore someone who is unconscious on the sidewalk? Diffusion of responsibility is one possible explanation.

The Influence of Apparently Calm Bystanders: When Faces Deceive

Sometimes it may not be clear that an actual emergency exists. Bystanders often hesitate to act until they are sure that intervention is appropriate (Clark & Word, 1972). They may stand there watching other apparently calm bystanders and conclude that nothing is really wrong and that no intervention is necessary (Darley & Latané, 1968b).

More than a few people have died while many potential helpers stood and watched passively because of the bystander effect. Picture an orthopedic surgeon's large waiting room in which eight patients are waiting to see the doctor. In one chair a middle-aged man sits slumped over, yet he does not appear to be sleeping. His position resembles that of a person who is unconscious. If you were a patient in such a setting, would you check on the man's condition or just continue sitting?

This was the actual scene one of the authors entered a few years ago as a patient. She sat down and immediately noticed the man slumped in his chair. She scanned the faces of the other waiting patients but saw no sign of alarm or even concern. Was there really no emergency, or was this a case of the bystander effect? Knowing that the reaction of onlookers is a poor indicator of the seriousness of a situation, she quickly summoned the doctor, who found that the man had suffered a heart attack. Fortunately, the doctor's office was attached to a large hospital complex, and almost immediately a hospital team appeared and rushed the victim to the emergency room.

IT HAPPENED IN CANADA

Canadian Heroes

Did you know that the Governor General of Canada presents Medals of Bravery to Canadians who are rewarded for their acts of heroism? Here are the stories of some of one year's recipients.

- The year's youngest recipient was seven-year-old Marie-Helène Etienne Rousseau, who saved her three-year-old brother from drowning in the St-Germain river in Québec. Despite the heavy current due to the spring thaw, Marie-Helène jumped in the river and managed to hold on to the bank with one hand while holding her brother until her mother rescued them both.
- Teresina Aniceto Batikayo of London, Ontario, received her award for helping a bus driver who was being stabbed near his vehicle. She grabbed the assailant from behind and pinned his arms to his sides, holding him down until others took over before the police arrived.
- Ian Goudy of Ilderton, Ontario, pulled a man from a burning car that had spun out of control. Mr. Goudy reached inside the burning vehicle.
- Barry Tait of B.C. made his way into his neighbour's smoke-filled house to rescue her 11-year-old son moments before the structure burned to the ground.

Are these people different from you and me? Would we rush to save someone from a burning fire or the frigid water of a river? Clearly, these people are among those who have performed extraordinary acts of heroism and altruism. Were they thinking of the possible rewards that might result from their act of heroism? Not likely. So how do social psychologists explain such incredible acts of prosocial behaviour? (Adapted from Canadian Press Newswire, April 5, 2000.)

People Who Help in Emergencies

There are many kinds of **prosocial behaviour**—behaviour that benefits others, such as helping, cooperation, and sympathy. Prosocial impulses arise early in life. Researchers agree that children respond sympathetically to companions in distress at least by their second birthday (Hay, 1994; Kochanska, 1993). The term **altruism** is usually reserved for behaviour aimed at helping others that requires some self-sacrifice, is not performed for personal gain, and carries no expectation of external reward (Bar-Tal, 1976). What motivates us to help or not to help in an emergency? Batson and colleagues (1988, 1989, 1998) believe that we help out of empathy—the ability to feel what another feels.

Cultures vary in their norms for social responsibility (i.e., for helping others). According to Miller and colleagues (1990), North Americans tend to feel an obligation to help family, friends, and even strangers in life-threatening circumstances, but only family in moderately serious situations. In contrast, in India social responsibility extends to strangers whose needs are only moderately serious or even minor.

We have heard accounts of people who have risked their lives to help others. During World War II in Nazi-occupied Europe, thousands of Christians risked their lives to protect Jews from extermination. What might explain such uncommon risks in the service of others? A study of 406 of these rescuers revealed that they did not consider themselves heroes and that different motives led to their altruistic behaviour. Some rescuers were motivated by strong convictions about how human beings should be treated, others by empathy for the individuals they were rescuing (Fogelman & Wiener, 1985; Oliner & Oliner, 1988). Still others were following the norms of their family or social group that emphasized helping others.

People are more likely to receive help if they are physically attractive (Benson et al., 1976), if they are perceived by potential helpers as similar to them (Dovidio, 1984), and if they are not considered responsible for their plight (Reisenzein, 1986; Schmidt & Weiner, 1988). Potential helpers are more likely to help if they have specialized training in first aid or police work, if they are not in a hurry, if they have been exposed to a helpful model (Bryan & Test, 1967), if they are in a positive mood (Carlson et al., 1988), and if the weather is good (Cunningham, 1979).

diffusion of responsibility: The feeling ampng bystanders at an emergency that the responsibility for helping is shared by the group, so that each individual feels less compelled to act than if he or she alone bore the total responsibility.

prosocial behaviour: Behaviour that benefits others, such as helping, cooperation, and sympathy.

altruism: Behaviour aimed at helping another, requiring some self-sacrifice, and not designed for personal gain.

Remember It!

Prosocial Behaviour

1. The bystander effect is influenced by all of the following *except*
   a. the number of bystanders.
   b. the personalities of bystanders.
   c. whether the bystanders appear calm.
   d. whether the situation is ambiguous.
2. As the number of bystanders to an emergency increases, the probability that the victim will receive help decreases. (true/false)
3. In an ambiguous situation, a good way to determine whether an emergency exists is to look at the reactions of other bystanders. (true/false)
4. Altruism is one form of prosocial behaviour. (true/false)

Answers: 1. b 2. true 3. false 4. true

Aggression: Intentionally Harming Others

We humans have a long history of **aggression**—intentionally inflicting physical or psychological harm on others. Consider the tens of millions of people killed by other humans in wars and even in times of peace. The rate of violent crime in Canada increased 65 percent between 1981 and 1991. In the latter year, 87 percent of violent crimes were assaults, and many of these were sexual assaults (Statistics Canada, 1992). Violence affects all of us.

What causes aggression? One of the earliest explanations of aggression was the instinct theory—the idea that human beings, along with other animal species, are genetically programmed for aggressive behaviour. Sigmund Freud believed that humans have an aggressive instinct that can be turned inward (as self-destruction) or outward (as aggression or violence toward others). Konrad Lorenz (1966), who won a Nobel Prize for his research in animal behaviour, maintained that aggression springs from an inborn fighting instinct common in many animal species. Most social psychologists, however, consider human behaviour too complex to attribute to instincts.

Biological Versus Social Factors in Aggression

What biological factors are thought to be related to aggression?

While rejecting the instinct theory of aggression, many psychologists believe that biological factors are involved. Twin and adoption studies suggest a genetic link for both aggression (Miles & Carey, 1997) and criminal behaviour (DiLalla & Gottesman, 1991).

Much research suggests there is a substantial sex difference in aggressiveness, especially physical aggressiveness (Eagly & Steffen, 1986). Some researchers believe that the male hormone testosterone is involved (Archer, 1991; Dabbs & Morris, 1990; Olweus, 1987). However, much of this gender difference in aggressiveness is likely due to socialization. In our culture, the "male role" encourages men to act in aggressive ways (Eagly & Steffen, 1986). The repercussions are often shocking. For instance, Statistics Canada (1989) reports that 90 percent of murders are committed by men. And over one million Canadian women are physically abused by their partners each year (MacLeod, 1989).

Alcohol and aggression are also frequently linked. Ito and others (1996) found that alcohol intoxication is particularly likely to lead to aggression in response to frustration. People who are intoxicated commit the majority of murders, spouse beatings, stabbings, and instances of physical child abuse.

Aggression in Response to Frustration: Sometimes, but Not Always

What is the frustration–aggression hypothesis?

Does **frustration**—the blocking of an impulse, or interference with the attainment of a goal—lead to aggression? The **frustration–aggression hypothesis** suggests that frustration produces aggression (Dollard et al., 1939; Miller, 1941). If a traffic jam kept you from arriving at your destination on time and you were frustrated, what would you do—lean on your horn, shout obscenities out of your window, or just sit patiently and wait? Berkowitz (1988) points out that even when a feeling of frustration is justified, it can cause aggression if it arouses negative emotions.

Aggression in response to frustration is not always aimed at the people causing it. If the preferred target is too threatening or not available, the aggression may

on the cutting edge in canada

Alcohol Consumption and Risky Behaviour

Alcohol consumption is a double-edged sword. On one hand, it is associated with parties and good times, perhaps because it is a social facilitator that causes people to be more relaxed and outgoing. But all of us certainly recognize the many negative personal consequences associated with too much alcohol consumption—poor decision-making process, risky behaviour, and the potential for increase in aggression. There is a common assumption among lay people and researchers alike that alcohol simply reduces inhibitions and that this process results in risky behaviours and thoughtless decision making. But recent research conducted by Tara MacDonald and her colleagues (1992, 2000a, 2000b) at Queen's University and the University of Waterloo suggests that the risky behaviours associated with alcohol consumption may not necessarily be the result of alcohol's capacity to make people less concerned about the consequences of their actions or be less inhibited. Instead, MacDonald suggests that when people are intoxicated, they may be more or less likely to act in risky ways depending on the cues provided by the situation. This "alcohol myopia" (Steele & Josephs, 1990) results in a restriction in cognitive capacity, so that people attend to the most salient cues in a situation.

In a series of complex and clever studies, MacDonald and her colleagues asked college-aged men who were in a dance club to indicate their attitudes and behavioural intentions toward engaging in unprotected sexual intercourse that evening. This information was collected under different conditions—when the men were sober or had not consumed alcohol, and when they were intoxicated. When the participants were sober, sexual arousal did not influence the participants' intentions. However, when participants were intoxicated, those who felt sexually aroused reported more favourable attitudes, thoughts, and intentions toward having unprotected sex. By contrast, participants who were intoxicated but who did not feel aroused indicated similar intentions to those who were sober.

MacDonald argues that the restriction in cognitive capacity associated with alcohol intoxication leads people to attend to the most salient cues in the situation. Variables such as sexual arousal, strong group pressure, and other factors commonly associated with situations where alcohol is consumed may provide such powerful cues that those who are intoxicated simply focus on these factors and not others. Perhaps these studies are worth considering next time you decide to have a drink.

be displaced. For example, children who are angry with their parents may take out their frustrations on a younger sibling. Sometimes minorities and others who have not been responsible for a frustrating situation become targets of displaced aggression—a practice known as **scapegoating** (Koltz, 1983).

Aggression in Response to Aversive Events: Pain, Heat, Noise, and More

What kinds of aversive events and unpleasant emotions have been related to aggression?

According to a leading researcher on aggression, Leonard Berkowitz (1988, 1989), aggression in response to frustration is only one special case of a broader phenomenon—aggression resulting from unpleasant or aversive events in general. People often become aggressive when they are in pain (Berkowitz, 1983), when they are exposed to loud noise or foul odours (Rotton et al., 1979), and even when they are exposed to irritating

aggression: The intentional infliction of physical or psychological harm on another.

frustration: Interference with the attainment of a goal or the blocking of an impulse.

frustration–aggression hypothesis: The hypothesis that frustration produces aggression.

scapegoating: Displacing aggression onto minority groups or other innocent targets who were not responsible for the frustration causing the aggression.

cigarette smoke. Extreme heat has been linked to aggression (Anderson, 1989; Anderson & Anderson, 1996; Anderson & DeNeve, 1992).

The Social Learning Theory of Aggression: Learning to Be Aggressive

According to social learning theory, what causes aggressive behaviour?

The social learning theory of aggression holds that people learn to behave aggressively by observing aggressive models and by having their aggressive responses reinforced (Bandura, 1973). It is well known that aggression is higher in groups and subcultures that condone violent behaviour and accord high status to aggressive members. A leading advocate of the social learning theory of aggression, Albert Bandura (1976) believes that aggressive models in the subculture, the family, and the media all play a part in the increasing levels of aggression in North American society.

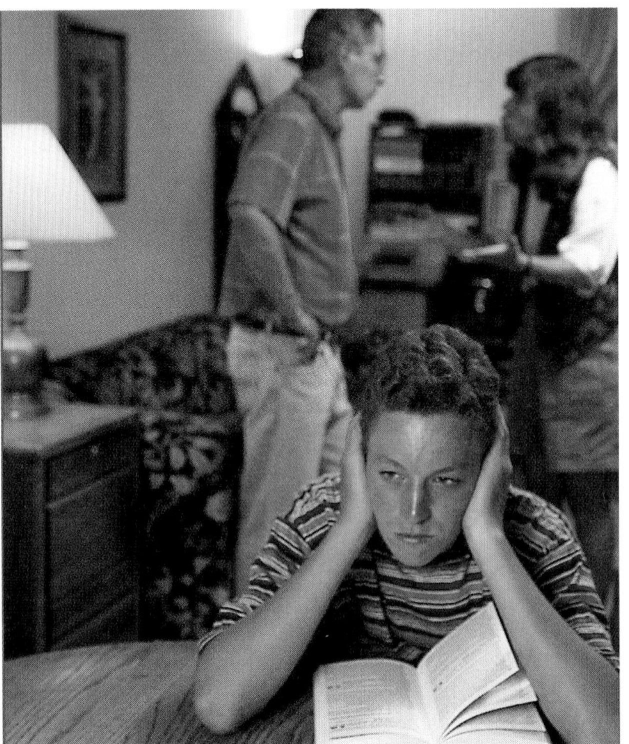

Children learn to behave aggressively by observing aggressive models, often their parents.

Abused children certainly experience aggression and see it modelled day after day. "One of the most commonly held beliefs in both the scholarly and popular literature is that adults who were abused as children are more likely to abuse their own children" (Widom, 1989b, p. 6). There is some truth to this belief. On the basis of original research and an analysis of 60 other studies, Oliver (1993) concludes that one-third of people who are abused go on to become abusers, and one-third do not; the final one-third may become abusers if the social stress in their lives is sufficiently high.

Most abusive parents, however, were not abused as children (Widom, 1989b). Although abused and neglected children run a higher risk of becoming delinquent, criminal, or violent, the majority do not take that road (Widom & Maxfield, 1996).

The Media and Aggression: Is There a Connection?

By the time the average North American child completes elementary school, he or she will have watched over 8000 murders and more than 100 000 violent acts (Huston et al., 1992). But is there a causal link between viewing aggressive acts and committing them? Some studies say no (Freedman, 1984; Milavsky et al., 1982) and suggest that laboratory studies cannot truly replicate real-life aggression. However, the evidence overwhelmingly reveals a relationship between TV violence and viewer aggression. Some research indicates that both adults and children as young as nursery school age show higher levels of aggression after they view media violence (Geen, 1978; Liebert et al., 1989). And the negative effects of TV violence are even worse for individuals who are highly aggressive by nature (Bushman, 1995).

Participants in a longitudinal study of 600 boys aged seven to nine, which was launched in 1960, were reinterviewed at age 19 and again at age 30 (Eron, 1987). Those participants who were most aggressive at 8 were still aggressive at 19 and at 30. Many of them showed antisocial behaviour ranging from traffic violations to criminal convictions and aggressiveness toward spouse and children (Huesmann et al., 1984). Did media influence play a part? "One of the best predictors of how aggressive a young man would be at age 19 was the violence of the TV programs he preferred when he was 8 years old" (Eron, 1987, p. 438). And the more frequently the participants had watched TV violence at that age, "the more serious were the crimes for which they were convicted by age 30" (p. 440). A similar study conducted in Finland found that the viewing of TV violence was related to criminality in young adulthood (Viemerö, 1996).

A review of 28 studies of the effects of media violence on children and adolescents revealed that "media violence enhances children's and adolescents' aggression in interactions with strangers, classmates, and friends" (Wood et al., 1991, p. 380). Media violence may stimulate physiological arousal, lower inhibitions, cause unpleasant feelings, and decrease sensitivity to violence and make it more acceptable to people (Wood et al., 1991).

Are violent episodes of TV shows in which the "good guys" finally get the "bad guys" less harmful? Not according to Berkowitz (1964), who believes that justified aggression is the type most likely to encourage the viewer to express aggression.

Remember It!

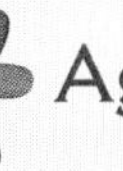

Aggression

1. Social psychologists generally believe that aggression stems from an aggressive instinct. (true/false)
2. Pain, extreme heat, loud noise, and foul odours have all been associated with an increase in aggressive responses. (true/false)
3. The social learning theory of aggression emphasizes all of the following *except*
   a. aggressive responses are learned from the family, the subculture, and the media.
   b. aggressive responses are learned through modelling.
   c. most aggression results from frustration.
   d. when aggressive responses are reinforced, they are more likely to continue.
4. According to the frustration–aggression hypothesis, frustration ______ leads to aggression.
   a. always
   b. frequently
   c. rarely
   d. never
5. The weight of research suggests that media violence is probably related to increased aggression. (true/false)
6. Research tends to support the notion that a person can drain off aggressive energy by watching others behave aggressively in sports or on television. (true/false)

Answers: 1. false 2. true 3. c 4. b 5. true 6. false

Apply It!

Sexual Harassment

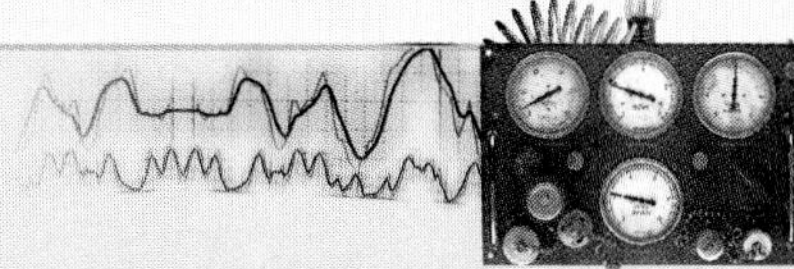

What is Sexual Harassment?

Sexual harassment on the job is very difficult to define. First, let's clarify what sexual harassment is *not*. It is not flirting with someone, asking for a date, flattery, and other similar behaviour. Sexual harassment lacks the elements of mutual choice found in normal relationships (Charney & Russell, 1994). It often involves unwelcome sexual remarks, lewd sexual comments or jokes, and sexual touching or deliberate brushing or rubbing against an intended victim.

The following standards on workplace sexual harassment have become widely accepted. Unwelcome sexual advances, requests for sexual favours, and other verbal or physical conduct of a sexual nature constitute sexual harassment when (1) submission to the conduct is made either explicitly or implicitly a term or condition of an individual's employment; (2) submission to or rejection of the conduct by an individual is used as a basis for employment decisions affecting the individual; or (3) the conduct has the purpose or effect of unreasonably interfering with an individual's work performance or creating an intimidating, hostile, or offensive working environment.

Sexual harassment in the workplace can take many forms, from mild to moderate to severe. In the most extreme form, a supervisor makes a raise, a promotion, conditions of employment, or other opportunities contingent upon an employee's compliance with sexual demands. Though we are more sensitive to it today, there is nothing new about sexual harassment.

How Prevalent Is Sexual Harassment?

In a random-sample survey of 24 000 U.S. federal employees conducted in 1981 and updated in 1988, 42 percent of the women and 15 percent of the men surveyed said that they had been sexually harassed during the two-year period prior to the survey.

In a more recent survey conducted by the *Harvard Business Review*, two-thirds of the men interviewed believed that reports of sexual harassment were exaggerated (Castro, 1992). But a survey by *Working Woman* magazine revealed that over 90 percent of the Fortune 500 companies had recorded employee complaints of sexual harassment, and over one-third of the companies had had sexual harassment lawsuits filed against them (Sandross, 1988).

Sexual harassment is also a problem on school campuses. According to the best data available, between 20 and 30 percent of female undergraduates have been sexually harassed while attending college or university (Charney & Russell, 1994). Similar rates have been reported in a study done in Canadian universities (DeKesseredy & Kelly, 1993). Note that the rates are said to be even higher for graduate students.

Not everyone who has been sexually harassed reports it. Experts today believe that as many as 50 percent of women in Canada and the United States experience some form of sexual harassment on campus, in the workplace, or elsewhere (Fitzgerald, 1993). And it does not appear that the incidence of sexual harassment has decreased (Ingrassia, 1993).

In the vast majority of cases, women are the victims of sexual harassment and men are the harassers. A survey of medical residents who had been sexually harassed found that for female victims, 96 percent of the harassers were male, and for male victims, 55 percent of the harassers were male (Komaromy et al., 1993).

What to Do about Sexual Harassment

If you were being sexually harassed by an employer, fellow worker, professor, or student, how would you handle it? Here are some practical suggestions, adapted from *Sex on Your Terms* by Elizabeth Powell (1996):

- *Maintain a strictly professional, businesslike manner.* Do not respond personally to acts of sexual harassment. Often a harasser seeks to get a personal, emotional response from his victims, and sometimes to shock, embarrass, or humiliate them. Let the harasser know that your relationship with him is strictly business.
- *Don't be alone with the harasser.* If the harasser on the job or on the campus asks or tries to coerce you to join him for lunch, for drinks, or in some other personal setting, refuse firmly and professionally.
- *Have a talk with the harasser.* If you can't avoid the harasser and he keeps coming on to you, it may help to talk directly with him about the situation. Point out his acts of sexual harassment and tell him directly that it must stop immediately.
- *Find support from friends, co-workers, or others you can trust for emotional support and advice.* Surveys indicate that more than 90 percent of sexual harassment victims suffer emotional distress (Charney & Russell, 1994). Victims are less likely to suffer emotional distress when there is a support group to help, but even then, some people may need professional counselling.
- *File a formal complaint if the harasser refuses to stop.* The law now requires companies (even relatively small ones) to respond to sexual harassment complaints. Large organizations and most colleges and universities have a designated professional to handle such complaints.
- *Seek legal advice if all else fails.* Sexual harassment is against the law, and you can take legal action against the harasser, or even against the company or institution that allowed the harassment to continue.

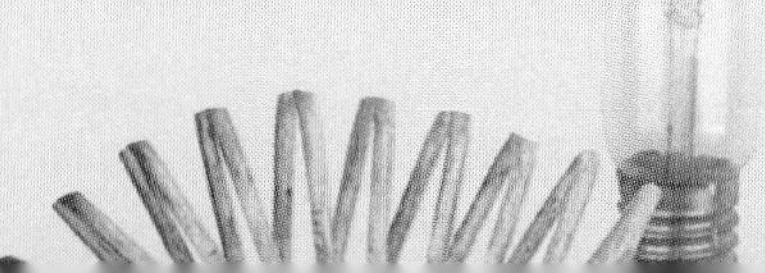

KEY TERMS

actor–observer bias, p. 446
aggression, p. 472
altruism, p. 471
attitude, p. 459
attribution, p. 445
audience effects, p. 456
bystander effect, p. 469
coaction effects, p. 456
cognitive dissonance, p. 460
compliance, p. 454
conformity, p. 450
contact hypothesis, p. 467
diffusion of responsibility, p. 470
discrimination, p. 463
dispositional attribution, p. 446
door-in-the-face technique, p. 455
foot-in-the-door technique, p. 454
frustration, p. 472
frustration–aggression hypothesis, p. 472
fundamental attribution error, p. 446
group polarization, p. 457
groupthink, p. 458
halo effect, p. 448
in-group, p. 464
low-ball technique, p. 455
matching hypothesis, p. 449
mere-exposure effect, p. 447
norms, p. 450
out-group, p. 464
persuasion, p. 461
prejudice, p. 463
primacy effect, p. 445
prosocial behaviour, p. 471
proximity, p. 447
realistic conflict theory, p. 464
reverse discrimination, p. 467
roles, p. 458
scapegoating, p. 473
self-serving bias, p. 446
situational attribution, p. 445
social cognition, p. 465
social facilitation, p. 456
social loafing, p. 456
social psychology, p. 444
stereotypes, p. 465

THINKING CRITICALLY

Evaluation

Many Canadians and Americans were surprised when the majority of the people in the Soviet Union rejoiced at the downfall of the communist system. Using what you have learned about attribution bias and conformity, try to explain why many Canadians mistakenly believed that the Soviet masses preferred the communist system.

Point/Counterpoint

Prepare a convincing argument supporting each of the following positions:

a. Aggression results largely from biological factors (nature).
b. Aggression is primarily learned (nurture).

Psychology in Your Life

Review the factors influencing impression formation and attraction as discussed in this chapter. Prepare a dual list of behaviours indicating what you should and should not do if you wish to make a better impression on other people and increase their liking for you.

SUMMARY & REVIEW

Social Perception

Why are first impressions so important and enduring?

First impressions are important because we attend more carefully to the first information we receive about a person, and because, once formed, an impression acts as a framework through which later information is interpreted.

What is the difference between a situational attribution and a dispositional attribution for a specific behaviour?

An attribution is our inference about the cause of our own or another's behaviour. When we use situational attributions, we attribute the cause of behaviour to some factor in the environment. With dispositional attributions, the inferred cause is internal– some personal trait, motive, or attitude.

How do the kinds of attributions we tend to make about ourselves differ from those we make about other people?

We tend to overemphasize dispositional factors when making attributions about the behaviour of other people, and to overemphasize situational factors in explaining our own behaviour.

Attraction

Why is proximity an important factor in attraction?

Proximity influences attraction because it is easier to develop relationships with people close at hand. Proximity also increases the likelihood of repeated contacts, and mere exposure tends to increase attraction (the mere-exposure effect).

How important is physical attractiveness in attraction?

Physical attractiveness is a major factor in attraction for people of all ages. People attribute other positive qualities to those who are physically attractive—a phenomenon called the halo effect.

Are people, as a rule, more attracted to those who are opposite or to those who are similar to them?

People are generally attracted to those who have similar attitudes and interests, and who are similar in economic status, ethnicity, and age.

Conformity, Obedience, and Compliance

What did Asch find in his famous experiment on conformity?

In Asch's classic study on conformity, 5 percent of the subjects went along with the incorrect, unanimous majority all the time; 70 percent went along some of the time; and 25 percent remained completely independent.

What did Milgram find in his classic study of obedience?

In Milgram's classic study of obedience, 65 percent of the subjects obeyed the experimenter's orders to the end of the experiment and administered what they believed were increasingly painful shocks to the learner up to the maximum of 450 volts.

What are three techniques used to gain compliance?

Three techniques used to gain compliance are the foot-in-the-door technique, the door-in-the-face technique, and the low-ball technique.

Group Influence

Under what conditions does social facilitation have either a positive or a negative effect on performance?

When others are present, either as an audience or as coactors, one's performance on easy tasks is usually improved, but performance on difficult tasks is usually impaired.

What is social loafing, and what factors can lessen or eliminate it?

Social loafing is the tendency of people to put forth less effort when they are working with others on a common task than when they were working alone. This is less likely to take place when individual output can be monitored or when people are highly involved with the outcome.

How are the initial attitudes of group members likely to affect group decision making?

Following group discussions, group decisions usually shift to a more extreme position in whatever direction the members were leaning toward initially—a phenomenon known as group polarization.

Attitudes and Attitude Change

What are the three components of an attitude?

Attitudes usually have a cognitive, an emotional, and a behavioural component.

What is cognitive dissonance, and how can it be resolved?

Cognitive dissonance is an unpleasant state that can occur when we become aware of inconsistencies between our attitudes or between our attitudes and our behaviour. We can resolve cognitive dissonance by changing the attitude or the behaviour, or by rationalizing away the inconsistency.

What are the four elements in persuasion?

The four elements in persuasion are the source, the audience, the message, and the medium.

What qualities make a source most persuasive?

Persuasive attempts are most successful when the source is credible (expert and trustworthy), attractive, and likable.

Prejudice and Discrimination

What is the difference between prejudice and discrimination?

Prejudice consists of attitudes (usually negative) toward others based on their gender, religion, race, or membership in a particular group. Discrimination consists of actions against others based on the same factors.

What is meant by the terms *in-group* and *out-group*?

An in-group is a social group with a strong sense of togetherness and from which others are excluded; an out-group consists of individuals or groups specifically identified by the in-group as not belonging.

How does prejudice develop, according to the social learning theory?

According to this theory, prejudice is learned in the same way as other attitudes–through modelling and reinforcement.

What are stereotypes?

Stereotypes are widely shared beliefs about the characteristics of members of various social groups (racial, ethnic, religious); they include the assumption that *they* are usually all alike.

What is reverse discrimination?

Reverse discrimination involves giving special treatment or higher evaluations to members of a group who have been the target of prejudice and discrimination.

What are several strategies for reducing prejudice and discrimination?

Several strategies for reducing prejudice include (1) arranging appropriate educational experiences for children, (2) providing situations where diverse social groups can interact under certain favourable conditions, and (3) extending the boundaries of narrowly defined social groups.

Prosocial Behaviour: Behaviour That Benefits Others

What is the bystander effect, and what factors have been suggested to explain why it occurs?

The bystander effect means that as the number of bystanders at an emergency increases, the probability that the victim will receive help decreases, and help, if given, is likely to be delayed. The bystander effect may be due in part to diffusion of responsibility or, in ambiguous situations, to the assumption that no emergency exists.

Aggression: Intentionally Harming Others

What biological factors are thought to be related to aggression?

Biological factors thought to be related to aggression are a genetic link (in criminal behaviour), high testosterone levels, low levels of serotonin, and brain damage.

What is the frustration–aggression hypothesis?

The frustration–aggression hypothesis holds that frustration produces aggression and that this aggression may be directed at the frustrater or displaced onto another target, as in scapegoating.

What kinds of aversive events and unpleasant emotions have been related to aggression?

Aggression has been associated with aversive conditions such as pain, heat, loud noise, and foul odours, and with unpleasant emotional states such as sadness, grief, and depression.

According to social learning theory, what causes aggressive behaviour?

According to the social learning theory, people acquire aggressive responses by observing aggressive models in the family, the subculture, and the media, and by having aggressive responses reinforced.

Glossary

absolute threshold: The minimum amount of sensory stimulation that can be detected 50 percent of the time.

accommodation: The changing in shape of the lens as it focuses objects on the retina, becoming more spherical for near objects and flatter for far objects.

accommodation: The process by which existing schemas are modified and new schemas are created to incorporate new objects, events, experiences, or information.

acetylcholine: A neurotransmitter that plays a role in learning, memory, and rapid eye movement (REM) sleep and causes the skeletal muscle fibres to contract.

actor–observer bias: The tendency of observers to make dispositional attributions for the behaviours of others but situational attributions for their own behaviours.

action potential: The firing of a neuron that results when the charge within the neuron becomes more positive than the charge outside the cell's membrane.

adolescent growth spurt: A period of rapid physical growth that peaks in girls at about age 12 and in boys at about age 14.

adoption method: A method researchers use to study the relative effects of heredity and environment on behaviour and ability in children adopted shortly after birth, by comparing them with their biological and adoptive parents.

adrenal glands (ah-DREE-nal): A pair of endocrine glands that release hormones that prepare the body for emergencies and stressful situations and also release small amounts of the sex hormones.

aerobic exercise (ah-RO-bik): Exercise that uses large muscle groups in continuous, repetitive action and requires increased oxygen intake and increased breathing and heart rates.

afterimage: The visual sensation that remains after a stimulus is withdrawn.

aggression: The intentional infliction of physical or psychological harm on another.

agoraphobia (AG-or-uh-FO-bee-uh): An intense fear of being in a situation in which immediate escape is not possible or help is not immediately available in case of incapacitating anxiety.

alarm stage: The first stage of the general adaptation syndrome, when there is emotional arousal and the defensive forces of the body are prepared for fight or flight.

alcohol: A central nervous system depressant.

algorithm: A systematic, step-by-step procedure, such as a mathematical formula, that guarantees a solution to a problem of a certain type if the algorithm is appropriate and executed properly.

alpha wave: The brain wave of 8 to 12 cycles per second that occurs when an individual is awake but deeply relaxed, usually with the eyes closed.

altered state of consciousness: A mental state other than ordinary waking consciousness, such as sleep, meditation, hypnosis, or a drug-induced state.

altruism: Behaviour aimed at helping another, requiring some self-sacrifice and not designed for personal gain.

amnesia: A partial or complete loss of memory resulting from brain trauma or psychological trauma.

amphetamines: A class of central nervous system stimulants that increase arousal, relieve fatigue, and suppress the appetite.

amplitude: Measured in decibels, the magnitude or intensity of a sound wave, determining the loudness of the sound; in vision the amplitude of a light wave affects the brightness of a stimulus.

amygdala (ah-MIG-da-la): A structure in the limbic system that plays an important role in emotion, particularly in response to aversive stimuli.

anal stage: Freud's second psychosexual stage (ages 12 or 18 months to three years), in which the child derives sensual pleasure mainly from expelling and withholding feces.

anterograde amnesia: The inability to form long-term memories of events occurring after brain surgery or a brain injury, although memories formed before the trauma are usually intact.

antidepressants: Drugs that are prescribed to treat depression and some anxiety disorders.

antipsychotic drugs: Drugs used to control severe psychotic symptoms, such as the delusions and hallucinations of schizophrenics; also known as neuroleptics or major tranquilizers.

antisocial personality disorder: A disorder marked by lack of feeling for others; selfish, aggressive, irresponsible behaviour; and willingness to break the law, lie, cheat, or exploit others for personal gain.

anxiety: A generalized feeling of apprehension, fear, or tension that may be associated with a particular object or situation or may be free-floating, not associated with anything specific.

aphasia (uh-FAY-zyah): A loss or impairment of the ability to understand or communicate through the written or spoken word, which results from damage to the brain.

applied research: Research conducted for the purpose of solving practical problems.

approach–approach conflict: A conflict arising from having to choose between desirable alternatives.

approach–avoidance conflict: A conflict arising when the same choice has both desirable and undesirable features; one in which you are both drawn to and repelled by the same choice.

archetype (AR-keh-type): Existing in the collective unconscious, an inherited tendency to respond in particular ways to universal human situations.

arousal: A state of alertness and mental and physical activation.

arousal theory: A theory suggesting that the aim of motivation is to maintain an optimal level of arousal.

assimilation: The process by which new objects, events, experiences, or information are incorporated into existing schemas.

association areas: Areas of the cerebral cortex that house memories and are involved in thought, perception, learning, and language.

attachment: The strong affectionate bond a child forms with the mother or primary caregiver.

attitude: A relatively stable evaluation of a person, object, situation, or issue.

attribution: An inference about the cause of our own or another's behaviour.

audience effects: The impact of passive spectators on performance.

audition: The sensation of hearing; the process of hearing.

authoritarian parents: Parents who make arbitrary rules, expect unquestioned obedience from their children, punish transgressions, and value obedience to authority.

authoritative parents: Parents who set high but realistic standards, reason with the child, enforce limits, and encourage open communication and independence.

automatic thoughts: Unreasonable and unquestioned ideas that rule a person's life and lead to depression and anxiety.

autonomy versus shame and doubt: Erikson's second psychosocial stage (ages one to three), when infants develop autonomy or shame depending on the way parents react to their expression of will and their wish to do things for themselves.

aversion therapy: A behaviour therapy used to rid clients of a harmful or socially undesirable behaviour by pairing it with a painful, sickening, or otherwise aversive stimulus until the behaviour becomes associated with pain and discomfort.

avoidance learning: Learning to avoid events or conditions associated with dreaded or aversive outcomes.

avoidance–avoidance conflict: A conflict arising from having to choose between equally undesirable alternatives.

axon (AK-sahn): The slender, tail-like extension of the neuron that transmits signals to the dendrites or cell body of other neurons or to the muscles or glands.

babbling: Vocalization of the basic speech sounds (phonemes), which begins between the ages of four and six months.

barbiturates: A class of central nervous system depressants used as sedatives, sleeping pills, and anesthetics; addictive, and in overdose can cause coma or death.

basic emotions: Emotions that are found in all cultures, that are reflected in the same facial expressions across cultures, and that emerge in children according to their biological timetable (examples: anger, disgust, happiness, sadness, distress).

basic research: Research conducted for the purpose of advancing knowledge rather than for its practical application.

basic trust versus basic mistrust: Erikson's first psychosocial stage (birth to 12 months), when infants develop trust or mistrust depending on the quality of care, love, and affection provided.

Beck's cognitive therapy: A brief cognitive therapy for depression and anxiety designed to help people recognize their automatic thoughts and replace them with more objective thoughts.

behaviour modification: The systematic application of the learning principles of operant conditioning, classical conditioning, or observational learning to individuals or groups in order to eliminate undesirable behaviour and/or encourage desirable behaviour.

behaviour therapy: A treatment approach that employs the principles of operant conditioning, classical conditioning, and/or observational learning theory to eliminate inappropriate or maladaptive behaviours and replace them with more adaptive responses.

behavioural genetics: The field of research that investigates the relative effects of heredity and environment on behaviour and ability.

behaviourism: The school of psychology founded by John B. Watson that views observable, measurable behaviour as the appropriate subject matter for psychology and emphasizes the key role of environment as a determinant of behaviour.

beta wave: The brain wave of 13 or more cycles per second that occurs when an individual is alert and mentally or physically active.

binocular depth cues: Depth cues that depend on two eyes working together; convergence and binocular disparity.

binocular disparity: A binocular depth cue resulting from differences between the two retinal images cast by objects at distances up to about six metres.

biofeedback: The use of sensitive equipment to give people precise feedback about internal physiological processes so that they can learn, with practice, to exercise control over them.

biological perspective: A perspective that emphasizes the role of biological processes and heredity as the keys to understanding behaviour.

biological therapy: A therapy, based on the assumption that most mental disorders have physical causes, that attempts to change or influence the biological mechanism involved (e.g., drug therapy, ECT, or psychosurgery).

biomedical model: A perspective that focuses on illness rather than health, explaining illness in terms of biological factors without regard to psychological and social factors.

biopsychosocial model: A perspective that focuses on health as well as illness, and holds that both are determined by a combination of biological, psychological, and social factors.

bipolar disorder: A mood disorder in which one has manic episodes alternating with periods of depression, usually with relatively normal periods in between.

bottom-up processing: Information processing in which individual components or bits of data are combined until a complete perception is formed.

brainstem: The structure that begins at the point where the spinal cord enlarges as it enters the brain and that includes the medulla, the pons, and the reticular formation.

brightness: The dimension of visual sensation that is dependent on the intensity of light reflected from a surface and that corresponds to the amplitude of the light wave.

brightness constancy: The tendency to see objects as maintaining the same brightness regardless of differences in lighting conditions.

Broca's aphasia: An impairment in the ability to physically produce speech sounds, or, in extreme cases, an inability to speak at all; caused by damage to Broca's area.

Broca's area: The area in the frontal lobe, usually in the left hemisphere, that controls production of speech sounds.

bystander effect: The fact that as the number of bystanders at an emergency increases, the probability that the victim will receive help decreases, and help, if given, is likely to be delayed.

Cannon-Bard theory: The theory that physiological arousal and the feeling of emotion occur simultaneously after an emotion-provoking stimulus is relayed to the thalamus.

cardinal trait: Allport's name for a personal quality that is so strong a part of a person's personality that he or she may become identified with that trait.

case study: An in-depth study of one or a few participants consisting of information gathered through observation, interview, and perhaps psychological testing.

catatonic schizophrenia (KAT-uh-TAHN-ik): A type of schizophrenia characterized by complete stillness or stupor and/or periods of great agitation and excitement; patients may assume an unusual posture and remain in it for long periods.

cell body: The part of the neuron, containing the nucleus, that carries out the metabolic functions of the neuron.

central nervous system (CNS): The brain and the spinal cord.

central trait: Allport's name for the type of trait you would use in writing a letter of recommendation.

centration: A preoperational child's tendency to focus on only one dimension of a stimulus and ignore other dimensions.

cerebellum (sehr-uh-BELL-um): The brain structure that executes smooth, skilled body movements and regulates muscle tone and posture.

cerebral cortex (seh-REE-brul KOR-tex): The grey, convoluted covering of the cerebral hemispheres that is responsible for higher mental processes such as language, memory, and thinking.

cerebral hemispheres (seh-REE-brul): The right and left halves of the cerebrum, covered by the cerebral cortex and connected by the corpus callosum.

cerebrum (seh-REE-brum): The largest structure of the human brain, consisting of the two cerebral hemispheres connected by the corpus callosum and covered by the cerebral cortex.

chromosomes: Rod-shaped structures in the nuclei of body cells, which contain all the genes and carry all the hereditary information.

circadian rhythm (sur-KAY-dee-un): Within each 24-hour period, the regular fluctuation from high to low points of certain bodily functions.

classical conditioning: A process through which a response previously made only to a specific stimulus is made to another stimulus that has been paired repeatedly with the original stimulus.

clinical psychologist: A psychologist, usually with a Ph.D., whose training is in the diagnosis, treatment, or research of psychological and behavioural disorders.

coaction effects: The impact on performance caused by the presence of others engaged in the same task.

cocaine: A stimulant that produces a feeling of euphoria.

cochlea (KOK-lee-uh): The snail-shaped, fluid-filled organ in the inner ear that contains the hair cells (the sound receptors).

cognitive dissonance: The unpleasant state that can occur when people become aware of inconsistencies between their attitudes or between their attitudes and their behaviour.

cognitive processes (COG-nuh-tiv): Mental processes such as thinking, knowing, problem solving, and remembering.

cognitive psychology: A specialty that studies mental processes such as memory, problem solving, decision making, perception, language, and other forms of cognition; often uses the information-processing approach.

cognitive therapy: Any therapy designed to change maladaptive thoughts and behaviour, based on the assumption that maladaptive behaviour can result from one's irrational thoughts, beliefs, and ideas.

collective unconscious: In Jung's theory, the most inaccessible layer of the unconscious, which contains the universal experiences of humankind transmitted to each individual.

colour blindness: The inability to distinguish some or all colours in vision, resulting from a defect in the cones.

colour constancy: The tendency to see objects as maintaining about the same colour regardless of differences in lighting conditions.

compliance: Acting in accordance with the wishes, the suggestions, or the direct request of another person.

compulsion: A persistent, irresistible, irrational urge to perform an act or ritual repeatedly.

concept: A label that represents a class or group of objects, people, or events sharing common characteristics or attributes.

concrete operations stage: Piaget's third stage of cognitive development (ages seven to eleven), during which a child acquires the concepts of reversibility and conservation and is able to apply logical thinking to concrete objects.

conditioned reflex: A learned reflex rather than a naturally occurring one.

conditioned response (CR): A response that comes to be elicited by a conditioned stimulus as a result of its repeated pairing with an unconditioned stimulus.

conditioned stimulus (CS): A neutral stimulus that, after repeated pairing with an unconditioned stimulus, becomes associated with it and elicits a conditioned response.

conditions of worth: Conditions upon which the positive regard of others rests.

cones: The receptor cells in the retina that enable us to see colour and fine detail in adequate light, but that do not function in dim light.

conformity: Changing or adopting an attitude or behaviour to be consistent with the norms of a group or the expectations of others.

conscious (KON-shus): Those thoughts, feelings, sensations, or memories of which we are aware at any given moment.

consciousness: The continuous stream of perceptions, thoughts, feelings, or sensations of which we are aware from moment to moment.

conservation: The concept that a given quantity of matter remains the same despite rearrangement or change in its appearance, as long as nothing has been added or taken away.

consolidation: The presumed process, believed to involve the hippocampus, by which a permanent memory is formed.

consolidation failure: Any disruption in the consolidation process that prevents a permanent memory from forming.

consumer psychology: A specialty concerned with studying, measuring, predicting, and influencing consumer behaviour.

consummate love: According to Sternberg's theory, the most complete form of love, consisting of three components–intimacy, passion, and decision/commitment.

contact hypothesis: The notion that prejudice can be reduced through increased contact among members of different social groups.

continuous reinforcement: Reinforcement that is administered after every desired or correct response; the most effective method of conditioning a new response.

control group: In an experiment, a group that is similar to the experimental group and that is exposed to the same experimental environment but is not exposed to the independent variable; used for purposes of comparison.

controlled drinking: A behavioural approach in the treatment of alcoholism, designed to teach alcoholics the skills necessary to drink socially without losing control.

conventional level: Kohlberg's second level of moral reasoning, in which right and wrong are based on the internalized standards of others; "right" is whatever helps or is approved of by others, or whatever is consistent with the laws of society.

convergence: A binocular depth cue in which the eyes turn inward as they focus on nearby objects–the closer an object, the greater the convergence.

conversion disorder: A somatoform disorder in which a loss of motor or sensory functioning in some part of the body has no physical cause but solves some psychological problem.

coping: Efforts through action and thought to deal with demands that are perceived as taxing or overwhelming.

cornea (KOR-nee-uh): The transparent covering of the coloured part of the eye that bends light rays inward through the pupil.

corpus callosum (KOR-pus kah-LO-sum): The thick band of nerve fibres that connects the two cerebral hemispheres and makes possible the transfer of information and the synchronization of activity between them.

correlation coefficient: A numerical value that indicates the strength and direction of the relationship between two variables; ranges from +1.00 (a perfect positive correlation) to −1.00 (a perfect negative correlation).

correlational method: A research method used to establish the relationship (correlation) between two characteristics, events, or behaviours.

counselling psychologist: A psychologist who helps people with problems that are considered less severe than those generally handled by a clinical psychologist; often provides vocational or academic counselling; usually works in a nonmedical setting.

crack: The most potent, inexpensive, and addictive form of cocaine, and the form that is smoked.

crash: The feelings of depression, exhaustion, irritability, and anxiety that occur following an amphetamine, cocaine, or crack high.

creativity: The ability to produce original, appropriate, and valuable ideas and/or solutions to problems.

critical period: A period that is so important to development that a harmful environmental influence can keep a bodily structure or behaviour from developing normally.

cross-sectional study: A type of developmental study in which researchers compare groups of subjects of different ages on certain characteristics to determine age-related differences.

CT scan (computerized axial tomography): A brain-scanning technique involving a rotating X-ray scanner and a high-speed computer analysis that produces slice-by-slice, cross-sectional images of the structure of the brain.

culture-fair intelligence test: An intelligence test designed to minimize cultural bias by using questions that will not penalize those whose culture or language differs from that of the urban middle or upper class.

dark adaptation: The eye's increasing ability to see in dim light; results partly from the dilation of the pupils.

decay theory: A theory of forgetting that holds that the memory trace, if not used, disappears with the passage of time.

decibel (DES-ih-bel): A unit of measurement of the intensity or loudness of sound based on the amplitude of the sound wave.

declarative memory: The subsystem within long-term memory that stores facts, information, and personal life experiences; also called *explicit memory*.

defence mechanism: An unconscious, irrational means used by the ego to defend against anxiety; involves self-deception and the distortion of reality.

delta wave: The slowest brain wave, having a frequency of 1 to 3 cycles per second and associated with slow-wave (deep) sleep.

delusion: A false belief, not generally shared by others in the culture, that cannot be changed despite strong evidence to the contrary.

delusion of grandeur: A false belief that one is a famous person or someone who has some great knowledge, ability, or authority.

delusion of persecution: An individual's false belief that a person or group is trying in some way to harm him or her.

dendrites (DEN-drytes): The branch-like extensions of a neuron that receive signals from other neurons.

denial: Refusing to consciously acknowledge the existence of a danger or a threatening condition.

dependent variable: The variable that is measured at the end of an experiment and that is presumed to vary as a result of manipulations of the independent variable.

depressants: A category of drugs that decrease activity in the central nervous system, slow down bodily functions, and reduce sensitivity to outside stimulation; also called "downers."

depth perception: The ability to see in three dimensions and to estimate distance.

descriptive research methods: Research methods that yield descriptions of behaviour rather than causal explanations.

developmental psychology: The study of how humans grow, develop, and change throughout the life span.

deviation score: A test score calculated by comparing an individual's score with the scores of others of the same age on whom the test was normed.

diathesis–stress model: The idea that people with a constitutional predisposition (diathesis) toward a disorder, such as schizophrenia, may develop the disorder if they are subjected to sufficient environmental stress.

difference threshold: The smallest increase or decrease in a physical stimulus required to produce a difference in sensation that is noticeable 50 percent of the time.

diffusion of responsibility: The feeling among bystanders at an emergency that the responsibility for helping is shared by the group, so each person feels less compelled to act than if he or she alone bore the total responsibility.

directive therapy: An approach to therapy in which the therapist takes an active role in determining the course of therapy sessions and provides answers and suggestions to the patient.

discrimination: Behaviour, usually negative, directed toward others based on their gender, religion, race, or membership in a particular group.

discrimination: The learned ability to distinguish between similar stimuli so that the conditioned response occurs only to the original conditioned stimulus but not to similar stimuli.

discriminative stimulus: A stimulus that signals whether a certain response or behaviour is likely to be followed by reward or punishment.

disorganized schizophrenia: The most serious type of schizophrenia, marked by inappropriate affect, silliness, laughter, grotesque mannerisms, and bizarre behaviour.

displacement: A defence mechanism. Substitution of a less threatening object for the original object of an impulse. Taking out frustrations on objects or people who are less threatening than those that provoked us.

displacement: The event that occurs when short-term memory is holding its maximum and each new item entering short-term memory pushes out an existing item.

display rules: Cultural rules that dictate how emotions should be expressed, and when and where their expression is appropriate.

dispositional attribution: Attribution of one's own or another's behaviour to some internal cause such as a personal trait, motive, or attitude; an internal attribution.

dissociative amnesia: A dissociative disorder in which there is a loss of memory for limited periods in one's life or for one's entire personal identity.

dissociative disorders: Disorders in which, under stress, one loses the integration of consciousness, identity, and memories of important personal events.

dissociative fugue (FEWG): A dissociative disorder in which one has a complete loss of memory for one's entire identity, travels away from home, and may assume a new identity.

dissociative identity disorder: A dissociative disorder in which two or more distinct personalities occur in the same person, each taking over at different times; also called multiple personality.

divergent thinking: Producing one or more possible ideas, answers, or solutions to a problem rather than a single, correct response.

dominant gene: The gene that is expressed in the individual.

door-in-the-face technique: A strategy in which someone makes a large, unreasonable request with the expectation that the person will refuse but will then be more likely to respond favourably to a smaller request at a later time.

dopamine (DOE-pah-meen): A neurotransmitter that plays a role in learning, attention, and movement; a deficiency of dopamine is associated with Parkinson's disease, and an oversensitivity to it is associated with some cases of schizophrenia.

double-blind technique: An experimental procedure in which neither the subjects nor the experimenter knows who is in the experimental or control groups until after the results have been gathered; a control for experimenter bias.

downers: A slang term for depressants.

drive: A state of tension or arousal brought about by an underlying need, which motivates one to engage in behaviour that will satisfy the need and reduce the tension.

drive-reduction theory: A theory of motivation suggesting that a need creates an unpleasant state of arousal or tension called a drive, which impels the organism to engage in behaviour that will satisfy the need and reduce tension.

drug dependence (physical): A compulsive pattern of drug use in which the user develops a drug tolerance coupled with unpleasant withdrawal symptoms when the drug is discontinued.

drug dependence (psychological): A craving or irresistible urge for a drug's pleasurable effects.

drug tolerance: A condition in which the user becomes progressively less affected by a drug so that larger and larger doses are necessary to maintain the same effect.

DSM-IV: *The Diagnostic and Statistical Manual of Mental Disorders (fourth edition)*, a manual published by the American Psychiatric Association which describes about 290 mental disorders and their symptoms.

Ecstasy (MDMA): A designer drug that is a hallucinogen-amphetamine and can produce permanent damage of the serotonin-releasing neurons.

ego : In Freudian theory, the rational, largely conscious system of personality, which operates according to the reality principle.

ego integrity versus despair: Erikson's eighth and final psychosocial stage, occurring during old age, when individuals look back on their lives with satisfaction or with major regrets.

eidetic imagery (eye-DET-ik): The ability to retain the image of a visual stimulus several minutes after it has been removed from view.

electroconvulsive therapy (ECT): A treatment in which an electric current is passed though the brain, causing a seizure; usually reserved for the severely depressed who are either suicidal or unresponsive to other treatment.

electroencephalogram (EEG) (ee-lek-tro-en-SEFF-uh-lo-gram): A record of brainwave activity made by the electroencephalograph.

embryo: The developing human organism during the period (week 3 through week 8) when the major systems, organs, and structures of the body develop.

emotion: A feeling state involving physiological arousal, a cognitive appraisal of the situation arousing the state, and an outward expression of the state.

emotional intelligence: A type of intelligence that includes an awareness of and an ability to manage one's own emotions, the ability to motivate oneself, empathy, and the ability to handle relationships successfully.

emotion-focused coping: A response aimed at reducing the emotional impact of the stressor.

encoding: Transforming information into a form that can be stored in short-term or long-term memory.

encoding failure: A cause of forgetting that results from material never having been put into long-term memory.

encounter group: An intense emotional group experience designed to promote personal growth and self-knowledge; participants are encouraged to let down their defences and relate honestly and openly to one another.

endocrine system (EN-duh-krin): A system of ductless glands in various parts of the body that manufacture and secrete hormones into the bloodstream or lymph fluids, thus affecting cells in other parts of the body.

endorphins (en-DOOR-fins): Chemicals produced naturally by the pituitary gland that reduce pain and affect mood positively.

episodic memory (ep-ih-SOD-ik): The subpart of declarative memory that contains memories of personally experienced events.

evolutionary perspective: A perspective that focuses on how humans have evolved and adapted behaviours required for survival against various environmental pressures over the long course of evolution.

exemplars: The individual instances of a concept that we have stored in memory from our own experience.

exhaustion stage: The final stage of the general adaptation syndrome, occurring if the organism fails in its efforts to resist the stressor.

existential therapy: A therapy that places an emphasis on finding meaning in life.

experimental group: In an experiment, the group of participants that is exposed to the independent variable or the treatment.

experimental method: The research method whereby researchers randomly assign participants to groups and control all conditions other than one or more independent variables, which are then manipulated to determine their effect on some behavioural measure—the dependent variable in the experiment.

experimenter bias: A phenomenon that occurs when the researcher's preconceived notions in some way influence the subjects' behaviour and/or the interpretation of experimental results.

exposure and response prevention: A behaviour therapy that exposes obsessive-compulsive disorder patients to stimuli generating increasing anxiety; patients must agree not to carry out their normal rituals for a specified period of time after exposure.

extinction: The weakening and often eventual disappearance of a learned response (in classical conditioning, the conditioned response is weakened by repeated presentation of the conditioned stimulus without the unconditioned stimulus; in operant conditioning, the conditioned response is weakened by the withholding of reinforcement).

extrasensory perception (ESP): Gaining awareness of or information about objects, events, or another's thoughts through some means other than the known sensory channels.

extraversion: The tendency to be outgoing, adaptable, and sociable.

extrinsic motivation: The desire to perform an act to gain a reward or to avoid an undesirable consequence.

facial-feedback hypothesis: The idea that the muscular movements involved in certain facial expressions trigger the corresponding emotions (for example, smiling makes us happy).

family therapy: Therapy based on the assumption that an individual's problem is caused and/or maintained in part by problems within the family unit, and so the entire family is involved in therapy.

fat cells: Numbering 30 to 40 billion, cells that serve as storehouses for liquefied fat in the body; with weight loss, they decrease in size but not in number.

fetal alcohol syndrome: A condition, caused by maternal alcohol intake during pregnancy, in which the baby is born mentally retarded, abnormally small, and with facial, organ, and limb abnormalities.

fetus: The developing human organism during the period (week 9 until birth) when rapid growth and further development of the structures, organs, and systems of the body take place.

figure–ground: A principle of perceptual organization whereby the visual field is perceived in terms of an object (figure) standing out against a background (ground).

five-factor theory: A trait theory that attempts to explain personality using five broad dimensions, each of which is composed of a constellation of personality traits.

fixation: Arrested development at a psychosexual stage occurring because of excessive gratification or frustration at that stage.

fixed-interval schedule: A schedule in which a reinforcer is given following the first correct response after a fixed period of time has elapsed.

fixed-ratio schedule: A schedule in which a reinforcer is given after a fixed number of non-reinforced correct responses.

flashback: The brief recurrence of effects a person has experienced while taking LSD or other hallucinogens, occurring suddenly and without warning at a later time.

flashbulb memory: An extremely vivid memory of the conditions surrounding one's first hearing the news of a surprising, shocking, or highly emotional event.

flavour: The combined sensory experience of taste, smell, and touch.

flooding: A behavioural therapy used to treat phobias, during which clients are exposed to the feared object or event (or asked to imagine it vividly) for an extended period until their anxiety decreases.

foot-in-the-door technique: A strategy designed to secure a favourable response to a small request at first, with the aim of making the subject more likely to agree later to a larger request.

formal operations stage: Piaget's fourth and final stage, characterized by the ability to apply logical thinking to abstract problems and hypothetical situations.

fovea (FO-vee-uh): A small area of the retina, 1/ 50 of an inch in diameter, that provides the clearest and sharpest vision because it has the largest concentration of cones.

fraternal (dizygotic) twins: Twins who are no more alike genetically than ordinary brothers and sisters; dizygotic twins.

free association: A psychoanalytic technique used to explore the unconscious by having patients reveal whatever thoughts or images come to mind.

frequency: Measured in the unit hertz, the number of sound waves or cycles per second, determining the pitch of the sound.

frequency theory: The theory that hair cell receptors vibrate the same number of times as the sounds that reach them, thereby accounting for the way variations in pitch are transmitted to the brain.

frontal lobes: The lobes that control voluntary body movements, speech production, and such functions as thinking, motivation, planning for the future, impulse control, and emotional responses.

frustration: Interference with the attainment of a goal or the blocking of an impulse.

frustration–aggression hypothesis: The hypothesis that frustration produces aggression.

functional fixedness: The failure to use familiar objects in novel ways to solve problems because of a tendency to view objects only in terms of their customary functions.

functionalism: An early school of psychology that was concerned with how mental processes help humans and animals adapt to their environments; developed as a reaction against structuralism.

fundamental attribution error: The tendency to overemphasize internal causes and underemphasize situational factors when explaining the behaviour of others.

gate-control theory: The theory that the pain signals transmitted by slow-firing nerve fibres can be blocked at the spinal gate if fast-firing fibres get their messages to the spinal cord first, or if the brain itself inhibits transmission of the pain messages.

gender identity disorders: Disorders characterized by a problem accepting one's identity as male or female.

general adaptation syndrome (GAS): The predictable sequence of reactions (the alarm, resistance, and exhaustion stages) that organisms show in response to stressors.

generalization: In classical conditioning, the tendency to make a conditioned response to a stimulus similar to the original conditioned stimulus; in operant conditioning, the tendency to make the learned response to a stimulus similar to the one for which it was originally reinforced.

generalized anxiety disorder: An anxiety disorder in which people experience excessive anxiety or worry that they find difficult to control.

generativity versus stagnation: Erikson's seventh psychosocial stage, occurring during for middle age, when the individual becomes increasingly concerned with guiding the next generation rather than becoming self-absorbed and stagnating.

genes: Within the chromosomes, the segments of DNA that are the basic units for the transmission of hereditary traits.

genital stage: The final of Freud's psychosexual stages (from puberty on), in which for most people the focus of sexual energy gradually shifts to the opposite sex, culminating in the attainment of full adult sexuality.

***g* factor:** Spearman's term for a general intellectual ability that underlies all mental operations to some degree.

Gestalt (geh-SHTALT): A German word roughly meaning "form" or "pattern."

Gestalt psychology: The school of psychology that emphasizes that individuals perceive objects and patterns as whole units and that the perceived whole is more than just the sum of its parts.

Gestalt therapy: A therapy originated by Fritz Perls that emphasizes the importance of clients fully experiencing, in the present moment, their feelings, thoughts, and actions and taking personal responsibility for their behaviour.

glial cells (GLEE-ul): Cells that help to make the brain more efficient by holding the neurons together, removing waste products such as dead neurons, making the myelin coating for the axons, and performing other manufacturing, nourishing, and clean-up tasks.

group polarization: The tendency of members of a group, after group discussion, to shift toward a more extreme position in whatever direction they were leaning initially—either more risky or more cautious.

group therapy: A form of therapy in which several clients (usually 7–10) meet regularly with one or two therapists to resolve personal problems.

groupthink: The tendency for members of a very cohesive group to feel such pressure to maintain group solidarity and to reach agreement on an issue that they fail to adequately weigh available evidence or to consider objections and alternatives.

gustation: The sensation of taste.

habituation: A decrease in response or attention to a stimulus as an infant becomes accustomed to it.

hair cells: Sensory receptors for hearing, found in the cochlea.

hallucination: A sensory perception in the absence of any external sensory stimulus; an imaginary sensation.

hallucinogens (hal-lu-SIN-o-jenz): A category of drugs, sometimes called psychedelics, that alter perception and mood and can cause hallucinations.

halo effect: The tendency to infer generally positive or negative traits in a person as a result of observing one major positive or negative trait.

hardiness: A combination of three psychological qualities shared by people who can undergo high levels of stress yet remain healthy: a sense of control over one's life, commitment to one's personal goals, and a tendency to view change as a challenge rather than as a threat.

hassles: Little stressors that include the irritating demands and troubled relationships that can occur daily and that, according to Lazarus, cause more stress than do major life changes.

health psychology: The field concerned with the psychological factors that contribute to health, illness, and recovery.

heritability: An index of the degree to which a characteristic is estimated to be influenced by heredity.

heroin: A highly addictive, partly synthetic narcotic derived from morphine.

heuristic (hyu-RIS-tik): A problemsolving method that offers a promising way to attack a problem and arrive at a solution, although it does not guarantee success.

hierarchy of needs: Maslow's theory of motivation, in which needs are arranged in order of urgency ranging from physical needs to security needs, belonging needs, esteem needs, and finally the need for selfactualization.

higher-order conditioning: Occurs when a neutral stimulus is paired with an existing conditioned stimulus, becomes associated with it, and gains the power to elicit the same conditioned response.

hippocampus (hip-po-CAM-pus): A structure in the limbic system that plays a central role in the formation of long-term memories.

homeostasis: The tendency of the body to maintain a balanced internal state with regard to oxygen level, body temperature, blood sugar, water balance, and so forth.

hormone: A substance manufactured and released in one part of the body that affects other parts of the body.

hue: The property of light commonly referred to as "colour" (red, blue, green, etc.), determined primarily by the wavelength of light reflected from a surface.

humanistic psychology: The school of psychology that focuses on the uniqueness of human beings and their capacity for choice, growth, and psychological health.

hypnosis: A trance-like state of concentrated, focused attention, heightened suggestibility, and diminished response to external stimuli.

hypochondriasis (HI-puh-kahn-DRY-uh-sis): A somatoform disorder in which persons are preoccupied with their health and convinced they have some serious disorder despite reassurance from doctors to the contrary.

hypothalamus (HY-po-THAL-uh-mus): A small but influential brain structure that controls the pituitary gland and regulates hunger, thirst, sexual behaviour, body temperature, and a wide variety of emotional behaviours.

hypothesis: A prediction about the relationship between two or more variables.

id: The unconscious system of the personality, which contains the life and death instincts and operates on the pleasure principle.

identical (monozygotic) twins: Twins with identical genes; monozygotic twins.

identity versus role confusion: Erikson's fifth psychosocial stage, when adolescents need to establish their own identity and to form values to live by; failure can lead to an identity crisis.

illusion: A false perception of actual stimuli involving a misperception of size, shape, or the relationship of one element to another.

imagery: The representation in the mind of a sensory experience—visual, auditory, gustatory, motor, olfactory, or tactile.

imaginary audience: A belief of adolescents that they are or will be the focus of attention in social situations and that others will be as critical or approving as they are of themselves.

inappropriate affect: A symptom common in schizophrenia in which a person's behaviour (including facial expression, tone of voice, and gestures) does not reflect the emotion that would be expected under the circumstances; for example, a person laughs at a tragedy, cries at a joke.

incentive: An external stimulus that motivates behaviour (examples: money, fame).

independent variable: In an experiment, the factor or condition that the researcher manipulates in order to determine its effect on another behaviour or condition known as the dependent variable.

industry versus inferiority: Erikson's fourth psychosocial stage (6 years to puberty), when children develop a sense of industry or inferiority depending on the way their parents and teachers react to their efforts to undertake projects.

infantile amnesia: The relative inability of older children and adults to recall events from the first few years of life.

in-group: A social group with a strong sense of togetherness and from which others are excluded.

initiative versus guilt: Erikson's third psychosocial stage (ages three to six), when children develop a sense of initiative or guilt depending on the way their parents react to their initiation of play, their motor activities, and their questions.

innate: Inborn, unlearned.

inner ear: The innermost portion of the ear, containing the cochlea, the vestibular sacs, and the semicircular canals.

insight therapy: Any type of psychotherapy based on the notion that psychological well-being depends on self-understanding.

insomnia: A sleep disorder characterized by difficulty falling or staying asleep or by light, restless, or poor sleep; causing distress and impaired daytime functioning.

instinct: An inborn, unlearned, fixed pattern of behaviour that is characteristic of an entire species.

instinct theory: The notion that human behaviour is motivated by certain innate tendencies, or instincts, shared by all individuals.

intelligence quotient (IQ): An index of intelligence originally derived by dividing mental age by chronological age and then multiplying by 100.

interference: Memory loss that occurs when information or associations stored either before or after a given memory hinder our ability to remember it.

interpersonal therapy (IPT): A brief psychotherapy designed to help depressed people understand their problems in interpersonal relationships and develop more effective ways to improve them.

intimacy versus isolation: Erikson's sixth psychosocial stage, when the young adult must establish intimacy in a relationship in order to avoid feeling isolated and lonely.

intrinsic motivation: The desire to perform an act because it is satisfying or pleasurable in and of itself.

introversion: The tendency to focus inward; to be reflective, retiring, and non-social.

inventory: A paper-and-pencil test with questions about a person's thoughts, feelings, and behaviours, which can be scored according to a standard procedure.

Jackson Personality Inventory (JPI): A highly regarded personality test used to assess the normal personality.

James-Lange theory: The theory that emotional feelings result when we become aware of our physiological response to an emotion-provoking stimulus (for example, we are afraid because we tremble).

just noticeable difference (JND): The smallest change in sensation that we are able to detect 50 percent of the time.

kinesthetic sense: The sense that provides information about relative position and movement of body parts.

latency period: The period following Freud's phallic stage (ages 5 or 6 years to puberty), in which the sex instinct is largely repressed and temporarily sublimated in school and play activities.

lateral hypothalamus (LH): The part of the hypothalamus that supposedly acts as a feeding centre and, when activated, signals an animal to eat; when the LH is destroyed, the animal refuses to eat.

lateralization: The specialization of one of the cerebral hemispheres to handle a particular function.

Lazarus theory: The theory that an emotion-provoking stimulus triggers a cognitive appraisal, which is followed by the emotion and the physiological arousal.

learned helplessness: The learned response of resigning oneself passively to aversive conditions, rather than taking action to change, escape, or avoid them; learned through repeated exposure to inescapable or unavoidable aversive events.

learning: A relatively permanent change in behaviour, capability, or attitude that is acquired through experience and cannot be attributed to illness, injury, or maturation.

left hemisphere: The hemisphere that controls the right side of the body, coordinates complex movements, and, in 95 percent of people, controls the production of speech and written language.

lens: The transparent structure behind the iris that changes in shape as it focuses images on the retina.

levels-of-processing model: A single-memory-system model in which retention depends on how deeply information is processed.

libido (lih-BEE-doe): Freud's name for the psychic or sexual energy that comes from the id and provides the energy for the entire personality.

limbic system: A group of structures in the brain, including the amygdala and hippocampus, that are collectively involved in emotion, memory, and motivation.

linguistic relativity hypothesis: The notion that the language a person speaks largely determines the nature of that person's thoughts.

lobotomy: A psychosurgery technique in which the nerve fibres connecting the frontal lobes to the deeper brain centres are severed.

locus of control: A concept used to explain how people account for what happens in their lives—people with an internal locus of control see themselves as primarily in control of their behaviour and its consequences; those with an external locus of control perceive what happens to be in the hands of fate, luck, or chance.

long-term memory: The relatively permanent memory system with a virtually unlimited capacity.

long-term potentiation: A longlasting increase in the efficiency of neural transmission at the synapses.

longitudinal study: A type of developmental study in which the same group of participants is followed and measured at different ages.

low-ball technique: A strategy to gain compliance by making a very attractive initial offer to get a person to agree to an action and then making the terms less favourable.

low-birth-weight baby: A baby weighing less than 2.5 kilograms.

LSD (lysergic acid diethylamide): A powerful hallucinogen with unpredictable effects ranging from perceptual changes and vivid hallucinations to states of panic and terror.

lucid dream: A dream during which the dreamer is aware of dreaming and is often able to influence the content of the dream while it is in progress.

mainstreaming: Educating mentally disabled students in regular rather than special schools by placing them in regular classes for part of the day or having special classrooms in regular schools.

major depressive disorder: A mood disorder characterized by feelings of great sadness, despair, guilt, worthlessness, and hopelessness and, in extreme cases, suicidal tendencies.

manic episode: A period of extreme elation, euphoria, and hyperactivity, often accompanied by delusions of grandeur and by hostility if activity is blocked.

marijuana: A hallucinogen with effects ranging from relaxation and giddiness to perceptual distortions and hallucinations.

massed practice: One long learning practice session as opposed to spacing the learning in shorter practice sessions over an extended period.

matching hypothesis: The notion that people tend to have spouses, lovers, or friends who are approximately equivalent in social assets such as physical attractiveness.

means–end analysis: A heuristic problem-solving strategy in which the current position is compared with the desired goal, and a series of steps are formulated and taken to close the gap between them.

meditation: A group of techniques that involve focusing attention on an object, a word, one's breathing, or body movement in order to block out all distractions and achieve an altered state of consciousness.

medulla (muh-DUL-uh): The part of the brainstem that controls heartbeat, blood pressure, breathing, coughing, and swallowing.

menarche: The onset of menstruation.

menopause: The cessation of menstruation, occurring between ages 45 and 55 and signifying the end of reproductive capacity.

mental disability: Subnormal intelligence reflected by an IQ below 70 and by adaptive functioning severely deficient for one's age.

mental set: The tendency to apply a familiar strategy to the solution of a problem without carefully considering the special requirements of the problem.

mere-exposure effect: The tendency of people to develop a more positive evaluation of some person, object, or other stimulus with repeated exposure to it.

metabolic rate (meh-tuh-BALL-ik): The rate at which the body burns calories to produce energy.

microelectrode: An electrical wire so small that it can be used either to monitor the electrical activity of a single neuron or to stimulate activity within it.

microsleep: A momentary lapse from wakefulness into sleep, usually occurring when one has been sleep-deprived.

middle ear: The portion of the ear containing the ossicles, which connect the eardrum to the oval window and amplify the vibrations as they travel to the inner ear.

Minnesota Multiphasic Personality Inventory-2 (MMPI-2): A revision of the most extensively researched and widely used personality test; used to screen and diagnose psychiatric problems and disorders.

model: The individual who demonstrates a behaviour or serves as an example in observational learning.

modelling: Another name for observational learning.

monocular depth cues (mah-NOK-yu-ler): Depth cues that can be perceived by only one eye.

mood disorders: Disorders characterized by extreme and unwarranted disturbances in feeling or mood.

morphemes: The smallest units of meaning in a language.

motivated forgetting: Forgetting through suppression or repression in order to protect oneself from material that is too painful, anxiety- or guilt-producing, or otherwise unpleasant.

motivation: The process that initiates, directs, and sustains behaviour to satisfy physiological or psychological needs.

motives: Needs or desires that energize and direct behaviour toward a goal.

motor cortex: The strip of tissue at the rear of the frontal lobes that controls voluntary body movement.

MRI (magnetic resonance imaging): A diagnostic scanning technique that produces high-resolution images of the structures of the brain.

myelin sheath (MY-uh-lin): The white, fatty coating wrapped around some axons that acts as insulation and enables impulses to travel much faster.

narcolepsy (NAR-co-lep-see): A serious sleep disorder characterized by excessive daytime sleepiness and sudden, uncontrollable attacks of REM sleep.

narcotics: Derived from the opium poppy, a class of depressant drugs that have pain-relieving and calming effects.

naturalistic observation: A research method in which the researcher observes and records behaviour in its natural setting without attempting to influence or control it.

nature–nurture controversy: The debate over whether intelligence and other traits are primarily the result of heredity or environment.

need for achievement: The need to accomplish something difficult and to perform at a high standard of excellence.

negative reinforcement: The termination of an unpleasant stimulus after a response in order to increase the probability that the response will be repeated.

neonate: Newborn infant up to 1 month old.

neuron (NEW-ron): A specialized cell that conducts impulses through the nervous system and contains three major parts–a cell body, dendrites, and an axon.

neurosis (new-RO-sis): An obsolete term for a disorder causing personal distress and some impairment in functioning but not causing loss of contact with reality or violation of important social norms.

neurotransmitter (NEW-ro-TRANS-mit-er): A chemical that is released into the synaptic cleft from the axon terminal of the sending neuron, crosses the synapse, and binds to appropriate receptor sites on the dendrites or cell body of the receiving neuron, influencing the cell either to fire or not to fire.

nightmare: A very frightening dream occurring during REM sleep.

non-declarative memory: The subsystem within long-term memory that consists of skills acquired through repetitive practice, habits, and simple classically conditioned responses; also called *implicit memory*.

non-directive therapy: An approach in which the therapist acts to facilitate growth, giving understanding and support rather than proposing solutions, answering questions, or actively directing the course of therapy.

nonsense syllable: A consonant-vowel-consonant combination that does not spell a word; used to control for the meaningfulness of the material.

norepinephrine: A neurotransmitter affecting eating and sleeping; a deficiency of norepinephrine is associated with depression.

norms: The attitudes and standards of behaviour expected of members of a particular group.

norms: Standards based on the range of test scores of a large group of people who are selected to provide the bases of comparison for those who will take the test later.

NREM dreams: Mental activity occurring during NREM sleep that is more thought-like in quality than REM dreams are.

NREM sleep: Non-rapid eye movement sleep, consisting of the four sleep stages and characterized by slow, regular respiration and heart rates, an absence of rapid eye movements, and blood pressure and brain activity that are at a 24-hour low point.

obesity: Excessive fatness; a term applied to men whose body fat exceeds 20 percent of their weight and to women whose body fat exceeds 30 percent of their weight.

object permanence: The realization that objects continue to exist even when they are no longer perceived.

observational learning: Learning by observing the behaviour of others and the consequences of that behaviour; learning by imitation.

obsession: A persistent, recurring, involuntary thought, image, or impulse that invades consciousness and causes great distress.

obsessive-compulsive disorder (OCD): An anxiety disorder in which a person suffers from obsessions and/or compulsions.

occipital lobes (ahk-SIP-uh-tul): The lobes that contain the primary visual cortex, where vision registers, and association areas involved in the interpretation of visual information.

Oedipus complex (ED-uh-pus): Occurring in the phallic stage, a conflict in which the child is sexually attracted to the opposite-sex parent and feels hostility toward the same-sex parent.

olfaction (ol-FAK-shun): The sensation of smell; the process of smell.

olfactory bulbs: Two matchstick-sized structures above the nasal cavities, where smell sensations first register in the brain.

olfactory epithelium: Two one-inch square patches of tissue, one at the top of each nasal cavity, which together contain about 10 million receptors for smell.

operant conditioning: A type of learning in which the consequences of behaviour tend to modify that behaviour in the future (behaviour that is reinforced tends to be repeated; behaviour that is ignored or punished is less likely to be repeated).

opponent-process theory: The theory that certain cells in the visual system increase their firing rate to signal one colour and decrease their firing rate to signal the opposing colour (red/green, yellow/blue, white/black).

optic nerve: The nerve that carries visual information from the retina to the brain.

oral stage: Freud's first psychosexual stage (birth to 12 or 18 months), in which sensual pleasure is derived mainly through stimulation of the mouth.

out-group: A social group specifically identified by the ingroup as not belonging.

outer ear: The visible part of the ear, consisting of the pinna and the auditory canal.

overextension: The act of using a word, on the basis of some shared feature, to apply to a broader range of objects than is appropriate.

overlearning: Practising or studying material beyond the point where it can be repeated once without error.

overregularization: The act of inappropriately applying the grammatical rules for forming plurals and past tenses to irregular nouns and verbs.

panic attack: An attack of overwhelming anxiety, fear, or terror.

panic disorder: An anxiety disorder in which a person experiences recurrent unpredictable attacks of overwhelming anxiety, fear, or terror.

paranoid schizophrenia: A type of schizophrenia characterized by delusions of grandeur or persecution.

paraphilia: A sexual disorder in which sexual urges, fantasies, and behaviour generally involve children, other non-consenting partners, non-human objects, or the suffering and humiliation of oneself or one's partner.

parapsychology: The study of psychic phenomena, which include extrasensory perception (ESP) and psychokinesis.

parasomnias: Sleep disturbances in which behaviours and physiological states that normally occur only in the waking state take place during sleep or the transition from sleep to wakefulness (e.g., sleepwalking, sleep terrors).

parasympathetic nervous system: The division of the autonomic nervous system that is associated with relaxation and the conservation of energy and that brings the heightened bodily responses back to normal after an emergency.

parietal lobes (puh-RY-uh-tul): The lobes that contain the somatosensory cortex (where touch, pressure, temperature, and pain register) and other areas that are responsible for body awareness and spatial orientation.

partial reinforcement: A pattern of reinforcement in which some portion, rather than 100 percent, of the correct responses are reinforced.

partial-reinforcement effect: The greater resistance to extinction that occurs when a portion, rather than 100 percent, of the correct responses have been reinforced.

participant modelling: A behaviour therapy in which an appropriate response is modelled in graduated steps and the client attempts each step, encouraged and supported by the therapist.

perception: The process by which sensory information is actively organized and interpreted by the brain.

perceptual constancy: The tendency to perceive objects as maintaining stable properties, such as size, shape, brightness, and colour despite differences in distance, viewing angle, and lighting.

peripheral nervous system (PNS) (peh-RIF-er-ul): The nerves connecting the central nervous system to the rest of the body; subdivided into the autonomic and the somatic nervous systems.

permissive parents: Parents who make few rules or demands and allow children to make their own decisions and control their own behaviour.

person-centred therapy: A non-directive, humanistic therapy in which the therapist creates a warm, accepting climate, freeing clients to be themselves and releasing their natural tendency toward positive growth; developed by Carl Rogers.

personal fable: An exaggerated sense of personal uniqueness and indestructibility, which may be the basis of risk taking common during adolescence.

personal unconscious: In Jung's theory, the layer of the unconscious containing all of the thoughts and experiences that are accessible to the conscious, as well as repressed memories and impulses.

personality disorder: A continuing, inflexible, maladaptive pattern of inner experience and behaviour that causes great distress or impaired functioning and differs significantly from the patterns expected in the person's culture.

personality: A person's unique and stable pattern of characteristics and behaviours.

persuasion: A deliberate attempt to influence the attitudes and/or behaviour of another.

PET scan (positron-emission tomography): A brain-imaging technique that reveals activity in various parts of the brain on the basis of on the amount of oxygen and glucose consumed.

phallic stage: Freud's third psychosexual stage (ages three to five or six), during which sensual pleasure is derived mainly through touching the genitals, and the Oedipus complex arises.

pheromones: Chemicals excreted by humans and other animals that act as signals to and elicit certain patterns of behaviour from members of the same species.

phi phenomenon: An illusion of movement occurring when two or more stationary lights are flashed on and off in sequence, giving the impression that the light is actually moving from one spot to the next.

phobia (FO-bee-ah): A persistent, irrational fear of an object, situation, or activity that the person feels compelled to avoid.

phonemes: The smallest units of sound in spoken language.

pituitary gland: The endocrine gland located in the brain and often called the "master gland," which releases hormones that control other endocrine glands and also releases a growth hormone.

place theory: The theory that sounds of different frequency or pitch cause maximum activation of hair cells at certain locations along the basilar membrane.

placebo (pluh-SEE-bo): Some inert substance, such as a sugar pill or an injection of saline solution, given to the control group in an experiment as a control for the placebo effect.

placebo effect: The phenomenon that occurs when a person's response to a treatment or response on the dependent variable in an experiment is due to expectations regarding the treatment rather than to the treatment itself.

plasticity: The ability of the brain to reorganize and compensate for brain damage.

pleasure principle: The principle by which the id operates to seek pleasure, avoid pain, and obtain immediate gratification.

population: The entire group of interest to researchers and to which they wish to generalize their findings; the group from which a sample is selected.

positive reinforcement: A reward or pleasant consequence that follows a response and increases the probability that the response will be repeated.

postconventional level: Kohlberg's highest level of moral reasoning, in which moral reasoning involves weighing moral alternatives; "right" is whatever furthers basic human rights.

posttraumatic stress disorder (PTSD): A prolonged and severe stress reaction to a catastrophic event characterized by anxiety, psychic numbing, withdrawal from others, and the feeling that one is reliving the traumatic experience.

preconscious: The thoughts, feelings, and memories that we are not consciously aware of at the moment but that may be brought to consciousness.

preconventional level: Kohlberg's lowest level of moral reasoning, based on the physical consequences of an act; "right" is whatever avoids punishment or gains a reward.

prejudice: Negative attitudes toward others based on their gender, religion, race, or membership in a particular group.

prenatal: Occurring between conception and birth.

preoperational stage: Piaget's second stage of cognitive development (ages two to seven), characterized by rapid development of language and thinking governed by perception rather than logic.

preterm infant: An infant born before the 37th week and weighing less than 2.5 kilograms; a premature infant.

primacy effect: The tendency for an overall impression or judgment of another to be influenced more by the first information received about that person than by information that comes later; the tendency to recall the first items on a list more readily than the middle items.

primary appraisal: Evaluating the significance of a potentially stressful event according to how it will affect one's well-being—whether it is perceived as irrelevant or as involving harm or loss, threat or challenge.

primary auditory cortex: The part of the temporal lobes where hearing registers in the cerebral cortex.

primary drive: A state of tension or arousal arising from a biological need; one not based on learning.

primary mental abilities: According to Thurstone, seven relatively distinct abilities that singularly or in combination are involved in all intellectual activities.

primary reinforcer: A reinforcer that fulfills a basic physical need for survival and does not depend on learning (examples: food, water, sleep, termination of pain).

primary visual cortex: The area at the rear of the occipital lobes where vision registers in the cerebral cortex.

problem-focused coping: A response aimed at reducing, modifying, or eliminating a source of stress.

projection: Attributing one's own undesirable thoughts, impulses, traits, or behaviours to others.

projective test: A personality test in which people respond to inkblots, drawings of ambiguous human situations, incomplete sentences, and the like, by projecting their own inner thoughts, feelings, fears, or conflicts onto the test materials.

prosocial behaviour: Behaviour that benefits others, such as helping, co-operation, and sympathy.

prototype: The example that embodies the most common and typical features of a particular concept.

proximity: Geographic closeness; a major factor in attraction.

psychiatrist: A medical doctor with a specialty in the diagnosis and treatment of mental disorders.

psychoactive drug: A drug that alters normal mental functioning–mood, perception, or thought; if used medically, called a "controlled substance."

psychoanalysis (SY-ko-ah-NAL-ih-sis): The term Freud used for both his theory of personality and his therapy for the treatment of psychological disorders; the unconscious is the primary focus of psychoanalytic theory; the psychotherapy that uses free association, dream analysis, and analysis of resistance and transference to uncover repressed memories, impulses, and conflicts thought to cause psychological disorder.

psychoanalyst (SY-ko-AN-ul-ist): A professional, usually a psychiatrist, with special training in psychoanalysis.

psychodrama: A group therapy in which one group member acts out personal problem situations and relationships, assisted by other members, to gain insight into the problem.

psycholinguistics: The study of the way in which language is acquired, produced, and used, and the way in which the sounds and symbols of language are translated into meaning.

psychology: The scientific study of behaviour and mental processes.

psychoneuroimmunology (sye-ko-NEW-ro-IM-you-NOLL-oh-gee): A field in which psychologists, biologists, and medical researchers study the effects of psychological factors on the immune system.

psychosexual stages: A series of stages through which the sexual instinct develops; each stage is defined by an erogenous zone that becomes the centre of new pleasures and conflicts.

psychosis (sy-CO-sis): A severe psychological disorder marked by loss of contact with reality and a seriously impaired ability to function.

psychosocial stages: Erikson's eight developmental stages through the lifespan, which are each defined by a conflict that must be resolved satisfactorily in order for healthy personality development to occur.

psychosurgery: Brain surgery to treat some severe, persistent, and debilitating psychological disorder or severe chronic pain.

psychotherapy: The treatment for psychological disorders that uses psychological rather than biological means and primarily involves conversations between patient and therapist.

puberty: A period of rapid physical growth and change that culminates in sexual maturity.

punishment: The removal of a pleasant stimulus or the application of an unpleasant stimulus, which tends to suppress a response.

random assignment: In an experiment, the assignment of participants to experimental and control groups through using a chance procedure, which guarantees that all participants have an equal probability of being placed in any of the groups; a control for selection bias.

rational-emotive therapy: A directive, confrontational psychotherapy designed to challenge and modify the client's irrational beliefs, which are thought to cause their personal distress; developed by Albert Ellis.

rationalization: Supplying a logical, rational, socially acceptable reason rather than the real reason for an action.

reaction formation: Denying an unacceptable impulse, usually sexual or aggressive, by giving strong conscious expression to its opposite.

realistic conflict theory: The notion that prejudices arise when social groups must compete for scarce resources and opportunities.

recall: A measure of retention that requires one to remember material with few or no retrieval cues, as in an essay test.

recency effect: The tendency to recall the last items on a list more readily than those in the middle of the list.

receptor site: A site on the dendrite or cell body of a neuron that will receive only specific neurotransmitters.

recessive gene: A gene that will not be expressed if paired with a dominant gene but will be expressed if paired with another recessive gene.

reciprocal determinism: Bandura's concept that behaviour, personal/cognitive factors, and environment all influence and are influenced by each other.

recognition: A measure of retention that requires one to identify material as familiar, or as having been encountered before.

reconstruction: A memory that is not an exact replica of an event but has been pieced together from a few highlights, with the use of information that may or may not be accurate.

reflex: An involuntary response to a particular stimulus, like the eye-blink response to a puff of air or salivation in response to food placed in the mouth.

reflexes: Inborn, unlearned, automatic responses to certain environmental stimuli (examples: coughing, blinking, sucking, grasping).

regression: Reverting to a behaviour characteristic of an earlier stage of development.

rehearsal: The act of purposely repeating information to maintain it in shortterm memory or to transfer it to long-term memory.

reinforcement: An event that follows a response and increases the strength of the response and/or the likelihood that it will be repeated.

reinforcer: Anything that strengthens a response or increases the probability that it will occur.

relearning method: Measuring retention in terms of the percentage of time or learning trials saved in relearning material compared with the time required to learn it originally; also called the *savings method.*

reliability: The ability of a test to yield nearly the same scores when the same people are tested and then retested using the same test or an alternative form of the test.

REM dreams: Having a dream-like and story-like quality; the type of dream that occurs almost continuously during each REM period; more vivid, visual, and emotional than NREM dreams.

REM rebound: The increased amount of REM sleep that occurs after REM deprivation; often associated with unpleasant dreams or nightmares.

REM sleep: Sleep characterized by rapid eye movements, paralysis of large muscles, fast and irregular heart rate and respiration rate, increased brain-wave activity, and vivid dreams.

representative sample: A sample of participants selected from the larger population in such a way that important subgroups within the population are included in the sample in the same proportions as they are found in the larger population.

repression: Removing from one's consciousness disturbing, guilt-provoking, or otherwise unpleasant memories so that one is no longer aware a painful event occurred.

resistance: In psychoanalytic therapy, the patient's attempts to avoid expressing or revealing painful or embarrassing thoughts or feelings.

resistance stage: The second stage of the general adaptation syndrome, during which there are intense physiological efforts to resist or adapt to the stressor.

resting potential: The membrane potential of a neuron at rest, about –70 millivolts.

reticular formation: A structure in the brainstem that plays a crucial role in arousal and attention, and that screens sensory messages entering the brain.

retina: The tissue at the back of the eye that contains the rods and the cones and onto which the retinal image is projected.

retinal image: The image of objects in the visual field projected onto the retina.

retrieval: The act of bringing to mind material that has been stored in memory.

retrieval cue: Any stimulus or bit of information that aids in the retrieval of particular information from long-term memory.

retrograde amnesia (RET-ro-grade): A loss of memory for events occurring during a time that preceding a brain trauma that caused a loss of consciousness.

reuptake: The process by which neurotransmitter molecules are taken from the synaptic cleft back into the axon terminal for later use, thus terminating their excitatory or inhibitory effect on the receiving neuron.

reverse discrimination: Giving special treatment or higher evaluations to individuals from groups that have been the target of discrimination.

reversibility: The realization that any change in shape, position, or order of matter can be reversed mentally.

right hemisphere: The hemisphere that controls the left side of the body and that, in most people, is specialized for visual-spatial perception and for understanding non-verbal behaviour.

rods: The light-sensitive receptors in the retina that provide vision in dim light in black, white, and shades of grey.

roles: The behaviours considered to be appropriate for individuals occupying certain positions within the group.

Rorschach Inkblot Test (ROR-shok): A projective test composed of 10 inkblots to which a participant responds; used to reveal unconscious functioning and the presence of psychiatric disorders.

sample: The portion of any population that is selected for study and from which generalizations are made about the entire larger population.

saturation: The degree to which light waves producing a colour are of the same wavelength; the purity of a colour.

savings score: The percentage of time or learning trials saved in relearning material over the amount of time or number of learning trials required for the original learning.

scapegoating: Displacing aggression onto minority groups or other innocent targets who were not responsible for the frustration causing the aggression.

Schachter-Singer theory: A two-stage theory stating that, for an emotion to occur, there must be (1) physiological arousal and (2) an explanation for the arousal.

schedule of reinforcement: A systematic program for administering reinforcements that has a predictable effect on behaviour.

schema: Piaget's term for a cognitive structure or concept used to identify and interpret information.

schemas: The integrated frameworks of knowledge and assumptions we have about people, objects, and events, which affect how we encode and recall information.

schizophrenia (SKIT-suh-FREE-nee-ah): A severe psychological disorder characterized by loss of contact with reality, hallucinations, delusions, inappropriate or flat affect, some disturbance in thinking, social withdrawal, and/or other bizarre behaviour.

seasonal affective disorder (SAD): A mood disorder in which depression comes and goes with the seasons.

secondary appraisal: Evaluating one's coping resources and deciding how to deal with a stressful event.

secondary reinforcer: A neutral stimulus that becomes reinforcing after repeated pairings with other reinforcers.

secondary sex characteristics: Those physical characteristics not directly involved in reproduction but distinguishing the mature male from the mature female.

selection bias: The assignment of participants to experimental or control groups in such a way that systematic differences among the groups are present at the beginning of the experiment.

selective attention: Focusing on one piece of information while placing other information in the background.

self-actualization: The development of one's full potential; the highest need on Maslow's hierarchy.

self-efficacy: A person's belief in his or her ability to perform competently in whatever is attempted.

self-serving bias: Our tendency to attribute our successes to dispositional causes, and our failures to situational causes.

semantic memory: The subpart of declarative memory that stores general knowledge; our mental encyclopedia or dictionary.

semantics: The meaning or the study of meaning derived from morphemes, words, and sentences.

semicircular canals: Three fluid-filled tubular canals in the inner ear that provide information about rotating head movements.

sensation: The process through which the senses pick up visual, auditory, and other sensory stimuli and transmit them to the brain; sensory information that has registered in the brain but has not been interpreted.

sensorimotor stage: Piaget's first stage of cognitive development (birth to age two), culminating in the development of object permanence and the beginning of representational thought.

sensory adaptation: The process of becoming less sensitive to an unchanging sensory stimulus over time.

sensory deprivation: A condition in which sensory stimulation is reduced to a minimum or eliminated.

sensory memory: The memory system that holds information coming in through the senses for a period ranging from a fraction of a second to several seconds.

sensory receptors: Specialized cells in each sense organ that detect and respond to sensory stimuli–light, sound, odours, etc.–and transduce (convert) the stimuli into neural impulses.

separation anxiety: The fear and distress shown by toddlers when their parent leaves, occurring from 8 to 24 months and reaching a peak between 12 and 18 months.

serial-position effect: The tendency to remember the beginning and ending items of a list better than the middle items.

serotonin: A neurotransmitter that plays an important role in regulating mood, sleep, aggression, and appetite; a serotonin deficiency is associated with anxiety, depression, and suicidal feelings.

set point: The weight the body normally maintains when one is trying neither to gain nor to lose weight (if weight falls below the normal level, appetite increases and metabolic rate decreases; if weight is gained, appetite decreases and metabolic rate increases so that the original rate is restored).

sex chromosomes: The 23rd pair of chromosomes, which carries the genes that determine one's sex and primary and secondary sex characteristics (XX in females and XY in males).

sexual dysfunction: A persistent or recurrent problem that causes marked distress and interpersonal difficulty and that may involve any or some combination of the following: sexual desire, sexual arousal or the pleasure associated with sex, or orgasm.

shape constancy: The tendency to perceive objects as having a stable or unchanging shape regardless of differences in viewing angle.

shaping: Gradually moulding a desired behaviour by reinforcing responses that become progressively closer to it; reinforcing successive approximations of the desired response.

short-term memory: The second stage of memory, which holds about seven (a range of five to nine) items for less than 30 seconds without rehearsal; working memory; the mental workspace we use to keep in mind tasks we are thinking about at any given moment.

signal detection theory: The view that detection of a sensory stimulus involves both discriminating a stimulus from background "noise" and deciding whether the stimulus is actually present.

situational attribution: Attribution of a behaviour to some external cause or factor operating in the situation; an external attribution.

size constancy: The tendency to perceive objects as the same size regardless of changes in the retinal image.

Skinner box: Invented by B.F. Skinner for conducting experiments in operant conditioning, a soundproof chamber with a device for delivering food and either a bar for rats to press or a disk for pigeons to peck.

sleep apnea: A sleep disorder characterized by periods when breathing stops during sleep and the person must awaken briefly to breathe; major symptoms are excessive daytime sleepiness and loud snoring.

sleep cycle: A cycle of sleep lasting about 90 minutes and including one or more stages of NREM sleep followed by a period of REM sleep.

sleep terror: A sleep disturbance in which a person partially awakens from Stage 4 sleep with a scream, in a dazed, groggy, and panicky state, and with a racing heart.

slow-wave sleep: Stage 3 and Stage 4 sleep; deep sleep.

social cognition: Mental processes that people use to notice, interpret, understand, remember, and apply information about the social world and that enable them to simplify, categorize, and order their world.

social facilitation: Any positive or negative effect on performance due to the presence of others, either as an audience or as co-actors.

social learning theory: A theory that explains the process of gender typing in terms of observation, imitation, and reinforcement.

social loafing: The tendency to put forth less effort when working with others on a common task than when working alone.

social motives: Motives acquired through experience and interaction with others.

social phobia: An irrational fear and avoidance of social situations in which people believe they might embarrass or humiliate themselves by appearing clumsy, foolish, or incompetent.

social psychology: The study of how the actual, imagined, or implied presence of others influences the thoughts, the feelings, and the behaviour of individuals.

Social Readjustment Rating Scale (SRRS): Holmes and Rahe's stress scale which ranks 43 life events from most to least stressful and assigns a point value to each.

social support: Tangible support, information, advice, and/or emotional support provided in time of need by family, friends, and others; the feeling that we are loved, valued, and cared for.

socialization: The process of learning socially acceptable behaviours, attitudes, and values.

sociocultural perspective: A perspective that emphasizes social and cultural influences on human behaviour and stresses the importance of understanding those influences when we interpret the behaviour of others.

somatoform disorders (so-MAT-uh-form): Disorders in which physical symptoms are present that are due to psychological rather than physical causes.

somatosensory cortex (so-MAT-o-SENS-or-ee): The strip of tissue at the front of the parietal lobes where touch, pressure, temperature, and pain register in the cortex.

somnambulism (som-NAM-bue-lism): Sleepwalking that occurs during a partial arousal from Stage 4 sleep.

source traits: Cattell's name for the traits that underlie the surface traits, make up the most basic personality structure, and cause behaviour.

specific phobia: A marked fear of a specific object or situation; a catch-all category for any phobia other than agoraphobia and social phobia.

spinal cord: An extension of the brain, reaching from the base of the brain through the neck and spinal column, that transmits messages between the brain and the peripheral nervous system.

split-brain operation: An operation, performed in severe cases of epilepsy, in which the corpus callosum is cut, separating the cerebral hemispheres and usually lessening the severity and frequency of grand mal seizures.

spontaneous recovery: The reappearance of an extinguished response (in a weaker form) when an organism is exposed to the original conditioned stimulus following a rest period.

Stage 4 sleep: The deepest NREM stage of sleep, characterized by an EEG pattern of more than 50 percent delta waves.

standardization: The establishment of norms for comparing the scores of people who will take the test in the future; administering tests using a prescribed procedure.

Stanford-Binet Intelligence Scale: An individually administered IQ test for those aged 2 to 23; Terman's adaptation of the Binet-Simon Scale.

state-dependent memory effect: The tendency to recall information better if one is in the same pharmacological or psychological (mood) state as when the information was encoded.

stereotypes: Widely shared beliefs about the characteristic traits, attitudes, and behaviours of members of various social groups (racial, ethnic, religious) and including the assumption that they are usually all alike.

stimulants: A category of drugs that speed up activity in the central nervous system, suppress appetite, and cause a person to feel more awake, alert, and energetic; also called "uppers."

stimulus (STIM-yu-lus): Any event or object in the environment to which an organism responds; plural is *stimuli*.

stimulus motives: Motives that cause us to increase stimulation and that appear to be unlearned (examples: curiosity and the need to explore, manipulate objects, and play).

stimulus satiation (say-she-A-shun): A behavioural technique in which a patient is given so much of a stimulus that it becomes something the patient wants to avoid.

storage: The act of maintaining information in memory.

stress: The physiological and psychological response to a condition that threatens or challenges a person and requires some form of adaptation or adjustment.

stressor: Any event capable of producing physical or emotional stress.

structuralism: The first formal school of psychology, aimed at analyzing the basic elements, or structure, of conscious mental experience through the use of introspection.

structure of intellect: The model proposed by Guilford consisting of 180 different intellectual abilities, which involve all of the possible combinations of the three dimensions of intellect–mental operations, contents, and products.

subjective night: The time during a 24-hour period when your body temperature is lowest and when your biological clock is telling you to go to sleep.

sublimation: Rechannelling of sexual or aggressive energy into pursuits that society considers acceptable or admirable.

subliminal perception: Perceiving sensory stimulation that is below the absolute threshold.

subliminal persuasion: Sending persuasive messages below the recipient's level of awareness.

successive approximations: A series of gradual training steps, with each step becoming more like the final desired response.

superego (sue-per-EE-go): The moral system of the personality, which consists of the conscience and the ego ideal.

suprachiasmatic nucleus (SCN): A tiny structure in the brain's hypothalamus that controls the timing of circadian rhythms; the biological clock.

surface traits: Cattell's name for observable qualities of personality, such as those used to describe a friend.

survey: A method whereby researchers use interviews and/or questionnaires to gather information about the attitudes, beliefs, experiences, or behaviours of a group of people.

sympathetic nervous system: The division of the autonomic nervous system that mobilizes the body's resources during stress, emergencies, or heavy exertion, preparing the body for action.

synapse (SIN-aps): The junction where the axon of a sending neuron communicates with a receiving neuron across the synaptic cleft.

syntax: The aspect of grammar that specifies the rules for arranging and combining words to form phrases and sentences.

systematic desensitization: A behaviour therapy, used to treat phobias, that involves training clients in deep muscle relaxation and then having them confront a graduated series of anxiety-producing situations (real or imagined) until they can remain relaxed while confronting even the most feared situation.

tactile: Pertaining to the sense of touch.

taste aversion: The dislike and/or avoidance of a particular food that has been associated with nausea or discomfort.

taste buds: The structures that are composed of 60 to 100 sensory receptors for taste.

telegraphic speech: Short sentences that follow a strict word order and contain only essential content words.

temporal lobes: The lobes that contain the primary auditory cortex, Wernicke's area, and association areas for interpreting auditory information.

teratogens: Harmful agents in the prenatal environment, which can have a negative impact on prenatal development or even cause birth defects.

thalamus (THAL-uh-mus): The structure located above the brainstem that acts as a relay station for information flowing into or out of the higher brain centres.

THC (tetrahydrocannabinol): The principal psychoactive ingredient in marijuana and hashish.

Thematic Apperception Test (TAT): A projective test consisting of drawings of ambiguous human situations, which the subject describes; thought to reveal inner feelings, conflicts, and motives, which are projected onto the test materials.

theory: A general principle or set of principles that explains how a number of separate facts are related to one another.

timbre (TAM-burr): The distinctive quality of a sound that distinguishes it from other sounds of the same pitch and loudness.

time out: A behavioural technique, used to decrease the frequency of undesirable behaviour, that involves withdrawing an individual from all reinforcement for a period of time.

token economy: A behavioural technique used to encourage desirable behaviours by reinforcing them with tokens that can be exchanged later for desired objects, activities, and/or privileges.

top-down processing: Application of previous experience and conceptual knowledge to first recognize the whole of a perception and thus easily identify the simpler elements of that whole.

trait: A personal characteristic that is used to describe or explain personality.

trait theories: Theories that attempt to explain personality and differences between people in terms of their personal characteristics.

tranquilizer (minor): A central nervous system depressant that calms the user.

transduction: The process by which sensory receptors convert sensory stimulation–light, sound, odours, etc.–into neural impulses.

transference: An intense emotional situation occurring in psychoanalysis when one comes to behave toward the analyst as one had behaved toward a significant figure from the past.

trial and error: An approach to problem solving in which one solution after another is tried in no particular order until a workable solution is found.

trial-and-error learning: Learning that occurs when a response is associated with a successful solution to a problem after a number of unsuccessful responses have been tried.

triangular theory of love: Sternberg's theory that three components–intimacy, passion, and decision/ commitment–singly and in various combinations produce seven different kinds of love.

triarchic theory of intelligence: Sternberg's theory that intelligence consists of three parts–the componential, the contextual, and the experiential.

trichromatic theory: The theory of colour vision suggesting that there are three types of cones, which are maximally sensitive to red, green, or blue, and that varying levels of activity in these receptors can produce all of the colours.

twin study method: Studying identical and fraternal twins to determine the relative effects of heredity and environment on a variety of characteristics.

unconditional positive regard: A condition required of person-centred therapists, involving a caring for and acceptance of clients regardless of their feelings, thoughts, or behaviour.

unconditioned response (UR): A response that is invariably elicited by the unconditioned stimulus without prior learning.

unconditioned stimulus (US): A stimulus that elicits a specific response without prior learning.

unconscious (un-KON-shus): For Freud, the primary motivating force of behaviour, containing repressed memories as well as instincts and wishes that have never been conscious.

underextension: Restricting the use of a word to only a few, rather than to all, members of a class of objects.

undifferentiated schizophrenia: A catch-all category; marked by symptoms that do not conform to the other types or conform to more than one type.

uplifts: The positive experiences in life, which can neutralize the effects of many of the hassles.

uppers: A slang term for stimulants.

validity: The ability of a test to measure what it is intended to measure.

variable-interval schedule: A schedule in which a reinforcer is given on the basis of an average time after the first correct response following a varying time of non-reinforcement.

variable-ratio schedule: A schedule in which a reinforcer is given on the basis of an average ratio after a varying number of non-reinforced responses.

ventromedial hypothalamus (VMH): The part of the hypothalamus that presumably acts as a satiety centre and, when activated, signals an animal to stop eating; when the area is destroyed, the animal overeats, becoming obese.

vestibular sense (ves-TIB-yu-ler): The sense that provides information about movement and our orientation in space through sensory receptors in the semicircular canals and the vestibular sacs, which detect changes in the movement and orientation of the head.

visible spectrum: The narrow band of electromagnetic rays, 380 to 760 nm in length, that are visible to the human eye.

visual cliff: An apparatus used to test depth perception in infants and young animals.

Weber's law: The law stating that the just noticeable difference (JND) for all our senses depends on a proportion or percentage of change in a stimulus rather than on a fixed amount of change.

Wechsler Adult Intelligence Scale (WAIS-R): An individual intelligence test for adults that yields separate verbal and performance (non-verbal) IQ scores as well as an overall IQ score.

Wernicke's aphasia: Aphasia resulting from damage to Wernicke's area, in which the patient's spoken language is fluent, but the content is either vague or incomprehensible to the listener.

Wernicke's area: The language area in the temporal lobe involved in comprehension of the spoken word and in formulation of coherent speech and written language.

withdrawal symptoms: The physical and psychological symptoms (usually the opposite of those produced by the drug) that occur when a regularly used drug is discontinued and that terminate when the drug is taken again.

working backward: A heuristic strategy in which a person discovers the steps needed to solve a problem by defining the desired goal and working backward to the current condition.

Yerkes-Dodson law: The principle that performance on tasks is best when arousal level is appropriate to the difficulty of the task–higher arousal for simple tasks, moderate arousal for tasks of moderate difficulty, and lower arousal for complex tasks.

References

Abbott, N. J., & Raff, M. C. (1991). Preface. *Annals of the New York Academy of Sciences*, 633, xiii–xv.

Abramov, I., & Gordon, J. (1994). Color appearance: On seeing red—or yellow, or green, or blue. *Annual Review of Psychology, 45*, 451–485.

Abrams, D., Wetherell, M., Cochrane, S., Hogg, M. A., & Turner, J. C. (1990). Knowing what to think by knowing who you are: Self-categorization and the nature of norm formation, conformity and group polarization. *British Journal of Social Psychology, 29*(Pt. 2), 97–119.

Abrams, R. (1988). *Electroconvulsive therapy*. New York: Oxford University Press.

Accurso, L. (1994, November 1). Your lucky stars. *Soap Opera Weekly*, p. 44.

Adelmann, P. K., & Zajonc, R. B. (1989). Facial efference and the experience of emotion. *Annual Review of Psychology, 40*, 249–280.

Ader, D. N., & Johnson, S. B. (1994). Sample description, reporting, and analysis of sex in psychological research: A look at APA and APA division journals in 1990. *American Psychologist, 49*, 216–218.

Adler, A. (1927). *Understanding human nature*. New York: Greenberg.

Adler, A. (1956). In H. L. Ansbacher & R. R. Ansbacher (Eds.), *The individual psychology of Alfred Adler: A systematic presentation in selections from his writings*. New York: Harper & Row.

Adler, A. (1964). *Social interest: A challenge to mankind*. New York: Capricorn. (Originally published 1933).

Adler, N., & Matthews, K. (1994). Health psychology: Why do some people get sick and some stay well? *Annual Review of Psychology, 45*, 229–259.

Aggleton, J. P. (1993). The contribution of the amygdala to normal and abnormal emotional states. *Trends in Neurosciences, 16*, 328–333.

Agras, W. S., Rossiter, E. M., Arnow, B., Telch, C. F., Raeburn, S. D., Bruce, B., & Koran, L. M. (1994). One-year follow-up of psychosocial and pharmacologic treatments for bulimia nervosa. *Journal of Clinical Psychiatry, 55*, 179–183.

Agras, W. S., Walsh, T., Fairburn, C. G., Wilson, G. T., & Kraemer, H. C. (2000). A multicenter comparison of cognitive-behavioral therapy and interpersonal psychotherapy for bulimia nervosa. *Archives of General Psychiatry, 57*(5), 459–466.

Ahmed, R., & Gray, D. (1996). Immunological memory and protective immunity: Understanding their relation. *Science, 272*, 54–60.

Aiken, L. R. (1997). *Psychological testing and assessment* (9th ed.). Boston: Allyn & Bacon.

Ainsworth, M. D. S. (1973). The development of infant-mother attachment. In B. Caldwell & H. Ricciuti (Eds.), *Review of child development research (Vol. 3)*. Chicago: University of Chicago Press.

Ainsworth, M. D. S. (1979). Infant-mother attachment. *American Psychologist, 34*, 932–937.

Ainsworth, M. D. S., Blehar, M. C., Walters, E., & Wall, S. (1978). *Patterns of attachment*. Hillsdale, NJ: Erlbaum.

Ajzen, I., & Fishbein, M. (1977). Attitude-behavior relations: A theoretical analysis and review of empirical research. *Psychological Bulletin, 84*, 888–918.

Åkerstedt, T. (1990). Psychological and psychophysiological effects of shift work. *Scandinavian Journal of Work and Environmental Health, 16*, 67–73.

Akiskal, H. S. (1989). New insights into the nature and heterogeneity of mood disorders. *Journal of Clinical Psychiatry, 50*(5, Suppl.), 6–10.

Albert, M. L., & Helm-Estabrooks, N. (1988a). Diagnosis and treatment of aphasia: Part I. *Journal of the American Medical Association, 259*, 1043–1047.

Albert, M. L., & Helm-Estabrooks, N. (1988b). Diagnosis and treatment of aphasia: Part II. *Journal of the American Medical Association, 259*, 1205–1210.

Aldrich, M. S. (1989). Cardinal manifestations of sleep disorders. In M. H. Kryger, T. Roth, & W. C. Dement (Eds.), *Principles and practice of sleep medicine* (pp. 313–331). Philadelphia: W. B. Saunders.

Alicke, M. D., & Largo, E. (1995). The role of the self in the false consensus effect. *Journal of Experimental Social Psychology, 31*, 28–47.

Allen, G., Buxton, R., Wong, E., & Courchesne, E. (1997). Attentional activation of the cerebellum independent of motor involvement. *Science, 275*, 1940–1943.

Allison, M. (1991, February). Improving the odds. *Harvard Health Letter, 16*, pp. 4–6.

Allport, G. W. (1935). Attitudes. In C. Murchison (Ed.), *Handbook of social psychology*. Worcester, MA: Clark University Press.

Allport, G. W. (1954). *The nature of prejudice*. Reading, MA: Addison-Wesley.

Allport, G. W. (1961). *Pattern and growth in personality*. New York: Holt, Rinehart & Winston.

Allport, G. W., & Odbert, J. S. (1936). Trait names: A psycho-lexical study. *Psychological Monographs, 47*(1, Whole No. 211), 1–171.

Alpert, B., Field, T., Goldstein, S., & Perry, S. (1990). Aerobics enhances cardiovascular fitness and agility in preschoolers. *Health Psychology, 9*, 48–56.

Altshuler, K. Z. (1989). Will the psychotherapies yield different results?: A look at assumptions in therapy trials. *American Journal of Psychotherapy, 43*, 310–320.

Amabile, T. M. (1983). *The social psychology of creativity.* New York: Springer-Verlag.

American Psychiatric Association. (1993). Practice guideline for eating disorders. *American Journal of Psychiatry, 150*, p. 212–228.

American Psychiatric Association. (1994). *Diagnostic and statistical manual of mental disorders* (4th ed.). Washington DC: Author.

American Psychological Association. (1984). Survey of the use of animals in behavioral research at U. S. universities. Washington, DC: Author.

American Psychological Association. (1993). Guidelines for providers of psychological services to ethnic, linguistic, and culturally diverse populations. *American Psychologist, 48*, 45–48.

American Psychological Association (1994). Interim report of the APA Working Group on Investigation of Memories of Childhood Abuse. Washington, DC.

Anand, B.K., & Brobeck, J.R. (1951). Hypothalamic control of food intake in rats and cats. *Yale Journal of Biological Medicine, 24*, 123–140.

Anastasi, A., & Urbina, S. (1997). *Psychological testing.* Upper Saddle River, NJ: Prentice Hall.

Anderson, B. L., Kiecolt-Glaser, J.K., & Glaser, R. (1994). A biobehavioral model of cancer stress and disease course. *American Psychologist, 49*, 389–404.

Anderson, C. A. (1989). Temperature and aggression: Ubiquitous effects of heat on occurrence of human violence. *Psychological Bulletin, 106*, 74–96.

Anderson, C. A., & Anderson, K. B. (1996). Violent crime rate studies in philosophical context: A destructive testing approach to heat and southern culture of violence effects. *Journal of Personality and Social Psychology, 70,* 740–756.

Anderson, C. A., & DeNeve, K. M. (1992). Temperature, aggression, and the negative affect escape model. *Psychological Bulletin, 111*, 347–351.

Anderson, S. M., Klatzky, R. L., & Murray, J. (1990). Traits and social stereotypes: Efficiency differences in social information processing. *Journal of Personality and Social Psychology, 59*, 192–201.

Andreasen, N. C. (1999). Understanding the causes of schizophrenia. *New England Journal of Medicine, 340,* 645–647.

Andreasen, N. C., & Black, D. W. (1991). *Introductory textbook of psychiatry.* Washington, DC: American Psychiatric Press.

Anisfeld, M. (1996). Only tongue protrusion modeling is matched by neonates. *Developmental Review, 16,* 149–161.

Annett, M. (1985). *Left, right hand and brain: The right shift theory.* London: Lawrence Erlbaum Associates.

Antonuccio, D. O., Danton, W. G., & DeNelsky, G. Y. (1995). Psychotherapy versus medication for depression: Challenging the conventional wisdom with data. *Professional Psychology: Research and Practice, 26*, 574–585.

Apgar, V., & Beck, J. (1982). A perfect baby. In H. E. Fitzgerald & T. H. Carr (Eds.), *Human Development 82/83* (pp. 66–70). Guilford, CT: Dushkin.

Archer, J. (1991). The influence of testosterone on human aggression. *British Journal of Social Psychology, 82*(Pt. 1), 1–28.

Archer, R. P., Maruish, M., Imhof, E. A., & Piotrowski, C. (1991). Psychological test usage with adolescent clients: 1990 survey findings. *Professional Psychology: Research and Practice, 22*, 247–252.

Aronson, E. (1973, May). The rationalizing animal. *Psychology Today*, pp. 46–52.

Aronson, E. (1976). Dissonance theory: Progress and problems. In E. P. Hollander & R. C. Hunt (Eds.), *Current perspectives in social psychology (4th ed.*, pp. 316–328). New York: Oxford University Press.

Aronson, E. (1990). Applying social psychology to desegregation and energy conservation. *Personality and Social Psychology Bulletin, 16*, 118–132.

Asch, S. E. (1946). Forming impressions of personality. *Journal of Abnormal and Social Psychology, 41*, 258–290.

Asch, S. E. (1951). Effects of group pressure upon the modification and distortion of judgments. In H. Guetzkow (Ed.), *Groups, leadership, and men.* Pittsburgh, PA: Carnegie Press.

Asch, S. E. (1955). Opinions and social pressure. *Scientific American, 193*, 31–35.

Atkinson, J. W. (1964). *An introduction to motivation.* Princeton, NJ: Van Nostrand.

Atkinson, R. C., & Shiffrin, R. M. (1968). Human memory: A proposed system and its controlled processes. In K. W. Spence & J. T. Spence (Eds.), *The psychology of learning and motivation (Vol. 2*, pp. 89–195). New York: Academic Press.

Ault, R. L. (1983). *Children's cognitive development (2nd ed.).* Oxford: Oxford University Press.

Avenoso, K. (1997, September 14). A decade of Prozac. *The Boston Globe,* pp. 12–13, 25–35.

Avraham, R. (1989). *The digestive system.* New York: Chelsea House.

Axelsson, A., & Jerson, T. (1985). Noisy toys: A possible source of sensorineural hearing loss. *Pediatrics, 76*, 574–578.

Ayed, N. (2000, May 18). Opposition slams 'Big Brother' database. No worries, official say. *The Canadian Press.*

Ayllon, T., & Azrin, N. H. (1965). The measurement and reinforcement of behavior of psychotics. *Journal of the Experimental Analysis of Behavior, 8*, 357–383.

Ayllon, T., & Azrin, N. H. (1968). *The token economy: A motivational system for therapy and rehabilitation.* New York: Appleton-Century-Crofts.

Azrin, N. H., & Holz, W. C. (1966). Punishment. In W. K. Honig (Ed.), *Operant behavior: Areas of research and application.* New York: Appleton-Century-Crofts.

Bach-y-Rita, P., & Bach-y-Rita, E. W. (1990). Biological and psychosocial factors in recovery from brain damage in humans. *Canadian Journal of Psychology, 44*, 148–165.

Baddeley, A. (1990). *Human memory.* Needham Heights, MA: Allyn & Bacon.

Baddeley, A. (1992). Working memory. *Science, 255*, 556–559.

Baddeley, A. D. (1982). *Your memory: A user's guide.* New York: Macmillan.

Baddeley, A. D. (1995). Working memory. In M. S. Gazzaniga (Ed.), *The cognitive neurosciences*. Cambridge, MA: MIT Press.

Baer, L. (1996). Behavior theory: Endogenous serotonin therapy? *Journal of Clinical Psychiatry, 57*(6), 33–35.

Bahrick, H. P., Bahrick, P. O., & Wittlinger, R. P. (1975). Fifty years of memory for names and faces: A cross-sectional approach. *Journal of Experimental Psychology: General, 104*, 54–75.

Bahrick, H. P., Hall, L. K., & Berger, S. A. (1996). Accuracy and distortion in memory for high school grades. *Psychological Science, 7*, 265–271.

Bahrick, H. P., & Phelps, E. (1987). Retention of Spanish vocabulary over 8 years. *Journal of Experimental Psychology: Learning, Memory, and Cognition, 13*, 344–349.

Baker, T. B. (1988). Models of addiction: Introduction to the special issue. *Journal of Abnormal Psychology, 97*, 115–117.

Ball, C. G., & Grinker, J. A. (1981). Overeating and obesity. In S. J. Mule (Ed.), *Behavior in excess* (pp. 194–220). New York: The Free Press.

Bandura, A. (1964). The stormy decade: Fact or fiction? *Psychology in the Schools, 1*, 224–231.

Bandura, A. (1967). Behavioral psychotherapy. *Scientific American, 216*, 78–82.

Bandura, A. (1969a). *Principles of behavior modification*. New York: Holt, Rinehart & Winston.

Bandura, A. (1969b). Social learning theory and identificatory processes. In D. A. Goslin (Ed.), *Handbook of socialization theory and research* (pp. 213–262). Chicago: Rand McNally.

Bandura, A. (1973). *Aggression: A social learning analysis*. Englewood Cliffs, NJ: Prentice Hall.

Bandura, A. (1976). On social learning and aggression. In E. P. Hollander & R. C. Hunt (Eds.), *Current perspectives in social psychology (4th ed.*, pp. 116–128). New York: Oxford University Press.

Bandura, A. (1977a). *Social learning theory*. Englewood Cliffs, NJ: Prentice Hall.

Bandura, A. (1977b). Self-efficacy: Toward a unifying theory of behavioral change. *Psychological Review, 84*, 191–215.

Bandura, A. (1986). *Social functions of thought and action: A social-cognitive theory*. Englewood Cliffs, NJ: Prentice-Hall.

Bandura, A. (1989). Social cognitive theory. *Annals of Child Development, 6*, 1–60.

Bandura, A. (1997a). Self-efficacy. *Harvard Mental Health Letter, 13*(9), 4–6.

Bandura, A. (1997b). *Self-efficacy: The exercise of control*. New York: Freeman.

Bandura, A., Adams, N. E., & Beyer, J. (1977). Cognitive processes mediating behavioral change. *Journal of Personality and Social Psychology, 35*, 125–139.

Bandura, A., Blanchard, E. B., & Ritter, B. J. (1969). The relative efficacy of desensitization and modeling therapeutic approaches for inducing behavioral, affective and attitudinal changes. *Journal of Personality and Social Psychology, 13*, 173–199.

Bandura, A., Jeffery, R. W., & Gajdos, E. (1975). Generalizing change through participant modeling with self-directed mastery. *Behaviour Research and Therapy, 13*, 141–152.

Bandura, A., Ross, D., & Ross, S. A. (1961). Transmission of aggression through imitation of aggressive models. *Journal of Abnormal and Social Psychology, 63*, 575–582.

Bandura, A., Ross, D., & Ross, S. A. (1963). Imitation of film-mediated aggressive models. *Journal of Abnormal and Social Psychology, 66*, 3–11.

Bar-Tal, D., 1976. *Prosocial behavior*. Washington, D.C.: Hemisphere.

Bar-Tal, D., & Saxe, L. (1976). Perceptions of similarly and dissimilarly attractive couples and individuals. *Journal of Personality and Social Psychology, 33*, 772–781.

Barber, T. X. (1970, July). Who believes in hypnosis? *Psychology Today*, pp. 20–27, 84.

Bard, P. (1934). The neurohumoral basis of emotional reactions. In C. A. Murchison (Ed.), *Handbook of general experimental psychology*. Worcester, MA: Clark University Press.

Bargh, J. A., & Chartrand, T. L. (1999). The unbearable automaticity of being. *American Psychologist, 54*(7), 462–479.

Bargmann, C. (1996). From the nose to the brain. *Nature, 384*, 512–513.

Barlow, D. (1997). Cognitive–behavioral therapy for panic disorder: Current status. *Journal of Clinical Psychiatry, 58*(6), 32–36.

Barr, H. M., & Streissguth, A. P. (1991). Caffeine use during pregnancy and child outcome: A 7-year prospective study. *Neurotoxicology and Teratology, 13*, 441–448.

Barr, H. M., Streissguth, A. P., Darby, B. L., & Samson, P. D. (1990). Prenatal exposure to alcohol, caffeine, tobacco, and aspirin: Effects on fine and gross motor performance in 4-year-old children. *Developmental Psychology, 26*, 339–348.

Barrett, A. (1999). Social support and life satisfaction among the never married. *Research on Aging, 21*, 46–72.

Barrett, J., Lack, L., & Morris, M. (1993). The sleep-evoked decrease of body temperature. *Sleep, 16*, 93–99.

Barron, F., & Harrington, D. M. (1981). Creativity, intelligence, and personality. *Annual Review of Psychology, 32*, 439–476.

Bartlett, F. C. (1932). *Remembering: A study in experimental and social psychology*. London: Cambridge University Press.

Bartoshuk, L. (1989). Taste: Robust across the age span? *Annals of the New York Academy of Sciences, 561*, 65–75.

Bartoshuk, L., Rifkin, B., Marks, L. E., & Bars, P. (1986). Taste and aging. *Journal of Gerontology, 41*, 51–57.

Bartoshuk, L. M., & Beauchamp, G. K. (1994). Chemical senses. *Annual Review of Psychology, 45*, 419–449.

Bartrop, R. W., Lazarus, L., Luckherst, E., et al. (1977). Depressed lymphocyte function after bereavement. *Lancet, 1*, 834–836.

Bassili, J. N. (1995). Response latency and the accessibility of voting intentions: What contributes to accessibility and how it affects vote choice. *Personality and Social Psychology Bulletin, 21*, 686–695.

Bateson, G. (1982). Totemic knowledge in New Guinea. In U. Neisser (Ed.), *Memory observed: Remembering in natural contexts*. San Francisco: W.H. Freeman.

Bateson, G., Jackson, D. D., Haley, J., & Weakland, J. (1956). Toward a theory of schizophrenia. *Behavioral Science, 1*, 214–264.

Batson, C. D. (1998). Altruism and prosocial behavior. In D. T. Gilbert, S. T. Fiske, & G. Lindzey (Eds.), *The handbook of social psychology* (4th ed., Vol. 2), (pp. 282–316). New York: McGraw-Hill.

Batson, C. D., Batson, J. G., Griffitt, C. A., Barrientos, S., Brandt, J. R., Sprengelmeyer, P., & Bayly, M. J. (1989). Negative-state relief and the empathy-altruism hypothesis. *Journal of Personality and Social Psychology, 56*, 922–933.

Batson, C. D., Dyck, J. L., Brandt, J. R., Batson, J. G., Powell, A. L., McMaster, M. R., & Griffitt, C. (1988). Five studies testing two new egoistic alternatives to the empathy-altruism hypothesis. *Journal of Personality and Social Psychology, 55*, 52–77.

Baumgardner, A. H., Heppner, P. P., & Arkin, R. M. (1986). Role of causal attribution in personal problem solving. *Journal of Personality and Social Psychology, 50*, 636–643.

Baumrind, D. (1967). Child care practices anteceding three patterns of preschool behavior. *Genetic Psychology Monographs, 75*, 43–88.

Baumrind, D. (1971). Current patterns of parental authority. *Developmental Psychology Monographs, 4*(1, Pt. 2).

Baumrind, D. (1978). Parental disciplinary patterns and social competence in children. *Youth and Society, 9*, 239–276.

Baumrind, D. (1980). New directions in socialization research. *American Psychologist, 35*, 639–652.

Baumrind, D. (1985). Research using intentional deception: Ethical issues revisited. *American Psychologist, 40*, 165–174.

Baumrind, D. (1991). The influence of parenting style on adolescent competence and substance use. *Journal of Early Adolescence, 11*, 56–95.

Beaman, A. L., Cole, C. M., Preston, M., Klentz, B., & Steblay, N. M. (1983). Fifteen years of foot-in-the-door research: A meta-analysis. *Personality and Social Psychology Bulletin, 9*, 181–196.

Beatty, J. (1995). *Principles of behavioral neuroscience.* Dubuque, IA: Brown & Benchmark.

Beck, A. T. (1967). *Depression: Causes and treatment.* Philadelphia: University of Pennsylvania Press.

Beck, A. T. (1976). *Cognitive therapy and the emotional disorders.* New York: New American Library.

Beck, A. T. (1991). Cognitive therapy: A 30-year retrospective. *American Psychologist, 46*, 368–375.

Beck, A. T. (1993). Cognitive therapy: Past, present, and future. *Journal of Consulting and Clinical Psychology, 61*, 194–198.

Beck, A. T., Brown, G., Berchick, R. J., Stewart, B. L., & Steer, R. A. (1990). Relationship between hopelessness and ultimate suicide: A replication with psychiatric outpatients. *American Journal of Psychiatry, 147*, 190–195.

Beck, A. T., & Emery, G. (with R. L. Greenberg) (1985). *Anxiety disorders and phobias: A cognitive perspective.* New York: Basic Books.

Beck, A. T., Sokol, L., Clark, D. A., Berchick, R., & Wright, F. (1992). A crossover study of focused cognitive therapy for panic disorder. *American Journal of Psychiatry, 149*, 778–783.

Beck, A. T., Steer, R. A., Beck, J. S., & Newman, C. F. (1993). Hopelessness, depression, suicidal ideation, and clinical diagnosis of depression. *Suicide and Life-Threatening Behavior, 23*, 139–145.

Beer ad gets 19,000 fans excited. (2000 April 15). Canada Press. Retrieved July 7, 2000 from the World Wide Web: www.canoe.ca/2000NHLPlayoffsOttTor/apr15_bee.html.

Beidler, L. M., & Smallman, R. L. (1965). Renewal of cells within taste buds. *Journal of Cell Biology, 27*, 263–272.

Beilin, H. (1992). Piaget's enduring contribution to developmental psychology. *Developmental Psychology, 28*, 191–204.

Békésy, G. von (1957). The ear. *Scientific American, 197*, 66–78.

Belitsky, R., & McGlashan, T.H. (1993). The manifestations of schizophrenia in late life: A dearth of data. *Schizophrenia Bulletin, 19*, 683–685.

Bell, J. (1991). *Evaluating psychological information: Sharpening your critical thinking skills.* Boston: Allyn & Bacon.

Bellas, D. N., Novelly, R. A., Eskenazi, B., & Wasserstein, J. (1988). Unilateral displacement in the olfactory sense: A manifestation of the unilateral neglect syndrome. *Cortex, 24*, 267–275.

Belsky, J. (1988). The "effects" of infant day care reconsidered. *Early Childhood Research Quarterly, 3*, 235–272.

Belsky, J., Rovine, M., & Fish, M. (1989). The developing family system. In M. Gunnar (Ed.), *Minnesota symposium on child psychology: Vol. 22. Systems and development.* Hillsdale, NJ: Erlbaum.

Belsky, J., Steinberg, L., & Draper, P. (1991). Childhood experience, interpersonal development, and reproductive strategy: An evolutionary theory of socialization. *Child Development, 62*, 647–670.

Bendich, A., & Keen, C. L. (1993). Influence of maternal nutrition on pregnancy outcome: Public policy issues: Introduction to Part V. *Annals of the New York Academy of Sciences, 678*, 284–285.

Benedict, M., & Cameron, A. (2000, July 24). Tornado terror. *Maclean's Online,* Retrieved December 28, 2000 from the World Wide Web: www.macleans.ca.

Bennett, W. I. (1990, November). Boom and doom. *Harvard Health Letter, 16*, pp. 1–4.

Bennett, W., & Gurin, J. (1982). *The dieter's dilemma.* New York: Basic Books.

Benson, H. (1975). *The relaxation response.* New York: Avon.

Benson, P. L., Karabenick, S. A., & Lerner, R. M. (1976). Pretty pleases: The effects of physical attractiveness, race, and sex on receiving help. *Journal of Personality and Social Psychology, 12*, 409–415.

Beratis, S., Gabriel, J., & Holdas, S. (1994). Age at onset in subtypes of schizophrenic disorders. *Schizophrenia Bulletin, 20*, 287–296.

Bergland, R. (1985). *The fabric of mind.* New York: Viking.

Berk, L. E. (1997). *Child development* (4th ed.). Boston: Allyn & Bacon.

Berkman, L. F., & Syme, S. L. (1979). Social networks, host resistance, and mortality: A nine-year follow-up study of Alameda County residents. *American Journal of Epidemiology, 109*, 186–204.

Berkowitz, L. (1964). The effects of observing violence. *Scientific American, 210*, 35–41.

Berkowitz, L. (1983). Aversively stimulated aggression: Some parallels and differences in research with animals and humans. *American Psychologist, 38*, 1135–1144.

Berkowitz, L. (1988). Frustrations, appraisals, and aversively stimulated aggression. *Aggressive Behavior, 14*, 3–11.

Berkowitz, L. (1989). Frustration-aggression hypothesis: Examination and reformulation. *Psychological Bulletin, 106*, 59–73.

Berkowitz, L. (1990). On the formation and regulation of anger and aggression: A cognitive-neoassociationistic analysis. *American Psychologist, 45*, 494–503.

Berlyne, D. E. (1971). *Aesthetics and psychobiology*. New York: Appleton-Century- Crofts.

Bernal, M., & Castro, L. (1994). Are clinical psychologists prepared for service and research with ethnic minorities? Report of a decade of progress. *American Psychologist, 49,* 797–805.

Bernstein, I. L. (1985). Learned food aversions in the progression of cancer and its treatment. *Annals of the New York Academy of Sciences, 443*, 365–380.

Bernstein, I. L., Webster, M. M., & Bernstein, I. D. (1982). Food aversions in children receiving chemotherapy for cancer. *Cancer, 50*, 2961–2963.

Berreby, D. (1994, January/February). Figures of speech: The rise and fall and rise of Chomsky's linguistics. *The Sciences*, 44–49.

Berscheid, E., Dion, K., Walster, E., & Walster, G. W. (1971). Physical attractiveness and dating choice: A test of the matching hypothesis. *Journal of Experimental Social Psychology, 7*, 173–189.

Bexton, W. H., Herron, W., & Scott, T. H. (1954). Effects of decreased variation in the sensory environment. *Canadian Journal of Psychology, 8*, 70–76.

Beyerstein, B., & Beyerstein, D. (Eds.). (1992). *The write stuff: Evaluations of graphology*. Buffalo, NY: Prometheus Books.

Bill, J. (2000, July 31). Car crash kills baby: Man, 44, faces drunk-driving charges causing death. *Toronto Sun,* p. 3.

Billiard, M., Pasquire-Magnetto, V., Heckman, M., Carlander, B., Besset, A., Zachariev, Z., Eliaou, J. F., & Malafosse, A. (1994). Family studies in narcolepsy. *Sleep, 17,* S54–S59.

Bird, H. (2000, June 1). Adieu, M. Richard: Rich and poor alike attend emotional funeral for hockey legend. *Toronto Sun,* pp. 1, 3.

Bisiach, E. (1996). Unilateral neglect and the structure of space representation. *Current Directions in Psychological Science, 5,* 62–65.

Bisiach, E., & Luzzati, C. (1978). Unilateral neglect of representational space. *Cortex, 14*, 129–133.

Bjorklund, D. F., & Green, B. L. (1992). The adaptive nature of cognitive immaturity. *American Psychologist, 47*, 46–54.

Bland, R. C., Newman, S. C., & Orn, H. (1986). Recurrent and nonrecurrent depression: A family study. *Archives of General Psychiatry, 43*, 1085–1089.

Blascovich, J., Wyer, N. A., Swart, L. A., & Kibler, J. L. (1997). Racism and racial categorization. *Journal of Personality and Social Psychology, 72*, 1364–1372.

Blatt, S., Sanislow, C., Zuroff, D., & Pilkonis, P. (1996). Characteristics of effective therapists: Further analysis of data from the National Institute on Mental Health Treatment of Depression Collaborative Research Program. *Journal of Consulting and Clinical Psychology. 64,* 1276–1284.

Bleuler, E. (1950). *Dementia praecox, or the group of schizophrenias.* (J. Zinkin & N. D. C. Lewis, Trans.). New York: International Universities Press, 1950. (Original work published 1911).

Bliss, T. V. P., & Lomo, T. (1973). Long-lasting potentiation of synaptic transmission in the dentate area of the anaesthetized rabbit following stimulation of the perforant path. *Journal of Physiology (London), 232*, 331–356.

Bloche, M. G., & Eisenberg, C. (1993). The psychological effects of state-sanctioned terror. *Harvard Mental Health Letter, 10*(5), 4–6.

Block, J. (1995). A contrarian view of the five-factor approach to personality description. *Psychological Bulletin, 117,* 187–215.

Bloomer, C. M. (1976). *Principles of visual perception.* New York: Van Nostrand Reinhold.

Blundell, J. E., Rogers, P. J., & Hill, A. J. (1988). Uncoupling sweetness and calories: Methodological aspects of laboratory studies on appetite control. *Appetite, 11*(Suppl.), 54–61.

Bogen, J. E., & Vogel, P. J. (1963). Treatment of generalized seizures by cerebral commissurotomy. *Surgical Forum, 14*, 431.

Bohannon, J. N., III. (1988). Flashbulb memories for the Space Shuttle disaster: A tale of two theories. *Cognition, 29*, 179–196.

Boivin, D. B., Czeisler, C. A., Dijk, J-J., Duffy, J. F., Folkard, S., Minors, D. S., Totterdell, P., & Waterhouse, J. M. (1997). Complex interaction of the sleep-wake cycle and circadian phase modulates mood in healthy subjects. *Archives of General Psychiatry, 54,* 145–152.

Bonanno, G., Keltner, D., Holen, A., & Horowitz, M. (1995). When avoiding unpleasant emotions might not be such a bad thing:Verbal-autonomic response dissociation and midlife conjugal bereavement. *Journal of Personality and Social Psychology, 69,* 975–989.

Bonnet, M. H., & Arand, D. L. (1995). We are chronically sleep deprived. *Sleep, 18,* 908–911.

Bootzin, R. R., & Perlis, M. L. (1992). Nonpharmacologic treatments of insomnia. *Journal of Clinical Psychiatry, 53*(6, suppl.), 37–41.

Borg, E., & Counter, S. A. (1989). The middle-ear muscles. *Scientific American, 261*, 74–80.

Bornstein, M. H., & Marks, L. E. (1982, January). Color revisionism. *Psychology Today*, pp. 64–73.

Bornstein, R. F. (1989). Exposure and affect: Overview and meta-analysis of research, 1968–1987. *Psychological Bulletin, 106*, 265–289.

Borrie, R. A. (1991). The use of restricted environmental stimulation therapy in treating addictive behaviors. *International Journal of the Addictions, 25*, 995–1015.

Bouchard, C. (1997). Human variation in body mass: Evidence for a role of the genes. *Nutrition Reviews, 55,* S21–S30.

Bouchard, T.J., Jr. (1994). Genes, environment, and personality. *Science, 264*, 1700–1701.

Bouchard, T. J., Jr. (1997, September/October). Whenever the twain shall meet. *The Sciences, 37*, 52–57.

Bouchard, T. J., Jr., Lykken, D. T., McGue, M., Segal, N. L., & Tellegen, A. (1990). Sources of human psychological differences: The Minnesota study of twins reared apart. *Science, 250*, 223–228.

Bouchard, T. J., Jr., Lykken, D. T., McGue, M., Segal, N. L., & Tellegen, A. (1991). IQ and heredity: Response. *Science, 252*, 191–192.

Bouchard, T.J., Jr., & McGue, M. (1981). Familial studies of intelligence: A review. *Science, 212*, 1055–1058.

Bouchard, T. J., Jr., & McGue, M. (1990). Genetic and rearing environmental influences on adult personality: An analysis of adopted twins reared apart. *Journal of Personality, 58*, 263–292.

Bovbjerg, D. H., Redd., W. H., Jacobsen, P. B., Manne, S. L., Taylor, K. L., Surbone, A., Crown, J. P., Norton, L., Gilewski, T. A., Hudis, C. F., Reichman, B. S., Kaufman, R. J., Currie, V. E., & Hakes, T. B. (1992). An experimental analysis of classically conditioned nausea during cancer chemotherapy. *Psychosomatic Medicine, 54*, 623–637.

Bower, B. (1988). Epileptic PET probes. *Science News, 133*, 280–281.

Bower, G. H. (1992). How might emotions affect learning? In S.-A. Christianson (Ed.). *Handbook of emotion and memory* (pp. 3–31). Hillsdale, NJ: Erlbaum.

Bower, G. H., Thompson-Schill, S., & Tulving E. (1994). Reducing retroactive interference: An interference analysis. *Journal of Experimental Psychology: Learning, Memory, and Cognition, 20*, 51–66.

Bowers, K. S., & Woody, E. Z. (1996). Hypnotic amnesia and the paradox of intentional forgetting. *Journal of Abnormal Psychology, 105*, 381–390.

Bowlby, J. (1951). Maternal care and mental health. *World Health Organization Monograph* (Serial No. 2).

Bradley, R. M. (1971). Tongue topography. In L. M. Beidler (Ed.), *Handbook of sensory physiology (Vol. 4*, Pt. 2). New York: Springer-Verlag.

Bradshaw, J. L. (1989). *Hemispheric specialization and psychological function*. New York: Wiley.

Brain imaging and psychiatry—Part 1. (1997, January). *Harvard Mental Health Letter, 13*(7), 1–4.

Bramblett, D. A. (1997, October). Personal communication.

Bransford, J., Sherwood, R., Vye, N., & Rieser, J. (1986). Teaching thinking and problem solving. *American Psychologist, 41*, 1078–1089.

Brantner, J. P., & Doherty, M. A. (1983). A review of time out: A conceptual and methodological analysis. In S. Axelrod & J. Apsche (Eds.), *The effects of punishment on human behavior* (pp. 87–132). New York: Academic Press.

Braun, S. (1996). New experiments underscore warnings on maternal drinking. *Science, 273*, 738–739.

Brawman-Mintzer, O., & Lydiard, R. (1997). Biological basis of generalized anxiety disorder. *Journal of Clinical Psychiatry, 58*(3, Suppl.), 16–25.

Bray, G. A. (1991). Weight homeostatis. *Annual Review of Medicine, 42*, 205–216.

Brazelton, T. B., Tronick, E., Adamson, L., Als, H., & Wise, S. (1975). Early mother-infant interaction. *In Parent-Infant Interaction, Ciba Symposium 33*. Amsterdam: Assoc. Science Publ.

Breckler, S. J. (1984). Empirical validation of affect, behavior, and cognition as distinct attitude components. *Journal of Personality and Social Psychology, 47*, 1191–1205.

Breggin, P. R. (1979). *Electroshock: Its brain-disabling effects*. New York: Springer.

Brems, C. (1991). Depression and personality disorder: Differential diagnosis with the MMPI. *Journal of Clinical Psychology, 47*, 669–675.

Brent, D. A., Perper, J. A., Moritz, G., Baugher, M., Roth, C., Baugher, M., Roth, C., Balach, L., & Schweers, J. (1993). Stressful life events, psychopathology, and adolescent suicide: A case control study. *Suicide and Life-Threatening Behavior, 23*, 179–187.

Breslow, L. (1999). From disease prevention to health promotion. *Journal of the American Medical Association, 28*, 1030–1033.

Brewer, W. F., & Nakamura, G. V. (1984). The nature and function of schemas. In R. S. Wyer & T. K. Sroll (Eds.), *Handbook of social cognition*. Hillsdale, NJ: Erlbaum.

Brickner, M. A., Harkins, S. G., & Ostrom, T. M. (1986). Effects of personal involvement: Thought-provoking implications for social loafing. *Journal of Personality and Social Psychology, 51*, 763–769.

Bridges, K. M. B. (1932). Emotional development in early infancy. *Child Development, 3*, 324–341.

Brigham, J. C., Maass, A., Snyder, L. E., & Spaulding, K. (1982). Accuracy of eyewitness identifications in a field setting. *Journal of Personality and Social Psychology, 42*, 673–681.

Broadbent, D. E. (1958). *Perception and communication*. New York: Pergamon Press.

Brody, L. R. (1985). Gender differences in emotional development: A review of theories and research. *Journal of Personality, 53*, 102–149.

Brody, L. R. (2000). The socialization of gender differences in emotional expression: Display rules, infant temperament, and differentiation. In A. H. Fischer et al. (Eds), *Gender and emotion: Social psychological perspectives. Studies in emotion and social interaction. Second series* (pp. 24–47). New York: Cambridge University Press.

Brooks-Gunn, J., & Furstenberg, F. F., Jr. (1986). The children of adolescent mothers: Physical, academic, and psychological outcomes. *Developmental Review, 6*, 224–251.

Brotman, A. W. (1994). What works in the treatment of anorexia nervosa? *Harvard Mental Health Letter, 10*(7), 8.

Brou, P., Sciascia, T. R., Linden, L., & Lettvin, J. Y. (1986). The colors of things. *Scientific American, 255*, 84–91.

Brown, A. (1990). Development of visual sensitivity to light and color vision in human infants: A critical review. *Vision Research, 30*, 1159–1188.

Brown, A. (1996). Mood disorders in children and adolescents. *NARSAD Research Newsletter*, 11–14.

Brown, J. (1958). Some tests of the decay theory of immediate memory. *Quarterly Journal of Experimental Psychology, 10*, 12–21.

Brown, J., & Pollitt, E. (1996). Malnutrition, poverty and intellectual development. *Scientific American, 274*, 38–43.

Brown, J. D., & Rogers, R. J. (1991). Self-serving attributions: The role of physiological arousal. *Personality and Social Psychology Bulletin, 17*, 501–506.

Brown, R. (1973). *A first language: The early stages*. Cambridge, MA: Harvard University Press.

Brown, R. J., & Donderi, D. C. (1986). Dream content and self-reported well-being among recurrent dreamers, past-recurrent dreamers, and nonrecurrent dreamers. *Journal of Personality and Social Psychology, 50*, 612–623.

Brown, R., & Kulik, J. (1977). Flashbulb memories. *Cognition, 5*, 73–99.

Brown, R., & McNeil, D. (1966). The "tip of the tongue" phenomenon. *Journal of Verbal Learning and Verbal Behavior, 5*, 325–337.

Brown, R., Cazden, C., & Bellugi, U. (1968). The child's grammar from I to III. In J. P. Hill (Ed.), *Minnesota symposium on child psychology (Vol. 2*, pp. 28–73). Minneapolis: University of Minnesota Press.

Brownell, K. (1991). Dieting and the search for the perfect body: Where physiology and culture collide. *Behavior Therapy, 22*, 1–12.

Bruce, K., Pihl, R., Mayerovitch, J., & Shestowsky, J. (1999). Alcohol and retrograde memory effects: Role of individual differences. *Journal of Studies on Alcohol, 60*, 130–136.

Bruce-Grey-Owen Sound Health Unit (2000, May 25). Walkerton e. coli outbreak (press release). Retrieved August 21, 2000 from the World Wide Web: www.srhip.on.ca/bgoshu2/index.html.

Bruner, J. S., Goodnow, J. J., & Austin, G. A. (1956). *A study of thinking*. New York: Wiley.

Bryan, J. H., & Test, M. A. (1967). Models and helping: Naturalistic studies in aiding behavior. *Journal of Personality and Social Psychology, 6*, 400–407.

Bryden, M. P., & McRae, L. (1988). Dichotic laterality effects obtained with emotional words. *Neuropsychiatry, Neuropsychology, and Behavioral Neurology 1*(3), 171–176.

Buchsbaum, M., Someya, T., Teng, C., Abel, L., Chin, S., Najafi, A., Haier, R., Wu, J., & Bunney, W. (1996). PET and MRI of the thalmus of never-medicated patients with schizophrenia. *American Journal of Psychiatry, 153*, 191–199.

Buck, L. B. (1996). Information coding in the invertebrate olfactory system. *Annual Review of Neuroscience, 19*, 517–544.

Buckhout, R., Eugenio, P., Licitra, T., Oliver, L., & Kramer, T. H. (1981). Memory, hypnosis and evidence: Research on eyewitnesses. *Social Action and the Law, 7*, 67–72.

Buis, J. M., & Thompson, D. N. (1989). Imaginary audience and personal fable: A brief review. *Adolescence, 24*, 773–781.

Burke, A., Heuer, F., & Reisberg, D. (1992). Remembering emotional events. *Memory and Cognition, 20*, 277–290.

Burke, R., & Greenglass, E. (1999). Work-family conflict, spouse support, and nursing staff well-being during organizational restructuring. *Journal of Occupational Health Psychology, 4*, 327–336.

Burtt, H. E. (1932). An experimental study of early childhood memory. *Journal of Genetic Psychology, 40*, 287–295.

Busch, C. Zonderman, A., & Costa, P. (1994). Menopausal transition and psychological distress in a nationally representative sample: Is menopause associated with psychological distress? *Journal of Aging and Health, 6*, 208–228.

Bushman, B. J. (1995). Moderating role of trait aggressiveness in the effects of violent media on aggression. *Journal of Personality and Social Psychology, 69*, 950–960.

Busnel, M. C., Granier-Deferre, C., & Lecanuet, J. P. (1992). Fetal audition. *Annals of the New York Academy of Sciences, 662*, 118–134.

Buss, D. M. (1984). Marital assortment for personality dispositions: Assessment with three different data sources. *Behavioral Genetics, 14*, 111–123.

Buss, D. M. (1994). The strategies of human mating. *American Scientist, 82*, 238–249.

Buss, D. M., Abbott, M., Angleitner, A., Asherian, A., Biaggio, A., Blanco-Villasenor, A., Bruchon-Schweitzer, M., et al. (1990). International preferences in selecting mates: A study of 37 cultures. *Journal of Cross-Cultural Psychology, 21*, 5–47.

Buss, D. M., & Kenrick, D. T. (1998). Evolutionary social psychology. In D. T. Gilbert, S. T. Fiske, & G. Lindzey (Eds.), *The handbook of social psychology* (4th ed., Vol. 2), (pp. 983–1026). New York: McGraw-Hill.

Butcher, J. N., Dahlstrom, W. G., Graham, J. R., Tellegen, A., & Kaemmer, B. (1989). *Manual for the restandardized Minnesota Multiphasic Personality Inventory: MMPI-2. An administrative and interpretive guide*. Minneapolis: University of Minnesota Press.

Butcher, J. N., & Graham, J. R. (1989). *Topics in MMPI-2 interpretation*. Minneapolis: Department of Psychology, University of Minnesota.

Butcher, J. N., & Hostetler, K. (1990). Abbreviating MMPI item administration: What can be learned from the MMPI for the MMPI-2? *Psychological Assessment: A Journal of Consulting and Clinical Psychology, 2*, 12–21.

Butcher, J. N., & Rouse, S. V. (1996). Personality: Individual differences and clinical assessment. *Annual Review of Psychology, 47*, 89–111.

Butler, R., & Lewis, M. (1982). *Aging and mental health* (3rd ed.). St. Louis: Mosby.

Byrne, D., Clore, G. L., & Smeaton, G. (1986). The attraction hypothesis: Do similar attitudes affect anything? *Journal of Personality and Social Psychology, 51*, 1167–1170.

Cahill, L., Babinsky, R., Markowitsch, H. J., & McGaugh, J. L. (1995). The amygdala and emotional memory. *Nature, 377*, 295–296.

Camp, D. S., Raymond, G. A., & Church, R. M. (1967). Temporal relationship between response and punishment. *Journal of Experimental Psychology, 74*, 114–123.

Campbell, A. (1975, May). The American way of mating: Marriage si, children only maybe. *Psychology Today*, pp. 37–43.

Campbell, D. T., & Sprecht, J. C. (1985). Altruism: Biology, culture, and religion. *Journal of Social and Clinical Psychology, 3*, 33–42.

Campbell, S. S. (1985). Spontaneous termination of ad libitum sleep episodes with special reference to REM sleep. *Electroencephalography & Clinical Neurophysiology, 60*, 237–242.

Campbell, S. S. (1995). Effects of timed bright-light exposure on shiftwork adaptation in middle-aged subjects. *Sleep, 18*, 408–416.

Campos, J. J., Langer, A., & Krowitz, A. (1970). Cardiac responses on the visual cliff in prelocomotor human infants. *Science, 170,* 196–197.

Canada praised for tough stand on illegal migrants. (2000, January 14). *Vancouver Sun.* Retrieved July 7, 2000 from the World Wide Web: www.amssa.org/migrants/news/news33.htm.

Canadian Centre for Occupational Health and Safety. (1988). Rotational Shiftwork: CCOHS Report. *Worklife 5*(6): 9–10.

Canadian Council on Animal Care. (1989). *Ethics of Animal Investigation.* Ottawa.

Canadian Parents for French (2000). Frequently asked questions about French second language programs. Retreived August 21 from the World Wide Web: www.cpf.ca/english/resources/frequently_%20asked_questions.htm.

Canadian Press (2000, July 25). Police officer drank, drove, killed three, pp. 1, 3.

Canadian Psychological Association. (1988). *Canadian Code of Ethics for Psychologists: Companion Manual: Preamble.* Ottawa.

Cannon, W. B. (1927). The James-Lange theory of emotions: A critical examination as an alternative theory. *American Journal of Psychology, 39,* 106–112.

Cannon, W. B. (1932). *The wisdom of the body.* New York: Norton.

Cannon, W. B., & Washburn, A. L. (1912). An explanation of hunger. *American Journal of Physiology, 29,* 441–454.

Carlat, D. J., Camargo, C. A., Jr., & Herzog, D. B. (1997). Eating disorders in males: A report on 135 patients. *American Journal of Psychiatry, 154,* 1127–1132.

Carlin, A., Hoffman, H., & Weghorst, S. (1997). Virtual reality and tactile augmentation in the treatment of spider phobia: A case report. *Behavior Research and Therapy, 35,* 153–158.

Carlson, E. B., & Rosser-Hogan, R. (1991). Trauma experiences, posttraumatic stress, dissociation, and depression in Cambodian refugees. *American Journal of Psychiatry, 148,* 1548–1551.

Carlson, M., Charlin, V., & Miller, N. (1988). Positive mood and helping behavior: A test of six hypotheses. *Journal of Personality and Social Psychology, 55,* 211–229.

Carlson, N. R. (1994). *Physiology of behavior* (5th ed.). Boston: Allyn & Bacon.

Carpi, J. (1996). Stress: It's worse than you think. *Psychology Today, 29,* 34–42, 68–76.

Carporael, L. R. (1989). Mechanisms matter: The differences between sociobiology and evolutionary psychology. *Behavioral and Brain Sciences 32,* 69–75.

Carskadon, M. A., & Dement, W. C. (1989). Normal human sleep: An overview. In M. H. Kryger, T. Roth, & W. C. Dement (Eds.), *Principles and practice of sleep medicine* (pp. 3–13). Philadelphia: W. B. Saunders.

Carskadon, M. A., & Rechtschaffen, A. (1989). Monitoring and staging human sleep. In M. H. Kryger, T. Roth, & W. C. Dement (Eds.), *Principles and practice of sleep medicine* (pp. 665–683). Philadelphia: W. B. Saunders.

Carson, R. C. (1989). Personality. *Annual Review of Psychology, 40,* 227–248.

Carver C. S., Pozo, C., Harris, S. D., Noriega, V., Scheier, M. F., Robinson, D. S., Ketcham, A. S., Moffat, F. L., Jr., & Clark, K. C. (1993). How coping mediates the effect of optimism on distress: A study of women with early stage breast cancer. *Journal of Personality and Social Psychology, 65,* 375–390.

Case, R. (1985). *Intellectual development: Birth to adulthood.* Orlando, FL: Academic Press.

Case, R. (1987). Neo-Piagetian theory: Retrospect and prospect. *International Journal of Psychology, 22,* 773–791.

Case, R. (Ed.). (1992). *The mind's staircase: Exploring the conceptual underpinnings of children's thought and knowledge.* Hillsdale, NJ: Erlbaum.

Casey, D. (1996). Side effect profiles of new antipsychotic agents. *Journal of Clinical Psychiatry, 57*(11), 40–45.

Cash, T. F., & Derlega, V. J. (1978). The matching hypothesis: Physical attractiveness among same-sexed friends. *Personality and Social Psychology Bulletin, 4,* 240–243.

Cash, T. F., & Janda, L. H. (1984, December). The eye of the beholder. *Psychology Today,* pp. 46–52.

Castro, J. (1992, January 20). Sexual harassment: A guide. *TIME,* p.37.

Cattell, R. B. (1950). *Personality: A systematic, theoretical, and factual study.* New York: McGraw-Hill.

Cattell, R. B., Eber, H. W., & Tatsuoka, M. M. (1977). *Handbook for the 16 personality factor questionnaire.* Champaign, IL: Institute of Personality and Ability Testing.

Cattell, R. B., Saunders, D. R., & Stice, G. F. (1950). *The 16 personality factor questionnaire.* Champaign, IL: Institute of Personality and Ability Testing.

Chaika, E. (1985, August). Crazy talk. *Psychology Today,* pp. 30–35.

Chaiken, S. (1979). Communicator physical attractiveness and persuasion. *Journal of Personality and Social Psychology, 37,* 1387–1397.

Chaiken, S. and C. Stanger. (1987). Attitudes and Attitude Change. *Annual Review of Psychology,* 38:575–630.

Chambless, D. L., & Goldstein, A. J. (1979). Behavioral psychotherapy. In R. J. Corsini (Ed.), *Current psychotherapies (2nd ed.,* pp. 230–272). Itasca, IL: F. E. Peacock.

Chang, E. (1998). Dispositional optimism and primary and secondary appraisal of a stressor: Controlling for confounding influences and relations to coping and psychological and physical adjustment. *Journal of Personality and Social Psychology, 74,* 1109–1120.

Chang, K. (2000, June 17). Einstein's wide brain. ABCNEWS.com.

Changeux, J-P. (1993). Chemical signaling in the brain. *Scientific American, 269,* 58–62.

Channouf, A., Canac, D., & Gosset, O. (1999). Les effets non specifiques de la publicite subliminale. *Revue Europeennes de Psychologie Appliquee, 49*(1), 13–21.

Charge stayed against man accused in slaying of UPS courier. (2000, March 20). *Canadian Press Newswire.*

Charness, N. (1989). Age and expertise: Responding to Talland's challenge. In L.W. Poon, D.C. Rubin, & B.A. Wilson (Eds.), *Everyday cognition in adulthood and old age.* New York: Cambridge University Press.

Charney, D. A., & Russell, R. C. (1994). An overview of sexual harassment. *American Journal of Psychiatry, 151,* 10–17.

Charney, D. S., & Woods, S. W. (1989). Benzodiazepine treatment of panic disorder: A comparison of alprazolam and lorazepam. *Journal of Clinical Psychiatry, 50*, 418–423.

Chase, M. H., & Morales, F. R. (1990). The atonia and myoclonia of active (REM) sleep. *Annual Review of Psychology, 41*, 557–584.

Checkley, H. (1941). *The mask of sanity*. St. Louis: Mosby.

Chipuer, H. M., Plomin, R., Pedersen, M. L., McClearn, G. E., & Nesselroade, J. R. (1993). Genetic influence on family environment: The role of personality. *Developmental Psychology, 29*, 110–118.

Chomsky, N. (1957). *Syntactic structures*. The Hague: Mouton.

Chomsky, N. (1968). *Language and mind*. New York: Harcourt, Brace & World.

Christensen, L. B. (1997). *Experimental methodology*, (7th ed). Boston: Allyn & Bacon.

Christianson, S-Å. (1992). Emotional stress and eyewitness memory: A critical review. *Psychological Bulletin, 112*, 284–309.

Christmas, J. T. (1992). The risks of cocaine use in pregnancy. *Medical Aspects of Human Sexuality, 26*(2), 36–43.

Chumlea, W. C. (1982). *Physical growth in adolescence. In B. B. Wolman (Ed.), Handbook of developmental psychology*. Englewood Cliffs, NJ: Prentice-Hall.

Church R. M. (1963). The varied effects of punishment on behavior. *Psychological Review, 70*, 369–402.

Church, R. M. (1989). Theories of timing behavior. In S. P. Klein & R. Mower (Eds.), *Contemporary learning theories: Instrumental conditioning theory and the impact of biological constraints on learning*. Hillsdale, NJ: Erlbaum.

Cialdini, R. B., Cacioppo, J. T., Basset, R., & Miller, J. A. (1978). Low-ball procedure for producing compliance: Commitment then cost. *Journal of Personality and Social Psychology, 36*, 463–476.

Cialdini, R. B., Vincent, J. E., Lewis, S. K., Catalan, J., Wheeler, D., & Darby, B. L. (1975). Reciprocal concessions procedure for inducing compliance: The door-in-the-fact technique. *Journal of Personality and Social Psychology, 31*, 206–215.

Cipolli, C., Bolzani, R., Cornoldi, C., De Beni, R., & Fagioli, I. (1993). Bizarreness effect in dream recall. *Sleep, 16*, 163–170.

Cipolli, C., & Poli, D. (1992). Story structure in verbal reports of mental sleep experience after awakening in REM sleep. *Sleep, 15*, 133–142.

Clark, D., Salkovskis, P., Ost, L-G., Breitholtz, E., Koehler, K., Westling, B., Jeavons, A., & Gelder, M. (1997). Misinterpretation of body sensations in panic disorder. *Journal of Consulting and Clinical Psychology, 65*, 203–213.

Clark, D. M., & Teasdale, J. D. (1982). Diurnal variation in clinical depression and accessibility of memories of positive and negative experiences. *Journal of Abnormal Psychology, 91*, 87–95.

Clark, R. D., III, & Word, L. E. (1972). Why don't bystanders help? Because of ambiguity? *Journal of Personality and Social Psychology, 24*, 392–400.

Clarkson-Smith, L., & Hartley, A. A. (1990). Structural equation models of relationships between exercise and cognitive abilities. *Psychology and Aging, 5*, 437–446.

Clayton, K. N. (1964). T-maze choice learning as a joint function of the reward magnitudes for the alternatives. *Journal of Comparative and Physiological Psychology, 58*, 333–338.

Clement, K., Vaisse, C., Lahlou, C., Cabrol, S., Pelloux, V., Cassuto, D., Gourmelen, M., Dina, C., Chambaz, J., Lacorte, J-M., Basdevant, A., Bougneres, P., Lubouc, Y., Froguel, P., & Guy-Grand, B. (1998). A mutation in the human leptin receptor gene causes obesity and pituitary dysfunction. *Nature, 392*, 398–401.

Coates, B., Pusser, H. E., & Goodman, I. (1976). The influence of "Sesame Street" and "Mister Rogers' Neighborhood" on children's social behavior in the preschool. *Child Development, 47*, 138–144.

Cobb S. (1976). Social support as a moderator of life stress. *Psychosomatic Medicine, 38*, 300–314.

Cohen, A. (1997, September 8). Battle of the binge. *Time*, 54–56.

Cohen, S. (1988). Psychosocial models of the role of social support in the etiology of physical disease. *Health Psychology, 7*, 269–297.

Cohen, S., Tyrrell, D. A .J., & Smith, A. P. (1993). Negative life events, perceived stress, negative affect, and susceptibility to the common cold. *Journal of Personality and Social Psychology, 64*, 131–140.

Cohen, S., & Williamson, G. M. (1991). Stress and infectious disease in humans. *Psychological Bulletin, 109*, 5–54.

Colapinto, J. (2000). *As nature made him: The boy who was raised as a girl*. Toronto: HarperCollins.

Colby, A., Kohlberg, L., Gibbs, J., & Lieberman, M. (1983). A longitudinal study of moral judgment. *Monographs of the Society for Research in Child Development, 48*(1–2, Serial No. 200).

Cole, J. O., & Chiarello, R. J. (1990). The benzodiazepines as drugs of abuse. *Journal of Psychiatric Research, 24*, 135–144.

Cole, P. M. (1986). Children's spontaneous control of facial expression. *Child Development, 57*, 1309–1321.

Coleman, R. M. (1986). *Wide awake at 3:00 a.m.: By choice or chance?* New York: W. H. Freeman.

Collins, W. A., & Gunnar, M. R. (1990). Social and personality development. *Annual Review of Psychology, 41*, 387–416.

Condon, W. S., & Sander, L. W. (1974). Neonatal movement is synchronized with adult speech: Interactional participation and language acquisition. *Science, 183*, 99–101.

Conjoined twins. (2000, October 19). BBC2. Retrieved December 7, 2000 from the World Wide Web: www.bbc.co.uk/science/horizon/conjoined.

Connidis, I., & McMullin, J. (1999). Permanent childlessness: Perceived advantages and disadvantages among older persons. *Canadian Journal on Aging, 18*, 447–465.

Conrad, R. (1964). Acoustic confusions in immediate memory. *British Journal of Psychology, 55*, 75–84.

Conway, M. A., Collins, A. F., Gathercole, S. E., & Anderson, S. J. (1996). Recollections of true and false autobiographical memories. *Journal of Experimental Psychology: General, 125*, 69–95.

Cook, M., Mineka, S., Wolkenstein, B., & Laitsch, K. (1985). Observational conditioning of snake fear in unrelated rhesus monkeys. *Journal of Abnormal Psychology, 94*, 591–610.

Cooper, J., & Fazio, R. H. (1984). A new look at dissonance theory. In L. Berkowitz (Ed.), *Advances in experimental social psychology, 17,* 229–266. New York: Academic Press.

Cooper, L. A., & Shepard, R. N. (1984). Turning something over in the mind. *Scientific American, 251*, 106–114.

Cooper, R. (1994). Normal sleep. In R. Cooper (Ed.), *Sleep.* New York: Chapman & Hall.

Coppen, A. (1994). Depression as a lethal disease: Prevention strategies. *Journal of Clinical Psychiatry, 55*(4, Suppl.), 37–45.

Corballis, M. C. (1989). Laterality and human evolution. *Psychological Review, 96*, 492–509.

Coren, S. (1997). *Sleep thieves: An eye-opening exploration into the science and mysteries of sleep.* New York: Free Press.

Coren, S. (1989). Left-handedness and accident-related injury risk. *American Journal of Public Health, 79*, 1–2.

Coren, S., & Halpern, D. F. (1991). Left-handedness: A marker for decreased survival fitness. *Psychological Bulletin, 109*, 90–106.

Coren, S., & Porac, C. (1977). Fifty centuries of right handedness: The historical record. *Science, 198*, 631–632.

Coren, S., Porac, C., & Ward, L. M. (1979). *Sensation and perception.* New York: Academic Press.

Coryell, W. (1996). Psychotic depression. *Journal of Clinical Psychiatry, 57*(3, Suppl.) 27–31.

Coryell, W. (1998). The treatment of psychotic depression. *Journal of Clinical Psychiatry, 59*(1), 22–27.

Costa, P. T., Jr., & McCrae, R. R. (1985). *The NEO Personality Inventory.* Odessa, FL: Psychological Assessment Resources.

Costa, P. T., Jr., & McCrae, R. R. (1986). Personality stability and its implications for clinical psychology. *Clinical Psychology Review, 6*, 407–423.

Costa, P. T., Jr., & McCrae, R. R. (1988). Personality in adulthood: A six-year longitudinal study of self-reports and spouse ratings on the NEO Personality Inventory. *Journal of Personality and Social Psychology, 54*, 853–863.

Costa, P. T., Jr., & McCrae, R. R. (1992). *NEO-PI-R: Revised NEO Personality Inventory (NEO-PI-R).* Odessa, FL: Psychological Assessment Resources. Costa, P.T., Jr., & McCrae, R.R. (1992b). Normal personality assessment in clinical practice: The NEO Personality Inventory. *Psychological Assessment*, *4*, 5–13.

Costa, P. T., Jr., & McCrae, R. R. (1997). Stability and change in personality assessment: The Revised NEO Personality Inventory in the year 2000. *Journal of Personality Assessment, 68*, 8694.

Costa E Silva, J. A., Chase, M. Sartorius, N., & Roth, T. (1996). Special report from the symposium held by the World Heath Organization and World Federation of Sleep Research Societies: An overview of insomnia and related disorders—recognition, epidemiology, and rational management. *Sleep, 19*, 412–416.

Cotman, C. W., & Lynch, G. S. (1989). The neurobiology of learning and memory. *Cognition, 33*, 201–241.

Courtney, S., Ungerleider, L., Keil, K., & Haxby, J.(1997). Transient and sustained activity in a distributed neural system for human working memory. *Nature, 386,* 608–611.

Cowan, C. P., & Cowan, P. A. (1992, July/August). Is there love after baby? *Psychology Today*, 58–63.

Cowan, N. (1988). Evolving conceptions of memory storage, selective attention, and their mutual constraints within the human information-processing system. *Psychological Bulletin, 104*, 163–191.

Coyle, J., & Draper, E. S. (1996). What is the significance of glutamate for mental health? *Harvard mental health Letter, 13*(6), 8.

Craik, F. I. M., & Lockhart, R. S. (1972). Levels of processing: A framework for memory research. *Journal of Verbal Learning and Verbal Behavior, 11*, 671–684.

Craik, F. I. M., & Tulving, E. (1975). Depth of processing and the retention of words in episodic memory. *Journal of Experimental Psychology: General, 104*, 268–294.

Craik, F. I. M., & Watkins, M. J. (1973). The role of rehearsal in short-term memory. *Journal of Verbal Learning and Verbal Behavior, 12*, 599–607.

Crasilneck, H. B. (1992). The use of hypnosis in the treatment of impotence. *Psychiatric Medicine, 10*, 67–75.

Cravens, H. (1992). A scientific project locked in time: The Terman Genetic Studies of Genius, 1920s–1950s. *American Psychologist*, *47*, 183–189.

Craver-Lemley, C., & Reeves, A. (1992). How visual imagery interferes with vision. *Psychological Bulletin*, *99*, 633–649.

Crespi, L. P. (1942). Quantitative variation of incentive and performance in the white rat. *American Journal of Psychology, 55*, 467–517.

Crews, F. (1996). The verdict on Freud. *Psychological Science*, *7*, 63–68.

Crick, F., & Koch, C. (1992). The problem of consciousness. *Scientific American*, *267*, 152–159.

Crick, F., & Mitchison, G. (1983). The function of dream sleep. *Nature, 304*, 408–416.

Crick, F., & Mitchison, G. (1995). REM sleep and neural nets. *Behavioural Brain Research, 69,* 147–155.

Crits-Christoph, P. (1992). The efficacy of brief dynamic psychotherapy: A meta-analysis. *American Journal of Psychiatry, 149*, 151–158.

Crosby, F., Bromley, S., & Saxe, L. (1980). Recent unobtrusive studies of black and white discrimination and prejudice: A literature review. *Psychological Bulletin, 87*, 546–563.

Crowder , R. (1992). Sensory memory. In L. Squire (Ed.), *Encyclopedia of learning and memory.* New York: Macmillan.

Crowe, L. C., & George, W. H. (1989). Alcohol and human sexuality: Review and integration. *Psychological Bulletin, 105*, 374–386.

Csikszentmihalyi, M. (1996, July/August). The creative personality. *Psychology Today*, *29*, 36–40.

Culbertson, F. (1997). Depression and gender: An international review. *American Psychologist, 52,* 25–31.

Cunningham, J., Sobell, L., & Sobell, M. (1999). Changing perceptions about self-change and moderate-drinking recoveries from alcohol problems: What can and should be done? *Journal of Applied Social Psychology, 29,* 291–299.

Cunningham, M. R. (1979). Weather, mood, and helping behavior: Quasi experiments with the sunshine Samaritan. *Journal of Personality and Social Psychology, 37*, 1947–1956.

Cunningham, M. R., Roberts, A. R., Barbee, A. P., Druen, P. B., & Wu, C-H. (1995). "Their ideas of beauty are, on the whole, the same as ours": Consistency and variability in the cross-cultural perception of female physical attractiveness. *Journal of Personality and Social Psychology, 68,* 261–279.

Cunningham, R. (2000, January 14). Jurisdictions in Canada with smoke-free laws for restaurants and bars. Canadian Cancer Society. Retrieved August 21, 2000 from the World Wide Web: www.ocat.org/body.

Curtis, R. C., & Miller, K. (1986). Believing another likes or dislikes you: Behaviors making the beliefs come true. *Journal of Personality and Social Psychology, 51,* 284–290.

Czeisler, C. A., Moore-Ede, M. C., & Coleman, R. M. (1982). Rotating shift work schedules that disrupt sleep are improved by applying circadian principles. *Science, 217*, 460–463.

Dabbs, J. M., Jr., & Morris, R. (1990). Testosterone, social class, and antisocial behavior in a sample of 4,462 men. *Psychological Science, 1*, 209–211.

Dale, N., & Kandel, E. R. (1990). Facilitatory and inhibitory transmitters modulate spontaneous transmitter release at cultured Aplysia sensorimotor synapses. *Journal of Physiology, 421*, 203–222.

Damasio, H., Grabowski, T., Frank, R., Galaburda, A. M., & Damasio, A. R. (1994). The return of Phineas Gage: Clues about the brain from the skull of a famous patient. *Science, 264*, 1102–1105.

Darley, J. M., & Latane, B. (1968a). Bystander intervention in emergencies: Diffusion of responsibility. *Journal of Personality and Social Psychology, 8*, 377–383.

Darley, J. M., & Latane, B. (1968b, December). When will people help in a crisis? *Psychology Today*, pp. 54–57, 70–71.

Darou, W. G. 1992. Native Canadians and intelligence testing. *Canadian Journal of Counselling, 26, 96*–99.

Darou, W. G., Kurtness, J., & Hum, A. (2000). The impact of conducting research with a First Nation. *Canadian Journal of Counselling, 34*(1), 43–54.

Darwin, C. (1859). *On the origin of species by means of natural selection.*

Darwin, C. (1965). *The expression of emotion in man and animals.* Chicago: University of Chicago Press. (Original work published 1872).

Dash, P. K., Hochner, B., & Kandel, E. R. (1990). Injection of the cAMP-responsive element into the nucleus of Aplysia sensory neurons blocks long-term facilitation. *Nature, 345*, 718–721.

Dashiell, J. F. (1925). A quantitative demonstration of animal drive. *Journal of Comparative Psychology*, 5, 205–208.

Davanloo, H. (Ed.). (1980). *Short-term dynamic psychotherapy.* New York: Jason Aronson.

Davidson, K., MacGregor, M. W., Stuhr, J., Dixon, K., & MacLean, D. (2000). Constructive anger verbal behavior predicts blood pressure in a population-based sample. *Health Psychology, 19,* 55–64.

Davis, K. L., Kahn, R. S., Ko, G., & Davidson, M. (1991). Dopamine in schizophrenia: A review and reconceptualization. *American Journal of Psychiatry, 148*, 1474–1486.

Davis, T. L. (1995). Gender differences in masking negative emotions: Ability or motivation? *Developmental Psychology, 31*(4), 660–667.

D'Azevedo, W.A. (1982). Tribal history in Liberia. In U. Neisser (Ed.), *Memory observed: Remembering in natural contexts.* San Francisco: W.H. Freeman.

Dean, G. A., Kelly, I. W., Saklofske, D. H., & Furnham, A. (1992). In B. Beyerstein, & D. Beyerstein (Eds.), *The write stuff: Evaluations of graphology*. Buffalo, NY: Prometheus Books.

DeCasper, A. J., & Fifer, W. P. (1980). Of human bonding: Newborns prefer their mothers' voices. *Science, 208*, 1174–1176.

DeCasper, A. J., & Spence, M. J. (1986). Prenatal maternal speech influences newborns' perception of speech sounds. *Infant Behavior and Development, 9,* 133–150.

de Castro, J. M. (1993). Genetic influences on daily intake and meal patterns of humans. *Physiology and Behavior, 53,* 777–782.

de Castro, J. M. (1998). Genes and environment have gender-independent influences on the eating and drinking of free-living humans. *Physiology & Behavior, 63*(3), 385–395

de Castro, J. M., & de Castro, E. S. (1989). Spontaneous meal patterns of humans: Influence of the presence of other people. *Journal of Clinical Nutrition, 50*, 237–247.

Deci, E. L. (1975). *Intrinsic motivation.* New York: Plenum.

Deese, J. (1959). On the prediction of occurrence of particular verbal intrusions in immediate recall. *Journal of Experimental Psychology, 58*, 17–22.

Degner, L. F., Kristjanson, L. J., Bowman, D., Sloan, J. A., et al. (1997). Information needs and decisional preferences in women with breast cancer. *Journal of the American Medical Association, 227*(18), 1485–1492.

DeJong, W. (1979). An examination of self-perception mediation of the foot-in-the-door effect. *Journal of Personality and Social Psychology, 37*, 2221–2239.

DeKesseredy, W. S., & Kelly, K. (1993). The incidence and prevalence of woman abuse in Canadian university and college dating relationships. *Canadian Journal of Sociology, 18,* 137–159.

Delgado, J. M. R. (1969). *Physical control of the mind: Toward a psychocivilized society*. New York: Harper & Row.

Delgado, J. M. R., & Anand, B. K. (1953). Increased food intake induced by electrical stimulation of the lateral hypothalamus. *American Journal of Physiology, 172*, 162–168.

Dement, W. C. (1974). *Some must watch while some must sleep.* San Francisco: W. H. Freeman.

Dement, W.C. (1992). The proper use of sleeping pills in the primary care setting. *Journal of Clinical Psychiatry, 53*(12, suppl.), 50–56.

Dement, W., & Kleitman, N. (1957). The relation of eye movements during sleep to dream activity: An objective method for the study of dreaming. *Journal of Experimental Psychology, 53*, 339–346.

Derry, P., Harnadek, M., McLachlan, R., & Sontrop, J. (1997). Influence of seizure content on interpreting psychopathology on the MMPI-2 in patients with epilepsy. *Journal of Clinical and Experimental Neuropsychology, 19,* 396–404.

Derry, P., & Wiebe, S. (2000). Psychological adjustment to success and failure following Epilepsy surgery. *Canadian Journal of Neurological Science, 27*(Suppl.1), s116–s120.

Des Jarlais, D.C., & Friedman, S.R. (1994). AIDS and the use of injected drugs. *Scientific American, 270*, 82–88.

Deslandes, R., Potvin, P., & Leclerc, D. (1999). Validation of the Quebec French version of the "Adolescent Autonomy Scale."/Validation quebecoise de l'"Echelle de l'Autonomie de l'Adolescent." *Science et Comportement, 27*(3), 37–51.

Detke, M. J., Brandon, S. E., Weingarten, H. P., Rodin, J., & Wagner, A. R. (1989). Modulation of behavioral and insulin responses by contextual stimuli paired with food. *Physiology and Behavior, 45*, 845–851.

Deutsch, J. A., & Deutsch, D. (1966). *Physiological psychology*. Homewood, IL: Dorsey.

DeValois, R. L., & DeValois, K. K. (1975). Neural coding of color. In E. C. Carterette & M. P. Friedman (Eds.), *Handbook of perception* (Vol. 5). New York: Academic Press.

Devanand, D. P., Dwork, A. J., Hutchinson, M. S. E., Bolwig, T. G., & Sackeim, H. A. (1994). Does ECT alter brain structure? *American Journal of Psychiatry, 151*, 957–970.

Devine, P. G. (1989a). Automatic and controlled processes in prejudice: The role of stereotypes and personal beliefs. In A. R. Pratkanis, S. J. Breckler, & A. G. Greenwald (Eds.), *Attitude structure and function* (pp. 181–212). Hillsdale, NJ: Erlbaum.

Devine, P. G. (1989b). Stereotypes and prejudice: Their automatic and controlled components. *Journal of Personality and Social Psychology, 56*, 5–18.

Devine, P. G., Monteith, M. J., Zuwerink, J. R., & Elliot, A. J. (1991). Prejudice with and without compunction. *Journal of Personality and Social Psychology, 60*, 817–830.

De Vito, G., Hernandez, R., Gonzalez, V., Felici, F., & Figura, F. (1997). Low intensity physical training in older subjects. *Journal of Sports Medicine and Physical Fitness*, 37, 72–77.

deVries, H. A. (1986). *Fitness after 50*. New York: Scribner's.

Diamond, M. E., Huang, W., & Ebner, F. F. (1994). Laminar comparison of somatosensory cortical plasticity. *Science, 265*, 1885–1888.

DiChiara, G. (1997). Alcohol and dopamine. *Alcohol Health and Research World, 21*, 108–114.

Dietz, W. H. (1989). Obesity. *Journal of the American College of Nutrition, 8*(Suppl.), 139–219.

Digman, J. M. (1990). Personality structure: Emergence of the five-factor model. *Annual Review of Psychology, 41*, 417–440.

Digman, J. M., & Inouye, J. (1986). Further specification of the five robust factors of personality. *Journal of Personality and Social Psychology, 50*, 116–123.

DiLalla, L. F., & Gottesman, I. I. (1991). Biological and genetic contributors to violence—Widom's untold tale. *Psychological Bulletin, 109*, 125–129.

Dimberg, U. (1990). Facial electromyography and emotional reactions. *Psychophysiology, 27*, 481–494.

Dinges, M. M., & Oetting, E. R. (1993). Similarity in drug use patterns between adolescents and their friends. *Adolescence, 28*, 253–266.

Dion, K., Berscheid, E., & Walster, E. (1972). What is beautiful is good. *Journal of Personality and Social Psychology, 24*, 285–290.

Dion, K. K. (1973). Young children's stereotyping of facial attractiveness. *Developmental Psychology* 9:183–188.

Dion, K. K. (1973). Physical attractiveness and interpersonal attraction. In M. Cook and G. Wilson (eds.), *Love and Attraction*. New York: Pergamon.

Dipboye, R. L., Fromkin, H. L., & Wilback, K. (1975). Relative importance of applicant sex, attractiveness, and scholastic standing in evaluation of job applicant resumes. *Journal of Applied Psychology, 60*, 39–43.

Dobb, E. (1989, November/December). The scents around us. *The Sciences, 29*, 46–53.

Dobie, R. A. (1987, December). Noise-induced hearing loss: The family physician's role. *American Family Physician*, pp. 141–148.

Dollard, J., Doob, L. W., Miller, N., Mowrer, O. H., & Sears, R. R. (1939). *Frustration and aggression*. New Haven: Yale University Press.

Dornbusch, S. M., Ritter, P. L., Leiderman, P. H., Roberts, D. F., et al. (1987). The relation of parenting style to adolescent school performance. *Child Development. Special Issue: Schools and development, 58*(5), 1244–1257.

Dovidio, J. F. (1984). Helping behavior and altruism: An empirical and conceptual overview. In L. Berkowitz (Ed.), *Advances in experimental social psychology (Vol. 17*, pp. 361–427). New York: Academic Press.

Dreikurs, R. (1953). *Fundamentals of Adlerian psychology*. Chicago: Alfred Adler Institute.

Drevets, W. C., Price, J. L., Simpson, J. R., Jr., Todd, R. D., Reich, T., Vannier, M., & Raichle, M. E. (1997). Subgenual prefrontal cortex abnormalities in mood disorders. *Nature, 386*, 824–827.

Drevets, W. C., Videen, T. O., Price, J. L., Preskorn, S. H., Carmichael, S. T., & Raichle, M. E. (1992). A functional anatomical study of unipolar depression. *Journal of Neuroscience, 12*, 3628–3641.

Drewnowski, A., Yee, D. K., Kurth, C. L., & Krahn, D. D. (1994). Eating pathology and DSM-III-R bulimia nervosa: A continuum of behavior. *American Journal of Psychiatry, 151*, 1217–1219.

Drigotas, S. M. (1993). Similarity revisited: A comparison of similarity/attraction versus dissimilarity/repulsion. *British Journal of Social Psychology, 32*(4), 365–377.

Dryden, J. (1994, September 8). Alcohol use by fathers may affect fetal development. *Washington University Record*, p. 2.

Dryer, D. C., & Horowitz, L. M. (1997). When do opposites attract? Interpersonal complementarity versus similarity. *Journal of Personality and Social Psychology, 72*, 592–603.

Duce, R. (2000, September 6). Sisters joined for 38 years back parents. *Sunday Times*. Retrieved December 7, 2000 from the World Wide Web: www.Sunday-times.co.uk/news/pages/tim/2000/09/06.

Duck, S. (1983). *Friends for life: The psychology of close relationships*. New York: St. Martin's Press.

Duffy, A., & Everson, R. (1996, December 14). Spinning out of control. *Ottawa Citizen*.

Duggan, J. P., & Booth, D. A. (1986). Obesity, overeating, and rapid gastric emptying in rats with ventromedial hypothalamic lesions. Science, 231, 609–611.

Dunkel-Schetter, C., Feinstein, L. G., Taylor, S. E., & Falke, R. L. (1992). Patterns of coping with cancer. *Health Psychology, 11*, 79–87.

Duong, T., Ades, A. E., Gibb, D. M., Tookey, P. A., & Masters, J. (1999). Vertical transmission rates for HIV in the British Isles: estimates based on surveillance data. *British Medical Journal, 319*(7219):1227–1229.

Dutton, D. G. (1971). Reactions of restaurateurs to blacks and whites violating restaurant dress requirements. *Canadian Journal of Behavioral Science, 3,* 298–331.

Dutton, D. G. (1973). The relationship of amount of perceived discrimination toward a minority group on behavior of majority group members. *Canadian Journal of Behavioral Science, 5,* 34–45.

Duyme, M. (1988). School success and social class: An adoption study. *Developmental Psychology, 24*, 203–209.

Dworkin, B. R. (1993). *Learning and physiological regulation.* Chicago: University of Chicago Press.

Dywan, J., & Bowers, K. (1983). The use of hypnosis to enhance recall. *Science, 222*, 184–185.

Eagly, A. H. (1987). *Sex differences in social behavior: A social-role interpretation.* Hillsdale, NJ: Erlbaum.

Eagly, A. H., Ashmore, R. D., Makhijani, M. G., & Longo, L. C. (1991). What is beautiful is good . . .: A meta-analytic review of research on the physical attractiveness stereotype. *Psychological Bulletin, 110*, 109–128.

Eagly, A. H., & Carli, L. (1981). Sex of researchers and sex-typed communications as determinants of sex differences in influence-ability: A meta-analysis of social influence studies. *Psychological Bulletin, 90*, 1–20.

Eagly, A. H., & Steffen, V. J. (1986). Gender and aggressive behavior: A meta-analytic review of the social psychological literature. *Psychological Bulletin*, *100*, 309–330.

Eating disorders—part II. (1997, November). *Harvard Mental Health Letter*, *14*(5), 1–5.

Ebbeck, V., & Weiss, M. R. (1988). The arousal-performance relationship: Task characteristics and performance measures in track and field athletics. *Sport Psychologist, 2,* 13–17.

Ebbinghaus, H. E. (1964). *Memory: A contribution to experimental psychology* (H. A. Ruger & C. E. Bussenius, Trans.). New York: Dover. (Original work published 1885).

Eckman, P. (1999). Basic emotions. In T. Dangleish, M. J. Power, et al. (Eds.), *Handbook of cognition and emotion,* (pp. 45–60). Chichester, England: John Wiley.

Edwards, K., & Smith, E. E. (1996). A disconfirmation bias in the evaluation of arguments. *Journal of Personality and Social Psychology, 71,* 5–24.

Efron, R. (1990). *The decline and fall of hemispheric specialization.* Hillsdale, NJ: Erlbaum.

Egeth, H. E. (1993). What do we *not* know about eyewitness identification? *American Psychologist*, *48*, 577–580.

Eibl-Eibesfeldt, I. (1973). The expressive behavior of the deaf-and-blind-born. In M. von Cranach & I. Vine (Eds.), *Social communication and movement.* New York: Academic Press.

Eich, E., Macaulay, D., & Ryan, L. (1994). Mood dependent memory for events of the personal past. *Journal of Experimental Psychology: General*, *123*, 201–215.

Eich, J. E. (1980). The cue dependent nature of state-dependent retrieval. *Memory and Cognition, 8*, 157–173.

Eichenbaum, H. (1997). Declarative memory: Insights from cognitive neurobiology. *Annual Review of Psychology, 48,* 547–572.

Eichenbaum, H., & Otto, T. (1993). LTP and memory: can we enhance the connection? *Trends in Neurosciences*, *16*, 163.

Eimas, P. D. (1985). The perception of speech in early infancy. *Scientific American, 252*, 46–52.

Ekman, P. (1972). Universals and cultural differences in facial expression of emotion. In J. Cole (Ed.), *Nebraska symposium on motivation* (Vol. 19). Lincoln: University of Nebraska Press.

Ekman, P. (1993). Facial expression and emotion. *American Psychologist*, *48*, 384–392.

Eckman, P. (1999). Basic emotions. In T. Dangleish, M. J. Power, et al. (Eds.), *Handbook of cognition and emotion,* (pp. 45–60). Chichester, England: John Wiley.

Ekman, P., & Friesen, W. V. (1975). *Unmasking the face: A guide to recognizing emotions from facial clues.* Englewood Cliffs, NJ: Prentice-Hall.

Ekman, P., Levenson, R. W., & Friesen, W. V. (1983). Autonomic nervous system activity distinguishes among emotions. *Science, 221*, 1208–1210.

Elkin, I., Gibbons, R. D., Shea, M. T., Sotsky, S. M., Watkins, J. T., Pikonis, P. A., & Hedeker, D. (1995). Initial severity and differential treatment outcome in the National Institute of Mental Health Treatment of Depression Collaborative Research Program. *Journal of Consulting and Clinical Psychology, 63*, 841–847.

Elkin, I., Shea, M. T., Watkins, J. T., et al. (1989). National Institute of Mental Health Treatment of Depression Collaborative Research Program: General effectiveness of treatments. *Archives of General Psychology, 46*, 971–982.

Elkind, D. (1967). Egocentrism in adolescence. *Child Development, 38*, 1025–1034.

Elkind, D. (1970, April 5). Erik Erikson's eight ages of man. *The New York Times Magazine*, pp. 25–27, 84–92, 110–119.

Elkind, D. (1974). *Children and adolescents: Interpretive essays on Jean Piaget (2nd ed.).* New York: Oxford University Press.

Elkins, R. L. (1991). An appraisal of chemical aversion (emetic therapy) approaches to alcoholism treatment. *Behaviour Research and Therapy, 29*, 387–413.

Ellason, J., & Ross, C. (1997). Two-year follow-up of inpatients with dissociative identity disorder. *American Journal of Psychiatry, 154,* 832–839.

Elliot, A. J., & Devine, P. G. (1994). On the motivational nature of cognitive dissonance: Dissonance as psychological discomfort. *Journal of Personality and Social Psychology, 67,* 382–394.

Ellis, A. (1961). *A guide to rational living.* Englewood Cliffs, NJ: Prentice-Hall.

Ellis, A. (1977). The basic clinical theory of rational-emotive therapy. In A. Ellis & R. Grieger (Eds.), *Handbook of rational-emotive therapy* (pp. 3–33). New York: Springer.

Ellis, A. (1979). Rational-emotive therapy. In R. J. Corsini (Ed.), *Current psychotherapies (2nd ed.*, pp. 185–229). Itasca, IL: F. E. Peacock.

Ellis, A. (1987). The impossibility of achieving consistently good mental health. *American Psychologist, 42*, 364–375.

Ellis, A. (1993). Reflections on rational-emotive therapy. *Journal of Consulting and Clinical Psychology, 61*, 199–201.

El-Shiekh, M., Klacynski, P. A., & Valaik, M. E. (1989). Stress and coping across the life course. *Human Development, 32*, 113–117.

Encarta, (2000). "Epilepsy." Microsoft Encarta Online Encyclopedia. Retrieved December 7, 2000 from the World Wide Web: http://encarta.msn.com.

Engel, G. L. (1977). The need for a new medical model: A challenge for biomedicine. *Science, 196*, 126–129.

Engel, G. L. (1980). The clinical application of the biopsychosocial model. *American Journal of Psychiatry, 137*, 535–544.

Engles, G. I., Garnefski, N., & Diekstra, R. F. W. (1993). Efficacy of rational-emotive therapy: A quantitative analysis. *Journal of Consulting and Clinical Psychology, 61*, 1083–1090.

Enns, M., & Reiss, J. (1992). Electroconvulsive therapy. *Canadian Journal of Psychiatry 37*(10), 671–678.

Epstein, J. (1983). Examining theories of adolescent friendships. In J. Epstein & N. Karweit (Eds.), *Friends in school.* New York: Academic Press.

Epstein, R. (1996, July/August). Capturing creativity. *Psychology Today, 29*, 41–43, 75–78.

Erikson, E. H. (1963). *Childhood and society (2nd ed.)*. New York: Norton.

Erikson, E. H. (1968). *Identity: Youth and crisis.* New York: Norton.

Erikson, E. H. (1980). *Identity and the life cycle.* New York: Norton.

Erikson, E. H., Erikson, J. M., & Kivnick, H. Q. (1986). *Vital involvement in old age: The experience of old age in our time.* New York: W. W. Norton.

Erlenmeyer-Kimling, L., & Jarvik, L. F. (1963). Genetics and intelligence: A review. *Science, 142*, 1477–1479.

Eron, L. D. (1987). The development of aggressive behavior from the perspective of a developing behaviorism. *American Psychologist, 42*, 435–442.

Erwin, E. (1996). A final accounting: Philosophical and empirical issues in Freudian psychology. Cambridge, MA: MIT Press.

Esses, V. M., Haddock, G., & Zanna, M. P. (1993). Values, stereotypes, and emotions as determinants of intergroup attitudes. In D. M. Mackie and D. C. Hamilton (Eds.), *Affect, cognition and stereotyping: Interactive processes in group perception.* New York: Academic Press.

Estes, W. K. (1994). *Classification and cognition.*. New York: Oxford University Press.

Ewin, D. M. (1992). Hypnotherapy for warts (Verruca Vulgaris): 41 consecutive cases with 33 cures. *American Journal of Clinical Hypnosis, 35*, 1–10.

Eyeferth, K. (1961). Leistungen verschiedener Gruppen von Besatzungskindern in Hamburg-Wechsler Intelligenztest für Kinder (HAWIK). *Archir für die Gesamte Psychologie, 113*, 224–241.

Eysenck, H. J. (1970). *The structure of human personality (3rd ed.)*. London: Methuen.

Eysenck, H. J. (1975). *The inequality of man.* San Diego: Educational and Industrial Testing Service.

Eysenck, H.J. (1981). *A model for personality.* Berlin: Springer-Verlag.

Eysenck, H. J. (1987). Behavior therapy. In H. J. Eysenck & I. Martin (Eds.), *Theoretical foundations of behavior therapy.* New York: Plenum Press.

Eysenck, H. J. (1990). Genetic and environmental contributions to individual differences: The three major dimensions of personality. *Journal of Personality, 58*, 245–261.

Eysenck, H. J. (1994). The outcome problem in psychotherapy: What have we learned? *Behaviour Research and Therapy, 32*, 477–495.

Fackelmann, K. (1997). Marijuana on trial: Is marijuana a dangerous drug or a valuable medicine? *Science News, 151,* 178–179.

Faedda, G. L., Tondo, L., Teicher, M. H., Baldessarini, R. J., Gelbard, H. A., & Floris, G. F. (1993). Seasonal mood disorders: Patterns of seasonal recurrence in mania and depression. *Archives of General Psychiatry, 50*, 17–23.

Fajardo, D. M. (1985). Author race, essay quality, and reverse discrimination. *Journal of Applied Social Psychology, 15*, 255–268.

Falbo, T., & Polit, D. F. (1986). Quantitative review of the only child literature: Research evidence and theory development. *Psychological Bulletin, 100*, 176–189.

Famighetti, R. (1997). *The world almanac and book of facts 1998.* Mahwah, NJ: World Almanac Books.

Farah, M. J. (2000). *The cognitive neuroscience of vision.* Malden, MA: Blackwell Press.

Faravelli, C., & Pallanti, S. (1989). Recent life events and panic disorder. *American Journal of Psychiatry, 146*, 622–626.

Farde, L. (1996). The advantage of using positron emission tomography in drug research. *Trends in Neurosciences, 19,* 211–214.

Fawcett, J. C. (1992). Intrinsic neuronal determinants of regeneration. *Trends in Neurosciences, 15*, 5–8.

Fazio, R. H. (1989). On the power and functionality of attitudes: The role of attitude accessibility. In A. R. Pratkanis, S. J. Breckler, & A. G. Greenwald (Eds.), *Attitude structure and function* (pp. 153–179). Hillsdale, NJ: Erlbaum.

Fazio, R. H., Sanbonmatsu, D. M., Powell, M. C., & Kardes, F. R. (1986). On the automatic activation of attitudes. *Journal of Personality and Social Psychology, 50*, 229–238.

Fazio, R. H., & Williams (1986). Attitude accessibility as a moderator of the attitude perception and attitude-behavior relations: An investigation of the 1984 presidential election. *Journal of Personality and Social Psychology, 51*, 505–514.

Fein, S., & Spencer, S. J. (1997). Prejudice as self-image maintenance: Affirming the self through derogating others. *Journal of Personality and Social Psychology, 73,* 31–44.

Feingold, A. (1988). Matching for attractiveness in romantic partners and same-sex friends: A meta-analysis and theoretical critique. *Psychological Bulletin, 104*, 226–235.

Feingold, A. (1990). Gender differences in effects of physical attractiveness on romantic attraction: A comparison across five research paradigms. *Journal of Personality and Social Psychology, 59*, 981–993.

Feingold, A. (1992). Good-looking people are not what we think. *Psychological Bulletin, 111*, 304–341.

Fenton, W. S., & McGlashan, T. H. (1991). Natural history of schizophrenia subtypes: I. Longitudinal study of paranoid, hebephrenic, and undifferentiated schizophrenia. *Archives of General Psychiatry, 48*, 969–977.

Fenton, W. S., & McGlashan, T. H. (1994). Antecedents, symptom progression, and long-term outcome of the deficit syndrome in schizophrenia. *American Journal of Psychiatry, 151*, 351–356.

Ferber, R. (1989). Sleepwalking, confusional arousals, and sleep terrors in the child. In M. H. Kryger, T. Roth, & W. C. Dement (Eds.), *Principles and practice of sleep medicine* (pp. 640–642). Philadelphia: W.B. Saunders.

Fern, E. F., Monroe, K. B., & Avila, R. A. (1986). Effectiveness of multiple request strategies: A synthesis of research results. *Journal of Marketing Research, 23,* 144–152.

Fernandez, A., & Glenberg, A. M. (1985). Changing environmental context does not reliably affect memory. *Memory and Cognition, 13,* 333–345.

Festinger, L. (1957). *A theory of cognitive dissonance.* Evanston, IL: Row, Peterson.

Festinger, L., & Carlsmith, J. M. (1959). Cognitive consequences of forced compliance. *Journal of Abnormal and Social Psychology, 58*, 203–210.

Festinger, L., Schachter, S., & Back, K. (1950). *Social pressures in informal groups: A study of a housing community.* New York: Harper & Row.

Fiatarone, M. A., Morley, J. E., Bloom, E. T., Benton, D., Makinodan, T., & Solomon, G. F. (1988). Endogenous opioids and the exercise-induced augmentation of natural killer cell activity. *Journal of Laboratory and Clinical Medicine, 112*, 544–552.

Fiatarone, M. A., O'Neill, E. F., Ryan, N. D., Clements, K. M., Solares, G. R., Nelson, M. E., Roberts, S. B., Kehayias, J. J., Lipsitz, L. A., & Evans, W. J. (1994). Exercise training and nutritional supplementation for physical frailty in very elderly people. *New England Journal of Medicine, 330*, 1769–1775.

Field, T. M., Cohen, D., Garcia, R., & Greenberg, R. (1984). Mother-stranger face discrimination by the newborn. *Infant Behavior and Development, 7*, 19–25.

Fiez, J. A. (1996). Cerebellar contributions to cognition. *Neuron, 16,* 13–15.

Finchilescu, G. (1988). Interracial contact in South Africa within the nursing context. *Journal of Applied Social Psychology, 18*, 1207–1221.

Fine, S., (1990, April 2). Disturbing number of teens seek solution in suicide. *The Globe and Mail*, pp. A2, A5.

Fink, M. (1997, June). What is the role of ECT in the treatment of mania? *Harvard Mental Health Letter, 13,* 8.

Finke, R. A. (1985). Theories relating mental imagery to perception. *Psychological Bulletin, 98*, 236–259.

Finkel, D., & McGue, M. (1997). Sex differences and nonadditivity in heritability of the Multidimensional Personality Questionnaire scales. *Journal of Personality and Social Psychology, 72,* 929–938.

Fiorito, G., & Scotto, P. (1992). Observational learning in *Octopus vulgaris. Science, 256*, 545–547.

Fischbach, G. D. (1992). Mind and brain. *Scientific American, 267,* 48–56.

Fiske, S. T. & Taylor, S. E. (1991). *Social cognition* (2nd ed.). New York: Random House.

Fitzgerald, L. F. (1993). Sexual harassment: Violence against women in the workplace. *American Psychologist, 48*, 1070–1076.

Flavell, J. H. (1985). *Cognitive development.* Englewood, NJ: Prentice-Hall.

Flavell, J. H. (1992). Cognitive development: Past, present, and future. *Developmental Psychology, 28*, 998–1005.

Flavelle, D. (2000, April). Rising stress contributes to workplace rage (Work Rage). *Canadian Press Newswire.*

Flegal, K. M. (1996). Trends in body weight and overweight in the U.S. population. *Nutrition Reviews, 54,* S97–S100.

Fleming, J. D. (1974, July). Field report: The state of the apes. *Psychology Today*, 31–46.

Fletcher, J. M., Page, B., Francis, D. J., Copeland, K., Naus, M. J., Davis, C. M., Morris, R., Krauskopf, D., & Satz, P. (1996). Cognitive correlates of long-term cannabis use in Costa Rican men. *Archives of General Psychiatry, 53,* 1051–1057.

Flood, J. F., Silver, A. J., & Morley, J. E. (1990). Do peptide-induced changes in feeding occur because of changes in motivation to eat? *Peptides, 11*, 265–270.

Florian, V., Mikulincer, M., & Taubman, O. (1995). Does hardiness contribute to mental health during a stressful real-life situation? The roles of appraisal and coping. *Journal of Personality and Social Psychology, 68*, 687–695.

Flynn, J. R. (1987b). Race and IQ: Jensen's case refuted. In S. Modgil, & C. Modgil (Eds.), *Arthur Jensen: Consensus and controversy.* New York: Palmer Press.

Foa, E. B. (1995). How do treatments for obsessive compulsive disorder compare? *Harvard Mental Health Letter, 12,* 8.

Fogelman, E., & Wiener, V. L. (1985, August). The few, the brave, the noble. *Psychology Today*, pp. 60–65.

Foley, D. J., Monjan, A. A., Brown, S. L., Simonsick, E. M., Wallace, R. B., & Blazer, D. G. (1995). Sleep complaints among elderly persons: An epidemiologic study of three communities. *Sleep, 18,* 425–432.

Folkard, S. (1990). Circadian performance rhythms: Some practical and theoretical implications. Philosophical Transactions of the Royal Society of London. Series B: *Biological Sciences, 327*, 543–553.

Folkman, S. (1984). Personal control and stress and coping processes: A theoretical analysis. *Journal of Personality and Social Psychology, 46*, 839–852.

Folkman, S., Chesney, M., Collette, L., Boccellari, A., & Cooke, M. (1996). Postbereavement depressive mood and its prebereavement predictors in HIV + and HIV- gay men. *Journal of Personality and Social Psychology, 70,* 336–348.

Folkman, S., & Lazarus, R. S. (1980). An analysis of coping in a middle-aged community sample. *Journal of Health and Social Behavior, 21*, 219–239.

Foreyt, J. P., Walker, S., Poston, C, II, & Goodrick, G. K. (1996). Future directions in obesity and eating disorders. *Addictive Behaviors, 21,* 767–778.

Forgas, J. P., & Bower, G. H. (1987). Mood effects on person-perception judgments. *Journal of Personality and Social Psychology, 53*, 53–60.

Foulkes, D. (1996). Sleep and dreams: Dream research 1953–1993. *Sleep, 19,* 609–624.

Fourn, L., Ducic, S., & Seguin, L. (1999). Smoking and intrauterine growth retardation in Republic of Benin. *Journal of Epidemiology and Community Health, 53,* 432–433.

Fowles, D. C. (1992). Schizophrenia: Diathesis-stress revisited. *Annual Review of Psychology, 43*, 303–336.

Frackowiak, R. S. J. (1994). Functional mapping of verbal memory and language. *Trends in Neurosciences, 17*, 109–115.

Frank, E., Kupfer, D. J., Wagner, E. F., McEachran, A. B., Cornes, C. (1991). Efficacy of interpersonal psychotherapy as a maintenance treatment of recurrent depression: Contributing factors. *Archives of General Psychiatry, 48*, 1053–1059.

Franz, C. E., McClelland, D. C., & Weinberger, J. (1991). Childhood antecedents of conventional social accomplishment in midlife adults: A 36-year prospective study. *Journal of Personality and Social Psychology, 60*, 586–595.

Frazer, A. (1997). Antidepressants. *Journal of Clinical Psychiatry, 58*, 9–25.

Frazier, P., Arikian, N., Benson, S., Losoff, A., et al., (1996). Desire for marriage and life satisfaction among unmarried heterosexual adults. *Journal of Social and Personal Relationships, 13*, 225–239.

Freedman, J. L. (1984). Effects of television violence on aggressiveness. *Psychological Bulletin, 96*, 227–246.

Freedman, J. L., & Fraser, S. C. (1966). Compliance without pressure: The foot-in-the-door technique. *Journal of Personality and Social Psychology, 4*, 195–202.

Freese, A. S. (1977). *The miracle of vision*. New York: Harper & Row.

French, C., French, F., & Rutherford, P. (2000). Applications of the WPPSI-R with a Canadian sample. *Canadian Journal of School Psychology, 15*, 1–10.

French, C. C., Fowler, M., McCarthy, K., & Peers, D. (1991). Belief in astrology: A test of the Barnum effect. *Skeptical Inquirer, 15*, 166–172.

Freud, A. (1958). *Adolescence: Psychoanalytic study of the child (Vol. 13)*. New York: Academic Press.

Freud, A. (1966). *The ego and the mechanisms of defense* (rev. ed.). New York: International Universities Press.

Freud, S. (1922). *Beyond the pleasure principle*. London: International Psychoanalytic Press.

Freud, S. (1953a). The interpretation of dreams. In J. Strachey (Ed. and Trans.), *The standard edition of the complete psychological works of Sigmund Freud (Vols. 4 and 5)*. London: Hogarth Press. (Original work published 1900).

Freud, S. (1953b). Three essays on the theory of sexuality. In J. Strachey (Ed. and Trans.), *The standard edition of the complete psychological works of Sigmund Freud (Vol. 7)*. London: Hogarth Press. (Original work published 1905).

Freud, S. (1960). Psychopathology of everyday life. In J. Strachey (Ed. and Trans.), *The standard edition of the complete psychological works of Sigmund Freud (Vol. 6)*. London: Hogarth Press. (Original work published 1901).

Freud, S. (1961). The ego and the id. In H. Strachey (Ed. and Trans.), *The standard edition of the complete psychological works of Sigmund Freud (Vol. 19)*. London: Hogarth Press. (Original work published 1923).

Freud, S. (1962). *Civilization and its discontents* (J. Strachey, Trans.). New York: W.W. Norton. (Original work published 1930).

Freud, S. (1963a). *An autobiographical study* (J. Strachey, Trans.). New York: W.W. Norton. (Original work published 1925).

Freud, S. (1963b). *A general introduction to psycho-analysis* (J. Riviere, Trans.). New York: Simon & Schuster. (Original work published 1920).

Freud, S. (1965). *New introductory lectures on psychoanalysis* (J. Strachey, Trans.). New York: W. W. Norton. (Original work published 1933).

Friedberg, J. M. (1976). *Shock treatment is not good for your brain*. San Francisco: Glide.

Friedberg, J. M. (1977). Shock treatment, brain damage, and memory loss: A neurological perspective. *American Journal of Psychiatry, 134*, 1010–1014.

Friedland, N., Keinan, G., & Regev, Y. (1992). Controlling the uncontrollable: Effects of stress on illusory perceptions of controllability. *Journal of Personality and Social Psychology, 63*, 923–931.

Friedman, M. I., & Ramirez, I. (1994). Food intake in diabetic rats: Relationship to metabolic effects of insulin treatment. *Physiology and Behavior, 56*(2), 373–378.

Friedman, M. I., Tordoff, M. G., & Ramirez, I. (1986). Integrated metabolic control of food intake. *Brain Research Bulletin, 17*, 855–859.

Fujita, F., Diener, E., & Sandvik, E. (1991). Gender differences in negative affect and well-being: The case for emotional intensity. *Journal of Personality and Social Psychology, 61*, 427–434.

Funder, D. C., & Colvin, C. R. (1991). Explorations in behavioral consistency: Properties of *persons, situations, and behaviors. Journal of Personality and Social Psychology, 60*, 773–794.

Furstenberg, F. F., Jr., Brooks-Gunn, J., & Chase-Lansdale, L. (1989). Teenaged pregnancy and childbearing. *American Psychologist, 44*, 313–320.

Fyer, A. J., Mannuzza, S., Chapman, T. F., Liebowitz, M. R., & Klein, D. F. (1993). A direct interview family study of social phobia. *Archives of General Psychiatry, 50*, 286–293.

Gabrenya, W. K., Jr., Latane, B., & Wang, Y-E (1983). Social loafing in cross-cultural perspective. *Journal of Cross-Cultural Psychology, 14*, 368–384.

Gabrieli, J. D. E. (1998). Cognitive neuroscience of human memory. *Annual Review of Psychology, 49*, 87–115.

Gabrieli, J. D. E., Desmond, J., Demb, J., Wagner, A., Stone, M., Viadya, C., & Glover, G. (1996). Functional magnetic resonance imaging of semantic memory processes in the frontal lobes. *Psychological Science, 7*, 278–283.

Gackenbach, J., & Bosveld, J. (1989, October). Take control of your dreams. *Psychology Today*, pp. 27–32.

Gaertner, S. L., & Dovidio, J. F. (1986). The aversive form of racism. In J. F. Dovidio & S. L. Gaertner (Eds.), *Prejudice, discrimination, and racism* (pp. 61–89). San Diego, CA: Academic Press.

Gaertner, S. L., Mann, J. A., Dovidio, J. F., & Murrell, A. J. (1990). How does cooperation reduce intergroup bias? *Journal of Personality and Social Psychology, 59*, 692–704.

Gaertner, S. L., Mann, J. A., Murrell, A., & Dovidio, J. F. (1989). Reducing intergroup bias: The benefits of recategorization. *Journal of Personality and Social Psychology, 57*, 239–249.

Galanter, M. C. (1988). Research on social supports and mental illness. *American Journal of Psychiatry, 145*, 1270–1272.

Gallagher, M., & Rapp, P. (1997).The use of animal models to study the effects of aging on cognition. *Annual Review of Psychology, 48,* 339–370.

Gallup, G., Jr., & Hugick, L. (1990). Racial tolerance grows, progress on racial equality less evident. *Gallup Poll Monthly, No. 297,* 23–32.

Galton, F. (1875). The history of twins as a criterion of the relative powers of nature and nurture. *Journal of the Royal Anthropological Institute, 5,* 391–406.

Gannon, L., Luchetta, R., Rhodes, K., Paradie, L., & Segrist, D. (1992). Sex bias in psychological research: Progress or complacency? *American Psychologist, 47,* 389–396.

Gardner, H. (1975). *The shattered mind: The person after brain damage.* New York: Knopf.

Gardner, H. (1981, February). How the split brain gets a joke. *Psychology Today,* pp. 74–78.

Gardner, H. (1983). *Frames of mind: The theory of multiple intelligence.* New York: Basic Books.

Gardner, L. I. (1972). Deprivation dwarfism. *Scientific American, 227,* 76–82.

Gardner, R., & Lysynchuk, L. (1990). The role of aptitude, attitudes, motivation, and language use on second-language acquisition and retention. *Canadian Journal of Behavioural Science, 22*(3), 254–270.

Gardner, R. A., & Gardner, B. T. (1969). Teaching sign language to a chimpanzee. *Science, 165,* 664–672.

Garfield, S. L. (1981). Psychotherapy: A 40-year appraisal. *American Psychologist, 36,* 174–183.

Gastil, J. (1990). Generic pronouns and sexist language: The oxymoronic character of masculine generics. *Sex Roles, 23,* 629–643.

Gauguelin, M. (1982). Zodiac and personality: An empirical study. *The Skeptical Inquirer, 6,* 57–65.

Gawin, F. H. (1991). Cocaine addiction: Psychology and neurophysiology. *Science, 251,* 1580–1586.

Gawin, F. H., & Ellinwood, E. H., Jr. (1988). Cocaine and other stimulants: Actions, abuse, and treatment. *New England Journal of Medicine, 318,* 1173–1182.

Gazzaniga, M. S. (1967). The split brain in man. *Scientific American, 217,* 24–29.

Gazzaniga, M. S. (1970). *The bisected brain.* New York: Appleton-Century-Crofts.

Gazzaniga, M. S. (1983). Right hemisphere language following brain bisection: A 20-year perspective. *American Psychologist, 38,* 525–537.

Gazzaniga, M. S. (1989). Organization of the human brain. *Science, 245,* 947–952.

Geen, R. G. (1978). Some effects of observing violence upon the behavior of the observer. In B. A. Maher (Ed.), *Progress in experimental personality research* (Vol. 8). New York: Academic Press.

Geen, R. G. (1984). Human motivation: New perspectives on old problems. In A. M. Rogers & C. J. Scheier (Eds.), *The G. Stanley Hall lecture series* (Vol. 4). Washington, DC: American Psychological Association.

Geiselman, R. E., Haight, N. A., & Kimata, L. G. (1984). Context effects on the perceived physical attractiveness of faces. *Journal of Experimental Social Psychology, 20,* 409–424.

Gemini Genomics (2000, February 14). *Gemini launches new genetics initiatives in Newfoundland and Labrador* (press release). Retrieved July 7, 2000 from the World Wide Web: www.gemini-research.co.uk/index1.htm.

Genesee, F. (1994). Bilingualism. In V. S. Ramachandran (Ed.), *Encyclopedia of human behavior* (Vol. 1, pp. 383–393). San Diego, CA: Academic.

George, M. S., Ketter, T. A., & Post, R. M. (1993). SPECT and PET imaging in mood disorders. *Journal of Clinical Psychiatry, 54*(11, Suppl.), 6–13.

Gergen, K., & Misra, G. (1996). Psychological science in cultural context. *American Psychologist, 51*(5), 496–504.

Geschwind, N. (1979). Specializations of the human brain. *Science, 241,* 180–199.

Gibbons, A. (1991). Déjà vu all over again: Chimp-language wars. *Science, 251,* 1561–1562.

Gibson, E., & Walk, R. D. (1960). The "visual cliff." *Scientific American, 202,* 64–71.

Gilbert, D. T., & Malone, P. S. (1995). The correspondence bias. *Psychological Bulletin, 117,* 21–38.

Gilligan, C. (1982). *In a different voice: Psychological theory and women's development.* Cambridge, MA: Harvard University Press.

Ginsberg, G., & Bronstein, P. (1993). Family factors related to children's intrinsic/extrinsic motivational orientation and academic performance. *Child Development, 64,* 1461–1474.

Ginty, D. D., Kornhauser, J. M., Thompson, M. A., Bading, H., Mayo, K. E., Takahashi, J. S., & Greenberg, M. E. (1993). Regulation of CREB phosphorylation in the suprachiasmatic nucleus by light and a circadian clock. *Science, 260,* 238–241.

Glanzer, M., & Cunitz, A. R. (1966). Two storage mechanisms in free recall. *Journal of Verbal Learning and Verbal Behavior, 5,* 351–360.

Glass, D. C., & Singer, J. E. (1972). *Urban stress: Experiments in noise and social stressors.* New York: Academic Press.

Glazer, W. M., Morgenstern, H., & Doucette, J. T. (1993). Predicting the long-term risk of tardive dyskinesia in outpatients maintained on neuroleptic medications. *Journal of Clinical Psychiatry, 54,* 133–139.

Gleaves, D. (1996). The sociocognitive model of dissociative identity disorder: A reexamination of the evidence. *Psychological Bulletin, 120,* 42–59.

Glover, J. A., & Corkill, A. J. (1987). Influence of paraphrased repetitions on the spacing effect. *Journal of Educational Psychology, 79,* 198–199.

Gluck, M. A., & Myers, C. E. (1997). Psychobiological models of hippocampal function in learning and memory. *Annual Review of Psychology, 48,* 481–514.

Godden, D. R., & Baddeley, A. D. (1975). Context-dependent memory in two natural environments: On land and underwater. *British Journal of Psychology, 66,* 325–331.

Godden, D. R., & Baddeley, A. D. (1980). When does context influence recognition memory? *British Journal of Psychology, 71,* 99–104.

Goebel, B. L., & Brown, D. R. (1981). Age differences in motivation related to Maslow's need hierarchy. *Developmental Psychology, 17,* 809–815.

Gold, M.S. (1994). The epidemiology, attitudes, and pharmacology of LSD use in the 1990s. *Psychiatric Annals, 24,* 124–126.

Goldberg, J. (1988). *Anatomy of a scientific discovery.* New York: Bantam.

Goldberg, P. A. (1965). A review of sentence completion methods in personality. In B. I. Murstein (Ed.), *Handbook of projective techniques.* New York: Basic Books.

Goldstein, A., & Kalant, H. (1990). Drug policy: Striking the right balance. *Science, 249,* 1513–1521.

Goldstein, R., Weissman, M., Adams, P., Horwath, E., Lish, J., Charney, D., Woods, S., Sobin, C., & Wickramaratne, P.(1994). Psychiatric disorders in relatives of probands with panic disorder and/or major depression. *Archives of General Psychiatry, 51,* 383–394.

Goleman, D. (1979, November). Positive denial: The case for not facing reality. *Psychology Today*, pp. 13, 44–60.

Goleman, D. (1991, September 17). Non-verbal cues are easy to misinterpret. The New York Times, pp. C1, C9.

Goleman, D. (1995). *Emotional intelligence.* New York: Bantam.

Goleman, D., Kaufman, P., & Ray, M. (1992). *The creative spirit.* New York: Dutton.

Gombu, H. (2000, March 9). Casino income explodes. *Toronto Star,* p. 13.

Gonzalez, R., Ellsworth, P. C., & Pembroke, M. (1993). Response biases in lineups and showups. *Journal of Personality and Social Psychology*, *64*, 525–537.

Goode, E. E. (1987, September 28). For a little peace of mine. *U.S. News & World Report,* pp. 98–102.

Goodglass, H. (1993). *Understanding aphasia.* San Diego, CA: Academic Press.

Goodman, W. K., Price, L. H., Rasmussen, S. A., Delgado, P. L., Heninger, G. R., & Charney, D. S. (1989). Efficacy of fluvoxamine in obsessive-compulsive disorder: A double-blind comparison with placebo. *Archives of General Psychiatry, 46,* 36–44.

Goodman, W. K., McDougle, C. J., & Price, L. H. (1992). Pharmacotherapy of obsessive compulsive disorder. *Journal of Clinical Psychiatry, 53*(4, Suppl.), 29–37.

Goodwin, D. W. (1985). Alcoholism and genetics: The sins of the fathers. *Archives of General Psychiatry, 42,* 171–174.

Goodwin, D. W. (1986). *Anxiety.* New York: Oxford University Press.

Goodwin, G. (1996). How do antidepressants affect serotonin receptors? The role of serotonin receptors in the therapeutic and side effect profile of the SSRIs. *Journal of Clinical Psychiatry, 57,* 9–13.

Gordon, N. P., Cleary, P. D., Parlan, C. E., & Czeisler, C. A. (1986). The prevalence and health impact of shiftwork. *American Journal of Public Health, 76,* 1225–1228.

Gorman, J. M., Liebowitz, M. R., Fyer, A. J., & Stein, J. (1989). A Neuroanatomical hypothesis for panic disorder. *American Journal of Psychiatry, 146,* 148–161.

Gormezano, I. (1984). The study of associative learning with CS-CR paradigms. In D. L. Alkon & J. Farley (Eds.), *Primary neural substrates of learning and behavioral change* (pp. 5–24). New York: Cambridge University Press.

Gosselin, P., Kirouac, G., & Dore, F. Y. (1995). Components and recognition of facial expression in the communication of emotion by actors. *Journal of Personality and Social Psychology 68*(1):83–96.

Gosselin, P., Kirouac, G., & Dore, F. Y. (1997). Components and recognition of facial expression in the communication of emotion by actors. In P. Ekman, E. L. Rosenberg, et al. (Eds.). *What the face reveals: Basic and applied studies of spontaneous expression using the Facial Action Coding System (FACS). Series in affective science,* (pp. 243–270). New York: Oxford University Press.

Gottesman, I. I. (1991). *Schizophrenia genesis: The origins of madness.* New York: W.H. Freeman.

Gottfried, A. E., Fleming, J. S., & Gottfried, A. W. (1994). Role of parental motivational practices in children's academic intrinsic motivation and achievement. *Journal of Educational Psychology, 86,* 104–113.

Graeber, R. C. (1989). Jet lag and sleep disruption. In M. H. Kryger, T. Roth, & W. C. Dement (Eds.), *Principles and practice of sleep medicine* (pp. 324–331). Philadelphia: W.B. Saunders.

Graham, S. (1992). "Most of the subjects were white and middle class": Trends in published research on African Americans in selected APA journals, 1970–1989. *American Psychologist, 47,* 629–639.

Grant , B., & Dawson, D. (1998). Age at onset of alcohol use and its association with DSM-IV alcohol and dependence: Results from the National Longitudinal Alcohol Epidemiologic Survey. *Journal of Substance Abuse, 9,* 103–110.

Grant, B. F., Harford, T. C., Chou, P., Pickering, M. S., Dawson, D. A., Stinson, F. S., & Noble, J. (1991). Prevalence of DSM-III-R alcohol abuse and dependence: United States, 1988. *Alcohol Health & Research World, 15,* 91–96.

Greden, J. F. (1994). Introduction Part III. New agents for the treatment of depression. *Journal of Clinical Psychiatry, 55*(2, Suppl.), 32–33.

Green, A. R., & Goodwin, G. M. (1996). Ecstacy and neurodegeneration: Ecstacy's long term effects are potentially more damaging than its acute toxicity. *British Medical Journal, 312,* 1493–1494.

Green, B. L., Lindy, J. D., Grace, M. C. (1985). Post-traumatic stress disorder: Toward DSM-IV. *Journal of Nervous and Mental Disorders, 173,* 406–411.

Green, J., & Shellenberger, R. (1990). *The dynamics of health and wellness: A biopsychosocial approach.* Fort Worth: Holt, Rinehart & Winston.

Greenberg, J. (1977, July 30). The brain and emotions: Crossing a new frontier. *Science News, 112,* 74–75.

Gregory, R. L. (1978). *Eye and brain: The psychology of seeing* (3rd ed.). New York: McGraw-Hill.

Greist, J. H. (1992). An integrated approach to treatment of obsessive compulsive disorder. *Journal of Clinical Psychiatry, 53*(4, Suppl.), 38–41.

Greist, J. H. (1995). The diagnosis of social phobia. *Journal of Clinical Psychiatry, 53*(4, Suppl.), 38–41.

Greist, J. H., & Jefferson, J. W. (1984). *Depression and its treatment.* Washington, DC: American Psychiatric Press.

Griffith, R. M., Miyago, O., & Tago, A. (1958). The universality of typical dreams: Japanese vs. Americans. *American Anthropologist, 60*, 1173–1179.

Griffitt, W., Nelson, J., & Littlepage, G. (1972). Old age and response to agreement-disagreement. *Journal of Gerontology, 27*, 269–274.

Grimm, R. J. (1976). Brain control in a democratic society. In W. L. Smith & A. Kling (Eds.), *Issues in brain/behavior control*. New York: Spectrum.

Grinker, J. A. (1982). Physiological and behavioral basis for human obesity.

Gronfier, C., Luthringer, R., Follenius, M., Schaltenbrand, N., Macher, J. P., Muzet, A., & Brandenberger, G. (1996). A quantitative evaluation of the relationships between growth hormone secretion and delta wave electroencephalographic activity during normal sleep and after enrichment in delta waves. *Sleep, 19*, 817–824.

Grossman, H. J. (Ed.). (1983). *Manual on terminology and classification in mental retardation*. Washington, DC: American Association on Mental Deficiency.

Grossman, M., & Wood, W. (1993). Sex differences in intensity of emotional experience: A social role interpretation. *Journal of Personality and Social Psychology, 65*, 1010–1022.

Grünbaum, A. (1994). Does psychoanalysis have a future? Doubtful. *Harvard Mental Health Letter, 11*(4), 3–6.

Grusec, J., & Goodnow, J. (1994). Impact of parental discipline methods on the child's internalization of values: A reconceptualization on current points of view. *Developmental Psychology 30*(1), 4–19.

Guerri, C., Riley, E., & Stroemland, K. (1999). Commentary on the recommendation of the Royal College of Obstetricians and Gynaecologists concerning alcohol consumption and pregnancy. *Alcohol and Alcoholism, 34*, 497–501.

Guilford, J. P. (1967). *The nature of human intelligence*. New York: McGraw-Hill.

Guilford, J. P. (1988). Some changes in the Structure-of-Intellect model. *Educational and Psychological Measurement, 48*, 1–4.

Guilleminault, C. (1993). Amphetamines and narcolepsy: Use of the Stanford database. *Sleep, 16*, 199–201.

Guimond, S., & Palmer, D. L. (1993). Developmental changes in ingroup favoritism among bilingual and unilingual francophone and anglophone students. *Journal of Language and Social Psychology, 12*(4), 318–351.

Gurin, J. (1989, June). Leaner, not lighter. *Psychology Today*, pp. 32–36.

Haaga, D. A. F., Dyck, M. J., & Ernst, D. (1991). Empirical status of cognitive theory of depression. *Psychological Bulletin, 110*, 215–236.

Haber, R. N. (1980, November). Eidetic images are not just imaginary. *Psychology Today*, pp. 72–82.

Haberlandt, D. (1997). *Cognitive psychology* (2nd ed.). Boston: Allyn & Bacon.

Hackel, L. S., & Ruble, D. N. (1992). Changes in the marital relationship after the first baby is born: Predicting the impact of expectancy disconfirmation. *Journal of Personality and Social Psychology, 62*, 944–957.

Hadjistavropoulos, T., & Malloy, D. C. (2000). Making ethical choices: A comprehensive decision-making model for Canadian psychologists. *Canadian Psychology, 41*(2), 104–115.

Hakuta, K. (1987). The second-language learner in the context of the study of language acquisition. In P. Homel, M. Palij, et al. (Eds.), *Childhood bilingualism: Aspects of linguistic, cognitive, and social development* (pp. 31–55). Hillsdale, NJ: Lawrence Erlbaum.

Hales, D. (1981). *The complete book of sleep: How your nights affect your days*. Reading, MA: Addison-Wesley.

Halford, G. S. (1989). Reflections on 25 years of Piagetian cognitive developmental psychology, 1963–1988. *Human Development, 32*, 325–327.

Hall, C. S., & Van de Castle, R. L. (1966). *The content analysis of dreams*. New York: Appleton-Century-Crofts.

Halligan, P. W., & Marshall, J. C. (1994). Toward a principled explanation of unilateral neglect. *Cognitive Neuropsychology, 11*, 167–206.

Halmi, K. A. (1996). Eating disorder research in the past decade. *Annals of the New York Academy of Sciences, 789*, 67–77.

Halperin, J. M., & McKay, K. E., (1998). Psychological testing for child and adolescent psychiatrists: A review of the past 10 years. *Journal of the American Academy of Child and Adolescent Psychiatry, 37*(6), 575–584.

Hamilton, M. C. (1988). Using masculine generics: Does generic "he" increase male bias in the user's imagery? *Sex Roles, 19*, 785–789.

Hammond, D. C. (1992). Hypnosis with sexual disorders. *American Journal of Preventive Psychiatry & Neurology, 3*, 37–41.

Handelman, S. (2000, September 2). One toke over the line. *Time Canada*.

Hansel, C. E. M. (1966). *ESP: A scientific evaluation*. New York: Charles Scribner's Sons.

Hansel, C. E. M. (1980). *ESP and parapsychology: A critical reevaluation*. Buffalo, NY: Prometheus.

Hare, R. (1985). Comparison of procedures for the assessment of psychopathy. *Journal of Clinical Psychology*, 53, 7–16.

Hare, R. D. (1970). *Psychopathy: Theory and research*. New York: Wiley.

Hare, R. D. (1995). Psychopaths: New trends in research. *Harvard Mental Health Letter, 12*, 4–5.

Harford, T. C., Parker, D. A., Grant, B. F., & Dawson, D. A. (1992). Alcohol use and dependence among employed men and women in the United States in 1988. *Alcoholism: Clinical and Experimental Research, 16*, 146–148.

Harkins, S. G., & Jackson, J. M. (1985). The role of evaluation in eliminating social loafing. *Personality and Social Psychology Bulletin, 11*, 456–465.

Harkins, S. G., & Szymanski, K. (1989). Social loafing and group evaluation. *Journal of Personality and Social Psychology, 56*, 941–943.

Harlow, H. F. (1950). Learning and satiation of response in intrinsically motivated complex puzzle performance by monkeys. *Journal of Comparative and Physiological Psychology, 43*, 289–294.

Harlow, H. F. (1953). Motivation as a factor in the acquisition of new responses. In M. R. Jones (Ed.), *Nebraska symposium on motivation*. Lincoln: University of Nebraska Press.

Harlow, H. F., & Harlow, M. K. (1962). Social deprivation in monkeys. *Scientific American, 207*, 137–146.

Harlow, R. E., & Cantor, N. (1996). Still participating after all these years: A study of life task participation in later life. *Journal of Personality and Social Psychology, 71*, 1235–1249.

Harper, T. (2000, June 8). Chinese boat people vanish: 75 percent abandon refugee claims. *Toronto Star.* Retrieved July 7, 2000 from the World Wide Web: www.thestar.com/back_...0000608/news/20000608NEW03b_NA-BOAT.html.

Harris, R. A., Brodie, M. S., & Dunwiddie, T. V. (1992). Possible substrates of ethanol reinforcement: GABA and dopamine. *Annals of the New York Academy of Sciences, 654*, 61–69.

Harrison, J. R., & Barabasz, A. F. (1991). Effects of restricted environmental stimulation therapy on the behavior of children with autism. *Child Study Journal, 21*, 153–166.

Hartmann, E. (1967). *The biology of dreaming*. Springfield, IL: Charles C. Thomas.

Hartmann, E. (1981, April). The strangest sleep disorder. *Psychology Today*, pp. 15, 14–18.

Hartmann, E. (1988). Insomnia: Diagnosis and treatment. In R. L. Williams, I. Karacan, & C. A. Moore (Eds.), *Sleep disorders: Diagnosis and treatment* (pp. 29–46). New York: John Wiley.

Hartmann, E. L. (1973). *The functions of sleep*. New Haven: Yale University Press.

Hatfield, E. (1988). Passionate and companionate love. In R. J. Sternberg and M. L. Barnes (Eds.), *The psychology of love*. New Haven, CT: Yale University Press.

Hatfield, E., & Sprecher, S. (1986). *Mirror, mirror . . . The importance of looks in everyday life*. Albany, NY: State University of New York Press.

Hauser, M.D. (1993). Right hemisphere dominance for the production of facial expression in monkeys. *Science, 261*, 475–477.

Have brain, will travel. (1999). ABC News. Retrieved from the World Wide Web: abcnews.com/science.

Hawkins, J. D., Catalano, R. F., & Miller, J. Y. (1992). Risk and protective factors for alcohol and other drug problems in adolescence and early adulthood: Implications for substance abuse prevention. *Psychological Bulletin, 112*, 64–105.

Hay, D. F. (1994). Prosocial development. *Journal of Child Psychology and Psychiatry, 35*, 29–71.

Hebb, D. O. (1949). *The organization of behavior*. New York: John Wiley & Sons.

Hefez, A., Metz, L., & Lavie, P. (1987). Long-term effects of extreme situational stress on sleep and dreaming. *American Journal of Psychiatry, 144*, 344–347.

Heikkinen, M., Aro, H., & Lönnqvist, J. (1993). Life events and social support in suicide. *Suicide and Life-Threatening Behavior, 23*, 343–358.

Heilbron, C., & Guttman, M. (2000). Traditional healing methods with First Nations women in group counselling. *Canadian Journal of Counselling, 34*, 3–13.

Heilman, K. M., Scholes, R., & Watson, R. T. (1975). Auditory affective agnosia: Disturbed comprehension of affective speech. *Journal of Neurology, Neurosurgery and Psychiatry, 38*, 69–72.

Held, J., Riggs, M., & Dorman, C. (1999). The effect of prenatal cocaine exposure on neurobehavioral outcome: A meta-analysis. *Neurotoxicology & Teratology, 21*, 619–625.

Held, R. (1993). What can rates of development tell us about underlying mechanisms? In C. E. Granrud (Ed.), *Visual perception and cognition in infancy* (pp. 75–89). Hillsdale, NJ: Erlbaum.

Hellige, J. B. (1990). Hemispheric asymmetry. *Annual Review of Psychology, 41*, 55–80.

Hellige, J.B. (1993). *Hemispheric asymmetry: What's right and what's left*. Cambridge, MA: Harvard University Press.

Hellige, J. B., Bloch, M. I., Cowin, E. L., Eng, T. L. Eviatar, Z., & Sergent, V. (1994). Individual variation in hemispheric asymmetry: Multitask study of effects related to handedness and sex. *Journal of Experimental Psychology: General, 123*, 235–256.

Hembree, W. C., III, Nahas, G. G., Zeidenberg, P., & Huang, H. F. S. (1979). Changes in human spermatozoa associated with high dose marihuana smoking. In G. G. Nahas & W. D. M. Paton (Eds.), *Marihuana: Biological effects* (pp. 429–439). Oxford: Pergamon Press.

Hendler, N. H., & Fenton, J. A. (1979). *Coping with pain*. New York: Clarkson N. Potter.

Henley, N. M. (1989). Molehill or mountain? What we know and don't know about sex bias in language. In M. Crawford & M. Gentry (Eds.), *Gender and thought: Psychological perspectives*. New York: Springer-Verlag.

Hennessey, B. A., & Amabile, T. M. (1988). The conditions of creativity. In R. J. Sternberg (Ed.), *The nature of creativity: Contemporary psychological perspectives*. New York: Cambridge University Press.

Henningfield, J. E., & Ator, N. A. (1986). *Barbiturates: Sleeping potion or intoxicant?* New York: Chelsea House.

Henningfield, J. E., Hariharan, M., & Kozlowski, L. T. (1996). Nicotine content and health risks of cigar. *Journal of the American Medical Association, 276*, 1857–1858.

Herkenham, M. (1992). Cannabinoid receptor localization in brain: Relationship to motor and reward systems. *Annals of the New York Academy of Sciences, 654*, 19–32.

Herman, L. M., Kuczaj, S. A., & Holder, M.D. (1993). Responses to anomalous gestural sequences by a language-trained dolphin: Evidence for processing of semantic relations and syntactic information. *Journal of Experimental Psychology: General, 122*, 184–194.

Hernandez, L., & Hoebel, B. G. (1989). Food intake and lateral hypothalamic self-stimulation covary after medial hypothalamic lesions or ventral midbrain 6-hydroxydopamine injections that cause obesity. *Behavioral Neuroscience, 103*, 412–422.

Herold, E. S., & Mewhinney, D. M. K. (1993). "Gender differences in casual sex and AIDS prevention: A survey of dating bars." *Journal of Sex Research, 30*(1), 36–42.

Herrnstein, R. J., & Murray, C. (1994). *The bell curve: Intelligence and class structure in American life*. New York: Free Press.

Hershenson, M. (1989). *The moon illusion*. Hillsdale, NJ: Erlbaum.

Hess, E. H. (1961). Shadows and depth perception. *Scientific American, 204*, 138–148.

Hess, E. H. (1965). Attitude and pupil size. *Scientific American, 212*, 46–54.

Hetherington, A. W., & Ranson, S. W. (1940). Hypothalamic lesions and adiposity in the rat. *Anatomical Record, 78*, 149–172.

Hilliker, N. A. J., Muehlbach, M. J., Schweitzer, P. K., & Walsh, J. K. (1992). Sleepiness/alertness on a simulated night shift schedule and morningness-eveningness tendency. *Sleep, 15*, 430–433.

Hinds, T. S., West, W. L., Knight, E. M., & Harland, B. F. (1996). The effect of caffeine on pregnancy outcome variables. *Nutritional Review, 54*(7), 203–207.

Hingson, R., Alpert, J. J., Day, N., Dooling, E., Kayne, H., Morelock, S., Oppenheimer, E., & Zuckerman, B. (1982). Effects of maternal drinking and marijuana use on fetal growth and development. *Pediatrics, 70*, 539–546.

Hobfoll, S. E., Spielberger, C. D., Breznitz, S., Figley, C., Folkman, S., Lepper-Green, B., Meichenbaum, D., Milgram, N. A., Sandler, I., Sarason, I., & van der Kolk, B. (1991). War-related stress: Addressing the stress of war and other traumatic events. *American Psychologist, 46*, 848–855.

Hobson, J. A. (1988). *The dreaming brain*. New York: Basic Books.

Hobson, J. A. (1989). *Sleep*. New York: Scientific American Library.

Hobson, J. A. (1996, February). How the brain goes out of its mind. *Harvard Mental Health Letter, 12*(8), 3–5.

Hobson, J. A., & McCarley, R. W. (1977). The brain as a dream state generator: An activation-synthesis hypothesis of the dream process. *American Journal of Psychiatry, 134*, 1335–1348.

Hobson, J. A., & Stickgold, R. (1995). The conscious state paradigm: A neurological approach to waking, sleeping, and dreaming. In M. S. Gazzaniga (Ed.), *The cognitive neurosciences.* Cambridge, MA: The MIT Press.

Hoekfelt, T., Broberger, C., Xu, D., Sergeyev, V., Ubink, R., & Diez, M. (2000). Neuropeptides—An overview. *Neuropharmacology, 39*(8), 1337–1356.

Hogan, E., & Barlow, C. (2000). Delivering counsellor training to First Nations: Emerging issues. *Canadian Journal of Counselling, 34,* 55–67.

Hokfelt, T., Johnasson, O., & Goldstein, M. (1984). Chemical anatomy of the brain. *Science, 225*, 1326–1334.

Holden, C. (1986). Depression research advances, treatment lags. *Science, 233*, 723–726.

Holden, C. (1996). Sex and olfaction. *Science, 273,* 313.

Holland, J. G. (1992). Obituaries: B.F. Skinner (1904–1990). *American Psychologist, 47*, 665–667.

Holland, J. G., & Skinner, B. F. (1961). *The analysis of behavior.* New York: McGraw-Hill.

Holmes, T. H., & Rahe, R. H. (1967). The social readjustment rating scale. *Journal of Psychosomatic Research, 11*, 213–218.

Hood, K. (1995). Social psychological and sociobiology: Which is the metatheory? *Psychological Inquiry, 6,* 54–56.

Horn, J. (1982). The aging of human abilities. In B. B. Wolman (Ed.), *Handbook of developmental psychology*. Englewood Cliffs, NJ: Prentice-Hall.

Horn, J. C., & Meer, J. (1987, May). The vintage years. *Psychology Today*, pp. 76–90.

Horn, J., & Donaldson, G. (1980). Cognitive development in adulthood. In O. Brim & J. Kagan (Eds.), *Constancy and change in human development*. Cambridge, MA: Harvard University Press.

Horn, J. L. (1982). The theory of fluid and crystallized intelligence in relation to concepts of cognitive psychology and aging in adulthood. In F. I. M. Craik & S. Trehub (Eds.), *Aging and cognitive processes* (pp. 201–238). New York: Plenum Press.

Horney, K. (1937). *The neurotic personality of our time.* New York: W. W. Norton.

Horney, K. (1939). *New ways in psychoanalysis.* New York: W. W. Norton.

Horney, K. (1945). *Our inner conflicts.* New York: W. W. Norton.

Horney, K. (1950). *Neurosis and human growth.* New York: W. W. Norton.

Horney, K. (1967). *Feminine psychology.* New York: W. W. Norton.

Horvitz, L. A. (1997, November 10). Aromachologists nose out the secret powers of smell. *Insight on the News, 13,* 36–37.

Horwath, E., Lish, J. D., Johnson, J., Hornig, C. D., & Weissman, M. M. (1993). Agoraphobia without panic: Clinical reappraisal of an epidemiologic finding. *American Journal of Psychiatry, 150*, 1496–1501.

Hothersall, D. (1984). *History of psychology*. Philadelphia: Temple University Press.

Hovdestad, W. E., & Kristiansen, C. M. (1996). A field study of "false memory syndrome": Construct validity and incidence. *Journal of Psychiatry and Law, 24*(2), 299– 338.

Hovland, C. I., Lumsdaine, A. A., & Sheffield, F. D. (1949). *Experiments on mass communication*. Princeton, NJ: Princeton University Press.

Howard, A. D., Feighner, S. D., Cully, D. F., Arena, J. P. Liberator, P. A., Rosenblum, C. L., et al. (1996). A receptor in pituitary and hypothalamus that functions in growth hormone release. *Science, 273,* 974–977.

Howard, J. A. Blumstein, P., & Schwartz, P. (1987). Social or evolutionary theories? Some observations on preferences in human mate selection. *Journal of Personality and Social Psychology, 53,* 194–200.

Hoy, E. A., Bill, J. M., & Sykes, D. H. (1988). Very low birthweight: A long-term developmental impairment? *International Journal of Behavioral Development, 11,* 37–67.

Hrushesky, W. J. M. (1994, July/August). Timing is everything. *The Sciences*, 32–37.

Hublin, C., Kaprio, J., Partinen, M., & Koskenvuo, M. (1999). Limits of self-report in assessing sleep terrors in a population survey. *Sleep, 22,* 89–93.

Hudspeth, A. J. (1983). The hair cells of the inner ear. *Scientific American, 248*, 54–64.

Huesmann, L. R., Eron, L. D., Lefkowitz, M. M., & Walder, L. O. (1984). The stability of aggression over time and generations. *Developmental Psychology, 20*, 1120–1134.

Hughes, J. R. (1992). Tobacco withdrawal in self-quitters. *Journal of Consulting and Clinical Psychology, 60*, 689–697.

Hull, C. L. (1943). *Principles of behavior.* New York: Appleton-Century-Crofts.

Hultsch, D., Hertzog, C., Small, B., & Dixon, R. (1999). Use it or lose it: Engaged lifestyle as a buffer of cognitive decline in aging? *Psychology and Aging, 14,* 245–263.

Hurley, G. (1988, January). Getting help from helping. *Psychology Today*, pp. 62–67.

Hurst, S. (1999). Legacy of betrayal: A grounded theory of becoming demoralized from the perspective of women who have been depressed. *Canadian Psychology, 40,* 179–191.

Huston, A. C., Donnerstein, E., Fairchild, H., Feshbach, N. D., Katz, P. A., Murray, J. P., Rubinstein, E. A.,Wilcox, B. L., & Zuckerman, D. (1992). *Big world, small screen: The role of television in American society.* Lincoln: University of Nebraska Press.

Hyman, A. (1983). The influence of color on the taste perception of carbonated water preparations. *Bulletin of the Psychonomic Society, 21,* 145–148.

Infante-Rivard, C., Fernandez, A., Gauthier, R., & Rivard, G. E. (1993). Fetal loss associated with caffeine intake before and during pregnancy. *Journal of the American Medical Association, 270*(24), 2940–2943.

International Association for Suicide Prevention (1999). I.A.S.P. guidelines for suicide prevention. *Crisis, 20,* 155–163.

Inglehart, R. (1990). *Culture shift in advanced industrial society.* Princeton, NJ: Princeton University Press.

Ingrassia, M. (1993, October 25). Abused and confused *Newsweek*, pp. 57–58.

Insel, T. R. (1990). Phenomenology of obsessive compulsive disorder. *Journal of Clinical Psychiatry, 51*(2, Suppl.), 4–8.

International Labour Organization. (1990). *Yearbook of labour statistics.* Geneva: Author.

Irwin, M., Daniels, M., Bloom, E. T., Smith, T. L., & Weiner, H. (1987). Life events, depressive symptoms, and immune function. *American Journal of Psychiatry, 144,* 437–441.

Isabella, R. A., Belsky, J., & von Eye, A. (1989). Origins of infant-mother attachment: An examination of interactional synchrony during the infant's first year. *Developmental Psychology, 25,* 12–21.

Isenberg, D. J. (1986). Group polarization: A critical review and meta-analysis. *Journal of Personality and Social Psychology, 50,* 1141–1151.

Ito, T. A., Miller, N., & Pollock, V. E. (1996). Alcohol and aggression: A meta-analysis on the moderating effects of inhibitory cues, triggering events, and self-focused attention. *Psychological Bulletin, 120,* 60–82.

Iverson, L. L. (1979). The chemistry of the brain. *Scientific American, 241,* 134–147.

Izard, C. E. (1971). *The face of emotion.* New York: Appleton-Century-Crofts.

Izard, C. E. (1977). *Human emotions.* New York: Plenum Press.

Izard, C. E. (1990). Facial expressions and the regulation of emotions. *Journal of Personality and Social Psychology, 58,* 487–498.

Izard, C.E. (1992). Basic emotions, relations among emotions, and emotion-cognition relations. *Psychological Review, 99,* 561–565.

Izard, C.E. (1993). Four systems for emotion activation: Cognitive and noncognitive processes. *Psychological Review, 100,* 68–90.

Jackson, B. B., Taylor, J., & Pyngolil, M. (1991). How age conditions the relationship between climacteric status and health symptoms in African American women. *Research in Nursing and Health, 14,* 1–9.

Jackson, D. N. (1976). *Jackson Personality Inventory Manual.* Goshen, NY: Research Psychologists Press.

Jackson, D.N. (1984). *Personality Research Form Manual.* Port Huron, MI: Research Psychologists Press.

Jacobs, G. H. (1993). The distribution and nature of colour vision among the mammals. *Biological Review, 68,* 413–471.

James, W. (1884). What is an emotion? *Mind, 9,* 188–205.

James, W. (1890). *The principles of psychology.* New York: Holt.

James, W. (1961). *Psychology: The briefer course.* New York: Harper and Row. (Original work published 1892).

Jamieson, D. W., & Zanna, M. P. (1989). Need for structure in attitude formation and expression. In A. R. Pratkanis, S. J. Breckler, & A. G. Greenwald (Eds.), *Attitude structure and function* (pp. 383–406). Hillsdale, NJ: Erlbaum.

Janis, I. L. (1982). *Groupthink: Psychological studies of policy decisions and fiascoes* (2nd ed.). Boston: Houghton Mifflin.

Janisse, M. P., & Peavler, W. S. (1974, February). Pupillary research today: Emotion in the eye. *Psychology Today*, pp. 60–63.

Janowitz, H. D., & Grossman, M. I. (1950). Hunger and appetite: Some definitions and concepts. *Journal of the Mount Sinai Hospital, 16,* 231–240.

Jaynes, J. (1976). *The origin of consciousness and the breakdown of the bicameral mind.* Boston: Houghton Mifflin.

Jellinek, E. M. (1960). *The disease concept of alcoholism.* New Brunswick, NJ: Hillhouse Press.

Jemmott, J. B., III., & Locke, S. E. (1984). Psychosocial factors, immunologic mediation, and human susceptibility to infectious diseases: How much do we know? *Psychological Bulletin, 95,* 78–108.

Jenike, M. A. (1990, April). Obsessive-compulsive disorder. *Harvard Medical School Health Letter, 15,* pp. 4–8.

Jenike, M. A., Baer, L., Ballantine, H. T., Martuza, R. L., Tynes, S., Giriunas, I., Buttolph, L., & Cassem, N. H. (1991). Cingulotomy for refractory obsessive-compulsive disorder: A long-term follow-up of 33 patients. *Archives of General Psychiatry, 48,* 548–555.

Jenkins, J. J., Jimenez-Pabon, E., Shaw, R. E., & Sefer, J. W. (1975). *Schuell's aphasia in adults: Diagnosis, prognosis, and treatment* (2nd ed.). Hagerstown, MD: Harper & Row.

Jensen, A. R. (1969). How much can we boost IQ and scholastic achievement? *Harvard Educational Review, 39,* 1–123.

Jensen, A. R. (1985). The nature of the black-white difference on various psychometric tests: Spearman's hypothesis. *Behavioral and Brain Sciences, 8,* 193–263.

Johnson, D. L. (1989). Schizophrenia as a brain disease: Implications for psychologists and families. *American Psychologist, 44,* 553–555.

Johnson, E. O., Roehrs, T., Roth, T., & Breslau, N. (1998). Epidemiology of alcohol and medication as aids to sleep in early adulthood. *Sleep, 21,* 178–186.

Johnson, L. A. (1996, June 5). Eye witness: New ATM technology identifies a customer by the iris. *St. Louis Post-Dispatch,* p. C5.

Johnson, M. P., Duffy, J. F., Dijk, D-J., Ronda, J. M., Dyal, C. M., & Czeisler, C. A. (1992). Short-term memory, alertness and performance: A reappraisal of their relationship to body temperature. *Journal of Sleep Research, 1,* 24–29.

Johnson, W. G., Tsoh, J. Y., & Varnado, P. J. (1996). Eating disorders: Efficacy of psychopharmacological and psychological interventions. *Clinical Psychological Review, 16,* 457–478.

Jones, D. (1999). Cogito in vitro. *Nature, 397,* 216.

Jones, E. E. (1976). How do people perceive the causes of behavior? *American Scientist, 64,* 300–305.

Jones, E. E. (1986). Interpreting interpersonal behavior: The effects of expectancies. *Science, 234,* 41–46.

Jones, E. E. (1990). *Interpersonal perception.* New York: Freeman.

Jones, E. E., & Davis, K. E. (1965). A theory of correspondent inferences: From acts to dispositions. In L. Berkowitz (Ed.), *Advances in experimental social psychology* (Vol. 2, pp. 219–266). New York: Academic Press.

Jones, E. E., & Nisbett, R. E. (1971). *The actor and the observer: Divergent perceptions of the causes of behavior.* New York: General Learning.

Jones, M. C. (1924). A laboratory study of fear: The case of Peter. *Pedagogical Seminary, 31,* 308–315.

Jorgensen, M., & Keiding, N. (1991). Estimation of spermarche from longitudinal spermaturia data. *Biometrics, 47,* 177–193.

Judd, C. M., Ryan, C. S., & Park, B. (1991). Accuracy in the judgment of in-group and out-group variability. *Journal of Personality and Social Psychology, 61,* 366–379.

Julien, R. M. (1995). *A primer of drug action* (7th ed.). New York: W.H. Freeman.

Jung, C. G. (1933). *Modern man in search of a soul.* New York: Harcourt Brace Jovanovich.

Jung, C. G. (1953). *The psychology of the unconscious* (R. F. C. Hull, Trans.), Collected works (Vol. 7). Princeton, NJ: Princeton University Press. (Original work published 1917).

Jung, C. G. (1961). *Memories, dreams, reflections* (R. Winston & C. Winston, Trans.). New York: Random House.

Jung, C. G. (1966). *Two essays on analytical psychology* (R. F. C. Hull, Trans.). Princeton, NJ: Princeton University Press.

Just say yes. (2000, May 16). *National Post.*

Kalb, C. (1997, Aug 25). Our embattled ears: Hearing loss once seemed a normal part of aging, but experts now agree that much of it is preventable. How to protect yourself. *Newsweek, 130,* 75–76.

Kalish, H. I. (1981). *From behavioral science to behavior modification.* New York: McGraw-Hill.

Kanaya, Y., Nakamura, C. and Miyake, D. (1989). Cross-cultural study of expressive behavior of mothers in response to their five-month-old infants' different emotion expression. *Research and Clinical Center for Child Development Annual Report, 11,* 25–31.

Kandel, E. R., Castellucci, V. F., Goelet, P., & Schacher, S. (1987). 1987 cell-biological interrelationships between short-term and long-term memory. *Research Publications—Association for Research in Nervous and Mental Disease, 65,* 111–132.

Kane, J.M. (1993). Understanding and treating psychoses: Advances in research and therapy. *Journal of Clinical Psychiatry, 54,* 445–452.

Kane, J. M. (1996). Treatment-resistant schizophrenic patients. *Journal of Clinical Psychiatry, 57*(9, Suppl.), 35–40.

Kaniasty, K., & Norris, F. H. (1993). A test of the social support deterioration model in the context of natural disaster. *Journal of Personality and Social Psychology, 64,* 395–408.

Kanner, A. D., Coyne, J. C., Schaefer, C., & Lazarus, R. S. (1981). Comparison of two modes of stress measurement: Daily hassles and uplifts versus major life events. *Journal of Behavioral Medicine, 4,* 1–39.

Kaplan, G., Wilson, T., Cohen, R., Kauhanen, J., Wu, M., & Salomen, J. (1994). Social functioning and overall mortality: prospective evidence from the Kuopi Ischemic heart Disease Risk Factor Study. *Epidemiology, 5,* 495–500.

Karacan, I. (1988). Parasomnias. In R. L. Williams, I. Karacan, & C. A. Moore (Eds.), *Sleep disorders: Diagnosis and treatment* (pp. 131–144). New York: John Wiley.

Karasu, T. B. (1986). The psychotherapies: Benefits and limitations. *American Journal of Psychotherapy, 40,* 324–342.

Karasu, T. B. (1990a). Toward a clinical model of psychotherapy for depression, I: Systematic comparison of three psychotherapies. *American Journal of Psychiatry, 147,* 133–147.

Karasu, T. B. (1990b). Toward a clinical model of psychotherapy for depression, II: An integrative and selective treatment approach. *American Journal of Psychiatry, 147,* 269–278.

Karau, S. J., & Williams, K. D. (1993). Social loafing; a meta-analytic review and theoretical integration. *Journal of Personality and Social Psychology, 65,* 681–706.

Karau, S. J., & Williams, K. D. (1995). Social loafing: Research findings, implications, and future directions. *Current Directions in Psychological Science, 4,* 134–140.

Karni, A., Tanne, D., Rubenstein, B. S., Askenasy, J. J. M., & Sagi, D. (1994). Dependence on REM sleep of overnight improvement of a perceptual skill. *Science, 265,* 679–682.

Kasper, S., Wehr, T. A., Bartko, J. J., Gaist, P. A., & Rosenthal, N. E. (1989). Epidemiological findings of seasonal changes in mood and behavior: A telephone survey of Montgomery County, Maryland. *Archives of General Psychiatry, 46,* 823–833.

Kastenbaum, R. (1992). *The psychology of death.* New York: Springer-Verlag.

Katon, W. (1996). Panic disorder: Relationship to high medical utilization, unexplained physical symptoms, and medical costs. *Journal of Clinical Psychiatry, 57*(10, Suppl.), 11–18.

Katzenberg, D., Young, T., Finn, L., Lin, L., King, D. P., Takahashi, J. S., & Mignot, E. (1998). A clock polymorphism associated with human diurnal preference. *Sleep, 21,* 569–576.

Kawachi, I., Colditz, G., Speizer, F., Manson, J., Stampfer, M., Willett, W., & Hennekens, C. (1997). A prospective study of passive smoking and coronary heart disease. *Circulation, 95,* 2374–2379.

Keating, C. R. (1994). World without words: Messages from face and body. In W. J. Lonner & R. Malpass (Eds.), *Psychology and culture,* (pp. 175–182). Boston: Allyn & Bacon.

Keefauver, S. P., & Guilleminault, C. (1994). Sleep terrors and sleepwalking. In M. Kryger, T. Roth, and W. C. Dement (Eds.), *Principles and practice of sleep medicine* (pp. 567–573).

Keesey, R. E. (1988). The body-weight set point. What can you tell your patients? *Postgraduate Medicine, 83,* 114–18, 121–122, 127.

Keesey, R. E., & Powley, T. L. (1986). The regulation of body weight. *Annual Review of Psychology, 37*, 109–133.

Keller, H., Schlomerich, A., & Eibl-Eibesfeldt, I. (1988). Communication patterns in adult-infant interactions in western and non-western cultures. *Journal of Cross-Cultural Psychology, 19*, 427–445.

Kelly, S. F., & Kelly, R. J. (1985). *Hypnosis: Understanding how it can work for you.* Reading, MA: Addison-Wesley.

Kelner, K. L. (1997). Seeing the synapse. *Science, 276*, 547.

Kendler, K.S., Gruenberg, A.M., & Kinney, D.K. (1994). Independent diagnoses of adoptees and relatives as defined by DSM-III in the provincial and national samples of the Danish Adoption Study of Schizophrenia. *Archives of General Psychiatry, 51*, 456–468.

Kendler, K. S., Kessler, R. C., Neale, M. C., Heath, A. C., & Eaves, L. J. (1993). The prediction of major depression in women: Toward an integrated etiologic model. *American Journal of Psychiatry, 150*, 1139–1148.

Kendler, K. S., Neale, M. C., Kessler, R. C., Heath, A. C., & Eaves, L. J. (1992). The genetic epidemiology of phobias in women. *Archives of General Psychiatry, 49*, 273–281.

Kendler, K. S., & Prescott, C. A. (1999). A population-based twin study of lifetime major depression in men and women. *Archives of General Psychiatry, 56*, 39–44.

Kerlinger, F. N. (1986). *Foundations of behavioral research* (5th ed.). New York: Holt, Rinehart & Winston.

Kessler, R. C., McGonagle, K. A., Zhao, S., Nelson, C. B., Hughes, M., Eshleman, S., Wittchen, H-U., & Kendler, K. S. (1994). Lifetime and 12-month prevalence of DSM-III-R psychiatric disorders in the United States: Results from the National Comorbidity Survey. *American Journal of Psychiatry, 51*, 8–19.

Kiecolt-Glaser, J. K., Fisher, L. D., Ogrocki, P., Stout, J., Speicher, C. E., & Glaser, R. (1987). Marital quality, marital disruption, and immune function. *Psychosomatic Medicine, 49*, 13–34.

Kiecolt-Glaser, J. K., & Glaser, R. (1992). Psychoneuroimmunology: Can psychological interventions modulate immunity? *Journal of Consulting and Clinical Psychology, 60*, 569–575.

Kiester, E. (1997, April 1). "Traveling light" has a new meaning for jet laggards. *Smithsonian, 28,* 110–119.

Kilbride, J. E., & Kilbride, P. L. (1975). Sitting and smiling behavior of Baganda infants. *Journal of Cross-Cultural Psychology, 6*, 88–107.

Kim, J. J., & Fanselow, M. S. (1992). Modality-specific retrograde amnesia of fear. *Science, 256*, 675–677.

Kim, S-G., Ashe, J., Hendrich, K., Ellermann, J. M., Merkle, H., Ugurbil, K., & Georgopoulos, A. P. (1993). Functional magnetic resonance imaging of motor cortex: Hemispheric asymmetry and handedness. *Science, 261*, 615–617.

Kimura, D. (1961). Cerebral dominance and the perception of verbal stimuli. *Canadian Journal of Psychology, 15,* 166–171.

Kimura, D. (1973). The asymmetry of the human brain. *Scientific American, 228,* 70–78.

King, L. A., Walker, L. M., & Broyles, S. J. (1996). Creativity and the five-factor model. *Journal of Research on Personality, 30,* 189–203.

King, N., Clowes-Hollins, V., & Ollendick, T. (1997). The etiology of childhood dog phobia. *Behavior Research and Therapy, 35,* 77.

Kingsbury, S. J. (1991). Why has the MMPI been revised? *Harvard Mental Health Letter, 7,* p. 8.

Kingsbury, S. J. (1993). Brief hypnotic treatment of repetitive nightmares. *American Journal of Clinical Hypnosis, 35,* 161–169.

Kinnamon, S. C. (1988). Taste transduction: A diversity of mechanisms. *Trends in Neurosciences, 11*, 491–496.

Kinsella, G., Prior, M. R., & Murray, G. (1988). Singing ability after right and left sided brain damage. A research note. *Cortex, 24*, 165–169.

Kisilevsky, B. S., Muir, D. W., & Low, J. A. (1992). Maturation of human fetal responses to vibroacoustic stimulation. *Child Development, 63*(6), 1497–1508.

Kite, M. E., Deaux, K., & Miele, M. (1991). Stereotypes of young and old: Does age outweigh gender? *Psychology and Aging, 6,* 19–27.

Klatzky, R. L. (1980). *Human memory: Structures and processes* (2nd ed.). New York: W. H. Freeman.

Klatzky, R. L. (1984). *Memory and awareness: An information-processing perspective.* New York: W. H. Freeman.

Kleinman, A., & Cohen, A. (1997, March). Psychiatry's global challenge. *Scientific American, 276,* 86–89.

Kleitman, N. (1960). Patterns of dreaming. *Scientific American, 203,* 82–88.

Klerman, G. L., Weissman, M. N., Rounsaville, B. J., & Chevron, E. S. (1984). *Interpersonal therapy of depression.* New York: Academic Press.

Klinnert, M. D., Campos, J. J., Sorce, J. F., Emde, R. N., & Suejda, M. (1983). Emotions as behavior regulators: Social referencing in infancy. In R. Plutchik & H. Kellerman (Eds.), *Emotions in early development: Vol. 2: The emotions* (pp. 57–86). New York: Academic Press.

Kluft, R. P. (1984). An introduction to multiple personality disorder. *Psychiatric Annals, 14*, 19–24.

Kluft, R. P. (1992). Hypnosis with multiple personality disorder. *American Journal of Preventative Psychiatry & Neurology, 3*, 19–27.

Kobasa, S. (1979). Stressful life events, personality, and health: An inquiry into hardiness. *Journal of Personality and Social Psychology, 37,* 1–11.

Kochanska, G. (1993). Toward a synthesis of parental socialization and child temperament in early development of conscience. *Child Development, 64*, 325–347.

Kohlberg, L. (1968, September). The child as a moral philosopher. *Psychology Today*, pp. 24–30.

Kohlberg, L. (1969). *Stages in the development of moral thought and action.* New York: Holt, Rinehart & Winston.

Kohlberg, L. (1981). *Essays in moral development, Vol. 1. The philosophy of moral development.* New York: Harper & Row.

Kohlberg, L. (1984). *Essays on moral development, Vol. 2. The psychology of moral development.* San Francisco: Harper & Row.

Kohlberg, L. (1985). *The psychology of moral development.* San Francisco: Harper & Row.

Kohlberg, L., & Gilligan, C. (1971). The adolescent as a philosopher: The discovery of the self in a postconventional world. *Daedalus, 100,* 1051–1086.

Kolb, B. (1990). Recovery from occipital stroke: A self-report and inquiry into visual processes. *Canadian Journal of Psychology, 44*(2), 130–147.

Kolodny, R. C., Masters, W. H., & Johnson, V. E. (1979). *Textbook of sexual medicine.* Boston: Little, Brown.

Koltz, C. (1983, December). Scapegoating. *Psychology Today,* pp. 68–69.

Komaromy, M., Bindman, A. B., Haber, R. J., Sande, M. A. (1993). Sexual harassment in medical training. *New England Journal of Medicine, 328,* 322–326.

Konishi, M. (1993). Listening with two ears. *Scientific American, 268,* 66–73.

Kopp, C. P., & Kaler, S. R. (1989). Risk in infancy: Origins and implications. *American Psychologist, 44,* 224–230.

Kosslyn, S. M. (1975). Information representation in visual images. *Cognitive Psychology, 7,* 341–370.

Kosslyn, S. M. (1981). The medium and the message in mental imagery: A theory. *Psychological Review, 88,* 46–65.

Kosslyn, S. M. (1983). *Ghosts in the mind's machine: Creating and using images in the brain.* New York: Norton.

Kosslyn, S. M. (1987). Seeing and imagining in the cerebral hemispheres: A computational approach. *Psychological Review, 94,* 148–175.

Kosslyn, S. M. (1988). Aspects of a cognitive neuroscience of mental imagery. *Science, 240,* 1621–1626.

Kosslyn, S. M. (1994). *Image and brain: The resolution of the imagery debate.* Cambridge, MA: MIT Press.

Kosslyn, S. M., & Ochsner, K. N. (1994). In search of occipital activation during visual mental imagery. *Trends in Neurosciences, 17,* 290–292.

Kozak, M. J., Foa, E. B., & McCarthy, P. R. (1988). Obsessive-compulsive disorder. In C. G. Last & M. Herson (Eds.), *Handbook of anxiety disorders* (pp. 87–108). New York: Pergamon Press.

Krantz, D. S., Grunberg, N. E., & Baum, A. (1985). Health psychology. *Annual Review of Psychology, 36,* 349–383.

Kranzler, H. R. (1996). Evaluation and treatment of anxiety symptoms and disorders in alcoholics. *Journal of Clinical Psychiatry, 57*(6, Suppl.).

Kraus, S. J. (1995). Attitudes and the prediction of behavior: A meta-analysis of the empirical literature. *Personality and Social Psychology Bulletin, 21,* 58–75.

Kristiansen, C.M. (1994). *Recovered memories of child abuse: Fact, fantasy, or fancy?* Invited address for the annual convention of the Canadian Psychological Association. Penticton, BC.

Kroger, W. S., & Fezler, W. D. (1976). *Hypnosis and behavior modification: Imagery conditioning.* Philadelphia: J. B. Lippincott.

Krosigk, M. von. (1993). Cellular mechanisms of a synchronized oscillation in the thalamus. *Science, 261,* 361–364.

Krueger, W. C. F. (1929). The effect of overlearning on retention. *Journal of Experimental Psychology, 12,* 71–81.

Krueger, J. M., & Takahashi, J. S. (1997). Thermoregulation and sleep: Closely linked but separable. *Annals of the New York Academy of Sciences, 813,* 281–286.

Krupnick, J., Sotsky, S., Simmens, S., Moyer, J., Elkin, I., Watkins, J., & Pilkonis, P. (1996). The role of the therapeutic alliance in psychotherapy and pharmacotherapy outcome: Findings in the National Institute of Mental health Treatment of Depression Collaborative Research Program. Journal of Counseling and Clinical Psychology, 64, 532–539.

Kubler-Ross, Elisabeth (1969). On death and dying. New York: Macmillan.

Kuch, K., & Cox, B. J. (1992). Symptoms of PTSD in 124 survivors of the Holocaust. *American Journal of Psychiatry, 149,* 337–340.

Kuczaj, S. A., III (1978). Children's judgments of grammatical and ungrammatical irregular past-tense verbs. *Child Development, 49,* 319–326.

Kuhl, P. K., Williams, K. A., Lacerda, F., Stevens, K. N., & Lindblom, B. (1992). Linguistic experience alters phonetic perception in infants by 6 months of age. *Science, 255,* 606–608.

Kuhn, D. (1984). Cognitive development. In M. H. Bernstein & M. E. Lamb (Eds.), *Developmental psychology.* Hillsdale, NJ: Erlbaum.

Kuhn, D., Kohlberg, L., Langer, J., & Haan, N. (1977). The development of formal operations in logical and moral judgment. *Genetic Psychology Monographs, 95,* 97–188.

Kuiper, N. A., & Martin, R. A. (1998). Is sense of humor a positive personality characteristic? In R. Willibald (Ed)., *The sense of humor: Explorations of a personality characteristic. Humor research: 3* (pp. 159–178). Berlin: Walter De Gruyter & Co.

Kukla, A. (1972). Foundations of an attributional theory of performance. *Psychological Review, 79,* 454–470.

Kunda, K., & Oleson, K. C. (1995). Maintaining stereotypes in the face of disconfirmation: Construction grounds for subtyping deviants. *Journal of Personality and Social Psychology, 68,* 565–579.

Kushner, M. G., Sher, K. J., & Beitman, B. D. (1990). The relation between alcohol problems and the anxiety disorders. *American Journal of Psychiatry, 147,* 685–695.

Labelle, R., Lachance, L., & Morval, M. (1996). Validation d'une version canadienne-francaise du "Reasons for Living Inventory." *Science et Comportement, 24*(3), 237–248.

La Berge, S. P. (1981, January). Lucid dreaming: Directing the action as it happens. *Psychology Today,* pp. 48–57.

Laferriee, S., & Bouchard, C. (1996). Illustration de la capacite discriminante du Questionnaire sur la resolution des conflicts dans la mesure de la violence parentale. *Canadian Journal of Behavioural Science, 28*(1), 70–73.

Lalonde, R., & Botez, M. I. (1990). The cerebellum and learning processes in animals. *Brain Research Reviews, 15,* 325–332.

Lambert, W. E., Genesee, F., Holobow, N., & Chartrand, L. (1993). Bilingual education for majority English-speaking children. *European Journal of Psychology Education, 8,* 3–22.

Lambert, W. E., Tucker, G. R., & D'Anglejan, A. (1973). Cognitive and attitudinal consequences of bilingual schooling. *Journal of Educational Psychology, 65*(2), 141–159.

Lamberti, R. (1998, January 26). Storm warnings. *Toronto Sun.*

Lamborn, S. D., Mounts, N. S., Steinberg, L., & Dornbusch, S. M. (1991). Patterns of competence and adjustment among adolescents from authoritative, authoritarian, indulgent, and neglectful families. *Child Development, 62,* 1049–1065.

Lamm, H. (1988). A review of our research on group polarization: Eleven experiments on the effects of group discussion on risk acceptance, probability estimation, and negotiation positions. *Psychological Reports, 62*, 807–813.

Landry, D. W. (1997, February). Immunotherapy for cocaine addiction. *Scientific American, 276,* 42–45.

Landy, D., & Sigall, H. (1974). Beauty is talent: Task evaluation as a function of the performer's physical attractiveness. *Journal of Personality and Social Psychology, 29*, 299–304.

Lange, C. G., & James, W. (1922). *The emotions* (I. A. Haupt, Trans.). Baltimore: Williams and Wilkins.

Lange, R. A., Cigarroa, R. G., Yancy, C. W., Jr., Willard, J. E., Popma, J. J., Sills, M. N., McBride, W., Kim, A. S., & Hillis, L. D. (1989). Cocaine-induced coronary-artery vasoconstriction. *New England Journal of Medicine*, 321, 1557–1562.

Langer, E. J., & Rodin, J. (1976). The effects of choice and enhanced personal responsibility for the aged: A field experiment in an institutional setting. *Journal of Personality and Social Psychology, 34*, 191–198.

Langevin, B., Sukkar, F., Léger, P., Guez, A., & Robert, D. (1992). Sleep apnea syndromes (SAS) of specific etiology: Review and incidence from a sleep laboratory. *Sleep, 15*, S25–S32.

Langlois, J. H., & Roggman, L. A. (1990). Attractive faces are only average. *Psychological Science, 1*, 115–121.

Lauber, J. K., & Kayten, P. J. (1988). Keynote address: Sleepiness, circadian dysrhythmia, and fatigue in transportation system accidents. *Sleep, 11*, 503–512.

Laurent, J., Swerdik, M., & Ryburn, M. (1992). Review of validity research on the Stanford-Binet Intelligence Scale: Fourth Edition. *Psychological Assessment, 4*, 102–112.

Lavie, P., Herer, P., Peled, R., Berger, I., Yoffe, N., Zomer, J., & Rubin, A-H. (1995). Mortality in sleep apnea patients: A multivariate analysis of risk factors. *Sleep, 18,* 149–157.

Lazarus, R. S. (1966). *Psychological stress and the coping process.* New York: McGraw-Hill.

Lazarus, R. S. (1991a). Cognition and motivation in emotion. *American Psychologist, 46,* 352–367.

Lazarus, R. S. (1991b). Progress on a cognitive-motivational-relational theory of emotion. *American Psychologist, 46,* 819–834.

Lazarus, R. S. (1995). Vexing research problems inherent in cognitive-mediational theories of emotion—and some solutions. *Psychological Inquiry, 6,* 183–187.

Lazarus, R. S., & DeLongis, A. (1983). Psychological stress and coping in aging. *American Psychologist*, 38, 245–253.

Lazarus, R. S., & Folkman, S. (1984). *Stress, appraisal, and coping.* New York: Springer.

Lazarus, R.S. (1993). From psychological stress to the emotions: A history of changing outlooks. *Annual Review of Psychology, 44,* 1–21.

Leckman, J. F., Grice, D. E., Boardman, J., Zhang, H., Vitale, A., Bondi, C., Alsobrook, J., Peterson, B. S., Cohen, D. J., Rasmussen, S. A., Goodman, W. K., McDougle, C. J., & Pauls, D. L. (1997). Symptoms of obsessive-compulsive disorder. *American Journal of Psychiatry, 154*, 911–917.

LeDoux, J. E. (1994). Emotional memory systems in the brain. *Behavioural Brain Research, 58*, 69–79.

LeDoux, J. E. (1995). Emotion, memory, and the brain. *Scientific American, 270*, 50–57.

Lee, J. A. (1973). *The colours of love.* Toronto: New Press.

Lee, J. A. (1988). Love-styles. In R. J. Sternberg and M. L. Barnes (Eds.), *The psychology of love*. New Haven, CT: Yale University Press.

Leenaars, A., & Lester, D. (1990). Suicide in adolescents: A comparison of Canada and the United States. *Psychological Reports, 67,* 867–873.

Lefcourt, H. M. (1966). Internal versus external control of reinforcement: A review. *Psychological Bulletin, 65,* 206–220.

Leichtman, M. D., & Ceci, S. J. (1995). The effects of stereotypes and suggestions on preschoolers' reports. *Developmental Psychology, 31*, 568–578.

Leland, J. (1996, August 26). The fear of heroin is shooting up. *Newsweek,* pp. 55–56.

Lenneberg, E. (1967). *Biological foundations of language.* New York: Wiley.

Lepper, M. R., Greene, D., & Nisbett, R. E. (1973). Undermining children's intrinsic interest with extrinsic rewards: A test of the "overjustification" hypothesis. *Journal of Personality and Social Psychology, 28*, 129–137.

Lerman, D. C., Iwata, B. A., Shore, B. A., & Kahng, S. W. (1996). Responding maintained by intermittent reinforcement: Implications for the use of extinction with problem behavior in clinical settings. *Journal of Applied Behavior Analysis, 29,* 153–171.

Leshner, A. I. (1999). Science is revolutionizing our view of addiction and what to do about it. *American Journal of Psychiatry, 156,* 1–3.

Lester, B. M., Hoffman, J., & Brazelton, T. B. (1985). The rhythmic structure of mother-infant interaction in term and preterm infants. *Child Development, 56*, 15–27.

Levav, I., Kohn, R., Golding, J. M., & Weissman, M. M. (1997). Vulnerability of Jews to affective disorders. *American Journal of Psychiatry, 154*, 941–947.

Levesque, L., Desharnais, R., & Godin, G. (1995). Validation canadienne-francaise du "self-control schedule." *Science et Comportement, 24*(2), 133–149.

Levenson, R.W., Carstensen, L. L., & Gottman, J. M. (1993). Long-term marriage: Age, gender, and satisfaction. *Psychology and Aging, 8*, 301–313.

Levenson, R.W., Ekman, P., & Friesen, W. (1990). Voluntary facial action generates emotion-specific autonomic nervous system activity. *Psychophysiology, 27*, 363–385.

Leventhal, H., & Tomarken, A. J. (1986). Emotion: Today's problems. *Annual Review of Psychology, 37*, 565–610.

Levine, C., Kohlberg, L., & Hewer, A. (1985). The current formulation of Kohlberg's theory and a response to critics. *Human Development, 28*, 94–100.

Levitt, A. G., & Wang, Q. (1991). Evidence for language-specific rhythmic influences in the reduplicative babbling of French- and English-learning infants. *Language and Speech, 34*, 235–249.

Levy, J. (1985, May). Right brain, left brain: Fact and fiction. *Psychology Today*, pp. 38–44.

Levy, J., & Nagylaki, T. (1972). A model for the genetics of handedness. *Genetics, 72*, 117–128.

Lewinsohn, P. M., & Rosenbaum, M. (1987). Recall of parental behavior by acute depressives, remitted depressives, and nondepressives. *Journal of Personality and Social Psychology, 52*, 611–619.

Lewis, M. (1995, January/February). Self-conscious emotions. *American Scientist, 83*, 68–78.

Lewis-Fernández, R., & Kleinman, A. (1994). Culture, personality, and psychopathology. *Journal of Abnormal Psychology, 103*, 67–71.

Leyens, J-P., Yzerbyt, V., & Olivier, C. (1996). The role of applicability in the emergence of the overattribution bias. *Journal of Personality and Social Psychology, 70*, 219–229.

Libb, J. W., Murray, J., Thurstin, H., & Alarcon, R. D. (1992). Concordance of the MCMI-II, the MMPI, and Axis I discharge diagnosis in psychiatric inpatients. *Journal of Personality Assessment, 58*, 580–590.

Lidz, T., Fleck, S., & Cornelison, A. R. (1965). *Schizophrenia and the family*. New York: International Universities Press.

Lieberman, J., Bogerts, B., Degreef, G., Ashtari, M., Lantos, G., & Alvir, J. (1992). Qualitative assessment of brain morphology in acute and chronic schizophrenia. *American Journal of Psychiatry, 149*, 784–794.

Lieberman, M. (1986). Self-help groups and psychiatry. *American Psychiatric Association Annual Review, 5*, 744–760.

Lieberman, M. A., Yalom, I. D., & Miles, M. B. (1973). *Encounter groups: First facts*. New York: Basic Books.

Liebert, R. M., Sprafkin, J. N., & Davidson, E. S. (1989). *The early window: Effects of television on children and youth* (3rd ed.). New York: Pergamon.

Lim, K. O., Tew, W., Kushner, M., Chow, K., Matsumoto, B., & Delisi, L. E. (1996). Cortical gray matter volume deficits in patients with first-episode schizophrenia. *American Journal of Psychiatry, 153*, 1548–1553.

Lincoln, R. (1986). Smoking and reproduction. *Family Planning Perspectives, 18*, 79–84.

Linton, M. (1979, July). I remember it well. *Psychology Today*, pp. 80–86.

Linville, P. W., Fischer, G. W., & Salovey, P. (1989). Perceived distributions of the characteristics of in-group and out-group members: Empirical evidence and a computer simulation. *Journal of Personality and Social Psychology, 57*, 165–188.

Lipsey, M. W., & Wilson, D. B. (1993). The efficacy of psychological, educational, and behavioral treatment: Confirmation from meta-analysis. *American Psychologist, 48*, 1181–1209.

Lipsitt, L. P. (1990). Learning processes in the human newborn: Sensitization, habituation, and classical conditioning. *Annals of the New York Academy of Sciences, 608*, 113–123.

Little, R. E., Anderson, K. W., Ervin, C. H., Worthington-Roberts, B., & Clarren, S. K. (1989). Maternal alcohol use during breast-feeding and infant mental and motor development at one year. *New England Journal of Medicine, 321*, 425–430.

Lloyd, G. G., & Lishman, W. A. (1975). Effect of depression on the speed of recall of pleasant and unpleasant experiences. *Psychological Medicine, 5*, 173–180.

Lockhart, R. S., & Craik, F. I. M. 1990. Levels of processing: A retrospective commentary on a framework for memory research. *Canadian Journal of Psychology, 44*, 87–112.

Loehlin, J. C., Horn, J. M., & Willerman, L. (1989). Modeling IQ change: Evidence from the Texas Adoption Project. *Child Development, 60*, 993–1004.

Loehlin, J. C., Horn, J. M., & Willerman, L. (1990). Heredity, environment, and personality change: Evidence from the Texas Adoption Project. *Journal of Personality, 58*, 221–243.

Loehlin, J. C., Lindzey, G., & Spuhler, J. N. (1975). *Race differences in intelligence*. San Francisco: Freeman.

Loehlin, J. C., Willerman, L., & Horn, J. M. (1987). Personality resemblance in adoptive families: A 10-year follow-up. *Journal of Personality and Social Psychology, 53*, 961–969.

Loehlin, J. C., Willerman, L., & Horn, J. M. (1988). Human behavior genetics. *Annual Review of Psychology, 39*, 101–133.

Loehlin, J.C. (1992). *The limits of family influence: Genes, experience, and behavior*. New York: Guilford.

Loehlin, J.C., Vandenberg, S., & Osborne, R. (1973). Blood group genes and Negro-White ability differences. *Behavior Genetics, 3*, 263–270.

Loftus, E. (1980). *Memory: Surprising new insights into how we remember and why we forget*. Reading, MA: Addison-Wesley.

Loftus, E. F. (1984, February). Eyewitnesses: Essential but unreliable. *Psychology Today*, pp. 22–27.

Loftus, E.F. (1993a). Psychologists in the eyewitness world. *American Psychologist, 48*, 550–552.

Loftus, E.F. (1993b). The reality of repressed memories. *American Psychologist, 48*, 518–537.

Loftus, E.F. (1994). The repressed memory controversy. *American Psychologist, 49*, 443–445.

Loftus, E. F. (1997). Creating false memories. *Scientific American, 277*, 71–75.

Loftus, E. F., & Hoffman, H. G. (1989). Misinformation and memory: The creation of new memories. *Journal of Experimental Psychology: General, 118*, 100–104.

Loftus, E. F., & Klinger, M. R. (1992). Is the unconscious smart or dumb? *American Psychologist, 47*, 761–765.

Loftus, E. F., & Loftus, G. R. (1980). On the permanence of stored information in the human brain. *American Psychologist, 35*, 409–420.

Logue, A. W. (1985). Conditioned food aversion learning in humans. *Annals of the New York Academy of Sciences, 443*, 316–329.

Logue, A. W., Ophir, I., & Strauss, K. R. (1981). The acquisition of taste aversions in humans. *Behaviour Research and Therapy, 19*, 319–333.

Lorenz, K. (1966). *On aggression*. New York: Harcourt, Brace, & World.

Lovaas, I. (1967). A behavior therapy approach to the treatment of childhood schizophrenia. In J. P. Hill (Ed.), *Minnesota symposia on child development* (Vol. 1, pp. 108–159). Minneapolis: University of Minnesota Press.

Lubin, B., Larsen, R. M., Matarazzo, J. D., & Seever, M. (1986). Psychological assessment services and psychological test usage in private practice and in military settings. *Psychotherapy in Private Practice, 4*, 19–29.

Luchins, A. S. (1957). Experimental attempts to minimize the impact of first impressions. In C. I. Hovland (Ed.), *Yale studies in attitude and communication*: Vol. 1. The order of presentation in persuasion (pp. 62–75). New Haven, CT: Yale University Press.

Lukeman, D., & Melvin, D. (1993). Annotation: The preterm infant: Psychological issues in childhood.f *Journal of Child Psychology and Psychiatry, 34*, 837–849.

Lundgren, C. B. (1986, August 20). Cocaine addiction: A revolutionary new treatment. *St. Louis Jewish Light*, p. 7.

Lyketsos, C., Chen, L., & Anthony, J. (1999). Cognitive decline in adulthood: An 11.5 year follow-up of the Baltimore Epidemiologic Catchment Area Study. *American Journal of Psychiatry, 156,* 56–58.

Lykken, D. T., Bouchard, T. J., Jr., McGue, M., & Tellegen, A. (1993). Heritability of interests: A twin study. *Journal of Applied Psychology, 78,* 649–661.

Lynch, S., & Yarnell, P. R. (1973). Retrograde amnesia: Delayed forgetting after concussion. *American Journal of Psychology, 86*, 643–645.

Lyons, M., Eisen, S., Goldberg, J., True, W., Lin, N., Meyer, J., Toomey, R., Faraone, S., Merla-Ramos, M., & Tsuang, M. (1998). A registry based twin study of depression in men. *Archives of General Psychiatry, 55,* 468–472.

Maccoby, E. E., & Martin, J. A. (1983). Socialization in the context of the family: Parent-child interaction. In P. H. Mussen (Ed.), *Handbook of child psychology* (4th ed., Vol. 4). New York: John Wiley.

MacDonald, T. K., Fong, G. T., Zanna, M. P., & Martineau, A. M. (2000a). Alcohol myopia and condom use: Can alcohol intoxication be associated with more prudent behavior? *Health Psychology, 19*(3), 290–298.

MacDonald, T. K., MacDonald, G., Zanna, M. P., & Fong, G. T. (2000b). Alcohol, sexual arousal, and intentions to use condoms in young men. Applying alcohol myopia theory to risky sexual behavior. *Health Psychology, 19*(3), 290–298.

MacDonald, T. K., Zanna, M. P., & Fong, G. T. (1998). Alcohol and intentions to engage in risky health-related behaviors: Experimental evidence for a causal relationship. In J. G. Adair & D. Belanger (Eds.), _Advances in psychological sicence, Vol. 1: Social, personal, and cultural aspects (pp. 407–428). Hove, UK: Psychology Press.

MacFarlane, A. (1978). What a baby knows. *Human Nature, 1*, 74–81.

MacLeod, L. (1989, October). *The city for women: No safe place.* Paper presented at the First European and North America Conference of urban Safety and Crime.

Macrae, C. N., Milne, A. B., & Bodenhausen, G. V. (1994). Stereotypes as energy-saving devices: A peek inside the cognitive toolbox. *Journal of Personality and Social Psychology, 66*, 37–47.

Magee, J., & Johnston, D. (1997). A synaptically controlled, associative signal for Hebbian plasticity in hippocampal neurons. *Science, 275,* 209–213.

Mahoney, J. (2000, July 17). Tornado death toll climbs in Alberta. *The Globe and Mail.* Retrieved August 21, 2000 from the World Wide Web: archives.theglobeand mail.com.

Maier, S. F., & Laudenslager, M. (1985, August). Stress and health: Exploring the links. Psychology Today, pp. 44–49.

Main, M., & Solomon, J. (1990). Procedures for identifying infants as disorganized/disoriented during the Ainsworth Strange Situation. In M. Greenberg, D. Cicchetti, & M. Cummings (Eds.), *Attachment in the preschool years: Theory, research, and intervention* (pp. 121–160). Chicago: University of Chicago Press.

Maj, M., Veltro, F., Pirozzi, R., Lobrace, S., & Magliano, L. (1992). Pattern of recurrence of illness after recovery from an episode of major depression: A prospective study. *Journal of Personality and Social Psychology, 62*, 795–800.

Malone, J. L. (2000). Working with Aboriginal women: Applying feminist therapy in a multicultural counselling context. *Canadian Journal of Counselling, 34*(1), 33–42.

Maratsos, M. (1983). Some current issues in the study of the acquisition of grammar. In P. H. Mussen (Ed.), Handbook of child psychology (Vol. 3). New York: Wiley.

Maratsos, M., & Matheny, L. (1994). Language specificity and elasticity: Brain and clinical syndrome studies. *Annual Review of Psychology, 45*, 487–516.

Marcus, G. F., Pinker, S., Ullman, M., Hollander, M., Rosen, T. J., & Xu, F. (1992). Overregularization in language acquisition. *Monographs for the Society for Research in Child Development, 57*(4, Serial No. 228).

Marder, S. R. (1996). Clinical experience with risperidone. *Journal of Clinical Psychiatry, 57*(9, Suppl.), 57–61.

Marder, S. R., & Meibach, R. C. (1994). Risperidone in the treatment of schizophrenia. *American Journal of Psychiatry, 161*, 825–835.

Marijuana as medicine: Parliament should make a useful drug available—and go a step further. (2000, August, 2). *The Globe and Mail.*

Marion, R. (1990). *The boy who felt no pain.* New York: Fawcett Crest Press.

Marks, G. A., Shatfery, J. P., Oksenberg, A., Speciale, S. G., & Roffwarg, H. P. (1995). A functional role for REM sleep in brain maturation. *Behavioral Brain Research, 69,* 1–11.

Marks, I. (1988). Blood-injury phobia: A review. *American Journal of Psychiatry, 145*, 1207–1213.

Marks, I. M. (1972). Flooding (implosion) and allied treatments. In W. S. Agras (Ed.), *Behavior modification.* New York: Little, Brown.

Marks, I. M. (1978). Behavioral psychotherapy of adult neurosis. In S. Garfield & A. E. Bergin (Eds.), *Handbook of psychotherapy and behavior change* (2nd ed.). New York: Wiley.

Marlatt, G. A. (1983). The controlled-drinking controversy: A commentary. *American Psychologist, 38*, 1097–1110.

Marshall, G. D., & Zimbardo, P. G. (1979). Affective consequences of inadequately explained physiological arousal. *Journal of Personality and Social Psychology, 37*, 970–988.

Marshall, J. (1997). Alcohol and substance abuse in panic disorder. *Journal of Clinical Psychiatry, 58*(2, Suppl.), 46–49.

Marshall, R. D., Schneier, F. R., Fallon, B. A., Feerick, J., & Liebowitz, M. R. (1994). Medication therapy for social phobia. *Journal of Clinical Psychiatry, 56*(6, Suppl.), 33–37.

Marshall, W., Serran, G., & Cortoni, F. (2000). Childhood attachments, sexual abuse, and their relationship to adult coping in child molesters. *Sexual Abuse: Journal of Research & Treatment, 12,* 17–26.

Marshall, W. L., & Segal, Z. (1988). Behavior therapy. In C. G. Last & M. Hersen (Eds.), *Handbook of anxiety disorders* (pp. 338–361). New York: Pergamon.

Martikainen, P., & Valkonen, R. (1996). Mortality after the death of a spouse: Rates and causes of death in a large Finnish cohort. *American Journal of Public Health, 86,* 1087–1093.

Martin, R. A. (1996) The situational humor response questionnaire (SHRQ) and coping humor scale (CHS): A decade of research findings. *Humor, 9,* 251–272.

Martin, R. A., Fitzsimmons, K., & Kuiper, N. A. (1997). Is humor always adaptive: *Individual differences in the stress-buffering effects of humor.* Conference of the International Society for Humor Studies, Oklahoma.

Martin, R. A., Kuiper, N. A., Olinger, J. & Dance, K. A. (1993). Humor, coping with stress, self-concept, and psychological well-being. *Humor 6*(1), 89–104.

Martin, S. K., & Eastman, C. I. (1998). Medium-intensity light produces circadian rhythm adaptation to simulated night-shift work. *Sleep, 21,* 154–165.

Martorano, S. C. (1977). A developmental analysis of performance on Piaget's formal operations tasks. *Developmental Psychology, 13,* 666–672.

Masand, P., Popli, A. P., & Weilburg, J. B. (1995). Sleepwalking. *American Family Physician, 51,* 649–654.

Maslow, A. H. (1970). *Motivation and personality* (2nd ed.). New York: Harper & Row.

Masters, J. C. (1981). Developmental psychology. *Annual Review of Psychology, 32,* 117–151.

Mathew, R. J., & Wilson, W. H. (1991). Substance abuse and cerebral blood flow. *American Journal of Psychiatry, 148,* 292–305.

Matlin, M. (1983). *Cognition.* New York: Holt, Rinehart & Winston.

Matlin, M. W. (1989). *Cognition* (2nd ed.). New York: Holt, Rinehart & Winston.

Matlin, M. W., & Foley, H. J. (1997). *Sensation and perception* (4th ed.). Boston: Allyn & Bacon.

Matsuda, L., Lolait, S. J., Brownstein, M. J., Young, A. C., & Bonner, T. I. (1990). Structure of a cannabinoid receptor and functional expression of the cloned CDNA. Nature, 346, 561–564.

Matthews, K. A., Wing, R. R., Kuller, L. H., Meilahn, E. N., et al. (1990). Influences of natural menopause on psychological characteristics and symptoms of middle-aged healthy women. *Journal of Consulting and Clinical Psychology, 58*(3), 345–351.

Mattson, S., & Riley, E. (2000). Parent ratings of behavior in children with heavy prenatal alcohol exposure and IQ-matched controls. *Alcoholism: Clinical and Experimental Research, 24,* 226–231.

Mayer, J. D., & Salovey, P. (1993). The intelligence of emotional intelligence. *Intelligence, 17,* 433–442.

Mayer, J. D., & Salovey, P. (1995). Emotional intelligence and the construction and regulation of feelings. *Applied and Preventive Psychology, 4,* 197–208.

Mayer, J. D., & Salovey, P. (1997). What is emotional intelligence? In P. Salovey & D. Sluyter (Eds.), *Emotional development, emotional literacy, and emotional intelligence.* New York: Basic Books.

Mazur, J. E. (1993). Predicting the strength of a conditioned reinforcer: Effects of delay and uncertainty. *Current Directions in Psychological Sciences, 2*(3), 70–74.

McAdams, D. P. (1992). The five-factor model in personality: A critical appraisal. *Journal of Personality, 60,* 329–361.

McCarthy, M. E., & Waters, W. F. (1997). Decreased attentional responsivity during sleep deprivation: Orienting response latency, amplitude and habituation, *Sleep, 20,* 226–237.

McCartney, K., Harris, M. J., & Bernieri, F. (1990). Growing up and growing apart: A developmental meta-analysis of twin studies. *Psychological Bulletin, 107,* 226–237.

McClearn, G. E., Johansson, B., Berg, S., Pedersen, N. L., Ahern, F., Petrill, S. A., & Plomin, R. (1997). Substantial genetic influence on cognitive abilities in twins 80 or more years old. *Science, 276,* 1560–1563.

McClelland, D. C. (1958). Methods of measuring human motivation. In J. W. Atkinson (Ed.), *Motives in fantasy, action and society: A method of assessment and study.* Princeton, NJ: Van Nostrand.

McClelland, D. C. (1961). *The achieving society.* Princeton, NJ: Van Nostrand.

McClelland, D. C. (1985). *Human motivation.* New York: Cambridge University Press.

McClelland, D. C., & Pilon, D. A. (1983). Sources of adult motives in patterns of parent behavior in early childhood. *Journal of Personality and Social Psychology, 44,* 564–574.

McClelland, D. C., Atkinson, J. W., Clark, R. W., & Lowell, E. L. (1953). *The achievement motive.* New York: Appleton-Century-Crofts.

McConnell, J. V., Cutler, R. L., & McNeil, E. B. (1958). Subliminal stimulation: An overview. *American Psychologist, 13,* 229–242.

McCormick, R. (1997). Healing through interdependence: The role of connecting in First Nations healing practices. *Canadian Journal of Counselling, 31*(3), 172–184.

McCormick, R. (2000). Aboriginal traditions in the treatment of substance abuse. *Canadian Journal of Counselling, 34*(1), 25–32.

McCourt, W. F., Gurrera, R. J., & Cutter, H. S. G. (1993). Sensation seeking and novelty seeking: Are they the same? *Journal of Nervous and Mental Disease, 181,* 309–312.

McCrae, R. R. (1993). Moderated analyses of longitudinal personality stability. *Journal of Personality and Social Psychology, 65,* 577–583.

McCrae, R. R. (1996). Social consequences of experiential openness. *Psychological Bulletin, 120,* 323–337.

McCrae, R. R., & Costa, P. T., Jr. (1987). Validation of the five-factor model of personality across instruments and observers. *Journal of Personality and Social Psychology, 52,* 81–90.

McCrae, R.R., & Costa, P.T., Jr. (1990). *Personality in adulthood.* New York: Guilford Press.

McCrae, R. R., & Costa, P. T., Jr. (1997). Personality trait structure as a human universal. *American Psychologist, 52,* 509–516.

McCrae, R. R., Costa, P. T., Jr., & Ostendorf, F. (2000). Nature over nurture: Temperament, personality and life-span development. *Journal of Personality and Social Psychology, 78*(1), 173–186.

McCrae, R. R., & John, O. P. (1992). An introduction to the five-factor model and its applications. *Journal of Personality, 60*, 175–215.

McCreary, D., Newcomb, M., & Sadava, S. (1999). The male role, alcohol use, and alcohol problems: A structural modeling examination in adult women and men. *Journal of Counseling Psychology, 46*, 109–124.

McCreary, D., & Sadava, S. (2000). Television viewing and self-perceived health, weight, and physical fitness: Evidence for the cultivation hypothesis. *Journal of Applied Social Psychology, 29*, 2342–2361.

McDaniel, M. A., Anderson, D. C., Einstein, G. O., & O'Halloran, C. M. (1989). Modulation of environmental reinstatement effects through encoding strategies. *American Journal of Psychology, 102*, 523–548.

McDonald, A. D., Armstrong, B. G., & Sloan, M. (1992). Cigarette, alcohol, and coffee consumption and prematurity. *American Journal of Public Health, 82*, 87–90.

McDonald, R. J., & White, N. M. (1993). A triple dissociation of memory systems: Hippocampus, amygdala, and dorsal striatum. *Behavioral Neuroscience, 107*(1), 3–22.

McGlashan, T. H., & Fenton, W. S. (1992). The positive-negative distinction in schizophrenia: Review of natural history validators. *Archives of General Psychiatry, 49*, 63–72.

McGue, M., Pickens, R. W., & Svikis, D. S. (1992). Sex and age effects on the inheritance of alcohol problems: A twin study. *Journal of Abnormal Psychology, 101*, 3–17.

McGuire, W. J. (1969). The nature of attitudes and attitude change. In G. Lindzey & E. Aronson (Eds.), *Handbook of social psychology* (Vol. 3). Reading, MA: Addison-Wesley.

McGuire, W. J. (1985). Attitudes and attitude change. In G. Lindzey & E. Aronson (Ed.), *Handbook of social psychology* (Vol. 2, 3rd ed.). New York: Random House.

McKellar, P. (1972). Imagery from the standpoint of introspection. In P. W. Sheehan (Ed.), *The function and nature of imagery* (pp. 36–63). New York: Academic Press.

McKelvie, S. J. (1984). Relationship between set and functional fixedness: A replication. *Perceptual and Motor Skills, 58*, 996–998.

McKinnon, M. (2000, October 2). Public not afraid to show its love. *The Globe and Mail*, p. 1.

McNaughton, M. E., Smith, L. W., Patterson, T. L., & Grant, I. (1990). Stress, social support, coping resources, and immune status in elderly women. *Journal of Nervous and Mental Disease, 178*, 460–461.

Medina, J. H., Paladini, A. C., & Izquierdo, I. (1993). Naturally occurring benzodiazepines and benzodiazepine-like molecules in brain. *Behavioural Brain Research, 58*, 1–8.

Mednick, S. A., & Mednick, M. T. (1967). *Examiner's manual, Remote Associates Test*. Boston: Houghton-Mifflin.

Medzerian, G. (1991). *Crack: Treating cocaine addiction*. Blue Ridge Summit, PA: Tab Books.

Meichenbaum, D. (1977). *Cognitive behavior modification: An integrative approach*. New York: Plenum.

Meichenbaum, D. (1985). *Stress Inoculation Training*. New York: Pergamon.

Meier, R. P. (1991). Language acquisition by deaf children. *American Scientist, 79* (1), 60–70.

Melamed, B. G., & Siegal, L. J. (1975). Reduction of anxiety in children facing hospitalization and surgery by use of filmed modeling. *Journal of Consulting and Clinical Psychology, 43*, 511–521.

Meltzer, E. O. (1990). Performance effects of antihistamines. *Journal of Allergies and Clinical Immunology, 86*, 613–619.

Meltzer, H. (1930). Individual differences in forgetting pleasant and unpleasant experiences. *Journal of Educational Psychology, 21*, 399–409.

Meltzoff, A. N. (1988). Imitation of televised models by infants. *Child Development, 59*, 1221–1229.

Meltzoff, A. N., & Moore, M. K. (1977). Imitation of facial and manual gestures by human neonates. *Science, 198*, 75–78.

Melzack, R. (1999a). Pain and stress: A new perspective. In R. J. Gatchel, D. C. Turk, et al. (Eds.). *Psychosocial factors in pain: Critical perspectives* (pp. 89–116). New York: Guilford Press.

Melzack, R. (1999b, August). From the gate to the neuromatrix. *Pain*, Suppl. 6, 121–126.

Melzack, R., & Wall, P. D. (1965). Pain mechanisms: A new theory. *Science, 150*, 971–979.

Melzack, R., & Wall, P. D. (1983). *The challenge of pain*. New York: Basic Books.

Menard, M. (1997). Vitamin and mineral supplement prior to and during pregnancy. *Obstetrics & Gynecology Clinics of North America, 24*, 479–498.

Mendelson, W. B. (1995). Long-term follow-up of chronic insomnia. *Sleep, 18*, 698–701.

Merckelbach, H., de Jong, P., Muris, P., & van den Hout, M. (1996). The etiology of specific phobias: A review. *Clinical Psychology Review, 16*, 337–361.

Merikle, P. M., & Skanes, H. (1992). Subliminal self-help audiotapes: A search for placebo effect. *Journal of Applied Psychology, 77*, 772–776.

Metter, E. J. (1991). Brain-behavior relationships in aphasia studied by positron emission tomography. *Annals of the New York Academy of Sciences, 620*, 153–164.

Meyer, P. (1972). If Hitler asked you to electrocute a stranger, would you? In R. Greenbaum & H. A. Tilker (Eds.), *The challenge of psychology* (pp. 456–465). Englewood Cliffs, NJ: Prentice-Hall.

Michaels, J. W., Bloomel, J. M., Brocato, R. M., Linkous, R. A., & Rowe, J. S. (1982). Social facilitation and inhibition in a natural setting. *Replications in Social Psychology, 2*, 21–24.

Middlebrooks, J. C., & Green, D. M. (1991). Sound localization by human listeners. *Annual Review of Psychology, 42*, 135–159.

Milavsky, J. R., Kessler, R., Stipp, H., & Rubens, W. S. (1982). Television and aggression: Results of a panel study. In D. Pearl, L. Bouthilet, & J. Lazar (Eds.), *Television and behavior: Ten years of scientific progress and implications for the eighties* (Vol. 2). Washington, DC: U.S. Government Printing Office.

Miles, D. R., & Carey, G. (1997). Genetic and environmental architecture of human aggression. *Journal of Personality and Social Psychology, 72*, 207–217.

Miles, R. (1999). A homeostatic switch. *Nature, 397,* 215–216.

Milgram, S. (1963). Behavioral study of obedience. *Journal of Abnormal and Social Psychology, 67,* 371–378.

Milgram, S. (1965). Liberating effects of group pressure. Journal of Personality and Social Psychology, 1, 127–134.

Miller, B. C. (1976). A multivariate developmental model of marital satisfaction. *Journal of Marriage and the Family, 38,* 643–657.

Miller, D. T., & Ross, M. (1975). Self-serving biases in the attribution of causality: Fact or fiction? *Psychological Bulletin, 82,* 213–225.

Miller, D. T., & Turnbull, W. (1986). Expectancies and interpersonal processes. *Annual Review of Psychology, 37,* 233–256.

Miller, G. A. (1956). The magical number seven, plus or minus two: Some limits on our capacity for processing information. *Psychological Review, 63,* 81–97.

Miller, G. A., & Gildea, P. M. (1987). How children learn words. *Scientific American, 257,* 94–99.

Miller, I. J., & Reedy, F. E., Jr. (1990). Variations in human taste bud density and taste intensity perception. *Physiological Behavior, 47,* 1213–1219.

Miller, J. G., Bersoff, D. M., & Harwood, R. L. (1990). Perceptions of social responsibilities in India and in the United States: Moral imperatives or personal decisions? *Journal of Personality and Social Psychology, 58,* 33–47.

Miller, L. (1988, February). The emotional brain. *Psychology Today,* pp. 34–42.

Miller, L. K. (1999). The savant syndrome: Intellectual impairment and exceptional skill. *Psychological Bulletin, 125,* 31–46.

Miller, M., & Kantrowitz, B. (1999, January 25). Unmasking Sybil: A re-examination of the most famous psychiatric patient in history. *Newsweek.* Retrieved July 7, 2000 from the World Wide Web: newsweek.washingtonpost.com/issue/04_99a/printed/us/st/front.htm.

Miller, N. E. (1941). The frustration-aggression hypothesis. *Psychological Review,* 48, 337–342.

Miller, N. S., & Gold, M. S. (1994). LSD and Ecstasy: Pharmacology, phenomenology, and treatment. *Psychiatric Annals, 24,* 131–133.

Millman, R. B., & Beeder, A. B. (1994). The new psychedelic culture: LSD, Ecstasy, "rave" parties and The Grateful Dead. *Psychiatric Annals, 24,* 148–150.

Milner, B. (1970). Memory and the medial temporal regions of the brain. In K. H. Pribram & D. E. Broadbent (Eds.), *Biology of memory.* New York: Academic Press.

Milner, B., Corkin, S., & Teuber, H. L. (1968). Further analysis of the hippocampal amnesic syndrome: 14-year follow-up study of H. M. *Neuropsychologia, 6,* 215–234.

Milner, B. R. (1966). Amnesia following operation on the temporal lobes. In C. W. M. Whitty & O. L. Zangwill (Eds.), *Amnesia* (pp. 109–133). London: Butterworth.

Miltner , W., Braun, C., Arnold, M., Witte, H., & Taub, E. (1999). Coherence of gamma band EEG activity as a basis for associative learning. *Nature, 397,* 434–436.

Mistlberger, R. E. (1991). Scheduled daily exercise or feeding alters the phase of photic entrainment in syrian hamsters. *Physiology and Behavior, 50,* 1257–1260.

Mistlberger, R. E., & Rusak, B. (1989). Mechanisms and models of the circadian timekeeping system. In M. H. Kryger, T. Roth, & W. C. Dement (Eds.), *Principles and practice of sleep medicine* (pp. 141–152). Philadelphia: W. B. Saunders.

Mistry, J., & Rogoff, B. (1994). Remembering in cultural context. In W.J. Lonner & R. Malpass (Eds.), *Psychology and culture* (pp. 139–144). Boston: Allyn & Bacon.

Mitchell, J. V. (1983). *Tests in Print III.* Lincoln, NE: Buros Institute of Mental Measurements.

Mitler, M. M., Aldrich, M. S., Koob, G. F., & Zarcone, V. P. (1994). Narcolepsy and its treatment with stimulants. *Sleep, 17,* 352–371.

Moldofsky, H., Gilbert, R., Lue, F. A., & MacLean, A. W. (1995). Sleep-related violence. *Sleep, 18,* 731–739.

Molin,, J., Mellerup, E., Bolwig, T., Scheike, T., & Dam, H. (1996). The influence of climate on development of winter depression. *Journal of Affective Disorders, 37,* 151–155.

Monk, T. H. (1989). Circadian rhythms in subjective activation, mood, and performance efficiency. In M. H. Kryger, T. Roth, & W. C. Dement (Eds.), *Principles and practice of sleep medicine* (pp. 163–172). Philadelphia: W. B. Saunders.

Monk, T. H., & Carrier, J. (1998). A parallelism between human body temperature and performance independent of the endogenous circadian rhythms. *Journal of Biological Rhythms, 13*(2), 113–122.

Montagu, A. (1962). *The humanization of man.* Cleveland: World.

Mookherjee, H. (1997). Marital status, gender and perception of well-being. *Journal of Social Psychology, 137,* 95–105.

Moore, D. (2000, Feb. 7). BC still battling smoking ban. The Canadian Press. Retrieved August 21, 2000 from the World Wide Web: www.canoe.ca/Health0002/07_smoking2.html.

Moore, M. K. (2000). Are you too hard on yourself? *Cosmopolitan Magazine On-Line.* Retrieved December 27, 2000 from the World Wide Web: cosmo.women.com/cos/you/quiz/c9quiz13.htm.

Moore, T. E. (1995). Subliminal self-help audiotapes: An empirical test of perceptual consequences. *Canadian Journal of Behavioral Science, 27*(1), 9–20.

Moore-Ede, M. (1993). *The twenty-four hour society.* Reading, MA: Addison-Wesley.

Moran, M. G., & Stoudemire, A. (1992). Sleep disorders in the medically ill patient. *Journal of Clinical Psychiatry, 53*(6, Suppl.), 29–36.

Moreno, J. L. (1959). Psychodrama. In S. Arieti et al. (Eds.), *American handbook of psychiatry* (Vol. 2). New York: Basic Books.

Morgan, C. (1996). Odors as cues for the recall of words unrelated to odor. *Perceptual and Motor Skills, 83,* 1227–1234.

Morgan, C. D., & Murray, H. A. (1935). A method for investigating fantasies: The Thematic Apperception Test. *Archives of Neurology and Psychiatry, 34,* 289–306.

Morgan, C. D., & Murray, H. A. (1962). Thematic Apperception Test. 530–545. In H. A. Murray et al. (Eds.), *Explorations in personality: A clinical and experimental study of fifty men of college age.* New York: Science Editions.

Morin, C. M., & Ware, C. (1996). Sleep and psychopathology. *Applied and Preventive Psychology, 5,* 211–224.

Morin, C. M., & Wooten, V. (1996). Psychological and pharmacological approaches to treating insomnia: Critical issues assessing their separate and combined effects. *Clinical Psychology Review, 16,* 521–542.

Morris, C. (2000a, August 30). Natives seek attempted murder charges against fisheries officers. The Canadian Press. Retrieved October 1, 2000 from the World Wide Web: www.canoe.ca/CNEWSTopNews/native_aug30.html.

Morris, C. (2000b, September 29). Rae prepares to resume mediation in native lobster fishing dispute. The Canadian Press. Retrieved October 1, 2000 from the World Wide Web: www.canoe.ca/CNEWSFishingCrisis/lobster_sep29-cp.html.

Morrison, T. L., Edwards, D. W., & Weissman, H. N. (1994). The MMPI and MMPI-2 as predictors of psychiatric diagnosis in an outpatient sample. *Journal of Personality Assessment, 62,* 17–30.

Mortensen, P., Pederson, C., Westergaard, T., et al., (1999). Effects of family history and place and season of birth on the risk of schizophrenia. *New England Journal of Medicine, 58,* 395–401.

Moscovici, S., & Zavalloni, M. (1969). The group as a polarizer of attitudes. *Journal of Personality and Social Psychology, 12,* 125–135.

Moscovitch, M., Behrmann, M., & Winocur, G. (1994). Do PETS have long or short ears? Mental imagery and neuroimaging. *Trends in Neurosciences, 17,* 292–294.

Mourtazaev, M. S., Kemp, B., Zwinderman, A. H. & Kamphuisen, H. A. C. (1995). Age and gender affect different characteristics of slow waves in sleep EEG. *Sleep, 18,* 557–564.

Mullington, J., & Broughton, R. (1993). Scheduled naps in the management of daytime sleepiness in narcolepsy-cataplexy. *Sleep, 16,* 444–456.

Munro, M. (1996, April 4). All we really need is sleep. *Toronto Star,* p. 26.

Muris, R., Steerneman, P., Merckelbach, H., & Meesters, C. (1996). The role of parental fearfulness and modeling in children's fear. *Behaviour Research and Therapy, 34,* 265–268.

Murphy, D. L., & Pigott, T. A. (1990). A comparative examination of a role for serotonin in obsessive compulsive disorder, panic disorder, and anxiety. *Journal of Clinical Psychiatry, 51*(4, Suppl.), 53–58.

Murray, D. (1995, July/August). Toward a science of desire. *The Sciences, 35,* 244–249.

Murray, H. (1938). *Explorations in personality.* New York: Oxford University Press.

Murray, H. A. (1965). Uses of the Thematic Apperception Test. In B. I. Murstein (Ed.), *Handbook of projective techniques* (pp. 425–432). New York: Basic Books.

Murray, T. (1999, June 11). Separation just one stage for Siamese twins. www.medicalpost.com.

Murtagh, D. R. R., & Greenwood, K. M. (1995). Identifying effective psychological treatments for insomnia: A meta-analysis. *Journal of Consulting and Clinical Psychology, 63,* 79–89.

Myers, D. G., & Lamm, H. (1975). The polarizing effect of group discussion. *American Scientist, 63,* 297–303.

Nadon, R., Hoyt, I. P., Register, P. A., & Kilstrom, J. F. (1991). Absorption and hypnotizability: Context effects reexamined. *Journal of Personality and Social Psychology, 60,* 144–153.

Nash, M., & Baker, E. (1984, February). Trance encounters: Susceptibility to hypnosis. *Psychology Today,* pp. 18, 72–73.

Nathans, J., Davenport, C. M., Maumenee, I. H., Lewis, R. A., Heitmancik, J. F., Litt, M., Lovrien, E., Weleber, R., Bachynski, B., Zwas, F., Klingaman, R., & Fishman, G. (1989). Molecular genetics of human blue cone monochromacy. *Science, 245,* 831–838.

Nation, J. R., & Woods, D. J. (1980). Persistence: The role of partial reinforcement in psychotherapy. *Journal of Experimental Psychology: General, 109,* 175–207.

National Institute of Mental Health. (1985, June 10–12). *Consensus development conference statement: Electroconvulsive therapy: Program and abstracts.* Washington, DC: National Institute of Mental Health.

National Institute of Neurological Disorders and Stroke (2000). Epilepsy. Retrieved August 21, 2000 from the World Wide Web: www.ninds.nih.gov/health_and_medical/disorders/epilepsy.htm.

National Research Council. (1993). *Losing generations: Adolescents in high risk settings.* Washington, DC: National Academy Press.

Neimark, E. D. (1981). Confounding with cognitive style factors: An artifact explanation for the apparent nonuniversal incidence of formal operations. In I. Sigel, D. Brodzinsky, & R. Golinkoff (Eds.), *New directions in Piagetian research and theory.* Hillsdale, NJ: Erlbaum.

Neimark, J., Conway, C., & Doskoch, P. (1994, September/October). Back from the drink. *Psychology Today,* 46–53.

Neisser, U., Boodoo, G., Bouchard, T., Boykin, A., Brody, N., Ceci, S., Halpern, D., Loehlin, J., Perloff, R., Sternberg, R., & Urbina, S. (1996). Intelligence: Knowns and unknowns. *American Psychologist, 51,* 77–101.

Neisser, U., & Harsch, N. (1992). Phantom flashbulbs: False recollections of hearing the news about *Challenger.* In E. Winograd & U. Neisser (Eds.), *Affect and accuracy in recall: Studies of "flashbulb" memories* (pp. 9-31). New York: Cambridge University Press.

Neitz, J., Neitz, M., & Kainz, M. (1996). Visual pigment gene structure and the severity of color vision defects. *Science, 274,* 801–804.

Neitz, M., & Neitz, J. (1995). Numbers and ratios of visual pigment genes for normal red-green color vision. *Science, 267,* 1013–1016.

Nelson, J. C. (1991). Current status of tricyclic antidepressants in psychiatry: Their pharmacology and clinical applications. *Journal of Clinical Psychiatry, 52,* 193–200.

Nelson, J. C. (1997). Safety and tolerability of the new antidepressants. *Journal of Clinical Psychiatry, 58*(6, Suppl.), 26–31.

Nelson, K. (1973). Structure and strategy in learning to talk. *Monographs of the Society for Research in Child Development, 38*(1–2, Serial No. 149).

Nelson, M., Saykin, A., Flashman, I., & Riordan, H. (1998). Hippocampal volume reduction in schizophrenia as assessed by magnetic resonance imaging: A meta-analytic study. *Archives of General Psychiatry, 55,* 430–455.

Nemeth, M. (1994). An alarming trend: suicide among the young has quadrupled. *Maclean's 107*(44), 14–16.

Nesbitt, M. N. (1990). The value of recombinant inbred strains in the genetic analysis of behavior. In D. Goldowitz, D. Wahlsten, et al. (Eds.), *Techniques in the behavioral and neural sciences: Vol. 8. Techniques for the genetic analysis of brain and behavior: Focus on the mouse* (pp. 141–146). Amsterdam: Elsevier.

Ness, R., Grisso, J., Hirschinger, N., Markovic, N., Shaw, L., Day, N., & Kline, J. (1999). Cocaine and tobacco use and the risk of spontaneous abortion. *New England Journal of Medicine, 340,* 333–339.

Neugarten, B. L. (1968). The awareness of middle age. In B. Neugarten (Ed.), *Middle age and aging* (pp. 93–98). Chicago: University of Chicago Press.

Neugarten, B. L. (1976). The psychology of aging: An overview. *Master lectures on developmental psychology*. Washington, DC: American Psychological Association.

Neugarten, B. L. (1982). Must everything be a midlife crisis? In T. H. Carr & H. E. Fitzgerald (Eds.), *Human development 82/83* (pp. 162–163). (Reprinted from Prime Time, February 1980, 45–48). Guilford, CT: Dushkin.

Neville, H., Bavelier, D., Corina, D., Rauschecker, J., Karni, A., Lalwani, A., Braun, A., Clark, V., Jezzard, P., & Turner, R. (1998). Cerebral organization for language in deaf and hearing subjects: Biological constraints and effects of experience. *Proceedings of the National Academy of Sciences, 95,* 922–929.

Newcomb, M. D. (1997). Psychosocial predictors and consequences of drug use: A developmental perspective within a prospective study. *Journal of Addictive Diseases, 95,* 922–929.

Newcomb, M. D., & Felix-Ortiz, M. (1992). Multiple protective and risk factors for drug use and abuse: Cross-sectional and prospective findings. *Journal of Personality and Social Psychology, 63,* 280–296.

Newcomb, T. M. (1956). The prediction of interpersonal attraction. *American Psychologist, 11,* 575–587.

Newell, A., & Simon, H. A. (1972). *Human problem solving*. Englewood Cliffs, NJ: Prentice-Hall.

Newport, F. (1993). Americans now more likely to say: women have it harder than men. *Gallup Poll Monthly*, No. 337, 11–18.

Newtson, R., & Keith, P. (1997). Single women in later life. In J. Coyle (Ed.), *Handbook on women and aging* (pp. 385–399). Westport, CT: Greenwood Press.

Ng, S. H. (1990). Androcentric coding of *man* and *his* in memory by language users. *Journal of Exprimental Social Psychology, 26,* 455–464.

Nguyen, P. V., Abel, T., & Kandel, E. R. (1994). Requirement of a critical period of transcription for induction of a late phase of LTP. *Science, 265,* 1104–1107.

Nickerson, R. S., & Adams, M. J. (1979). Long-term memory for a common object. *Cognitive Psychology, 11,* 287–307.

Nicol, S. E., & Gottesman, I. I. (1983). Clues to the genetics and neurobiology of schizophrenia. *American Scientist, 71,* 398–404.

Nisbett, R. E., & Wilson, T. D. (1977). The halo effect: Evidence for unconscious alteration of judgments. *Journal of Personality and Social Psychology, 35,* 250–256.

Nishimura, H., Hashikawa, K., Doi, K., Iwaki, T., Watanabe, Y., Kusuoka, H., Nishimura, T., & Kubo, T. (1999). Sign language "heard" in the auditory cortex. *Nature, 397,*116.

Nogrady, H., McConkey, K. M., & Perry, C. (1985). Enhancing visual memory: Trying hypnosis, trying imagination, and trying again. *Journal of Abnormal Psychology, 94,* 195–204.

Nordentoft, M., Lou, H. C., Hansen, D., Nim, J., Pryds, O., Rubin, P., & Hemmingsen, R. (1996). Intrauterine growth retardation and premature delivery: The influence of maternal smoking and psychosocial factors. *American Journal of Public Health, 86,* 347–354.

Novello, A. C. (1990). The Surgeon General's 1990 report on the health benefits of smoking cessation: Executive summary. *Morbidity and Mortality Weekly Report, 39* (No. RR-12).

Nowak, M. A., & McMichael, A. J. (1995). How HIV defeats the immune system. *Scientific American, 273,* 58–65.

Noyes, R., Jr., Burrows, G. D., Reich, J. H., Judd, F. K., Garvey, M. J., Norman, T. R., Cook, B. L., & Marriott, P. (1996). Diazepam versus alprazolam for the treatment of panic disorder. *Journal of Clinical Psychiatry, 57,* 344–355.

Noyes, R., Jr., Garvey, M. J., Cook, B. L., & Samuelson, L. (1989). Problems with tricyclic antidepressant use in patients with panic disorder or agoraphobia: Results of a naturalistic follow-up study. *Journal of Clinical Psychiatry, 50,* 163–169.

Nyberg, L., Cabeza, R., & Tulving, E. (1996a). PET studies of encoding and retrieval: The HERA model. *Psychonomic Bulletin and Review, 2,* 134–147.

Nyberg, L., McIntoch, A., Cabeza, R., Harib, R., Houle, S., & Tulving, E. (1996b). General and specific brain regions involved in encoding and retrieval of events: What, where, and when. *Proceedings of the National Academy of Science, 93,* 11280–11285.

Oatley, K., & Jenkins, J. M. (1992). Human emotions: Function and dysfunction. *Annual Review of Psychology, 43,* 55–85.

O'Brien, C. P. (1996). Recent developments in the pharmacotherapy of substance abuse. *Journal of Consulting and Clinical Psychology, 64,* 677–686.

O'Brien, C. P., Childress, A. R., McLellan, A. T., & Ehrman, R. (1992). Classical conditioning in drug-dependent humans. *Annals of the New York Academy of Sciences, 654,* 400–415.

Ohzawa, I., DeAngelis, G. C., & Freeman, R. D. (1990). Stereoscopic depth discrimination in the visual cortex: Neurons ideally suited as disparity detectors. *Science, 249,* 1037–1041.

Olds, J. (1956). Pleasure centers in the brain. *Scientific American, 195,* 105–116.

O'Leary, A. (1990). Stress, emotion, and human immune function. *Psychological Bulletin, 108,* 363–382.

O'Leary, K. D., & Smith, D. A. (1991). Marital interactions. *Annual Review of Psychology, 42,* 191–212.

Oliner, S. P., & Oliner P. M. (1988). *The altruistic personality: Rescuers of Jews in Nazi Europe*. New York: Free Press.

Oliver, J. E. (1993). Intergenerational transmission of child abuse: Rates, research, and clinical implications. *American Journal of Psychiatry, 150,* 1315–1324.

Olweus, D. (1987). Testosterone and adrenaline: Aggressive antisocial behavior in normal adolescent males. In S. A. Mednick, T. E. Moffitt, & S. A. Stack (Eds.), *The causes of crime: New biological approaches* (pp. 263–282). Cambridge, England: Cambridge University Press.

Orne, M. (1983, December 12). Hypnosis "useful in medicine, dangerous in court." *U.S. News & World Report*, pp. 67–68.

Ostrom, T. M., Carpenter, S. L., Sedikides, C., & Li, F. (1993). Differential processing of in-group and out-group information. *Journal of Personality and Social Psychology, 64,* 21–34.

Otto, M. W., Pollack, M. H., Sachs, G. S., Reiter, S. R., Meltzer-Brody, S., & Rosenbaum, J. F. (1993). Discontinuation of benzodiazepine treatment: Efficacy of cognitive-behavioral therapy for patients with panic disorder. *American Journal of Psychiatry, 150,* 1485–1490.

Overmeier, J. B. & Seligman, M. E. P. (1967). Effects of inescapable shock upon subsequent escape and avoidance responding. *Journal of Comparative and Physiological Psychology, 67,* 28–33.

Page, S. (1999). Accommodating persons with AIDS: Acceptance and rejection in rental situations. *Journal of Applied Social Psychology, 29,* 261–270.

Panksepp, J. (1992). A critical role for "affective neuroscience" in resolving what is basic about basic emotions. *Psychological Review, 99,* 554–560.

Panksepp, J., Knutson, B., & Pruitt, D. L. (1998). Toward a neuroscience of emotion: The epigenetic foundations of emotional development. In M. F. Mascolo, S. Griffin, et al. (Eds.), *What develops in emotional development: Emotions, personality, and psychotherapy* (pp. 53–84). New York: Plenum Press.

Papalia, D., & Bielby, D. D. (1974). Cognitive functioning in middle and old age adults. *Human Development, 17,* 424–443.

Pappas, T. N., Melendez, R. L., & Debas, H. T. (1989). Gastric distension is a physiologic satiety signal in the dog. *Digestive Diseases and Sciences, 34,* 1489–1493.

Park, B. (1986). A method for studying the development of impressions of real people. *Journal of Personality and Social Psychology, 51,* 907–917.

Park, B., & Judd, C. M. (1990). Measures and models of perceived group variability. *Journal of Personality and Social Psychology, 59,* 173–191.

Park, K. A., & Waters, E. (1989). Security of attachment and preschool friendships. *Child Development, 60,* 1076–1081.

Parke, R. D. (1977). Some effects of punishment on children's behavior—revisited. In E. M. Hetherington, E. M. Ross, & R. D. Parke (Eds.), *Contemporary readings in child psychology.* New York: McGraw-Hill.

Parker, G. H. (1922). *Smell, taste, and allied senses in the vertebrates.* Philadelphia: Lippincott.

Parkinson, W. L., & Weingarten, H. P. (1990). Dissociative analysis of ventromedial hypothalamic obesity syndrome. *American Journal of Physiology, 259,* 829–835.

Parloff, M. B., London, P., & Wolfe, B. (1986). Individual psychotherapy and behavior change. *Annual Review of Psychology, 37,* 321–349.

Parrott, A. C. (1993). Cigarette smoking: Effects upon self-rated stress and arousal over the day. *Addictive Behaviors, 18,* 389–395.

Partinen, M., Hublin, C., Kaprio, J. Koskenvuo, M., & Guilleminault, C. (1994). Twin studies in narcolepsy. *Sleep, 17,* S13–S16.

Pascual-Leone, A., Dhuna, A., Altafullah, I., & Anderson, D. C. (1990). Cocaine-induced seizures. *Neurology, 40,* 404–407.

Pascual-Leone, A., & Torres, F. (1993). Plasticity of the sensorimotor cortex representation of the reading finger in Braille readers. *Brain, 116,* 39–52.

Pattison, E. M. (1982). The concept of alcoholism as a syndrome. In E. M. Pattison (Ed.), *Selection of treatment for alcoholics.* New Brunswick, NJ: Rutgers Center of Alcohol Studies.

Paul, G. L., & Lentz, R. J. (1977). *Psychosocial treatment of chronic mental patients.* Cambridge, MA: Harvard University Press.

Paunonen, S. V., Keinonen, M., Trzebinski, J., Forsterling, F., Grishenko-Roze, N., Kouznetsova, L., & Chan, D. W. (1996). The structure of personality in six cultures. *Journal of Cross-Cultural Psychology, 27,* 339–353.

Paunonen, S. V., Zeidner, M., Engvik, H. A., Oosterveld, P, & Maliphant, R. (2000). The nonverbal assessment of personality in five cultures. *Journal of Cross Cultural Psychology, 31*(2), 220–239.

Pavlov, I. P. (1960). *Conditioned reflexes: An investigation of the physiological activity of the cerebral cortex* (G. V. Anrep, Trans.). New York: Dover. (Original translation published 1927).

Pedersen, D. M., & Wheeler, J. (1983). The Müller-Lyer illusion among Navajos. *Journal of Social Psychology, 121,* 3–6.

Pederson, D. R., Moran, G., Sitko, C., Campbell, K., Ghesquire, K., & Acton, H. (1990). Maternal sensitivity and the security of infant-mother attachment: A Q-sort study. *Child Development, 61,* 1974–1983.

Peele, S. (1992). Alcoholism, politics, and bureaucracy: The consensus against controlled-drinking therapy in America. *Addictive Behaviors, 17,* 49–62.

Penfield, W. (1969). Consciousness, memory, and man's conditioned reflexes. In K. Pribram (Ed.), *On the biology of learning* (pp. 129–168). New York: Harcourt Brace Jovanovich.

Penfield, W. (1975). *The mystery of the mind: A critical study of consciousness and the human brain.* Princeton, NJ: Princeton University Press.

Perls, F. S. (1969). *Gestalt therapy verbatim.* Lafayette, CA: Real People Press.

Perry, P. (1996). Pharmacotherapy for major depression with melancholic features: Relative efficacy of tricyclic versus selective serotonin reuptake inhibitor antidepressants. *Journal of Affective Disorders, 39,* 1–6.

Pert, C. B., Snowman, A. M., & Snyder, S. H. (1974). Localization of opiate receptor binding in presynaptic membranes of rat brain. *Brain Research, 70,* 184–188.

Peters, M. (1995a). Does brain size matter? A reply to Rushton and Ankney. *Canadian Journal of Experimental Psychology, 49,* 570–576.

Peters, M. (1995b). Race differences in brain size: Things are not as clear as they seem to be. *American Psychologist, 50,* 947–948.

Petersen, A.C., Compas, B.E., Brooks-Gunn, J., Stemmier, M., Ey, S., & Grant, K.E. (1993). Depression in adolescence. *American Psychologist, 48,* 155–168.

Peterson, L. R., & Peterson, M. J. (1959). Short-term retention of individual verbal items. *Journal of Experimental Psychology, 58,* 193–198.

Petitto, L. A., & Marentette, P. R. (1991). Babbling in the manual mode: Evidence for the ontogeny of language. *Science, 251,* 1493–1496.

Petty, R. E., & Wegener, D. T. (1998). Attitude change: Multiple roles for persuasion variables. In D. T. Gilbert, S. T. Fiske, & G. Lindzey (Eds), *The handbook of social psychology* (4th ed., Vol. 1), (pp. 323–390). New York: McGraw-Hill.

Petty, R. E., Wegener, D. T., & Fabrigar, L. R. (1997). Attitudes and attitude change. *Annual Review of Psychology, 48,* 609–647.

Phillips, K., Fulker, D. W., Carey, G., & Nagoshi, C. T. (1988). Direct marital assortment for cognitive and personality variables. *Behavioral Genetics, 18*, 347–356.

Phillips, S. D., & Blustein, D. L. (1994). Readiness for career choices: Planning, exploring, and deciding. *The Career Development Quarterly, 43*, 63–75.

Phillips, S. T., & Ziller, R. C. (1997). Toward a theory and measure of the nature of nonprejudice. *Journal of Personality and Social Psychology, 72*, 420–434.

Piaget, J. (1960). *The child's conception of physical causality.* Patterson, NJ: Littlefield, Adams.

Piaget, J. (1963a). *The child's conception of the world.* Patterson, NJ: Littlefield, Adams.

Piaget, J. (1963b). *Psychology of intelligence.* Patterson, NJ: Littlefield, Adams.

Piaget, J. (1964). *Judgment and reasoning in the child.* Patterson, NJ: Littlefield, Adams.

Piaget, J. (1972). Intellectual evolution from adolescence to adulthood. *Human Development*, 15, 1–12.

Piaget, J., & Inhelder, B. (1969). *The psychology of the child.* New York: Basic Books.

Pich, E. M., Pagliusi, S. R., Tessari, M., Talabot-Ayer, D., Van Huijsduijnen, R. H., & Chiamulera, C. (1997). Common neural substrates for the addictive properties of nicotine and cocaine. *Science, 275*, 83–86.

Pigott, T. (1996). OCD: Where the serotonin selectivity story begins. *Journal of Clinical Psychiatry, 57*(6, Suppl.), 11–20.

Pihl, R. O., Lau, M. L., & Assaad, J-M. (1997). Aggressive disposition, alcohol, and aggression. *Aggressive Behavior, 23*, 11–18.

Pihl, R. O., Peterson, J. B., & Finn, P. R. (1990a). Inherited predisposition to alcoholism. *Journal of Abnormal Psychology, 99*(3), 291–301.

Pihl, R. O., Peterson, J. B., & Finn, P. R. (1990b). An heuristic model for the inherited predisposition to alcohol. *Psychology of Addictive Behaviors, 4*(1), 12–25.

Pilcher, J. J., & Huffcutt, A. I. (1996). Effects of sleep deprivation on performance: A meta analysis. *Sleep, 19*, 318–326.

Pillemer, D. B. (1990). Clarifying the flashbulb memory concept: Comment on McCloskey, Wible, and Cohen (1988). *Journal of Experimental Psychology: General, 119*, 92–96.

Pillow, D. R., Zautra, A. J., & Sandler, I. (1996). Major life events and minor stressors: Identifying mediational links in the stress process. *Journal of Personality and Social Psychology, 70*, 381–394.

Pinel, J. P. J. (1993). *Biopsychology* (2nd ed.). Boston: Allyn & Bacon.

Plomin, R. (1989). Environment and genes: Determinants of behavior. *American Psychologist, 44*, 105–111.

Plomin, R. (1990). The role of inheritance in behavior. *Science, 248*, 183–188.

Plomin, R., & Bergeman, C. S. (1991). The nature of nurture: Genetic influence on "environmental" measures. *Behavioral and Brain Sciences, 14*, 373–427.

Plomin, R., DeFries, J. C., & Fulker, D. W. (1988). *Nature and nurture during infancy and early childhood.* New York: Cambridge University Press.

Plomin, R., DeFries, J. C., McClearn, G. E., & Rutter, M. (1997). *Behavioral genetics* (3rd ed.). New York: Freeman.

Plomin, R., Owen, M. J., & McGuffin, P. (1994). The genetic basis of complex human behaviors. *Science, 264*, 1733–1739.

Plomin, R., & Rende, R. (1991). Human behavioral genetics. *Annual Review of Psychology, 42*, 161–190.

Plummer, D., & Slane, S. (1996). Patterns of coping in racially stressful situations. *Journal of Black Psychology, 22*, 302–315.

Polich, J. M., Armor, D. J., & Braiker, H. B. (1981). *The course of alcoholism: Four years after treatment.* New York: Wiley.

Pomerleau, O. F., & Pomerleau, C. S. (1989). A biobehavioral perspective on smoking. In T. Ney & A. Gale (Eds.), *Smoking and human behavior* (pp. 69–93). New York: Wiley.

Porac, C. (1993). Are age trends in adult hand preference best explained by developmental shifts or generational differences? *Canadian Journal of Experimental Psychology 47*(4), 697–713.

Porter, F. L., Porges, S. W., & Marshall, R. E. (1988). Newborn pain cries and vagal tone: Parallel changes in response to circumcision. *Child Development, 59*, 495–505.

Posner, M. I. (1996, September). Attention and psychopathology. *Harvard Mental Health Letter, 13*(3), 5–6.

Postman, L., & Phillips, L. W. (1965). Short-term temporal changes in free recall. *Quarterly Journal of Experimental Psychology, 17*, 132–138.

Potts, N. L. S., Davidson, J. R. T., & Krishman, K. R. R. (1993). The role of nuclear magnetic resonance imaging in psychiatric research. *Journal of Clinical Psychiatry, 54*(12, Suppl.), 13–18.

Powell, E. (1996). *Sex on your terms.* Boston: Allyn & Bacon.

Pozzulo, J. & Lindsay, R. (1999). Elimination lineups: An improved identification procedure for child eyewitnesses. *Journal of Applied Psychology, 84*, 167–176.

Pratkanis, A. R. (1989). The cognitive representation of attitudes. In A. R. Pratkanis, S. J. Breckler, & A. G. Greenwald (Eds.), *Attitude structure and function* (pp. 71–93). Hillsdale, NJ: Erlbaum.

Pratkanis, A. R., Eskenazi, J., & Greewald, A. G. (1994). What you expect is what you believe (but not necessarily what you get): A test of the effectiveness of subliminal self-help audiotapes. *Basic and Applied Social Psychology, 15*, 251–276.

Pratt, M., & Arnold, M. L. (1995). Families tell their stories. Parenting style and family narratives of moral socialization.

Premack, D. (1971). Language in chimpanzees. *Science, 172*, 808–822.

Premack, D., & Premack, A. J. (1983). *The mind of an ape.* New York: Norton.

Prescott, C. A., & Kendler, K. S. (1999). Age at first drink and risk for alcoholism: A noncausal relation. *Alcoholism: Clinical and Experimental Research, 23*, 101–107.

Prescott, C. A., & Kendler, K. S. (1999). Genetic and environmental contributions to alcohol abuse and dependence in a population-based sample of male twins. *American Journal of Psychiatry, 148*, 52–56.

Pressley, M. & Woloshyn, V. (Eds). (1997). *Cognitive strategies that really improve children's learning.* Brookline Press.

Pribor, E. F., & Dinwiddie, S. H. (1992). Psychiatric correlates of incest in childhood. *American Journal of Psychiatry, 148*, 52–56.

Price, R. A., Cadoret, R. J., Stunkard, A. J., & Troughton, E. (1987). Genetic contributions to human fatness: An adoption study. *American Journal of Psychiatry, 144,* 1003–1008.

Price, R. A., Stunkard, A. J., Ness, R., Wadden, T., Heshka, S., Kanders, B., & Cormillot, A. (1990). Childhood onset (age less than 10) obesity has a high familial risk. *International Journal of Obesity, 14,* 185–195.

Prien, R. F., & Kocsis, J. H. (1995). Long-term treatment of mood disorders. In F. Bloom & D. Kupfer (Eds.), *Psychopharmocology: The fourth generation of progress* (pp. 1067–1079). New York: Raven.

Prien, R. F., Kupfer, D. J., Mansky, P. A., Small, J. G., Tuason, V. B., Voss, C. B., & Johnson, W. E. (1984). Drug therapy in the prevention of recurrences in unipolar and bipolar affective disorders. *Archives of General Psychiatry, 41,* 1096–1104.

Priest, R. F., & Sawyer, J. (1967). Proximity and peership: Bases of balance in interpersonal attraction. *American Journal of Sociology, 72,* 633–649.

Prinz, P. N., Vitiello, M. V., Raskind, M. A., & Thorpy, M. J. (1990). Geriatrics: Sleep disorders and aging. *New England Journal of Medicine, 323,* 520–526.

Provine, R. R. (1996, January/February). Laughter. *American Scientist, 84,* 38–45.

Provins, K. (1997). Handedness and speech: A critical reappraisal of the role of genetic and environmental factors in the cerebral lateralization of function. *Psychological Review, 104,* 544–571.

Pushkar, D. , Etezadi, J., Andres, D., Arbuckle, T., Schwartzman, A., & Chaikelson, J. (1999). Models of intelligence in late life: Comment on Hultsch et al. *Psychology and Agining, 14,* 520–527.

Putnam, F. W. (1989). *Diagnosis and treatment of multiple personality disorder.* New York: Guilford Press.

Putnam, F. W. (1992). Altered states: Peeling away the layers of a multiple personality. *The Sciences, 32,* 30–36.

Putnam, F. W., Guroff, J. J., Silberman, E. K., Barban, L., & Post, R. M. (1986). The clinical phenomenology of multiple personality disorder: Review of 100 recent cases. *Journal of Clinical Psychiatry, 47,* 285–293.

Quadrel, M. J., Fischhoff, B., & Davis, W. (1993). Adolescent (In)vulnerability. *American Psychologist, 48,* 102–116.

Quattrone, G. A. (1986). On the perception of a group's variability. In S. Worchel & W. Austin (Eds.), *The psychology of intergroup relations* (Vol. 2, pp. 25–48). Chicago: Nelson-Hall.

Rachman, S. J., & Wilson, G. T. (1980). *The effects of psychological therapy* (2nd ed.). New York: Pergamon.

Rahe, R. J., Meyer, M., Smith, M., Kjaer, G., & Holmes, T. H. (1964). Social stress and illness onset. *Journal of Psychosomatic Research, 8,* 35–44.

Raichle, M. E. (1994a). Images of the mind: Studies with modern imaging techniques. *Annual Review of Psychology, 45,* 333–356.

Raichle, M. E. (1994b). Visualizing the mind. *Scientific American, 270,* 58–64.

Ralph, M. R. (1989, November/December). The rhythm maker: Pinpointing the master clock in mammals. *The Sciences, 29,* 40–45.

Ramsay, D. S., & Woods, S. C. (1997). Biological consequences of drug administration: Implications for acute and chronic tolerance. *Psychological Review, 104,* 170–193.

Randi, J. (1980). *Flim-Flam: The truth about unicorns, parapsychology, and other delusions.* New York: Lippincott & Crowell.

Rao, S. C., Rainer, G., & Miller, E. K. (1997). Integration of what and where in the primate prefrontal cortex. *Science, 276,* 821–824.

Rapoport, J. L. (1989). The biology of obsessions and compulsions. *Scientific American, 260,* 83–89.

Rasmussen, S. A., & Eisen, J. L. (1990). Epidemiology of obsessive compulsive disorder. *Journal of Clinical Psychiatry, 51*(2, Suppl.), 10–13.

Rasmussen, S. A., & Eisen, J. L. (1992). The epidemiology and differential diagnosis of obsessive compulsive disorder. *Journal of Clinical Psychiatry, 53*(4, Suppl.), 4–10.

Rasmussen, S. A., Eisen, J. L., & Pato, M. T. (1993). Current issues in the pharmcologic management of obsessive compulsive disorder. *Journal of Clinical Psychiatry, 54*(6, Suppl.), 4–9.

Rauch, S. L., Jenike, M. A., Alpert, N. M., Baer, L., Breiter, H. C. R., Savage, C. R., & Fischman, A. J. (1994). Regional cerebral blood flow measured during symptom provocation in obsessive-compulsive disorder using oxygen 15-labeled carbon dioxide and positron emission tomography. *Archives of General Psychiatry, 51,* 62–70.

Regestein, Q. R., & Monk, T. H. (1991). Is the poor sleep of shift workers a disorder? *American Journal of Psychiatry, 148,* 1487–1493.

Reiman, E. M., Fusselman, M. J., Fox, P. T., & Raichle, M. E. (1989). Neuroanatomical correlates of anticipatory anxiety. *Science, 243,* 1071–1074.

Reinke, B. J., Ellicott, A. M., Harris, R. L., & Hancock, E. (1985). Timing of psychosocial changes in women's lives. *Human Development, 28,* 259–280.

Reis, H. T., Wilson, I. M., Monestere, C., Bernstein, S., Clark, K., Seidl, E., Franco, M., Gioioso, E., Freeman, L., & Radoane, K. (1990). What is smiling is beautiful and good. *European Journal of Social Psychology, 20,* 259–267.

Reisberg, D., Heuer, F., McLean, J., & O'Shaughnessy, M. (1988). The quantity, not the quality, of affect predicts memory vividness. *Bulletin of the Psychonomic Society, 26,* 100–103.

Reisenzein, R. (1986). A structural equation analysis of Weiner's attribution-affect model of helping behavior. *Journal of Personality and Social Psychology, 50,* 1123–1133.

Renzetti, C. M., & Curran, D. J. (1992). *Women, men, and society.* Boston: Allyn & Bacon.

Rescorla, R. A. (1967). Pavlovian conditioning and its proper control procedures. *Psychological Review, 74,* 71–80.

Rescorla, R. A. (1968). Probability of shock in the presence and absence of CS in fear conditioning. *Journal of Comparative and Physiological Psychology, 66,* 1–5.

Restak, R. (1988). *The mind.* Toronto: Bantam.

Restak, R. (1993, September/October). Brain by design. *The Sciences,* 27–33.

Reyner, A., & Horne, J. A. (1995). Gender- and age-related differences in sleep determined by home-recorded sleep logs and actimetry from 400 adults. *Sleep, 18,* 127–134.

Reznick, J. S. (1999). Can prenatal caffeine exposure affect behavioral inhibition? *Review of General Psychology, 3*(2), 118–132.

Rhodes, N., & Wood, W. (1992). Self-esteem and intelligence affect influenceability: The medicating role of message reception. *Psychological Bulletin, 111,* 156–171.

Rice, F. P. (1992). *Intimate relationships, marriages, and families.* Mountain View, CA: Mayfield.

Rice, P. L. (1987). *Stress and health: Principles and practice for coping and wellness.* Monterey, CA: Brooks/Cole.

Riedel, G. (1996). Function of metabotropic glutamate receptors in learning and memory. *Trends in Neurosciences, 19,* 219–224.

Robberson, M. R., & Rogers, R. W. (1988). Beyond fear appeals: Negative and positive persuasive appeals to health and self-esteem. *Journal of Applied Social Psychology, 18,* 277–287.

Robertson, G. L. (1983). Thirst and vasopressin function in normal and disordered states of water balance. *Journal of Laboratory and Clinical Medicine, 101,* 351–371.

Robins, R. W., Gosling, S. D., & Craik, K. H. (1999). An empirical analysis of trends in psychology. *American Psychologists, 54,* 117–128.

Roche, A. F., & Davila, G. H. (1972). Late adolescent growth in stature. *Pediatrics, 50,* 874–880.

Rodin, J. (1981). Current status of the internal-external hypothesis for obesity: What went wrong? *American Psychologist, 36,* 361–372.

Rodin, J. (1985). Insulin levels, hunger, and food intake: An example of feedback loops in body weight regulation. *Health Psychology, 4,* 1–24.

Rodin, J. (1986). Aging and health: Effects of the sense of control. *Science, 233,* 1271–1276.

Rodin, J., & Salovey, P. (1989). Health psychology. *Annual Review of Psychology, 40,* 533–579.

Rodin, J., & Wing, R. R. (1988). Behavioral factors in obesity. *Diabetes/Metabolism Reviews, 4,* 701–725.

Rodin, J., Slochower, J., & Fleming, B. (1977). The effects of degree of obesity, age of onset, and energy deficit on external responsiveness. *Journal of Comparative and Physiological Psychology, 91,* 586–597.

Rodin, J., Wack, J., Ferrannini, E., & DeFronzo, R. A. (1985). Effect of insulin and glucose on feeding behavior. *Metabolism, 34,* 826–831.

Roediger, H.L., III. (1991). They read an article? A commentary on the everyday memory controversy. *American Psychologist, 46,* 37–40.

Roediger, H. L., III, & McDermott, K. B. (1995). Creating false memories: Remembering words not presented in lists. *Journal of Experimental Psychology: Learning, Memory, and Cognition, 21,* 803–814.

Roehrich, L., & Kinder, B. N. (1991). Alcohol expectancies and male sexuality: Review and implications for sex therapy. *Journal of Sex and Marital Therapy, 17,* 45–54.

Rogers, C. R. (1951). *Client-centered therapy: Its current practice, implications, and theory.* Boston: Houghton Mifflin.

Rogers, C. R. (1959). A theory of therapy, personality, and interpersonal relationships, as developed in the client-centered framework. In S. Koch (Ed.), *Psychology: A study of a science, Vol. III. Formulations of the person and the social context* (pp. 184–256). New York: McGraw-Hill.

Rogers, C. R. (1961). *On becoming a person: A therapist's view of psychotherapy.* Boston: Houghton Mifflin.

Rogers, C. R. (1977). The case of Mary Jane Tilden. In S. J. Morse & R. I. Watson, Jr. (Eds.), *Psychotherapies: A comparative casebook* (pp. 197–222). New York: Holt, Rinehart & Winston.

Rogers, C. R. (1981). Notes on Rollo May. *Perspectives, 2*(1), 16.

Rogers, M. P., & Reich, P. (1988). On the health consequences of bereavement. *New England Journal of Medicine, 319,* 510–512.

Rogers, P. J. (1990). Why a palatability construct is needed. *Appetite, 14,* 167–170.

Rogoff, B., & Mistry, J. (1985). Memory development in cultural context. In M. Pressley & C. Brainerd (Eds.) *The cognitive side of memory development.* New York: Springer-Verlag.

Roik, R. (2000, June 22). Dad pleads guilty in crash that killed daughter. *Ottawa Sun,* p. 5.

Roland, P. E., & Gulyás, B. (1994). Visual imagery and visual representation. *Trends in Neurosciences, 17,* 281–287.

Rollins, B. C., & Feldman, H. (1970). Marital satisfaction over the family life cycle. *Journal of Marriage and the Family, 32,* 20–28.

Roorda, A., & Williams, D. R. (1999). The arrangement of the three cone classes in the human eye. *Nature, 397,* 520–521.

Rosch, E. H. (1973). Natural categories. *Cognitive Psychology, 4,* 328–350.

Rosch, E. H. (1978). Principles of categorization. In E. H. Rosch & B. Lloyd (Eds.), *Cognition and categorization.* Hillsdale, NJ: Erlbaum.

Rosekind, M. R. (1992). The epidemiology and occurrence of insomnia. *Journal of Clinical Psychiatry, 53*(6, suppl.), 4–6.

Rosen, R. C., Rosekind, M., Rosevear, C., Cole, W. E., & Dement, W. C. (1993). Physician education in sleep and sleep disorders: A national survey of U.S. medical schools. *Sleep, 16,* 249–254.

Rosenbaum, J. F., Biederman, J., Pollock, R. A., & Hirshfeld, D. R. (1994). The etiology of social phobia. *Journal of Clinical Psychiatry, 55*(6, Suppl.), 10–16.

Rosenbaum, M. E. (1986). The repulsion hypothesis: On the nondevelopment of relationships. *Journal of Personality and Social Psychology, 51,* 1156–1166.

Rosenheck, R., Cramer, J., Xu, W., et al, (1997). A comparison of clozapine and haloperidol in hospitalized patients with refractory schizophrenia. *New England Journal of Medicine, 337,* 809–815.

Rosenthal, A. M. (1964). *Thirty-eight witnesses.* New York: McGraw-Hill.

Rosenthal, N. E., Carpenter, C. J., James, S. P., Parry, B. L., Rogers, S. L. B., & Wehr, T. A.. (1986). Seasonal affective disorder in children and adolescents. *American Journal of Psychiatry, 143,* 356–358.

Rosenthal, N. E., Sack, D. A., Carpenter, C. J., et al. (1985). Antidepressant effects of light in seasonal affective disorder. *American Journal of Psychiatry, 142,* 163–170.

Rosenzweig, M. R. (1961). Auditory localization. *Scientific American, 205,* 132–142.

Ross, C. A., Miller, S. D., Reagor, P., Bjornson, L., Fraser, G. A., & Anderson, G. (1990). Structured interview data on 102 cases of multiple personality disorder from four centers. *American Journal of Psychiatry, 147,* 596–601.

Ross, C. A., Norton, G. R., & Wozney, K. (1989). Multiple personality disorder: An analysis of 236 cases. *Canadian Journal of Psychiatry, 34,* 413–418.

Ross, L. (1977). The intuitive psychologist and his shortcomings: Distortions in the attribution process. In L. Berkowitz (Ed.), *Advances in experimental social psychology* (Vol. 10). New York: Academic Press.

Roth, D. L., Wiebe, D. J., Filligim, R. B., & Shay, K. A. (1989). Life events, fitness, hardiness, and health: A simultaneous analysis of proposed stress-resistance effects. *Journal of Personality and Social Psychology, 57,* 136–142.

Roth, W. T., Margraf, J., Ehlers, A., Taylor, B., Maddock, R. J., Davies, S., Argras, W. S. (1992). Stress test reactivity in panic disorder. *Archives of General Psychiatry, 49,* 301–310.

Rotter, J. B. (1966). Generalized expectancies for internal versus external control of reinforcement. *Psychological Monographs, 80*(1, Whole No. 609).

Rotter, J. B. (1971, June). External control and internal control. *Psychology Today*, pp. 37–42, 58–59.

Rotter, J. B. (1990). Internal versus external control of reinforcement: A case history of a variable. *American Psychologist, 45,* 489–493.

Rotton, J., Frey, J., Barry, T., Milligan, M., & Fitzpatrick, M. (1979). The air pollution experience and physical aggression. *Journal of Applied Social Psychology, 9,* 397–412.

Rovee-Collier, C. K., & Lipsett, L. P. (1982). Learning, adaptation, and memory in the newborn. In P. Stratton (Ed.), *Psychobiology of the human newborn.* New York: Wiley.

Rozin, P., & Zellner, D. (1985). The role of Pavlovian conditioning in the acquisition of food likes and dislikes. *Annals of the New York Academy of Sciences, 443,* 189–202.

Rubenstein, C. (1982, July). Psychology's fruit flies. *Psychology Today*, pp. 83–84.

Ruggero, M. A. (1992). Responses to sound of the basilar membrane of the mammalian cochlea. *Current Opinion in Neurobiology, 2,* 449–456.

Rushton, J. P., Fulker, D. W., Neale, M. C., Nias, D. K. B., & Eysenck, H. J. (1986). Altruism and aggression: The heritability of individual differences. *Journal of Personality and Social Psychology, 50,* 1192–1198.

Rushton, P. J. (1991). Mongoloid-caucasoid differences in brain size from military samples. *Intelligence, 15,* 351–359.

Rushton, P. J. (1992). Contributions to the history of psychology: XC evolutionary biology and heritable traits (with reference to oriental-white-black differences). *Psychological Reports, 71,* 811–821.

Russell, J.A. (1994). Is there universal recognition of emotion from facial expression? A review of the cross-cultural studies. *Psychological Bulletin, 115,* 102–141.

Russell, J.A., Suzuki, N., & Ishida, N. (1993). Canadian, Greek, and Japanese freely produced emotion labels for facial expressions. *Motivation and Emotion* 17(4):337–351.

Sackeim, H. A. (1992). The cognitive effects of electroconvulsive therapy. In W. H. Moos, E. R. Gamzu, & L. J. Thal (Eds.), *Cognitive disorders: Pathophysiology and treatment.* New York: Marcel Dekker.

Sackeim, H. A., Gur, R. C., & Saucy, M. (1978). Emotions are expressed more intensely on the left side of the face. *Science, 202,* 434–436.

Sackeim, H.A., Prudic, J., Devanand, D.P., Kiersky, J.E., Fitzsimmons, L., Moody, B.J., McElhiney, M.C., Coleman, E.A., & Settembrino, J.M. (1993). Effects of stimulus intensity and electrode placement on the efficacy and cognitive effects of electroconvulsive therapy. *New England Journal of Medicine, 328,* 839–846.

Sakai, K., & Miyashita, Y. (1994). Visual imagery: an interaction between memory retrieval and focal attention. *Trends in Neurosciences, 17,* 287–289.

Salama, A. A. A., & England, R. D. (1990). A case study: Schizophrenia and tactile hallucinations, treated with electroconvulsive therapy. *Canadian Journal of Psychiatry, 35,* 86–87.

Salovey, P., & Mayer, J. D. (1990). Emotional intelligence. *Imagination, cognition, and personality, 9,* 185–211.

Sanbonmatsu, D. M., & Fazio, R. H. (1990). The role of attitudes in memory-based decision making. *Journal of Personality and Social Psychology, 59,* 614–622.

Sandou, F., Amara, D. A., Dierich, A., LeMeur, M., Ramboz, S., Segu, L., Buhot, M-C., & Hen, R. (1994). Enhanced aggressive behavior in mice lacking 5-HT_{1B} receptor *Science, 265,* 1875–1878.

Sandross, R. (1988, December). Sexual harassment in the Fortune 500. *Working Woman*, p. 69.

Sanna, L. J., & Shotland, R. L. (1990). Valence of anticipated evaluation and social facilitation. *Journal of Experimental Social Psychology, 26,* 82–92.

Sapolsky, R. M. (1994). *Why zebras don't get ulcers: A guide to stress, stress-related diseases, and coping.* San Francisco: W.H. Freeman.

Saufley, W. H., Jr., Otaka, S. R., & Bavaresco, J. L. (1985). Context effects: Classroom tests and context independence. *Memory and Cognition, 13,* 522–528.

Savage-Rumbaugh, E. S. (1986). *Ape language.* New York: Columbia University Press.

Savage-Rumbaugh, E. S. (1990). Language acquisition in a nonhuman species: Implications for the innateness debate. *Developmental Psychology, 26,* 599–620.

Savage-Rumbaugh, E. S., Sevcik, R. A., Brakke, K. E., & Rumbaugh, D. M. (1992). Symbols: Their communicative use, communication, and combination by bonobos (Pan paniscus). In L.P. Lipsitt & C. Rovee-Collier (Eds.). *Advances in infancy research* (Vol. 7, pp. 221–278). Norwood, NJ: Ablex.

Scarr, S., & Weinberg, R. (1976). IQ test performance of black children adopted by white families. *American Psychologist, 31,* 726–739.

Scarr, S., & Weinberg, R. A. (1986). The early childhood enterprise: Care and education of the young. *American Psychologist, 41,* 1140–1146.

Scarr, S., Pakstis, A., Katz, S., & Barker, W. (1977). Absence of a relationship between degree of White ancestry and intellectual skills within a Black population. *Human Genetics, 39,* 69–86.

Scattolon, Y., & Stoppard, J. (1999). "Getting on with life": Women's experiences and ways of coping with depression. *Canadian Psychology, 40,* 205–219.

Schab, F. R. (1990). Odors and the remembrance of things past. *Journal of Experimental Psychology: Learning, Memory, and Cognition, 16,* 648–655.

Schachter , D., Norman, K., & Koutstaal, W. (1998). The cognitive neuroscience of constructive memory. *Annual Review of Psychology, 49,* 289–318.

Schachter, S., & Singer, J. E. (1962). Cognitive, social, and physiological determinants of emotional state. *Psychological Review, 69,* 379–399.

Schaie, K. W. (1990). Late life potential and cohort differences in mental abilities. In M. Perlmutter (Ed.), *Late life potential* (pp. 43–61). Washington, DC: Gerontological Society.

Schaie, K. W. (1993). Ageist language in psychological research. *American Psychologist, 48,* 49–51.

Schaie, K. W. (1994). The course of adult intellectual development. *American Psychologist, 49,* 304–313.

Scheier, M. F., & Carver, C. S. (1985). Optimism, coping, and health: Assessment and implications of generalized outcome expectancies. *Health Psychology, 4,* 219–247.

Scheier, M. F., & Carver, C. S. (1992). Effects of optimism on psychological and physical well-being: Theoretical overview and empirical update. *Cognitive Therapy and Research, 16,* 201–228.

Scheier, M. F., Matthews, K. A., Owens, J., Magovern, G. J., Sr., Lefebvre, R. C., Abbott, R. A., & Carver, C. S. (1989). Dispositional optimism and recovery from coronary artery bypass surgery: The beneficial effects on physical and psychological well-being. *Journal of Personality and Social Psychology, 57,* 1024–1040.

Scheier, M. F., Weintraub, J. K., & Carver, C. S. (1986). Coping with stress: Divergent strategies of optimists and pessimists. *Journal of Personality and Social Psychology, 51,* 1257–1264.

Scherer, K.R., & Wallbott, H.G. (1994). Evidence for universality and cultural variation of differential emotion response patterning. *Journal of Personality and Social Psychology, 66*, 310–328.

Scherer, K. R., Wallbott, H. G., & Summerfield, A. B. (1986). *Experiencing emotion: A cross-cultural study*. Cambridge, England: Cambridge University Press.

Schieber, M. H., & Hibbard, L. S. (1993). How somatotopic is the motor cortex hand area? *Science, 261,* 489–492.

Schiff, M., & Lewontin, R. (1986). *Education and class: The irrelevance of IQ genetic studies*. Oxford: Clarendon.

Schildkraut, J. (1970). *Neurophychopharmacology of the affective disorders*. Boston: Little, Brown.

Schiller, F. (1993). *Paul Broca: Explorer of the brain*. Oxford: Oxford University Press.

Schindler, L.W. (1988). *Understanding the immune system* (NIH Publication No. 88–529). Washington, DC: Department of Health and Human Services.

Schlaug, G., Jancke, L., Huang, Y., & Steinmetz, H. (1995). In vivo evidence of structural brain asymmetry in musicians. *Science, 267,* 699–700.

Schleifer, S. J., Keller, S. E., Camerino, M., et al. (1983). Suppression of lymphocyte stimulation following bereavement. *Journal of the American Medical Association, 250,* 374–377.

Schleifer, S. J., Keller, S. E., Siris, S. G., Davis, K. L., & Stein, M. (1985). Depression and immunity: Lymphocyte function in ambulatory depressed patients, hospitalized schizophrenic patients, and patients hospitalized for herniorraphy. *Archives of General Psychiatry, 42*, 129–133.

Schlenker, B. R., Weigold, M. F., & Hallam, J. R. (1990). Self-serving attributions in social context: Effects of self-esteem and social pressure. *Journal of Personality and Social Psychology, 58*(5), 855–863.

Schlesinger, B. (1996). The sexless years of sex rediscovered. *Journal of Gerontological Social Work, 26*(1–2), 117–131.

Schmidt, G., & Weiner, B. (1988). An attributional-affect-action theory of behavior: Replications of judgments of helping. *Personality and Social Psychology Bulletin, 14*, 610–621.

Schooler, N. R., Keith, S. J., Severe, J. B., Matthews, S. M., Bellack, A. S., Glick, I. D., Hargreaves, W. A., Kane, J. M., Ninan, P. T., Frances, A., Jacobs, M., Lieberman, J. A., Mance R., Simpson, G. M., & Woerner, M. G. (1997). Relapse and rehospitalization during maintenance treatment of schizophrenia: The effects of dose reduction and family treatment. *Archives of General Psychiatry, 54*, 453–463.

Schou, M. (1989). Lithium prophylaxis: Myths and realities. *American Journal of Psychiatry, 146*, 573–576.

Schreurs, B. G. (1989). Classical conditioning of model systems: A behavioral review. *Psychobiology, 17*, 145–155.

Schrieber, F. R. (1973). *Sybil*. Chicago: Henry Regnery.

Schuetze, P., & Zeskind, P. (1997). Relation between reported maternal caffeine consumption during pregnancy and neonatal state and heart rate. *Infant Behavior and Development, 20,* 559–562.

Schulz, R., & Tompkins, C. (1990). Life events and changes in social relationships: Examples, mechanisms, and measurement. *Journal of Social and Clinical Psychology, 9*, 69–77.

Schuman, E. M., & Madison, D. V. (1994). Locally distributed synaptic potentiation in the hippocampus. *Science, 263,* 532–536.

Schwartz, G. E. (1982). Testing the biopsychosocial model: The ultimate challenge facing behavioral medicine? *Journal of Consulting and Clinical Psychology, 50*, 1040–1052.

Schwartz, J. (1997, August 14). Gambling—the dark side. *Montreal Gazette.*

Schwartz, R. H., & Miller, N. S. (1997). MDMA (Ecstacy) and the rave: A review. *Pedriatrics, 100,* 705–708.

Schwarz, N. (1999). Self-reports: How the question shape the answers. *American Psychologist, 54*, 93–105.

Scott, J. (1996). Cognitive therapy of affective disorders: A review. *Journal of Affective Disorders, 37,* 1–11.

Scott, S. K., Young, A. W., Calder, A. J., Hellawell, D. J., Aggleton, J. P., & Johnson, M. (1997). Impaired auditory recognition of fear and anger following bilateral amygdala lesions. *Nature, 385,* 254–257.

Searles, J. S. (1988). The role of genetics in the pathogenesis of alcoholism. *Journal of Abnormal Psychology, 97*, 153–167.

Seeman, M., & Seeman, A. Z. (1992). Life strains, alienation, and drinking behavior. *Alcoholism: Clinical and Experimental Research, 16*, 199–205.

Seeman, M. V. (1994). Schizophrenia: D4 receptor elevation. What does it mean? (editorial). *Journal of Psychiatry and Neuroscience, 19*(3), 171–176.

Segal, S. J., & Fusella, V. (1970). Influence of imaged pictures and sounds on detection of visual and auditory signals. *Journal of Experimental Psychology, 83*, 458–464.

Segall, M. H., Campbell, D. T., & Herskovitz, M. J. (1966). *The influence of culture on visual perception*. Indianapolis: Bobbs-Merrill.

Segall, R. (2000). Online shrinks: The inside story. *Psychology Today, 32*(3), 38–43.

Sejnowski, T. (1997). The year of the dendrite. *Science, 275*, 178–79.

Seligman, M. E. P. (1975). *Helplessness: On depression, development and death.* San Francisco: Freeman.

Seligman, M. E. P. (1990). *Learned optimism: How to change your mind and your life.* New York: Simon & Shuster.

Seligman, M.E.P. (1991). *Learned optimism*. New York: Knopf.

Selye, H. (1956). *The stress of life*. New York: McGraw-Hill.

Selye, H. (1974). *Stress without distress*. Philadelphia: Lippincott.

Senecal, C. B., & Vallerand, R. J. (1999). Construction and validation of the Family Activities Motivation Scale/Construction et validation de l'Echelle de Motivation envers les Activites Familiales (EMAF). *European Review of Applied Psychology, 49*(3), 261–274.

Separate lives. (2000, August 29). Kensington Communications. Retrieved July 2000 from the World Wide Web: www.kensingtontv.com.

Servos, P., Engel, S., Gati, J., & Menon, R. (1999). fMRI evidence for an inverted face representation in human somatosensory cortex. *NeuroReport, 10,* 1393–1395.

Seta, J. J., Crisson, J. E., Seta, C. E., & Wang, M. A. (1989). Task performance and perceptions of anxiety: Averaging and summation in an evaluation setting. *Journal of Personality and Social Psychology, 56*, 387–396.

Seto, M., Lalumiere, M., & Kuban, M. (1999). The sexual preferences of incest offenders. *Journal of Abnormal Psychology, 108,* 267–272.

Shah, M., & Jeffery, R. W. (1991). Is obesity due to overeating and inactivity, or to a defective metabolic rate? A review. *Annals of Behavioral Medicine, 13,* 73–81.

Shatz, M. (1983). Communication. In P. H. Mussen (Ed.), *Handbook of child psychology* (Vol. 3). New York: Wiley.

Shaw, D. W., & Thoresen, C. E. (1974). Effects of modeling and desensitization in reducing dentist phobia. *Journal of Counseling Psychology, 21*, 415–420.

Shaw, J. S., III. (1996). Increases in eyewitness confidence resulting from postevent questioning. *Journal of Experimental Psychology: Applied, 2*, 126–146.

Shear, M., & Weiner, K. (1997). Psychotherapy for panic disorder. *Journal of Clinical Psychiatry, 58*(2, Suppl.), 51–58.

Sheehan, D. V. (1983). *The anxiety disease*. New York: Scribner's.

Sheehan, D. V., & Raj, A. B. (1988). Monoamine oxidase inhibitors. In C. G. Last & M. Hersen (Eds.), *Handbook of anxiety disorders* (pp. 478–506). New York: Pergamon Press.

Shepard, R. J. (1986). Exercise in coronary heart disease. *Sports Medicine*, 3, 26–49.

Shepard, R. N., & Metzler, J. (1971). Mental rotation of three-dimensional objects. Science, *171,* 701–703.

Sherbourne, C., Weels, K., & Judd, I. (1996). Functioning and well-being of patients with panic disorder. *American Journal of Psychiatry, 153,* 213–218.

Sherif, M. (1956). Experiments in group conflict. *Scientific American, 195*, 53–58.

Sherif, M. (1958). Superordinate goals in the reduction of intergroup conflict. *American Journal of Sociology, 63*, 349–358.

Sherif, M., & Sherif, C. W. (1967). The Robbers' Cave study. In J. F. Perez, R. C. Sprinthall, G. S. Grosser, & P. J. Anastasiou, *General psychology: Selected readings*, (pp. 411–421). Princeton, NJ: Van Nostrand.

Sherman, C. (1994, September/October). Kicking butts. *Psychology Today*, pp. 41–45.

Shiffrin, R. M. (1970). Forgetting: Trace erosion or retrieval failure? *Science, 168*, 1601–1603.

Shiffrin, R. M., & Atkinson, R. C. (1969). Storage and retrieval processes in long-term memory. *Psychological Review, 76*, 179–193.

Shimamura, A., Brerry, J., Mangela, J., Rusting, C., & Jurica, P. (1995). Memory and cognitive abilities in university professors: Evidence for successful aging. *Psychological Science, 6,* 271–277.

Shneidman, E. (1989). The Indian summer of life: A preliminary study of septuagenarians. *American Psychologist, 44*, 684–694.

Shneidman, E. S. (1987, March). At the point of no return. *Psychology Today*, pp. 54–58.

Shneidman, E. S. (1994). Clues to suicide reconsidered. *Suicide and Life-Threatening Behavior, 24,* 395–397.

Shulman, H. G. (1972). Semantic confusion errors in short-term memory. *Journal of Verbal Learning and Verbal Behavior, 11*, 221–227.

Siegel, S., Hinson, R. E., Krank, M. D., & McCully, J. (1982). Heroin "overdose" death: Contribution of drug-associated environmental cues. *Science, 216*, 436–437.

Siegler, R. S. (1991). *Children's thinking* (2nd ed.). Englewood Cliffs, NJ: Prentice-Hall.

Sigurdson, E., Staley, D., Matas, M, Hildahl, K., et al. 1994. A review of youth suicide in Manitoba. *Canadian Journal of Psychiatry, 39*(8), 397–403.

Silva, C. E., & Kirsch, I. (1992). Interpretive sets, expectancy, fantasy proneness, and dissociation as predictors of hypnotic response. *Journal of Personality and Social Psychology, 63*, 847–856.

Simon, H. B. (1988, June). Running and rheumatism. *Harvard Medical School Health Letter, 13*, pp. 2–4.

Simon, L., Greenberg, J., & Brehm, J. (1995). Trivialization: The forgotten mode of dissonance reduction. *Journal of Personality and Social Psychology, 68,* 247–260.

Singh, D. (1995). Female health, attractiveness, and desirability for relationships: Role of breast asymmetry and waist-hip ratio. *Ethology and Sociobiology, 16,* 445–481.

Sivacek, J., & Crano, W. D. (1982). Vested interest as a moderator of attitude-behavior consistency. *Journal of Personality and Social Psychology, 43*, 210–221.

Skinner, B. F. (1938). *The behavior of organisms.* New York: Appleton-Century-Crofts.

Skinner, B. F. (1948a). "Superstition" in the pigeon. *Journal of Experimental Psychology, 38*, 168–172.

Skinner, B. F. (1948b). *Walden two*. New York: Macmillan.

Skinner, B. F. (1953). *Science and human behavior*. New York: Macmillan.

Skinner, B. F. (1957). *Verbal behavior*. New York: Appleton-Century-Crofts.

Skinner, B. F. (1967). Autobiography. In E. G. Boring & G. Lindzey (Eds.), *A history of psychology in autobiography* (Vol. 5, pp. 387–413). New York: Appleton.

Skinner, B. F. (1971). *Beyond freedom and dignity*. New York: Knopf.

Skinner, B. F. (1987). Whatever happened to psychology as the science of behavior? *American Psychologist, 42*, 780–786.

Skinner, B. F. (1988). The operant side of behavior therapy. *Journal of Behavior Therapy and Experimental Psychiatry, 19*, 171–179.

Slawinski, E.B., Hartel, D.M., & Kline, D.W. (1993). Self-reported hearing problems in daily life throughout adulthood. *Psychology and Aging, 8*, 552–561.

Slobin, D. (1972, July). Children and language: They learn the same all around the world. *Psychology Today*, pp. 71–74, 82.

Slopek, D. (2000, July 25). Manager, Corporate Communications, The TDL Group Ltd. Tim Hortons- smoke-free information. Personal communication.

Smart, R. G., & Adlaf, E. M. (1992). Recent studies of cocaine use and abuse in Canada. *Canadian Journal of Criminology, 34*, 1–13.

Smeaton, G., Byrne, D., & Murnen, S. K. (1989). The repulsion hypothesis revisited: Similarity irrelevance or dissimilarity bias? *Journal of Personality and Social Psychology, 56*, 54–59.

Smith, D. (1982). Trends in counseling and psychotherapy. *American Psychologist*, 37, 802–809.

Smith, M. L., Glass, G. V., & Miller, T. I. (1980). *The benefits of psychotherapy*. Baltimore, MD: Johns Hopkins University Press.

Snarey, J. R. (1985). Cross-cultural universality of social-moral development: A critical review of Kohlbergian research. *Psychological Bulletin, 97*, 202–232.

Snarey, J. R. (1995). In communitarian voice: The sociological expansion of Kohlbergian theory, research, and practice. In W. M. Kurtines & J. L. Gerwirtz (Eds.), *Moral development: An introduction* (pp. 109–134). Boston: Allyn & Bacon.

Snow, C. E. (1993). Bilingualism and second language acquisition. In J. B. Gleason & N. B. Ratner (Eds.), *Psycholinguistics*. Fort Worth, TX: Harcourt.

Snyder, F. (1971). Psychophysiology of human sleep. *Clinical Neurosurgery, 18*, 503–536.

Snyder, S. H. (1984, November). Medicated minds. *Science 84*, pp. 141–142.

Sobell, M. B., & Sobell, L. C. (1978). *Behavioral treatment of alcohol problems*. New York: Plenum.

Sobin, C., & Sackheim, H. (1997). Psychomotor symptoms of depression. *American Journal of Psychiatry, 154*, 4–17.

Sobol, M. P., & Cardiff, J. (1983). A sociopsychological investigation of adult adoptees' search for birth parents. *Family Relations: Journal of Applied Family & Child Studies, 32*(4), 477–483.

Sobol, M. P., & Daly, K. J. (1992). The adoption alternative for pregnant adolescents: Decision making, consequences, and policy implications. *Journal of Social Issues, 48*(3), 143–161.

Sobol, M. P., Daly, K. J., & Kelloway, E. K. (2000). Paths to the facilitation of open adoption. *Family Relations, 49*, 419–424.

Solomon, R. L. (1964). Punishment. *American Psychologist, 19*, 239–253.

Solso, R. (1991). *Cognitive psychology* (3rd ed.). Boston: Allyn & Bacon.

Somers, M. (1993). A comparison of voluntarily child-free adults and parents. *Journal of Marriage and the Family, 55*, 643–650.

Sommer, R., & Shutz, H. (1991). The consumer psychologist. In R. Gifford (Ed.), *Applied psychology: Variety and opportunity* (pp. 195–214). Boston: Allyn & Bacon.

Spanos, N. (1991). A sociocognitive approach to hypnosis. In S. J. Lynn & J. R. Ruhe (Eds.), *Hypnosis theories: Current models and perspectives* (pp. 324–361). New York: Guilford Press.

Spanos, N., Perlini, A., Patrick, L., Bell, S., & Gwynn, M. (1990). The role of compliance and hypnotic and nonhypnotic analgesia. *Journal of Research in Personality, 24*, 433–453.

Spearman, C. (1927). *The abilities of man*. New York: Macmillan.

Sperling, H. (1960). The information available in brief visual presentations. *Psychological Monographs: General and Applied, 74*(Whole No. 498), 1–29.

Sperry, R. W. (1964). The great cerebral commissure. *Scientific American, 210*, 42–52.

Sperry, R. W. (1966). Brain bisection and consciousness. In J. Eccles (Ed.), *Brain and conscious experience*. New York: Springer-Verlag.

Sperry, R. W. (1968). Hemisphere deconnection and unity in conscious experience. *American Psychologist, 23*, 723–733.

Spetch, M. L., Wilkie, D. M., & Pinel, J. P. J. (1981). Backward conditioning: A reevaluation of the empirical evidence. *Psychological Bulletin, 89*, 163–175.

Spitz, R. A. (1946). Hospitalism: A follow-up report on investigation described in volume I, 1945. *The Psychoanalytic Study of the Child, 2*, 113–117.

Spitzer, M. W., & Semple, M. N. (1991). Interaural phase coding in auditory midbrain: Influence of dynamic stimulus features. *Science, 254*, 721–724.

Spooner, A., & Kellogg, W. N. (1947). The backward conditioning curve. *American Journal of Psychology, 60*, 321–334.

Springer, S. P., & Deutsch, G. (1985). *Left brain, right brain* (rev. ed.). New York: W. H. Freeman.

Squire, L. R. (1986). Memory functions as affected by electroconvulsive therapy. *Annals of the New York Academy of Sciences, 462*, 307–314.

Squire, L. R. (1992). Memory and the hippocampus: A synthesis from findings with rats, monkeys, and humans. *Psychological Review, 99*, 195–231.

Squire, L. R., & Zola-Morgan, S. (1991). The medial temporal lobe memory system. *Science, 253*, 1380–1386.

Squire, L. R., Knowlton, B., & Musen, G. (1993). The structure and organization of memory. *Annual Review of Psychology, 44*, 453–495.

Stack, D. M., & Arnold, S. L. (1998). Changes in mothers' touch and hand gestures influences infant behavior during face-to-face interchanges. *Infant Behavior and Development, 21*(3), 451–468.

Stack, D. M., & LePage, D. E. (1996). Infants' sensitivity to manipulations of maternal touch during face-to-face interactions. *Social Development, 5*(1), 41–55.

Stanovich, K. E. (1989). *How to think straight about psychology* (2nd ed.). Glenview, IL: Scott, Foresman.

Stark, E. (1984, October). Answer this question: Responses: To sleep, perchance to dream. *Psychology Today*, p. 16.

Stark-Adamec, C., & Kimball, M. (1984). Science free of sexism: A psychologist's guide to the conduct of non-sexist research. *Canadian Psychology, 25*(1), 23–34.

Statistics Canada. (1992) *Canadian Crime Statistics, 1991*. Ottawa: Ministry of Supply and Services.

Statistics Canada. (1995) *Earnings of Men and Women, 1993*. Cat. 13–217. Ottawa: Ministry of Supply and Services.

Statistics Canada. (1989) *Homicide in Canada, 1988*. A Statistical Perspective. Ottawa: Ministry of Supply and Services.

Statistics Canada. (1996). 1996 Census, First official language spoken as defined by Official Languages Regulations. Retrieved July 7, 2000 from the World Wide Web: www.ocol-clo.gc.ca/map_e.htm.

Steele, C. M., & Josephs, R. A. (1990). Alcohol myopia: Its prized and dangerous effects. *American Psychologist, 45*(8), 921–933.

Steffens, A. B., Scheurink, A. J., & Luiten, P. G. (1988). Hypothalamic food intake regulating areas are involved in the homeostasis of blood glucose and plasma FFA levels. *Physiology and Behavior, 44,* 581–589.

Stein, L., Xue, B.G., & Belluzzi, J.D. (1993). Cellular targets of brain reinforcement systems. *Annals of the New York Academy of Sciences, 702,* 41–45.

Steinberg, L., Elman, J. D., & Mounts, N. S. (1989). Authoritative parenting, psychosocial maturity, and academic success among adolescents. *Child Development, 60*, 1424–1436.

Steinman, L. (1993). Autoimmune disease. *Scientific American, 269*, 106–114.

Stern, K., & McClintock, M. K. (1998). Regulation of ovulation by human pheromones. *Nature, 392,* 177–179.

Stern, L. D. (1981). A review of theories of human amnesia. *Memory & Cognition, 9*, 247–262.

Stern, W. (1914). *The psychological methods of testing intelligence.* Baltimore: Warwick and York.

Sternberg, G., & Hagekull, B. (1997). Social referencing and mood modification in 1-year-olds. *Infant Behavior & Development, 20*(2), 209–217.

Sternberg, R. J. (1985a). *Beyond IQ: A triarchic theory of human intelligence.* New York: Cambridge University Press.

Sternberg, R. J. (1985b). Human Intelligence: The model is the message. *Science, 230*, 1111–1118.

Sternberg, R. J. (1986a). *Intelligence applied: Understanding and increasing your intellectual skills.* San Diego: Harcourt Brace Jovanovich.

Sternberg, R. J. (1986b). A triangular theory of love. *Psychological Review, 93*, 119–135.

Sternberg, R. J. (1987). Liking versus loving: A comparative evaluation of theories. *Psychological Bulletin, 102,* 331–345.

Sternberg, R. J. (1997). Construct validation of a triangular love scale. *European Journal of Social Psychology, 27*(3), 313–335.

Sternberg, R. J., Wagner, R. K., Williams, W. M., & Horvath, J. A. (1995). Testing common sense. *American Psychologist, 50,* 912–927.

Stone, A. A., Bovbjerg, D. H., Neale, J. M., Napoli, A., Valdimarsdottir, H., Cox, D., Hayden, F. G., & Gwaltney, J. M. (1992). Development of the common cold symptoms following experimental rhinovirus infection is related to prior stressful life events. *Behavioral Medicine, 18,* 115–120.

Stone, M. (2000, May 22). Canadians distrust Big Brother Database. *Newsbytes.*

Strack, F., Martin, L. L., & Stepper, S. (1988). Inhibiting and facilitating conditions of facial expressions: A nonobtrusive test of the facial feedback hypothesis. *Journal of Personality and Social Psychology, 54,* 768–777.

Strakowski, S., Lonczak, H., Sax, K., West, S., Crist , A., Mehta, R., & Theinhaus, O. (1995). The effects of race on diagnosis and disposition from a psychiatric emergency service. *Journal of Clinical Psychiatry, 56,* 101–107.

Streissguth, A. P., Barr, H. M., Sampson, P. D., Darby, B. L., & Martin, D. C. (1989). IQ at age 4 in relation to maternal alcohol use and smoking during pregnancy. *Developmental Psychology, 25,* 3–11.

Strentz, H. (1986, January 1). Become a psychic and amaze your friends! *Atlanta Journal*, p. 15A.

Stretch, R. H. (1990). Post-traumatic stress disorder and the Vietnam veteran. *Journal of Traumatic Stress, 3*(2), 239–254.

Stricker, E. M., & Verbalis, J. G. (1987). Biological bases of hunger and satiety. *Annals of Behavioral Medicine, 9,* 3–8.

Strome, M., & Vernick, D. (1989, April). Hearing loss and hearing aids. *Harvard Medical School Health Letter, 14*, pp. 5–8.

Stromeyer, C. F., III. (1970, November). Eidetikers. *Psychology Today*, pp. 76–80.

Stryer, L. (1987). The molecules of visual excitation. *Scientific American, 257*, 42–50.

Stunkard, A. J., Harris, J. R., Pedersen, N. L., & McClearn, G. E. (1990). The body-mass index of twins who have been reared apart. *New England Journal of Medicine, 322,* 1483–1487.

Stuss, D. T., Gow, C. A., & Hetherington, C. R. (1992). "No longer Gage": Frontal lobe dysfunction and emotional changes. *Journal of Consulting and Clinical Psychology, 60,* 349–359.

Sue, D. (1994). *Counseling the culturally different: Theory and practice.* New York; Wiley.

Suedfeld, P. (1990). Restricted environmental stimulation and smoking cessation: A 15-year progress report. *International Journal of the Addictions, 25,* 861–888.

Suedfeld, P., & Borrie, R. A. (1999). Health and therapeutic applications of chamber and flotation restricted environmental stimulation therapy (REST). *Psychology & Health, 14*(3), 545–566.

Suedfeld, P., & Coren, S. (1989). Perceptual isolation, sensory deprivation, and REST: Moving introductory psychology texts out of the 1950s. *Canadian Psychology, 30,* 7–29.

Sullivan, P., Chu, S., & Fleming, L. (1997). Changes in AIDS incidence for men who have sex with men: United States 1990–1995. *AIDS, 11*(13), 1641–1646.

Sumnerfeldt, L., Richter, M., Antony, M., & Swinson, R. (1999). Symptom structure in obsessive compulsive disorder: A confirmatory factor-analytic study. *Behavior Research and Therapy, 37,* 297–311.

Suppes, T., Baldessarini, R. J., Faedda, G. L., & Tohen, M. (1991). Risk of recurrence following discontinuation of lithium treatment in bipolar disorder. *Archives of General Psychiatry, 48,* 1082–1088.

Swanson, L. W. (1995). Mapping the human brain: past, present, and future. *Trends in Neurosciences, 18,* 471–474.

Swap, W. C. (1977). Interpersonal attraction and repeated exposure to rewarders and punishers. *Personality and Social Psychology Bulletin, 3,* 248–251.

Sweatt, J. D., & Kandel, E. R. (1989). Persistent and transcriptionally-dependent increase in protein phosphorylation in long-term facilitation of Aplysia sensory neurons. *Nature, 339,* 51–54.

Swedo, S. E., Rapoport, J. L., Leonard, H., Lenane, M., & Cheslow, D. (1989). Obsessive-compulsive disorder in children and adolescents: Clinical phenomenology of 70 consecutive cases. *Archives of General Psychiatry, 46,* 335–341.

Sweller, J., & Levine, M. (1982). Effects of goal specificity on means-end analysis and learning. *Journal of Experimental Psychology: Learning, Memory, and Cognition, 8,* 463–474.

Swets, J. A. (1992). The science of choosing the right decision threshold in high-stakes diagnostics. *American Psychologist, 47,* 522–532.

Swets, J. A. (1998). Separating discrimination and decision in detection, recognition, and matters of life and death. In D. Scarborough, S. Sternberg et al. (Eds.). *Methods, models and conceptual issues: An invitation to cognition sciences,* Vol. 4, (pp. 635–702). Cambridge, MA: MIT Press.

Symons, C. S., & Johnson, B. T. (1997). The self-reference effect in memory: A meta analysis. *Psychological Bulletin, 121*(3), 371–394.

Szymanski, K., & Harkins, S. G. (1987). Social loafing and self-evaluation with a social standard. *Journal of Personality and Social Psychology, 53,* 891–897.

Tajfel, H. (1982) Social psychology of intergroup relations. *Annual Review of Psychology, 33,* 1–39.

Tan, D. T. Y., & Singh, R. (1995). Attitudes and attraction: A developmental study of the similarity-attraction and dissimilarity-repulsion hypotheses. *Personality & Social Psychology Bulletin, 21*(9), 975–986.

Tanda, G., Pontieri, F. E., & Di Chiara, G. (1997). Cannabinoid and heroin activation of mesolimbic dopamine transmission by a common μ1 opioid receptor mechanism. *Science, 276,* 2048–2050.

Tanner, J. M. (1961). *Education and physical growth.* London: University of London Press.

Tanner, J. M. (1990). *Fetus into man* (2nd ed.) Cambridge MA: Harvard University Press.

Taylor, E. (1996, July/August). Peace Timothy Leary. *Psychology Today, 29,* 56–59, 84.

Taylor, S. E. (1991). *Health psychology* (2nd ed.). New York: McGraw-Hill.

Taylor, S. E., & Brown, J. D. (1988). Illusion of well-being: A social psychological perspective on mental health. *Psychological Bulletin, 103,* 193–210.

Teasdale, J. D., & Fogarty, S. J. (1979). Differential effects of induced mood on retrieval of pleasant and unpleasant events from episodic memory. *Journal of Abnormal Psychology, 88,* 248–257.

Tellegen, A., Lykken, D. T., Bouchard, T. J., Jr., Wilcox, K. J., Segal, N. L., & Rich, S. (1988). Personality similarity in twins reared apart and together. *Journal of Personality and Social Psychology, 54,* 1031–1039.

Templeton, R. D., & Quigley, J. P. (1930). The action of insulin on the motility of the gastrointestinal tract. *American Journal of Physiology, 91,* 467–474.

Terman, G. W., Shavit, Y., Lewis, J. W., Cannon, J. T., & Liebeskind, J. C. (1984). Intrinsic mechanisms of pain inhibition: Activation by stress. *Science, 226,* 1270–1277.

Terman, L. M. (1925). *Genetic studies of genius, Vol. 1: Mental and physical traits of a thousand gifted children.* Stanford, CA: Stanford University Press.

Terman, L. M., & Oden, M. H. (1947). *Genetic studies of genius, Vol. 4: The gifted child grows up.* Stanford, CA: Stanford University Press.

Terman, L. M., & Oden, M. H. (1959). *Genetic studies of genius, Vol. 5: The gifted group at mid-life.* Stanford, CA: Stanford University Press.

Termine, N. T., & Izard, C. E. (1988). Infants' responses to their mother's expressions of joy and sadness. *Developmental Psychology, 24,* 223–229.

Terry, W. S. (1988). Everyday forgetting: Data from a diary study. *Psychological Reports, 62,* 299–303.

Tesser, A. (1988). Toward a self-evaluation maintenance model of social behavior. *Advances in experimental social psychology,* Vol 21, pp. 181–227, San Diego, CA: Academic Press.

Tesser, A. (1993). The importance of heritability in psychological research: The case of attitudes. *Psychological Review, 100,* 129–142.

Teuting, P., Koslow, S. H., & Hirschfeld, R. M. A. (1981). *Special report on depression research.* Rockville, MD: U.S. Department of Health & Human Services.

Thase, M. E., Frank, E., Mallinger, A. G., Hammer, T., & Kupfer, D. J. (1992). Treatment of imipramine-resistant recurrent depression, III: Efficacy of monoamine oxidise inhibitors. *Journal of Clinical Psychiatry, 53*(1, Suppl.), 5–11.

Thase, M. E., & Kupfer, D. (1996). Recent developments in the pharmacotherapy of mood disorders. *Journal of Consulting and Clinical Psychology, 64,* 646–659.

Thase, M. E., & Shipley, J. E. (1988). Tricyclic antidepressants. In C. G. Last & M. Hersen (Eds.), *Handbook of anxiety disorders* (pp. 460–477). New York: Pergamon Press.

Thessing, V. C., Anch, A. M., Muehlbach, M. J., Schweitzer, P. K., & Walsh, J. K. (1994). Two- and 4-hour bright-light exposures differentially effect sleepiness and performance the subsequent night. *Sleep, 17,* 140–145.

Thompson, M. G., & Heller, K. (1990). Facets of support related to well-being: Quantitative social isolation and perceived family support in a sample of elderly women. *Psychology and Aging, 5,* 535–544.

Thompson, S. C., Sobolew-Shubin, A., Galbraith, M. E., Schwankovsky, L., & Cruzen, D. (1993). Maintaining perceptions of control: Finding perceived control in low-control circumstances. *Journal of Personality and Social Psychology, 64,* 293–304.

Thorndike, E. L. (1920). A constant error in psychological ratings. *Journal of Applied Psychology, 4,* 25–29.

Thorndike, E. L. (1970). *Animal intelligence: Experimental Studies.* New York: Macmillan. (Original work published 1911).

Thornhill, R., & Gangestad, G. W. (1994). Human fluctuating asymmetry and sexual behavior. *Psychological Science, 5,* 297–302.

Thorpe, G. L., & Olson, S. L. (1990). *Behavior therapy: Concepts, procedures, and applications.* Boston: Allyn & Bacon.

Thurstone, L. L. (1938). *Primary mental abilities.* Chicago: University of Chicago Press.

Thyer, B. A., Parrish, R. T., Curtis, G. C., Neese, R. M., & Cameron, O. G. (1985). Ages of onset of DSM-III anxiety disorders. *Comprehensive Psychiatry, 26,* 113–122.

Tomaka, J., Blascovich, J., Kelsey, R. M., & Leitten, C. L. (1993). Subjective, physiological, and behavioral effects of threat and challenge appraisal. *Journal of Personality and Social Psychology, 65,* 248–260.

Tomkins, S. (1962). *Affect, imagery, and consciousness: The positive effects* (Vol. 1). New York: Springer.

Tomkins, S. (1963). *Affect, imagery, and consciousness: The negative effects* (Vol. 2). New York: Springer.

Tordoff, M. G. (1988). Sweeteners and appetite. In G. M. Williams (Ed.), *Sweeteners: Health effects* (pp. 53–60). Princeton: Princeton Scientific.

Torrey, E. F. (1983). *Surviving schizophrenia: A family manual.* New York: Harper & Row.

Torrey, E. F., & Bowler, A. (1990). Geographical distribution of insanity in America: Evidence for an urban factor. *Schizophrenia Bulletin, 16,* 591–604.

Tousignant, M., Bastien, M. F., & Hamel, S. (1993). Suicidal attempts and ideations among adolescents and young adults: The contribution of father's and mother's care and of parental separation. *Social Psychiatry and Psychiatric Epidemiology, 28*(5), 256–261.

Travis, J. (1994). Glia: The brain's other cells. *Science, 266,* 970–972.

Triandis, H. C. (1994). *Culture and social behavior.* New York: McGraw-Hill.

Triplett, N. (1898). The dynamogenic factors in pacemaking and competition. *American Journal of Psychology, 9,* 507–533.

Trotter, R. J. (1986, August). Three heads are better than one: Profile: Robert J. Sternberg. *Psychology Today,* pp. 56–62.

Tulving, E. (1972). Episodic and semantic memory. In E. Tulving & W. Donaldson (Eds.), *Organization of memory* (pp. 382–403). New York: Academic Press.

Tulving, E. (1974). Cue-dependent forgetting. *American Scientist, 62,* 74–82.

Tulving, E. (1985). How many memory systems are there? *American Psychologist, 40,* 385–398.

Tulving, E. (1987). Multiple memory systems and consciousness. *Human Neurobiology, 6,* 67–80.

Tulving, E. (1989). Remembering and knowing the past. *American Scientist, 77,* 361–367.

Tulving, E., Kapur, S., Craik, F. I. M., Moscovitch, M., & Houle, S. (1994). Hemispheric encoding/retrieval asymmetry in episodic memory: Positron emission tomography findings. *Proceedings of the National Academy of Sciences, 91,* 2016–2020.

Tulving, E., Schacter, D. L., McLachlan, D. R., & Moscovitch, M. (1988). Priming of semantic autobiographical knowledge: A case study of retrograde amnesia. *Brain and Cognition, 8,* 3–20.

Tulving, E., & Thompson, D. M. (1973). Encoding specificity and retrieval processes in episodic memory. *Psychological Review, 80,* 352–373.

Turner, J. C., Hogg, M. A., Oakes, P. J., Reicher, S. D., & Wetherell, M. S. (1987). *Rediscovering the social group: A self-categorization theory.* Oxford: Blackwell.

Turner, T. J., & Ortony, A. (1992). Basic emotions: Can conflicting criteria converge? *Psychological Review, 99,* 566–571.

Tzu-Chin, W., Tashkin, D. P., Djahed, B., & Rose, J. E. (1988). Pulmonary hazards of smoking marijuana as compared with tobacco. *New England Journal of Medicine, 318,* 347–351.

Uchino, B. N., Cacciopo, J. T., Kiecolt-Glaser, J. K. (1996). The relationship between social support and physiological processes: A review with emphasis on underlying mechanisms and implications for health. *Psychological Bulletin, 119,* 488–531.

Underwood, B. J. (1957). Interference and forgetting. *Psychological Review, 64,* 49–60.

Underwood, B. J. (1964). Forgetting. *Scientific American, 210,* 91–99.

Vaillant, G. E. (1977). *Adaptation to life.* Boston: Little, Brown.

Vaillant, G. E. (1983). *The natural history of alcoholism: Causes, patterns, and paths to recovery.* Cambridge, MA: Harvard University Press.

Vaillant, G. E. (1994). Ego mechanisms of defense and personality psychopathology. *Journal of Abnormal Psychology, 103,* 44–50.

Vaillant, G. E. (1998). Where do we go from here? *Journal of Personality, 66*(6), 1147–1157.

Vaillant, G. E. (2000). Adaptive mental mechanisms: Their role in a positive psychology. *American Psychologist, 55*(1), 89–98.

Vallerand, R. G., Pelletier, L. G., Blais, M. R., Briere, N. M., et al. (1993). On the assessment of intrinsic, extrinsic, and amotivation in education: Evidence on the concurrent and construct validity of the Academic Motivation Scale. *Educational & Psychological Measurement, 53*(1), 159–172.

van den Hout, M., & Merckelbach, H. (1991). Classical conditioning: Still going strong. *Behavioural Psychotherapy, 19,* 59–79.

Vandell, D. L., & Mueller, E. C. (1980). Peer play and friendships during the first two years. In H. C. Foot, A. J. Chapman, & J. R. Smith (Eds.), *Friendship and social relations in children.* New York: Wiley.

Van de Perre, P. (1999). HIV and AIDS in Africa: Impact on mother and child health. *European Journal of Medical Research, 4*(8), 341–344.

Van Lancker, D. R., Cummings, J. L., Kreiman, J., & Dobkin, B. H. (1988). Phonagnosia: A dissociation between familiar and unfamiliar voices. *Cortex, 24*, 195–209.

Vargha-Khadem, F., Gadian, D., Watkins, D., Connellly, A., Van Paesschen, W., & Mishkin, M. (1997). Differential effects of early hippocampal pathology on episodic and semantic memory. *Science 277,* 376–380.

Veleber, D. M., & Templer, D. I. (1984). Effects of caffeine on anxiety and depression. *Journal of Abnormal Psychology, 93*, 120–122.

Vener, K. J., Szabo, S., & Moore, J. G. (1989). The effect of shift work on gastrointestinal (GI) function: A review. *Chronobiologia, 16*, 421–439.

Viemerö, V. (1996). Factors in childhood that predict later criminal behavior. *Aggressive Behavior, 22,* 87–97.

Vilberg, T. R., & Keesey, R. E. (1990). Ventromedial hypothalamic lesions abolish compensatory reduction in energy expenditure to weight loss. *American Journal of Physiology, 258*, 476–480.

Vincent, M., & Pickering, M. R. (1988). Multiple personality disorder in childhood. *Canadian Journal of Psychiatry, 33*, 524–529.

Viney, W. (1993). *A history of psychology: Ideas and context*. Boston: Allyn & Bacon.

Vinokur, A., & Burnstein, E. (1978). Depolarization of attitudes in groups. *Journal of Personality and Social Psychology, 36*, 872–885.

Vogel, G. (1992). Clinical uses and advantages of low doses of benzodiazepine hypnotics. *Journal of Clinical Psychiatry, 53*(6, Suppl.), 19–22.

Vogel, G. W. (1975). A review of REM sleep deprivation. *Archives of General Psychiatry, 32*, 749–761.

Volkow, N. D., & Tancredi, L. R. (1991). Biological correlates of mental activity studied with PET. *American Journal of Psychiatry, 148*, 439–443.

Volkow, N. D., Wang, G. J., Fischman, M. W., Foltin, R. W., Fowler, J. S., Abumrad, N. N., Vitkun, S., Logan, J., Gatley, S. J., Pappas, N., Hitzemann, R., & Shea, C. E. (1997a). Relationship between subjective effects of cocaine and dopamine transporter occupancy. *Nature, 386,* 827–830.

Volkow, N. D., Wang, G. J., Fowler, J. S., Logan, J., Gatley, S. J., Hitzemann, R., Chen, A. D., Dewey, S. L., & Pappas, N. (1997b). Decreased striatal dopaminergic responsiveness in detoxified cocaine-dependent subjects. *Nature, 386,* 830–833.

von Mayrhauser, R. T. (1992). The mental testing community and validity: A prehistory. *American Psychologist, 47,* 244–253.

Wahba, M. A., & Bridwell, L. G. (1976). Maslow reconsidered: A review of research on the need hierarchy theory. *Organization Behavior and Human Performance, 15*, 212–240.

Wald, G. (1964). The receptors of human color vision. *Science, 145*, 1007–1017.

Wald, G., Brown, P. K., & Smith, P. H. (1954). Iodopsin. *Journal of General Physiology, 38*, 623–681.

Walker, L. (1989). A longitudinal study of moral reasoning. *Child Development, 60*, 157–166.

Wallabaum, A. B., Rzewnicki, R., Steele, H., & Suedfeld, P. (1991). Progressive muscle relaxation and restricted environmental stimulation therapy for chronic tension headache: A pilot study. *International Journal of Psychosomatics, 38,* 33–39.

Wallach, H. (1985a). Learned stimulation in space and motion perception. *American Psychologist, 40*, 399–404.

Wallach, H. (1985b). Perceiving a stable environment. *Scientific American, 252*, 118–124.

Wallach, M. A., & Wallach, L. (1983). *Psychology's sanction for selfishness: The error of egoism in theory and therapy*. New York: W. H. Freeman.

Walsh, W. B., & Betz, N. E. (1990). *Tests and assessment* (2nd ed.). Englewood Cliffs, NJ: Prentice-Hall.

Walster, E., & Walster, G. W. (1969). The matching hypothesis. *Journal of Personality and Social Psychology, 6*, 248–253.

Wark, G., & Krebs, D. (1996). Gender and dilemma differences in real-life moral judgement. *Developmental Psychology, 32,* 220–230.

Warren, R. M. (1999). *Auditory perception: A new analysis and synthesis.* New York, NY: Cambridge University Press.

Wasserman, E. A., & Miller, R. R. (1997). What's elementary about associative learning? *Annual Review of Psychology, 48,* 573–607.

Watson, J. B., & Rayner, R. (1920). Conditioned emotional reactions. *Journal of Experimental Psychology, 3*, 1–14.

Waugh, N. C., & Norman, D. A. (1965). Primary memory. *Psychological Review, 72*, 89–104.

Wayment, H. A., & Peplau, L. E. (1995). Social support and well-being among lesbian and heterosexual women: A structural modeling approach. *Personality & Social Psychology Bulletin, 21*(11), 1189–1199.

Webb, W. (1995). The cost of sleep-related accidents: A reanaysis. *Sleep, 18,* 276–280.

Webb, W. B. (1975). *Sleep: The gentle tyrant*. Englewood Cliffs, NJ: Prentice-Hall.

Webb, W. B. (1994). Sleep as a biological rhythm: A historical review. *Sleep, 17,* 188–194.

Webb, W. B., & Campbell, S. S. (1983). Relationships in sleep characteristics of identical and fraternal twins. *Archives of General Psychiatry, 40*, 1093–1095.

Webb, W. B., & Cartwright, R. D. (1978). Sleep and dreams. *Annual Review of Psychology, 29*, 223–252.

Wechsler, D. (1975). Intelligence defined and undefined: A relativistic appraisal. *American Psychologist, 34*, 135–139.

Wegner, D. M., & Bargh, J. A. (1998). Control and automaticity in social life. In D. T. Gilbert, S. T. Fiske, et al. (Eds.), *The handbook of social psychology* (4th ed.), (pp. 446–496). Boston: McGraw-Hill.

Wehr, T. A., & Rosenthal, N. E. (1989). Seasonality and affective illness. *American Journal of Psychiatry, 146*, 829–839.

Wehr, T. A., Jacobsen, F. M., Sack, D. A., et al. (1986). Phototherapy of seasonal affective disorder. *Archives of General Psychiatry, 43*, 870–875.

Weiner, B. (1972). *Theories of motivation: From mechanism to cognition*. Chicago: Rand McNally.

Weiner, B. (Ed.) (1974). *Achievement motivation and attribution theory*. Norristown, NJ: General Learning Press.

Weiner, B. (1980). *Human motivation*. New York: Holt, Rinehart & Winston.

Weiner, B. (1985). "Spontaneous" causal thinking. *Psychological Bulletin, 97*, 74–84.

Weiner, I. B. (1994). The Rorschach Inkblot Method (RIM) is not a test: Implications for theory and practice. *Journal of Personality Assessment, 62,* 498–504.

Weiner, I. B. (1997). Current status of the Rorschach Inkblot Method. *Journal of Personality Assessment, 68*, 5–19.

Weingartner, H., Adefris, W., Eich, J. E., & Murphy, D. L. (1976). Encoding-imagery specificity in alcohol state-dependent learning. *Journal of Experimental Psychology: Human Learning and Memory, 2*, 83–87.

Weinstein, S. (1968). Intensive and extensive aspects of tactile sensitivity as a function of body part, sex, and laterality. In D. R. Kenshalo (Ed.), *The skin senses*. Springfield, IL: Charles C. Thomas.

Weinstock, S. (1954). Resistance to extinction of a running response following partial reinforcement under widely spaced trials. *Journal of Comparative and Physiological Psychology, 47*, 318–322.

Weiss, L., Saklofske, D., Prifitera, A., Chen, H., & Hildebrand, D.(1999). The calculation of the WISC-III General Ability Index using Canadian norms. *Canadian Journal of School Psychology, 14,* 1–9.

Weissman, M. M. (1993). The epidemiology of personality disorders. A 1990 update. *Journal of Personality Disorders, 1*(Spring Supplement), 44–62.

Weissman, M. M., Bland, R. C., Canino, G. J., Greenwald, S., Hwu, H-G., Lee, C. K., Newman, S. C., Oakley-Browne, M. A., Rubio-Stipec, M., Wickramaratne, P. J., Wittchen, H-U., & Yeh, E-K. (1994). The cross national epidemiology of obsessive compulsive disorder. *Journal of Clinical Psychiatry, 55*(3, Suppl.), 5–10.

Weissman, M. M., Bland, R., Joyce, P. R., Newman, S., Wells, J. E., & Wittchen, H-U. (1993). Sex differences in rates of depression: cross-national perspectives. *Journal of Affective Disorders, 29*, 77–84.

Weissman, M. M., Gershon, E. S., Kidd, K. K., et al. (1984). Psychiatric disorders in the relatives of probands with affective disorders: The Yale University–National Institute of Mental Health Collaborative Study. *Archives of General Psychiatry, 41*, 13–21.

Weissman, M. M., Klerman, G. L., Markowitz, J. S., & Ouellette, R. (1989). Suicidal ideation and suicide attempts in panic disorder and attacks. *New England Journal of Medicine, 321*, 1209–1214.

Weissman, M. M., Klerman, G. L., Prusoff, B. A., Sholomskas, D., & Padian, N. (1981). Depressed outpatients: Results one year after treatment with drugs and/or interpersonal psychotherapy. *Archives of General Psychiatry, 41*, 51–55.

Weissman, M. M., Wickramartne, P., Merikangas, K. R., Leckman, J. F., Prusoff, B. A., Caruso, K. A., Kidd, K. K., & Gammon, G. D. (1984). Onset of major depression in early adulthood. *Archives of General Psychiatry, 41*, 1136–1143.

Weldon, E., & Gargano, G. M. (1988). Cognitive loafing: The effects of accountability and shared responsibility on cognitive effort. *Personality and Social Psychology Bulletin, 14,* 159–171.

Wells, G. L. (1993). What do we know about eyewitness identification? *American Psychologist, 48,* 553–571.

Wertheimer, M. (1958). Principles of perceptual organization. In D. C. Beardslee & M. Wertheimer (Eds.), *Readings in perception* (pp. 115–135). Princeton, NJ: D. Van Nostrand.

Westen, D. (1998). The scientific legacy of Freud: Toward a psychonomically informed psychological science. *Psychological Bulletin, 124*(3), 333–371.

Wetzel, R. D., & Reich, T. (1989). The cognitive triad and suicide intent in depressed in-patients. *Psychological Reports, 65*, 1027–1032.

Wever, E. G. (1949). *Theory of hearing*. New York: Wiley.

Wheeler, M. A., Stuss, D. T., & Tulving, E. (1997). Toward a theory of episodic memory: The frontal lobes and autonoetic consciousness. *Psychological Bulletin, 121*(3), 331–354.

Whelan, E. M., & Stare, F. J. (1990). Nutrition. *Journal of the American Medical Association, 263*, 2661–2663.

White, D. P. (1989). Central sleep apnea. In M. H. Kryger, T. Roth, & W. C. Dement (Eds.), *Principles and practice of sleep medicine* (pp. 513–524). Philadelphia: W. B. Saunders.

White, S. D., & DeBlassie, R. R. (1992). Adolescent sexual behavior. *Adolescence, 27,* 183–191.

Whitehurst, G. J., Fischel, J. E., Caulfield, M. B., DeBaryshe, B. D., & Valdez-Menchaca, M. C. (1989). Assessment and treatment of early expressive language delay. In P. R. Zelazo & R. Barr (Eds.)., *Challenges to developmental paradigms: Implications for assessment and treatment* (pp. 113–135). Hillsdale, NJ: Erlbaum.

Whitney, D., Sharma, V. & Kueneman, K. (1999). Seasonality of manic depressive illness in Canada. *Journal of Affective Disorders, 55,* 99–105.

Whittal, W. L., Agras, W. S., & Gould, R. A. (1999). Bulimia nervosa: A meta-analysis of psychosocial and pharmacological treatments. *Behavior Therapy, 30*(1), 117–135.

Who owns life? (2000, March 20). *This Morning,* CBC Radio. Retrieved July 7, 2000 from the World Wide Web: www.radio.cbc.ca/programs/thismorning/features/life_1.html.

Whorf, B. L. (1956). Science and linguistics. In J. B. Carroll (Ed.), *Language, thought, and reality: Selected writings of Benjamin Lee Whorf.* Cambridge, MA: MIT Press.

Wickelgren, I. (1996). For the cortex, neuron loss may be less than though. *Science, 273,* 58–50.

Wickelgren, I. (1997). Getting a grasp on working memory. *Science, 275*, 1580–1582.

Wickens, B. & Hawkes, C. (2000, June 5). Tragedy in Walkerton. *Maclean's Online.* Retrieved August 21, 2000 from the World Wide Web: www.macleans.ca.

Wicker, A. W. (1969). Attitudes versus action: The relationship of verbal and overt behavioral responses to attitude objects. *Journal of Social Issues, 25*, 41–78.

Widiger, T. A., Frances, A., Spitzer, R. L., & Williams, J. B. W. (1988). The DSM-III-R personality disorders: An overview. *American Journal of Psychiatry, 145*, 786–795.

Widom, C. S. (1989a). The cycle of violence. Science, 244, 160–166.

Widom, C. S. (1989b). Does violence beget violence? A critical examination of the literature. *Psychological Bulletin, 106*, 3–28.

Widom, C. S., & Maxfield, M. G. (1996). A prospective examination of risk for violence among abused and neglected children. *Annals of the New York Academy of Sciences, 794,* 224–237.

Wiebe, S. & Derry, P. (2000). Measuring quality of life in epilepsy surgery patients. *Canadian Journal of Neurological Science, 27*(Suppl.1), s111–s115.

Wierson, M., Long, P. J., & Forehand, R. L. (1993). Toward a new understanding of early menarche: The role of environmental stress in pubertal timing. *Adolescence, 28,* 13–24.

Wigfield, A., & Eccles, A. (2000). Expectancy-value theory of achievement motivation. *Contemporary Educational Psychology. Special Issue: Motivation and Educational Processes, 25*(1), 68–81.

Wiggins, J. E. (Ed.). (1996). *The five-factor model of personality: Theoretical perspectives.* New York: Guilford.

Williams, J. E., Satterwhite, R. C., & Saiz, J. L. (1998). *The importance of psychological traits: A cross-cultural study.* New York: Plenum.

Williams, K., Harkins, S. G., & Latane, B. (1981). Identifiability as a deterrent to social loafing: Two cheering experiments. *Journal of Personality and Social Psychology, 40,* 303–311.

Williams, K. D., & Karau, S. J. (1991). Social loafing and social compensation: The effects of expectations of co-worker performance. *Journal of Personality and Social Psychology, 61,* 570–581.

Williams, S. R. (1986). *Essentials of nutrition and diet therapy* (4th ed.). St. Louis: Times Mirror/Mosby.

Willoughby, T., Wood, E., McDermott, C., & McLaren, J. (2000). Enhancing learning through strategy instruction and group interaction: Is active generation of elaborations critical? *Applied Cognitive Psychology, 14,* 19–30.

Wills, T. A., McNamara, G., Vaccaro, D., & Hirky, A. E. (1996). Escalated substance use: A longitudinal grouping analysis from early to middle adolescence. *Journal of Abnormal Psychology, 105,* 166–180.

Wilson, M. A., & McNaughton, B. L. (1993). Dynamics of the hippocampal ensemble code for space. *Science, 261,* 1055–1058.

Wink, P., & Helson, R. (1993). Personality change in women and their partners. *Journal of Personality and Social Psychology, 65,* 597–605.

Winn, P. (1994). Schizophrenia research moves to the prefrontal cortex. *Trends in Neurosciences, 17,* 265–268.

Winokur, G., Coryell, W., Akiskal, H.S., Endicott, J., Keller, M., & Mueller, T. (1994). Manic-depressive (bipolar) disorder: The course in light of a prospective ten-year follow-up of 131 patients. *Acta Psychiatrica Scandinavica, 89,* 102–110.

Winokur, G., Coryell, W., Keller, M., Endicott, J., & Akiskal, H. S. (1993). A prospective follow-up of patients with bipolar and primary unipolar affective disorder. *Archives of General Psychiatry, 50,* 457–465.

Winsor, H. (2000, October 22). Mourners pour out respect for Trudeau. *The Globe and Mail,* pp. 1, 2.

Winston, A. S. (1996). The context of correctness: A comment on Rushton. *Journal of Social Distress and the Homeless, 5*(2), 231–250.

Witelson, S. F. (1985). The brain connection: The corpus callosum is larger in left-handers. *Science, 229,* 665–668.

Witelson, S. (1990). Structural correlates of cognition in the human brain. In A. B. Scheibel, A. F. Wechsler, et al. (Eds.). *Neurobiology of higher cognitive function. UCLA forum in medical sciences, No. 29* (pp. 167–183). New York: Guilford Press.

Witty, P. A., & Jenkins M. D. (1936). Intra-race testing and Negro intelligence. *Journal of Psychology, 1,* 188–191.

Wolfson, J. & Causkadon, M. A. (1998). Sleep schedules and daytime functioning in adolescents. *Child Development, 69*(4), 875–887.

Wolkin, A., Barouche, F., Wolf, A. P., Rotrosen, J., Fowler, J. S., Shiue, C-Y., Cooper, T. B., & Brodie, J. D. (1989). Dopamine blockade and clinical response: Evidence for two biological subgroups of schizophrenia. *American Journal of Psychiatry, 146,* 905–908.

Woloshyn, V., Willoughby, T., Wood, E., & Pressley, M. (1990). Elaborative interrogation facilitates adult learning of factual paragraphs. *Journal of Educational Psychology, 82,* 513–524.

Wolpe, J. (1958). *Psychotherapy by reciprocal inhibition.* Stanford, CA: Stanford University Press.

Wolpe, J. (1973). *The practice of behavior therapy* (2nd ed.). New York: Pergamon Press.

Wolpe, J. (1981). Behavior therapy versus psychoanalysis: Therapeutic and social implications. *American Psychologist, 36,* 159–164.

Wood, E., Presley, M., & Winne, P. (1990). Elaborative interrogation effects on children's learning of factual content. *Journal of Educational Psychology, 82,* 741–748.

Wood, E., Woloshyn, V., & Willoughby, T. (1995). *Cognitive strategies for middle and high schools.* Brookline Press.

Wood, J. M., & Bootzin, R. (1990). The prevalence of nightmares and their independence from anxiety. *Journal of Abnormal Psychology, 99,* 64–68.

Wood, J. M., Lilienfeld, S. O., & Garb, H. N. (2000). The Rorschach test in clinical diagnosis: A critical review with a backward look at Garfield (1947). *Journal of Clinical Psychology, 56*(3), 395–420.

Wood, W., Lundgren, S., Ovellette, J. A., Busceme, S., & Blackstone, T. (1994). Minority influence: A meta-analytic review of social influence processes. *Psychological Bulletin, 115,* 323–345.

Wood, W., Rhodes, N., & Whelan, M. (1989). Sex differences in positive well-being: A consideration of emotional style and marital status. *Psychological Bulletin, 106,* 249–264.

Wood, W., Wong, F. Y., & Chachere, J. G. (1991). Effects of media violence on viewers' aggression in unconstrained social interaction. *Psychological Bulletin, 109,* 371–383.

Woods, J. H., Katz, J. L., & Winger, G. (1987). Abuse liability of benzodiazepines. *Pharmacological Reviews, 39,* 251–413.

Woolley, C., Weiland, N., McEwen, B., & Schwartzkroin, P. (1997) Estradiol increases the sensitivity of hippocampal CA1 pyramidal cells to NMDA receptor-mediated synaptic output: Correlation with dendritic spine density. *Journal of Neuroscience,17,* 1848–1859.

Wright, S., Taylor, D., & Macarthur, J. (2000). Subtractive bilingualism and the survival of the Inuit language: Heritage- versus second-language education. *Journal of Educational Psychology, 92,* 63–84.

Wright, S. C., Taylor, D. M., & Moghaddam, F. (1990). Responding to membership in a disadvantaged group: From acceptance to collective protest. *Journal of Personality and Social Psychology, 58,* 994–1003.

Wrong man tried for murder (1985, October 27). *St. Louis Post-Dispatch,* p. 9A.

Wu, C., & Shaffer, D. R. (1987). Susceptibility to persuasive appeals as a function of source credibility and prior experience with the attitude object. *Journal of Personality and Social Psychology, 52*, 677–688.

Wurtman, R. J., & Wurtman, J. J. (1989). Carbohydrates and depression. *Scientific American, 260*, 68–75.

Wyrostock, N., & Paulson, B. (2000). Traditional healing practices among First Nation students. *Canadian Journal of Counseling, 34*(1), 14–24.

Yarmey, A. D., & Yarmey, M. J. (1997). Eyewitness recall and duration estimates in field settings. *Journal of Applied Social Psychology, 27*(4), 330–344.

Yarmey, A. D., Yarmey, M. J., & Yarmey, A. L. (1996). Accuracy of eyewitness identification in showups and lineups. *Law and Human Behavior, 20*(4), 459–477.

Yazigi, R. A., Odem, R. R., & Polakoski, K. L. (1991). Demonstration of specific binding of cocaine to human spermatozoa. *Journal of the American Medical Association, 266,* 1956.

Yonkers, K. A., & Hamilton, J. A. (1995, May). Do men and women need different doses of psychotropic drugs? *Harvard Mental Health Letter, 11*(11), 8.

Yuille, J. C., & Marschark, M. (1983). Imagery effects on memory: Theoretical implications. In A. A. Sheikh (Ed.), *Imagery: Current theory, research, and application* (pp. 131–155). New York: Wiley.

Yuille, J. C., & Tollestrup, P. A. (1992). A model of the diverse effects of emotion in eyewitness memory. In S.A. Christianson (Ed.), *The handbook of emotional learning: Research and theory.* Hillsdale, NJ: Erlbaum.

Zajonc, R. B. (1965). Social facilitation. *Science, 149*, 269–274.

Zajonc, R. B. (1968). Attitudinal effects of mere exposure. *Journal of Personality and Social Psychology, Monographs Supplement, 9*(Pt. 2), 1–27.

Zajonc, R. B. (1980). Feeling and thinking: Preferences need no inferences. *American Psychologist, 35,* 151–175.

Zajonc, R. B. (1984). On the primacy of affect. *American Psychologist, 39,* 117–123.

Zajonc, R. B. (1998). Emotions. In D.T. Gilbert, S. T. Fiske, et al. (Eds.), *The handbook of social psychology* (4th ed.), (pp. 591–632). Boston: McGraw-Hill.

Zajonc, R. B., & Sales, S. M. (1966). Social facilitation of dominant and subordinate responses. *Journal of Experimental Social Psychology, 2*, 160–168.

Zanna, M. P., & Rempel, J.K. (1988). Attitudes and attidude change. *Annual Review of Psychology, 38,* 575–630.

Zelnik, M., Kim, Y. J., & Kantner, J. F. (1979). Probabilities of intercourse and conception among U.S. teenage women, 1971 and 1976. *Family Planning Perspectives, 11*, 177–183.

Zilbergeld, B. (1986, June). Psychabuse. *Science 86*, pp. 48–52.

Zimbardo, P. G. (1972). Pathology of imprisonment. *Society, 9,* 4–8.

Zimbardo, P. G., Haney, C., & Banks, W. C. (1973, April 8). A Pirandellian prison. *The New York Times Magazine*, pp. 38–60.

Zivian, M., Larsen, W., Knox, J., Gekoski, W., & Hatchette, V. (1992). Psychotherapy for the elderly: Psychotherapists' preferences. *Psychotherapy, 29*(4), 668–674.

Zivian, M., Larsen, W., Knox, J., Gekoski, W., & Hatchette, V. (1994). Psychotherapy for the elderly: Public opinion. *Psychotherapy, 31*(3), 492–502.

Zubin, J., & Spring, B. J. (1977). Vulnerability: A new view of schizophrenia. *Journal of Abnormal Psychology, 86*, 103–126.

Zuckerman, M., Miyake, K., & Hodgins, H. S. (1991). Cross-channel effects of vocal and physical attractiveness and their implications for interpersonal perception. *Journal of Personality and Social Psychology, 60*, 545–554.

Name Index

Subject Index

Photo Credits

3 (top): Gabe Palmer/The Stock Market. 3 (bottom): Canadian Press CP 6: Michael Newman/PhotoEdit. 17: Steve Winter/Black Star 26: Jeff Greenberg/Photo Edit. 28: Andy Levin/Photo Researchers Inc. 33: Tony Stone Images/Med. Illus. SBHS. 34: Canadian Press TRSTR. 44: PhotoDisc, Inc. 47: A. Glauberman/Photo Researchers Inc. 49: Photosynthesis Archives. 52: Richard Gross/ The Stock Market. 55: Paul Derry. 58: Alexander Tsiaras/Photo Researchers Inc. 59 (left): Tony Stone Worldwide. 59 (right): Dr. Michael Phelps and Dr. John Mazziota/UCLA School of Medicine. 60: Courtesy Wood, Wood, Wood, and Desmarais. 64: Robert Brenner/Photo Edit. 71: Nathan Benn/Woodfin Camp & Associates. 75: Serguel Fedoror/Woodfin Camp & Associates. 76: Peter Arnold/J & L Weber. 82: T. Farmer/Tony Stone Worldwide. 84: T. Svensson/The Stock Market. 87: G. Gardner/The Image Works. 92: Debbie Rogow/PhotoEdit. 94: Gerard Vandeystadt/Photo Researchers Inc. 99 (top): Bill Horsmon/Stock Boston. 99 (bottom): Ernest Braun/Bonnie Kamin. 101: Ron Pretzer. 104: Rashid/Monkmeyer. 111 (top): Alan Becker/Image Bank. 111 (bottom): Associated Press/Watertown Daily Times. 114: Charles Gupton/Tony Stone Images. 116: Photo Researchers Inc. 119: Esbin Anderson/The Image Works. 120: Bohdan Hrynewych/Stock Boston. 121: Woods/First Light. 125: Louis Psihoyos/Matrix. 127: Francoise Sauze, Science Photo Library/Photo Researchers Inc. 133: R. Hutchings/PhotoEdit 137: Esbin Anderson/The Image Works. 143 (top): Tony McCarthy/PhotoEdit. 143 (bottom): Liaison Agency, Inc. 145: Photosynthesis Archives. 149: Tony Freeman/Photo Edit. 150: Bettman. 151: Photosynthesis Archives. 153: Ullmann/Monkmeyer. 154 (bottom): Ed Kashi. 156 (top): Christopher Johnson/Stock Boston. 156 (bottom): Nina Leen/Time Magazine. 160: Chris Thomaidis/Tony Stone Images. 169: Tony Freeman/PhotoEdit 177: D. Littell Greco/Stock Boston. 178: Eileen Wood. 180: Kent Wood/Photo Researchers Inc. 185 (left): Nicholas Desciose/Photo Researchers Inc. 185 (right): Karin Cooper/Gamma Liaison. 194: Grantpix/Monkmeyer. 197: Jerome DeLay/Associated Press. 199: M & E Bernheim/Woodfin Camp & Associates. 213: Sam Ogden/Science Photo Library/Photo Researchers Inc. 214: Associated Press AP. 216 (left): Bernard Wolf/Monkmeyer. 216 (middle): Rafael Macia/Photo Researchers Inc. 216 (right): B & C Alexander/Photo Researchers Inc. 217: Photosynthesis Archives. 224: Porterfield/Chickering/Photo Researchers Inc. 228: Collins/Monkmeyer. 232 (left): Jim Simncen/Tony Stone Worldwide. 232 (right): Art Wolfe/Tony Stone Worldwide. 242: CNN/A&B Archives. 251 (top): Charles Thatcher/Tony Stone Images. 251 (bottom): Reuters/Bettmann. 256 (left): Francis Leroy/Photo Researchers Inc. 256 (centre and right): Lennart Nilsson/Bonniers. 260: Enrico Fercrelli. 263: Yves De Braine/Black Star. 270: Elizabeth Brooks/A & B Archives. 273: Martin Rogers/Stock Boston. 275: Smith/Monkmeyer. 280: Michael Sobol. 282: Jayne Kamin. 289 (top): Ron Dahlquist/Tony Stone Images. 289 (bottom): Canadian Press VKA. 292: Anthony Neste/A&B Archives. 295: Courtesy McGill University. 296: Photosynthesis Archives. 297: Arthur Beck/Photo Researchers Inc. 301: Robert Harbison. 309 (left): Paul Ekman 1975. 309 (right): Mark M. Lawrence/The Stock Market. 312: Penny Gentieu. 314: William Thompson/The Picture Cube. 321: Lori Adamski Peek/Tony Stone Images. 322: Stone. 328: Prettyman/PhotoEdit. 330: Bettmann. 332: Bob Daemmrich/Stock Boston. 339: Bettmann. 349: Bob Daemmrich/The Image Works. 353: Burt Glinn/Magnum Photos, Inc. 354: Michael Newman/PhotoEdit. 356: AP Wide World Photo. 361: Mark Richards/PhotoEdit. 362: David Leifer/Offshoot Stock. 365: David Leifer/Offshoot Stock. 370: Tony Freeman/Photo Edit. 373: Robert Harbison. 375: Perlstein/Jerrican/Photo Researchers Inc. 381: Bonnie Kamin. 383 (left): Robert Harbison/A&B Archives. 383 (right): Russ Schleipman /Offshoot Stock. 388: Will Hart. 396: Will Hart. 399: Gordon Willitt/Tony Stone Worldwide. 401: J. Griffin/The Image Works. 407: Will Hart. 413 (top): Bob Daemmrich/The Image Works. 415: Bettmann. 416: Michael Rougier/Life Magazine. 419: Will Hart. 424 (left and right): Georgia Tech Telephoto. 425: Andrew Sacks. 428: Leif Skoogfors/Woodfin Camp and Associates. 443: Bob Carroll. 444: Dick Hemingway. 445: C. Gatewood/The Image Works. 448: J. Christopher Briscoe/Photo Researchers Inc. 451: William Vandevert/Scientific American. 453 (left and right): Courtesy of Milgram Estate. 457: Timothy Eagan/Woodfin Camp and Associates. 470: Dan Miller/Woodfin Camp and Associates. 474: David Young-Wolff/PhotoEdit.